Studies in the Scriptures 1930-31

Volume 5
of
17 Volume Set

Studies in the Scriptures 1930-31

Volume 5
of
17 Volume Set

Arthur W. Pink

Sovereign Grace Publishers, Inc.
P.O. Box 4998
Lafayette, IN 47903
2001

A. W. Pink's Studies in the Scriptures,
Volume 5 of 17 Vols - 1930-31 - Paperback Edition
Copyright © 2001
By Jay P. Green, Sr.
All Rights Reserved

Volume 1 = ISBN 1-58960-234-X

Studies in the Scriptures -- 1930
Index

The Epistle to the Hebrews	Heb. 6:4-6	2
The Satisfaction ("Atonement") of Christ		8
The Everlasting Covenant		13
Christian Experience		18
The Epistle to the Hebrews	Heb. 6:7, 8	26
The Satisfaction ("Atonement") of Christ		32
The Everlasting Covenant Administered		37
Satanic Assaults		43
The Epistle to the Hebrewa	Heb. 6:9-11	50
The Satisfaction ("Atonement") of Christ		56
The Work of the Spirit		62
Prayer Perverted		65
The Snare of Service		68
Assurance		70
Quietness		71
The Epistle to the Hebrews	Heb. 6:12-15	74
The Satisfaction ("Atonement") of Christ		80
Mortification of Sin		86
Divine Warnings		90
A Request		94
The Epistle to the Hebrews	Heb. 6: 16-20	98
The Satisfaction ("Atonement") of Christ		104
Sanctification of the Spirit		110
Profiting from the Word		114
Filled Vessels		118
The Epistles to the Hebrews	Heb. 7:1-3	122
The Satisfaction ("Atonement") of Christ		128
Gorwth in Grace		133
The Cross and Self	Matt. 16:24	138
Good Cheer		141
A Personal Word		143
The Epistle to the Hebrews	Heb. 7:4-10	146
The Satisfaction ("Atonement") of Christ		152
The Life of Faith		158
Profiting from the Word		162
The Epistle to the Hebrews	Heb. 7:11-16	170
The Satisfaction ("Atonement") of Christ		176
The Believer's Blessedness in Glory		182
Welcome Tidings		186
An Exposition of Psalm 1		188
The Epistle to the Hebrews	Heb. 7:17-19	194

The Satisfaction ("Atonement") of Christ		200
The Brazen Sea	2 Chron. 4:2-6	210
The Epistle to the Hebrews	Heb. 7:20-24	218
The Satisfaction ("Atonement") of Christ		224
Profiting rom the Word		230
Simon Peter		234
Xmas	Jer. 10:1-3	236
Danger!	Matt. 26:41	239
The Epistles to the Hebrews	Heb. 7:25-28	242
The Satisfaction ("Atonement") of Christ		248
The Intercession of Christ		254
The Radio		259
The Supremacy of God		260
A Mighty Saviour	Isa 63:1	263
The Epistle to the Hebrews	Heb. 8:1-5	266
The Satisfaction ("Atonement") of Christ		272
The Christian's Warfare	Rom. 7:22-25	278
The Intercession of Christ		281
A Personal Word		286
Review		287

Studies in the Scriptures -- 1931
Index

The Epistle to the Hebrews	Heb. 8:6-9	2
The Satisfaction ("Atonement") of Christ		9
The Intercession of Christ (Continued)		15
God's hold on Us and Our Hold on Him		22
The Epistle to the Hebrews	Heb. 8:10-13	26
The Satisfaction ("Atonement") of Christ		33
The Intercession of Christ		39
Sound the Alarm		44
The Epistle to the Hebrews	Heb. 9:1-5	50
The Satisfaction ("Atonement") of Christ		56
Subjection to God	Rom. 6:22	67
Faith Triumphant	Isa. 12:2	69
Praise the Lord		71
The Epistles to the Hebrews	Heb. 9:6-10	74
The Satisfaction ("Atonement") of Christ		80
Husbands		87
Regeneration, or, The New Birth		90
Pride		93
Faith	Heb. 11:6	94
The Epistle to the Hebrews	Heb. 9:11-14	98

The Satisfaction ("Atonement") of Christ	104
Regeneration, or, The New Birth	111
Profiting from the Word	115
The Epistle to the Hebrews	122
The Satisfaction ("Atonement") of Christ	128
Regeneration, or, The New Birth .... John 3:6	134
Caring for the Children	138
Communion .... 1 Pet. 5:7	142
A Personal Word	143
The Epistle to the Hebrews .... Heb. 9:16-22	146
The Satisfaction ("Atonement") of Christ	152
Regenration, or, The New Birth .... 1 John 5:19	158
Welcome Tidings	163
Following Christ .... John 8:12	165
The Epistle to the Hebrews .... Heb. 9:23-28	170
The Satisfaction ("Atonement") of Christ	176
Regeneration, or, The New Birth	182
Sound the Alarm	186
Is Christ Your Lord?	189
Important Notice	190
The Epistle to the Hebrews	194
The Satisfaction ("Atonement") of Christ	200
Depravity .... Psa. 58:3:5	206
Repentance .... 2 Tim. 3:13	208
Preservation and Perseverance .... Phil 1:6	213
The Epistle to the Hebrews .... Heb. 10:5-7	218
The Satisfaction ("Atonement") of Christ	224
Profiting from the Word	230
Repentance .... Luke 13:3	234
A Personal Word	238
The Epistle to the Hebrews .... Heb. 10:7-10	242
The Satisfaction ("Atonement") of Christ	248
Love: Divine and Human	254
The Mighty Breaker .... Micah 2:13	261
Prayer .... Mark 11:24	262
The Epistle to the Hebrews	266
The Satisfaction ("Atonement") of Christ	272
Repentance	278
Profiting from the Word	282
A Personal Word	285

VOL. IX.   JANUARY, 1930   No. 1

STUDIES IN THE SCRIPTURES

"Search the Scriptures" John 5 : 39

Copyright in all English-speaking Countries.

Editor: Arthur W. Pink, Morton's Gap, Ky., U. S. A.
Hon. Agent in England: Mr. A. Winstone, 2, Lennox Villas, Hewlett Road, Cheltenham.
Hon. Agent in Australia: Mr. G. Ardill, The Christian Workers' Depot.
Commonwealth and Reservoir Streets, Sydney.

The Solitariness of God.

The title of this article is perhaps not sufficiently explicit to indicate its theme. This is partly due to the fact that so few today are accustomed to meditate upon the personal perfections of God. Comparatively few of those who occasionally read the Bible are aware of the awe-inspiring and worship-provoking grandeur of the Divine character. That God is great in wisdom, wondrous in power, yet full of mercy, is assumed by many to be almost common knowledge; but, to entertain anything approaching an adequate conception of His being, His nature, His attributes, as these are revealed in Holy Scripture, is something which very, very few people in these degenerate times have attained unto. God is solitary in His excellency. "Who is like unto Thee, O Lord, among the gods? Who is like Thee, glorious in holiness, fearful in praises, doing wonders?" (Ex. 15:11).

"In the beginning, God" (Gen. 1:1). There was a time, if "time" it could be called, when God, in the unity of His nature (though subsisting equally in three Divine Persons), dwelt all alone. "In the beginning, God". There was no heaven, where His glory is now particularly manifested. There was no earth to engage His attention. There were no angels to hymn His praises; no universe to be upheld by the word of His power. There was nothing, no one, but God; and **that**, not for a day, a year, or an age, but "from everlasting". During a past eternity, God was alone: self-contained, self-sufficient, self-satisfied; in need of nothing. Had a universe, had angels, had human beings been necessary to Him in any way, they also had been called into existence from all eternity. The creating of them when He did, added nothing to God essentially. He changes not (Mal. 3:6), therefore His essential glory can be neither augmented nor diminished.

God was under no constraint, no obligation, no necessity **to** create. That He chose to do so was purely a sovereign act on His part, caused by nothing outside Himself, determined by nothing but His own mere good pleasure; for He "worketh all things after the counsel of His own will" (Eph. 1:11). That He did create was simply for His **manifestative** glory. Do some of our readers imagine that we have gone beyond what Scripture warrants? Then our appeal shall be to the Law and the Testimony: "Stand up and bless the Lord your God forever and ever: and blessed be Thy glorious name, which is exalted **above all blessing** and praise" (Neh. 9:5). God is no gainer even from our worship. He was in no need of that external glory of His grace which arises from His redeemed, for He is glorious enough in Himself without that. What was it moved Him to predestinate His elect to the praise of the glory of His grace? It was, as Eph. 1:5 tells us, "according to the good pleasure of His will".

We are well aware that the high ground we are here treading is new and strange to almost all of our readers; for that reason it is well to move slowly. Let our appeal again be to the Scriptures. At the end of Rom. 11, where the apostle brings to a close his long argument on salvation by pure and sovereign grace, he asks, "For who hath known the mind of the Lord? Or who hath been His counsellor? Or who hath first given to Him, and it shall be recompensed to him again?" (vv. 34, 35). The force of this is, It is impossible to bring the Almighty under obligations to the creature; God gains nothing from us. 'If thou be righteous, what givest thou **Him**? Or what receiveth He of thine hand? Thy wickedness may hurt a man as thou art; and thy righteousness may profit the son of man" (Job 35:7, 8), but it certainly cannot affect God, who is all-blessed **in Himself.**

(Continued on Page 24)

IMPORTANT NOTICES

Please advise promptly of change of address, otherwise copies will be lost in the mails.

We are glad to send a sample copy to any of our friends whom you believe would be interested in such a publication.

Send to Mr. I. C. Herendeen, 433-435, The Arcade, Cleveland, Ohio, for a list of our publications. He has published many of our books and booklets.

This Magazine is published as a work of faith and labour of love. The Editor and his wife gladly give their services. It is freely sent to all who will read it. No charge is made for it.

Christians who feel definitely lead to do so, may have fellowship with us in this ministry. Those outside the U. S. A., please send only INTERNATIONAL Money Orders made out to Morton's Gap, Kentucky, U. S. A. See that it is made out in American money.

CONTENTS

The Epistle to the Hebrews 2

The Satisfaction ("Atonement") of Christ 8

The Everlasting Covenant 13

Christian Experience 18

THE EPISTLE TO THE HEBREWS

25. The Twofold Working of the Spirit: Heb. 6:4-6.

In our last article we attempted little more than an explication of the terms used in Heb. 6:4-6. Lack of space prevented us from throwing upon these verses the light which other portions of God's Word affords, yet this is necessary if we are to form anything like a true and adequate conception of the particular characters which are there in view. One chief reason why students of Scripture continue to experience difficulty in ascertaining the meaning of any verse therein, is because they fail to prayerfully and **patiently** compare "spiritual things with spiritual" (1 Cor. 2:13). All of us are in far too much a hurry, and for this reason miss the best of what God has provided—true both of temporal and spiritual things. Probably few of our readers considered that we had succeeded in clearing away all the difficulties raised by this solemn passage, therefore the need of a further article thereon.

On the present occasion we propose to take up our passage more from a topical viewpoint than an expository, seeking (as God may be pleased to graciously enable) to open up more fully that in it which has caused the most trouble, namely, the precise relation of the Holy Spirit to the characters therein mentioned. They who "fall away" and whom it is "impossible to renew again unto repentance", are said to have been "made partakers of the Holy Spirit". We ask now, On what has the Spirit wrought? What was the character of His work toward them? **How** had they been made "partakers" of Him? To what extent? This leads us to point out that Scripture reveals a twofold working of God's Spirit with men: with the elect, **and** with the non-elect. It is of the latter we shall here treat.

Concerning the Spirit's work with the non-elect, we begin by enquiring, Upon what does He work? We answer, Upon the faculties of men's souls. First, He works upon the **understanding**. There are in all men natural faculties of understanding, will, and affection. A man could not love God unless he had in him the faculty of affection—a stone could never love God! So a man could never understand spiritual things unless he had the faculty of understanding. With the elect, the Holy Spirit "renews" the understanding (Rom. 12:2 compared with Titus 3:5); but with the non-elect, He only enlightens or educates it. The understanding of fallen and unregenerate men, which is enlightened by the Spirit, **is** capable of knowing, in some measure, both the Godhead, and parts of His law. Let us give Scriptural proof of this.

In Rom. 1:18 we read of men who "hold the truth in unrighteousness", and what is there referred to is explained in what follows: "Because that which may be known of God is manifest in them; for God hath showed unto them. For the invisible things of Him from the creation of the world are clearly seen, being understood by the things that are made: His eternal power and Godhead" (vv. 19, 20). The reference there, as the later verses show, is to the Heathen. Now what we would press upon the attention of the reader is, that in addition to poor fallen nature, God has granted to men a manifestation of Himself; that which "may be known of God", which He "hath **showed** unto them".

It is not merely that creation reveals a Creator, but that the Creator **has revealed Himself**—"when they **knew** God" (v. 21), and that must have been by the Spirit's enlightening their natural understanding.

Again, in Rom. 2:14, 15 we read, "For when the Gentiles, which have not the law, do by nature the things contained in the law, these, having not the law are a law unto themselves: Which show the work of the law written in their hearts, their conscience also bearing witness". The Holy Spirit is speaking here of men according to "nature", not grace. In his natural heart there is **written** "the work of the law"—by whom? but by the finger of God! Except for this, man would be destitute of moral light, for the Fall robbed him of all light.

The understanding in man, or the principle of reason, may, by education and contact with others, be developed to a considerable extent, so that a man may become exceeding wise; nevertheless, his knowledge and wisdom is only **natural**, even though his understanding be exercised upon super-natural objects. But let now the light of reason and the light of conscience be brought to the Scriptures for instruction, and man's knowledge will be much further increased, yet still his light is but **natural**, it rises not to the level of what grace produces. Proof of this is seen in the case of the Jews: "Behold, thou art called a Jew, and restest in the law, and makest thy boast of God; and knowest His will, and approvest the things that are more excellent, being instructed out of the law; and art confident that thou thyself art a guide of the blind, a light of them which are in darkness" (Rom. 2:17-19). How like thousands of unregenerate souls in Christendom today!

From the last-quoted passage we learn what is the effect of the light of nature (reason) being brought to the law of God: it is increased and improved. As we have seen above, a man has some light by nature that there is a God; let that light be brought to Scripture, and he becomes "confident" there is. A man by nature has some light about the duties which God requires of him; let him bring that light to the Scriptures and he will have "the **form** (systematised) of knowledge, and of the **truth** in the law" (Rom. 2:20). When the understanding of the natural man is illumined by the Scriptures, his light is both rarified and added unto, yet is it still **natural** light which he has; it is but the educating of his natural reason.

Second, the Holy Spirit works upon the **affections** of the natural man. There is in fallen man a natural devotion to a deity. This is evidenced by the fact that practically all of the heathen worship some god or other. In Acts 13:50 we read of "devout women" being stirred up against Paul and Barnabas: they had a devotion in them which is common to mankind. Now let men bring their natural devotion to the Scriptures and they will come to know of the true God, and learn to reverence Him too; yet is that only nature improved. Through the Word, the Holy Spirit may (usually, does) convince its reader that the Maker of heaven and earth is the true God, and therefore worthy of honour and homage. The fact is, though very few indeed recognize it, the identical principle which causes a Hindoo to worship Buddha, causes an Anglo-Saxon to worship the Father of Jesus Christ.

Again; there is in every sinner the natural recognition that his sins deserve eternal death, and that God, unless He be appeased, will punish him. Doubtless many of our readers will feel inclined to call into question this last statement; let our appeal again be to the Word of Truth. There we read, "Who, **knowing** the judgment of God, that they which commit such things are **worthy of death**" (Rom. 1:32). That, be it noted, is said of the heathen. Now bring one having such knowledge to the law of God, and what will follow? This, "But we **are sure** that the judgment of God is according to truth against them which commit such things" (Rom. 2:2). There it is the Jews speaking. The natural man enlightened from the Word has his conviction deepened.

Again; if a man is conscious of his sins, and realizes that the justice of God calls for their punishment, is it not natural for him to think next of a **mediator**, to desire someone to intercede for him to God? Such a concept is by no means a sure evidence of regeneration. This too is found in mere nature. Every heathen religion, with the propitiatory offerings which are brought to their gods, exemplifies it. Romanism with its mediating priests demonstrates the same fact in this land. Illustrations are also to be found in the Holy Scriptures. When Pharaoh was convicted of his sins, he entreated Moses to intercede for him (Ex. 10:16, 17). So too wicked Simon Magus desired Peter to pray for him (Acts 8:24).

Once more; there is in the heart of every natural man a desire for happiness, and for a greater happiness than this poor world can provide. It is plainly evident that man rests not in anything down here, for like a bee which goes from one flower to another, so the heart of man cannot be satisfied with any earthly object. When Balaam saw the blessedness of God's people, he exclaimed, "Let **me** die the death of the righteous" (Num. 23:10). The most abandoned wretch does not want to go to hell, and to the very end he hopes that he will be taken to heaven.

So likewise in the matter of believing that a man really **is** a child of God. There is such self-love and self-flattery in the fallen heart that if an unregenerate man hears, out of the Word of God, the good news that Christ Jesus came into the world to save sinners, he at once concludes that **he** is the man God will honour, as wicked Haman imagined that **he** was the man king Ahasuerus would honour. So when the Holy Spirit has terrified a man's conscience, by giving it a sight of sin as it is before a holy God, when he learns about remission of sins through Christ, he at once fondly imagines that his own sins are pardoned. Alas, in the vast majority of cases it has to be said, "the pride of thine heart hath deceived thee" (Obad. 3).

Now let us take note of how the Holy Spirit may work upon these **natural** principles of the human soul, mightily raising them, and yet **not** changing a man's heart. Just as the rays of the sun shining upon plants in a garden adds no new nature to them, but serves to aid their best development, so the Holy Spirit when He deals with the reprobate communicates nothing new to them, yet raises their natural faculties to their highest point. The principles or faculties of man's soul **are** capable of being wrought upon **without** the impartation of regenerating grace. As we have seen, man's understanding is illuminated by the light of conscience, but let the Holy Spirit—**without** imparting a new eye—still further enlighten that conscience, bring before it the exalted claims of the thrice holy God, and its knowledge will be greatly increased. Nevertheless, this educated conscience falls far below the level of the spiritual discernment possessed by one who has been brought out of death into life. Let us particularise:

1. The Spirit restrains the Corruptions of men.

In Gen. 20:6 we read of how God bound the lust of Abimeleck when Sarah was at his mercy, "I also withheld thee from sinning against Me: therefore suffered I thee not to touch her". So in 2 Peter 2:20 we read of some "having escaped the pollutions of the world through the knowledge of our Lord and Saviour Jesus Christ", yet from what follows in the next two verses it is clear they were never regenerated. There the apostle uses the similitude of a sow being washed from her filth, and being kept for a while, after she is washed, from going back again into the mire; yet is there no changing or "renewing" of the swine's nature.

Contrast now what is said of the Lord's people in 2 Peter 1:3, 4, "According as His Divine power hath given unto us all things that pertain unto life and godliness, through the knowledge of Him that hath called us to glory and virtue: Whereby are given unto us exceeding great and precious promises; that by these ye might be partakers of the Divine nature, having escaped the corruption that is in the world through lust". In 2 Peter 2:20 the Greek word for the "pollutions" of the world, signifies the gross and outward defilements into which the irreligious run; but in 2 Peter 1:4 the regenerated are said to have escaped "the **corruption**" that is in the world **through lust** or "desire", i.e. the inward disposition toward evil. Moreover, the Lord's people are made "partakers of the Divine nature", which means, the Divine image is stamped upon them: "life and godliness" are seen in them.

Again; in the similitude used in 2 Peter 2:20 the apostle likens those who have known "the way of righteousness" to a dog that has been made sick, but which turns to its own vomit again. The figure is very striking and forceable. When the Holy Spirit brings the Word of God to bear upon an unregenerate man's conscience, he is made sick at heart. Of Christians it is said, "For ye have not received the Spirit of bondage again to fear" (Rom. 8:15), but to the non-elect He often becomes a Spirit **of** "bondage" by binding their sins upon their conscience. Whereas before they had a glimmering light that the judgment of God is against sinners, their conscience now is set on fire, and the temporary consequence is that sins are refused with loathing, vomitted out. Yet, like a dog, such an one loves them still, and ultimately returns thereto.

2. The Spirit causes men to turn naturally toward the Redeemer.

When conscience is wrought upon by a few sparks of God's wrath falling upon it, what saith the soul next? This, O for a physician! There is, as we have pointed out above, a natural principle in men which causes them to make use of a mediator unto God—a witch-doctor, a priest, or a preacher, as the case may be. Now a man who has lived under the sound of the Gospel learns that Christ is the one Mediator. Scriptural education has taught him this, just as the heathen education teaches a Turk that Mahomet is the one mediator. And, by the same principle that Agrippa believed Moses and the prophets, the unregenreate "Christian" (?) **believes** in Christ. Nay further, the light of the Spirit shining upon him, as the sun on the plants, develops his natural understanding and causes him to now remember that Redeemer which before he ignored.

A scripture clearly to the point of what we have just said above is Psa. 78:34, 35, "When He slew them, then they sought Him: and they returned and enquired early after God. And they remembered that God was their Rock, and the high God their Redeemer". Yet what immediately follows? This, "Nevertheless they did flatter Him with their mouth". And what signifies this "flattering"? Why, they sought Him merely out of **self-love**, simply because they felt their very lives were in imminent danger. There is a seeking out of friendship, out of love to the object. But if one seek unto an enemy because he hath need of him, **that** is but "flattery" or self-love. So if sinful man feels he is in extremity, if his conscience remains sick, mere nature will call for the Physician.

Self-love is the predominant principle in the natural man; he loves himself more than he loves God; it is this which lies at the root of depravity and sin. Now when a man's conscience is convicted so that he perceives his need of a physician, and recognizes that happiness comes from Christ, such good news appeals to his self-love. Satan, who knows human nature so well, was right when he said, "skin for skin yea, all that a man hath will he give for his life" (Job 2:4). Make the self-love of the natural man conscious of the wrath of God, and he is ready to "accept Christ", or do anything else which the preacher bids him; yet that is only the workings of nature, he is still unregenerate.

When the storm arose and threatened to sink the ship in which Jonah lay asleep, we read, "Then the mariners were afraid, and cried every man unto his god"; then the captain awoke Jonah and said, "Arise, call upon thy God, if so be God will think upon us that we perish not" (1:5, 6). So a conscience terrified by the prospect of Hell, will cause a man to seek Christ after a natural way. It is but the instinct of self-preservation at work. Add to this, the craving for happiness which self-love ever seeks, and hearing that such happiness is to be found only in Christ, little wonder that multitudes seek Him now for what they can get **from** Him, as of old they sought Him for the sake of the loaves and fishes.

In John 6:33 we are told that Christ announced, "For the bread of God is He which cometh down from heaven, and giveth life unto the world". What was their response? This, "Then they said unto Him, Lord, evermore **give us** this bread". Yet their eager request sprang not from a renewed heart, but from the corrupt spring of self-love. Proof of this is found in the immediate sequel. In v. 36 the Lord tells them plainly, ye "believe not". In v. 41 we are told that they "murmured at Him". Yet that very same people said to the Lord, "Evermore give us this Bread"! Ah, all is not gold that glitters.

An enlightened understanding, moved by self-love, is prepared to take up Divine duties never practiced before, yea, to walk in the commandments of God. This was demonstrated plainly at Sinai. When Jehovah appeared before Israel in His awesome majesty, and their conscience was smitten by His manifested holiness, they said to Moses, "Go thou near, and hear all that the Lord our God shall say; and speak thou unto us all that the Lord our God shall speak unto thee; and we will hear and **do**". They were prepared to receive and obey the Lord's statutes. Yet mark what God said of them, "Oh, that there were such a heart in them, that they would fear Me, and keep all My commandments always". They still lacked the principle of regeneration!

3. The Spirit elevates the natural faculties of man.

Just as the shining of the sun causes plants to grow higher and fruits to be sweeter than would be the case were the heavens to remain cloudy and overcast, so the Spirit works upon the faculties of the unregenerate and causes them to bring forth that which, left to themselves, they would not produce. Or, just as fire will raise the temperature and level of water, causing it to bubble up and ascend in steam, though the principle of heat is in the fire and not in the water, for when the fire is withdrawn the water returns to its natural coldness again; so the Spirit enlightens the understandings of the non-elect, stirs their affections, and moves their wills to action, without communicating a new principle to them, without regenerating them.

He elevates the **understanding**. In Num. 24:2 we read that the Spirit of God came upon Balaam, the consequence of which he has told us: "The man who had his eyes shut, but now opened, hath said: he hath said, which heard the words of God, which saw the vision of the Almighty, falling but having his eyes opened: How goodly are thy tents, O Jacob, thy tabernacles, O Israel!" (vv. 3-5). Thus Balaam had a vision of the Almighty, and perceived the blessed estate of His people; yet was he still unregenerate!

He elevates the **affections**. In 1 Sam. 11:1-3 we read of how the enemies of Jehovah insulted His people. Then we are told, "And the Spirit of God came upon Saul when he heard these tidings, and his **anger was kindled** greatly" (v. 6). That was holy indignation, yet it proceeded from a reprobate! As the winds blowing upon the sea will, at times, raise its waters to a great height, so the Spirit, under a faithful sermon, will blow upon the affections of the unregenerate, and elevate them to nobler objects and occupations. Yet, He stops short of making them new creatures in Christ Jesus.

Again; as we have seen, there is in man a natural desire for real happiness, hence, when Christ is presented in the Gospel, many receive Him "with joy"; yet, are they, for the most part, but **stony-ground** hearers, destitute of any root of vital godliness (Matt. 13:20, 21). Nature may be so raised by the light which the Holy Spirit brings to it, that unregenerate men may taste of the heavenly gift, Christ, see John 4:10. So too they are enabled to **taste** of the "powers of the world to come". As in their conscience, they get a taste of Hell, and so know for a certainty that there is a Hell, the same natural principle which desires a happiness which is beyond this world, is **confirmed** and comforted when they have a "taste" of what belongs to the world to come.

He elevates the **will** and sets it to work in the way of obedience to God. The Holy Spirit is the Author of all moral and civil righteousness which there is in the world. The Lord stirred up the spirit of Cyrus to issue a proclamation for the building of His house (Ezra 1:1, 2); and He also moved Caiaphas to prophesy of Christ (John 11:51). Of wicked Herod we read that, when he heard John "he **did** many things, and heard him gladly" (Mark 6:20). And God will be no man's Debtor: every act of obedience, performed by him in obedience to His Word, shall be rewarded: a temporary joy shall be the portion of such. The tragic thing is that so many conclude from such an experience that they are in a state of grace, and therefore become loud in their professions of assurance, being fully persuaded that **they** are really born-again persons.

Now we trust that what has been said will enable some of our readers to understand the better what is found in Heb. 6:4-6. One eminent commentator suggested that these verses describe neither the regenerate nor the unregenerate, but a third condition, midway between; because there must be a third state between that of mere nature and that of supernatural grace. Nor are we at all surprised that he arrived at this conclusion. Few indeed have perceived the force of 1 Cor. 12:6, "And there are **diversities of operations,** but it is the same God which worketh all in all".

There **are** operations of the Spirit upon men's hearts which are above nature, which are works of Divine power, which produces that in and from unregenerate men which leads multitudes of them to fondly imagine that they have been actually born again, and yet **this** work of the Spirit falls far short of that "**exceeding greatness** of His power to usward who believe" (Eph. 1:19). Heb. 6:4-6 supplies a most striking example of this, for there we have men who are made "partakers of the Holy Spirit". There we see a work which is above nature, for they taste of the "heavenly Gift". It is a work of power, for they taste of the "**powers** of the world to come". As 1 Cor. 12:4 tells us, "There are diversities of gifts, but the same Spirit". And why is this? 1 Cor. 12:11 answers, "But all these worketh that one and the selfsame Spirit, dividing to every man severally **as He will**": He proportions His power as He pleases, to an inferior or a superior work. Note carefully, there are "good gifts" from above, as well as "perfect gifts" (James 1:17)!

Of old Jehovah said, "My Spirit shall not always strive with man" (Gen. 6:3). There we find the Spirit putting forth power upon man, for He "strives" with him; yet, not in the fulness of His power, or it had not been resisted. In other cases He puts forth power and men yield thereto (as did Balaam), yet is that power simply directed to the winding up of man's natural faculties to their greatest height, and comes far short of regenerating them. This is clearly illustrated in the parable of the Sower. There is the stony-ground hearer, who received the Word with joy, yet falls away in time of persecution. There is also the thorny-ground hearer, who withstands persecution, and brings forth fruit, yet **not** "to perfection". And both of them represent unregenerate souls.

And **why** does God put forth His power upon the reprobate, yet not the "exceeding greatness" of His power? God has seen well to **test** men in various ways. First, He gave them the light of nature, the work of the law written in their hearts, augmented by the light of conscience—a light which enabled men to know there was a God and of their duties toward Him. And Socrates, who knew nothing of the Scriptures, went so far as to die for the truth that there was One God. But this light of nature did not regenerate men, nor enable them to bring forth the fruit of the Spirit.

Again; He tried the Jews with His Law. He would make it evident how far the light of nature, improved by the light of His Law, would go. And let it not be forgotten that of Israel under the Law it is said, "Thou gavest **also** Thy good Spirit to instruct them" (Neh. 9:20). Nevertheless, the law was "weak through the flesh" (Rom. 8:3): it could not bring forth that which was truly spiritual. And just as God gave Socrates as the highest product of what the light of nature could produce, so He gave Saul of Tarsus—a man who walked **blamelessly** (Phil. 3:6)—as the highest product under the Law.

But now He is trying men with the Gospel, to show how far human nature as such can go. That Gospel is accompanied with the Spirit, and Heb. 6:4-6 shows us the highest point which can be attained under it, by man in the flesh. He may be enlightened, renewed unto repentence, enjoy the Word of God, be made a partaker of the Holy Spirit, and yet apostatise and perish forever. So too the same characters are said to have "done despite unto the Spirit of grace" (Heb. 10:26). The tragic thing is that the vast majority in Christendom look upon these inferior workings of the Spirit as evidence of His new-creating grace.

And **what**, we may enquire, is **God's purpose** in these secondary operations of His Spirit? It is manifold. We can barely mention the leading designs. First, it is **to exhibit the excellency of Grace.** Everything in nature hath either its counterfeit or counterfoil. If there are stationary stars, there are also shooting stars. If there are precious stones, there are pebbles which closely resemble yet differ widely from them. The one serves to set off the other. So there is a natural faith—"many believed in His name when they saw the miracles which He did. But Jesus did not commit Himself unto **them**" (John 2:23, 24); "The demons believe" (James 2:19)—and there is a supernatural faith, "the faith of God's elect" (Titus 1:1), called "**precious** faith" (2 Peter 1:1)! So there are common operations of the Spirit, and special operations; inferior workings upon the flesh, and superior workings that beget "spirit" (John 3:6). By virtue of this contrast, God says to each of His elect, See how much I have wrought on mere nature in the reprobate! yet it was not grace; I might have done no more for you, but I showed the "exceeding greatness of My power" (Eph. 1:19) toward **you.**

Second, to show **the depravity of human nature.** No matter under what trial God places man, that which is born of the flesh remains naught but flesh. The Law was weak through the flesh; so too is the Gospel, notwithstanding the shining of God's Spirit upon men. The conscience may be convicted, the understanding enlightened, the affections raised, and the will moved, yet it still remains true that "every man at his **best** state is altogether **vanity**" (Psa. 39:5). Men may be instructed in the truth, believe in the living God, "accept Christ as their personal Saviour", contend for the faith once delivered to the saints, and pass among men for devout Christians, yet be no better than "whited sepulchres, full of dead men's bones".

Third, to **place bounds upon sin.** The general workings of God's Spirit upon the reprobate serve to curb the risings of man's corrupt nature. As it is His presence here upon earth which hinders the full manifestation of the mystery of iniquity in the appearing of the Anti-christ (2 Thess. 2), so His operations upon the non-elect prevent many outbursts of wickedness. In the time of Israel's apostasy the Holy Spirit (the "glory") withdrew gradually, stage by stage (Ezek. 11), so as the apostasy of Christendom increases, the restraining operations of the Spirit are decreasing, and hence the rising tide of lawlessness.

Fourth, to **afford protection for the elect.** God's flock is only "the **little**" one (Luke 12:32), very, very much smaller than is commonly supposed. Christ Himself declared that only "FEW" are in the **Narrow** Way which leadeth "unto life" (Matt. 7:14). Nor must Rev. 7:9 be made to contradict these clear passages; instead, the "great multitude which no man could number" is to be compared with and interpreted by the expressions found in Judges 6:5, 7:12; 2 Chron. 12:3; Joel 1:6. Now suppose that only the elect had been reformed by the Gospel, and all the rest of the world had remained in utter enmity against it, then the fruits of the Gospel had been too bare, being without leaves. The leaves of a tree, though not fit for the table, **are** serviceable to the fruit, and ornamental to the tree, for without them the fruit would be exposed to ripen on bare twigs.

An acknowledgement of the doctrine of the Gospel, where it is not accompanied by regeneration of heart, may indeed be suitably compared to the leaves of a tree which shelter and protect the fruit. Thus they are serviceable, though not valuable in God's account. The leaf of the vine does more good to the grapes against a scorching sun, than the leaf of any other fruit tree—how much we may yearn from God's creatures if only we have eyes to see! So God's elect have been outwardly shaded by the multitude of nominal christians around them. For this we may well thank the kind providence of our Lord. Moreover, God has rewarded the doctrinal faith of the great crowd of unregenerate professors by preserving our public liberties, which the little handful of the regenerate could never, humanly speaking, have enjoyed, without the others.

Again; the operations of the Spirit upon the reprobate have shamed the wicked, increased sobriety, promoted morality, and caused nominal professors to support externally the preaching of the Gospel, the carrying on of the ministry, and thus providing for the benefit of common hearers. This is all useful in its season, but will reap no reward in eternity. The writer most seriously doubts if there be a single church on earth today, having in it sufficient of God's elect to support a preacher, were all the unregenerate in it excluded. Yea, most probably, most of God's own sent-servants, would be so completely dismayed if they could but see into the hearts of those who have a name to live and are dead, that they would be in despair. Yet though we cannot see into the hearts of professors, we **can** form an accurate idea of what is in them, for "out of the abundance of the heart the mouth speaketh". And the worldliness and emptiness of the ordinary speech of the majority shows plainly **Who** is **not** in their hearts.

We sincerely trust and earnestly pray that it may please our God to strike terror into the souls of many who read this article, that their false peace may be disturbed, and their worthless profession be exposed. Should some of the more thoughtful exclaim with the apostles, "Who then can be saved"? we answer in the words of our Lord, "With men this is **impossible**" (Matt. 19:26). Conclusive proof is this, my reader, that no sinner can be saved by **any** act of his own; and faithfulness requires us to tell you frankly that if your hope of Heaven is resting upon **your** act of "accepting Christ", then your house is built upon the sand. But blessed be His name, the Redeemer went on to say, "But with God all things **are** possible". "Salvation is of the Lord" (Jonah 2:9), not of the creature (Rom. 9:16). Then marvel not that Christ said, "Except a man be **born again**, he cannot see the kingdom of God" (John 3:3).

—ARTHUR W. PINK.

THE SATISFACTION ("ATONEMENT") OF CHRIST

1. Introduction.

The death of Christ, the incarnate Son of God, is the most remarkable event in all history. Its uniqueness was demonstrated in various ways. Centuries before it occurred it was foretold with an amazing fulness of detail, by those men whom God raised up in the midst of Israel to direct their thoughts and expectations to a fuller and more glorious revelation of Himself. The prophets of Jehovah described the promised Messiah, not only as a person of high dignity and as one who should perform wondrous and blessed miracles, but also as one who should be "despised and rejected of men", and whose labours and sorrows should be terminated by a death of shame and violence. In addition, they affirmed that He should die not only under human sentence of execution, but that "it pleased the Lord to bruise Him, **He** hath put Him to grief" (Isa. 53:10), yea, that Jehovah should cry, "Awake, O sword, against My Shepherd, and against the man that is My Fellow, saith the Lord of hosts: smite the Shepherd" (Zech. 13:7).

The supernatural phenomena which attended Christ's death clearly distinguishes it from all other deaths. The obscuration of the sun at midday without any natural cause, the earthquake which clove asunder the rocks and laid open the graves, and the rending of the vail of the temple from top to bottom, proclaimed that He who was hanging on the cross was no ordinary sufferer. So too that which followed the death of Christ is equally noteworthy. Three days after His body had been placed in Joseph's tomb and the sepulchre securely sealed, He, by His own power (John 2:19; 10:18), burst asunder the bonds of death and rose in triumph from the grave, and is now alive forevermore, holding the keys of death and hades in His hands. Forty days later, after having appeared again and again, in tangible form before His friends, He ascended to heaven from the midst of His disciples. Ten days after, He poured out the Holy Spirit, by whom they were enabled to publish to men out of every nation in their respective languages, the wonders of His death and resurrection.

As another has said, "The effect was not less surprising than the means employed to accomplish it. The attention of Jews and Gentiles was excited; multitudes were prevailed upon to acknowledge Him as the Son of God, and the Messiah; and a church was formed, which, notwithstanding powerful opposition and cruel persecutions, subsists at the present hour. The death of Christ was the great subject on which the apostles were commanded to preach, although it was known beforehand that it would be offensive to all classes of men; and they actually made it the chosen theme of their discourses. 'I determined', Paul said, 'not to know anything among you, save Jesus Christ and Him crucified' (1 Cor. 2:2). . . . In the N. T., His death is represented as an event of the greatest importance, as a fact on which Christianity rests, as the only ground of hope to the guilty, as the only source of peace and consolation, as, of all motives, the most powerful to excite us to mortify sin and devote ourselves to the service of God" (Dr. John Dick).

Not only was the death and resurrection of Christ the central theme of apostolic preaching and the principal subject of their writings, but it is remembered and celebrated in heaven: the theme of the songs of the redeemed in glory is the person and blood of the Saviour: "Saying with a loud voice, Worthy is the Lamb that was slain to receive power, and riches, and wisdom, and strength, and honour, and glory, and blessing" (Rev. 5:12). "The Atonement made by the Son of God, is the beginning of the ransomed sinner's hope, and will be the theme of his exultation, when he shall cast his crown before the throne, singing the song of Moses and of the Lamb" (Mr. James Haldane).

Now it is evident from all these facts that there is something peculiar in the death of Christ, something which unmistakeably separates it from all other deaths, and therefore rendering it worthy of our most diligent, prayerful, and reverent attention and study. It behooves us by all that is serious, solemn, and salutary, to have just and right conceptions of it; by which is meant not merely that we should know when it happened, and with what circumstances it was attended, but that we should most earnestly endeavour to ascertain what was the Saviour's **design** in submitting to die upon the cross, why it was that Jehovah smote Him, and exactly what has been accomplished thereby.

But as we attempt to approach a subject so important, so wonderful, yet so unspeakably solemn, let us remember that it calls for a heart filled with awe, as well as a sense of our utter unworthiness. To touch the very fringe of the holy things of God ought to inspire reverential fear, but to take up the innermost secrets of His covenant, to contemplate the eternal counsels of the blessed Trinity, to endeavour to enter into the meaning of that unique transaction at Calvary, which was vailed with darkness, calls for an especial degree of grace, fear, and humility, of heavenly teaching and the humble boldness of faith. Our prayerful hope is that He who is pleased to use ciphers (1 Cor. 1:28) to promote His glory, may condescend to grant us now a special measure of the guidance of the Holy Spirit, and deign to bless these articles to not a few of those whom God has loved with an everlasting love.

What has Christ done in order to secure the salvation of sinners? what is the import of that death of His on which salvation hinges? In the outset we may be fairly warned of what must be the consequences of submitting the question to human reason or of bringing the world's wisdom into the inquiry. "The preaching of the cross is to them that perish **foolishness**, but unto us which are saved it is the power of God" (1 Cor. 1:18). To which the apostle added, "But we preach Christ crucified, unto the Jews a stumblingblock, and unto the Greeks foolishness; but unto them which are called, both Jews and Greeks, Christ the power of God, and the wisdom of God". In view of these statements, it was an easy matter for by-gone generations of the saints to anticipate what would be the inevitable result when the wisdom of the world, which was fully arrayed against the Gospel which Paul preached, should be constituted its interpreter, or should presume to accommodate it to worldly principles.

Sixty years ago Mr. James Inglis writing in "The Waymarks of the Wilderness" on "The Atonement", said, "There is one question which underlies all theological controversy; and as we approach the crisis, it is coming more and more to the surface. The question in it all really is; whether God or man is to be the supreme; whether the glory of God or the supposed interest of man is the center around which all is to revolve; whether the will of God is to be supreme and unquestioned, or whether every expression of it is to be brought to the bar of human reason; and whether everything in theology, as in morals, is to be judged by its reasonableness and its apparent usefulness to man. Those who claim to be the most advanced theologians and moralists, exalt human nature to the place of the sovereign arbitrator of truth and right, and seek to apply their favourite maxim regarding earthly governments to the Divine government also: that it exists only for the sake—as yet they would scarcely have the hardihood to say by the **consent**—of the governed.

'This fundamental question of Divine or human supremacy underlies the views men adopt of the inspiration and authority of Scripture. On one side the question is simply, What is written? on the other side a right is claimed to decide what ought to be written—the very presumption which Satan taught our first parents regarding what God had said. When this claimed right is exercised, little of revelation is left unmodified. One of the first points on which proud reason comes into conflict with what is written, is the natural condition of man. Nor need we be surprised if it should revolt against the Divine estimate of fallen man, and against the sentence under which he lies—as by nature a child of wrath, dead in trespasses and sins, vile, polluted, helpless, and hopeless in himself. It is only the Spirit of God that can convince a man of sin in the Scriptural sense; and so long as the appeal is to human reason, the Scriptural view of man's condition must be rejected. Though it cannot be denied that the facts in the case, whether in the history of an individual or of mankind, most painfully corroborate the Scriptural view, and though the most humbling descriptions of human depravity in the Word of God seem to be only history condensed, there is a wonderful facility in off-setting these sad realities by an ideal excellence, and in covering them up by glowing delineations of the possibilities of human progress. The power of self-deception and self-flattery in the human heart is amazing. The admirable sentiments which are elegantly expressed in the writings of men whose lives were very far from exemplifying them, serve to cover up the deep and general depravity of the age in which they lived. Their modern admirers estimate themselves rather by their admiration of these virtuous sentiments, than by what they know themselves to be in life and character. Never is this power of self-deception and self-flattery more signally illustrated than when it comes into the sphere of Christianity, substituting the Sermon on the Mount for the discourses of heathen moralists, and reckoning all the graces of the renewed man, if not the living perfections of the Word made flesh, among the possibilities of human cultivation. That man is fallen, may not be denied; but we are taught that the evil is incidental, not inherent, and may be traced to physical degeneracy, the influence of a disordered world, of bad example and defective education. While undeveloped and dormant in the soul, there is inherent nobility, the germ of all excellence, which only needs to be aroused and cherished, until it expands into a perfection which renders it meet for the inheritance of the saints in light.

"Such views of the natural condition of man lead to a corresponding modification of the Scriptural doctrine of **regeneration,** which, according to our liberal theologians, is but the awakening of the dormant excellence of man, giving a new turn to misdirected affections and powers, and is the first step in the development of his inherent nobility. The testimony of Scripture as to the utter ruin of man, and the necessity of being born again, in the singularly emphatic terms used with reference to the one as well as the other, might seem to present an insuperable objection to the self-exalting scheme; but an evasion of the objection has already been provided for in a theory of inspiration which permits every thing in the Scriptures which is irreconcilable with their theology, to be explained away as the exaggeration of enthusiasts or the daring imagery of Eastern poets.

"In such a system of doctrine the mission of Christ can have no place, except as it provides for this moral development, or aids it. For, first of all, in the daring exaltation of man, the revealed character of God is tampered with; His perfections are rendered tributary to the supposed interest of His creatures; His righteousness, holiness, and truth are resolved into benevolence; so that there are no claims of justice to be satisfied, no holiness and truth to be vindicated, and sin is only to be taken cognizance of in so far as it may interfere with the well-being of the creature. The humiliation, suffering, and death of the Son of God furnished but an impressive spectacle, by which the evil effects of an unconditional pardon of sin might be averted, and by which the heart of the sinner might be melted and conciliated. The life and death of Christ, in short, are the moral influences by which the dormant excellence of the soul is aroused, love to God and man engendered, and by which the wanderer is to be won into the path of virtue. The 'influence' of the Holy Spirit, rather than His **personal agency,** now comes in to give effect to the truth and to aid the moral development, just as in the natural world the influence of the sun's rays change the desolation of winter into the verdure of spring".

When we remember that the Atonement is the most important subject which can engage the minds of either men or angels: that it not only secures the eternal happiness of all God's elect, but also gives to the universe the fullest view of the perfections of the Creator: that in it are hid all the treasures of wisdom and knowledge, while by it are revealed the unsearchable riches of Christ: that through the very Church which has been purchased thereby is being made known to principalities and powers in the heavenlies manifold wisdom of God (Eph. 3:10)—then, of what supreme moment must it be to understand it aright! But how is fallen man to apprehend these truths to which his depraved heart is **so** much opposed? All the force of intellect is less than nothing when it attempts, in its own strength, to comprehend the deep things of God. Since a man can receive **nothing** except it be given him from heaven (John 3:26), much more is a special enlightenment by the Holy Spirit needed if he is to enter at all into this highest mystery.

"Great is the mystery of godliness" (1 Tim. 3:16). Amazing beyond all finite conception is that transaction which was consummated at Golgotha. There we behold the Prince of life dying. There we gaze upon the Lord of glory made a spectacle of unutterable shame. There we see the Holy One of God made sin for His people. There we witness the Author of all blessing made a curse for worms of the earth. It is the mystery of mysteries that He who is none other than Immanuel, should stoop so low as to join together the infinte majesty of Deity with the lowest degree of abasement that was possible to descend into. He could not have gone lower and be God. Well did the Puritan Sibbes say, "God, to show His love to us, showed Himself God in this: that He could be God and go so low as to die" (Vol. 5, p. 327).

To what source then can we appeal for light, for understanding, for an explanation and interpretation of the Cross? Human reasoning is futile, speculation is profane, the opinions of men are worthless. Thus, we are absolutely shut up to what God has been pleased to make known to us in His Word. If it be true that we can know nothing about the origin of the old creation save what the Holy Scriptures reveal—the wild and conflicting guesses of science "falsely so called" (1 Tim. 6:20)—only serving to make this the more evident; then much more are we entirely dependent upon the teaching of Holy Writ concerning the foundation on which the new creation rests. In his splendid work on "The Atonement" (1867) Dr. A. A. Hodge rightly affirmed, "I insist that, as the Gospel is wholly a matter of Divine revelation, the answer to the question, What did Christ do on earth in order to reconcile us to God? be sought **exclusively** in a full and fair induction from **all** the Scriptures teach upon the subject. From a survey of all the matter revealed on the subject, what, in the judgment of a mind unprejudiced by theories, did the sacred writers intend us to believe? The result of such an examination, unmodified by philosophy or secular analogies, is alone, we insist, the true redemptive work of Christ".

Well did this deeply-taught servant of God say, "unmodified by secular analogies". The truth of God has been grossly perverted, the honour of Christ grievously sullied, and the people of God (who were too lazy to diligently study the Scriptures for themselves) have often been misled by the superficial efforts of irreverent preachers, who sought "illustrations" from the imaginary analogies in human relations. For example: the case of a criminal is supposed, in whose character there is no redeeming trait, who is condemned to death for his aggravated crimes. When he stands upon the scaffold, the Queen of

England is supposed to send her son and heir to die in the villian's stead, that he may again be turned loose upon society. Yet this monstrous and revolting supposition was offered last century as an illustration of John 3:16 in the discourse of a popular preacher of wide reputation.

"The plan of redemption, the office of our Surety, and the satisfaction which He rendered to the claims of justice against us, have no parallel in the relations of men to one another. We are carried above the sphere of the highest relations of created beings into the august counsels of the eternal and independent God. Shall we bring our own line to measure them? We are in the presence of Father, Son, and Holy Spirit; one in perfections, will, and purpose. If the righteousness of the Father demands a sacrifice, the love of the Father provides it. But the love of the Son runs parallel with that of the Father; and not only in the general undertaking, but in every act of it, we see the Son's full and free consent. In the whole work we see the love of the Father as clearly displayed as the love of the Son; and again, we see the Son's love of righteousness and hatred of iniquity as clearly displayed as the Father's, in that work of which it were impossible to tell whether the manifestation of love or righteousness is most amazing. In setting out upon the undertaking we hear the Son say with loving delight, 'Lo, I come to do Thy will'; as he contemplates its conclusion, we hear Him say, 'Therefore doth My Father love Me, because I lay down My life, that I might take it again'. They are one in the glorious manifestation of common perfections, and in the joy of all the blessed results. The Son is glorified by all that is for the glory of the Father. And while, in the consummation of this plan, the wisdom of God—Father, Son, and Holy Spirit—shall be displayed, as it could not otherwise have been, to the principalities and powers in heavenly places, ruined man will, in Christ, be exalted to heights of glory and bliss otherwise unattainable".

But while no parallel to the great transaction of the Atonement, or to the relations of the Father, Son and Holy Spirit as to its accomplishment, can be found in any of the relations of mere creatures to one another, God has graciously adopted a series of types, historical and ceremonial, to the illumination of His great plan, and especially to the illustration of the various aspects of the offices and work of Christ. In these, Divine wisdom is signally displayed. By means of the typical system God was educating men for the "good things to come", and preparing human language to be a fitting medium for the revelation of His grace in Christ. By introducing the Levitical system God has shown us the sense in which such words (in the N. T.) as sacrifice, priesthood, propitiation and redemption, are to be understood. We cannot here give an exposition of these types (D. V. a separate article will be devoted to them), our purpose in referring to them here simply being to call attention to the fact that **they** supply the needed key to unlock this N. T. mystery.

That which is outstandingly prominent in the typical sacrifices of the O. T. is, first, that they were offered to God, having Him for their object and end, instead of being pageants for making impressions on men. Second, that they were expiatory, atoning for sin, blotting out iniquities. Third, that just as the sins of the offerer were imputed to the victim, so the excellency of the victim was ascribed to the offerer. Fourth, that something more was effected by these offerings than an atonement being made for sins—a **satisfaction** was offered to God's holiness and justice. This leads us to call attention to the heading or title for this series of articles, and here we cannot do better than give below a digest from Dr. Hodge's able comments on this point:—

During the latter part of the nineteenth century the word "Atonement" became commonly employed to express that which Christ wrought in order to the salvation of His people. But before then, the term used since the days of Anselm (1274), and habitually employed by all the Reformers, was "Satisfaction". The older term is much to be preferred, first, because the word, "Atonement" is **ambiguous.** In the O. T. it is used for an Hebrew word which signifies "to cover by making expiation". In the N. T. it occures but once, Rom. 5:11, and there it is given as the rendering for a Greek word meaning "reconciliation". But reconciliation is the **effect** of the sin-expiating and God-propitiating work of Christ. On the other hand, the word "Satisfaction" is not ambiguous. It always signifies that complete work which Christ did in order to secure the salvation of His people, as that work stands related to the will and nature of God.

Again; the word "Atonement" is **too limited** in its signification for the purpose assigned to it. It does not express **all** that Scripture declares Christ did in order to meet the complete demands of God's law. It properly signifies, the expiation of sin, and nothing more. It points to that which Christ rendered to the justice of God, in vicariously bearing the **penalty** due the sins of His people; but it does not include that vicarious **obedience** which Christ rendered to the precepts of the law, which obedience is imputed to all of the elect. On the other hand, the term "Satisfaction" naturally includes both of these. "As the demands of the law upon sinful men are both preceptive and penal —the condition of life being 'do this and live', while the penalty denounced upon disobedience is, 'the soul that sinneth it shall die'—it follows that any work which shall fully satisfy the demands of the Divine law in behalf of men must include (1) that obedience which the law demands as the condition of life, and (2) that suffering which it demands as the penalty of sin".

May the Lord graciously fit both writer and reader to contemplate and apprehend this wondrous theme in such a way that much fruit may issue to His glory and praise.

—ARTHUR W. PINK.

THE EVERLASTING COVENANT

Dr. H. Martin began his invaluable work on the Atonement by saying: "If we would investigate the very doctrine of Atonement which God's Word sets forth, —avoiding arbitrary and capricious speculations, and illegitimate and useless trains of thought,—it must be laid down at the outset, as a proposition of transcendent importance,—That the Doctrine of the Atonement ought to be discussed and defended as inside the Doctrine of the Covenant of Grace". Alas that so many have failed to do so, with the result that the foundations of faith have been undermined, Truth has been perverted, the people of God perplexed, and the enemies of the Lord afforded every opportunity to attack with no little success an, otherwise, impregnable fortress.

The Satisfaction or Atonement of Christ ought never to be separated from its **source**, that source being the eternal agreement entered into by the Persons of the Godhead. That which Christ wrought out in time was what had been determined upon in the timeless counsels of the Holy Trinity. That which was accomplished here in this world was what had been decided upon and ordained in heaven before ever this earth had an existence. Christ did not propose the plan of reconciliation or offer to carry it into execution. Instead, it was proposed unto Him. The Father drew the plan and proposed it unto Christ as the God-man, the Mediator. He most cheerfully engaged to carry out that plan. The Holy Spirit was a witness unto that great transaction between the Father and the Son, and He recorded it in the eternal volume of the Divine decrees, and has accurately and authentically stated it in the Holy Scriptures, in which we read of "the blood of **the everlasting covenant**" (Heb. 13:20).

In summarising the evangel of God's grace Mr. S. E. Pierce (1814), than whom few have proclaimed the everlasting Gospel so blessedly since the days of the apostles, said, "The Three in Jehovah are co-equal, co-essential, co-eternal. They have loved the elect with an everlasting love: They are jointly engaged towards the persons of the elect, and have an interest in them. Their love for them is all expressed in Christ: in Him they were chosen, in Him they were blessed with all spiritual blessings, in Him they were predestinated to the adoption of children, in Him they were accepted; and all this before the foundation of the world. Also on the foreviews of the fall, a covenant was entered into betwixt the Eternal Three, concerning the salvation of the elect, and how they should be raised up, above and beyond all the ruins of the fall, by the undertakings of their eternal Head; who, becoming their Surety, engaged to become incarnate, and by His obedience unto death, even the death of the cross, would save them in Himself, and by Himself alone, with an everlasting salvation".

When writing or thinking of the work of redemption, we ought to ascend to its **source**, and begin with the consideration of that eternal agreement between the Persons of the Godhead, on which the whole dispensation of Divine grace to the elect is founded. It is through failure to recognize or refusal to believe what is revealed in the Scripture of Truth concerning the relation of Christ's mediatorial work to the everlasting covenant, which has engendered so many fruitless controversies upon the Atonement. Once we are enabled to discern the fact of, the terms of, the immutability of the Covenant of Grace, then such questions as the injustice of an Innocent person suffering for the guilty, of the certain efficacy or contingent inefficacy of Christ's sacrifice securing what it was designed to effect, and of the scope or extent of the Atonement— whether for all mankind or only the elect of God—are settled once for all.

That Scripture expressly reveals an organic connection between the Covenant of Grace and the sacrifice of Christ is plain from the words of Heb. 13:20, "The blood of the everlasting covenant". So again in Zech. 9:11 we find God saying to the Mediator, "By the blood of Thy covenant I have sent forth Thy prisoners out of the pit wherein is no water". Our blessed Lord Himself when instituting the memorial Supper, said, "This cup is the new covenant in My blood" (1 Cor. 11:25). It is the blood which maketh an atonement for the soul (Lev. 17:11), but it does so because that blood is "the blood of the everlasting covenant". In Heb. 8:6 Christ is expressly denominated the "Mediator of a better covenant", and in Heb. 7:22 "A Surety of a better covenant". Yea, Scripture represents Him as the very **substance** of the covenant. "I the Lord have called Thee in righteousness and will hold Thine hand, and will keep Thee, and give Thee for a **covenant** of the people, for a light of the Gentiles" (Isa. 42:6).

Now a covenant is an agreement between two parties who are under mutual engagements. Something is to be done by one of the parties, in consequence of which the other party binds himself to do something in return. When a master, for example, enters into an agreement or covenant with a servant, he prescribes certain duties to be performed by the servant, and promises to recompense him with suitable wages. By consenting to the compact, the servant becomes bound to perform the stipulated work, and the master is bound to bestow the reward when the term of labour is finished. In a covenant therefore there are two parts, a condition and a promise. When the condition of the covenant is met, the performer is by right entitled to the reward.

In his truly excellent work "The Satisfaction of Christ" (1650), Dr. J. Owen, the prince of the Puritans, when treating of the everlasting covenant pointed out, "There are five things required to the complete establishing and accomplishing of such a compact and agreement: 1. That there be sundry persons, two at least, namely, a promiser and undertaker, agreeing voluntarily together in counsel and design, for the accomplishment, and bringing about some common end, acceptable to them both, so agreeing together; being both to do somewhat, that they are not otherwise obliged to do; there must be some common end agreed on by them, wherein they are delighted; and if they do not both voluntarily agree to what is on each hand incumbent, it is no covenant or compact, but an imposition of one upon the other. 2. That the person promising, who is the principal engager in the covenant, do require something at the hand of the other, to be done or undergone, wherein he is concerned. He is to prescribe something to him, which is the condition, whereon the accomplishment of the end aimed at, is to depend. 3. That he make to him who doth undertake, such promises as are necessary for his supportment and encouragement, and which may fully balance in his judgment, all that is required of him, or prescribed to him. 4. That upon the consideration of the condition and promise, the duty and reward prescribed and engaged for, as formerly mentioned, the undertaker do voluntarily address himself to the one, and expect the accomplishment of the other. 5. That the accomplishment of the condition being pleaded by the undertaker, and approved by the promiser, the common end originally designed, be brought about and established.

"These five things are required to the entering into, and complete accomplishment of such a covenant, convention, or agreement, as is built on personal performances; and they are all eminently expressed in the Scripture, to be found in the compact between the Father and the Son". Let us adopt these statements as our divisions:—

1 The Agreement between the Father and the Son.

God and the Mediator agreed together in counsel for the accomplishment of a common end, namely, the promotion of the manifested glory of God in the salvation of His elect. In Zech. 6:13 we read, "And the counsel of peace shall be between them both": the reference here is to the Lord Jehovah, and the Man whose name is "The Branch" of the previous verse. The "counsel of peace" signifies the compact or agreement between Them as to the reconciliation between God and His sinful people. There was a voluntary concern of the Father and the Son for the accomplishment of the work of peace in bringing us to God. It is to this that Isa. 9,6 also refers: there Christ is called the "Wonderful Counsellor", as concurring in the design of His Father, and with Him, to be the Child born and the Son given "to **us**", that He might be the Prince of peace. In that connection, and in that passage (only) is Christ called "the everlasting Father", because His everlasting "children" (Heb. 2:13) were being covenanted for. So too in Zech. 13:7 the Mediator is addressed by Jehovah as "My Fellow", because they had taken counsel together about the work of our salvation.

The Mediator's voluntary acceptance of the Father's proposal is clearly seen from His own language in that great Messianic Psalm, "Lo, I come—in the volume of the book it is written of Me—I delight to do Thy will, O My God; yea, Thy law is within My heart" (Psa. 40:7). These words express His cheerful compliance with the terms of the covenant, and those terms—God's "will"—are recorded in the volume of the Divine decrees concerning the salvation of God's elect, and transcribed in the Holy Scriptures. "Animated with zeal for the glory of His God, and with intense love for those who have been given to Him, He 'rejoiced in the habitable parts of the earth' (Prov. 8:31), taking the highest pleasure to assume the character of our Redeemer, although He was fully cognizant of the unparalleled humiliation and sufferings to which it would be necessary to submit in order to accomplish His design.

"In consequence of His consent to the terms of the covenant, He was constituted the Head or Representative of His people. He became a public person, who acted in the name of others" (Dr. Dick). Therefore is Christ called the "Surety of the covenant" (Heb. 7:22). A "surety" is a person who gives security for another that he will perform something which the other is bound to do; that is, in case of failure, will perform it for him. This work, as given to our Saviour, signifies that He came under obligation to fulfill the conditions of the covenant for His people. He undertook to yield that obedience unto the law which they owed, and to make satisfaction to Divine justice for their sins. A surety for a bankrupt is one who engages to satisfy his creditors, by paying his debts. Hence, when the Lord Jesus is called the Surety of the new covenant, it denotes that He undertook to discharge the whole debt which His people owed to the Law of God, the debt of obedience, the debt of suffering.

As we have seen above, our Saviour is also called the "Mediator" of the covenant. This title imports that He interposes between God and men to reconcile them: "There is one God, and one Mediator between God and men, the man Christ Jesus" (1 Tim. 2:5). For this office He is qualified by the constitution of His person. Possessed of the Divine nature, He agreed to assume the human, that He might be allied to both parties. As this will come before us, D.V., in the fourth of our articles on "The Atonement" we will not enlarge upon it now. Very similar in force to the "Mediator" of the new covenant, is Christ's title of "the last Adam" (1 Cor. 15:45), which points both a comparison (Rom. 5:14) and a contrast (Rom. 5:15, 18) between Him and the first Adam. This designation of our Saviour's declares that He is a **federal Head,** by whose conduct others are affected.

2. The Work the Father gave the Son to do.

There are many expressions used in both Old and New Testaments which, when carefully weighed, oblige us to conclude that there was an eternal transaction between the Father and the Son: the former assigning to the latter a certain task in order to securing the salvation of His elect. First, it was required of the Surety that He should take on Him the nature of those whom He was to bring to God; therefore do we find Him saying, "A body hast Thou prepared Me" (Heb. 10:5)—that is, appointed for Me. Hence it is said, "God sent forth His son, made of a woman" (Gal. 4:4).

Second, it was required of Him that in this 'body" or human nature, He should be a **servant**, and yield obedience to God; therefore we hear the Father saying of Him, "Behold, My servant" (Isa. 42:1). The Father required from the Mediator perfect obedience to all the precepts of His law, therefore are we told in Gal. 4:4 that He was "made under the law"; and so we hear Him expressing, in view of His future incarnation, His intention to fulfill it—"I delight to do Thy will, O My God; yea, Thy law is within My heart" (Psa. 40:8). He knew and loved the law, and came into this world to honour it by submission to its authority. From the beginning He was ever ready to recognize His obligations to God. As a Boy He was "subject unto" His parents (Luke 2:51). By receiving baptism at the hands of His forerunner, He solemnly and publicly dedicated Himself unto the service of His Father, saying, "Thus it becometh us to fulfill all righteousness" (Matt. 3:15); and His whole conduct was a commentary upon His declaration "I must work the works of Him that sent Me" (John 9:4). Though He were a Son "Yet learned He obedience" (Heb. 5:8).

Third, it was required of Him that He should suffer and undergo what in justice was due those He came to deliver. Satisfaction had to be made for their sins. The glory of the Gospel is, that "grace reigns through righteousness" (Rom. 5:21). Salvation is of grace, but this grace comes to us in a way of **righteousness.** It is grace to us, but it was brought about in such a way that all our debt was paid. Thus God is seen to be both just and merciful: just, in requiring full compensation to His broken law; merciful, because it was He, and not the sinner, who furnished the ransom. The redeemed are saved without any injury to justice. Now Christ was "foreordained before the foundation of the world" as the Lamb whose precious blood was to be shed (1 Peter 1:19, 20). He had received "commandment" to lay down His life (John 10:18). Therefore was He "obedient unto death" (Phil. 2:8), and hence, when the bitter cup, which had been appointed, was presented to Him, He said, "Not My will, but Thine, be done".

3. The Promises the Father made the Son.

The promises of the covenant may be distinguished into two classes: the one, those which immediately respected Christ; the other, which respected His elect. Let us consider the former first. In relation to Christ Himself, God promised to furnish Him with all necessary **preparation for** the arduous work which He had undertaken to perform. Let the reader carefully consult Isa. 11:2, 3; 49:1-3. Again, the Father promised to support Him **in** that work. That work was attended with such difficulties, that created power, although unimpaired by sin, would have been totally inadequate to it. It was to be performed in human nature, and **that** had failed in an easier undertaking, even when possessed of untainted innocence, and of faculties in all their freshness and vigour. Our Saviour was encouraged by the assurance of the Divine presence and assistance: see Isa. 42:1-7.

Blessed is it to behold the Lord Jesus firmly depending upon those promises in the most trying occasions. "For the Lord God **will** help Me; therefore shall I not be confounded: therefore have I set My face like a flint, and I know that I shall not be ashamed. He is near that justifieth Me" (Isa. 50:7, 8). In the spirit of unshaken faith, when His enemies were conspiring against Him, and His few friends were about to forsake Him, He said, "Behold, the hour cometh, yea, is now come, that ye shall be scattered, every man to his own, and shall leave Me alone: and yet I am not alone, because **the Father is with Me**" (John 16:32).

Once more, the Father promised to confer a glorious **reward** upon His Son's **accomplishment** of the work. He promised to invest Him with honour and power: Psa. 110:1; 89:27; 72:8. These promises were fulfilled after His resurrection from the dead, when God gave Him a name above every name: Phil. 2:9-11. He promised too to accomplish and secure the salvation of that people for whom He had obeyed, suffered and died: see Isa. 53:10-12. He would have an offspring, who would arise to call Him blessed, and rejoice in the wondrous benefits which He had purchased and procured for them.

Concerning the promises which respect the elect, they were made in the first instance, **to Christ,** with whom alone God transacted in the Covenant of Grace. Those promises were made to the Surety, for the persons in whose favour they were to be performed had no actual existence, for that transaction took place before Gen. 1:1. A remarkable proof of this is found in Titus 1:2: 'In hope of eternal life, which God, that cannot lie, **promised** (not simply "purposed") before the world began". If eternal life was 'promised before the world began", it follows that it must have been promised to Christ, who was then constituted the federal Head of His people. "Eternal life" is **the** promise, including all others: see 1 John 2:26. With Titus 1:2 should be carefully compared 2 Tim. 1:9.

4. The Son's acceptance of the Conditions.

The covenant engagement into which our Saviour entered was entirely **voluntary** on His part. There existed no previous obligation, nor was there any authority by which He could be compelled to do it. As a Divine person He was subject to no one and acknowledged no superior: "He thought it not robbery to be equal with God" (Phil. 2:6). By a free action of His own will He consented to execute that work which the Father had proposed to Him. Proof of this is found in Psa. 40:6, "Mine ears hast Thou digged", language which takes us back to the servant of Ex. 21:5, 6, who willingly relinquished his rights. So Christ freely and cheerfully undertook to do and suffer the will of His father.

It is important to be clear upon and hold fast this point. Whatever was the will of the Father was the will of the Son; whatever the Father proposed, the Son consented unto. If there are many verses in the N. T. which speak of the Father **sending** the Son, there are also many others which affirm His own voluntariness therein: "The Son of man is **come** to seek and to save that which was lost" (Luke 19:10), "Christ Jesus **came** unto the world to save sinners" (1 Tim. 1:15), etc. His words, "I **delight** to do Thy will, O My God" (Psa. 40:7) forever settle this point.

5. The Father's acceptance of the Work performed.

When Christ had completed on earth the work which had been given Him to do, He "offered Himself without spot to God" (Heb. 9:14). The Lord God evidenced His acceptance of the Mediator's sacrifice, First, by preserving His body in the grave. With absolute trust the Saviour said, "Thou wilt not leave My soul in hades; neither wilt Thou suffer Thine Holy One to see corruption" (Psa. 16:10). Nor did He. Second, by raising Him from the dead: "Whom God hath raised up, having loosed the pains of death" (Acts 2:24). In bringing forth the crucified Saviour from the tomb, God showed to all created intelligences that He **was** well pleased with the work His incarnate Son had performed. Moreover, He was raised not as an act of grace or mercy, but "According to the spirit of **holiness**" (Rom. 1:4). Thus the death of Christ was the payment of His peoples' debt; His resurrection, was God's receipt. Third, God evidenced His acceptance of Christ's mediatorial work by exalting His Servant-Son above all creatures: Phil. 2:9-11.

6. The Son's claim to the promised Reward.

This is what Christ's present intercession on High consists of. It is not through strong crying and tears, in earnest pleadings and supplications, as in the days of His humiliation, but in **laying claim** to His rightful remuneration, namely, that God shall now save "unto the uttermost" all those for whom He acted as Surety. The whole of His high priestly prayer in John 17 is to be regarded in **that** light. There we behold the Mediator demanding the accomplishment of the whole compact and the fulfilment of all the promises which have been made to Him, when He undertook to become a Saviour (vv. 1-4, 9, 12-16); concluding by saying, "Father, **I will** that they also, whom Thou hast given Me, be with Me where I am; that they may behold My glory, which Thou hast given Me" (v. 24).

In the 2nd Psalm there is a remarkable unfolding of our present theme, which is understood by very few of the Lord's people today. It contains a series of prophecies, which, like all others, are to receive a **double** fulfillment. We confine ourselves now to the original accomplishment of them. First, we behold the leaders of the Gentiles and the rulers of the Jews taking counsel together against Jehovah and against His Christ (vv. 1-3). This found its fulfillment at the cross, as Acts 4:25-28 plainly shows. Second, we have Jehovah's response (vv. 4-6): His derision against them, His threat to visit them in wrath—which was fulfilled at the destruction of Jerusalem (Matt. 22:7); His exaltation of Christ (v. 6). Third, we hear Jehovah saying, "I will **declare** the decree" (v. 7), i.e., I will now make known, publish abroad, the mystery of the everlasting Covenant. He owns Christ in resurrection: see Acts 13:33. Then He says, "**Ask** of Me and I shall give Thee the Gentiles for Thine inheritance" etc (v. 8). "Ask of Me"—put in your claim for the fulfillment of that promise to which Thou art now justly entitled.

7. The Immutability of the Covenant.

From all that has been before us it should be evident, beyond all possibility of contradiction, that the Covenant of Grace is entirely **unconditional** so far as man is concerned, for it was made long before he drew his first breath. The elect themselves cannot be a party to it, though their salvation was the purpose of it. How far, far below the glorious Truth of God are the wretched thoughts and opinions of people today! The idea which now prevails, is that Christ's death has merely made possible the salvation of men, that it has simply afforded sinners an opportunity of becoming reconciled to God. Instead, the death and resurrection of Christ was the ratification of an eternal agreement between the Father and the Son, which infallibly ensures the salvation of all named in it. Therefore did Christ affirm, "And this is the Father's will which hath sent Me, that of **all** which He hath given Me I should lose **nothing**" (John 6:39).

The covenant-work of Christ not only gave full and final satisfaction to God for the failed responsibilities of His people, atoning for all their sins and securing a perfect righteousness for them, but it also procured for them the gift of the regenerating Spirit, and with Him, the gifts of repentance, faith, preservation and glorification. God "**hath** blessed us with **all** spiritual blessings in the heavenlies in Christ" (Eph. 1:3). When? When we believed? No, "**according** as He hath chosen us in Him **before** the foundation of the world". That was not merely an election **to** those blessings, but an actual **bestowment** of them upon us in Christ, and this secures the actual communication of them to us now **through** Christ. In like manner we are told, "Who hath saved us ... according to His own purpose and grace, which was given us in Christ Jesus before the world began" (2 Tim. 1:9). The "grace" there, is in addition to God's "purpose", and that "grace" **included** regenerating grace, justifying grace, sanctifying grace, believing grace, preserving grace, glorifying grace: compare 2 Tim. 1:1.

The salvation of God's elect is not left contingent on their repenting and believing, but is made certain by God's promise to Christ that He "**shall** see of the travail of His soul and be **satisfied**" (Isa. 53:10). And that promise is made good by giving the Holy Spirit to each of those for whom Christ fulfilled His covenant-engagements. Though God's elect be yet in a state of nature, some of them dead in trespasses, wallowing in the mire of this world, yet has the Father assured His Son, "By the blood of Thy covenant I have sent forth **Thy** prisoners out of the pit wherein is no water" (Zech. 9:11). Christ by His death ransomed and made those captives, yet in the pit, **His own.** He acquired a legal right to their persons, and therefore, in His own appointed time, does God, by His Spirit, bring them forth on to resurrection ground. Assured of this, Christ declared, "Other sheep I have, which are not of this fold: them also I must bring, and they **shall** hear My voice; and they **shall** be one flock, one Shepherd" (John 10:16).

How invincibly certain then is the salvation of every one for whom Christ covenanted! Each of them shall yet say with David, "He hath made with me (in Christ) an everlasting covenant, ordered in all things and **sure**: for this is all my salvation, and all my desire" (2 Sam. 23:5). And as good old Matthew Henry said of this covenant: "It was **from** everlasting in the counsel and contrivance of it, and **to** everlasting in the continuance and consequences of it". This covenant is based on God's own promise and confirmed by His oath: "Wherein God, willing more abundantly to show unto the heirs of promise the immutability of His counsel, confirmed it by an oath: That by two immutable things, in which it was impossible for God to lie, we might have a strong consolation who have fled for refuge to lay hold upon the hope set before us: Which we have as an anchor of the soul, both sure and steadfast, and which entereth into that within the vail; Whither the Forerunner is **for us** entered, Jesus, made an hight priest, forever after the order of Melchizedek" (Heb. 6:17-20).

—ARTHUR W. PINK.

CHRISTIAN EXPERIENCE

In the good providence of God, and through the courtesy and kindness of one of our English brethren, we had the loan of a small book which has long been out of print. It was written by a servant of the Lord comparatively very little known, who laboured in London and Devonshire more than a century ago. Samuel Eyles Pierce was a man exceptionally favoured and deeply taught of the Holy Spirit. The reading of his book brought such blessing to our own soul, we felt constrained to copy out more than half of it for insertion in "Studies". The book is entitled "Growth in Grace". It treats of true Christian spiritual experience, and shows that this consists solely of a Holy-Spirit-communicated knowledge to the understanding and heart of the "new man", of the Divine perfections in the person and work of the God-man.

After an introduction, which contains a summary of the contents of the twelve sections that follow, in chapter one Mr. Pierce treats of "the eternal designs of the Father, Son and Holy Spirit towards the elect, with some account of, their distinctive and respective outgoings of love towards them in Christ Jesus from everlasting". As we have ourselves written, in the past, so freely on Election and Predestination, we have omitted this section. In chapter two of "How the Eternal Three, as the God of all grace, displayed their love and mercy towards and on the elect in their fallen state and circumstances". The ground covered by this section is fully dealt with by us in the present series on "The Atonement". Chapter three is on "Regeneration", which we have explained in our booklet on "The New Birth". Saving one chapter on "Communion", which we hope to quote from freely in a future series of articles on this subject, D.V., from our own pen, we have reprinted, with only a few brief omissions, the whole of the remainder of the book. If the Lord is pleased to bless these to our readers as richly as He has to us, we shall be amply repaid for our toil.

The first of eight articles follows. They will well bear reading and re-reading, again and again. But let each one first lift up his or her heart in prayer to God, humbly but earnestly beseeching Him for Christ's sake, to sanctify and bless them to your own soul, to open your understanding to receive their blessed teachings, to write them upon your heart. May He get great praise and glory to Himself by them.—A. W. P.

It requires much Divine light and unction from the Spirit of God to treat of His sacred influence and operations within and upon the souls of the regenerate. In all attempts on a subject of such vast and eternal importance great attention ought to be given to what is revealed concerning His work in the written Word. For though the Holy Spirit works like Himself, as an Almighty agent, yet He works always agreeably to the written Word. To talk of His operations apart from the Word is wholly enthusiastic. And to talk of the **Word** without His own life-giving energy accompanying it to our hearts, is to neglect Him who only can make it unto us "spirit and life". We can never fully conceive the infinite delight which the Father hath in His Son as Mediator, and in His finished work. The everlasting acceptance, which Christ's person, righteousness, and sacrifice have found with Jehovah the Father, exceeds our utmost conception. In consequence of which our Saviour appears on His mediatorial throne, as "the Lamb newly slain", with His heart burning with love to His redeemed. He remembers them with everlasting kindness. He looks on them with inexpressible complacency, rejoicing in them and over them to do them good. As enthroned in glory, and invested with all power in heaven and in earth, He sends down His Holy Spirit to bring home "His banished ones", whose work and office in the souls of the regenerate are wholly of grace, the fruit and effects of the everlasting covenant. The Holy Spirit works within and upon them as "the travail of Christ's soul". He views them as the objects of the Father's everlasting love, and out of His own free and sovereign love towards them, He works most freely and effectually within them.

Like as the Father gave the greatest evidence of His everlasting love to the elect by the gift of His son, to live and to die for them, when they were sinners, enemies, and ungodly (Rom. 5:8); and as Christ manifested His love, when we were in our sins and in our blood, for He loved us and gave Himself for us, and was made sin and a curse for us, and washed us from our sins in His own blood; so the Holy Spirit, whose love is fixed on the persons of His people, and who loves them as the elect of God and members of Christ's mystic body with the same everlasting love, with which the Father and the Son do, is also on His part pleased to give such a demonstration of it, when they are dead in trespasses and sins, as proves it to be wholly of **grace**. His whole work within them and on them is but the fruit and effects of His love. God's election is an election of **persons**. Christ died for **persons**. The Holy Spirit works on **persons**. And His work is eternal and will last forever. His work, when truly and scripturally explained, is strictly pure Gospel. It consists in bringing the elect into the state of knowing the Lord, in furnishing them by His new-creation within them with those spiritual and supernatural faculties, which capacitate them for the enjoyment of the Father's love, and for communion with Christ in all the benefits and blessings of His salvation, and in leading them off entirely from every hope, but **in the Lord alone**. The foundation of which is laid in Jesus, of whom the believer says, "He is the rock, His work is perfect" (Deut. 32:4). The work of the Holy Spirit in the souls of the regenerate is great and glorious, worthy of Himself. It is perfect, and truly Divine. As the Spirit of the living God, He enters into the souls of His people, making them alive to God (Eph. 2:1). Having quickened them, He abides in them forever. He is a witness to us for the Lord Jesus (Heb. 10:15), and sets His seal to the eternal value, virtue and efficacy of His obedience and sacrifice, and testifies that all the sins of all the elect are freely and fully forgiven by the Father in consequence thereof (1 John 1:7).

He shows how Christ's obedience unto death is the everlasting righteousness of His church, that His people are complete in Him; that He works effectually on them in consequence of it, and forms them in regeneration for Jehovah's praise.

At which time they are born sons of God, heirs of God, and joint-heirs with Christ, interested in, and effectually introduced into the kingdom of grace, which cannot be moved. As the new-born, they are brought into a state of grace openly and **manifestatively**. In their new birth also they are furnished with all those spiritual faculties, perceptions, and affections, which qualify them for those spiritual enjoyments which belong to this state. The Holy Spirit is pleased to enlarge those faculties. He shines upon, quickens, and draws forth the senses and affections of the **inner man**, and exercises them on Christ and God in Him. The state into which the child of God is brought by regeneration and conversion, is a state of perfect acceptance with God, perfect justification before God, and of free and full pardon of all sins. God's eternal purpose of grace toward His people now begins to take place actually **in** them (2 Tim. 1:9).

The believer hath a new understanding given him in regeneration to know the Lord his God. He hath spiritual ears to hear the voice of God in His Word speaking unto him and saying, "I am the Lord **thy** God". He hath spiritual eyes, the eyes of his understanding, which are opened by the Holy Spirit, that he may have a spiritual sight and perception of Jesus Christ, as made by the Father unto him, 'Wisdom and righteousness, sanctification, and redemption" (1 Cor. 1:30). He hath spiritual hands to handle the Word of life, a spiritual appetite to feed on the bread of life, a thirst for Christ the water of life, and feet to walk in Christ, who is the way, the truth, and the life. In brief, the believer is exactly suited by the work of the Holy Spirit within him to take in Christ, and to have fellowship with Him, who is all-sufficient to fill every faculty of the new-born soul, and to give and continue perfect joy and satisfaction to every one of his spiritual senses thereof.

One of the greatest blessings, and which includes all others, which the Lord God bestows on His people, is contained in these declarations of His, "I will be thy God", "I am the Lord thy God", "I am thine"; which contain the utmost expressions of grace, that can be revealed on earth or made known in heaven, where the Lord will be our everlasting light, and our God our glory. God is the God of His people, and as such He hath bestowed Himself in all His persons; and He exercises all His perfections on their behalf. His love is the fountain and spring of all their happiness in time and eternity. His mercy, which is but the exercise of His love to them in their fallen state, encompasses them as with a shield. His compassions are expressed towards them every moment. His eye is continually upon them. His ear is open to their cry; and that greatest of all promises, which contains in it all others, He fulfills in them: "I will give them an heart to know Me, that I am the Lord, and they shall be My people, and I will be their God" (Jer. 24:7).

The prophet Isaiah gives us a beautiful account of the Divine procedure, and how the Lord acts with His regenerate ones: "I will pour water upon him that is thirsty, and floods upon the dry ground", which Jehovah Himself thus explains, saying, "I will pour My Spirit upon thy seed, and My blessing upon thine offspring". The effect follows, "And they (under the out-pouring of the Holy Spirit) shall spring up as among the grass, as willows by the watercourses" (44:3, 4). The Holy Spirit, by putting forth His life-giving power through the Word in their souls, by opening their renewed minds to receive the true knowledge of God in Christ from the Word, and by anointing them with His own unctuous influences, constrains them to acknowledge the Lord **to be** their God: "One shall say, I am the Lord's; and another shall call himself by the name of Jacob; and another shall subscribe with his hand unto the Lord, and surname himself by the name of Israel" (Isa. 44:5). Thus God is pleased to acknowledge His people, to call them by name, to bring them near Himself, to induce them to acknowledge Him, and call Him the God of their salvation. Thus He is pleased to speak unto them by the prophet, "Ye shall be My people, and I will be your God" (Jer. 30:22). And speaking of them and of His grace which should take place in them, He says, **see** Jer. 32:38-41.

Now it is one great part of the Holy Spirit's work and office in the souls of the regenerate to open and explain the Scriptures to their understanding, to open their understanding to know the Gospel as contained in them, so as to make them the foundation of their faith, and the experience of their hearts, and by this means to bring them to a scriptural and saving knowledge of God the Father and His Son Jesus Christ, which knowledge contains. "Eternal life". So saith our blessed Lord: see John 17:3. And this knowledge is entirely received from the Word through the Divine teachings of the Lord the Spirit. It is a point of vast moment in experience to know, that what is revealed in the written Word belongs to us, that God speaks to us in it, that He makes known to us His everlasting love by it, and that what He speaks to **one** belongs to **all** His saints. He said to His great favourite Moses, "Thou hast found grace in My sight, and I know thee by name" (Ex. 33:17). It is equally true of all His people, that they have found grace in His sight; and it proves to a demonstration that He knows them by name, when in the day of His power He brings them to an effectual knowledge of **themselves** and of **Himself** as the Lord their God. As the Lord's people are the high favourites of His grace, so He delights to acknowledge them to be His peculiar ones. He says of them, "This people have I formed for Myself, they shall show forth My praises". He opens His whole soul unto them, "Thou wast precious in My sight, and I have loved thee". Which expressions the Holy Spirit fills with Divine energy, sets home upon the mind, and through them conveys such ideas of the Father's love as fill the believer with unutterable joy.

All the communion which saints have with the Father and the Son, is carried on by this means, which brings them most highly to prize and esteem the sacred Word of inspiration. In it they read that, "God is love". By mixing faith with the revealed account of it, they have the actual experience and enjoyment of it in their souls. By which means they become witnesses for God; setting their seals to the truth of what the mouth of the Lord hath spoken. They see Christ in the Word, have a spiritual perception of Him from it, believe in Him by it, rest on Him from the warrant they have for so doing in it, and have an inward knowledge of what He saith in John 5:24. They have a spiritual knowledge of Christ in their renewed understanding: see 1 John 5:20. And what they know of Christ in their understanding, they believe concerning Him in their hearts: Rom. 10:10; and by believing, Christ dwells in their hearts (Eph. 3:17). And thus faith, which John makes the evidence of the new birth (1 John 5:1), is exercised upon our Lord Jesus Christ, as our righteousness and atonement; and on God our heavenly Father, as reconciled unto us by the death of His Son; so that the state of the believer before God is truly blessed.

He is **manifestatively** justified from all things. God hath forgiven him all trespasses. He is freed from all condemnation. "The law of the Spirit of life in Christ Jesus hath made him free from the law of sin and death" (Rom. 8:2). He shines in Christ, and outshines the angels in glory. Having received life from the Spirit of Christ, he is quickened up unto life eternal. The whole body of sin within him has received its death-wound; the heart and life-giving influence in and throughout every one of his corrupt affections, are mortified. So that he can sing (though he feels them struggling within him), "There is therefore now no condemnation to them which are in Christ Jesus" (Rom. 8:1). And he rejoices at seasons in hope of the promised glory, which the God of all grace hath by Jesus Christ called him unto, having fully invested him with a right and title to it, and a complete meetness for it: and He saith, by way of encouragement to him (let him see and feel what he may of his inward corruptions and spiritual enemies), "Fear not, I am thy shield and thy exceeding great reward" (Gen. 15:1).

As it respects the **experience** of a regenerate and believing person, especially when first brought home to God by effectual calling, it consists in, and may be expressed as containing, the following important inward perceptions. The person feels, and is sensible of the effectual change wrought in the mind, viz. that he is passed from a state of darkness into a state in which God's marvelous light shines and enlightens him. He finds himself "a new creature in Christ Jesus", in a new world, and entered on a new and spiritual state; that he hath a new heart given him, new affections and desires formed within him; that old things are passed away, and all things are become new. He clearly perceives that he once was darkness, but now he is **light in the Lord** (Eph. 5:8). In the light of everlasting life he clearly sees the whole world out of Christ is in the arms of the wicked one; that all have sinned and come short of the glory of God, and that by the deeds of the law no flesh living can be justified. Which truths enter into his very soul, form a true part of his experience, and lead him to admire the grace of God in opening his eyes, in awakening his mind, and in showing him the way to experience the blessings of pardoning salvation by faith in Christ Jesus. A true sight of sin comes from the teaching of the Holy Spirit, and is the fruit of spiritual life imparted in regeneration. And believing on the Lord Jesus Christ is the **best**, and may be said to be the **only evidence** of our regeneration, because all other fruits and effects truly spiritual flow from it: see 1 John 5:1.

Regeneration is faith in the habit; and the experience of it **in believing on the**

Son of God is the evidence and manifest proof of inward regeneration. Now it forms and constitutes a peculiar part of the experience of one who is new-born to think much of Christ, of His love, and most precious blood-shedding. The Holy Spirit forms in the newly enlightened mind some precious thoughts of Christ, and draws them forth as He leads him to meditate on some portions of Scripture, in which Christ is revealed; so that he is by the secret and mysterious influence of the Holy Spirit engaged in thinking on Christ as most exactly suited to his case. And the subject is found in real experience, especially at first, to be **Christ crucified.** Jesus in His bloody sweat, as made sin, as having been wounded in soul and body, when He sustained the whole curse and punishment due to the sins of all His people, is what the mind chiefly dwells on. The new-born soul takes its life from Christ's death, its health and cure from Christ's wounds, its purity from Christ's blood-shedding, and its consolations from Christ's sorrows and bitter passion. By these views of Christ, and as the mind is engaged in spiritual meditations thereon, the Holy Spirit exalts Christ in the heart, and makes Him ineffably precious. So that Paul's high prizings of Christ now suit the frame of the new-born soul: Gal. 6:14.

The Holy Spirit lets in a view, and gives a sense and enjoyment of the Father's everlasting love upon the mind, as He creates views of it in the conceptions of the new-born soul from the following passage: John 3:16. On this inestimable love, expressed in this ineffable gift, the mind is for a season swallowed up, lost in wonder, and filled with admiration. What he sees in this love, feels, and enjoys of it, exceeds all expression. In the enjoyments of it, sin is perfectly hated, self perfectly hid, the world trampled on, and the soul is filled with joy unspeakable and full of glory. Thus the Holy Spirit is pleased to reveal Christ, and in due season to shed forth the perfections of His righteousness, and to lead the mind of the believer to fix itself on Him for ever and ever.

In believing on the Lord Jesus, it pleases the Father to **manifest** His pardoning mercy, which is received and enjoyed in the hearing and believing of God in the simplicity of His own Word; wherein He says, "I have blotted out as a thick cloud thy transgressions" etc (Isa. 40:22). Which as it was uttered upon the footing of Christ's atonement, so it is made known in its Divine efficacy to the regenerate in their believing on Jesus: see Acts 10:43. When these words, "I will be merciful to your unrighteousness, and your sins and your iniquities will I remember no more", are received by faith through the influence of the Holy Spirit, the soul hath a manifestative apprehension of God's pardoning mercy, and from the experience of it is led to break forth thus, "Who is a God like unto Thee, that pardoneth iniquity" etc (Micah 7:19). As a partaker of a spiritual birth, he hath a nature inherent in his soul, which cannot sin; in which all grace and holiness are contained. He is sanctified by the indwelling of the Holy Spirit. He is justified, and therefore he is **blessed**, for the Lord Himself says, see Psa. 32:1, 2. He is favoured with a spiritual view of the righteousness of Christ, which leads him to count all things but loss and dung in comparison with Him and His obedience unto death.

The blessing of adoption belongs to him, and he cannot but admire this marvelous grace, which God has bestowed most freely upon him. He has union with Christ and God in Him, which the Holy Spirit makes manifest by the communion which the believer hath with the Son and with the Father, through His Divine indwelling in the soul. In Christ the believer is built up, and builded together for an habitation of God through the Spirit. And his comforts are the fruits and effects of these blessings, which he is made a free partaker of, and put into actual possession of, when it is given unto him to believe in the Lord Jesus for everlasting life. "The God of hope" fills him with all joy and peace in believing, and he abounds in hope through the power of the Holy Spirit. These peculiar comforts, which the soul hath the first enjoyment of upon its return to God, flow from the sight and sense it hath of its salvation from sin, of its deliverance from its former state, and of its being delivered from the wrath to come. They chiefly consist in a sense of God's pardoning mercy, in an enjoyment of His peace which surpasses all understanding, in an apprehension of free and full redemption in the blood of the Lamb, and in sweet intercourse with Christ, which produces warm frames, and truly comfortable impressions and feelings. So that from the testimony of sense, as well as from the record which God hath given of His Son, the believer cries out with rapture, "Behold, God is my salvation, I will trust and not be afraid; for the Lord Jehovah is my strength and my song; He is become my salvation" (Isa. 12:2). The soul

see the things of God (John 3:3), still less apprehend them (1 Cor. 2:14). The Holy Spirit has to shine in our hearts (not intellects) in order to give us "the knowledge of the glory of God in the face of Jesus" (2 Cor. 4:6). And even that spiritual knowledge is but fragmentary. The regenerated soul has to **grow** in grace and in the knowledge of the Lord Jesus (2 Pet. 3:18).

The principal prayer and aim of Christians should be that we "walk worthy of the Lord unto all pleasing, being fruitful in every good work and **increasing** in the knowledge of God" (Col. 1:10).

—ARTHUR W. PINK.

---

is now admitted to know and feel that the Love of Christ passeth knowledge.

Thus, **the kingdom**, which consists in "righteousness, and peace, and joy in the Holy Spirit", is enjoyed in the believer's heart. He brings down into the mind and sheds abroad therein the love of God. He reveals Christ in the Word and by the Word to the believer, as his hope of glory, opens to his view the unsearchable riches of Christ, and shows him that the whole body of sin has received its death-wound, giving him to experience that "They that are Christ's have crucified the flesh with its affections and lusts" (Gal. 5:24), that the death of Christ extends its influence over the whole body of sin and death, and gives him to see that living by faith on Christ is the life and spring of all spirituality. He opens to his view this inestimable truth, that whom Jehovah did "predestinate, them He also called, and whom He called, them He also justified, and whom He justified, them He also glorified", teaching him therefrom that effectual calling proceeds from, and is the first evidence of election, that manifestative justification follows upon effectual calling, and that such are as fully entitled to heaven, as though they were instated in glory; which blessed lessons the Holy Spirit accompanies with Divine power and comfort, so that the believer rejoices in God (Rom. 5:11).

O my soul! here is matter for wonder, gratitude, and praise, which thou mayest well exercise thyself in. Yet when thou hast done thy best, the subject and the grace of it will exceed all blessing and praise. Thou canst not express thy sense of the subject better than by an address to the Holy Trinty for Their inestimable grace. O Thou God and Father of all Thy family in heaven and earth! They are all one in Christ Jesus, and Thou lovest them all in Him with one and the same everlasting and invariable affection. Thou art pleased to bring them in Thine own good time into the kingdom of Thy dear Son. I praise Thee for Thy love to me in **Christ.** I adore Thee for Thy mercy in sending down the Holy Spirit into my heart, and for making me a partaker of a spiritual birth, whereby I am capacitated for the enjoyment of Thy love, and to hold communion with Thee by faith in Christ Jesus through the gracious influences of Thine eternal Spirit. I would present my best praises to Thee. O Thou blessed Saviour! who art the Son of the Father, that I am born into Thy kingdom of grace, made a partaker of Thee, and brought into communion with Thee. O Thou Spirit of Jehovah! it is to Thee I owe my second birth and every faculty of the new man. O Thou Divine Spirit of all grace I bless Thee for quickening me with new and spiritual life, for enlightening the eyes of my mind to know Jesus, and the Father's love in Him; for revealing Christ in me, and giving me a view of Him as the everlasting treasury of grace and glory. Secure all the praise to Thyself, and go on to show me more of the riches of the Father's love and glory, and exalt in my heart the Saviour's work and fulness. Grant this, Holy Spirit, to the honour of the Father and the Son, to whom as co-equal and co-eternal in one Jehovah be everlasting praise. Amen.

—S. E. PIERCE, 1804.

"When ye shall have done all those things which are commanded you, say, We are unprofitable servants" (Luke 17:10)—our obedience has profited God nothing.

Nay, we go further: our Lord Jesus Christ added nothing to God in His essential being and glory, either by what He did or suffered. True, blessedly and gloriously true, He **manifested** the glory of God **to us,** but He added nought to God. He Himself expressly declares so, and there is no appeal from His words: "My goodness extendeth not to Thee" (Psa. 16:2). The whole of that Psalm is a Psalm of Christ. Christ's goodness or righteousness reached unto His saints in the earth (Psa. 16:31), but God was high above and beyond it all, God only is "the Blessed One" (Mark 14:61, Gr.).

It is perfectly true that God is both honoured and dishonoured by men; not in His essential being, but in His official character. It is equally true that God has been "glorified" by creation, by providence, and by redemption. This we do not and dare not dispute for a moment. But all of this has to do with His manifestative glory and the recognition of it by us. Yet had God so pleased, He might have continued alone for all eternity, **without making known** His glory unto creatures. Whether He should do so or not, was determined solely by His own will. He was perfectly blessed in Himself before the first creature was called into being. And what are all the creatures of His hands **unto Him** even now? Let Scripture again make answer:—

"Behold, the nations are as a drop of a bucket, and are counted as the small dust of the balance: behold, He taketh up the isles as a very little things; and Lebanon is not sufficient to burn, nor the beasts thereof sufficient for a burnt offering. All nations before Him are as **nothing**; and they are counted to Him less than nothing, and vanity. To whom then will ye liken God? or what likeness will ye compare unto Him?" (Isa. 40:15-18). **That** is the God of Scripture; alas, He is still "the **unknown** God" (Acts 17:23) to the heedless multitudes. "It is He that sitteth upon the circle of the earth, and the inhabitants thereof are as grasshoppers; that stretcheth out the heavens as a curtain, and spreadeth them out as a tent to dwell in: that bringeth the princes to nothing; He maketh the judges of the earth as vanity" (Isa. 40:22, 23). How vastly different is the God of Scripture from the "god" of the average pulpit!

Nor is the testimony of the New Testament any different from that of the Old: how could it be, seeing that both have one and the same Author! There too we read, "What in His times He shall show, who is the blessed and **only** Potentate, the King of kings, and Lord of lords: Who only hath immortality, dwelling in the light which no man can approach unto; whom no man hath seen, nor can see; to whom be honour and power ever more, Amen" (1 Tim. 6:16). Such an One is to be revered, worshipped, adored. He **is** solitary in His majesty, unique in His excellency, peerless in His perfections. He sustains all, but is Himself independent of all. He gives to all, but is enriched by none.

Such a God cannot be found out by searching; He can be known, only as He is **revealed** to the heart by the Holy Spirit through the Word. It is true that creation demonstrates a Creator, and that, so plainly, men are "without excuse"; yet, we still have to say with Job, "Lo, these are parts of His ways: but **how little** a portion is heard of Him? But the thunder of His power who can understand?" (26:14). The so-called argument from design by well-meaning "Apologists" has, we believe, done much more harm than good, for it has attempted to bring down the great God to the level of finite comprehension, and thereby has lost sight of His solitary excellence.

Analogy has been drawn between a savage finding a watch upon the sands, and from a close examination of it he infers a watch-maker. So far so good. But attempt to go further: suppose that savage sits down on the sand and endeavours to form to himself a conception of this watch-maker, his personal affections and manners; his disposition, acquirements, and moral character—all that goes to make up a personality; could he ever think or reason out a real man—**the** man who made the watch, so that he could say, "I am acquainted with him"? It seems trifling to ask such questions, but is the eternal and infinite God so much more within the grasp of human reason? No, indeed. The God of Scripture can only be known by those to whom He **makes Himself known.**

Nor is God known by the intellect. "God is Spirit" (John 4:24), and therefore can only be known spiritually. But fallen man is not spiritual, he is carnal. He is dead to all that is spiritual. Unless he is born again, supernaturally brought from death unto life, miraculously translated out of darkness into light, he cannot even

(Continued on Page 23)

STUDIES IN THE SCRIPTURES

"Search the Scriptures" John 5 : 39

Copyright in all English-speaking Countries.

Editor: Arthur W. Pink, Morton's Gap, Ky., U. S. A.
Hon. Agent in England: Mr. A. Winstone, 2, Lennox Villas, Hewlett Road, Cheltenham.
Hon. Agent in Australia: Mr. G. Ardill, The Christian Workers' Depot.
Commonwealth and Reservoir Streets, Sydney.

The Decrees of God.

The decree of God is His purpose or determination with respect to future things. We have used the singular number as Scripture does (Rom. 8:28, Eph. 3:11), because there was only one act of His infinite mind about future things. But **we** speak as if there had been many, because our minds are only capable of thinking of **successive** revolutions, as thoughts and occasions arise, or in reference to the various **objects** of His decree, which being many seem to us to require a distinct purpose for each one. But an infinite understanding does not proceed by steps, from one stage to another: "Known unto God are **all** His works from the beginning of the world" (Acts 15:18).

The Scriptures make mention of the decrees of God in many passages, and under a variety of terms. The word "decree" is found in Psa. 2:7 etc. In Eph. 3:11 we read of His "eternal purpose". In Acts 2:23 of His "determinate counsel and foreknowledge". In Eph. 1:9 of the mystery of His "will". In Rom. 8:29 that He also did "predestinate". In Eph. 1:9 of His "good pleasure". God's decrees are called His "counsel" to signify they are consummately wise. They are called God's "will" to show He was under no control, but acted according to His own pleasure. When a man's will is the rule of his conduct, it is usually capricious and unreasonable; but **wisdom** is always associated with "will" in the Divine proceedings, and accordingly, God's decrees are said to be "the counsel of His own will" (Eph. 1:11).

The decrees of God relate to all future things without exception: whatever is done in time, was foreordained before time began. God's purpose was concerned with everything, whether great or small, whether good or evil, although with reference to the latter we must be careful to state that while God is the Orderer and Controler of sin, He is **not** the Author of it in the same way that He is the Author of good. Sin could not proceed from a holy God by positive and direct creation, but only by decretive permission and negative action. God's decree is as comprehensive as His government, extending to all creatures and all events. It was concerned about our life and death; about our state in time, and our state in eternity. As God works **all** things after the counsel of His own will, we learn from His works what His counsel is (was), as we judge of an architect's plan by inspecting the building which was erected under his directions.

God did not merely decree to make man, place him upon the earth, and then leave him to his own uncontrolled guidance; instead, He fixed all the circumstances in the lot of individuals, and all the particulars which will comprise the history of the human race from its commencement to its close. He did not merely decree that general laws should be established for the government of the world, but He settled the **application** of those laws to all particular cases. Our days are numbered, and so are the hairs of our heads. We may learn what is the **extent** of the Divine decrees from the dispensations of providence, in which they are executed. The care of Providence reaches to the most insignificant creatures, and the most minute events—the death of a sparrow, and the fall of a hair.

Let us now consider some of the **properties** of the Divine decrees. First, they are **eternal**. To suppose any of them to be made in time, is to suppose that some new occasion has occurred, some unforeseen event or combination of circumstances has arisen, which has induced the Most High to form a new resolution. This would argue that the knowledge of the Deity is limited, and that He is growing wiser in

(Continued on Page 48)

IMPORTANT NOTICES

Please advise promptly of change of address, otherwise copies will be lost in the mails.

We are glad to send a sample copy to any of our friends whom you believe would be interested in such a publication.

Send to Mr. I. C. Herendeen, 433-435, The Arcade, Cleveland, Ohio, for a list of our publications. He has published many of our books and booklets.

This Magazine is published as a work of faith and labour of love. The Editor and his wife gladly give their services. It is freely sent to all who will read it. No charge is made for it.

Christians who feel definitely lead to do so, may have fellowship with us in this ministry. Those outside the U. S. A., please send only INTERNATIONAL Money Orders made out to Morton's Gap, Kentucky, U. S. A. See that it is made out in American money.

CONTENTS

The Epistle to the Hebrews	26
The Satisfaction ("Atonement") of Christ	32
The Everlasting Covenant	37
Satanic Assaults	43

THE EPISTLE TO THE HEBREWS

26. The Two Classes of Professors: Heb. 6:7, 8.

Our preceding article was entitled "The Twofold Working of the Spirit". This was suggested by the contents of the first six verses of Heb. 6. In them we find persons belonging to two entirely different classes are spoken of. The former, one in whom a work of Divine grace had been wrought, effectually applying to them the "great salvation" of God. The latter, one upon whom a work of Divine grace was also wrought, transforming its objects to a considerable degree, yet falling short of actually regenerating them. "The Lord is good to all: and His tender mercies are over all His works" (Psa. 145:9), but the **richness** of His "mercy" is reserved for the objects of His great love (Eph. 2:4). So too God puts forth His power in **varying** degrees, proportioned to the work which He has before Him. Thus, Christ referred to His casting out of demons "with the **finger** of God" (Luke 11: 20). Speaking to Israel, Moses said. "With a strong **hand** hath the Lord brought thee out of Egypt" (Ex. 13:9). When referring to the amazing miracle of the Divine incarnation Mary said, "He hath showed strength with His **arm**" (Luke 1:51). But when Paul prayed that God would enlighten His saints to apprehend His stupenduous miracle of grace in salvation, it was that they might know "the **exceeding greatness** of His power to usward".

God's power was put forth and is displayed in the natural creation (Rom. 1:20). It will be made known in Hell, upon the vessels of wrath fitted to destruction (Rom. 9:22). It is exercised upon the reprobate in this life (in some more than in others, according to His sovereign pleasure) in subduing their corruptions, restraining their sins, reforming their characters, causing them to receive the doctrine of the Gospel. But the greatest excellency and efficacy of His power is reserved for His beloved people. His power toward **them** is such that it exceedeth all our thoughts: "Now unto Him that is able to do exceeding abundantly above all that we ask or think, **according to the power** that worketh **in us**" (Eph. 3:20).

The recognition of only one of the two distinct operations of God's Spirit upon men has divided theologians into two opposing camps. On the one hand, are the Arminians, who insist that Scripture teaches a **common** grace of God toward all men, a grace which may be despised. So far they are right, for Jude 4 expressly speaks of a class who turn "the **grace** of our God into lasciviousness". But they err when they teach there is no special grace, which is always efficacious upon those in whom it works. On the other side, the majority of modern Calvinists (the older ones did not) deny a common grace of God to all men, and insist in **distinguishing** grace to the elect only. In this they are wrong, and hence their unsatisfactory interpretations of Heb. 6:4-6 and 10:26.

Now as we have shown in our last article, James 1:17 tells us "Every good gift and every perfect gift is from above" etc. Two distinct "gifts" are here referred to. Scripture draws a clear line of distinction between that which God calls "good", and that which He designates "perfect". The main difference between them being that, usually, "good" is applied to something which is temporal, "perfect" to that which is spiritual. The operations of the Spirit upon the non-elect produces that which is "good", that which accomplishes a useful purpose in time, that which is serviceable to God's elect. But His operations upon the children of God produces that which is "perfect", i.e. spiritual, supernatural, eternal. The difference between these two classes and their relation to God in time, was clearly foreshadowed in the Old Testament. The commonwealth of Israel was the type of Christendom as a whole; the "remnant according to the election of grace" in Israel (Rom. 11:5), represented the regenerated people of God now. Hence in both the Tabernacle and the Temple there were two distinct grades of worshippers; so there are today. Those who are merely nominal christians are the outer-court worshippers; the regenerated Christians, who have been made "kings and **priests** unto God" (Rev. 1:6), worship in the holy place (Heb. 10:19). Both classes are contemplated in Heb. 6.

In the short passage which is to be before us on this present occasion, the apostle sums up and makes a searching application of all that he has been writing about in the preceding verses, and this in the form of a parable or similitude. In the context two different classes of people are viewed, though at first it is by no means easy to distinguish between them, the reason for this being that they have so much in common. They had both enjoyed the same external privileges, had been enlightened under the same Gospel ministry, had alike been made "partakers of the Holy Spirit", and had all made a good profession. Yet, of the second class it had to be said, as Christ said to the young ruler, "One thing thou lackest", namely, the shedding abroad of God's love in their hearts, evidenced by **leaving all** and following Christ.

The first class is addressed in the opening verses of our chapter, where the apostle bids the truly regenerated people of God "Go on unto perfection", i.e. having left the temporal shadows, seek to apprehend that for which they had been apprehended—live in the power and enjoyment of the spiritual, supernatural, and eternal. This, the apostle had said, "will we do, if God permit" (v. 3). Divine enablement was needed if they were to "possess their possessions" (Obad. 17), for the regenerate are just as dependent upon God as are the unregenerate. The second class are before us in vv. 4-6, where we have described the principal effects which the common operations of the Spirit produce upon the natural faculties of the human soul. Though those faculties be wound up to their highest pitch, yet the music which they produce is earthly not heavenly, human not Divine, fleshly not spiritual, temporal not eternal. Consequently, they are still liable to apostatise, and even though they should not, they are certain to perish eternally.

The apostle's design in this 6th chapter was to exhort the Hebrews to **progress** in the Christian course (vv. 1-3), and to **persevere** therein (vv. 12-20). The first exhortation is presented in v. 1 and qualified in v. 3. The **motive** to obedience is drawn from the danger of apostacy: (vv. 4-6, note the opening "for"). His purpose in referring to this second class (of unregenerate professors, who apostatise) was, to warn against the outcome of a continuance in a state of slothfulness. Here in the similitude found in vv. 6, 7, he continues and completes the same solemn line of thought, showing what is the certain and fearful doom of all upon whom a regenerating work of grace is not wrought. First, however, he describes the blessedness of the true people of God.

"For the earth which drinketh in the rain that cometh oft upon it and bringeth forth herbs meet for them for whom it is dressed, receiveth blessing from God; But that which beareth thorns and briers is rejected, and is nigh unto cursing; whose end is to be burned" (vv. 7, 8). In taking up these verses we shall endeavour to give, first, an interpretation of them; second, make an application of their contents. The interpretation respects, in its direct and local reference the **Jews,** or rather, two classes among the Jews; the application belongs to all who come under the sound of the Gospel.

The two verses quoted above are designed to illustrate and confirm the solemn admonition found in the six preceding verses, therefore are they introduced with the word "for". In the context two classes of people are in view, both of which were, according to the flesh, Jews. This we have sought to establish in our previous expositions. With the first class the apostle identified himself, note the "we" in v. 3; from the second class Paul dissociates himself, note the words "those" in v. 4 and "they" in v. 6. So, too, two different pieces of ground are now described: first, fruitful ground, which depicts those who have been truly regenerated, and who in consequence, had received the Word into good and honest hearts. Second, unfruitful ground, which represents that class against whose sin and doom the apostle was warning the Hebrews; namely, those who, however great their privileges and fair their professions, bring forth only thorns and briers, who, being rejected by God, are overtaken with swift and terrible destruction.

"For the earth which drinketh in the rain". The prime reference is to the Jewish nation. They were God's vineyard (see Isa. 5:7, 8; Jer. 2:21 etc.). It was unto them God had sent all His servants, the prophets, and last of all His Son (see Matt. 21:35-37). The "rain" here signifies the Word, or Doctrine which the Lord sent unto Israel: "My doctrine shall drop as the rain" (Deut. 32:2 and cf. Isa. 55:10, 11). Note how when Ezekiel was to prophesy or preach, his message would "drop" as the rain does (21:2 and cf. Amos 7:16). The figure is very beautiful. The rain is something which no man can manufacture, nor is the Word of human origin. Rain comes down from above, so is the Gospel a heavenly gift. The rain refreshes vegetation, and causes it to grow, so too the Doctrine of God revives His people and makes them fruitful. The rain quickens living seeds in the ground, though it imparts no life to dead ones; so the Word is the Spirit's instrument for quickening God's elect (John 3:5; James 1:18), who previously had (federal) life in Christ.

There is nothing in nature that God assumes the more into His own prerogative than the giving of rain, The first reference to it in Scripture is as follows, "For the Lord God had not caused it to rain upon the earth" (Gen. 2:5). All rain is from God, who gives or withholds it at His pleasure. The sending of rain He appeals to as a great pledge of His promises and goodness: "Nevertheless He left not Himself without witness, in that He did good, and gave us rain from heaven" etc. (Acts 14:17). Whatever conclusions men may draw from the commonness of it, and however they may imagine they are acquainted with its causes, nevertheless God distinguishes Himself from all the idols of the world in that none of them can give rain: "Are there any among the vanities of the Gentiles that can cause rain?" (Jer. 14:22). Hence the prophet said, "Let us now fear the Lord our God, that giveth rain" (Jer. 5:24).

The high sovereignty of God is also exhibited in the manner of His bestowal and non-bestowal of rain: "Also I have withholden the rain from you, when there were yet three months to the harvest: and I caused it to rain upon one city, and caused it not to rain upon another city: one piece was rained upon, and the piece whereon it rained not withered" (Amos 4:7). Thus it is absolutely in connection with His providential sending of the Gospel to nations, cities, and individuals: it is of God's disposal alone, and He exercises a distinguishing authority thereon. "Now when they had gone throughout Phrygia and the region of Galatia, and were **forbidden** of the Holy Spirit to preach the Word in Asia. After they were come to Mysia, they assayed to go into Bithynia: **but** the Spirit suffered them not" (Acts 16:6, 7). God sends His Gospel to one nation and not to another, to one city and not to another—there are many large towns both in England and U. S. A. where there is no **real** Gospel preached today—and at one season and not at another.

The natural is but a shadowing forth of the spirtiual. What a contrast was there between Egypt (figure of the world), and Canaan (type of the Church)! "For the land, whither thou goest in to possess it, is not as the land of Egypt, from whence **ye came out,** where thou sowedst thy seed, and waterest with thy foot, as a garden of herbs. But the land, whither ye go to possess it, is a land of hills and valleys, and drinketh water of the rain of heaven: A land which the Lord thy God careth for; the eyes of the Lord thy God are always upon it, from the beginning of the year unto the end of the year . . . I will give you the rain of your land in his due season, the first rain and the latter rain" (Deut. 11:11, 12, 14). Thus, there were two special wet seasons: the first in October (the beginning of Israel's year), when their seed was cast into the ground: the other in March when their corn was nearly grown. Hence we read, "Jordan overfloweth all his banks all the time of harvest" (Josh. 3:15, and cf. 1 Chron. 12:15). Besides these, were many "showers" (Psa. 65:10).

"The rain that cometh oft upon it". The reference is to the repeated and frequent ministerial showers with which God visited Israel. To them He had called, "O earth, earth, earth, hear the Word of the Lord!" (Jere. 22:29). It was looking back to these multiplied servants which Jehovah had sent to His ancient people that Christ said, "O Jerusalem, Jerusalem, that killest the prophets, and stonest them which are sent unto thee, **how often** would I have gathered thy children together" (Matt. 23:37). This then was the "earth" in which were the plants of God's husbandry.

In what follows to the end of the passage the apostle distributes the plants into two classes: "herbs" (v. 7), "thorns and briers" (v. 8). The former, represent those who, having believed and obeyed the Gospel, brought forth the fruits of practical godliness. These constituted that "remnant according to the election of grace" (Rom. 11:5), which obtained mercy, when the rest of their brethren according to the flesh were blinded. These still continued to be the vineyard of the Lord, a field which He cared for. They formed the first Gospel church, gathered out from the Hebrews, which brought forth fruit to the glory of God, and was blessed by Him. The latter, were made up of obstinate unbelievers on the one hand, who persistently rejected Christ and His Gospel; and on the other hand, of those who embraced the profession of the Gospel, but after a season returned again to Judaism. These were rejected of God, fell under His curse, and perished.

"And bringeth forth herbs". Several have noted the close resemblance which our present passage bears to the parable of the Sower, recorded in the Gospels. There are some noteable parallels between them; the one of most importance being, to observe that in both places we have men looked at, not from the standpoint of God's eternal counsels (as for example, Eph. 1:3-11), but according to **human responsibility**. The earth which receives the rain, is a figure of the hearts and minds of the Jews, to whom the Word of God had been sent, and to whom, in the days of Christ and His apostles, the Gospel had been preached. So our Lord compared His hearers unto several sorts of ground into which the seed is cast—observe how the word "dressed" or "tilled" presupposes the seed. What response, then, will the earth make to the repeated rains? or, to interpret the figure, What fruit is brought forth by those who heard the Gospel? That is the particular aspect of truth the Holy Spirit here has before Him.

"And bringeth forth herbs". The verb here properly signifies the bringing forth of a woman that hath conceived with child, cf. Luke 1:31. So here the earth is said to bring forth as from a womb impregnated, the rains causing the seeds to issue in fruit. The Greek word for "herbs" occurs nowhere else in the N. T. It appears to be a general term for vegetables and cereals. It is found frequently in the Sept. as the equivalent of the Heb. "eseb", which has the same extensive meaning. Now just as the cultivator of land has a right to expect that, under the providential blessings of God, his toils shall be rewarded, that the seed he has sown and the ground he has tilled, should yield an increase, so had Jehovah the right to expect fruit from Israel: "And He looked that it (His vineyard) **should** bring forth grapes" (Isa. 5:4).

"Meet for them by whom it is dressed". The Greek may be rightly rendered thus: equally so, as in the margin, "for whom" it is dressed: either makes good sense. "By whom" would look to the actual cultivator; "for whom", the proprietor. The apostle's design here is to show the importance of making a proper use of receiving God's Word: a "meet" or suitable response should be forthcoming. The ministry of the Gospel tests the state of the hearts of those to whom it comes, just as the fallen rain does the ground which receives it; tests it by exhibiting its character from what is brought forth by it. As it is in nature, so it is in grace; the more frequently the rain falls, and the more the ground be cultivated, the better and heavier should be the yield. Thus it is with God's elect. The more they sit under the ministry of the Word, and the more they seek grace to improve what they hear, the more fruit will they yield unto God. Thus it had been with the godly in Israel.

"Receiveth blessing from God". The "blessing" here is not antecedent in the communication of mercies, for that we have at the beginning of the verse; rather is it a consequent upon the bringing forth of "herbs" or fruit. What we have here is God's acceptation and approbation, assuring His care unto a further improvement: "A vineyard of red wine: I the Lord do keep it; I will water it every moment; lest any hurt it, I will keep it night and day" (Isa. 27:2, 3). Three things then are included in God's blessing of this fruitful field: first, His owning of it: He is not ashamed to acknowledge it as His. Second, His watchcare over it, His pruning of the branches that they may bring forth more fruit (John 15:2). Third, His final preservation of it from evil, as opposed to the destruction of barren ground. All this was true of that part of Israel spoken of in Rom. 11:5.

"But that which beareth thorns and briers is rejected" (v. 8). It is important to note that in the similitude there is a common subject of the whole, which is then divided into two parts, with very different events ascribed unto each. The common subject is "the earth", of the nature whereof both parts are equally participant. Originally, and naturally, they differ not. On this common subject, on both parts or branches of it, the "rain" equally falls. And too both are equally "dressed". The difference between them lies, first, in what each part of "the earth" (Israel) produced; and secondly, God's dealings with each part. As we have seen, the one part brought forth "herbs" meet for the dresser or owner: a suitable response was made to the rain given and the care expended upon it. The other, which we are now to look at, is the very reverse.

"But that which beareth thorns and briers is rejected". Everything here is in sharp antithesis from the terms of the preceding verse. There, the good ground, "bringeth forth", the Greek word signifying a natural conception and production of anything in due order and season. But the evil ground "**beareth**" thorns and briers, the Greek verb signifying an unnatural and monstrous production, a casting out in abundance of that which is not only without the use of means, but actually against it. As God said of His Israelitish vineyard, "He looketh that it should bring forth grapes, and it brought forth **wild** grapes" (Isa. 5:2). The Greek for "thorns and briers" is identical with the Sept. rendering of Gen. 3:18, which, in our Bibles, is rendered, "thorns and thistles". Three thoughts seem suggested by the term here given to the product of this evil ground. First, it brought forth that which was of no profit to its owner, that which promoted not the glory of God. Second, "thorns and briers" are of a hurtful and noxious nature: see Ezek. 28:2 etc. Third, these terms tell us that all which is brought forth by the natural man is under the **curse** of God: Gen. 3:18, 4:11, 12.

"But that which beareth thorns and briers is rejected". Land which, after cultivation, brings forth only such products, is abandoned by the farmer as worthless. The Greek word here for "rejected", signifies the setting aside as useless after trial has been made of a thing. The application of it here is to by far the greater part of the Jewish people. First, Christ had warned them "the kingdom of God shall be taken from you and given to a nation bringing forth the fruits thereof" (Matt. 21:43). Second, after their full and open rejection of Himself and His Gospel, Christ told them, "Behold, your house is left unto you desolate" (Matt. 23:38). Third, proof that the Nation as a whole **had been** "rejected" by God, is found in Acts 2:40, when, on the day of Pentecost, Peter bade the believing remnant, "Save yourselves from this untoward generation".

"And is nigh unto cursing". This is in sharp contrast from what was said of the good ground: "receiveth blessing from God". The word "cursing" here, means, "given over to execration", or "devoted to destruction". It was given over to be "burned", which, according to the analogy of faith, means, it would be visited with Divine judgment. Israel had become a barren tree, a cumberer of the ground, and the word had gone forth, "Cut it down" (Luke 12:7). Further proof that Israel as a nation **was** given over to "execration", is found in the solemn incident of Christ's **cursing** of the "fig tree" (Matt. 21:19), figure of the Jews, see Matt. 24:32. True, a short respite had been granted—another "year" (Luke 12:8)—hence the "**nigh** unto cursing".

"Whose end is to be burned". In Eastern lands, when a husbandman discovers that a piece of ground is worthless, he neglects it, abandons it. Next, he breaks down its fences, that it may be known it is outside the bounds of his possession. Finally, he sets fire to its weeds, to prevent their seeds being blown on to his good ground. Thus it was with Israel. In the last chapter of Acts we see how the apostle Paul warned the Jews how that God had set them aside (Acts 28:25-28), and shortly after, the solemn words of Christ in Matt. 22:7 were fulfilled, "He sent forth His armies, and destroyed those murderers, and **burned up** their city".

The contents of Heb. 6:7, 8 are not be restricted to the regenerated and unregenerated Jews, for "as in water face answereth to face, so the heart of man to man" (Prov. 27:19). "This is a similitude most appropriate to excite a desire to make progress in due time; for as the earth cannot bring forth a good crop in harvest except it causes the seed as soon as it is sown to germinate, so if we desire to bring forth good fruit, as soon as the Lord sows His Word, it ought to strike roots in us without delay; for it cannot be expected to fructify, if it be either choked or perish. But as the similitude is very suitable, so it must be wisely applied to the design of the apostle.

"The earth, he says which be sucking in the rain produces a blade suitable to the seed sown, at length by God's blessing produces a ripe crop; so they who receive the seed of the Gospel into their hearts and bring forth genuine shoots, will always make progress until they produce ripe fruit. On the contrary, the earth, which after culture and irrigation, brings forth nothing but thorns, affords no hope of a harvest; nay, the more that grows which is its natural produce, the more hopeless is the case. Hence the only remedy the husbandman has is to burn up the noxious and useless weeds. So they who destroy the seed of the Gospel, either by their indifference or by corrupt affections, so as to manifest no sign of good progress in their life, clearly show themselves to be reprobates, from whom no harvest can be expected. The apostle then, not only speaks here of the fruit of the Gospel, but also exhorts us promptly to embrace it, and he further tells us, that the blade appears presently after the seed is sown, and that grain follows the daily irrigations". (Dr. John Calvin).

The Lord Jesus completed His parable of the Sower by saying, "Take heed therefore **how ye hear**" (Luke 8:18): how you profit by it, what use you make of it; be sure that **you** are a good-ground hearer. **Such**, are those in whom, first, the Word falls, as into "a good and honest heart" (Luke 8:15) i.e. they bow to its authority, judge themselves by it, are impartial and faithful in applying it to their own failures. Second, they "receive" the Word (Mark 4:20): they make personal appropriation of it, they take it home to themselves, they apply it to their own needs. Third, they "understand" it (Matt. 13:23): they enter into a spiritual and experimental acquaintance with it. Fourth, they "keep" it (Luke 8:15): they retain, heed, obey, practice it. Fifth, they "bring forth fruit with patience" (Luke 8:15), they persevere, overcome all discouragements, triumph over temptations, and walk in the paths of obedience. Upon such the "blessing" of God rests.

Now in contrast from the good-ground hearer, are the wayside, stony, and thorny-ground hearers. These, we believe, are they who come under the common or inferior operations of the Holy Spirit, spoken of in our last article. Let it be carefully noted, first, that even of the wayside hearer (the lowest grade of all) Christ said the Seed was "sown in his **heart**" (Matt. 13:19). Second, that of the stony-ground hearers it is said, "the same is he that heareth the Word, and anon with joy receiveth it" (Matt. 13:20), and "for a while believeth, and in time of temptation falls away" (Luke 8:13). Third, that of the stony-ground hearer Christ said, "Which when they have heard, go forth, and are choked with cares and riches and pleasures of this life, and bring no fruit to perfection" (Luke 8:14). Yet none of them had been born of the Spirit. All that they had brought forth, under His gracious operations, was but the works of the flesh —"thorns and briers".

Above, in our interpretation, we called attention to the difference between the "bringeth forth" of herbs in v. 7, and the "beareth" thorns in v. 8. There is a like producing, but an unlike manner and measure. The former "Bring forth in their lives what was before conceived and cherished in their hearts. They had the **root** in themselves of what they bring forth. So doth the word here used signify, viz., to bring forth the fruit of an inward conception. The doctrine of the gospel as cast into their hearts, is not only rain but seed also. This is cherished by grace, as precious seed, and as from a spiritual root or principle in their hearts, bringeth forth precious fruit. And herein consists the difference between the fruitbearing of the true believers, and the works of hypocrits or false professors. These latter bring forth fruit **like mushrooms**, they come up suddenly, have oft-times great bulk and goodly appearance, but are merely a forced excrescence, they have no natural seed or root in the earth. They do not proceed from a living principle in the heart". (Dr. John Owen).

Thus, it should be most carefully borne in mind that the "thorns and **briers**" of v. 8 have reference not to sins and wickedness as men view things, but to the **best** products of the flesh, as cultivated by "religion", and that, as instructed out of the Scriptures, and "enlightened" by the Holy Spirit. This is evident from the fact that the thorns and briers, equally with the "herbs", are occasioned by the same "rain" which had come oft upon the earth, and from which they sprang. However fair the professions of the unregenerate may appear in the eyes of their fellows, no matter what proficiency they may reach in an understanding of the letter of Scripture, nor what their zeal in contending for the faith, loyalty to their church, self-sacrifice in their service; yet, in the sight of Him who searcheth the heart and taketh note of the **root** from which things spring, all is worthless. These products or works are only the fruits of a nature which is under the curse of a holy God.

"But that which beareth thorns and briers is **rejected**" i.e of God. Little did the Jews believe this when Paul penned those words. Their great boast was that they **were** God's people, that He preferred **them** above all others. Nevertheless, though He yet withheld His wrath for a little space, He **had** disowned them. The sad analogy to this is found everywhere in Christendom today. Countless thousands who bear the name of Christ, and who have no doubts but that **they** are among the true people of God, are yet "rejected" by Him. Are you, my reader, among them?

What need is there for every professing Christian to heed that word in 2 Peter 1: 10, "**Give diligence** to make **your** calling and election **sure**"! Those who sit under the ministry of God's Word are upon trial, and it is high time that many of us who have been so long privileged, should call on ourselves to a strict account with respect to our improvement thereof. **What** are we bringing forth? Are we producing "the fruits of righteousness which are by Jesus Christ, unto the glory and praise of God" (Phil. 1:11)? If so, all praise to Him who has made us fruitful. Or are we, though not notoriously wicked persons, yet so far as fruit for God is concerned, cumberers of the ground? If upon inquiry we find ourselves at a loss to be sure of which sort of ground we belong unto, and this because of our barrenness and leanness, unless we are hardened by the deceitfulness of sin, we shall give ourselves no rest until we have bettter evidences of our bearing spiritual fruit.

O let these solemn words search our hearts: "And is nigh unto cursing, whose end is to be burned". Such is the awful fate confronting multitudes of professing Christians in the churches today, who resist all exhortations to produce the fruit of godly living. Corrupt desires, pride, worldliness, coveteousness, are as plainly to be seen in their lives, as are thorns and briers on abandoned ground. O what a thought! professing **Christians**, "nigh unto **cursing**"! Soon to hear their last sermon. Soon to be cut off out of the land of the living. Afterwards to hear from the lips of Christ the fearful sentence, "Depart from Me, ye cursed, into everlasting fire, prepared for the Devil and his angels" (Matt. 25:41).

—ARTHUR W. PINK.

THE SATISFACTION ("Atonement") OF CHRIST.

2. Its Source.

"In approaching this solemn and sacred mystery we should do so with awe and reverence, remembering it is rather a subject of faith and adoration than of reasoning and arguing; a sanctuary open indeed to the meek and sorrowful, to the earnest and contrite, but always to be approached with solemnity and godly fear" (A. Saphir). It is written, "The meek will He guide in judgment and the meek will He teach His way" (Psa. 25:9). The "meek" are they who have no confidence in the flesh, who lean not unto their own understanding, whose dependence is in and upon God alone.

The source of the Atonement or Satisfaction of Christ, is **God**. This of necessity, for only God can produce that which satisfies Himself. Men can no more provide that which will meet the requirements of God's holiness and justice against their sins than they can create a universe: "None of them can by any means redeem his brother, nor give to God a ransom for him" (Psa. 49:7). A perfect law can only be kept by a perfect creature. One who has been rendered impotent by sin is "without strength" (Rom. 5:6) to do anything which is good; therefore deliverance must come from without himself: "For what the law could not do, in that it was weak through the flesh, God sending His own Son in the likeness of sinful flesh, and for sin, condemned sin in the flesh: that the righteousness of the law might be fulfilled in us" (Rom. 8:3, 4).

"In the beginning, God" (Gen. 1:1). Such words at the commencement of Holy Writ are worthy of their Divine Author. God is both the Alpha and Omega. He is the Beginning and the End of everything, for "of Him and through Him, and to Him, are all things" (Rom. 11:36). Nothing can exist apart from God. In creation, in providence, and in redemption, God is the Beginning. But for God, not a creature would have had being. But for God, not a creature could continue for a moment, for "in Him we live, and move, and have our being". But for God's direct permission, sin could not have entered the world; and but for His will in determining, His grace in providing, His power in securing, His Spirit in applying, there had been no satisfaction made for the failed responsibilities of His people.

Yes, God and God alone is the Source of the great and glorious Atonement. His will was the determining factor, His love the motive-spring, His righteousness the incentive, His manifested glory the end. In humbly attempting to amplify the several members of the preceding sentence, we earnestly cry with one of old, "That which I see not teach Thou me" (Job 34:32). May it please the God of all grace to prepare the hearts of both writer and reader to contemplate the supernal glories of the Divine character.

1. The Will of God.

Of necessity this must be the starting-point when considering the ultimate source of anything, for God "worketh all things after the counsel of His own **will**" (Eph. 1:11). It is nowhere said that He worketh all things according to "the requirements of His holiness", though God does not and cannot do that which is unholy. There is no conflict between the Divine will and the Divine nature, yet it needs to be insisted upon that God is a law unto Himself. God does what He does, not simply because righteousness requires Him so to act, but what God does **is** righteous simply because **He** does it. All the Divine works issue from mere sovereignty.

"Creation could be nothing else but a sovereign act. To deny sovereignty here, would be to deny sovereignty altogether: for, if the created universe came into being, and is what it is, as a necessary consequence of a 'First Cause', that first cause could not be a person, could not be endowed with freedom of will, could not be God. Besides, if the existence of this first cause necessitated the existence of the universe, it must have done so from all eternity. There could have been no beginning of the created universe.

"Redemption, as well as creation, must also be a purely sovereign determination of the Divine will. This is required by the necessities of the case, as well as plainly declared in Scripture. No doctrine of Redemption that in any way casts the slightest shadow over the high mountain of Divine Sovereignty can be tolerated for a moment. All theologies that in any manner teach or imply that there was any obligation upon God to do this or that for fallen, rebellious subjects of law, are unscriptural, unreasonable, if not blasphemous. Divine sovereignty is to be recognized as determined to save any fallen ones, in determining who should be saved, in 'chosing', 'raising up', and 'delivering up the Saviour, and in the Saviour's giving of Himself; but this Sovereign Redemption once determined, was wrought out under law, and in exact accordance with law"

(Dr. J. Armour, "Atonement and Law", 1917; published by Moody Inst., Chicago).

What follows may be deemed to savour of metaphysics, yet do we feel it to be called for in view of modern slanderers of God. Even some who are regarded as quite orthodox have drawn a broad distinction, almost a gulf, between the nature of God and the will of God, failing to perceive that God's will is an **essential part of His nature**. Some have descended so low as to affirm there is in the very nature of things a standard of right which exists independently and apart from God, according to which He Himself acts, must act. Such a conception is not only degrading, but blasphemous. Others who have not adopted this insulting figment, have, nevertheless, been injuriously infected by it, and suppose that God's nature, as quite distinct from His will, is what determines His actions.

There is nothing determined by the nature of God which is not determined by the will of God. "When we affirm that God is holy, we do not mean that He makes right right, by simply willing it, but that He wills it because it is right. There must be, therefore, some absolute standard of righteousness"—is how a so-called Bible teacher has recently expressed himself. Even if it be said that the "absolute standard of righteousness" is the Divine nature, if by this be meant God's nature as separate from His determining will, the expression is, to say the least, faulty and misleading. The will of God is an essential part **of** His nature, and therefore His **will** is "the absolute standard of right". The will of God is not something related, dependent, and determined; but is sovereign, imperial, regnant.

God Himself is the ultimate and absolute standard of righteousness. **Man** is commanded to recognize a standard of righteousness outside of and above himself, and his will and conduct must conform thereto. That standard of righteousness is the revealed will of God. But shall we reason from this that **God** also recognizes a standard of righteousness to which His will must be conformed, a standard which makes right right, and right being made right, He wills it **because** it is right? No, indeed. The truth is, that we best discover what the nature of God requires Him to do, by noting what He, by His will, **actually does.** When God says, "I will have mercy on whom I will have mercy" (Rom. 9:15), He assuredly sets before us His will, in its utmost freedom and sovereignty. But this supreme act of sovereign grace, is the act of God Himself, an act into which the whole nature of God (His will being included in that nature) moved Him.

We fail to trace anything to its original source unless we track it right back to the sovereign will of God. This is true alike of creation, of providence, and of redemption. God was not obliged to have created this world; He did so, simply because it so pleased Him (Rev. 4:10). Having created it, when Adam fell, He could have well left the whole race to perish in its sins, and **would** have done so, unless His sovereign will had, previously, determined otherwise. **Justice** did not require Him to intervene in mercy, for as the righteous Governor of the world, He might have proceeded to uphold the authority of His law by exacting its penalty upon all the disobedient, and thus have given to the unfallen angels a further example of His awful vengeance. Nor did His **goodness** require that He should rescue any of His rebellious subjects from the misery which they had brought upon themselves, for He had already given a complete display of **that** in creation. Nor did His **love**, abstractly considered, demand that a Saviour should be provided; had that been the case one must also have been given to the angels which fell.

It needs to be pointed out that the manifestative glory of God does not depend upon ifestive glory of God does not depend upon the display of any particular attribute, but rather upon the exhibition of them all, in full harmony, and on proper occasions. He is glorified when He bestows blessings upon the righteous, and is equally glorified when he inflicts punishment on the wicked. God's manifestative glory consists in the **revelation** of His character to His creatures; yet is this purely **optional** on His part: it is quite voluntary, and contributes nothing to His happiness, and might have been withheld had He so pleased. Yet, as God always acts consistently with Himself, if He shows Himself at all to His creatures, the discovery will ever correspond to the greatness and excellency of His nature.

That the atoning death of Christ **had** its source in the will of God, is plainly declared in Acts 2:23, "Him being delivered by the determinate counsel and foreknowledge of God". Though accomplished in the fulness of time, it was resolved upon before time, decreed and enacted in heaven by the Eternal Three. Therefore do we read in Rev. 13:8 of "The Lamb slain from the foundation (or "founding") of the earth". Christ was "the Lamb slain" **determinately,** in the counsel and decree of God (Acts 2:23); **promissorily,** in the word of God passed to Adam after the fall (Gen. 3:15); **typically,** in the sacrifices appointed immediately after the promise of redemption (Gen. 3:21; 4:4); **efficaciously,** in regard of the merit of it, applied by God to believers before the actual sufferings of Christ (Rom. 3:25; Heb. 9:15).

"He (God) made Him (Christ, the Mediator) to be sin for us" (2 Cor. 5:21): "made" or "constituted" by a Divine statute; i.e. He was ordained to enter the place of the penal condition of sinners. Had not God appointed it, the death of Christ had had no meritorious value. Once more in Heb. 10 the efficacy of Christ's sacrifice unto the elect is traced back and directly ascribed to the eternal and sovereign will of God. In v. 7, we find Christ Himself saying, as He was about to become incarnate and enter this world, "Lo, I come to do **Thy** will, O God"; while in v. 10 we are told, "**by the which will** we are sanctified (consecrated to God) through the offering of the body of Jesus Christ once for all". That which saves, or sanctifies, us, is not simply the offering of Christ—for that had availed us nought, if it had not been Divinely appointed—but the "will" and decree of the Eternal Three concerning that offering.

2. The Love of God.

Love was, or better is, the motive-spring of all God's goodness and grace toward His people. He has for them an "everlasting love" (Jer. 31:3). It was "in love" that He "predestinated us unto the adoption of children by Jesus Christ to Himself" (Eph. 1:5). Proof of this is, that, from all eternity He, "accepted us in (not "Christ", but) the Beloved" (Eph. 1:6)—note carefully that this declaration is given **before** reference is made to the forgiveness of our sins in v. 7. Had it so pleased God, He could have prevented the entrance of sin into this world, He could have restricted the progeny of Adam to the persons of His elect, and He could have taken them to heaven without their having been polluted by sin and redeemed from it, there to enjoy eternal bliss forever. **That** would have been an astonishing demonstration of His love for us. Yet it pleased God to grant unto His people still further, fuller, deeper, higher, manifestations of His love to and for them.

God loved His people in ordaining them to eternal life (Acts 13:48, Rom. 9:11-13), but He gave yet grander proof by suffering them to fall into a state of spiritual death, and then sending His own dear Son to redeem them out of it. Three hundred years ago Dr. Thos. Goodwin, in his incomparable exposition of Eph. 1, pointed out that, "Had we at first been brought to that communion with Christ which we shall have in heaven after the day of judgment, without having known either sin or misery, it had been a good and blessed condition indeed; we should have infinitely rejoiced in it, and had reason to so have done. But certainly heaven will be sweeter to us by reason of our having once fallen into sin and misery, and then having a Redeemer that came and freed us from all, and then brought us to heaven. Oh how sweet will this make heaven to be unto you!

"I would have you observe this that it may mightily and wonderfully instance the love of God toward us. The last words of Eph. 1:6 are that God hath accepted us in His Beloved, while the first of v. 7 are 'In whom we have redemption through His blood'. What! was He God's Beloved, and have you redemption in Him too? Shall God sacrifice His Beloved! God chose us to be holy in heaven with Himself (v. 4), to be sons with Him there (v. 5), to delight in us there (v. 6). Let that purpose stand: let them never come to be sinful, let Me have them up in heaven presently with My Son. One would have thought God might have said this. No, God would **commend** His love yet further. He would let them fall into sin; to redeem them, He would sacrifice this Beloved. He had so much love in His heart that He could commend it to us no way but by sacrificing His Beloved. How wondrously has He displayed His love!"

That love **was** the motive-spring which caused God to provide for His people an atoning sacrifice for their sins, is clear from the well-known words of John 3:16, "For God so loved the world that He gave His only begotten Son". So too in 1 John 4:9, 10, "In this was manifested the love of God toward us, because that God sent His only begotten Son into the world, that we might live through Him. Herein is love, not that we loved God, but that He loved us, and sent His Son to be the propitiation for our sins". Thus the sacred oracles celebrate the work of redemption as the highest and most remarkable instance and exhibition of Divine love, and direct us to behold it acted out in the highest degree and to the utmost advantage, to be seen and admired by all the elect as an exhaustless and endless source of gratitude and praise. The more unworthy and ill-deserving the objects of that love were in themselves—sinners, enemies (Rom. 5:7—10)—the more amazing that love. The greater the deliverance effected by it, and the costlier the sacrifice to procure that deliverance, the more is such love crowned. The greater the difficulties to be overcome—sin, death, the grave—the more was that love magnified. The greater the blessings bestowed—justification, sanctification, glorification—the more is that love to be adored.

"Herein was the **emphasis** of Divine love to us, that 'He sent His Son to be the propitiation for our sins' (1 John 4:10). It was love that He would restore men after the Fall; there was no more necessity of doing this, than of creating the world. As it added nothing to the happiness of God, so the want of it had detracted nothing from it. There was no more absolute necessity of setting up man again after his breaking with God, than a new repair of the world after the destructive deluge. But that He might wind up His love to the highest pitch, He would not only restore man, but rather than let him lie in his deserved misery, would punish His own bowels to secure man from it. It was purely His grace (which is **love** bestowing **favours** on the hell-deserving—A. W. P.) which was the cause that His Son 'tasted death for every' son, Heb. 2:9" (S. Charnock, 1635).

3. The Righteousness of God.

The Atonement of Christ directs our thoughts toward God as One whose governmental holiness demanded satisfaction, whose inflexible justice insisted that its claim be fully met, and whose righteous law must be magnified and made honourable, before any resultant blessings could flow to His elect, considered as the guilty and depraved children of Adam. God can "by no means clear the guilty" (Ex. 34:7). Unlike so much that passes for it in the human realm, the love of God is not lawless; it is not exercised in defiance of righteousness. God is "light" (1 John 1:5), as well as love; and because He is such, sin cannot be ignored, its heinousness minimized, nor its guilt cancelled. True it is that, where sin abounded, grace did much more abound. Yet, grace did not abound at the expense of righteousness, rather does "grace reign **through** righteousness" (Rom. 5:21).

But could not God remit the sins of His people **without** an atoning satisfaction? This question is explicitly and authoritatively answered for us in Heb. 9:22, "Without shedding of blood is **no** remission". Commenting on this in his remarkable book "The Atonement" (1871), the late Hugh Martin said, "No doubt, at first sight, this seems merely to allege a fact, without assigning a reason. It seems to intimate nothing more than the historical truth, that in point of fact God never has remitted the sins of men without shedding of blood. But if emphasis is placed on the word **remission**, and if a true idea is entertained of the transaction which that word represents, the proposition, 'without shedding of blood is no remission', will be found not merely to allege the fact, but also assign a reason for that fact—to embody not only the historical verity, but the underlying principle which justifies it, and which only needs to be carefully investigated and apprehended to furnish a satisfactory answer to the question,—Why should not God remit the sins of men without an Atonement?

"For, when the inspired writer affirms that without shedding of blood is no remission, it is as if he had said:—You may imagine a forgiveness without shedding of blood, if you will; you may conjecture, or conjure up, some other scheme or principle of pardon; you may conceive of God as dealing with the sinner, and delivering him from the punishment due to his iniquities, without these iniquities being expiated,—without the penalty incurred by them being exacted,—without the law of which they are transgressions being relieved from the stain of dishonour which they had cast upon it,—without any costly sacrifice, any solemn propitiation, any priceless ransom. But whatever this transaction might be, it would not be **remission**. Granting that it were quite possible for God to let the sinner off; to wipe out, by a mere arbitrary decree, and without any satisfaction to divine justice, the debt which the sinner had contracted; to cease from His anger toward His enemies and return to a state of friendship; to say, Your sins be forgiven you, you have nothing now to fear;—all this, 'without shedding of blood', without any sacrifice, or atonement, or expiation: still all this, whatever it might amount to, does not amount to **remission**. Call it what you please: be it what it may; it is not remission. It may be held up as an equivalent for it; it may be in room and lieu of it; it may be all that multitudes care to inquire after, or have ever felt the need of, or troubled themselves to seek. But, however possible it might be on God's part, however satisfactory it might be on their part, it is not **remission**. It may look like it. It may seem to carry with it all that the unenlightened have any thought of when thinking of remission; but real remission it is not. Without shedding of blood it is not remission.

"What the enlightened conscience of an anxious inquirer longs for **is** 'remission'—remission of sin. And what is that? It is removal of guilt; removal of liability to the wrath of God; removal of criminality or ill-desert. It is a sentence of 'Not Guilty'. It is a recognition of blamelessness before the Holy One of Israel; a position and relation toward God, therefore, in which His wrath would be undue, unrighteous, impossible. That would be Remission."

We must not anticipate the ground which we hope to cover in later articles, except to say here that, the great problem which confronted God, and which we make so bold as to say could never have been solved by either human or angelic intelligence, was, How mercy might act freely without justice being insulted, of how justice might exact its full due without mercy's hands being tied. A marvelous, perfec,t and completely satisfactory solution to this problem has been found and furnished in the Satisfaction made to God by the mediatorial Redeemer. It is in this satisfaction that "Mercy and truth are met together; righteousness and peace have kissed each other" (Psa. 85:10). It is this satisfaction which has enabled God to be "Just, **and** the Justifier of him which believeth in Jesus" (Rom. 3:26).

4. The Glory of God.

Rightly has it been said that "The ultimate reason and motive of all God's actions are within Himself. Since God is infinite, eternal and unchanging, that which was His first motive in creating the universe must ever continue to be the ultimate motive or chief end in every act concerned in its preservation and government. But God's first motive must have been just the **exercise** of His own essential perfections, and in their exercise the **manifestation** of their excellence. This was the **only** end which could have been chosen by the Divine mind in the beginning, before the existence of any other object" (The Atonement, Dr. A. A. Hodge). The Scriptures are very explicit on this point, "The Lord hath made all things, **for Himself**" (Prov. 16:4). "For of Him, and through Him, and **to Him**, are all things" (Rom. 11:36). "Thou hast created all things, and for **Thy pleasure** they are and were created" (Rev. 4:11).

The ultimate motive, therefore, which moved God to ordain Christ as Satisfaction for the failed responsibilities of His people must have been the Divine glory, and not the effects intended to be produced in the creature. But glory is manifested excellence, and moral excellence is manifested only by being exercised. The infinite justice and love of God both find their highest conceivable exercise in the sacrifice of His own Son as the Substitute of guilty men. God did ordain to have other sons beside Christ (Rom. 8:29), but it was in order that they might behold His glory (John 17:24), and that **He** might "be glorified in them" (John 17:10). To ordain Christ to come into this world as Man, **only** upon the occasion of man's sin and for the work of redemption, would be to subject Christ unto us, and to make **our** good the "end" of God's actions. Such a conception is not only extremely absurd, but terribly impious. Adam was not made for Eve, but Eve for Adam; and as the woman is "the glory of the man" (1 Cor. 11:7) so the saints are called "the glory of Christ" (2 Cor. 8:23); and as the saints are Christ's, so is Christ, the Mediator, "God's" (1 Cor. 3:23).

5. The Covenant of God.

Though we have made this a heading distinct from the preceding four, yet we would point out that it is in the Everlasting Covenant we find the will, the love, the righteousness, the glory of God, united, as the moving cause or causes of the perfect provision found in the Satisfaction of Christ. As this article is followed by a separate one on the covenant, (in this issue of the Magazine) we shall not now enter into any details concerning it.

As we have insisted in previous paragraphs, had God so pleased He might never have created a single being to admire His perfections. When creatures were admitted to that wondrous spectacle, and then became guilty of dishonouring Him, He might have further revealed Himself only in wrath, pouring out the vials of His indignation upon the spot which they inhabited, and turning it into a scene of desolation. What would be the loss of a world to Him in whose eyes it is as nothing, yea, less than nothing and vanity (Isa. 40:17)?

It follows from these premises, the truth of which cannot be gainsaid, that the plan which God designed for the salvation of His elect, who by nature, also shared in the ruins of Adam's fall, originated not only in His sovereign grace, but was determined solely by His own imperial will. Therefore, in contemplating the work of redemption we need to ascend to its source, and begin with the consideration of that **eternal agreement** between the Persons of the Godhead, on which the whole dispensation of grace to fallen men is founded. That agreement is spoken of in Scripture as "The everlasting covenant" (Heb. 13:20). To the article which immediately follows this we would now refer the reader.

—ARTHUR W. PINK.

THE EVERLASTING COVENANT ADMINISTERED.

The Salvation of God's people originated in the covenant acts of the Eternal Three. The Covenant of Grace comprises all the Divine designs and transactions respecting the redemption of the elect. In it we learn the eternal purpose of Father, Son, and Spirit, fixing the manner of redemption, and everything relating thereto, and entering into a mutual agreement, in which the part each Divine person should perform, as distinguished from the Others, was fixed and voluntarily undertaken. A proper apprehension of these covenant-transactions is of vast importance, for when the Holy Spirit reveals to a soul the reality of them, he is at once brought off from all creature-acts, for he then perceives that the salvation of God's people is the **certain** consequence of that Covenant. He now discerns that it was the will of God from all eternity to save His people from all their sins and miseries, and out of the hands of all their enemies, by Jesus Christ alone. He now knows that in the sight of God he was saved in Christ and by Christ from all sin.

The God-given blessing of an eye of faith enables the recipient of it to see that his salvation was from eternity, wholly dependent upon the responsibility of his Surety, and He being sufficient and all-sufficient for them for whom He engaged, and He having completed the whole by His incarnation, life and death, has obtained "eternal redemption" (Heb. 9:12). He now sees for himself the truth of the apostle's words that, God made Christ to be sin for His people, that they might be made the righteousness of God in Him (2 Cor. 5:21). This causes the Spirit-taught soul to admire and adore the Lord Jesus Christ for His righteousness and sacrifice; he sees such worth, such perfection, such virtue and efficacy in His merits and blood, as causes him to rest his heart with holy contentment and delight thereon. As the Spirit grants him clearer spiritual apprehension of these Divine realities, he sees his righteousness in the sight of God is Christ Himself.

The Everlasting Covenant is **published** in the Gospel of God's grace. As we read in Rom. 16:25, 26, "Now to Him that is of power to stablish you according to my gospel, and the preaching of Jesus Christ, according to the revelation of the mystery, which was kept secret since the world begain, But now is made manifest, and by the Scriptures of the prophets, according to the commandment of the everlasting God, made known to all nations for the obedience of faith". Notice, first, the Gospel is here said to be a "**revelation** of the mystery". This "mystery" had been "kept secret", not from all men, but from "all nations". Second, it was revealed, "by the Scriptures of the prophets", but that which had for centuries been known only to Israel, was now to be "made known to all nations". Third, mark the title here given to the Deity, "the **everlasting** God"! This attribute of eternity is hereby ascribed to Him because the "everlasting covenant" is here in view.

Above we have said that the Gospel is a **revelation** of a Divine mystery. Clear proof of this is found in 1 Cor. 2. There the apostle declared, "But we speak the wisdom of God in a mystery, the hidden, which God ordained before the world unto our glory" (v. 7). The apostle here calls the Gospel (see 1 Cor. 1:17, 18 and cf. 2: 2-6) the "wisdom of God", because in it the wondrous wisdom of God is made known. But more, he affirms that the Gospel exhibits a "**hidden** wisdom" (cf. "kept secret" Rom. 16:25) yea, that which God had predestinated to the glory of His people. That the whole of this passage in 1 Cor. 2 concerns the eternal grace of God toward His elect, is clear from "the things which God hath **prepared** for them that love Him" (v| 9), which things "God hath revealed unto us by His Spirit: for the Spirit searcheth all things, yea, the **deep** things of God" (v. 10) i.e. the Spirit is thoroughly cognizant of and conversant with the secret counsels of the Eternal Three in the "everlasting Covenant".

The words "kept secret since the world began" in Rom. 16:25 are not to be taken absolutely as the very next verse clearly shows. This "mystery" or "hidden wisdom" had, to a considerable degree, been made known in the Scriptures of Israel's prophets, but as 1 Cor. 2:8 tells us, it was something which "none of the princes of this world knew". "But now is made manifest" (Rom. 16:26) is explained in the last clause of the verse: "made known to all nations for the obedience of faith". Parallel with this is Eph. 3:3-9. There Paul again refers to "the mystery", the "mystery of Christ" which "in other ages had not been made known to **the sons of men**" (though it **had** to Israel); but now he was to "preach among the **Gentiles** the unsearchable riches of Christ". So in Col. 1:25-27: note "this mystery **among the Gentiles**" (v. 27).

Reverting once more to Rom. 16:26, the apostle declares this mystery, or hidden wisdom, concerning the Everlasting Covenant, had been "made manifest by the Scriptures of the prophets". Many are the Old Testament passages which might be cited in illustration of this fact. This Covenant is expressly mentioned in Psa. 89:3, 4, "I have made a covenant with My chosen, I have sworn unto David My servant, Thy seed will I establish forever, and build up thy throne to all generations". The direct and local reference is to David and his descendants, but, without doubt, a greater than David is here in view, viz., his illustrious Son and Lord, who is sometimes called by this very name (see Ezek. 37:24, 25; Hos. 3:5), and in whom this promise has been fulfilled—Luke 1: 32, 33; Acts 13:34-37. A careful reading of the whole Psalm will show its language is too sublime, and the things foretold are too great, to admit of being limited to any earthly monarch or succession of monarchs.

In Psa. 119:122 David prays, "Be **surety** for Thy servant for good; let not the proud oppress me". In Isa. 38:14 Hezekiah supplicates God thus, "O Lord, I am oppressed, undertake (Heb. "Be Surety") for me". When these men prayed thus, to be delivered from their enemies and afflictions, by addressing their Deliverer in **this** particular character, it is evident that they understood He had undertaken to be Surety for His people. The **mediatorial** work and character of Christ was well known to the Old Testament saints.

In Isa. 49 we have what may be called a **draught** of the Covenant, or **deed** of gift between Christ and His Father for us; wherein Christ first begins and shows His commission as the ground of the treaty between Them; intimating to His Father that He had called Him unto this great work: "Listen, O isles, unto Me; and hearken, ye people, from far; The Lord hath called Me from the womb; from the bowels of My mother hath He made mention of My name" (v. 1). Then He refers to God's having fitted Him for this work: "And He hath made My mouth like a sharp sword; in the shadow of His hand hath He hid Me, and made Me a polished shaft; in His quiver hath He hid Me" (v. 2). In what follows the triune God has condescended to employ expressions taken from a human manner of speaking, that we may the better comprehend this mysterious transaction:

First, the Father offers, as it were, **only** "Israel" as Messiah's portion: "Thou art My Servant: O Israel, in whom I will be glorified" (v. 3). To which Christ is represented as fore-seeing how few of Israel would believe in Him, and that such sparce gleanings would be a poor recompense for all His toil; yet He is prepared to leave the issue with the Lord: "Then I said, I have laboured in vain, I have spent My strength for nought, and in vain: yet, surely My judgment is with the Lord, and My work with My God" (v. 4). God therefore answers Him again, and **enlarges the grant**: "And now, saith the Lord, that formed Me from the womb to be His Servant, to bring Jacob again to Him, Though Israel be not gathered, yet shall I be glorious in the eyes of the Lord, and My God shall be My strength. And He said, It is a light thing that Thou shouldest be My Servant to raise up the tribes of Jacob, and to restore the preserved of Israel; I will **also** give Thee for a light to the Gentiles, that Thou mayest be My salvation unto the end of the earth: In an acceptable time have I heard Thee, in a day of salvation have I helped Thee: and I will preserve Thee, and give Thee **for a covenant** of the people" (vv. 5, 6, 8). Thus we see that this Covenant which God made with Christ was to save both Jews and Gentiles as the reward for His work.

That by Divine agreement and covenant settlement Christ had been set up as Mediator **before** He entered this world, is plainly taught in the New Testament too. In John 6:27 we hear Christ saying, "Labour . . . for that meat which endureth unto everlasting life, which the Son of man shall give unto you: for Him hath God the Father **sealed**". So again in John 6:38, "For I came down from heaven not to do Mine own will, but the will of Him that sent Me". In John 10:18 He speaks of a "power" or "commandment" which He had received from the Father to lay down His life and take it again, so that He might answer the great end of redemption thereby. In John 10:36 He refers to Himself as Him "whom the Father hath **sanctified** (consecrated to a Divine service) and sent into the world": "sanctified" before "sent"! In Luke 22:29 He declared to His disciples, "**I appoint** unto you a kingdom, as My Father hath **appointed** unto Me".

The Everlasting Covenant of grace was typified, or more correctly speaking, adumbrated (shadowed forth in this lower or visible sphere) in the covenant which the Lord made with Abram. This will be easier for us to grasp if we bear in mind the fact that the Gospel is a revelation of the Covenant of Grace. Now in Acts 3:25 we read that Peter said, "Ye are the children of the prophets, and of the **covenant** which God made with our fathers, saying unto Abraham, And in thy Seed shall all the kindreds of the earth be blessed". Now link up this with Gal. 3:8: "And the scripture, foreseeing that God would justify the heathen through faith, preached before the **gospel** unto Abraham, In thee shall all nations be blessed". Note well that what is called "the covenant" in the former passage, is called "the gospel" in the latter; and that "all kindreds of the earth" in one, becomes "all nations" in the other; while the "blessing" mentioned in both is explained to be the justification of the ungodly by faith.

The all-conclusive proof that the Abrahamic covenant shadowed forth in time the covenant of Grace which had been made in eternity, is found in Gal. 3:16, "Now to Abraham and his Seed were the promises made, He saith not, And to seeds, as of many; but as of one, And to thy Seed, which is Christ", not only Christ personal, but "Christ" **mystical**, i.e., the Head and His members. This is clear from Gal. 3:29, "And if ye be Christ's, then are **ye** Abraham's **seed**, and heirs according to the promise".

The Abrahamic covenant was followed by the Siniatic, which was the very antithesis of the other: the former being one of pure grace, the latter one of works. The Abrahamic was one of unconditional promise: the Siniatic was conditional—blessing being determined by Israel's obedience to the law. Now as the Abrahamic adumbrated the Everlasting Covenant, so the Siniatic exemplified the Adamic. The first man had been constituted by God the federal head of his race, and God entered into a covenant with him (see Hos. 6:6 margin), and thus he was "the figure of Him that was to come" (Rom. 5:14). That Covenant was one of works, blessing for Adam and his posterity being conditioned upon the obedience of the federal head.

It has been well said that, "God deals with men only by Covenant. What is a covenant? It is a promise made upon conditions to be fulfilled. This being so, it is clear that there can be but two, and only two covenants possible between God and man—a covenant founded upon what **man shall do**, and a covenant founded on what **God shall do for him;** in other words, a Covenant of Works, and one of Grace" (Dr. G. S. Bishop). The Covenant of Works was made with Adam, the Covenant of Grace with Christ. Israel according to the flesh was under the one, the spiritual "Israel of God" (Gal. 6:16) are the beneficaries of the other. The one was revealed by the Law, the other is made known by the Gospel. As the law preceded the Gospel, the Covenant of Grace, is termed "the **new** covenant" (Heb. 8:8), not because it is "new" in its constitution, but in its **manifestation** and **proclamation** abroad.

Coming now to the **administration** of the Covenant, we would observe, first, that the blessings of it are committed into the hands of the Saviour, that He may distribute them according to His own will, which in this, as in everything else, harmonises perfectly with the will of the Father, This high honour has been conferred upon the Mediator that, the blessings which were purchased with His infinitely perfect Satisfaction, should be at His own disposal, and that hell-deserving sinners should be reminded of their incalculable obligations to Him, by receiving every blessing immediately from His hands. His fulfilment of the conditions which the Everlasting Covenant had required of Him, gave Him a right to the promises, and the possession of their inestimable treasures. The Scriptural proof for these assertions are clear and convincing.

After His resurrection, the triumphant Surety declared to His disciples, "All power (authority) is given unto Me in heaven and in earth" (Matt. 28:18), evidently meaning, that such right of administration was bestowed upon Him in consequence of His obedience unto death. Centuries before, the Psalmist, moved by the Spirit of prophecy, said, "Thou hast ascended on high, Thou hast led captivity captive, Thou hast received gifts for men; yea, for the rebellious also" (68:18). Those words of David's were explained by Peter to the Jews, who were amazed at the miracles of Pentecost: "This Jesus hath God raised up, whereof we all are witnesses. Therefore being by the right hand of God exalted, and having received of the Father the **promise** of the Holy Spirit, **He** hath shed forth this, which ye now see and hear" (Acts 2:32, 33). Three things are observable in these words: first, the gift of the Spirit to Christ was the performance of a "promise" that had been made to Him by the Father. Second, the Spirit was given to Christ that He might pour Him out upon men, like the refreshing rains which fall upon the earth. Third, the subjection of the Spirit to the Mediator in the economy of grace (Mark 1:8), demonstrates that "all authority" is Christ's **in heaven** as well as upon earth.

Anticipating His resurrection, our great High Priest declared to His disciples on the eve of His death, "As Thou hast given Him power (authority) over all flesh" (John 17:2). And for what purpose was that grant made unto Him? The same verse tells us, "that He should give eternal life to as many as Thou **hast** given Him". That was the equivalent of saying, that **He** would administer the promised blessings of the Covenant of Grace to those for whom He had covenanted, whose Surety and Mediator He was. So, again, in Matt. 11:27 He declared, "All things are delivered unto Me of My Father". Now it is upon this donation or gift to Him (as Mediator) is founded the whole dispensation of grace, which was established by His authority and will be continued until the end. Hence, follows, immediately after, the gracious promise of the Gospel: "Come unto Me, all ye that labour and are heavy laden, and I will give you rest" (Matt. 11:28). This important truth is more fully expressed in Eph. 4:8, 11-16.

Now the administration of the Covenant has taken the form of a will or "testament", or deed, by which a person bequeaths his property to his heirs, to be enjoyed by them after his decease; thus the blessings of the covenant are conveyed to its beneficaries in a testamentary form. The Greek word "diatheke" occurs forty times in the Authorized Version. It has been rendered "covenant" twenty times, and "testament" twenty times. The

Greek word has this double meaning, yet it is of great importance to distinguish between its two significations in order to a right understanding of each passage in which it is found. Unfortunately our English translators have not always succeeded in doing this. For example in Heb. 7:22 Jesus is termed "a Surety of a better testament" or "will", which is a quite meaningless expression. It should have been "Surety of a better covenant", the more so as it is there contrasted from the Siniatic covenant, which certainly was not a "testament". So again, "the Mediator of the new testament" (Heb. 9:15) conveys no intelligible concept: "covenant" is the proper word there.

But in Heb. 9:16, 17 it should be observed that "testament" is the proper rendition: "For where a testament is, there must also of necessity be the death of the testator. For a testament is of force after men are dead, otherwise it is of no strength at all while the testator liveth". This idea of a "testament" naturally follows after mention of the "eternal **inheritance**" in the previous verse. 'As an inheritance is conveyed from one person to another by testament, this designation may be given to the Covenant of Grace, because it conveys to us the inheritance of eternal life, and conveys it in virtue of the death of the Surety. It was with the Covenant of Grace as it was with a testament. As the death of the testator is necessary to render a testament valid, so the death of Christ was necessary to ratify the Covenant, and to make its promises sure to His spiritual seed. It is the necessity of the death of Christ which the apostle intended to establish, and the notice of a testament is incidentally introduced, solely for the purpose of illustrating this point. Salvation comes to us through His death, as an inheritance comes to the legatees through the death of a testator" (Dr. John Dick).

In treating of the **administration** of the Covenant of Grace it is essential that we should consider it, severally, under **two distinct economies**, of which the one preceded and the other succeeded the coming of Christ in the flesh. That there **was a** dispensation of grace prior to the Divine incarnation should be evident to every careful reader of the O. T.. It commenced immediately after the Fall, when the first intimation of mercy was made (Gen. 3:15), and it continued till the death of the Saviour, when it was formally abolished. That it was virtually and vitally the same with the present dispensation, and differed from it only in form, may be proved from a number of considerations. Abel's offering of a bleeding lamb "by faith" (Heb. 11:4), which necessarily presupposes a revelation of the Divine will (Rom. 10:17), evidences that the Gospel of Divine grace was made known at a very early date. The same blessed Evangel was preached to the patriarchs, and later to Israel, by their typical institutions and the voice of their prophets. Therefore is the mision of Christ said to be the fulfillment of the ancient predictions: "Blessed be the Lord God of Israel: for He hath visited and redeemed His people, and hath raised up an horn of salvation for us in the house of His servant David; **As** He spake by the mouth of His holy prophets, which have been since the world began" (Luke 1:68-70).

When before Aggripa, Paul declared, "Having therefore obtained help of God, I continue unto this day, witnessing both to small and great, saying **none other** things than those which the prophets and Moses did say should come: That Christ should suffer, that He should be the first that should rise from the dead, and should show light unto the people, and to the Gentiles" (Acts 26:22, 23). To the Hebrews he declared the "Gospel" had been "preached" to Israel in the wilderness (4:2). To the Galatians he insisted (when rebutting the errors of Judaisers) that the Gospel he proclaimed had, long before, been preached to Abraham, and that those who believed it were admitted to a participation in the same privileges with the patriarchs: "And the Scripture foreseeing that God would justify the Gentiles through faith, preached before the Gospel unto Abraham, In thee shall all nations be blessed. So then they which be of faith are blessed **with** faithful Abraham" (3:8, 9).

There are at least two passages in the New Testament which expressly affirm that the dispensation of grace under which the Old Testament saints lived, was founded upon that atonement of Christ by which the covenant was ratified. First, Rom. 3:25: "Whom God hath set forth a propitiation through faith in His blood, to declare His righteousness for the remission of sins that are past, through the forebearance of God". Note carefully the expression "for the passing over of sins that are past". Here the apostle is obviously referring to the sins of the Old Testament saints, which God had remitted prior to the manifestation of Christ. But how had it been consistent with His justice to do so, seeing that no expiatory sacrifice of efficacy had been offered for them? The answer is, The Satisfaction of the Redeemer was of such infinite value, that its virtue reaches back to the beginning of time, as well as forward to the end of it. God acted like a creditor who lets his debtor go free, although the payment had not been made by the surety, because he has full confidence in him that he **will** fulfill his engagement.

The second passage is in Heb. 9:15, "And for this cause He is the Mediator of the new covenant, that by means of death for the redemption of the transgressions under the first covenant, they which are called might receive the promise of eternal inheritance." The "transgressions which were under the first covenant" has reference to the sins of God's (spiritual) elect, who lived, dispensationally, under the Siniatic covenant, the typical sacrifices for which then offered up, delivering **only** from the **temporal** penalties of the law; yet some of them obtained the full and eternal forgiveness of their sins, namely, the "called" of Israel; and that too, was on the ground of the great Sacrifice which was to be offered in the fulness of time. Christ was the Mediator of the new covenant for the redemption of **their** sins, as well as for the sins of His saints who have lived since the Cross. Thus we see that the elect of God who lived under the law of Moses, were as truly saved by the grace of our Lord Jesus Christ, as they who are saved under the Gospel.

Christ, in fact, sustained the office and performed the duties of Mediator **before** His incarnation. "It was not a vain opinion of the Jews that it was the second Person of the Trinity who gave the promise of mercy to our first parents in Paradise, appeared to the patriarchs, published the law from Sinai, conducted the church in the wilderness, and managed its affairs during the ages which followed. It is certain that a Divine Person **did** often appear under the ancient economy, and as there is no reason to think it was the Father, whom no man has seen, we conclude it was the Son, who assumed the form of that nature in which He was after to sojourn upon earth. He was the Angel of God's presence, and the Angel of the covenant, concerning whom these three particulars are worthy of attention: that He was a Divine Person, for the name of God was in Him, and the power of pardoning or not pardoning sin belonged to Him: that He acted in an official capacity, for He was an angel or messenger; and that His office was connected with the gracious dispensation which was then established, for He was the Messenger of the covenant. As far as that dispensation was carried on by the revelation of the Divine will, we are expressly assured, that it was under His direction and superintendence. It was the Spirit of the Messiah, Peter says, 'who testified beforehand' in the prophets 'the sufferings of Christ and the glory that should follow', 1 Peter 1:11" (Dr. J. Dick).

Concerning the administration of the everlasting covenant **since** the coming of Christ, it is the Gospel which makes known to us the eternal council between the Father and the Son, which displays the richness and freeness of Divine grace, which proclaims salvation to all who believe, and comforts its recipients by its promises of present and future refuge. The present dispensation is distinguished from the past by the superior clearness of its manifestation. What was formerly exhibited under the vail of types, is now openly revealed: "The darkness, is past, and the true light now shineth" (1 John 2:8). It is distinguished, too, by the more abundant supply of the Spirit: Acts 2, 2 Cor. 3, Rom. 8:15 etc.

The great **design** in the administration of the Covenant of Grace is to impart its benefits to those for whom they were intended. This is accomplished by the Holy Spirit, who works faith in the hearts of those who were chosen in Christ to eternal life. It is only by faith we can learn our individual interest in that Covenant, and that God-given faith causes its recipient to "take hold of His covenant" (Isa. 56:6), yea, to enter into covenant with God. Where God acts there is a reciprocal action from those in whom He works. Does God love His people; they love Him in return. Has He called them; they call upon Him. Has He made a covenant (in Christ) with them; they too dedicate themselves to a covenant-God, with a real sense of their binding obligations to render Him that obedience which they are thereby engaged to.

It concerns each person, therefore, to enquire whether God hath made with **him** a covenant "ordered in all things and sure". It is an enquiry intimately connected with his eternal wellfare, for salvation comes to any sinner only on the basis of this Covenant. How then shall the point be ascertained? First, he who has entered into a covenant with God, is an awakened and convicted sinner. None others feel their need of God's great salvation. Peace with God is only prized by those who have been made conscious of death, and of the Divine displeasure and vengeance. Careless worldlings are unconcerned about reconciliation with God. The Spirit's application of the law to the heart and conscience is the first step by which men are led to take hold of God's covenant, and "make peace with God" (Isa. 27:5).

Second, he who has entered into this Covenant has "fled for refuge, to lay hold on the hope set before him" (Heb. 6:18). That "hope" is set before him in the Gospel. The word "refuge" looks back to the cities of refuge in Israel (Num. 33, Josh. 20), entry into which secured from the avenger of blood. The awakened and convicted sinner, aroused and terrified by his sins, and the wrath of God, **flees** for refuge to Christ, and, by a God-given faith, lay hold of, believes in, appropriates, the Saviour as his.

Third, he who has entered into this Covenant rests his hope of salvation upon the righteousness of Christ, by which it was fulfilled, and on that alone. He has no confidence in the flesh, he repudiates his own righteousness as filthy rags, he relies not on any works, performances, or acts of his own; neither his repentance, faith, or obedience. The language of his heart and lips is, "My mouth shall show forth Thy righteousness, Thy salvation all the day ... I will go in the strength of the Lord God: I will make mention of Thy righteousness, of **Thine only**" (Psa. 71:15, 16).

Lastly, he who is in covenant with a holy God is a holy person. God's promise to Christ concerning His people is, "I will put My laws into their mind, and write them in their hearts: and I will be to them a God, and they shall be to Me a people" (Heb. 8:10). The effects of this are clearly and unmistakeably manifested in their daily lives. True, while they are left in this world, the flesh is still there, and it annoys and hinders them, so that they are prevented from fully realizing the desires of their hearts. Nevertheless, their faith overcomes the world (1 John 5:4). The Spirit in them, which is mightier than Satan (1 John 4:4), subdues the flesh, and produces in and through them **His** "fruit". They are taught that they have no strength of their own, and so they look to the Lord for enablement. They depend upon His grace, and He works in them (notwithstanding all the opposition of the flesh, which is as nothing to Him) "both to will **and to do** of His good pleasure" (Phil. 2:13), and thus they ascribe **to Him** all the praise of their success.

—ARTHUR W. PINK.

2. SATANIC ASSAULTS.

It is the Lord's revealed will, that His beloved and called ones should honour Him chiefly in a way of believing His testimony, receiving His record concerning His Son, and setting their seal to His immutable and infallible truth. Therefore He permits them, in the course of their walking with Him as their reconciled God and Father, to be opposed, assaulted, and resisted by Satan, to the intent they may have full experience, and learn practically, that salvation is wholly out of themselves, that it resides wholly in the person and is contained in the finished work of Christ, and that it is treasured up with all its blessings in the fulness of Him who "filleth all in all," and that they are to receive the whole of it, and be happy in the enjoyment of it, entirely in believing on Christ, to the saving of the soul. When this love hath been manifested to a poor sinner, it draws out the implacable malice and hatred of the Devil. It is a sufficient motive with him to hate with a peculiar hatred those whom the Lord loves.

When a sinner is turned from darkness to light, and from the power of Satan unto God, all hell is alive. Satan immediately begins to rage; and though for a season he may be restrained from making a formal combat with the new-born person, yet he only forebears, because under restraint, or, that he may work the more craftily and successfully against him. It pleases the Lord for a season to screen His child, newly brought into His family, from Satan's temptations and assaults, to the end he may be the better prepared for them, when he shall be exercised with them. At the believer's first entrance into the state of grace, and on the enjoyment of those blessings which belong to the called of God in Christ Jesus, he knows but little of that body of sin and death, which he is the subject of. It is with him, when newly converted and turned to the Lord, as though all sin were entirely dead in him. He feels no stirrings of corruptions. God is his exceeding joy. He draws near to Him, approaches the throne of grace with great frequency and delight, prays with great freedom and affections, enjoys much sensible comfort, reads the Word and finds his heart sweetly melted, and his affections sensibly stirred within him, especially when Christ and His sufferings are the subjects contained in those portions of it before him. The promises make a divine impression on his mind. The ordinances are greatly prized by him. His heart is warm. His language is, "Come and hear, all ye that fear God, and I will declare what He hath done for my soul." (Psa. 66:16).

And thus, like as when the Lord brought His people out of Egypt, He led them not through the land of the Philistines, although that was near, that they might not be discouraged. So it pleases Him, in His spiritual dealings with a new convert, to be very gracious to him in keeping out of sight those trials and sorrows which will more or less befal him in his walk heavenward. He sees no danger, he fears no evil. The Lord goes before him as his guide. The God of Israel is His re-reward. And like as the Israelites, when they had passed safely through the Red Sea, looked and saw their enemies dead on the shore, believed the Lord and sang His praise; so does the believer in Christ. He says, "I will sing unto the Lord, for He hath triumphed gloriously. The Lord is my strength and my song, and He is become my salvation. He is my God and I will exalt Him." This confounds Satan and provokes him to withstand him; for the appropriating language, "My God," he hates with the most implacable hatred. For a season he is forced to forebear, but he only waits for what he considers a suitable occasion to make an assault on the converted person. And in like manner as when God bore His testimony to the divine Sonship of Christ, and the Holy Spirit sealed that testimony by His inward witness to the Messiah's mind concerning it, He was soon questioned by Satan, who put an **if** upon it, "**If** Thou be the Son of God"; so, the same evil one, on the testimony of the Spirit's being received into the heart, "Thou art a Son of God and an heir of glory," the Devil aims to call this into question. It is one of his peculiar and almost universal temptations, with which he more or less assaults the holy brethren: and there are seasons in the believer's experience, which suits Satan to make such a temptation very successful.

The believer, after a while, is permitted by the Lord to feel what he is in himself. He sees and feels that in his fallen nature dwelleth nothing that is good. This gives great occasion of grief, damps the believer's holy joy in the Lort, lessens those lively affections, which the child of God has experienced, and thus a way is opened for Satan's renewed temptations; which peculiarly consist in fighting against the believer's faith and joy in God. At first, the believer being in a new world, experiencing such a powerful change in his soul, and finding nothing but light and joy in the Lord, is very greatly affected. When those sensible affections to Divine and heavenly enjoyments abate (some of which are not so much supernatural as natural), he begins to feel a strange alteration in his mind; at which Satan begins to suit his temptations accordingly. He puts on the appearance of an angel of light, compliments him upon what he has enjoyed, and suggests that it looks as though he had been more than highly favoured of the Lord, seeing his affections have been highly raised after heavenly things, his zeal very great, his joys super-abundant, his sins mightily subdued, and his mind quite deadened to the world. But, at the same time, he darts this thought into the mind, that, allowing all this to be strictly true, yet the case is very greatly altered, that old corruptions are still inherent, that it is a matter of question, if they were truly mortified, that, if God loved, surely His love, being unchangeable, the enjoyment of it would be so also, and in short that things are not what they were. Then, together with this, he insinuates, it is a possible case that the soul may have been deceived, that its apprehensive sense of pardoning mercy may have been notional, its views of Christ altogether delusion, and its joys all fanciful; which so secretly operates on the mind and influences the heart and affections, as to add great force to the energy of his temptations. For, in all this, Satan's hand is not seen. The converted person reasons on, concludes it is his case, looks into himself, and searches to find some good thing there towards the Lord God; but, in his old nature he finds no change.

Now Satan breathes with his hellish breath on the inward corruption of the mind; by which means it is excited, quickened, and drawn forth. He draws the eye of the mind to look on it. Then he pretends to preach the exceeding sinfulness of it. This alarms the believer who looks so much at it as to be overcome by it, which makes the way for the Devil to accuse. He knows that the conscience being defiled with guilt will breed ten thousand jealousies in the heart. Now he throws off his appearance of an angel of light, and proceeds boldly to charge home actual sin on the converted person, asks, what he thinks of himself and states now,—if this is the fruit of his pretended conversion,—if he can now be bold to call God his Father, which being accomplished with much hellish influence, puzzle and perplex the believer, and cause him to doubt his adoption into the family of God.

Thus the Devil, having made a breach in the spirit goes on working from time to time secretly and imperceptibly upon the body of sin in every faculty, sense and affection of it, with a design to draw the believer into the actual commission of evil. He is very attentive to the believer, marks him well, studies him accurately, makes conclusions concerning him, tries experiments on him, discharges his whole artillery against him, and is in no part of his skill and practice more successful, than by his sly, legal insinuations. From the moment he can perceive any souls to be truly translated into the kingdom of God's dear Son, he attends very particularly to what their views of Gospel-grace are, with their profession, experiences, and enjoyments of the same. He feels the pulse of their minds to find out particularly what their besetting sins and weaknesses are. And having discovered this, he knows the better how to suit his temptations.

That variety of experience, which the Lord's people have of the wiles and malice of this their sworn and constant adversary, may be ascribed and attributed to this personal application of his for finding out the peculiar constitution, inclination, and besetting sin of every individual believer, together with his various modes of temptations and assaults upon them. To sum up the peculiar temptations and assaults of the regenerate and believing child of God: Satan tempts him to doubt, concerning his regeneration, telling him plainly by his secret workings on the mind, that it is very difficult for him to prove that **he is born of God;** as it is expressly said, "He that is born of God cannot commit sin"; whereas he has sinned since he professed to be born again. He adds also, that all allow, "If any man be in Christ, he is a new creature"; which, with all his profession, he cannot find himself to be, seeing he has the same old heart and spirit, the same lusts and corruptions within him as ever. As it respects his profession of being a justified and pardoned person, Satan suggests this is very doubtful, because the believer himself hath at times his inward doubts concerning it. This, says, Satan, thou knowest, that after the sweet seasons of refreshment, as thou callest them, thou hast lost the relish and sense of the same: yea, to thy knowledge and thy shame, thou hast fallen by thy besetting sin. Satan assaults the soul in the very use of God's ordinances. If the soul enjoys liberty in prayer, freedom in spirit, and exercises the mind without bondage and distress, then he will try to prevail on it to be well pleased with its own performances. If much comfort and joy be bestowed, he will try to get the child of God to live **on** them, and rest **in** them. If there be no freedom in prayer, then he will make use of this circumstance by way of distress.

When God is pleased, on some peculiar seasons of grace, to shine upon the regenerate, and enlighten the mind with some high, supernatural, and exalted use of His love, the person of Christ, His glories, work, salvation, grace, fulness and perfection, so that the believer enjoys more than ordinary communion with the Father, Son and Holy Spirit; immediately Satan will make an attack upon the child of God. He will either aim to puff him up thereby, and fill him with spiritual pride; or he will by his secret wiles stir up corruption within him, and cast in some of his fiery darts to inflame and scorch the mind, and then ask the believer, what he thinks of himself now, what **he is** more than others, what sort of communion with God he can have, when his corruptions are as easily stirred and drawn forth, as ever. Satan has an art, and most frequently exercises it towards the person born of God; and it is this, viz, to turn the very Scriptures themselves against the believer, by putting his own glosses and comments on them, and by his subtle and false applications of them to the mind: and hereby he prevails most with the regenerate. Because it is not so easy to detect him, when he works like an angel of light, as when he falls upon his hellish projects and assaults like a roaring lion.

When we review his titles, and what is related of his power, rage, and wrath, in the written Word; and how he is indefatigable night and day to distress to the uttermost the child of God, it leads us to consider that we are in continual danger from him. He is called, "the old Serpent," the "god of this world", "Satan", "the Devil", "and the deceiver which deceiveth the whole world" i. e. the world of persons out of Christ, who are said to be in the arms of the wicked one, 1 John 5:19. He is filled with great rage against the saints: all the persecutions which have been raised against them are a proof of it. The immutable enmity between his seed and the seed of the woman is a continual evidence of it. He is "the prince of the power of the air," and has whole legions of fallen spirits at his command and under his control. He is "that spirit which worketh in the children of disobedience." There is not a sin they commit, but his hand is in it.

Peter, though an apostle of Jesus Christ, was so fiercely assaulted by this common adversary, who wanted to swallow him up, that he gives us a solemn warning to be on the watch and guard against him, saying, "Be sober, be vigilant, because your adversary the devil, as a roaring lion, walketh about seeking whom he may devour. Whom resist steadfast in the faith, knowing that the same afflictions are accomplished in your brethren, that are in the world" 1 Peter 5:8, 9. Satan's temptations are **to saints** "affections". Yet we are never tempted, but sin is quickened, even though we may be preserved from falling by it. Sometimes Satan engages the soul in a particular combat. He attacks it on a particular season. In a short time he departs, and seems to leave the soul without any further assaults on it; when, after a long cessation, and the believer has been kept going on with a high hand towards the city of habitation, all on a sudden he returns, renews his assaults, interrupts the believer's communion with God and then preaches to him in this legal manner, saying, You cannot be the Lord's; do not be presumptuous; hast thou never heard that despair hath slain its thousands, and presumption its ten thousands? Knowest thou not that it is written, "Without holiness no man shall see the Lord"? Sure, says this arch-deceiver, you cannot look into your heart and say, you are holy.

In such insinuations as these consist the very depths of Satan's wiles and stratagems, as it respects his assaults on a child of God; which suggestions operate on the believer's mind to his very great distress. He forgets the one everlasting Foundation, neglects the exercise of his faith on the perpetual virtue and efficacy of Christ's most precious blood shedding, is led off from the simplicity that is in Christ Jesus, has his eye off Christ, looks into himself for that which can only be found in the Lord Jesus, legalises the word of the Gospel, makes use of it against himself, and thus Satan gains his end by keeping him at a distance from Christ. Hereby the believer's mind is affected, shut up, and contradicted, in consequence of harbouring some secret jealousies concerning the love of Christ. The child of God in such a case, says, O what a depth of corruption! what a fountain of impurity is within me! I once thought myself among the number of the renewed and called people of God, looked on myself as sanctified by faith which is in Christ Jesus, but alas! such a sight and sense of my inward sinfulness and corruption have been discovered to me in the hour of temptation, that I know not what to say or think of myself and state. I am vile in my own eyes, so that I cannot but most heartily loathe and abhor myself. And if I be thus exceedingly sinful, vile, and loathsome in my own sight, what must I be in the eyes of an Holy God? Sure I am, the language of Job well becomes me, and fitly expresses my experience: "Behold, I am vile, I abhor myself, I will lay mine hand upon my mouth."

The mind, thus deeply affected with the experience it hath of the body of inward corruption, and inwardly oppressed by the devil through his temptations and fiery assaults, is in heaviness for a season; and there is necessity for it. By this means the believer **learns to know himself.** He feels his **great need of Christ.** Those words from the mouth of his Lord, serve to sustain him, "My grace is sufficient for thee". The temptations and assaults of Satan, with which the believer has been exercised, through the divine influence of the Holy Spirit, have done him good; they have produced such frames and feelings, as will serve to humble and keep him low in his own eyes. His mind is emptied of all high thoughts concerning himself. His frame of heart is meek and lowly. He views himself to be the least of saints and the chief of sinners. The publican's prayer suits his feelings as well as his case, and he offers it up with the energy of the spirit, "God be merciful unto me a sinner", through the propitiatory sacrifice of Thy co-equal Son.

In the valley of humiliation he prizes Christ's refreshings. When under darkness and in soul-distress without spiritual consolations, such a Scripture as this is prized beyod the gold of Ophir: "For a small moment have I forsaken thee, but with great mercies will I gather thee. In a little wrath I hid My face from thee for a moment; but with everlasting kindness will I have mercy on thee, saith the Lord thy Redeemer" Isa. 54:7, 8. He experiences that the flesh lusteth against the spirit. He feels the effects of it, which leads him to see that his salvation is all of grace, and that he needs Christ **every moment** and **for everything.** The experience which he hath

to fly to in the hour of need and trial? None at all. There would be nothing better than the black darkness and abject horror of atheism. O my reader, how thankful should we be that everything **is** determined by Infinite wisdom and goodness! What praise and gratitude are due unto God **for** His Divine decrees. It is because of them that "**we know** that all things work together for good to them that love God, to them who are the called according to His purpose" (Rom. 8:28). Well may we exclaim, "For of Him, and through Him, and to Him, are all things: **to whom be glory** forever. Amen." (Rom. 11:36).

—ARTHUR W. PINK.

---

of himself, with the rage and malice of Satan against him, only increases his importunity at the throne. He is poor and needy, and as such he betakes himself to the Lord, and finds a promise which ex-- actly suits his case, frame, and feelings, "Fear not, thou worm Jacob, I will help thee. When the poor and needy seek water, and there is none, and their tongue faileth for thirst, I the Lord will hear them, I will open rivers in high places, and fountains in the midst of the valleys. I will make the wilderness a pool of water, and the dry land springs of water" Isa. 41:14, 17, 18. The fulfilment of this promise to the believer, in a time of spiritual need, renders the grace contained in it almost inestimably precious. It gives a proof of God's being **his God**, and shows how His eye is on His child, and is an expression of His mercy, and draws out the faith and hope of the believer into fresh act and exercise; so that he saith, "Truly my soul waiteth upon God, from Him cometh my salvation. In God is my salvation and my glory: the rock of my strength and my refuge is in God. Trust in Him at all times; ye people, pour out your hearts before Him."

Thus, in course of the believer's experience, a way is opened for his knowing God more fully, as his covenant God, and for trusting in Him under that character. Looking on the promises and declarations of grace in Christ Jesus, as so many parts of the covenant, he finds, that, as there is a time for the execution of all God's purposes, so there is for the fulfilment of all His exceeding great and precious promises, and that some of them would remain unknown to him, if he were not brought into soul-distress. Moreover, in some circumstances, he prizes spiritual strength more than divine consolations; and he sees ground for faithfulness for this promise **at all times,** let his frame and feelings be ever so uncomfortable: "He giveth power to the faint, and to them that have no might He increaseth strength." From his own experinece he can give God the honour of saying concerning Him, "He is faithful which promised": and may add, "He will not leave me nor forsake me". I have His word for it. To live thus by faith on God, as He hath been pleased to reveal Himself in the Word, and to hold communion wtih Him by mixing faith therewith, is the glory of our most holy profession: it is doing God the utmost honour, and giving Him the highest glory we can possibly render Him on this side heaven.

O my soul; learn thou to improve this subject daily. Seek to put honour in His Word by steadfast faith continually. O, thou blessed God and Father, who keepest covenant forever, blessed be Thy holy Name! Thou art ever mindful of it. O, look upon the glorious Mediator of it, and upon me in Him! And, for His sake, bestow on me Thy Holy Spirit, as the Spirit of promise to put life into it; and send Him to explain and apply Thy promises, as my various cases may require. I thank Thee for appointing Christ to be the Captain of salvation, and for calling me to fight under His banner against sin, the world and devil. Thou hast provided me with armour of proof. Lord, clothe me with it. Teach me the proper use of every part, and let me go forward, fighting the good fight of faith, laying hold of eternal life. I ask it for the honour of thy grace, and would ascribe all praise to the Father, the Son and the Holy Spirit; to whom, as co-equal and co-eternal in the unity of one undivided Godhead, be everlasting glory, blessing, and worship. Amen.

S. E. PIERCE, 1804.

We are now writing on the International Sunday School Lessons. Send to us for sample copy of "Sunday School Helps", published by Mr. Herendeen of Cleveland, at 50 cents a year.

the progress of time—which would be horrible blasphemy. No man who believes that the Divine understanding is infinite, comprehending the past, the present, and the future, will ever assent to the erroneous doctrine of temporal decrees. God is not ignorant of future events which will be executed by human volitions; He has foretold them in innumerable instances, and prophecy is but the **manifestation** of His eternal prescience. Scripture affirms that believers were chosen in Christ before the world began (Eph. 1:4), yea, that grace was "given" to them then (2 Tim. 1:9).

Second, the decrees of God are **wise**. Wisdom is shown in the selection of the best possible ends and of the fittest means of accomplishing them. That this character belongs to the decrees of God is evident from what we know of them. They are disclosed to us **by their execution**, and every proof of wisdom in the works of God is a proof of the wisdom of the **plan**, in conformity to which they are performed. As the Psalmist declared, "O Lord, how manifold are Thy works! in wisdom hast Thou made them all" (Psalm 104:24). It is indeed but a very small part of them which falls under our observation, yet, we ought to proceed here as we do in other cases, and judge of the whole by the specimen, of what is unknown, by what is known. He who perceives the workings of admirable skill in the parts of a machine which he has an opportunity to examine, is naturally led to believe that the other parts are equally admirable. In like manner should we satisfy our minds as to God's works when doubts obtrude themselves upon us, and repel the objections which may be suggested by something which we cannot reconcile to **our** notions of what is good and wise. When we reach the bounds of the finite and gaze toward the mysterious realm of the Infinite, let us exclaim "O the depth of the riches, both of the wisdom and knowledge of God" (Rom. 11:33).

Third, they are **free**. "Who hath directed the Spirit of the Lord, or being His counsellor hath taught Him? With whom took He counsel, and who instructed Him, and taught Him in the path of judgment, and taught Him knowledge, and showed to Him the way of understanding"? (Isa. 40:13, 14). God was alone when He made His decrees, and His determinations were influenced by no external cause. He was free to decree or not to decree, and to decree one thing and not another. This liberty we must ascribe to Him whom is supreme, independent, and sovereign in all His doings.

Fourth, they are **absolute and unconditional**. The execution of them is not suspended upon any condition which may, or may not be, performed. In every instance where God has decreed an end, He has also decreed every means to that end. The One who decreed the salvation of His elect, also decreed to work faith in them (2 Thess. 2:13). "My counsel shall stand, and I will do **all** My pleasure" (Isa. 46:10): but that could not be, if His counsel depended upon a condition which might not be performed. But God "worketh all things after the counsel of His own will" (Eph. 1:11).

Side by side with the immutability and invincibility of God's decrees, Scripture plainly teaches that man is a responsible creature and answerable for his actions. And if our thoughts are formed from God's Word the maintenance of the one will not lead to the denial of the other. That there is a real difficulty in defining where the one ends and the other begins, is freely granted. This is ever the case where there is a conjunction of the Divine and the human. Real prayer is indited by the Spirit, yet it is also the cry of a human heart. The Scriptures are the inspired Word of God, yet were they written by men who were something more than machines in the hand of the Spirit. Christ is both God and man. He was Omniscient, yet "increased in wisdom" (Luke 2:52). He was Almighty, yet was "crucified through weakness" (2 Cor. 13:4). He was the Prince of life, yet He died. High mysteries are these, yet faith receives them unquestioningly.

It has often been pointed out in the past that, every objection made against the eternal decrees of God applies with equal force against His eternal foreknowledge. "Whether God has decreed all things that ever come to pass or not, all that own the being of a God, own that He knows all things beforehand. Now, it is self-evident, that if He knows all things beforehand, He either doth approve of them or doth not approve of them; that is, He either is willing they should be, or He is not willing they should be. But to will that they **should be**, is to decree them" (Dr. Jonathan Edwards).

Finally, attempt to assume and then contemplate the opposite. To **deny** the Divine decrees would be to predicate a world and all its concerns regulated by **un**-designed chance or blind fate. Then what peace, what assurance, what comfort would there be for our poor hearts and minds? What refuge would there be

(Continued on Page 47)

VOL. IX.   MARCH, 1930   No. 3

STUDIES IN THE SCRIPTURES

"Search the Scriptures" John 5 : 39

Copyright in all English-speaking Countries.

Editor: Arthur W. Pink, Morton's Gap, Ky., U. S. A.
Hon. Agent in England: Mr. A. Winstone, 2, Lennox Villas, Hewlett Road, Cheltenham.
Hon. Agent in Australia: Mr. G. Ardill, The Christian Workers' Depot.
Commonwealth and Reservoir Streets, Sydney.

THE KNOWLEDGE OF GOD

God is omniscient. He knows everything: everything possible, everything actual; all events, all creatures, of the past, the present and the futre. He is perfectly acquainted with every detail in the life of every being in heaven, in earth and in hell. "He knoweth what is in the darkness" (Dan. 2:22). Nothing escapes His notice, nothing can be hidden from Him, nothing is forgotten by Him. Well may we say with the Psalmist, "Such knowledge is too wonderful for me; it is high, I cannot attain unto it" (Psa. 139:6). His knowledge is perfect. He never errs, never changes never overlooks anything. "Neither is there any creature that is not manifest in His sight: but all things are naked and open unto the eyes of Him with whom we have to do" (Heb. 4:13). Yes, such is the God with whom we "have to do"!

"Thou knowest my downsitting and mine uprising, Thou understandest my thoughts afar off. Thou compassest my path and my lying down, and art acquainted with **all** my ways. For there is not a word in my tongue but, lo, O Lord, Thou knowest it altogether" (Psa. 139:2-4). What a wondrous Being is the God of Scripture! Each of His glorious attributes should render Him honourable in our esteem. The apprehension of His omniscience ought to bow us in adoration before Him. Yet how little do we meditate upon this Divine perfection! Is it because the very thought of it fills us with uneasiness?

How solemn is this fact: nothing can be concealed from God! "For I know the things that come into your mind, every one of them" (Ezek. 11:5). Though He be invisible to us, we are not so to Him. Neither the darkness of night, the closest curtains, nor the deepest dungeon can hide any sinner from the eyes of Omniscience. The trees of the garden were not able to conceal our first parents. No human eye beheld Cain murder his brother, but his Maker witnessed his crime. Sarah might laugh derisively in the seclusion of her tent, yet was it heard by Jehovah. Achan stole a wedge of gold and carefully hid it in the earth, but God brought it to light. David was at much pains to cover up his wickedness, but ere long the all-seeing God sent one of His servants to say to him "Thou art the man!" And to writer and reader is also said, "Be sure **your** sin will find you out". (Num. 32:23).

Men would strip Diety of His omniscience if they could—what a proof that "the carnal mind **is** enmity against God" (Rom. 8:7)! The wicked do as naturally hate this Divine perfection as much as they are naturally compelled to acknowledge it. They wish there might be no Witness of their sins, no Searcher of their hearts, no Judge of their deeds. They seek to banish such a God from their thoughts: "They consider not in their hearts that I remember all their wickedness" (Hosea 7:2). How solemn is Psa. 90:8! good reason has every Christ-rejecter for trembling before it: "Thou hast set our iniquities before Thee, our **secret** sins in the light of Thy countenance".

But to the believer, the fact of God's omniscience is a truth fraught with much comfort. In times of perplexity, he says with Job, "But **He knoweth** the way that I take" (23:10). It may be profoundly mysterious to me, quite incomprehensible to my friends, but "**He knoweth**"! In times of weariness and weakness believers assure themselves "**He knoweth** our frame; He remembereth that we are dust" (Psa. 103:14). In times of doubt and suspicion they **appeal to** this very attribute, saying, "**Search me**, O God, and know my heart: try me, and know my thoughts: and see if there be any wicked in me, and lead me in the way everlasting" (Psa. 139:23, 24). In time of sad failure, when our actions have belied our hearts, when our deeds

(Continued on Page 72)

IMPORTANT NOTICES

Please advise promptly of change of address, otherwise copies will be lost in the mails.

We are glad to send a sample copy to any of our friends whom you believe would be interested in such a publication.

Send to Mr. I. C. Herendeen, 433-435, The Arcade, Cleveland, Ohio, for a list of our publications. He has published many of our books and booklets.

This Magazine is published as a work of faith and labour of love. The Editor and his wife gladly give their services. It is freely sent to all who will read it. No charge is made for it.

Christians who feel definitely lead to do so, may have fellowship with us in this ministry. Those outside the U. S. A., please send only INTERNATIONAL Money Orders made out to Morton's Gap, Kentucky, U. S. A. See that it is made out in American money.

CONTENTS

The Epistle to the Hebrews 50
The Satisfaction ("Atonement")
  of Christ 56
The Work of the Holy Spirit 62
Prayer Perverted 65
The Snare of Service 68
Assurance 70
Quietness 71

THE EPISTLE TO THE HEBREWS

27. True Christians Described: Heb. 6:9-11

The passage which is to be before us is in strong and blessed contrast from what we found in vv. 4-6. There we beheld a class of people highly favoured, blest with grand external privileges, richly gifted, and wrought upon by the Holy Spirit. There we see the faculties of the natural man's soul wound up to their highest pitch: the conscience searched, the understanding enlightened, the affections drawn out, and the will moved to action. There we have described the character of a class which constitutes a very large proportion of those who profess the name of Christ. Yet, though they have never been born again, though they are unsaved, though their end is destruction, nevertheless, it is by no means an easy matter for a real child of God to identify them. Oftentimes their head-knowledge of the truth, their zeal for religion, their moral qualities, put him to shame. Still, if he weigh them in the balances of the sanctuary, they will be found wanting.

The careful reader of the four Gospels, will discover that in the days of His flesh, the Lord Jesus healed those concerning whom nothing is recorded of their faith. The blessings which He dispensed were not restricted to His disciples. Temporal mercies were bestowed upon natural men as well as upon spiritual. And, be it carefully noted, this was something more, something in addition to, the providential goodness of the Creator, which is extended to all of Adam's race: "He maketh His sun to rise, on the evil and on the good, and sendeth rain on the just and on the unjust" (Matt. 5:45). Rather did those gracious acts of Christ unto the unbelieving, foreshadow that which we designated in the preceding article, the interior operations of His Spirit. On a few Christ bestowed spiritual blessings, saving mercies; to others, He imparted temporal blessings, mercies which came short of saving their recipients.

In our last article we made reference to James 1:17: "Every good gift and every perfect gift is from above". We believe that, in keeping with the character, theme and purpose of that epistle, those words have reference to two distinct classes of gifts, for two different classes of people: the "good" referring to those bestowed, under Gospel-ministry on the non-elect; the "perfect" imparted to God's own people. A scripture which we believe supplies strong corroboration of this is found in Psa. 68:18. There, in a Messianic prophecy concerning the ascension of Christ, we read, "Thou hast received gifts for men; yea, for the rebellious also": gifts are bestowed by Christ on two distinct classes. It is to be particularly observed that a part of this verse is quoted by the Spirit in Eph. 4:8; part of it we say, for its closing words, "the rebellious also" are there omitted. And why? Because in Ephesians it is the elect of God (see 1:3, 4 etc) who are in view. Yet, in addition to them, Christ has received "gifts" for the "rebellious also"; that is, for the non-elect too.

Few indeed have perceived that there is **a double work of** GOD being prosecuted under the ministry of the Gospel. Plain intimation of this is found in the words of Christ in Matt. 22:14, "For many are called, but few chosen." Half of the human race has never heard the Gospel; those who have, are divided into four classes, as Christ has taught us in His parable of the Sower. The "wayside" hearers are those upon whom the preaching of the Gospel produces no effect. The "stony" and the "thorny" ground hearers are they which form a very large percentage of "church members" or who are "in fellowship" with those known as "the Brethren". Of these it is said that they "for a while believe" (Luke 8:13); nor are they unproductive, yet they "bring no fruit to perfection" (Luke 8:14). In them the "enmity" of the carnal mind is, to a considerable extent, subdued; yet it is not vanquished. There is a work of the Spirit upon them, yet it falls short of the new creation. They are "called" but not "chosen".

Only as due attention is paid to the distinction just noted, are we really able to appreciate the point and meaning of the qualifying language which the Spirit of God has used when speaking of the saving call of God's elect. For example, in Rom. 8:28 they are denominated the called "according to His purpose", which notes a distinction from others who receive an inferior "call" according to His providence, under the general proclamation of the Gospel. So too in 2 Tim. 1:9 we read of those "called with a holy calling... according to His own purpose and grace", which is the language of discrimination, signifying there are others called yet not with "a holy calling". So again in 1 Peter 5:10, "The God of all grace, who hath called **us** unto His eternal glory", is in antithesis from the many who are only called unto a temporal righteousness in this world.

It needs to be very carefully noted that the "us" of the Epistles is frequently used with a far narrower discrimination than from all the rest of the world: very often the "us" is in contrast from the great crowd of lifeless professors which ever surrounds the little handful of God's true people—professors which, though spiritually lifeless, are yet to be distinguished from the vast multitudes of non-professors; distinguished by a real work of the Holy Spirit upon them, but still an abortive work. Of this class the Epistle of James has much to say. Concerning them John, in his first Epistle, declares "They went out from **us**, but they were not of **us**; for if they had been of **us**, they would have continued with **us**" (2:19). A work of "calling" must have been wrought upon them, for they had once separated from the world and united themselves with the true people of God. Moreover, that work of "calling" must have produced such a change in them that **they** had been accounted real Christians, or otherwise they had not been admitted among such.

The occasion of Christ's uttering those words "For many are called, but few chosen" (Matt. 22:14) is exceedingly solemn and searching. The context records the parable of the wedding-feast of the King's Son. First, the invitation to it had been given to the Jews, but they despised it, mistreated God's servants, and, in consequence, their city was destroyed. Then God's servants are sent forth into the Gentile highways to bring in others. But when the King inspects the guests. He sees a man "which had not on a wedding-garment". The awful sentence goes forth, "Bind him hand and foot, and take him away, and cast him into outer darkness." Immediately after, Christ said, **"For** many are called, but few chosen".

Now in sharp and blessed contrast from the many professing the name of Christ who have received only the inferior call of God through the Gospel—a call which, yet, leads them to assent to the doctrine of His word, which brings them to espouse the outward cause of Christ in this world, which produces a real reformation in their ways, so that they become respectable and useful members of their community, as well as provide a measure of protection to the **few** of God's "chosen" from the openly antagonistic world;—our present passage treats of "the **remnant** according to the election of grace" (Rom. 11:5). This is clear from its opening words, "But, beloved, we are persuaded better things of you." The "But" sets these "beloved" ones in opposition from those mentioned in v. 8. The "better things" also points an antithesis. "Better" is an adjective in the comparative degree, set over against something which is merely "good". Those described in vv. 4, 5 had good things yet these possessed something far better. Mark how this confirms what we have said on James 1:17!

In vv. 9-12 we find the apostle doing three things: first, he expresses his good will towards the Hebrew saints; second, he declares his judgment concerning their state; third, he gives the grounds upon which his judgment was based. His aim was that they should make a proper use of what he had set before them in the first eight verses, so that on the one hand they might not be discouraged, and on the other hand not become careless. We subjoin Dr. J. Brown's summary of our passage. "The general meaning of this paragraph, all the parts of which are closely connectetd together, plainly is: The reason why I have made these awful statements about apostates, is not because I consider you whom I am addressing as apostates for your conduct proves that this is not your charactetr, and the promise of God secures that this doom shall not be yours; but that you may be stirred up to persevering steadiness in the faith, and hope, and obedience of the truth, by a constant continuance in which alone you can, like those who have gone before you, obtain in all their perfections the promised blessings of the Christian salvation."

"But, beloved" (v. 9). This term testified to the apostle's good will toward and affection in the Hebrew saints. Such an expression was more than the formal language of courtesy; it revealed the warmth of Paul's heart for God's people. Though he had spoken severely to them in 5:11-14, it was not because he was unkindly disposed toward them. Love is faithful, and because it seeks the highest good of its objects, will reprove, rebuke, admonish, when occasion calls for it. Spiritual love is regulated not by impulse, but by principle. Herein it differs from the backboneless amiability and affability of the flesh, and from the maudlin sentimentality of the day. "We hence conclude, that not only the reprobates ought to be reproved, severely, and with sharp earnestness, but also the elect themselves, even those whom we deem to be children of God" (J. Calvin).

"The apostle hastens to comfort and encourage, lest the Hebrews should be overwhelmed with fear and sorrow, or least they should think that their condition was regarded by him as hopeless. The affection of the writer is now eager to inspire hope, and to draw them with the cords of love. The word 'beloved' is introduced here most appositely, a term of endearment which occurs frequently in other epistles, but only once in ours; not that the apostle was not filled with true and fervent love to the Hebrew Christians, but that he felt obliged to restrain as it were his feelings, by reason of the prejudices against him. But here the expression bursts forth, as in a moment of great danger or of anxious suspense the heart **will** speak out in tender language" (A. Saphir).

"But, beloved, we are persuaded better things of you". In these words the apostle sets forth his judgment concerning the spiritual state of the Hebrews (cf. 3:1). The "persuasion" here did not amount to an infallible certitude, but was a strong confidence based on good grounds. It is similar to what we find in Rom. 15:14, "I myself also am persuaded of you my brethren, that ye also are full of goodness, fil.ed with all knowledge, able also to admonish one another". So again in 2 Tim. 1:5, "When I call to remembrance the unfeigned faith that is in thee, which dwelt first in thy grandmother Lois, and thy mother Eunice; and I am persuaded that in thee also." However low the spiritual condition of these Hebrews (5:11-14), there had been, and still was found in them, fruit, such as manifested them to be truly regenerated souls. It ever holds good that a tree is known by its fruits, hence, the genuineness of my Christian profession is evidenced by what I bring forth, or its worthlessness by what I fail to produce. There may be a "form of godliness" (2 Tim. 3:5), but if the power thereof be "denied" by my works (Titus 1:16) then is it profitless and vain.

"But, beloved, we are persuaded better things of you." It is the bounden duty of every pastor to ascertain the spiritual condition of his people: "Be thou diligent to know **the state** of thy flocks" (Prov. 27:23). This is very necessary if the servant of God is to minister suitably and seasonably. While he is ignorant of their state, he knows not when or how to rebuke or console, to warn or encourage. A general preaching at random is little more than a useless formality. A physician of bodies must acquaint himself with the condition of his patients, otherwise he cannot prescribe intelligently or effectually. Equally so it is with a physician of souls. The same principle holds good in the fellowship of Christians one with another. I cannot really love a brother with the Gospel-love which is required of me, unless I have a well-grounded persuasion that he **is** a brother.

"And things that accompany salvation" (v. 9). The word "accompany" signifies "conjoined with", or inseparable from, that which has a sure connection with "salvation". The principal things that "accompany salvation" are sorrow for and hatred of sin, humility or self-abnegation, the peace of God comforting the conscience, godly fear or the principle of obedience, a diligent perseverance in using the appointed means of grace and pressing forward in the race set before us, the spirit of prayer, and a joyous expectation of being conformed to the image of Christ and spending eternity with Him. True Gospel faith and sincere obedience are far "better things" than the most dazzling gifts ever bestowed on unregenerate professors.

To believe on Christ is very much more than my understanding assenting and my will consenting to the fact that He is a Saviour for sinners, and ready to receive all who will come to Him. To be received by Christ, I must come to Him renouncing all my own righteousness (Rom. 10:3), as an empty-handed beggar (Matt. 19:21). But more; to be received by Christ, I must come to Him forsaking my self-will and rebellion against Him (Psa. 2:11, 12; Prov. 28:13). Should an insurrectionist and seditionist come to an earthly king seeking his sovereign favour and pardon, then, obviously, the very law of his coming to him for forgiveness requires that he should come on his knees, laying aside his hostility. So it is with a sinner who comes to Christ for pardon; it is against the law of faith to do otherwise.

An "unfeigned faith" (2 Tim. 1:5) in Christ, is one which submits to His yoke and bows to His authority. There is no such thing in Scripture as receiving Christ as Saviour **without also** receiving Him as Lord: "As ye have therefore received Christ Jesus **the Lord**, walk ye in Him" (Col. 2:6). If it be an honest and genuine faith, it is inseparably connected with a spirit of obedience, a desire to please Him, a resolve to not henceforth live unto self, but unto Him which died for me (2 Cor. 5:15). The man who really thinks he has a saving faith in Christ, but yet has no concern for His glory and no heart for His commandments, is blinded by Satan. There are things which **"accompany** salvation", that have a certain connection therewith. As light iis inseparable from the shining of the sun, as heat is inseparable from fire, so good works are inseparable from a saving faith.

"Though we thus speak" (v. 9). The reference is to what the apostle had said about apostates in vv. 6, 8, and which had been written to these Hebrews as a solemn and searching warning for them to take to heart. "In the visible professing church, all things outwardly seemed to be equal. There are the same ordinances administered unto all, the same profession of faith is made by all, the same outward duties are attended unto, and scandalous offences are by all avoided. But yet things are not internally equal. In a great house, there are vessels of wood and stone, as well as of gold and silver. All that eat outwardly of the bread of life, do not feed on the hidden manna. All that have their names enrolled in the church's book, may yet not have them written in the Lamb's book. There are yet better things than gifts, profession, participation of ordinances and whatever is of the like nature. And the use hereof in one word is to warn **all** sorts of persons, that they rest not in, that they take not up with an interest in, or participation of the privileges of the church, with a common profession, which may give them a name to live; seeing they may be dead or in a perishing condition in the mean time" (Dr. J. Owen).

"For God is not unrighteous to forget your work" (v. 10). Here the apostle makes known the ground on which his "persuasion" rested, and that was, the unchanging faithfulness of God toward His covenant promises unto His people, and why he believed that these Hebrews were numbered among them. The foundation on which confidence should rest concerning my own security unto eternal glory, as that of my fellow-Christians, is nothing in the creature. "It is of the Lord's mercies that we are not consumed" (Lam. 3:22). The believer's perseverance is not the cause but the consequence of God's preservation.

"For God is not unrighteous to forget your work". A scripture which enables us to understand the force of these words is 1 John 1:9, "If we confess our sins, He is faithful and just to forgive us our sins". God is "faithful" to His covenant engagements with us in the person of His Son; "just", to the full satisfaction which He rendered unto Him. The very justice of God is engaged on the behalf of those whom Christ redeemed. His veracity towards us is pledged: "In hope of eternal life, which God, that cannot lie, **promised** before the world began" (Titus 1:2). And because God is immutable, without variableness or shadow of turning, He cannot go back on His own oath: "For I am the Lord, I change not; **therefore** ye sons of Jacob are not consumed" (Mal. 3:6). Therefore have we the absolute assurance that "He which hath begun a good work in you will **finish it**" Phil. 1:6).

"For God is not unrighteous to forget your work". Some have found a difficulty here, because these words seem to teach that heaven is a reward earned by good works. But the difficulty is more apparent than real. What God rewards is only what He Himself hath wrought in us: it is the Father's recognition of the Spirit's fruit. "The act of a benefactor in entering into engagements with his beneficiary may be wholly gratuitous, and yet, out of his act, rights may grow up to the beneficiary. The advantages thus acquired are not the less gracious, because they have become rights; for they originated in free grace" (Dr. Sampson, 1857).

It may look now as though God places little value on sincere obedience to Him, that in this world the man who lives for self gains more than he who lives for Christ; yet, in a soon-coming day it shall appear far otherwise.

"For God is not unrighteous to forget your works". "God does not pay us a debt, but performs what He has of Himself freely promised, and not so much on our works, as on His own grace in our works; nay, He looks not so much on our works, as on His own grace in our works. And this is to be 'righteous', fo rHe cannot deny Himself... God is righteous in recompensing works, because He is true and faithful; and He has made Himself a debtor to us, not by receiving anything from us, but, as Augustine says, by freely promising all things" (John Calvin). They who imagine there is an inconsistency between the God of all grace "rewarding" His people, will do well to ponder carefully the Reformer's words.

"Your work". We believe the reference here is to their **faith.** First, because he is here speaking of the "things that accompany salvation", and faith is inseparable therefrom. Second, because faith "worketh by love" (Gal. 5:6), and the very next thing mentioned in our verse is their "labour of love". Third, because in 1 Thess. 1:3 we read of the "work of faith, and labour of love, and patience of hope", and in Heb. 6:11, we have their "hope" mentioned. Should it be inquired, Why did the apostle omit the express mention of "faith" here? We answer, Because their faith was so small and feeble. To have commended their faith directly, would have weakened the force of his repeated exhortations in 3:12, 4:1, 2, 6:12, 12:1 etc. "Your work" refers not to any single work, but to a course of working, i. e. the whole course of obedience to God, of which faith is the principle moving thereunto. Evangelical obedience is thus denominated "your work" because this is what they had been regenerated unto (see Eph. 2:10), and because such a course calls for activity, pains, toil; cf. "all diligence" (2 Peter 1:5).

A living faith is a **working** faith (James 2:17). Two things are plainly and uniformly taught throughout the N. T. Justification is by faith, and not by works, (Rom 4 etc.). Yet, such justifying faith is a living, operative, fruitful faith, evidencing itself by obedience to the commands of God (1 John 2:4 etc.). Christ gave Himself for us that "He might redeem us from all iniquity, and purify unto Himself a peculiar people, **zealous of good works**" (Titus 2:14). This greatly needs emphasising today and pressing repeatedly upon those professing to be believers in the Lord Jesus, for multitudinous of these have a name to live, but "are dead" (Rev. 3:1). Their faith is not that of God's elect (Titus 1:1), but nothing better or different than that which the demons have (James 2:19).

"Your faith and the labour of love", for so the Greek reads. These were the evidences upon which the apostle grounded his confidence concerning the Hebrew saints. Five things are to be noted. First this distinguishing grace, their "labour of love": let the reader turn to and ponder carefully 1 John 3:16-19; 4:7-12. "Mutual love among believers is a fruit of the Spirit of holiness, and an effect of faith, whereby being knit together in the bond of entire spiritual affection, on the account of their joint interest in Christ; and participation of the same, new, divine, spiritual nature from God, they do value, delight and rejoice in one another, and are mutually helpful in a constant discharge of all those duties whereby their eternal, spiritual and temporal good may be promoted" (Dr. J. Owen). Note **"labour** of love": a lazy love, like that of James 2:15, 16, is no evidence of saving faith. True love is active, diligent, untiring.

"Which ye have showed". This gives us the second feature of their love. It was not a secret and unmanifested love: but one that had been plainly evidenced in a practical way. In James 2:18 the professor is challenged to "show" his faith, today it would also be pertinent to ask many of those who bear the name of Christ to "show" their love, especially along the line of 1 John 5:2. "Which ye have showed toward His name," defines, third, the **end before them** in the exercise of their ardent love in ministering to the saints. The words last quoted have a three-fold force. **Objectively,** because God's name is upon His people (Eph. 3:15). It is both blessed and solemn to know that whatever is done unto the people of God, whether it be good or evil, is done toward the name of Christ: Matt. 25:34-45. **Formally:** they ministered to the saints **as** the people of God. This it is which gives spiritual love its distinctive character: when it is exercised to souls **because** God's name is on them. **Efficiently:** the "name of God" stands for His authority. God requires His people to love one another, and when they do so out of obedience to Him, it is, necessarily, done "toward His name", having respect to His will.

"In that ye have ministered to the saints, and do minister". This tells us, fourth, the **manner** in which their love had been exercised: in an untiring service. Fifth, it announces, the objects of their love, God's "saints". Many of God's people are in various kinds of temporal distress, and one reason why their loving Father permits this is, that their brethren and sisters in Christ may have the holy privilege of ministering to them: see Rom. 15:25-27, 2 Cor. 8:21, 9:11-15. But let such ministry be rendered not from sentimental considerations, nor to satisfy an uneasy conscience, still less with the object of vain glory, to gain a reputation for benevolence; rather let it be **"shown toward** His name". It is the owning of His authority, the conscious performance of His will, which alone gives life, spirituality and acceptance unto all those duties of love which we are able to perform to others.

In summing up the teaching of vv. 9, 10, let us observe **how** the apostle justified the Hebrews according to his Master's rule in Matt. 7:15-20. Genuine Christians give plain evidence that **their** profession of the Gospel **is** accompanied by transforming grace. The obedience of faith and the labour of love toward the saints—not from human instincts, but out of submission to the revealed will of God —both in the past and in the present, were the visible ground of Paul's good persuasion concerning them. It is important to note **what** were the particular graces singled out for mention. The apostle says nothing about their clear views of the truth, their missionary activities, zeal for "their church"—which are the things that many formal professors boast in.

"And we desire that every one of you do show the same diligence to the full assurance of hope unto the end" (v. 11). The apostle looks back to the exhortation of v. 1 and also the solemn warning pointed in vv. 4-8. His purpose had been to excite them unto a diligent persevering continuance in faith and in love, with the fruits thereof. All he had said was unto this end. The closer connection of this verse with the preceding one is: having expressed his conviction about their spiritual state, and having assurd them of a blessed issue of their faith from the fidelity of God, he now presses upon them their responsibility to answer to the judment he had formed of them, by diligent progress unto the end.

In this verse (11) the apostle, with heavenly wisdom, makes known the proper use and end of Gospel threatenings (vv. 6-8), and Gospel promises (vv. 9, 10): either may be, and often are, abused. Many have looked upon threatenings as serving no other purpose than a terrifying of the minds of men, causing them to despair; as if the things threatened must inevitably be their portion. Few have known how to make a right application of them to their consciences. On the other hand, many have abused the promises of God: those who had no title to such have suffered themselves to be deceived, and to be so falsely comforted by them to lie down in a carnal security, imagining that no evil could befal them. But here the apostle reveals the proper end of each, both to believers and unbelievers: the threatenings should stir up to earnest examination of the foundation of our hope; the promises should encourage unto a constant and patient diligence in all the duties of obedience. What wisdom is needed by a minister of the Gospel to make a proper and due use of both upon his hearers!

"And", or rather (Greek) "But we desire". In vv. 9, 10 the apostle had told them what was **not** his object in making to them the statements of vv. 4-8; now he tells them what it **was.** The word "desire" here signifies an intense longing; without this, preaching is cold, formal, lifeless. "That every one of you": the loving care and untiring efforts of the minister should be extended to all the members of his flock. The oldest, as much as the youngest, is in need of constant exhortation. "Do show the same diligence . . . unto the end'" Unless this be done, our profession will not be preserved nor God glorified. Paul knew nothing of that half-heartedness and sluggish neglect of the means of grace which today satisfies the generality of those bearing the name of Christ. "Give thyself **wholly** to them" (1 Tim. 4-15).

Many are very "diligent" in their worldly business, still more are most punctual in prosecuting their round of pleasure and fleshly gratification; but there are very few indeed who exercise a godly concern for their souls. To an earnest endeavor after personal holiness, the work of faith and labour of love, the vast majority of professors are strangers, nor can they be persuaded that any such things are required or expected from them. They may be regular attenders of "church" from force of custom; they may perform certain acts of charity for the sake of their reputation; but to be really exercised in heart as to how they may please and honour God in the details of their lives, they know nothing and care still less. Such are **destitute** of those things which "accompany salvation"; they are deluded and lost souls. Make no mistake, my reader, unless there is in you a work of faith in keeping God's commandments, and a labour of love toward His saints as such, then "the root of the matter" (Job 19:28) is **not** in you. This is the test of profession, and the rule whereby each of us shall be measured.

Nor can this work of faith and labour of love be persisted in without studious diligence and earnest endeavour. It calls for the daily searching of the scriptures, and that, not for intellectual gratification, but to learn God's will for my walk. It calls for watchfulness and prayer against every temptation which would turn me aside from following Christ. It requires that I should rigidly abstain from "fleshly lusts that war against the soul" 1 Peter 2:11), yielding myself unto God as one that is passed from death unto life, and my members "as instruments of righteousness unto God" (Rom. 6:13). It requires that I "lay aside every weight" (whatever hinders vital godliness) and the sin which doth so easily beset (the love of self), and run (which calls for the putting forth of all our energies) the race that is set before us" (Heb. 12:2), and that race is a fleeing from the things of this doomed world, with our faces set steadfastly towards God. Those who despise, or even continue to neglect such things, are only nominal Christians.

This "diligence" is to be shown "to the full assurance of hope". Full assurance here signifies a firm conviction or positive persuasion. "Hope" in the N. T. means an ardent desire for and strong expectation of obtaining its object. Faith looks to the Promiser, hope to the things promised. Faith begets hope. God has promised H's people perfect deliverance from sin and all its troubles, and full enjoyment of everlasting glory with Himself. Faith rests on the power and veracity of God to make good His word. The heart ponders these blessings, and sees them as yet future. Hope values and anticipates the realization of them. Like faith, "hope" has its degrees. "Full assurance of hope" signifies a steady prevailing persuasion, a persuasion which issues from faith in the promises made concerning "good things to come". The "diligence" before mentioned, is God's appointed **means** toward this full assurance: compare 2 Peter 1:10, 11. To cherish a hope of Heaven while I am living to please self is wicked presumption. "Unto the end": no furloughs are granted to those called upon to "fight the good fight of faith" (1 Tim. 6:12); there is no discharge from that warfare as long as we are left upon the field of battle. No spiritual state is attainable in this life, where "reaching forth unto those things which are before" (Phil. 3:13) becomes unnecessary.

—ARTHUR W. PINK.

THE SATISFACTION ("ATONEMENT") OF CHRIST

3. Its Necessity

In employing this term, the **necessity** of the Atonement, we are making use of an expression which calls for careful definition and explanation. Unfortunately, many writers have failed to perform this duty, with the consequence that loose and, oftentimes, most God-dishonouring views are entertained upon this aspect of our subject. To say that God must or must not do certain things, is the language of fearful impiety, unless expressly warranted by the very words of Holy Writ. We are living in a day which is strongly marked by irreverence, and the most degrading views of the Almighty are now entertained by some who imagine their views are quite orthodox. It would be a simple matter for us to give illustrations and proofs of this, but we refrain from defiling our readers (1 Cor. 15:33). Suffice it now to point out, once more, that never was there a time when God's people more earnestly needed to heed that word, "Prove all things" (1 Thess. 5:21).

"The Lord of hosts is excellent in counsel and excellent in working" (Isa. 28:29). Infinite wisdom never acts aimlessly. God, who is perfect in knowledge, does nothing without good reason. All His works are proportioned according to His unerring designs. This is true alike in His acts of creation, providence, and grace. At the close of the six days' work we read, "And God saw everything that He had made, and behold, it was **very good**" (Gen. 1:31). Concerning His government over us, "We know that all things work together **for good** to them that love God, to them who are the called according to His purpose" (Rom. 8:28). And as for the operations of His grace, faith unhesitatingly affirms "He hath done all things **well**" (Mark 7:37).

Now the most wondrous of all God's works is that which was performed by His Son here upon earth. When we attempt to contemplate what that Work involved, we are lost in amazement. When we seriously endeavour to guage the depths of unutterable shame and humiliation into which the Beloved of the Father entered, we are awed and staggered. That the eternal Son of God should lay aside the robes of His ineffable glory and take upon Him the form of a servant, that the Ruler of heaven and earth should be "made **under** the law" (Gal. 4:4), that the Creator of the universe should tabernacle in this world and "have not where to lay His head" (Matt. 8:20), is something which no finite mind can comprehend; but where carnal reason fails us, a God-given faith believes and worships.

As we trace the path which was trode by Him who was rich yet for our sake became poor, we cannot but feel that we are entering the realm of mystery; the more so when we learn that every step in His path had been ordered in the eternal counsels of the Godhead. Yet, when we find that path entailing for the One in whom the Father was well pleased, immeasurable sorrow, unutterable anguish, ceaseless ignominy, bitterest hatred, relentless persecution, both from men and Satan, we are made to marvel. And, when we find that path leading to Calvary, and there behold the Holy One nailed to the cross, our wonderment deepens. But, when Scripture itself declares that God not only delivered up Christ into the hands of earth's vilest wretches to be reviled and blasphemed, that God Himself was not merely a spectator of that awful scene, that He not only beheld the sufferings of Heaven's Darling, but that HE also smote Him, scourged Him with the rod of His indignation, and called upon the sword to smite His "Fellow" (Zech. 13:7) we are moved to reverently inquire into the needs-be for such an unparalleled event.

That the incarnation, humiliation and crucifixion of the Son of God were **necessary,** no one who (by grace) bows implicitly before the Word of Truth can doubt for a moment. The language of Christ Himself on this point is too plain to be misunderstood. To Nicodemus He said, "As Moses lifted up the serpent in the wilderness, even so **must** the Son of man be lifted up: that whosoever believeth in Him should not perish, but have eternal life" (John 3:14, 15). To His disciples He declared, "how that He **must** go to Jerusalem, and suffer many things of the elders and chief priests and scribes, and be killed, and be raised again the third day" (Matt. 16:21). So too on the day of His resurrection, He asked, **Ought not** Christ to have suffered these things, and to enter into His glory?" (Luke 24:26). Nevertheless, plain and positive as is the language of these verses, we need to be much upon our guard lest we draw from them a conclusion which will clash with other scriptures and lead us to a most dishonouring conception of God.

From the passages just quoted, and others of a similar character, not a few good men have drawn the inference that the sufferings of Christ were an **absolute** necessity, that the very nature of God rendered them so indispensable that apart from them the salvation of sinners was impossible; yea, that no other possible alternative presented itself to the omniscience of God. To such assertions we cannot assent, for they go beyond the express language of Holy Writ. However plausible the reasoning may be, however logical the deduction, we must, where Scripture is silent, resist a conclusion so momentous. To say that the all-wise God Himself could find no other way of saving sinners, consistently with His holiness and justice, than the one He has, is highly presumptuous. To declare that Omniscience was helpless, that God was obliged to adopt the means which He did, is perilously nigh unto blasphemy.

To affirm that God has selected the best possible way to magnify **all** His perfections in the redemption of His people, is to affirm that which is honouring to Diety, but to assert that this was the **only** way, is going beyond what Scripture declares. That supremest wisdom and supremest love would seek the noblest means to achieve the most glorious ends, we firmly believe; but to conclude that God was unable to contrive any other method is mere fatalism, and, we might add, semi-atheism. According to the theorisings of some theologians we ought to change Eph. 1:11 so that it reads, "He worketh all things **after the necessities** of His own nature." Not so did Christ reason in Gethsemane: He did not accept the bitter cup because of the inexorableness of God's nature, but out of submission to His will.

From the words of our Saviour's in the Garden, "If it be possible let this cup pass from Me," it has been inferred that it was **impossible** it should do so. In one sense that is true: God had **ordained** that Christ should die, the terms of the everlasting covenant required it, the will of God demanded it; so die He **must**. But this is a very different thing from saying that when the Godhead held Their councils no other alternative could be devised, that the death of Christ was an absolute and unavoidable necessity. It is indeed most striking to note, and worthy of our most reverent attention, that at the very time our agonizing Saviour presented His petition, He said, "Abba, Father, **all things are possible** unto Thee; take away this cup from Me: nevertheless not what I will, but what Thou wilt" (Mark 14:36).

In summing up this point, let us never forget that the Atonement originated in the mere good pleasure of God. He was not obliged to save any sinners; He was under **no** obligations to provide a Redeemer at all. That He did so, was purely a matter of grace, and, in the very nature of things, the bestower of "grace" is **free**, absolutely free, to bestow or withhold it, otherwise it would cease to be "grace", and because a debt owed to its recipient. As to the **method** by which God chose to manifest His grace, we can only say that the appointed Mediator has answered to every perfection of God and superlatively magnified all His attributes; and that this Saviour is both the gift of His **love**, and the appointment of His **will**.

Once again we would remind ourselves that we are within the realm of mystery, mystery deep and insoluable to finite intelligence. The entrance of **sin** into the world, God's infinite abhorrence of it, the moral requirements of His government concerning its punishment, the saving of His own people from it, the magnifying of His own name by it, are some of the principal elements entering into this mystery; and the relation which the whole mediatorial scheme of Divine grace has thereunto, is what is now to engage our attention. Conscious of our own utter incapacity to even grapple with, much less solve, a problem so profound; conscious that reasoning thereon is worse than futile, we would prayerfully turn, in humble dependence upon the Spirit of Truth, to the Holy Scriptures, to ascertain what light God has been pleased to throw upon this mystery of mysteries.

1. The Atonement was necessitated by the Will of God

Unless this be our starting point we are certain to err. God's Word implicitly declares that He "worketh **all** things after the counsel of His own will" (Eph. 11:11). The whole extent of this passage contains a revelation of God's eternal counsels concerning His own people. It takes us back before the foundation of the world to the time when He chose them in Christ. While it makes known that it was in **love** He predestinated them unto the adoption of children by Jesus Christ unto Himself, it at once adds, that this purpose was "according to the good pleasure of His **will**" v. 5). It is in Christ that we have "redemption through His blood, the forgiveness of sins, according to the riches of His grace" (v. 7), yet right after we are told, "Having made known unto us the mystery of **His will**, according to His good pleasure which He hath purposed in Himself" (v. 9).

The above passage ought to make it abundantly plain to every impartial mind, that the Atonement or Redemption which God has so graciously provided for His elect, sprang from **no obligation** either in His own nature or from any claims which His creatures had upon Him. There have been not a few writers and preachers who have blasphemously asserted, that the fall of man **obliged** God to provide a Redeemer. They have had the effrontery to affirm, that since the Creator permitted Adam to bring ruin upon himself and his descendants, the least He could do was to raise up a Restorer. They say the exegencies of the situation which sin introduced into the world, **required** that some remedy be given that would neutralize its baneful effects. In short, these traducers of the Most High have argued that the Atonement was **imperative**, if God was to justify His creation of man and vindicate Himself for allowing him to lose his original uprightness. It is to such arrogant rebels that Jude 10 refers: "But these speak evil of those things which they know not."

Others, who gave vent to the enmity of the carnal mind against God in a more moderated form, have insisted that the **benevolence** of God required Him to provide a Saviour for sinners. While allowing that man himself is to shoulder the full blame for the condition in which he now finds himself, while granting that God has justly punished the disobedience of our first parents in ordaining that all their descendants shall taste the bitterness of sin's wages, yet they imagine that God's pity for Adam's fallen children **obliged** Him to provide a Saviour for sinners. A sufficient refutation of this widely-held error is found in the Creator's treatment of the angels that fell: no Saviour was provided for them! "God spared not the angels which sinned" (2 Peter 2:4). There is plain proof that the benevolence of God did not render the Atonement imperative.

Whatever claims an unfallen creature may have upon God, certainly a rebel against Him is entitled to nothing but summary judgment. Nor can offenders against His moral government by anything **they** perform, lay Him under obligation to furnish them with a legal ground of deliverance from sin. To say that they can, would be investing guilty sinners with the power to control the divine Lawgiver, and would completely divest God's grace of its character of sovereign free, and unmerited favour. No there was nothing either in the perfections of God's character nor in the claims of His creatures, which rendered the Atonement an absolute necessity. God's purpose to save a remnant according to the election of grace arose solely out of His own free and sovereign will: the provision of a Saviour to save His people from their sins sprang from naught but God's own determination.

2. The Atonement was necessitated by the Law of God

In saying that the Atonement was necessitated by the Law, we are not contradicting what has been said above, as will plainly appear if close attention be given to the sentences immediately following. The sovereign will of God was exercised in at least two things with respect to the Atonement: first, in His original purpose **to save** sinners, for that was solely His mere good pleasure; second, in the **process decreed** whereby they **should be** saved, namely, through the vicarious work of a Redeemer. Having purposed to save His people from the wrath to come, it pleased God to resolve that their sins should be remitted in a way whereby His Law should be honoured and magnified. But let it be carefully remembered that in this too God acted quite freely, and not from any constraint. The Law itself is of His own appointment, and not something superior to Himself.. Having purposed **to** save, the Everlasting Covenant was drawn up, and the Mediator having freely accepted its terms and having voluntarily placed Himself under the Law, thenceforward all was done in obedience to the Law. Thus, the Eternal Three having elected that redemption should be effected under the Law, all was wrought out in perfect accordance with the Law.

It is in the light of these facts that the passages quoted in an earlier paragraph respecting the relative necessity of the Atonement, are to be interpreted. "As Moses lifted up the serpent . . . so must the Son of man be lifted up". There was no **absolute** necessity in either case. It was sovereign grace, pure and simple, which provided a way of life for the guilty Israelites who were dying in the wilderness. It was by Divine **appointment** that both the brazen serpent and the Antitype were "lifted up"' So of Matt. 16:21. Christ "must" go up to Jerusalem and be killed. Why? Because God had so ordained, because the terms of the Everlasting Covenant so required. So it was not possible for the "cup" to pass from the agonizing Saviour. Why? Because God had willed that salvation should come to His people via His drinking it; thus it had been unalterably determined. "Without shedding of blood there could have been no remission" is what Scripture nowhere affirms. But under the regime God has instituted, "without shedding of blood is no remission" (Heb. 9:22).

It has been well said that, "The work of redemption as well as the course of Nature proceeds in accordance with a predetermined plan, and under absolute and invariable law, law quite as exact as that which governs the material universe. Every end contemplated by the divine mind in the realm of the spiritual, and all the means for its attainment under the reign of absolute law, were determined, with infinite exactness, from the beginning" (Dr. J. Armour).

The analogies between the reign of law in the natural and in the moral spheres are both close and numerous, the former serving to adumbrate the latter. For example, first, every law in the natural world, such as that of the recurring seasons or of gravitation, has been ordained and imposed by the Creator according to His own sovereign will. So too has every law in the moral realm, as that of sowing and reaping, sin and its punishment, been appointed by God. Second, the reign of law, as such, is invariable and inexorable: it knows of no exceptions. If the dearest child on earth drinks poison by mistake, it produces precisely the same effects as though the vilest wretch had deliberately taken in to end his earthly existence. Third, yet, though law and its demands cannot be defied with impunity, a **higher** law may be set in motion reversing the action of an inferior. Poisons have their antidotes. The law of gravity may be overcome by lifting an object from the ground. Law is never suspended, but higher power may intervene and deliver from the effects of a lower by magnifying a superior law. This was the case with the Atonement.

Law requires conformity to its precepts. The more perfect a law, the greater the obligations to respect it. Given a law which is "holy and just and good" (Rom. 7:12), and obedience to it becomes imperative. For God to repeal or even suspend it, would be tantamount to acknowledging there was some defect in it. This could never be. Therefore, creatures made under that law must, of necessity, render obedience to it. In case of their failure, then, before it were possible to justify them, that is, pronounce them righteous, up to the required standard, another must fulfill that law on their behalf, and his righteousness or obedience be imputed to their account. This has actually been done. Christ was "made under the law" (Gal. 4:4), "fulfilled" it (Mat. 5:17), and His obedience has been placed to the legal credit of all His people (Rom. 5:19), so that they are now made "the righteousness of God in Him" (2 Cor. 5:21).

The law not only requires obedience to its precepts, but demands the punishment of its transgressors. Its invariable sentence is "The soul that sinneth, it shall die" (Ezek. 18:4). Inasmuch as God Himself declared this, and He "cannot lie", it inevitably ensues that wherever sin is found, death with all that it includes, must certainly follow. The Lord has expressly affirmed that He "will by no means clear the guilty" (Ex. 34:7). The only way of escape for law's transgressors is for Another to suffer the penalty in their stead. Under the regime which God has instituted, were He to pardon without satisfaction made to His broken law by a Substitute being paid sin's wages, then, God would not only trample upon His own law, but disregard His solemn threatening, and scripture says "He cannot deny Himself" (2 Tim. 2:13). Therefore did God Himself provide that wondrous sacrifice upon which the righteous penalty of the law fell.

To understand aright the work of Redemption, it is all-important that we should hold correct views of the Law of God under which man has transgressed, and the state into which he, by rebellion, has fallen. The law of God points out the duty of man, requiring from him that which is right and just. It cannot be altered in the least degree to exact more or less. It is therefore an unalterable rule of righteousness. This law necessarily implies, as essential to it, a sanction and a penalty—a penalty exactly fitted to the magnitude of the crime in transgressing it. Every creature who is under this law is bound by infinite obligations to obey it, without the slightest deviation from it throughout the whole of his existence. But by transgessing it, man has righteously incurred its penalty and fallen under its curse: "Cursed is every one that continueth not in all things which are written in the book of the law to do them" (Gal. 3:10).

Now the curse under which sinners have fallen, cannot be removed nor the transgressor released until full satisfaction has been made to it. Such satisfaction the sinner himself is utterly unable to render: "By the deeds of the law there shall **no** flesh be justified in His sight" (Rom. 3:20). Because the law of God is an unalterable expression of His will and moral character, neither its demands nor threatenings can be abated. The authority of the law must be maintained. To pardon without a satisfaction, would be acting contrary to law. This insuperable barrier in the way of the sinner's deliverance is what underlay the relative necessity for the Mediator and Deliverer.

In order for the curse of the law to be removed from him who had incurred its anathema, it must fall upon another who is made a curse in his stead. It is at this point the amazing riches of Divine grace have been displayed. Not only was the Christ of God "made under the law", not only did He render perfect obedience to its precepts, but in addition—O wonder of wonders—He was "made a curse for us" (Gal. 3:13). Him did God Himself foreordain to be "a propitiation through faith in His blood to declare His righteousness . . . that He might be (not merely 'merciful", but) **just**, and the Justifier of him which believeth in Jesus" (Rom. 3: 25, 26).

3. The Atonement was necessitated by Sin

In asserting that the Atonement was necessitated by sin, let it not be supposed for a moment that the entrance of sin into this world was a calamity unanticipated by the Creator, and that the Atonement is His means of remedying a defect in His handiwork. Far, far from it. So far from man's fall being unforseen by God, the Lamb was "foreordained before the foundation of the world" (1 Peter 1:19, 20). The tragedy of Eden was no unlooked for catastrophe, but foreknown and permitted by God for His own wise reasons. No, we employ the term used in this third heading in the sense of a **conditional** necessity. As we sought to show in the previous article, the ultimate reason and motive of all God's acts are found within Himself, and that reason and motive is ever His own glory. But "glory" is manifested excellency, therefore God magnifies His manifestative glory by the exercise and exhibition of His manifold perfections.

Wondrously has God used sin as an occasion for displaying His own attributes. He has employed it as a dark background from which has shone forth the more resplendently the beauties of His wisdom, His holiness, His faithfulness, His grace. Thus He **has** made the very wrath of man to "praise Him" (Psa. 76:10). God is ineffably holy. As such, He is absolutely free from every vestige of moral pollution. He delights in whatever is pure, and, therefore He hates whatever is impure: "Thou art of purer eyes than to behold evil, and canst not look on iniquity" (Hab.) 1:13). Now sin is directly opposed to the holiness of God, for it is essentially impure, filthy, abominable; therefore is it the object of His unceasing detestation. How then shall God's abhorrence of sin be manifested by His punishment of it?

The Atonement relatively necessitated by sin is obvious from other considerations. Had the creature never fallen, he had never merited sin's wages. Had he never transgrssed against God's law, no satisfaction had been required for its outraged honour. Sin being obnoxious to both the nature and the law of God renders those who have committed it subject to His displeasure. Again; sin is a grevious dishonour to the manifested glory of God (Rom. 3:22), a direct insult offered to the high Majesty of Heaven, and were sin pardoned without an adequate satisfaction, it would be tantamount to saying that God may be insulted with impunity. But if the holiness of God requires that sin shall be punished, if the law of God requires a satisfaction should be rendered its honour, how can its transgressors possibly escape? Sin has imposed a gulf between the thrice holy One and those who have rebelled against Him (Isa. 59:2). Man is utterly incapable of filling up that gulf or of passing over it.

Well might Job exclaim, "For He is not a man, as I am, that I should answer Him, and we should come together in judgment. Neither is there any Daysman betwixt us, that might lay his hand upon us both" (9:32, 33). Ah, a "Daysman," a **Mediator**, one able to come "betwixt", is what was so urgntly required. And what the terrible condition of fallen sinners needed, the matchless grace of God freely provided. Christ is the Divine answer to the Devil's overthrow of our first parents. And in Christ, and by Christ, every attribute of God has been glorified and every requirement of His law satisfied. Through the incarnation, life and death, of His blessed Son, God has shown to all created intelligences what a terrible thing sin is, what a dreadful breach it had made between Himself and His creatures, how impartial is His justice, what an ocean of love is in His heart to promote the happiness of His people, and, above all, He has secured and advanced His own manifestative glory by the honouring of all His attributes. Through the Atonement God has been vindicated.

But let the final thought of our article be this: it was **sin** which required the Antonement. Let each truly Christian reader make it individual: it was **my** sins that brought down the eternal Son of God to this world of darkness and death. Had there been no other sinner on earth but me, Christ had certainly come here. Yes, it was **my** dreadful and excuseless sins which caused the Lord of glory to become "the Man of sorrows." It was **my** sins which required the Beloved of the Father to descend into such unfathonable depths of shame and suffering. It was for **me** the ineffably Holy One was "made a curse". It was for **me** He endured the cross, suffered separation from God, and tasted the bitterness of death. O may the realization of this make me **hate sin,** and cry daily to God for complete deliverance from it. May the realization of grace so amazing constrain me to **live only** for Him "who loved me and gave Himself for me" (Gal. 2:20).

—ARTHUR W. PINK.

For the benefit of new readers we may say that we have a few sets of the 1928 and 1929 "Studies" on hand. They are in bound form, for future use and reference. They contain our exposition of Hebrews from the beginning. We can supply them at $1.00 each post paid.

3. THE WORK OF THE SPIRIT

When Solomon at the dedication of the temple considered the immensity, blessedness and majesty of the Eternal Three, he broke out with astonishment, saying, "But will God indeed dwell on the earth? Behold, the heaven and heaven of heavens cannot contain Thee, how much less this house that I have builded" (1 Kings 8:27). The temple was a symbol of Christ's body, and solemn pledge of His incarnation. It was an astonishing subject to contemplate, that the second person in the divine Essence would become man and appear in our world, "God manifest in the flesh". And it is equally stupendous grace, that the third person in God should, according to the economy of the covenant, which obtained between the divine person, dwell in His people, and thereby consecrate them for fellowship with the Father and Son. This is one of the great **miracles of grace,** as truly great and divine as the incarnation of the Son of God. By it believers are the temples of God: "your bodies are the temples of the Holy Spirit" (1 Cor. 6:19).

When we view and consider the various frames of mind which the believer hath the inward experience of, with the inward sight, sense and feeling, which he hath from time to time of his own sin, guilt, filth, wounds, and miseries, with the spiritual perception which he hath of his heart's apostacy and departure from the Lord in his daily walk and warfare, it is altogether wonderful to contemplate how the Holy Spirit is pleased to carry on His work of grace with power in the regenerate in defiance of all opposition. It pleases this Divine Teacher to let the believer have a real sight of what he is, as one with the first Adam in the total corruption of his nature, the rebellion of his will, and the alienation of his heart from God, that he may feel every moment his need of Christ and his complete salvation: which is the only antidote for him from all the bitings of the old serpent. And all the experience which the believer hath, from the first moment of his new birth to his investiture with eternal glory, consists in his feeling and knowing, that in his fallen nature dwelleth nothing that is good, and that without Christ he cannot in any one single instance do that which is spiritually good.

This makes way for **grace,** free, sovereign grace, to be exalted in the soul. Indeed it is the good pleasure of the Lord to pursue such a method with the sinner who is called in Christ Jesus with a holy calling, as will leave him to renounce himself in every point of view, and cause him to learn this truth so as to practice it on earth and in heaven forever that "he who glorieth must glory in the Lord". To this very end he is led into the dark chambers of imagery in his heart, and left to feel the plague of it, deprived of sensible manifestations of divine love, that he may know his standing is all of grace. As in the whole economy of the Eternal Three, in their distinct offices and displays of mercy towards the heirs of glory, all is of grace: so it is Their ultimate design and end to exalt the exceeding riches of it in Their kindness to the elect in Christ Jesus. Salvation may be said to be founded on the Father's eternal purpose in Christ Jesus, on the personal mediation of the God-man, and on the indwelling of the Holy Spirit and His internal operations in the called, regenerate, and believing people of God.

As election in Christ, which is the fruit of the Father's everlasting love and His evidence of it to His elect, is vast, mysterious, and divine; so is redmption, as wrought out and eternally completed by the Son of God in the nature and on the behalf of His people. Nor is it less ineffable grace, which is manifested in the office and work of the Holy Spirit, originating from and founded in the covenant settlements of the Three in Jehovah. God the Spirit is in the souls of the regenerate, and dwells in them in an inexplicable way as the spring and fountain of all spiritual life and quickening, and of all holy and Divine influences within and upon them. Thus they have God Himself dwelling in them, and making His abode with them, working in them both to will and to do His good pleasure.

The eternal Spirit dwells in us to give us a sight and feeling of our sinfulness and wounds, that we may be led continually to Christ for the whole of our salvation, and for every grace and benefit thereof. The various cases and frames which the called have the experience of, serve as an occasion for the Holy Spirit to prove and manifest the immutability of His love to them. O how transcendent is this grace! for Him to dwell in us, notwithstanding we are in our fallen nature the subjects of sin and death. It is His great work and office in the souls of the regenerate to give a comprehensive sight and sense of what they are; and He shows the believer by a variety of experiences how the Word of God suits him, and how sweetly and suitably the Lord speaks to him in it. He gives the soul an inward relish of the sweetness of it, and thus leads it to Christ by the Word, and into real communion with Christ by faith in it. Hereby He sweetly shows, that like is all the sweets scattered throughout the whole creation are in their utmost perfection in Christ; so all the grace contained in the Word and promises of God is treasured up in Him who filleth all in all.

As the Holy Spirit carries on His most blessed work in the soul, according to His most faithful and true promise in the Word, so He does it likewise by and with the Word, which He continues to put life and light into. There are various acts and influences performed and put forth by the Holy Spirit in the soul, which faith hath not the least perception of, nor are the effects immediately perceived. Nothing is more sure that the gifts and calling of God are without repentance, that the Lord doth not forsake the work of His hands, and that He will accomplish in His people all the good pleasure of His will. In the whole work of the Holy Spirit within us and upon us we are entirely passive. As we could not live a natural life **one single moment**, unless the Lord by His continual act did breathe in at our nostrils the breath of life; so we could not have spiritual life continued in us, if the Holy Spirit did not continually breathe within us; though this is to us imperceptible. The Psalmist confesseth this truth, saying, "Who holdeth our soul in life" (Psa. 66:9).

As the whole work of God on the soul in regeneration, conversion, sanctification, and perseverance to the end, is the fruit of the new creation: so it is styled by the apostle "a new creature" (Gal. 6:15). Now, as no creature can support itself, but must receive its support and continuance in being from the Lord; so must also the new creature. And, as the sustentation of the universe and preservation of it from falling into its chaotic state are as great a proof of Godhead as creation is itself, being equal to a continued act of it; so the maintaining of spiritual life in the newborn soul, and the drawing of it forth into an exercise in carrying on the work of faith with power, are a standing proof and constant evidence in the regenerate of the eternal power and Godhead of the Holy Spirit. We should study and seek to gain from the inspired Word a spiritual knowledge of His personal, relative, and covenant offices, titles, names and characters, that from hence we might learn to worship Him, to give Him the glory of His distinct personality, and honour Him for the part and office, which He exercises on our behalf agreeably to the transactions of the Divine and co-essential Three in the well-ordered covenant.

The Holy Spirit, as given by the Father, and sent by Christ, is to supply the want of His bodily presence with His church on earth. Hereby our Lord fulfilled His most blessed promise, "Lo, I am with you alway, even unto the end of the world. Amen" (Matt. 28:20). This He makes good by His Spirit, who is spiritually present with His church, and equal to all the concerns of it. He is the Author and Bestower of all spiritual gifts on it. He rears up and builds it on the one everlasting foundation. As His voice was uttered under the O. T. dispensation, so it hath also been under the New. He is Lord and God, who dispenses to all the members of Christ's visible church severally as He will. He is the one living Spirit, who, as the Spirit of life, quickens, animates, and enlivens the whole mystic body of Christ. He is fully acquainted with all the wants of His people. He knows the whole mind and will of the Father and the Son concerning them; for He searcheth all things, yea, the deep things of God; which proves His co-equality with the Father and the Son by essential union with the Godhead.

Christ having opened the way into the Holy of Holies by His most precious bloodshedding, the Holy Spirit descended to dwell and abide in us forever, and to testify the everlasting worth and eternal efficacy of our Lord's obedience and sacrifice, that the Father hath accepted Him, and is infinitely well pleased with His finished work, and that He is at perfect peace with all whom He sees in the Beloved, and saith to them in the everlasting Gospel, "I will be merciful to your unrighteousness, and your sins and your iniquities will I remember no more". Christ said to His disciples, "When the Comforter is come, whom I will send unto you from the Father, even the Spirit of truth, which proceedeth from the Father, He shall testify of Me" (John 15:26). It is very meet, right, and our bounden duty, to get a truly scriptural acquaintance with these truths, and to view and consider the names and titles, which the Holy Spirit sustains in the economy of grace, as they serve to encourage and increase our faith and hope in Him, the Author of all grace in us: and we should consider Him as the fountain and spring of all our spirituality more than we usually do.

It is, perhaps, an almost universal case to be looking more at what we call His work in us, than at **Him,** "Who worketh all our works in us and for us": which leads us frequently to talk more of ourselves than of Him, and to admire ourselves as the subjects of His grace, more than **Himself,** the Worker and Bestower of all we are and have, except sin. The Holy Spirit often works and produces most effects, when we are least sensible thereof. He works passively within and on the regenerate, by giving such views of the inconceivable holiness, purity, and majesty of God, by showing them the exceeding guilt and pollution of sin, and permitting them to have such an inward sense and feeling of it, as make way for an acknowledgment of their own vileness, and lead them to self-abhorrence; the experience of which is made use of by the Holy Spirit to make more room for Christ in the heart. Hereby they are made humble and contrite, meek and lowly of heart: and when they are most humble and broken in spirit, then are they in the highway to be exalted. Thus they are conformed to Christ, who was perfectly humbled as the very preparation to His being exalted far above all heavens, that He might fill all things.

It is the Father's will concerning those whom He foreknew, to "predestinate them to be conformed to the image of His Son". The Holy Spirit is to effect this Divine conformity, which He doth by His inward convictions, teachings, and renewings. Hereby He fits the soul for the fulfillment of the following promise, "Thus saith the high and lofty One that inhabiteth eternity, whose name is holy, I dwell in the high and holy place: with him also that is of a contrite and humble spirit, to revive the heart of the contrite ones" (Isa. 57:15). And like as the Father manifested His love when we were in our lost and low estate; and the Son **His** by laying down His life for us, when we were in our sins: so the eternal Spirit displays His love by dwelling in the regenerate, and revealing and applying the word and promises, work and grace of our Lord Jesus, exactly as the case is, and as the experience of the believer requires. When He is most shut up in his mind, being cold in his affections, dead in his praise, without enlargement at heart, destitute of all spiritual consolation, incapable as he thinks of prayer, and as unable by any effort of his own to **pray** in **prayer,** as he is to make a world: even then he is secretly and imperceptibly led to pour out his heart at the throne of grace, and often **prays most** and **best** when he thinks he prays least. It is at such seasons, that the Holy Spirit according to His office of Intercessor "maketh intercession for him with groanings which cannot be **(fully)** uttered'; but are, nevertheless, partially expressed by the bitter exclamations made by the believer concerning his own inherent vileness, his want of spirituality, and his utter inability to worship God, or perform any spiritual service by any power of his own, or from himself. Hence he renounces all confidence for life and salvation, for blessedness and glory, but in the immutable will and eternal purpose of the Essential Three, expressed in the everlasting covenant; and is led to pray on the consideration of it, and also in agreement with it: which prayer is altogether supernatural, and produced by the secret power and influence of the Holy Spirit. **This** is His making intercession for the saints according to the will of God (Rom. 8:27). As the Spirit of grace and supplication, He engages the heart in prayer, teaches the believer how to pray, and what to pray for; helps him to offer up his supplications with energy, and leads him into spiritual worship, as He directs him in his approach to come in the name of Jesus to the Father, as the God of all grace. All which is through His own secret influence, which the believer is made acquainted with in subsequent experience, as he grows into a more clear and distinct apprehension of the work of the Holy Spirit in His own personal case and experience. Then he hath a clear proof that 'through Christ he hath access by the Spirit unto the Father".

As "the Spirit of the Lord", He leads the believer into real communion with the Lord. As "the good Spirit", He is pleased to bestow on the regenerate such blessings as are spiritual, substantial, durable, and supernatural. As the "Holy Spirit," He sheds His holy, heavenly, and life-giving influences on the regenerate in the use of the Divine means. In prayer, reading, hearing the Gospel, in the observance of the Lord's Supper, in spiritual meditation, and holy conversation, He sanctifies the mind and spiritualizes it thereby. Thus He is to the believer the holy-making Spirit. As "The Spirit of Truth," He guides into all necessary truth. He makes it precious to the soul. He seals it home upon the heart, and therby quickens the believer into spiritual communion with the Lord. As "the Spirit of Christ," He takes of the things which are His; and manifests to him his interest in Christ and His great salvation. As "the Comforter", or **Advocate,** He comforts the heart when cast down, gives fresh v of Christ to the dejected mind, and His cause, His work and worth court of conscience. As "the Spirit of Christ and g'ory," He rests upon the believer, and often gives him a foretaste of glory. And as He dwells by personal inhabitation in the regenerate, He sometimes brings down the real blessedness of heaven into the heart, and enriches the mind with such Divine, supernatural, and exalted views of the love of God in Christ Jesus, as fill the soul with transporting wonder and holy joy, so that the promise is accomplished, "My people shall be satisfied with My goodness, saith the Lord".

O my soul! consider these things. Pray the Lord to give thee an understanding in these experimental points, which concern the office of the Holy Spirit; and how He carries on His work in the soul, when thou canst not sensibly feel nor perceive it. Learn to believe in the personality, deity, work and office of the Holy Spirit, and to honour Him in His relation to the Father and the Son, and for the part He bears in the covenant of grace for thee; and for His names and titles, which He sustains to point out this unto thee. Look up unto Him, saying, O Holy Spirit! I beseech Thee to shine on my mind, and enlighten me from Thy Word, to apprehend spiritually what is revealed therein concerning Thyself, that I may give Thee equal worship and glory with the Father and the Son. Teach me to honour Thee by committing myself wholly to Thee for carrying on, perfecting and crowning with eternal glory what Thou hast already begun in me, and the glory shall be ascribed to Thee, as co-equal and co-eternal with the Father and the Son in one Jehovah, to whom be unceasing praise. Amen.

—SAMUEL E. PIERCE, 1804.

PRAYER PERVERTED

Prayer is the highest privilege which God has granted to His people on earth. It is appointed as the grand means by which they may converse and communicate with their Father. By it they have access to His throne of grace. By it they may b'ess and adore God for His excellencies, praise and magnify Him for all His goodness to them, acknowledge and thank Him for His manifold gifts. By it they may unburden their hearts and cast all their care upon Him. By it they may obtain mercy and find grace to help in time of need. By it they may secure fulfillment of His promises, receive fresh tokens of His love, and make fresh discoveries that He is "a very present help in trouble". But, like other blessings of God, prayer may be, and is, sadly abused.

"In an idle tale, which amused the childhood of many of our readers, there is a worse than foolish fancy of a wishing-cap, which, when the possessor wore it, invested him with the power of obtaining, instantaneously, whatever he desired. Men sometimes appear to regard the promises of God to answer prayer, as serving a similar purpose. As though they meant, that a man. whatever his character, had only to work himself up to a blind and presumptuous confidence, and Omnipotence stood pledged to the accomplishment of his wishes, and that unless his selfish desires were gratified, he would be almost entitled to impugn the Divine veracity" (Mr. James Inglis).

Nowhere does the terrible irreverence of the present generation evidence itself more blatantly than in much of the so-called "praying" of our day. Instead of humbly bowing before the great Jehovah in lowliness and godly fear, many presume to dictate to Him and demand His response to their petitions. Instead of first confessing their own sins, and acknowledging their utter unworthiness to approach the thrice holy God save through the merits of His Son, they consider themselves fully qualified to act as intercessors on behalf of the needs of others. Instead of begging Him to work in them those spiritual graces which are required prerequisites for obtaining an audience with the Most High, there are thousands who call upon God without any apparent concern for their state of soul.

Today the prayer-realm is looked upon by many as affording a legitimate field in which to make experiments. They seize upon some promise of Scripture, "claim" it as theirs, repeat it to God, and imagine that He will grant their request. But the prayer-promises of Holy Writ need to be carefully pondered in the light of their connections and qualifications. If this were done, it would then be seen that they are far from teaching the Almighty has made His will subservient to the caprice of a worm of the earth; that they are far from affirming God has bound Himself to gratify every fleshly whim of sinful creatures. We shall now point out four ways in which prayer is perverted.

1. By the wicked addressing a holy God

Much that has the sound of prayer in human ears falls dead and ineffectual, for

God is not deceived by words upon the lips when there is not behind them a heart that is intent in the performing of His will and the promotion of His manifested glory. Beasts, when in pain, will cry out; so too, man, when in distress, will seek unto God for relief. But that is not prayer. "And they have not cried unto Me with their heart, when they **howled** upon their beds" (Hos. 7:14). Parrots may learn by rote and repeat accurately the words of man. So too, "religious" persons may go through a mechanical performance of uttering some pious expression composed by others. But that is not prayer.

The wicked have no access to God: "No man cometh unto the Father, but by Me"—Christ (John 14:6), makes that unmistakeably plain. Not until a man takes the place of a lost sinner, and intreats mercy for the Mediator's sake, will God regard him with favour. It is true that God is sovereign, and that sometimes He deigns to hear the cries of the unregenerate (Gen. 16:11; 21:17), as He does that of inanimate creatures (Job 38:11; Psa. 147:9); yet that is a vastly different thing from saying the wicked obtain answers to prayer. They do not.

Scripture is too clear on this point to allow of any mistake. "The Lord is far from the wicked: but He heareth the prayer of the righteous" (Prov. 15:29). "He that turneth away his ear from hearing the law, even his prayer shall be abomination" (Prov. 28:9). To apostate Israel God said, "When ye spread forth your hands, I will hide Mine ears from you; yea, when ye make many prayers, I will not hear: your hands are full of blood" (Isa. 1:15). And again, "Behold, I will bring evil upon them, which they shall not be able to escape; and though they shall cry unto Me, I will not hearken unto them" (Jer. 11:11). For God to answer the prayers of those who despise His commands and live only to please themselves, woul be setting a premium on sin and encouraging the wicked in their evil doings. This an holy God cannot do.

2. By attempting to make God the Servant of our lusts

Above we have said, that prayer is the highest privilege which God has granted to His children on earth; but, like every other Divine blessing, it may be, and often is, sadly abused. It is just at this point we may behold the sad havoc which sin has wrought upon the human constitution, in that man so frequently perverts and prostitutes Divine favours and mercies to unworthy ends and base uses. Instead of seeking God's will (for which prayer is designed), the common custom is for man to press for the accomplishment of his own will. Instead of bowing before the throne of grace as a lowly suppliant, the proud creature desires to mount it, and direct its activities. Instead of seeking those gifts which will be for God's glory and our own highest good, only too often we have no immediate concern for His honour, nor even of our deepest spiritual blessing; but think only of our fleshly comforts and present ease.

A solemn confirmation of what we have just written is found in James 4:3, "Ye ask, and receive not, **because** ye ask amiss, that ye may consume it upon your lusts". How this exhibits the leprous depravity of our hearts! How it manifests that self-love which dominates the fallen creature! The prayer-promises of Scripture open to God's people a wondrous door of blessing. "Ask, and it shall be given you; seek, and ye shall find; knock, and it shall be opened unto you" (Matt. 7:7) says Christ. But **what** is the well-nigh general response that is made to this royal invitation? This: an asking for those things which will minister to the flesh, a seeking of what will gratify the carnal nature, an attempting to make God Himself minister to our selfish wishes.

God has bidden us, "Covet earnestly the **best** gifts" (1 Cor. 12:31); but alas, only too often our hearts are set upon the perishing things of time and sense. Christ taught His disciples to "seek **first** the kingdom of God and His righteousness" (Matt. 6:33), and assured them that if they did so, their temporal needs **would be** supplied. Yet, sad to say, instead of yearning for and seeking after spiritual blessings, we think mainly of material mercies. Instead of petitioning God about the needs of our souls, we are more concerned about the good of our bodies, and that, not that God may be glorified, but rather that we may be suffered to enjoy our ease. Ah, my reader, when we make **self** the object and end of our prayers, we are guilty of "asking amiss" (James 4:3).

Before we supplicate God at all, we need to faithfully search our hearts, and ascertain the **end** we have in view for the mercies we are about to request. Suppose we are going to ask God for a reasonable measure of temporal prosperity: let us first examine our motive, and discover **why** we desire this. If we are on the point of asking Him for health and strength, pause and ascertain **why** we seek them. If it is the salvation of our children which is to be the burden of our petition, ask, Why **our** children rather than somebody else's? O how much **sin** there is in our prayers! Any prayer which has self for its end, rather than the glory of God, is obviously wrong. If I ask God for my daily bread in order that I may be able to serve Him more freely and cheerfully, that is well; but if I have no higher motive than that my lot in this world may be more comfortable and congenial, that is ill. How much we need the help of the Holy Spirit in our praying!

Reader, if you really wish to do so, you may **test** the state of your own soul by making an application **to yourself** of what has been said above. What **are** the things for which you most frequently supplicate God? The carnal-minded yearn for carnal things. The worldling desires that which pertains to the world, but a spiritual person pants after spiritual blessings. God has never promised to satisfy fleshly desires, so be not surprised that you "have not" when you "ask amiss" (James 4:3). Unanswered prayers ought ever to lead us to serious self-examination. It is possible to ask for **spiritual** mercies, and yet not obtain them. I may seek from God a deeper knowledge of His Word, an increase of faith, or more patience and fortitude. So far, so good; but **what** was my motive and end? Was it that my Christian reputation might be advanced? God knows, and He regulates His answers accordingly. Holy desires have a sure answer. "Lord, Thou hast heard the desire of the humble: Thou wilt prepare their heart, Thou wilt cause Thine ear to hear" (Psa. 10:17). "He will fulfill the desire of them that **fear** Him. He also **will** hear **their** cry" (Psa. 145:19).

3. By ignoring the character of our walk

In these degenerate times there are not a few who suppose, or at any rate take for granted, that no matter how their daily lives may be lived, no matter how much self-will and self-pleasing there may be, nor how little true concern for God's honour and glory; yet, that He stands pledged to hear their cries and answer their prayers. This is a horrible error, and discovers a fearfully degrading conception of the Holy One. Scripture teaches plainly that there is a most intimate connection between the character of our walk and obtaining answers to our prayers.

"If I regard iniquity in my heart, the Lord will **not** hear" (Psa. 66:18). "Your iniquities have turned away these things, and your sins have **withholden** good from you" (Jer. 5:25). "Therefore it is come to pass, that as He cried, and they would not hear, so they cried, and I would not hear, saith the Lord of hosts" (Zech. 7:13). Perhaps some readers will say in reply to these solemn passages, These are all from the O. T.! Our answer is, True, and what difference does that make? Does the great God act one way in the past and another way in the present? Do the principles of His government change? Does He regard the walk of His people in one age and disregard it in another age? If **this** is the outcome of your "dispensational" study of God's Word, then it has done you great harm. But as a matter of fact, the teaching of the N. T. on this subject is in perfect accord with that of the Old. Of course it is!

In John 15:7 we find Christ saying, "If ye abide in Me, and My words abide in you, ye shall ask what ye will, and it shall be done unto you". Here is a double restriction or qualifying of the promise. First, to have his petitions granted, the supplicant must abide in Christ. All through John's writings, the word "abide" has reference to **communion**. Second, Christ's words are to abide in the believer: affecting his heart, searching his conscience, forming his thoughts, regulating his ways; only thus can communion with Christ be maintained. "If ye keep My commandments, ye shall abide in My love; even as I have kept My Father's commandments and abide in His love" (John 15:10).

"For let not that man think that he shall receive any thing of the Lord" (James 1:7). **What** "man"? The one mentioned at the close of the preceding verse and described in the verse that follows. In v. 6 this particular character is spoken of as one who "wavereth" and is like "a wave of the sea, driven with the wind and tossed". It is a character lacking in stability; one who, instead of being regulated by the Word, is actuated by impulse, or the everchanging opinions and standards of the world. Thus, in v. 8 he is spoken of as "A double-minded man, unstable in all his ways".

"And whatsoever we ask, we receive of Him, **because** we keep His commandments, and do those things that are pleasing in His sight" (1 John 3:22). What could be plainer than this? In the light of such a Divine declaration, who will dare deny that there **is** a most intimate connection between the character of our walk and God's response to our prayers? Let any who might have been inclined to quarrel with this article as being "legalistic", pause and tremble, lest they be found guilty of replying wickedly against God. In connection with this verse let us link together and note the order of, two statements concerning Christ: "I do **always** those things that please Him" (John 8:29); "Thou hearest Me **always**" (John 11:42).

4. By carnalizing God's promises

"Ask and it shall be given you" (Matt. 7:7). From these words many carnal souls draw the inference Christ here taught that anybody may have anything he pleases from God just for the asking, providing he asks in faith; and in their estimation, asking in faith is simply working themselves up to a firm persuasion that they **shall** obtain what they ask. But this blessed verse affirms no such absurdity. The passage, as a whole, teaches that if Christians ask their Heavenly Father for "**good** things", they shall have them; but **He** must decide what **is** for their good. To pray "in faith" is not to pray expecting God will give us whatever we desire, but that He will give us what He has **promised**. The Christian duty of "praying in faith" rests on the plain principle that "if we ask anything according to **His will**, He heareth us" (1 John 5:14).

The last quoted passage is one that greatly needs pressing upon people today. First, it shows the great **design** of prayer, and that is, the bringing of our rebellious wills into subjection to God's. Second, it makes known the **nature** of true prayer, and that is, a seeking of those things which God has promised, for it is His **revealed** will (in the Word) which is mainly, though not solely, in view. God requires to be "inquired of" (Ezek. 36:37). But let it be said very emphatically that, prayer in accord with the will of God, can only really proceed from a heart whose ruling desire and aim is that His will **may be done**. Third, it announces the **limits** of prayer: God will not grant us what is contrary to His will: He would not Moses (Deut. 3:26), nor Paul (2 Cor. 12:8).

"If ye ask any thing in My name, I will do it" (John 14:14). How often has it been said that, Christ here gave a blank check, signed it, and now leaves us to fill it in. Such a statement betrays a woeful ignorance of what it means to ask God "in the name of His Son". It ought not to be necessary to point out that it means something else than merely **saying** at the close of our prayer, "Hear me for Christ's sake". To pray in the name of Christ signifies, asking by virtue of our union with Him, as **identified** with Him; and therefore, asking only for that which is in keeping with **His** perfections and what will be for **His** glory. We can only rightly ask God for that which will magnify His Son.

Lest this article be perverted, a final warning needs to be added. Let no reader form the conclusion that God hears us and answers our prayers **because of** our goodness, faithfulness, or obedience to Him. Not so; that is Phariseeism. The ground upon which God hears His people is that of the **merits** of His blessed Son. Hence, in Rev. 8:3 we are shown the Angel of the Covenant "adding" (see margin) the "much incense" (the fragrance of His own perfections) to the "prayers of **all** saints". Thus, to pray to the Father in Christ's name means, first of all, to plead **His** righteousness, to beseech Him to hear us for **His** sake. Let it not be forgotten that Christians are invited to approach the "Throne of **grace**"; yet let them also remember it ever remains true, that grace reigns ''through **righteousness**'' Rom. 5: 21), and never at the expense of it.

—ARTHUR W. PINK.

THE SNARE OF SERVICE

The main business and the principal concern of the Christian should be that of thanking, praising, and adoring that blessed One who has saved him with an everlasting salvation, and who to secure that salvation left Heaven's glory and came down to this sin-curst earth, here to suffer and die the awful death of the Cross, that His people might be "delivered from this present evil world" (Gal. 1:4). "Praise is comely for the upright" (Psa. 33:1). But to see the upright praising God is something which Satan cannot endure, and he will employ every art and device to turn aside the happy Christian from such blissful occupation.

Our great Enemy is very, very subtle in the methods and means he uses. He cares not what the object may be, as long as it serves to engross the believer and hinder his giving to **Christ** that consideration (Heb. 3:1) and adoration (Rev. 5:12) which are His due. Satan's aim is gained if he can occupy the believer with perishing sinners rather than with the Lord of glory. The tactics which the Devil follows towards the saints are the same he uses so successfully with the unsaved. What is the chief thing he employs to shut out Christ from the vision of the lost (2 Cor. 4:4)? Is it not getting them occupied with **their own** deeds and doings? Assuredly it is. In like manner, he deals with God's people: he seeks to get them engaged in "service" as a substitute for **communing with Christ.** It is the dragon of darkness posing as an angel of light, stirring up the feverish nature and restless energy of the flesh, to find some outlet that appears to be pleasing to God.

Above we have said that, the great aim and chief exercise of the Christian should be that of worshipping and adoring his wondrous and blessed Saviour, which is, really, heaven begun on earth. Yet, let it be pointed out that this ought not to terminate at the lips—our very lives ought to show forth His praise (1 Peter 2:9), our daily walk ought to be pleasing and honouring to Him (1 Cor. 10:31), our every act needs to be brought into conformity to His holy will (Prov. 3:6). To these statements many, perhaps all Christians, will assent. But do they perceive what is necessarily involved? We fear not. It involves a **life's task.** And what is that? This is a constant searching of the Scriptures, with a prayerful and earnest desire to find out **what is** pleasing to Him, a holy determination to discover the **details** of His revealed mind.

This is the service to which God has called each of His people: to serve **Himself,** to take His yoke upon them, to submit to His rule over them, to be in all things in subjection to His holy will. But, we say again, the learning of what His will really **is,** in all its fulness, is a life's task, which requires and calls for the utmost attention in the cultivation of our own soul's garden. "Exercise **thyself** unto godliness" (1 Tim. 4:7), "Take heed unto **thyself**" (1 Tim 4:16), "Keep **thyself** pure" (1 Tim. 5:22), "Study to show **thyself** approved unto God" (2 Tim. 2:15), are some of the exhortations of Holy Writ which much need to be taken to heart by God's dear people in these hustling, bustling days. But, alas, they are unheeded by many.

And what is one of the chief causes of hindrance? What is it that in these times so often prevents the child of God **from** "taking heed" unto himself? This, he is far too much engrossed in attempting to "take heed" for others. The woman who has spent much of the day in attending to domestic duties, the man who has been toiling for his daily bread, instead of spending the evening quietly in spiritual devotions, prayerfully studying God's Word, giving "attendance to reading" (1 Tim. 4:13), and thus feeding his soul, removing the world's stains acquired through the day, and conversing with his family upon the things of God, has a round of religious meetings which he must attend, numerous church duties he must perform. So it is with many on the Holy Sabbath. Instead of that being, as God has designed, chiefly a day of **rest,** only too often it becomes the busiest of the whole week. No wonder that so many are litttle better than nervous wrecks! And all because departing from God's arrangements.

It is greatly to be feared that when the saints shall stand before the judgment-seat of Christ "that everyone may receive the things done in the body" (2 Cor. 5:10), that many of the redeemed will have to make the sad lament, "they made me the keeper of the vineyards; mine own vineyard have I **not kept**" (Song of Sol. 1:6). Note carefully the first word, it is not **"He** made me the keeper of the vineyard"—no. **His** yoke is "easy", His burden is "light" (Matt. 11:30); but "they". Ah, it is the Egyptian-taskmakers who spur on the people of God to engage in works which the Lord has never called them to do. Martha is not alone in being "cumbered" (weighted down) with "**much** serving" (Luke 10:40).

The witness of our **lives** is far more weighty than that of our lips. If we spent more time in secret communings with Christ, people would take knowledge of us that we had "been with Jesus" (Acts 4:13). If we were more diligent and painstaking to find out and **put into practice** the precepts and commands which God has recorded in His Word for the regulation of our lives; if, in consequence, we were really walking with Him, filled with that peace which passeth all understanding, rejoicing in the Lord; then instead of our going to the people, and pressing upon all and sundry the precious things of Christ —thus **disobeying** Him who has bidden His disciples, "Give not that which is holy unto the dogs" (Matt. 7:6)—some, at least, would come to us and **ask** "a reason of the hope" that is "in us" (1 Peter 3:15).

But, as we have said above, the restless energy of the flesh longs to find some outlet, and our hearts are only too eagerly inclined to substitute service toward others for personal dealings with God for ourselves. It calls for less exercise of soul to memorize a few texts for the purpose of quoting them to some one else, than it does to measure myself by the Scriptures, confess my sad failures, and beg God to write His Word upon my heart. Ah, it is a comforting sop for our conscience, to persuade ourselves that, though our **walk** is so far from being what it should be, yet we **can** "do our duty" in warning the wicked, or engage in some form of "christian service." Yes, and Satan will whisper in our ears, you **have** been "faithful" there, and instead of being humbled and chastened before God for our miserable failures to **live** Christ, our evil hearts are puffed up by the Devil's flatteries that we have, at least, faithfully **preached** Christ.

Let not the reader conclude from what has been said, that the writer is opposed either to public worship or the Christian's being engaged in **any** good works for the benefit of others. Not so, though we would earnestly warn against any attempt to worship with those who are not walking with God, or engaging in works which are not really glorifying to Him. Our main design has simply been to show the need of putting first things first. Our first great need is not seeking to minister to others, but ourselves being ministered unto by the Lord. Our highest privilege is not that of being engaged in service **for** Christ, but of enjoying daily communion **with** Him. Our first obligation is not that of being concerned over the welfare of our neighbours, but making our own calling and election sure. Our first great task is not to serve our fellow men, but to serve our God, by studying His Word, learning His will, and then **doing** it. Our first circle of responsibility is not towards strangers and distant acquaintances, but our own home. Our chief ambition should not be the proclamation of Christ with our lips, but the preaching of Him by our lives.

If we have not learned to worship God in the secret place, we cannot do so in the public assembly. If we are not ourselves really following Christ, walking and communing with Him, it is but a mockery to speak of Him to others. If we preach Him in words but deny Him in our works, then we are only a stumblingblock to those who hear us. If our "service" for Christ is robbing us of the time so urgently needed for the cultivation of our personal vineyard, then it is a snare and a curse to us. Then, "take heed **unto thyself**", "**lay aside** every weight" (Heb. 12:1) which hinders you from running the race which **God** "has set before us". As a well-known hymn says, "Take time to be holy", or, better still, as Scriptures says, "The kingdom of God is . . . righteousness, and peace, and joy in the Holy Spirit. For He that in **these** things serveth Christ is acceptable to God, and approved of men" (Rom. 14:17, 18).

—ARTHUR W. PINK.

ASSURANCE

We desire to say a plain word on the perplexing subject of "feeling". We meet with it everywhere. The mistake into which so many fall, is that of confounding the enjoyment of truth, when believed, with the mere feeling or impression of their own minds. When persons say, "I can't feel that God loves me—that Christ died for me—that my sins are forgiven", we believe they simply mean, "I do not enjoy or feel the power of these blessed truths". But how can these or any other truths be enjoyed, or their power felt, until they are believed? Faith never refers to self, but always to the Word of God. We meet with many who want to **feel** that they are believers, before they have believed the truth, and to **feel** that they are safe before they trust in Christ.

Now, this is all confusion. The truth to be believed is **outside** of self, the enjoyment of it is **within**. "The Lord direct your hearts", says the apostle, "into the love of God, and into the patient waiting for Christ" (2 Thess. 3:5). These blessed central truths are ever the same—unchangeable, outside, and independent of the believer; nevertheless, they are to be enjoyed in the heart. But if we at times fail to realize their power, and to enjoy them in our hearts, they remain unchangeably the same. The object of faith is ever outside of self—the enjoyment within. Our failure to enjoy the object, can never lessen its value, or change its character.

The truth as to pardon, peace, and acceptance must be received in faith before it can be enjoyed, or its power felt. The same moment that the sinner is brought to the Lord Jesus in faith, the whole need of the soul is met—fully, perfectly, and forever met. When this is believed, the soul has rest; not, observe, in its own feelings, but in the word of Christ believed. He never says to one who comes to Him, "I will forgive". No, blessed be His name; but, in plainest terms, "son, daughter, thy

of us knows what a day may bring forth, but all futurity is open to His omniscient gaze. The infinite knowledge of God ought to fill us with holy **awe**. Nothing we do, say, or even think, escapes the cognizance of Him with whom we have to do: "The eyes of the Lord are in every place, beholding the evil and the good" (Prov. 15:3). What a curb this would be unto us, did we but meditate upon it more frequently! Instead of acting recklessly, we should say with Hagar, "Thou God seest me" (Gen. 16:13). The apprehension of God's infinite knowledge should fill the Christian with **adoration**. The whole of my life stood open to His view from the beginning. He foresaw my every fall, my every sin, my every blacksliding; yet, nevertheless, fixed His heart upon me. Oh, how the realization of this should bow me in wonder and worship before Him! —ARTHUR W. PINK.

---

sins **are** forgiven, thy faith **hath** saved thee; go in peace" (Mark 2:5).

The only question now is, Can the troubled one receive it as the truth of God? If so, the voice of Christ has spoken peace to that soul. And if the ear be kept open only for Him, its peace will be as complete and settled as the word of Christ can make it. Did the Lord ever send away a seeking soul from His presence in a state of uncertainty? No! never! and He never will. His word is pledged: "Him that cometh to Me, I will in no wise cast out". When He says, "Thy sins **are** forgiven", should the soul have another doubt as to the blessed fact? When He says, "Thy faith **hath** saved thee", should the slightest feeling of uncertainty remain? When He says, "Go in **peace**", should the soul go in trouble? Assuredly not. And assuredly it will not, if only it looks to Him, and not within—if only it hears His word, and listens not to the voice of its own feelings. Oh! that anxious, troubled souls, would only cease from looking within, and from judging of their state before God from their own feelings. The blessed consequences of faith in Christ, are fully and plainly revealed in God's Word. Let the eye of faith rest on it, and let the heart of faith count it most surely, and forever, true, and then peace, like a river, will flow into your soul. "Therefore being justified by faith we have peace with God, through our Lord Jesus Christ. By whom also we have access into this grace wherein we stand, and rejoice in hope of the glory of God" (Rom. 5:1, 2).

—Extracts from C. H. M.

QUIETNESS

One of the N. T. commands is, "Study to **be quiet**" (1 Thess. 4-11). It must be for our good that we prayerfully seek grace to practice it, otherwise God had not recorded it in His Word. Moreover, a "meek and quiet spirit is, in God's sight, of great price" (1 Peter 3:4). Here again God's estimates are the opposite of man's, perhaps never more evident than in these evil days. What man despises, God esteems; and what man admires, He abominates. The world is mad, and **speed** is one of the "gods" which is now worshipped by the multitudes. And living as we yet are in the world, God's own people are infected with its evil spirit. Much need has each of us to beg the Lord to lay His cooling and calming hand upon the feverish "flesh" in us. Rush, hurry, and hustle are the terms which best describe modern activities; but "stand", "sit", and "wait" are words that have a promient place in the Scriptures.

To those who disobey the above command, God, oftentimes, afflicts His people in their bodies, so that a season of "quiet" is enforced. He has many ways of **making** us "rest awhile" (Mark 6:31). Yet is it ever our highest welfare which He has in view. We ought to be exercised in our hearts, humbled before God, whenever He sets us aside, asking with Job, "Show me wherefore Thou contendest with me" (10:2). It is the one who is "exercised" under the chastening rod of God (Heb. 12:11) who afterward brings forth "the **peaceable** fruit of righteousness". Let the reader prayerfully ponder Ex. 14:13, Psa. 46:10, Eccl. 9:17, Isa. 30:15, 32:17, 18, Lam. 3:26, Luke 10:39, 2 Thess. 3:12.

—A. W. P.

have repudiated our devotion, and the searching question comes to us, "Lovest thou Me?"; we say, as Peter did, "Lord, Thou knowest **all** things; Thou **knowest** that I love Thee" (John 21:17).

Here is encouragement to prayer. There is no cause for fearing that the petitions of the righteous will not be heard, or that their sighs and tears shall escape the notice of God, since He knows the thoughts and intents of the heart. There is no danger of the individual saint being overlooked amidst the multitude of supplicants who daily and hourly present their various petitions, for an **infinite** Mind is as capable of paying the same attention to millions as if only one individual were seeking its attention. So too the lack of appropriate language, the inability to give expression to the deepest longing of the soul, will not jeopardise our prayers, for "It shall come to pass, that before they call, I will answer; and while they are yet speaking, I will hear" (Isa. 65:24).

"Great is our Lord, and of great power: His understanding is infinite" (Psa. 147:5). God not only knows whatsoever has happened in the past in every part of His vast domains, and He is not only thoroughly acquainted with everything that is now transpiring throughout the entire universe, but He is also perfectly cognizant with every event, from the least to the greatest, that ever will happen in the ages to come. God's knowledge of the future is as complete as is His knowledge of the past and the present, and that, because the future depends entirely upon Himself. Were it in anywise possible for something to occur apart from either the direct agency or permission of God, then that something would be independent of Him, and He would at once cease to be Supreme.

Now the Divine knowledge of the future is not a mere abstraction, but something which is inseparably connected with and accompanied by His purpose. God has Himself designed whatsoever shall yet be, and what He has designed **must** be effectuated. As His most sure Word affirms, "He doeth according to His will in the army of heaven, and the inhabitants of the earth, and **none** can stay His hand" (Dan. 4:35). And again, "There are many devices in a man's heart; nevertheless the counsel of the Lord that **shall** stand" (Prov. 19:21). The wisdom and power of God being alike infiinite, the accomplishment of whatever He hath purposed is absolutely guaranteed. It is no more possible for the Divine counsels to fail in their execution than it would be for the thrice holy God to lie.

Nothing relating to the future is in anywise uncertain so far as the actualization of God's counsels are concerned. None of His decrees are left contingent either on creatures or secondary causes. There is no future event which is only a mere possibility, that is, something which may or may not come to pass, **"Known** unto God are **all** His works from the beginning" (Acts 15:18). Whatever God has decreed is inexorably certain, for He is without variableness, or shadow of turning (James 1:17). Therefore we are told at the very beginning of that book which unveils to us so much of the future, of "Things which **must** shortly come to pass" (Rev. 1:1).

The perfect knowledge of God is exemplified and illustrated in every prophecy recorded in His Word. In the O. T. are to be found scores of predictions concerning the history of Israel, which were fulfilled to their minutest detail, centuries after they were made. In them too are scores more foretelling the earthly career of Christ, and they too were accomplished literally and perfectly. Such prophecies could only have been given by One who knew the end from the beginning, and whose knowledge rested upon the unconditional certainty of the accomplishment of everything foretold. In like manner, both Old and New Testament contain many other announcements yet future, and they too **"must** be fulfilled" (Luke 24:44), must because foretold by Him who had decreed them.

It should, however, be pointed out that neither God's knowledge nor His cognition of the future, considered simply in themselves, are causative. Nothing has ever come to pass, or ever will, merely because God knew it. The **cause** of all things is the **will** of God. The man who really believes the Scriptures knows beforehand that the seasons will continue to follow each other with unfailing regularity to the end of earth's history (Gen. 8:22), yet his knowledge is not the cause of their succession. So God's knowledge does not arise from things because they are or will be, but because He has **ordained** them to be. God knew and foretold the crucifixion of His Son many hundreds of years before He became incarnate, and this, because in the Divine purpose, He was a Lamb slain from the foundation of the world: hence we read of His being "delivered by the determinate counsel and foreknowledge of God" (Acts 2:23).

A word or two by way of application. The infinite knowledge of God should fill us with **amazement.** How far exalted above the wisest man is the Lord! None

(Continued on Page 71)

STUDIES IN THE SCRIPTURES

"Search the Scriptures" John 5 : 39

Copyright in all English-speaking Countries.

Editor: Arthur W. Pink, Morton's Gap, Ky., U. S. A.
Hon. Agent in England: Mr. A. Winstone, 2, Lennox Villas, Hewlett Road, Cheltenham.
Hon. Agent in Australia: Mr. G. Ardill, The Christian Workers' Depot.
Commonwealth and Reservoir Streets, Sydney.

THE FOREKNOWLEDGE OF GOD

What controversies have been engendered by this subject in the past! But what truth of Holy Scripture is there which has not been made the occasion of theological and ecclesiastical battles? The deity of Christ, His virgin birth, His atoning death, His second advent; the believer's justification, sanctification, security; the church, its organization, officers, discipline; baptism, the Lord's supper, and a score of other precious truths might be mentioned. Yet, the controversies which have been waged over them, did not close the mouths of God's faithful servants; why, then, should we avoid the vexed question of God's Foreknowledge, because, forsooth, there are some who will charge us with fermenting strife? Let others contend if they will, our duty is to bear witness according to the light vouchsafed us.

There are two things concerning the Foreknowledge of God about which many are in ignorance: the **meaning** of the term, its Scriptural **scope**. Because this ignorance is so widespread, it is an easy matter for preachers and teachers to palm off perversions of this subject, even upon the people of God. There is only one safeguard against error, and that is to be established in the faith; and for that, there has to be prayerful and diligent study, and a receiving with meekness the engrafted Word of God. Only then are we fortified against the attacks of those who assail us. There are those today who are **mis**-using this very truth in order to discredit and deny the absolute sovereignty of God in the salvation of sinners. Just as higher critics are repudiating the Divine inspiration of the Scriptures; evolutionists, the work of God in creation; so some pseudo Bible-teachers, are perverting His foreknowledge in order to set aside His unconditional election unto eternal life.

When the solemn and blessed subject of Divine foreordination is expounded, when God's eternal choice of certain ones to be conformed to the image of His Son is set forth, the Enemy sends along some man to argue that election is based upon the foreknowledge of God, and this "foreknowledge" is interpreted to mean that God foresaw certain ones would be more pliable than others, that they would respond more readily to the strivings of the Spirit, and that because God knew they **would** believe, He, accordingly, predestinated **them** unto salvation. But such a statement is radically wrong. It repudiates the truth of total depravity, for it argues that there **is** something good in some men. It takes away the independency of God, for it makes His decrees **rest upon** what He discovers in the creature. It completely turns things upside down, for in saying God foresaw certain sinners would believe in Christ, and that because of this, He predestinated them unto salvation, is the very reverse of the truth. Scripture affirms that God, in His high sovereignty, singled out certain ones to be recipients of His distinguishing favours (Acts 13:48), and therefore He determined to bestow upon them the gift of faith. False theology makes God's foreknowledge of our believing the **cause** of His election to salvation; whereas, God's election is the cause, and our believing in Christ is the **effect**.

Ere proceeding further with our discussion of this much misunderstood theme, let us pause and define our terms. What is meant by "foreknowledge"? "To know beforehand", is the ready reply of many. But we must not jump to conclusions, nor must we turn to Webster's dictionary as the final court of appeal, for it is not a matter of the etymology of the term employed. What is needed is to find out how the word is **used** in Scripture. The Holy Spirit's usage of an expression always defines its meaning and scope. It is failure to apply this simple rule which is responsible for so much confusion and error. So many people assume they already know the

(Continued on Page 96)

IMPORTANT NOTICES

Please advise promptly of change of address, otherwise copies will be lost in the mails.

We are glad to send a sample copy to any of our friends whom you believe would be interested in such a publication.

Send to Mr. I. C. Herendeen, 433-435, The Arcade, Cleveland, Ohio, for a list of our publications. He has published many of our books and booklets.

This Magazine is published as a work of faith and labour of love. The Editor and his wife gladly give their services. It is freely sent to all who will read it. No charge is made for it.

Christians who feel definitely lead to do so, may have fellowship with us in this ministry. Those outside the U. S. A., please send only INTERNATIONAL Money Orders made out to Morton's Gap, Kentucky, U. S. A. See that it is made out in American money.

CONTENTS

The Epistle to the Hebrews	74
The Satisfaction ("Atonement") of Christ	80
Mortification of Sin	86
Divine Warnings	90
A Request	94

THE EPISTLE TO THE HEBREWS

28. Christian Perseverance: Heb. 6:12-15

Two exhortations were set before the Hebrew Christians in the 6th chapter of this epistle. First, they were bidden to turn their backs upon Judaism and go on unto a full embracing of Christianity (v. 1). The application to God's people today of the principle contained in this exhortation is, Abandon everything which enthralled your hearts in your unregenerate days, and find your peace, joy, satisfaction in Christ. In contemplating the peculiar temptation of the Hebrews to forsake the Christian position and path for a return to Judaism, let us not lose sight of the fact that a danger just as real menaces the believer today. The flesh still remains within him, and all that Satan used in the past to occupy his heart, still exists in the present. Though Israel came forth from the House of Bondage, passed through the Red Sea, and started out joyfully (Ex. 15:1) for the promised land, yet it was not long ere their hearts went back to Egypt, lusting after its fleshpots (Ex. 16:3).

It is worse than idle to reply to what has been pointed out above by saying, Real Christians are in no "danger", for God has promised to preserve them. True, but God has promised to preserve His people in a way of holiness, not in a course of sinful self-will and self-gratification. Those whom Christ has declared shall "never perish" are they who "hear His voice and follow Him" (John 10:27, 28). The apostles were not fatalists, neither did they believe in a mechanical salvation, but one that required to be worked out "with fear and trembling" (Phil. 2:12). Therefore Paul, moved by the Holy Spirit, did not hesitate to refer to the Israelites who were "overthrown" in the wilderness, and say, "Now these things were **our** examples to the intent that **we** should not lust after evil things as they also lusted. Neither be ye idolators, as were some of them; . . . Neither let us tempt Christ, as some of them also tempted, and were destroyed of serpents. . . Now all these things happened unto them for ensamples: and they are written for **our admonition.** . . Wherefore let him that thinketh he standeth **take heed** lest he fall" (1 Cor. 10:6-12)

The second exhortation of Heb. 6 is found in vv. 11, 12, the first part of which was before us at the close of our last article. There the apostle says, "And we desire that everyone of you do show the same diligence". This, together with the verses that follow, is a call to perseverance in the path of godliness. To a church which had left its "first love" Christ said, "Repent, and do the first works" (Rev. 2:4, 5). What are these "first works"? A submitting of ourselves unto God, an humbling of ourselves before Him, a throwing down of the weapons of our hostility against Him. A turning unto Christ as our only hope, a casting of ourselves upon Him, a trusting in the merits of His precious blood. A taking of His yoke upon us, bowing to His Lordship, owning His authority, earnestly seeking grace to do His commandments.

Now the Christian is to continue as he began. He is to daily own his sins before God. He is to daily renew the same acts of faith and trust in Christ which he exercised at the first. Instead of counting upon some experience in the past, he is to maintain a **present** living upon Christ. If he continues to cast himself upon the Redeemer, putting his salvation wholly in His hands, then He will not, cannot, fail him. But in order to cast myself upon

Christ, I must be **near** Him; I cannot do so while I am following Him afar off. To be near Him, I must be in separation from all that is contrary to Him. Communion is based upon an obedient walk: the one cannot be without the other. For the maintenance of this, I must "show the **same** diligence" I did when I was first convicted of my lost estate, saw Hell yawning at my feet ready to receive me, and fled to Christ for refuge.

This same diligence which marked my state of heart and regulated my actions when I first sought Christ, is to be continued "unto the end" This means persevering in a holy living, and unto this the servants of God are to be constantly urging their hearers. "Ministerial exhortation unto duty, is needful even unto them who are sincere in the practice of it, that they may abide and continue therein. It is not easy to be apprehended how God's institutions are despised by some, neglected by others, and by how few, duly improved; all for want of taking right measures for them. Some there are, who, being profoundly ignorant, are yet ready to say, that they know as much as the minister can teach them, and therefore, it is to no purpose to attend unto preaching. These are the thoughts, and this is too often the language, of persons profane and profligate, who know little, and practise nothing of Christianity. Some think that exhortations unto duty, belong only unto them who are negligent and careless in their performance; and unto them, indeed they do be'ong, but not unto them only, as the whole Scripture testifieth. And some, it may be, like well to be exhorted unto what they do, and do find satisfaction therein, but **how few are there** (it was the same then! A. W. P.) who look upon it as a means of God whereby they are enabled for, and kept up unto their duty, wherein, indeed, their use and benefit doth consist. They do not only direct unto duty, but through the appointment of God, they are means of communicating grace unto us, for the due performance of duties" (Dr. J. Owen, 1680).

"Do show the same diligence to the full assurance of hope unto the end". Hope is a spiritual grace quite distinct from faith or love. Faith casts me upon God. Love causes me to cleave to and delight in pleasing Him. Hope sustains under the difficulties and discouragements of the way. It supports the soul when the billows of trouble roll over it, or when we are tempted to despair, and give up the fight. That is why, in the Christian's armour, Hope is called "the helmet" (Eph. 5:8), because it wards off the sharp blows or bears the weight of those strokes which befall the saint in trials and afflictions. Hope values the things promised, looks forward to the day of their realization, and thus is nerved to fresh endeavour. Hope views the Promised Land, and this gives alacrity to the weary pilgrim to continue pressing forward. Hope anticipates the welcome and the glorious fare awaiting us at the Heavenly Port, and this gives courage to go on battling against adverse winds and waves. There is the test.

Many pretend to the possession of a good hope who yet have no faith. Others make a profession of faith who yet have no real hope. But real faith and real hope are inseparable. A spiritual faith eyes the Promiser, and is assured that He cannot lie. A spiritual hope embraces the promises, esteems them above all silver and gold, and confidently anticipates their fulfillment. But between the present moment and the actual realization of our hope lies a rugged path of testing, in which we encounter much that wearies, disheartens and retards us. If we are really walking in the path of God's appointment, there will be oppositions to meet, fierce persecutions to be endured, grievous troubles to be borne. Yet, if our valuation of God's promises be real, if our anticipation of their fulfi'ment be genuine, the comfort and joy they afford will more than offset and over-balance the effects of our trials. The exercise of hope will alone deliver from fainting and despondency under continued afflictions.

Now to be in the enioyment of "the full assurance of hope unto the end", the Christian must continue giving "the **same** diligence" to the things of God and the needs of his soul, as he did at the beginning. When the terrors of God first awakened him from the sleep of death, when he was made to feel his own awful danger of being cast into the eternal burnings, when he learned that Christ was the only Refuge, no half-hearted seeker was he. How diligently he searched the Word! How earnestly he cried unto God! How sincere was his repentance! How gladly he received the Gospel! How radical was the change in his life! How real did Heaven seem unto him, and how he longed to go there! How bright was his "hope" then! Alas, the fine gold has become dim; the manna has lost much of its sweetness, and he has become as one who "cannot see afar off" (2 Peter 1:9). Why? Ah, cannot the reader supply the answer from his own experience?

But we dare not stop short at the point reached at the close of the preceding paragraph. Backsliding is dangerous, so dangerous that if it be persisted in, it is certain to prove fatal. If I continue to neglect the Divine means of grace for spiritual strength and support, if I go back again into the world and find my delight in its pleasures and concerns, and if I am not recovered from this sad state, then that will demonstrate that I was only the subject of the Holy Spirit's **inferior** operations, that I was not really regenerated by Him. The difference between thorny-ground and the good-ground hearer is, that the one brings forth no fruit "to perfection" (Luke 8:14), whereas the other brings forth fruit "with patience" or perseverance (Luke 8:15). It is **continuance** in Christ's word which proves us His disciples indeed (John 8:31). It is **continuing** in the faith, grounded and settled, and being "not moved away from the hope of the Gospel" (Col. 1:23) which demonstrates the reality of our profession.

"He said **to the end** that they might know they had not yet reached the goal, and were therefore to think of further progress. He mentioned **diligence** that they might know they were not to sit down idly, but to strive in earnest. For it is not a small thing to ascend above the heavens, especially for those who hardly creep on the ground, and when innumerable obstacles are in the way. There is, indeed, nothing more difficult than to keep our thoughts fixed on things in heaven, when the whole power of our nature inclines towards, and when Satan by numberless devices draws us back to earth" (John Calvin).

Once more would we press upon our hearts that it is only as "diligence" in the things of God is continually exercised that a scriptural "hope" is preserved, and the full assurance of it attained. First, because there is an inseparable connection between these two which is of Divine institution: God Himself has appointed "diligence" as the means and way whereby His people shall arrive at this assurance: cf. 2 Peter 1:10, 11. Second, because such "diligence" has a proper and necessary tendency unto this end. By diligence our spiritual faculties are strengthened, grace is increased in us, and thereby we obtain fuller evidence of our interest in the promises of the Gospel. Third, by a faith l attention to the duties of faith and love we are preserved from sinning, which is the principal evil that weakens or impairs our hope.

"That ye be not slothful, but followers of them who through faith and patience inherit the promises" (v. 12). These words confirm what we have said above concerning the force of the exhortation found in v. 11. There the apostle is giving a call to perseverance in the path of practical holiness. But there are multitudes of professing Christians that cherish a hope of heaven, who nevertheless continue in a course of self-will and self-pleasing. "There is a generation that are pure in their own eyes, and yet is not washed from their filthiness" (Prov. 30:12), Christ came here to save His people "**from** their sins" (Matt. 1:21), not in them. No presumption is worse than entertaining the idea that I am bound for Heaven while I live like a child of Hell.

"That ye be not slothful, but followers of them who through faith and patience inherit the promises". This verse forms the connecting link between the preceding section and the closing one of this chapter. The apostle here warns against any evil, indolence and inertia, which stands opposed to giving "diligence": they are the opposite virtue and vice. Slothfulness persisted in would effectually prevent the performance of the duty just enjoined. In 5:11 Paul had charged the Hebrews with being "dull (slothful—the same Greek word) of hearing", not absolutely, but relatively; they were not as industrious in heeding "the Word of **righteousness**" (5:13) as they ought to have been. Here he bids them be not slothful in good works, but emulators of the saints who had gone before.

"That ye be not slothful". "He knew that the utmost intention of our spirits, the utmost diligence of our minds, and endeavours of our whole souls, are required unto a useful continuance in our profession and obedience. This, God requireth of us; this, the nature of things themselves about which we are conversant, deserveth; and necessary it is, unto the end which we aim at. If we faint or grow negligent in our duty, if careless or slothful, we shall never hold out unto the end; or if we do continue in such a formal course as will consist with this sloth, we shall never come unto the blessed end which we expect or look for. The oppositions and difficulties which we shall assuredly meet with, from within and without, will not give way unto feeble and languid endeavours. Nor will the holy God prostitute eternal rewards unto those who have no more regard unto them, but to give up themselves unto sloth in their pursuits. Our course of obedience is called running in a race, and fighting as in a battle, and those who are slothful on such occasion will never be crowned with victory. Wherefore, upon a due compliance with this caution, depends our present perseverance, and our future salvation" (Dr. J. Owen).

The slothfulness against which the apostle warns, is in each of us by nature. The desires of the "old man" are not toward, but away from the things of God. It is the "new man" which is alone capacitated to love and serve the Lord. But in addition to the two natures in the Christian, there is the individual himself, the possessor of those natures, the "I" of Rom. 7:25, and **he** is held responsible to "make not provision for the flesh" (Rom. 13:14) on the one hand, and to "desire" the sincere milk of the Word that he may grow thereby" (1 Peter 2:2) on the other. It is the consciousness of this native sloth, this indisposition for practical holiness, which causes the real saint to cry out, "Draw me, we will run after Thee" (Song of Sol. 1:4); "Make me to go in the path of Thy commandments, for therein do I delight"; "Order my steps in Thy Word, and let not any iniquity have dominion over me" (Psa. 119:35, 133). It is **this** which distinguishes the true child of God from the empty professor—his wrestling with God in secret for grace to enable him to press forward in the highway of holiness.

"But followers of them who through faith and patience inherit the promises". The reference here is to the believing forefathers of the Hebrews, who, by continuing steadfast in faith and persevering in hope amidst all the trials to which they were exposed, had now entered into the promised blessings—Heaven. Dr. J. Brown has pointed out that there is no conflict between this declaration and what is said in 11:13. Though during their lives they had "not received the promises", yet at death, they **had** entered into their rest, and are among "the spirits of just men made perfect" (12:23). The word "inherit" denotes their right thereto.

The example which the apostle here sets before the Hebrews was that of the O. T. patriarchs. Just as in the 3rd chapter he had appealed to one portion of the history of their fathers in warning, so now he makes reference to another feature of it in order to encourage. Two things are here to be taken to heart: the happy goal reached by the patriarchs and the path of testing which led thereto. Two things were required of them: faith and patience. Their faith was something more than a general faith in God and the inerrancy of His Word (James 2:19); it was a special faith which laid hold of the Divine promises concerning the covenant of grace in Christ Jesus. Nor was this a mere notional faith, or bare mental assent to the Truth: it was marked by a practical and influential acknowledgement that they were "strangers and pilgrims on the earth" see 11:13. Such is the faith which God requires of us today.

The second grace ascribed unto the patriarchs is their "patience" or "longsuffering" as the word is usually rendered. A different word is employed in 10:36 and 12:1, where an active grace is in view. Here it is more of a passive virtue, hence it is used of the "longsuffering" of God in Rom. 9:22, 1 Peter 3:20 etc. "It is a gracious sedate frame of soul, a tranquility of mind on holy grounds with faith, not subject to take provocation, not to be wearied with opposition" (Dr. J. Owen). It is a spirit which refuses to be daunted by the difficulties of the way, which is not exasperated by trials and oppositions encountered, so as to desert the course or flee from the path of duty. In spite of man's hatred, and of the seeming slowness of God's deliverance, the soul is preserved in a quiet waiting upon Him.

"These were the ways whereby they came to inherit the promises. The heathen of old fancied that their heroes, or patriarchs, by great, and, as they were called, heroic actions, by valour, courage, the slaughter and conquest of their enemies, usually attended with pride, cruelty and oppression, made their way into heaven. The way of God's heroes unto their rest and glory, unto the enjoyment of the Divine promises, was by faith, longsuffering, humility, enduring persecution, self-denial, and the spiritual virtues generally reckoned in the world unto pusillanimity, and so despised. So contrary are the judgments and ways of God and men even about what is good and praiseworthy" (Dr. J. Owen).

As reasons **why** the apostle was moved to set before the Hebrews the noble example of their predecessors, we may suggest the following. First, that they might know he was exhorting them to nothing but what was found in those who went before them, and whom they so esteemed and admired. This, to the same end, he more fully confirms in chapter 11. Second, he was urging them to nothing but what was needful to all who shall inherit the promises. If "faith and patience" were required of the patriarchs, persons who were so high in the love and favour of God, then how could it be imagined that these might be dispensed with as **their** observance! Third, he was pressing upon them nothing but what was practicable, which others had done, and which was therefore possible, yea, easy for them through the grace of Christ.

Ere turning from this most important verse, we will endeavour to anticipate and dispose of a difficulty. Some of our readers who have followed attentively what has been said in the last few paragraphs, may be ready to object. But this is teaching salvation by works; you are asking us to believe that Heaven is a wage which we are required to earn by **our** perseverance and fidelity. Observe then how carefully the Holy Spirit has, in the very verse before us, guarded against such a perversion of the gospel of God's grace. First, in the preposition He used: it is **not** "who **for** faith and patience inherit the promises", but "through". Salvation is not bestowed because of faith and patience, in return for them; yet it **does** come "through" them as the Divinely appointed **channel**, just as the sun shines into a room through its windows. The windows are in no sense the cause of the sun's shining; they contribute nothing whatever to it; yet are they **necessary** as the means by which it enters.

Another word here which precludes all ground of human attainment and completely excludes the idea of earning salvation by anything of ours, is the verb used. The apostle does **not** say "purchase" or "merit", but **"inherit"**. And how come we to "inherit"? By the same way as any come to an inheritance, namely, by being the true heirs to it. And **how** do we become "heirs" of this inheritance? By God's gratuous adoption. "Ye have received the Spirit of adoption, whereby we cry, Abba, Father. The Spirit Himself beareth witness with our spirit, that we are the children of God: and if children, then heirs" (Rom. 8:15-17). God, by an act of His sovereign will, made us His children (Eph. 1:4, 5). This Divine grace, this free assignment, is the foundation of all; and God's faithfulness is pledged to preserve us unto our inheritance (v. 10). Yet, we are **such** heirs as have **means** assigned to us for obtaining our inheritance, and we are required to apply ourselves thereunto.

"For when God made promise to Abraham, because He could swear by no greater, He sware by Himself" (v. 13). The opening "For" denotes that the apostle is here giving a reason why he had appealed to the example of the patriarchs, as those who "through faith and patience inherit the promises": that they really did so, he now proves by a most illustrious instance. Paul here cites the case of one whom he knew would be most notable and forceable. God made promise to Abraham, but he did not obtain the fulfillment thereof until after he had "patiently endured" (v. 15).

The one to whom God made promise was Abraham. He was originally called "Abram", which signifies "an exalted father". Upon Jehovah's renewal of the covenant to him, his name was changed to Abraham, God giving as the reason "for a father of many nations have I made thee" (Gen. 17:5). The reference was not only to those nations which should proceed naturally from him—the descendarts of Ishmael (Gen. 17:20) and of Keturah's sons (Gen. 25:1-4)—but to the elect of God scattered throughout the world, who should be brought to embrace his faith and emulate his works. Therefore is he designated "the father of all them that believe", and "the father of us all" (Rom. 4:11, 16).

"Because he could sware by no greater, He sware by Himself". The assurance which was given to Abraham was the greatest that Heaven itself could afford: a promise and an oath. We say the greatest, for in v. 16 the apostle declares that amongst men an "oath" is an end of strife; how much more when the great God Himself takes one! Moreover, observe He swear "by Himself": He staked Himself; it was as though He had said, I will cease to be God if I do not perform this. The Lord pledged His veracity, declared the event should be as certain as His existence, and that it should be secured by all the perfections of His nature. Dr. J. Brown has rightly pointed out, "The declaration was not in reality made more certain by the addition of an oath, but so solemn a form of assevation was calculated to give a deeper impression of its certainty."

"Saying, Surely blessing I will bless thee, and multiplying I will multiply thee" (v. 14). It seems strange that almost all of the commentators have quite missed the reference in the preceding verse. There we read, "God made promise to Abraham". Some have regarded this as pointing back to the first promise Jehovah made to the patriarch in Gen. 12:2, renewed in 15:5; others have cited Gen. 17:2, 6; still others, the promise recorded in Gen. 17:15, 16; and thus they limit the "patiently endured" (Heb. 6:15) to a space of twenty-five years, and regard the "he obtained the promise" as finding its fulfillment at the birth of Isaac. But these conjectures are completely set aside by the words of our present verse, which are a direct quotation from Gen. 22:17, and that was uttered **after** Isaac was born.

That which God swear to was to bless Abraham with all blessings, and that unto the end: "Surely, blessing I will bless thee". The phrase is a Hebrew mode of expression, denoting emphasis and certainty. Such reduplication is a vehement affirmation, partaking of the nature of an oath: where such is used, it was that men might know God is in earnest in that which He expressed. It also respects and **extends** the thing promised or threatened: I will do without fail, without measure, and eternally without end. It is indeed solemn to note the first occurrence in Scripture of this mode of expression. We find it in the awful threat which the Lord God made unto Adam: "But of the tree of the knowledge of good and evil, thou shalt not eat of it: for in the day that thou eatest thereof dying thou shalt die" (Gen. 2:17).

It is Gen. 2:17 which supplies the first key that unlocks the meaning of Gen. 22:17. These are the first two occurrences in Holy Writ of this unusual form of speech. They stand in direct antithesis the one to the other. The first concerned the curse, the second respected the blessing. The one was the sentence of irrevocable doom, the other was the promise of irreversible bliss. Each was uttered to an individual who stood as the head and representative of a family, upon whose members the curse and the blessing fell. Each head sustained a **double** relationship. Adam was the head of the entire human family, and the condemnation for his sin has been imputed to all his descendents (Rom. 5:12, 18, 19). But in a narrower sense Adam was the head of the non-elect, who not only share his condemnation, partake of his sinful nature, but also suffer his eternal doom. In like manner, Abraham was the head of a natural family, that is, all who have descended from him; and they share in the temporal blessings which God promised their father. But in a narrower sense Abraham (type of Christ as the "everlasting Father" Isa 9:6 and cf. Isa. 53:10 "His seed", and His "children" in Heb. 2:13) was the head of God's elect, who are made partakers of his faith, performers of his works, and participants of his spiritual and eternal blessings.

It was through their failing to look upon Abraham as the type of Christ as the Head and Father of God's elect, which caused the commentators to miss the deeper and spiritual significance of God's promise and oath to him in Gen. 22. In the closing verses of Heb. 6 the Holy Spirit has Himself expounded the type for us, and in our next article (D. V.) we shall seek to set before the reader some of the supporting proofs of what we have here little more than barely asserted. The temporal blessings wherewith God blessed Abraham—"God hath blessed Abraham in all things" (Gen. 24:1 and cf. v. 35)—were typical of the spiritual blessings wherewith God has blessed Christ. So too the earthly inheritance guaranteed unto Abraham's seed, was a figure and pledge of the Heavenly inheritance which pertains to Christ's seed. Let the reader ponder carefully Luke 1:70-75 where we find the type merging into the antitype.

"Surely, blessing I will bless thee" is further interpreted for us in Gal. 3:14, where we read, "That the blessing of Abraham might come on the Gentiles through Jesus Christ". Thus, in blessing Abraham, God blessed all the heirs of promise, and pledges Himself to bestow on them what He had sworn to give unto him: "If ye be Christ's then are ye Abraham's seed, and heirs according to the promise" (Gal. 3:29). That the deeper and ultimate signification of Gen. 22:17 had reference to spiritual and future "blessing" is not only established, unequivocally, by Rom. 9:7, 8, but also by the fact that otherwise there had been **no relevancy** in Paul's setting before the Hebrews, and us, the example of Abraham.

That with which God promised to bless Abraham and his seed was faith, holiness, perseverance, and at the end, salvation (Gal. 3:14). That which God pledged Himself unto with an oath was that His power, His long-suffering, should be engaged to the uttermost to work upon the hearts of Abraham and his spiritual children, so that they would effectually attain unto salvation. Abraham was to live on the earth for many long years after God appeared unto him in Gen. 22. He was to live in an adverse world where he would meet with various temptations, much opposition, many discouragements; but God undertook to deliver, support, succor, sustain him unto the end, so that His oath should be accomplished. Proof of this is given in our next verse.

"And so after he had patiently endured, he obtained the promise" (v. 15). This means that, amid all the temptations and trials to which he was exposed, Abraham studiously persevered in believing and expecting God to make good His word. The emphatic and all-important word here is "And **so**" which joins together what was said in vv. 13, 14 and what follows here in v. 15. It was in **this** way and manner. of God's dealing with him; it was in **this** way of conducting himself. He "patiently endured", which covers the whole space from the time that God appeared to him in Gen. 22 until he died, at the age of one hundred and seventy-five years (Gen. 25:7). It is this exercise of hope unto the end which Paul was pressing upon the Hebrews. They professed to be Abraham s children, let them, then, manifest Abraham's spirit.

"He obtained the promise": by installments. First, an earnest of it in this life, having the blessing of God in his own soul; enjoying communion with Him and all that that included—peace, joy, strength, victory. By faith in the promise, he saw Christ's day, and was glad (John 8:56). Second, a more complete entering into the blessing of God when he left this world of sin and sorrow, and departed to be with Christ, which is "far better" (Phil. 1:23) than the most intimate fellowship which may be had with Him down here. Abraham had now entered on the peace and joy of Paradise, obtaining the Heavenly Country (Heb. 11:16), of which Canaan was but the type. Third, following the resurrection, when the purpose of God shall be fully realized in perfect and unending blessing and glory.

—ARTHUR W. PINK.

THE SATISFACTION ("ATONEMENT") OF CHRIST

4. Its Pre-requisites

Before we are in the position to discern what was required in order for an atonement to be made for the sins of believers, or more specifically, what were the **qualifications** which must be possessed by him who should render an acceptable satisfaction to God, it is essential that we should know something of the actual **nature** of the Atonement itself. This we shall endeavour to define at length in the articles which (D. V.) are to immediately follow this one; but, to pave the way for a more intelligent consideration of the perfections of the Mediator, let us briefly state **what it was** that Christ came here to do. The Son of God became the Son of man in order that sons of men might become sons of God. But these sons of men were not merely creatures, they were fallen and sinful creatures, and, as such, hateful to God, and under the condemnation of His inexorable law.

Sin has produced a tremendous gulf between the thrice holy God and the rebellious children of Adam. Man has no ability whatever to fill in or pass over that gulf. Not only is he alienated from his Maker (Eph. 4:18), but that law which he has broken, insists upon full reparation, and this, man is incompetent to render. Thus, his case is desperate indeed. His only hope, as we sought to show near the close of our last article, lies in a mediator espousing his cause, a mediator acceptable to that God whom man has so grossly and grievously offended, a mediator both willing and qualified to undertake for him. But where was such an one to be found? where was one who could bridge the awful gulf sin had made, who was fitted to be entrusted with the interests of the Godhead, and who was capable of representing those who were, in the scale of being, so far, far below Him?

"Although man had remained immaculately innocent, yet his condition would have been too mean for him to approach to God without a Mediator. What, then, can he do, after having been plunged by his fatal fall into death and hell, defiled with so many blasphemies, putrefying in his own corruptions; in a word, overwhelmed by every curse? Since our iniquities, like a cloud, intervening between us and God, entirely alienating us from Heaven, no one that could not approach to God could be a mediator for the restoration of peace. But who could have approached Him? Could any of the children of Adam? No; they, with their first parent, dreaded the Divine presence. What, then, could be done? Our situation was truly deplorable, unless the Divine majesty itself would descend to us; for we could not ascend to it. Thus it was necessary (as arising from the heavenly decree) that the Son of God should become Immanuel, that is, God with us" (Calvin's Institutes, book 2, chapt. 12).

Yet instead of removing, this only seems to increase, the difficulty. As we have pointed out above, atonement could only be effected by a full satisfaction rendered to the Law; and this involved two things: first, a perfect obedience given to all its precepts; second, a full endurance of its unrelenting punishment. But how could a Divine Person enter the place of subserviency and become subject to the Law's demands? And again, How could a Divine person suffer and die? This seems an insoluable problem, yet Divine wisdom provided a glorious solution. One of the Eternal Three, without in anywise ceasing to be God, took upon Him the form of a Servant and became Man. The Divine incarnation was undertaken in order to sin's expiation. The eternal Word's becoming flesh was a gracious means to a glorious end: it was that He might mediate between God and His people.

A mediator is one who intervenes between two parties at variance and makes peace. He must of necessity be a different person from each of the parties whom it is his design to reconcile; he can neither be the party which is offended, nor the party which has given offence. The party offended may forgive the offender; but in such a case, a mediator is not wanted. The party offending may be sorry for his conduct, and earnestly desire that peace be made; but he may have no access to the party offended, or the latter may reject his advances, because he does not deem the proffered satisfaction to be adequate. In this case a third party may interpose to adjust the difference, by the proposal of terms in which both will acquiesce.

What has just been pointed out raises a further difficulty: was not God the Son the party offended by the sinner, equally with the Father and the Spirit? Assuredly, for in His essential being, He is one with Them. But the Scriptures not only reveal the absolute unity of nature and essence in the three persons of the Godhead, they also make known an economy or arrangement among those Persons, by which different characters and offices were assigned to Each, and new **relations** are sustained by Them toward one another and towards us. In the economy of Redemption and its connection with the world, the Father appears in the character of the Supreme Governor of heaven and earth, the Son as Mediator, and the Spirit as the Applier of Redemption. In His office of Mediator, Christ does not press the claims of justice against sinners, but stands forth as their Friend, rescuing them from their perilous situation by rendering satisfaction for them to their offended Sovereign.

"The necessity of the mediation of Christ arises from the existence of sin; which being contrary to the nature and revealed will of God, renders those who have committed it obnoxious to His displeasure. As they had no means of appeasing His anger, the interposition of another person was requisite to atone for their guilt, and lay the foundation of peace. This is the great design of His office; but it extents to all the acts, by which sinners are actually brought into a state of reconciliation, are fitted for holding communion with God, and are raised to perfection and immutable felicity in the world to come. It comprehends the particular offices which our Saviour is represented as sustaining, the prophetical, the sacerdotal, and the regal; and it is by executing these that He completely performs the duties, and realizes the character of a Mediator" (Dr. J. Dick). Let us now particularise by endeavoring to point out what was required in the one who should make atonement for sinners to God.

1. The Mediator must be Man

"The mediator between God and men cannot be God only, or man only. This is taught in Gal. 3:20. 'A mediator is not of one, but God is one'. A mediator supposes two parties between whom he intervenes; but God is only one party. Consequently, the Mediator between God and men must be related to both, and be the equal of either. He cannot be simply God, who is only one of the parties, and has only one nature. Therefore the eternal Word must take man's nature into union with Himself if He would be a mediator between God and men. The same truth is taught in 1 Sam. 2:25, 'For if one man sin against another, the judge shall judge him; but if a man sin against the Lord, who shall intreat for him?'. 'Therefore when He (the mediator) cometh into the world, He saith, A body hast Thou prepared Me' (Heb. 10:5)", Dr. J. Shedd.

Relationship of nature to those for whom Atonement was made, is an essential element in its validity. Christ required to be real and proper **man**, as well as true **God**. To qualify Him for the work of redemption, He needed to possess opposite attributes: a frail and mortal nature, combined with ineffable dignity of person. Humanity was requisite to fit the Messiah for suffering, to render Him susceptible of pain and death, to make it possible for Him to offer Himself as a sacrifice. Equally so was the possession of human nature required in order to impart validity to what He **did**, to give to His obedience and sufferings an essential value in the estimation of God's law. The work of our redemption being a moral satisfaction to the Law of God for the sins of men, there existed a moral fitness that the satisfaction should be made by one in the nature of those who had sinned. It is striking to note in the types how that redemption had to be effected by a near kinsman" (Lev. 25:25-27; Ruth 4:7)!

Unless the Redeemer Himself possesses the nature of those to be redeemed the moral government of God had not been vindicated, nor the glory of the divine Lawgiver been maintained, nor the principles of the law been upheld. The law in its precept was suited to man, and in its curse had a claim upon man. Its requirements were such as man only could fulfill; its penalty such as one possessing the nature of man only could bear. The penalty was **suffering unto death;** and no angel could die (Luke 20:36). The death only of a man could possess a moral and legal congruity to the cause of a law given to man and broken by man. Thus, it was not only to qualify Him for suffering that the Messiah took upon Him the nature of man, but to qualify Him for **such** sufferings as should possess validity in the eye of the divine law. "For both He that sanctifieth and they who are sanctified, are all of one . . . Wherefore in all things it behooved Him to be made like unto His brethren . . . to make propitiation for the sins of the people" (Heb. 2:11, 17). "Since by man came death, by man **also** the resurrection of the dead" (1 Cor. 15:21).

The law required that its subject should love God with all his soul and serve Him with all the members of his body, seeing both are God's. Now none can do this but man, who consists of soul and body. Again; the law required the love of our neighbour, but none is our neighbour but man, who is of the same blood with us: hence the force of those words, "that thou hide not thyself from thine own flesh" (Isa. 58:7). Hence our Surety must cherish us, as one does his own flesh, and consequently we have to be, "members of His body, of His flesh, and of His bones" (Eph. 4:30). Therefore, has the Holy Spirit joined together these two things about Christ: "made of a woman, made under the law" (Gal. 4:4), intimating the principal end of His incarnation was that He might be subject to the law.

"It is not without reason that Paul, when asked to exhibit Christ in the character of a Mediator, expressly speaks of Him as a man: 'There is one Mediator between God and men, the man Christ Jesus' (1 Tim. 2:5). He might have called Him God, or might indeed have omitted the appellation of man, as well as that of God; but because the Spirit, who spake by him knew our infirmity, He has provided a very suitable remedy against it, by placing the Son of God familiarly amongst us (Christians, A. W. P.) as though He were one of us. Therefore, that no one may distress himself where he is to seek the Mediator or in what way he may approach Him, the apostle, by denominating Him a man, apprizes us that He is near, and even close to us, since He is our own flesh. He certainly intends the same in Heb. 4:15" (J. Calvin).

2. The Mediator must be Sinless

He who makes atonement for others must himself be entirely free from that which renders the atonement necessary. That which made atonement necessary was sin. The redeemer must be sinless, otherwise he would require redeeming. A sinner cannot expiate his own sins, still less can he be a saviour of others. Thus it was a prime pre-requisite that the substitionary victim should himself be undefiled, pure. This was plainly foreshadowed in the types. The lamb used in sacrifice must be "without blemish". The red heifer must not only be flawless, but also one "upon which never came yoke" (Num. 19:2). The levitical high priest was required to possess a high degree of ceremonial purity.

"Legal obligation to the curse may arise from one or both of two things: either from being born under the curse, that is to say, from original sin; or from becoming exposed to the penalty in consequence of a personal breach of its requirements, that is by actual transgression. Infants of the human family are under it in the former way; adults in both; but Jesus was neither the one nor the other" (Dr. W. Symington on "The Atonement", 1854). Jesus was never under the Adamic covenant, and therefore the sin of our first father was never imputed to Him. He was supernaturally conceived of a virgin, and therefore, the virus of sin never entered His veins.

3. The Mediator must be Holy

More than a sinless nature was required by the redeemer. Satan, was, originally, created without sin; yet he fell, Adam had no impurity in his nature when he left his Maker's hands, yet he transgressed. But Jesus Christ was not merely negatively sinless, He was, in His very humanity, positively **holy**—"that holy thing, which shall be born of thee" (Luke 1:35) were the words of God to His mother. It is striking and blessed to note that when the Holy Spirit exhibits, from the human side, the personal perfections of our High Priest, He speaks of Him first as "holy", which refers to the intrinsic excellency of His nature; then as "harmless" which speaks of His entire freedom from evil in respect to conduct; "undefiled", which denotes the absolute purity of His official qualification and administration (Heb. 7:26). The intrinsic and unsullied purity of the Mediator was necessary to the acceptance of His services.

Beautifully has Dr. Dick pointed out, "This primitive purity He retained during the course of His life, conversing and familiarly associating with sinners, but not learning their ways. He died, indeed, as a criminal, but He died for sins not His own: He 'suffered, the Just for the unjust, that He might bring us to God' (1 Peter 3:18). Nay, He was not only free from actual transgression, He was incapable of sin; so fortified against temptation, that He could not be seduced .. He stood firm in the severest trial. No argument, however subtle, could perplex His reason; no solicitation, however powerful, could seduce His affections. Satan exhausted his arts associating with Him in vain". To which we may add: He touched the leper, but was uncontaminated. He came into contact with death, but remained undefiled. He bare our sins in His own body on the tree, yet it was the "Holy One", unsullied, that was laid in the grave (Psa. 16:10).

4. The Mediator must be Master of himself

The one whose work it is to reconcile two parties at variance must not be under personal obligations to either. None could offer a satisfaction to Law if he himself owed a debt unto it. A mediator must be independent, having full power over himself, possessing complete right to act on the part of others. Those who are subject to the authority of another, cannot dispose of themselves and their services without his consent. Now angels and men are the absolute property of their Creator, and must wait His command before they may venture to engage in any enterprise not comprehended in the original law of their nature. The life of man is God's gift, and must not be thrown away nor surrendered, no matter what good might be anticipated from the sacrifice, without the direct permission of the giver. In a word, a Mediator between God and man must have full power over his own life, to lay it down and take it again.

"It is not enough that the substitute be innocent, is free from the claims of the law to which he gives satisfaction to others. He may be under obligations to another law, the fulfillment of whose demand may render it impossible to occupy the place of surety. His whole time and energies may be thus, as it were, previously engaged, so as to put it out of his power to make a transfer of any part of them for the behoof of others. This is, indeed, the case with all creatures, whatever service they are capable of performing, they owe originally and necessarily to God. They are, from their very nature, incapable of meriting for **themselves**, much less for **others**. The right of self-disposal belongs not to creatures. Themselves and all that pertains to them, are the property of Him who made and preserves the same. They are under law to God. They are not under the covenant which God made with man, to be sure; but the law under which they exist demands all their energies, it has a claim upon them for the full amount of the service which they are capable of performing, and thus denies them all right of giving satisfaction to another law, in behalf of a different order of creatures" (Dr. W. Symington).

5. The Mediator must act Voluntarily

This is so self-evident it should need no arguing. Without this qualification, all others would be worthless. Let an appointed mediator be ever so dignified in his person, let him be most intimately related to man, let him be entirely free from all moral contamination, let him be completely at his own disposal; yet, it is manifest that, unless he choose actually to dispose of himself for the good of others, no validity could attach to what he did. Vicarious satisfaction can never be compulsory: willingness enters into its very essence. To **compel** one to suffer for another would be the height of injustice. Moreover, God will not accept any sacrifice which is reluctantly offered to Him: the heart must be in it: "My son, give Me thine heart" (Prov. 23:26) is His first request from His children, for when He has **that,** He has everything.

Inexpressibly blessed is it to observe how plainly and how frequently this very element is seen in the great Mediator. To the proposal in the eternal covenant He gave His cheerful consent: "Lo, I come: in the volume of the book it is written of Me, I **delight to do** Thy will, O My God" (Psa. 4:6-8). In all that He did to make atonement for sin, the Lord Jesus manifested no degree of reluctance. His meat was to do the Father's will (John 4:34). He was "led (not "driven") as a lamb to the slaughter" (Acts 8:32); He **"gave** His back to the smiters, and His cheeks to them that plucked off the hair" (Isa. 50:6). "He **poured out** His soul unto death" (Isa. 53:12); He **gave up** the spirit" (John 19:30). Let the interested reader turn to the Song of Sol. and behold how blessedly He is there represented as "leeping" and "skipping" over the mountains of separation as He hastens to His people!

6. The Mediator must be federally united to His people.

In his defense of the Satisfaction of Christ, Turretin pointed out how that there are three kinds of union known to us in human relations which justifies the imputation of sin one to another; natural, as between a father and his child; moral and political, as between a king and his subjects; voluntary, as between friends, or between an arraigned criminal and his sponsor. But the union of Christ with His people rests on far stronger ground than any of these considered alone. It was voluntary on His part, for He spontaneously assumed all the obligations He bore. But it was also a **covenant** ordinance, decreed by the three Divine persons in counsel, whose behests are alone the foundation of all law, all rights, and of all obligations. "The scriptures plainly teach that God has established between Christ and His people a union **sui-generis,** transcending all earthly analogies in its intimacy of fellowship and reciprocal co-partnership both federal and vital" (Dr. C. Hodge).

The mediatorial position assumed by Christ and the redemptive work which He performed cannot be rightly understood till they are viewed in connection with the Everlasting Covenant. It is not difficult to see that the death of the cross was only made possible for the Son of God by His becoming Man. But we need to go farther back and ask, What was the relation between Christ and His people that made it meet for Him to become incarnate and die for them? It is not enough to say that He was their Surety, and Substitute, True, blessedly true, He wrought and suffered for them because He was their Surety to the offended Law-giver and Judge. But **what** rendered it proper that He should occupy such a place? No satisfactory answer can be given till we go right back to the counsels of the Godhead. **Covenant oneness** accounts for all, vindicates all, explains all.

Christ was substituted **for** His people because He was and is one **with** them—identified with us and we with Him; not merely as decreed by the sovereign authority of the Godhead, but as **covenanted** between the eternal Father and the eternal Son. Christ "bore the sins of many" because in His covenant identification with them, their sins became sinlessly but truly His sins; and unto the sons and daughters of the covenant, the Father imputes the righteousness of His Son, because, in their **covenant oneness** with Him, His righteousness is undeservedly but truly their own righteousness. This alone explains all Christ's history as the incarnate Son of God; all His interposition as the Saviour of His people; and it places the career of Christ on earth in its true relations to the eternal purpose of God. In its completeness, as bearing on the covenant-clients as well as the covenant-Head, it is the formal instrument by which faith comes into sure possession of Christ Himself and the benefits of redemption.

Christ is expressly denominated "the last Adam" (1 Cor. 15:45), and therefore are we told that the first Adam was "the figure of Him that was come" (Rom. 5:14). Adam was a "figure" of Christ in quite a number of ways, but supremely in this, that he stood as the federal head of a race. God entered into a covenant with him (Hos. 6:6, margin), and therefore he stood and fell as the legal representative of all his family: when he sinned, they sinned; when he died, they died (Rom. 5:12-19). So was it with the "last Adam": He stood as the covenant Head and federal Representative of all His people, being legally one with them, so that He assumed and discharged all their responsibilities. The birth of Christ was the begun **manifestation** of the eternal union between Him and His people.

In the Covenant, Christ had said to the Father, "I will declare Thy name unto My brethren, in the midst of the Church will I sing praise unto Thee. And again, I will put My trust in Him. And again, Behold I and the children which God hath given Me" (Heb. 2:12, 13) Most blessedly is this explained in what immediately follows: "Forasmuch then as the children are partakers of flesh and blood, He also Himself likewise took part of the same", and therefore "He is not ashamed to call them brethren". **Federation** is the root of this amazing mercy, covenant-identification is the key which explains it.

Christ came not to strangers, but to "brethren"; He came here not to procure a people for Himself, but to secure a people already His (Eph. 1:4, Matt. 1:21).

Such a union has existed between Christ and His people from all eternity it inevitably followed that, when He came to earth, He **must** bear their sins, and now that He has gone to heaven they **must** be clothed (Isa. 61:10) with all the rewardableness of His perfect obedience. **This** is the strongest buttress of all in the walls of Truth, yet the one which has been most frequently assailed by its enemies. Men have argued that the punishment of the Innocent **as though He were** guilty, was an outrage upon justice. In the human realm, to punish a man for something of which he is neither responsible nor guilty, is, beyond question, unjust. But this principle did not apply to Christ, for He had **voluntarily** identified Himself with His people in such an intimate way that it could be said, "For both He that sanctifieth, and they who are sanctified, are **all of one**" (Heb. 2:11).

When we say that the union between Christ and His people is a **federal** one, we mean that it is of such a nature as to involve an **identification** of legal relations and reciprocal obligations and rights: "By the obedience of One shall many be made (legally constituted) righteous" (Rom. 5:19). God's elect were "chosen **in** Christ" (Eph. 1:4). They are "created **in** Christ Jesus" (Eph. 2:10). They were circumcised in Him (Col. 2:11). They are "made the righteousness of God **in Him**" (2 Cor. 5:21). In view of this ineffable union, scripture does not hesitate to say, "We are members of His body, of His flesh, and of His bones" (Eph. 4:30).

7. The Mediator must be Divine.

Think of the **work** the Mediator had to perform. He was to restore to divine favour those who were under the curse. He had to render unto the Law an obedience which one created sinless (Adam) had failed to perform. He was required to present unto God a satisfaction possessing **infinite** merits, which procured infinite blessings for His people. This a finite creature could not do. He was to endure the full weight of God's outpoured wrath upon all the sins of His people, as they were concentrated upon the Surety. He was to vanquish the Devil, so as to deliver his captives. He was to overcome sin, so that its sting was destroyed. He was to swallow up death and bestow eternal life on all those the Father had given him.

Finally, He was to give the Holy Spirit unto His people, who would apply to them the redemption purchased. Who but a Divine person was competent for **such** an undertaking?

Again; think of what has been **effected** by the Mediator's work. It has restored God's people to true liberty (Gal. 5:1). Now as Witsius rightly pointed out, if any mere **creature**, however exalted, had redeemed us, we should have become the personal property of that creature, for he who sets us free, makes a purchase of us for his possession (1 Cor. 6: 19, 20). But it is a manifest contradiction to be freed and be free, and yet at the same time be the property of any creature, for true liberty consists in subjection alone. Thus, our Lord says. "If **the Son** therefore shall make you free, ye shall be free **indeed**" (John 8:36). Again; for the redeemed to glory in anyone as their Saviour, to say to him, Thou art our Lord, to render to him adoring homage, is an honour to which no mere creature could have the slightest claim. Thus, the Mediator, **must be** a Divine person.

"It is not possible that the blood of bulls and goats should take away sins" (Heb. 10:4). Why? In the first place, those typical sacrifices could not, in the nature of them, magnify the **precepts** of the Law: they were totally incapable of rendering that perfect obedience which was required. Nor, secondly, could they endure the full **penalty** of the Law: "Lebanon is not sufficient to burn, nor the beasts thereof for a burnt offering" (Isa. 40:16). The fires of God's wrath had utterly annihilated the cattle upon a thousand hills, and would still wait for something else to consume. Therefore did God "lay help upon One that is **mighty**" (Psa. 89:19). Christ **was able** not only to perfectly keep the law, but to suffer the full extent of its unbated curse.

It is, "The altar that sanctifieth the gift" (Matt. 23:19), the reference being to the type of Ex. 29:37: "it shall be an altar most holy, whosoever toucheth the altar shall be holy". Upon this Dr. T. Ridgley (1815) well said, "From whence it is inferred, that the altar was more holy than the gift which was laid upon it, and it signifies, that the altar on which Christ was offered, added an excellency to His offering. Now nothing could be said to do so, but His divine nature's being personally united to His humanity, which rendered it infinitely valuable". For this reason, the mercy-seat was made not of wood, but of "pure gold" (Ex. 25:17).

How often does the Holy Spirit give supreme emphasis to **this** fact. Before He tels us in Heb. 1 that Christ has "by Himself purged our sins", He first presents this vicarious Sufferer as God's "Son", the "Heir of all things" the "Brightness of God's glory", yea, the "express image of His person"! So in Phil 2, the One who "humbled Himself and became obedient unto death", is first set before us as Him who subsisted "in the Form of God", and "thought it not robbery to be **equal** with God". So again in Col. 1 He is described as the Creator of all things (v. 16), ere we read of the peace which He made by the blood of His Cross. It is because Christ was who He was which gave an infinite value to what He did.

We close this somewhat lengthy article with the concluding words of Dr. Symington on this enthralling subject: "From the perfection of His atonement, arising out of the circumstances specified above, does it proceed, that He makes intercession for us within the veil of the upper sanctuary, that He dispenses with a munificent hand the gifts of His purchase and causes the prey of a great spoil to be divided. And pardon and peace, redemption and holiness, eternal glory and bliss are, among the rich fruits of the royal and triumphal conquest He achieved, when by His infinitely meritorious death, He spoiled principalities and powers, and made a show of them openly. With the most entire confidence, then, may the needy sinner, smitten with the deepest sense of conscious unworthiness, rely for salvation on this all-sufficient atonement."

—ARTHUR W. PINK.

MORTIFICATION OF SIN

The apostle Paul expressly says that "If any man have not the Spirit of Christ, he is none of His" (Rom. 8:9). None who know anything of the Christ, will venture to deny it. God hath revealed no possible way to eternal life in His most Holy Word, but the free, sovereign gift which He hath made of it in His Son; nor any other way of conveying spiritual and eternal life to us, but by His Spirit. The record of testimony, which the Lord has given us in the Bible of His ways with His people, is from the beginning to the end of it so full of the same Spirit, that there is no getting rid of the term without absolutely rejecting the whole Word of God. The fountain of eternal life is in God. "With Thee", says the Psalmist, "is the fountain of life" (36:9). It is conveyed through Jesus Christ, by whom all things are and were created. The free grant of it is recorded in the everlasting Gospel, which is the only way whereby we come to the knowledge of it, of our title to it, and also to the possession and enjoyment of it. It is the eternal Spirit who is called the Spirit of God and of Christ, that makes the conveyance of it effectual to us. Our eternal life consists in the abiding and indwelling of the Holy Spirit. This eternal life is conveyed to us in and with our new and second birth: which is styled, a "being born again", a "new creation", and the "workmanship" of God. And the effect of it is styled, "**a new creature**".

Mortification of sin proceeds from this, as the effect from the cause. It is the fruit of this spiritual life, thus communicated to the regenerate soul. It most naturally and necessarily follows upon it. The "man in Christ", who is by regeneration and conversion to the Lord a new creature in Christ Jesus, hath in his new nature received from the Holy Spirit a perfect hatred, an entire aversion, and contrariety to all the sin, impurity, and sinfulness inherent in his fallen nature. And as life is opposite to death, purity to impurity, holiness to sin, spirituality to carnality; so there is now felt and experienced a severe combat between sin and grace, which reside and dwell in one and the same person: from henceforward therefore, the inward conflict is perpetual, as each strives for mastery. Hence proceeds the absolute necessity for the believer to be sober and to watch unto prayer.

The apostle suits his exhortation most exactly to the case: "This I say then, walk in the Spirit, and ye shall not fulfill the lusts of the flesh. For the flesh lusteth against the Spirit, and the Spirit against the flesh; and these are contrary the one to the other: so that ye cannot do the things which ye would. But if ye be led by the Spirit, ye are not under the law" (Gal. 5:16-18). It is of vast importance to the believer in Jesus to have clear and scriptural views of what he is, as the subject of both sin and grace. We have Paul's personal experience of it recorded in Romans 7. He says he saw another law in his members warring against the law of his mind, and bringing him into captivity to the law of sin which was in his members. This caused him most bitterly to exclaim, "O wretched man that I am". As the child of God is led to view and consider what actually passes within himself, and as he compares it with what the apostle has declared, he finds that the one case is explanatory of the other. This leads him to study himself in the various motions and operations of **inherent sin,** and **inherent grace.** From hence he will practica.ly learn that in himself, in his fallen nature, dwelleth nothing that is good. Grace does not sanctify sinful nature, but leaves it as it was.

Our Lord gives us a most exact account of this when He says, "That which is born of the flesh is flesh, and that which is born of the Spirit is spirit" (John 3:6). Nothing but sin and corruption is introduced into our nature by the one life; nothing but holiness, grace, and purity by the other. There is no holiness in our fallen nature, nor sinfulness in our new. It is absolutely necessary that the believer should see and acknowledge the truth of this; because although sin received its death-wound in him the first moment he was quickened by the Holy Spirit with spiritual life, and though he hungers and thirts after Chirst, has real communion with Him, and is under the influence and reign of grace, at seasons he feels that, notwithstanding with the mind he serves the law of God, yet with the flesh he serves the law of sin; so that every experience proves to him that he is, every moment in his fallen nature, carnal, sold under sin; and that, when he would do good, sin which dwelleth in him acts under one form or other to prevent him; so that the good he would, he does not; but the evil which he would not, that he does. This is matter of the greatest grief, and it creates much perplexity to the mind of the new born soul how to account for it. He learns from it the necessity of attending to what the apostle says, "If ye live after the flesh, ye shall die; but if ye through the Spirt do mortify the deeds of the body ye shall live" (Rom 8:13).

He sees how absolutely necessary it is for him to die to sin, and to have it perfectly mortified within him, that he may get above its love, power, deceit, and influence. He finds, that, though his affections to sin are deadened as to sinful pleasures, and though the old man is indeed put off concerning the former conversation, yet he is not put to death. He still remains alive, and is sometimes very active, though he lies in chains, and is under the power and dominion of mighty and victorious grace; yet as he plainly perceives, this does not amount to a mortification, a killing and destroying of the inward principles of sin within him. He is led to consider the nature of that mortification, which the Scriptures speak most generally of, and exhort to, which is a mortification of the outward acts of sin, and of an external course of living in iniquity. And as these are but the effects of an inward mortification, which is the consequence of eternal life begun in the soul by the Holy Spirit, he considers more distinctly and applies himself to search more closely into this very important subject.

From the Scriptures he finds, that the spiritual mortification of sin by the efficacy of Christ's death consists not in a partial abstinence from this or the other corruption, nor in being kept from partial falling into sin, nor in being without sin; but that it extends its influence over the whole body of sin, in its life, love, guilt, power and dominion:—that this is not effected by anything without us, nor any performance of ours; but that we must look wholly to Christ for it, and can only partake of the fruits and effects of it, as we have actual communion with Him in His death by the influence of the Holy Spirit. The apostle is upon this great subject in Romans 6. This is an important truth, that, as believers in Christ, we are transplanted into Christ, into the likeness of His death, and have an actual participation of the blessed consequences thereof. He saith, "Know ye not that so many of us as were baptized into Jesus Chr.st were baptized into His death"? You are by virtue of your union with Jesus **interested in** His crucifixion, death, burial and resurrection. Baptism is a solemn memorial of this: verse 4. Baptism is but once administered, because regeneration is but once wrought. And Christ being once revealed by the Holy Spirit, His great salvation is **applied,** and the regenerate are partakers of all the blessings contained in His death and resurrection: "For if we have been planted together in the likeness of His death, we shall be also in the likeness of His resurrection" (v. 5). And being quickened by virtue of our union with Christ, and interest in His resurrection, up to a spiritual and endless life, we receive therefrom an eternal blow and death to all our inward sin, lusts, and corruptions: "Knowing this, that our old man is crucified with Him, that the body of sin might be destroyed, that henceforth we should not serve sin" (v. 6).

By virtue of Christ bearing our sins in His own body on the tree, our old man being then and there nailed to the cross and crucified with Him, we have an eternal discharge from the **imputation** of all our sin, inherent and external, with the complete mortification of the whole body of it, and an everlasting victory over all its guilt, love, power, and dominion, in the one perfect offering and everlasting efficacious death of our great High Priest, Christ Jesus. (This is the **judicial** side of truth, and as it is "mixed with faith" (Heb. 4:2), we live in the **experimental** power and enjoyment of it. A. W. P.). To which the apostle adds, by way of confirmation, "For he that is dead is freed from sin" (v. 7); i. e. believers in Christ, as united to Him and one with Him in His death, are dead to the law by the body of Christ. This is the doctrine of Paul in Romans 6.

Our Lord Jesus represented all His people, and acted as their Substitute. The Father laid on Him all their sins, both original and actual. He was clad and wrapped about with the whole body of the sins of the elect. He bore the whole guilt, impurity, and demerit contained in them, as truly as He was clothed with a body of flesh. And He died for that, which we by nature are in, and for which we could never make atonement. He died, **but once**, because the sacrifice of Himself, as God-man Mediator, was everlastingly effectual to answer every end, and accomplish every design, for which the Father in His infinite wisdom appointed. And His people were **in union with Him**, represented by Him, and interested in all the virtue and efficacy of His mediation. His death is the death and everlasting destruction of all the sins of His people. By it He conquered the damning, and also the reigning power of it. The whole body of sin and death received its death-wound when Jesus died, "the Just for the unjust". There is not any part, member, affection or corruption in the body of sin, but what was actually mortified by the obedience of our Lord unto death. All its heartstrings were broken when Christ expired on the Cross.

Hence the apostle saith, "I am crucified with Christ" (Gal. 2:20). Herein consists the believer's perfection. He is a member of Christ, a partaker of all the benefits of His death, eternally complete in Him, and without all fault before the throne of God. This must be truly known, spiritually understood, received and believed from the testimony of God in His Word, to the intent that the believer may enjoy the benefit of it. He cannot get above sin and its guilt, nor overcome its power, until he has received his perfect discharge from his original and actual guilt, by believing in the blood and righteousness of Jesus. The apostle puts believers on considering what they are in Christ: "Likewise reckon ye yourselves to be dead indeed unto sin" (Rom. 6:11). A believer should view himself one with Christ in His death, and reckon himself to be what Christ is. Did He die the death? die to sin? The believer is discharged from the **imputation** of all sin, guil , and condemnation, on the footing thereof; so that he may well say, "Blessed is the man to whom the Lord will not impute sin" (Rom. (4:8). The believer is legally represented by Christ, is what He is, dead to sin in Him, holy as He is holy, righteous as He is righteous; and, as thus viewed by his Heavenly Father, shines in His sight, in the person and work of Christ, holy, pure and complete in Him. So saith the apostle, "And you, that were sometime alienated and enemies in your minds by wicked works, yet now hath He reconciled in the body of His flesh through death, to present you holy, unblameable and unreproveable in His sight" (Col. 1:21, 22). Christ is the representative of His people, and He represents them in Himself, holy, unblameable, and unreproveable in the sight of **His** Father and **our** Father, **His** God and **our** God.

When it is given to the believer to view the everlasting perfection and sufficiency of Christ's salvation, and when He is led by the Holy Spirit to look on himself as one in Christ and with Him in all the perfection of His holiness, righteousness, and oblation, and to trust thereon for his eternal discharge from all his sin, and for his everlasting perfection before the Lord, then he triumphs as being justified from all things. He believes that "there is therefore now no condemnation to them which are in Christ Jesus" (Rom. 8:1). This leads him to seek for real and growing fellowship with Him in His death, in all the benefits of it. The Holy Spirit gives the believer clear and spiritual conceptions of these truths. The believing mind is exercised in spiritual contemplations of them; and thereby, through the influence of the Holy Spirit, the believer is led into actual communion with Christ, and experiences the power and efficacy of His death, which produces in him such effects as these: his heart is purified from the guilt of sin by faith in the virtue and value of our Lord's most precious bloodshedding. His mind is at peace with God, believing He hath freely forgiven him all trespasses. And having in the light of the Word and Spirit a believing perception of Christ as his holiness, purity, and perfection, he feels the influence thereof in all his spiritual faculties, and throughout his whole spiritual frame. It leaves its sanctifying influence on the mind and affections. It leads the believer to hate all sin both inward and outward, carnal and spiritual wickedness, with a perfect and immutable hatred. He loathes, and most sincerely mourns at, the least rising of inward corruption. He longs for perfect conformity to Christ, and to be delivered from the very in-being of sin; which will be the case with him, when he is delivered from his present state of warfare, and introduced by Christ into the kingdom of glory. These are the fruits and effects of our being (legally) dead to all sin, in Christ. Our union with Christ in His death, and our communion with Christ by faith therein are the foundation of all our death to sin. Here is our complete mortification of it. It is in Christ's obedience unto death, as our surety.

The believer is without all sin in Christ. Like as Immanuel was perfectly free from all sin inherently, though He once was made sin, and bore all the sins of His people in His own body; so the believer, notwithstanding he has a body of sin inherent in his fallen nature, is yet in God's sight as perfect in Christ, as if he were entirely without it; because he is wholly absolved from it, and it is not imputed to him: "The blood of Jesus Christ God's Son cleanseth us from all sin" (1 John 1:7). And in the union of the believer with Christ, and in interest in and communion with Him in His death, is founded his complete mortification; and all the strength which he receives from Christ to mortify sin in its fruits, is the effect of it. The believer from the Word by the Spirit learns to know that he is accepted in the Beloved, that he is beloved by the Father with the same love wherewith Christ is loved, that we appear in His view, and are in His sight, what Jesus is, and are justified freely and fully.

From the spiritual belief of these eternal truths, that whole body of sin inherent in the believer receives its deathwounds; which will one day, namely, at the disunion of soul and body by death, end in his complete deliverance from it, so that he will be as truly without sin in him as Christ Himself. The believer is led by the Spirit to see that all exhortations concerning mortification of sin are built on these Gospel truths, as their foundation; and finds in real experience, that nothing saves him from the love, power, guilt and dominion of sin, so much as the knowledge and belief of his perfect deliverance from the guilt and filth of the whole body of sin by virtue of his union **with** and interest **in Christ Jesus.** As the believer hath, in the light of the Holy Spirit, a clear knowledge and belief of his union with Jesus, he is led to seek intimate fellowship with Him. And, as this is carried on by the Holy Spirit in the believer's mind, corruptions are subdued, and he experiences the truth of this apostolic assertion, that "They that are Christ's have crucified the flesh with the affections and lusts" (Gal. 5:24). They were first crucified in Christ, as they were nailed to the cross with Him. And they are crucified in the believer by virtue of Christ's death. The influences of which are put forth in the soul through the gracious energy of the Lord the Spirit; which the believer gives open evidence and manifestative proof of by his putting off of the old man with his deeds.

The apostle having set forth the true and perfect mortification of sin in Christ, and shown how the believer is dead to all sin **in H m,** proceeds to exhortation; "Let not sin therefore reign in your mortal body that ye should obey it in the lusts thereof. Neither yield ye your members as instruments of unrighteousness unto sin, but yield yourselves unto God as those that are alive from the dead, and your members as instruments of righteousness unto God" (Rom. 6:12, 13). Which is founded on the union and communion which believers have with Christ: and it is set on with energy by the encouragement which the apostle gives in v. 14: "For sin shall not have dominion over you: for ye are not under law, but under grace". The believer is led by the blessed Spirit to mix faith with His word of promise, and he derives strength in believing the faithfulness of God to fulfill it; moreover, as long as there is an inward rising against and inward groaning and mourning on account of it, this promise cannot fail of being accomplished to him; and these are, and should be looked on, as indisputable evidences thereof.

His clear apprehensions of his state in Christ makes spiritual exhortations very sweet and suitable to him. "For ye are dead, and your life is hid with Christ in God. When Christ who is our life shall appear then shall ye also appear with Him in glory" (Col. 3:4, 5). We see from hence, that we should believe more concerning our being **in Christ** dead to all sin than we feel an experience of it in ourselves. Then follows the exhortation, "Mortify therefore your members which are upon the earth; fornication, uncleanness, inordinate affection, evil concupisence, and covetousness, which is idolatry". The believer feels the weight and sees the importance of these apostolic exhortations. They are set home and applied to his heart by the Spirit of God. The believer renounces his former conversation and walk before conversion, which were corrupt according to his deceitful lusts. He walks in the Lord's good ways, and runs with alacrity in the paths of Divine commands. His outward walk and conversation are the true and real fruit of the secret and inward communion which he hath with Jesus. He walks before the Lord unto all well-pleasing, because he walks with God, as his God and Father in Christ Jesus, in secret and spiritual communion. (This is realised in our experience just so far as real fellowship with the Lord is maintained.—A. W. P.).

O Thou holy and blessed Spirit! from whom proceed all spiritual life and light, Thou art the Conveyor of them from Christ, the fountain and Head thereof to Thy church. I bless Thee, O Holy Spirit! that Thou hast communicated this life and light to my soul. I beseech Thee to lead me to look to and believe on Jesus for my complete and everlasting discharge from all sin, and for everlasting purity and perfection before the Lord. Teach me the true Scriptural doctrine concerning the spiritual mortification of sin. Thou hast set it before me in Thy Word, teach me the true method and practice of it. Lead me by faith to view the everlasting virtue and perfection of Christ's most precious bloodshedding. Help me to see my eternal completeness in Him. Lead me into constant fellowship with Jesus in His death. Help me to believe without the least doubt or wavering my union with Christ, and enable me to improve it in receiving continual virtue and influence from Him in believing, to the deadening and mortifying of every corrupt lust and affection. Do Thou help me to put off the old man with his deeds in my daily walk. Thus may I act as the redeemed of the Lord, and go forward with renewed strength. I ask it for the honour of Thy name, to whom with the Father and the Son be everlasting praise. Amen.

—S. E. PIERCE, 1804.

DIVINE WARNINGS

It is both unwise and irreverent to philosophise about spiritual things. It is unwise, because spiritual things lie outside the province and transcend the grasp of our intellect. It is irreverent, because for a finite creature to attempt the dragging down of the Truth of the Infinite to the bar of human reason is most impious. The natural man receiveth not the things of the Spirit of God. The Kingdom of Heaven cannot be entered except we become as little children. We are exhorted to "lean not" unto our own understanding (Prov. 3:5). Humbling lessons are these to flesh and blood, never more so than in this day of intellectual pride and arrogance. Nevertheless they have to be learned—learned by submitting to them—if we are to spiritually apprehend the things of God. If His Word is to be engrafted into our souls, it has to be received "with meekness" (James 1:21).

There is a certain type of mind which finds it peculiarly difficult to abstain from carnal reasoning. Just as there are those who are constitutionally prone to gluttony, or sloth, or immorality; just as there are those who are temperamentally inclined to be melancholy, impatient, or hilarious, as the case may be; so there are others whose peculiar temptations lie mainly in the mental realm, and such people are far less likely to be conscious of their danger than the others we have mentioned. Instead of their tendency being looked upon as a weakness, it is more often regarded as strength of mind. Instead of being something to mourn before God, it is more likely to be boasted of before men. "**Be not** highminded, but fear" (Rom. 11: 20) is well-suited to them.

The wondrous and glorious Truth of God, as unfolded to us in the Holy Scriptures, cannot be reduced to a series of human propositions, logical and self-consistent. Those very Scriptures are inspired of God, so completely, that every jot and tittle of the original manuscripts was written under the immediate superintendency of the Holy Spirit. The human penmen were not free to express their own opinions, nor even select their own words; every syllable they used, was given them by God, and given in such a way they could use none other. Nevertheless, as every attentive reader of that Word is aware, the personalities of the writers are plainly impressed upon their handiwork. But how was that possible? The same phenomenon is observable in the incarnate Word. As the Holy One, it was impossible for him to sin. How then could He be "tempted" by Satan? Christ died only for God's elect; why, then, is the Gospel to be preached to every creature? The real child of God is eternally secure, why, then, is he sometimes addressed as though he is in real danger of perishing? Such questions might be extended almost indefinitely. Our purpose in asking them is to show the futility of **reasoning** about the things of God, and the need of meekly receiving **all** that God has revealed, whether we can perceive the harmony of one thing with another, or not; whether we are able or unable to discern their perfect agreement.

Now there are those who are attempting to blunt the searching point of some of the solemn warnings of Holy Writ by a process of carnal reasoning. Because there are plain declarations that none of those who are fully trusting the merits of Christ's obedience and blood can possibly miss Heaven, the inference is (logically) drawn that, those passages which speak of the danger of apostasy and describe the fearful doom of apostates, have no direct application to God's own people. Let those who are of this opinion ponder carefully what is recorded in Acts 27. There we find God positively promising His servant that "there should be **no** loss of life among you" (v. 22); but a little later, when the shipmen were about to flee out of the ship, Paul unhesitatingly declared, "**Except** these abide in the ship, ye **cannot** be saved" (v. 31). How could God's assurance to Paul, and Paul's warning to the mariners stand together?

Let the above incident be attentively weighed. God had given His word that not a life should be lost, yet, when the shipmen thought to betake themselves to the boats, Paul did not fatalistically reason that there was no occasion for him to be concerned, and no need for him to caution them about their imminent danger. If they were to be saved, they **must** remain on the ship. Does, then, the purpose of God depend upon the will and actions of man? Not as a cause from which it receives force and strength; but as a **means appointed** unto the execution of His decree, it does, God has instituted means whereby His ends shall be accomplished. Having made known to us His appointed means, there rests a **duty** upon the Christian to **use** those means, and not to expect the end without them. God hath united the two together, and woe be unto the man who attempts to separate them.

Not a few create their own difficulties by losing sight of the fact that "salvation" is set forth in the Scriptures from various angles; there is **both** a legal and an experimental side to it. In the epistles of Paul, especially the Romans, the legal or judicial side of salvation is most prominent. In Hebrews, James, and the epistles of Peter and John, it is the experimental aspect of salvation which is, mainly, contemplated. Unless each writer's **special viewpoint** be kept in mind, the reader fails to appreciate his perspective; and unless we **combine** in our thoughts their joint-teachings, a most inadequate and faulty conception will be ours. They are not contradictory, but complementary, and supplementary.

Because Paul is treating (mainly) of the believer's position in Christ, his perfect standing before God, his flawless legal title to Heaven, he emphasises the fact that there is **no** condemnation resting upon believers, that nothing can separate them from the love of God in Christ Jesus (Rom 8:35-39); that they are "complete in Him" (Col. 2:10). Because Peter is dealing (largely) with the experimental side of our salvation, he bids us **add to** our faith virtue, knowledge, self-control etc., and exhorts us to make our calling and election **sure** (2 Peter 1:5-10), and speaks of the **difficulty** with which the righteous are saved (1 Pet. 4:18).

In Romans the believer is spoken of as already "glorified" (8:30); in Ephesians, as already seated in the heavenlies in Christ (2:6). But in Hebrews the believer is contemplated as still in the Wilderness, and in Peter's epistles, as yet in the place of fiery trials and testings. Legally, the one who really trusts in Christ, is, even now, as blameless before the high court of Heaven (Col. 1:22) as though he were already in the Glory. But experimentally, he has within him an evil heart of unbelief, and so urgently needs to be warned against "**departing from** the living God" (Heb. 3:12). Experimentally, the believer's present lot is cast in a world lying in the Wicked one, where dangers, real and perilous, menace him on every side; and, therefore, the utmost care and caution is to be exercised, lest his very soul be placed in jeopardy.

Rightly has it been said, "There is a one-sided and unscriptural forgetfulness of the actual position of the believer (or professing believer), as a man who is still on the road in the battle; who has still the responsibility of trading with the talent entrusted, of watching for the return of the Master. Now there are many byepaths, dangers, precipices on the road, and we must persevere to the end. Only they who overcome and are faithful unto death shall be crowned. It is not spiritual, but carnal, to take the blessed and solemn doctrines of our election in Christ and of the perseverance of the saints, given us as a cordial for fainting hours, and as the inmost and ultimate secret of the soul in its dealings with God, and place them on the common and daily road of our duties and trials, **instead of** the precepts and warnings of the Divine Word. It is not merely that God keeps us through these warnings and commandments, but the attitude of soul which neglects or hurries over these portions of Scripture is not child-like, humble, and sincere. The attempts to explain away the fearful warnings of Scripture against apostasy are rooted in a very morbid and dangerous state of mind. A precipice is a precipice, and it is folly to deny it. 'If ye live after the flesh', says the apostle, 'ye shall die'. Now, to keep people from falling over a precipice, we do not put up a slender and graceful hedge of flowers, but the strongest barriers we can; and piercing spikes or cutting pieces of glass to prevent calamities. But even this is only the surface of the matter. Our walk with God and our perseverance to the end are great and solemn realities. We are dealing with the living God, and only life with God, and in God, and **unto** God, can be of any avail here. He who brought us out of Egypt is now guiding us and **if** we follow **Him,** and follow Him to the end, we shall enter into the final rest" (A. Saphir).

A God-given faith dwells in a lowly heart. Such a faith is humble and child-like, whereas unbelief and self-will are proud and presumptuous. Faith never reasons: where reasoning begins faith ends, and where faith begins to be exercised, reasoning ceases. "Trust in the Lord with all thine heart" (Prov. 3:5), is at once followed by "And lean not unto thine own understanding", because it is acting on the principles of "common sense" and following the dictates of logical acumen, which is one of the greatest hindrances to a walk of faith. In Matt. 16:7 we are told that the disciples **"reasoned** among themselves" immediately following we read, "which when Jesus perceived, He said unto them, O ye of **little faith**"! Again in Luke 24:15, it is said of the two disciples journeying to Emmaus, "While they communed and **reasoned,** Jesus Himself drew near, and went with them". Most solemn and searching is the immediate sequel: "But their eyes were **holden** that they should **not know** Him"!

Nor can any part of God's truth be known so long as we "reason" upon it. "The **meek** will He teach His way" (Psa. 25:9).

Returning to the subject of a preceding paragraph, let it be pointed out that God's decrees, or foreordinations, include **both** the ends and means thereto, for all His counsels are executed by fit means. Another incident which strikingly illustrates and exemplifies this principle is recorded in 2 Kings 20:5-7. There we learn that God absolutely resolved to add fifteen years to Hezekiah's life (which according to the course of mere **nature** was then on the point of expiring), yet **he must** take a lump of figs and lay on his boil. Had he leaned unto his own understanding and gone to reasoning, such a course had appeared quite needless, yea, entirely inconsistent; in such a case he had argued that, inasmuch as Divine assurance was given that he **would** recover, there was no occasion for him to apply a remedy **in order to** a recovery. Hezekiah's case shows plainly that no promise of God, nor assurance of man, renders the use of means superfluous; God works **by** them, and rarely without them.

It is a grievous sin of presumption, a tempting of God, to count on the end while we ignore the means which He has appointed us to use. Yet not a few are guilty at this point. We have personally met those who have sat under hyper-Calvinistic teaching that have fallen into a fatalistic lethargy. They reason that if God has predestinated them unto salvation, there is no need to be concerned about their eternal destiny, no need for them to earnestly seek the Lord: for when God's appointed time comes He **will** save them. Some who profess to be Christians, never give the Gospel to their children, arguing that such is needless and useless, for if they are among God's elect, sooner or later they **will be** brought in. Such people need to be reminded that the very God who has, from the beginning chosen unto salvation, has also ordained that we shall be saved **through** sanctifiaction of the Spirit and **belief** of the truth" (2 Thess. 3:13). Without the means, the end cannot be attained.

There are those who will grant that the use of means is necessary in connection with the unsaved obtaining the pardon of their sins, but who will not allow that the use of means is just as requisite, necessary, and indispensible for Christians if they are to keep on the Narrow Way that "leadeth unto life". They will acknowledge there is real danger menacing the unbeliever and that it is a part of

Christian duty to **warn** him, yet they do not see that there is a real danger menacing the believer, and that it is the part of the preacher's duty to **warn** him against it. This appears inconsistent to them. If God's people are eternally secure, there may be danger which threatens to rob them of communing with Him, which threatens to spoil their reward in the Day to come; but, that there are dangers threatening their very spiritual life, they will not allow.

To say that warnings to real Christians against apostasy partake of the character of a "bogey" or "boogerman", seems to the writer akin to reasoning that because God has **promised** to supply all our need, there is no occasion for us to **ask Him** to do so. Rather do we believe that just as prayer is one of the ordained channels **through which** God graciously supplies the needs of His people, so warnings are one of the instituted means **by which** He preserves His saints from apostasy. "The Scripture says, 'If any man destroy the temple of God'. 'Lest I myself should be a castaway'. What are these but wise and reasonable barriers set along the way, beacons against presumption, helps, by the alarm they sound, to a proper avoidance of these things which, if persisted in, would ruin, but which by the very caution are avoided". (Dr. G. S. Bishop).

Whether our explanation of the Divine warnings to believers be the correct one or no, certain it is that such warnings are found again and again on the pages of Holy Writ. The Lord Jesus bade His **disciples,** "Fear Him, which after He hath killed hath power to cast into Hell; yea, I say unto **you,** Fear Him" (Luke 12:5). Who will dare to suggest that Christ was **needlessly** alarming them? Who will have the impious temerity to challenge His wisdom in giving such a caution? Similar was the practice of the apostles: "For if ye live after the flesh, ye shall die; but if ye through the Spirit do mortify the deeds of the body, ye shall live" (Rom. 8:13); upon which Dr. Stifler rightly said, "Mark how Paul implies not only that the flesh still exists, but also that there is a danger from it".

"Destroy not him with thy meat, for whom Christ died" (Rom. 14:15). The Greek word here for "destroy" is the very one used by the demons when they asked Christ, "Art Thou come to destroy us?" (Mark. 1:24), and the one employed in Jude 5: "afterward destroyed them that believed not". Has a single one for whom Christ died **been** "destroyed"? No, a thousand times, No. Then why bid us "destroy not" a brother? Because the Holy Spirit is thereby pointing out to me that I **may** act in such a way **as tends to** the destruction of a fellow-Christian. Against such a course I am admonished, warned, reproved. Christ knew full well that the Father **would** preserve to the end every one He had given to Him, nevertheless, He did not deem it useless or needless to pray", **keep** through Thine own name those whom Thou hast given Me" (John 17:11).

It is true, blessedly true, that the saints are "kept by the power of God". But how? In a **mechanical** way? In a way that absolves them from all personal responsibility? Nay, verily; we are "kept by the power of God **through faith**" (1 Peter 1:5), and faith not only feeds on, God's promises, but it also heeds His warnings. The apostle John did not hesitate to say to God's people, "Ye **shall** abide in Him", and yet he immediately follows this by the exhortation, "And now, little children, **abide** in Him" (1 John 2:27, 28). The apostle Jude assured the saints that the Lord "is able to keep you **from** falling, and to present you faultless before the presence of His glory" (v. 24); nevertheless, he did not deem it superfluous to say, "**Keep yourselves** in the love of God" (v. 21).

None of the apostles wrote more frequently and plainly upon the eternal security of believers than did Paul, yet we find him holding up before the Corinthians the fearful warning furnished by the history of Israel in the wilderness. To those saints he said, "neither be ye idolators as some of them (v. 7). Some would reason that such an exhortation was altogether uncalled for, that there is no more possibility of a real child of God becoming an idolator than there is of the sun's ceasing to shine, and that therefore it is needless, yea, highly inconsistent, to **so** address God's people. Not so did Paul think. The flesh still remains within us, and must be **denied**, otherwise, Christ will yet deny us as belonging to Him.

The solemn warning given by Paul in 1 Cor. 10 concludes with these words, "Wherefore let him that thinketh he standeth take heed lest he fall". In his sermon on this verse the late C. H. Spurgeon began by saying, "It is a singular fact, but nevertheless most certain, that the vices are the counterfeits of virtues. Whenever God sends from the mint of Heaven precious coin of genuine metal, Satan will imitate the impress, and utter a vile production of no value. God bestows courage, and it is a good thing to be able to look one's fellow in the face, fearless of all men in doing our duty: Satan inspires foolhardiness, stiles it courage, and bids the man rush to the cannon's mouth for the bubble 'reputation'. Though we cannot be too confident of the might of the Most High, there is a thing so near akin to true confidence, that unless you use the greatest discernment you cannot tell the difference. Unholy presumption is that against which I shall speak this morning".

When one preaches or writes in such a strain as this article, he is usually reminded that Scripture says the sheep of Christ shall never perish. We too believe that with all our heart. Yet that is not all that Scripture says, and to prefer the promises to the precepts of Holy Writ evidences a most unhealthy state of soul. But waiving that now, let it be pointed out that one of the means God uses in the preserving of His "sheep" is the **warnings** He has given them. Without further amplifying that fact it remains to ask, **Who are** His "sheep"? John 10 describes them: they are those who "hear", not disregard, the voice of Christ; they are those who "follow" **Him** (John 10: 27), not follow the desires of the **flesh** and the ways of the world.

The deplorable and tragic thing is that today there are countless thousands who profess to be Christ's sheep, and many of them sincerely believe they **are** such, who have **no** scriptural warrant for their hope. It is true that many of them, like the stony-ground hearers (Matt. 13:20, 21), began by receiving the Word with joy, and for a while they ran well; but the course appointed by God was too exacting, too flesh-withering, for their tastes, and they have forsaken it; yet, resting on some experience in the past, they are quite sure that **they** are still bound for Heaven. The awful thing is that there is almost nothing in present-day preaching which is calculated to dis-illusion them. Even many "Fundamentalists" will affirm, "once in grace, always in grace", **without** presenting the balancing truth that the Highway of Grace is also the Path of practical Godliness. It is just as true that "without faith" (Heb. 11:6) and "without holiness" (Heb. 12:14) no man shall see the Lord, as it is that without Chirst's atonement and the Holy Spirit's regeneration no one can be saved.

—ARTHUR W. PINK.

A REQUEST

What strange methods God sometimes employs in teaching His children much needed lessons! This has recently been the writer's experience. He has been approached by a "University" to accept from them a degree of "D. D.". Asking for time to be given so that he might prayerfully seek from God, through His written Word, a knoweldge of His will, fuller light came than was expected. He had very serious doubts as to the permissibility of one of God's servants accepting a title of (fleshly) honour. He now perceives that it is wrong for him to receive it even complimentarily. Various friends, as a mark of respect, have addressed us as "Dr. Pink". We now ask them to please **cease** from doing so. Let it not be understood that we hereby condemn other men for what they allow. No, to their own Master they stand or fall. The principal passages which have helped us we now mention, praying that it may please God to also bless them to others.

First, to the false comforters of Job, Elihu (God's representative) said, "Let me not, I pray you, accept any man's person, neither let me give **flattering titles** unto man" (32:21). Second, "Be **not** ye called Rabbi" or "Teacher" (Matt. 23:8), which is what "Doctor" signifies. Third, John 5:44 reproves those who "receive honour one of another", and bids us seek "the honour that cometh from God **only**". Fourth, none of the Lord's servants in the N. T. ever employed a title: "Paul, an apostle", but never "the apostle Paul". Fifth, the Son of God "made Himself of **no** reputation" (Phil. 2:7), is it fitting then that His servants should now follow an opposite course? Sixth, Christ bids us learn of Him who was "meek and **lowly**" (Matt. 11:29). Seventh, one of the marks of the Apostacy is "having men's persons in admiration because of advantage" (Jude 16). Eighth, we are bidden to go forth unto Christ outside the camp "bearing His **reproach**" (Heb. 13:13). For these reasons it does not seem to us to be fitting that one who is here as a representative and to witness for a "despised and rejected" Christ should be honoured and flattered of men. Please address us as "Brother Pink".

tion? The answer is, None whatever. Scripture **never** speaks of repentance and faith as being foreseen or foreknown by God. Truly, He **did** know from all eternity that certain ones **would** repent and believe, yet this is not what Scripture refers to as the **object** of God's "foreknowledge". The word uniformly refers to God's foreknowing **persons**; then let us "hold fast the form of sound words" (2 Tim 1:13).

Another thing to which we desire to call particular attention is that the first two passages quoted above show plainly and teach implicitly that God's "foreknowledge" **is not causative,** that instead, something else lies behind, precedes it, and that something is His own **sovereign decree**. Christ was "delivered by the (1) determinate counsel and (2) foreknowledge of God" (Acts 2:23). His "counsel" or decree, was the ground of His foreknowledge. So again in Rom. 8:29. That verse opens with the word "for", which tells us to look back to what immediately precedes. What, then, does the previous verse say? This, "all things work together for good to them . . . who are the called according to His purpose". Thus God's "foreknowledge" is **based upon** His "purpose" or decree (see Psa. 2:7).

God foreknows what **will be** because He has decreed what **shall be**. It is therefore a reversing of the order of Scripture, a putting of the cart before the horse, to affirm that God elects because He foreknows people. The truth is, He "foreknows" because He has **elected**. This removes the ground or cause of election from outside the creature, and places it in God's own sovereign will. God purposed in Himself to elect a certain people, not because of anything good in them or from them, either actual or foreseen, but solely out of His own mere pleasure. As to **why** He chose the ones He did, we do not know, and can only say, "Even so, Father, for so it seemed good in **Thy** sight." The plain truth of Rom. 8:29 is that God, before the foundation of the world, singled out certain sinners and appointed them unto salvation (2 Thess. 2:13). This is clear from the concluding words of the verse: "Predestinated to be conformed to the image of His Son" etc. God did not predestinate those whom He foreknew **were** "conformed", but, on the contrary, those whom He "foreknew" (i. e. loved and elected) He predestinated **"to be** conformed". Their conformity to Christ is not the cause, but the effect of God's foreknowledge and predestination.

God did not elect any sinner because He foresaw that he would believe, for the simple but sufficient reason that **no** sinner ever does believe until God gives him faith; just as no man can see until God gives him sight. Sight is God's gift, seeing is the consequence of my using His gift. So faith is God's gift (Eph. 2:8, 9), believing is my using His gift. If it were true that God had elected certain ones to be saved **because** in due time they would believe, then that would make believing a **meritorious act,** and in that event the saved sinner **would** have ground for "boasting", which Scripture emphatically denies: Eph. 2:9.

Surely God's Word is plain enough in teaching that believing is **not** a meritorious act. It affirms that Christians are a people "who have believed **through grace**" (Acts 18:27). If, then, they have believed "through grace", there is absolutely nothing meritorious about "believing", and if nothing meritorious, it could not be the ground or cause which moved God to choose them. No; God's choice proceeds not from anything in **us,** or anything from us, but solely from His own sovereign pleasure. Once more, in Rom. 11:5, we read of "a remnant according to the election of grace". There it is, plain enough: election itself is **of grace,** and grace is **unmerited** favour, something for which we had **no claim** upon God whatsoever.

It thus appears that it is highly important for us to have clear and scriptural views of the "foreknowledge" of God. Erroneous conceptions about it lead inevitably to thoughts most dishonouring to Him. The popular idea of Divine foreknowledge is altogether inadequate. God not only knew the end from the beginning, but He planned, fixed, predestinated everything from the beginning. And, as cause stands to effect, so God's purpose is the ground of His pre-science. If then the reader be a real Christian, he is so because God chose him in Christ before the foundation of the world (Eph. 1:4), and chose not because He foresaw you **would** believe, but chose simply because it pleased Him to choose; chose you notwithstanding your natural unbelief. This being so, **all** the glory and praise belongs alone to Him. You have **no** ground for taking **any** credit to yourself. You have "believed **through grace"** (Acts 18:27), and that, because your very election was "of grace" (Rom. 11:5).

—ARTHUR W. PINK.

signification of a certain word used in Scripture, and then they are too dilitary to **test** their assumptions by means of a concordance. Let us amplify this point.

Take the word "flesh". Its meaning appears to be so obvious that many would regard it as a waste of time to look up its various connections in Scripture. It is hastily assumed that the word is synonymous with the physical body, and so no inquiry is made. But, in fact, "flesh" in Scripture frequently includes far more than what is corporeal; all that is embraced by the term can only be ascertained by a diligent comparison of **every** occurrence of it and by a study of each separate context. Take the word "world". The average reader of the Bible imagines this word to be the equivalent for the human race, and consequently, many passages where the term is found are wrongly interpreted. Take the word "immortality". Surely it requires no study! Obviously it has reference to the indestructibility of the soul. Ah, my reader, it is foolish and wrong to assume anything where the Word of God is concerned. If the reader will take the trouble to carefully examine each passage where "moral" and "immortality" are found, it will be seen these words are never applied to the soul, but always to the body.

Now what has just been said, on "flesh", the "world", "immortality", applies with equal force to the terms "know" and "foreknow". Instead of imagining that these words signify no more than a simple cognition, the different passages in which they occur require to be carefully weighed. The word "foreknowledge" is not found in the Old Testament. But "know" occurs there frequently. When that term is used in connection with God, it often signifies **to regard with** favour, denoting **not mere** cognition but an **affection** for the object in view. "I **know** thee by name" (Ex. 33-17). "Ye have been rebellious against the Lord from the day that I **knew** you" (Deut. 9:24). "Before I formed thee in the belly I **knew** thee" (Jer. 1:5). They have made princes and I **knew not**" (Hos. 8:4). "You only have I **known** of all the families of the earth" (Amos 3:2). In these passages "knew" signifies either **loved** or **appointed**.

In like manner, the word, "know" is frequently used in the New Testament, in the same sense as in the Old Testament. "Then will I profess unto them, I **never knew** you" (Matt. 7:23). "I am the good shepherd and **know** My sheep and am **known** of Mine" (John 10:14). "If any man love God, the same is **known** of Him" (1 Cor. 8:3). "The Lord **knoweth** them that are His" (2 Tim. 2:19).

Now the word, "foreknowledge" as it is used in the N. T. is less ambiguous than in its simple form "to know". If every passage in which it occurs is carefully studied, it will be discovered that it is a moot point whether it ever has reference to the mere perception of events which are yet to take place. The fact is that "foreknowledge" is **never** used in Scripture in connection with events or actions, instead, it always has reference to **persons**. It is persons God is said to "foreknew", not the actions of those persons. In proof of this we shall now quote each passage where this expression is found.

The first occurrence is in Acts 2:23. There we read, "Him being delivered by the determinate counsel and foreknowledge of God, ye have taken, and by wicked hands have crucified and slain". If careful attention is paid to the wording of this verse it will be seen that the apostle was not there speaking of God's foreknowledge of the **act** of the crucifixion, but of the **Person** crucified: "Him (Christ) being delivered **by**" etc.

The second occurrence is in Rom. 8:29, 30. "For **whom** He did foreknow, He also did predestinate to be conformed to the image of His Son, that He might be the Firstborn among many brethren. Moreover **whom** He did predestinate, them He also called" etc. Weigh well the pronoun that is used here. It is not **what** He did foreknow, but **whom** He did. It is not the surrendering of their wills nor the believing of their hearts, but the **persons** themselves, which is here in view.

"God hath not cast away His people which He foreknew" (Rom. 11:2). Once more the plain reference is to persons, and to persons only.

The last mention is in 1 Peter 1:2: "Elect according to the foreknowledge of God the Father". **Who** are "elect" according to the foreknowledge of God the Father"? The previous verse tells us: the reference is to the "strangers scattered" i. e. the Diaspora, the Dispersion, the believing Jews. Thus, here too the reference is to persons, and not to their foreseen acts.

Now in view of these passages (and there are no more) **what scriptural ground** is there for any one saying God "foreknew" the **acts** of certain ones, viz, their "repenting and believing", and that because of those acts He elected them unto salva-

(Continued on Page 95)

STUDIES IN THE SCRIPTURES

"Search the Scriptures" John 5 : 39

Copyright in all English-speaking Countries.

Editor: Arthur W. Pink, 1139 Alameda Ave., Glendale, Calif.
Hon Agent in England: Mr. A. Winstone, 2, Lennox Villas, Hewlett Road, Cheltenham.
Hon. Agent in Australia: Mr. G. Ardill, The Christian Workers' Depot.
Commonwealth and Reservoir Streets, Sydney.

THE SUPREMACY OF GOD

In one of his letters to Erasmus, Luther said, "Your thoughts of God are too human". Probably that renowned scholar resented such a rebuke, the more so, since it proceeded from a miner's son; nevertheless, it was thoroughly deserved. We too, though having no standing among the religious leaders of this degenerate age, prefer the same charge against the vast majority of the preachers of our day, and against those who, instead of searching the Scriptures for themselves, lazily accept their teachings. The most dishonouring and degrading conceptions of the rule and reign of the Almighty are now held almost everywhere. To countless thousands, even among those professing to be Christians, the God of Scripture is quite unknown.

Of old, God complained to an apostate Israel, "Thou thoughtest that I was altogether as thyself" (Psa. 50:21). Such must now be His indictment against an apostate Christendom. Men imagine that the Most High is moved by sentiment, rather than actuated by principle. They suppose that His omnipotency is such an idle fiction that Satan is thwarting His designs on every side. They think that if He has formed any plan or purpose at all, then it must be like theirs, constantly subject to change. They openly declare that whatever power He possesses must be restricted, lest He invade the citidel of man's "free will" and reduce him to a "machine". They lower the all-efficacious Atonement, which has actually redeemed every one for whom it was made, to a mere "remedy", which sin-sick souls may use if they feel disposed to; and they enervate the invincible work of the Holy Spirit to an "offer" of the Gospel which sinners may accept or reject as they please.

The "god" of this twentieth century no more resembles the Supreme Sovereign of Holy Writ than does the dim flickering of a candle the glory of the midday sun. The "god" who is now talked about in the average pulpit, spoken of in the ordinary Sunday school, mentioned in much of the religious literature of the day, and preached in most of the so-called Bible-conferences, is a figment of human imagination, an invention of maudlin sentimentality. The heathen outside of the pale of Christendom form "gods" out of wood and stone, while the millions of heathen inside Christendom manufacture a "god" out of their own carnal mind. In reality, they are but atheists, for there is no other possible alternative between an absolutely supreme God, and no God at all. A "god" whose will is resisted, whose designs are frustrated, whose purpose is checkmated, possesses no title to Diety, and so far from being a fit object of worship, merits nought but contempt.

The supremacy of the true and living God might well be argued from the infinite distance which separates the mightiest creatures from the almighty Creator. He is the Potter, they are but the clay in His hands, to be moulded into vessels of honour. or to be dashed into pieces (Psa. 2:9) as He pleases. Were all the denizens of heaven and all the inhabitants of earth to combine in open revolt against Him, it would occasion Him no uneasiness, and would have less effect upon His eternal and unassailable Throne than has the spray of Mediterranian's waves upon the towering rocks of Gibraltar. So purile and powerless is the creature to affect the Most High, Scripture itself tells us that when the Gentile heads unite with apostate Israel to defy Jehovah and His Christ, "He that sitteth in the heavens shall **laugh**" (Psa. 2:4).

The absolute and universal supremacy of God is plainly and positively affirmed in many scriptures. "Thine, O Lord, is the greatness, and the power, and the glory,

(Continued on Page 120)

IMPORTANT NOTICES

Please advise promptly of change of address, otherwise copies will be lost in the mails.

We are glad to send a sample copy to any of our friends whom you believe would be interested in such a publication.

Send to Mr. I. C. Herendeen, Swengel (Union County), Penna., for a list of our publications. He has published many of our books and booklets.

This Magazine is published as a work of faith and labour of love. The Editor and his wife gladly give their services. It is freely sent to all who will read it. No charge is made for it.

Christians who feel definitely lead to do so, may have fellowship with us in this ministry. Those outside the U. S. A., please send only INTERNATIONAL Money Orders made out to Glendale, California, U. S. A.

CONTENTS

The Epistle to the Hebrews	98
The Satisfaction of Christ	104
Sanctification of the Spirit	110
Profiting from the Word	114
Filled Vessels	118

THE EPISTLE TO THE HEBREWS

29. The Anchor of the Soul: Heb. 6: 16-20

In our last article we saw that the Holy Spirit through Paul exhorted the people of God to "be not slothful, but followers of them who through faith and patience inherit the promises" (v. 12). This declaration was illustrated and exemplified from the history of one who has been highly venerated both by Jews and believing Gentiles, namely, Abraham, of whom it is here declared, "after he had patiently endured, he received the promise" (v. 16). We cannot but admire again the heavenly wisdom given to the apostle, inspiring him to bring in Abraham at this particular point of his epistle. In chapter 3 we saw how that, before he set forth the superiority of Christ over Moses, he first made specific mention of the typical mediator's **faithfulness** (v. 5); so here, ere setting forth the superiority of Christ over Abraham (which is done in 7:4), he first records his triumphant **endurance**. How this shows that we ought to use every lawful means possible in seeking to remove the prejudices of people against God's truth!

The mention of Abraham in Heb. 6 should occasion real searchings of heart before God on the part of all who claim to be Christians. Abraham is "the father of all them that believe" (Rom. 4:11), but as Christ so emphatically declared to those in His day who boasted that Abraham was their father, "If ye were Abraham's children ye **would do** (not merely "ye ought to do"!) the **works** of Abraham" (John 8:39), and as Rom. 4:12 tells us, Abraham is "the father of circumcision (i.e. spiritual circumcision: Col. 2:11) to those who are not of the (natural) circumcision only, but who also **walk** in the steps of that faith of their father Abraham". In his day (1680) J. Owen said, "It is a sad consideration which way and by what means some men think to come to Heaven, or carry themselves as if they think so. There are **but few** who deem more than a naked profession to be necessary thereunto, but living in all sorts of sins, they yet suppose they shall inherit the promises of God. This was not the way of the holy men of old, whose example is proposed to us. True, some think that faith at least be necessary hereunto, but by faith they understand little more than a mere profession of true religion".

It behooves us, if we value our souls, to examine closely the Scriptural account of the nature and character of Abraham's faith. It was far more than a bare assenting to the veracity of God's Word. It was an operative faith, which caused him to separate himself from the world (Heb. 11:8, 9), which led him to take the place of a stranger and pilgrim down here (Heb. 11:13), which enabled him to patiently endure under severe trials and testings. In the light of other scriptures, the words, "patiently endured" (Heb. 6:15) enable us to fill in many a blank in the Genesis history. Patiently "endured" what? Mysterious providences, the seeming slowness of God to make good His promises, that which to sight and sense appeared to repudiate His very love (Gen. 22:2). Patiently "endured" what? The attacks of Satan upon his faith, the insinuations of the Serpent that God had ceased to be gracious, the temptation of the Devil to be enriched by the king of Sodom (Gen. 14:21). Patiently "endured" what? The cruel sneers, the biting taunts, the persecution of his follow-men, who hated him because his godly walk condemned their ungodly ways. Yes, like his Redeemer afterwards, and like each one of his believing children today, "he endured the contradiction of sinners against himself".

But the Holy Spirit had another design here in referring to the case of Abraham. Having so faithfully warned us of the danger of apostasy, having so earnestly set before us the imperative need of faithful perseverance, He now closes this lengthy parenthesis with a most glorious message of **comfort,** which is designed to set the hearts of God's children at perfect rest, allay their fears of uncertainty as to their ultimate issue, strengthen their faith, deepen their assurance, and cause them to look forward to the future with the most implicit confidence. It is ever God's way to wound before He heals, to alarm the conscience before He speaks peace to it, to press upon us our responsibility ere He assures of His preserving power. "For it is God which worketh in you both to will and to do of His good pleasure", is preceded by "work out your own salvation with fear and trembling" (Phil. 2:12, 13).

And **what** is it that the Holy Spirit here uses **to comfort** the hearts of God's tried and troubled and trembling people? Why, the wondrous and glorious Gospel of His grace. This He does by now making known the deeper design and significance of His reference to Abraham. He shows that the promise which God made to "the father of all that believe", to which promise He designed to add His oath, concerned not Abraham alone, but is, without fail, to be made good to all his spiritual seed. Yea, He shows how God's dealings with Abraham in time, were but a shadowing-forth on this earth-plane of His covenant-transactions with Christ and His seed in Heaven ere time began. May the Lord grant the much-needed wisdom, guidance and grace, that both the writer and reader may be led to a right and clear apprehension of this most blessed subject.

Ere turning to v. 16 let us attempt to show the connection of our present passage with its context, by giving a brief analysis of the verses which were before us in the preceding article. 1. Abraham is set before us as an example: v. 12 and the opening "For" of v. 13. 2. God made promise to Abraham: v. 13. 3. That promise had immediate reference to Christ and the benefits of His mediation: Gal. 3:16. 4. In addition to His promise, God placed Himself on oath to Abraham: v. 13. 5. The peculiar nature of that oath: v. 13. God sware by Himself: v. 13. 6. God sware by Himself because there was none greater to whom He might appeal: v. 13. 7. Abraham's faith, resting on the ground of God's promise and oath, patiently endured and obtained the promise: v. 15.

The emphatic and important words of v. 15 are its opening "And so", or "And **thus**", the reference being to the absolute faithfulness of the divine promise, followed by the divine oath, namely, "Surely, blessing I will bless thee" (v. 14). In other words, God's oath to Abraham was the guarantee that He would continue to effectively work in him and invincibly preserve him to the end of his earthly course, so that he should infallibly enter into the promised blessing. Though Abraham was to be left in the place of trial and testing for another seventy-five years, his entrance into heaven was not left contingent upon his own mutable will. Though it is only through "faith and patience" any inherit the promises (v. 12), yet God has solemnly pledged Himself to sustain these graces in His own unto the end of their wilderness journey and right across Jordan itself, until entrance into Canaan is secured, "These **all** died in faith" (Heb. 11:13).

"For men verily sware by the greater: and an oath for confirmation is to them an end of all strife" (v. 16). The design of this verse is to give us an explanation of **why** it is that the great God has placed Himself on oath. When we consider who He is and what He is, we may well be amazed at His action. When we remember His exalted majesty, that He "humbles" Himself to so much as "behold" the things that are in heaven (Psa. 113:6), there is surely cause for wonderment to find Him "swearing" by Himself. When we remember that He is the God of Truth, who cannot lie, there is reason for us to enquire why He deemed not His bare word sufficient.

"For men verily sware by the greater: and an oath for confirmation is to them an end of all strife". The opening "for" looks back to God "sware by Himself" of v. 13. The apostle here appeals to a custom which has obtained among men in all ages. When one party avers one thing, and another, another, and each stands firmly by what he says, there is not only mutual contradiction, but endless strife. Where matters of interest and importance are concerned between two or more men, the difference between them can only be settled by them being placed on oath. In such cases an oath is necessary for the governing and peace of mankind, for without it strife must be perpetual, or else ended by violence. Thus, the purpose or design of oaths among men is to place bounds upon their contradictions and make an end of their contentions.

Strikingly has Dr. J. Owen pointed out in his remarks upon v. 16: "As these words are applied to or are used to illustrate the state of things between God and our souls, we may observe from them: First, that there is, as we are in a state of nature (looking at the elect as the descendants of fallen Adam—A. W. P.), a difference and strife between God and us. Second, the promises of God are gracious proposals of the only way and means for the ending of that strife. Third, the oath of God interposed for the confirmation of these promises (better, "in addition to" the promises—A. W. P.) is every way sufficient to secure believers against all objections and temptations in all straits and trials, about peace with God through Jesus Christ".

"Wherein God, willing more abundantly to show unto the heirs of promise the immutability of His counsel, confirmed it by oath" (v. 17). The relative "wherein" or "wherefore" has, we believe, both an immediate connection with v. 16, and a more remote one to what had been declared in v. 13. Regarding it, first, as a conclusion drawn from the general principle enunciated in the preceding verse, its force is this: since an oath serves to establish man's words among his fellows, the great God has condescended to employ this means and method to confirm the faith of His people. Because an oath gives certainty among men unto the point sworn to, God has graciously designed that the heirs of promise shall have the comfort of a Divine dual certainty. The more remote connection with v. 13 will appear in the course of our exposition: it is to here give assurance that what God so solemnly pledged Himself to do for and give unto Abraham, is equally sure and certain to and for all his children—the "wherein" signifies "in which" **oath**.

God's design in swearing by Himself was not only that Abraham might be fully persuaded of the absolute certainty of His blessing, but that the "heirs of promise" should also have pledge and proof of the immutability of His counsel concerning them; for the mind and will of God was the same toward all of the elect as it was toward the patriarch himself. Though we are lifted to a much greater height in these closing verses of Heb. 6, yet the application which the apostle is here led to make of God's dealings with Abraham, is identical in principle with what we find in Rom. 4. There we read of Abraham believing God and that it was counted unto him for (better "unto") righteousness, and in v. 16 the conclusion is drawn: "Therefore it is of faith, that it might be by grace; to the end the promise might be sure to **all** the seed"; while in vv. 23, 24 we are told, "Now it was not written for his sake alone, that it was reckoned to him, but for **us also**, to whom it shall be reckoned, if we believe on Him that raised up Jesus our Lord from the dead"—cf. Gal. 3:29.

We come now to enquire, What is the "immutability of His counsel" which God determined to show the more abundantly unto the heirs of promise? To ascertain this, we need first to consider God's "counsel". Like the expression the "will of God", His "counsel" has a **double** reference and usage in the N. T. There is the revealed "will" of God, set forth in the Scriptures, which defines and measures human responsibility (1 Thess. 4:3, e. g.), but which "will" is perfectly done by none of us; there is also the secret and invincible will of God (Rom. 9:19 etc), which is wrought out through each of us. So we read, on the one hand, that "the Pharisees and lawyers **rejected** the counsel of God against themselves" (Luke 7:30); while on the other hand, it is said of the crucifiers of Christ, they "were gathered together **for to do** whatsoever Thy hand and Thy counsel determined before **to be done**" (Acts 4:27, 28). The "**immutability** of His counsel" declares plainly in which of the two senses the term is to be taken in Heb. 6.

The "counsel" of God in Heb. 6:17 signifies His everlasting decree or eternal purpose. It is employed thus of Christ's death in Acts 2:23, "Him, being delivered by the determinate counsel, and foreknowledge of God". It bears the same meaning in Eph. 1, as is abundantly clear if v. 9 be compared with v. 11: in the former we read, "Having made known unto us the mystery of His will, according to His good pleasure which He hath **purposed** in Himself"; in the latter it is said, "being predestinated according to the purpose of Him who worketh all things after **the counsel** of His own will". Both of those verses take us back to the Divine determination before this world was created; equally plain is it that both of them are treating of the eternal resolutions of God concerning the **salvation** of His people: cf. 1 Thess. 2:13.

Still more specially the "counsel" of God in Heb. 6:17 concerns the holy and wise purpose of His will to give His Son Jesus Christ to be of the seed of Abraham for the salvation of all the elect, and that, in such a way, and accompanied by such blessings, as would infallibly secure their faith, perseverance, and entrance into Glory. In other words, the "counsel" of God respects the agreement which He entered into with Christ in the Everlasting Covenant, that upon His fulfillment of the stipulated conditions, the promises made to Him concerning His seed should most certainly be fulfilled. Proof of this is found in comparing Luke 1:72, 73, with Gal. 3:16, 17. In the former we read of Zacharias prophesying that God was "to remember His holy **covenant**, the **oath** which He sware to our father Abraham". In the latter, the Holy Spirit brings out the hidden meaning of God's dealings with the patriarch: "Now to Abraham and his seed were the **promises** made. He saith not, And to seeds, as of many; but as of one, And to thy seed, which is Christ. And this I say, the covenant, that was confirmed before of God **in Christ**".

Referring to the covenants made by Jehovah with the patriarchs, as affording so many types of that Everlasting Covenant (Heb. 13:20) made with Christ, Mr. Hervey (1756) when refuting the terrible heresies of John Wesley, wrote, "True, it is recorded that God made a covenant with Abraham, with Isaac, with Jacob, and with David: but were they in a capacity to enter into a covenant with their Maker? to stand for themselves or be surety for others? I think not. The passages mean no more than the Lord's **manifesting**, in an especial manner, the grand Covenant to them, ratifying and confirming their personal interest in it, and further assuring them that **Christ**, the great Covenant-Head, should spring from their seed. This accounts for that remarkable and singular mode of expression which often occurs in Scripture: 'I will make a covenant with them'. Yet there follows no mention of any conditions but only a promise of unconditional blessings".

Now what it is particularly important to note here is, that God was "willing more abundantly **to show** unto the heirs of promise the **immutability** of His counsel", and therefore, "confirmed it by (or as the margin much more accurately renders it "interposed Himself by") an oath". This leads us to call attention to the distinction between God's "counsel" and His "promise". His "counsel" is that which, originally, was a profound and an impenetrable secret in Himself; His "promise" is an open and declared revelation of His will. It is most blessed to perceive that God's promises are but the transcripts of His eternal decrees; His promises now make known to us in words the hitherto secret counsels of His heart. Thus, "the immutability of His counsel" is that from which His sure promises proceed and by which it is expressed.

But in addition to His promise, God was willing "more abundantly" to "show", or reveal, or make known to His people, the unchangeableness of His counsel. All proceeds from the **will** of God. He freely purposed to give unto the elect, while they are in this world, not only abundant, but "more abundant" proofs of His everlasting love (Jer. 31:3), His gracious concern for their assurance, peace and joy. This He did by "interposing Himself by an oath". The Greek word which the A. V. has rendered in the text "confirmed", has for its prime meaning "to mediate" or "intervene". This at once directs our thoughts to the Mediator, of whom Abraham was the type. It was **to Christ** that the original Promise and Oath were made. Hence, in Titus 1:2 we read, "In hope of eternal life, which God, that cannot lie, promised before the world began": as the elect were not then in existence, the promise must have been made to their Head. Concerning God's oath to Christ we read, "The Lord hath sworn, and will not repent, Thou art a priest forever after the order of Melchizedek" (Psa. 110:4).

Now it is not unto all mankind, but only unto a certain number of persons to whom God designs to manifest the immutability of His counsel, and to communicate the effects thereof. These are here denominated "the heirs of promise" which includes all the saints of God both under the Old and N. T. They are called "heirs of promise" on a double account: with respect unto the promise itself, and the thing promised. They are not yet the actual possessors, but waiting in expectation (cf. 1:14): proof of this is obtained by comparing Heb. 11:13, 17, 19. In this the members are conformed to their Head, for though Christ is the "Heir of all things" (1:2), yet He, too, is "expecting" (see 10:13). The "heirs of promise" here are the same as "the children of promise" in Rom. 9:8.

"That by two immutable things in which it was impossible for God to lie, we might have a strong consolation, who have fled for refuge to lay hold upon the hope set before us" (v. 18). In order to simplify our exposition of this verse, we propose taking up its contents in their inverse order, and doing so under a series of questions. First, what is "the hope set before us"? Where is it thus "set before us", What is meant by "fled for refuge to lay hold upon the hope"? What is the "strong consolation"? How do the "two immutable things" supply this strong consolation?

In seeking to ascertain the character of "the hope" of v. 18 it needs to be carefully distinguished from the "strong consolation", which at once intimates that it is not the grace of hope within the heart of the believer. Further corroboration of this is found in the words, "set before us", which clearly speaks of what is objective rather than subjective; and too, it is to be "laid hold of". Moreover, what is said of this "hope" in v. 19 excludes the idea of an internal expectation. The needed help is found in 7:19 where of the "better hope" it is said, "by the which we draw nigh unto God": John 14:6, Eph. 2:18 etc. In 1 Tim. 1:1 the Lord Jesus Christ is distinctly designated "our Hope", and is He not the One whom God hath "set before" His people? Is not "that blessed Hope" for which we are to be "looking" (Titus 2:13), Christ Himself?

Where is it that Christ is "set before us" as "the hope"? Surely, in the Gospel of God's grace. It is there that the **only** hope for lost sinners is made known. The Gospel of God is "the Gospel of Christ" (Rom. 1:16), for it exhibits the excellencies of His glorious person and proclaims the efficacy of His finished work. Therefore in Rom. 3:25 it is said of Christ Jesus, "Whom God hath **set forth** a propitiation through faith in His blood"; while to the Galations Paul affirmed, "before whose eyes Jesus Christ hath been evidently (openly) **set forth** among you—crucified". In the Gospel, Christ is presented both as an Object of Faith and an Object of Hope. As an Object of Faith it is what He has done for the elect, providing for them a perfect legal standing before God: this is mainly developed in Romans. As an Object of Hope it is what Christ will yet do for His people, bring them out of this wilderness into the Promised Land. In Hebrews we are seen as yet in the place of trial, moving toward the Inheritance.

What is meant by "fled for refuge to lay hold upon the hope set before us"? It expresses that which the Gospel requires from those who hear it—appropriating it unto one's self. Saving faith is explained under various figures. Sometimes as "believing", which means the heart resting upon Christ and His finished work. Sometimes as "Coming to Christ", which means a turning from every other refuge and closing with Him as He is set forth in the Gospel. Sometimes as a "setting to our seal that God is true" (John 3:33 cf. Isa. 44:5), which means ratifying His testimony by our receiving it. Sometimes as the committal of our soul and its eternal interests into the hands of the Lord (2 Tim. 1:12). Sometimes as a "submitting ourselves unto the righteousness of God" (Rom. 10:3), which means repudiating our own works and resting upon the vicarious obedience and sacrifice of Christ. Here, it is pictured as a 'fleeing for refuge", the figure being taken from an O. T. type.

Under the Law, God made merciful provision for the man who had unintentionally slain another: that provision was certain cities appointed for refuge for such. Those cities are spoken of in Num. 35, Deut. 19, Josh. 20. Those cities were built on high hills or mountains (Josh. 20:7), that those seeking asylum there, might have no difficulty in keeping them in sight. So the servants of Christ who hold Him up, are likened unto "a city which is set upon a hill" (Matt. 5:14). They were a refuge from "the avenger of blood" (Josh 20:3); cf. "flee from the wrath to come" (Matt. 3:7). They had a causeway of stones approaching them as a path to guide thereto (Deut. 19:3); so in the Gospel a way of approach is revealed unto Christ. Those who succeeded in entering these cities secured protection and safety (Num. 35:15): so Christ has declared "him that cometh to Me I will in no wise cast out" (John 6:37).

Now the particular point to be noted in the above type is that the one who desired shelter from the avenger of blood had to personally **flee to** the city of refuge. The figure is very impressive. Here was a man living in peace and comfort, fearing none; but having now slain another at unawares, everything is suddenly changed. Fear within, and danger without, beset on either hand. The avenger of blood threatens, and nothing is left but to flee to the appointed place of refuge, for there alone is peace and safety to be found. Thus it is with the sinner. In his natural condition, a false serenity and comfort are his. Then, unawares to him, the Holy Spirit convicts him of sin, and he is filled with distress and alarm, till he cries, "What must I do to be saved"?

The Divine answer is, "Flee for refuge and **lay hold of** the hope set before us".

But let us not fail to note here the immeasurable superiority of Christianity over Judaism as seen in the vast difference between the "refuge" under the Law, and that made known in the Gospel. The cities of refuge were available only for those who had unintentionally killed a person. But we have been conscious, deliberate, lifelong rebels against God; nevertheless Christ says, "Come unto Me **all** ye that labour and are heavy-laden, and I will give you rest". Again, the manslayer in the city was safe, yet his very refuge was a **prison**: it is the very opposite with the believer—Christ opened for him the prison-door and set him at liberty (Isa. 61:2), Christ "makes free" (John 8:36). Again, in entering the city of refuge he turned away from his inheritance, his land and cattle; but the one who lays hold of Christ obtains an inheritance (1 Peter 1:4). For the manslayer to return to his inheritance meant death; for the Christian, death means going to his inheritance.

Those who have fled to Christ to "lay hold on eternal life" (1 Tim. 6:12), are entitled to enjoy "strong consolation". On this the Puritan Manton said, "There are three words by which the fruits and effects of certainty and assurance is expressed, which imply so many degrees of it: peace, comfort, and joy. Peace, denotes, rest from accusations of conscience. Comfort, a temperate and habitual confidence. Joy, an actual feeling, or hightide of comfort, an elevation of the saints". Strong consolation is a firm and fixed persuasion of the love of God toward us, and the assurance that "our light affliction, which is but for a moment, worketh for us a far more exceeding eternal weight of glory" (2 Cor. 4:17). "David encouraged himself in the Lord **his** God" (1 Sam. 30:6).

It remains for us now to consider what it is which supplies and supports the "strong consolation" in the believer. This is stated at the beginning of our verse: "That by two immutable things in which it is impossible for God to lie". These are, His promise and His oath. The assurance of the believer rests upon the unchanging veracity of God. Were He influenced by His creatures, God would be constantly changing His plans (as we do), willing one thing today and another to-morrow; in such case who could confide in Him? None, for no one would know what to expect; thus, all certainty would be at an end. But, blessed be His name, our God is "without variableness or shadow of turning" (James 1:17), and therefore the immutability of His counsel is the very life of our assurance.

For the stay of our hearts and the full assurance of our faith, God has graciously given to us an irrevocable 'deed of settlement'. namely, His promise, followed by His oath, whereby the whole inheritance is infallibly secured unto every heir of promise. Heaven and earth shall pass away, but God's words never shall (Luke 21:23). All the promises recorded in Scripture are but copies of God's assurances made **to Christ** for us from everlasting, so that the Divine oaths and covenants mentioned in Holy Writ are but transcripts of the original Covenant and Oath between God and Christ before the foundation of the world. Note how the words "impossible for God to lie", link up with "in hope of eternal life, which God, that cannot lie, promised before the world began" (Titus 1:2)!

Near the close of the previous article we pointed out how that the deeper and spiritual significance of God's promise and oath to Abraham in Gen. 22 has been missed by most of the commentators, through their failure to see in him a type of Christ as the Head and Father of God's elect. There we find God swearing to the patriarch, "Blessing I will bless thee." The application of these words to Christ as the Representative of His people is clearly seen in Psa. 45:2, where God says to Him who is Fairer than the children of men, "God hath **blessed** Thee **forever**". Let it also be pointed out that God's promise and oath to David in Psa. 89 also gives an adumbration of His transactions with the Mediator before the world began: "My Covenant will I not break . . . His seed shall endure forever" (vv. 34-36). Thus, our "strong consolation" issues from the implicit assurance that God has bound Himself in Christ **to** "bless" His people. "For all the promises of God **in Him** (Christ) are Yea, and in Him Amen" (2 Cor. 1:20)!

"Which (hope)) we have as an anchor of the soul, both sure and steadfast, and which entereth into that within the veil" (v. 19). We deeply regret that we feel obligated to part company with every commentator that we have consulted on this verse. Owing to the general mistake of making the "hope" of v. 18 a subjective one, hardly any two are agreed upon the meaning of the "anchor" here. Some regard it as God's promise; others, His oath; others, Christ's priesthood; others, the believer's assurance; and so on. The only point upon which there is common consent is, that the figure is **dropped** in the very next clause!—"entereth into that within the veil". Below we give the literal rendering of Bagster's Interlinear.

"Which as an anchor we have of the soul both certain and firm, and entering into that within the veil". Now an anchor is used for securing a ship, particularly in times of storm, to prevent it from **drifting**. It is an **invisible** thing, sinking down beneath the waters and gripping firmly the ground beneath. The winds may roar and the waves lash the ship, but it rides them steadily, being held fast by something outside itself. Surely the figure is plain. The "anchor" is **Christ Himself,** sustaining His people down here in this world, in the midst of the wicked, who, are likened unto "the troubled sea, when it cannot rest" (Isa. 57:20). Did He not declare, "Neither shall any pluck them out of My hand" (John 10:28)? Certainly there is nothing in us "both sure and steadfast": it is the love (John 13:1), power (Matt. 28:18,20), and faithfulness (Heb. 7:25) of Christ which is in view.

"Whither the Forerunner is for us entered, Jesus, made an High Priest forever, after the order of Melchizedek" (v. 20). Surely this explains for us the previous verse: it was the entrance of Christ into Heaven which settles fast the "Anchor" within the veil! It was **for us** Christ has gone on High! A "forerunner" is one who has already traversed every step of the race which is set before us (12:1, 2), and who has entered into possession of that toward which he ran. Because Christ has been where we now are, we shall soon be where He now is. Thus, the force of this figurative title of our Redeemer is not only designed to give assurance of our security, but to show us **where** that security lies—entirely outside of ourselves: held fast by a triumphant and ascended Christ. Hence the force of His name here: "Jesus", who "**shall** save His people from their sins" (Matt. 1:21).

Condensing from Dr. Owen's excellent remarks:—Christ is a "Forerunner" **for us,** first, by way of **declaration.** It belongs unto a forerunner to carry tidings and declare what success has been obtained in the affair of which he is to render account. So when the Lord Christ entered Heaven, He made an open declaration of His victory by spoiling principalities and leading captivity captive: see Psa. 47:5-7, 68:18, 24-26. Second, by way of **preparation.** This He did by opening the way for our prayers and worship: 10:19-22 and making ready a place for us, John 14:2, 3. Third, by way of **occupation.** He has gone into Heaven, in our name, to take possession and reserve it for us: Acts 26:18, 1 Peter 1:4.

"Made an high priest forever, after the order of Melchizedek". Having warned us of our danger (5:11 to 6:8), having exhorted us to continue pressing forward (6:11-15), having assured our hearts of infallible preservation (6:16-19), the apostle now returns to the very point he had dropped at 5:10. This final clause of Heb. 6 forms a pertinent and perfect transition between the apostle's digression at 5:11 and onwards, and the description of Christ's priesthood which follows in chapter 7, etc. He now declares who and what that "Forerunner" was, who **for us has** gone on High, even Jesus, our great High Priest. Thus the apostle **has** led us on to the "perfection" which he mentioned at the beginning of this chapter (6:1, 3)—Christ within the veil!

—ARTHUR W. PINK.

THE SATISFACTION
("Atonement")
OF CHRIST

5. Its Nature.

An inadequate conception of the terrible enormity of sin necessarily results in a faulty view of the Atonement. In reading through scores of books which were written at varying intervals during the last four hundred years, we have been struck by the fact that side by side with the modifying of the immeasurable heinousness of sin there has been a whittling down of the most essential features comprised in the character of Christ's redemptive work. The more lightly sin be regarded, the less will appear the need for such a stupenduous undertaking as that which the Son of God entered upon and triumphantly carried through. Sin is an evil of **infinite** magnitude, for it is committed against an **infinite** Person, unto whom every creature is under infinite obligations of rendering unceasing and joyful obedience. This is why God's punishment of sin unatoned for will be **eternal:** necessarily so, for nothing less will fit the case, nothing less will satisfy Divine justice. And this is why God could receive no satisfaction to His broken law save from one that possessed infinite merits.

Rom. 3:22 defines sin as a "coming short of the glory of God", i.e., His manifestative or declarative glory. Sin is failing to render unto God that to which His high honour is entitled, namely, implicit, perfect, constant homage and service. God's **essential** blessedness cannot be affected by the creature: were He to so please, He has merely to utter the words and every rebel throughout the entire universe would immediately cease to exist. But His declarative glory can be affected, yea, **is** so, by our sins. Sin dishonours God, and fallen man is utterly unable to restore His honour, yet this inability so to do is criminal and increases his guilt. Not only does sin dishonour God, but it cannot be remitted by Him and the transgressor pardoned, till every claim of His law has been met. This the creature cannot do. As we showed in our last article, none but a mediator who was Divine as well as human, was competent to render full satisfaction unto God. This is what Christ has done: His Atonement has brought back to God's declarative glory that revenue of honour and praise to which He is entitled.

Now the life and death of Christ are historical facts which are, practically, universally admitted, but the "**word** of the cross" (1 Cor. 1:18, R. V.), i.e., the scriptural explanation of His atoning work is purely a matter of Divine revelation, and is to be received with uncavilling humility and rested upon with peaceful assurance, simply because it is made known to us on the authority of God. Reasoning thereon is utterly vain, and speculating thereabout is profane. Moreover, as we stated in the opening article, all attempts to **illustrate** from supposed analogies in human relations dishonour God and grossly pervert His Truth. The Atoning Work of Christ is unique. It stands alone in its solitary grandeur. There is nothing in all history which in anywise resembles it. When a preacher attempts to "simplify" the mystery of the three Persons of the Godhead by some illustration from "nature", he only exhibits his own foolishness, and helps nobody. So too every effort to explain the Atonement with what is outside Scripture, is only turning from light to darkness. Divine mysteries cannot be understood by means of those things which come within the range of our physical senses.

It has been rightly said that "Accuracy of terms clarifies thought", to which we may add, Accuracy of thought is essential to right views of any portion of the Truth, and right views of the Truth are honouring to God. Therefore, no effort should be spared in seeking to attain unto the utmost possible precision of language when seeking to set forth the things of God. Many a reader has obtained only a cloudy view of a subject because the writer confused **effects** with the nature of the thing he was dealing with. For example, **assurance** of salvation is one of the fruits of faith (as well as a gift of the Spirit), yet it has often been regarded as an essential element of faith itself. In consequence, because they lacked assurance, some real Christians have been plunged into what Bunyan termed the Slough of Despond, because they imagined they were not saved at all. In like manner, many writers on the Atonement, have carelessly jumbled together some of its leading effects and fruits with the nature of it.

A pertinent example of what we have just said is seen in the now almost current idea that the Atonement of Christ signifies "at-one-ment", the bringing of God and the sinner together. But **that** is not the meaning of the term at all, either as used in Scripture or as employed in sound theology. Reconciliation is one of the many effects or fruits of Christ's Atonement, but was not a part of the work He did. Many others have failed to distinguish between the Atonement of Christ and the Redemption which is one of its fruits. It is vitally important to distinguish between what Christ did and that which has resulted therefrom. To understand what He did, let us now attempt to define the **nature** of His Atonement.

1. It was a Federal work.

By the term "federal" we mean that there was an official oneness existing between the Mediator and those for whom He mediated, or, in simpler language, that there is a **legal union** between Christ and His people. "When, in the O. T., the elect are spoken of as the party with whom God makes a covenant, they are viewed as in Christ and one with Him. The covenant is not made with them as alone and apart from Christ. This is taught in Gal. 3:16. 'To Abraham and his seed were the promise made', but this seed 'is Christ'. The elect are here (as also in 1 Cor. 12:12) called 'Christ', because of the union between Christ and the elect. And in like manner, when Christ, as in Isa. 42:1-6, is spoken of as the party with whom the Father covenants, the elect are to be viewed as in

Him. As united and one with Him, His atoning suffering is looked upon as their atoning suffering: 'I am crucified with Christ', Gal. 2:20" (Wm. Shedd, 1889).

"Christ is not only the Substitute, but the Surety of His people. The Gospel is founded on the fact Adam and Christ are covenant heads and representatives of their respective families. Hence they are termed 'the first man' and 'the second man' (1 Cor. 15:47), as if there had been none other but themselves, for the children of each were entirely dependent on their head. In Adam all die; in Christ all are made alive (1 Cor. 15:22). The first **all** includes every individual of mankind, the last **all** is explained by the apostle to mean 'they that are Christ's' (1 Cor. 15:23)" (James Haldane, Doctrine of the Atonement).

It was as the Head of His elect that God covenanted with Christ, so that, in a very real sense, that covenant was made with them. This it is which explains all those passages that speak of the saints' oneness with Christ, as that, they were "crucified with Christ" (Gal. 2:20), "died with Him" (Rom. 6:8), were "buried with Him" as Scriptural baptism symbolises (Rom. 6:4), were "quickened" with Him (Col. 2:12), "raised with Him" (Eph. 2:6), and made to "sit together in the heavenlies in Christ Jesus" (Eph. 2:6). So they were legally one with Him, and He with them, in all that He did in rendering a full Satisfaction to God. On this vitally important point we cannot do better than give a synopsis of the last section from chapter two of H. Martin's invaluable work:

"How are we to formulate and establish the relation subsisting between Christ and His, as Redeemer and redeemed, unless we fall back upon the doctrine of the Covenant? **Some** relation, it is evident, must be acknowledged as subsisting between Christ and those on whose behalf He dies, else we do not even come within sight of the idea of a vicarious sacrifice. The possibility of real atonement absolutely postulates and demands a conjuncture between Him who atones and those for whom His atonement is available. This is beyond the need of proof. And as there is an absolute and obvious necessity for **some** conjuncture or relation, so in searching for the **the** conjunction or relation which actually subsists, our search cannot terminate satisfactorily till we reach and recognize the covenant oneness. The same reason that demands **a** relation, remains unsatisfied till it meets with **this** relation".

It does not meet the necessities of the case to refer to the union between Christ and His people which is effected in their regeneration by the agency of the Holy Spirit and the instrumentality of that faith which is His gift. True, this is indispensible before any can enjoy any of the blessings of His purchase. But there must have been a relation between Christ and His people before He ransomed them. Nor are the necessities of the case met by a reference to the Incarnation. True, the Redeemer must take upon Him flesh and blood before He **could** redeem, yet there must be a bond of union more intimate than that which Christ holds alike to the saved and the unsaved. He took hold of "the seed of **Abraham**" (Heb. 2:16), not the "seed of Adam"! Nor is it sufficient to say that the relation is that of suretyship and substitution, for the question still calls for answer, **What** rendered it fit and righteous that the Son of God **should** suffer for others, the Holy One be made sin? It is to **this** point the inquiry must be narrowed.

Christ was the Surety of His people because He was their Substitute. He acted **on their behalf** because He stood **in their** room. The relation of a substitute justifies the suretyship; but **what** shall justify the substitution? There is the hinge upon which everything turns. We heartily concur with Dr. Martin when he says, "We can obtain no satisfaction on this point, no sufficient answer to this question, and therefore no satisfactory conclusion to our whole line of investigation, till the doctrine of the everlasting **covenant-oneness** comes into view. That is the grand underlying relation. That is the grand primary conjunction between the Redeemer and the redeemed, which alone bears up and accounts for all else in respect of relation which can be predicated as true concerning them. 'Both He that sanctifieth and they who are sanctified are **all of one**: for **which** cause He is not ashamed to call them brethren' (Heb. 2:11). He is substituted **for us**, because He is one **with us**—identified with us and we with Him".

Promoted by infinite love, Christ, as the God-man, freely accepted the terms of the Everlasting Covenant which had been proposed to Him, and voluntarily assumed all the legal responsibilities of His people. As their Head He came down to this earth, lived, wrought, and died as their vicarious Representative. He obeyed and suffered as their Substitute. By His obedience and sufferings He discharged all their obligations. His sufferings remitted the penalty of the law, and His obedience merited infinite blessings for them. Rom. 5:12-19 explicitly affirms that the elect of God are, legally, "made righteous" on precisely the same principle by which they were first "made sinners". "Our union with Christ is of the same order, and involves the same class of effects, as our union with Adam. We call it a union both **federal and vital.** Others may call it what they please, but it will nevertheless remain certain that it is of such a nature as to involve **an identity** of legal relations and reciprocal obligations and rights" (A. A. Hodge). "For **as** by one man's disobedience many were made sinners, **so** by the obedience of One shall many be made righteous" (Rom. 5:19)—"made the righteousness of God **in Him**" (2 Cor. 5:21).

More than a thousand years ago, Augustine remarked, "Such is the ineffable closeness of this transcendental union, that we hear the voice of the members suffering, when they suffered in their Head, and cried through the Head on the cross, 'My God, my God, why hast Thou forsaken me'? And, in like manner, we hear the voice of the Head suffering, when He suffered in His members, and cried to the persecutor on the way to Damascus 'Saul, Saul, why persecutest thou Me'? (Acts 9:4)"

The **federal** relation of Christ to His people was a **real** one, upon which the infallible God deemed it just to punish Christ for the sins of His people, and to credit them with His righteousness, and thus completely satisfy all the demands of His law upon them. As the result of that union, Christ was in all things "made like unto His brethren" (Heb. 2:17), being "numbered (reckoned one) with transgressors" (Isa. 53:12); and they, in turn, are "members of His body, of His flesh, and of His bones" (Eph. 5:30). In consequence of this federal union, Christ is also made "a quickening Spirit" (1 Cor. 15:45) so that, in due time, each of His people becomes a living and vital member of that spiritual body of which He is the Head (Eph. 1:19-23).

The relation between Christ and those who benefit from His Atonement was, therefore, no vague, indefinite haphazard one, but consisted of an actual covenant oneness, legal identity, vital union. Suretyship presupposes it. Strict substitution demands it. Real imputation proceeds upon it. The penalty Christ endured could not otherwise have been inflicted. They for whom Satisfaction was made do, by inevitable necessity, share its benefits and receive what was purchased for them. This alone meets the objection of the injustice of the Innocent suffering for the guilty, as it alone explains the transfer of Christ's sufferings and merits to the redeemed.

2. It was a Substitutionary work.

The terms "substitutionary" and "vicarious" are often used very loosely. Many who have sought to gain a reputation for orthodoxy and thereby ingratiate themselves into the confidence of God's people have made use of the bare terms, yet intended by them nothing more than that Christ suffered on the behalf of others, for the benefit of others. But **that** is only a half truth, and therefore close akin to a lie. Vicarious suffering or punishment is more than suffering endured for the good of others. The suffering of martyrs for the good of their cause, of patriots for their country, of philanthropists for mankind, are **not** "vicarious", for they are not **substitutionary.** Vicarious suffering is suffering endured not only of behalf of others, but in the stead of others, in the actual **place of** others. It therefore carries with it, of necessity, the **exemption** of the party in whose place the suffering is endured. What a substitute does for the person whose place he fills, absolves that person from the need of himself doing or suffering the same thing. Thus, when we affirm that the sufferings of Christ were "vicarious" we mean that He substituted Himself in the room of sinners and satisfied the Law in their behalf, and that, in such a way, the Law can now make no claim whatever upon them. Christ's sufferings were "vicarious" in identically the same way that the death of animals in the O. T. sacrifices was in lieu of the death of the transgressor offering them.

The Scriptures teach that Christ was in a strict and exact sense the Substitute of His people, i. e., that by Divine appointment and of His own free will, He assumed all their liabilities, took their Law-place, and bound Himself to do in their stead all that the Law demanded, rendering to it that obedience upon which their wellbeing depended, and suffering its penalty which their sins deserved. Christ became their vicarious Sponsor, assuming their obligations and undertaking to satisfy Divine justice on their behalf. So real was His substitution in their place, that what He did and suffered for them precluded all necessity of their meeting the demands of the Law in their own persons. Thus, the Satisfaction which Christ made was far more than an expedient for "removing those obstacles" which prevented God from justifying the ungodly: it was that which **required** Justice to remit the sins of all for whom it was made. The Satisfaction of Christ was infinitely more than a means for "opening a way" whereby the grace of God could flow forth: it was that which **necessitated** all for whom it was made being vested with all its meritorious efficacy.

In becoming the Substitute of His people, in placing Himself under their liabilities, in engaging to discharge all their responsibilities, Christ was, necessarily, "made under the Law" (Gal. 4:4), so that He might keep its statutes, fulfill its requirements, and thus "magnify" and render it "honourable" (Isa. 42:21). The Scriptures plainly teach that Christ's **obedience** was as truly "vicarious" as was His suffering, and that He reconciled the elect to God by the one as well as the other—that is why we insist on using the wider term "the **Satisfaction** of Christ", for "atonement", strictly speaking, covers only the expiation of our guilt by His vicarious suffering. The active obedience of Christ to the Law was required as the meritorious condition upon which the Divine favour and the promised reward of the Covenant might come upon all whose Surety He was. We must never attempt to separate between the active obedience and the passive sufferings of Christ, either when contemplating His mediatorial work, or when considering the effect of that work upon the covenant-standing of His people. Christ's vicarious obedience is an intrinsic part of that "righteousness" which He wrought in our stead, and which is imputed to us as the ground of our justification. **All** that Christ did on earth He did **as Mediator**. He was acting in our stead just as truly when He was obeying God as when He was enduring His wrath. It is in reference to both of these conjointly that He is designated "the Lord **our righteousness**" (Jer. 23:6).

It needs to be pointed out that the "obedience" of Christ is not to be restricted to what He wrought prior to the cross, nor are His "sufferings" to be limited to what He endured during the crucifixion and immediately preceding it. No, He suffered all through His life, and obeyed throughout His dying. "The whole earth life of Christ, including His birth itself, was one continued self-emptying, even unto death. His birth, and every moment of His life, in the form of a servant, was of the nature of holy sufferings. Every experience of pain during the whole course of His life, and eminently in His death on the cross, was, on His part, a voluntary and meritorious act of obedience. He lived His whole life, from His birth to His death, as our Representative, obeying and suffering in our stead, and for our sakes; and during this whole course, all His suffering was obedience, and all His obedience was suffering. The righteousness which He wrought out for His people consisted precisely in this suffering and obedience. The righteousness of Christ, which is imputed severally to each believer, as the ground of his justification, consists precisely of this suffering and obedience. His earth life as **suffering** cancels the penalty, and as **obedience**, fulfills the precepts and secures the promised reward of the Law; but the suffering and the obedience were not separated in fact, and are inseparable in principle, and equally necessary to satisfy the law of the covenant and to secure the salvation of the elect" (A. A. Hodge).

The Law, as a covenant of life, was accompanied by two sanctions. First, the promise of "life" or Divine favour and eternal wellbeing, conditioned upon perfect obedience: see Lev. 18:5, Matt. 19:17, Rom. 10:5, Gal. 3:12. Second, the penalty of "death" suspended on disobedience. Now the object for which Christ became incarnate was "**that the righteousness** of the law might be fulfilled in us" (Rom. 8:4), and therefore is Christ declared to be "the end of the law for righteousness to every one that believeth" (Rom. 10:4). And this was only made possible by His fulfilling all the Law's conditions. Had not Christ vicariously obeyed the Law, had He merely suffered its penalty, due our sins, then we should be destitute of any positive righteousness, and would be left just where Adam was before he fell. But the Scriptures emphatically affirm that Christ saved by His obedience as well as by His sufferings: "For as by one man's disobedience, many were made sinners, so by the obedience of One shall many be made righteous" (Rom. 5:19)—Christ's "obedience" is to be interpreted here in the same natural and obvious way as the "disobedience" of Adam. Thus our **twofold** obligation to God, as creatures and as sinners, was met and discharged by Christ.

"As our Representative, He bore in the union of His divine personality our nature impersonally ('a true body and a reasonable soul'), in order that He might thus be **made vicariously under the Law,** to the end that by His purely vicarious obedience He might 'redeem them that are under the law, **that** we might receive the adoption of sons' (Gal. 4:4, 5). This means necessarily (a) that Christ was **made** under the law, that He did not belong there naturally, but was transferred to that position by an act of divine sovereignty. (b) That He was placed there, not for Himself but in **our stead.** (c) That He was made under the law for the purpose of securing for us not only the remission of sins, but also the **adoption of sons,** whereby we become 'heirs of God **through Christ**' (Gal. 4:7); all of which is conditioned not upon suffering, but upon obedience. All that Christ did on earth He did as our Mediator, and all that He did as Mediator, He did in the stead of those for whom He acted as Mediator. Therefore He said (Matt. 3:15). 'for thus it becometh us to fulfill all righteousness', that is, all that God requires of His peopeople" (A. A. Hodge).

In Rom. 8:3 (the context should be carefully weighed) we read of "what the law could not do, in that it was weak through the flesh". That which the law was unable to do was **justify the ungodly.** The reason for this was that the law demands perfect obedience, and this the flesh, because of sin, makes it impossible for the sinner to render. In view of this, God sent His own Son in the likeness of sinful flesh and for sin. Sent Him into the Law-place of His people and by His executing the penalty upon Him "condemned sin in the flesh", and by accepting His vicarious obedience the "righteousness of the law" is fulfilled in us. The phrase "the righteousness of the law" is used in the N. T. to express the totality of that which the law demands as the condition of favour. In Adam, before he fell, the righteousness of the law was perfect obedience. In the case of all his descendants, it is perfect obedience plus the suffering of its penalty; hence the impossibility of our achieving a legal righteousness by our own personal agency.

Now "the righteousness of the law" is placed in antithesis from "the righteousness of faith", Rom. 10:5, 6. That is to say (see context) the futile attempts of the sinner to satisfy the requirements of the law in his own person, is contrasted from the vicarious satisfaction of Christ which faith apprehends and appropriates. "To them that have obtained like precious faith with us through the **righteousness** of our God and Saviour Jesus Christ" (2 Peter 1:1). To the same effect our worthless righteousness is contrasted from God's perfect righteousness in Christ: see Rom. 3:20-26. Obedience is therefore the essence of righteousness, and that obedience, the obedience **of Christ.** Therefore we read that He is "made unto us wisdom and righteousness" (1 Cor. 1:30). And therefore Paul declares his desire to "be found in Him, not having mine own righteousness, which is of the law, but that which is through the faith of Christ, the righteousness which is of God by faith" (Phil. 3:9). The endurance of penalty by Christ demanded that our sins should be remitted; the performing of obedience by Christ demanded that His righteousness be imputed to us and that we should be eternally established in God's favour.

In the above passage (Rom. 8:3) we are told that God sent His own Son "in the likeness of sinful (literally "sin's") flesh". This remarkable expression needs to be carefully investigated, lest we err by overstatement, or come short of its meaning by defective statement. First, it affirms the **reality** of Christ's humanity. Second, inasmuch as that humanity was united to Godhead, it must be **sinless** humanity: generated by the Holy Spirit it was pure and holy. This was secured by the fact that though He took flesh from Adam through the Virgin, **He** was **not** in Adam's covenant. Third, its "likeness" or appearance was after the order of "sin's flesh": between Him and sinful men there was **no perceptible** difference that could be traced: in weariness and exhaustion, sorrow and heaviness, Christ was in all respects, "made like unto His brethren". But toil and sorrow, weakness and pain, came not on Him as the inevitable consequence of the Incarnation, but resulted from His coming here as the Surety of His people.

Christ was **personally** exempt from all the consequences of Adam's sin, but **officially** He was subject to them. Personally, He was a Divine person assuming a sinless humanity, and had He not come here as the Head of God's elect (considered as fallen creatures), He had doubtless appeared in a humanity as glorious as that of unfallen Adam's. But officially He assumed "the likeness of **sin's** flesh", an expression referring to the effects of which sin was the cause: namely, subject to suffering and mortality and this from the moment of His birth. O infinite stoop! O marvel of condescension! He bore in His body the weight of imputed sin, a body bearing the sad marks of sin, for "**His** visage was so marred more than any man, and **His** form more than the sons of men" (Isa. 52:14). There was no **perceptible** difference between His humanity and ours, **not** because precisely the same flesh had been transmitted to Him from Adam, but because as our Sin-bearer He voluntarily assumed the burden of imputed guilt, which carried with it abasement and degradation, suffering and death: it was officially assumed, not personally inherited.

Christ came in the likeness of sin's flesh **for** sin" (Rom. 8:3), i. e., on account of sin: **that** is why God "sent" Him. "Condemned sin in the flesh": sin is still **personified**, as in Rom. 5, 6, 7: see 5:21, 6:14, etc.—the potentate having men in bondage. God "condemned sin" speaks of sin as a person judged before the highest tribunal and righteously condemned. In consequence of God's judgment, sin has no further claim on those over whom he had tyrannized: they are set free. "Condemned sin in the flesh" means condemned it in **Christ's** humanity, as the sinless Sin-offering—cf. 2:1, 5:18—a condemnation freeing His people from condemnation: 8:1. Christ was "condemned", visited with penal suffering, because He appeared before God only in the guise of our accursed sins. And, this, in order that, "the righteousness of the law might be fulfilled **in us**", i. e., as if **we** personally had done it.

Rightly did Mr. J. Inglis point out, "The fact that God sent forth His Son in the likeness of sinful flesh and for sin, intimates that He entered into the condition of His people, which, with all its evils, is the consequence of sin. If we find Him poor and despised, hungry and thirsty, subject to toil and fatigue, a man of sorrows and acquainted with grief, not exempt from the fear of death nor from actual mortality, to say nothing of all else that He endured at the hands of Satan and of man; all these are indubitably the consequences of sin, and He could be exposed to them **only** as He **represented** sinners" (Waymarks Vol. 10).

A fuller light shines forth from the four Gospels when we perceive that they are not the biography of a private individual, but the history of the Surety of God's people. Christ was the Representative Head of an elect company: from Bethlehem to Calvary He was their Vicarious Victim. The appearing of the Son of God on earth was the direct consequence of sin. The Incarnation and the Cross are inseparable; both were a means to an end—the vindication of Divine justice, the expiation of sin, the rendering of meritorious obedience to the law. We cannot survey the meanness of His birth, made lower than the angels; the poverty of His condition; His manual occupation, earning His bread by the sweat of His brow, according to the curse upon His people; His temptation by Satan; His privations, the enduring of hunger and thirst and having not where to lay His head; His public execution; these, we say, cannot be contemplated without the firm conviction that they were all included in **our** guilt and related to **our** punishment.

—ARTHUR W. PINK.

5 SANCTIFICATION OF THE SPIRIT

Sanctification, or Gospel-holiness, without which no man shall see the Lord, comprehends the whole work of the Spirit of God within and upon us, from our regeneration to our eternal glorification. It is the fruit and blessed consequence of His in-dwelling in us, and the continued effect of spiritual regeneration: i. e., in begetting within us a nature suited to take in spiritual things, and be properly affected by them. Regeneration is the root, and sanctification is the bud, blossom and fruit which it produces. In our regeneration by the Holy Spirit we are made alive to God, and this is manifested by our faith in Christ Jesus. Our lusts are mortified, because we are quickened together with Christ. And what we style the Sanctification of the Spirit, which follows after regeneration hath taken place within us, consists in drawing forth that spiritual life which is conveyed to our souls in our new birth, into act and exercise on Christ and spiritual things, in quickening our graces, and in leading us to walk in the paths of holiness, by which proof is given that we are alive to God through Jesus Christ our Lord".

The Old Testament is the foundation of the New. There is nothing in the latter but what may be found in the former. The one serves to explain the other. Nothing can be more safe than to search the Scriptures, that we may clearly see what they say and testify concerning Sanctification. The generality of real Christians seem to be mistaken concerning it, as they most commonly fit their ideas of their own personal sanctification, on what they see, feel, and are in themselves, more than on what they are in Christ. They overlook what the Spirit of Christ hath wrought in them in regeneration by looking at what they are, simply considered in themselves. The word "sanctification" both in the Old and New Testament, in its primitive meaning and simplicity, signifies **separation.** To sanctify is to consecrate, to separate, or set apart, from a common to a higher or sacred use. Hence persons, things, and places, when separated from others, and set apart for the service and worship of God, are said to be **sanctified.** Thus in the Old Testament, God is said to sanctify the "seventh day" (Gen. 2:3), the "first born" among the Israelites (Ex. 13:2), and "the mount" on which the law was given (Ex. 19). Also the tabernacle, the temple, the priests, the altar, and the sacrifices, were sanctified thus, i. e., by a separation to the immediate worship and service of God. And the proofs concerning the meaning of the word "sanctification", namely, that it signifies in the New Testament just what it does in the Old, may be seen in the following Scriptures: Matt. 23:17, 19; John 10:36; 17:9 compared with 17; Heb. 10:29, 13:12 compared with 1 Cor. 7:14.

I will endeavour to briefly set forth the truth of this doctrine in its proper light from the figures and shadows of it under the Old Testament dispensation: which may conduce to form in our minds right and scriptural conceptions of it. Let us view and consider it in the following particulars: a separation from the profane community, in which men are naturally lying, is **sanctification.** Thus the Lord chose Israel, though they were according to His own declaration, the fewest and most perverse of all people: see Deut. 7:6-8. In consequence of this separation, they are styled "A kingdom of priests, an holy nation" (Ex. 19:6). It should be observed that the word, "sanctification" is taken in the original language from the shadows and figures of it under the O. T. dispensation of it. Thus washing, purifying, and cleansing those who were thus separated, from defilement and pollution, (which they had naturally, or which they had contracted) by the blood of the sacrifices, which was performed by the **application** of it in some shape or other to the person who was to be "sanctified", were a shadow and figure of Gospel-sanctification. There was no remission of sin without shedding of blood, nor any purification from the guilt and filth of it without the application of that blood (Lev. 14:14). Persons thus separated and cleansed, were solemnly devoted and set apart to God for that particular station to which they were separated, and the service and business which belonged to it, as was the case with Aaron and his sons (Lev. 8). Such persons thus separated were qualified for what they were separated unto with proper gifts; and some of them anointed with oil, as a symbol and sign of the Divine anointing. All these shadows and figures are so easily to be applied to the true sanctification of the regenerate by the blood and Spirit of our Lord Jesus Christ, that we see the one illustrated by the other.

Let us now see how sanctification is expressed in the New Testament by separation, ordination, and setting apart to the Lord. Christ, God-man, the Head, Mediator, and Saviour of His people is said to be "sanctified" by His designation to His office. In His address to the Jews he speaks thus, "Say ye of Him whom the Father hath **sanctified,** and sent into the world, Thou blasphemest: because I said, I am the Son of God" (John 10:36). Christ, God-man, could be, "sanctified" no other way than by His being set apart to His mediatorial work and office; He being essentially, personally, and transcendently holy, the "Holy One of God", and the very fountain and spring of holiness to elect angels and saints. Again: in His intercessory prayer to His Father, speaking on the behalf of His people, He says, "For their sakes I **sanctify** Myself" (John 17:19), which can be understood no otherwise, than of His being separated and set apart for His office by Jehovah the Father, which our most Divine Lord voluntarily devoted Himself unto, and performed to the eternal honour of law and justice. The Son of God, Christ Jesus, is said to be "sanctified", hallowed and consecrated, **by His own blood**; called "the blood of the covenant" (Heb. 10:29). This is in allusion to Aaron and his sons, who were sanctified by the sacrifices of slain beasts, to minister in the priest's office (Lev. 8). So Christ offered Himself, and shed His most precious blood, by which the covenant of grace was ratified; and, being brought back from the dead through "the blood of the everlasting covenant" (Heb. 13:20), He sat down at the right hand of the Majesty on high, to exercise His priesthood in heaven, **for which** He was "sanctified" by His own blood.

As the word **sanctification**, when used of Christ Himself, means **separation**, so it may be further added that the N. T. fully proves that those O. T. types of purification from sin contained in them the nature of Gospel-sanctification. So says the apostle in his epistle to the Hebrews: see 9:22, 23. And they are so: "Wherefore Jesus also, that He might sanctify the people with His own blood, suffered without the gate" (13:12). To sum up what is said of the sanctification effected by the sacrifices and sprinklings of blood under the law, and as expressive of the true sanctification by the blood and Spirit of Christ, observe what he says in Heb. 9:13, 14. From these observations before us it appears to me that, "sanctification" consists in God's effectually calling His people out of darkness into His marvelous light, separating them from others, their former state, and life, by an holy calling; sprinkling them with the blood of Christ, putting His Holy Spirit within them, and working in them all the good pleasure of His will, and the work of faith with power. It is our common misfortune to confound causes and effects together. It should be our study to keep these apart, and to apply our minds to obtain from the Word and Spirit, clear and scriptural views and ideas of every part of Divine truth. We should never venture to receive any conception concerning Divine realities, but from the inspired volume. If we receive **from it** a right understanding of the doctrine of sanctification, it will save us from much error. It will clear our judgments, and lead us to give the whole glory of it to the co-equal and co-essential Three.

The great and leading title peculiar to "the Spirit of Christ" as considered in His economical office-capacity, is "the Spirit of life". He is the Spirit of life from God in these following most eminent instances and respects to His people. First, as He conveys life to them in regeneration, and therein quickens them up unto life eternal. Secondly, as He continues, maintains, and supports the same; yea, brings it to its full maturity and perfection in the full fruition and enjoyment of Christ in His kingdom of glory. There is a spiritual and real union between Christ and His people. They are united to Him the fountain of life. The Holy Spirit descends on them and enters within them, **in consequence of** this union. He comes from heaven to make known this union between Christ and them. He is the Divine Manifester of it. He conveys Himself into our hearts, and we receive Him, that we may obtain from His Divine teaching the knowledge of those things which are freely given to us of God. He dwells in us as a well of water, springing up into everlasting life. He abides with us as our Divine Comforter, and will be our Guide even unto death, and continue His life-giving influences to us and dwell in us, filling us with all the fullness of God in heaven forever.

The believer, as united to Christ, is a partaker of His Spirit. That same Spirit which dwells in Jesus the Mediator and Head of His church, which He received without measure, that very **anointing**, from whence He receives His name and title, "The Messiah" or "the Christ", dwells and abides **in, on** and **with** all the called people of God. Hence they derive their name "Christians", which signifies **anointed ones**, because they are anointed with the Spirit of Christ. The apostle John says to them, "Ye have an unction from the Holy One" (1 John 2:20). The allusion is to the anointing oil under the law, with which the high priest was anointed, or christened; and which was a symbol of the Holy Spirit. And Paul says, "He that is joined to the Lord is one Spirit" (1 Cor. 6:17). As Christ's human nature was formed by the Holy Spirit, who overshadowed His virgin mother; so we receive our new birth and every faculty of the new man from the new-creating power of the Holy Spirit; and every grace which was in Christ is wrought therein. So says the apostle: "Of His fulness have all we received, and grace for grace" (John 1:16).

The new creature is a conformity to the image of Christ. Hereby we are fitted for Divine communion with Him. He is the vine, and we are branches in Him, and He conveys sap and spiritual nourishment to us, that we may grow and increase with the increase of God. Like as a single drop of water is of the same nature with the ocean, so spiritual graces wrought in our new nature by the Spirit of Christ, are of the same nature and kind with those which were wrought in Jesus by the same Holy Spirit. Hence the apostle says to the renewed and called people of God, "Ye are washed, ye are sanctified, ye are justified, in the name of the Lord Jesus, and by the Spirit of our God" (1 Cor. 6:11). The regenerate have received through the virtue of Christ's death, put forth in their souls through the energy of the Spirit, a death unto sin, and a life unto righteousness, and are in that state where "grace reigns through righteousness unto eternal life through Jesus Christ our Lord" (Rom. 5:21).

The apostle in Romans 6 treats of the subject of **sanctification** in both its parts: mortification of sin, and living unto God. In this great discourse on the believer's union with Christ and communion with Him in His death, burial, and resurrection, he sets before us the state of grace which the believer is in, how he stands in

Christ, what his state in Christ is before God, how permanent and immutable it is, and calls on believers to reckon themselves to be what Christ is: "Knowing that Christ being raised from the dead dieth no more; death hath no more dominion over him. For in that he died, he died unto sin once; but in that he liveth, he liveth unto God. **Likewise reckon ye also** yourselves to be dead indeed unto sin; but alive unto God through (or "in") Jesus Christ our Lord" (Rom. 6:9-11). The apostle in these words draws a parallel between our state by regeneration, signified by baptism into Christ's death and resurrection, and the actual death and resurrection of Christ. As the change wrought in us by regeneration is once for all; so the state, which we are brought into thereby, is an eternal and immutable one. As Christ died once and lives forever, and death hath no more dominion over Him; so we, being planted by regeneration and baptism into the likeness of His death and resurrection, are saved from wrath through Him. As such we should view the comparison between what was wrought in Christ for us, and what is wrought by the Spirit of Christ within us; and also the permanency of our state in Christ, it being as unchangeable as His. As He lives forever, and death hath no more dominion over Him; so neither sin, nor death, shall have final dominion over us. Hence the apostle saith, "Sin shall not have dominion over you" (v. 12).

Being born again into Christ, we are born forever: we are translated into the kingdom of grace, and introduced by the Holy Spirit into actual communion with Christ, and partake with Him in His death, and in the virtues and glories of His resurrection. We have a real participation in all the blessings and benefits of it. As at His resurrection He was declared thereby to be the Son of God, so regeneration is our evidence that we are sons of God (1 John 3:1). The apostle would have us look on ourselves in Christ, as one with Him in His death, burial, and resurrection, and live and act in the full belief of it (Rom. 6:11). Thus He shows us that our state in Christ is the same with the state of Christ Himself, equally unchangeable; and that our being quickened by the Spirit of God and made alive in Christ and to Him are real, spiritual, supernatural, Gospel-sanctification and holiness, and that the whole thereof is the fruit of union with the person of Christ, God-man. "He who sanctifieth and they who are sanctified are all of one; for which cause He is not ashamed to call them brethren" (Heb. 2:11). On account of which they are called "Holy brethren" (Heb. 3:1).

The life of sanctification consists in **living unto God.** The Holy Spirit is sent by Christ to dwell in the new creature, and to abide with it forever. The whole secret of the Christian's life, consists in Christ's living in him: so saith Paul, "Christ liveth in me" (Gal. 2:20). As Christ liveth unto God, so doth the **man in Christ.** He lives to Him by faith on the person, righteousness, and atonement of His co-equal Son. The glory of God is his one supreme end; the will of God in Christ is his great delight. This is the whole sanctification of saints on earth, and the very essence of it in heaven, to prefer God's glory above all things, and to acquiesce in the whole good pleasure of His eternal will. Christ being in us is the spring and fountain of all inward sanctification and holiness; and our living **in Him** and **on Him** produces all the blessed fruits thereof in our hearts, lives and conversation. The whole fulness and perfection of our sanctification are in Christ. He is our Head and Representative, in whom we are immutably holy. He is the Holy One of Israel, from whom all our holiness is derived. He imparts it out of His fulness unto us. He is made by the Father "sanctification" unto us (1 Cor. 1:30). We are never more sanctified than whilst we look to and live on Him. A real spiritual view of Christ sanctifies the mind; and the perfection of our sanctification in heaven will consist in seeing Him as He is. The believer receives his all out of the infinite fulness of the God-man.

Having real communion with Christ in His death, and a growing acquaintance with Him and the power of His resurrection, he lives Christ, and thereby gives outward proof and evidence of his being alive to God by the power of the Holy Spirit. This is manifested in bringing forth "The fruits of righteousness, which are by Jesus Christ unto the glory and praise of God". The fruits of sanctification and holiness, which flow from inward principles implanted in the soul in regeneration, are generally treated and considered **as** sanctification; though, properly speaking, they are but the **effects** of that true spirituality of mind, **which is** inward sanctification and holiness. "To be spiritually-minded is life and peace": it leads to, produces, and regulates the outward conversation, so that it is such as "becometh the Gospel of Christ". This is external: and by an open walking in the paths of holiness, as marked out in the written Word, evidence is given that such **are** renewed in the spirit of their mind. This is farther evidenced by putting on "the new man" which after God is "created in righteousness and true holiness". And, the new man being put on, the faculties of it with the graces and gifts bestowed are exercised, as our own cases, the good of others, and the glory of God require, and as the latter may be promoted thereby.

On the oneness of believers with Christ, and their actual communion with Him, all those exhortations, which are given in the Scriptures for **practical** sanctification and holiness, are built. Hence John speaks thus, "He that saith he abideth in Him ought himself also to walk, even as He walked". Peter saith, "As He who hath called you is holy, so be ye holy in all manner of conversation. Because it is written, Be ye holy for I am holy". Paul says, "Follow peace with all men, and holiness, without which no man shall see the Lord". In his epistle to the Colossians he most sweetly excites believers to be exercised of their graces in an outward manifestative way towards each other: **see** Col. 3:12-17. The Holy Spirit puts life into these exhortations which are perfectly spiritual and evangelical; and applies and makes them effectual to the sanctified in Christ Jesus. He draws their minds off all other considerations, and fixes them on Christ and spiritual things. He sweetly inclines their wills, and most powerfully influences them to the putting on of the new man, as their proper garment, in the exercise of every grace in their walk before God and man.

O my soul! meditate on this subject. Seek for a growing acquaintance with it, that thou mayest live, think, speak, and act under the influence of it, and turn the whole of it for thyself into prayer. O God, the Spirit! Thou art essential in Thy personality and co-equality with the Father and the Son, the one living and incomprehensible Jehovah. Thou art, in Thy covenant office and work, God the sanctifier, the Spirit of life, of holiness, of Christ, and glory. Thou hast conveyed life to my soul from Christ the fountain of it; in whom all the springs of it are contained. Thou hast separated me by Thy holy and effectual calling to the Lord. Thou hast made me a new creature in Christ Jesus. Thou hast wrought in it all spiritual graces, and implanted therein all the seeds and principles of holiness and life everlasting. Shine, Holy Spirit! on Thy own work in my soul. Draw forth Thy grace implanted in me into constant act and exercise. Give me a clear view and apprehension of my union with Christ, and of my state in Him; and lead me into fellowship with Him in the blessings, benefits, and glories of His resurrection. As Christ is the life of all my grace and spirituality, teach me how to live continually **on Him**, that I may in all things live **to Him**.

Do Thou, O Holy Spirit! strengthen what Thou hast wrought in me. Quicken, lead, guide, and continually influence me; that God in Christ may **in me** and **by me** be glorified **in all things.** Sanctify my will by the belief of the truth. Enable me to exercise every grace, that I may so walk in Thy good ways, that sinners may have no evil thing justly to say against me, that saints may be edified, and Christ magnified. O, Holy Father! I believe Thou dost, as the God of peace, (who art at peace with all Thou seest in the Beloved through the blood of His cross) sanctify Thy church by the blood of Thy Son and the grace of Thy Spirit, I beseech Thee to sanctify me wholly in spirit and soul and body. Keep me blameless in life, temper and conversation unto the coming of Christ to receive me to His everlasting embraces. In health, in sickness, in life, and in death, let me be wholly devoted to Thee. And the praise shall be given to Thee, O Thou Holy and Eternal Three! Amen.

—S. E. PIERCE, 1804.

PROFITING FROM THE WORD

1. The Scriptures and Sin.

There is grave reason to believe that much Bible-reading and Bible-study of the last few years has been of no spiritual profit to those who engaged in it. Yea, we go farther: we greatly fear that in many instances it has proved a curse rather than a blessing. This is strong language we are well aware, yet no stronger than the case calls for. Divine gifts may be mis-used, and Divine mercies abused. That this has been so in the present instance is evident by the fruits produced. Even the natural man may (and often does) take up the study of the Scriptures with the same enthusiasm and pleasure as he might one of the sciences. Where this is the case, his store of knowledge is increased, and so also is his pride. Like a chemist engaged in making interesting experiments, the intellectual searcher of the Word is quite elated when he makes some discovery in it; but the joy of the latter is no more spiritual than would be that of the former. So too, just as the successes of the chemist generally increases his sense of self-importance and causes him to look with disdain upon others more ignorant than himself, such, alas, is often the case, with those who have investigated the subjects of Bible-numerics, typology, prophecy, etc.

The Word of God may be taken up from varied motives. Some read it to satisfy their literary pride. In certain circles it has become both the respectable and popular thing to obtain a general acquaintance with the contents of the Bible, simply because it is regarded as an educational defect to be ignorant thereof. Some read it to satisfy their sense of curiosity, as they might any other book of note. Others read it to satisfy their sectarian pride. They consider it a duty to be well-versed in the particular tenets of their own denomination, and so search eagerly for proof-texts in support of "**our** doctrines". Yet others read it for the purpose of being able to argue successfully with those who differ from them. But in all this there is no thought of **God**, no yearning for **spiritual** edification, and therefore no real benefit to the **soul**.

Of what, then, does a true profiting from the Word consist? Does not 2 Tim. 3:16, 17 furnish a clear answer to our question? There we read, "All Scripture is given by inspiration of God, and is profitable for doctrine, for reproof, for correction, for instruction in righteousness: that the man of God may be perfect, thoroughly furnished unto all good works". Observe what is here omitted: the Holy Scriptures are given us not for intellectual gratification and carnal speculation, but to furnish unto "all good works", and that, by teaching, reproving, correcting us. Let us endeavour to amplify this by the help of other passages.

1. An individual is spiritually profited when the Word **convicts him of sin**. This is its first office: to reveal our depravity, to expose our vileness, to make known our wickedness. A man's moral life may be irreproachable, his dealings with his fellows, faultless; but when the Holy Spirit applies the Word to his heart and conscience, opening his sin-blinded eyes to see his relation and attitude **to God**,

he cries "Woe is me, for I am undone". It is in this way that each truly saved soul is brought to realize his need of Christ. They that are whole need not a physician, but they that are sick". Yet it is not until the Spirit applies the Word in Divine power that any individual is made to feel he **is** sick, sick unto death.

Such conviction that brings home to the heart the awful ravages which sin has wrought in the human constitution, is not to be restricted to the initial experience which immediately precedes conversion. Each time that **God** blesses His Word to my heart, I am made to feel how far, far short I come of the standard which He has set before me, namely, "Be ye holy in **all** manner of deportment" (1 Peter 1:15). Here then, is the first test to apply: as I read of the sad failures of different ones recorded in Scripture, does it make me realize how sadly like unto them **I** am? As I read of the blessed and perfect life of Christ, does it make me recognize how terribly unlike Him I am?

2. An individual is spiritually profited when the Word works in him **sorrow for sin**. Of the stony-ground hearer it is said, he "heareth the Word and anon with **joy** reviveth it, yet hath he no root in himself" (Matt. 13:20, 21); but of those who were convicted under the preaching of Peter, it is recorded, "they were **pricked** in their hearts" (Acts 2:37). The same contrast exists today. Many will listen to a flowery sermon or an address on "Dispensational truth" that displays the oratorical powers or exhibits the intellectual skill of the speaker, but which, usually, contains no searching application to the conscience, and it is received with approbation; but no one is humbled before God or brought into a closer walk with Him through it. But let a faithful servant of the Lord (who by grace, is not seeking to acquire a reputation for his "brilliance") bring the teaching of Scripture to bear upon character and conduct, exposing the sad failures of even the best of God's people, and though the crowd will despise the messenger, the truly regenerate will be thankful for the message which causes them **to** mourn before God and cry "O wretched man that I am". So it is in the private reading of the Word. It is when the Holy Spirit applies it in such a way that I am made to see **and feel** my inward corruptions, that I am really being blest.

What a word is that in Jer. 31:19: "After that I was instructed, I smote upon my thigh: I was ashamed, yea, even confounded"! Do you, my reader, know anything of such an experience? Does your study of the Word produce a broken heart and lead to an **humbling** of yourself before God? Does it convict you of your sins in such a way that you are brought to **daily** repentance before Him? The paschal lamb had to be eaten with "bitter herbs" (Ex. 12:8); so as we really feed on the Word, the Holy Spirit makes it "bitter" to us **before** it becomes sweet to our taste. Note the order in Rev. 10:8, "And I went unto the angel, and said unto him, Give me the little book. And he said unto me, Take, and eat it up; and it shall make thy belly bitter, but it shall be in thy mouth sweet as honey". This is ever the experimental order: there must be "mourning" before "comfort" (Matt. 5:4). Humbling before exalting (1 Peter 5:6).

3. An individual is spiritually profited when the Word leads to **confession of sin**. The Scriptures are profitable for "reproof" (2 Tim. 3:16), and an honest soul will acknowledge its faults. Of the carnal it is said, "For every one that doeth evil hateth the light, neither cometh to the light lest his deeds should be reproved" (John 3:20). "God be merciful to me the sinner" is the first cry of a renewed heart, and every time we are "quickened" by the Word (Psa. 119), there is a fresh revealing to us and a fresh owning by us of our transgressions before God. "He that covereth his sins shall not prosper: but whoso confesseth and forsaketh them shall have mercy" (Prov. 28:13). There can be no spiritual prosperity or fruitfulness (see Psa. 1:3) while we conceal within our breasts our guilty secrets; only as they are freely owned before God, and that, in detail, shall we enjoy His mercy.

There is no real peace for the conscience and no rest for the heart while we carry the burden of unconfessed sin. Relief comes when it is fully unbosomed to God. Mark well the experience of David, "When I kept silence, my bones waxed old through my roaring all the day long. For day and night Thy hand was heavy upon me: my moisture is turned into the drought of summer" (Psa. 32:4, 5). Is this figurative but forceible language unintelligible to you? Or does your own spiritual history explain it? Ah, there is many a verse of Scripture which no commentary, save that of personal experience, can satisfactorily interpret. Blessed indeed is the immediate sequel here: "I acknowledged my sin unto Thee, and mine iniquity have I not hid. I said, I will confess my transgressions unto the Lord: and Thou **forgavest** the iniquity of my sin" (Psa. 32:5).

4. An individual is spiritually profited when the Word produces in him **a deeper hatred of sin**. "Ye that love the Lord, hate evil" (Psa. 97:10). "We cannot love God without hating that which He hates. We are not only to avoid evil, and refuse to continue in it, but we must be in arms against it, and bear towards it a hearty indignation" (Mr. C. H. Spurgeon). One of the surest tests to apply to a profest conversion is the heart's attitude toward sin. Where the principle of holiness has been planted, there will necessarily be a loathing of all that is unholy. If our hatred of evil be genuine, we are thankful when the Word reproves even the evil which we suspected not.

This was the experience of David: "Through Thy precepts I get understanding: therefore I hate every false way" (Psa. 119:104). Observe well, it is not merely I "abstain from", but "I hate"; not only "some", or "many", but "every false way"; and not only "every evil", but "every **false** way". "Therefore I esteem all Thy precepts concerning all things to be right, and I hate every false way" (Psa. 119:128). But it is the very opposite with the wicked: "Seeing thou hatest instruction, and castest My words behind thee" (Psa. 50:17). In Prov. 8:13 we read, "The fear of the Lord is to hate evil", and this godly fear comes through reading of the Word: see Deut. 17:18, 19. Rightly has it been said, "Till sin be hated, it cannot be mortified; you will never cry against it, as the Jews did against Christ, Crucify it. crucify it till sin be really abhorred as He was" (E. Reyner 1635).

5. An individual is spiritually profited when the Word causes **a forsaking of sin**. "Let every one that nameth the name of Christ depart from iniquity" (2 Tim. 2:19). The more the Word is read with the definite object of discovering what is pleasing and what is displeasing to the Lord, the more will His will become known; and if our hearts are right with Him, the more will our ways be conformed thereto. There will be a **walking** "in the Truth" (3rd John 4). At the close of 2 Cor. 6 some precious promises are given to those who separate themselves from unbelievers. Observe, there, the **application** which the Holy Spirit makes of them. He does not say, "Having these promises be comforted and become complacent thereby"; but, "Having these promises, dearly beloved, let us

cleanse ourselves from all filthiness of the flesh and spirit" (2 Cor. 7:1).

"Now ye are **clean** through the Word which I have spoken unto you" (John 15:3). Here is another important rule by which I should frequently test myself: is the reading and studying of God's Word producing a **purging** of my ways? Of old the question was asked, "Wherewithal shall a young man cleanse his way? and the Divine answer is, "by taking heed thereto according to Thy Word". Yes, not simply by reading, believing, or memorising it, but by the personal application of the Word to my "way". It is by "taking heed" to such exhortations as **"flee fornication"** (1 Cor. 6:18), **"flee** from idolatry" (1 Cor. 10:14), **"flee** these things" —a covetous love of money (1 Tim. 6:11). **"flee** also youthful lusts" (2 Tim. 2:22), that the Christian is brought into practical separation from evil; for sin has not only to be "confessed", but **"forsaken"** (Prov. 28:13).

6. An individual is spiritually profited when the Word **fortifies against sin**. The Holy Scriptures are given to us not only for the purpose of revealing our innate sinfulness, and the many, many ways in which we "come short of the glory of God" (Rom. 3:23), but also to teach us how to obtain deliverance from sin, how to be kept from displeasing God. "Thy Word have I hid in mine heart, that I **might not sin** against Thee" (Psa. 119:11). This is what each of us is required to do: "Receive, I pray thee, the law from His mouth, and lay up His words in thine heart" (Job 22:22). It is particularly the commandments, the warnings, the exhortations, we need to make our own and treasure: to memorize them, meditate upon them, pray over, and put into practice. The only effective way of keeping a plot of ground from being covered with weeds, is to sow good seed therein: "Overcome evil with good" (Rom. 12:21). So, the more Christ's Word dwells in us "richly" (Col. 3:16), the less room will there be for the exercise of sin in our hearts and lives.

It is not sufficient to barely assent to the veracity of the Scriptures, they require to be received into the affections. It is unspeakably solemn to note that the Holy Spirit specifies as the ground of apostacy, "because **the love** of the Truth they **received not**" (2 Thess. 2:10, Greek). "If it lie only in the tongue or in the mind, only to make it a matter of talk and speculation, it will soon be gone. The seed which lies on the surface, the fowls of the air will pick up. Therefore hide it deeply; let it get from the ear into the mind, from the mind into the heart; let it soak in further and further. It is only when it hath a prevailing sovereignty in the heart that we receive it in the love of it—when it is dearer than our dearest lust, then it will stick to us" (Thos. Manton).

Nothing else will preserve from the infections of this world, deliver from the temptations of Satan, and be so effective a preservative against sin, as the Word of God received into the affections. "The law of his God is in his heart; none of his steps shall slide" (Psa. 37:31)! As long as the Truth is active within us, stirring the conscience, and is really loved by us, we shall be kept from falling. When Joseph was tempted by Potiphar's wife, he said, "How then can I do this great wickedness and sin against God?" (Gen. 39:9). The Word was in his heart, and therefore had prevailing power over his lusts. The Word had taught him the sovereign majesty, the infinite goodness, the ineffable holiness, the mighty power of God, who is able both to save and to destroy. None of us know when we may be tempted; therefore it is necessary to be prepared against it. "Who among you will give ear, and hear **for the time to come?**" (Isa. 42:23). Yes, we are to anticipate the future and be fortified against it, by storing up the Word in our hearts for coming emergencies.

7. An individual is spiritually profited when the Word causes him to **practice the opposite of sin**. "Sin is the transgression of the law" (1 John 3:4). God says, "Thou shalt", sin says "I will not"; God says "Thou shalt not", sin says "I will". Thus, sin is rebellion against God, the determination to have my own way (Isa. 53:6). Therefore sin is a species of anarchy in the spiritual realm, and may be likened unto a waving of the red flag in the face of God. Now the opposite of sinning against God is submission to Him, as the opposite of lawlessness is subjection to law. Thus, to practice the opposite of sin is to walk in the path of obedience. This is another chief reason why the Scriptures were given: to **make known** the path which is pleasing to God for us. They are profitable not only for reproof and correction, but also for "instruction in righteousness".

Here, then, is another important rule by which I should frequently test myself: are my thoughts being formed, my heart controlled, and my ways and works regulated by God's Word? This is what the Lord requires: "Be ye **doers of** the Word, and not hearers only, deceiving your own selves" (James 1:22). This is how gratitude to and affection for Christ is to be expressed: "If ye love Me, **keep** My commandments" (John 14:15). For this, Divine assistance is needed. David prayed, **"Make me to go** in the path of Thy commandments" (Psa. 119:35). "We need not only light to know our way, but a heart to walk in it. Direction is necessary because of the blindness of our minds; and the effectual impulsions of grace are necessary because of the weakness of our hearts. It will not answer our duty to have a naked notion of truths, unless we embrace and persue them". (Thomas Manton). Note it is "the **path** of Thy commandments": not a self-chosen course, but a definitely-marked one; not a public "road", but a private and narrow "path"!

There are other ways of being spiritually profited from God's Word than those we have named, and some of them we hope to consider, D. V. in a future article. But let both writer and reader honestly and diligently seek to measure himself, as in the presence of God, by the seven things here enumerated. Has your study of the Bible made you more humble or more proud—proud of the knowledge you have acquired? Has it raised you in the estimate of your fellow-men, or has it led you to take a lower place before God? Has it produced in you a deeper abhorrence and loathing of self, or has it made you more complacent? Has it caused those you mingle with, or perhaps teach, to **say,** I wish I had your **knowledge** of the Bible; or does it cause them to **pray,** Lord give me the faith, the grace, the **holiness,** Thou has granted to my friend or teacher? "Meditate upon these things; give thyself wholly to them; that thy profiting **may appear** to all" (1 Tim. 4:15).

—ARTHUR W. PINK.

FILLED VESSELS

Yes, this is the great need of the present hour—"filled vessels". The Church needs them: the world needs them. Many times in Scripture we read of "filled vessels", and the filling is always significant and important. No one would attempt to water a horse out of an empty bucket or feed him out of an empty sack, and the attempt to meet the requirements of the Church and world out of empty vessels is just as futile. Yet empty vessels are necessary, and in a spiritual sense the great difficulty is to find them empty. If they are kept full of pride, vanity, selfishness, or worldliness, they cannot be filled with that which is good. They **must be emptied in order to be filled.**

In the days of Elisha empty vessels were needed, but he never for one moment expected to meet the need of the creditor from empty vessels. He asked for them in order that they might be filled. Perhaps a little consideration of this subject may be profitable and opportune, especially so in view of the widespread desire for another Pentecost ere the Church is taken home. There does appear to be a burning desire in many hearts today for a real and extensive work of God such as has been going on locally in Wales, and we are persuaded that the first demand is for filled vessels. Thousands who have not been permitted to see the grace of God in Wales have rejoiced unfeignedly over it, and are longing now that it may become world-wide. Many of the vessels used there have been small and insignificant from a worldly or popular point of view, but we doubt not they have all been "filled", and that is our one point just now.

Let us, then, turn to 2 Kings 4 with the desire to learn an important lesson. Here we read of a certain woman of the wives of the sons of the prophets who in her distress cried to Elisha for help. Her statement is very melancholy, yet we fear it may, but too truly typify the spiritual condition of many today. To Elisha she says: "Thy servant my husband is dead; and thou knowest that thy servant did fear the Lord: and the creditor is come to take unto him my two sons to be bondmen". Death in the house is bad enough, especially when it is the "head" that is taken, but to lose the sons as bondmen also would indeed add sorrow to sorrow. However, she did the wisest and best thing under the circumstances in appealing to Elisha, for his name means "God that saves", and this was about to be made good in her case. In verse 2 Elisha asks: "What shall I do for thee? tell me, what hast thou in the house? And she said, Thine handmaid hath not anything in the house, save a pot of oil". To this he replies, "Go borrow thee vessels abroad of all thy neighbours, even empty vessels;

borrow not a few. And when thou art come in, thou shalt shut the door upon thee and upon thy sons, and thou shalt pour out into all those vessels, and thou shalt **set aside that which is full.**"

Here we get some important and interesting lessons. First we have the law and grace in contrast. The law, typified in the creditor, demands even of a widow, and is prepared to lay hold with its iron hand: while grace, manifested in Elisha—or "God that saves"—is prepared to give expecting nothing in return. This is ever true of law and grace. One demands (Matt. 12:35-40), the other gives (Rom. 5:21; Matt. 11:28; John 3:16, etc.); therefore they must never be confounded. The poverty of the woman is seen here in that, in reply to Elisha's question, she is only able to speak of possessing a single pot of oil. Thank God, she had that much! for it was enough for the divine purpose; and thank God the single pot is possessed by every true believer. She had that which typified the Holy Spirit, while we have the antitype Himself (Rom. 8:9; 1 Cor. 3:16, etc.). She is next told to borrow vessels of her neighbours, empty vessels, and **borrow not a few**. Here reason might have stepped in and asked, What is the use of empty vessels? The demands of the creditor cannot be met from empty vessels? Certainly not, neither can the needs and demands of the great harvest-field today be met by such things. Where God does find an empty vessel, He is prepared to fill it out of His own infinite fulness, but in order to do this the vessel must be surrendered to Him (Rom. 12:1).

From the one pot of oil the woman is instructed to "pour into all the vessels and **set aside that which is full**" (v. 4). Here again, reason is not allowed to act, for she might have said, One vessel cannot fill all these, and this, of course, in a natural way would have been true. Thank God, she arose above nature and obeyed the prophet, as the disciples obeyed the Lord in carrying the bread to the hungry multitude. According to her faith she borrowed, and by faith she poured out from her own little vessel until all were filled; **then the oil stayed**. Elisha now says: "Go sell the oil, and pay thy debt, and live thou and thy children of the rest".

We get here two divine principles of immense importance. The first is that from the filled vessels her need was met and the creditor satisfied: the second is that when God supplies the need He does it exceedingly abundantly. These principles are manifest through the woman and Elijah (1 Kings 17), the servants and the waterpots (John 2), the disciples and the multitude (Matt. 14), and are displayed to the full on the divine side of Calvary. Here the infinite resources of our God are seen, the love of His heart is told out, and human need met to the uttermost. When He undertakes there is enough and more than enough to meet the creditor. From the abundance of His supply the family is provided for, the disciples are fed, and their unbelief rebuked. Ruth ate of the portion Boaz gave her at meal time, and was **sufficed and left thereof.** The portion left over after she was satisfied was doubtless used to the restoration of Naomi (Ruth 2:18). From this moment she becomes a "filled vessel" and the means of blessing to the one she had previously sought to hinder. Compare Ruth 1:8-15 with 2:22, etc.

Oh, for filled vessels today! Emptied of self-righteousness, self-seeking, self-pleasing, self-will, self-glory, "and filled" with the antitype of the widow's oil. If there is to be a Pentecost, there must be a pentecostal filling. Again and again, we read in the beginning of the Acts, "They were filled with the Holy Ghost". Their emptiness was filled out of His infinite fulness, therefore no wonder we read, "They spake the Word of God with boldness". They could not help themselves. The fountain was within and it had to bubble over. From the filled vessels the need was supplied, and it must be so today. Let us, beloved, seek to get filled like the widow's vessels, and like some whom God in His infinite wisdom and grace is using in Wales, then we shall have little relish for anything that is unprofitable. The command in 2 Kings 4:4 was, "**Set aside that which is full**", and the Lord still sets apart "him that is godly for Himself". Through such alone the need will be supplied and through Spirit-led believers alone the Lord will be glorified.

—The Witness, 1905.

If, under God's blessing, you are receiving help from these "Studies", is it not a duty to make them known to other Christians? Sample copies gladly sent.

and the victory, and the majesty: for all in the heaven and in the earth is Thine; Thine is the Kingdom, O Lord, and Thou art exalted as Head above all . . . And Thou reignest over all" (1 Chron. 29:11, 12)—note "reignest" now, not "will do so in the Millennium". "O Lord God of our fathers, art not Thou God in heaven? and rulest not Thou over all the kingdoms of the heathen? and in Thine hand is there not power and might, so that none (not even the Devil himself) is able to withstand Thee"? (2 Chron. 20:6). Before Him presidents and popes, kings and emporers, are less than grasshoppers.

"But He is in one mind, and who can turn Him? and what His soul desireth, **even that** He doeth" (Job. 23:13). Ah, my reader, the God of Scripture is no make-believe monarch, no mere imaginary sovereign, but King of kings, and Lord of lords. "I know that Thou canst do everything, and that **no** thought of Thine can be hindered (Job 42:3, margin), or, as another translator, "no purpose of Thine can be frustrated". All that He has designed, He does. All that He has decreed, He perfects. All that He has promised, He performs. "But our God is in the heavens: He hath done **whatsoever** He hath pleased" (Psa. 115:3); and why has He? Because "there is no wisdom, nor understanding, nor counsel against the Lord" (Prov. 21:30).

God's supremacy over the works of His hands is vividly depicted in Scripture. Inanimate matter, irrational creatures, all perform their Maker's bidding. At His pleasure, the Red Sea divided and its waters stood up as walls (Ex. 14); the earth opened her mouth, and guilty rebels went down alive into the pit (Num. 14). When He so ordered, the sun stood still (Josh. 10); and on another occasion went **backward** ten degrees on the dial of Ahaz (Isa. 38:8). To exemplify His supremacy, He made ravens carry food to Elijah (1 Kings 17), iron to swim on top of the waters (2 Kings 6:5), lions to be tame when Daniel was cast into their den, fire to burn not when the three Hebrews' were flung into its flames. Thus "Whatsoever the Lord pleased, that did He in heaven, and in earth, in the seas, and all deep places" (Psa. 135:6).

God's supremacy is also demonstrated in His perfect rule over the **wills** of men. Let the reader ponder carefully Ex. 34:24. Three times in the year all the males of Israel were required to leave their homes and go up to Jerusalem. They lived in the midst of hostile people, who hated them for having appropriated their lands. What, then, was to hinder the Canaanites from seizing their opportunity, and, during the absence of the men, slaying the women and children and taking possession of their farms? If the hand of the Almighty was not upon the wills even of wicked men, how could He make this promise beforehand, that none **should** so much as "desire" their lands? Ah, "The king's heart is in the hand of the Lord, as the rivers of water: He turneth it whithersoever He will" (Prov. 21:1).

But, it may be objected, do we not read again and again in scripture how that men defied God, resisted His will, broke His commandments, disregarded His warnings, and turned a deaf ear to all His exhortations? Certainly we do. And does this nullify all we have said above? If it does, then plainly the Bible contradicts itself. But that cannot be. What the objector refers to is simply the wickedness of man against the **external** word of God, whereas what we have mentioned above is what God has **purposed in Himself.** The rule of conduct He has given us to walk by, is perfectly fulfilled by none of us; His own eternal "counsels" are accomplished to their minutest details.

The absolute and universal supremacy of God is affirmed with equal plainness and positiveness in the N. T. There we are told that God "worketh **all** things after the counsel of His own will" (Eph. 1:11)—the Greek for "worketh" means "to work effectually". For this reason we read, "For of Him, and through Him, and to Him, are all things: to whom be glory forever. Amen" (Rom. 11:36). Men may boast that they are free agents, with a will of their own, and are at liberty to do as they please, but Scripture says to those who boast "we will go into such a city, and continue there a year, and buy and sell. . . . Ye ought to say, **If the Lord** will" (James 4:13, 15)!

Here then is a sure resting-place for the heart. Our lives are neither the product of blind fate nor the result of capricious chance, but every detail of them was ordained from all eternity, and is now ordered by the living and reigning God. Not a hair of our heads can be touched without His permission. "A man's heart deviseth his way: **but the Lord** directeth his steps" (Prov. 16:9). What assurance, what strength, what comfort this should give the real Christian! "My times are in **Thy** hand" (Psa. 31:15). Then let me "**Rest in the Lord,** and wait patiently for Him" (Psa. 37:7).

—ARTHUR W. PINK.

Vol. IX.   JUNE, 1930   No. 6

STUDIES IN THE SCRIPTURES

"Search the Scriptures" John 5 : 39

Copyright in all English-speaking Countries.

Editor: Arthur W. Pink, 1139 Alameda Ave., Glendale, Calif.
Hon Agent in England: Mr. A. Winstone, 2, Lennox Villas, Hewlett Road, Cheltenham.
Hon. Agent in Australia: Mr. G. Ardill, The Christian Workers' Depot.
. Commonwealth and Reservoir Streets, Sydney.

THE SOVEREIGNTY OF GOD.

The sovereignty of God may be defined as the **exercise** of His supremacy—see preceding editorial. Being infinitely elevated above the highest creature, He is the Most High, Lord of heaven and earth. Subject to none, influenced by none, absolutely independent; God does as He pleases, only as He pleases, always as He pleases. None can thwart Him, none can hinder Him. So His own Word expressly declares: "My counsel shall stand, and **I will do** all My pleasure" (Isa. 46:10); "He doeth according to **His** will in the army of heaven, and the inhabitants of the earth: and none can stay His hand" (Dan. 4:35). Divine sovereignty means that God is God in fact, as well as in name, that He is on the Throne of the universe, directing all things, working all things "after the counsel of His own will" (Eph. 1:11).

Rightly did the late Mr. Spurgeon say in his sermon on Matt. 20:15, "There is no attribute more comforting to His children than that of God's Sovereignty. Under the most adverse circumstances, in the most severe trials, they believe that Sovereignty has ordained their afflictions, that Sovereignty overrules them, and that Sovereignty will sanctify them all. There is nothing for which the children ought more earnestly to contend than the doctrine of their Master over all creation —the Kingship of God over all the works of His own hands—the Throne of God and His right to sit upon that Throne. On the other hand, there is no doctrine more hated by worldlings, no truth of which they have made such a football, as the great, stupendous, but yet most certain doctrine of the Sovereignty of the infinite Jehovah. Men will allow God to be everywhere except on His throne. They will allow Him to be in His workshop to fashion worlds and make stars. They will allow Him to be in His almonry to dispense His alms and bestow His bounties. They will allow Him to sustain the earth and bear up the pillars thereof, or light the lamps of heaven, or rule the waves of the ever-moving ocean; but when God ascends His throne, His creatures then gnash their teeth, and we proclaim an **enthroned** God, and His right to do as He wills with His own, to dispose of His creatures as **He** thinks well, without consulting them in the matter; then it is that we are hissed and execrated, and then it is that men turn a deaf ear to us, for God on His throne, is not the God they love. But it is God upon the throne that we love to preach. It is God upon His throne whom we trust."

"Whatsoever the Lord pleased, that did He in heaven, and in earth, in the seas, and all deep places" (Psa. 135:6). Yes, dear reader, such is the imperial Potentate revealed in Holy Writ. Unrivalled in majesty, unlimited in power, unaffected by anything outside Himself. But we are living in a day when even the most "orthodox" seem afraid to admit the proper Godhood of God. They say that to press the sovereignty of God excludes human responsibility; whereas human responsibility is based upon Divine sovereignty, and is the product of it.

"But our God is in the heavens: He hath done whatsoever **He** hath pleased" (Psa. 115:3). He **sovereignly** chose to place each of His creatures on that particular footing which seemed good in His sight. He created angels: some He placed on a conditional footing, others He gave an immutable standing before Him (1 Tim. 5:21), making Christ their head (Col. 2:10). Let it not be overlooked that, the angels which sinned (2 Peter 2:5) were as much His creatures as the angels that sinned not. Yet God foresaw they **would** fall, nevertheless He placed them on a mutable, creature, conditional footing, and suffered them to fall, though He was not the Author of their sin.

(Continued on Page 144)

IMPORTANT NOTICES

Please advise promptly of change of address, otherwise copies will be lost in the mails.

We are glad to send a sample copy to any of our friends whom you believe would be interested in such a publication.

Send to Mr. I. C. Herendeen, Swengel (Union County), Penna., for a list of our publications. He has published many of our books and booklets.

This magazine is published as a work of faith and labour of love. The Editor and his wife gladly give their services. It is freely sent to all who will read it. No charge is made for it.

Christians who feel definitely lead to do so, may have fellowship with us in this ministry. Those outside the U. S. A., please send only INTERNATIONAL Money Orders made out to Glendale, California, U. S. A.

CONTENTS

The Epistle to the Hebrews 122
The Satisfaction of Christ 128
Growth in Grace 133
The Cross and Self 138
Good Cheer 141
A Personal Word 143

THE EPISTLE TO THE HEBREWS

30. Melchizedek: Heb. 7:1-3.

In 2:17 the apostle announced that the Lord Jesus is "a merciful and faithful High Priest in things pertaining to God", while in 3:1 he calls on those who are partakers of the heavenly calling to "Consider the Apostle and High Priest of our profession". Having shown in chapters 3 and 4 the superiority of Christianity's Apostle over Judaism's, viz, Moses, whose work was completed by Joshua, Paul then declared that "We have a great High Priest, that is passed through the heavens, Jesus the Son of God", an High Priest who can be touched with the feeling of our infirmities, seeing that He also was tempted in all points like us (in His spirit, His soul, and His body), sin excepted; for which reason we are bidden to "Come boldly unto the throne of grace, that we may obtain mercy, and find grace to help in time of need" (4:14-16).

In the opening verses of Heb. 5 we are shown how Christ fulfilled the Aaronic type, and how that He possessed every necessary perfection to qualify Him for filling the sacerdotal office, see articles 19 to 21. But while the Holy Spirit there shows how Christ provided the substance of what was foreshadowed by the Levitical priests, He is also particular to exhibit how that Christ excelled them at every point. Finally, he declares that the Lord Jesus was, "Called of God an High Priest after the order of Melchizedek" (v. 10). We have previously called attention to it, but as this detail is so important and so little understood, we repeat: it is highly essential to observe that Christ is **not** there said to be "High Priest **of** the order of Melchizedek", but " **after** the order of", etc. The difference between the two expressions is real and radical: "of" would have **limited** His priesthood to that particular order; "after" simply shows that there is a **resemblance** between them, as there also was between Aaron's and Christ's.

At 5:11 the apostle declared, "Of whom we have many things to say and hard to be uttered, seeing ye are dull of hearing". The **difficulty** lay in the strong disinclination of man to relinquish that which has long been cherished, which nowhere appears more evident than in connection with religious things. To say that Christ was a High Priest "after the order **of Melchizedek**" was tantamount to affirming that the **Aaronic** order was Divinely set aside, and with it, all the ordinances and ceremonies of the Mosaic law. "This", as we said in an earlier article, "was the hardest thing of all for a Hebrew, even a converted one, to bow to, for it meant repudiating everything that was seen, and cleaving to that which was altogether invisible. It meant forsaking that which their fathers had honoured for fifteen hundred years, and espousing that which the great majority of their brethren according to the flesh denounced as Satanic.

The Hebrews had become "dull of hearing". They were too slothful to make the effort needed for a proper understanding of the nature of Christ's priestly office and work. In 3:1 the apostle had called on them to, "**Consider** the Apostle and High Priest of our profession", and in 7:4 he again says, "Now **consider**". The Greek word means to "ponder intensely" to "behold diligently", to "weigh thoroughly" the things proposed unto us. It is at this point so many fail: they imagine all that is required of them is to **hear** the Word of God expounded, and if anything appears to them hard to understand, they conclude it is not for them; hence, they make little progress in Divine things and fail to "increase in the knowledge of God" (Col. 1:10). And this is not simply an "infirmity", it reveals a sad state of soul; it shows a lack of **interest** in spiritual things. This was the state of the Hebrews: they had gone back.

The condition of soul in which a Christian is has very much to do with his spiritual receptivity. He may hear the best of preaching and read the soundest of books, yet if his heart be not right with God, he will not be profited. His head knowledge of Truth may be increased and his pride puffed up, but his soul is not fed, nor is his walk influenced Godwards. It was thus with the Corinthians, therefore we find the apostle writing to them, "And I, brethren, could not speak unto you as unto spiritual, but as unto carnal, as babes in Christ" (1 Cor. 3:1). It was thus with the Hebrews: the spirit of the apostle was straitened. He longed to expound to them the excellency of the glories of Christ's priesthood, but he had to pause and address himself to their sorrowful state of heart. In this he has left an example which all teachers do well to weigh and imitate.

As we have seen, at 5:11 the apostle makes a digression, which is continued to the end of the 6th chapter. It is most instructive to observe the **order** he followed. The better to appreciate it, let us review the contents of this parenthetical section in their inverse order. In chapter 7, he sets forth the official glories of Christ. But what immediately precedes? This: at the close of 6 (vv. 16-20) he presents the sure ground which true Christians occupy for having a "strong consolation". Thus, it is only as the heart is set at perfect rest before God, fully assured of His favour, of His unchanging grace, that the soul is in any condition to ponder, to appreciate, to revel in the glories of Christ. It is faith's realization of the unceasing and effectual intercession of our great High Priest within the veil, which keeps the heart in peace. The contemplation of the essential Holiness of God would fill the soul with despair, but it is turned into hope and joy by seeing **Jesus** at His right hand "for us". The secret of victory is to be, in spirit, where our Forerunner is.

And what precedes the blessed assurance which the closing verses of 6 are designed to convey to the believer? This: a call to faithful perseverance in running the race set before us; a bidding of us "be not slothful, but followers of them who through faith and patience inherit the promises" (vv 9-15) We are not entitled to the comfort which comes from resting upon the immutability of the Divine counsels while we are following a course of self-will and self-pleasing. Only those who are really walking with God have any right to the **joy** of His salvation. To talk of our certainty of reaching Heaven while out of the path of obedience, is nothing but a carnal presumption.

And what, in turn, precedes the call to a steady continuance in welldoing, to the exercise of faith and love? This: a solemn warning against the danger of apostasy (vv. 4-7). The sluggards of 5:11-14 must be aroused, the careless plainly told of what the final outcome would be were indifference to the righteous claims of God persisted in. There are some who refuse to allow that vv. 4-7 contain a warning given to real Christians against the danger of apostasy. They say it would be quite inconsistent for the Holy Spirit to so warn them, while in vv. 16-20 He gives the most absolute assurance of their security. Ah, but mark it well, the assurance in vv. 16-20 is for "the heirs of promise", and not for all professing believers. The warning is to make us examine ourselves and make sure that we **are** "heirs". This, the truly regenerate **will** do; whereas the self-complacent and presumptuous will ignore it, to their own eternal undoing.

In confirmation of what has been pointed out above, we quote the following from J. Owen: "As the minds of men are to be greatly prepared for the communication of spiritual mysteries unto them, so the best preparation is by the cure of their sinful and corrupt affections, with the removal of their barrenness under what they have already heard and been instructed in. It is to no purpose, yea, it is but the putting of new wine into old bottles to the loss of all, to be daily leading men into the knowledge of higher mysteries, whilst they live in a neglect of the practice of what they have been taught already".

At the close of his hortatory digression, the apostle returns to the precise point at which his orderly argument had been interrupted, as will immediately appear by comparing 5:10 and 6:20. Jesus was, and is for ever, High Priest. This was an entirely new doctrine for the Hebrews. Our Lord Himself had made no specific reference to it during the days of His earthly ministry, nor is there any record of it in the preaching of the apostles. Yet the teaching of both the One and the others was based upon and assumed this fundamental fact. But now the Holy Spirit was pleased to give a clear unfolding of this precious truth. It was "hard" for even converted Jews to receive. Their chief objection would be that, to assert Christ was High Priest, yea, the **only** High Priest of His Church, was affirming something inconsistent with and contrary to the Law, for He did not (according to the flesh) belong to the Levitical tribe, He was not in the line of the priests.

It is most important for us to take account of this difficulty which presented itself to the minds of the Hebrews, for unless we recognise that one of the chief objects before the apostle in chapter 7 was to **remove** this very difficulty, we are certain to err in our understanding of the details of his argument. It was not the design of the apostle to teach that the nature and functions of Christ's priesthood had no resemblance to that of the Aaronic. Far from it. He could not now contradict all that he has so explicitly set forth in 5:1-9. There he had plainly shown that the Lord Jesus **had** fulfilled the Aaronic type by Himself offering to God a perfect and final Sacrifice for the sins of His people. To this he again returns in chapter 9, where he declares that Christ had (as Aaron foreshadowed) "by His own blood entered into the Holy Place, having obtained eternal redemption" (v. 12). Let it not be forgotten that the atoning ministry of Israel's high priest was consummated **within** the veil, Lev. 16: 12-14.

In Heb. 7 the apostle proves that so far from the priestly office and work of the Lord Jesus conflicting with what God had instituted through Moses, it was the fulfilment of His own counsels as made known in the O. T. scriptures. At the same time he takes occasion to submit the proof that the priesthood of Christ was far more glorious than that of Aaron's. This he does by an appeal to an ancient oracle, the mystical meaning of which had been hidden from the Jews, yea, the very letter of which appears to have been quite forgotten by them. We refer to the 110th Psalm, which will come before us in the course of examining our present chapter.

"For this Melchizedek, king of Salem, priest of the most high God" (v. 1). At the close of chapter 6 the Holy Spirit directs our gaze into the Holiest, whither for us the Forerunner hath entered, even Jesus, our great High Priest. He now proceeds to emphasise the **dignity** of His priesthood, showing that it is accompanied by royal majesty, that it is intransmissible, and that it abideth forever. Thus our confidence in Him should be complete and entire, unwavering and unceasing. Thus too we may perceive again the immeasurable superiority of Christianity over Judaism by the super-excellency of its Priest.

"For this Melchizedek, king of Salem, priest of the most high God". The opening "For" has, we believe, a double connection. More immediately, it forms the closest possible link between what is declared in 6:20, and what is to immediately follow. There it was affirmed that "Jesus is made an High Priest **forever**, after the order of Melchizedek"; here it will be shown that thus it was ,**mystically**, with Melchizedek himself. This will be the more apparent if the second half of v. 2 and the whole of v. 3, saving its final clause, be placed in a parenthesis, reading it thus: "For this Melchizedek, king of Salem, priest of the most high God, abideth a priest continually". More remotely the opening "For" of this verse, looks back to 5:10, 11: he now brings forth the "many things" he had to say of him.

"For this Melchizedek, king of Salem, priest of the most high God". Two things are here affirmed of Melchizedek: he was king, and he was priest. Almost endless conjectures have been made as to the **identity** of Melchizedek. Questions have been raised as to what order of beings he belonged to. Some have insisted that he was a Divine person, others that he was an angel, still others that he was Christ Himself in theophanic manifestation—as when He appeared to Joshua (Josh. 5:14), or in Babylon's furnace (Dan. 3:25), etc. Others, allowing that he was only a man, have speculated as to his nationality, family connections, and so on. But as the Holy Spirit has not seen fit to give us any information on these points, we deem it irreverence (Deut. 29:29) to indulge in any surmises thereon.

The first time Melchizedek is brought before us on the pages of Holy Writ is in Gen. 14. There he confronted Abraham, without introduction, in the land of Canaan. At that time all the world had fallen into the grossest of idolatry and the most awful immorality: Rom. 1:19-31. Even the progenitors of Abraham worshipped false gods: Josh. 24:2. At that time Canaan was inhabited chiefly by the Sodomites on the one hand (Gen. 13), and by the Amorites (Gen. 15:16) on the other. Yet, in the very midst of these people who were sinners above others,

God was pleased to raise up a man who was an illustrious type of Christ! A signal instance was this of the absolute sovereignty of God. He can raise up instruments for His service and unto His glory, when, where, and as it pleases Him. He can raise up the greatest light in the midst of the greatest darkness: Matt. 4:16.

Melchizedek was "king of Salem": in the light of Psa. 76:2 there can be no doubt but what this was the earlier or original name for Jerusalem: "In Salem also is His tabernacle, and His dwelling-place in Zion". Only **Jerusalem** can there be intended. Further, Melchizedek was "priest of the most high God", and this in the days of Abraham! Thus, Jerusalem had a king many centuries before David, and God had a priest which He owned long ere Aaron was called! It has been rightly pointed out that, "The argument of the apostle, deducing and illustrating the superiority of Christ's priesthood over the Aaronic, from and by the relation of Melchizedek to the Levitical priesthood, is in some respects analogous to the argument of the apostle with regard to the law, and its parenthetical and inferior position, as compared with the Gospel . . . the Jews were shocked when the apostle Paul taught that it was not necessary for the Gentiles to observe the law; that for the new covenant church the law of Moses was no longer the rule and form of life. And therefore the apostle in his epistle to the Galatians, tells them that the law was given four hundred years after the promise had been made unto Abraham, and that therefore there was no injustice, and no inconsistency, in the bringing in of a new dispensation, which was in fact only a return in a fuller and more perfect manner to that which was from the beginning in the mind of God" (A. Saphir).

There is, indeed, a still closer analogy than has been pointed out by Mr. Saphir between Paul's argument in Heb. 7 and that which he used to the Galatians. Melchizedek was the king-priest of Jerusalem. Now in Gal. 4:26 we are told that, "Jerusalem which is above, is free, which is the mother of us all". The word "above" there has misled almost all of the commentators. The primary reference is not to location, but to **time**; it is antithetical from "now is", **not**, from "below"! In the immediate context the apostle contrasts two covenants, each of which was associated with a city. Paul there calls attention to the fact that the "promise" which God made to Abraham both preceded and outlasted the law! so too does the "Jerusalem" of the promise. Melchizedek was connected with Jerusalem before the Law was first given, and it was a type of Heaven: Heb. 11:10, etc.

It is indeed striking to discover that God's first priest was this king of Salem—which signifies "peace", Jerusalem meaning "the foundation of peace". Jerusalem was to be the place where the incarnate Son of God was to begin the exercise of His sacredotal office; moreover, it was to be the seat of His local church (Acts 1 to 15) until the significance of the type had been effected. In the history of that unique city we see the sovereign pleasure of God again exercised and exemplified, for He appoints various intervals of blessing unto places. Jerusalem was first privileged with the presence of this priest of the most high God. Afterwards, for a long season, it was given over to the idolatrous Jebusites: see Josh. 15:63, 2. Sam. 5:6, etc. Then, in process of time, it was again visited with Divine favour and made the headquarters of the solemn worship of Jehovah. Now, as for centuries past, it is "trodden down of the Gentiles" (Luke 21:24). But in the future it will again be the centre of Divine blessing on earth: Isa. 2:1-4. In like manner God hath dealt with many another place and city.

"Who met Abraham returning from the slaughter of the kings, and blessed him" (v. 1). The historical reference is to Gen. 14:18, 19. "Whether any intercourse had previously taken place between these two venerable men, or whether they afterwards continued to have occasional intercourse, we cannot tell; though the probability seems to be, that Melchizedek was not a stranger to Abraham when he came forth to meet him, and that, in an age when the worshippers of the true God were comparatively few, two such men as Abraham and Melchizedek did not live in the same district and country without forming a close intimacy" (Dr. J. Brown).

"And blessed him". This was a part of the priestly office as we learn from Deut. 21:15: "And the priests the sons of Levi shall come near for the Lord thy God hath chosen to minister unto Him, and **to bless** in the name of the Lord". The "blessing" Abraham received, is recorded in Gen. 14:19: "Blessed be Abraham of the most high God, Possessor of heaven and earth". Absolutely, only God can either bless or curse, for He only has sovereign power over all good and evil. This power He exercises directly (Gen. 12:3): yet by a gracious concession and by His institution, God also allows men to invoke blessings on others. In the O. T. we find parents blessing their children (Gen. 9:26, 27:27, 48:15, etc.), and the priests blessing the people (Num. 6:24-26).

In both instances it was **Christ** that was typically, in view. "In the blessing of Abraham by Melchizedek, all believers are virtually blessed by Jesus Christ,— Melchizedek was a type of Christ, and represented Him in what He was and did, as our apostle declares. And Abraham in all these things, bare the person of, or represented, all his posterity according to the faith. Therefore doth our apostle in the foregoing chapter entitle all believers, unto the promises made unto him, and the inheritance of them. There is, therefore, more than a bare story in this matter. A blessing is in it conveyed unto all believers in the way of an ordinance forever (J. Owen). It deserves to be noticed that the final act of Christ ere leaving this earth was that "He led them out as far as to Bethany, and He lifted up His hands, and **blessed** them" (Luke 24:50).

"To whom also Abraham gave a tenth part of all" (v. 2). Melchizedek's "blessing" of Abraham was the **exercise** of his priesthood; Abraham's paying him tithes was the **recognition** of it. Abraham had just obtained a most memorable victory over the kings of Canaan, and now in his making an offering to Melchizedek, he acknowledged that it was God who had given him the victory and owned that Melchizedek was His servant. Under the Mosaic dispensation we find that the Levitical priests were supported by the tithes of the people: Num. 18:24. In like manner, God's servants today ought to be so maintained: 1 Cor. 9:9, 10. Melchizedek's receiving of Abraham's tithe was a sacerdotal act: it was given as **to God,** and received by **His** officer in this world. This comes out plainly in the apostle's reasoning thereon in the later verses.

"First being by interpretation King of righteousness, and after that also King of Salem, which is King of peace" (v. 2). The Holy Spirit now gives us the mystical signification of the proper names used in the previous verse, which conveys more than a hint to us that there is nothing meaningless or superfluous in the perfect Word of God. Everything has an "interpretation". "In the scripture everything is of importance; we cannot read and interpret the Scripture as any other book, since Scripture is not like any other book, even as no other book is like the Scripture. The Scripture is among books what the man Christ Jesus is among men . . . These quotations and expositions of Scripture in Scripture are 'grapes of Eshcol', examples of, not exceptions to, the fruitful Carmel, whence they come. Thus who can fail to see the significance of the name Seth, who was given instead of Abel, one who was 'firm and enduring' in the place of him who 'vanished'? or of the name of Joshua (God's Saviour), who brought Israel into the promised land"? (A. Saphir).

This 2nd verse of Heb. 7 furnishes a clear and decisive proof of the **verbal** inspiration of the Scriptures. The revelation which God has given to us was not communicated in the rough, and then left to men to express it in their own words. No; so far from that being the case, every "jot and title" of the originals were given under the immediate superintendence of the Holy Spirit. "Hence the names of persons and places, the omissions of circumstances, the use of the singular or plural number, the application of a title—all things are under the control of the all-wise and gracious Spirit of God. Compare Paul's commentary on the word 'all' in Psa. 8:7, and the important deductions from it in Heb. 2:8 and 1 Cor. 15:27; on the word 'new' Jer. 31, Heb. 8:13; the singular 'seed' Gal. 3:16. What a wonderful superstructure is built on Psa. 110:4! Each word is full of most important and blessed meaning. In Psa. 32:1, 2 no mention is made of works, hence Rom. 4:6" (A Saphir).

Let us consider now the "interpretation" which is here given us. Melchizedek means "king of righteousness" and Salem "king of peace". But observe it well that the Holy Spirit has also emphasized the **order** of these two: "first" king of righteousness, "after that also" king of peace. This calls attention to another important and blessed detail in our type. Doubtless, the historical Melchizedek was both a righteous and peaceable king, but what the apostle here takes up is not the personal characteristics of this man, but how he represented Christ in His mediatorial office and work. Now the "**King** of righteousness" and "of peace" is the Author, Cause, and Dispenser of righteousness and peace. Christ is the Maker and Giver of peace because He is "the Lord our righteousness" (Jer. 23:6). Righteousness must go first, and then peace will follow after. This is the uniform order of Scripture wherever the two are mentioned together: peace never precedes righteousness. Mark well the following passages:

"Surely His salvation is nigh them that fear Him; that glory may dwell in our land. Mercy and truth are met together:

righteousness and peace have kissed" (Psa. 85:9, 10). "And the work of righteousness shall be peace; and the effect of righteousness quietness and assurance forever" (Isa. 32:17). "In His days shall the righteous flourish; and abundance of peace so long as the moon endureth" (Psa. 72:7). Jesus Christ is "the Righteous" One (1 John 2:1). He came here to "fulfill all righteousness" (Matt. 3:17), to "magnify the law and make it honourable" (Isa. 42:21). He came here as the vicarious Representative of His people, being made under the law for them (Gal. 4:4), obeying the law for them (Matt. 5:17), and thus wrought out a perfect obedience for them (Rom. 5:19). Therefore are they made "the righteousness of God in Him" (2 Cor. 5:21). He also came here to pacify the wrath of God against His peoples' sins (Eph. 2:3) to be a propitiation (Rom. 3:25), to "make peace through the blood of His cross" (Col. 1:20). Hence we are told, "Therefore being justified by faith we have peace with God through our Lord Jesus Christ" (Rom. 5:1).

How minutely accurate, then, how Divinely perfect was the type! The very word Melchizedek means "King of righteousness", while the name of his capitol signifies "peace". Well did J. Owen remark: "I am persuaded that God Himself, by some providence of His, or other intimation of His mind, gave that name of 'peace' first unto that city, because there He designed not only to rest in His typical worship for a season, but also in the fulness of time, there to accomplish the great work of peace-making between Himself and mankind. . . Wherefore our apostle doth justly argue from the signification of those names which were given, both to the person and place, by divine authority and guidance, that they might teach and fore-signify the things whereunto by him they are applied".

Christ is not only the Producer of righteousness and the Maker and Giver of peace, but He is also the **King** of both. All authority has been given to Him in heaven and in earth (Matt. 28:18). He is, even now, upholding all things by the word of His power (Heb. 1:3). He is expressly declared to be "the blessed and only Potentate, the King of kings and Lord of lords" (1 Tim. 6:15). In the Millennium this will be openly demonstrated here upon earth. Then it will appear to all that He is a **righteous** Branch, for as King He shall "reign and prosper, and shall execute judgment and justice in the earth" (Jer. 23:5), and, as Isa. 9:7 tells us, "Of the increase of His government **and peace** there shall be no end". Meanwhile, faith views Him today as King, King of righteousness and King of peace.

"Without father, without mother, without pedigree, having neither beginning of days, nor end of life; but made like unto the Son of God" (v. 3). Up to this point everything has been plain and simple, but here, judging from the labourious strugglings of most expositors, we enter deep water. Yet, in reality, it is not so. Men, as usual, have created their own difficulty; and, as is generally the case, they have done so through ignoring the immediate context. Had these statements in v. 3 referred to him as a **man**, it would surely be quite impossible to understand them. But it is not as man he is referred to, but as **priest**. Once this is clearly seen and firmly grasped little or no difficulty remains.

That Melchizedek was not a superhuman creature, a divine or angelic being, is unequivocally established by Heb. 5:1, where we are expressly told, "For **every** high priest taken **from among men** is ordained for men in things pertaining to God". To be possessed of human nature is an essential prerequisite in order for one to occupy and exercise the sacredotal office. The Son of God could not serve as Priest till He became incarnate. Observe carefully how that in v. 4 Melchizedek is expressly declared to be a "man". What, then, it may be asked, is the meaning of the strange statements about him in v. 3? We answer, their meaning is to be explained on the principle of the apostle's subject in this passage.

"Without father, without mother, without descent". Now in connection with the Aaronic priesthood, personal genealogy was a vital prerequisite, hence the great care with which they preserved their pedigree: see Ezra 2:61, 62. But, in contradistinction from them, Melchizedek was priest of an order where natural descent was not regarded, an order free from the restrictions of the Levitical, Num. 3:10, etc; therefore was he an accurate type of Christ, who belonged not to the tribe of Levi. Neither the book of Genesis, nor any of the later scriptures, say a word about Melchizedek's parentage, and this **silence** was a part of the type.

"Having neither beginning of days nor end of life" is to be explained on the same principle. The Jewish priests "began" their "days" **as priests** at the age of twenty-five, when they were permitted to wait upon their brethren: Num. 8:24 and cf. 1 Chron. 23:27, 28. At the age of thirty they began their regular priestly duties: Num. 4:3. At the age of fifty their **priestly** "life" ended: "from the age of fifty years they shall **cease** waiting upon the service, and shall serve no more" (Num. 8:25). But no such restriction was placed upon the sacerdotal ministry of Melchizedek: so, in this too, he was an eminent type of Christ.

"But made like unto the Son of God", or, more literally "but assimilated to the Son of God". It is very striking to note that it is not the Son of God who was "assimilated to Melchizedek", but vice versa. In the order of **time** Christ subsisted before Melchizedek; in the order of **nature**, Melchizedek was a priest before Christ was. The priesthood of the Son of God, ordained and appointed by the Eternal Three, was the **original**, and Melchizedek's priesthood furnished the **copy**, and a copy **given in advance** is the same thing as the type. Melchizedek was "assimilated to the Son of God" as a type. First, as priest of the most high God. Second, as being a royal priest, possessing personal majesty and authority. Third, as being the king of righteousness. Fourth, as king of peace. Fifth, as the one who "blessed Abraham". Sixth, as the one who received the grateful gifts of God's people, represented by Abraham. Seventh, as not owing his priesthood to natural genealogy. Eighth, as abiding a priest beyond the bounds of the Levitical limitations.

"Abideth a priest continually" (v. 3). Note carefully it is not that the **natural** life of Melchizedek had no end, but that his **priestly** life did not cease at the age of fifty: in other words, he continued a priest to the very end of his earthly existence, which shows he had no vicar or successor, deriving a priesthood from his. "The expression 'abideth a priest **continually**', therefore, is the equivalent to saying that he had a **perpetual priesthood** in contradistinction from those whose office terminated at a definite period, or whose office passed over into the hands of others" (A Barnes). In the verses that follow, the apostle reasons from these facts and shows the superiority of Melchizedek as a priest to Aaron and his sons. This, D. V. will come before us in our next article.

—ARTHUR W. PINK.

THE SATISFACTION
("Atonement")
OF CHRIST

6. Its Nature (Continued).

The particular aspect of the Satisfaction of Christ which is now before us leads into the very heart of this wondrous theme. It is most important for the honouring of God and the establishing of our souls in the Truth that the nature of the Atonement should be Scripturally and clearly defined. Mistake at this point is fatal. Until we apprehend aright **what** it was that Christ did, we are not prepared to contemplate the design, the efficacy, the extent, or the fruits and results of it, still less are we equipped to proclaim and expound it. For these reasons we must proceed slowly and endeavour to make quite sure of our ground. The great majority of the errors of men upon the Atonement are the consequences of an unscriptural conception of the nature of it. We would therefore beg the reader to prayerfully and patiently read and re-read what we are writing on this vital phase of our subject, testing all by God's Word.

In our last article we pointed out that the atoning work of Christ was, first, a **federal** one: that there was an official union existing between the Mediator and those for whom He mediated, that there is a **legal oneness** between Christ and His people. Before the foundation of the world God's elect were "chosen in Christ" (Eph. 1:4), "promised" eternal life (Titus 1:2), and were "given grace in Him (2 Tim. 1:9). It was therefore as their covenant Head, and, because of this, as their covenant Surety, that when the fulness of time was come God sent forth His Son to transact on their behalf. All that Christ did and all that He suffered was as their legal Representative. Unless this be firmly grasped as what lies at the very foundation of the redemptive sacrifice of Christ, we are certain to err when attempting to interpret its scope and application. Christ and His people together formed one mystical Person in the repute of God.

Second, the atoning work of Christ was a **substitutionary** one. What Christ did and suffered was not only on the behalf of others, but it was also expressly in the stead of others. True, blessedly true, that His obedience and His sufferings have benefitted others, but it needs to be emphatically said and firmly held to that His obedience was performed and His sufferings were endured in the actual room of others. Christ took the law-place of His people, assuming their liabilities, became their Sponsor, and undertook to satisfy Divine justice for them. This, Christ **engaged** to do, when He accepted the terms of the Everlasting Covenant. This, Christ **came** to do, when He became incarnate. From Bethlehem to Calvary He is to be regarded as having taken the place of His guilty people, suffering and doing, doing and suffering, what the righteous Law of God required at their hands.

"When the fulness of the time was come, God sent forth His Son, made of a woman, made under the law" (Gal. 4: 4). Christ's derivation of real humanity through His mother is no unimportant matter, concerning the Atonement, for His fraternity, as our kinsman Redeemer, absolutely depends upon the fact that He derived His humanity from the substance of His mother; for without this He would neither possess the natural nor legal union with His people, which must be at the foundation of His representative character. To be our Redeemer His humanity could neither be brought from heaven, nor immediately created by God, but derived as ours is, from a human mother; but with this difference, His humanity never existed in Adam's covenant, to entail either guilt or taint. He must be within the pale of mankind. Nevertheless, Christ was "made under the law" not by the condition of creaturehood, but for the ends of Suretyship: hence the imputative value of His obedience: (Condensed from G. Smeaton).

The words "made under the law" need to be very carefully defined. "Christ became subject to the law by a special Divine constitution. He was not born under it as all men are; their subjection to the law follows upon their being the natural descendants of Adam, to whom the Law was originally given, and his being to them a representative. But Christ was not a natural descendant of Adam, nor was the first Adam a representative of the second Adam, for He was the Lord from heaven. His obligation to the law ariseth not from His birth, but He was made under it by an **appointment** peculiar to Himself, to answer a specific end, viz., the redemption of sinful men. And therefore what the law required of men, either in a way of suffering or obedience, He became obliged by this Divine constitution to undergo and perform" (John Brine, 1743), "The Certain Efficacy of the Death of Christ").

Christ was both "born" and "given" to the people of God (Isa. 9:6), and that with a view to their salvation: what He did and suffered was for the sake of and in the room of those on whose account He came into the world. Some have sought to evade the vicarious character of His obedience by arguing that as Man Christ was **under obligation** to keep the law. But this is to deny, if not implicitly yet explicitly that He was the Son of God. Great care needs to be exercised at this point. The humanity of Christ, as such. was **impersonal**, and therefore owed no obedience to the law. The God-man is **not** two persons in one: He is one person with two natures. As the Son of God He was a person before He became incarnate. In becoming incarnate He took to Himself humanity, but not a second personality. Therefore the manhood of Christ being united to the Son of God, He was not and could not be **obligated** to obey the law. It was by a Divine constitution, by covenant agreement, that He was "made under the law", with a view to the redemption and justification of God's elect.

Now the moment Christ **was** "made under the law" He entered the place occupied by His people, considered as fallen creatures. This alone explains the experiences He encountered, the degradation He suffered, the injustice He met with at the hands of men, and the punishment He received from God Himself. We harbour the most dishonoring and degrading views of God if we imagine for a moment that He would allow an innocent person to suffer, still less so that He would permit His beloved Son to unrighteously suffer at the hands of human wretches. We shall never view aright the manger-cradle, the necessity for the flight into Egypt, the labouring at the carpenter's bench, the having not where to lay His head, the horrible indignities He endured from His enemies, and the wicked treatment He received from those who passed sentence of death upon Him, till we recognise that from Bethlehem to Calvary He was the vicarious Victim of His people, that He was bearing their sins, and suffering the due rewards of their iniquities.

"No good thing will He withhold from them that walk uprightly" (Psa. 84:11) But as the descendants of fallen Adam, God's people, in their unregenerate days, did the very reverse from walking uprightly. They forsook the way of God's commandments and followed a course of self-will, and that, not occasionally, but constantly. In consequence, many good things were withheld from them. Though addressed directly to Israel, the words of Jer. 5:25 contain a principle of wide application: "Your iniquities have turned away these things, and your sins have withholden good things from you". Therefore, when Christ came here as the Sinbearer of His people, Divine justice required that He should be deprived of many "good things".

As a wanderer from the Father's house (Luke 15:13), man has forfeited all right to so much as an earthly abode, hence we find Christ taking the place of the homeless Stranger here. Inasmuch as fallen man prefers the "world" to anything that God sets before him, we find Christ carried down into Egypt (the outstanding symbol of "the world" in Scripture), and therefore did God say "Out of Egypt have I called My Son" (Matt. 2:15). In consequence of the Fall, God pronounced the following curse upon man, "In the sweat of thy face shalt thou eat bread" (Gen. 3:19), therefore do we find Christ toiling for His (Mark 6:3). Because the elect in their unregenerate days failed to love their neighbours, we find Christ experiencing the hatred of men. Because we have been guilty of gluttony, He was made to hunger. Because we have been intemperate in drinking, He thirsted. Because we have mis-used our money, He was penniless (Matt. 17:27). Because we have spoken ill of God, He was spoken against; because we have denied Him. He was denied. "Not one throb of pain did He feel, not one pang of sorrow did He experience, not one sigh of anguish did He heave, not one tear of grief did He shed, for Himself. All were for men; all were for us. If not one of His sufferings was personal, it follows that they were all substitutionary, that they were all, of course, included in the matter or substance of His atoning sacrifice. During the whole period of His mortal life the victim was a-slaying. At the moment of His birth, the sword of justice was unsheathed against the man who is Jehovah's fellow, and returned not to its scabbard till it had been bathed in the blood of Calvary.

"It may be deemed at variance with this view of the subject, that the redemption of man is sometimes in Scripture ascribed simply to the blood of Christ, or to His death alone. But such language is not to be understood as limiting the atonement of Christ to the simple act of dying, or to those sufferings in which there was an effusion of literal blood. The bloody agony of the garden, and the accursed death of the cross, were prominent and concluding parts of His sufferings, and, by a common figure, were fit representatives of the whole. They were the last portions, so to speak, the completion of His humiliation, without which all that went before must have been in vain; and may be regarded as having procured salvation, in the same way as that last instalment of a sum which is paid by degrees, may be supposed to cancel the debt and procure a discharge. But, as when Christ is said to have been 'obedient unto death', we are to understand the phrase, not of a **single act,** but of the **duration** of His obedience throughout the whole period of His life, so may it be said that He **suffered unto death,** as expressive of the duration of His suffering throughout the whole of His earthly course" (W. Symington).

It is in the closing scenes of "the days of His flesh" that we may the more fully discover Christ occupying the place of His sinful people, and receiving from God that which was due them. Even where we behold Him before men, that which transpired is to be read and interpreted in the light of His vicarious position and His complete identification with His guilty people. What took place here on earth was but the visible adumbration of the trial and verdict of the Higher Court. Take His appearance before Caiaphas and Pilate. We venture to say that all the annals of human history will be searched in vain not only for a parallel but for anything approaching a resemblance. Nevertheless, the deeper meaning of the unprecedented treatment meted out to Christ has been perceived by but few. Here, as almost everywhere else, men have been occupied with the **human** instead of with the Divine side of things. Many a writer has marvelled at the iniquitous conduct of Israel's high priest and Judea's Roman governor, and have scathingly condemned their unrighteous actions; but apparently it never occurred to them to ask, Why did **God** not only suffer, but ordain it all? (Acts 4:27, 28).

The Romans were renowned for their respect for law, the equity of their dealings, the generosity with which they treated those whom they conquered. How then is Pilate's unjust treatment of Christ to be accounted for? True, from the human side, he feared that if he resisted the demands of the Jewish leaders, a complaint would be made to Caesar, and then he would probably lose his position. Nevertheless, this still leaves unsolved the deeper and more important question: Why should **God** require His Son to be mocked by submitting to a trial which appears to us worse than a farce, really, a travesty of justice? We submit that one consideration alone supplies the key to this mighty problem, and that, the twofold relation which Christ sustained:—personally innocent, officially guilty; in Himself, without sin, by virtue of His identification with His people, "made sin". It was the Sinner who was arraigned for sentence. "He was (judicially) **reckoned** (by God) among the transgressors" (Luke 22:37): this applies equally to His trial, His buffetings in the judgment-hall, and His actual crucifixion. John 18:8 proves this: If the Representative be seized, then those whom He represented **must** go free.

As the Substitute of His sinful people, Christ had to be found innocent and yet pronounced guilty! Though personally spotless, Divine justice required that He should be dealt with as officially deserving of condemnation. What occurred in Jerusalem was but the **visible** expression of the great Assize which had been held in Heaven. The sentence pronounced by the human judges was but the intimation or announcement of the sentence which had been passed by the Divine Judge upon the Sin-bearer. Christ hid not His face from shame and spitting. Why? Because as guilty criminals, as convicted outlaws, as the vilest of wretches, **that** is what our sins deserved. When before His accusers, He was "dumb", making no reply to the charges brought against Him (Matt. 26:60). Why? Because though **personally** innocent, He occupied the place of **guilty** sinners, therefore was there nothwhich He could adduce in extenuation.

A marvelous flood of light does this throw upon the Gospel narratives. The charge which was laid against Christ as He stood before the Sanhedrin, as brought against **those whom He represented**, was not false! Guilty of blasphemy against God each of us most certainly is. Therefore as the official Representative of His sinful people, the Lord Jesus stood silent, putting in no plea to arrest judgment. So true was the accusation **against us**, there was no need of witnesses (Matt. 26:65)! We say again, the earthly court, dealing with the charge of blasphemy, or dishonour done to the name and word of God, and in sentencing to death our Surety, was the pronouncement on **our** sins, much in the same way as the shadow on the sundial registers the movements which are taking place in another sphere! Christ's holy person was there in the room of guilty persons, and the human judge but expressed the verdict of the Divine Judge! It was the Sinner who was arraigned for sentence. At the beginning, the Judge of all the earth had formally pronounced sentence, "Thou shalt surely die", and that sentence was now fully and finally executed, **vicariously**, on elect sinners.

It were an insult to His moral government to suppose for a moment that the inflexibly righteous and ineffably holy God would permit a perfectly innocent and pure Man to endure the indignities, the sufferings, and the sentence which Christ received. His own infallible Word assures us, "When a man's ways please the Lord, He maketh even his enemies to be at peace with him" (Prov. 16:7). Ah, it was **no** innocent person that stood before Caiaphas and Pilate; instead, it was **the sinner** who was on trial—there in the person of his sinless and immaculate Substitute. The earthly court of judgment was but the foreground; in reality it was the Bearer of sin making a **real** appearance before **the Bar of God**! Hence, there could only be one decision possible: though personally sinless He was officially guilty, and nothing remained but sentence of condemnation and the prompt execution of it. Thus may we, and thus should we **admire** the over-ruling providence of God, which caused the lower court on earth to shadow forth so clearly the action of the Supreme Court on High.

What we have attempted to bring out above is so little apprehended, yea is so completely unknown to almost all of our readers—so superficial to the last degree are the pulpit-ministrations of the best today!—that we trust they will bear with our repetitions, and even go to the trouble of re-reading what has been written. So we say again, that there is no possible explanation of that (seemingly) anomalous trial, which passed through the due forms of law and order, unless we recognise that it was a symbolical representation, yea, a Divinely-arranged tableau, of a spiritual mystery, setting forth the altogether unique, because **dual**, relation which Christ occupied. Thus was Pilate obliged to affirm the absolute innocence of that blessed One who stood before him: seven times over he declared "I find **no** fault in Him." Nevertheless, he sentenced Him to death! Christ was **personally** innocent, yet as the vicarious Victim, as the Representative of His criminal people, He was **officially** guilty. Thus, Christ was **rightously** pronounced personally spotless, but offcially condemned to death. **That** is why God caused His beloved to endure such mockery, ignominy and suffering.

> "Bearing shame and scoffing rude,
> In **my** place condemned He stood;
> Sealed my pardon with His blood,
> Hallelujah **what** a Saviour."

The passages of Scripture which expressly set forth the vicarious character of Christ's atoning work are so numerous that we can here but make a selection from them. It was predicted that, "After three score and two weeks shall Messiah be cut off, **but not for Himself**" (Dan. 9:26). Then for whom was He "cut off"? Hear the answer of God's Spirit-taught people, "He was wounded **for our** transgressions, bruised **for our** iniquities: the chastisement of our peace was upon Him; and with His stripes we are healed" (Isa. 53:5). From His own declarations we may cite the following, "The Son of man came not to be ministered unto, but to minister, and to give His life a ransom **for** many" (Matt.20:28); "The Good Shepherd giveth His life **for** the sheep" (John 10:11). From the writings of the apostles, the following may be taken as samples: "Christ died **for** the ungodly" (Rom. 5:6); "Christ also hath once suffered for sins, the Just **for** the unjust" (1 Peter 3:18); "God ... sent His Son to be the propitiation **for** our sins" (1 John 4:10).

Enemies of the Truth, anxious to repudiate the substitutionary nature of Christ's obedience and death have pointed out the word "for" is not conclusive. It **may** signify "in the stead of", or it may also mean only "on the behalf of". Thus: the soldier dies "for", or on behalf of his country. The sufficient answer to this is that though in some passages the Greek preposition "huper" is used, which also has the same double meaning as our English "for", yet there are other passages where the Holy Spirit has employed the term "anti" and this cannot signify anything else than "in the stead of". **This** is the word used in Mark 10:41, "This is My body which is given **for** (anti) you".

In the Septuagent Greek translation of the O. T. the word "anti" is used to express the setting of one thing or person over against another. This may be seen by a reference to the following passages, where "anti" is used for the words we place in bold type: "God hath appointed me another seed **instead** of Abel" (Gen. 4:25). "Joseph gave them bread **in exchange for** horses and flocks and cattle" (Gen. 47:17). "Aaron died, and Eli his son ministered in the priest's office **in his stead**" (Deut. 10:6). These passages are so clear and the scope of the preposition is so obvious that comment thereon would be superfluous.

This Greek preposition is also used in the N. T. in passages other than where Christ is in view, which define its meaning unequivocally. Take the following instances where "anti" is the Greek equivalent for the English words placed in bold type: "Archelaus reigned in Judea **in the room of** his father Herod" (Matt. 2:22). "Ye have heard that it hath been said, An eye **for** an eye, and a tooth **for** a tooth" (Matt. 5:38). "If he ask for a fish, will he **for** a fish give him a serpent"? (Luke 11:11). "Recompense no man evil **for** evil" (Rom. 12:17). In none of these passages can "anti" possibly mean "on behalf of". No, it has—except in those cases where it is used in the sense of **against**, as in "anti-christ"—the uniform significance of "in the stead of".

Thus, after a minute examination of the passages where this Greek preposition is found, we are thoroughly satisfied that we are fully warranted in saying with A. A. Hodge, "If the Holy Spirit intended us to understand that Christ was strictly substituted in the Law-place of His people, He could have used no language more exactly adapted to express His meaning. If this were **not** His meaning, we may well despair of arriving at the understanding of His meaning on any subject through the study of His words in any department of Scripture".

Though the Greek preposition "huper" has the double meaning which our English "for" possesses, that is no reason for allowing the enemies of Truth to wrest from our hands those passages which treat of Christ's Atonement, where this particular term occurs. That "huper" sometimes has **the same** force as "anti" no honest scholar will deny. That we are obliged to understand it as signifying "in the stead of" in many places, may be clearly shown and definitely established by various considerations. Take just one passage: "For the love of Christ constraineth us; because we thus judge, that if One died **for** (huper) all, therefore all died" (2 Cor. 5:14 R. V.). Here the fact of substitution is plain: since Christ died in the room and place of the "all", then the "all" are legally regarded as having died too. In other words, the vicarious atonement of Christ is reckoned as the personal atonement of the believer. It would be mere nonsense to say, "If one died for the benefit of all, then all died". Should it be asked, Why has the Holy Spirit used the somewhat ambiguous "huper" in some passages rather than the unequivocal "anti", the answer is, Because Christ not only died in His people's stead, but **also** for their benefit!

Summing up what has been before us under this second division of the **nature** of Christ's Satisfaction, we would say: The Sufferings to which the Lord Jesus was exposed, from the hour of His birth until He committed His spirit into the hands of the Father, were strictly and definitely vicarious, borne as the Substitute of His people—not only for their advantage, but actually in their room and stead. He came here as their Representative and federal Head, undertaking and discharging all their obligations, receiving in His spirit and soul and body, all that was due them. He was their Ransom, paying their debts. He was their Mediator, coming in between God and them, receiving from Him and rendering to Him, whatever was due to and from them. He was their High Priest offering for them. He was abased because of our pride. He was made poor to atone for our covetousness, He was an hungered because, we in Adam, eat of the forbidden fruit. He thirsted, because we have drunken from forbidden fountains. He died, because we were dead in sins.

Though it be an anticipation of what belongs, strictly speaking, to a later aspect of our theme, we cannot close this paper without calling attention to the clear, unescapable, and inexpressibly blessed **implication** of what has been before us. Christ not only died in our stead, He died to secure our salvation. He not only died in our room, He died for our benefit. Because He became poor, we are enriched. Because He was forsaken of God, we are reconciled to God. Because He was stripped of His garments, we are clothed with the robe of His righteousness. He was abased that we might be exalted. He came to earth that we might go to heaven. He became servant that we might be "made free". He was troubled that we might be comforted. He was tempted that we might triumph. He was scourged that we might be healed. He was dishonoured that we might be glorified. And there is no contingency or uncertainty about it. That His people should reap the benefits of Christ's satisfaction is not made dependent on their fulfilling any conditions. Repentance and faith were **purchased** by Christ for every one for whom He obeyed and suffered. Divine justice **requires** that Christ shall see of the travail of His soul and be satisfied. The law of God **demands** that its reward should be bestowed on all for whom Christ obeyed it. The very righteousness and faithfulness of God **insist** that, because the Captain of their salvation was made perfect through suffering, He **shall** bring the "many sons **to Glory**".

"Payment God cannot twice demand
First at my bleeding Surety's hand
And then again at mine.
Complete atonement Thou hast made,
And to the utmost farthing paid
What e'er Thy people owed.
How then can wrath on me take place
If sheltered in Thy righteousness
And sprinkled with Thy blood?
Turn, then, my soul, unto thy rest,
The merits of thy Great High Priest
Speak peace and liberty.
Trust in His efficacious blood,
Nor fear thy banishment from God
Since Jesus died for thee." (Toplady).

—ARTHUR W. PINK.

---

6. GROWTH IN GRACE.

Growth in grace is inseparably connected with an **increasing knowledge** of our Lord and Saviour Jesus Christ: "Grow in grace and in the knowledge of our Lord and Saviour Jesus Christ" (2 Peter 3:18). It is commonly asserted, even by some champions for the free and sovereign grace of God and doctrinal divinity, that sanctification is a progressive work in the soul. There is, say they, something wanting in our faith, hope, and love; and consequently there are increase and growth in sanctification. To which I would reply, if regeneration be at once complete, and personal holiness be the real fruit of it, then what is commonly styled growth in sanctification will be found, on the strictest examination, to be but the **fruit** of faith. In that case, though there be a growth in faith, it will not follow that it can be strictly and properly said, that there is a growth in sanctification and holiness; unless bringing forth the fruits of it in our life and walk be called by that name. To this it may be objected, that the apostle John speaks of babes in Christ, also of young men, and fathers in Christ, which evidently proves that all God's children are not of one and the same spiritual growth and advancement in the school of Christ: and that consequently there must be allowed to be a spiritual growth in real Christians.

It is most readily acknowledged that the Scriptures treat of true, real, and spiritual growth in the called people of God, which is styled in the infallible Word "growth in grace", "Growing up into Christ", etc. But though there are innumerable circumstantial differences in the cases and experiences of the called people of God, and though there is a growth which is suited to them, considered as "babes, young men, and fathers"; yet there is but one **common life** in the various stages and degrees of the **same life** carried on to its perfection by the Holy Spirit, until it issues in glory eternal. The work of God the Holy Spirit in regeneration is **eternally complete.** It admits of no increase nor decrease. It is one and the same in all believers. There will not be the least addition to it in heaven, not one grace, holy affection, desire, or disposition **then**, which is not in it **now**. The whole of the Spirit's work, therefore from the moment of regeneration to our glorification, is to draw out those graces into act and exercise, which He hath wrought within us. And, though one believer may abound in the fruits of righteousness more than another, yet there is not one of them **more** regenerated than another.

This work of the Spirit, in which our meetness for the eternal fruition of God consists, is like in all, in each, and every one, that is born of the Spirit. The babe in Christ, dying as such, is as capable of as high communion with God, as Paul in the state of glory. Because all depends on the eternal Spirit's drawing out the graces of the new creature into an actual exercise on God in Christ as his eternal joy. The regenerate soul cannot have any addition to the holiness of that new principle imparted from the Spirit to eternity. He cannot be a partaker of every grace of the Holy Spirit more completely than he is already. He **is** in Christ "complete" (Col. 2:10), and he can be but "complete" in glory. So that it appears to me to be most Scriptural to say, that though there is a **"growth in grace"**, yet none in inward sanctification and holiness.

The believer's view of his spiritual state, as a new creature in Christ Jesus, hath a Divine influence on his Growth in Grace. He should consider his heavenly Father's love to him to be without increase or diminution; as one eternal and consummate act in the infinite mind, which knows no change towards him. He should view the finished work of the Son to be his everlasting salvation, in which he stands before the throne eternally complete. He should remember that the revelation of the Father's love and the Son's redemption is once for all made and applied to him by the Holy Spirit; so that, **in all these respects**, he cannot have greater evidence than he has of his union with Christ, and of his title to all spiritual blessings in Him; and that the Father's love and these inestimably precious truths are made realities to his spiritual mind by the witness and testimony of the Holy Spirit.

This leads into an **acquaintance with grace** in its **original**:—with grace in the doctrine, influence, and efficacy; which is, as considered in God the fountain, His free, sovereign, and royal favour, wherein there is life. All the blessings flowing from it are the expressions of God's eternal delight and complacency in His beloved ones. The whole doctrine of it as recorded in the Word, is one grand display of the love and bounty of the Three Persons in the one ever blessed **Jehovah** towards the elect. It declares how freely God loved them. It sets forth how He bestows every blessing of His love on them out of His hearty good-will unto them, and how He continues the blessings He bestows with the same everlasting good-will both in time and in eternity. The influence and efficacy of Divine grace on the mind of the believer are divinely quickened and powerful; and there is a rich variety of expressions made use of in the volume of inspiration to set this forth.

The communications of spiritual and eternal life being the immediate consequence of union with the person of Christ, believers are said to live "through Him", sometimes "by Him", and at other times, "on Him"; and sometimes Christ is said to be "their life", to live in them, to be in them. Our Lord in John 6 sets Himself before us as the giver of life, and also as the giver of the bread or meat which endures unto eternal life,—as that bread which came down from heaven, the proper sustenance of spiritual life; and as sent into the world by the Father for that very purpose. The exercise and actings of spiritual life are all under His immediate direction and influence. The preservation, continuance, growth, and increase of it in its acts and exercises are wholly from Him. By His Holy Spirit He carries on all the operations of grace in the souls of His people: and as they are the objects of His love and mercy, so He fulfills in them all the good pleasure of His will, agreeably to what He hath uttered in His most precious promises. Hereby He promotes spiritual growth and vigour in their souls. It is an everlasting truth, that it is wholly impossible that a regenerate person should be kept alive to God and His Son Jesus Christ in heart and affections, let him be already favoured with ever so great and supernatural a knowledge of and communion with the Father and the Son, **unless** the Holy Spirit be pleased **continually to give** new light and life to the mind by setting home afresh with His own Divine unction, power and energy, what is known. Hence in the soul's real experience it is found, that though Divine truth dwell in the mind, yet the person is shut up, and remains dull, barren, and low in spiritual activity, notwithstanding what is already known hath been received through the channel of regeneration and from the Word and Spirit, except the same truths receive a **fresh** light, life, and influence from the Holy Spirit. If we be kept alive to God, if the Lord Jesus be increasingly precious to us, it must be owing to the Holy Spirit's opening the mind to perceive fresh glories and perfections in Him and His great salvation, and to His giving us such apprehensions of the Father's love in Him as exceed all ever before discovered.

As it respects Growth in Grace, it consists in growing into a greater acquaintance with ourselves, with Christ and spiritual things, and in growing **out of ourselves into Christ**, rooted, grounded and settled **in Him**. This will appear, if we consider those scriptures which treat of it, the promises which refer to it, and the prayers offered for it. That spiritual growth consists in growing into a greater acquaintance with ourselves appears from the case of Paul, who, as he learnt to know himself and the grace of God exercised **towards** and bestowed **on** him, styles himself "The least of the apostles", "less than the least of all saints", and "the chief of sinners". This was the fruit of his high advancement in Divine fellowship with the Lord Jesus.

In treating on this subject, Growth in grace, and in showing what it consists in, and how it is manifested, I will briefly cite some scriptures which treat of it. I will begin with Peter's words, "Grow in grace". I conceive that by **grace** here, all those faculties, graces, habits, and dispositions, which are wrought in us by the Holy Spirit, are to be understood. And to have our spiritual faculties, graces, habits, and dispositions exercised distinctly and supernaturally on their proper objects and subjects **is** to "grow in grace". What follows in the text is explanatory: "and in the knowledge of our Lord and Saviour Jesus Christ". He is the object on which all our graces are to be exercised. He is the life of all our grace. Therefore growing into a greater knowledge of Him, and of the Father's love in Him, **is** to grow in grace; for hereby all our graces are quickened, strengthened, exercised, and drawn forth to the praise and glory of God. It is of vast importance on this subject to know that all apostolical exhortations, as also the apostolical prayers on Divine record are founded on Divine promises, in which the interest of the Holy Trinity in the elect is included. Paul, speaking of spiritual growth, says to the Ephesians: see 4:15, 16.

In the above passage the relation of believers unto Christ is stated. He is the Head, and they have union and relation to Him as members of His mystic body. As in the natural body, there are supplies of nourishment and natural spirits communicated from the head unto the members by the subserviency of all the different parts of the body, to the growth and increase of every part; so from Christ, the Head of His church, there is a supply of spiritual life, strength, and nourishment administered unto every member of the body unto the increase, growth, and edification of it. Col. 2:19 affirms the same. So did our Lord in John 15:1, 4, 5. The in-being of the branches in the vine is the mean of communicating life, sap, and nourishment, from it to them. So the in-being of believers in Christ, the holy-making vine, is the mean whereby they receive that influx of light, life, grace, and influence from Him, which makes them holy and fruitful. The fulness of Christ, God-man, is for the use and benefit of His people. All those gifts and graces, in all their extent and diversity, which He received, are for their edification: see Eph. 4:13. These Scriptures show what spiritual growth **is**: so do those promises which follow. The grace of the Holy Spirit implanted in regeneration is incorruptible. It cannot become extinct. It is of heavenly extraction. Concerning which **the** Lord saith, "I the Lord do keep it, I water it every moment; lest any hurt it, I will keep it night and day" (Isa. 27:3). **How** the Lord is pleased to nourish and make His people fruitful, is set forth in Hosea 14:5, 6. "Dew" is of the fructifying nature: see also Mal. 4:2. Thus spiritual growth is wholly of the Lord.

The apostle's prayers for spiritual growth on behalf of the Ephesians runs thus; **see** 1:17; 3:14-19. For the Philippians he pleads thus: 1:9-11. For the Colossians: see 1:9-10. These prayers contain the very essence of grace. They are indited by the Holy Spirit. They are all offered up for knowledge, as the mean of increasing faith, experience, and a true walk with God. They are not presented to God for inherent grace and holiness, but for the strengthening and exercise thereof; for communion with God, for being strengthened with all might by the Spirit in the inner man, that we may have Christ dwelling in our hearts by faith, and have it exercised distinctly and particularly on Him, that we may abound in the knowledge of the Lord's will in all wisdom and spiritual understanding, so as to approve things that are excellent, and be filled with the fruits of righteousness. These are the blessings requested; of which I may boldly say, greater cannot be requested **for us**, nor can God Himself bestow greater **on us**. In them we may see what it is to "grow in grace", what promotes spiritual growth, and that really spiritual prayer is founded on our true knowledge of the persons in God, Their relation to and interest in us, and Their everlasting love and favour towards us. In the view of these Divine truths, which serve to draw out our hearts, and increase our confidence in the Lord our God, believers pray in the Holy Spirit; and, under His Divine unction and influence, enjoy such communion with God and His Son Jesus Christ, as affords them a real foretaste of heaven and eternal glory.

But although the Scripture treats of growth in grace, though the promises, which are so many expositions of the covenant, refer to it, and though the apostolical prayers show what it consists in; yet there are some of the Lord's people, in whom the essence and reality of holiness dwell, who do not perceive in themselves any spiritual growth. It should, therefore, be remembered that there is real growth in grace where it is not perceived. We should judge of it, not by what we experience of it in ourselves, but by the Word. It is a subject for faith to be exercised on. The seasons of spiritual growth are seasons of soul distress, when we are in heaviness through manifold temptations, and when we feel and mourn most on account of a body of sin. It is common for us to think, that when we enjoy most of God in a manifestative way, then we thrive most. No. When we are favoured with the clear sunshine of Divine favour, our spiritual graces and fruits are ripened; but they thrive and grow most, when we are in our own views in the lowest cases and frames.

Spiritual growth is a mystery, and is more evident in some than in others. The more the Holy Spirit shines into the mind, and puts forth His life-giving influences in the heart, so much the more sin is seen, felt and loathed, as the greatest of all evils. And this is an evidence of spiritual growth, namely, to hate sin, as sin, and to abhor it on account of its contrareity to the nature of God. The quick perception and insight which we have of inherent sin, and our feeling of it, so as to look on ourselves as most vile, to renounce ourselves and all we can do for ourselves, and look wholly and immediately to Christ for relief, and strength, are growth in grace, and a sure, and most certain evidence of it. To see more into the excellency and spirituality of spiritual truths and to prize and esteem them with an increasing pleasure, on account of their sublimity and divinity, are real growth in grace. To see more of our need of depending continually on the person, work, intercession, and word, of the Lord Jesus, is the effect of spiritual growth, To become more spiritual in worship, esteeming means more by divine quickenings, and by God-glorifying and Christ-exalting thoughts created in our minds by the Holy Spirit, and not being contented with the use of means, unless we have real communion with the Father, and the Son through the Spirit, is to grow in grace.

A young convert is much taken with his own importunity in prayer, with his own enlargements, and affections (they being very warm and lively), with the multitude of means, and the much time he spends in the use and observance of them: whereas a believer of longer standing and greater measure of spiritual growth, values those discoveries, which the Holy Spirit gives him in prayer and inward converse with the Lord, of the Father's free love, and the Son's personal, particular, and prevalent intercession on his behalf; and he is more taken with those, than with his own fervour and his own supplications at the throne of grace. There is indeed a spiritual growth in all the called people of God, suited to and corresponding with their age and state in Christianity, "as babes, young men, and fathers".

The "babes" in Christ are particularly affected with a sense and enjoyment of pardoning mercy, and with calling God, Father. Hence it must necessarily follow, that the blessings of pardon of sin, peace with God, the spirit of adoption, whereby they cry, "Abba Father" i. e., Father, Father, and advancement in an increasing spiritual perception of these inestimably precious realities, must be a Growth in Grace, such as is quite suited to their spiritual stature and circumstances.

The "young men" in Christ, whose graces are particularly active, resist unto blood, striving against sin. The glory of young men is their strength, says Solomon, And the spiritual strength of these young men in Christ is exercised in fighting the Lord's battles against the world, the devil, and the flesh; so that their growing strong in the grace which is in Christ Jesus, or their growing strong in the Lord and in the power of His might, is quite suited to their spiritual state, case, and experience. The apostle writing to these saith, "Ye are strong, and the Word of God abideth in you, and ye have overcome the wicked one" (1 John 2:14). And then he gives them the following exhortation: see 1 John 2:15-17. Their learning the use of every part of their spiritual armour, fighting the good fight of faith, weilding the sword of the Spirit, which is the Word of God, looking wholly **to** and depending entirely **on** Christ, the Captain of salvation, for strength, success, and victory over all their enemies, are Growth in Grace.

To know Christ more clearly, spiritually, and distinctly, in the eternity, glory, and excellencies of His person, as God-man, the Head and Mediator of His church, and the perfection, worth, and eternal excellency of His righteousness and atonement, is the signal honour, and the peculiar distinction of the "fathers" in Christ from the "babes" and "young men". And, as peculiarly suited to their age and state in Christianity, their Growth in Grace, in the very essential part and proof of it, consists in their increasing in the knowledge of Jesus and of the Father in Him, through the grace of the Holy Spirit, and in growing up into Christ, viz. into real and personal communion with Him, whereby they become more deeply rooted in Him, and more firmly grounded on Him. Thus by the sacred unction of the Holy Spirit leading the believer on from strength to strength, Growth in Grace is promoted, increased, and carried on in fellowship with God. Agreeably to which the apostle says, "But we all with open face, beholding as in a glass the glory of the Lord, are changed into the same image, from glory to glory, even as by the Spirit of the Lord" (2 Cor. 3:18). It is by a supernatural light shining on the Word and reflecting on the renewed mind that the believer takes in views of Christ from the Word. The glory of His person is viewed, and the believer apprehends Christ, as He is in truth, "the Only-begotten of the Father, full of grace and truth". And the beholding of Christ in the light of the Word and Spirit is quickening. It fills the mind with wonder, the heart with love, the conscience with peace, and the affections with holy delight. And the believer is hereby changed into the same image, from glory to glory, even as by the Spirit of the Lord.

In the Gospel, as in a mirror, is Christ set forth as the brightness of His Father's glory and the express image of His person. In the face, or person, of Jesus Christ revealed in the Gospel, the glory of God shines forth. Believers have a clear view of it as they in a spiritual way take into their enlightened minds Jesus Christ. He dwells in their hearts by faith; and by the Holy Spirit's thus revealing Christ in the Word **to** them and **in** them, they are changed into the same image, which consists in a conformity to Him. Yet it is by degrees; for, from our regeneration to our glorification, we are growing up into Christ. When He first manifested Himself to us He apprehended us as His beloved ones, and took hold of us, as the objects of His Father's love, to work, **in** us and to bestow all grace **on** us. And as He shines in us and reflects His glory on us, and as we take in increasing apprehensions **of Him**; so we are in a gradual way changed from one degree of glory to another. This glorious image of Christ is perfected little by little, till we come to the measure of the stature of the fulness of Christ. Paul, speaking of his own conversion to the Lord, says, "It pleased God, who separated me from my mother's womb, and called me by His grace, to reveal His Son in me" (Gal. 1:15, 16).

Paul was a perfect man in Christ on the first day of his translation into the kingdom of God's dear Son. He had a full and complete knowledge of Christ. Whereas **we**, even **all** of us, are but growing by degrees, and sometimes very slowly, into the knowledge of our Lord and Saviour. And **thus** "The path of the just is as the shining light, which shineth more and more unto the perfect day". This evidently refers to Growth in Grace, and it receives its accomplishment as the Holy Spirit is pleased to lead us into more enlarged views **of** and acquaintance **with** Christ and spiritual things, which is effected by spiritual revelation, or a new creating act of God within us; see 2 Cor. 4:6. The believer finds the reality of Divine things, and that they carry their own evidence to the mind; and by comparing his experience with the Word, which treats on spiritual growth, he hath a knowledge and spiritual perception of his own growth in the things of God. He finds, as he is enabled to center in Christ and live on Him as the fountain and spring of all his spiritual and eternal life and light, that the Holy Spirit is pleased to put forth His influential power and energy. In consequence of which, such measure of life, light, holiness, consolation and joy, are produced, as evidently manifest growth in the fruits of faith, grace and holiness. The believer's high prizing of Christ, his increasing estimation of the person of the Lord Jesus, and his spiritual desires after close and intimate fellowship with Him, are expressed by the apostle Paul in Phil. 3-8-10.

O my soul! here is a subject which requires close consideration, and should lead thee to self examination, that thou mayest know what thy real state is respecting spiritual Growth in Grace in the exercise of thy graces; and what real communion **with** Christ and growth **into** Him thou hast in thine own experience. Look up to the Eternal Three, saying, O, Thou incomprehensible, essential, and ever-blessed Jehovah, Thou God of all grace! I beseech Thee to look down from the habitation of Thy holiness and glory, and behold me, holy Father, **in the Beloved**, and help me to view and consider Thee in Thy high title, "The God of all grace". Teach me from Thy Word and by Thy Spirit what grace is. Give me to conceive rightly how freely Thou dost bestow all the blessings of Thy love on me in Christ Jesus. Thou hast been pleased to show forth Thy greatness and goodness, the exceeding riches of Thy grace, and Thy kindness toward me in Christ Jesus, in the holy Gospel. Thou hast made me Thine forever; and Thou, Lord, art become my God. According to Thine own heart Thou hast done all these great things for Thy Word's sake; and Thou hast made Thy servant to know them. Teach me, I beseech Thee, more effectually to apprehend what Thy Word promises respecting Growth in Grace. Let me view Thy promises concerning it. Grant me to mix faith with them, that I may receive them by that grace which shall enable me to live on the fulness of Jesus. Send down Thy Holy Spirit afresh into my heart to glorify Thy Son, and lead me into communion with **Thyself in Him**. O Holy Spirit! be unto my soul all that is contained in Thy own word of promise, wherein Thou sayest, "I will be as the dew unto Israel". Make fresh discoveries of Christ, as He is revealed in the Word, to my understanding. Let me, under Thy own Divine and most gracious influences grow into an increasing knowledge of His person, and into more bright views of His worth and excellencies. Breathe, O Holy Spirit, on my soul, water me every moment, and make me as a fruitful garden, whose waters fail not, that I may appear to be the blessed of the Lord. I ask it, Holy Father, for the honour of Thy co-equal Son, to whom with Thee and the Holy Spirit be unceasing praise. Amen, and Amen.

—S. E. PIERCE, 1804.

THE CROSS AND SELF.

"Then said Jesus unto His disciples, If any will come after Me let him deny himself, and take up his cross, and follow Me" (Matt. 16:24).

Ere developing the theme of this verse let us comment on its terms. "If any": the duty enjoined is for **all** who would join Christ's followers and enlist under His banner. "If any will": the Greek is very emphatic, signifying not only the consent of the will, but full purpose of heart; a determined resolution. "Come after Me": as a servant subject to his Master, a scholar his Teacher, a soldier his Captain. "Deny": the Greek means "deny utterly". Deny himself: his sinful and corrupt nature. "And take up": not passively bear or endure, but voluntarily assume, actively adopt. "His cross": which is scorned by the world, hated by the flesh, but is the distinguishing mark of a real Christian. "And follow Me": live as Christ lived—to the glory of God.

The immediate context is most solemn and striking. The Lord Jesus has just announced to His apostles, for the first time, His approaching death of humiliation (v. 21). Peter was staggered, and said, "Pity Thyself, Lord" (v. 22 mar.). That expressed the policy of the carnal mind. The way of the world is self-seeking and self-shielding. "Spare **thyself**", is the sum of its philosophy. But the doctrine of Christ is not "save thyself" but **sacrifice** thyself. Christ discerned in Peter's counsel a temptation from Satan (v. 23), and at once flung it from Him. Then turning to Peter, He said: v. 24. Not only "must" Jesus go up to Jerusalem and die, but everyone who would be a follower of His **must** take up **his** cross. The "must" is as imperative in the one case as in the other. Mediatorially the cross of Christ stands alone, but **experimentally** it is shared by all who enter into life.

What is a "Christian"? One who holds membership in some earthly church? No. One who believes an orthodox creed? No. One who adopts a certain mode of conduct? No. What, then, is a Christian? He is one who has renounced self and received Christ Jesus as **Lord** (Col. 2:6). He is one who takes Christ's yoke upon him and learns of Him who is "meek and lowly in heart" (Matt. 11:29). He is one who has been "called unto the fellowship of God's Son, Jesus Christ our Lord" (1 Cor. 1:9): fellowship in His obedience and suffering now, in His reward and glory in the endless future. There is no such thing as belonging to Christ and living to please self. Make no mistake on that point. "Whosoever doth not bear his cross, and come after Me, **cannot** be My disciple" (Luke 14:27) said Christ. And again He declared, "But whosoever shall (instead of denying himself) deny Me before men (**not** "unto" men: it is conduct, the walk which is here in view), him will I also deny before My Father which is in heaven" (Matt. 10:33).

The Christian life begins with an act of self-renunciation, and is continued by self-mortification (Rom. 8:13). The first question of Saul of Tarsus, when Christ apprehended him, was, "Lord, what wouldst **Thou** have me to do?" The Christian life is likened unto a "race", and the racer is called upon to "lay aside every weight, and the sin which doth so easily beset" (Heb. 12:2), which "**sin**" is the **love of self**, the desire and determination to have our "own way" (Isa. 53:6). The one great aim, end, task, set before the Christian is to **follow Christ**: to follow the example He has left us (1 Peter 2:21), and **He** "pleased not Himself" (Rom. 15:3). But there are difficulties in the way, obstacles in the path, the chief of which is SELF. Therefore this **must be** "denied". This is the first step toward "following" Christ.

What does it mean for a man to utterly "deny **himself**"? First, it signifies the complete repudiation of his own **goodness**. It means ceasing to rest upon any works of our own to commend us to God. It means an unreserved acceptance of God's verdict that "**all** our righteousnesses (our best performances) are as filthy rags" (Isa. 64:6). It was at this point that Israel failed: "For they being ignorant of God's righteousness, and going about to establish their **own** righteousness, have not submitted themselves unto the righteousness of God" (Rom. 10:3). But contrast the declaration of Paul: "And be found in Him, **not** having mine own righteousness" (Phil. 3:9).

For a man to utterly "deny himself" is to completely renounce his own **wisdom**. None can enter the kingdom of heaven except they become "as little children" (18:3). "Woe unto them that are wise in their own eyes and prudent in their own sight" (Isa. 5:21). "Professing themselves to be wise, they became fools" (Rom. 1:21). When the Holy Spirit applies the Gospel in power to a soul, it is to the "Casting down imaginations, and every high thing that exalteth itself against the knowledge of God, and bringing into captivity every thought to the obedience of Christ" (2 Cor. 10:5). A wise motto for each Christian to adopt is "Lean not unto thine own understanding" (Prov. 3:5).

For a man to utterly "deny himself" is to completely renounce his own **strength**. It is to have "**no** confidence in the flesh" (Phil. 3:3). It is the heart bowing to Christ's positive declaration "Without Me ye can do nothing" (John 15:5). It was at this point Peter failed: Matt. 26:33. "Pride goeth before destruction, and an haughty spirit before a fall" (Prov. 16:18). How necessary it is, then, that we heed 1 Cor. 10:12: "Let him that thinketh he standeth take heed lest he fall"! The secret of spiritual strength lies in realizing our personal weakness: see Isa. 40:29; 2 Cor. 12:9. Then let us "be strong in the grace that is in Christ Jesus" (2 Tim. 2:1).

For a man to utterly "deny himself" is to completely renounce his own **will**. The language of the unsaved is, "We will not have this Man to reign over us" (Luke 19:14). The attitude of the Christian is, "For to me to live is Christ"

(Phil. 1:21)—to honour, please, serve Him. To renounce our own wills means heeding the exhortation of Phil. 2:5, "Let **this** mind be in you, which was also in Christ Jesus", which is defined in the verses that immediately follow as that of self-abnegation. It is the practical recognition that "ye are not your own, for ye are bought with a price" (1 Cor. 6:19, 20). It is saying with Christ, "Nevertheless not what I will, but what Thou wilt" (Mark 14:36).

For a man to utterly "deny himself" is to completely renounce his own **lusts** or fleshly desires. "A man's self is a bundle of idols" (Thos. Manton, Puritan), and those idols must be repudiated. Non-christians are "lovers of their own selves" (2 Tim. 3:1); but the one who has been regenerated by the Spirit says with Job, "I am vile" (40:4), "I abhor myself" (42:6). Of non-christians it is written, "all seek their own, not the things which are Jesus Christ's" (Phil. 2:21); but of God's saints it is recorded, "they loved not their own lives unto the death" (Rev. 12:11). The grace of God is "Teaching us that, denying ungodliness and worldly lusts, we should live soberly, righteously, and godly in this present world" (Titus 2:12).

This denial of self which Christ requires from all His followers is to be **universal.** There is to be no reserve, no exceptions made: "Make not provision for the flesh, to the lusts" (Rom. 13:14). It is to be **constant,** not occasional: "If any man will come after Me, let him deny himself, and take up his cross **daily,** and follow Me" (Luke 9:35). It is to be **spontaneous** not forced, performed gladly, not reluctantly: "And whatsoever ye do, do **heartily,** as to the Lord" (Col. 3:23). O how wickedly has the standard which God sets before us been lowered! How it condemns the easy-going, flesh-pleasing, worldly lives of so many who profess, (but vainly) that **they** are "Christians"!

"And take up his cross." This refers to the cross not as an object of faith, but as an experience in the soul. The **legal** benefits of Calvary are received through believing, when the guilt of sin is cancelled, but the **experimental** virtues of Christ's Cross are only enjoyed as we are, in a practical way, "made conformable unto His death" (Phil. 3:10). It is only as we really apply the cross to our daily lives, regulate our conduct by its principles, that it becomes efficacious over the **power** of indwelling sin. There can be no resurrection where there is no death, and there can be no practical walking "in newness of life" until we "bear about in the body the **dying** of the Lord Jesus" (2 Cor. 4:10). The "cross" is the badge, the evidence, of Christian discipleship. It is his "cross" and not his creed, which distinguishes a true follower of Christ from religious-worldlings.

Now in the N. T. the "cross" stands for definite realities. First, it expresses **the world's hatred.** The Son of God came here not to judge, but to save; not to punish but to redeem. He came here "full of grace and truth". He was ever at the disposal of others: ministering to the needy, feeding the hungry, healing the sick, delivering the demon-possessed, raising the dead. He was full of compassion: gentle as a lamb; entirely sinless. He brought with Him glad tidings of great joy. He sought the outcast, preached to the poor, yet scorned not the rich; He pardoned sinners. And how was He received? What welcome did men accord Him? They "despised and rejected" Him (Isa. 53:3). He declared, "They hated Me without a cause" (John 15:25). They thirsted for His blood. No ordinary death would appease them. They demanded that He should be crucified. The Cross, then, was the manifestation of the world's inveterate hatred of the Christ of God.

The world has not altered, any more than the Ethiopian has changed his skin or the leopard his spots. The world and Christ are still in open antagonism. Hence it is written, "Whosoever therefore will be a friend of the world is the enemy of God" (James 4:4). It is impossible to walk with Christ and commune with Him until we have **separated from** the world. To walk with Christ necessarily involves sharing His humiliation: "Let us go forth therefore unto Him without the camp, bearing His **reproach**" (Heb. 13:13). This is what Moses did: see Heb. 11:24-26. The closer I am walking with Christ, the more shall I be misunderstood (1 John 3:2), ridiculed (Job 12:4) and detested by the world (John 15:19). Make no mistake here: it is utterly impossible to keep in with the world and have fellowship with the Holy Christ. Thus, to "take up" my "cross" means, that I deliberately court the enmity of the world through my refusing to be "conformed" to it (Rom. 12:2). But what matters the world's frowns if I am enjoying the Saviour's smiles!

Taking up my "cross" means a life **voluntarily surrendered to God.** As the act of wicked men, the death of Christ was a murder; but as the act of Christ Himself, it was a voluntary sacrifice, offering Himself to God. It was also an act of obedience to God. In John 10:18 He said, "No man taketh it (His life) from Me, but I lay it down of Myself". And why did He? His very next words tell us: "This commandment have I received of My Father". The cross was the supreme demonstration of Christ's obedience. Herein He was our Exemplar. Once again we quote Phil. 2:5, "Let this mind be in you, which was also in Christ Jesus". In what follows we see the Beloved of the Father taking upon Him the form of a Servant, and becoming "**obedient unto death, even the death of the cross**". Now the obedience of Christ must be the obedience of the Christian—voluntary, gladsome, unreserved, continuous. If that obedience involves shame and suffering, reproach and loss, we must not flinch, but set our face "like a flint" (Isa. 50:7). The cross is more than the object of the Christian's faith, it is the badge of discipleship, the principle by which his life is to be regulated. The "cross" stands for surrender and dedication to God: "I beseech you therefore, brethren, by the mercies of God, that ye present **your** bodies a living sacrifice, holy, acceptable to God, your reasonable service" (Rom. 12:1).

The "cross" stands for **vicarious service and suffering.** Christ laid down His life for others, and His followers are called on to be willing to do the same: "We ought to lay down our lives for the brethren" (1 John 3:16): that is the inevitable logic of Calvary. We are called to follow Christ's example, to the fellowship of His sufferings, to be partners in His service. As Christ made Himself "of no reputation" (Phil. 2:7) we must not. As He "came not to be ministered unto, but to minister" (Matt. 20:28), so must we. As He "pleased not Himself" (Rom. 15:3), no more must we. As He ever thought of others, so must we: "Remember them that are in bonds, as bound with them; them which suffer adversity, as being yourselves in the body" (Heb. 13:3).

"For whosoever will save his life, shall lose it; and whosoever will lose his life for My sake, shall find it" (Matt. 16:25). Words almost identical with these are found again in Matt. 10:39, Mark 8:35, Luke 9:24; 17:33, John 12:25. Surely, such repetition argues the deep importance of our noting and heeding this saying of Christ's. He died that we might live (John 12:24), so must we (John 12:25). Like Paul we must be able to say, "Neither count I my life dear unto myself" (Acts 20:24). The "life" that is lived for the gratification of self in this world, is "lost" for eternity; the life that is sacrificed to self-interests and yielded to Christ, will be "found" again, and preserved through eternity. A young university graduate, with brilliant prospects, responded to the call of Christ to a life of service for Him in India among the lowest cast of the natives. His friends exclaimed, What a tragedy! a life thrown away! Yes, "lost" so far as this world is concerned, but "found" again in the world to come!

—ARTHUR W. PINK.

GOOD CHEER.

"Be of good cheer" (Matt. 9:2; John 16:33; Mark 6:51). When taken together these three Scriptures set forth the rich grace of God as it meets at different stages the soul's deep need. They are as windows through which the eye of faith looks upon the sweet unfoldings of Divine love.

1. Reconciliation of the Sinner.

"Be of good cheer, thy sins be forgiven thee" (Matt. 9:2). This points back to an experience through which each child of God has passed, to a time never to be forgotten, when God in grace forgave us our sins and brought us as beggars from the dunghill to set us among princes and make us inherit the Throne of Glory. That day is past, but the results abide. Nothing can change the Divine decree: "Their sins and their iniquities will I remember no more" (Heb. 8:12). Nothing can separate us from His love, "I will never leave thee, nor forsake thee" (Heb. 13:5).

Were this all that grace bestowed, it would be much. Life knows no heavier burden than sins unforgiven. It is this which gives to death its sting, and fills the future with a "fearful looking for of judgment." The forgiveness of sins is a grace which sweetens earth's bitterest cup, robs the grave of its gloom, and gilds with glory the eternity which lies beyond. Much as this is, it is but a foretaste or first instalment of Heaven's "Good Cheer." An abiding blessing, which unlike the goods of earth which perish with the using, becomes more precious as the passing years reveal its worth. This blessing the world's wealth can never buy and human effort can never procure. It is God's gift to man, with which the poorest on earth is rich, and without which the richest is poor indeed.

According to the law of Heaven, "it is more blessed to give than to receive." So Christ hath done the better part. His joy is not measured by our appreciation of His gift, but rather by the bounteous liberality of His giving. This is indeed "Good Cheer," which brings to the sinner such blessing and to the Saviour such joy.

2. Rest of the Saint.

"Be of good cheer, I have overcome the world" (John 16:33). The portion of the saints in this life is varied; no two share alike. Upon some the favours of earth fall in showers from the hand of a bountiful Giver; with others it is not so. They are as children "born to adversity," seldom free from pain—from poverty never. Tribulation in some form is the common lot of all. "The course of this world" is against the child of God in whatever rank of life his lot is cast. He who knows best has said it:—"In the world ye shall have tribulation."

Concerning the future we have but little trouble. We know that the anchor of our soul is not cast in the shifting sands of outer circumstances. Our hope is not built below the watermark of Time's troubled sea. Our faith enters into that within the veil, and our hope is set on Him whose throne is far above the withering touch of sin, or the mightiest wave of earthly woe. It is here we are tried amid the cares and troubles of this life. Prayers unanswered, purest desires ungratified, best designs demolished, all **seem** to say "God cares not for His child." We look at the waves and begin to sink. It would be wrong to expect our rest here, or to escape the trials which are the common lot of all. But times of difficulty and bitter experiences which at the first seem like barren sands may afterwards yield good results. At the very least they serve as tools in the hand of the Master to shape and mould our character more perfectly according to the destined end.

The cutting and grinding may be hard to bear, but like the diamond, we gain by losing, and others who know nothing of the price paid or the pain endured, as they see the light of Heaven reflected on the more polished surface, will acknowledge that the hand of God has been at work. Better than this, we have been brought into closer intimacy with our best Friend; we have gained a truer estimate of His faithfulness, as we discover when the cloud lifts that He has been with us all the while.

"Peace in HIM" is our portion now. This promise is for present use. May we still say, "God is our refuge and strength—a very present help in trouble. Therefore will not we fear though the earth be removed, and though the mountains be carried into the sea" (Psa. 46:1, 2). Here may our faith rest. "Be of good cheer, I have overcome the world."

3. Return of the Saviour.

"Be of good cheer, it is I; be not afraid" (Mark 6:50). Good as it is to have peace in tribulation, there is something better. As the way is not the end, and the gift is not the giver, so the "Good Cheer" of the **promise** shall pass away in the presence of Him who gave it, as grace gives place to glory.

"BE OF GOOD CHEER, IT IS I." Here the context is instructive—each line seems aglow with prophetic light. Christ is yet "alone on the land." Not now as the Man of Sorrows despised and rejected. As Lord and King, He fills the throne amid the wealth of Heaven's glory. "His own" are still on the deep. Surely the night has come, the darkness falls, the winds are contrary, many are toiling in rowing.. He who saw through the darkness of midnight still sees. He who came treading the waves beneath His feet will come again. Above the noise of earth's strife His voice shall be heard: "be of good cheer, IT IS I." Then shall we have peace without tribulation. Fullness of joy shall fill each heart, and love's deepest longings shall be met in the presence of His Glory.

Does the darkness deepen?—it is nearer daybreak. Are the toilers weary?—rest is at hand. "Cast not away therefore your confidence, which hath great recompense of reward. For yet a little while and He that shall come will come, and will not tarry" (Heb. 10:35, 37). Then in the clear light of Heaven we shall read the meaning of earth's cross. The mystery of suffering shall yield its secret, and we shall know the **why** of every dark day.

In the assurance of this may we possess our souls in peace, knowing that even though clouds of earth's trouble may hide from our vision the brightness of the glory of things heavenly, they are but as dust from the chariot wheels. "The Lord of Hosts is with us. The God of Jacob is our refuge."

—The Witness, 1903.

a reward: Isa. 53:10-12. He was to be the Firstborn among many brethren; He was to have a people who should share His glory. Blessed be His name forever, He fulfilled those conditions, and because He did so, the Father stands pledged, on solemn oath, to preserve through time and bless throughout eternity everyone of those for whom His incarnate Son mediated. Because He took their place, they now share His. His righteousness is theirs, His standing before God is theirs, His life is theirs. There is not a single condition for them to meet, not a single responsibility for them to discharge in order to their eternal bliss. "By one offering He **hath perfected** forever them that are set apart" (Heb. 10:14).

Here then is the sovereignty of God openly displayed before all, displayed in the **different** ways in which He has dealt with His creatures. Part of the angels, Adam, Israel, were placed upon a conditional footing, continuance in blessing being made dependent upon **their** obedience and fidelity to God. But in sharp contrast from them, the "little flock" (Luke 12:32) have been given an unconditional, an immutable standing in God's covenant, God's counsels, God's Son; their blessing being made dependent upon what **Christ** did for them. "The foundation of God standeth sure, having this seal: The Lord knoweth them that are His" (2 Tim. 1:19). The foundation on which God's elect stand, is a perfect one: nothing can be added to it, nor anything taken from it (Eccl. 3:14). Here, then, is the highest and grandest display of the absolute sovereignty of God. Verily, He **has** "mercy on whom He will have mercy, and whom He will He hardeneth" (Rom. 9:18).

—ARTHUR W. PINK.

A PERSONAL WORD

"I will instruct thee and teach thee in the way which thou shalt go: I will guide thee with Mine eye" (Psa. 32:8). What a precious promise is this! How thankful Christians should be that He who, by day and by night, guided Israel across the trackless desert, is **our** God! Sometimes He conducts us through some strange and rough places, but He makes no mistakes. He is working in us both to will and to do of His good pleasure (Phil. 2:13), and, at the end of the journey each believer will praise Him for "**all** the way which the Lord thy God led thee" (Deut. 8:2).

Many of the Lord's people are unduly exercised about the future, anxious to know for sometime ahead what God has designed for them. This is wrong. Our responsibility is defined in Psa. 37:5. "Commit thy way unto the Lord; trust also in Him; and He shall bring to pass". Following this are the words, "Rest in the Lord, and wait patiently for Him" (v. 7). If by Divine grace we really heed these important exhortations, then our hearts will be kept in perfect peace, and the Lord will open up **His** way for us in His own good time and manner, and that, **without** our having to take the initiative. Until He does so, the word for us is, "Fear ye not, stand still" (Ex. 14:13). But we can no more do this of ourselves than we can create a world. **Much** earnest waiting upon God for a quiet spirit is needed.

For sometime past we have been resting in the Lord, quietly waiting for the pillar of cloud to move, mercifully preserved from all anxiety. On March 10 a letter arrived from a dear Brother in N. Calif. saying, (for the first time) that he hoped the Lord would **soon** bring us out to the Coast. On March 13 the text on our daily calendar was, "Are ye still? Be not slothful to go, to enter to possess the land" (Judges 18:9). It made a deep impression on our dear wife, and several times during the day she said, "I feel strongly that it is a message from the Lord". The same night we received a letter from a Brother in S. Calif., from whom we had not heard for over a year, urging us to come out to Glendale—a suburb of Los Angeles. Still other indications the Lord gave us that **this** was what He would have us do.

God willing we shall continue publishing this magazine. We hope to spend most of our time in prayerful study and in writing: in additions to articles, letters to many of God's perplexed and distressed people "scattered abroad". We shall continue walking in separation from the apostate "churches", for today the Lord is on the outside of practically everything that bears His name (Rev. 3:20). But we hope to conduct some Bible classes, and shall greatly value the prayers of God's people about this. Please note our new address on the front cover page.—A. W. P.

So too, God **sovereignly** placed Adam in the garden of Eden upon a **conditional** footing. Had He so pleased, He could have placed him upon an unconditional footing; He could have placed him on a footing as firm as that occupied by the unfallen angels, He could have placed him upon a footing as sure and as immutable as that which His saints have in Christ. But, instead, He chose to set him in Eden on the base of creature responsibility, so that he stood or fell according as he measured or failed to measure up to his responsibility—obedience to his Maker. Adam stood accountable to God by the law which his Creator had given him. Here was responsibility, unimpaired responsibility, tested out under the most favourable conditions.

Now God did not place Adam upon a footing of conditional, creature-responsibility, because it was right He **should** so place him. No, it was right because God did it. God did not even give creatures being because it was right for Him to do so, i. e., because He was under any obligations **to** create; but it was right because He did so. God is sovereign. His will is supreme. So far from God being under any law of "right", He is a law unto Himself, so that whatsoever **He** does **is** right. And woe be to the rebel that calls His sovereignty into question: "Woe unto him that striveth with his Maker. Let the potsherd strive with the potsherds of the earth. Shall the thing say to Him that fashioned it, What makest Thou?" (Isa. 45:9).

Again; the Lord God **sovereignly** placed Israel upon a **conditional** footing. The 19th, 20th and 24th chapters of Exodus afford a clear and full proof of this. They were placed under a covenant of works. God gave to them certain laws, and made national blessing for them depend upon their observance of His statutes. But Israel were stiffnecked and uncircumcised in heart. They rebelled against Jehovah, forsook His law, turned unto false gods, apostatised. In consequence, Divine judgment fell upon them, they were delivered into the hands of their enemies, dispersed abroad throughout the earth, and remain under the heavy frown of God's displeasure to this day.

It was God in the exercise of His high sovereignty that placed Satan and his angels, Adam, Israel, in their respective **responsible** positions. But so far from His sovereignty taking away responsibility from the creature, it was by the exercise thereof that He placed them on this conditional footing, under such responsibilities as He thought proper; by virtue of which sovereignty, He is seen to be God over all. Thus, there is perfect harmony between the sovereignty of God and the responsibility of the creature. Many have most foolishly said that it is quite impossible to show where Divine sovereignty ends and creature accountability begins. **Here** is where creature responsibility begins: in the sovereign ordination of the Creator. As to His sovereignty, there is not and never will be any "end" to it!

Let us give further proofs that the responsibility of the creature **is** based upon God's sovereignty. How many things are recorded in Scripture which were right because God **commanded** them, and which would **not** have been right had He not so commanded! What right had Adam to "eat" of the trees of the Garden? The permission of his Maker (Gen. 2:16), without such, he had been a thief! What right had Israel to "borrow" of the Egyptians' jewels and raiment (Ex. 12:35)? None, unless Jehovah had authorized it (Ex. 3:22). What right had Israel to slay so many lambs for sacrifice? None, except that God commanded it. What right had Israel to kill off all the Canaanites? None, save as Jehovah had bidden them. What right has the husband to require submission from his wife? None, unless God had appointed it. And so we might go on. Human responsibility is **based upon** Divine sovereignty.

One more example of the exercise of God's absolute sovereignty. God placed His elect upon a **different** footing from Adam or Israel. He placed them upon an **un**conditional footing. In the Everlasting Covenant Jesus Christ was appointed their Head, took their responsibilities upon Himself, and wrought out a righteousness for them which is perfect, indefeasible, eternal. Christ was placed upon a conditional footing, for He was "made under the law, to redeem them that were under the law", only with this infinite difference: the others failed, He did not and could not. And **who** placed Christ upon that conditional footing? The Triune God. It was sovereign will that appointed Him, sovereign love that sent Him, sovereign authority that assigned Him His work.

Certain conditions were set before the Mediator. He was to be made in the likeness of sin's flesh; He was to magnify the law and make it honorable; He was to bear all the sins of all God's people in His own body on the tree; He was to make full atonement for them; He was to endure the outpoured wrath of God; He was to die and be buried. On the fulfillment of those conditions He was promised

(Continued on Page 143)

STUDIES IN THE SCRIPTURES

"Search the Scriptures" John 5 : 39

Copyright in all English-speaking Countries.

Editor: Arthur W. Pink, 1139 Alameda Ave., Glendale, Calif. 'Phone: Burbank 2155
Hon. Agent in England: Mr. A. Winstone, "Shalom", Old Bath Road, Leckhampton, Cheltenham.
Hon. Agent in Australia: Mr. G. Ardill, The Christian Workers' Depot. Commonwealth and Reservoir Streets, Sydney.

THE IMMUTABILITY OF GOD.

This is one of the Divine perfections which is not sufficiently pondered. It is one of the excellencies of the Creator which distinguishes Him from all His creatures. God is perpetually the same: subject to no change in His being, attributes, or determinations. Therefore God is compared to a **rock** (Deut. 32:4 etc.) which remains immovable, when the entire ocean surrounding it is continually in a fluctuating state; even so, though all creatures are subject to change, God is immutable. Because God has no beginning and no ending, He can know no change. He is everlastingly "the Father of lights, with whom is no variableness, neither shadow of turning" (James 1:17).

First, God is immutable in His **essence**. His nature and being are infinite, and so, subject to no mutations. There never was a time when He was not; there never will come a time when He shall cease to be. God has neither evolved, grown, nor improved. All that He is today, He ever has been, and ever will be. "I am the Lord, I change not" (Mal. 3:6) is His own unqualified affirmation. He cannot change for the better, for He is already perfect; and being perfect, He cannot change for the worse. Altogether unaffected by anything outside Himself, improvement or deterioration is impossible. He is perpetually the same. He only can say, "I am that I am" (Ex. 3:14). He is altogether uninfluenced by the flight of time. There is no wrinkle upon the brow of eternity. Therefore His power can never diminish nor His glory ever fade.

Second, God is immutable in His **attributes**. Whatever the attributes of God were before the universe was called into existence, they are precisely the same now, and will remain so forever. Necessarily so; for they are the very perfections, the essential qualities of His being. Semper idem (always the same) is written across every one of them. His power is unabated, His wisdom undiminished, His holiness unsullied. The attributes of God can no more change than Deity can cease to be. His veracity is immutable, for His Word is "forever settled in heaven" (Psa. 119:89). His love is eternal: "I have loved thee with an everlasting love" (Jer. 31:3) and "Having loved His own which were in the world, He loved them unto the end" (John 13:1). His mercy ceases not, for it is "everlasting" (Psa. 100:5).

Third, God is immutable in His **counsel**. His will never varies. Perhaps some are ready to object that we read "It **repented** the Lord that He had made man" (Gen. 6:6). Our first reply is, Then, do the Scriptures contradict themselves? No, that cannot be. Num. 23:19 is plain enough: "God is not a man, that He should lie; neither the son of man, that He should repent". So also in 1 Sam. 15:19, "The Strength of Israel will not lie nor repent: for He is not a man, that He should repent". The explanation is very simple. When speaking of Himself, God frequently accomodates His language to our limited capacities. He describes Himself as clothed with bodily members, as eyes, ears, hand, etc. He speaks of Himself as "waking" (Psa. 78:65), as "rising early" (Jer. 7:13); yet He neither slumbers nor sleeps. When He institutes a **change in His dealings** with men, He describes His course of conduct as "repenting".

Yes, God is immutable in His counsel. "The gifts and calling of God are **without** repentance" (Rom. 11:29). It must be so, for "He is in one mind, and who can turn Him? and what His soul desireth, even that He doeth" (Job 23:13). Change

(Continued on Page 168)

IMPORTANT NOTICES

Please advise promptly of change of address, otherwise copies will be lost in the mails.

We are glad to send a sample copy to any of your friends whom you believe would be interested in such a publication.

Send to Mr. I. C. Herendeen, Swengel (Union County), Penna., for a list of our publications. He has published many of our books and booklets.

This magazine is published as a work of faith and labour of love. The Editor and his wife gladly give their services. It is freely sent to all who will read it. No charge is made for it.

Christians who feel definitely led to do so, may have fellowship with us in this ministry. Those outside the U. S. A., please send only INTERNATIONAL Money Orders made out to Glendale, California, U. S. A.

CONTENTS

The Epistle to the Hebrews 146
The Satisfaction of Christ 152
The Life of Faith 158
Profiting From the Word 162

THE EPISTLE TO THE HEBREWS

31. Melchizedek, Continued: Heb. 7:4-10.

The chief design of the apostle in this chapter was not to declare the **nature** of Christ's priesthood, nor to describe the exercise thereof; instead, he dwells upon the **excellency** of it. The nature of Christ's sacerdotal office had been treated of in the first half of chap. 5 and is dealt with again, at length, in chap. 9. But here he occupies us with the great **dignity** of it. His reason for so doing was to display the immeasurable superiority of Christianity's High Priest over that of Judaism's, and that, the faith of the Hebrews might be established and their hearts drawn out in love and worship to Him. Unless the scope of the apostle's theme in this chapter be clearly apprehended, it is well-night impossible to appreciate and undertsand the details of his argument.

The proof for the **excellency** of Christ's priesthood is drawn from the O. T. In His written Word God had given hints of an alteration from the Levitical priesthood, and the introduction of another more efficacious and glorious. It is true that those hints were of such a character that their signification could not be perceived at the time, for it is "the glory of God to **conceal** a thing" (Prov. 25:2), and this (in part) that His creatures may be taught their complete dependency upon Him, and that He may have the honour of **revealing** what they by mere searching cannot find out. He has chosen to make known His counsels gradually, so that "the path of the just is as the shining light, that shineth **more and more** unto the perfect day" (Prov. 4:19).

As "life and immortality", so all spiritual truth, was brought to light by the Gospel (2 Tim. 1:10). Much truth was enfolded in the prophecies, promises, and institutions of the O. T., yet in such a way as that it was in a great measure incomprehensible until God's time came to unfold them (1 Peter 1:10, 11). The great secret of the manifold wisdom of God was hidden in Himself from the beginning of the world (Eph. 3:9, 10), yet not so absolutely so, that no intimation of it had been given. But it had been given in **such** a way in the Scriptures that much was obscure to the understanding of the saints in all generations till it was interpreted and displayed by the Gospel. More than once we read of Israel's chief seer and singer speaking of inclining his ear unto a "parable" and opening his "**dark** saying" upon the harp (Psa. 49:4, 78:2). In sharp contrast therefrom, in the N. T. dispensation, "the darkness is past, and the true light **now** shineth" (1 John 2:8).

In consequence of the fuller revelation which God has made to us through the Gospel, all the glorious evidences of His grace which now appear unto us in the O. T. Scriptures, is in consequence of a **reflection** of light upon them from the N. T. This it is which supplies the key to our present Epistle. In Luke 24:27 we read of how Christ began at Moses and the prophets, expounding unto the two disciples who were journeying to Emmaus, "the things concerning Himself", while in v. 45 we are told that He "opened the understanding" of the eleven "that they might understand the Scriptures". It has been thought by some (and we deem it quite probable) that in this very Hebrews' Epistle the Holy Spirit has recorded for **our** instruction and joy the very things which the risen Saviour communicated to those two favoured disciples. Whether this be the case or no, certain it is that the leading design of the Spirit in this Epistle is to give us light on many O. T. mysteries by means of the fuller revelation which God has now made by and through Jesus Christ.

A notable illustration and example of this principle appears in the case of Melchizedek, the priest-king. That strange and striking individual is first introduced to us in the sacred narrative in Gen. 14. Then a single verbal reference is made to him again in the 110th Psalm, and nothing more is said of him in the O. T. Therefore we need not be surprised that the Jews appear to have given little or no consideration to him. It is not until he is contemplated in the light of the N. T. that we are able to discern in him an eminent type of Christ. This we sought to examine in our last article. all that we now emphasise is that the chief points which the apostle dwells upon are that Melchizedek had neither predecessor nor successor in his sacred office. Melchizedek did not belong to a **line** of priests as did Eleazar, Eli, etc. It was in **this** respect, more especially, that he was "made like unto the Son of God", our great High Priest.

The various appellations under which our Lord is referred to in this Epistle call for due attention. They are not used at haphazard, but with precision and design. In 2:9 it is "Jesus" that faith beholds—the humiliated but now glorified Saviour. In 3:6 it is "Christ", the Anointed One, who is over God's house. But in 7:3 it is "the Son of God", as High Priest, unto whom Melchizedek was made a similitude. The Spirit here jealously guards the honour of Him whom it is His office and delight to glorify. He hereby intimates to the Hebrews that though Melchizedek were such an excellent person, yet he was infinitely beneath Him whom he represented. The typical person was but man; the antitype, Divine! Furthermore, one who was more than mortal was required in order to fulfil that which Melchizedek foreshadowed: he who should be capable of discharging an always-living, constant-abiding, uninterrupted priesthood, **must** be "the Son of God"!

In the first three verses of Heb. 7 the apostle mentions those details in which Melchizedek resembled the great and glorious Priest of Christianity; in vv. 4 to 10 he **applies** the type unto his immediate purpose and design. Having affirmed that Christ, the promised Messiah, was a Priest after the order of Melchizedek (6:20), and having given a description of the person and office of that typical character from the inspired narrative of Moses (Gen. 14:), he now dwells upon various details in the type in order to establish the argument which he has in hand. That which the apostle particularly designed to prove, was that a more excellent priesthood than that of Aaron's, having been introduced according to the purpose and promise of God, it necessarily followed that the ceremonies and institutions connected with it had now been abolished.

"Now consider how great this man was, unto whom even the patriarch Abraham gave the tenth of the spoils" (v. 4). The apostle here calls upon the Hebrews to attentively mark and seriously ponder the official dignity of this ancient servant of God. The word "man" has been supplied by the translators, and should have been placed in italics. In the Greek it is simply "now consider how great this", i.e. royal priest. Think of how great he "must have been", seems preferable to "was". His exalted rank appears from the fact that none other than Abraham, the father and head of Israel, had shown him deference.

The force of the apostle's reasoning here is easily perceived. To give tithes to another who is the servant of God is a token of official respect, it is the recognition and acknowledgement of his superior status. The value of such official tokens is measured by the dignity and rank of the person making them. Now Abraham was a person of very high dignity, both naturally and spiritually. Naturally he was the founder of the Jewish nation; spiritually he was the "father" of all believers (Rom. 4). In his person was concentrated all the sacred dignity belonging to the people of God. How "great" then must be Melchizedek, seeing that Abraham himself owned his official superiority! And therefore how "great" must be that **order** of priesthood to which he belonged!

That upon which the Jews insisted as their chief and fundamental privilege, and which they were unwilling to forego, was the greatness of their ancestors, considered as the high favorites of God. They so gloried in Abraham and their being **his** children, that they opposed this to the person and doctrine of Christ Himself (John 8:33, 53). With regard to official dignity, they looked upon Aaron and his successors as to be preferred above all the world. Whilst they clung to such fleshly honours, the Gospel of Christ, which addressed them as lost sinners, could not be but distasteful to them. To disabuse their minds, to demonstrate that those in whom they trusted came far short in dignity, honour and greatness, of the true High Priest, the apostle presses upon them the eminence of him who was a type of Christ, and shows that the greatest of all their ancestors paid obeisance to him.

Three proofs of the eminence of Melchizedek are found in the verse before us. First, in the nomination of the person that was subject unto him: "**even** Abraham". Second, in the dignity of Abraham: "the patriarch". Third, in that Abraham gave him a tenth of the spoils. Abraham was not only the root and stock of the Israelitish people, but he was the one who first received the promise of the covenant (Gen. 12:17); therefore they esteemed him next unto God Himself. A "patriarch" is a father, prince or ruler of a family. The sons of Jacob are thus denominated (Acts 7:8, 9), for the twelve tribes descended from them. None else is termed a "patriarch" except David (Acts 2:29), and he, because the royal family came from his loins. But David and Jacob's sons, all sprang from Abraham, thus was he, pre-eminently, "**the** patriarch". Yet great as Abraham was, Melchizedek was still greater, for he was "priest of the most high God", and as such the father of the faithful owned him.

Let us not miss the **practical** lesson which the above facts teach us. Therein we learn of what **true** "greatness" consists. The Christian is to measure things by a different standard from that which worldlings employ. They look upon those who occupy prominent social and political positions as being the eminent of the earth. The vulgar mind esteems the wealthy and opulent as those who are most to be envied. But the anointed eye sees things in another light: the fashion of this world passeth away. Death levels all distinctions. Presidents and millionaires, kings and queens, are no more than the poorest beggar when their bodies are reduced to lifeless clay. And what of their souls? Ah, what concern have such after **eternal** interests? Learn, my reader, that true "greatness" consists in the favour of God and our nearness to Him. The meanest of His saints have been made "kings and priests unto God" (Rev. 1:6).

Ere leaving this verse, a few words need to be said upon the subject of **tithing**. There are few things on which many of the Lord's people are more astray than the matter of giving to His cause and work. Are our offerings to be regulated by sentiment and impulse, or by principle and conscience? That is only another way of asking, Does God leave us to the promptings of gratitude and generosity, or has He definitely specified His mind and stated **what** portion of His gifts to us are due Him in return? Surely He has not left this important point undefined. He has given us His Word to be a lamp unto our feet, and therefore He cannot have left us in darkness concerning any obligation or privilege that pertains to our dealings with Him.

At a very early date the Lord made it known that a definite portion of the saints' income should be devoted to Him who is the Giver of all. There was a period of twenty-five centuries from Adam until the time that God gave the law to Israel at Sinai, but it is a great mistake to suppose that His people were, at that time, without a definite communication from Him upon their several duties. A careful study of the book of Genesis reveals clear traces of a primitive revelation, which seems to have centered about these things: the offering of sacrifices to God, the observance of the Sabbath, and the giving of tithes. While we cannot today place our finger upon any positive enactment or command of God for any of those three things in those early days, nevertheless, from what **is** recorded we are **compelled** to assume that such must have been given.

No one can point to a "thus saith the Lord" requiring Noah to offer a sacrifice to Him, nor can we assign chapter and verse giving a command for the saints to tithe ere the law was given; yet is it impossible to account for either without presupposing a revelation of God's mind on those points. The fact that Abraham **did** give a tithe or tenth to Melchizedek, intimates that he acted in accordance with God's will. So too the words of Jacob in Gen. 28:22 suggest the same thing. This principle of recognizing God's ownership and owing His goodness, was later incorporated into the Mosaic law: Lev. 27:30. Finally, it is taken note of here in Heb. 7, and in the humble judgment of the writer the passage which is before us presents an argument which admits of no refutation. Abraham paid tithes to Melchizedek, and Abraham is the father of all that believe (Rom. 4; Gal. 3). He is the pattern man of faith. He is the outstanding exemplar of the stranger and pilgrim on earth whose Home is in Heaven. Melchizedek is the type of Christ. If then Abraham gave the tithe to Melchizedek, most assuredly every Christian should give tithes to Christ, our great High Priest.

"And verily they that are of the sons of Levi, who receive the office of the priesthood, have a commandment to take tithes of the people according to the law, that is, of their brethren, though they come out of the loins of Abraham; But he whose descent is not counted from them received tithes of Abraham, and blessed him that had the promises" (vv. 5, 6). In these verses the apostle strengthens the argument drawn from the important fact presented in v. 4, while at the same time he anticipates and obviates any counter argument which might be advanced against him. His argument consists of two parts: Abraham gave tithes to Melchizedek, Abraham was blest by him. In response, the Jews might reply, **That** does not establish the superiority of Melchizedek over the Levitical order, for the Aaronic priesthood also received tithes. To this the apostle answers by pointing out that Aaron's sons were all descended from Abraham, and therefore they, in their progenitor, paid tithes to the royal priest of Jerusalem, and by so doing owned his pre-eminence. Let us amplify this analysis.

In v. 5 the apostle acknowledges that God had granted the Levitical priests the right to receive tithes from His people (Num. 18:21-24), and thus they were set above all other Israelites; nevertheless, they too had "come out of the loins of Abraham", and inasmuch as **he** had given a tenth to a priest of another order, his descendants were therefore inferior to **that** priest. Moreover, the Levites had "received" the priestly office, and accepted tithes by command "according to the law". Thus, the Aaronic priesthood was wholly **derived** in its functions and privileges. But not so Melchizedek's. **He** was under no law. He was "king", as well as priest, and therefore belonged to a superior order. In this also he was a type of Christ, who, by virtue of His Divine nature, has authority **in Himself**, to receive and to bless. The words "take tithes ... of their brethren" finds its counterpart in 1 Cor. 9:11-14. The Aaronic priesthood was not supported by a tax levied on the idolatrous Canaanites, but by the gifts of the Lord's people!

The manner in which the apostle expresses himself in v. 5 deserves our closest notice, his language plainly intimating that his eye was on the high sovereignty of God. Observe that he did not simply say, "the priests have a commandment to take tithes", but "they that are **of** the sons of Levi". God distributed dignity and bestowed office in His Church (Acts 7:38) as it pleased Him. Not all the posterity of Abraham were set apart to receive tithes, and not all who belonged to the tribe of Levi; but only the family of Aaron was called to the priesthood. This appointment of His imperial will God required all to submit to: Num. 16:9, 10. It was something new to Israel to see the whole tribe of Levi taken into peculiar (official) nearness to Jehovah; yet to it they submitted. But when the "priests" were taken **out of** the tribe of Levi and exalted above all, some rebelled: Num. 16:1-3, etc.

The same principle holds good today. It is true, blessedly true, and God forbid that we should say a word to weaken it, that all believers enjoy **equal** nearness to God, that every one of them belongs to that "holy priesthood" who are to "offer up spiritual sacrifices acceptable to God by Jesus Christ" (1 Peter 2:5). Nevertheless, all believers are **not** called by God to occupy the same position of ministerial honour, all are not called to be preachers of His Gospel or teachers of His Word (James 3:1). God calls and equips whom He pleases to engage in His public service, and bids the rank and file of His people "obey them that have the rule over you, and submit yourselves" (Heb. 13:17). Yet, sad to say, in some circles the sin of Korah is repeated. They demand an ecclesiastical socialism, where any and all are allowed to speak. They "**heap** to themselves teachers" (2 Tim. 4:3). This ought not to be.

In v. 6 the apostle repeats the same thing he had said in v. 2. The Levitical priesthood received tithes from those descended from Abraham, and that was an evidence of official dignity conferred upon them by God's appointment. But Melchizedek received tithes of Abraham himself, which not only manifested his superiority to Aaron but to him from whom Aaron sprang. The apostle's insisting on this so particularly shows how difficult a matter it is to dispossess the minds of men of those things which they have long held and in which they boast. The Jews clung tenaciously to their descent from Abraham, in fact rested upon it for salvation. Much patience is required in order to deal faithfully but lovingly with those in error. "In **meekness** instructing those that oppose themselves" (2 Tim. 2:25) is a needed word for every teacher.

Melchizedek not only received tithes from Abraham, but he actually pronounced blessing upon him, which was a further evidence of his official superiority to the patriarch. To make this detail the more emphatic, the apostle stresses the dignity of Abraham, for the more glorious he was, the more illustrious the dignity of the one qualified to pronounce a benediction upon him. Thus Abraham is here referred to as he who "had the promises". He was the first of the Israelitish race with whom God made the covenant of life. It was no ordinary honour which Jehovah conferred upon the father of the faithful. As the immediate result of his receiving the promises, Abraham "saw" the Day of Christ (John 8:56). Yet great as was the privilege and honour bestowed upon Abraham it did not hinder him from showing subjection to Melchizedek, God's vicegerent.

There is an important practical lesson for us in v. 6. The one who had received the "promises" of God was now blest! Ah, we may have the promises of God stored in our minds and at our tongue's end, but unless we also have the blessing of God, what do they avail us? Moreover, it is particularly, the blessing **of Christ** (typified by Melchizedek) which makes the promises of God effectual to us. Christ is Himself the great subject of the promises (2 Cor. 1:20), and the whole blessing of them comes forth from Him alone (Eph. 1:3). In Him, from Him, and by Him, are all blessings to be obtained. Apart from Christ all are under the curse.

"And without all contradiction the less is blessed of the better" (v. 7). This verse summarises the argument contained in vv. 4-6. "These words are plainly to be understood with limitations. It does not follow that, because a priest under the law blessed the king, he was in a civil capacity the king's superior, any more than that a Christian minister instructing or even reproving a man of high civil rank who is a member of the church of which he is pastor, is civilly his superior. The apostle's argument is: The person who accepts of priestly benediction from an individual acknowledges his spiritual superiority, just as the highest authority in the land, if he were becoming a member of a voluntary Christian society, would acknowledge that its pastor was 'over him in the Lord'" (John Brown).

"Let us first know what the word **blessed** means here. It means indeed a solemn praying, by which he who is invested with some high and public honour, recommends to God men in private stations and under his ministry. Another way of blessing is when we pray for one another, which is commonly done by all the godly. But this blessing mentioned by the apostle was a symbol of greater authority. Thus Isaac blessed his son Jacob, and Jacob himself blessed his grandsons (Gen. 27:27, 48:15). This was not done mutually, for the son could not do like the father; but a higher authority was required for such a blessing as this. And this appears more evident still from Num. 6:23, where a command is given to the priest to bless the people, and then a promise is immediately added, that they would be blessed whom they blessed. It hence appears that the blessing of the priest depended on this,—that it was not so much man's blessing as that of God. For as the priest in offering sacrifices represented Christ, so in blessing the people he was nothing more than a minister and legate of the supreme God" (John Calvin).

The application of the principles expressed by the above writers to the case in hand is apparent. The blessing of the priest in O. T. times (type of Christ's blessing His people now), though pronounced as the minister of God, was an evidence of high honour of the one uttering it. Though Abraham was more eminent than any of his descendants, yet he himself was indebted to the royal priest of Jerusalem.

"And here men that die receive tithes; but there he of whom it is witnessed that he liveth" (v. 8). Here the apostle advances a further argument to support his demonstration of the inferiority of the Aaronic order of priesthood to the Melchizedekean: the "here" referring to the former, the "there" to the latter as stated in Gen. 14. The point singled out for notice is that, the Levitical order of office was but temporary, not so of that priest who blest Abraham. "The type is described as having no end: the order of priesthood which it represents is therefore eternal" (Calvin). The Scripture makes no mention of the death of Melchizedek when it relates that tithes were paid to him; so the authority of his priesthood is limited to no time, but on the contrary there is given an intimation of perpetuity.

Some have stumbled over the statement here made about Melchizedek: "it is witnessed that he liveth". These words have been appealed to in proof that he was a superhuman being. But if this statement be interpreted in the light of its context, there is no difficulty. It was not absolutely and personally that Melchizedek still lived, but typically and as a representation of Christ. Scripture frequently attributes to the type what is found alone in the antitype. Thus, the paschal lamb was expressly called **God's** passover (Ex. 12:11), when in reality it was only a pledge and token thereof. So the emblems on the Lord's table are denominated the body and blood of Christ, because they **represent** such. The blessedness of this detail will come before us, D. V., in the later verses.

"And as I may so say, Levi also, who receiveth tithes, paid tithes in Abraham. For he was yet in the loins of his father, when Melchizedek met him" (vv. 9, 10). In these verses the apostle meets the last objection which a carping Jew could make upon the subject. Against what the apostle had been saying, it might be advanced: Granting that Abraham himself paid tithes to Melchizedek, it does not follow that Melchizedek was superior to all Abraham's descendants. Abraham was, in some sense, a priest (Gen. 12:7), yet he was not so by virtue of any office which God had instituted in His Church. But in the days of Moses, Jehovah did institute an order and office of priesthood in the family of Aaron, and were not they, by Divine appointment, superior, because superceding the earlier order of Melchizedek? This the apostle makes reply to.

Many find it difficult to follow his line of thought, and that, because they are so ill-acquainted with the most important truth of headship and representation. Let us quote here from F. S. Sampson. "Abraham was truly the covenant-head of his posterity in the line of Isaac and Jacob, in whose descendants the promises made to him were fulfilled. It was in virtue of this covenant with Abraham, that the Jews inherited their distinguished privileges as a nation. It was the transaction with Abraham which brought them into the relation of a 'peculiar people' to Jehovah: and hence, in his patriarchal character and acts, he stood forth as the representative or federal head of the nation, so far as all the promises, privileges, and institutions of the Judaicial were concerned. He was both their natural progenitor and their covenant-head, by the appointment of God. We must remember that He was concerned, through His providence and promises, in all this business. Therefore, when Abraham paid tithes to Melchizedek as a priest of the most High God, and received a blessing from him, it was a historical fact intentionally introduced by God's providence, with a view to its becoming a feature of the type (so to speak) which Melchizedek, in his history and functions, was foreordained to

present, of the supreme and eternal High Priest. This providential incident prefigured and represented, by the Divine intention, the supremacy of the antitype; and in it Abraham acknowledged the official superiority of the type, not only over himself, but over his posterity then in his loins, represented by and acting in him".

The principle of federal representation lies at the very base of all God's dealings with men, as a careful study of Rom. 5: 12-19 and 1 Cor. 15:45-47 reveals. Adam stood for and transacted on the behalf of the whole human race, so that what he did, they **legally** did; hence his sin, guilt and death, are imputed to all his posterity, and God deals with them accordingly. So too Christ stood for and transacted on the behalf of all His seed, so that what He did, they **legally** did; hence, His meeting the demands of the law, His death and resurrection-life, are imputed to all who believe on Him. In like manner, Abraham stood for and transacted on the behalf of all his posterity, so that God's covenanting with him, is to be regarded as His covenanting with them also. Proof of this is found in the title **here** (and nowhere else) given to Abraham, viz., "the patriarch" (v. 4), which means, head or father of a people.

Thus the apostle here brings to a head his argument by pointing out that, virtually and representatively (not personally and actually), Levi himself had paid tithes to Melchizedek. We repeat, that Abraham in Genesis is not to be considered only as a private individual, but also as the head and representative of all his children. When Abraham gave tithes he did so not only in his own name, but also in that of all his descendants. Abraham had been called of God and separated to His service as the head of His elect people. There was more than a natural relation between him and his descendants. Jehovah promised to be a God unto him and to his seed after him, and therefore Abraham covenanted with God in the name of and as the representative of his seed. What God gave unto Abraham He gave unto his children, but he received the grant of it as the representative of his children, who, four hundred years later, took possession of it.

The typical teaching of Gen. 14 is exceedingly rich, but difficult to apprehend through lack of familiarity with the leading principles which interpret it. In Melchizedek's blessing of Abraham, we have a foreshadowing of Christ, as our great High Priest, blesing the whole election of grace (Luke 24:50). Abraham's owning Melchizedek as priest of the most high God by giving him tithes, we have prefigured the subjection to Christ of all His believing people. It lay outside the apostle's scope to fully expound this type in Heb. 7 (cf. 9:5). Here he practically confines himself to a single point, viz., showing that the High Priest of Christianity far exceeded in honour and glory that of Judaism's. His argument in vv. 9, 10 is to the effect that Melchizedek had been as much and as truly honoured by Abraham as though the whole Levitical priesthood had personally done him homage.

The all-important and inexpressibly blessed truth for us to lay hold of is that in vv. 9, 10 we have an **illustration** of the most soul-satisfying truth revealed in Holy Writ. Just as Levi was "**in** Abraham", not only seminally but representatively, so every one of God's children was "**in** Christ" when He wrought out that glorious work which has honoured and pleased God high above everything else. When the death-sentence of the law fell upon Christ, it fell upon the believer, so that he can unhesitatingly say, "I was crucified with Christ" (Gal. 2:20). So too when Christ arose in triumph from the tomb, all His people shared His victory (Eph. 2:5, 6). When He ascended on high, they ascended too. Let all Christian readers pray earnestly that God may be pleased to reveal to them the meaning, blessedness, and fulness of those words "In Christ".

—ARTHUR W. PINK.

THE SATISFACTION
("Atonement")
OF CHRIST

7. Its Nature (Continued).

Rightly has it been said that, "The doctrine of the Atonement is put in its proper light only when it is regarded as the central truth of Christianity, the great theme of Scripture. The principal object of Revelation was to unfold this unique method of reconciliation by which men, once alienated from God, might be restored to a right relation, and even to a better than their primeordial standing. But the doctrine is simply **revealed**, or, in other words, is taught us by Divine authority alone" (G. Smeaton). If it be a fact that the great Atonement is the central luminary in the firmament of God's truth, it is equally true that the **nature** of the Atonement is the very heart of this vital subject. Therefore it behoves us to give it our most prayerful and careful consideration.

In seeking to set forth the **nature** of that Satisfaction which the Mediator rendered to God on behalf of His people, we have seen, first, that His work was a **federal** one: that Christ entered this world not as a private individual, but in an official character, as the covenant-Head of God's elect, as their legal Representative. Remarkably does this appear in His first ministerial utterance. In Luke 2:49 we have the first **personal** word which Scripture records as proceeding from those lips into which **grace** had been "poured" (Psa. 45-2), viz., "Wist ye not that I must be about My Father's business?" There He expressed His relation to **God**, to the One who had sent Him: He had come here to do that business or work the Father had assigned Him. Those words were uttered by Him as a Boy of twelve. An interval of eighteen years pass before we hear another utterance from Him who spake as never man did, viz., "Suffer it to be so now: for thus it becometh **us** to fulfill all righteousness" (Matt. 3:15). Here He expresses His relation to His **people**, to those on whose behalf He was sent.

The Saviour had now come forth from the seclusion of Nazareth and presented Himself for baptism at the hands of His forerunner. John is to be regarded as the living expression and culminating point of the Law and the Prophets (Luke 16:16), who had for long centuries witnessed to the Coming of Messiah, and which now, by their great representative (Matt. 11:11), was to induct Christ into His office (John 1:31). As Christ recognized **them** (by coming to John), so **they** (in him, their representative) were to authenticate Him as the **truth** of the Prophets and the **substance** of the Law's types. At first John demurred, and Christ said "suffer it to be so **now**". In the Greek the "now" is emphatic: suffer it in My **present** state of humiliation, as an act suited to My office **as Substitute**. The reason given was: "for thus it becometh US", not "Me" personally, but "us"—Christ **one with** those whom He had come to save! There is the federal relationship seen from the beginning!

"**Thus** it becometh us to fulfill all righteousness". Those words are not to be limited to the act of baptism: the language is more general in its scope, though particular in its terms. The words "becometh" signified, It is not unworthy of the Son of God to stoop so low, for "righteousness" requires it. His language intimated it is suitable that I should appear in the "likeness of sin's flesh", identifying Myself with them in "confessing their sins" (Mark 1:5). It was becoming that He should be immersed in that river which spoke of death (Jer. 12:5), at the very outset of His public ministry, for it symbolized that "baptism" of **suffering** which He would undergo (Luke 12:50), and showed His **willingness** to endure it. Passing beneath the waters of Jordan was a fitting emblem of all those "waves and billows" (Psa. 42:7) of God's wrath which would shortly break over Him. It was meet that He **should** "fulfil all righteousness", submit to all that the Law had foreshadowed and the Prophets predicted, and thus meet all the demands of God upon His people.

Second, we have seen that the Satisfaction which Christ rendered unto God was a **vicarious** one. Now as the Substitute of His people the Law exacted two things from Christ: first, that He should render that obedience which was required from them as creatures; second, that He should endure that penalty which they merited as sinners. Thus, the mediatorial work which was given to Christ to perform involved two things, which though inseparably connected, yet are clearly separable in thought, namely a work of obedience distinguished from the sufferings He bore. In all His obedience He suffered; in all His sufferings He obeyed. Hence, it is of first importance to recognize that throughout His earhtly course Christ sustained a twofold relation to the Law: personally sinless, officially under its curse. The very fact of His putting on "the likeness of **sin's** flesh" (Rom. 8:3) evidences that sin had been transferred to Him from the moment He was conceived in the Virgin's womb. Nevertheless, He who "bore sin" all through the days of His flesh, was also the sinless Doer of a Divine work.

The very sinlessness of Christ was the necessary basis of His work of sin-bearing (2 Cor. 5:21). He must be innocent to stand for the guilty; He must be holy to take the place of the unholy, otherwise, He too had needed a Saviour. It was the Just who suffered for the unjust (1 Peter 3:18). Thus the wondrous life of Christ is far more than a spectacle to be gazed at in admiration, and more than an example for His people to follow (1 Peter 2:21); it must be regarded as the Work of **one for the many.** Unique, glorious, perfect, was His lovely life. "I seek not Mine own will, but the will of the Father which hath sent Me" (John 5:30), sets forth the guiding principle which ever regulated Him: cf. John 4:34. "I do always those things that please Him" (John 8:29). His was a life of constant service to God: uninterrupted in duration, perfect in degree, flawless in its balance. One grace neither excluded nor marred another: all was there, all was perfectly blended. Such a life, such obedience, such service, **merited reward**, and is actually bestowed on all He represented, on all whose substitute He was. We are now ready to contemplate.

3. It was a Penal work.

Scripture plainly teaches that God is both holy and righteous, and that "Justice and judgment (**not** "love and pity") are the establishment of God's "throne" (Psa. 89:14). Thus there is that in the Divine Essence which abhors sin for its intrinsic sinfulness, both in its aspect of pollution and in its aspect of guilt. The perfections of God are therefore displayed both by forbidding and punishing the same. He has pledged Himself that "the soul that sinneth, it shall die" (Ezek. 18:4). Therefore, in order to a full Satisfaction being rendered unto God, sin must be punished, the penalty of the Law must be enforced. Consequently, as Saviour of His Church, Christ had to vicariously suffer the infliction of the Law's curse.

What we shall now seek to show is that, the sufferings and death of Christ were a satisfaction to Divine justice on behalf of the sins of His people. In case any should object against our use of the term "satisfaction", let us point out that this very word is found in our English Bibles, being given by the translators as the equivalent for the Hebrew word which is ordinarily rendered "Atonement": "Moreover ye shall take no **satisfaction** for the life of a murderer, which is guilty of death: but he shall surely be put to death. And ye shall take no **satisfaction** for him that is fled to the city of his refuge, that he should come again to dwell in the land, until the death of the priest" (Num. 35: 31, 32).

The deep humiliation to which the Son of God was subjected in taking upon Him the form of a servant, and being made "in the likeness of sin's flesh", was a judicial infliction imposed upon Him by the Father, yet voluntarily submitted to by Himself. The very **purpose** of His humiliation, His obedience, His sufferings, makes them **penal**, for they were unto the satisfying of the claims of God's law upon His people. In being "made under the law" (Gal. 4:4), Christ became **subject to** all that the Law enjoins: "Now we know that what things soever the law saith, it saith to them who are under the law" (Rom. 3: 19), which means the law calls for the fulfilment of its terms. "Christ in our room and stead, did both by doing and suffering, **satisfy Divine justice**, both the legislatory, the retributive, and the vindictive, in the most perfect manner, fulfilling all the righteousness of the law, which the law otherwise required of us, in order to impugnity, and to our having a right to eternal life" (H. Witsius, 1693).

"For Christ also hath once suffered for sins, the Just for the unjust" (1 Peter 3: 18). The reference here must not be restricted to what Christ endured at the hands of God while He hung upon the cross, nor to all He passed through during that day and the preceding night. Beware of **limiting** the Word of God! No; the entirety of His humiliation is here included. The whole life of Christ was one of sufferings, therefore was He designated the Man of Sorrows, not simply, "sorrow". From His birth to His death, suffering and sorrow, marked Him as their legitimate Victim. While yet an Infant, He was driven into exile, to escape the fury of those who sought His life. That was but the prophetic fore-runner of His whole earthly course. The cup of woe, put to His lips at Bethlehem, was never removed till He drained its bitter dregs at Calvary.

Every variety of suffering was experienced by Him. He tasted **poverty** in its severest rigor. Born in a stable, never owning any property on earth, dependent upon the charity of others (Luke 8:3), oftentimes being worse situated than the inferior orders of creation: Matt. 8:20. He suffered **reproach** in all its bitterness. The most malignant accusations, the vilest asperations, the most cutting sarcasms, were directed against His person and character. He was taunted with being a glutton, a winebibber, a deceiver, a blasphemer, a devil. Therefore do we hear Him crying, "Reproach hath broken My heart" (Psa. 69:20). He experienced **temptation** in all its malignity. The Prince of darkness assailed Him with all his ingenuity and power, causing his infernal legions to attack Him, coming against Him like "strong bulls of Bashan", gaping on Him with their mouths like ravening and roaring lions (Psa. 22:12, 13). Above all, He suffered the **wrath** of God, so that He was "exceeding sorrowful, even unto death" (Matt. 26:38), in "an agony" (Luke 22:44), and ultimately, "forsaken of God".

What then is the explanation of these unparalleled "sufferings"? Why was the most perfect obedience followed by the most terrible punishment? Why was unsullied holiness visited with unutterable anguish? David declared, "Yet have I not seen the righteous forsaken" (Psa. 37:25); why, then was the Righteous One abandoned by God? Only one answer is possible; only one answer fully meets all the facts of the case; only one answer clears the government of God. In taking the place of offending sinners, Christ became obligated to discharge all their liabilities, and this involved bearing their sins, being charged with their guilt, suffering their punishment. Accordingly, God dealt with Him as the Representative of His criminal people, inflicting upon Him all that their sins merited. As the sin-bearing Substitute of His people, Christ was justly exposed to all the dreadful consequences of God's manifested displeasure.

Of old the question was asked, "Who ever perished being innocent?" (Job 4:7), to which we may, without the slightest hesitation, answer, None. God never has and never will smite the innocent. Therefore before His punitive wrath could fall upon Christ, the sins of His people must first be transferred to Him, and this is precisely what Scripture affirms. Remarkably was this foreshadowed of old in the great type of Israel's annual Day of Atonement, "And Aaron shall lay both his hands upon the head of the live goat, and confess over him all the iniquities of the children of Israel, and all their transgressions with all their sins, **putting them upon** the head of the goat" (Lev. 16:21). So too was it plainly prophesied, "The Lord hath laid **on Him** the iniquity of us all . . . He **bare** the sin of many" (Isa. 53: 6, 12). So also is it expressly affirmed in the N. T., "So Christ was once offered to **bear** the sins of many" (Heb. 9:28). Once again we would point out there is not a hint in these passages that Christ bore the sins of His people **only** while He was hanging upon the cross. We are aware that many have so affirmed, but in doing so they have not only been guilty of adding to the Word of God, but also of flatly contradicting it.

We have already pointed out that the expression of Rom. 8:3, "made in the likeness of sin's flesh", clearly pre-supposes the **transfer** of His people's sins **to** Christ, and that what happened immediately after His birth was in full keeping with this fact, and cannot be understood apart from it. That He was "circumcised" (Luke 2:21) not only proved that He had been "made in the likeness of men" (Phil. 2:7), but also evidenced that He **had** been made "in the likeness of **sin's flesh**". So too the ceremonial "purification" of His mother (Luke 2:22) and her presentation of a "**sin**-offering" (Lev. 12:2, 6), was in perfect keeping with the fact that, though His humanity was immaculate, yet He had entered this world officially guilty.

As little children we sinned—"the wicked are estranged from the womb: they go astray as soon as they be born, speaking lies" (Psa. 58:3)—and therefore as a Child Christ suffered, suffered not only as our Substitute, but because our sins had been transferred to Him. In our youth we sinned, and as a Youth Christ suffered, and suffered at the hands of God, as His own words clearly testify: "I am afflicted and ready to die from youth up: I suffer Thy terrors, I am distracted" (Psa. 88:15). In the prime of our manhood, we sinned, and in the prime of His manhood Christ suffered. Let us refer once more to His being assailed by Satan. Heb. 2:18 tells us that He "**suffered** being tempted", and that very suffering was **penal**. That Christ's "suffering" under Satan was designed and appointed as an infliction **from God**, is proved by the statement that "Jesus was led up **of the Spirit** into the wilderness **to be** tempted of the Devil" (Matt. 4:1).

Man having allowed himself to be overcome by Satan, God has, by a just sentence, delivered him up as a slave to his tyrrany; therefore was it necessary that Christ, as His sinful people's Substitute, should be exposed to the harrassings of the Devil, that in **this** respect also He might satisfy Divine justice. Most assuredly Satan and his agents could never have assailed Christ, had He not been so (legally) charged with the guilt of our crimes, that God righteously exposed Him to injuries from them (Acts 2:23). The elect themselves, as sinners, were subject to Satan's power (Col. 1:13), and that by the righteous sentence of the Judge of all the earth; therefore were they not only the "prey of the mighty", but also were "**lawful** captives" (Isa. 49:24). Therefore, as Christ came here as Surety in their room, He, by virtue of God's sentence, also became subject to the buffetings of Satan.

"Christ's passive, or suffering obedience, is not to be confined to what He experienced in the garden and on the cross. This suffering was the culmination of His piacular sorrow, but not the whole of it. Everything in His human and earthly career that was distressing belongs to His passive obedience. It is a true remark of Jonathan Edwards, that the blood of Christ's circumcision was as really a part of His vicarious atonement, as the blood that flowed from His pierced side. And not only His suffering proper, but His humiliation, also, was expiatory" (W. Shedd). "The satisfaction or propitiation of Christ consists either in His suffering evil, or His being subject to abasement... Whatever Christ was subject to which was the judicial fruit of sin, had the nature of satisfaction for sin. But not only proper suffering, but all abasement and depression of the state and circumstances of mankind (human nature) below its primitive honour and dignity, such as his body remaining under death, and body and soul remaining separate, are the judicial fruits of sin" (Jno. Edwards, 1743).

When the Scriptures speak of the satisfaction of Christ, it ascribes it to His sufferings in general, as Isa. 53:4, "Surely He hath borne our griefs and carried our sorows", that is, He suffered all the pains and sorrows due to us from sin. It is to be most carefully noted that the inspired declaration "the Lord hath laid on Him the iniquity of us all" (Isa. 53:6) comes **before** "He was oppressed" and before "He is brought as a lamb to the slaughter"; as it was at the commencement of His public ministry, and **not** while He hung upon the cross that God moved one of His servants to cry, "Behold the Lamb of God" which taketh away the sin of the world. Christ was brought "to the slaughter" before the three hours of darkness, yet even then "affliction" lay upon Him, and our iniquity was exacted of Him. So too this very chapter (Isa. 53) ascribes our "healing" to the **stripes** which He received from **men**, as plainly as other passages attribute our being delivered from the curse of the law through **God's** visiting Him with its curse.

"For even hereunto were ye called: because Christ also suffered for us, leaving us an example" (1 Peter 2:21). "To **suffer** here denotes to be in affliction; for all those sufferings are here intended, in which Christ has left us an example of patience. These sufferings he affirms to be **for** us, that is, undergone as well in our stead, as for our good. For this is ordinarily the signification of the word **huper,** and that this is the true meaning of Peter, we conclude hence. that in 3:18 he says. 'Christ suffered **for sins**', namely, that He might be the propitiation for our sins" (H. Witsius).

When the sovereign rights of God are emphasized there is generally raised the objection that we are hereby "reducing man to a mere machine". Many are they who are prepared to hold a brief for human responsibility. But rare indeed is it that we ever hear anything about **transferred responsibility.** Yet it is at this very point lies one of the chief wonders and glories of the Gospel. The responsibility of God's people was transferred to Christ: He assumed their liabilities, made Himself chargeable with their debts, answerable to every demand of the law against them. Had this not been the case, how could God have righteously laid the iniquities of His people upon the head of His holy Son? Still less could He have called for the sword of Justice to smite Him. It was because Christ was "made **sin**" for us, that He was also "made a curse" for us: the latter could not be without the former. As this is a point of such vital importance we must amplify a little further.

Heb. 7:22 declares that Christ is "Surety of a better covenant": He was the Sponsor of His people, as Judah undertook to be for Benjamin, "I will be **surety** for him; of my hand shalt thou require him; if I bring him not unto thee, and set him before thee, then let **me** bear the blame for ever" (Gen. 43:9). Or, as Paul was for Onesimus, "If he hath wronged thee, or oweth ought, put that on **mine account,** I Paul have written it with mine own hand, I will **repay**" (Phil. 18, 19). Just so did Christ engage Himself unto His Father for us: reckon to Me whatever they owe Thee, and I will satisfy for it. "A surety, whose name is put into a bond, is not only bound to pay the debt, but he makes it his **own** debt also, even as well as it is the principal's, so that **he** may be sued and charged for the debt. So Christ, when He once made Himself a Surety, He so put Himself in the room of sinners, that what the law could lay to their charge, it might lay to His" (T. Goodwin, 1680).

Christ must take on Him the guilt of our transgressions before He could take our punishment upon Him, and so satisfy Divine justice on our behalf. That He **did so**, is demonstrated by His own words. It is indeed remarkable to find how that Christ actually **owned** our sins as being **His**. First, in the 40th Psalm. That this Psalm is a Messianic one we know from its quotation in Heb. 10. That it contains the very words of Christ, is plainly evident from vv. 7-11. He is still the Speaker in v. 12, where He declared "For innumerable evils have compassed Me about: **Mine** iniquities have taken hold upon Me, so that I am not able to look up; they are more than the hairs of Mine head: therefore My heart faileth Me". What a proof that the sins of His people **had been** transferred to Him! Second, in the 69th, another great Messianic Psalm. There too we find Him saying, "O God, Thou knowest **My** foolishness; and **My** sins are not hid from Thee" (v. 5). How unmistakably do those words show our sins had been reckoned to Him! Those sins were His not by perpetration, but by imputation.

"Who His own self bare our sins in His own body on (to) the tree" (1 Peter 2:24). "'Our sins' here are our liabilities to punishment on account of our violations of the Divine Law, and the necessary consequences of those liabilities; in other words, guilt in the sense of binding over to punishment, and punishment itself" (J. Brown). Those sins Christ "bare", endured as a heavy load. The prime meaning of the Greek verb is "to carry up", the allusion being to the typical animal which was carried up to the altar, which was always erected on an elevated place. The margin gives the preferable rendering—"**to** the tree": the preposition is the same as in the next verse, "ye are returned **to** the Shepherd". The reason why the cross is here termed "the tree" we will state a little later.

There was a needs-be for Christ taking on Him the guilt of our transgressions in order for Divine justice to punish Him, for "we are sure that the judgment of God is according to truth" (Rom. 2:2). Whomsoever God punishes for sin, must be guilty **of** sin. Therefore we read, "For He hath made Him sin for us, who knew no sin" (2 Cor. 5:21). Each word here calls for a separate paragraph. The opening "for" assigns the ground on which the message of reconciliation (vv. 19, 20) rests. V. 19 states that God does not impute trespasses unto His people; v. 21 tells us why: because they were imputed to Christ. Here the Atonement is traced back to its Source, "God was in Christ reconciling": **He** made Christ to be sin— when? In the everlasting covenant, by the mutual agreement of the Father and the Son. Then we behold the **fitness** of Christ to make atonement: He was personally sinless, it was **God** who so adjudged Him! "Who knew no sin" is the negative way of saying that His obedience was perfect. The Law had no fault against Him, either of omission or commission. Nevertheless, "He (God) made Him (legally constituted Christ) to be sin for us", not in mere semblance, but in awful reality, and this, from the moment of His incarnation.

In entering the Law-place of His people, Christ became **answerable** to the righteousness of God on their behalf: whatever they owed, must be exacted from their Sponsor: He must pay their debts, suffer the full penalty of their iniquities, receive sin's wages in their room. Christ now became exposed to all that the holiness of God must inflict upon sin. Therefore we read, "Christ hath redeemed us from the curse of the law, being made a curse for us: for it is written, Cursed is every one that hangeth on a tree" (Gal. 3:13). "The cross was accursed, not only in the opinion of men, but by the decree of the Divine law. Therefore when Christ was lifted up upon it, He rendered Himself obnoxious to the curse" (Calvin).

The very **mode** of death which God appointed for His Son reveals to us the **penal** nature of it. The cross was no mere "accident", as though it made no difference what form His death took. Fundamental reasons rendered it expedient and necessary that the Surety should die a death which was **accursed of God**; hence the frequent reference in the N. T. to the "cross" and the "tree"—cf. John 12: 32, 33. At Calvary God's terrible curse on sin was publicly displayed, of which the **cross** was not the cause but the symbol: cf. John 3:14. Under the Mosaic law (to which the apostle refers in Gal. 3:13), hanging on a tree was a death reserved for great criminals. Hence the force of the word "tree" in 1 Peter 2-24. Christ hanging upon the Tree was the **public** testimony to **God's** curse on Him. "The **cause** of the curse was not the hanging on the tree, but the sin with which He was charged; and that mode of punishment exhibited that He was the object of God's holy displeasure; not indeed because He was suspended on the tree, but because He was the sin-bearer, and the punishment of the offences for which that ignominious penalty was allotted was then inflicted. Divine wisdom appointed that He who bore the sin of the world should be exposed as a curse, for the Divine displeasure was there most awfully displayed" (G. Smeaton).

As to why **this** means and method of death was selected by God out of all others possible—poisoning, stoning, beheading, etc.—Gen. 3 supplies the answer: "As the fatal sin which diffused the curse over the human race was connected with the forbidden 'tree' God wisely ordered that the last Adam should expiate sin by being suspended on a tree: and He appointed in the law (Deut. 21:22, 23), such a symbol of the curse as reminded all men of the **origin** of the Divine curse on the world. He would not have the curse removed in any other way" (G. Smeaton). Among the Romans, death by crucifixion was the deepest possible humiliation. It was the most degrading of punishments, inflicted only on slaves and the lowest of the people, and if freemen were at any time subjected to crucifixion for great crimes, such as robbery, high treason, or sedition, the sentence could not be executed till they were put into the catalogue of slaves, and that, by the utmost humiliation. Their liberty was taken from them by servile stripes and scouraging, as was done to Christ. Thus the Curse of God's Law was executed upon the Head, and Substitute of His people. To "preach Christ crucified" (1 Cor. 1:23) is to proclaim and expound His being "made a curse for us".

Because Christ was "made sin" and "made a curse" for His people, the wrath of God's holiness flamed against Him and the sword of His justice pierced Him. "Awake, O sword, against My Shepherd, against the man that is My Fellow, saith the Lord of hosts: **smite** the Shepherd" (Zech. 13:7), and cf. Matt. 26:31. God inflicted punishment on Christ as if He had been the personal offender. "It pleased the Lord to bruise Him; **He** hath put Him to grief: when **Thou** shalt make His soul an offering for sin" (Isa. 53:10). As all the sufferings of men, whether inflicted immediately by God or mediately by Satan or men (Jer. 2:15-17), arise from the demerits of sin; so **all** the sufferings of Christ, from man, Satan, God, arose from the demerits of His peoples' sins imputed to their Substitute.

The punishment which God meted out to Christ was the **very** punishment which was due His people. That He was accursed of God is seen from His hanging on the tree. That He received sin's wages was evidenced by God's forsaking Him. That He was numbered with transgressors was exhibited by His dying between two theives. True, He did not suffer eternally, for the eternity of our punishment was only a circumstance arising from **our incapacity** to suffer the whole weight of

God's wrath in a brief season, and therefore the brevity of duration of Christ sufferings is no valid objection against the **identity** of penalty which He received. Moreover, the infinite dignity of **His** person more than compensated the law. "To the enlightened eye, there is found on the cross another inscription besides that which Pilate ordered to be written there: The Victim of guilt. The Wages of sin" (J. Brown).
—ARTHUR W. PINK.

7. THE LIFE OF FAITH

Our Lord explains this great and sublime subject in its original and connections thus: "As the living Father hath sent Me, and I live by the Father; so he that eateth Me, **even he** shall live by Me" (John 6:57). Which words imply, that like as Christ, the Head and Mediator of His Church, lives **by** the Father, **in** Him, and **on** Him: so Christ united to His people communicates His life unto them so far, as freely and fully, as is communicable in their life of grace, and in their life of glory. Believers thus live **by** Christ, **in** Him and **on** Him, as He does by the Father. This union, life, and communion of believers with Christ, and with the Father in Him through the Spirit, are incomprehensibly high and divine. They have such an union with God, the fountain of life, in the person and through the mediation of our Lord Jesus Christ, by His standing between God and them, that they are most closely and indissolubly united to God, and He to them in the person of the God-man, Mediator; so that the life of God is conveyed **to** and maintained **in** them.

"He that hath the Son hath life" (1 John 5:12). Thus the believer is most nearly united in Christ, so as to have one life with Him and to live "by Christ living in him": moreover, Jesus is the immediate object of his faith, on whom he lives as his Saviour and God. The apostle Paul expresses the whole life of faith thus, "I live by the faith of the Son of God". The Son of God, Christ Jesus, as Mediator, lived by faith. His walk was the walk of faith. He died in the exercise of faith. And He is the grand pattern and exemplar to all His believing people, who are called upon to be looking unto Him, the Author and Finisher of faith. "To me to live is Christ" (Phil. 1:21). To **live Christ** contains the very essence of the life of faith. It is the fruit of knowing Christ and of receiving Him by faith in the Word, as life everlasting. Our Lord saith, "I am the resurrection and the life". Paul calls Christ "our life" (Col. 3:4). By faith the believer lives, and he only lives so far as faith is kept in constant exercise. Spiritual life, supported and maintained in all its strength and vigour by the Spirit of life in Christ Jesus, is manifested in believing, which in spiritual life, the very consciousness of all the actings and exercises of it is this Christ living in us.

Faith in Christ is inseparably connected with faith in God the Father, and in the Holy Spirit. Our Lord assures us that, "he that believeth on Him believeth not on Him, but on the Father who sent Him". "Through Him we believe in God" (1 Pet. 1:21). The faith of Christ leads us necessarily to faith in the Holy Spirit, who dwells in Him without measure, and which He communicates unto every believer; and thus faith terminates equally on the whole adorable Trinity, and raises up the heart into Divine admiration of Their unutterable love. Faith is a spiritual and supernatural knowledge of Christ received **from** the Word and **by the Spirit.** The Word of God is the ground of the believer's faith. The revelation which God hath made of Christ therein is the subject on which faith is exercised. "This is the record, that God hath given to us eternal life, and this life is in His Son". In that record the whole of Christ is set before us, viz. His person, love, covenant-engagements, incarnation, life, sacrifice, salvation, offices, fulness of grace, and riches of mercy, with the testimony of God concerning Him.

The God and Father of our Lord Jesus Christ gives us in His Word, His own thoughts of Immanuel, declares His everlasting acceptance of Him, and His infinite complacency in Him and His finished work. He records in it the inestimable perfection, the eternal virtue, and the perpetual efficacy of the life and death of His co-equal Son. He presents His Son to us in the Word of His grace in the very same light and point of view, in which He beholds Him; proclaiming Him to be His Elect, in whom His soul delighteth, and testifying that His blood cleanseth us from all sin. The Holy Spirit takes of the things of Christ thus revealed, and shows them to the believer; and by this way and means exalts Him in the mind and heart, and makes Him supremely glorious in the view of faith. The views which faith takes in of Christ are real and true, being founded on the account which God hath given of His Son. What is revealed of Christ in the Word must have its existence in the mind, and be there stated just as it is in the Scriptures, or, we cannot make a proper advantage of it. The apprehensions which the believer takes in of Christ by faith must be strong and lively to influence his heart, and to enable him to live a life of faith on the Son of God. The gift and grant of eternal life must be understood, or he cannot set his seal to it by believing.

The life of faith consists in the believer's living on Christ, in the exercise of his spiritual faculties on Him, as set forth in the Word; and the highest lesson in the school of Christ is to learn to live on Christ in the Word, as exactly suited to every want, wound, weakness, and misery, which we feel ourselves to be the subject of. The believer reads, and through the power of the eternal Spirit he believes it to be an immutable truth, that there are three that bear record in heaven, the Father, the Word, and the Holy Spirit, and that they testify there is life and salvation for every one that believeth in Jesus; that the gift of God is eternal life, and that this life is in His Son. He considers that his receiving God's testimony and believing the record which he hath given of His Son, is a real evidence of **his** interest in Jesus. Faith gives a real subsistance or existence to Christ and the things of Christ in the believer's mind. From what he receives from the Word concerning Him he is led to exercise his mind in spiritual contemplations on Him. And his life of faith consists in living over in his own mind the great thoughts which God the Father hath of His Son.

The believer's mind is fed in spiritual contemplations on the Father's everlasting love, which He bears to His co-equal Son, and the delight which He takes in Him. What he beholds in Christ and His work of salvation fills him with real satisfaction: so that what the believer apprehends of Christ is the life of his soul. His faith is just what **his knowledge of Christ** is. What he takes in concerning what is revealed of the Lord Jesus feeds, sustains, and strengthens his faith. The believer finds it his duty to renounce self constantly, and to make use of Christ continually. This is what **practical godliness** consists in: so far as he lives on Christ in the Word, exercises his mind on Him as set forth therein, and brings Him into all things which concern him, both for soul and body, for life and death, for time and eternity. Whilst the believer is living **thus**, he gets above himself. He finds nothing in himself to encourage his heart and hope in God. His whole salvation is in the finished work of Christ. The whole foundation of his hope in God is **without** him.

The Christian's faith produces great experience, but it is not nourished and increased by it. No; Christ is the immediate object of his faith. God's promises are the means of nourishing it; and faith is the exercise of the spiritual mind on Christ irrespective of anything felt or experienced in us. It is going **off** and **out of** ourselves to Christ for all things. It is trusting to Him **to be** unto us just what He hath promised to be, and to fulfill His Word to us, so far as it will be for His glory and our good. Faith is both passive and active; it takes in the knowledge of Christ from the Word, and is exercised on Him accordingly. It is the eye of the mind, and Christ is the object; the Word is the mean, and the Holy Spirit is the Enlightener. He sets forth Christ in His own light in the Word, and thereby gives the believer a clear and spiritual knowledge of Him; and it is by what faith sees in Christ that it is supported: not by any of its acts or fruits. He finds himself most exactly suited to Christ, and Christ to him; and that his faith is most Divinely suited to take in all that is revealed concerning His most precious and perfect salvation. This causes the believer to flee to Him with full purpose of heart. Having received Christ Jesus he walks in Him by the same faith with which he received Him (Col. 2:6). Believing in Christ and walking in Him are but the repeated acts of one and the same faith. The testimony of God the Father is always one; and faith is also **at all times one.** There is never more ground for believing at one time than another. Therefore the believer should be always exercising the same faith on Christ as set forth in the Word. This living is wholly spiritual and supernatural.

In our walking by faith, it is of vast importance to preserve in the mind a remembrance of what we are to believe, namely, the record of God; i. e. that John 3:16, John 6:40, etc. To study the Divine record as containing a perfect warrant for believing, and making continual use of Christ, is a point on which the life, peace, and comfort of the believer in his walk with God greatly depends. Whilst he views the will, counsel, covenant, and oath of the eternal Trinity, which are his security for everlasting life and salvation, and believes himself hereby secured from eternal condemnation, he hath strong consolation and good hope through grace. In the knowledge and belief of the everlasting virtue and efficacy of the blood of the Lamb his conscience is purged from guilt, and his mind is filled with the peace of God. In the belief of the everlasting perfection of Immanuel's righteousness he hath hope in God. Thus he enters with boldness into the holiest by the blood of Jesus, and is hereby prepared to walk with God in the full belief that the blood of Jesus Christ His Son cleanseth from all sin, that the obedience of Jesus is his everlasting perfection, and that all grace is treasured up for his use in the fulness of the Saviour. And he apprehends that, as he is receiving out of it, he hath all things necessary for his holy and happy walk and successful warfare, such as strength against corruptions, victory over his spiritual enemies, and triumphs over death. These truths, **thus believed**, animate the believer in his walk with God, as his reconciled Father.

The spiritual knowledge which the true believer hath of the Lord God, as his covenant God, from the Word of grace, is the foundation of his inwardly and outwardly holy walk **with** God and **before** Him unto all pleasing. The experience which the believer hath of the outward and inward cross is sanctified to him by the inward teaching of the Holy Spirit; and it tends to his increasing profit. From the outward cross he learns these truths, viz., that man is born unto trouble as the sparks fly upward; that all things out of Christ are under the curse, that nothing out of Christ can yield him the least real joy; that self must be brought down; that, in all its shapes and various workings, it must be renounced and denied: that if he live Christ, he must be a martyr; (which he may be without dying at a stake), that he must die to all things below Christ, good and bad; and that he must live above all the schemes, maxims, ways, joys and sorrows, of this present evil world, by faith on the Son of God. The believer clearly sees that he cannot otherwise walk and act as a stranger and pilgrim here below. He perceives that all the joys and comforts, which the creature and things of time and sense propose, are not to be compared with the happiness enjoyed in one single moment's communion with God. All the misery in the world does not deserve a single sigh; because the sorrow of worldlings is confined **to** and concerned **about** things which perish in their using.

The believer being in Adam a fallen creature, and having received from him a sinful nature, hath his personal cross, a continual one, which he will never outlive, though he may so live above it as to sing and make melody to the Lord with it on his back. It may be bodily disease, domestic trials, loss of friends and property, straitened circumstances, persecutions for Christ's sake, loss of good name and character, particular and strong corruptions, or some singular dispensation in providence, which may last long, touch to the very quick, and reach even to the soul. Yet these things are so well-suited by the Lord to the believer, that there are times when he cannot but be thankful to his heavenly Father for all that He hath been pleased to exercise him with. On a retrospective view of all his trials, afflictions, temptations, or whatsoever may have been his lot and portion assigned him by the Lord, he cannot but say when in his right mind, good is the whole will of my heavenly Father concerning me. He is certain that no trials could have suited him so well. From them he reaps much and real instruction, profit, and good. The believer is taught **to bring Christ into all things**, and to hold communion with Him whilst under the cross; and finds, as he looks to Him for supports and a sanctified use of it, that it may produce the peaceable fruits of righteousness: see 2 Cor. 4:17, 18.

The believer is exercised also with the inward cross, which consists in his knowing and feeling the exceeding sinfulness of his fallen nature. Though it is painful beyond expression to feel what he is **in, of,** and **from** himself, and though he fetches many a deep sigh and groan from his heart, yet it is most truly profitable. He learns from it, through the Divine influence of the Holy Spirit, to renounce himself and walk humbly with his God, to look continually to Christ, to depend wholly on the **finished work** of God his Saviour, and to triumph in His complete conquest over sin, Satan, the world, death, and hell. The inward cross serves in the hand of the Spirit to keep him continually looking out of himself, and to be every moment dependent on Jesus. To live, walk, and hold communion by faith with God in Christ. The believer learns in his walking with God that **self** is a monster in religion. It will not live and thrive under spiritual means, unless communion with Christ be enjoyed in them. Nothing short of supernatural views of Immanuel will prove **the death of self**. The believer learns to know from his own experience that it is possible to be dead to all the pleasures which sin can propose to the outward senses, and yet be alive to himself, and **live on** what he finds **in** himself. Thus he finds it, in his daily walk with God, and in his communion with Him, to be absolutely necessary to **live out of self** and utterly to renounce it.

All that the Holy Spirit hath taught him concerning himself under the inward cross, and all that he knows and hath believed of Christ from the Word concerning Him and His great salvation, serve to bring him to this one single and settled point, viz., that he cannot make a proper use of all, but by **bringing in Christ** into all things, i.e., into the whole of his experience, walk and warfare. He clearly sees from the teaching of the Holy Spirit that no one can be in more need of Christ than himself, and that Christ cannot be more suited to anyone; and he learns to **make use of what He is,** to live in an entire dependence on Him. His faith being maintained by the Word of promise, and exercised on Christ as his righteousness, he goes on heavenward, fighting the good fight of faith, and laying hold on eternal life. In his going forward, all the hosts of Satan, with all the inward sinfulness of his fallen nature, in conjunction with the world, will secretly, continually, and most violently oppose him. Yet in prospect of all the triumphs, saying "Jehovah is **my** banner". In the full belief of the everlasting victory of Christ over all His foes, and in constant dependence on His word of promise, he goes forth to fight **the Lord's battles**; and clothed with the whole armour of God, and attending to the commands of Christ, the Captain of his salvation, he is "strong in the Lord, and in the power of His might". In these wars of the Lord he is, in Christ, "more than conqueror".

His loins are "girt about with truth". That saving knowledge of God in Christ, which the Holy Spirit hath taught him, is a **spiritual military girdle,** which connects or binds together all the graces which are to be exercised in the field of battle. He sees to the need of "the breastplate of righteousness", and he puts on in the exercise of faith, **the imputed righteousness of the God-man Christ Jesus**. It is a protection for the vital parts, from every stroke. He wears it on his heart. Faith in the everlasting efficacy of the life and death of Immanuel, is armour of proof against all the strength of sin, Satan, earth, death, and hell. Thus accoutred the believer may march on with undaunted courage. "Having his feet shod with the preparation of the Gospel of peace", the believer, maintaining in his conscience peace with God, by faith in Jesus Christ our Lord, goes on with holy boldness. He marches on fearless, conquering, taking "the shield of faith wherewith he is able to quench all the fiery darts of the wicked one". Let those darts fly ever so thick about the believer, faith in the blood of the Lamb will quench them all. The believer may lift up his head with joy, because he has "the helmet of salvation" on it. And having "the sword of the Spirit, which is the Word of God", he overcomes Satan in the same way and by the same weapons, whereby the great company which is now before the throne was victorious; of which it is recorded, that they overcame Satan, "by the blood of the Lamb, and by the word of their testimony". When the believer has all his armour of invincible proof on, he looks up to His Divine Saviour in prayer and faith, for orders, courage, strength, victory: "Praying always with all prayer and supplication in the spirit, and watching thereunto with all perseverance". And the views which the Holy Spirit gives him of the triumphs and complete conquest which the ever-blessed God-man obtained in His own person over all the power of the enemy, fill him with gladness of heart, cause him to shout for joy, give him a prospect of his complete redemption in Christ, and help him to go on with growing strength, longing for the time when he shall be absent from the body and present with the Lord.

Thus the believer "kept by the power of God through faith unto salvation" goes on singing to the praise of Him, "who led His people through the wilderness; for His mercy endureth forever". He perseveres in his walk and warfare overcoming himself, sin, and all his spiritual enemies, by faith **in the Son of God**. As the truth of the everlasting Gospel enters through believeing more and more into his experience, and influences his understanding, affections and will, he becomes daily more and more victorious. He receives soul-content and real satisfaction from them. He rests his whole hope of heaven and eternal glory on the infallibility of them. He sees enough in Christ to bear him up and carry him infinitely above and beyond himself and all the miseries of this present life. In the knowledge of the Lord Jesus he hath a perfect antidote against the fears of death. He feels the mortality of his body. He finds that the sentence, "Dust thou art, and unto dust thou shalt return", begins to take place in him, but he triumphs in the victory of Christ, who conquered death and him that had the power of death, that is, the devil.

In the prospect of a speedy dissolution he is most graciously supported through the knowledge which the Holy Spirit has given him from the Word of the covenant-engagements of the eternal Three on his behalf. He receives the record of the Divine persons concerning it, and sets his own seal to the truth of it. He believes himself safe in the hands of Christ. He perceives every part of his salvation to be without himself. He sees that his vast obligations to the Holy Spirit for what He hath wrought in him, for what He hath taught him, and for leading him from time to time into communion with Christ and His Father in Him, surpass all his thoughts.

The time comes that he must die. The Lord sends death to take down the tabernacle of his body. The believer has nothing to do but to die. He says, "to me to live is Christ, and to die is gain" (Phil. 1:21). As he lived by faith, so he must die in faith; as **all**, who went to heaven before, **did**: "these all die in faith" (Heb. 11:13). In his dying case and circumstances he finds the Word of our Lord sweet to him, "If a man keep My saying, he shall never see death". He mixes faith with it, and receives strength and consolation thereby. Death is to him only his body falling asleep in the arms of Jesus. Our Lord hath **abolished** "death". He hath taken out the sting of it. There is in the very article of death everlasting life for the believer. As soon as his connection is broken with the elements of this visible system, he enters through the consecrated passage of death, on that same spiritual and eternal life which Christ lives in glory.

The Lord, having finished all the good pleasure of His will in and with the believer in a time-state, is his guide unto death, **over** and **beyond** it. He resigns his soul to his divine Saviour saying, "Lord Jesus, receive my spirit". Thus he dies in faith, dies in Christ, under the blessing of the holy Trinity. "Blessed are the dead which die in the Lord". From the very moment of their death believers are blessed. From henceforth their eternal blessedness begins. The Holy Spirit sets His seal to this truth: "yea, saith the Spirit" (Rev. 14:13). The soul of the believer being absent from the body, is present with the Lord, whilst the corpse sleeps in the arms of Jesus to be raised, in the future appointed time, from the grave of death: when it will be fashioned like unto Christ's glorious body.

—S. E. PIERCE, 1804.

PROFITING FROM THE WORD

2. The Scriptures and God.

The Holy Scriptures are wholly supernatural. They are a Divine revelation. "All Scripture is given by inspiration **of God**" (2 Tim. 3:16). It is not merely that God elevated men's minds, but that He directed their thoughts. It is not simply that He communicated concepts to them, but that He dictated the very words they used. "The prophecy came not in old time by the will of man: but holy men of God spake moved by the Holy Spirit" (2 Peter 1:21). Any human "theory" which denies their **verbal** inspiration, is a device of Satan's, an attack upon God's truth. The Divine image is stamped upon every page. Writings so holy, so heavenly, so awe-producing, could not have been created by man.

The Scriptures make known a **supernatural God**. That may appear a very trite remark, yet today it needs making. The "god" which is believed in by many professing Christians is far too human. This is only one more evidence that modern Christendom is becoming more and more paganised. The prominent place which "sport" now has in the nation's life, the excessive love of pleasure, the abolition of home-life, the brazen immodesty of women, are so many symptoms of the same disease which brought about the downfall and death of the empires of Babylon, Persia, Greece, and Rome. And, the twentieth-century idea of God which is entertained by the bulk of the people in lands nominally "Christian", is rapidly approximating to the character ascribed to the gods of the ancients. In sharp contrast therefrom, the God of Holy Writ is clothed with such perfections and vested with such attributes that no carnal intellect could possibly have invented them.

God can only be known by means of **a**

supernatural revelation of Himself. Apart from the Scriptures, even a theoretical acquaintance with Him is impossible. It still holds true that "the world by wisdom knew not God" (1 Cor. 1:21). Where the Scriptures are ignored, God is "The unknown God" (Acts 17:23). But something more than the Scriptures are required before the soul can **know** God, know Him in a real, personal, vital way. This seems to be recognized by few today. The prevailing practice assumes that a knowledge of God can be obtained through studying the Word, in the same way as a knowledge of chemistry may be secured by mastering its text-books. An intellectual knowledge of God may be; not so a spiritual one. A supernatural God can only be known supernaturally (i. e., known in a manner **above** that which mere nature can acquire), by a supernatural revelation of Himself to the heart. "God who commanded the light to shine out of darkness, hath shined in our hearts, **to** the light of the knowledge of the glory of God in the face of Jesus Christ" (2 Cor. 4:6). The one who has been favoured with this supernatural experience has learned that only "in Thy light shall we see light" (Psa. 36:9).

God can only be known through **a supernatural faculty.** Christ made this clear when He said, "Except a man be born again he **cannot see** the kingdom of God" (John 3:3). The unregenerate have **no spiritual knowledge** of God. "The natural man receiveth not the things of the Spirit of God, for they are foolishness unto him; neither can he know them, because they are **spiritually** discerned" (1 Cor. 2:14). Water, of itself, never rises above its own level. So the natural man is incapable of perceiving that which transcends mere nature. "This is life eternal, that they might **know Thee**, the only true God" (John 17:3). Eternal life must be imparted before the "true God" can be known. Plainly is this affirmed in 1 John 5:20, "We know that the Son of God is come, and hath given us an understanding, **that we may know** Him that is true". Yes, an "understanding", a **spiritual** understanding, by new creation, must be given **before** God can be known in a spiritual way.

A supernatural knowledge of God produces **a supernatural experience.** And this is something to which multitudes of church-members are total strangers. Most of the "religion" of the day is but a touching up of "old Adam". It is merely a garnishing of sepulchres full of corruption. It is only an outward "form". Even where a sound creed is held, only too often it is a dead orthodoxy. Nor should this be wondered at. It has ever been thus. It was so when Christ was here upon earth. The Jews were very orthodox. At that time they were free from all idolatry. The Temple stood at Jerusalem, the Law was expounded, Jehovah was worshipped. And yet Christ said to them, "He that sent Me is true, whom ye **know not**" (John 7:28). "Ye neither know Me, nor My Father: if ye had known Me, ye should have known My Father also" (John 8:19). "It is My Father that honoureth Me; of whom ye say, that He is your God. Yet **ye have not known Him**" (John 8:54, 55). And mark it well, this was said to a people who had the Scriptures, searched them diligently, and venerated them as **God's** Word! They were well acquainted with God theoretically, but a spiritual knowledge of Him they had not.

As it was in Judaism, so it is in Christendom. Multitudes who "believe" in the Holy Trinity are completely devoid of a supernatural or spiritual knowledge of God. How are we so sure of this? In this way: the character of the fruit reveals the character of the tree that bears it; the nature of the waters make known the nature of the fountain from which they flow. A supernatural knowledge of God produces a supernatural experience, and a supernatural experience results in **supernatural fruit.** That is to say, God actually dwelling in the heart revolutionises, transforms the life. There is that brought forth which mere nature cannot produce, yea, that which is directly contrary thereto. And this is noticeably absent from the lives of perhaps ninety-five out of every hundred now professing to be God's children. There is nothing in the life of the average professing Christian except what can be accounted for on natural grounds. But in the genuine child of God it is far otherwise. He is, in truth a **miracle** of grace; he is a "**new creature** in Christ Jesus" (2 Cor. 5:17). **His** experience, his life, **is** supernatural.

The supernatural experience of the Christian is seen in his **attitude toward God.** Having within him the life of God, having been made a "partaker of the divine nature" (2 Peter 1:4), he, necessarily, loves God, loves the things of God, loves what God loves; and, contrariwise, he hates what God hates. This supernatural experience is wrought in him by the Spirit of God, and that, by means of the Word of God. The Spirit never works apart from the Word. By that Word He quickens. By that Word He produces conviction of sin. By that Word He sanctifies. By that Word He gives assurance. By that Word He makes the saint to grow. Thus, each one of us may ascertain the extent to which we are profiting from our reading and studying of the Scriptures by the **effects** which they are, through the Spirit's application of them, **producing in us**. Let us enter now into details. He who is truly and spiritually profiting from the Scriptures has:

1. A clearer recognition of God's claims.

The great controversy between the Creator and the creature has been whether He or they should be God, whether His wisdom or theirs should be the guiding principle of their actions, whether His will or theirs should be supreme. That which brought about the fall of Lucifer was his resentment at being in subjection to his Maker: "Thou hast said in thine heart, I will ascend into heaven, I will exalt **my** throne above the stars of God . . . . I will be like the Most High" (Isa. 14:13, 14). The lie of the Serpent which lured our first parents to their destruction was, "Ye shall be **as gods**" (Gen. 3:5). And ever since then the heart-sentiment of the natural man has been, "Depart from us; for we desire not the knowledge of Thy ways. What is the Almighty, that we should serve Him?" (Job 21: 14, 15). "Our lips are our own, who is Lord over us?" (Psa. 12:4). "We are lords; we will come no more unto Thee" (Jer. 3:31).

Sin has alienated man from God: Eph. 4:18. His heart is averse to Him, his will is opposed to His, his mind is at enmity against Him. Contrariwise, **salvation** is being restored to God: "For Christ also hath once suffered for sins, the Just for the unjust, that He might **bring us to God**" (1 Peter 3:18). Legally that has already been done; experimentally, it is in process of accomplishment. Salvation means being reconciled to God; and that involves and includes sin's dominion over us being broken, enmity within us being slain. The heart being won to God. This is what true conversion is: it is a tearing down every idol, a renouncing the empty vanities of a cheating world, and taking God for our Porton, our Ruler, our All in all. Of the Corinthians we read they, "First gave their own selves to the Lord" (2 Cor. 8:5). The desire and determination of those truly converted is that they "should not henceforth live unto themselves, but unto Him who died for them and rose again" (2 Cor. 5:15).

God's claims are now recognized, His rightful dominion over us is acknowledged, He is owned **as** God. The converted yield themselves "unto God as those that are alive from the dead", and their members as "instruments of righteousness unto God" (Rom. 6:13). This is the demand which He makes upon us: to **be** our **God**, to be served as such by us; for us to be and do, absolutely and without reserve, whatsoever He demands, surrendering ourselves fully to Him: see Luke 14:26, 27, 33. It belongs to God as God to legislate, prescribe, determine for us; it belongs to us as a bounden duty to be ruled, governed, disposed of by Him at His pleasure.

To own God as our God is to give Him the throne of our hearts. It is to say in the language of Isa. 26:13 "O Lord our God, other lords beside Thee have had dominion over us: by Thee **only** will we make mention of Thy name". It is to declare with the Psalmist, not hypocritically, but sincerely, "O God, Thou art **my** God; early will I seek Thee" (Psa. 63:1). Now it is in proportion as this becomes our actual experience that we profit from the Scriptures. It is in them, and in them alone, that the claims of God are revealed and enforced, and just so far as we are obtaining clearer and fuller views of God's rights, and are **yielding ourselves** thereto, are we really being blest.

2. A greater fear of God's majesty.

"Let all the earth fear the Lord; let all the inhabitants of the world stand in awe of Him" (Psa. 33:8). God is so high above us, that the thought of His majesty should make us tremble. His power is so great that the realization of it ought to terrify us. He is so ineffably holy and His abhorrence of sin is so infinite, that the very thought of wrongdoing ought to fill us with horror. "God is greatly to be feared in the assembly of the saints, and to be had in reverence of all about Him" (Psa. 89:7).

"The fear of the Lord is the beginning of wisdom" (Prov. 9:10), and "wisdom" is a right use of "knowledge". Just so far as God is truly **known** will He be duly feared. Of the wicked it is written, "There is **no** fear of God before their eyes" (Rom. 3:18). They have no realization of His majesty, no concern for His authority, no respect for His commandments, no alarm that He shall yet judge them. But concerning His covenant-people God has promised "I will put My fear in their hearts, that they shall not depart from Me" (Jer. 32:40). Therefore do they tremble at His Word (Isa. 66:5), and walk softly before Him.

"The fear of the Lord is to hate evil" (Prov. 8:13). And again, "By the fear of the Lord men depart from evil" (Prov. 16:6). The man who lives in the fear of God is conscious that "The eyes of the Lord are in every place, beholding the evil and the good" (Prov. 15:3), therefore is he as conscientious about his private conduct as of his public. The one who is deterred from committing certain sins because the eyes of men are upon him, and who hesitates not to commit them when alone, is destitute of the fear of God. So too the man who moderates his language when Christians are about him, but does not so at other times, is devoid of God's fear. He has no awe-inspiring consciousness that GOD sees and hears him at all times. The truly regenerate soul is **afraid** of disobeying and defying God. Nor does he want to. No, his real and deepest desire is to **please Him** in all things, at all times, and in all places. His earnest prayer is "unite my heart to fear Thy name" (Psa. 86:11).

Now even the saint has to be **taught** the fear of God (Psa. 34:11). And here, as ever, it is through the Scriptures, this teaching is given us (Prov. 2:5). It is through them we learn that God's eye is ever upon us, marking our actions, recording our words, weighing our motives. As the Holy Spirit **applies** the Scripture to our hearts, we give increasing heed to that command "be thou in the fear of the Lord all the day long" (Prov. 23:17). Thus, just so far as we are awed by God's awful majesty, are made conscious that "Thou God seest me" (Gen. 16:13), and work out our salvation with "fear and trembling" (Phil. 2:12) are we truly profited from our reading and study of the Bible.

3. A deeper reverence for God's commandments.

Sin entered this world by Adam's breaking of God' law, and all his fallen children are begotten in his depraved likeness (Gen. 5:3). "Sin is the transgression of the law" (1 John 3:4). Sin is a species of high treason, spiritual anarchy. It is a repudiating God's dominion, the setting aside of His authority, rebelling against His will. Sin is having my own way. Now salvation is deliverance from sin, from its dominion as well as its guilt, from its power as well as its penalty. The same Spirit who convicts of the need of God's grace, also convicts of the need of God's government to rule us. God's promise to His covenant people is, "I will put My laws into their mind, and write them in their hearts; and I will be to them a God" (Heb. 8:10).

A spirit of obedience is communicated to every regenerated soul. Said Christ, "If a man love Me, he **will** keep My words" (John 14:23). There is the test: "Hereby we do know that we know Him, if we keep His commandments" (1 John 2:3). None of us keep them perfectly, yet every real Christian both desires and strives to do so. He says with Paul "I delight in the law of God after the inward man" (Rom. 7:22). He says with the Psalmist, "I have **chosen** the way of truth", "Thy testimonies have I **taken** as an heritage forever" (Psa. 119:30, 111). And teaching which lowers God's authority, which ignores His commands, which affirms that the Christian is, in **no** sense, under the Law, is of the Devil, no matter how oily-mouthed his human instrument may be. Christ has redeemed His people from the curse of the law and not from the command of it: He has saved them from the wrath of God, but not from His government. "Thou shalt love the Lord thy God with all thine heart" never has and never will be repealed.

1 Cor. 9:21 expressly affirms that we **are** "under the law to Christ". "He that saith he abideth in Him ought himself also so to walk, even as He walked" (1 John 2:6). And **how** did Christ "walk"? In perfect obedience to God; in complete subjection to His law, honouring and obeying it in thought and word and deed. He came not to destroy the law, but to fulfill it (Matt. 5:17). And our love for Him is expressed not in pleasing emotions or beautiful words, but in keeping His commandments (John 14:15); and the commandments of Christ are the commandments of God; cf. Ex. 20:6. The earnest prayer of the real Christian is, "**Make me to go** in the path of Thy commandments; for therein do I delight" (Psa. 119:35). Just so far as our reading and study of Scripture is, by the Spirit's application, begetting within us a greater love and a deeper respect for, and a more punctual keeping of God's commandments, are we really profiting thereby.

4. A firmer trust in God's sufficiency.

Whatsoever or whomsoever a man most trusts in is his "god". Some trust in health, others in wealth; some in self, others in their friends. That which characterises all the unregenerate is that they lean upon an arm of flesh. But the Election of Grace have their hearts drawn from all creature supports, to rest upon the living God. God's people are the Children of Faith. The language of their hearts is, "O my God, I trust in Thee: let me not be ashamed" (Psa. 25:2). And again, "Though He slay me yet will I trust in Him" (Job 13:15). They rely upon God to provide, protect and bless them. They look to an unseen Resource, count upon an invisible God, lean upon a hidden Arm.

True, there are times when their faith wavers, but though they fall, they are not utterly cast down. Though it be not their uniform experience, yet Psa. 56:11 expresses the general state of their souls: "In God have I put my trust, I will not be afraid what man can do unto me". Their earnest prayer is, "Lord, increase our faith". "Faith cometh by hearing, and hearing by the Word of God" (Rom. 10:17). Thus, as the Scriptures are pondered, its promises received in the mind, faith is strengthened, confidence in God increased, assurance deepened. By this we may discover whether or no we are profiting from our study of the Bible.

5. A fuller delight in God's perfections.

That in which a man most delights is his "god". The poor worldling seeks satisfaction in his pursuits, pleasures and possessions. Ignoring the Substance, he vainly pursues the shadows. But the Christian delights in the wondrous perfections of God. To really own God as **our** God, is not only to submit to His sceptre, but it is to love Him more than the world, to value Him above everything and everyone else. It is to have with the Psalmist an experimental realization that "all my springs are in Thee" (Psa. 89:7). The redeemed have not only received a joy from God such as this poor world cannot impart, but they "rejoice **in** God" (Rom. 5:11) such as the poor worlding knows nothing about. The language of such is "the Lord is **my Portion**" (Lam. 3:24).

Spiritual exercises are irksome to the flesh. But the real Christian says, "it is **good** for me to draw near to God" (Psa. 73:28). The carnal man has many cravings and ambitions: the regenerate soul declares, "**One** thing have I desired of the Lord, that will I seek after; that I may dwell in the house of the Lord all the days of my life, to behold the beauty of the Lord" (Psa. 27:4). And why? Because the true sentiment of his heart is, "whom have I in heaven but Thee? and there is none upon earth that I desire beside Thee' (Psa. 73:25). Ah, my reader, if your heart has not been drawn out to love and **delight in** God, then it is still dead toward Him.

The language of the saints is, "Although the fig tree shall not blossom, neither shall fruit be in the vines; the labour of the olive shall fail, and the fields shall yield no meat; the flocks shall be cut off from the fold, and no herd in the stalls; **yet** I will rejoice in the Lord, I will **joy** in the God of my salvation" (Hab. 3:17, 18). Ah, that **is** a supernatural experience indeed! Yes, the Christian can rejoice when all his worldly possessions are taken from him: see Heb. 10:34. When he lies in a dungeon with back bleeding, he can still sing praises to God: see Acts 16:25. Thus, to the extent that you are being weaned from the empty pleasures of this world, are learning that there is no blessing outside of God, are discovering He is the Source and Sum of excellency, and your heart is being drawn out to Him, your mind stayed upon Him, your soul finding its joy and satisfaction in Him, are you really profiting from the Scriptures.

6. A larger submission to God's providences.

It is natural to murmur when things go wrong, it is supernatural to hold our peace (Lev. 10:3). It is natural to be disappointed when our plans miscarry, it is supernatural to bow to **His** appointment. It is natural to want our own way, it is supernatural to say, "Not my will, but Thine be done". It is natural to rebel when a loved one is taken from us by death, it is supernatural to say from the heart "The Lord gave, and the Lord hath taken away, **blessed be** the name of the Lord" (Job 1.21). As God is truly made our Portion, we learn to admire His wisdom and to know that He doeth all things well. Thus the heart is kept in "perfect peace" as the mind is stayed on Him (Isa. 26:3). Here, then is another sure test: if your Bible-study is teaching you that **God's** way is best, if it is causing you to submit unrepiningly to all His dispensations, if you are enabled to give thanks for **all** things (Eph. 5:20), then are you profiting indeed.

7. A more fervent praise for God's goodness.

Praise is the outflow of a heart which finds its satisfaction in God. The language of such an one is, "I will bless the Lord at all times, His praise shall continually be in my mouth" (Psa. 34:1). What abundant cause have God's people for praising Him! Loved with an everlasting love, made sons and heirs, all things working together for their good, their every need supplied, an eternity of bliss assured them. Their harps of gladness ought never to be silent. Nor will they be while they enjoy fellowship with Him who is "Altogether Lovely". The more we are "increasing in the knowledge of God" (Col. 1:10), the more shall we adore Him. But it is only as the Word dwells in us richly that we are filled with spiritual songs (Col. 3:16) and make melody in our hearts to the Lord. The more our souls are drawn out in true worship, the more we are found thanking and praising our great God, the clearer evidence we give that our study of His Word is profiting us.

—ARTHUR W. PINK.

To live Christ, is to live in the full belief that God hath made Christ to be unto us, wisdom and righteousness, and sanctification and redemption; you will, as far as you thus live, triumph in Christ indeed. And it is your birthright so to do; for Christ, and all His salvation, and all the blessings of it belong to you, as much and as truly as any saint in glory. Therefore be not slack to praise Him, and in praising Him your faith will be strengthened, and you will increase in the knowledge of Him, and this will endear Him more and more unto you, and He will be increasingly precious unto you.

It is good for us to be always looking to, believing in, and living by the faith of the Son of God. It is well with us when Christ dwells in our hearts by faith. For whilst our minds are spiritually, properly, distinctly, and truly exercised on Him, He is then most truly our all: we cannot be more blessed, happy, and holy than at such seasons. We are at all seasons what our minds are; if Jesus is the subject of our thoughts, then they are spiritually influenced according to the subject. I should be glad to have it as natural to think on Christ, as it is natural to be sinful; and I think indeed it is natural to the renewed mind, where Christ has been revealed from the Word and by the Holy Spirit to it, to be exercised on Him, as for the natural mind to be exercised on natural things. It is generally objected to this, that we have all in our fallen natures which is opposite to all this; we have, but the body of grace is as complete as the body of sin, and the Holy Spirit dwells in us to quicken every grace; to put the whole into spiritual act; to draw it all forth, to exercise it all on Christ Jesus. It is the very element of the new creature to live on Christ; the new creation does not live on itself, or its own acts; no, nor on any comforts neither. The whole being and the well-being of the new creature is in Christ.

When we live on Christ, we live out of ourselves, without thinking anything about ourselves. Neither interest in Christ, nor comforts flowing from Christ, are what faith is exercised on. The person of Christ, the love of Christ, the undertakings of Christ, the incarnation of Christ, the life of Christ, the sacrifice, death, burial, resurrection, and ascension of Christ, His love to us, and life in heaven for us, are what faith, true faith, Gospel faith, that which is of the operations of the Spirit, is exercised on. Think on this; then all creature acts, and affections, towards Christ are nothing worth; indeed they are not. We must be dead to self, and all which belongs to it, or we cannot live to Christ. We must know more of Christ than we do of sin and self, or we shall never renounce self and live above sin; and we must know the value and virtue of Christ's blood, or we shall never get above the guilt of sin. we must get above the guilt of sin, or we shall never live above the love and power of sin. Say you to me, why I know all this; well, then, I say, put it all into practice.

—S. E. PIERCE, 1809.

We shall value the prayers of the Christian readers at this time that the Lord will graciously make it clear whether He would have us engage in oral ministry in and around Los Angeles; and that if so, He will direct and provide some place for us.

and decay in all around we see, may He who changeth not abide with thee. God's purpose never alters. One of two things causes a man to change his mind and reverse his plans: want of foresight to anticipate everything, or lack of power to execute them. But as God is both omniscient and omnipotent there is never any need for Him to revise His decrees. No, "The counsel of the Lord standeth forever, the thoughts of His heart to all generations" (Psa. 33:11). Therefore do we read of "The immutability of His counsel" (Heb. 6:17).

Herein we may perceive the infinite distance which separates the highest creature from the Creator. Creaturehood and mutability are correlative terms. If the creature was not mutable by nature, it would not be a creature; it would be God. By nature we tend to nothing, as we came from nothing. Nothing stays our annihilation but the will and sustaining power of God. None can sustain himself a single moment. We are entirely dependent on the Creator for every breath we draw. We gladly own with the Psalmist Thou "holdest our soul in life" (Psa. 66:9). The realization of this ought to make us lie down under a sense of our own nothingness in the presence of Him "in whom we live and move, and have our being".

As fallen creatures we are not only mutable, but everything in us is **opposed** to God. As such we are "wandering stars" (Jude 13), out of our proper orbit. The wicked are "like the troubled sea, when it **cannot rest**" (Isa. 57:20). Fallen man is inconstant. The words of Jacob concerning Reuben apply with full force to all of Adam's decendants: "Unstable as water" (Gen. 49:4). Thus it is not only a mark of piety, but also the part of wisdom to heed that injunction, "cease ye **from man**" (Isa. 2:22). No human being is to be depended on. "Put not your trust in princes, in the son of man, in whom is **no help**" (Psa. 146:3). If I disobey God, then I deserve to be deceived and disappointed by my fellows. People who like you today, may hate you tomorrow. The multitude who cried "Hosanna to the Son of David", speedily changed to "Away with Him, Crucify Him".

Herein is solid **comfort**. Human nature cannot be relied upon; but God can! However unstable I may be, however fickle my friends may prove, God changes not. If He varied as we do, if He willed one thing today and another tomorrow, if He were controlled by caprice, who could confide in Him? But, all praise to His glorious name, He is ever the same. His purpose is fixed, His will stable, His word is sure. Here then is a **rock** on which we may fix our feet, while the mighty torrent is sweeping away everything around us. The permanence of God's character guarantees the fulfillment of His promises: "For the mountains shall depart, and the hills be removed; but My kindness shall not depart from thee, neither shall the covenant of My peace be removed, saith the Lord that hath mercy on thee" (Isa. 54:10).

Herein is **encouragement to prayer**. "What comfort would it be to pray to a god that, like the chameleon, changed colour every moment? Who would put up a petition to an earthly prince that was so mutable as to grant a petition one day, and deny it another"? (S. Charnock, 1670). Should some one ask, But what is the use of praying to One whose will is already fixed? We answer, Because He so requires it. What blessings has God promised without our seeking them? "If we ask anything according to His will, He heareth us" (1 John 5:14), and He **has** willed everything that is for His child's good. To ask for anything contrary to His will, is not prayer, but rank rebellion.

Herein is terror **for the wicked**. Those who defy Him, break His laws, have no concern for His glory, but live their lives as though He existed not, must not suppose that, when at the last they shall cry to Him for mercy, He will alter His will, revoke His word, and rescind His awful threatenings. No, He has declared, "Therefore will I also deal in fury: Mine eye shall not spare, neither will I have pity: and though they cry in Mine ears with a loud voice, yet will I not hear them" (Ezek. 8:18). God will not deny Himself to gratify their lusts. God is holy, unchangingly so. Therefore God hates sin, eternally hates it. Hence the **eternality** of the punishment of all who die in their sins.

"The Divine immutability, like the cloud which interposed between the Israelites and the Egyptian army, has a dark as well as a light side. It insures the execution of His threatenings, as well as the performance of His promises; and destroys the hope which the guilty fondly cherish, that He will be all lenity to His frail and erring creatures, and that they will be much more lightly dealt with than the declarations of His own Word would lead us to expect. We oppose to these deceitful and presumptuous speculations the solemn truth, that God is unchanging in veracity and purpose, in faithfulness and justice" (J. Dick, 1850).

—ARTHUR W. PINK.

VOL. IX.　　　　　AUGUST, 1930　　　　　No. 8

STUDIES IN THE SCRIPTURES

"Search the Scriptures" John 5 : 39

Copyright in all English-speaking Countries.

Editor: Arthur W. Pink, 1139 Alameda Ave., Glendale, Calif. 'Phone: Burbank 2155
Hon. Agent in England: Mr. A. Winstone, "Shalom", Old Bath Road, Leckhampton, Cheltenham.
Hon. Agent in Australia: Mr. G. Ardill, The Christian Workers' Depot. Commonwealth and Reservoir Streets, Sydney.

THE HOLINESS OF GOD.

"Who shall not fear Thee, O Lord, and glorify Thy name? for Thou only art holy" (Rev. 15:4). He only is independently, infinitely, immutably holy. In Scripture He is frequently styled "The Holy One": He is so because the sum of all moral excellency is found in Him. He is absolute Purity, unsullied even by the shadow of sin. "God is light, and in Him is no darkness at all" (1 John 1:5). Holiness is the very excellency of the Divine nature: the great God is "glorious in holiness" (Ex. 15:11). Therefore do we read, "Thou art of purer eyes than to behold evil, and canst not look on iniquity" (Hab. 1:13). As God's power is the opposite of the native weakness of the creature, as His wisdom is in complete contrast from the least defect of understanding or folly, so His holiness is the very antithesis of all moral blemish or defilement. Of old God appointed singers in Israel "that they should praise for the beauty of holiness" (2 Chron. 20:21). "Power is God's hand or arm, omniscience His eye, mercy, His bowels, eternity His duration, but holiness is His beauty". (S. Charnock). It is this, supremely, which renders Him lovely to those who are delivered from sin's dominion.

A chief emphasis is placed upon this perfection of God. "God is oftener styled Holy than Almighty, and set forth by this part of His dignity more than by any other. This is more fixed on as an epithet to His name than any other. You never find it expressed 'His mighty name' or 'His wise name', but His **great** name, and most of all His **holy** name. This is the greatest title of honour; in this latter doth the majesty and venerableness of His name appear" (S. Charnock). This perfection, as none other, is solemnly celebrated before the Throne of Heaven, the seraphim crying, "Holy, holy, holy, is the Lord of hosts" (Isa. 6:3). God Himself singles out this perfection, "Once have I sworn by My holiness" (Psa. 89.35). God swares by His "holiness" because that is a **fuller** expression of Himself than anything else. Therefore are we exhorted, "Sing unto the Lord, O ye saints of His, and give thanks at the remembrance of His holiness" (Psa. 30:4). "This may be said to be a transcendental attribute, that, as it were, runs through the rest, and casts lustre upon them. It is an attribute of attributes" (J. Howe, 1670). Thus we read of "the **beauty** of the Lord" (Psa. 27:4), which is none other than "the beauty of holiness" (Psa. 110:3).

"As it seems to challenge an excellency above all His other perfections, so it is the glory of all the rest: as it is the glory of the Godhead, so it is the glory of every perfection in the Godhead; as His power is the strength of them, so His holiness is the beauty of them; as all would be weak without almightiness to back them, so all would be uncomely without holiness to adorn them. Should this be sullied, all the rest would lose their honour; as at the same instant that the sun should lose its light, it would lose its heat, its strength, its generative and quickening virtue. As sincerity is the lustre of every grace in a Christian, so is purity the splendour of every attribute in the Godhead. His justice is a holy justice, His wisdom a holy wisdom, His arm of power a 'holy arm' (Psa. 98:1), His truth or promise a 'holy promise' (Psa. 105:42). His name, which signifies all His attributes in conjunction, 'is holy', Psa. 103:1" (S. Charnock).

God's holiness is manifested in His **works**. "The Lord is righteous in all His ways, and holy in all His works" (Psa. 145:17). Nothing but that which is excellent can proceed from Him. Holiness is the rule of all His actions. At the beginning He

(Continued on Page 192)

IMPORTANT NOTICES

Please advise promptly of change of address, otherwise copies will be lost in the mails.

We are glad to send a sample copy to any of your friends whom you believe would be interested in such a publication.

Send to Mr. I. C. Herendeen, Swengel (Union County), Penna., for a list of our publications. He has published many of our books and booklets.

This magazine is published as a work of faith and labour of love. The Editor and his wife gladly give their services. It is freely sent to all who will read it. No charge is made for it.

Christians who feel definitely led to do so, may have fellowship with us in this ministry. Those outside the U. S. A., please send only INTERNATIONAL Money Orders made out to Glendale, California, U. S. A.

CONTENTS

The Epistle to the Hebrews	170
The Satisfaction of Christ	176
The Believer's Blessedness in Glory	182
Welcome Tidings	186
An Exposition of Psalm 1	188

THE EPISTLE TO THE HEBREWS.

32. The Priesthood Changed: Heb. 7:11-16

In 5:1-9 the apostle had shown (in part, for he returns to the same theme again in chap. 9) how Christ fulfilled that which Aaron had foreshadowed of Him as the High Priest of His people. Then, in 5:11 he declares Christ had been hailed by God as High Priest "after the order of Melchizedek". Immediately following, the apostle adds that, though he had "many things" to say of him, he was restrained through the Hebrews' dullness. After a lengthy parenthesis in which he corrects their faulty condition, return is made to the subject of Christ's priesthood in 6:20, which is amplified in chap. 7. The main object now before him was to show that Christ is superior to the Jewish high priest, and, in proof, he appeals to the striking type of Melchizedek. Concerning that type he pointed out that not only was Melchizedek greater in his own person than Aaron, but that his superiority had been **owned** by the whole Levitical stock, inasmuch as they, represented by Abraham, had done homage to him.

In the second section of chap. 7 which begins at v. 11, the apostle points out the inevitable inferences which must be drawn from and the certain corollaries which are involved in what had just been shown. The fact that the Messiah was Priest after the order of Melchizedek, necessarily set aside the Levitical order. The fact that God had sent His Son to perform a sacerdotal work, plainly signified that the ministry of Aaron and his successors was inadequate. The fact that "perfection" was not brought in till Christ offered Himself as a sacrifice to God, clearly showed that imperfection attached to those who preceded Him. To bring this out the more clearly was the great design of the apostle in the verses which are to be before us. He had now reached that which was the most difficult for the Jews to receive, viz., that what had been so long venerated by their fathers had now been set aside by God.

To announce that the Mosaic economy was temporary, inadequate, defective, was unbelievable to a pious but unregenerate Israelite, and it was something which was far from easy to prove to a regenerated Jew. They believed that the Levitical system of priesthood **was** "perfect". It had been instituted by Jehovah Himself, so surely it must be sufficient and permanent! If the whole Aaronic system was of Divine appointment how could it possibly be, **in itself**, so unsatisfactory that it must now be discarded? The apostle might have reasoned from the analogies supplied by Nature. Many things made by God—such as the chrysalis for the butterfly—serve a temporary purpose and then become useless when a more perfect stage of development is reached. But the apostle takes much higher ground and proves by invincible logic that the Levitical system **was** imperfect, and therefore had been superceded by something else.

God had raised up a Priest who belonged not to the Levitical tribe. This the believing Hebrews freely granted: that Jesus Christ had by His sacrifice put away their sins and brought them nigh unto God, was the glorious truth they espoused when they received the Gospel. But they were slow to perceive and acknowledge the necessary **implications** of it. That the Lord Jesus was Priest "after the order of Melchizedek", intimated unequivocally that the priesthood which preceded His was incapable of producing "perfection", for there was no need of introducing something new if the old met all the requirements of God. But more: not only did Christ's bringing in "perfection" presuppose the imperfection of the old order, but it necessarily involved a **change of economy** i.e. all that was distinctly associated with the Levitical system was now effete, out of date. It is **this** which the apostle proceeds to show.

It was never the intention of God that the Levitical priesthood should remain forever, for in the **Old** Testament Scriptures He gave intimation of **another** Priest, of another order, rising to supercede the former. That intimation was to be found, first, in Gen. 14, where the head and representative of the whole Jewish race had owned Melchizedek as the priest of the most High God. Still plainer was the prophecy which God gave to David. In the 110th Psalm He had greeted the Messiah with these words, "Sit Thou at My right hand" (v. 1), and then He had declared "The Lord hath sworn, and will not repent, Thou art a priest forever after the order of Melchizedek" (v. 4). This the apostle here cites, and by so doing bases his argument on a ground which no pious Jew could gainsay: the inspired and infallible testimony of Holy Scripture. Therefore if Christ was Priest "after the order of Melchizedek", the Aaronic **must be** imperfect, or there had been no need for introducing this change.

"If therefore perfection were by the Levitical priesthood (for under it the people received the law), what further need that another priest should rise after the order of Melchizedek, and not be called after the order of Aaron?" (v. 11). The apostle now points out some of the **consequences** of Christ's being a Priest "after the order of Melchizedek". The first he mentions is that the Levitical was unable to bring in "perfection". This was evident. Had it done so there was no need for introducing another. But wherein was it that the Levitical system fell short? What was it that it failed to procure? To answer these questions we need to carefully weigh the expression "perfection".

The term "perfection" is one of the characteristic and key-words of this Epistle. It has a different shade of meaning than it has in the other Pauline Epistles. Unless careful attention be paid to its immediate connections, we are almost certain to fall into an erroneous conception of its force. It has to do more with **relationship** than experience, though as the relationship is spiritually apprehended a corresponding experience follows. It concerns the **objective** side of things rather than the subjective. It looks to the judicial and vital aspect rather than to the experimental and practical. Its first occurrences are in 2.10 and 5:9, used of Christ Himself, where the obvious reference is what pertained to Him officially rather than personally. Then it is found in 6:1—compare our comments thereon. In 9:9 we are told that in O. T. times the gifts and sacrifices offered "could not make him that did the service perfect as pertaining to the conscience". The same thing is affirmed in 10:1. But in blessed contrast therefrom we read, "For by one offering He hath perfected forever them that are sanctified" (10:14).

"Perfection" means, the bringing of a thing to that completeness of condition designed for it. Doctrinally it refers to the producing of a satisfactory and final relation between God and men. It speaks of that unchangable standing in the favour and blessing of God which Christ has secured for His people. In 12:23 we read of "the spirits of just men **made perfect**", which does not mean that the O. T. saints had been perfected in holiness and happiness (though that, of course, was true of them), but that they had been "made perfect" as their **title** to heavenly glory. This did not take place till the sacrifice of Christ had been offered, though, in the certain prospect of its accomplishment, they had received the blessings which flow from it long before: cf. 11:40.

In our present section the apostle insists that "perfection" could not be produced by the Levites, and that a priesthood which **did** bring in perfection must be superior. It therefore remains for us to enquire next, What are the great ends of priesthood? What is it that the priest should effect? The priest was the mediator who drew near unto God on behalf of others. His work was to present to Him a sacrifice for the satisfying of Divine justice. It was to effect such a procuring of His favour and such a securing of a standing-ground before Him for those whom he represented, that their conscience might be at peace. It was to come forth from His presence that he might pronounce blessing. **Had** the Levitical priesthood been able to obtain these things? Had Aaron and his successors obtained God's remission from all the consequences of sin and brought in a complete and abiding redemption? No, indeed.

The office and work of a priesthood may be considered two ways: first, as it respects **God**, who is the prime and immediate object of all the proper acts of that office; second, as it respects **His people**, who are the subject of its blessings and the beneficiaries of its administration. As priesthood respects God, its chief design was to make expiation of sin by means of an atoning sacrifice. But this the Levitical priesthood was unable to do. A typical, ceremonial, and temporary value attached to their sacerdotal ministrations; but an effectual, vital, and permanent did not. This is positively stated in 10:4, "For it is not possible that the blood of bulls and of goats should take away sins". Why, then, were such appointed? To exhibit the holy claims of God and the requirements of His justice; to prefigure the great Sacrifice yet to come.

Let us next inquire, **What** was the "perfection" which **Christ** hath brought in? And here we cannot do better than give a summary of the most helpful exposition of J. Owen. That which Christ hath produced to the glory of God and the blessing of His people is, first, **righteousness**. The introduction of all imperfection was by sin. This made the law weak (Rom. 8:3) and sinners to be "without strength" (Rom. 5.7). Therefore perfection must be introduced by righteousness. **That** was the fundamental of the new covenant: see Isa. 60:21, Psa. 72:7, etc. Therefore do the saints speak of Christ as "The Lord our righteousness" (Jer. 23:6). Christ has brought in an "everlasting righteousness" (Dan. 9:24), and therefore are believers "made the righteousness of God in Him" (2 Cor. 5:21).

Second, **peace** is the next thing which belongs to the evangelical "perfection" of Christianity. As the High Priest of the covenant it pertained to the Lord Jesus to make peace between God and sinners. "When we were enemies, we were reconciled to God by the death of His Son" (Rom 5:10). Therefore is He denominated "The Prince of peace" (Isa. 9:6): He is such because He has "made peace through the blood of His cross" (Col. 1:20). The result of this is that believers have "peace with God through our Lord Jesus Christ" (Rom. 5.1). Thus the evangel we proclaim is "The Gospel of peace" (Eph. 6:15).

Third, **light**. God designed for Christians a greater measure of spiritual light and knowledge of the mysteries of His wisdom and grace than were attainable under the law. God reserved for His Son the honour of making known the **fulness** of His counsels (John 1:18, Heb. 1:1, 2). There was under the Levitical priesthood but a "**shadow** of good things to come" (Heb. 10:1), but the mystery of them remained hid in God (Eph. 3:9). The prophets themselves perceived not the depths of their own predictions (1 Peter 1:11, 12). Hence, the attitude of the O. T. Church was a looking forward unto a fuller revelation: "till the day break, and the shadows flee away" (Song of Sol. 2:17, 4:6). The contrast between the two economies is seen in 1 John 2:8, "The darkness is past, and the true light **now** shineth".

Fourth, **access to God**. There belongs to the "perfection" which Christ hath brought in, a liberty and boldness of approach unto the throne of grace that was not only unknown but expressly forbidden under the law. At Sinai the people were fenced off at the foot of the mount, when Jehovah appeared to Moses on its summit. In the tabernacle, none save the priests were suffered to go beyond the outer court, and they not at all into the holy of holies where God dwelt. How blessed is the contrast today. "For through Him we both **have access** by one Spirit into the Father" (Eph. 2:18)! To us the word is, "Having therefore, brethren, boldness to enter into the holiest by the blood of Jesus, let us draw near with a true heart in full assurance of faith" (Heb. 10:19, 22).

Fifth, the **unveiling of the future state**. Christ hath "brought life and immortality to light through the Gospel" (2 Tim. 1:10). Whatever knowledge of resurrection and eternal blessedness individual saints enjoyed in O. T. times, it was **not** conveyed to them by the ministrations of the Levitical priesthood. That which characterized the people under the Mosaic law was that they "through fear of death were all their lifetime subject to bondage" (Heb. 2:15). Nor could it be otherwise while the curse of the law hung over them. But now our great High Priest has endured the curse for us. He entered the devouring jaws of death. But He did not remain there. He triumphed over the grave, and in the resurrection of Christ His people have the evidence, guarantee, and pattern, of their own victory too. He has gone on High, and that as **our** "Forerunner" (6:20). And His request is, "Father, I will that they also, whom Thou hast given Me, be with Me where I am" (John 17:24).

Sixth, **joy**. "The kingdom of God is, . . . righteousness and peace and joy in the Holy Spirit" (Rom. 14:17). True it is that many of the O. T. saints rejoiced greatly in the Lord, yet it was not by virtue of the Levitical priesthood. The ground of their joy was that death would be swallowed up in victory (Isa. 25:8), and that awaited the death and resurrection of Christ. Therefore did Abraham rejoice to see **His** day (John 8:56). But ordinarily their joy was mixed and allayed with a respect unto temporal things: see Lev. 23.39-41, Deut. 12:11, 12, 18, etc. But the Christian has a joy "unspeakable, and full of glory" (1 Peter 1:8). It is that inexpressible satisfaction which is wrought in his mind by the Holy Spirit, from the knowledge of his interest in the love of God by Jesus Christ. This gives the soul a repose in all trials, refreshment when it is weary, peace in trouble, delight in tribulations: Rom. 5:1-5.

Seventh, **glorying in the Lord**. This is the fruit of joy. One chief design of the Gospel is to exclude all human boasting, to empty us of glorying in self (Rom. 3:27, Eph. 2:9). God has so ordered things that no flesh should now glory in His presence, so that he that glorieth must glory in the Lord (1 Cor. 1:29, 31). Thus it was promised of old: see Isa. 45:25. Glorying in the Lord is that high exultation of spirit which causes believers to esteem their interest in heavenly things high above things present, to despise and condemn all that is contrary thereto, to say with the apostle, "God forbid that I should glory save in the cross of our Lord Jesus Christ". If the reader desires to follow up more fully the contrast between the glory and excellency of the two economies, the Mosaic and the Christian, let him study 2 Cor. 3.

Ere leaving this blessed subject, let us make a brief practical application of what has been before us. To be a real Christian is to have a personal and vital interest in and be an actual participant of those blessings which the "perfection" of Christ has brought in. Multitudes make an outward profesion of the same; few have an experimental acquaintance with them. Again; the pre-eminence of Christianity over Judaism is entirely spiritual and cannot be discerned by the carnal eye: wherein it excels has been pointed out above—it consists of a clearer knowledge of God, a freer approach to Him, a fuller enjoyment of Him. Finally, let it be said that the attempts to find glory and satisfaction in outward forms and ceremonies is to prefer the Levitical priesthood before that of Christ's. **That** is the outstanding sin of all ritualists.

A brief word needs to be added upon the parenthetic clause of v. 11: "For under it the people received the law". Its evident design was to strengthen the apostle's argument. It is brought in as a subsidiary proof that "perfection" could not be by the Levitical priesthood. We are therefore disposed to regard "the law" here as referring to the whole system of the Mosaic economy. The passive "received the law" is a single word in the Greek, and really means "were legalized". The reference is not to the actual giving of the law, but to the state of the people under it, their being brought beneath its power. The law demanded perfect righteousness, but fallen man was incapable of producing it (Rom. 3:19, 20; 8-3); nor could the Levitical priesthood effect it. Thus the only hope lay outside of themselves. "**Christ** is the end of the law for righteousness to every one that believeth" (Rom. 10:4).

"For the priesthood being changed, there is made of necessity a change also of the law" (v. 12). Here the apostle names the second **consequence** which must be drawn from the facts stated in vv. 1-10. First, the Levitical priesthood was inadequate, incapable of producing "perfection". Second, therefore it was but a temporary institution, and the whole economy connected with it must be set aside. In other words, Judaism as such, was now defunct. Thus "a change of the law" means a change of dispensation, a change of Divine administration. This at once fixes the meaning of "law" in the parenthetic clause of the previous verse. The reference is not to the ten commandments, but to the Mosaic system.

The "change also of the law" or setting aside of the Mosaic system was that to which the Jews were so strenuously opposed. They stoned Stephen (Acts 6:14), and vented their rage upon Paul, on this very charge (Acts 21:28). Yea, many who professed the faith of the Gospel continued to obstinately contend that the Mosaic law remained in force (Acts 21:20). It was this same contention which caused so much trouble in the early churches, the Judaisers harassing the Gentile converts with their insistence upon circumcision and subjection to the ceremonial law. Difficult as it was for a pious Jew to believe that God should have set aside as dead and useless the whole solemn system of worship, which He had appointed in so glorious a manner and accepted for so many centuries, yet the proof that He **had** done so was abundant and clear. The law and the Gospel could not mix. Works and grace are antithetical. Moses must disappear when Christ was revealed: carefully compare Mark 9:5-8! So far from God's people being the losers they are immeasurably the gainers by His bringing in the "better hope" (7:19).

"For He of whom these things are spoken pertaineth to another tribe, of which no man gave attendance at the altar" (v. 13). The argument of this verse, introduced by the "for", makes it plain that it is **not** the moral law which the apostle had reference to at the close of the preceding verse: the closing words of the next verse make this still more evident. We mention this because certain "Dispensationalists" have appealed to Heb. 7:12 in their misguided efforts to show that Christians are, in no sense, under the ten commandments. The moral law is not at all under discussion in this passage. 1 Cor. 9:21. 1 John 2:6, etc., are quite sufficient to prove that the moral law has not been (and never will be) repealed.

"For He of whom these things are spoken pertaineth to another tribe, of which no man gave attendance at the altar". The apostle's object here is to give further proof that the Levitical priesthood, and the entire ceremonial law, had been set aside by God. He appeals to the fact that our Lord, according to the flesh, belonged not to the tribe of Levi, and therefore His sacerdotal office was not according to the Aaronic order. The expresion "attendance at the altar" signifies, "exercising priestly functions". The "these things" looks back to what is said at the end of v. 11, which receives amplification in vv. 17, 21.

The honour of the Aaronic order of priesthood continued, by Divine appointment and privilege, within the bounds of the Levitical tribe: Ex. 40:12-16. None belonging to any other tribe in Israel was suffered to officiate at the altar or minister in the holy place. So strictly was this institution observed, that when one of Israel's kings dared to violate it, the judgment of God fell immediately upon him (2 Chron. 26:18-21). In smiting Uzziah with leprosy God maintained the sanctity of His law, and gave a most solemn warning against any obtruding into holy office who have received no Divine call to it. Furthermore, this exercise of God's severity should have been more than a hint to Israelites that when **He** did introduce a priest of another tribe then the priesthood of the old order **must** have been Divinely set aside.

"For it is evident that our Lord sprang out of Judah; of which tribe Moses spake nothing concerning priesthood" (v. 14). The opening "for" at once denotes the apostle is here continuing his proof that the Levitical priesthood and economy was now a thing of the past so far as God's recognition of it was concerned. His words here contain a double assertion: our Lord, according to His humanity, belonged to the tribe of Judah; of that tribe Moses revealed nothing concerning priesthood. All that was needed to complete the proof of his argument was that Christ **was** a Priest: this he shows in the ensuing verses. The appeal made to this verse by those who deny that the Lord Jesus entered upon His priestly office till after His ascension, proceeds from such gross ignorance or malice that it deserves no direct refutation.

First, it was "evident" that our Lord "sprang"—as the "Rod" out of Jesse's stem—from Judah. This was included in the faith of believers that the Messiah was to come out of the royal tribe. Such prophecies as Gen. 49:8-10, 2 Sam. 7:12, Isa. 11:1-5, Micah 5.2 had made that very plain. The genealogy recorded in Matt. 1 established the same fact. Whoever therefore acknowledge the Lord Jesus to be the true Messiah, as all to whom the apostle was directly writing did, (though most of them still clung to the ceremonial law), granted that He was of the tribe of Judah. Nor did the unbelieving Jews deny it. In passing, we may note that Judah signifies "praise": Christ still dwells in the midst of His people's praises!

Second, about Judah Moses spake nothing concerning priesthood. The apostle's object is to render it conclusive that God's raising up of a Priest out of the royal tribe, must necessarily exclude all the house of Aaron from sharing His office. Moses did specify that the priesthood should be exercised by those belonging to the tribe of Levi, but he nowhere intimated that a time would come when it should be transferred to the royal family. Here again we may take note of the significance of the **silences** of Scripture, and the justification of arguing therefrom. As, for example, no mention is made of the month in which the Saviour was born, intimating that God did not intend us to celebrate the anniversary of His birth: cf. Jer. 7:31. Paul here reasons from the silence of Moses as being quite sufficient to show that the legal or Aaronic priesthood could not be transferred to the tribe of Judah.

"And it is yet far more evident: for that after the similitude of Melchizedek there ariseth another priest" (v. 15). In this and the next verse the apostle presents the third **consequence** which follows from the facts set forth in vv. 1-10. First, he had pointed out from those facts that, it necessarily followed the Levitical priesthood was inadequate, for it was unable to bring in "perfection". Second, therefore it was evident that the Levitical priesthood could only be a temporary institution, and that the whole economy connected with and based upon it must be set aside. Third, he now insists that the priesthood of Christ must be radically different from and be immeasurably superior to the Levitical order. So much for the general scope of these two verses. Let us now attend to their details.

"And it is yet far more evident". **What** is it that was "far more evident"? What was the particular point to which the apostle was here calling the Hebrews' attention? Not that Christ had sprung from the tribe of Judah, nor that He fulfilled the Melchizedek type, but that the Levitical priesthood and economy was now obsolete. The proof that this **was** so obvious is presented in what immediately follows. That proof may be expressed thus: the priesthood of Christ was no temporary expedient, brought in only to supply the deficiency of the Levitical order. No; it was a permanent office and abiding ministry. Therefore as God would not own two separate and different priesthoods, the former and inferior must give place to the latter. The second, "consequence" had been drawn from the tribal humanity of Christ; this third "consequence", from the character of His priesthood.

"And it is yet far more evident". It is to be carefully noted that the apostle did not say "it is far more **certain**". No, he was not absolutely comparing one thing with another, but comparing them only with respect to their evidential significance, the relative force of those facts to all who were capable of weighing them. The fact that God had caused our great "High Priest" to spring from the tribe of Judah rather than from that of Levi, made it obvious that the Aaronic order could no longer continue. But the further fact that He had been made "after the similitude of Melchizedek", rendered this still more obvious. The apostle is but adding argument to argument, in order to show how wrong it was for the Hebrews to still cling to Judaism.

"For that after the similitude of Melchizedek there ariseth another priest". The Greek word for "similitude" means "likeness" and occurs elsewhere only in 4:15. The emphatic term here is "**another** priest". It is not "allos" which means another of the same species, but "heteros", another of a totally different order: one who was a stranger to the house of Aaron. Let the reader consult Ex. 29:33, Lev. 22: 10, Num. 16.40, and he will see how imposible it was for one from the tribe of Judah to perpetuate the Levitical priesthood. The word "ariseth" is also very emphatic. It means to be brought forth after an extraordinary manner: cf. Judges 5:7, Deut. 18:18, Luke 1:69. The arising of Christ in His priestly office put an end to the Aaronic, just as His arising in the hearts of His people (2 Peter 1:19) puts an end to their looking to anything or anyone else for salvation.

"Who is made, not after the law of a carnal commandment, but after the power of an endless life" (v. 16). This completes the sentence begun in v. 15. The apostle is still showing how manifest it was that the Levitical priesthood had been set aside, for one infinitely superior had now been set up by God. The contrast here made between the two is very striking. The Aaronic was constituted "according to the law of commandment fleshly". The same expresion is used in Eph. 2:15 to designate the whole system of worship under Judaism. This emphatic denomination may be accounted for by the fact that under it commandments were so multiplied, and because of the severity wherewith obedience was exacted. The Levitical priesthood was "carnal", first, inasmuch as the sacrifices offered at their consecration were the bodies of beasts. Second, inasmuch as the priesthood was by fleshly propagation, from father to son. Third, inasmuch as their ministrations availed **only** to the "purifying of the flesh" (9:13). In sharp contrast, Christ was not dedicated to His office by the sacrifice of beasts, nor did He claim any right to it by His natural descent.

"Who is made . . . after the power of an endless life". Let the reader compare our remarks on 5:5. The Lord Christ did not merely on His own authority and power take the priestly office upon Himself, but by the appointment of His Father The way or manner in which He **was** "made priest" is here stated: according to the power of an indissoluable life". These words have been grossly wrested by those who seek to prove by them that Christ never entered upon the priestly office until after His resurrection. It is truly pitiable to find those who ought to know better echoing the errors of "annihiliationists". Christ officiated as priest before His resurection, or He could not have offered Himself as a sacrifice to God. As this will, D. V., come before us again in the 9th. chapter we will say no more thereon at the present juncture.

Christ's "indissoluable life" here has unquestionable reference to His life as **the Son of God.** Upon **that** depended His own mediatorial life forever, and His conferring eternal life upon His people: John 5. 26, 27). It was only by the Mediator being made priest "after **the power of** an indissoluable life" that He was qualified to discharge that office, whereby **God** was to redeem His church with His own blood (Acts 20:28)—i. e. here called "His blood" because the humanity had been taken up into union with the second person in the Godhead. Should it be objected? But Christ died! True, yet his **person** still lived: though actually dead in His human nature, He was still alive in His indissoluable person, and therefore there was **no** interruption whatever to the discharge of His sacerdotal office; no, not for a moment. Thus the contrast between Aaron and Christ is that of a mortal man and "The King eternal, imortal, invisible" (1 Tim. 1:17).

How deeply thankful should every Christian be for **such** a Priest. The eternal Word became flesh. The Lord of glory stooped to become man. As the God-man He mediates between the ineffably holy God and sinful creatures. The Saviour is none other than Immanuel (Matt. 1:21, 23). In His humanity, He suffered, bled and died. But in His Divine-human person He Himself quickened that humanity (John 2:19, 10:18). We profess not to understand the mystery, but by grace, we believe what the Scriptures record concerning Him. The "life" that was given to Christ as the Mediator (unlike that of His humanity) was an indestructible one. Therefore He is "a Priest **forever**", and therefore "He ever liveth to make intercession" (7:25). Hallelujah!

—ARTHUR W. PINK.

THE SATISFACTION
("Atonement")
OF CHRIST

8. Its Nature: concluded.

We have pointed out in the preceding articles that the particular aspect of Christ's Satisfaction which is now before us constitutes the very heart of this mighty subject. As the physical heart is to the human body, so is the **nature** of the Atonement to the whole of this wondrous theme. When a man's heart becomes seriously affected, the whole of his constitution suffers. In like manner, when we err in our views of the precise **character** of Christ's obedience and sufferings, the whole of our system of truth suffers injury in exact proportion. The acid test of a theologian's views and a preacher's capability to expound the Gospel, is his orthodoxy at this particular point. Hence, because, **this** part of the Truth is of such vital importance we have prayerfully sought to examine it with sevenfold thoroughness, and set before our readers at some length the results of our investigation.

First, we have shown that the Work of Christ was **federal** in its character: that is, Christ became legally one with His people. He came here not to strangers, but to His "brethren" (Heb. 2.12). He came here not to procure a people for Himself, but to secure a people already His (Eph. 1:4, Matt. 1:21). The place we occupied was "under the law". We were placed under it at creation, and perfect obedience was made the condition of our well-being. By our fall in Adam we became incapable of obeying the demands of the law and subject to its unrelaxable penalty. The law remained over us, therefore, as an inexorable taskmaster, demanding the impossible, and as the organ of immutable justice, insisting upon our death. Therefore to be our Saviour the Son of God was "made under the law" (Gal. 4:4): He was, by God's ordination, transferred to that position. Thus, the place He took was our law-place. In taking that place He necessarily assumed all our responsibilities: obedience as a condition of life, suffering as a penal consequence of disobedience.

Second, we have shown that the work of Christ was **vicarious** in its character. Substitution has been thus defined: "A 'substitute' is one who does or suffers the same thing which the person or persons for whom he is substituted would have done or suffered". The Scriptures teach us plainly that Christ's obedience was as truly vicarious as was His suffering, and that He reconciled us to the Father by the one as well as the other. It is for this reason we have chosen the term "Satisfaction" in preference to the more popular "Atonement". "The word Atonement signifies only the expiation of our guilt by Christ's vicarious sufferings, but expresses nothing concerning the relation which His obedience sustains to our salvation, as that meritorious condition upon which the Divine favour and the promised reward have by covenant been suspended. On the other hand, the word Satisfaction exactly expresses **all** that Christ has done as our Substitute, in our stead, and for our sakes, to the end of satisfying in our behalf the federal demands of the law, and of securing for us the rewards conditioned upon their fulfillment. His whole work was of the nature of a satisfaction" (A. A. Hodge).

Third, we have shown that, the Work of Christ was **penal** in its character. This follows of inevitable necessity. In becoming one with His criminal people, Christ entered their law-place before God. In acting as the Substitute of His people, Christ must receive that which was due them from God. Because the sins of His Church were transferred to Christ, He must be paid their wages. Because He took our law-place, the curse of the law must fall upon Him. Because He was "made sin" for us, the sword of Divine justice must smite Him. As 1 Cor. 15:3 declares, the God-man not only died "for us", but "Christ died for **our sins**", which was only made possible by our sins having been federally placed upon Him. Because our sins were imputed to Him, the wroth of God fell upon Him, and He was visited with all that our sins merited. We are now ready to show,

4. It was a Sacrificial Work.

From the many passages which set forth this aspect of Christ's redemption, we may cite the following. "When Thou shalt make His soul **an offering** for sin" (Isa. 53:10). "Christ our passover is **sacrificed** for us" (1 Cor. 5:7). "Christ also hath loved us, and hath given Himself for us an offering and a sacrifice to God for a sweetsmelling savour" (Eph. 5:2). "Who needeth not daily, as those high priests, to offer up sacrifice . . . for this He did once, when He offered up Himself" (Heb. 7.27). "How much more shall the blood of Christ, who through the eternal Spirit **offered Himself** without spot to God, purge your conscience from dead works to serve the living God?" (Heb. 9:14).

Ere attempting to define the character of Christ's sacrifice, let us first remind ourselves that He presented Himself a sacrifice to God **by covenant argeement.** As we are told in Rom. 3:25 "Whom God hath **foreordained** a propitiation, through faith in His blood". God can be pleased only with that which He has appointed.

The Everlasting Covenant furnishes the key to many a verse of Scripture. For instance, when Christ was about to go to the cross, He said, "Now is the Son of Man **glorified**" (John 13:31). But how could that be? Was it not rather His degradation? No, for the Eternal Three had assigned to the God-man the work of mediation, and **that** was a high honour. So the Son of man viewed it. It is our "glory" too to bow to God's will and keep His appointments.

Second, though Christ offered Himself a sacrifice according to Divine appointment, it was also by His own **free consent.** As in all our obedience there are two principal ingredients to the true and right constitution of it, namely, the matter of the obedience itself, and the principle or fountain of it in us; in other words, the deed, and the will behind it—which latter God accepts in us, oftentimes without (2 Cor. 8:12) and always more than the outward deed—so in Christ's obedience, which is both the pattern and measure of ours, there are these two eminent parts which complete it:—the obedience itself, His willingness thereto. First, Christ was willing from all eternity. This is clear from the Covenant, for **that** is a mutual agreement between two parties. It is also necessarily implied in His being made "a Surety" (Heb. 7:22), an undertaking on His part: a surety is a plighter of his throth, by 'striking hands' as the phrase is in the original: Prov. 22:26. Again; His willingness from everlasting unto the time of His incarnation is evidenced from Prov. 8:30, which shows in what or whom He delighted all that while.

Again: His willingness is seen in those words "He humbled Himself" (Phil. 2.8) actively, not "He was humbled", passively. Remarkably and blessedly is this also brought out in Heb. 10:5-7. There we find His dedication of Himself unto His great work. "When He cometh into the world, He saith, Sacrifice and offering Thou wouldest not, but a body hast Thou prepared Me... Lo, I come ... to do Thy will, O God". Very, very remarkable is this: the Holy Spirit has here been pleased to make known to us (as the great Secretary of the Covenant) the very words the Son used as He left the Father's presence to come to earth. To which we may add—amazing, heart-thrilling fact—the Holy Spirit has also been pleased to reveal to us the first words which were uttered by the Father when His Son returned to Him, "The Lord said unto My Lord, Sit Thou at My right hand" (Psa. 110:1).

The point we are now dealing with is so precious that we would feign dwell upon it. There was no constraint laid upon Christ: all that He did was done freely and gladly. From the beginning of the days of His flesh He said, "Thou art My God from My mother's belly" (Psa. 22:9), and that, by His perfect choice. So too as He neared the end He could say, "I was not rebellious, neither turned away back. I **gave** My back to the smiters, and My cheeks to them that plucked off the hair: I hid not My face from shame and spitting" (Isa. 50:5, 6). Yes, Christ "**gave** Himself" (Gal. 2:20) for us.

Third, as it was of the Father's appointment, and the God-man's willing consent that He presented Himself a sacrifice, so also was it **by the Spirit's agency**. "How much more shall the blood of Christ, who through the eternal Spirit offered Himself without spot to God" (Heb. 9:14). The discharge of His entire Messianic office was by the enduement of the Holy Spirit. The very title, "Christ" means "the **anointed** One", and was given to Him because of the peculiar unction of the Spirit conferred upon Him, an unction which was unique in nature and degree. At the beginning of His public ministry He declared, "The Spirit of the Lord is upon Me" (Isa. 61:1). He was "full of the Holy Spirit" (Luke 4.1), and the same Spirit which led Him into the wilderness (Matt. 4:1), also led Him as a willing Victim, to the Cross. We shall now take note of the various characteristics of Christ's Sacrifice:

It was a **ransoming** one. "There are three several generic forms of conception under which the work wrought by Christ for the salvation of men is set forth. These are (a) that of an expiatory **offering** for sin; (b) that of the redemption of the life and liberty of a captive by the payment of a **ransom** in his stead, and (c) the satisfaction of the **law** by the vicarious fulfilment of its demands. These different conceptions are designed both to limit and to supplement each other in a manner strictly analogous to the combination of the different perceptions of the same object by the different bodily senses. The sense of sight, although when educated in connection with the concurrent and mutually limiting and supplementing perceptions of the organs of touch and hearing, is unmatched as to the extent and accuracy of its information, yet would, if left to itself never have risen beyond an infant's vague perception of a surface variously shaded, without any sense of relation in space.

"All our knowledge of the material world, considered as an object of sense, arises from the education of our minds in the use of our bodily senses **in combination**, and the habits of judgment and inference to which are thus produced. Men learn to interpret the impressions made upon them through their eyes by means of other impressions made upon them in connection with the same object, through the senses of touch and hearing, and vice versa. In like manner our knowledge of the true nature of the work of Christ and its bearing upon us results from all the various forms in which the Scriptures set it forth in **combination**, each at on limiting, modifying and supplementing all the others.

"It should be noticed, moreover that the Scriptures do not present these several views as different sides of the same house to be taken in succession, but habitually present them in combination, as lights and shades blend together in the same picture in producing the same intelligible expression. Thus, in the same sentences it is said, 'We are **redeemed** with the precious blood of Christ, **as of a lamb** without blemish and without spot'. 'Christ hath **redeemed** us from the **curse of the law** being made a curse for us' (Gal. 3:13). That is, He redeems us not in the sense of making a pecuniary payment in cancellation of our debts, but by His vicarious suffering, like the bleeding sacrifices of the Mosaic ritual, of the penalty due our sins.

"The fact here noticed, that the same inspired sentences represent Christ at the same instance and in the same relations as a 'ransom' and as a 'sin-offering', and as made to endure 'the curse of the law' for us, is worthy of careful study. The teaching of Scripture is not that Christ is a sacrifice, **and** a ransom, **and** a bearer of the curse of the law, but it is that He is that particular species of sacrifice which **is** a ransom; that His redemption is of that nature which is effected by His bearing the curse of the law in our stead, and that He redeems us by offering Himself a bleeding sacrifice to God. Thus, the teaching of the Holy Spirit is as precise as any ecclesiastical theory of Atonement. Christ saves us by being a sacrifice. He is specifically a sin-offering in the Jewish sense. More specifically yet, the offering of Himself a ransom for us, and to His bearing the curse of the law in our stead, and the design and effects of this ransom-paying, curse-bearing sacrifice of His, that He redeems us from the curse of the law. It is not any kind of a sacrifice, but a ransom-paying, curse-bearing sacrifice. It is not any kind of redemption, but a sacrificial redemption" (A. A. Hodge).

That the sacrifice of Christ was a **ransoming** one is clear, first, from Matt. 20:28, "Even as the Son of man came not to be ministered unto but to minister, and to give His life a ransom for many". This remarkable declaration calls for our closest attention. Christ came here not to be ministered unto as the Lord of all, but to give His life, not only in and by dying, but throughout the whole course of His earthly **service**. The word "give" emphasises the fact that He acted voluntarily, without compulsion of any kind. The reason for His saying that He came to give His "life" or "soul" appears from the sacrificial language of Lev. 17:11, "For the life of the flesh is in the blood: and I have given it to you upon the altar to make atonement for your souls". The life of the typical sacrifice represented the life of its offerer: the death-sentence executed on the former was what the latter had incurred. That was the fundamental idea of all the O. T. sacrifices.

Christ came here to give His life "a ransom". This term necessarily connotes that the many for whom the ransom was paid were **captives**, in bondage, the slaves of sin (Titus 3:3), and as such, obnoxious to God's holy displeasure. There is an important distinction between "ransom" and "redemption": the former is the price paid to secure the latter. The first mention of a "ransom" in Scripture is in Ex. 21:30, where a valuable price was required for the deliverance of one who, through guilt, was worthy of death, cf Ex. 30:12 etc. Christ's ransom was paid to satisfy God's justice: a life for a life; the ransom being a penal infliction. Christ gave His life "a ransom **for** many"; the Greek preposition is "anti" which, except in the few instances where it means "against", is always used in a **substitutionary** sense. His life was not "given" in any vague, indefinite way for the good of others, but was a specific quid pro quo, dying in the very room of His people. The "many" is in contrast from the one life.

"The church of God, which He hath **purchased** with His own blood" (Acts 20: 28). The prominent idea of "ransom" is that of payment, of vicarious substitution, of one thing standing in the place of another. No figure can so fully convey this idea as of one drawn from purchases with money. The very idea of **purchase** necessarily involves that of substitution. I go into a shop and ask the price of a book. It is one dollar. I put down the money, and I am at liberty at once to take up the book. It is mine. On what principle? Of substitution. I substitute the money for the book. In **this** way Christ bought His people. To the Corinthian saints Paul wrote, "Ye are not your own; for ye are **bought** with a price" (1 Cor. 6:19, 20).

"Ye were not redeemed with corruptible things, as silver and gold . . . but with the precious blood of Christ" (1 Peter 1: 18, 19). Sinners are the prisoners of Divine justice. True, they are the captives of the Devil; but **who** delivered them up to him? The Lord: Satan is but the executioner of His righteous sentence. And their salvation is not a simple discharge without compensation. Neither is the salvation of guilty sinners an act of power only, effected by the interposition of an arm full of might to secure their escape. Gratuitous favour and all-mighty power **are** both concerned in it, but there is more: there is a price paid, a ransom laid down, every way equivalent to the redemption for which it is offered; and that price was Christ's satifaction.

Christ's satisfaction was a **priestly** one. This has been denied by Socinians, and it is sad to see those who believe in the Deity of Christ adopting the vain reasoning of "unitarians" upon the sacerdotal nature of our Saviour's oblation. Through a misunderstanding of Heb. 8:4, they insist that Christ only entered upon His priestly office consequent upon His ascension. That Christ was High Priest and **acted** as such while He was here on earth is abundantly plain from Heb. 2:17, for He made "propitiation" for the sins of His people on the cross! It is true that others besides priests offered sacrifices to God in O. T. times, but the N. T. represents Christ not only as Priest, but as the great **"High** Priest" of His people, and if the character, purpose and scope of that office be interpreted (as it must be) in the light of the inspired types, then there is no room left for doubt as to the meaning of the antitype.

Israel's high priest represented the people before God. Taken from among men, he was ordained to act in the behalf of men in those matters which related **to God,** so that he might bring near to God both gifts and sacrifices (Heb. 5.1). As the general character of the prophet was that of one qualified and authorized to speak from God to men, so the general idea of the priest is that of one qualified and authorized to treat in matters of men with God. The high priest was he in whom the entire priesthood culminated, and he, especially, acted in all respects as the literal representative of the entire holy (separated) Nation. First, he bore the names of each tribe graven on the stones on his shoulders, and on the breastplate over his heart (Ex. 28:9-29). Second, he made atonement in behalf of all the people, confessing over the head of the scapegoat all their sins (Lev. 16:15-21). Third, if he sinned, it was regarded as the sin of all the people (Lev. 4:3). His chief function was to offer bleeding sacrifices for propitiation and to make intercession for the people. The antitypical fulfillment of this is shown us in the epistle to the Hebrews, where Christ is called Priest six times, and High Priest twelve times. Let us, very briefly, point out the several details of this.

First, in 2:17, 18 we are told that Christ became incarnate "**That He might be** a mercifull and faithful High Priest," etc. Second, in 5:4-6 we learn that Christ was chosen by God **to this office**... Third, 5:7, 8:3, 9:11-15, 25-28, 10:10-12 etc. show that Christ literally discharged the functions of a priest, offering to God a sacrifice for all His people, which, through God's acceptance thereof, brought to an end all the typical offerings. Conclusive proof of this was furnished by God in rending the veil of the temple, thereby setting aside the whole system of the Levitical priesthood. The priestly sacrifice of Christ's had now superceded theirs.

That Christ **was** High Priest on earth is also clear from Heb. 4:14. "Seeing then we have a great High Priest, that is passed into the heavens" etc. Aaron was high priest when he entered the holy of holies, yet he was also a high priest **before**, or he could not have entered at all. If Christ be a priest He must have a sacrifice, for the very nature of the sacerdotal office required it. The entire employment of the high priest, as priest, consisted in offering sacrifice, with the performance of those things which did necessarily precede and follow it. Now Christ was both Priest and Sacrifice. He offered Himself to God. What could be plainer than Eph. 5.2, "Christ ... hath given Himself for us an offering and a sacrifice **to God** for a sweet-smelling savour"? He had to do with God as He stood in the relation and respect of a "sacrifice". In His dual person He was Priest: in His human nature, He was the sacrifice offered. In the term "flesh" —"condemned sin in the flesh" (Rom. 8:3) —the Holy Spirit refers to the whole manhood of Christ, and **it** was the "sacrifice" for sin **by which** sin was "condemned".

"For every high priest is ordained to offer gifts and sacrifices: wherefore of necessity that this Man have somewhat also to offer" (Heb. 8:3). And **what** was it that He did "offer"? His "own blood" (Heb. 9:12), His "body" (Heb. 10:10), His "soul" or "life" (Isa. 53:10), "Himself" (Heb. 9:14). In Christ's sacrifice there was an "altar" too, namely, His Godhead: "The altar that sanctifieth the gift" (Matt. 23:19). The Deity of Christ not only sustained and strengthened His human nature in being a sacrifice therein, but it also gave merit and efficacy to His sacrifice. How did that **one** Sacrifice avail for all the sins of all God's people, but from the fact that He who offered up Himself was God as well as man! Christ abides in His office of priesthood (Heb. 8.1), not to offer fresh sacrifice (10:12), but to intercede (7:25).

Christ's sacrifice was a **propitiatory** one. By Adam's fall a sad breach was made between God and man. Sin greatly incensed the Holy God against His rebellious creatures, nay, there was a mutual enmity constrained between them. On the one hand, we read of God, "Thou **hatest** all workers of iniquity" (Psa. 5:5); "But they rebelled, and vexed His Holy Spirit: therefore He was turned to be their **Enemy**, He fought against them" (Isa. 63:10). Of man we read, "The carnal mind is **enmity against** God" (Rom. 8:7); "You that were sometimes alienated and **enemies in your mind** by wicked works, yet now hath He reconciled" (Col. 1:21). Now Christ came here to effect reconciliation between these alienated parties, to bring God and men together again in amity and love. By His bloodshedding, Christ appeased the righteous wrath of God. By His sacrifice, He pacified the claims of Divine justice. Some have asked, How could the elect be "by nature the children of **wrath**" (Eph. 2:3), seeing that God always **loved** them (Jer. 31:3)? In the language of John Owen we reply, "He loved us, in respect of the free purpose of His will to send Christ to redeem us and satisfy for our sins; He was angry with us, in respect of His violated law, and provoked justice by sin".

The leading N. T. scriptures which present this particular aspect of Christ's sacrifice are the following: "Whom God hath foreordained **a propitiation** through faith in His blood to declare His righteousness" (Rom. 3:25). "For if, when we were enemies, we were **reconciled** to God by (not the Holy Spirit's work in us, nor by our laying down the weapons of our warfare but) **by the death of His Son**" (Rom. 5:10). We were "reconciled" through Christ's averting God's anger from us and procuring our acceptance in

His legal favour. "All things are of God, who hath **reconciled** us to Himself by Jesus Christ" (2 Cor. 5:18). "And having **made peace** through the blood of His cross" (Col. 1:20). "That He might be a merciful and faithful High Priest in things pertaining to God to **make propitiation** for the sins of the people" (Heb. 2:17). "If any one sin, we have an Advocate with the Father, Jesus Christ the righteous: And He is the **propitiation** for our sins" (1 John 2:2).

Now the above passages are best understood in the light of the O. T. types. There we read, "And Moses said unto Aaron, Take a censer, put fire therein from off the altar, and put on incense, and go quickly unto the congregation and **make an atonement** for them: FOR there is **wrath** gone out from the Lord; the plague is begun. And Aaron took as Moses commanded . . . and made an atonement for the people . . . and the plague was stayed" (Num. 16:46-48). Again, we read, "The Lord said to Eliphaz the Temanite, My **wrath** is kindled against thee, and against thy two friends: . . . therefore take unto you now seven bullocks and seven rams, and go to My servant Job, and offer up for yourselves a burnt offering; and My servant Job shall pray for you: for him will I accept" etc. (Job 42.7-9). What could be plainer?—the wrath of God was appeased by bloodshedding! It remains to be pointed out that the Hebrew word for "atonement" and the Greek word for "propitiation" are one and the same.

Christ's sacrifice was an **expiatory** one. The whole of Christ's humiliation and suffering from His birth to the cross were invested with a priestly and sacrificial character, as constituting His once-offering up of Himself a sacrifice, as propitiatory of God and expiatory of His peoples' sins; yet the emphasis of Scripture shows that Christ's oblation of Himself as victim was principally manifested and concentrated in His pouring out of His soul unto death. Faith is directed to the cross, as presenting not merely the historical terminus and climax, but the logical and indispensable completion of all that preceded, for sin not only entails suffering but **death.**

"Propitiation" defines the bearing which Christ's sacrifice had **Godwards:** it placated Him. "Expiation" has reference to the bearing which Christ's sacrifice had **manwards:** it removed the sins of His people.

"This is My blood of the new covenant, which is shed for many for the **remission** of sins" (Matt. 26:28). "Remission" is a judicial term, and signifies the annuling of guilt, the removal of all ground of punishment. "Once in the end of the age hath He appeared to **put away** sin by the sacrifice of Himself"(Heb. 9:26). Christ has so "put away" all the sin of His people that they are perfectly and finally acquitted in the High Court of God, so that **no** charge can evermore be laid against them: (Rom. 8:33). Blessedly and gloriously has the O. T. type been fulfilled, "On that day shall the priest make an atonement for you, to **cleanse** you, that ye may be clean from **all** your sins **before the Lord**" (Lev. 16:30). Thus are God's believing children able to say, "The blood of Jesus Christ His Son **cleanseth** us from **all sin**" (1 John 1:17).

This was one of the chief ends of Christ's Satisfaction saintwards: to take upon Him the sins of His people, and so atone for them that an **end** was made of them. Those who are not sheltering beneath the precious blood of Christ have to say, "Thou hast set our iniquities before Thee, our secret sins in the light of Thy countenance" (Psa. 90:8). But they who, by marvelous sovereign grace, have been brought to trust in the Lamb, may exclaim, "As far as the east is from the west, so far hath He **removed** our transgressions from us" (Psa. 103.12). Our guilt has all been annuled. We have been completely freed from a deserved punishment. No longer is there a single charge on God's docket against us. Proof of this is that, "This Man, after He had offered one sacrifice for sins forever, **sat down** on the right hand of God" (Heb. 10:12). Therefore "unto them that look for Him shall He appear the second time **without sin** unto salvation" (Heb. 9:28) Hallelujah!

—ARTHUR W. PINK.

Never have we written upon a more important, vital, profound, and wondrous theme than the atoning Satisfaction of Christ. We have spared no pains in the earnest endeavour to be equipped for this weighty task. Nevertheless, unless the Holy Spirit constantly guides us, we are certain to err. We feel a deel need of being "taught **of God**," and shall greatly value the definite prayers of His people until the end (D. V.) of this series of articles.—A. W. P.

8. THE BELIEVER'S BLESSEDNESS IN GLORY.

The ever-blessed God, whose **infinite blessedness** flows from His essential nature and perfections, hath loved His elect with an everlasting love. He hath manifested it by setting them apart in His own eternal decree to a super-creation union and communion with Himself. It hath pleased Him to open His vast designs respecting them; and He executes His internal and eternal purposes towards them, within and upon them, in a vast variety of ways and means, and by successive degrees. As the **"God of all Grace,"** He brings them out of their natural and sinful state, calls them unto, and invests them with a title to, and works in them in regeneration a meetness for, His eternal glory by Christ Jesus. As they are prepared for it by regeneration, so He gives them many sweet foretastes of it in their communion with Him by faith in His beloved Son, through the grace and influence of the Holy Spirit. As they know Him to be their portion and shield; so He hath given them His promise, that He will be in all His persons, perfections, and blessedness "their exceeding great reward". He is their Guide through life, their hope and consolation in death, and will continue to be to them in heaven their "everlasting light and glory".

God is styled, **"The God of Glory"**. What God is essentially, that He is as personally considered. The Father is called "the Father of glory". Christ "The Lord of glory". The Spirit "the Spirit of glory". And the state of blessedness, into which believers immediately enter on the disunion of their souls and bodies by death, is a state of glory. The apostle speaks of it as "an exceeding, eternal weight of glory". As the title "the God of all Grace is most justly due to our Covenant-God, and taken by Him to express what He is to us, and what an all-sufficiency of grace He hath displayed towards us in Christ Jesus, and treasured up in His fulness for us; so the title "The God of Glory" expresses what He hath prepared for us, what He will bestow upon us, and what He will be to us in "the house eternal in the heavens".

It is an important truth and an immutable reality, whether it be perceived by us or not, that the Lord is in a most particular manner very present with His people in their dying moments. They are then most truly blessed, because they "die in the Lord", in union and in communion with Him. They are "blessed", as in general they die in the free and full exercise of their faith, and hope, and love on Him. They are "blessed", the moment they cease to breathe, the whole body of sin with all its lusts inherent within it expires, and they are eternally delivered from it. They are "blessed", as they have a prospect of the glory which they are entering upon. They are "blessed", as the Spirit of glory rests on them, and an "abundant entrance is ministered to them into the everlasting kingdom of our Lord and Saviour Jesus Christ". He admits them into it, and, "presents them faultless before the presence of His glory with exceeding joy". This is a great and most peculiar solemnity. Every individual believer at his entrance into heaven **doth** and **will** share in it. Like as when the soul regeneration was made by the Holy Spirit the subject of His graces and gifts, and was then introduced into the state of grace, and spiritual joys suited hereunto were imparted; so it is now admitted into the state of eternal glory and joys equal to it are imparted.

The complacency which the eternal Three will express on the arrival of the elect in heaven, far exceeds all expression, yea, infinitely transcends all conception. On the soul's first conversion and open espousals to Christ, all the persons in the Godhead made an open manifestative discovery of their respective loves; so upon its arrival at the city of habitation, there will be fresh, most free, and most glorious expressions of it. God the Father as "The Father of spirits", receives the soul into the open embraces of His everlasting love; and gives new and unspeakable views, proofs and enjoyments of it. He fills the soul with so much of it in communion with Himself, as exceeds all that was ever known of it on earth. Our Divine Jesus, the Head of His church, and its most precious and adorable Mediator, presents the soul to its Divine Father, **faultless;** and receives it with unutterable joy to the continued and perpetual enjoyment of all the love wherewith He hath loved it, and to an uninterrupted communion with Himself in all the fruits and blessings of His eternal redemption and glory. God the Holy Spirit expresses His love in a fresh and most transcendent manner, viz. by filling the soul with eternal glory, and by leading it into such views, and into such a participation of the Father's love expressed in His immutable act of election and acceptance in the person of the Beloved, as fill the understanding with knowledge and enjoyment ineffable.

All the love of the Father and all the grace of the Holy Spirit flow through the person of the God-man into the soul; and thus it is filled with all the fulness of God. The Holy Spirit, as the Spirit of Glory dwelling in and fully possessing the disembodied soul, fills it inwardly through every faculty with unutterable and eternal glory. As heaven was prepared from the foundation of the world for the elect; so we find in the accounts given of saints both in the Old and N. T., that they have all been prepared for this state, and most earnestly long for the enjoyment of it. It is expressly said, of the O. T. saints, that at their death they were gathered to their people, viz. to the congregation above,—"the spirits of just men made perfect" (Heb. 12:35). After their death God is expressly called "**their** God" (Heb. 11: 16), for this reason because "they all live unto Him", and appear before Him complete in the righteousness of His Son. In the name of all N. T. saints Paul saith; see 2 Cor. 5:1-4.

In persuing this subject concerning the state and blesedness to which the believer is advanced when admitted to eternal glory, and in which the riches of glory will be made known on the vessels of mercy, it will be suitable and necessary to speak briefly of the place where this will be, of the state itself, and then wherein this unspeakable blesedness may be conceived to consist.

For the place: it is Heaven. This is the habitation into which disembodied spirits are received immediately on their departure from their bodies, and where they exist and dwell. The subject which is before us concerns the place where Jehovah is pleased to manifest Himself in the greatest displays of His persons, and perfections, and in the richest communications of His love to elect angels and saints, where **on this account** He is said to "dwell", and on no other; because His essence cannot be bounded—"Do'st not Thou fill heaven and earth"? The word "heaven" is in an especial manner given to the habitation of the Most High (Isa. 63:15); where Jehovah in all the full blaze, majesty, and perfection in His deity, shines forth in the utmost display of His manifestative glory in the person of the God-man (in whom all the fulness of the Godhead dwelleth) on His elect church in heaven.

The apostle Paul speaks of the "third heaven", as the place where God resides in all the glory of His majesty. And when Jesus sat down on the right hand of the Majesty on high, He is said to have been exalted "above all heavens". He spoke of the habitation of the blessed immediately after death as "Abraham's bosom", "everlasting habitations", "paradise", "His Father's house", in which are many mansions. Heaven is a place, the city of the living God, where Christ lives and shines forth in an inconceivable display of His essential, personal, mediatorial, and relative glories, before and unto the view of that innumerable company of elect angels and saints who surround His throne, casting their crowns before Him, saying; see Rev. 5:12, 13. In the apostolic writings, heaven bears the titles of an "house eternal in the heavens", and "a city which hath foundations (which denotes the perpetuity of it) whose builder and maker is God".

I will next speak of the **state** of the blessed in heaven. This is set before us in such expressions as "an exceeding, eternal weight of glory", a being "present with the Lord", "the inheritance of the saints in light", "an inheritance incorruptible, and undefiled which fadeth not away", and "a glory to be revealed in us". Which considered, may lead us to some spiritual conceptions and faith-views of this most blessed state which awaits us. **It is a state of immortality.** The soul is "swallowed up of life". It is pure and eternal life that the soul now lives. It is perpetual activity. No sooner is the soul taken up into heaven, than it is all life, joy, and activity in God the fountain of life. Whilst the soul is in its present embodied state, its life even in spiritual acts is greatly cramped. On its dismission from it, its mortality is swallowed up of life. Hereby it is delivered from all the misery and imperfection which adhered to it whilst in the body. It now lives an heavenly life.

It is also a state of **perfect happiness.** The apostle makes a distinction between the present and the future state of glory: see 1 Cor. 13:10, 12. Our imperfection consists in our "seeing through a glass darkly". Our perfection in the heavenly state consists in seeing God "face to face" in the person of our all-glorious Immanuel. This is also a state of unutterable perfection in **knowledge and enjoyment.** The understanding will be filled with the knowledge of God, and with the whole good pleasure of His will, in all His vast designs, in all His acts of grace. The will shall rest perfectly satisfied with God, as the fountain of essential happiness, who in His persons and communications, in the blessings and consolations of His love, and in uninterrupted communion with the soul, will bestow on it such enjoyments as surpass all thought on earth, and exceed all praise in heaven. God is the glory of it, and the Lamb is the light thereof. The Holy Spirit dwells in every member of it. In their knowledge and enjoyment of the God-man, and of communion with the Eternal Three in Him, God becomes to them their **all in all**. Hence their understandings and wills are so swallowed up in God, and they are so filled with all the fulness of God, that they are incapable of sinning to all eternity. All this is of **grace**.

The state of the blessed is also a **state of glory**. The soul will be in the enjoyment of glory, it will encircle him. He will be, as it were, immersed in it. It is an "exceeding, eternal weight of glory". The soul will have fellowship with Christ in His glory. And the being with Christ will be everlasting perfection and blessedness. It is "the inheritance of the saints in light". They are "heirs of God and joint-heirs with Christ". As the created sun shines equally through every part of this visible system; so the uncreated Sun of everlasting righteousness, the God-man Christ Jesus, the Lord of glory, shines on saints in heaven, and puts His own glory on them; and they shine therein, bright and pure as the light. This effectually fixes them in their state of bliss; so that their inheritance, or the state into which they are introduced, is immutable.

Before attempting to show wherein consists that unspeakable blessedness the separated soul enters upon at death, let me fix my mind on such scripture declarations as these: Christ is said "to receive us to the glory of God" (Rom. 15:7). We are "called of God unto His kingdom and glory" (1 Thess. 2:12). We are "called to the obtaining of the glory of our Lord Jesus Christ" (2 Thess. 2:14). Peter entitles himself "a partaker of the glory that shall be revealed", and writing to all the holy brethren tells us that, "the God of all grace hath called us unto His eternal glory by Christ Jesus" (1 Pet. 5:10). These important, soul-quickening, and eternal realities, concerning the state and blessedness of saints in heaven, will, as I conceive, receive fresh light, and shine with redoubled splendour on our minds by a due and proper consideration of these great and glorious declarations.

Our Lord Jesus Christ is our Head in glory, and we are to receive our glory from Him, i. e. out of His immense fulness, by seeing Him as He is and by having fellowship with Him in all His communicable glory. The word **glory**, in the O. T., in its highest acceptation, is given to that person in Jehovah, who was to become incarnate; of whom the prophet had a vision, and of whom he prophesied, "The glory of the Lord shall be revealed" (Isa. 40:5). He, as God-man, is the glory of Jehovah. The word "glory", as used in the O. T., is also expressive, of a supernatural and visible appearance of fire, light, and splendour, which showed Jehovah to be peculiarly present, see Ex. 24:16, 17; 40:34, 35; 1 Kings 8:11. This glory appeared sometimes in a human form, prefiguring the future incarnation of the second Person in Jehovah: as, for instance, that over the cherubim, Ezek. 1:28. In the N. T. we have all this realized in the person of Jesus Christ. He is "the Lord of glory", "the brightness of the Father's glory, and the express image of His person".

Christ's personal glory, as God-man, is the glory of the Godhead, dwelling personally in Him. This glory is founded on the union of the human nature with the Son of God. This glory of Christ's person is His birthright, as the essential God. "This glory breaks forth and shines through His human nature, as if the sun were encompassed with a case of crystal; how glorious would that crystal be!" (Dr. T. Goodwin). Christ's glory, as to the very essence of it, consists in this, (He hath it so inherently and essentially in Himself) that He is "the Lord of glory". To this He referred in John 17:5: this He prayed to be glorified with, and put into the full possession of, on His performance of the work of redemption: and it was granted, when He was "received up into glory" (1 Tim. 3:16). The glory which Christ had with the Father "before the world was" is His **personal** glory, or the glory due to Him, and which belongs to Him, as God-man, the "Fellow" or equal of the Lord of hosts. The utmost perfection of Christ's glory now at the right hand of the Majesty on high is purely personally, His own, and for Himself alone. He shines forth in it, and lives in heaven, "the Image of the invisible God". It is a glory which He hath **in** God and **with** God alone in the enjoyment of all that God is. Our Lord's own words express wherein the very life and essence of it consists: see John 17:5.

Christ, as God-man, hath God Himself, as the fountain and spring of all His joys and blessedness. He hath the glory of being crowned with many crowns. He is the Head of the whole election of grace, in whom their whole life of grace and glory is treasured up. He is their Head of union, and the Medium of all their communion with God. He hath also together with the glory of His being Head over all things to His church, which is His body, the fulness of Him that filleth all and in all, a Mediatorial, relative, and communicable glory. In all which He shines forth with transcendent majesty, infinitely beyond our utmost conception to the everlasting joy of all His saints. Speaking of His people to His Father He says, "And the glory which Thou gavest Me I have given them" (John 17:22). This was bestowed by the Father on Him, as the Head, which He is to communicate to His members. It flows from Him. It is the fruit of their union with Him. It is of the same kind with His, though not to the same degree. It is not inherently in them. And thus His glory is revealed in them, and reflected on them; and hereby Christ is their everlasting light, and their everlasting glory. Christ is said, "to receive us to the glory of God"; that is, to the participation of that glory which is to be had in the ever-blessed God. We are "heirs of God and co-heirs with Christ" (Rom. 8:17). He communicates it to us in His own right. He is personally the proprietor and inheritor of it.

This glory consists in a beholding His glory in heaven: **see** John 17:24. Here we have the utmost blessedness of heaven set before us. It consists in the beatific vision of the person of Christ in His kingdom and glory. It should be observed from the last clause of John 17:24 that the God-man values His Father's "love", the spring and fountain from whence His personal glory and our election originated, **beyond all**: it being the original of all. So then, to bring this subject to its point, the unspeakable blessedness of the elect in heaven consists in being with Christ, in seeing Christ as He is, and in beholding His glory. In which vision of Christ, and in communion with Him in His glory, consist the eternal life and everlasting perfection of the saint admitted within the vail; where he has such communion with Christ in an intuitive way and manner, as fills the soul **in every faculty** with the knowledge of God to a Divine satiety, and with such an enjoyment as gives the most complete satisfaction. As there will be a most blessed communion with the Head of saints, so there will be also a most perfect fellowship with glorified saints. They will all worship in the same perfection of holiness. They will all unite in the same song to the Lamb that was slain.

I conceive the glory, happiness, and blessedness of the saints in heaven are increasing, and will continue to increase throughout the ages of eternity. Although there is no want in the happiness which each of the blessed enjoys, yet they being but finite, and God in Christ infinite, there must be a succession and gradation in their knowledge, enjoyment and communion. I conceive with respect to the present state of saints in glory that, though they see Christ in His **personal** glory, and have communion with Him in a certain degree, in His mediatorial and relative glory, as their Head, Saviour, and Lord, yet their chief subject is His **mediatorial** glory; and their constant praise is to Him, as "the Lamb that was slain". And through Him, as such, all the love of the Father, and all the grace and consolation of the Holy Spirit flow into their souls, and will continue so to do, till, "the Lord my God shall come and all His saints with Him". At which time the trumpet being sounded, the bodies of the elect-dead being raised and re-united to their souls, and the living-elect changed in a moment, in the twinkling of an eye, from mortality to immortality, His glory will shine on the bodies and souls of all His saints to a far greater degree than what it does now in heaven. And this will increase their enjoyment of blessedness beyond the conception of saints by any former communion which they had with Christ in glory.

In **the new Jerusalem state** (as it is very justly styled by divines, to distinguish it from the **present** state of saints in glory, and also from what is most properly styled the **ultimate** glory-state, where and when Christ will dwell personally with all His saints together), Jesus and His Church will have such communion suited to this state, as will far surpass the blessedness of their present communion with Him now in glory. This New Jerusalem-state of the blessed is thus expressed: see Rev. 21:23. And further it is said of it: see Rev. 22:3-5. And even this will be exceeded by what will be more fully manifested and enjoyed in the state of ultimate glory, when God in His Divine persons and perfections in the God-man shall be so clearly and fully known and enjoyed, as to be **all in all.** Then the Father, the Son, and the Holy Spirit, will be enjoyed by the saints to the uttermost perfection of blessedness. O, my soul! are these things so? Are these truths Divine realities? Has the Holy Spirit made them so to thee? Astonishing grace! Let them then, O my soul! sink down into thy heart. Meditate on them. Pray over them. Seek to digest them inwardly and spiritually;

and labour to bring them into daily use and practice.

Look up to the Eternal Three, saying, **Holy Father!** I present myself at Thy throne, in the name and person of the God-man, Christ Jesus, praying Thee to shine upon me **in Him.** Thou art the Father of glory, and out of the riches of Thy glory Thou hast loved me in Christ Jesus, before the foundation of the world, with the same love wherewith Thou lovedst Him. Eternal thanks be given unto Thee for the evidence which Thou hast given me of this from Thy Word and by Thy Spirit, that "Thou art my exceeding great reward". O, **Thou matchless Jesus.** Thou art all-glorious:—the true Immanuel.—the Fellow of the Lord of hosts. Blessings on Thee! It is Thy will that I should be where Thou art to behold Thy glory, and to see Thee as Thou art. This will be my everlasting perfection, my inconceivable bliss, and my eternal heaven and feast in glory. O Thou almighty Jesus! It affords me a present heaven to contemplate Thy essential, personal, mediatorial, and communicable glories. It leads me spiritually to perceive, that personal communion with Thee in Thy kingdom will everlastingly engage all my spiritual faculties and fix my mind eternally on Thee. O, Thou **Holy Spirit.** Thou dwellest in my soul as my earnest of glory. Thou hast given me to experience in communion with the Father and the Son joys unspeakable and full of glory. O, thou holy, blessed, and Essential Three, I rejoice in the prospect of personal, uninterrupted and eternal communion with Thee in the state of glory, in the new Jerusalem-state, and in the state of ultimate glory. Blessed be Thy name, Thou eternal Three, for the revelation, prospects, and foretastes which Thou hast given me hereof. And for these Thy blessings, and for the experience which Thou hast given me, I desire to most earnestly on earth and in heaven join with the whole election of grace in giving unceasing glory to Thee as the **One Jehovah,** who art essential blessedness, and the fountain of all blessedness to Thy saints. To whom be praise, and glory in the highest. Amen.

—S. E. PIERCE (1804).

WELCOME TIDINGS.

Once a year we take the liberty of publishing extracts out of letters received from those who get this little monthly messenger. Our object in so doing is threefold. First, that our gracious God, who deigns to use such unprofitable and unworthy instruments, may receive honour and praise. Second, that the many who are so faithfully helping us by their daily prayers, may know that our blessed heavenly Father does not refuse their petitions but is granting answers. May what is recorded below evoke much thanksgiving and praise. Third, that those who are having financial fellowship in this ministry may know that God is giving rich returns. Lest this should be regarded by any as an indirect appeal for money, we wish to state that at this date of writing (June 1) we have several hundred dollars on hand, and are in no need whatever. So please **do not send** in gifts till the Lord clearly prompts you to do so.

Our God is indeed kind to us in granting so many encouragements along the way. Truly **His** yoke is "easy" and His burden is "light". It is sin's slaves who groan under cruel taskmasters. The number of cheering and praise-provoking letters received during the last few months have far exceeded in number those which came to hand formerly. Our difficulty is to make a selection. Though our circulation is a very small one, yet its influence is, under God's good hand, far reaching, as the following excerpts bear witness. The Lord's people are "scattered abroad" (John 11:52) but each one is known to Him, is dear to Him, and is ministered to by Him.

"In these days the mails are full of religious journals of all shades and descriptions. Some shade the Word of God to suit the people of the day; many cater to sensationalism; others go to seed on outlines and alliteration, and still others openly deny the fundamentals of our faith. There is none more strictly Biblical and rich in spiritual food than 'Studies in the Scriptures'. Please accept this humble word of appreciation from one who, in a land of spiritual darkness, receives much inspiration and strength from the pages of your magazine. May the only wise God give you much wisdom in preparing these expositions". Missionary in El Salvador.

"I profit more by the reading of these 'Studies' than any other Religious (so-called) literature, and when the magazines arrive a joy comes into my heart, saying, Now I have something good and profitable to read. I have two Bible Classes for girls and young women in my home, and I have borrowed much from your writings". A Sister in England. "I thank you from the depth of my heart for your precious magazine; I always find things very suitable to my case in them": one of the poor of the flock in Scotland. "Your publication is so very superior to the type of religious literature now disseminated. Such writings are greatly needed these days": A Brother in Wales.

"I thank you for the sending of the 'Studies'. I have learned by them and received blessing. God give you grace to write, His name to honour": preacher in Holland. "Your 'Studies' are a great help to us, even though they need much time in working through their contents": Preacher in Germany. "I thank you for the 'Studies'. I have wished many times that I had money to send you. But I am poor (not in faith). The messages of the magazine are food for my soul. I thank my God that I heard about the magazine and wrote after it. It has helped me in faith": A Brother in Sweden.

"I want to write you a few lines of thanks for sending to my wife and myself of 'Studies'. We have found them a great help to a better understanding of the Word of God. I enjoyed very much the articles on Abraham. Hebrews too is very precious. I trust you may be spared to continue this kind of exposition, which is very lacking in the Christian magazines of today". Missionary in Morocco. "Regularly I receive the magazine, and get many blessings from it. Thank God and you. I pray the Lord to be with you always and help you to continue this precious magazine": A Brother in Syria. "Thank you so much for the 'Studies' you so kindly send me. They have been a real blessing": Missionary in Japan.

"Many thanks for the 'Studies'. These are very helpful and my wife especially has made very definite use of them in her work": Missionary in India. "I cannot begin to express what help and blessing I have received through perusal of these 'Studies'—not to mention the hundreds who in different parts of China have profited in the ministry and blessing passed on to them. Your labours are **not** in vain in the Lord": Missionary in China. "We enjoy your writings more than any others, because they are so clear, and no statements are made without Scripture authority. You may be sure much from your writings is passed on to Native Christians here": Missionary in Guatemala.

"I have been much refreshed in reading the 'Studies'. I have found them 'profitable for doctrine, for reproof, for correction, for instruction in righteousness'. I have been reproved and corrected many times, while the instruction has been of much blessing to my soul. I continue in prayer that your work may be greatly blessed of God". A Brother in Australia. Such tidings as this afford ample compensation for the many long but happy hours we spend in preparing each article. Our earnest prayer is that both writer and readers may be brought into a closer walk and more sustained communion with the Lord Himself.

"I have been reading with much profit the 'Studies': A Brother in Canada. "Your blessed Paper is a feast to the soul for those of us who love God's Word. Particularly did I find great help in your article on 'Apostacy' on Heb. 6:4-6": A bed-ridden Christian. "All the ministry I received during my two years' affliction was reading your Paper. It was so much comfort to me. I got so much food while reading it": A lonely widow. "I receive great blessing and new light from God's holy Word by reading the Studies. May the God of grace and love continue to bless you with the gift He has bestowed upon you": An aged Brother in Mo. "I do not feel I can get along without your 'Studies'. They are a wonderful help to me. My desire is to know more of Him and His Word. I feel I am one of the least of His and thank Him for your paper which provides a real food": A Sister in New York.

"My soul has been blessed immeasurably by the exposition of Hebrews": A Brother in Mich. "My spiritual life has been so deepened and my reading of the Scriptures so enriched through the help of Studies that I want to express my gratitude to you. I thank my Father for you both, and pray that He may continue to bless you": A Sister in Wisc. "Thank God that He has some faithful servants who are led by the Holy Spirit to expound Bible truth to hungry souls": An aged Pilgrim in Wash. "I would not know how to get on without 'Studies' these days, for there is so little food in the literature we get": An isolated Christian.

"Please accept my heartfelt thanks and appreciation for your kindness in sending me the 'Studies'. They are very helpful and soul and mind enriching, and just what is needed in these days of apostacy". Preacher in New Jersey. "I have been reading Studies for three years, and can say without hesitancy they have meant more to me in the feeding of my own soul and ministry to others than anything else aside from the Word itself. Words cannot express the blessings conveyed to my life and ministry through your writings": Preacher in Mich. "I find Studies very clear. Your articles on the Covenant made some phrases and clauses of Scripture pregnant with meaning, which were before but words": Another Preacher in Mich. "The heart is saddened by so much that comes to hand bearing the stamp of 'Christian', that it is refreshing to see the Word so clearly expounded and our Lord exalted": Preacher in Canada. "The 'Studies' stimulate to a study of the Word itself, and that is a most desirable thing, for about every book written today centers one's thoughts on the writer and not on the Scriptures—man's opinions and not God's revelation. I thank God for Studies": Preacher in Mich.

"I am greatly benefited by your various articles in Studies. They have provoked me to a more diligent study of His precious Word. They have enabled me to see His Christ in many of the O. T. Scriptures where I had not seen Him. They have magnified the obligation upon me to grow in grace and in the knowledge of our Lord Jesus Christ. They have clearly taught me my duty to use His Word more in my preaching": Preacher in Alabama. It is much cause for thankfulness that the Lord has seen fit to give our little paper favour in the eyes of quite a number of preachers. They, more than every body else today, urgently need the prayers of God's people that they may be kept faithful.

We sincerely hope the reading of these unsolicited testimonies will bow many before the Lord in fervent thanksgiving, that in these awful days He is still graciously ministering to His own. As the darkness deepens our responsibility to send forth His light increases! Will you not **pray daily** that the Lord will deepen His work of grace in the editor and so teach him, experimentally, that he may be able to teach others. That God will mercifully preserve him from all error, and guide and help in the preparation of every article. Also that He will, if it be His holy pleasure, bring us into touch with many more of His scattered and hungry people, that they may enjoy with us some of the wondrous riches of His grace. Above all, that **God's** blessing may continue upon this ministry to His own glory and the good of His beloved saints.

—ARTHUR W. PINK.

AN EXPOSITION OF PSALM 1.

"**Blessed**" (v1). See how this book of Psalms opens with a benediction, even as did the famous Sermon of our Lord upon the Mount! The word translated "blessed" is a very expressive one. The original word is plural, hence we may learn the multiplicity of the blessings which shall come upon the man whom God hath justified, and the perfection and greatness of the blessedness he shall enjoy. We might read it, "Oh, the blessedness-es"! And we may well regard it as a joyful acclamation of the gracious man's felicity. May the like benediction rest on us.

Here the gracious man is described both negatively (v. 1) and positively (v. 2). He is a man who "walketh not in the counsel of the ungodly". He takes wiser counsel, and walks in the commandments of the Lord his God. To him the ways of piety are paths of peace and pleasantness. His footsteps are ordered by the Word of God, and not by the cunning and wicked devices of carnal man. It is a rich sign of inward grace when the outward walk is changed and when ungodliness is put far from our actions. Note next, he "standeth not in the way of sinners". His company is of a choiser sort than it was. Although a sinner himself, he is now a blood-washed sinner,, quickened by the Holy Spirit, and renewed in heart. Standing by the rich grace of God in the congregation of the righteous, he dares not herd with the multitude that do evil. Again it is said, "Nor sitteth in the seat of the scornful". He finds no rest in the atheist's scoffings. Let others make a mock of sin, of eternity, of heaven and hell, and of the eternal God; this man has learned better philosophy than of the infidel. and has too much sense of God's presence to endure to hear His name blasphemed. The seat of the scorner may be very lofty, but it is very near to the gate of hell; let us flee from it, for it shall soon be empty, and destruction shall swallow up the man who sits therein. Mark the gradation in the first verse: he does not

Walk in the "council" of the **ungodly,**
Nor **stand** in the "way" of **sinners,**
Nor **sit** in the "seat" of **scorners.**

When men are living in sin they go from bad to worse. At first they merely **walk** in the counsel of the careless and "ungodly", who forget God—the evil is rather practical than habitual—but after that, they become habituated to evil, and they **stand** in the way of open "sinners" who wilfully violate God's commandments; and if let alone, they go one step further and become themselves pestilent teachers and tempters of others, and thus they "**sit** in the seat of the scornful". They have taken their degree in vice, and as true Doctors of Damnation they are enstalled, and are looked up to by others as Masters in Belial. But the blessed man, the man to whom the blessings of God belong, can hold no communion with such characters as these. He keeps himself pure from such lepers; he puts away evil things from him as garments spotted by the flesh; he comes out from among the wicked, and goes without the camp, bearing the reproach of Christ. Oh for grace to be thus separate from sinners.

And now mark his positive character: "His delight is in the Law of the Lord". He is not **under** the law as a curse and condemnation, but he is **in** it, and delights to be in it as his rule of life; he delights, moreover, to **meditate** in it, to read it "by day", and think upon it "by night". He takes a text and carries it with him all day long; and in the night-watches, when sleep forsakes his eyelids, he museth upon the Word of God. In the **day** of his prosperity he sings "psalms" out of the Word of God, and in the **night** of his affliction he comforts himself with "promises" out of the same book. The "Law of the Lord" is the daily bread of the true believer. And yet, in David's day, how small was the volume of inspiration, for they had scarcely anything save the first five books of Moses! How much more, then, should we prize the whole written Word which it is our privilege to have in all our homes! But, alas, what ill-treatment is given to this angel from heaven! We are not all Berean searchers of the Scriptures. How few among us can lay claim to the benediction of the text! Perhaps some of you can lay claim to the benediction of the text! Perhaps some of you can claim a sort of negative purity, because you do not walk in the way of the ungodly; but let me ask you—Is your delight in the law of God? Do you make it the man of your right hand—your best companion and hourly guide? If not, this blessing belongeth not to you.

"And he shall be like a tree planted"; not a wild tree, but "a tree **planted**", chosen, considered as property, cultivated and secured from the last terrible uprooting, for "every plant, which My heavenly Father hath not planted, shall be rooted up" (Matt. 15:13). "By the rivers of water" so that even if one river should fail, he hath another. The rivers of pardon and the rivers of grace, the rivers of the promise and the rivers of communion with Christ, are never-failing sources of supply. He is "like a tree planted by the rivers of water, that bringeth forth his fruit **in his season**"; not unseasonable graces, like untimely figs which are never ful-flavoured. But the man who delights in God's Word, being taught by it, bringeth forth patience in the time of suffering, faith in the day of trial, and holy joy in the hour of prosperity. Fruitfulness is an essential quality of a gracious man, and that fruitfulness should be seasonable. "His leaf also shall not wither"; his faintest word shall be everlasting; his little deeds of love shall be had in remembrance. Not simply shall his fruit be preserved, but his **leaf also.** He shall neither lose his beauty nor his fruitfulness.

"And whatsoever he doeth **shall prosper**". Blessed is the man who hath such a promise as this. But we must not always estimate the fulfilment of a promise by our own eye-sight. How often, my brethren, if we judge by feeble sense may we come to the mournful conclusion of Jacob, "All these things are against me"! For though we know our interest in the promise, yet are we so tired and troubled, that sight seems the very reverse of what that promise foretells. But to the eye of faith this word is sure, and by it we perceive that our works **are** prospered, even when everything seems to be against us. It is not outward prosperity which the Christian most desires and values; it is soul prosperity which he longs for. We often, like Jehosaphat, make ships to go to Tarshish for gold, but they are broken at Ezion-geber; but even here there is a true prospering, for it is often for the soul's health that we should be poor, bereaved, and persecuted. Our worst things are often our best things. As there is a curse wrapped up in the wicked man's mercies, so there is a blessing concealed in the righteous man's crosses, losses, and sorrows. The trials of the saint are a Divine husbandry, by which he grows and brings forth abundant fruit.

V. 4. We have now come to the second head of the Psalm. In this verse the contrast of the ill estate of the wicked is employed to heighten the colouring of that fair and pleasant picture which precedes it. The more forceable translation of the Vulgate and the Septuagint version is—"Not so the ungodly, not so". And we are hereby to understand that whatever good thing is said of the righteous is not true in the case of the ungodly. Oh! how terrible is it to have a double negative put upon the promises! and yet this is just the condition of the ungodly. Mark the use of the term "ungodly", for, as we have seen in the opening of the Psalm, these are the beginners in evil, and are the least offensive of sinners. Oh! if such is the sad state of those who quietly continue in their morality, but neglect their God, what must be the condition of open sinners, and shameless infidels? The first sentence is a negative description of the ungodly, and the second is the positive picture. Here is their **character**—"they are like the chaff", intrinsically worthless, dead, unserviceable, without substance, and easily carried away. Here, also, mark their **doom**—"which the wind driveth away": death shall hurry them with its terrible blast into the fire in which they shall be utterly consumed.

"Therefore the ungodly shall not stand in the judgment, nor sinners in the congregation of the righteous" (v.5). They shall stand there to be judged, but not to be acquitted. Fear shall lay hold upon them; they shall not stand their ground; they shall flee away; they shall not stand in their own defense; for they shall blush and be covered with eternal contempt. Well may the saints long for heaven, for no evil man shall dwell there: "nor sinners in the congregation of the righteous". All our congregations upon earth are mixed. Every church hath one devil in it. The tares grow in the same furrows as the wheat. There is no floor which is as yet thoroughly purged from chaff. Sinners mix with saints, as dross mingles with gold. God's precious diamonds still lie in the same field with pebbles. Righteous Lots are this side heaven continually vexed by the men of Sodom. Let us rejoice then, that in "the general assembly and church of the firstborn" above, there shall by no means be admitted a single unrenewed soul. Sinners cannot live in heaven. They would be out of their element. Sooner could a fish live upon a tree than the wicked in Paradise. Heaven would be an intolerable hell to an impenitent man, even if he could be allowed to enter; but such a privilege shall never be granted to the man who perseveres in his iniquities. May God grant that we may have a name and a place in His courts above!

"For the Lord knoweth the way of the righteous: but the way of the ungodly shall perish" (v. 6). Or, as the Hebrew hath it yet more fully, "The Lord is **knowing** the way of the righteous". He is constantly looking on their way, and though it may often be in mist and darkness, yet the Lord knoweth it. If it be in the clouds and tempests of affliction, He understandeth it. He numbereth the hairs of our heads; He will not suffer any evil to befall us. "He knoweth the way that I take: when He hath tried me I shall come forth as gold" (Job 23:10). **"But the way of the ungodly shall perish."** Not only shall **they** perish themselves, but **their way** shall perish too. The righteous carves his name upon the rock, but the wicked writes his remembrance in the sand. The righteous man ploughs the furrows of earth, and sows a harvest here, which shall never be fully reaped till he enters the enjoyment of eternity; but as for the wicked, he ploughs the sea, and though there may seem to be a shining trail behind his keel, yet the waves shall pass over it, and the place that knew him shall know him no more forever. The very "way" of the ungodly shall perish. If it exist in remembrance, it shall be in the remembrance of bad; for the Lord will cause the name of the wicked to rot, to become a stench in the nostrils of the good, and to be only known to the wicked themselves by its putridity.

May the Lord cleanse our hearts and our ways, that we may escape the doom of the ungodly, and enjoy the blessedness of the righteous!

—C. H. SPURGEON.
"Treasury of David".

For the benefit of our new readers we may say that we have a few sets of the 1928 and 1929 "Studies" on hand. They are in bound form, neat and strong, for (D. V.) future use and reference. They contain our expositions of Hebrews from the beginning. We can supply them at $1.00 post paid.

Because God is holy, acceptance with Him on the ground of creature doings is utterly impossible. A fallen creature could sooner create a world than produce that which would meet the approval of infinite Purity. Can darkness dwell with Light? Can the Immaculate One take pleasure in "filthy rags" (Isa. 64:6)? The best that sinful man brings forth is defiled. A corrupt tree cannot bear good fruit. God would deny Himself, vilify His perfections, were He to account as righteous and holy that which is not so in itself; and nothing is so which has the least stain upon it contrary to the nature of God. But blessed be His name, that which His holiness demanded, His grace has provided in Christ Jesus our Lord. Every poor sinner who has fled to Him for refuge stands "accepted in the Beloved" (Eph. 1:6). Hallelujah!

Because God is holy the utmost reverence becomes our approaches unto Him. "God is greatly to be feared in the assembly of the saints, and to be had in reverence of all about Him" (Psa. 89:7). Then "Exalt ye the Lord our God, and worship at His footstool; He is holy" (Psa. 99:5). Yes, "At His **footstool**", in the lowest posture of humility, prostrate before Him. When Moses would approach unto the burning bush, God said, "put off thy shoes from off thy feet" (Ex. 3:5). He is to be served "with fear" (Psa. 2:11). Of Israel His demand was, "I will be sanctified in them that come nigh Me, and before all the people I will be glorified" (Lev. 10:3). The more our hearts are awed by His ineffable holiness, the more acceptable will be our approaches unto Him.

Because God is holy we should desire to be conformed to Him. His command is, "Be ye holy, for I am holy" (1 Peter 1:16). We are not bidden to be omnipotent or omniscient as God is, but we are to be holy, and that "in **all** manner of deportment" (1 Peter 1:15). "This is the prime way of honouring God. We do not so glorify God by elevated admirations, or eloquent expressions, or pompous services of Him, as when we aspire to a conversing with Him with unstained spirits, and live **to** Him in living **like** Him" (S. Charnock). Then as God alone is the Source and Fount of holiness, let us earnestly seek holiness from Him; let our daily prayer be that He may "sanctify us **wholly**; and our whole spirit and soul and body be preserved blameless unto the coming of our Lord Jesus Christ" (1 Thess. 5:23).

—ARTHUR W. PINK.

"For every woman that prayeth or prophesieth with head uncovered dishonoureth her head" (1 Cor. 11:5). Observe, first, there is nothing in this verse (or in any other verse of Holy Writ) which **limits** the injunction to any particular time or place. What is here said applies to women whether engaged in prayer in some public meeting, at family worship, or in the privacy of her own room. In other words, the Divine requirement for a woman to have some "covering" over her head when she engages in prayer, holds good at **all** seasons and in **all** places. The needs-be for our pointing this out here is because this word is almost universally disregarded today, even by professing sisters in Christ. Doubtless, in many instances, this is due to ignorance; yet is there no excuse, for the Scripture is plain enough.

When attention is called to this Divine requirement, not a few seek to evade its force by saying that their "hair" is given them for a covering. That is true, but it is not all the truth. If 1 Cor. 11 be read attentively, and with an honest desire to learn and do God's will, there will be no difficulty in perceiving that God requires the woman to place something (a hat or "veil") on her hair. First, observe that it is said in v. 5 "every woman that prayeth or prophesieth with her head uncovered dishonoureth her head": for that is **even all one** as if she were shaved". In other words, it is just as shameful for a woman to pray without any headgear as it is for her to have her head completely shaved. Second, in v. 6 it is said, "If the woman be not covered, let her **also** be shorn": the word "also" removes all doubt that there must be another "covering" in addition to the hair.

It should be obvious that there can be nothing in vv. 14, 15 to weaken what has been said in vv. 4 to 6, for the apostle would not contradict himself. No, rather is appeal made unto the natural to **illustrate** the spiritual. If "nature" teaches that it is more becoming and decorous for the woman to have "**long** hair" (alas that many have sunk so low morally as to be deaf even to the voice of human propriety), then none should murmur because the Spirit requires an additional head covering (in token of submission) when bowing before God in prayer.—A. W. P.

pronounced all that He made "very good" (Gen. 1:31), which He could not have done had there been anything imperfect or unholy in them. Man was made "upright" (Eccl. 7:29), in the image and likeness of his Creator. The angels that fell were created holy, for we are told that they "kept not their first habitation" (Jude 6). Of Satan it is written, "Thou wast perfect in thy ways from the day that thou wast created, till iniquity was found in thee" (Ezek. 28:15).

God's holiness is manifested in His **law**. That law forbids sin in **all** of its modifications: in its most refined as well as its grossest forms, the intent of the mind as well as the pollution of the body, the secret desire as well as the overt act. Therefore do we read, "The law is holy, and the commandment holy, and just, and good" (Rom. 7:12). Yes, "the commandment of the Lord is pure, enlightening the eyes. The fear of tthe Lord is clean, enduring forever: the judgments of the Lord are true and righteous altogether" (Psa. 19:8, 9).

God's holiness is manifested **at the Cross**. Wondrously and yet most solemnly does the Atonement display God's infinite holiness and abhorrence of sin. How hateful must sin be to God for Him to punish it to its utmost deserts when it was imputed to His Son! "Not all the vials of judgment that have or shall, be poured out upon the wicked world, nor the flaming furnace of a sinner's conscience, nor the irreversible sentence pronounced against the rebellious demons, nor the groans of the damned creatures, give such a demonstration of God's hatred of sin, as the wrath of God let loose upon His Son. Never did Divine holiness appear more beautiful and lovely than at the time our Saviour's countenance was most marred in the midst of His dying groans. This Himself acknowledges in Psa. 22. When God had turned His smiling face from Him, and thrust His sharp knife into His heart, which forced that terrible cry from Him, 'My God, My God why hast Thou forsaken Me?' He adores this perfection—'Thou art holy' v. 3" (S. Charnock).

Because God is holy He **hates all sin**. He loves everything which is in conformity to His laws, and loathes everything which is contrary to it. His Word plainly declares, "The froward is an abomination to the Lord" (Prov. 3:32). And again, "The thoughts of the wicked are an abomination to the Lord" (Prov. 15:26). It follows, therefore, that He must necessarily punish sin. Sin can no more exist without demanding His punishment than without requiring His hatred of it. God has often forgiven sinners, but He never forgives sin; and the sinner is only forgiven on the ground of Another having borne his punishment; for "without shedding of blood is no remission" (Heb. 9:22). Therefore we are told "The Lord will take vengeance on His adversaries, and He reserveth wrath for His enemies" (Nahum 1:2). For one sin God banished our first parents from Eden. For one sin all the posterity of Ham fell under a curse which remains over them to this day. For one sin Moses was excluded from Canaan, Elisha's servant smitten with leprosy, Ananias and Sapphira cut off out of the land of the living.

Herein we find proof for the Divine inspiration of the Scriptures. The unregenerate do not really believe in the holiness of God. Their conception of His character is altogether one-sided. They fondly hope that His mercy will override everything else. "Thou thoughtest that I was altogether as thyself" (Psa. 50.21) is God's charge against them. They think only of a "god" patterned after their own evil hearts. Hence their continuance in a course of mad folly. Such is the holiness ascribed to the Divine nature and character in Scripture that it clearly demonstrates their superhuman origin. The character attributed to the "gods" of the ancients and of modern heathendom, are the very reverse of that immaculate purity which pertains to the true God. An ineffably holy God, who has the utmost abhorrence of all sin, was never invented by any of Adam's fallen descendants! The fact is that nothing makes more manifest the terrible depravity of man's heart and his enmity against the living God, than to have set before him One who is infinitely and immutably holy. His own idea of **sin** is practically limited to what the world calls "crime". Anything short of that, man palliates as "defects", "mistakes", "infirmities", etc. And even where sin is owned at all, excuses and extenuations are made for it.

The "god" which the vast majority of professing Christians "love", is looked upon very much like an indulgent old man, who himself has no relish for folly, but leniently winks at the "indiscretions" of youth. But the Word says, "Thou hatest **all** workers of iniquity" (Psa. 5:5). And again, "God is angry with the wicked every day" (Psa. 7:11). But men refuse to believe in **this** God, and gnash their teeth when His hatred of sin is faithfully pressed upon their attention. No, sinful man was no more likely to devise a holy God than to create the Lake of fire in which he will be tormented for ever and ever.

(Continued on Page 191)

"Search the Scriptures" John 5 : 39

Copyright in all English-speaking Countries.

Editor: Arthur W. Pink, 1339 Bates Ave., Los Angeles, Calif, U. S. A.
Hon. Agent in England: Mr. A. Winstone, "Shalom", Old Bath Road, Leckhampton, Cheltenham.
Hon. Agent in Australia: Mr. G. Ardill, The Christian Workers' Depot. Commonwealth and Reservoir Streets, Sydney.

THE POWER OF GOD.

We cannot have a right conception of God unless we think of Him as all-powerful, as well as all-wise. He who cannot do what he will and perform all his pleasure cannot be God. As God hath a will to resolve what He deems good, so has He power to execute His will. "The power of God is that ability and strength whereby He can bring to pass whatsoever He pleases, whatsoever His infinite wisdom may direct, and whatsoever the infinite purity of His will may resolve . . . As holiness is the beauty of all God's attributes, so power is that which gives life and action to all the perfections of the Divine nature. How vain would be the eternal counsels, if power did not step in to execute them. Without power His mercy would be but feeble pity, His promises an empty sound, His threatenings a mere scare-crow. God's power is like Himself: infinite, eternal, incomprehensible; it can neither be checked, restrained, nor frustrated by the creature" (S. Charnock).

"God hath spoken once; twice have I heard this, that power belongeth unto God" (Psa. 62:11). "God hath spoken once": nothing more is necessary! Heaven and earth shall pass away, but His word abideth forever. "God hath spoken once": how befitting His Divine majesty! We poor mortals may speak often and yet fail to be heard. He speaks but once and the thunder of His power is heard on a thousand hills. "The Lord also thundered in the heavens, and the Highest gave His voice; hailstones and coals of fire. Yea, He sent out His arrows, and scattered them; and He shot out lightnings, and discomfited them. Then the channels of waters were seen and the foundations of the world were discovered at Thy rebuke, O Lord, at the blast of the breath of Thy nostrils" (Psa. 18:13-15).

"God hath spoken once": behold His unchanging authority. "For who in the heaven can be compared unto the Lord? who among the sons of the mighty can be likened unto the Lord?" (Psa. 89:6). "And all the inhabitants of the earth are reputed as nothing: and He doeth according to His will in the army of heaven, and among the inhabitants of the earth: and none can stay His hand, or say unto Him, What dost Thou?" (Dan. 4:35). This was openly displayed when God became incarnate and tabernacled among men. To the leper He said, "I will, be thou clean, and immediately his leprosy was cleansed" (Matt. 8:3). To one who had lain in the grave four days He cried, "Lazarus, come forth", and the dead came forth. The stormy wind and the angry wave were hushed at a single word from Him. A legion of demons could not resist His authoritative command.

"Power belongeth unto God", and to Him alone. Not a creature in the entire universe has an atom of power save what God delegates. But God's power is not acquired, nor does it depend upon any recognition by any other authority. It belongs to Him inherently. "God's power is like Himself, self-existent, self-sustained. The mightiest of men cannot add so much as a shadow of increased power to the Omnipotent One. He sits on no buttressed throne and leans on no assisting arm. His court is not maintained by His courtiers, nor does it borrow its splendor from His creatures. He is Himself the great central source and Originator of all power" (C. H. Spurgeon). Not only does all creation bear witness to the great power of God, but also to His entire independency of all created things. Listen to His own challenge: "Where wast thou when I laid the foundations of the earth? declare, if thou hast understanding. Who hath laid the measures thereof, if thou knowest? or who hath stretched the line upon it? Whereupon are the foundations thereof

(Continued on Page 216)

IMPORTANT NOTICES

Please advise promptly of change of address, otherwise copies will be lost in the mails.

We are glad to send a sample copy to any of your friends whom you believe would be interested in such a publication.

Send to Mr. I. C. Herendeen, Swengel (Union County), Penna., for a list of our publications. He has published many of our books and booklets.

This magazine is published as a work of faith and labour of love. The Editor and his wife gladly give their services. It is freely sent to all who will read it. No charge is made for it.

Christians who feel definitely led to do so, may have fellowship with us in this ministry. Those outside the U. S. A., please send only INTERNATIONAL Money Orders made out to Los Angeles, California, U. S. A.

CONTENTS

The Epistle to the Hebrews	194
The Satisfaction of Christ	200
The Power of God	205
The Brazen Sea	210
Godly Companions	213

THE EPISTLE TO THE HEBREWS.

33. Judaism set aside: Heb. 7:17-19.

As stated in the opening paragraphs of the preceding article, the apostle had now reached (in the second section of Heb. 7) the most difficult and delicate part of his task, namely, to satisfy believing Jews that God had set aside the entire system which He had Himself instituted in the days of Moses. It is exceedingly difficult for us to form any adequate estimate of what that meant to them; in truth, it was the severest test to which the faith of God's people has ever been put. To be assured that God had discarded as dead and useless the entire order of solemn worship which He had appointed in so glorious a manner and which He had accepted for so many generations, was indeed a sore trial of faith. To acquiesce in His sovereign pleasure in this momentous matter called for no ordinary measure of grace. To establish the truth thereof Paul was led of the Spirit to enter into such detail that every valid objection was fairly met and clearly refuted.

There are many today who quite fail to appreciate the reason why the apostle should here pursue his argument so laboriously and enter into so many minute details. That these should strike anyone as "dry", uninteresting and unprofitable, is because he is insensible of the vast importance of what the apostle had before him. Rightly did John Owen affirm that "he hath the greatest argument in hand that was ever controverted in the church of God, and upon the determination whereof the salvation or ruin of the church did depend. The worship he treated of was immediately instituted by God Himself, and had now continued near fifteen hundred years in the church. All that while it had been the certain rule of God's acceptance of the people, or of His anger toward them; for whilst they complied with it, His blessing was continually upon them, and the neglect of it was still punished with severity".

The final exhortation which God had given to Israel through the last of His prophets was, "Remember ye the law of Moses My servant . . . lest I come and smite the earth with a curse" (Mal. 4:4-6). **Those** are the closing words of the Old Testament! So highly did the Jews esteem their great and singular privileges above all other nations, that they would rather die than part with them. So high ran their feelings against those who pressed upon them the claims of Christ that, the charge preferred against the first Christian martyr was, "We have heard him speak blasphemous words **against Moses** and God . . . This man ceaseth not to speak blasphemous words against the holy place **and the law**" (Acts 7:11, 13); and though he remonstrated so faithfully, earnestly, and tenderly with them, they "gnashed on him with their teeth" and "stoned" him (Acts 7:54, 59). It was therefore most necessary that Paul should proceed cautiously, carefully and slowly, omitting nothing that was of any force in favour of the cause he was pleading.

The truth of God requires no vindication from us, nor are we called upon to attempt any justification for what may strike some as being unnecessarily tedious. Yet, in addition to intimating the needs be for Paul to enter so microscopically into the signification and application of the details of the Melchizedek type, we may most profitably observe how that he has left an example which servants of

God today need to take to heart. The course here followed by this beloved teacher supplies a most helpful illustration of what is meant by believers being "established in the **present** truth" (2 Peter 1:12). All truth is eternal, and in itself is equally valuable and applicable to each age and generation. Yet portions of it are especially so from their timely pertinency to particular seasons, and that because of the opposition made against them. Thus Paul's teaching here about the abolishing of the Mosaic ceremonies with the introduction of a new priesthood and new ordinances of worship was then the **"present** truth" in the knowledge and confirmation of which the people of God were vitally concerned. The same principle holds good continuously. Each portion of God's truth may become of peculiar urgency by virtue of some special opposition thereto.

In His sovereign wisdom God is pleased to exercise and try the faith of His saints by various heresies which are fierce, persistant, and subtle oppositions to His Truth. None of the Devil's agents, while posing as the champions of the Cause of Christ or as revealing new and fuller "light" from Heaven, reject **all** the Gospel or repudiate **all** the fundamentals of the faith. No, Satan is far too clever to show his hand so openly. Rather do his wolves, who aim at robbing God's children of their inheritance, appear in sheep's clothing, and pretend to great reverence for the Scriptures. Instead of repudiating the entire faith delivered to the saints, they insidiously direct their attacks upon some single portion thereof; and thus a defense of what is directly opposed becomes the "present truth" for that day, in which the saints need establishing, because of the Enemy's attempt to overthrow them.

Though Satan hates all Truth, yet he is far too wary to send his satallites among the people of God and openly deny **all** that they hold dear. Nor can he gain **any** advantage over them while they are really walking **with God,** in humble, dependant, obedient submission to Him. No, he has to watch and wait until he discovers what professing Christians, because of their lusts and prejudices, are most inclined to receive. As the spirit of worldliness increases among them, then he presses that which is most calculated to hide from their view the **heavenly** calling of God's people and its inseparable consequence of walking down here as "**strangers and pilgrims**". As the spirit of egotism and pride is allowed a large place, then that which humbles and abases the flesh is withheld and a species of intellectualism which puffs up, is substituted.

It is indeed solemn and saddening to review the course which Christendom has followed during the last two or three generations in the light of the above principle. As the denying of self and the daily taking up of the cross declined, the heart was prepared for the Satanic delusion that because salvation is by grace alone, that therefore obedience to God, submission to His law, and the actual **doing** of His Word, are quite unnecessary; and thus Paul has been pitied against James, and the teaching of the latter ignored. That there is a Strait gate to be entered and a Narrow way to be traversed, before "life" is actually reached, is almost universally denied by those who pose as the servants of God; yet that only solemnly confirms our Lord's words, "Few there be that find it" (Matt. 7:14).

Again; as the "professing Church" became more infected with the **lawlessness** abounding in the world, the teaching that the Sabbath is "Jewish" and that the Law of God has been totally abolished, became very acceptable to those intent on pleasing themselves. As the exalted standard of holiness which God has set before His people became lowered by those professing to speak in His name, the monstrous idea that **repentance** belongs only to the "Kingdom age" was readily espoused. As the masses of those who bore the name of Christ refused to take upon them His **yoke** and learn of Him who was "meek and lowly in heart", the horrible heresy that the searching precepts of the Sermon on the Mount (found in Matt. 5-7) are not addressed to Christians living today, was greedily devoured. Ah, it is just these things which are now being opposed that have become the "present truth", in which numbers of God's people most need to be "established". It is at these very points that God is now causing the faith of His people to be tested, and the true servants of the Lord will seek grace, wisdom and courage, to emulate the example here left by Paul, and spare no pains to root and ground the saints in what is most needful for them. Such is the **practical application** we need to make of the principle exemplified by the apostle in Heb. 7.

In the verses immediately preceding our present passage, the apostle had shown that the abolition of the Levitical order was inevitable. First, he pointed out that **before** Aaron had been called, God Himself had owned another priesthood which was far more execellent, namely, that of Melchizedek's. Second, the introduction of that more excellent priesthood for a season, was designed to prefigure what was afterwards to be established, therefore another priesthood had to arise and be given unto the Church in answer to that ancient type. Third, the new priest after the order of Melchizedek could not consist side by side with that of Levi's, for He belonged to another tribe, and His sacrifice was of another kind. Hence, inasmuch as the Aaronic priesthood could not take away sins nor make the worshipper perfect before God, and because Christ's sacerdotal work effected these, therefore the former must give place to the latter. Still further reasons for the necessity of this the apostle continues to advance.

"For He testifieth, Thou art a priest forever after the order of Melchizedek" (v. 17). This verse completes the sentence begun at v. 15, the design of the whole being to afford a demonstration of what had been said in v. 11. In v. 11 a deduction is drawn from the signification of the Melchizedek type. That type announced the rising of a Priest distinct from and superior to the order of Aaron. From that fact the apostle points out, first, that the Levitical order must be inadequate, imperfect, and therefore must give way before that which was more excellent; and second, that the revocation of the Aaronic order necessarily involved the setting aside of the whole dispensation or economy connected therewith.

Though the "logic" of his argument was perfect and could not be gainsaid, the apostle does not ask the Hebrews to rest their faith on mere reasoning, but proceeds to **prove** what he has said by an appeal to those Scriptures which they owned as the inspired and authoritative Word of God. He reminds them that not only had the Lord given them more than a hint in the historical narrative of Genesis, that One should arise and fulfill the priestly type recorded therein, but he points out that in one of the great Messianic Psalms Jehovah Himself addresses the Messiah as "A Priest forever after the order of Melchizedek". We cannot but marvel at the wondrous and perfect ways of our God. At the very time when the church of Israel was in the highest enjoyment of the Levitical priesthood, whose office depended wholly on their genealogy, the Holy Spirit deemed it well to inform them through David that a Priest was to come and be independent of any line of fleshly descent, namely, after the order of Melchizedek, who had none, Psa. 110:4.

Well may we reverently ponder and admire the sovereign wisdom of the Holy Spirit in bringing forth truth unto light according as the state of God's people require. Here again we see exemplified that basic principle in all God's dealings with men: "first the blade, then the ear, after that the full corn in the ear" (Mark 4:28). First, He inserted in Genesis a very brief account of a person who was a type of Christ. Second, almost a thousand years afterwards, when, it **may** be, all understanding of the Genesis type had been lost, and the people of God were fully satisfied in a priesthood of quite another nature, the Holy Spirit in one word of prophecy intimated that, what Moses had recorded of him to whom Abraham paid tithes, was a foreshadowing of another Priest who was afterwards to arise. Thus God not only gave Israel light upon an important piece of ancient history, but also signified to them that the priesthood which they then enjoyed was not always to continue, but would be superceded by one of another and better nature.

But notwithstanding the plain prophecy recorded in the 110th Psalm, it is evident that at the coming of the Saviour and the fulfillment of both type and prophecy, the Jews had lost all knowledge and understanding of the mystery of Gen. 14 and the promises renewed through David. They thought it strange that there should be a Priest that had no genealogy, no solemn consecration at the hands of man, and no formal investiture with His office. Therefore does the apostle proceed so slowly and carefully in the opening of this mystery, prefacing the same not only by the assertion of how hard it was to understand it aright (5:10), but also with a lengthy discourse (5:11 to 6:20) to prepare their hearts for a diligent attention thereto. The difficulty before him was not only because the true understanding of Gen. 14 and Psalm 110 had been lost, but because of the carnality of those to whom he wrote made them reluctant to admit that the raising up of Christ as Priest after the order of Melchizedek necessarily involved the termination of the Levitical priesthood and the whole system of worship connected therewith.

Difficult as it was for the Jew to be weaned from that system in which he had been brought up and to which he was so deeply attached, nevertheless, his very salvation turned thereon. Therefore we are not to wonder at the apostle's insisting so much on the setting aside of

Judaism, for that was the very hinge on which the eternal salvation or destruction of the whole Nation did turn. If they would not forego their old priesthood and worship, their ruin was unavoidable. Christ would either be received by them, or "profit them nothing" (Gal. 5:2). Thus it was that it fell out with the great majority of them! turning away from the Lord Jesus, they clung tenaciously to their ancient institutions and perished in their unbelief.

Nor should we lose sight of the analogy and parallel furnished by the Jews in connection with salvation today. While it be true that salvation is wholly of grace, and in nowise obtained by any efforts or works of the creature, nevertheless, it is equally true that none can obtain that salvation until there be a complete break from the world and their old manner of life in it. Conversion is a turning **to** God, and to turn to God there must be a turning **from** all that is opposed to Him. None are saved till they "come" to Christ, and the very term "coming to Christ" implies a **leaving** of what is contrary to Him. The Lord Jesus does not save men **in** their sins, but **from** their sins, and before He saves them from their sins, there must be a **repenting** of sin (Luke 13:3), and no man savingly repents of his sins while he lives in and loves them. The wicked have to **forsake** their "way" **before** God will "pardon" (Isa. 55:7). The sinner has to turn his back on the far country, yea, leave it behind him, before he can approach the Father and receive the "best robe" (Luke 15)!

Should any object to what has just been said, But **that** is to make man, in part, his own saviour! We reply, Not at all. There is nothing whatever meritorious about repentance, any more than there is about faith. Neither of them are virtues entitling a sinner to salvation, yet they **are** required qualifications, in the same way that an empty-handed beggar is qualified for my charity or a sick person is fit to receive the attention of a physician. Scripture does not teach that a man must reform his life in order to win God's approval, but it does affirm "he that covereth his sins shall not prosper; but whoso confesseth and forsaketh them shall have mercy" (Prov. 28:13).

"For He testifieth, Thou art a priest forever after the order of Melchizedek. Note "He testifieth", not simply "He said". The words of the Holy Spirit through David are here appealed to by the apostle in support of what he had said. Brief as is that citation, it nevertheless substantiates all the principal points Paul had made: first, here was proof that there **should be** another priest not of the tribe of Levi, for Jehovah here affirms of Christ, who sprang from Judah, "Thou art a priest". Second, He was a priest "after the order of Melchizedek". Third, God Himself owned Him as such. Fourth, He was so "after the power of an endless life" (v. 16), for He is priest "forever".

Perhaps one more word needs to be added upon Christ's being "a priest forever after the order of Melchizedek". The priesthood of Christ was, in the mind of God, the eternal idea and original exemplar. Accordingly, God called forth Melchizedek, and invested him with his office in such a manner that he might fitly foreshadow Christ. Hence he and his priesthood became an external adumbration of the priesthood of Christ, and therefore is He said to remain a priest "after" his "order", that is suitably unto the representation made thereof in him.

"For there is verily a disannulling of the commandment going before for the weakness and unprofitableness thereof" (v. 18). In v. 12 the apostle had affirmed that the priesthood being changed, there was of necessity a change made of the law also. Having, in vv. 15-17, proved the former, he now proceeds to confirm the unescapable inference from it, and this he does by showing that the Priesthood promised and now given, was in all things inconsistent with the Levitical. In v. 12 he had used the milder term "change"; now he insists that the old regime could not be altered and adjusted to the new order of things, but had been altogether "disannulled".

"For there is verily a disannulling of the commandment going before". The reference here is to the entire system of the Mosaic institutions. That system is here spoken of as "the commandment going before". It was of Divine appointment and authority, yet was it only designed "until the time of reformation" (9:19). The "going before" signifies the introduction of the new Priest in fulfillment of the promise in Psalm 110. The commandment going before was that which regulated the worship of God and obedience to Him prior to the Christian dispensation; but this had now been cancelled and a new law of worship given.

It is indeed striking to note the **warnings** which God gave to Israel of the disannulling of the law. First, at the very beginning He gave a clear intimation that it **had not** a perpetuity annexed to it. Immediately after the giving of the law **as a covenant** to Israel, they broke the covenant by setting up the golden calf at Horeb; whereupon Moses break the tables of stone, whereon the law was given. Had God intended that that covenant should be perpetuated, He would not have suffered its first constitution to have been accompanied with an express emblem of its abolition. Second, Moses implicitly declared after the giving of the law that, God would provoke Israel to jealousy by a foolish people (**see** Deut. 33:21), which was by calling of the Gentiles (Rom. 10:19); whereupon the law of commandments contained in ordinances, was of necessity to be taken out of the way! Third, through Jeremiah (chap. 31, etc.) Jehovah made known that, following the revocation of the old, a **"new** covenant" should be established with the Church! In these and other ways was Israel forewarned that the time would come when the whole Moasic law, as to its covenant **efficacy**, would be repealed, unto the unspeakable advantage of God's people.

If it be asked how and when the commandment respecting Judaism was "disannulled", the answer is, First, virtually and really by Christ Himself. He had fulfilled and accomplished it in His own person, and by so doing took away its obligatory power. Second, formally, by the new ordinances which Christ instituted. The Lord's supper (Matt. 26:26-29) and Christian baptism (Matt. 28:19) were altogether inconsistent with the ordinances of the law, for these declared that was passed and done, which they directed unto as future and yet to come. Third, declaratively by the revealed will of God: in Acts 15 we learn how the Holy Spirit through the apostles (v. 28) expressly declared that the Gentile converts were **not** under obligations to heed the Moasic law (v. 24). Fourth, providentially, in A. D. 70, when God caused Jerusalem and the temple to be destroyed.

"For the weakness and unprofitableness thereof". Here the apostle assigns the reason why God had annulled the Moasic law. In v. 11 the apostle had asked, If "perfection" were obtainable by the Levitical priesthood what need was there for another priesthood to arise? Here he plainly declares that the whole system was, relatively speaking, worthless. This raises a difficulty of no small dimension, namely, in assigning such imperfections to a system which had been given by God Himself. How can it be supposed that the good and holy Jehovah should prescribe such a law unto His people as was always weak and unprofitable?

Absolutely considered no reflection can be made upon the Mosaic law, for it was the product of Divine wisdom, holiness and truth. But with respect unto the **people** to whom it was given, and the **end** for which it was given, imperfection **did** attach to it. It was given to **sinners** who were defiled and guilty, and therefore was the law "weak through the flesh" (Rom. 8:3), its subject having no power to meet its high demands. Moreover, it was (in itself) incapable of meeting their deep needs; taking away their sins, bestowing life on them, conforming them to God's holiness. Why, then, was it given? It was "added because of transgressions, till the Seed should come to whom the promise was made" (Gal. 3:19). It discovered the nature of sin, so that the conscience of man might be sensible thereof. It restrained sin by prohibitions and threatenings, so that it did not run out to an excess of riot. It represented, though obscurely, the ways and means by which sin could be expiated. Finally, it made known the imperative need for the coming of Christ to do for men what they could not do of and for themselves.

"For the law made nothing perfect, but the bringing in of a better hope did; by the which we draw nigh unto God" (v. 19). There are three things for us to note in this verse. First, the apostle names a particular instance in which the law was "weak and unprofitable". Second, he specifies what had been introduced in the room of that which had been disannulled. Third, he mentions the design and end of this change. The failure of the law was that it "made nothing perfect". "It did not make the church-state perfect, it did not make the worship of God perfect, it did not perfect the promises given to Abraham in their accomplishment, it did not make a perfect covenant between God and man; it had a shadow, an obscure representation, of all these things, but it made nothing perfect" (John Owen).

Above, we sought answer to the question, Why should God have given His people a law which made nothing perfect? It may further be pointed out that in all things the sovereignty of God is to be submitted unto; and for humble souls there is beauty and blessedness in Divine sovereignty. When the Lord Jesus rejoiced in spirit and returned thanks because heavenly mysteries had been hid from the wise and prudent and revealed unto babes, He assigned no other reason than, "Even so Father, for so it seemed good in Thy sight" (Luke 10:21). And until we recognize an excellency in **all** God's dispensations, simply because they are **His,** who giveth no account of His matters, we shall never admire His ways.

Again, men have sinned, and apostatised from God, and therefore it was but just and equal that they should not be re-instated in their reparation at once. "As God left the generality of the world without the knowledge of what He intended, so He saw good to keep the Church in a state of expectancy, as to the condition of liberty and deliverance intended. He could have created the world in an hour or moment; but He chose to do so in the space of six days, that the glory of His works might be distinctly represented unto angels and men. And He could, immediately after the fall, have introduced the promised Seed, in whose advent the Church must of necessity enjoy all the perfection which it is capable of in this world. But to teach the Church the greatness of their sin and misery, and to work in them an acknowledgement of His unspeakable grace, God proceeded gradually in the very revelation of Him, and caused them to wait under earnest desires and expectations many ages for Christ's coming" (John Owen).

Finally and primarily, God designed that the Lord Jesus should in **all** things have the pre-eminence. This was due Him because of the glory of His person and the transcendent excellency of His work. But if the law could have made anything perfect, it is evident that this could not have been. Christ is the centre of all God's counsels, the key to every problem. All things are being directed to His ultimate honour and praise. The system of Judaism, with its mysteries and shadows, served as a suitable background, from which might shine forth the more gloriously the full blaze of God's perfections made manifest by His incarnate Son. "The darkness is past, and the true light now shineth" (1 John 2:8).

"But the bringing in of a better hope did". When a sufficient discovery had been made of the insufficiency of the law to make things "perfect", God introduced that which did. A parallel passage is found in Rom. 8:3, 4. There too we read of the law being "weak", and, that, through the faultiness of those to whom it was addressed. There too we read of the law being followed by God's sending something "better", namely, His own Son. There too we read of the "perfection" which Christ has brought in for His people. The same thing will come before us again, D. V., when we arrive at Heb. 10:1-10.

"Hope" is used metonymically, that is to say, for the object itself, the thing hoped for. From the giving of the first promise in Gen. 3:15, renewed in Gen. 12:3 and 17:8, the coming of Christ into this world was the great thing which believers longed for. Abraham rejoiced to see His day (John 8:56), as did the prophets search diligently concerning it (1 Peter 1:11, 12). Hence, we read of Simeon "waiting for the Consolation of Israel" (Luke 2:35) and of aged Anna speaking of the newly-born Saviour to "all them that **looked for** redemption in Jerusalem" (Luke 2:38). In like manner, the "blessed hope" set before God's saints throughout this dispensation is the "appearing of the glory of the great God and our Saviour Jesus Christ" (Titus 2:13).

By the introduction of the "better hope" believers now "draw nigh unto God". The verb here is a sacerdotal term, denoting the approach of priests to God in His worship. By nature we were unable so to do, for we were "alienated from the life of God" (Eph. 4:18). Sin separated between us and the thrice Holy One. But now we who once were far off "are made nigh by the blood of Christ" (Eph. 2:13), in consequence whereof both believing Jews and Gentiles "have access by one Spirit unto the Father" (Eph. 2:18), for the whole election of grace have been made "a holy priesthood, to offer up spiritual sacrifices, acceptable to God by Jesus Christ" (1 Peter 2:5). The right and privilege of believers drawing nigh unto God Himself and the throne of His grace, is further opened in Heb. 10, particularly vv. 19-22. Everything which kept us at a distance from God has been removed by the bringing in of the Better Hope.

In its complete realisation and ultimate fulfillment, it is still the "better **hope**". Believers are yet here on earth; there is much within and without which mars and interrupts their communion with God. Their being "made perfect" in their state and experience (Heb. 11:40), and their being actually conducted into the Father's presence (John 14:1-3) is yet future. But blessed be God, our sins have been put away, we already have "**access** by faith into this grace wherein we stand" (Rom. 5:2). The Forerunner has "**for us** entered" within the veil (Heb. 10:19, 20). Then, in the meantime, "Let us therefore come boldly unto the throne of grace, that we may obtain mercy, and find grace to help in time of need" (Heb. 4:16). The Lord grant it for His name's sake.

—ARTHUR W. PINK.

THE SATISFACTION
("Atonement")
OF CHRIST.
9. Its Design.

What was the purpose of the Eternal Three in sending Christ Jesus into this world? What was the incarnation of the Son of God intended to accomplish? What were His sufferings and obedience ordained to effect? Concerning this all-important matter the most erroneous ideas have been entertained, ideas at direct variance with Holy Scripture, ideas most dishonouring to God. Even where these awful errors have not been fully espoused, sufficient of their evil leaven has been received to corrupt the pure truth which many good men have held. In other instances, where this great subject has been largely neglected, only the vaguest and haziest conceptions are entertained. Sad it is to see what a very small place this vital theme now has in most pulpits, and in the thoughts and studies of the majority of professing Christians.

"Known unto God are all His works from the beginning of the world" (Acts 15:18). Everything God does is according to design: all is the working out of "the eternal purpose which He purposed in Christ Jesus our Lord" (Eph. 3:11). God had a design in creation: Rev. 4:10. He has a design in providence: Rom. 8:28. And He has a design or purpose in the Satisfaction which was wrought by Christ: 1 Peter 1:20. What, then, was that purpose? This is not a speculative question, but one of the utmost moment. Surely the right answer to it must be the one which upholds the glory of God. Therefore any answer which carries with it the inevitable corollaries of a dishonoured Father, a disgraced Saviour, and a defeated Holy Spirit, **cannot** be the right one. Redemption is the glory of all God's works, but it would be an everlasting disgrace of them if it should fail to effect whatsoever it was ordained to accomplish.

The Arminian conception, now so widely held, is that, Christ came here to remove certain barriers which stood in the way of God's grace flowing forth to fallen creatures. Their theory is that Christ's death took away that hindrance which the Divine justice interposed to mercy being extended to transgressors of the law. They suppose the great Atonement was merely the procuring unto God a right for His pardoning of sin. The words of Arminius are: "God had a mind and will to do good to humankind, but could not by reason of sin, His justice being in the way; whereupon He sent Christ to remove that obstacle, so that He might, upon the prescribing of what condition He pleased, and its being by them fulfilled, have mercy on them". Sad it is to find so many today echoing the blasphemies of this arch-heretic.

The error in the above theory is easily exposed. If it were true that the design of Christ's satisfaction was to acquire a right unto His Father, that notwithstanding His justice He might save sinners, then did He rather die to redeem a liberty **unto God**, than a liberty **from evil** unto His people; that a door might be opened for God to come out in mercy to us, rather than that a way should be opened for us to go in unto Him. This is certainly a turning of things upside down. And where, we may ask, is there a word in Scripture to support such a grotesque idea? Does Scripture declare that God sent His Son out of love to Himself or out of love unto us? Does Scripture affirm that Christ died to procure something for God, or for His people? Does Scripture teach that the obstacles thrown out by Divine justice or that our sins were what Christ came here to remove? There can be only one answer to these questions.

Again; the Arminian theory would reduce the whole Work of Christ to a costly experiment which might or might not succeed, inasmuch as according to them there is still some condition which the sinner himself must fulfil ere he can be benefited by that mercy which God would bestow upon him. But **that** is a flat denial of the fatal effects of the Fall, a repudiation of the total depravity of man. Those who are spiritually dead in sins are quite **incapable** of performing any spiritual conditions. As well offer to a man who is stone blind a thousand dollars on condition that he sees, as offer something spiritual to one who has **no** capacity to discern it: see John 3:3, 1 Cor. 2:14. Such a view as this is as far removed from the truth as is light from darkness. Such a view, reduced to plain terms, comes to this; if the sinner believes, then Christ died for him; if the sinner does not believe, then Christ did not die for him; thus the sinner's act is made the cause of its own object, as though his believing would make that **to be** which otherwise was not. To such insane absurdities are the opposers of Grace driven.

How different the plain teaching of the Word! Christ came here to fulfill His agreement in the Everlasting Covenant. In that covenant a certain work was prescribed. Upon His performance of it a certain reward was promised. That work was that Christ should make a perfect satisfaction unto God on behalf of each and all of His people. That reward was that all the blessings procured and purchased by Him should be infalliby bestowed on each and all of His people. "God out of His infinite love to His elect, sent His dear Son in the fulness of time, whom He had promised in the beginning of the world; to pay a ransom of infinite value and dignity, for the purchasing of eternal redemption, and bringing unto Himself all and every one of those whom He had before ordained to eternal life, for the praise of His own glory. So that freedom from all the evil from which we are delivered, and an enjoyment of all the good things that are bestowed on us, in our traduction from death to life, from hell and wrath to heaven and glory, are the proper issues and effects of the death of Christ, as the meritorous cause of them all" (John Owen). We are now ready to answer our opening question. The Design of Christ's Satisfaction was,

1. That God might be magnified

"The Lord hath made all things for Himself" (Prov. 16:4). The great end which God has in all His works is the promotion of His own declarative glory: "For of Him, and through Him, and to Him, are all things: to whom be glory forever. Amen" (Rom. 11:36). It must be so, There is nothing outside Himself which can possibly supply any motive for Him to act. To assert the contrary would be to deny His self-sufficiency. The aim of God in creation, in providence, and in redemption, is the magnifying **of Himself.** Everything else is subordinate to this paramount consideration. We press this, because we are living in an age of infidelity and practical atheism.

God predestinated His people unto "the glory of His grace" (Eph. 1:6). Christ has "received us to the glory of God" (Rom. 15:7). All the Divine promises for us are in Christ "Amen, to the glory of God" (2 Cor. 1:20). The inheritance which we have obtained in Christ is in order that "we should be to the praise of His glory" (Eph. 1:12). The Holy Spirit is given us as the earnest of our inheritance "unto the praise of His glory" (Eph. 1:14). The very rejoicing of the believer is "in hope of the glory of God" (Rom. 5:2). Our thanksgiving is that it may "redound to the glory of God" (2 Cor. 4:15). This is the one design of all the benefits which we obtain from the Satisfaction of Christ, for "we are filled with the fruits of righteousness which are by Jesus Christ unto the glory and praise of God" (Phil. 1:11). While every tongue shall yet "confess that Jesus Christ is Lord to the glory of God the Father" (Phil. 2:11).

God hath both a subservient and a supreme design in sending Christ into this world: the supreme design was to display His own glory, the subservient design was to save His elect unto His own glory. The former was accomplished by the manifestation of His blessed attributes, which is the chief design in all His works, preeminently so in His greatest and grandest Work of all. The remainder of the article might well be devoted to the extension of this one thought. Through Christ's obedience and death God magnified His **law**: Isa. 42:21. The Law of God was more honoured by the Son's subjection to it, than it was dishonoured by the disobedience of all of Adam's race. God magnified His **love** by sending forth the Darling of His bosom to redeem worthless worms of the earth. He magnified His **justice,** for when sin (by imputation) was found upon His Son, He called for the sword to smite Him: Zech. 13:7. He magnified His **holiness**: His hatred of sin was more clearly shown at the cross than it will be in the lake of fire. He magnified His **power** by sustaining the Mediator under such a load as was laid upon Him. He magnified His **truth** by fulfilling His covenant engagements and bringing forth from the dead the great Shepherd of the sheep: Heb. 13:20. He magnified His **grace** by imputing to the ungodly all the merits of Christ. This, then, was the prime purpose of God in the Atonement: to magnify Himself.

2. That the God-man might be glorified.

Christ is the Center of all the counsels of the Godhead. He is both the Alpha and Omega of Their designs. All God's thoughts concerning everything in heaven and in earth begin and end in Christ. "God created all things by Jesus Christ" (Eph. 3:9), and all things were created "for Him" (Col. 1:16). As Mediator He is the alone medium of union and communion between God and the creature. "That in the dispensation of the fulness of times He might gather together in one all things **in Christ**, both which are in heaven, and which are on earth; in Him" (Eph. 1:10). Christ is the one universal Head in which God has summed up all things. Therefore was the stupenduous work of redemption given to Him that He might reconcile all things in heaven and earth unto Himself, and this, that a revenue of glory might come to Him.

The man Christ Jesus was taken up into union with the essential and eternal Word, God the Son, so that He might be Jehovah's "Fellow" (Zech. 13:7). The man Christ Jesus was predestinated unto the ineffable honour of union with the second person in the Trinity. As such He is the Head of the whole election of grace, called by the Father, "Mine Elect, in whom My soul delighteth" (Isa. 42:1). As the God-man, the Father covenanted with Him, appointed Him as Surety, and assigned Him His work. As God-man, He had a covenant subsistence before He became incarnate. This is clear from John 6:62. "What and if ye shall see the Son of **man** ascend up where He was **before**?" It was as the God-man the Father "sent" forth Christ on His errand of mercy, and that for His personal glory.

As Judas went out to betray Him Christ said, "Now is the Son of man glorified" (John 13:31). Within a few hours His stupenduous undertaking would be accomplished. The Mediator was honoured, supremely honoured, by God's having committed to His care the mightiest Work of all, a work which none other was capable of performing. To Him was entrusted the task of glorifying God here on earth; of vanquishing His arch-enemy, the Devil; of redeeming His elect. To this He makes reference in John 17:4, "I have glorified Thee on earth; I have finished the work which Thou gavest Me to do". He had completed God's vast design, executed His decrees, fulfilled all His will.

Having so gloriously glorified the Father, the Father has proportionately glorified the Mediator. He has been exalted high above "all principality and power, and might and dominion, and every name that is named, not only in this world, but also in that which is to come" (Eph. 1:21). He has been elevated to "the right hand of the Majesty on high" (Heb. 1:3). He has been given all authority in heaven and in earth (Matt. 28:18). He has been given "power over all flesh, that He should give eternal life to as many as the Father hast given Him" (John 17:2). He has been given a name which is above every name, before which name every knee shall yet bow (Phil. 2:11). Speaking of Christ's finished Work and the Father's rewarding thereof, the Psalmist said, "His glory is great in Thy salvation: honour and majesty hast Thou laid upon Him. For Thou hast made Him most blessed forever: Thou hast made Him exceeding glad with Thy countenance" (Psa. 21:5, 6). This was the grand design of the Trinity: that the God-man should thus be glorified.

3. That God's elect might be saved.

"For the Son of man is come to seek and to save that which was lost" (Luke 19:10). How different is this plain, positive, and unqualified statement from the tale which nearly all preachers tell today! The story of the vast majority is that Christ came here to make salvation **possible** for sinners: He has done His part, now they must do theirs. There is considerable difference of opinion as to exactly **what** the sinner must do in order to win salvation, but from the pope of Rome to the street-corner evangelist, almost all are agreed that man must perform some work or some act or otherwise Christ cannot save him. To reduce the wondrous, finished, and glorious work of Christ to a merely making salvation possible is most dishonouring and insulting to Him.

Christ came here to carry into effect God's sovereign purpose of election, to save a people already "His" (Matt. 1:21) by covenant settlement. There are a people whom God hath "from the beginning chosen unto salvation" (2 Thess. 2:13), and redemption was in order to the **accomplishing** of that decree. And if we believe what Scripture declares concerning the person of Christ, then we have indubitable proof that there can be no possible failure in connection with **His** mission. The Son of man, the Child born, was none other than "the mighty God" (Isa. 9:6). Therefore is He omniscient, and knows where to look for each of His lost ones; He is also omnipotent, and so cannot fail to deliver when they are found.

Observe that Luke 19:10 does not say that Christ came here to seek and to save **all** the lost. Of course it does not. Two thirds of human history had already run its course before Jesus was born. Half the human race was already in Hell when He entered Bethlehem's manger. It was for "**the** lost" (see Greek) for which He became incarnate. That is the awful condition in which God's elect are by nature. Lost! They have lost all knowledge of the true God, all liking for Him, all desires after Him. They have lost His image in which they were originally created, and have contracted the image of Satan. They have lost all knowledge of their own actual condition, for their understanding is darkened (Eph. 4:18), they are spiritually dead in trespasses and sins (Eph. 2:1). Totally unconscious of their terrible state they neither seek Christ nor realise their need of Him.

Christ did not come here to see if there were any who would seek after Him. Of course not. Rom. 3:11 emphatically declares "there is **none** that seeketh after God". **Christ** is the seeker. Beautifully is that brought out by Him in His parable of the lost sheep. A strayed dog or a lost horse will usually find its way back home. Not so a sheep: the longer it is free, the farther it strays from the fold. Hence, if that sheep is ever to be recovered, one must go after it. This is what Christ did, and which by His Spirit He is still doing. As Luke 15:4 declares, He goes "after that which is lost until He **find** it". But more: Christ came here not only to seek and find, but also to **save**. His words are, "For the Son of man is come to seek and to save that which was lost". Note it is not merely that He offers to, nor helps to, but that He actually **saves**. Such was the emphatic and unqualified declaration of the angel to Joseph, "Thou shalt call His name Jesus, for He **shall save** His people from their sins"—not try to, not half do so, but actualy **save** them. Reader, do you really believe this?

Christ came here with a definitely defined object in view, and being who He is there no possible room for any failure in His mission. Hence, before He came here, God declared that He should "see of the travail of His soul and **be satisfied**" (Isa. 53:10). As the Mediator He solemnly covenanted with the Father **to** save His people from their sins. He actually **purchased** them with His blood (Acts 20:28). He has wrought out for them a perfect salvation, therefore is He "mighty to save" (Isa. 63:1). Blessedly is this illustrated in the immediate context of Luke 19:10. To Zacchaeus He said, "Make haste, and come down; for today I **must** abide at thy house... This day is salvation come to this house, forsomuch as he also is a son of Abraham" (vv. 5, 9). Yes, "a son of Abraham", one of the elect seed. Therefore we boldly say to the reader, If you belong to the sheep of Christ, you **must** be saved, even though now you may be quite unconscious of your lost condition. Though, like Saul of Tarsus, you may yet "kick against the pricks", invincible grace **shall** conquer you, for it is written, "Thy people shall be willing in the day of Thy power" (Psa. 110:3).

"I am come **that** they might have life, and that they might have it more abundantly. I am the good Shepherd: the good Shepherd giveth His life for the sheep" (John 10:10, 11). Here again we have clearly defined the **design** of Christ's mission and satisfaction. His sheep once possessed "life", possessed it in their natural head, Adam. But when he fell, they fell; when he died, they died. As it is written, "In Adam all die" (1 Cor. 15:22). But by Christ, through His work, and in Him their spiritual Head, they obtain not only "life", but "more abundant "life; that is, a "life" which as far excells what they lost in their first father, as the last Adam excells in His Person, the first Adam. Therefore is it written, "The first Adam was made a living soul; the last Adam a quickening spirit" (1 Cor. 15:45).

"As the Father hath life in Himself, so hath He given to the Son to have life in Himself" (John 6:26), which speaks of Christ as the God-man, the Mediator, as is clear from the words "given to". But that "life" had to be 'laid down" (John 10:17) and received again in resurrection before it could be, efficaciously, bestowed on His people: John 12:24. It was as the Risen One that Christ was made " a quickening spirit". The first Adam was "made a living soul" that he might communicate natural life to his posterity; the last Adam was "made a quickening spirit" that He might impart spiritual life to all His seed. As the soul dwelling in Adam's body animated it and so made him to be a "living soul", so the man Christ Jesus being united to the second of the Trinity, has constituted Him a "quickening spirit", i.e. quickening His mystical body, both now and hereafter. The life of the Head is the life of His members.

The Christian first has a federal life **in** Christ before he has a vital life **from** Christ. Being legally one with Christ, this must be so. When Christ died His people died, when Christ was quickened His people were quickened 'together with" Him (Eph. 2:5). It is to this union with the life of Christ that Rom. 5:17 refers, "For if by one man's offence death reigned by one; much more they which receive abundance of grace and of the gift of righteousness shall reign in life by one, Jesus Christ". Yes, there is a "much more": the abundance of grace is greater than the demerits of sin, and the gift of righteousnes exceeds that which was lost in Adam. The righteousness of God's elect far surpasses that which they possessed in innocence by the first Adam, for it is the righteousness of Christ, who is God. To this, neither the righteousness of Adam nor of angels can be compared. Those redeemed by Christ are not only recovered from the fall, but they are made to "**reign** in life" to which they had no title in their first parent. Since Christ is King, His people are made "kings" too (Rev. 1:6).

The same aspect of truth is brought before us again in 2 Cor. 5:14, 15, "For the love of Christ constraineth us: because we thus judge **that** if one for all died, then all died. And for all He died, **that** they who live no longer to themselves should live, but to Him who for them died and was raised again" (Bagster's Interlinear). The A. V. is very misleading here. Many have supposed that the last clause of v. 14 refers to those who are "dead in sins", but **that** was true apart from the death of Christ! Nor does the spiritual death of Adam's fallen descendants render them capable of "living unto" Christ, but the very reverse. No, it is, "If one for all died" i.e. for all His people, then they all died **in Him**. Then in v. 15 we have stated the consequence and fruit of this: as the result of His rising from the dead, they "live". His act was, representatively, their act. The atoning death of Christ, on the ground of federal union and substitution, was also our death; see Gal. 2:20. So too His resurrection was, representatively our resurrection: see Col. 3:1. Thus, in Christ, God's elect have a "more abundant" life than they ever had in unfallen Adam.

The same truth is set before us in 1 Peter 2:24, "Who His own self bare our sins in His own body on the tree, **that** we, being dead to sins, should live unto righteousness". The first part of this verse has been before us in a previous article. The second half of it expresses the Divine design in appointing Christ to be federally and vicariously the Bearer of His peoples' sins. Christ's death was their death: they are "dead to sins", not to "sinning"! Let the reader compare Rom. 6:2 and the apostle's exposition in the next nine verses. Further, Christ's resurrection was their resurrection: they "live", legally and representatively, "unto righteousness" in Christ their risen Head, of whom it is written "He liveth unto God" (Rom. 6:10). We quote below from John Brown's lucid exposition of 1 Peter 2:24.

"To be 'dead in sins' is to be delivered from the condemning power of sin; or, in other words, from the condemning sentence of the law, under which, if a man lies, he cannot be holy; and from which, if a man is delivered, his holiness is absolutely secured. To 'live unto righteousness' is plainly just the positive view of that, of which 'to be dead to sins' is the negative view. 'Righteousness', when opposed to 'sin', in the sense of guilt or liability, to punishment, as it very often is in the writings of the apostle Paul, is descriptive of a state of justification. A state of guilt is a state of condemnation by God; a state of righteousness is a state of acceptance with God. To live unto righteousness, is in this case to live under the influence of a justified state, a state of acceptance with God; and the apostle's statement is: Christ Jesus, by His sufferings unto death, completely answered the demands of the law on us by bearing, and bearing away our sins, that we, believing in Him, and thereby being united to Him, might be as completely freed from our liabilities to punishment, as if we, in our own person, not He himself, in His own body, had undergone them; and that we might as really be brought into a state of righteousness, justification, acceptance with God, as if we, not He, in His obedience to death, had magnified the law and made it honourable".

"God sending His own Son in the likeness of sin's flesh, and for sin, condemned sin in the flesh: **that** the righteousness of the law might be fulfilled in us" (Rom. 8:3, 4). Here again the **design** of Christ's mission is clearly stated. God sent His Son here in order that (1) the punishment of His peoples' guilt should be inflicted upon their Head, (2) that the righteous requirements of the law—perfect obedience—might be met by Him for us. This righteousness is said to be "fulfilled **in** us" because representatively, we were "in Christ" our Surety: He obeyed the law not only "for" our good, but so that His obedience should become actually ours by imputation: and thus Christ purchased for us a **title** to Heaven.

A parallel passage to Rom. 8:3, 4 is found in 2 Cor. 5:21, "For He hath made Him sin for us, who knew no sin; **that** we might be made the righteousness of God in Him". The purpose of Christ's vicarious life and death was that a perfect righteousness should be wrought out for His people and imputed to them by God, so that they might exclaim, "**In the Lord** have I righteousness" (Isa. 45:24). This will come before us (D. V.) more fully when we take up the **results** of Christ's satisfaction, yet a few words upon it are here in place. The righteousness of the believer is wholly **objective;** that is to say, it is something altogether outside of himself. This is clear from the antithesis of 2 Cor. 5:21. Christ was "made sin" not inherently, but imputatively, by the guilt of His people being legally transferred to Him. In like manner, they are "made the righteousness of God **in Him**", not "in themselves", by Christ's righteousness being legally reckoned to their account. In the repute of God, Christ and His people constitute one mystical person, hence it is that their sins were imputed to Him, and that His righteousness is imputed to them, and therefore we read "Christ is the end of the law for righteousness to every one that believeth". (Rom. 10:4)

"For Christ also hath once suffered for sins, the Just for the unjust, **that** He might bring us to God" (1 Peter 3:18). This wondrous declaration gives us a remarkably clear view of the substitutionary punishment which Christ endured, with the design thereof, namely, to restore His people to priestly nearness and service to God. Four things in it are worthy of our most close attention. First, Christ "suffered". Sin was the cause of His suffering. Had there been no sin, Christ had never suffered. To "suffer" means "to bear punishment", as in ordinary speech we say, a child suffers for the sins of its parents. Christ suffered for "us", the whole election of grace: it was for their sins He was penalized. Second, He suffered "once". This must not be understood to signify that His suffering was confined to the three hours of darkness, but means "once for all" as in Heb. 9:27, 28. The "suffering" which pervaded the whole of Christ's earthly life, culminated at the cross. That suffering was final. His all-sufficient Atonement possesses eternal validity.

Third, Christ Himself was personally sinless: it was the "Just" or "Righteous" One who suffered. To affirm that He was "righteous" means that He was approved of God as tested by the standard of the law. He was not only sinless, but One whose life was adjusted to the Divine requirements. As such, He suffered, the Pure for the impure, the Innocent for the guilty. His sufferings were not on His own account, nor were they from the inevitable course of events or laws of evil in a sinful world; but they were the direct and necessary consequence of His vicariously taking the place of His guilty people. Christ received the punishment they ought to have suffered. He was paid sin's wages which were due them.

Fourth, the end in view of Christ's substitutionary sufferings was to bring His people **to God**. This was only possible by the removal of their sins, which separated them from the thrice Holy One: Isa. 59:2. By His sufferings Christ has procured for us access to God. "But in Christ Jesus ye who sometimes were far off, are **made nigh** by the blood of Christ" (Eph. 2:13). "That He might bring us to God" is the most comprehensive expression used in Scripture for stating the design of Christ's Satisfaction. It includes the bringing of His people out of darkness into marvelous light: out of a state of alienation, misery, and wrath, into one of grace, peace, and eternal communion with God. By nature they were in a state of enmity, but Christ has reconciled them by His death: Rom. 5:10. By nature they were "children of wrath" (Eph. 2:3), obnoxious to God's judicial displeasure; but by grace they have been accepted into His favour: (Rom. 5:2). By nature they were spiritual lepers, but by one offering Christ hath "perfected forever them that are sanctified" (Heb. 10:14).

Here then, in brief, is the Divine **design** in the Satisfaction of Christ; that God Himself might be honoured; that Christ might be glorified; that the elect might be saved, by their sins being put away, an abundant life being given them, a perfect righteousness imputed to them, and their being brought into God's favour, presence, and fellowship.

—ARTHUR W. PINK.

THE POWER OF GOD.

"Twice have I heard this, that power belongeth unto God" (Psa. 62:11). In our first article upon this glorious theme, we practically confined our attention to the omnipotence of God as it is seen in and through the old creation. Here we propose to contemplate the exercise of His might in and on the new creation. That God's people are much slower to perceive the latter than they are the former is plain from Eph. 1:19 where the apostle prayed that the saints might know "**what is** the exceeding greatness of His power to usward who believe, according to the working of His mighty power". Very striking indeed is this. When Paul speaks of the Divine power in creation he mentions "His power and Godhead" (Rom. 1:20), but when he treats of the work of grace and salvation, he calls it "the exceeding greatness of His power".

God proportions His power to the nature of His work. The casting out of demons is ascribed to His "finger" (Luke 11:20); His delivering of Israel from Egypt, to His "hand" (Ex. 13:9); but when the Lord saves a sinner it is His "holy **arm**" which gets Him the victory (Psa. 98:1, 2). It is to be duly noted that the language of Eph. 1:19 is so couched as to take in the **whole** work of Divine grace in and upon the elect. It is not restrained to the past—"who have believed according to"; nor to the time to come—"the power that shall work in you"; but instead, it is "the exceeding greatness of His power to usward **who believe**". It is the "effectual working" of God's might from the first moment of illumination and conviction, till their sanctification and glorification are completed.

So dense is the darkness which is now fallen upon the people (Isa. 60:2), that the vast majority of those even in the "churches" deem it by no means a hard thing to become a Christian. They seem to think it is almost as easy to purify a man's heart (James 4:8), as it is to wash his hands; that it is as simple a matter to admit the light of Divine truth into the soul, as it is the morning-sun into our chambers by opening the shutters; that it is no more difficult to turn the heart from evil to good, from the world to God, from sin to Christ, than to turn a ship round by the help of her helm. And this in the face of Christ's emphatic statement, "With men this is impossible" (Matt. 19:26).

To mortify the lusts of the flesh (Col. 3:5), to be crucified daily to sin (Luke 9:23), to be meek and gentle, patient and kind, in a word, **to be Christlike**, is a task altogether beyond our powers: it is one on which we should never venture, or having ventured on, would soon abandon, but that God is pleased to perfect His strength in our weakness, and is "mighty to save" (Isa. 63:1). That this may be the more clearly evident to us, we shall now consider some of the features of God's powerful operations in the saving of His people.

1. **In regeneration.** Little as even real Christians may realise it, a far greater power is put forth by God in the new creation than in the old, in re-fashioning the soul and conforming it to the image of Christ than in the original making of it. There is a greater distance between sin and righteousness, corruption and grace, depravity and holiness, than there is between nothing and something, or non-entity and being; and the greater the distance there is, the greater the power in producing something. The miracle is greater according as the **change** is greater. As it is a more signal display of power to change a dead man to life than a sick man to health, so it is a far more wonderful performance to change unbelief to faith and enmity to love, than simply to create out of nothing. Therefore we are told, "The Gospel of Christ is **the power of God** unto salvation to every one that believeth" (Rom. 1:16).

The Gospel is the instrument which the Almighty uses when accomplishing the most wondrous and blessed of all His works, i.e. the picking up of a wretched worm of the earth and making him "**meet** to be a partaker of the inheritance of the saints in light" (Col. 1:12). When God formed man out of the dust of the ground, though the dust contributed nothing to the act whereby God made him, so it had in it no principle **contrary to** His design. But in turning the heart of a sinner toward Himself, there is not only the lack of any principle of assistance from him in this work, but the whole strength of fallen nature unites to combat the power of Divine grace. When the Gospel is presented to the sinner, not only is his understanding completely ignorant of its glorious contents, but the will is utterly perverse against it. Not only is there no desire for Christ, but there is inveterate hostility against Him. Nothing but the Almighty power of God can overcome the enmity of the carnal mind. To turn back the ocean from its course would not be such an act of power as to change the turbulent bent of man's wicked heart.

2. **In convicting us of sin.** "For ye were sometimes darkness" (Eph. 5:8). Such was the Christian's fearful condition before Divine grace laid hold of him. He was not only **in** darkness, but he himself **was** "darkness". He was utterly devoid of a single ray of spiritual light. The "light of reason" of which men boast so much, and the "light of conscience" which others value so highly, were utterly worthless, so far as giving any intelligence in the things of God was concerned. It was to this awful fact that Christ referred when He said, "If therefore the light that **is** in thee **be darkness**, how great is that darkness" (Matt. 6:23). Yes, so "great" is that darkness that men "call evil good, and good evil; put darkness for light, and light for darkness; put bitter for sweet, and sweet for bitter" (Isa. 5:20). So "great" is that darkness, spiritual things are "foolishness" unto them (1 Cor. 2:14). So "great" is that darkness, they are completely **ignorant of it** (Eph. 4:18), and utterly blind to their own actual state. Not only is the natural man unable to deliver himself from this darkness, but he has **no** desire whatever for such deliverance, for being spiritually dead he has no consciousness of any **need for** deliverance.

It is because of their fearful state that, until the Holy Spirit actually regenerates, **all** who hear the Gospel are totally incapacitated for any **spiritual** understanding of it. The majority who hear it imagine that they are already saved, that **they** are real Christians, and no argument from the preacher, no power on earth, can ever convince them to the contrary. Tell them that "There is a generation that are pure in their own eyes, and yet is not washed from their filthiness" (Prov. 30:12), and it makes no more impression than does water on a duck's back. Warn them that "Except ye repent, **ye** shall all likewise perish" (Luke 13:3), and they are no more moved than are the rocks by the ocean's spray. No, they either suppose they have nothing to repent of, or that they have already repented, and know not **their** repentance needs "to be repented of" (2 Cor. 7:10). They have far too high an opinion of their religious profession to allow that **they** are in any danger of Hell. Thus, unless a mighty miracle of grace is wrought within them, unless Divine power shatters their complacency, there is no hope at all for them.

For a soul to be **savingly convicted** of sin is a greater wonder than for a putrid fountain to send forth sweet waters. For a soul to be brought to realise that "**every** imagination of the thoughts of his heart was only evil continually" (Gen. 6:5), requires the power of Omnipotence to produce. By nature man is independent, self-confident, self-sufficient: what a miracle of grace has been wrought when he now feels and owns his helplessness! By nature a man thinks well of himself: what a miracle of grace has been wrought when he acknowledges "in me . . . dwelleth **no** good thing" (Rom. 7:18)! By nature men are "**lovers** of their own selves" (2 Tim. 3:2): what a miracle of grace has been wrought when they **abhor** themselves (Job 42:6)! By nature man thinks he is doing Christ a favour to espouse His Gospel and patronise His cause: what a miracle of grace has been wrought when he discovers that he is so utterly unfit for **His** holy presence, he cries "Depart from me, for I am a sinful man, O Lord" (Luke 5:8). By nature man is proud of his own abilities, accomplishments, attainments: what a miracle of grace has been wrought when he can truthfully declare, "I count **all** things but loss for the excellency of the knowledge of Christ Jesus . . . and do count them but dung, that I may win Christ" (Phil. 3:8).

3. In casting out the Devil. "The whole world lieth in the Wicked one" (1 John 5:19), bewitched, fettered, helpless. As we go over the Gospel narratives and read of different ones who were possessed of demons, thoughts of pity for their unhappy victims stir our minds, and when we behold the Saviour delivering these wretched creatures we are full of wonderment and gladness. But does the Christian reader realise that we too were once in that same awful plight? Before conversion, we were the slaves of Satan; the Devil wrought in us his will (Eph. 2:2), and so we "walked according to the prince of the power of the air". What ability had we to deliver ourselves? Less than we have to stop the rain from falling or the wind from blowing. A picture of man's helplessness to deliver himself from Satan's power is drawn by Christ in Luke 11:21: "When a strong man armed keepeth his palace his goods are in peace". The "strong man armed" is Satan; his "goods" are his helpless captives.

But blessed be His name, "The Son of God was manifested that He might destroy the works of the devil" (1 John 3:8). This too was pictured by Christ in the same parable: "But when a stronger than he shall come upon him, and overcome him, He taketh from him all his armour wherein he trusted, and divideth his spoils" (Luke 11:22). Christ is mightier than Satan, He overcomes him in "the day of His power" (Psa. 110:3), and emancipates "His own" who were bound (Isa. 61:1). He still comes by His Spirit to "set at liberty them that are bruised" (Luke 4:18), therefore is it said of God "who hath delivered us from the power of darkness, and hath translated into the kingdom of His dear Son" (Col. 1:13). The Greek word for "delivered" signifies freeing by violence, a plucking or snatching out of a power that otherwise would not yield its prey.

4. In producing repentance. Man without Christ cannot repent: "Him hath God exalted with His right hand to be a Prince and a Saviour, for to give repentance" (Acts 5:31). Christ gives it as a "Prince", and therefore, to none but His subjects, those who are in His kingdom, in whom He rules. Nothing can draw men to repentance but the regenerating power of Christ, which He exercises at God's right hand; for the acts of repentance are hatred of sin, sorrow for it, determination to forsake it, an earnest and constant endeavour after its death. But sin is so transcendently dear and delightful to a man out of Christ, that nothing but an infinite power can draw him to these acts.

Sin is more precious to an unregenerate soul than anything else in heaven or earth. It is dearer to him than liberty, for he gives himself up to it entirely, and becomes its servant and slave. It is dearer to him than health, strength, time, or riches, for he spends all these upon sin. It is dearer to him than his own soul whether shall a man lose his sins or his soul? Ninety-nine out of a hundred vote for the latter, and lose their souls on that account.

Sin is a man's self. Just as "I" is the central letter of "sin", so sin is the center, the moving-power, the very life of self. Therefore did Christ say, "If any man will come after Me, let him **deny himself**" (Matt. 16:24). Men are "lovers of their own selves" (2 Tim. 3:2), which is the same as saying, Their hearts are wedded to sin. Man "drinketh iniquity like water" (Job 15:16):) he cannot exist without it, he is ever thirsting for it, he must have his fill of it. Now since man so doates on sin, what is going to turn his delight into sorrow, his love for it into loathing of it? Nothing but almighty power.

Here then we may mark the folly of those who cherish the delusion that they can repent whenever they get ready to do so. But evangelical repentance is **not** at the beck and call of the creature. It is the gift of God: "If God peradventure will give them repentance to the acknowledging of the truth" (2 Tim. 2:25). Then what insanity is it that persuades multitudes to defer the effort to repent till their deathbeds! Do they imagine that when they are so weak they can no longer turn their bodies, that they will have strength to turn their souls from sin? Far sooner could they turn themselves back to perfect physical health. What praise, then, is due to God if He has wrought a saving repentance in us.

5. In working faith in His people. Saving faith in Christ is not the simple matter that so many vainly imagine. Countless thousands suppose it is as easy to believe in the Lord Jesus as it is in Caesar or Napoleon, and the tragic thing is that hundreds of preachers are helping forward this lie. It **is** as easy to believe on Him as on them in a **natural**, historical, intellectual way; but not so in a spiritual and saving way. I may believe in all the heroes of the past, but such belief effects no change in my life! I may have unshaken confidence in the historicity of George Washington, but does my belief in him abate my love for the world and cause me to hate even the garment spotted by the flesh? A supernatural and saving faith in Christ purifies the life. Is **such** a faith easily attained? No, indeed. Listen to Christ Himself, "How can ye believe, which receive honour one of another, and seek not the honour that cometh from God only?" (John 5:44). And again we read, "They could not believe" (John 12:39).

Faith in Christ is receiving Him as He is offered or presented to us by God (John 1:12). Now God presents Christ to us not only as Priest, but as King; not only as Saviour, but "Prince" (Acts 5:31)—note that "Prince" **precedes** "Saviour", as taking His "yoke" upon us goes before finding "rest" to our souls (Matt. 11:29)! Are men as willing for Christ to **rule** as save them? Do they pray as earnestly for purity as pardon? Are they as anxious to be delivered from the **power** of sin as they are from the fires of Hell? Do they desire holiness as much as they do Heaven? Does the filthiness of sin grieve them as much as the guilt and damnation of it? Is the dominion of sin as dreadful to them as its wages? The man who divides what God has joined together when He offers Christ to us, **has not** "received" Him at all.

Faith is the gift of God (Eph. 2:8, 9). It is wrought in the elect by "the operation of God" (Col. 2:12). To bring a sinner from unbelief to saving faith in Christ, is a miracle as great and wondrous as was God's raising Christ from the dead (Eph. 1:19, 20). Unbelief is far, far more than entertaining an erroneous conception of God's "way of salvation": it is a species of hatred against Him. So faith in Christ is far more than the mind assenting to all that is said of Him in the Scriptures. The demons do that (James 2:19), but it does not save them. Saving faith is not only the heart being taken off from every other object of confidence as the ground of my acceptance before God, but it is also the heart being weaned from every other object that competes with Him for my affections. Saving faith is that which "worketh by love" (Gal. 5:6), a love which is evidenced by keeping His commandments (John 14:23); but by nature all men hate His commandments. Therefore, where there is a believing heart which is devoted to Christ, esteeming Him high above self and the world, a mighty miracle of grace has been wrought in the soul.

6. In communicating a sense of pardon. When a soul has been sorely wounded by the "arrows of the Almighty" (Job 6:4); when the ineffable light of the thrice holy God has shone into our dark hearts, revealing its unspeakable filthiness and corruption; when our innumerable iniquities have been made to stare us in the face, until the convicted sinner has been made to realise he is fit only for Hell, and sees himself even now on the very brink of it: when he is brought to feel that he has provoked God so sorely, that he greatly fears he has sinned beyond all possibility of forgiveness (and unless **your** soul has passed through such experiences, my reader, you have never been born again); then nothing but Divine power can raise that soul out of abject despair and create in it a hope of mercy. To lift the stricken sinner above those dark waters that have so terrified him, to bestow the light of comfort as well as the light of conviction into a heart filled with worse than Egyptian darkness, is an act of Omnipotence. God only can heal the heart which He has wounded, and speak peace to the raging tempest within.

Men may count up the promises of God and the arguments of peace till they are as old as Methusalah, but it will avail them nothing, until a Divine hand shall pour in "the balm of Gilead". The sinner is no more able to **apply to himself** the word of Divine comfort when he is under the terrors of God's law, and writhing beneath the strokes of God's convicting Spirit, than he is able to resurrect the molding bodies in our cemeteries. To "restore the **joy of salvation**" was in David's judgment an act of sovereign power equal to that of "creating a clean heart" (Psa. 51:10). All the Doctors of Divinity put together are as incapable of healing a wounded spirit, as are the physicians of medicine to animate a corpse. To silence a tempestuous conscience is a mightier performance than the Saviour's stilling of the stormy winds and raging waves, though it is not to be expected that any will grant the truth of this who are themselves **strangers** to such an experience. As nothing but infinite power could remove the guilt of sin, so nothing but infinite power can remove the despairing sense of it.

7. In actually converting a soul. "Can the Ethopian change his skin, or the leopard his spots?" (Jer. 13:23). No, indeed; though he may paint or cover them over. So, one out of Christ may restrain the outward acts of sin, but he cannot **mortify** the inward principle of it. To turn water into wine was indeed a miracle, but to turn fire into water would be a yet greater one. To create men out of the dust of the ground was a work of Divine power, but to re-create man, so that a sinner becomes a saint, a lion is changed into a lamb, an enemy is transformed into a friend, hatred is melted into love, is a far greater wonder of Omnipotence. The miracle of conversion, which is effected by the Spirit through the Gospel, is described thus, 'For the weapons of our warfare (i' e., of the preachers) are not carnal, but mighty **through His God** to the pulling down of strong-holds; Casting down imaginations, and every high thing that exalteth itself against the knowledge of God, and bringing into captivity every thought to the obedience of Christ" (2 Cor. 10:4, 5).

Well has it been said that, "To dispossess a man, then, of his self-esteem and self-excellency, to make room for God in the heart where there was none but for sin, as dear to him as himself; to hurl down the pride of nature, to make stout imaginations stoop to the cross, to make designs of self-advancement sink under a zeal for the glory of God and an overruling design for His honour, is not to be ascribed to any but to an out-stretched Arm wielding the sword of the Spirit. To have an heart full of the fear of God that was just before filled with contempt of Him, to have a sense of His power, an eye to His glory, admiring thoughts of His wisdom; to have a hatred of his habitual lustings that had brought him in much sensitive pleasure; to loath them as much as he loved them; to live by faith in and **obedience to** the Redeemer, who before was so heartily under the dominion of Satan and self, is a triumphant act of infinite power that can 'subdue all things' to itself" (S. Charnock).

8. In preserving His people. "Who are kept **by the power of God** through faith unto salvation, ready to be revealed in the last time" (1 Peter 1:5). "Kept" **from what**? Ah, what mortal is capable of returning a full answer? A whole article might profitably be devoted to this one aspect of our subject. Kept from the dominion of sin which still dwells within us. Kept from being drawn out of the Narrow Way by the enticements of the world. Kept from the horrible heresies which ensnare thousands on every side. Kept from being overcome by Satan, who ever seeks our destruction. Kept from departing from the living God so that we do not make shipwreck of the faith. Kept from turning His grace into lasciviousness. Weak as water in ourselves, yet enabled to endure as seeing Him who is invisible. This "is the Lord's doing, and it is marvelous in our eyes".

Sin is a mighty monarch which none of his subjects can withstand. There was more in Adam while innocent to resist sin than in any other man since, for sin has an ally within the fallen creature that is ever ready to betray him to temptation from without. But sin had no such advantage over Adam, nevertheless it overwhelmed him. The non-elect angels were yet better able to withstand sin than Adam was, having a more excellent nature and being nearer to God, yet sin prevailed against them, and threw them out of heaven into hell. Neither reason nor resolution, innocence nor creature-perfection, can resist sin. Then what a **mighty** power is required to subdue it! Only He who "led captivity captive" can make His people more than conquerors.

"As the providence of God is a manifestation of His power in a continued creation, so the preservation of grace is a manifestation of His power in a continued regeneration. God's strength abates and modifies the violence of temptations, His staff supports His people under them, His might defeats the power of Satan. The counterworkings of indwelling corruption, the reluctancies of the flesh against the breathings of the Spirit, the fallacies of the senses and the rovings of the mind would quickly stifle and quench grace if it were not maintained by the same all-powerful blast that first inbreathed it. No less power is seen in perfecting it, than in implanting it, 2 Peter 1:3; no less in fulfilling the work of faith, than in engrafting the word of faith, 2 Thess. 1:11" (S. Charnock).

The preservation of God's people in this world greatly glorifies the power of God. To preserve those with so many corruptions within and so many temptations without, magnifies His ineffable might more than if He were to translate them to Heaven the moment they believed. In a world of suffering and sorrow, to preserve the **faith** of His people amid so many and sore testings, trials, buffetings, disappointments, betrayals by friends and professed brethren in Christ, is infinitely more wonderful than if a man should succeed in carrying an unsheltered candle alight, across an open moor, when a hurricane was blowing. To the glory of God the writer bears witness that but for **omnipotent grace** he had become an infidel years ago as the result of the treatment which he has received from those who pose as preachers of the Gospel. Yes, for God to supply strength to His fainting people, and enable them to "hold the beginning of their confidence steadfast unto the end" (Heb. 3:14), is more marvelous than though He were to keep a fire burning in the midst of the ocean.

How the contemplation of the power of God should deepen our confidence and trust in Him: "Trust ye in the Lord forever: **for** in the Lord Jehovah is everlasting **strength**" (Isa. 26:4). The power of God was the ground of Abraham's assurance (Heb. 11:19), of the three Hebrews in Babylon (Dan. 3:17), of Christ's (Heb. 5:7). O to bear constantly in mind that "**God is able** to make all grace abound toward" us (2 Cor. 9:8). Nothing is so calculated to calm the mind, still our fears, and fill us with peace, as faith's appropriation of God's strength and sufficiency. "If God be for us, who **can** be against us?" (Rom. 5:3). His infallible promise is, "Fear thou not; for I am with thee; be not dismayed; for I am thy God; I will strengthen thee; yea, I will help thee; yea, I will uphold thee with the right hand of My righteousness" (Isa. 41:10). He who brought a Nation through the Red Sea without any ships and led them across the Desert for forty years where was neither bread nor water, still lives and reigns!

—ARTHUR W. PINK.

THE BRAZEN SEA.
(2 Chron. 4:2-6).

In order to a clear understanding of the doctrine taught us in this beautiful and significant figure, three things demand our attention, namely, the material, the contents, the object. May God the Spirit guide our thoughts and speak to our hearts as we dwell upon these things.

1. The Material

Solomon's molten sea was made of brass, which is the apt symbol of divine righteousness demanding judgment upon **sin**, as in the brazen **altar;** or demanding judgment upon **uncleanliness,** as in the brazen **sea.** The Lord Jesus is spoken of, in the first chapter of Revelation as having His feet" like unto fine **brass** as if they burned in a furnace." It is thus He is seen walking amongst the candlesticks. He cannot tolerate evil, but must, in the exercise of judgment, trample it beneath His feet. This will explain the reasons why the altar where sin was expiated, and the sea where defilement was washed away, were both made of brass. Everything in scripture has its meaning, and we should seek, in the spirit of prayer, to ascertain what that meaning is.

Now it is most comforting and establishing to the heart to be assured of this, that the sin which God freely pardons, and the uncleanness which He freely removes, has been both fully and forever judged and condemned in the cross. Not a single jot or tittle of guilt—not a single trace of uncleanness has been passed over; all has been divinely judged. "Mercy rejoiceth against judgment"; and "Grace reigns through righteousness" (James 2:13; Rom. 5:21). The believer is pardoned and cleansed; but his guilt and uncleanness were judged on the cross. The knowledge of this most precious truth works in a double way—it sets the heart and conscience perfectly free, while, at the same time, it causes us to abhor sin and uncleanness, with an ever-growing intensity. The altar of brass told forth in mute yet impressive eloquence, its double story: guilt **had been** divinely condemned and therefore **could be** divinely pardoned. The molten sea gave silent but clear testimony to the fact that uncleanness **had been** divinely judged, and, on that ground, **could be** divinely washed away.

What deep consolation for the heart, in all this! And yet it is **holy** consolation. I cannot gaze upon the antitype of the altar and lightly commit sin. I cannot muse upon the antitype of the molten sea, and indifferently contract defilement. My consolation is deep and solid, because I know I am pardoned and cleansed; but my consolation is holy, because I know that Jesus had to yield up His life to procure my pardon and cleansing. God has been perfectly glorified; sin and uncleanness have been perfectly condemned; I am set eternally free; but the death of Christ is the basis of all. Such is the consolatory yet holy lesson taught us in the material of the brazen altar and the molten sea. Nothing is passed over by God; and yet nothing is imputed to me, because Christ was judged for all.

2. The Contents

Let us now consider in the second place, the **contents** of Solomon's molten sea. "It received and held three thousand baths" **of water.** If at the altar I see **brass** in connection with **blood,** at the sea I find **brass** in connection with **water.** Both point to Christ. "This is He that came by water and blood, Jesus Christ; not by water only, but water and blood" (1 John 5:6). "But one of the soldiers with a spear pierced His side, and forthwith came thereout blood and water" (John 19:34). The blood that expiates, and the water that cleanses, both flow from a crucified Saviour. Precious and solemn truth! Precious because we have expiation and cleansing; solemn, because of the way in which we get them.

But the brazen sea contained water, not blood. Those who approached thereto had already proved the power of the blood, and therefore only needed the washing of water. Thus it was in the type, and thus it is in the antitype. A priest, under the law, whose hands and feet had become defiled, did not need to go back to the brazen altar; but forward to the brazen sea. He did not need again to apply the blood, in order to constitute him a priest, but only to wash with water, to enable him to discharge his priestly functions. So now, if a believer falls, if he commits sin, if he contract defilement, he does not need to be again washed in the blood, as at the first, but simply the cleansing action of the Word, whereby the Holy Spirit doth apply to the soul the remembrance of what Christ has done, so that the defilement is removed, the communion is restored, and the spiritual priest fitted, afresh, to discharge his priestly functions. "He that is **washed** needeth not, save to wash his feet, but is clean every whit" (John 13:10). "The worshippers **once purged** should have no more conscience for sins" (Heb. 10:2). Does this make little of defilement? The very opposite. Did the provision of a molten sea, with its three thousand baths of water, make little of priestly defilement? Did it not rather prove how much was made of it—what a serious matter it was in the judgment of God—how impossible it was to go on with a single soil upon the hands and feet.

Let my reader ponder this matter. Let him examine it in the light of scripture. Let him see that he really understands it. There is, in many cases, a great want of clearness as to the doctrine set forth in the brazen altar and the molten sea. Hence it is that so many earnest Christians get into spiritual darkness and trouble as to the question of daily sins and daily defilement. They do not see the divine completeness of their purgation by the blood of Christ, and they therefore entertain the idea that they must, on every fresh occasion, betake themselves, as at the beginning, to the brazen altar, as if they had not been washed at all. This is a mistake. When once a man is purged by the blood of Jesus, he is clean forever.

If Christ has cleansed me, I am divinely, and, therefore, eternally clean. I am introduced into a condition to which perfect cleanness attaches, and I can never be out of it. I may lose the sense of it, the power of it, the enjoyment of it. Peter speaks of some forgetting that they were purged from their old sins. If sin be trifled with, and if **self** be not judged, it is hard to say what a Christian may come to. The Lord give us to walk softly and tenderly, before Him, every day, so that we may not come under the blinding and hardening influence of sin!

But, be it remembered, that the most effectual safeguard against the working and the influence of sin, is to have the heart established in grace, and to be clear in the apprehension of our standing in Christ. To be dark or doubtful as to these things is the sure way of falling into Satan's snares. If I am seeking to live a holy life in order to establish my position before God, I shall either be propped up in pharisaism, or plunged into some horrible sin. But when I know that all my sins and all my defilements were judged and condemned in the cross, and that I am justified and accepted in a risen Christ, then I stand on the true ground of holiness. And, if I fail, as, alas! I do constanly, I can bring my failure to God in confession and self-judgment, and know Him as faithful and just to forgive my sins, and to cleanse me from all unrighteousness. I judge myself on the ground of this, that Christ has been already judged before God for the very thing which I confess in His presence. If it were not so, my confession would be of no use. The only ground on which God can be "faithful and just to forgive and cleanse" is that Christ has already been judged on my behalf; and most assuredly, God will not execute judgment twice for the same thing. True it is—blessedly true, I must confess and judge myself, if I have gone wrong. A single sinful thought is sufficient to interrupt my communion. Every such thought must be judged, ere my communion can proceed. But it is as a purged one that I confess. I am no longer viewed as a sinner, having to do with God as Judge. I am now in the position of a child having to do with God as a Father. He has made provision for my daily need, a provision which does not involve a denial of my place and portion, or an ignoring of the work of Christ; but a provision which tells me at once of the holiness and grace of Him who made it. I am not to ignore that altar because I need the sea, but I am to adore the grace of Him who provided both the one and the other.

3. The Object

Having said thus much on the material and the contents of Solomon's molten sea, very few words will suffice as to the **object** thereof. "The sea was for the priests to wash in". Thither came the priests from day to day, to wash their **hands** and **feet**, so that they might always be in a fit condition to go through their priestly work. A striking type, this, of God's spiritual priests, that is to say, of all true believers whose **works** and **ways** need to be cleansed by the action of the Word. Both the brazen laver, in the tabernacle, and the brazen sea in the temple, foreshadowed that "washing of water by the Word" which Christ is now carrying on by the power of the Holy Spirit. Christ, in Person, is acting up in heaven **for** us; and, by His Spirit and Word, He is acting **in** us and **on** us. Thus, and only thus, are we enabled to get on. He restores us when we wander; He cleanses us from every soil; He corrects our every error. He ever liveth in us. We are saved by His life. He maintains us in the full power and integrity of the position in which His precious blood has set us. All is secured in Him. "Christ loved the church, and gave Himself for it; that He might sanctify and cleanse it with the washing of water by the Word, that He might present it to Himself a glorious church, not having spot or wrinkle or any such thing; that it should be holy and without blemish" (Eph. 5:25-27).

And, now, one more word as to the "oxen" which sustained the brazen sea. The ox is used in scripture as the symbol of patient labour; and hence their significant place beneath the brazen sea. From whatever side the priest approached, he was met by the apt expression of patient labour. It mattered not how often or in what way he came, he could never exhaust the patience that was devoted to the work of cleansing him from all his defilements. What a precious figure! And we have the substance in Christ. We can never weary Him by our frequent coming. His patience is **exhaustless. He will not** tire until He presents us to Himself without spot or wrinkle or any such thing. May our hearts adore Him who is our Altar, our Laver, our Sacrifice, our Priest, our Advocate, our All.—Things New and Old, Vol. 5.

GODLY COMPANIONS

"I am a companion of all that fear Thee, and of them that keep Thy precepts" (Psa. 119:63).

In the above verse we have a description of God's people according to the course of their lives and conduct. They are a people marked by two things: fear and submission, the latter being the fruit of the former. Regenerated souls obey God conscientiously, out of reverence to His majesty and goodness, and from a due regard of His will as made known in His Word. The same description is given of them in Acts 10:35, "In every nation he that feareth God and worketh righteousness is accepted with Him". It is a filial fear which is awed by God's greatness and is careful not to offend Him, which is constrained by His love and is anxious to please Him. Such are the only ones fit to be a Christian's "companions".

A "companion" is, properly speaking, one whom I choose to walk and converse with in a way of friendship. Inasmuch as the companions we select is an optional matter, it is largely true that a person may be known by the company he or she keeps; hence the old adage, "Birds of a feather flock together". Scripture asks the searching question, "Can two walk together except they be agreed"? (Amos 3:3). A Christian, before his conversion, was controlled by the Prince of darkness and walked according to the course of this world (Eph. 2:2, 3), and therefore did he seek and enjoy the company of worldlings. But when he was born again the new nature within him prompted new tastes and desires, and so he seeks a new company, delighting only in the saints of God. Alas that we do not always continue as we began.

The Christian is to have a good-will toward all with whom he comes in contact, desiring and seeking their best interests (Gal. 6:10), but he is not to be yoked to (2 Cor. 6:14) nor have any fellowship with (Eph 5:11) those who are unbelievers, nor is he to delight in or have complacency toward those who despise his Master. "Shouldest thou help the ungodly, and love them that hate the Lord"? (2 Chron. 19:2). Would you knowingly take a viper into your bosom? "The wicked is an abomination unto the righteous" (Prov. 29:26). So said David, "Do I hate them, O Lord, that hate Thee? and am not I grieved with those that rise up against Thee? I hate them with perfect hatred: I count them mine enemies" (Psa. 139:21, 22). That holy man could not be confederate with such.

Evil company is to be sedulously avoided by the Christian lest he become defiled by them. "He that walketh with wise men shall be wise; but a companion of fools shall be destroyed" (Prov. 13:20). Nor is it only the **openly** lawless and criminal who are to be shunned, but even, yea, especially, those professing to be Christians yet who **do not live the life** of Christians. It is this latter class particularly against which the real child of God needs most to be on his guard: namely, those who say one thing and do another; those whose talk is pious, but whose walk differs little or nothing from the non-professor. The Word of God is plain and positive on this point: "Having a form of godliness, but denying the power thereof: **from such turn away**" (2 Tim. 3:5). This is not merely good advice, but a Divine command which we disregard at our peril.

In selecting your "companions" let not a pleasing personality deceive you. The Devil himself often poses as "an angel of light", and sometimes his woolfish agents disguise themselves in **"sheep's clothing"** (Matt. 7:15). Be most careful in seeing to it that what draws you toward and makes you desire the companionship of Christian friends is their **love and likeness to Christ** and not their love and likeness to you. Shun as you would a deadly plague those who are not awed by the fear of God, i. e. a trembling lest they offend Him. Let not the devil persuade you that you are too well established in the faith to be injured by intimacy with worldly "Christians" (?). "Be not deceived: evil communications corrupt good manners" (1 Cor. 15:33). Rather "follow righteousness, faith, love, peace, with them that call on the Lord out of a pure heart" (2 Tim. 2:22).

"Be not deceived: evil communications corrupt good manners" (1 Cor. 15:33). The Greek word here for "communications" properly means "a bringing together, companionships". And evil companionships "corrupt". All evil is contagious, and association with evil-doers, whether they be "church-members" or open infidels, has a defiling and debasing effect upon the true child of God. Mark well how the Holy Spirit has prefaced this warning: "be not deceived". Evidently there is a real danger of God's people imagining that they can play with fire without getting burned. Not so; God has not promised to protect us when we fly in the face of his danger-signals. Observe too the next verse, which is inseparably connected with the one to which we have directed attention.

"Awake to righteousness, and sin not; for some have not the knowledge of God: I speak (this) to your shame" (1 Cor. 15:34). The word "awake" signifies to arouse as from a torpor or state of lethargy. It is a call to shake off the delusive spell that a Christian may company with Christless companions without being contaminated by them. "And sin not", in this respect. To cultivate friendship with religious-worldings **is** SIN, for such "have not the knowledge of God": they have no experimental acquaintance with Him, His fear is not on them, His authority has no weight with them. "I speak (this) to your shame". The child of God ought to be abashed and filled with confusion that he needs such a word as this.

"I am a companion of all that fear Thee, and of them that keep Thy precepts". Such are the only "companions" worth having, the only ones who will give you any encouragement to continue pressing forward along the "**Narrow** Way". It is not those who merely pretend to "believe" God's precepts, or profess to "stand for" them, but those who **actually** "keep" them. But where are such to be found these days? Ah, where indeed. They are but "few" in number (Matt. 7:14) one here, and one there. Yea, so very "few" are they that we are constrained to cry, "Help, Lord, for the **godly** man ceaseth; for the **faithful** fail from among the children of men" (Psa. 12:1).

It is indeed solemn to read the words that immediately follow the last-quoted scripture and find how aptly they apply to and how accurately they describe the multitude of God-less professing "Christians" all around us: "They speak vanity every one with his neighbour, with flattering lips, with a double heart do they speak" (v. 2). Note three things about them. First, they "speak vanity" or "emptiness". Their words are like bubbles, there is nothing edifying about them. It cannot be otherwise "out of the abundance of the heart the mouth speaketh" (Matt. 12:34). Their poor hearts are **empty** (Matt. 12:44). So their speech is empty too. Second, they have "flattering lips", which is the reason why they are so popular with the ungodly. They will seek to puff you up with a sense of your own importance, pretend to admire the "much light" you have, and tell you it is your duty to "give it out to others". Third, they have a "double heart". They are (vainly) seeking to serve **two** masters: cf. 2 Kings 17:32, 33.

"I am a companion of all that fear Thee, and of them that keep Thy precepts". There is a very real sense in which this is true even where there is no outward contact with such. Faithfulness to God, obedience to His Word, **keeping** His precepts, companying only with those who do so, turning away from everybody else, has always involved a **lonely** path. It was thus with Enoch (Jude 14). It was thus with Abraham (Isa. 51:2). It was thus with Paul (2 Tim. 1:15). It is the same today. Every city in the land is filled with "churches", "missions", "Gospel halls", "Bible Institutes" etc., etc., but where are those who give plain evidence that they are living in this world as "strangers and pilgrims" and as such abstaining "from fleshly lusts which war against the soul" (1 Peter 2:11)?

But, thank God, though the path of faithfulness to Him be a lonely one, it brings me into **spiritual** fellowship **with** those who have gone before. We are to walk by faith and not by sight, and faith perceives that walking with Christ "**outside** the camp" (Heb. 13:13) necessarily brings into communion with "all" His redeemed, be they on earth or be they in heaven. Thus the apostle John in his lonely exile on Patmos referred to himself as "your brother and **companion** in tribulation, and in the kingdom and **patience** of Jesus Christ" (Rev. 1:9). Yes, Christian reader, for a little while it means companionship "in" **tribulation**", but praise God, it will not mean enduring the throes of the swiftly-approaching Great Tribulation—the portion of the Christless professors left behind when Christ comes for His own (2 Thess. 2:10-12). For a little while it means companionship in "the kingdom and **patience** of Jesus Christ", soon it will be in the kingdom and **glory** of Christ. May Divine grace enable us so to live now that in that Day we shall receive **His** "Well done."

—ARTHUR W. PINK.

We solicit the prayers of fellow-Christians that our God will continue to graciously guide, help and bless us in this printed ministry.

wherein He first lodged it, continuing its channel, without overflowing the earth and dashing in pieces the lower part of the creation? The natural situation of the water is to be above the earth, because it is lighter, and to be immediately under the air, because it is heavier. Who restrains the natural quality of it? Certainly man does not, and cannot. It is the fiat of its Creator which alone bridles it: "And said, Hitherto shalt thou come, but no further: and here shall thy proud waves be stayed" (Job 38:11). What a standing monument of the power of God is the preservation of the world!

Consider God's power **in government**. Take His restraining the malice of Satan. "The devil, as a roaring lion, walketh about, seeking whom he may devour" (1 Peter 5:8). He is filled with hatred against God, and with fiendish enmity against men, particularly the saints. He that envied Adam in paradise, envies us the pleasure of enjoying any of God's blessings. Could he have his will, he would treat all the same way he treated Job: he would send fire from heaven on the fruits of the earth, destroying the cattle, cause a wind to overthrow our houses, and cover our bodies with boils. But, little as men may realise it, God bridles him to a large extent, prevents him from carrying out his evil designs, and confines him within **His** ordinations.

So too God restrains the natural corruption of men. He suffers sufficient outbreakings of sin to show what fearful havoc has been wrought by man's apostasy from his Maker, but who can conceive the frightful lengths to which men would go were God to remove His curbing hand? "Their mouth is full of cursing and bitterness, their feet are swift to shed blood" (Rom. 3). This is the nature of **every** descendant of Adam. Then what unbridled licentiousness and headstrong folly would triumph in the world, if the power of God did not interpose to lock down the flood-gates of it! See Psa. 93:3, 4.

Consider God's power **in judgment**. When He smites, none can resist Him: see Ezek. 22:14. How terribly this was exemplified at the Flood! God opened the windows of heaven and broke up the great fountains of the deep, and (excepting those in the ark) the entire human race, helpless before the storm of His wrath, was swept away. A shower of fire and brimstone from heaven, and the cities of the plain were exterminated. Pharaoh and all his hosts were impotent when God blew upon them at the Red Sea. What a terrific word is that in Rom. 9:22: "What if God, willing to show wrath, and to make His **power** known, endured with much longsuffering the vessels of wrath fitted to destruction". God is going to display His mighty power upon the reprobate not merely by incarcerating them in Gehenna, but by supernaturally preserving their bodies as well as souls amid the eternal burnings of the Lake of Fire.

Well may all **tremble** before such a God! To treat with impunity One who can crush us more easily than we can a moth, is a suicidial policy. To openly defy Him who is clothed with omnipotence, who can rend us in pieces or cast into Hell any moment He pleases, is the very height of insanity. To put it on its lowest ground, it is but the part of wisdom to heed His command, "Kiss the Son, lest He be angry, and ye perish from the way, when His wrath is kindled but a little" (Psa. 2:12).

Well may the enlightened soul **adore** such a God! The wondrous and infinite perfections of such a Being call for fervent worship. If men of might and renown claim the admiration of the world, how much more should the power of the Almighty fill us with wonderment and homage. "Who is like unto Thee O Lord, among the gods, who is like Thee, glorious in holiness, fearful in praises, doing wonders" (Ex. 15:11).

Well may the saint **trust** such a God! He is worthy of implicit confidence. Nothing is too hard for Him. If God were stinted in might and had a limit to His strength we might well despair. But seeing that He is clothed with omnipotence, no prayer is too hard for **Him** to answer, no need too great for Him to supply, no passion too strong for Him to subdue; no temptation too powerful for Him to deliver from, no misery too deep for Him to relieve. "The Lord is the strength of my life; of whom shall I be afraid?" (Psa. 27:1). "Now unto Him that is able to do exceeding abundantly above all that we ask or think, according to the power that worketh in us, Unto Him be glory in the church by Christ Jesus throughout all ages, world without end. Amen" (Eph. 3:20, 21).

—ARTHUR W. PINK.

fastened or who laid the cornerstone thereof?" (Job 38:4-6). How completely is the pride of man laid in the dust!

"Power is also used as a name of God, 'the Son of man sitting at the right hand of power' (Mark 14:62), that is, at the right hand of God. God and power are so inseparable that they are reciprocated. As His essence is immense, not to be confined in place; as it is eternal, not to be measured in time; so it is almighty, not to be limited in regard of action" (S. Charnock). "Lo, these are parts of His ways: but how little a portion is heard of Him? but the thunder of His power who can understand?" (Job 26:14). Who is able to count all the monuments of His power? Even that which **is** displayed of His might in the visible creation is utterly beyond our powers of comprehension, still less are we able to conceive of omnipotence itself. There is infinitely more power lodged in the nature of God than is expressed in all His works.

"Parts of His ways" we behold in creation, providence, redemption, but only a "little part" of **His** might is seen in them. Remarkably is this brought out in Hab. 3:4: "and **there** was the hiding of His power". It is scarcely possible to imagine anything more grandiloquent than the imagery of this whole chapter, yet nothing in it surpasses the nobility of this statement. The prophet (in vision) beheld the mighty God scattering the hills and overturning the mountains, which one would think afforded an amazing demonstration of His power. Nay, says our verse, **that** is rather the "hiding" than the displaying of **His** power. What is meant? This: so inconceivable, so immense, so uncontrollable is the power of Deity, that the fearful convulsions which He works in nature conceal more than they reveal of His infinite might!

It is very beautiful to link together the following passages: "He walketh upon the waves of the sea" (Job 9:8), which expresses God's uncontrollable power. "He walketh in the circuit of Heaven" (Job 22:14), which tells of the immensity of His presence. "He walketh upon the wings of the wind" (Psa. 104:3), which signifies the amazing swiftness of His operations. This last expression is very remarkable. it is not that "He flieth", or "runneth", but that He "walketh" and that, on the very "wings of the wind"—on the most impetuous of the elements, tossed into utmost rage, and sweeping along with almost inconceivable rapidity, yet they are **under** His feet, beneath His perfect control!

Let us now consider God's power **in creation**. "The heavens are Thine, the earth also is Thine, as for the world and the fulness thereof, Thou hast founded them. The north and the south Thou hast created them" (Psa. 89:11, 12). Before man can work, he must have both tools and materials, but God began with nothing, and by His word alone out of nothing made all things. The intellect cannot grasp it. God "spake and it was done, He commanded and it stood fast" (Psa. 33:9). Primeval matter heard His voice. "God said, Let there be . . . and **it** **was** so" (Gen. 1). Well may we exclaim, "Thou hast a mighty arm: strong is Thy hand, high is Thy right hand" (Psa. 89:13).

"Who, that looks upward to the midnight sky; and, with an eye of reason, beholds its rolling wonders; who can forbear enquiring, Of **what** were their mighty orbs **formed**? Amazing to relate, they were produced without materials. They sprung from emptiness itself. The stately fabric of universal nature emerged out of **nothing**. What instruments were used by the Supreme Architect, to fashion the parts with such exquisite niceness, and give so beautiful a polish to the whole? How was all connected into one finely-proportioned and nobly-finished structure? A **bare fiat** accomplished all. **Let them be**, said God. He added no more; and at once the marvelous edifice arose, adorned with every beauty, displaying innumerable perfections, and declaring, admist enraptured seraphs its great Creator's praise. 'By the **word** of the Lord were the heavens made, and all the host of them by the **breath** of His mouth', Psa. 150:1" (James Hervey, 1789).

Consider God's power **in preservation**. No creature has power to preserve itself. "Can the rush grow up without mire? can the flag grow up without water? (Job 8:11). Both man and beast would perish if there were not herbs for food, and herbs would wither and die if the earth were not refreshed with fruitful showers. Therefore is God called the Preserver of "man and beast" (Psa. 36:6). He "upholdeth all things by the word of His power" (Heb. 1:3). What a marvel of Divine power is the pre-natal life of every human being! That an infant can live at all, and for so many months, in such cramped and filthy quarters, and that without breathing, is unaccountable without the power of God. Truly He "holdeth our soul in life" (Psa. 66:9).

The preservation of the earth from the violence of the sea is another plain instance of God's might. How is that raging element kept pent within those limits

(Continued on Page 215)

Vol. IX　　　　　　OCTOBER, 1930　　　　　　No. 10

STUDIES IN THE SCRIPTURES

"*Search the Scriptures*" *John 5 : 39*

Copyright in all English-speaking Countries.

Editor: Arthur W. Pink, 1339 Bates Ave., Los Angeles, Calif, U. S. A.
Hon. Agent in England: Mr. A. Winstone, "Shalom", Old Bath Road, Leckhampton, Cheltenham.
Hon. Agent in Australia: Mr. G. Ardill, The Christian Workers' Depot. Commonwealth and Reservoir Streets, Sydney.

THE FAITHFULNESS OF GOD.

Unfaithfulness is one of the most outstanding sins of these evil days. In the business world, a man's word is, with exceedingly rare exceptions, no longer his bond. In the social world, marital infidelity abounds on every hand, the sacred bonds of wedlock being broken with as little regard as the discarding of an old garment. In the ecclesiastical realm, thousands who have solemnly covenanted to preach the truth make no scruple to attack and deny it. Nor can reader or writer claim complete immunity from this fearful sin: in how many ways have we been unfaithful to Christ, and to the light and privileges which God has entrusted to us! How refreshing, then, how unspeakably blessed, to lift our eyes above this scene of ruin, and behold One who **is** faithful, faithful in all things, faithful at all times.

"Know therefore that the Lord thy God, He is God, the **faithful** God" (Deut. 7:9). This quality is essential to His being, without it He would not be God. For God to be unfaithful would be to act contrary to His nature, which were impossible: "If we believe not, yet He abideth faithful; He cannot deny Himself" (2 Tim. 2:13). Faithfulness is one of the glorious perfections of His being. He is as it were clothed with it: "O Lord God of hosts, who is a strong Lord like unto Thee? or to Thy faithfulness **round about** Thee?" (Psa. 89:8). So too when God became incarnate it was said, "Righteousness shall be the girdle of His loins, and faithfulness the girdle of His reins" (Isa. 11:5).

What a word is that in Psa. 36:5, "Thy mercy, O Lord, is in the heavens; and Thy faithfulness unto the clouds". Far above all finite comprehension is the unchanging faithfulness of God. Everything about God is great, vast, incomparable. He never forgets, never fails, never falters, never forfeits His word. To every declaration of promise or prophecy the Lord has exactly adhered, every engagement of covenant or threatening He will make good, for "God is not a man, that He should lie; neither the son of man, that He should repent: hath He said, and shall He not do it? or hath He spoken, and shall He not make it good?" (Num. 23:19). Therefore does the believer exclaim, "His compassions fail not, they are new every morning: **great** is Thy faithfulness" (Lam. 3:22, 23).

Scripture abounds in illustrations of God's faithfulness. More than four thousand years ago He said, "While the earth remaineth, seedtime and harvest, and cold and heat, and summer and winter, and day and night shall not cease" (Gen. 8:22). Every year that comes furnishes a fresh witness to God's fulfilment of this promise. In Gen. 15 we find that Jehovah declared unto Abraham, "thy seed shall be a stranger in a land that is not theirs, and shall serve them . . . But in the fourth generation they shall come hither again" (vv. 13-16). Centuries ran their weary course. Abraham's descendants groaned amid the brick-kilns of Egypt. Had God forgotten His promise? No, indeed. Read Ex. 12:41, "And it came to pass at the end of the four hundred and thirty years, even the selfsame day it came to pass, that all the hosts of the Lord went out from the land of Egypt". Through Isaiah the Lord declared, "Behold, a virgin shall conceive, and bear a son, and shall call His name Immanuel" (7:14). Again centuries passed, but "When the fulness of the time was come, God sent forth His Son, made of a woman" (Gal. 4:4).

God is true. His Word of Promise is sure. In all His relations with His people God is faithful. He may be safely relied upon. No one ever yet really trusted Him in vain. We find this precious truth expressed almost everywhere in the Scriptures. for His people need to know that faithfulness is an essential part of the Divine character. This is the basis of our confidence in Him. But it is one thing to accept

(Continued on Page 240)

IMPORTANT NOTICES

Please advise promptly of change of address, otherwise copies will be lost in the mails.

We are glad to send a sample copy to any of your friends whom you believe would be interested in such a publication.

Send to Mr. I. C. Herendeen, Swengel (Union County), Penna., for a list of our publications. He has published many of our books and booklets.

This magazine is published as a work of faith and labour of love. The Editor and his wife gladly give their services. It is freely sent to all who will read it. No charge is made for it.

Christians who feel definitely led to do so, may have fellowship with us in this ministry. Those outside the U. S. A., please send only INTERNATIONAL Money Orders made out to Los Angeles, California, U. S. A.

CONTENTS

The Epistle to the Hebrews - - - - - 218
The Satisfaction of Christ - - - - - - 224
Profiting From the Word - - - - - - 230
Xmas - - - - - - - - - - - - - - - - - 236
Danger - - - - - - - - - - - - - - - - 239

THE EPISTLE TO THE HEBREWS

34. Judaism set aside: Heb. 7:20-24

It may be well for us to recall the principal design of the apostle in this section of his epistle. This was twofold; first, to demonstrate that the great High Priest of Christianity is far more excellent than was the typical high priest of Judaism, and that, that the faith of the Hebrews might be established and their hearts drawn out in love and worship to Him. Second, to show that it necessarily followed God's bringing in of the new order of priesthood, the old order was completely set aside. The method of proof which the Spirit moved the apostle to pursue was, an appeal to a notable O. T. type, confirmed by the citation of a Messianic prophecy. From this there was no possible appeal by any who really bowed to the Divine authority of Holy Writ. Blessed it is to see how graciously God has always provided a sure foundation for the faith of His people to rest upon. Yet it is only as His Word is diligently searched that this foundation is fully discovered, and even that, by the directing and illuminating guidance of the Holy Spirit.

An analysis of our chapter reveals that Christ's superiority over Aaron appears in the following points. First, Aaron was but a man; Christ was "the Son of God" (v. 3—and note the repetition of this item at the close of the argument in v. 28!). Second, Aaron belonged to the tribe of Levi; Christ, according to the flesh, sprang from the royal tribe (v. 14), and is the Priest-King. Third, Aaron was made "after the law of a carnal commandment"; Christ, "after the power of an endless life" (v. 16). Fourth, Aaron "made nothing perfect"; Christ did (v. 19). Fifth, Aaron was unable to bring the sinner, "nigh unto God" (v. 19); Christ has (v. 25). Sixth, Aaron was not inducted into his priestly office by a Divine oath; Christ was (v. 21). Seventh, Aaron had many successors (v. 23); Christ has none. Eighth, Aaron died (v. 23); Christ "ever liveth" (v. 25). Ninth, Aaron was a sinner (v. 27); Christ was "separate from sinners" (v. 26). Tenth, Aaron was only the priestly head of an earthly people; Christ has been "made higher than the heavens" (v. 26). Eleventh, Aaron had to offer sacrifice "daily" (v. 27); Christ's sacrifice is "once for all", Twelfth, Aaron was filled with "infirmity" (v. 28); Christ is "perfected forevermore". Well may we praise God for "**such** a High Priest" (v. 26).

In view of the introduction of this Priest par excellent, what room was there for another? No longer was there any need of the type, for the Antitype had appeared. Symbols and shadows have served their purpose when the substance itself is manifested. The things of childhood are put away when manhood is reached. A crutch is dispensed with when the limb is restored. When that which is perfect is come, then that which is in part is done away with. This is the unescapable inference which the apostle dwells upon here. "For there is **verily**—of a truth which cannot be gainsaid, as a fact which cannot be controverted—a disannulling of the commandment going before". And why? Because "the priesthood being changed, there is made of necessity a change also of the law". The whole system of Judaism had been set aside by God.

One cannot read through the O. T. without marvelling at the long-suffering of the Lord. Notwithstanding the many and great provocations of Israel, He did not set Judaism aside until the end for which He had appointed it had actually been reached. When the promised Messiah appeared, the temple still stood in Jerusalem, its priesthood still functioned, the sacrifices were still offered. But now its purpose had been served, its mission accomplished. The antitype of the temple was seen in the person of God incarnate (John 2:21); that which Aaron foreshadowed was fulfilled in the great High Priest of Christianity; and all the sacrifices found their perfected sequel in the final offering of the Lord Jesus. Therefore did God take "the law of commandments contained in ordinances" and nailed it to the cross (Col. 2:14), where He left it completely accomplished.

In the verses which are to be before us the apostle dwells upon two things. First, he calls attention to a most significant and deeply important item in the prophecy given through David, and this, that Christ was constituted Priest by Divine oath, which exalts Him high above priesthood under the law. The profound meaning and inestimable value of this fact will come before us in what follows. Second, he affirms that Christ is Priest forever, and this in order to show that there should never more be any need of another priest, nor any possibility of a return of the Levitical priesthood. Marvelously full and comprehensive was that brief word in Psa. 110, supplying for us an example of what unsearchable stores of wisdom and truth are laid up in every verse of Scripture, if we are given spiritual sight in their investigation. Signal proof also is this of the **verbal** inspiration of Scripture: every phrase, every word, was indited by Divine wisdom and has its own value and meaning.

"And inasmuch as not without an oath He was made priest" (v. 20). The opening word has the force of "Moreover": it is not that the apostle is here drawing a conclusion from a promise previously laid down; instead he moves forward in the argument before him. He here introduces a new consideration for the confirmation of the leading design before him. That the contents of the verse depend upon what follows was the conviction of the translators, as may be seen from the fact that they supply the ellipsis (the words in italics) from v. 21. That which the apostle now insisted upon was, that the dignity of Christ's sacerdotal office was commensurate with the solemnity of His appointment to it.

Nothing was lacking on the part of God to give eminency and stability unto the priesthood of Christ: "Not without an oath". This was due unto the glory of His person. The Son of God, in infinite grace, condescending to take upon Him the priestly office and discharge all the duties of it, it was meet that any thing which would contribute unto the glory or efficacy of it, should accompany His undertakings. In this God showed how jealous He is for the honour of His Beloved; in all things He must have the pre-eminence. In everything that He undertook, He was preferred above all others who were ever employed in the service of God, or who ever shall be; and therefore was He made a Priest "not without an oath".

Moreover, God deemed it needful to encourage and secure the faith of His people. There were many things defective in the priesthood under the law, and it suited the design of God that it should be so. He never intended that the faith of the church should terminate in those priests. But upon the introduction of the priesthood of Christ God has exhibited all that faith is to look unto and lean upon, and therefore did He, in infinite wisdom and grace, grant the highest and most specific evidence of the everlasting continuation of His priesthood. In this manner has He shown that this appointment of His will and mercy is absolutely unchanging, so that if we comply not therewith we must perish forever. (Condensed from John Owen).

The priesthood of Aaron was not instituted with an oath; Christ's was. Now that which is connected with an oath can never be changed, for God is immutable. "In the same way as He sware unto Abraham, 'Surely blessing I will bless thee', in order that by two immutable things in which it is impossible for God to lie, we might have abundant assurance of hope; even thus is it that because the High Priesthood of Jesus can never be altered, because it is based upon the eternal decree and counsel of God, and because it is essentially connected with the very nature and purpose of God Himself, it is introduced with an oath. The Lord hath sworn, and will not repent" (A. Saphir).

"For those priests were made without an oath; but this with an oath, by Him that said unto Him, the Lord sware and will not repent, Thou art a priest forever after the order of Melchizedek" (v. 21). It should be particularly noted that God never solemnly interposed Himself with an oath with respect unto privilege or mercy but that in each instance it had **Christ** in view. Thus, He sware by Himself unto Abraham that in his seed all the nations of the earth should be blessed, whereby He announced the immutability of His counsel to send His Son to take His seed upon Him. So also He sware unto David by His holiness that his seed, Christ, should sit on his throne forever'

"For those priests were made without an oath, but this with an oath". Although there is never the slightest alteration in the internal acting of God's will nor the least changing of His purpose, for with Him there is **no** "variableness or shadow of turning", yet, He frequently alters His works, His providences, and even some of the things which He appoints unto men at different times, unless they be confirmed with an oath. The Levitical priests were by Divine appointment, and therefore the people of Israel were obligated to obey them. But they did not enter their office by Divine oath, the absence of this intimating that God reserved to Himself the liberty to make an alteration when He saw good.

"But this with an oath, by Him that said unto Him, The Lord sware and will not repent, Thou art a Priest forever after the order of Melchizedek". The person swearing is God the Father, the One unto whom He speaks is God the Son: "The Lord said unto my Lord" (Psa. 110:1). The oath of God is the open declaration of His eternal purpose and unchanging decree. Thus is the same act and counsel of God's will spoken of in Psa. 2:7. "I will **declare** the **decree**". Therefore when God is pleased to unveil His decree or reveal His purpose, testifying it to be absolute and unchanging, He does it by way of oath: see 6:13, 14, 17 and our comments thereon.

Should it be asked, **When** did God thus sware unto Christ? We must distinguish between two things, or more accurately, two aspects of the same thing, namely: the Divine decree or purpose itself, and the revelation or declaration of it, for the "oath" includes both. As to the decree itself, that takes us back to those eternal federal transactions between the Father and the Son, when the "Everlasting Covenant" was entered into. As to the revelation of it, that was through David. Thus, the many modern commentators who regard this oath as being made with Christ upon His ascension into heaven are seriously mistaken, for that would completely invalidate the apostle's argument here. Had Christ offered His sacrifice **before** God sware unto Him, He had no pre-eminence herein over the Aaronical priests. The oath must precede His entrance upon and discharge of His priestly office, or otherwise the force of the apostle's reasoning here would utterly break down.

Not only did God's oath to Christ make manifest the exalted dignity of Christianity's High Priest, but it also denoted the great importance of the economy which He introduced and now administers. "No wise or good man interposes his oath in a matter of trivial consequence. If he voluntarily gives his oath, it is a plain proof that he considers that matter as one of importance. That economy must then be a high and holy one indeed with regard to which Jehovah swares; and this circumstance must elevate it far above every other economy, though Divine in its origin, that is not distinguished by this highest conceivable mark of its importance in the estimation of Him who alone hath wisdom. But the oath of God marks not only the importance, but the **stability** of the economy in reference to which it is made. God is never represented in Scripture as swaring to anything but what was fixed and immutable" (John Brown).

"By Him that said unto Him, The Lord sware and will not repent, Thou art a Priest forever after the order of Melchizedek". As this is the final reference in Scripture to Melchizedek perhaps we had better summarise the cardinal features in which he foreshadowed Christ. First, Melchizedek was the only priest of his class or order, and thus pointed to the solitariness of Christ's priesthood—He shares it with none. Second, Melchizedek had no predecessor, and therefore his right to office depended not on fleshly descent: foreshadowing the fact that Christ's priesthood was quite distinct from the Aaronic. Third, Melchizedek had no successor: typifying the fact that Christ's priesthood is final and eternal. Once again we would stress the fact that it is not said Christ is priest **of** the order of Melchizedek, had He been so, the resemblance between them had been destroyed in a vital particular. Christ did not succeed Melchizedek, but was his Antitype. Unto those who object that nothing is said in the O. T. about Melchizedek's offering sacrifice to God, we would reply, Neither is there anything said of his **making intercession!** It was not in **those** things that God designed him to prefigure Christ, but in the particulars pointed out above.

"By so much was Jesus made a surety of a better testament" (v. 22). The "by so much" answers to the "in as much" of v. 20, hence our present verse is in immediate connection with v. 20, thus: "And inasmuch as He was not made a priest without an oath, He is by so much made the surety of a better testament". V. 21, though containing the confirmation or proof of the principal assertion, is rightly placed in a parenthesis. On the close connection between vv. 20 and 22, J. Owen said:

"There may be a twofold design in the words. 1. That His being made a priest by an oath, made Him meet to be the surety of a better testament; or, 2. That the testament whereof He was the surety, must needs be better than the other; because He who was the surety of it was made a priest by an oath. In the one way, he proved the dignity of the priesthood of Christ from the new testament; and in the other, the dignity of the new testament from the priesthood of Christ. And we may reconcile both these verses by affirming that really and efficiently the priesthood gives dignity unto the new testament, and declaratively the new testament sets forth the dignity of the priesthood of Christ".

"By so much was Jesus made a surety of a better testament". These words clearly presuppose three things. First, that another covenant had existed between God and His people prior to the appearing of Christ. This is dealt with more expressly in Heb. 8, where the old and the new covenants are compared and contrasted. Second, that in some respect or re-respects the old covenant was good—implied by the contrastive "better". The old covenant **was** good in itself, as the product of God's wisdom and righteousness; it served a good purpose, for its statutes restrained sin and promoted godliness; its design was good, for it pointed forward to Christ. Third, that the old covenant had a "surety". Many have erred at this point through failing to distinguish between a "mediator" and a "surety". Moses was the typical mediator; Aaron, the typical surety, for he it was who offered solemn sacrifices in the name and on behalf of the people, making atonement for them according to the terms of the covenant.

"By so much was Jesus made a surety of a better covenant." Here for the first time in this chapter the apostle expressly names the person who had been referred to and described. Declaration had been made of the nature of the priesthood of Him who was to fill the office according to the Melchizedek type, but now definite application of the whole is made unto the Saviour. Two questions had long engaged the attention of the Jews: the nature of the Messiah's office, and who that person should be. The apostle had demonstrated from their own Scriptures that the Messiah was to be a Priest, yet not of the Levitical stock; as he had also shown the necessary consequences of this. Now he asserts that it was **Jesus** who is this Priest, for He alone has fulfilled the type and discharged the principal duty of that office. Concerning "Jesus" it is here affirmed that He was "made a Surety". He was "made so" or appointed so by the will and act of God the Father: compare 1:4, 3:2, 5:5 and our comments thereon for the force of this term "made". The whole undertaking of Christ, and the efficacy for the discharge of His office, depended entirely upon the appointment of God the Father.

"The Greek word for 'surety' properly means a bondsman: one who pledges his name, property or influence, that a certain thing shall be done. When a contract is made, a debt contracted, or a note given, a friend often becomes the **security** in the case, and is himself responsible if the terms of the contract are not complied with" (A. Barnes). A "surety" is one who agrees to undertake for another who is lacking in ability to discharge his own obligations. Whatever undertaking the surety makes, whether in words of promise, or in the depositing of real security in the hands of the arbitrator, or by any other personal engagement of life or body, it implies the **defect** of the person for whom any one becomes surety. The surety is **sponsor for** another, standing in the room of and acting for one who is incompetent to act for himself: he represents that other person, and pledges to make good his engagements. Thus, Christ was not a Surety for God, for **He** needed none; but for His own poor, failing and deficient people, who were unable to meet their obligations, incapable of discharging their liabilities. In view of this, Christ agreed to undertake for them, fully pay all their debts, and completely satisfied every demand which God had against them.

A beautiful illustration of the "surety" is found in Gen. 43:8, 9, "And Judah said unto Israel his father, send the lad with me, and we will arise and go; that we may live, and not die, both me and thou, and also our little ones. I will be **surety** for him; of **my** hand shalt thou require him: if I bring him not unto thee, and set him before thee, then let **me** bear the blame forever". Blessed is it to find how faithful Judah was to his agreement. Later, Joseph's cup was found in Benjamin's sack (44:12), and on their return into Egypt and re-appearance before Joseph the governor, we hear him saying, "For thy servant became surety for the lad unto my father, saying, If I bring him not unto thee, then I shall bear the blame, to my father forever. Now therefore, I pray thee, let thy servant abide **instead of** the lad, **a bondman** to my lord; and let the lad go with his brethren" (44:32, 33).

A blessed N. T. example is found in the case of Paul who volunteered to be surety for Onesimus: "If he hath wronged thee, or oweth thee ought, **put that on mine account**; I Paul have written it with mine own hand, **I will repay**" (Philemon 18, 19). In like manner Christ engaged Himself unto the Father for His elect, saying, Charge to My account whatsoever My people owe Thee, and I will fully discharge their debts. This is an office in which Christ sustains a **representative character** in relation to those sinners for whom He interposed. It was Christ pledging Himself, or making Himself responsible, for the fulfilment of all that the Everlasting Covenant required on the part of those who are to share its provisions. It is as the Surety of the Covenant that Christ is called the "Second Man", the "Last Adam" (1 Cor. 15:47). This title, then, views Christ as **identifying Himself** with those whom the Father gave to Him, and on whose behalf He accomplished the great work assigned Him (see John 6:38, 39 etc.) in their room and stead, making full satisfaction to God.

Let us now observe that Jesus was made "a Surety of a better testament", or "covenant", as the term should be rendered, for the word denotes an arrangement or constitution, a dispensation or economy. It signifies that order of things introduced by Christ, in contrast from the order of things which obtained under the Mosaic regime. The Mosaic covenant was administered by the instrumentality of the Levitical priesthood, but the better covenant by Jesus, the Son of God: that was transitory and changing; this is permanent and eternal. It is so because those who enjoy its blessings receive an enablement to comply with its terms, fulfill its conditions, and yield the obedience which God requires therein. For by the ordination of God, our Surety merited and procured for them the Holy Spirit, and all the needed supplies of grace to make them new creatures, and empower to yield obedience to God from a new principle of spiritual life, and that, faithfully to the end.

It is the **Surety** by the Divine oath which gives stability unto the covenant. God entered into a covenant with the first Adam (see Hos. 6:6 margin), but it had no "surety"! And therefore though our first parent had all the tremendous advantages of a sinless nature filled with holy inclinations, and free from all evil imaginations, desires and habits, yet he broke the covenant and forfeited all the benefits thereof. God made a covenant with Israel at Sinai (Ex. 19 and 24), and appointed the high priest to act as the typical surety of it; yet, as we have seen, that covenant and that surety, made nothing perfect. The purpose of that covenant was to demonstrate the need of another and better one. In contradistinction from these God has made with His elect, in Christ, a covenant "ordered in all things and sure", for "He laid help upon One that is mighty" (Psa. 89:19).

And what is the practical application to God's children today of what has been before us? Surely this, that just so far as the new covenant surpasses the old, are we under greater obligations unto God, "for unto whomsoever much is given, of him shall be much required" (Luke 12:48). That just so far as the Surety of the better covenant exceeds in dignity and glory the surety under the old regime, are we under higher obligation of rendering to Him more complete submission, deeper devotion, fuller obedience. O my brethren, **what is due** unto that blessed One who left heaven's glory and came here to this sin-curst world to discharge our obligations, pay our debts, suffer and die in our room and stead! May His love truly "constrain" us to gladsome and whole-hearted surrender to Him, no longer seeking to please ourselves, but living to and for **His** honour and praise. If we do not, that is certain proof that we are yet in our sins, strangers to the Surety of the better covenant.

"And they truly were many priests, because they were not suffered to continue by reason of death" (v. 23). In this and the following verse the apostle advances his last argument from the consideration of Christ's priesthood as represented by that of Melchizedek. His design is to present further proof of the excellency of it above the Levitical, and of His person above theirs. That Paul is still looking back to Melchizedek as a type of Christ, is evident from the description which he had given of him in the earlier verses, namely, that he "abideth a priest continually" (v. 3), and that "it is witnessed that he liveth" (v. 8), for his priesthood did not terminate at the age of fifty as did that of the Levitical. This is the particular detail of the type which is here siezed and improved upon, for it was that which gives virtue and efficacy to everything else he had insisted upon. Set **this** aside and all the other advantages and excellencies he had named would be quite ineffectual to secure "perfection". What lasting profit could it be to the Church to have so glorious a Priest for a season, and then be deprived of Him by the expiration of His office?

Just as what the apostle declares of Christ in v. 24 hath respect to what he had before observed concerning Melchizedek, so what he affirms in v. 23 of the Levitical priests looks back to what he had before declared about them, namely, that they were all mortal men, and nothing more, for they actually died in their successive generations: see v. 8. The apostle expresses himself very emphatically "and truly". It was not a dubious point he was now handling, but one which was well known and could not be controverted. "They truly were **many** priests". It is of the **high** priest's only, Aaron and his successors, of whom he speaks. Jewish records inform us that there were no fewer than eighty-three high priests from Aaron, the first, to Phinehas, who perished with the temple. Thirteen lived under the tabernacle prior to Solomon, eighteen under the first temple before its destruction by the Babylonians, the remainder under the second temple till A. D. 70.

The reason for this multiplication of priests was "because they were not suffered to continue by reason of death". Notwithstanding the great dignity of their office, and the solemnities with which they were installed in it, they were but men, subject to infirmity and dissolution, like those for whom they ministered. Mortality suffered them not to continue in the execution of their office. It forbade them so to do in the name of the great sovereign Lord of life and death. A signal instance of this was given in Aaron himself, the first of them. God, to show the nature of that priesthood unto the people, and to manifest that the everlasting Priest was yet to come, commanded Aaron to die **in the sight of** all the congregation: Num: 20:25-29! In like manner, death seized upon each of his successors. Thereby did God intimate unto Israel that **imperfection** attached to that office which was so frequently interrupted in its administration.

"But this man, because He continueth ever, hath an unchangeable priesthood" (v 24). This is the final proof in our present passage for the immeasurable superiority of our great High Priest over the Levitical priests. The Surety of the better covenant has an unchanging priesthood. The reason for and the ground on which this rests is here stated: "because He continueth ever". The apostle is not here proving the absolute perpetuity of Christ's sacerdotal office, but the continuous and uninterrupted administration of it. This was the faith of the Jews concerning the Messiah and His office: "We have heard out of the law that Christ abideth forever" (John 12:34), which was interposed as a difficulty and said by them in reply to our Lord's declaration that He was to be lifted up in death. It was this perpetuity of office that was principally typed out in Melchizedek.

Against this it might be replied, But Jesus Christ died also, no less truly and really than did Aaron and his successors, and thus it would follow that He had no more an uninterrupted priesthood than they. To obviate this difficulty, many of our moderns have fallen back on the error of the Socinians, that Christ did not become a Priest at all until after His resurrection. But such a reply cuts the knot, instead of untieing it. This figment we have already confuted in previous articles. Nor is there anything here in Heb. 7 which warrants the idea that the administration of Christ's priesthood is in heaven only. The whole context here shows plainly to all who are not blinded by prejudice that the apostle is treating of the **whole** of Christ's sacerdotal office.

The death of Christ was a vastly different thing from the death of the Levitical priests, for His death did not prevent Him abiding a priest, as theirs did. First, He died **as** a Priest; they died **from** being priests; He died in His office, they died out of office. Second, personal death was no part of their **work**, whereas to die was the chief priestly duty incumbent upon the Lord Jesus. Third, when they fell under the power of death, they could not extricate themselves from it and return to life and the service of the sanctuary, but the Son of God had power to lay down His life and take it again. So far from death putting an end to His priesthood, it did not even interrupt the exercise of it. Christ died as a priest, because He was also the Sacrifice for sins, yet through the indissoluableness of His person, His soul and body still subsisting in the person of the Son of God, He abode active in His office without any break: "He **continueth forever**".

It necessarily follows from what has been pointed out above that Christ hath "an unchangeable priesthood", subject to no alteration, that cannot pass away. The entire office of the priesthood pertaining and belonging to the new covenant, with its administration, are strictly confined unto the person of Jesus, the Son of God. There are none that succeed, any more than any (except typically) preceded Him. This at once exposes and gives the lie to the abominable blasphemy of the Papists who call their ministers "priests", affirming that they perform the proper work of such by offering sacrifice. It is highly derogatory to the honour of Christ, and subversive of the whole teaching of Scripture, to maintain that any person is now invested with priestly office and performs its proper work. They who wickedly assume this character encroach upon Christ's lone prerogative, and to suppose them to be what they pretend, would be to regard our Redeemer as a priest, not after the order of Melchizedek, but after the order of Aaron, which admitted of successors.

The abiding of Christ as Priest manifests the continuance of His care for His people. The same love which caused Him, as Priest, to lay down His life for them, remains unchanged within Him. Therefore each one may, with the same confidence, go unto Him with all their concerns, as poor and afflicted people went to Him while He was here upon earth. Again: it is upon the perpetuity of Christ's priesthood that the **security** of His Church rests. "Do we meet with troubles, trials, difficulties, temptations, and distresses? Hath not the church done so in former ages? But was any one true believer ever lost forever? Did not Satan rage, and the world gnash their teeth, to see their power broken by the faith, patience, and suffering of them whom they hated? And was it from their own wisdom and courage that they were so preserved? Did they overcome the enemy by their own blood, or were they delivered by their own power? No; instead, all their preservation and success, their deliverance and eternal salvation, depended solely on the care and power of their merciful High Priest". Blessed be His name, He is "the Same yesterday, and today, and forever". Hallelujah, what a Saviour! what a Surety! what a Priest!

—ARTHUR W. PINK.

THE SATISFACTION
("Atonement")
OF CHRIST

10. Its Efficacy

In our last article we considered the Divine design in Christ's Satisfaction; in this we propose to show from Scripture that that design **must be** accomplished. Two widely differing views have been taken concerning the effectuation of what the mediatorial work of the Lord Jesus was meant to achieve. Some have affirmed that the Atonement possesses only a **conditional** efficacy, others that it is vested with an **infallible** efficacy. These two views are known as the Arminian and the Calvinistic interpretations. They are completely antagonistic and utterly irreconcilable. The difference between them is that of Truth and error, Light and darkness, Jehovah and Baal, God and the Devil. Before attempting to set forth some of the sure grounds on which rests the certain accomplishment of God's purpose in the obedience and suffering of Christ, we will first glance briefly at the contrary view and expose its fallacy.

It is high time that some voice was raised in protest against the fearful perversions of Divine truth which are now being given out by many, who, though posing as the champions of orthodoxy, are nothing more than wolves in sheep's clothing, blind, leading those who follow their pernicious heresies into the ditch. The omnipotency of God is now frittered down to a persuasive power which He brings to bear upon sinners, but which is so feeble that it fails to move the great majority who are subject to it: more than this "persuasion" must not be affirmed, lest man be reduced to a "mere machine". The all-efficacious Atonement, which has actually redeemed everyone for whom it was made, is degraded to a "remedy" which sin-sick souls may use if they feel disposed to. The invincible work of the Holy Spirit is supposed to be nothing more than an "offer" of the Gospel which sinners may accept or reject as they please. That such frightful errors should now be accepted in "churches" calling themselves "Fundamentalists", only shows how far the Apostacy has advanced.

The horrible and blasphemous idea of Arminians is, that the wondrous and perfect Atonement of Christ has made sure and certain the salvation of none, that it has only made possible the salvation of all who hear the Gospel. When this "possibility" is carefully examined it is found to be an impossibility! The supposed "possibility" is that fallen man, while dead in trespasses and sins, must fulfill a certain condition, must of himself perform a certain act which God is said to require of him, before the Sacrifice of Christ can be of any avail. That "condition" is faith; that "act" is that he must believe. Now to reduce the "great salvation" which Christ procured and secured to a bare possibility, as something which is available for everybody but sure for nobody, is to say that Christ did no more for Peter and Paul than He did for Pilate and Judas. Everything is thus left to chance and uncertainty.

To make the efficacy of Christ's Atonement depend upon an act of man's will is highly dishonouring to our blessed Saviour. To say that the success of the greatest of all God's works is left contingent upon the creature's pleasure is most insulting to the Almighty, impeaching as it does His wisdom, goodness, and justice. To teach that salvation lies within the sinner's own power to secure, is to flatly deny Christ when He said "with men this is **impossible**" (Mat. 19:26). Alas, nearly all preachers today speak of faith in Christ as a comparatively easy matter, as though it were well within the range of the sinner's own ability. But the Scriptures teach far otherwise. They teach that man by nature is spiritually bound with fetters, such as none but God can break (Gal. 5:1), that he is shut up in darkness (Eph. 4:18), and is in a prison-house (Isa. 61:1). The salvation of no man is "possible" apart from the effectual operations of God's invincible grace.

To affirm the "possibility" of an unregenerate sinner believing in Christ to the saving of his soul, is to deny that "men loved darkness rather than light" (John 3:19) that "they that are in the flesh **cannot** please God" (Rom. 8:8), that the "carnal mind is enmity against God". In short, it is to repudiate the fact that man is, by nature, a fallen creature, **dead** in trespasses and sins. Carnality cannot thirst after holiness. An evil tree cannot produce good fruit. A corpse cannot quicken itself. Man's will, like all his other faculties, has been disabled by the fall. His only hope is the intervention of sovereign and omnipotent grace: that God will perform upon and within him a miracle of mercy; that Divine power will lift him out of the grave of sin and make him a new creature in Christ Jesus. Until he is born again he can no more love God, savingly believe in Christ, or walk in the Spirit, than he can create a world.

We have not said that faith is unnecessary, nor that God does not call on man to believe the Gospel. What we do say is that faith is God's gift, that this gift was **purchased** by Christ for all for whom He died, and that in due time this gift is imparted to them. As this will come before us again we shall say no more upon it now; instead, we proceed to call attention to some of the many infallible proofs which demonstrate the certain efficacy of Christ's Satisfaction.

1. The Purpose of God

All the designs of a Being possessed of infinite wisdom and allmighty power must be fulfilled. It is impossible that they should be frustrated. In Eph. 3:11 we read of "the eternal purpose which He purposed in Christ Jesus our Lord." The context shows what that "eternal purpose" concerned. It was a "dispensation of the grace of God (v. 2) toward poor sinners. It was that elect Jews and elect Gentiles should be "fellow heirs and of the same body, and partakers of His promise in Christ by the gospel" (v. 6). It was that these should be partakers of "the unsearchable riches of Christ" (v. 8). It was that by means of the Church the "manifold wisdom of God" should be exhibited (v. 10). This same "eternal purpose" of God is revealed in 1 Thess. 5:9, "For God hath not appointed us to wrath, but to obtain salvation by our Lord Jesus Christ."

Now the purpose of God is absolutely certain of fulfillment. He Himself emphatically declares, "My counsel shall stand, and I will do all My pleasure" (Isa. 46:10). He insists that, "There is **no** wisdom nor understanding nor counsel against the Lord" (Prov. 21:30). Neither the malice of man nor the enmity of Satan can prevent the infallible accomplishment of whatsoever God hath ordained. To affirm the contrary is blasphemy. In Prov. 19:21 we are told that "there are many devices in a man's heart, nevertheless the counsel of the Lord, that shall stand". There were many "devices" in the heart of Pharaoh against Jehovah and His people, nevertheless the "counsel" of the Lord stood fast. There were many "devices" in the heart of Saul of Tarsus against Christ and His church, and though he kicked against the pricks, nevertheless, the "counsel" of the Lord was accomplished.

"The counsel of the Lord standeth forever, the thoughts of His heart to all generations" (Psa. 33:11). This is the firm and glorious confidence of His saints. No ingenuity of man and no plotting of the Devil can overthrow it, no, nor so much as hinder it. "Our God is in the heavens: He hath done **whatsoever** He hath pleased" (Psa. 115:3). Hath He "from the beginning chosen us unto salvation" (2 Thess. 2:13)? then saved we must be. Hath He "predestinated us unto the adoption of children by Jesus Christ to Himself, according to the good pleasure of His will" (Eph. 1:5)? then that will must be fulfilled. God's purpose is immutable (Heb. 6:17), invincible (Psa. 2:6), triumphant (Isa. 14:26, 27). Before there can be the slightest failure in the accomplishment of the Divine design in the Atonement of Christ, God must cease to be! But this is impossible.

2. The Covenant of God.

Now it is obviously impossible to have any clear views of what the Lord Jesus died to achieve, if we have no real knowledge of the Eternal Agreement between the Father and the Son **in fulfillment of which** His death took place. Yet, today, deplorable to say, even the great majority of those considered evangelical—to mention no others—have scarcely any such knowledge. The very fact that that Covenant was proposed, accepted, and drawn up before the foundation of the world, proves beyond all shadow of doubt that it was unconditional so far as man is concerned, for **he** then had no existence! Therefore he cannot be a party to it, even though his eternal wellbeing is the object of it.

It must be admitted that, in effecting salvation God acts agreeably to a preconceived plan or designed arrangement. We say "must", for to deny this is to impute to the infinitely wise God conduct such as is found only among the most thoughtless and foolish among men, conduct such as is exemplified in no other department of His works, for in all of them we discover such order and regularity as clearly evince the existence of an original plan or design. Hence, to direct attention to the Everlasting Covenant is but to show that God is now working according to an eternal purpose. The Scriptures plainly represent the Divine persons as entering into a federal agreement for the salvation of men. In that covenant the Father is the representative of the Godhead, and the Son the representative of those who are to be redeemed. He is, on that account, called the "Surety" (Heb. 7:22) and "Mediator" (Heb. 8:6) of the covenant. Whatever He did as Surety or Mediator must, therefore, have been done in connection with the covenant.

The great Architect of the universe drew up His plans before ever a creature was brought into existence. Everything concerning Christ and His Church was firmly settled beyond possibility of alteration. All that concerns the being and wellbeing of His people is done according to God's covenant-enactment. As Eph. 1:11 declares God "worketh all things after the counsel of His own will". Yes, "He will ever be mindful of His covenant" (Psa. 111:5). There were no contingencies, no uncertainties, no peradventures. All the affairs of the elect were settled by the mutual consent of all the persons of Deity. The Father made choice of the elect (Eph. 1:4), the Son accepted that choice (John 17:10), the Spirit recorded it in the Lamb's book of life (Rev. 13:8). The Father decreed salvation, the Son consented to purchase it, the Spirit pledged Himself to the communication of it.

Now as stated in an earlier article, a covenant is an agreement between two parties who are under mutual engagements. Something is to be done by one of the parties, in consequence of which the other party binds himself to do something in return. When a master, for example, enters into an agreement or covenant with a servant, he prescribes certain duties to be performed by the servant and promises to recompense him with suitable wages. By consenting to the compact, the servant becomes bound to perform the stipulated work, and the master is bound to bestow the reward when the term of labour is finished. Such an agreement, such a compact, was entered into between the Father and the Son before the foundation of the world. Clear proof of this is found in Isa. 49:1-9, 2 Tim. 1:9. In Isa. 53:10-12 we have recorded the promises which God made to the Mediator. In John 17:24 we hear Christ putting in His claim to the fulfilment of that promise.

The covenant is "ordered in all things and sure" (2 Sam. 23:5). It is "sure" in its ordinations, operations, communications, preservations, and consummations. Yes, it is a salvation **worthy of God!** Well might the late Joseph Irons say, "O the vast importance of getting at and possessing an infallible Christianity! The Devil knew well of what worth and importance that word was, and, therefore, he carried it off to Rome, that the vilest of wretches might claim it as theirs and talk about infallible heads, and infallible decrees, and infallible councils, and infallible vicars of Christ. I wonder the earth does not swallow them up as it did Korah, Dathan, and Abiram; it is such blasphemous presumption. They talk about infallibility, and then run away to Gaeta to take care of it; they talk about infallibiliy, and then are obliged to have an army of infidels from France to reestablish and to preserve it. I would not give a straw for such infallibility. I want the infallibi'ity of the throne of God, the infallibility of the existence of Deity, the infallibility that is sworn to by the Persons of Godhead, that is ratified in the oaths of His Word, embraced and enjoyed in my own soul; all the members of Christ secure in His hands, so that none shall pluck them thence; all the purposes of grace infallibly settled; and all that the Father gave Him be infallibly brought home, to behold His glory and see Him as He is".

The Satisfaction of Christ was the one and only "condition" of the Covenant. It was stipulated as the condition of His having a seed to serve Him, that He should make His soul an offering for sin, that He should bear their iniquities, that He should pour out His soul into death. In reference to this, we find Him saying to His apostles on the eve of His crucifixion, "This is My **blood of the new covenant**, which is shed for many for the remission of sins" (Matt. 26:28). The b'ood of Christ was not shed by accident, nor was it poured out at random or on a venture. No, He laid down His life by commandment: He had received orders from His Father so to do: John 10:18. The blood of Christ was the **sealing** of the Covenant, and by it He has—not as the Arminians say, simply secured the possibility of salvation for all of Adam's race, but—actually **purchased** to Himself the Church of God: Acts 20:28.

At the close of His earthly career we find Christ saying to the Father, "I have glorified Thee on the earth: I have finished the work which **Thou gavest** Me to do" (John 17:4). On the ground of this He prays, "And now, O Father, glorify Thou Me with Thine own self" (v. 5). Furthermore He said, "Father, I will that they may behold My glory" (v. 24). Having faithfully discharged His part of the Contract, the Father is now in honour bound to bring to Heaven every one for whom Christ died. So far as the elect are concerned, the design of the Mediator's work, was not that God might, if He would, but that He **should**, by virtue of His engagement with the Surety, actually **bestow** on the Church all that He merited for it. Therefore we boldly affirm that, before there can be the slightest failure in the Divine design of the Atonement, the Father must betray the Son's confidence in Him and prove false to His own stipulation with Him. That is impossible.

3. The Veracity of God.

In the past eternity the Father made definite promises to the Meditor. From these we may cite the following: "I the Lord have called Thee in righteousness, and will hold Thine hand, and will keep Thee, and give Thee for a covenant of the people, for a light of the Gentiles; To open the blind eyes, to bring out the prisoners from the prison" (Isa. 42: 6, 7). "In the Lord **shall** all the seed of Israel (namely "the Israel of God", Gal. 6:16) be justified, and shall glory" (Isa. 45:25). "Thus saith the Lord, the Redeemer of Israel, His Holy One, to Him whom man despiseth, to Him whom the nations abhorreth, to a Servant of rulers, Kings shall see and arise, princes also **shall** worship, because of the Lord that is **faithful**" (Isa. 49:7). "He **shall** see of the travail of His soul, and be satisfied: by His knowledge **shall** My righteous Servant justify many: for He shall bear their iniquities. Therefore will I divide Him a portion with the great, and He **shall** divide the spoil with the strong" (Isa. 53: 11, 12). "Ask of Me, and I **shall give** the heathen for Thine inheritance, and the uttermost parts of the earth for Thy possession" (Psa. 2:8). In view of these promises, Christ had a joy "set before Him", for which joy He endured the cross and despised the shame (Heb. 12:2).

Now if one man enters into a solemn engagement with another which is duly ratified, signed, sealed, and witnessed to, for him to attempt to break it would be to violate his honour, forfeit his good name, and make him an object of contempt to all righteous people. But the man who is honourable and upright, respects his pledges: his word is his bond. Infinitely more so does all this hold good of Him who is the God of Truth. "God is not a man, that He should lie; neither the Son of man, that He should repent: hath He said, and shall He not do it? or hath He spoken, and shall He not make it good?" (Num. 23:19). God not only entered into formal covenant with Christ, not only made Him definite promises, but solemnly placed Himself on oath to the certain fulfillment of them: "My covenant will I not break, nor alter the thing that is gone out of My lips. Once have I sworn by My holiness that I will not lie unto the Beloved" (Psa. 89:34, 35).

Here then is another sure and unchanging ground of confidence. The very perfections of Deity stand pledged unto the triumphant issue of Christ's Satisfaction. The honour of God is involved in it. His faithfulness is at stake. His veracity is eternally pledged for the fulfillment of every iota of the grand Charter between Himself and the Mediator of His people. Therefore not a promise can fail, not one elect vessel of mercy be cast out. There can be no failure, for nothing is left contingent on the creature. As Psa. 111:5 declares "He will ever **be mindful of** His covenant". Here is security indeed. God will not change His mind, revoke His choice, or violate His pledge. Therefore we boldly affirm that, before there can be the slightest failure in the Divine design concerning the Atonement, the Father would have to falsify His promises, lie to His Son, and go back upon His most solemn oath. Such is utterly impossible.

4. The Power of God

The Work of Christ, of itself, never did, never will, and never can, save a single soul. God must carry that death into effect. If the efficacy of Christ's sacrifice should be, as blind leaders tell the people it is, left for men to receive or reject, men to help forward or impede the prosperity thereof, then His death would be utterly in vain. But the Lord Jesus did not leave the virtues of His Atonement to depend upon the creature. No, He committed His cause and interests unto the Father. Hear Him saying, "And now I am no more in the world, but these are in the world, and I come to Thee. Holy Father, **keep** through Thine own name those whom Thou hast given Me, that they may be one, as We" (John 17:11). Unto the keeping power of the Father did Christ entrust those for whom He died.

We have shown in previous articles that Christ died not as a private person, but as the federal Head of the whole election of grace; therefore His final act on the cross must be understood as signifying "Father, unto **Thy** hands I commend **My** (mystical) spirit" (Luke 23:46). And what was the Father's response? Psa. 110 tells us. The Father not only exalted Christ to His own right hand, but solemnly assured Him that, "The Lord shall send the rod of Thy strength out of Zion... Thy people shall be willing in the day of Thy power" (vv. 2, 3). Thereby He promised to make the preaching of the Gospel successful unto the saving of His "people". Invincible grace should open hearts to the reception of its message (Acts 16:14), and they should be **"kept** by the **power** of God through faith unto salvation" (1 Peter 1: 5). Therefore we boldly say that, before there can be the slightest failure in the Divine design concerning the Atonement, God must be stript of His omnipotence. But that is impossible.

5. The Justice of God

"There are many who plead for the atonement of Chirst, who, in effect, deny it, as well as its open opposers. They suppose that it is a conditional atonement, of efficacy only to those who comply with certain terms. It is evident, however, that a conditional atonement is no atonement in the proper sense of the word; for an atonement **must** expiate the sins atoned for, just as a payment cancels a debt. Where, then, there has been an actual atonement made, the sins atoned for never can be punished again, more than a debt once paid can be charged a second time. It would be unjust in God to charge the debt to the account of man that was fully paid by man's Surety. It may be alleged that one man may pay another man's debts upon certain conditions; and that if those conditions are not fulfilled, the debt will be still chargeable upon the debtor. But it is evident that, in such a case, the surety either does not actually pay the debt till the conditions are fulfilled, or if he has conditionally paid it, he is refunded before it is chargeable upon the debtor. In every such case, the debt is not really paid. But Jesus **has paid** the debt. He has already made atonement; and if they for whom He dies are not absolved, the debt is charged a second time. Christ can never be **refunded.** His blood has been shed; and there is no possibility that what He suffered can be now either more or less. They, then, who suspend the efficacy of the atonement of Christ upon conditions to be complied with by man, in effect **deny** that atonement has been truly made" (Alex. Carson, 1847).

Shall not the Judge of all the earth do right? Assuredly. His very perfections move Him to give every one His due. This principle is exemplified time after time in Holy Writ. Then shall God make an exception of His Son? No, indeed. God ever acts sovereignly, but He never acts unrighteously. Just as He will not, cannot (Ex. 34:7), remit sin without satisfaction, so He will not, cannot (Job. 4:7), punish sin where satisfaction **has been** received. To condemn one for whom an atonement has been accepted, would be as incompatible with perfect equity as to ignore sin without an atonement. If the punishment of sin has been borne, the remission of the offense follows of course. God never punishes twice for the same crime. Thus, inasmuch as the oblation of Christ was a legal satisfaction for sin, all for whom it was offered **must** enjoy the remission of their transgressions.

It is a matter of bare justice that those blessings which Christ intended to procure for His people **should be** actually bestowed upon them. First, because this was promised Him as the reward of His obedience and sufferings; that reward has been fully earned. Second, because He actually **purchased** salvation for them. The enmity of the carnal mind may object that such a conception is a "commercialising" of Divine love, but Scripture does not hesitate to employ pecuniary terms: "Ye are bought with a price" (1 Cor. 6:20). What has been paid for, the purchaser has a right to. To deny that to him would be unjust. Again, the Word speaks of our sins as "debts" (Matt. 6:12): if then Christ has discharged them, He has the right to demand the exemption of all for whom He acted as Sponsor. Therefore we boldly affirm that, before there can be the slightest failure in the Divine design of the Atonement, God must cease to hate iniquity, and love righteousness. But that is impossible.

6. The Government of God

The law of substitution, which is a principle appointed by the Divine government, requires the salvation of all those whom Christ represented. "Perfect suretyship, whether we regard the supreme instance and exemplification of it in the work of Christ in our behalf, or the most common and familiar instances of it as exemplified among men, is always and manifestly suretyship which, in its own nature, **secures** and **necessitates**, the re-instatement of every one in whose behalf it is undertaken" (John Armour). Now as Christ fully met every demand of the Law, both preceptive and penal, against His people, its claims having been satisfied, cannot be again enforced.

In the fifth article of this series we sought to define with care the meaning of the term "substitution". We pointed out that substitutionary suffering is that which is endured in the stead of others, in their actual place. Such suffering inevitably carries with it the **exemption** of the party or parties in whose room it is endured. What is done or suffered by a substitute, completely absolves those whom he represents from doing or suffering the same thing. Christ so satisfied the law of God in behalf of His people that the law can now make no claim whatsoever upon them. The death of Christ was as truly and actually a substitutionary one as was the death of those animals sacrificed in old O. T. times in lieu of the death of the transgressor offering them. Thus the substitutionary satisfaction of Christ **requires** Divine justice **to** remit the sins and to reinstate in Divine favour all for whose sake it was made.

Substitution necessarily involves two parties: an offender and one who takes his place, a debtor and one who discharges it for him. It is equally self-evident that substitution involves a two-fold effect; the position of **each** is changed in relation to the law. The one who before was innocent now becomes guilty, and the one who before was guilty now becomes innocent. This is a palpable fact and not a fine-spun theory. If then Christ bore the sins of His people, no sin can rest on them. If on their behalf He was made a curse, the law cannot now curse them. With the apostle we triumphantly exclaim, "Who shall lay any thing to the charge of God's elect?—God that justifieth! Who is he that condemneth?—Christ that died" (Rom. 8:33, 34). Therefore we boldly affirm that, before there can be the least failure in the Divine design of Christ's Atonement, the Throne of God, which is founded upon "righteousness and judgment", (Psa. 97:2), must be overturned. But that is impossible.

7. The Glory of God

No lengthy argument is needed to establish the fact that the glory of God **requires** the mediatorial work of Christ should be completely efficacious, i. e. that it should infallibly accomplish all it was designed to effect. If there were any failure in the **fruits** or **results** of the Atonement, then the purpose of God would be foiled, His covenant broken, His veracity forfeited, His power defeated, His justice sullied, and His glory dishonoured. Few seem to realise the fearful implications which necessarily follow the principles they hold and advocate. To predicate an Atonement which fails to atone, a Redemption which does not redeem, a Sacrifice which secures not the actual remission of sins, is a horrible reflection upon all the attributes of God. To make the efficacy or success of the greatest of all God's works dependent upon the choice of fallen and depraved creatures, is to magnify man at the cost of dethroning his Maker.

The manifestative glory of God is bound up in the person and work of Christ. Our Lord Jesus revealed this very plainly when, facing the crucial hour, He cried, "Father glorify **Thy** name" (John 12:28). Again

He declared, "Now is the Son of man glorified, and God is glorified **in Him**" John 13:31). Compare also John 14:13. If then Christ be dishonoured, God is dishonoured. But if Christ be glorified by the Father's acceptance of His work and by the Spirit's infallible application thereof, so that every effect is produced which it was intended to bring forth, then is God supremely glorified. Therefore we boldly declare that, before there can be the slightest failure in the Divine design of the Atonement, God must cease to have any respect for His own honour. But that can never be.

—ARTHUR W. PINK.

PROFITING FROM THE WORD

3. The Scriptures and Christ

The order we are following in this series of articles is that of **experience.** It is not until man is made thoroughly displeased with himself that he begins to aspire after God. The fallen creature, deluded by Satan, is self-satisfied till his sin-blinded eyes are opened to get a sight of himself. The Holy Spirit first works in us a sense of our ignorance, vanity, poverty, depravity, before He brings us to perceive and acknowledge that in God alone are to be found true wisdom, real blessedness, perfect goodness, unspotted righteousness. We must be made conscious of our imperfections ere we can really appreciate the Divine perfections. As the perfections of God are contemplated, man becomes still more aware of the infinite distance that separates him from the Most High. As he learns something of God's pressing claims upon him, and his own utter inability to meet them, he is prepared to hear and welcome the good news that Another has fully met those claims for all who are led to believe on Him.

"Search the Scriptures" said the Lord Jesus, and then He added "for they are they which testify **of Me**" (John 5:39). They testify of Him as the only Saviour for perishing sinners, as the only Mediator between God and men, as the only One through whom the Father can be approached. They testify to the wondrous perfections of His person, the varied glories of His offices, the sufficiency of His finished work. Apart from the Scriptures, He cannot be known. In them alone is He revealed. When the Holy Spirit takes of the things of Christ and shows them unto His people, in thus making Him known to the soul, He uses naught but what is written. While it is true that Christ is the key to the Scriptures, it is equally true that only in the Scriptures do we have an opening-up of the "mystery of Christ" (Eph. 3:4).

Now the measure in which we profit from our reading and study of the Scriptures may be ascertained by the extent to which **Christ** is becoming more real and more precious unto our hearts. To "grow in grace" is defined as "and in the knowledge of our Lord and Saviour Jesus Christ" (2 Peter 3:18): the second clause there is not something in addition to the first, but it is an explanation of it. To "know" Christ (Phil. 3:10) was the supreme longing and aim of the apostle Paul, a longing and an aim to which he subordinated all other interests. But mark it well, the "knowledge" which is spoken of in these verses is not intellectual but spiritual, not theoretical but experimental, not general but personal. It is a supernatural knowledge, which is imparted to the regenerate heart, by the operations of the Holy Spirit, as He interprets and applies to us the Scriptures concerning Him.

Now the knowledge of Christ which the blessed Spirit imparts to the believer through the Scriptures profits him in different ways, according to his varying frames, circumstances and needs. Concerning the bread which God gave to the children of Israel during their wilderness wanderings, it is recorded that "some gathered more, some less" (Ex. 16:17). The same is true in our apprehension of Him of whom the manna was a type. There is that in the wondrous person of Christ which is exactly suited to our every condition, every circumstance, every need, both for time and for eternity; but we are slow in realising it, and slower still to act upon it. There is an inexhaustible "fulness" in Christ (John 1:16) which is available for us to draw from, and the principle regulating the extent to which we become "strong in the grace that is in Christ Jesus" (2 Tim. 2:1) is, "according unto your faith be it unto you" (Matt. 9:29).

1. An individual is profited from the Scriptures when they reveal to him **his need of Christ.** Man in his natural estate

deems himself self-sufficient. True, he has a dim perception that all is not quite right between himself and God, yet has he no difficulty in persuading himself that **he** is able to do that which will please Him and offer that which will propitiate Him. **That** lies at the foundation of all man's "religion", begun by Cain, in whose "way" (Jude 11) the multitudes still walk. Tell the devout religionist that "they that are in the flesh **can not** please God" (Rom. 8:8), and he is at once offended. Press upon him the fact that "all our righteousnesses are as filthy rags" (Isa. 64:4), and his hypocritical urbanity at once gives place to anger. So it was when Christ was on earth. The most religious people of all, the Jews, had no sense that **they** were "lost" and in dire need of an almighty Saviour.

"They that be whole need not a physician, but they that are sick" (Matt. 9:12). It is the peculiar office of the Holy Spirit, by His application of the Scriptures, to convict sinners of their desperate condition, to bring them to see their state is such that "from the sole of the foot even unto the head there is no soundness" in them, but "wounds and bruises and putrifying sores" (Isa. 1:6). As the Spirit convicts us of our sins—our ingratitude to God, our murmuring against Him, our wanderings from Him; as He presses upon us the claims of God—His right to our love, obedience, adoration, and our sad failure to render Him His due; then are we made to recognize that Christ is our only hope, and that except we flee to Him for refuge, the righteous wrath of God will most certainly fall on us.

Nor is this to be limited to the initial experience of conversion. The more the Spirit deepens His work of grace in the regenerated soul, the more that individual is made conscious of his pollution, his sinfulness, his vileness; and the more does he discover his need of and learn to value that precious, precious Blood which cleanses from all sin. The Spirit is here to glorify Christ, and one chief way in which He does so is by opening wider and wider the eyes of those for whom He died, to see how suited Christ is for such wretched, foul, and Hell-deserving creatures. Yes, the more we are truly profiting from our reading of Scripture the more do we feel our need of Him.

2. An individual is profited from the Scriptures when they **make Christ more real** to him. The great mass of the Israelitish nation saw nothing more than the outward shell in the rites and ceremonies which God instituted, but a regenerated remnant were privileged to behold Christ Himself. "Abraham rejoiced to see My day" said Christ (John 8:56). Moses esteemed "the reproach of Christ" greater riches than the treasures in Egypt (Heb. 11:26). So it is in Christendom. To the multitudes Christ is but a name, or at most a historical character. They have no personal dealings with Him, have no experimental acquaintance with Him, enjoy no spiritual communion with Him. Should they hear one speak in raptures of His excellency, they regard him as an enthusiast or fanatic. To them Christ is unreal, vague, intangible. But with the real Christihn it is far otherwise. The language of his heart is,

"I have heard the voice of Jesus,
Tell me not of aught beside,
I have seen the face of Jesus,
All my soul is satisfied".

Yet such a blissful sight is not the consistant and unvarying experience of the saints. Just as clouds come in between the sun and the earth, so failures in our walk interrupt our communion with Christ and serve to hide from us the light of His countenance. "He that hath My commandments, and keepeth them, he it is that loveth Me: and he that loveth Me shall be loved of My Father, and I will love him, and will **manifest** Myself to him" (John 14:21). Yes, it is the one who by grace is treading the path of obedience to whom the Lord Jesus grants manifestations of Himself. And the more frequent and prolonged these manifestations are, the more real He becomes to the soul, until we are able to say with Job, "I have heard of Thee by the hearing of the ear: **but now** mine eye **seeth Thee**" (42:2). Thus, the more Christ is becoming a living reality to me, the more I am profiting from the Word.

3. An individual is profited from the Scriptures when he becomes **more engrossed with Christ's perfections**. It is a sense of need which first drives the soul to Christ, but it is the realization of His excellency which draws me to run after Him. The more real Christ becomes to us, the more are we attracted by His perfections. At the beginning, He is viewed only as a Saviour, but as the Spirit continues to take of the things of Christ and show them unto us, we discover that upon His head are "many crowns" (Rev. 19:12). Of old it was said, "His name shall be called Wonderful" (Isa. 9:6): His "name" signifies all that He is as made known in Scripture. "Wonderful" are His offices, in their number, variety, sufficiency. He is the Friend that sticketh closer than a brother, to help in every time of need. He

is the great High Priest, who is touched with the feeling of our infirmities. He is the Advocate with the Father, who pleads our cause when Satan accuses us.

Our great need is to be occupied with Christ, to sit at His feet as Mary did, and receive out of His fulness. Our chief delight should be to "**Consider** the Apostle and High Priest of our profession" (Heb. 3:1): to contemplate the various relations which He sustains to us, to meditate upon the many promises He has given, to dwell upon His wondrous and changeless love for us. As we do this, we shall so delight ourselves in the Lord, that the siren voices of this world will lose all their charm for us. Ah, my reader, do you know anything about this in your own actual experience? Is Christ the Chief among ten thousand to your soul? Has He won your heart? Is it your chief joy to get alone and be occupied with Him? If not, your Bible-reading and study has profited you little indeed.

4. An individual is profited from the Scriptures as **Christ becomes more precious** to him. Christ is precious in the esteem of all true believers (1 Peter 2:7). They count all things but loss for the excellency of the knowledge of Christ Jesus their Lord (Phil. 3:8). His name is to them as ointment poured forth (Song of Sol. 1:3). As the glory of God that appeared in the wondrous beauty of the temple, and in the wisdom and splendour of Solomon, drew worshippers to him from the uttermost parts of the earth, so the unparalleled excellency of Christ, which was prefigured thereby, does more powerfully attract the hearts of His people. The Devil knows this full well, therefore is he ceaselessly engaged in blinding the minds of them that believe not, by placing between them and Christ the allurements of this world. God permits him to assail the believer too, but it is written, "Resist the Devil, and he will flee from you". Resist him by definite and earnest prayer, entreating the Spirit to draw out your affections to Christ.

The more we are engaged with Christ's perfections, the more we love and adore Him. It is the lack of experimental acquaintance with Him that makes our hearts so cold toward Him. But where real and daily fellowship is cultivated the Christian will be able to say with the Psalmist, "Whom have I in heaven but Thee? and there is none upon earth I desire beside Thee" (Psa. 73:25). This it is which is the very essence and distinguishing nature of true Christianity. Legalistic zealots may be busily engaged in tithing mint and annice and cummin, they may encompass sea and land to make one proselite, and yet have no love for God in Christ. It is the heart which God looks at: "My son, give Me thine heart" (Prov. 23:26) is His demand, and only the one to whom Christ is more than life is able to meet that demand. The more precious Christ is to us, the more delight does He have in us.

5. An individual who is profited from the Scriptures has an **increasing confidence in Christ**. There is "little faith" (Matt. 14:3) and "great faith" (Matt. 8:10). There is the "full assurance of faith" (Heb. 10:22), and trusting in the Lord "with all the heart" (Prov. 3:5). Just as there is a growing "from strength to strength" (Psa. 84:7), so we read of "from faith to faith" (Rom. 1:17). The stronger and steadier our faith, the more the Lord Jesus is honoured. Even a cursory reading of the four Gospels reveals the fact that nothing more pleased the Saviour than the firm reliance which was placed in Him by the few who really counted upon Him. He Himself walked and lived by faith, and the more we do so, the more are the members being conformed to their Head. Above everything else there is one thing to be aimed at and diligently sought by earnest prayer: that our faith may be increased. Of the Thessalonian saints Paul was able to say, "Your faith groweth exceedingly" (2 Thess. 1:3).

Now Christ cannot be trusted at all until He be known, and the better He is known, the more will He be trusted: "And they that know Thy name **will** put their trust in Thee" (Psa. 9:10). As Christ becomes more real to the heart, as we are increasingly occupied with His manifold perfections and He becomes more precious to us, confidence in Him is deepened until it becomes as natural to trust Him as it is to breathe. The Christian life is a **walk** of faith (2 Cor. 5:7), and that very expression denotes a continual progress, an increasing deliverance from doubts and fears, a fuller assurance that all He has promised He will perform. Abraham is the father of all them that believe, and thus the record of his life furnishes an illustration of what a deepening confidence in the Lord signifies. First, at His bare word he turned his back upon all that was dear to the flesh. Second, he went forth in simple dependence on Him and dwelt as a stranger and sojourner in the land of promise, though he never owned a single acre of it. Third, when promise was made of a seed in his old age, he considered not the obstacles in the way of its fulfillment, but was strong in faith giving glory to God. Finally, when called on to offer up Isaac through whom the promises were to be realized, he accounted that God was able also "to raise him up even from the dead" (Heb. 11:19).

In the history of Abraham we are shown how grace is able to subdue an evil heart of unbelief, how the spirit may be victorious over the flesh, how the supernatural fruits of a God-given and God-sustained faith may be brought forth by a man of like passions with us. This is recorded for our encouragement, for us to pray that it may please the Lord to work in us what He wrought in and through the father of the faithful. Nothing more pleases, honours and glorifies Christ than the confiding trust, the expectant confidence, the childlike faith, of those to whom He has given every cause to trust in Him with all their hearts. And nothing more evidences that we are being profited from the Scriptures than by an increasing faith in Christ.

6. An individual is profited from the Scriptures when they beget within him **a deepening desire to please Christ.** "Ye are not your own. For ye are bought with a price" (1 Cor. 6:19, 20), is the first great fact that Christians need to apprehend. Henceforth they are not to "live unto themselves, but unto Him which died for them, and rose again" (2 Cor. 5:15). Love delights to please its object, and the more our affections are drawn out to Christ, the more shall we desire to honour Him by a life of obedience to His known will. "If a man love Me, he will keep My words" (John 14:23). It is not in happy emotions nor in verbal professions of devotion, but in the actual assumption of His yoke and the practical submitting to His precepts that Christ is most honoured.

It is at this point, particularly, that the genuineness of our profession may be tested and proved. Have they a faith in Christ which make no effort to learn His will? What a contempt of the king if his subjects refuse to read his proclamation! Where there is faith in Christ there will be a delight in His commandments, and a sorrowing when they are broken by us. When we displease our Christ we shall mourn over our failure. It is impossible to seriously believe that it was my sins which caused the Son of God to shed His precious blood without me hating them. If Christ groaned under sin, we shall too. And the more sincere those groanings be, the more earnestly shall we seek grace for deliverance from all that displeases, and strength to do that which pleases our blessed Redeemer.

7. An individual is profited from the Scriptures when they cause him to **long for the return of Christ.** Love can be satisfied with nothing short of a sight of its object. True, even now, we behold Christ by faith, yet it is "through a glass darkly". But at His second advent we shall behold Him "face to face" (1 Cor. 13:12). Then will be fulfilled His own prayer for us, "Father, I will that they also, whom Thou hast given Me, be with Me where I am; that they may behold My glory, which Thou hast given Me, for Thou lovedst Me before the foundation of the world" (John 17:24). Only this will fully meet the longings of His heart, and only this will meet the longings of those redeemed by Him. Only then will He "see of the travail of His soul and be satisfied" (Isa. 53:10)., and "as for me, I will behold Thy face in righteousness: I shall be satisfied, when I awake, with Thy likeness" (Psa. 17:15).

At the return of Christ we shall be done with sin forever. The elect are predestinated to be conformed to the image of God's Son, and that Divine purpose will only be realised when Christ comes to receive His people unto Himself. "We shall be like Him, for we shall see Him as He is" (1 John 3:2). Never again will our communion with Him be broken; never again shall we groan and moan over our inward corruptions; never again shall we be harassed with unbelief. He will present His Church to Himself "a glorious church, not having spot, or wrinkle, or any such thing" (Eph. 5:27). For that hour we eagerly wait. For our Redeemer we lovingly look. The more we yearn for the Coming One, the more we are trimming our lamps in earnest expectation of His imminent appearing, the more do we give evidence that we are profiting from our knowledge of the Word.

Let writer and reader honestly search himself as in the presence of God. Let us seek truthful answers to these questions. Have we a deeper felt sense of our need of Christ? Is He Himself becoming to us a brighter and living reality? Are we finding increasing delight in being occupied with His lovely perfections? Is Christ Himself becoming daily more precious to us? Is our faith in Him growing so that we confidently trust Him for everything? Are we really seeking to please Him in all the details of our lives? Are we so yearning for His return that we would be filled with joy did we know for certain that He would come during the next twenty-four hours? May the Holy Spirit search our hearts with these pointed questions.

—ARTHUR W. PINK.

SIMON PETER

A recent "Sunday School" lesson on Simon Peter was given the following title, "How a weak man became strong". Much depends upon how the contrastive terms are understood, whether naturally or spiritually: if in the former sense, then it would be far more accurate to designate it, "How a strong man became weak." The world looks upon self-assurance, self-reliance, and self-sufficiency as the marks of a strong character; but not so God. His thoughts and ways are ever the opposite of man's (Isa. 55:8, 9), therefore hath God "made foolish the wisdom of this world" (1 Cor. 1:20), for "that which is highly esteemed among men is an abomination in the sight of God" (Luke 16:15). Therefore it is written, "let no man deceive himself. If any man among you seemeth to be wise in this world, let him become a fool, that he may be wise" (1 Cor. 3:18).

Instead of giving an exposition of the passages selected, we propose taking up one point only, namely, Peter's sad fall, and this in a more or less topical way. Some have wondered why the awful defection of such an eminent servant of Christ as Simon Peter should have been recorded in Holy Writ. A few have impiously imagined that it had been better to have drawn the curtain of silence over such an event. Not so the Holy Spirit; He deemed otherwise. It is recorded to the glory of God, demonstrating His faithfulness, His love, His grace. It is recorded for our instruction, to take to heart as a warning, to reveal to us the terrible tendency of the flesh which is still within us.

Matt. 26:69-74 presents to us one of the most heart-searching and fear-provoking passages in God's Word—O that it may be prayer-provoking too. There we behold one of the most highly favoured from among the sons of men: one who had not only been called out of darkness into God's marvelous light, but to be an apostle of the Lamb; one who had lived in blessed intimacy with Him for three years. Now that his beloved Master had been taken by wicked hands, and Peter was challenged with being one of His disciples, he denied it with oaths. How is such a sin to be accounted for? Every effect must have a previous cause. To answer that it was the breaking forth of indwelling sin is only too true, yet such a reply is not sufficiently specific. The Saviour prayed that Peter's faith should not fail (Luke 22:32), why had He not prayed that he should not fail at all?

If we go back to Matt. 26:31-35 we discover the root from which the bitter fruit of Peter's denial sprang. The Saviour announced that that night all the Eleven would be offended because of Him. Instead of bowing before the Lord in brokenness of heart, beseeching Him to preserve His frail disciple from such a terrible thing, Peter boastfully declared. "Though all shall be offended because of Thee, I will never be offended". Ah, there we see the seat of the whole trouble: self-confidence was what led to and occasioned his fearful fall. Because it is nearly always overlooked we turn back to a yet earlier incident which symbolically forecast Peter's sin in the high priest's palace, as well as the cause of it and his subsequent restoration.

In Matt. 14:22-33 we read of the disciples on the storm-tossed sea, the Saviour walking to them on the waters and saying, "Be of good cheer it is I, be not afraid". Then we are told that Peter said, "Lord, if it be Thou, bid me come unto Thee on the water". The more closely these words are pondered, the more do they appear to exhibit a strange mingling of motives. On the other hand, it is blessed to note that Peter would not make a move until Christ had bidden him; on the other hand, it seems to us that there was even then, the desire to manifest his **superior** devotion to Christ—or why the "bid **me**" rather than "us"? Moreover, was there not self-confidence expressed too? Was it not for the purpose of checking this, as a warning to him, that Christ suffered Peter to do as he desired? The whole incident is rich with spiritual lessons.

Two things are absolutely necessary if we are to walk in triumph upon the waters of life and not sink beneath them. First, we must have the authority of the Word for all which we engage to do: we must not take a step or attempt anything unless we have Divine warrant for it. Second, there must be an abiding realisation of the Divine presence and a constant staying of ourselves upon the living God. Unless our eye be fixed steadfastly on Him, unless we are really depending upon Him moment by moment for wisdom, strength, everything, we are certain to fall. It was precisely here that Peter failed. He did not fail in obedience, but in full dependence on Christ. He acted or His word in leaving the ship, but he did not lean on His arm while walking on the water, hence his fear and "beginning to sink". Mere authority is not enough; we need **power** as well. To act without Divine authority is self-will; to act without Divine power is certain failure. It is striking and blessed to see the two joined together in Matt. 28:19, 20: first, Christ's command giving us authority; second, His promised presence for us to look to for all needed grace.

Returning now to Matt. 26:33. There we see a **strong** man, strong in his own estimation, strong in his resolutions, strong in self-confidence. Yet man is never so weak as when he is filled with a sense of his own sufficiency. The writer has no doubt in his mind of Peter's sincerity. We are fully persuaded that he meant what he said, and that he had not the slightest suspicion about the awful sin he was on the eve of committing. The fact is that he **was ignorant of himself,** and it is ignorance of self (experimental ignorance, we mean, not theoretical) which lies behind all self-confidence. The more fully self is known—known as God has diagnosed it in His unerring Word—the more will it be distrusted. The man who deems himself incapable of committing Peter's sin is ignorant of himself.

"Let him that thinketh he standeth take heed lest he fall" (1 Cor. 10:12), fall into the fearful sins mentioned in the immediate context. The believer is here warned against the abominations committed by Israel in the wilderness: self-will, murmurings, idolatry, fornication. And why is such a warning needed by us? Because there is within us precisely the same evil nature that was in them. "The heart is deceitful above all things, and desperately wicked" (Jer. 17:9), such is **our** heart, and unless Divine power subdue it, any of the fearful things mentioned by Christ in Mark 7:21, 22 are liable to issue from it. Unless the grace of God keeps us moment by moment we are fully capable of committing **every** sin mentioned in Scripture. The more this is **realised** by us, the more earnestly and frequently shall we cry, "Lead us not into temptation, but deliver us from evil".

The **effect** of Peter's self-confidence was his failure to heed the exhortation which Christ gave Him, "Watch and pray, lest ye enter into temptation" (Matt. 26:41). Had he felt his utter weakness, he had waited on God for Divine strength. Had he suspected that he was fully capable and in eminent danger of denying his beloved Master, he had earnestly cried to God for "grace to help in time of need". But instead of so doing, he disregarded Christ's warning, and went to sleep. Ah my reader, little as you may realize it, your prayerlessness is due to **pride,** to the self-sufficiency of your haughty heart, to a **lack** of conscious weakness and helplessness. If you believed what God says of your evil heart, and felt your utter impotency to suppress its risings, your daily prayer would be, "Hold Thou me up, and I shall be safe" (Psa. 119:117).

It is God's way to empty us of ourselves before He fills us with Himself. Those who imagine they can subdue the power of evil within them, sustain themselves under their afflictions, or serve the Lord in their own wisdom and strength, God **leaves** to their own resources, as He did Peter. But unto those who feel and acknowledge their weakness He communicates Divine strength. What a word is that in Isa. 40:29, "He giveth power to the faint; and to **no might** He increaseth strength"! Yes, it is when we come to the end of ourselves that He works in and through us. So of the O. T. worthies it is said, "Out of weakness were made strong" (Heb. 11:34). In sharp and solemn contrast from these Scriptures is the case recorded in 2 Chron. 36:15, 16, "And his name spread far abroad; for he was marvelously helped **till he was strong.** But when he was strong, his heart was lifted up to his destruction".

What a solemn admonition does the record of Uzziah's life contain for us! Any attempt to expound those words is only calculated to hide their weighty message, blunt their sharp point, and dull their keen edge. O that the same Spirit who inspired them of old might apply them to our hearts and cause them to "work effectually" in us by His mighty power. As we read the whole chapter it seems as though Uzziah's chief object was to be "strong". But alas! it was with him as it is with many of us: the strength we covet is in dependency of God; whereas we are exhorted, "Be strong **in the Lord** and in the power of His might" (Eph. 6:10). There is no real strength apart from Him: all else is utter weakness. The apostle gave proof of this when he said, "For when I am weak, then am I strong" (2 Cor. 12:10).

How often the Lord's people mourn over their weakness, unmindful of the fact that consciousness of their weakness should make them rejoice and praise God. It is only when we have been brought to realise **our** powerlessness that we are in a position and condition to hear His voice saying, "My grace is made perfect in weakness" (2 Cor. 12:9). It is the desire of the flesh to be self-sufficient, to have some resources in ourselves, instead of crying unto the Lord, "all my springs are in Thee" (Psa. 87:7). We want to be strong in ourselves, but God will not trust His people with any strength out of Christ! O for the Spirit to impress upon each of our hearts the fact that the place of blessing is the place of confessed need: the place of strength, our felt weakness. It was when we were "without strength" that Christ died for us (Rom. 5:6), and it is only as we are kept in the consciousness that we are still "without strength" in ourselves that we learn how truly Christ lives in us.

If God does not use some of us it is probably because we are too big and too strong in our own estimation and would be sure to take some of the credit of the work to ourselves. There is a question asked in the Talmud, "Why did God create man last"? and the answer is, "Because man would have claimed some share in the work if God had done so". Look at some of the **weak and small** things God has used at different times. A baby's tear was used to confound the wisdom of Egypt and deliver Israel out of the house of bondage (Ex. 2:6 and cf. 1:10). One man, and he "left handed", delivered Israel from the captivity of Moab (Judg. 3:15). An "ox goad" was used to deliver Israel from the Philistines (Judg. 3:31). A weak woman was used to deliver Israel from the king of Canaan (Jud. 4:4), while a "tent peg" in the hands of another woman disposed of the commander of his forces (Judg. 4:21). Earthen vessels in the hands of a reduced company put to flight the armies of the aliens (Jud. 7:20). The "jawbone of an ass", in the hands of a man made strong by God, delivered Israel from the Philistines (Judg. 15:16). A sling and a stone were sufficient to overthrow the mighty Goliath.

The same principle has been exemplified again and again since Bible times. It was Luther, a miner's son, who was raised up by God to bring the inestimable blessing of the Reformation to the world. It was Calvin, a cooper's son in Picardy, who was used to open up the Word of God as it had not been for a thousand years. It was Zwingle, a shepherd's son in the Alps, who waged war so successfully against sacramentarianism. It was Melancthon, an armourer's son, who stood by Luther, and was so wondrously used of God. It was John Knox, the son of a common burgess of a country town, who did for Scotland what Luther had done for Germany. The mightiest preacher of the last century, C. H. Spurgeon, had neither college education nor a seminary course.

O to realize the truth of the Lord's own words, "without Me ye can do **nothing**" (John 15:5). May He so write those words on the hearts of both writer and reader that we may be kept in the place of conscious weakness, and thus prove it to be the place of strength and blessing. To have "**no** confidence in the flesh" (Phil. 3:3), is an experience which cannot be gained merely by reading good books, nor is it attained in a few days. It is the result of the Spirit's mighty operation within us, bringing home to our hearts the Word of power, or causing us to profit from our failures and falls, and thus empty us of self-confidence.

N. B. We are much indebted to an article in "Things to Come" (Vol. 10) for part of the above.

XMAS.

"Thus saith the Lord, Learn not the way of the heathen... for the CUSTOMS of the people are vain" (Jer. 10:1-3).

Christmas is coming! Quite so; but what is "Christmas"? Does not the very term itself denote its source—"Christmass". Thus it is of Romish origin, brought over from Paganism. But, says some one, Chirstmas is the time when we commemorate the Saviour's birth. Is it? And **who** authorised such commemoration? Certainly God did not. The Redeemer bade His disciples "remember" Him in His death, but there is not a word in Scripture, from Genesis to Revelation, which tells us to celebrate His birth.

Moreover, who knows when, in what month, He was born? The Bible is silent thereon. Is it without reason that the **only** "birthday" commemorations mentioned in God's Word are Pharaoh's (Gen. 40:20) and Herod's (Matt. 14:6)! Is this recorded "for our learning"? If so, have we prayerfully taken it to heart?

And **who** is it that celebrates "Christmas"? The whole "civilized world". Millions who make no profession of faith in the blood of the Lamb, who "despise and reject Him", and millions more who while claiming to be His followers yet in works deny Him, join in merry-making under the pretense of honouring the birth of the Lord Jesus. Putting it on its lowest ground, we would ask, Is it fitting that His friends should unite with His enemies in a worldly round of fleshly gratifications? Does any truly born-again soul really think that He whom the world cast out, is either pleased or glorified by such participation in the world's joys? Verily, "the customs of the people **are vain**"; and it is written, "thou shalt not follow a multitude to do evil" (Ex. 23:2).

Some will argue for the "keeping of Christmas" on the ground of "giving the kiddies a good time". But why do this under the cloke of honouring the Saviour's birth? Why is it necessary to drag in **His** holy name in connection with what takes place at that season of carnal jollification? Is this taking the little ones with you **out of** Egypt (Ex. 10:9, 10) a type of the world, or is it not plainly a mingling with the present-day Egyptians in their "pleasures of sin for a season" (Heb. 11: 25)? Scripture says, "Train up a child in the way he should go: and when he is old, he will not depart from it" (Prov. 22:6). Scripture does command God's people to bring up their children "in the nurture and admonition of the Lord" (Eph. 6:4), but where does it stipulate that it is our duty to give the little ones a "good time"? Do we ever give the children "a **good** time" when we engage in anything upon which we cannot fittingly ask **the Lord's** blessing?

There are those who **do** abstain from some of the grosser carnalities of the "festive season", yet are they nevertheless in cruel bondage to the prevailing custom of "Christmas", namely, that of exchanging "gifts". We say "exchanging" for that is what it really amounts to in many cases. A list is kept, either on paper or in memory, of those from whom gifts were received last year, and that for the purpose of returning the compliment this year. Nor is this all: great care has to be taken that the "gift" made to the friend is worth as much in dollars and cents as the one they expect to receive from him or her. Thus, with many who can ill afford it, a considerable sum has to be set aside each year with which to purchase things simply to send them out **in return** for others which are likely to be received. Thus a burden has been bound on them which not a few find it hard to bear.

But what are we to do? If we fail to send out "gifts" our friends will think hard of us, probably deem us stingy and miserly. The honest course is to go to the trouble of notifying them—by letter if at a distance—that from now on you do not propose to send out any more "Christmas gifts" as such. Give your reasons. State plainly that you have been brought to see that "Christmas merry-making" is entirely a thing **of the world,** devoid of any scriptural warrant; that it is a Romish institution, and that now you see this, you dare no longer have any fellowship with it (Eph. 5:11); that you are the Lord's "free man" (1 Cor. 7:22), and therefore you refuse to be in bondage to a costly custom imposed by the world.

What about sending out "Christmas cards" with a text of Scripture on them? That also is an abomination in the sight of God. Why? Because His Word expressly forbids all **un-**holy mixtures; Deut. 22:10, 11 typified this. What do we mean by an "unholy mixture"? This: the linking together the pure Word of God with the Romish "Christ-**mass**." By all means send out cards (preferably at some other time of the year) to your ungodly friends, and Christians too, with a verse of Scripture, but **not** with "Christmas" on it. What would you think of a printed program of a vaudeville show having Isa. 53:5 at the foot of it? Why, that it was altogether **out of place,** highly incongruous. But in the sight of God the circus and the theatre are far less obnoxious than the "Christmas celebrations" of Romish and Protestant "churches". Why? Because the latter are done under the cover of the holy name of Christ; the former are not.

"But the path of the just is as the shining light, that shineth more and more unto the perfect day" (Prov. 4:18). Where there is a heart that really desires to please the Lord, He graciously grants increasing knowledge of His will. If He is pleased to use these lines for opening the eyes of some of His dear people to recognize what is a growing evil, and to show them that they have been dishonouring Christ by linking the name of the Man of Sorrows (and such He **was,** when on earth) with a "**merry** Christmas", then join with the writer in a repentant confessing of this sin to God, seeking His grace for complete deliverance from it, and praise Him for the light which He has granted you concerning it.

Beloved fellow-Christian, "The coming of the Lord draweth nigh" (Jas. 5:8). Do we really believe this? Believe it not because Mussolini is dictator of Italy, or because the Papacy is regaining its lost temporal power, but because **God** says so— "for we walk by faith, and **not** by sight" (2 Cor. 5:7). If so, what effect does such believing have upon our walk? This **may be** your last Christmas on this earth. During it the Lord Himself may descend from heaven with a shout to gather His own unto Himself. Would you like to be summoned from a "Christmas party" to meet Him in the air? The call for the moment is, "Go ye **out** to meet Him" (Matt. 25:6): out from a Godless Christendom, out from the Christ-deserted "churches", out from the horrible burlesque of "religion" which now masquerades under His name.

"For we must all appear before the judgment-seat of Christ; that every one may receive the things done in the body, according to that he hath done, whether good or bad" (2 Cor. 5:10). How solemn and searching! The Lord Jesus declared that "every idle word that men shall speak, they shall give account thereof in the day of judgment" (Matt. 12:36). If every "idle word" is going to be taken note of, then most assuredly will be every wasted energy, every wasted dollar, every wasted hour! Should we still be on earth when the closing days of this year arrive, let writer and reader earnestly seek grace to live and act with the judgment-seat of Christ before us. **His** "well done" will be ample compensation for the sneers and taunts which we may now receive from Christless souls.

Does any Christian reader imagine for a moment that when he or she shall stand before their holy Lord, that they will then regret having lived "too strictly" on earth? Is there the slightest danger of **Him** reproving any of His own because they were "too extreme" in "abstaining from fleshly lusts, which war against the soul"? (1 Peter 2:11). We may gain the good-will and good-word of worldly religionists to-day by our compromisings on "little (?) points", but shall we receive **His** smile of approval in that Day? O to be more concerned of what **He** thinks, and less concerned about what perishing mortals think.

"Thou shalt not follow a multitude to do evil" (Ex. 23:2). Ah, it is an easy thing to float with the tide of popular opinion; but it takes much grace, diligently sought from God, to swim against it. Yet that is what the heir of Heaven is called on to do: to "Be not conformed to this world" (Rom. 12:2), to deny self, take up the cross, and follow a rejected Christ. How sorely does both writer and reader need to heed that word of the Saviour's, "Behold, I come quickly: hold that fast which thou hast, that no man take thy crown" (Rev. 3:11). O that each of us may be able to truthfully say, "I have refrained my feet from **every** evil way, that I might keep **Thy Word**" (Psa. 110:101).

Our final word is to the Pastors to a goodly number of whom this little magazine is being sent. To you the Word of the Lord is, "Be thou **an example** of believers, in word, in deportment, in love, in spirit, in faith, in purity" (1 Tim. 4:12). Is it not true that the most corrupt "churches" you know of, where almost every fundamental of the faith is denied, will have their "Christmas celebrations"? Will you imitate them? Are you consistant to protest against unscriptural methods of "raising money", and then to sanction unscriptural "Christmas services"? Seek grace to firmly but lovingly set God's Truth on this subject before your people, and announce that you can have no part in following Pagan, Romish, and Worldly customs.

—ARTHUR W. PINK.

N. B. The following extract is from the late C. H. Spurgeon's exposition on Psa. 81 in the Treasury of David. "'Blow ye the trumpet in the new moon, in the **time appointed**, on our solemn feast day' (v. 3). Obedience is to direct our worship, not whim and sentiment: God's appointment gives a solemnity to rites and times which no ceremonial pomp or hierarchial ordinance could confer. The Jews not only observed the ordained month, but that part of the month which had been Divinely set apart. The Lord's people in the olden time welcomed the times appointed for worship; let us feel the same exultation, and never speak of the Sabbath as though it could be other than a 'delight' and 'honourable'. Those who plead this passage as an authority for their man-appointed feasts and fasts must be moonstruck. We will keep such feasts as **the Lord** appoints, but not those which Rome or Canterbury may ordain.

'For this was a statute for Israel, and a law of the God of Jacob' (v. 4). It was a precept binding upon all the tribes that a sacred season should be set apart to commemorate the Lord's mercy, and truly it was but the Lord's due. He had a right and a claim to such special homage. When it can be proved that the observance of Christmas, Whitsuntide and other Popish festivals were ever instituted by a Divine statute, we also will attend to them, **but not till** then. It is as much our duty to reject the traditions of men as to observe the ordinances of the Lord".

God's love plighted in the everlasting covenant, but they are parts of the administration of the same. God is not only faithful notwithstanding afflictions, but faithful in sending them. Then will I visit their transgression with the rod, and their iniquity with stripes: My loving kindness will I not utterly take from him nor suffer My faithfulness to fail" (Psa. 89:32, 33). Chastening is not only reconcilable with God's loving kindness, but it is the effect and expression of it. It would much quieten the minds of God's people if they would remember that His covenant love binds Him to lay on them seasonable correction. Afflictions are necessary for us: "In their affliction they will seek Me early" (Hos. 5:15).

God is faithful in **glorifying** His people. "Faithful is He which calleth you, who also will do" (1 Thess. 5:24). The immediate reference here is to the saints being "preserved blameless unto the coming of our Lord Jesus Christ". God treats with us not on the ground of our merits (for we have none), but for His own great name's sake. God is constant to Himself and to His own purpose of grace "whom He called ... them He also glorified" (Rom. 8:30). God gives a full demonstration of the constancy of His everlasting goodness toward His elect by effectually calling them out of darkness into His marvelous light, and this should fully assure them of the certain continuance of it. "The foundation of God **standeth sure**" (2 Tim. 2:19). Paul was resting on the faithfulness of God when he said, "I know whom I have believed, and am persuaded that He is able to keep that which I have committed unto Him against that day" (2 Tim. 1:12).

The apprehension of this blessed truth will **preserve us from worry**. To be full of care, to view our situation with dark forebodings, to anticipate the morrow with sad anxiety, is to reflect upon the faithfulness of God. He who has cared for His child through all the years, will not forsake him in old age. He who has heard your prayers in the past, will not refuse to supply your need in the present emergency. Rest on Job 5:19, "He **shall** deliver thee in six troubles; yea, in seven there shall no evil touch thee".

The apprehension of this blessed truth will **check our murmurings**. The Lord knows what is best for each one of us, and one effect of resting on this truth will be the silencing of our petulant complainings. God is greatly honoured when, under trial and chastening, we have good thoughts of Him, vindicate His wisdom and justice, and recognise His love in His very rebukes.

The apprehension of this blessed truth will beget increasing **confidence in God**. "Wherefore let them that suffer according to the will of God commit the keeping of their souls to Him in well doing, as unto a faithful Creator" (1 Peter 4:19). When we trustfully resign ourselves and all our affairs into God's hands, fully persuaded of His love and faithfulness, the sooner shall we be satisfied with His providences and realise that "He doeth **all** things well".—ARTHUR W. PINK.

DANGER!

"Watch and pray that ye enter not into temptation" (Matt. 26:41). This exhortation of our Saviour's is utterly ignored by those who go to hear preachers and teachers of error. No matter how strong the spirit of curiosity may be in us, no matter how urgent the persuasive pleas of friends to accompany them, we cannot count upon God preserving us if we deliberately expose ourselves to what is contrary to His Word. Satan may tell us that **we** are too well established in the faith to be in any danger of injury, but Christ says, "**Take heed** what ye hear" (Mark 4:24). And again, God says, "Cease, My son, to hear the instruction that causeth to err from the words of knowledge" (Prov. 19:27). It is at our imminent peril that we disregard these plain warnings. Peter was self-confident and imagined he needed not this faithful word. "Watch and pray lest ye enter into temptation", but the sequel proved he had been spared a fearful fall if he heeded it. Remember Peter, then!

The above has been suggested to our mind from reading the following words of J. Owen, written about 1680: "How many professors have I known that would plead for their liberty, as they called it. They could hear anything, all sorts of men; they would try all things, whether they come to them in the way of God or no; and on that account would run to hear every broacher of false opinions; every seducer, though stigmatized by the generality of the saints. I scarce ever knew any come off without a wound; the most have had their faith overthrown; let no man then pretend to fear sin, that doth not fear temptation to it. They are too nearly alike to be separated".
—A. W. P.

the faithfulness of God as a Divine truth, it is quite another to **act upon it**. God has given us many "exceeding great and precious promises", but are we really counting on His fulfilment of them? Are we actually **expecting** Him to do for us all that He has said? Are we resting with implicit assurance on these words, "He is **faithful** that promised" (Heb. 10:23)?

There are seasons in the lives of all when it is not easy, no not even for Christians, to believe that God **is** faithful. Our faith is sorely tried, our eyes bedimmed with tears, and we can no longer trace the outworkings of His love. Our ears are distracted with the noises of the world, harassed by the atheistic whisperings of Satan, and we can no longer hear the sweet accents of His still small voice. Cherished plans have been thwarted, friends on whom we relied have failed us, a profest brother or sister in Christ has betrayed us. We are staggered. We sought to be faithful to God, and now a dark cloud hides Him from us. We find it difficult, yea, impossible, for carnal reason to harmonise His frowning providence with His gracious promises. Ah, faltering soul, severely-tried fellow-pilgrim, seek grace to heed Isa. 50:10, "Who is among you that feareth the Lord, that obeyeth the voice of His servant, that walketh in darkness and hath no light? let him trust in the name of the Lord, and **stay upon his God**".

When you are tempted to doubt the faithfulness of God cry out, "Get thee hence, Satan". Though you cannot now harmonise God's mysterious dealings with the avowals of His love, wait on Him for more light. In His own good time He will make it plain to you. "What I do thou knowest not **now**, but thou shalt know hereafter" (John 13:7). The sequel will yet demonstrate that God has neither forsaken nor deceived His child. "And therefore will the Lord **wait** that He may be gracious unto you, and therefore will He be exalted, that He may have mercy upon you: for the Lord is a God of judgment: blessed are all they **that wait for Him**" (Isa. 30:18).

"Judge not the Lord by feeble sense,
But trust Him for His grace,
Behind a frowning providence
He hides a smiling face.
Ye fearful saints, fresh courage take,
The clouds ye so much dread,
Are rich with mercy, and shall break
In blessing o'er your head".

"Thy testimonies which Thou hast commanded are righteous and very faithful" (Psa. 119:138). God has not only told us the best, but He has not withheld the worst. He has faithfully described the ruin which the Fall has effected. He faithfully diagnosed the terrible state which sin has produced. He has faithfully made known His inveterate hatred of evil, and that He must punish the same. He has faithfully warned us that He is "a consuming fire" (Heb. 12:29). Not only does His Word abound in illustrations of His fidelity in fulfilling His promises, but it also records numerous examples of His faithfulness in making good His threatenings. Every stage of Israel's history exemplifies that solemn fact. So it was with individuals: Pharaoh, Korah, Achan and a host of others are so many proofs. And thus it will be with **you**, my reader: unless you have fled or do flee to Christ for refuge, the everlasting burning of the Lake of Fire will be your sure and certain portion. God **is** faithful.

God is faithful in **preserving** His people. "God is faithful, by whom ye are called unto the fellowship of His Son" (1 Cor. 1:9). In the previous verse promise was made that God would confirm unto the end His own people. The apostle's confidence in the absolute security of believers was founded not on the strength of their resolutions or ability to persevere, but on the veracity of Him that cannot lie. Since God has promised to His Son a certain people for His inheritance, to deliver them from sin and condemnation, and to become the participants of eternal life in glory, it is certain that He will not allow any of them to perish.

God is faithful in **disciplining** His people. He is faithful in what He withholds, no less than in what He gives. He is faithful in sending sorrow as well as in giving joy. The faithfulness of God is a truth to be confessed by us not only when we are at ease, but also when we are smarting under the sharpest rebuke. Nor must this confession be merely of our mouths, but of our hearts too. When God smites us with the rod of chastisement, it is **faithfulness** which wields it. To acknowledge this means that we humble ourselves before Him, own that we fully deserve His correction, and instead of murmuring, thank Him for it. God never afflicts without a reason: "For **this cause** many are weak and sickly among you" (1 Cor. 11:30), illustrates this principle. When His rod falls on us let us say with Daniel, "O Lord, righteousness belongeth unto Thee, but unto us confusion of faces" (9:7).

"I know, O Lord, that Thy judgments are right, and that Thou **in faithfulness** hast afflicted me" (Psa. 119:75). Trouble and affliction are not only consistant with

(Continued on Page 239)

Vol. IX.   NOVEMBER, 1930   No. 11

STUDIES IN THE SCRIPTURES

"Search the Scriptures" John 5 : 39

Copyright in all English-speaking Countries.

Editor: Arthur W. Pink, 1339 Bates Ave., Los Angeles, Calif, U. S. A.
Hon. Agent in England: Mr. A. Winstone, "Shalom", Old Bath Road, Leckhampton, Cheltenham.
Hon. Agent in Australia: Mr. G. Ardill, The Christian Workers' Depot. Commonwealth and Reservoir Streets, Sydney.

THE GOODNESS OF GOD.

"The goodness of God endureth continually" (Psa. 52:1). The "goodness" of God respects the perfection of His nature: "God is light, and in Him is **no** darkness at all" (1 John 1:5). There is such an absolute perfection in God's nature and being that nothing is wanting to it or defective in it, and nothing can be added to it to make it better. "He is originally good, good of Himself, which nothing else is; for all creatures are good only by participation and communication from God. He is essentially good; not only good, but goodness itself: the creature's good is a superadded quality, in God it is His essence. He is infinitely good; the creature's good is but a drop, but in God there is an infinite ocean or gathering together of good. He is eternally and immutably good, for He cannot be less good than He is; as there can be no addition made to Him, so to subtraction from Him" (Thos. Manton). God is summum bonum, the chiefest good.

The original Saxon meaning of our English word "God" is "The Good." God is not only the Greatest of all beings, but the Best. All the goodness there is in any creature has been imparted from the Creator, but God's goodness is underived, for it is the essence of His eternal nature. As God was infinite in power from all eternity, before there was any display thereof, or any act of omnipotency put forth; so He was eternally good before there was any communication of His bounty, or any creature to whom it might be imparted or exercised. Thus, the first manifestation of this Divine perfection was in giving being to all things. "Thou art good, and **doest** good" (Psa. 119:68). God has in Himself an infinite and inexhaustible treasure of all blessedness enough to fill all things.

All that eminates from God—His decrees, His creation, His laws, His providences—cannot be otherwise than good: as it is written, "And God saw everything that He had made, and, behold, it was **very good**" (Gen. 1:31). Thus, the "goodness" of God is **seen**, first, in creation. The more closely the creature is studied, the more the beneficence of its Creator becomes apparent. Take the highest of God's earthly creatures, man. Abundant reason has he to say with the Psalmist, "I will praise Thee, for I am fearfully and wonderfully made: marvelous are Thy works, and that my soul knoweth right well" (139:14). Everything about the structure of our bodies attests the goodness of their Maker. How suited the hands to perform their allotted work! How good of the Lord to appoint sleep to refresh the wearied body! How benevolent His provision to give unto the eyes lids and brows for their protection! And so we might continue indefinitely.

Nor is the goodness of the Creator confined to man, it is exercised toward all His creatures. "The eyes of all wait upon Thee; and Thou givest them their meat in due season. Thou openest Thine hand, and satisfiest the desire of every living thing" (Psa. 145:15, 16). Whole volumes might be written, yea have been, to amplify this fact. Whether it be the birds of the air, the beasts of the forest, or the fish in the sea, abundant provision has been made to supply their every need. God "giveth food to all flesh, for His mercy endureth forever" (Psa. 136:25). Truly, "The earth is full of the goodness of the Lord" (Psa. 33:5).

The goodness of God is seen in the variety of natural pleasures which He has provided for His creatures. God might have been pleased to satisfy our hunger without the food being pleasing to our palates—how His benevolence appears in the varied flavours which He has given to meats, vegetables, and fruits! God has

(Continued on Page 264)

IMPORTANT NOTICES

Please advise promptly of change of address, otherwise copies will be lost in the mails.

We are glad to send a sample copy to any of your friends whom you believe would be interested in such a publication.

Send to Mr. I. C. Herendeen, Swengel (Union County), Penna., for a list of our publications. He has published many of our books and booklets.

This magazine is published as a work of faith and labour of love. The Editor and his wife gladly give their services. It is freely sent to all who will read it. No charge is made for it.

Christians who feel definitely led to do so, may have fellowship with us in this ministry. Those outside the U. S. A., please send only INTERNATIONAL Money Orders made out to Los Angeles, California, U. S. A.

CONTENTS

The Epistle to the Hebrews	242
The Satisfaction of Christ	248
The Intercession of Christ	254
The Radio	259
The Supremacy of God	260
A Mighty Saviour	263

THE EPISTLE TO THE HEBREWS

35. The perfect Priest: Heb. 7:25-28.

The principal subject in the verses which are to be before us is the same as that which has engaged the apostle throughout this 7th. chapter, namely, the pre-eminent excellency of the great High Priest of Christianity. That which he is setting forth is the superiority of our Lord's High Priesthood over that of the Levitical. The various proofs may be expressed thus. First, because Christ is called of God after the order of Melchizedek, 5:10. In enlarging upon that fact, here in chapter 7, the apostle did three things: evidenced the superiority of Melchizedek over the order of Aaron. 7:1-10; appealed to the Messianic prediction of Psa. 110:4 in proof that Christ **had been** called after the order of Melchizedek; showed that the fulfillment of this prophecy necessarily involved the setting aside of the Levitical order.

The second proof of the superiority of Christ's Priesthood over the Aaronic order was, the distinguishing solemnity of its institution, namely, by the Divine oath, 7:20-22. Third, it was proved by the perpetual permanency of His Priesthood, 7:23, 24. Fourth, it is proved by the saving efficacy of His priestly work, 7:25. Fifth, it is proved by the personal qualifications which He possesses to serve as Priest, 7:26-28. Sixth, it is proved by the Heavenly Sanctuary in which He now ministers, 8:1-5. Seventh, it is proved by the New Covenant with which it is connected, 8:6-13.

Or again, we may view the contents of Heb. 7 as a setting forth of the **results** from God's having brought in Christ as Priest after the order of Melchizedek. First, it necessarily follows that the Levitical order of priesthood has been abrogated, for that order could not possibly consist side by side with His, v. 11. Second, in consequence of this change of priesthood, the whole Mosaic ritual has been repealed, v. 12. The reason of this is obvious, the entire ceremonial law presupposed the Aaronic priesthood, to which it was adapted and on which it was based—remove the foundation and the whole structure falls. Third, the introduction of Christ as Priest ushered in an entirely new and immeasurably better economy, vv. 19-24. Finally, the providing of such a great High Priest infallibly secures the salvation of all God's people, vv. 25-28.

In the closing verses of our chapter the apostle brings the whole preceding discourse unto an issue, by making application of it unto the faith and comfort of the Church. His object was not only to open-up mysterious Old Testament Scriptures, nor only to demonstrate the glory and pre-eminence of Christianity over Judaism, by virtue of the priesthood of Christ; but his chief design was to make evident the efficacy and eternal advantages of all true believers by these things. The climax to which he had been leading up is before us in v. 25, which he enlarges upon in the end of the chapter. That which Christians ought to seek and what they should expect from the blessed and glorious priesthood of Christ is what he now undertakes to make known. In like manner, in all his epistles the apostle makes it clear that the purpose of God in the whole mystery of redemption by Jesus Christ and the institutions of the Gospel, is the salvation of His elect unto the praise of the glory of His grace.

"Wherefore He is able also to save them

to the uttermost that come unto God by Him, seeing He ever liveth to make intercession for them" (v. 25). First, let us endeavour to ponder this inexpressibly precious word in the light of its context. The opening "Wherefore" denotes that an inference is here drawn from that which had previously been said. What then is the premise, or what are the premises, on which this conclusion rests? Or, in plainer language, **Why** is it that Christ is here said to be able to "save unto the uttermost"? "Wherefore"—because of the oath of His consecration (v. 20), because of the immutability of the Father's purpose (He "will not repent") v. 21, because of the better covenant of which He is "Surety" (v. 22), and because He "continueth ever" an unchanging Priest (v. 24)—"He is able also to save them unto the uttermost". This, we take it, is the connection between v. 25 and its context.

From the consideration of the glorious truth and office of Christ as Priest, the apostle, to strengthen the faith and increase the consolation of God's people, points out the infallible corollary: "He is able". All power is His, abundant sufficiency of ability to accomplish His design of grace. This is the second time we are reminded of the capability of our High Priest. First, in 2:18 it was said, "For in that He Himself hath suffered being tempted, He is able to succor them that are tempted", and see our comments thereon. That which is particularly in view is not the ability of His nature, but of his office. It is still the pre-eminency of Christ above the legal high priests which is chiefly intended. By reason of their personal infirmities and the limited tenure of their office, they were unable to effect that which those desiring to approach unto God most stood in need of. But our great High Priest, being free from all such imperfections, "is able". Because His priesthood is indissoluable and perpetual, His office is all-sufficient to meet every need of God's people.

"Wherefore He is able also to save them to the uttermost". It is no mere temporal or transcient deliverance which Christ effects for His people, but a supernatural, spiritual and eternal one. The word "save" denotes some evil and danger from which deliverance is secured. This is sin, with all its terrible consequences—pollution, guilt, the curse of the law, the captivity of Satan, the wrath to come. Wherefore it is written of Christ that He saves His people "from their sins" (Matt. 1:21), "from the curse" (Gal. 3:13), "from the wrath to come" (1 Thess. 1:10). "He is **able** also to save". It was no easy matter to subdue Satan, fulfill the law, take away sin, placate God, procure pardon, purchase grace and glory, with all that belongs unto God's great salvation. But God "laid help upon One that is mighty" (Psa. 89:19), and He who hath undertaken this work is able to accomplish it, and that by the means He hath designed to use and the way wherein He will proceed.

Now the way in which He has designed to save His people, is by the discharge of Christ's priestly office. God has appointed no other means to that end. We must look for it therein, or go without it. Alas, multitudes are like those sons of Belial who said of Saul when God had anointed him king, "how shall this man save us, and despised him" (1 Sam. 10:21). They understand not (nor do they desire to know) **how** Christ is able to save sinners by His priestly work, and therefore, under various pretences, they trust to themselves, and despise Him. "All false religion is but a choice of other things for men to place their trust in with a neglect of Christ. And all superstition, instances of it, be they great or small" (John Owen).

"Wherefore He is able also to save unto the uttermost". The last word here may have a double sense: it may respect either the perfection of the work, or its duration, so it is variously rendered, completely and entirely or forevermore and forever. Take its first meaning: Christ will not effect part of our salvation and then leave what remains to ourselves or to others. "He does not relinquish it by reason of death, but He lives on as long as it is necessary that anything should be done for the salvation of His people (A. Barnes). Consider its second meaning: whatever hindrances and difficulties lie in the way of the salvation of believers, the Lord Jesus is fully competent, by virtue of the exercise of His priestly office, to carry out the work for them unto eternal perfection. No matter what oppositions may arise, He is more than sufficient to cope with and overcome them all. Combining the two meanings: a complete salvation is a never-ending one.

"Them that come unto God by Him". This clause defines who are the partakers of His salvation. Christ is able to save unto the uttermost, yet all are not saved by Him, yea, they are few indeed that are saved. Multitudes hear of Him, but, loving more the things of time and sense, refusing to forsake all and follow Him, they "will not come" to Him that they "might have life" (John 5:40). Only those who come unto God by Him, does He save. To come to God means, first, to believe on Him (Heb. 11:6); second, to draw nigh to Him in worship (10:1, 22). It is the latter sense which is here principally in view, for the apostle is speaking of the state of the Church under the new covenant, and its advantage over that of Judaism, by virtue of its relation unto the priesthood of Christ. "They that come unto God by Christ are such, as believing in Him, do give up themselves in holy obedience to worship God in and by Him" (John Owen).

To come unto God by Jesus Christ is holy worship. So as to be therein interested in His saving power as the High Priest of His people is to come, first, in **obedience** unto His authority, as to the way or manner of it. There must be a bowing to His sceptre and a practical owning of His lordship, otherwise we are rebels and idolators, not worshippers. Second, with **reliance** upon His meditation as to the acceptance of it, counting on the sufficiency of His sacrifice to atone for our sins and His intercession to procure the acceptance of our persons and offerings. Third, with **faith** in His person as the foundation of it; so to believe in Him as vested with His holy office that the discharge of it **will** save even to the uttermost them that come unto God by Him. Unless we are true believers, our worship will not be accepted.

First, the quickened sinner comes to Christ, is **drawn** to Him by the Father (John 6:44), and through Christ he comes unto God; cf. 1 Peter 3:18. In His priestly office Christ saves from sin unto God. His righteousness carries them beyond Himself as Mediator unto God Himself: cf. Heb. 10:22. Thus "coming to God" is the fruit and consequence of "coming to Christ". God is a just and holy God, yet may the believing sinner, in and through Christ, have communion with Him. Suppose I am under an awakening sense of the terrible majesty and consuming holiness of God: I tremble, and dare not approach unto Him—alas, where are they these days who ever have such an experience? But, later, the Holy Spirit takes of the things of Christ and shows them unto me—His compassion for sinners, His mediatory office, His all-sufficient love: then my fears are silenced, and I draw near unto God praising Him for His unspeakable gift. Nor does Christ's "ability" to save depend upon my coming to Him, rather does it lie in His power to overcome the reluctance of "His own"

and incline them **to** come: see John 17:20.

"Seeing that He ever liveth to make intercession for them". These words express the reason why Christ is able to effectually save His people: that which secures them is His perpetual life—"He ever liveth"; His perpetual work—"to make intercession". This is what gives efficacy to priesthood of Christ. The Lord Jesus lives a mediatorial life in Heaven for His people: as He died for them, so He lives **for them**, and therefore does He assure them "because I live, ye shall live also" (John 14:19). Comparatively few today either understand or appreciate this blessed fact. That Christ died for them, all who assent to the Gospel profess to believe; but that there is an equally vital necessity for Him to now live for and make intercession for them, is something which they perceive not. Nevertheless, Scripture is clear on this point: "If Christ be not raised, your faith is vain; ye are yet in your sins" (1 Cor. 15:17).

"There are many Christians who dwell on the crucifixion of Jesus in a one-sided way. We cannot dwell too much on the glorious truth that Jesus Christ was crucified for our sins. Yet it is not on the crucifixion, but on Christ the Lord, that our faith rests; and not on Christ as He was on the cross do we dwell, but on Christ who was dead and is risen again, and liveth at the right hand of God, making intercession for us. . . . When Jesus died upon the cross He put away our sins, but this was only removing an obstacle. The ultimate object of His death upon the cross was His resurrection and ascension, that through suffering He should enter into glory, that He should be the perfect Mediator between God and man, presenting us unto God and bestowing upon us all the blessings which He has purchased for us with His precious blood. He has obtained eternal redemption on the cross, He **applies** the blessings of eternal redemption from the holy of holies. If Christ was not risen we should still be in our sins; and if such a thing were possible, though we might be forgiven, we should be dead and without the Spirit" (A. Saphir).

So stupenduous is the work of saving believers unto the uttermost, it is necessary for the Lord Jesus to live a mediatory life in heaven for the perfecting and accomplishing thereof. It is indeed generally acknowledged by professing Christians that sinners could not be saved without the death of Christ, but that believers could not be saved without the resurrection-ministry of Christ is not so freely owned or considered. Yet, Rom. 5:10 is very explicit on the point: "For if, when we were enemies we were reconciled to God by the death of His Son, **much more**, being reconciled, we shall be saved by His life". Let Rom. 8:33-35 also be duly weighed. It is one thing to recognise that, by the once offering of Himself, Christ has "obtained eternal redemption for us" (9:12), it is quite another to perceive that His intercession is required in order to the **fruits** of His oblation **being applied** to those for whom it was made.

It appears to many that, seeing Christ fulfilled all righteousness for His people, redeemed them by His blood, made full atonement for their sins, nothing more was needed. But had Christ left us to build our eternal safety on the foundation which He laid, had He ascended on High to enjoy His reward **without** continuing to exercise His priestly office on our behalf, had He merely secured our right and title unto the heavenly inheritance and left us to press forward to it unaided by Him, everyone of us would quickly fall a prey to the powerful adversaries which constantly seek our destruction. When God "laid the **foundations** of the earth", the "morning stars sang together, and all the sons of God (angels) shouted for joy" (Job 38:4, 7), yet were the **continued** actings of God's creative power required unto the perfection of the earth. So the foundation of the new creation was laid gloriously in the death and resurrection of Christ, causing triumphant praise unto God (Col. 2:15, 1 Tim. 3:16), yet that praise is founded upon the guarantee of Christ's unchanging love, care, and power, to complete the work He has undertaken.

Those for whom Christ died are not taken to Heaven the moment they believe, but are still left here in the Enemy's country; nor are they yet glorified, instead, the "flesh", with all its defiling influences, is still left within them. Therefore do they stand in urgent need of the priestly care of Christ, that, in answer to His intercession, God might send them His Spirit, grant them renewed supplies of grace, deliver them from their foes, keep them in communion with the Father, answer the accusations of Satan, preserve them unto the end of their earthly course, and, then receive them unto Himself and "present them faultless before the presence of His glory" (Jude 24). "Who can express the opposition that continues to be made unto this work of completing the salvation of believers? What power is able to conflict and conquor the remaining strength of sin, the opposition of Satan and the world? How innumerable are the temptations which every individual believer is exposed unto, each of them in its own nature pernicious and ruinous" (John Owen).

"The most glorious prospect that we can take into the things that are within the veil, into the remaining transactions of the work of our salvation in the most holy place, is in the representation that is made unto us of the intercession of Christ. Our High Priest has entered within the veil where no eye can pierce unto Him, yet is He there as High Priest, which makes Heaven itself to be a glorious temple. Herein we see Him by faith still vested with the office of the priesthood, and continuing with the discharge of it. Hence, in His appearance to John, He was clothed with a garment down to the foot and girded about the paps with a golden girdle; both of which were sacerdotal vestments, Rev. 1:13" (Condensed from John Owen).

"The intercession of Christ is the great evidence of the continuance of His love and care, His pity and compassion towards His Church. . . . But how shall we know that the Lord Christ is thus tender, loving, compassionate, that He continueth so to be; what evidence or testimony have we of it? It is true, He was eminently so when He was upon the earth in the days of His flesh, and when He laid down His life for us. We know not what changes may be wrought in nature itself, by its investiture with glory; nor how inconsistent those affections which in us cannot be separated from some weakness and sorrow, are with His present state and dignity. But herein we have an infallible demonstration of it, that He yet continueth in the exercise of that office, with respect thereunto all those affections of love, pity and compassion are ascribed unto Him" (John Owen).

"For such an High Priest became us-holy, harmless, undefiled, separate from sinners, and made higher than the heavens" (v. 26). In this verse the apostle shows that in order for sinners to come unto God, they have need of an High Priest to encourage and enable them so to do. Not only is a high priest necessary, but there must be one possessed of certain qualifications or excellencies, if ever we are to obtain access to the thrice Holy One. Such a Priest is here described; such a Priest "became us", was requisite for and suited to poor sinners.

None other could expiate our sins, purge our conscience from dead works, procure acceptance with God for us, purchase eternal redemption, administer supplies of grace enabling us to live unto God in all the duties of faith, obedience and worship, comforting us in trials, delivering from temptations, preserving us unto eternal glory.

The only high priest fitted to officiate before God on the behalf of desperately-wicked sinners was one who was "holy". That which is here in view is the absolute purity of Christ's **nature**. He was entirely free from the slightest spot or taint of our original defilement. Instead of being, as we were, "conceived in sin and shapen in iniquity", His humanity was "that **holy** thing" (Luke 1:35). His conception being miraculous, by the immediate operation of the Holy Spirit, and not derived to Him by natural generation, He was completely exempt from the pollutions which corrupts every one of Adam's descendants. He could say, "the prince of this world cometh, and hath nothing in Me" (John 14:30): there was nothing within Him to which the Evil one could make a successful appeal. And such an High Priest "became us". Had His nature been defiled, He had been disqualified either to be Priest or Sacrifice. This holiness of His nature was imperative in order to answer for the unholiness of our nature.

Second, He was "harmless". "Holy" tells of what Christ was Godwards: perfectly conformed to the Divine will inwardly, evidenced by His perfect outward conduct. "Harm'ess" tells of what He was manwards. He is the only one who has ever walked this earth who never contaminated, tempted, injured, those with whom He came into contact. As "holy", He loved the Lord His God with all His heart; as "harmless" He loved His neighbour as Himself. He lived not for self, but was ever at the disposal of others. He went about doing good. When reviled, He reviled not again. When ill-treated, He never retaliated. He was the Lamb in the midst of wolves. He was the Sun of righteousness with healing in His wings. How perfectly adapted was He, then, to serve as Priest and meet the exegiencies of His people!

Third, "undefiled". He not only entered this world "holy" and "harmless", but He was so when He left it. Tabernaciing for thirty-three years in a world under the curse, mingling daily with sinners, He contracted no defilement. Just as the rays of the sun may shine into the foulest stream without losing any of their purity, so Christ moved in and out amongst the vilest without the glory of His holiness being sullied in the slightest degree. Christ was "undefiled" morally, as the priests under the law were required to be ceremonially. He was never infected by the evils around Him. He touched the leper, and the leper was cleansed. He came into contact with death, and death was conquered. He was in the presence of the Devil for forty days, and was as spotless at the close as He was at the beginning of them.

Fourth, "separate from sinners". The position of this clause in our verse must govern its interpretation. It has a double force. It is intimately related to what precedes, as it is closely connected with the words immediately following. As it comes after the "holy, harmless, undefiled", it gives a summary of what Christ was in Himself, emphasising His uniqueness and demonstrating His fitness to officiate as Priest. **He** was the "Blessed" Man of the first Psalm: He walked not in the counsel of the ungodly, stood not in the way of sinners, sat not in the seat of scorners. He was the true Nazarite of Numbers 6. Though He lived amongst sinners, He was infinitely apart from them, in nature and character, motive and conduct. He was in the world, but **not** "of" it. Thus was He qualified to act as Mediator between God and sinners.

"Separate from sinners". As this clause prepares the way for "made higher than the heavens", it stands in sharp antithesis from "He was numbered with transgressors". On the cross, we behold Him in the place of sinners, but He occupies that place no longer. Death is for ever behind Him. He is now, in the absolute sense, "separate from sinners", that is, distinguished from those for whom He is interceeding. He has been removed from their society unto another sphere. Thus, this clause points another contrast from the high priest under the law. Aaron offered atonement for sinners, and continued amongst them afterwards. Not so Christ.

"Made higher than the heavens". This refers to the present place and state of our great High Priest. "He was for a season made lower than the angels, and descended into the lower parts of the earth, and that, for the discharge of the principal part of His priestly office, namely, the offering of Himself for a sacrifice unto God. But He abode not in that state, nor would He discharge His whole office, and all the duties of it, therein. And therefore He was made higher than the heavens. He was not made higher than the heavens, that He might be a Priest; but **being** our High Priest, and **as** our High Priest, He was so made, for the discharge of that part of His office which yet remained to be perfected; for He was to live forever to make intercession for us" (John Owen).

"Absolute perfection of character is not the only requisite in a high priest suited to our circumstances; he must be possessed also of dignified station, or high authority, of unlimited power. He must be one 'made higher than the heavens'. The phrase is peculiar. It nowhere else occurs in Scripture; but its meaning is obvious enough. He must occupy a place of the highest honour and power. And He must be '**made** higher than the heavens'. Those words plainly imply that His elevation above the heavens is something conferred on Him. It intimates that our High Priest must be beneath the heavens in order to the discharge of some of the functions of His office, and that in consequence of the successful discharge of of them, He must be exalted far above all heavens, for the discharge of other functions, and for gaining the grand object, the ultimate end, of His office" (John Brown).

"Jesus went into the holy of holies, which was typified in the tabernacle. Above all created heavens, above angels and principalities, Jesus is now in the true Sanctuary, in the presence of God, and there He is enthroned as our perfect High Priest. His position in Heaven demonstrates that when He offered up Himself He put away sin forever, even as it sets forth His divine glory. For who but the Son of God can sit at the right hand of the Majesty on High? As it is written, 'Be Thou exalted, O God, above the heavens' (Psa. 57:5)" (A Saphir). "**Made** higher than the heavens" by God: this proves that complete expiation has already been made. It emphasises the fact that Christ has entered the Heavenly Sanctuary on our behalf: see 4:14, 8:1, 2, 9:24 and Eph. 1:20-23. It announces that He has been exalted above every order of created things. It makes known how immeasurably superior is our High Priest over Aaron.

Ere passing from this verse let us take to heart its searching practical application. The perfections of our High Priest are what we ought to be conformable to. "If we give up ourselves to the conduct of this High Priest, if by Him alone we design to approach unto God, then conformity unto Him in holiness of nature and life, according to our measure, is indispensibly required of us. None can more dishonour the Lord Christ, no more perniciously deceive and betray their own souls, than by professing Him to be **their** Priest, with their trust thereby to be saved by Him, and yet **not endeavour to be** holy, harmless, undefiled, separate from sinners, like unto Him" (John Owen).

"Who needeth not daily, as those high priests, to offer up sacrifice (first for his own sins, and then for the people's:) for this He did once, when He offered Himself" (v. 27). Let the reader note carefully our punctuation of this verse: by placing the central clause in a parenthesis (as it obviously should be) we are relieved of a difficulty which has baffled most of the commentators. In this and the next verse the apostle names other instances in which our High Priest is preeminent over those of the order of Aaron. His perfections, described in v. 26, exempted Him from all the infirmities of the Levitical priests, which disqualified them from making personal atonement. The design of the apostle is to show that Christ was infinitely well-pleasing unto God, and because He was under no necessity to sacrifice for Himself, the offering which He made for His people is of eternal validity. "This he did **once**" announces there is no need of any further repetition.

The apostle is still contrasting Christ from the Levitical high priests. How could they pacify the declarative holiness of God which had been outraged by others, when God was justly displeased with them for their own sins? They were obliged to offer "daily" from time to time, "day by day" or again and again, by periodical repetition, for their own sins—cf. "from year to year" (10:1), and note that the Heb. of Ex. 13:10 "from year to year" is, literally, "days to days". Not only did the legal high priest have to sacrifice for his own sins, the offering which he presented on behalf of the people had no abiding efficacy, but had to be repeated annually. Whereas Christ, being perfect, needed no sacrifice for Himself; and His offering being perfect, there is no need for any further one. Christ's sacrifice abides "a new and living" one (10:20).

"For the law maketh men high priests which have infirmity; but the word of the oath which was since the law, maketh the Son, who is perfected forevermore" (v. 28). In this verse the apostle sums up the whole of His preceding discourse, evidencing the true foundation on which he had built. Those who still adhered to the Mosaic institutions allowed that there must be a priest over God's people, for without such there could be no approach unto Him. So it was under the law, and if the same order be not continued, then the Church must needs be under a great disadvantage. As Owen rightly said, "To lose the high priest of our religion, is to lose the Sun out of the firmament of the Church."

Now the apostle has granted that the high priests who officiated in the tabernacle and temple were appointed by God to that office. His opponents were persuaded that these priests would continue in the church without change or alteration. God had designed a time when they were to be removed, and a Priest of another order introduced in their room. This change, so far from being regretable, was to the great advantage, safety, blessedness, glory of the Church. First, the Levitical priests were appointed under, by "the law"; but the new and perfect Priest "**since** the law" (i. e. in Psa. 110:4), showing Christ had superceded them. Second, they were but "men"; Christ was the "Son of God".

Third, they were "made" by "the law"; Christ by "the word of the oath". Fourth, they had "infirmity"; the Son had none. Fifth, they served only in their day and generation; He "for evermore".

"But the word of the oath, which was since the law. maketh the Son, who is perfected for evermore". "The apostle turns again, in a most emphatic and conclusive manner, unto the key-note which he had struck at the beginning of the epistle. The law of Moses constitutes priests that were changing continually. But the Word which came with the oath after the law, consecrated forevermore as High Priest Him who is the **Son**: compare the same emphasis on 'Son' in 1:1, 2. Only the Son could be the High Priest, and He **became** the High Priest. Through His incarnation, through all the experiences of His life of sorrow and of faith, through His death on the cross, through His resurrection and ascension, Jesus is perfected for evermore" (A. Saphir). Chirst abides perpetually in His priestly office because of the validity of His perfect Sacrifice. Hallelujah

—ARTHUR W. PINK.

THE SATISFACTION
("Atonement")
OF CHRIST

II. Its Application

"If the righteous scarcely (literally "with difficulty") be saved where shall the ungodly and the sinner appear?" (1 Peter 4:18). It seems that comparatively few of the Lord's people have an adequate conception of the obstacles in the way of their salvation, of all that is involved in God's overcoming of them, and of the manner in which His salvation becomes theirs. Rightly did John Owen affirm, "So great and glorious is the work of saving believers unto the utmost, that it is necessary that the Lord Christ should lead a mediatory life in heaven, for the perfecting and accomplishment of it". Yet how few today recognize the needs-be for this. There has been such a one-sided emphasis laid upon the death of Christ, that the relation of His resurrection, ascension, and intercession to the **salvation** of His people is now little understood even in orthodox circles.

If it were more clearly grasped that the redemptive work of Christ is a strictly **priestly** one, and if His **priestly** work were interpreted in the light of the Old Testament types we should experience less difficulty in perceiving the necessity, the meaning, and the value of His present intercession on High. At the cross Christ offered Himself to God, in all the merits of His life of perfect obedience, as a Satisfaction for His failing people. But what Christ did for His people, and their actual entering into the good of what He did for them, are two totally different things. That which He **purchased** for them, has to be **applied** to them. It is at this point that so much confusion exists in the minds of many. God has left nothing uncertain, nor is anything contingent on the creature. Full provision was made by the wisdom of God for securing the results or fruitage of His Son's work: "He **shall** see of the travail of His soul and be **satisfied**" (Isa. 53:11) guarantees this. It is by the present ministry of Christ on High and by the operations of His Spirit on earth that this is attained. The first of these will now engage our attention.

The offices of Christ, the great Mediator between God and men, are the foundation of our hopes and the springs of our peace and joy; His priestly office particularly so. The exercise of His priestly office concerns two principal parts: His making full satisfaction to God by dying for His people, and His intercession at the right hand of God. "To offer and to intercede, to sacrifice and to pray, are both acts of the same sacerdotal office, and both required of him who is high priest, so that if he omit either of these, he cannot be a faithful **priest** for them; if either he doth not offer for them, or not intercede for the access of his oblation on their behalf, he is wanting in the discharge of this office by him undertaken" (John Owen). To which we may add that the **third** act of the high priest is his coming forth to "bless" those for whom he has offered an atonement: Lev. 9:22, 1 Chron. 23:13, Heb. 9:28.

But, as we have said above, through a one-sided conception of the death of Christ many fail to see the need for His present intercession as being requisite to their **salvation**. Their difficulty may be expressed thus: If our salvation was secured by the "one offering" of Christ, why must He now intercede for us? On the other hand, if our salvation "unto the uttermost" (Heb. 7:25) be obtained by Christ's intercession, what need was there for His atonement? We will answer in the words of H. Martyn, "**Apparently** they mutually exclude each other, because they do **really** mutually and reciprocally **include** each other. The offering by which alone we are perfected is not passive endurance or suffering of the cross, but that **active** priestly offering of the cross which is prolonged without suffering into the function of intercession. And the Intercession, by which alone we are saved even unto the uttermost, is just the **perpetual presentation** of the 'continual burnt offering' of Calvary, which, as an active **offering**, subsists in perpetuity, and belongs to eternity, while the **suffering** of the cross belongs to the history of the past, and the Atonement, had it been mere suffering would have belonged to the past too".

The last-made quotation places the emphasis where it rightfully belongs. Had the Satisfaction of Christ consisted merely of His passively enduring the wrath of God, then everything required of Him as Mediator had been accomplished when He died. But in such case the "much more" of Rom. 5:10 and the "yea rather" of Rom. 8:34 had been rendered nugatory. Moreover, the sacrificial types of the Old Testament had been emptied of their meaning. Yea, the whole plan devised by God for the glorifying of Himself and the saving of His elect had been thrown into confusion. But allow that the Satisfaction of Christ is a **priestly** work, in which He is **active** throughout, and these difficulties are at once removed, for the types and the exposition of them in the epistle to the Hebrews show plainly enough that the work of atonement is not, in all respects, completed at the death of the victim. The intercession of Christ is just as requisite, just as vitally necessary, in order to save His people, as were His incarnation, obedience, and death.

In support of what has just been said, we would call careful attention to one or two of the details found in Lev. 16, where we have the fullest Old Testament type of Christ's high priestly office and work. As we hope to devote a separate article to the subject, in a later one of this series, we shall now confine ourselves to that which bears immediately upon the present aspect of our theme. First, in v. 11 we read of Aaron **killing** the bullock for a sin-offering, then, in v. 14, of his taking its blood within the veil and **sprinkling** it upon the mercyseat. In like manner, in v. 15 we find the goat treated in the same way; something more than its blood being shed at the altar, namely brought within the veil. The antitype of this is found in Heb. 9:12, where we read of Christ, entering heaven "by His own blood", and in 9:24, where we are told that He has gone there "to appear in the presence of God for us".

Again, "The two altars of Sacrifice and of Incense were combined and corrrelative instruments of official action to the priest in the one complete office of his priesthood; and they constituted component and indispensable factors of one complete act of sacrificial worship. The same functionary or officebearer transacted at both: he transacted for the self-same person or persons, the blood of the self-same sacrifice that he had slain and offered on the altar, he sprinkled or put upon the horns of the other. To dislocate or derange this co-ordination would be to negative his official action in its intrinsic import, to annihilate the gracious results of his priestly intervention, and indeed to evert his office utterly. His action at the altar of Atonement was pre-requisite to his approach to the altar of Incense: and the successful achievement which signalized his action at the latter, revealed beyond the possibility of doubt the nature and efficacy of the services which he had accomplished at the former; while only in virtue of the two, in their combination and synthesis, was Aaron's priesthood a real priesthood at all (H. Martin).

The intimate relation which existed between the brazen and the incense altars of Israel may be seen from their being linked together Psa. 84:3. "Thine **altars**, O Lord of hosts". The close connection between them is revealed in a number of scriptures. for instance, we gather from Lev. 16:12, 13, and Num. 16:46 that the fire on which the incense was laid upon the golden altar, was taken from the brazen altar, where the sin-offering was consumed. Thus, the activities of the one were based upon those of the other, the incense being kindled by that fire which had first fed upon the sacrifice; thus identifying the priest's service at both. This, in figure, tells us that our great High Priest pleads for no blessings which His blood has not purchased, and asks pardon from Divine justice for no sins for which He did not atone. The measure of the blessings for which Christ pleads is God's estimate of the life which He gave.

The wondrous scene portrayed in Isa. 6 shows us again the inseparable connection between the two altars. There the prophet beheld the Lord of hosts, in His ineffable majesty and exalted glory, seated upon the throne in His heavenly temple, above which stood the seraphim, with veiled faces, crying, "Holy, holy, holy". What he saw and heard was so overwhelming that he said, "Woe is me for I am undone; because I am a man of unclean lips, and I dwell in the midst of a people of unclean lips: for mine eyes have seen the King, the Lord of hosts" (v. 5). Blessed is it to mark the sequel: "Then flew one of the seraphims unto me, having a live coal in his hand, which he had taken with the tongs from off the altar: And he laid it upon my mouth, and said, Lo, this hath touched thy lips; and thine iniquity is taken away, and thy sin purged" (vv. 6, 7). As another remarked, "The emblem of Divine holiness had already consumed the sacrifice and was also consuming the sweet incense. Thus, symbolically, the prophet's lips were cleansed according to God's estimate of the value of the sacrifice and person of our Lord."

1. The Nature of His Intercession

"Christ maketh intercession, by His appearing in our nature, continually before the Father in heaven, in the merit of His obedience and sacrifice on earth, declaring His will to have it applied to all believers, answering all accusations against them, procuring for them quiet of conscience, notwithstanding daily failure, access with boldness to the throne of grace, and acceptance of their persons and sacrifices" (T. Ridgley). This definition seems to embody the essential features of the present intercession of our great High Priest. Having done everything on earth which God required from the Surety of our salvation, both in the removing of what would hinder it (sins and the curse) and procuring what would effect it (perfect obedience or righteousness), He has now gone into heaven, there "to appear in the presence of God for us" (Heb. 9:24).

First, He "appears" in our nature. The Mediator is "the Man Christ Jesus" (1 Tim. 2:5) and to "intercede" **is to mediate**. He did not cast off the human nature when He left this earth, but carried it into heaven, retaining the same body, though glorified, as He had in the days of His humiliation. The same body in which He offered Himself as a sacrifice to God, he now **presents** in heaven—"a Lamb as it had been slain" (Rev. 5:6). The apostle does not say in Heb. 9:24 that Christ entered heaven, to appear there in glory and majesty, as if His appearance there had been for Himself only; but "to appear in the presence of God **for us**." As He was born, lived and died for us, so He ascended to heaven, and appears in our nature at the right hand of God **for us**. cf. Heb. 6:20.

Second, He appears as our "Advocate" to present His people and their cause unto God. When Aaron was to enter the most holy place to intercede for Israel, he was to bear the names of the twelve tribes upon his heart and shoulders (Ex. 28:12, 29): thus he went there not in his own name, but in the name and behalf of his people. As our Advocate (1 John 2:1) Christ replies to the accusations of Satan (Rev. 12:10). A typical adumbration of this is found in Zech. 3, where we see Joshua— type of the Church—charged by Satan. Christ, "the Lord", by His intercession with the Father, pleads that instead of Joshua, his accuser might be rebuked and confounded; acquitting and justifying the accused. No charge will have any better success which is formed against those for whom Christ appears as Advocate: see Rom. 8:33, 34.

Third, He presents His meritorious sacrifice to God, pointing to His obedience and death in the stead of His people, to His blood which was shed for them. The typical high priest, when he was to mediate for Israel before God, brought in the blood of sacrifice and solemnly presented it (Heb. 9:7); so Christ, "by His own blood" has gone into heaven, thereby to "make intercession for the transgressors" (Isa. 53:12). Christ's blood **"speaketh** better things than Abel" (Heb. 12:24), crying for mercy, as Abel's did for vengeance. Its efficacy is so potent, and has as much the virtue of intercession, as if it had an articulate voice. The virtue of Christ's blood is still as fresh and powerful as if it were but just now shed—note "new and living" in Heb. 10:20.

Fourth, He presents His will and desire that His people might have all which He purchased for them: the will of the Divine nature as He is God, the desires of His human nature as He is man. This is revealed to us most fully in that wondrous 17th of John, where we are permitted to hear the breathings of our great High Priest. There we find Him asking of the Father those things which are most requisite for His people in their time-state. There we behold Him putting in His claim on their behalf: "Father, **I will** that they also, whom Thou hast given Me, be with Me where I am; that they may behold My glory, which Thou hast given Me" (John 17:24).

Fifth, by the intercession of Christ **access** to the throne of grace is obtained for His people. Though they have been delivered from the curse of the law, the flesh still remains within them, daily producing its evil fruit, defiling their service and interrupting their communion. As the conscience is made aware of this, the thought of drawing nigh unto the ineffably holy God would terrify, were it not that the Scriptures assure us we have One at His right hand pleading our cause. It is the realization of this blessed fact that gives us "boldness to enter into the Holiest by the blood of Jesus" (Heb. 10:19). Imperfect as are our approaches, unworthy as we are in ourselves, feeble though our petitions be, yet, there is One on High who has been given "**Much incense**" and that "that He should add it to the prayers of all saints upon the golden altar which was before the throne" (Rev. 8:3). Thus may we "offer up spiritual sacrifices acceptable to God **by Jesus Christ**" (1 Peter 2:5).

2. The Necessity of His Intercession

In an humble endeavour to ascertain the reasons why God has appointed the intercession of Christ respect should be had unto the Divine honour, the Mediator's glory, and His people's peace and security. Underlying the whole plan of redemption God has determined that we should be saved in a way and manner which most contributed to His own honour and praise, in a way which would most glorify His Son, and in a way which should make our salvation most sure and steadfast. Let us seek, then, to reverently ponder the needs-be for our Saviour's present mediation in the light of these basic considerations.

The first reason, then, respects God Himself. "In general, God will be dealt with withal like Himself, in and throughout the whole way of our salvation, from first to last, and carry it all along as a superior wronged, and so keep a distance between Himself and sinners; who still are to come to Him by a Priest and a Mediator (Heb. 7:25), upon whose mediation and intercession their salvation doth depend; and therefore through Christ, in His dispensation of all **to us downward** doth carry is as a **king**, as one having all power to justify and condemn, yet **upward toward God**, He carries it as a **priest**, who still must intercede to do all that which He has power to do as king. Therefore, in the 2nd Psalm after that God has set Him as 'King upon His holy hill' (v. 6), namely, in heaven, and so has committed all power in heaven and earth to Him; then He must yet 'ask' all that He would have done—'**Ask** of Me and I will give Thee' (v. 8) God says to Him; for though He be a king, yet He is God's king—'I have set **My** King', and by asking from Him God will be acknowledged to be above Him—i. e., above Him **as Mediator.**

"More particularly, God hath two attributes which He would have most eminently appear in their highest glory by Christ's effecting our salvation, namely, justice and free grace; and therefore hath so ordered the bringing about of our salvation, as that Christ might apply Himself in a more especial manner unto each of them, by way of satisfaction to the one, of entreaty to the other. Justice will be known to be justice, and dealt with upon its own terms; and grace will be acknowledged to be free grace, throughout the accomplishment of our salvation. You have both of them joined together in Rom. 3:24, 26: 'Being justified **freely by His grace** through the **redemption** that is in Christ Jesus; that He might be **just**, and the Justifier of him that believeth'. Here is highest justice and freest grace both met to save us, and both ordered by God to be 'declared' and 'set forth'.

"Our salvation depending and being carried on, even in the application of it, by a continuation of grace in a free way, notwithstanding satisfaction unto justice, therefore His free grace must be sought to, and treated with like itself, and applied upon in all, and the sovereignty and freeness of it acknowledged in all, even as well as God's justice had the honour to be satisfied by a price paid to it, that so the severity of it might appear and be held forth in our salvation. Thus God having two attributes eminently to be dealt with, His justice and His free grace, it was meet that there should be two eminent actions of Christ's priesthood, wherein He should apply Himself to each, according to their kind, and as the nature and glory of each doth require. And accordingly in His death He deals with justice, by laying down a sufficient price; and in His intercession He entreateth free grace, and thus both come to be alike acknowledged" (T. Goodwin).

What has been said above supplies the key which unlocks the blessed meaning of Heb. 4:16, where Christians are encouraged to "come boldly to the throne of grace", and that, because they have "a great High Priest that is passed into the heavens", the "therefore" of v. 16 looking back to what is said there in v. 14. Observe well that it is called "the **throne of grace**" at which our High Priest now officiates: it is so designated because it is **chiefly** "grace" which His sacerdotal office now deals with and sues unto: therefore does He there treat with God by way of intercession. Of this throne of grace in heaven the mercy-seat in the holy of holies was the type, and as Aaron brought the b'ood and the mercy-seat together (Lev. 16:14), so has Christ. But more: Aaron not only entered the holiest with blood, but with incense too (Lev. 16:12)—the figure of prayer (Rev. 8:3)—to show that heaven is opened unto God's people not by mere justice (bloodshedding), but by grace also, yet grace which must be intreated.

Thus it is that there is the unfinished work of Christ in heaven, as well as His finished work on earth. In the one He dea't with justice here below, in the other He is treating with mercy in heaven. All the grace which Christ now bestows on His people, He first **receives** from God, and that, in answer to His petitions. In Acts 2:33 it is said that, consequent upon His ascension, "He **received** of the Father the promise of the Holy Spirit, which He (Christ) hath shed forth", namely, on the day of Pentecost. Yet, if we go back to John 14:16 we learn that Christ received the Spirit (that as Mediator He might send Him forth) in answer to His intercession: "And I will **pray** the Father, and He shall give you another Comforter". So too in Eph. 4:11 we read that the ascended Christ "gave" gifts unto His Church, but, if we go back to Psa. 68:18, we learn that He "**received** (from the Father those) gifts for men", and that, as the fruit of His intercession.

In the second place, God had respect unto the glory of His beloved Son. In ordering our salvation to be accomplished by His work of intercession, God had in view the honour and praise of Christ too, that "all might honour the Son even as they honour the Father" (John 5:23). Thus, for the maintaining of His honour and the manifestation of His glory, it was appointed that He shou'd continue to intercede. None of His offices were to lie idle. All offices have work assigned them, and all work (properly done) has honour as its reward. When, then, Christ had finished His work here upon earth, as pertained to the **meriting** of our salvation, God appointed this perpetual work in heaven for the applying and bringing His people **into possession of** His salvation, and that, as a Priest, by praying in the virtue of the one oblation of Himself: see Heb. 7:24.

For the same reason it became Him that the whole work of salvation from first to last, in every step and degree of its accomplishment, should be so ordered that **Christ** wou'd still continue to have as great a hand in its application and consummation as He had in laying the first foundation thereof. This we have expressed in Heb. 12:2, "Looking unto Jesus the Author **and Finisher** of faith". In what immediately follows two things are said of Him, as the two causes of two effects, concerning each of which faith needs to be "looking unto" Him. First, He is to be "looked" at as dying—"enduring the cross"; second, as "set down at the right hand of the Majesty on high", there interceding. We need to look to Him as dying as the "Author", or "Beginning of our faith", and at His sitting at God's right hand as an Intercessor, for the "finishing of our faith", and so of our final salvation. Christ is both the Alpha and Omega.

In the third place, God had respect unto the comfort and security of His people. "God would have our salvation made sure, and us saved all manner of ways, over and over. First, by ransom and price (as captives are redeemed), which was done by His death, which of itself was enough. Second, by power and rescue; so in His resurrection, ascension, and sitting at God's right hand, which a'so was sufficient. Third, by intercession, a way of favour and entreaty, and this likewise would have been enough, but God would have all things concur in it, whereof notwithstanding not one could fail; a threefold cord, whereof each strand was strong enough, but all together must of necessity hold". (T. Goodwin).

The whole **application** of Christ's Satisfaction, both in justifying and saving us, first and last, has a special dependence upon His intercession. The leading difference between the influence of His death, and that of His intercession, unto our salvation, is this: the one was the means of procuring or obtaining it for us, the other the means of securing and applying it unto us. Christ purchased salvation by the one, but we are possessed of it by the other. It was not until Christ was "perfected through suffering" that He became "the Author (or "applying cause") of eternal salvation" (Heb. 5:7). The two things were united at the cross: "He bear the sins of many **and** made intercession for the transgressors" (Isa. 53:12). That while the death of Christ procured our salvation, it did not (of itself) secure it, seems very evident from 1 Cor. 15:17: "If Christ be not raised your faith is vain, ye are yet in your sins".

Those for whom Christ intercedes are they whose sin He bore (Isa. 53:12), namely, those given to Him by the Father (John 17:9). That for which He intercedes is what He purchased for them by His Satisfaction, namely, "eternal redemption" (Heb. 9:12), which includes the gift of the Holy Spirit to apply unto them all the virtues of His perfect work. That which the Holy Spirit communicates to them is life, light, love, faith, repentance, and perseverance in obedience. As we shall devote the whole of the next article to an amplification of this deeply important yet greatly neglected aspect of our theme, only the briefest statement thereon can now be made. By His death Christ meritoriously procured for all of His people an actual participation in the blessings of redemption, and this is infallibly applied to them by His Spirit. By the operations of the Spirit the elect are brought to saving faith and repentance, so that every requirement of God's government is fully met.

3. The Efficacy of His Intercession

First, this is fully assured by the fact that Christ's petitions are grounded upon indisputable **merit,** and therefore must prevail in the high court of Justice. His obedience unto death was infinitely meritorious and did deserve for His people that which, as Intercessor on their behalf, He pleads for. He fully satisfied every demand of the law, perfectly performed the work which He came to do, paid to the last mite all His people owed, and therefore, because of the intrinsic value of what He did, He must, in very righteousness, be granted that which He purchased.

Second, the success of Christ's intercession is fully assured by the fact that He sues only for that which is agreeable to His Father, and therefore is He entirely ready to grant His requests. He pleads for nothing but what is according to the will of God: Heb. 10:7-9. God's will was that Christ should be a sacrifice, and it is upon the ground of having perfectly performed His will, that His plea proceeds; such being the ground, it **must** prevail. Were it not effectual, the will of God were ineffectual. But, it is **God** that justifieth, so as none can condemn. How so? It is Christ that maketh the intercession: Rom. 8:33, 34.

Third, the success of Christ's intercession is fully assured because it is a commemoration of His sacrifice. That which Christ pleads before God is His own blood, which is "precious" in His sight. The sacrifice of Christ is a "sweet-smelling savour" unto God (Eph. 5:2). He is infinitely pleased with it, and in view of it He cannot but grant Christ, upon His personal application, that which it was offered to procure. If the blood of bulls and of goats, and the ashes of an heifer sprinkling the unclean sanctified to the purifying of the flesh, "how much more shall the blood of Christ" prevail as He pleads its merits before God (Heb. 9: 12, 13)!

Fourth, the success of Christ's intercession is fully assured by the fact that He is the Beloved of the Father. In Him the Father is so well pleased that He can deny Him naught that He asks Him. Christ Himself declared, "Thou hearest Me always" (John 11:42). When Esther appeared before king Ahasuerus to intercede for her people condemned to destruction, he gave her this assurance, "What is thy request? it shall be given even to thee to the half of the kingdom" (5:2). Christ was given still greater assurance before He entered upon His sacrificial work, "ask of Me", God said, "and **I will** give Thee the Gentiles for thine inheritance and the uttermost parts of the earth for Thy possession" (Psa. 2:8). This is the greatest thing for which Christ does ask, the sum of all He intercedes for.

Finally, the success of Christ's intercession is fully assured by the fact that nothing, in, of, from, or by His people can possibly countervail it. "Wherefore He is able also to save them **to the uttermost** that come unto God by Him, seeing He ever liveth to make intercession for them (Heb. 7:25). If Christ has once taken a person into His prayers, He will never, under any circumstances, cast him out. A man may be cast out of good men's hearts and prayers as Saul was out of Samuel's, and apostate Israel was out of Jeremiah's, but no man was ever cast out of Christ's prayers when He once took him in. The only possible danger could be through **sinning**, but Christ's prayers see to it and prevail and prevent them from apostatising (John 17:15), which is the only sin for which there is no forgiveness. "If any one (of the family) sin, we **have** an Advocate with the Father, Jesus Christ the righteous" (1 John 2:1).

How infallibly certain it is, then, that Christ shall "see of the travail of His soul and **be satisfied**" (Isa 53:11). He sees to it Himself that nothing which He purchased by His obedience unto death shall be lost. The application of His Satisfaction is as sure as the impetration of it. He is Himself constantly engaged in maintaining the interests of those for whom He died. There is not only an "access" into the grace of God "through our Lord Jesus Christ," but there is also a **standing** in the same (Rom. 5:1, 2), and that continued "standing" is expressly attributed to His "life" (Rom. 5:10), which, as it is interpreted for us in Heb. 7:25, means His ever living to intercede. "We owe our standing in grace every moment to His sitting in Heaven and interceding every moment. There is no fresh act of justification goes forth, but there is a fresh act of intercession. And as though God created the world once for all, yet every moment He is said to create, every new act of Providence being a new creation; so likewise is Jesus continually, through His continuing out free grace to justify us at the first, and this Christ doeth by continuing His intercessions; He continues "a Priest forever', and so we continue to be justified for ever" (T. Goodwin).

—ARTHUR W. PINK.

THE INTERCESSION OF CHRIST

That the Lord Jesus, now in heaven, ever liveth to make intercession for His people, is a truth which is tacitly owned by them; but as to the reasons **why** He is so engaged, as to the relation which it bears to their salvation, as to what it is He is obtaining for them, few indeed have any clear or Scriptural ideas. Yea, to those who do not give it any serious thought at all, the subject presents serious difficulty, for the views which they hold of the death of Christ appear to render His intercession quite unnecessary. Nor is any real help to be obtained from current literature. Very little has been written on this theme during the past fifty years, and what has been is superficial and unsatisfactory to the last degree, marred as it is by Socinian error. Thus we feel there is a real need for casting ourselves upon God and entreating Him to grant us needed wisdom and grace to write something thereon which will be acceptable to Him and profitable to His people.

That Christ should fill the office of Intercessor was plainly foretold in O. T. prophecy. First, in Job 33. There we are given to hear that sorely-afflicted saint speaking of one whose "soul draweth near the grave" (v. 22). He feels the need of a mighty Deliverer, "one among a thousand to show unto men His uprightness" (v. 23). Then follows a remarkable passage which finds its fulfillment in none other but Christ: concerning Him God says, "Deliver Him from going down to the pit: I have found an atonement" (v. 24). Then He declares, "His flesh shall be fresher than a child's: He shall return to the days of His youth" (v. 25), referring to Christ's resurrection: cf. Psa. 102:24-27. Finally He adds, "He shall **pray unto** God, and He will be favourable unto Him: and He will see His face with joy: for He will render unto man His righteousness" (v. 26).

The second Psalm announced that after God should exalt His Son to His "holy hill of Zion" (cf. Heb. 12:22), He would "**Ask** of Him" and should be given the Gentiles for His inheritance and the uttermost parts of the earth for His possession" (v. 8). Again, in Psalm 21:2 it was prophesied of Christ, "Thou hast given Him His heart's desire, and hast not withholden the request of His lips"—the whole Psalm is a commentary upon Psalm 2. Isa. 53, which gives such a vivid account of the sufferings and death of Christ—the first main act of His priestly office, whereby He made satisfaction unto Divine justice—concludes with the explicit declaration that He should make "intercession for the transgressors" (v. 12), which is the other principal part of His priestly office.

There is also a remarkable passage in Jer. 30 on this point, which is little understood today. There we learn that God has given Christ a commission authorizing Him to act as our Advocate: "And their Governor (the same word as in Psalm 22:28 and as rendered "Ruler" in Micah 5:2) shall proceed from the midst of them, and will cause Him to draw near, and He shall approach unto Me" (v. 21). Then God breaks forth with, "For who is this that engaged His heart to approach unto Me? saith the Lord": the Hebrew verb here signifies, literally, "Who hath **become a Surety** in His heart?", the same word being rendered "surety" in Gen. 44:32 and Prov. 6:1. As the King-Priest, the "Governor-Surety", Christ approaches unto God, the prime reference being to His mediatory intercession, Christ pleading with God for our sakes; the result of this is, "and ye shall be My people and I will be your God" (v. 22).

"The intercession of Christ was under the Old Testament **typified** in three ways. First, by the **living fire** that was continually on the altar. Herewith were all sacrifices to be kindled and burned, which thence were called 'firings'. But this principally typified His prayers, when He offered Himself unto God through the eternal Spirit, which He did with strong cries and supplications or intercessions, Heb. 5:7. Hereby, and the actings of the eternal Spirit therein, He kindled and fired in Himself a sacrifice of sweet-smelling savour to God, Eph. 5:2. Second, by the **daily sacrifice** of morning and evening for the whole people, Ex. 29:38-42. For although that sacrifice had in it the nature of an expiatory oblation because it was by blood, yet the principal end of it was to make continual application of the great solemn annual expiation, unto the consciences of the people. Third, by **the incense** that was burned in the sanctuary. And this was of two sorts:

(a). That wherewith the high priest entered once a year into the most holy place on the day of expiation. For he might not enter in, yea, he was to die if he did, unless in his entrance he filled the place, and covered the ark and mercyseat with a cloud of incense, Lev. 16:12, 13; which incense was to be fired with burning coals from the altar of burnt offerings. So did our High Priest: He filled heaven at His entrance with the sweet savour of His intercession, kindled with the coals of that eternal fire, wherewith He offered Himself unto God.

(b). The incense that was burned every day in the sanctuary by the priests in their courses. This represented prayer. Psa. 141:12, and was always accompanied with it, Luke 1:9, 10. This also was a type of the continual efficacy of the intercession of Christ, Rev. 8:4. But the most solemn representation of it, was in that anniversary sacrifice, whereof we must treat afterward at large; in this there was atonement made for all the sins and transgressions of the people, Luke 16:21. And it was consummated by carrying some of the blood as a representation of it into the most holy place. This was done but once in the year. To keep this in remembrance, and to make application of the benefits of it unto the consciences of the worshippers, the daily sacrifice was appointed. So doth the intercession of Christ make continual application of His great sacrifice and atonement, whence it derives its efficacy. And as the fire on the altar kindled all the renewed sacrifices, which were to be repeated and multiplied, because of their weakness and imperfection; so doth the intercession of Christ make effectual the one perfect sacrifice, which He offered once for all, in the various applications of it unto the consciences of believers, Heb. 10:12" (John Owen).

1. Its Necessity

Seeing that Christ made an end of His people's sins at the cross (1 Peter 3:18, Heb. 9:26), wherein is an Intercessor and Advocate required? Great care needs to be taken that we obtain a Scriptural conception of the precise sense in which our sins **have been** "made an end of". Sin still indwells the Christian (1 John 1:8) and daily brings forth sins (Luke 11:3, 4) which need to be confessed to God, if they are to be forgiven (1 John 1:9). Moreover, it is a serious mistake to affirm that God so beholds the believer in Christ that He sees no sin in him: the fact that He "chastens" us, proves otherwise—Heb. 12:5-11. Our sins were judged at the cross, and every demand of Divine justice against them was fully and finally settled, so that "there is therefore now no **condemnation** to them which are in Christ Jesus" (Rom. 8:1). Nevertheless, we are still the subjects of God's government, as well as members of His family, over which He maintains a righteous discipline. Furthermore, our daily sins defile and unfit us for the presence of the thrice holy God, and without a Priest on High to mediate for us, we would not, in our present state, draw nigh unto Him.

Both the character of God and the actual condition of His people require the intercessory ministry of the Lord Jesus: the Divine nature and our imperfections render it essential. If believers, who are defiled by inward corruption and outward transgression, are to enter (in spirit) the Holiest, the mediation of Christ is necessary. A third reason is to be found in the accusations of the devil (Rom. 12:10). Were it not for the advocacy of Christ, while there is so much within and about us unfitted for Heaven, Satan would effectually bar our access to God. But blessed be His name, we are told, that Christ has entered "into heaven itself, now to appear in the presence of God for us" (Heb. 9:24). As the once-slain Lamb, Christ refutes every charge of the Adversary, not by denying the truth of them, but by showing that the very sins which he mentions against the people of God, were atoned for at Calvary.

It must not be forgotten that in Rom. 8:33, 34 the Spirit challenges all creation, in the light of that infinite holiness of the Divine glory, to lay anything to the charge of God's elect: first, because it is God Himself that "justifieth". Second, because of the all-sufficient ground on which He does so. That ground is not only that Christ "died" but as the apostle added, "yea rather, that is risen again, who is even at the right hand of God, who also maketh intercession for us". Thus the argument is clinched by the fact of Christ's intercession in the presence of God. It is clear, then, from this passage alone, that Christ's intercession respects our **standing**, i. e. the **maintaining** of it before God, thereby meeting the requirements of His holiness.

The **advocacy** of Christ brings in another line of things altogether. That relates to our **state**. Here it is not our standing before God as the subjects of His government, but our condition before the Father as His children. It is mentioned only in John's first Epistle, which treats of "fellowship" (1:3, 7). The Greek word "Advocate" in 1 John 2:2 is the same as that translated "Comforter" in John 14:16, "And I will pray the Father, and He shall give you **another** Comforter, that He may abide with you forever". The fundamental thought in each case is that of a **Helper**. It is the fallen child, and not the Father, who needs the help. When a child falls, it needs lifting up, and if soiled by the fall, for the filth to be removed. The Father does not need to be entreated to forgive the child. John 14:26, 27 gives the main thought connected with the "Paraclete".

Christ's advocacy consists of keeping us right with the Father, and not the Father with us. The Paraclete with the believer and the Paraclete with the Father act in perfect harmony. The Holy Spirit in the believer leads the erring one to confession, and directs his eye to the Paraclete or "Comforter" above, and Christ as the Helper, who is with the Father, takes the penitent child by the hand (so to speak) and leads him back to the Father's presence, who is ever ready to forgive and cleanse (1 John 1:9) and restore to fellowship. The restored soul then learns that, although sin had shut him out from enjoying the Father's love, yet His love had never changed. Mark that the advocacy of Christ is also based upon His propitiatory work: 1 John 2:2.

Our deliverance from Hell is attributed more directly unto the death of Christ, our preservation in grace, as we pass through this hostile wilderness-scene on our way to Heaven, is ascribed more particularly to His intercession . H. Martin rightly said, "The Intercession of Christ is essentially an Atonement or substitutionary oblation, once perfected of Calvary, now perpetually presented and undergoing a perpetual acceptance in heaven". While it is true that "By one offering He hath perfected forever them that are sanctified" (Heb. 10:14), we are also told in the same Epistle that, "He is able also **to save** them to the uttermost that come unto God by Him, **seeing** He ever liveth to make intercession for them" (7:25). The two passages need to be borne in mind. After Christ's righteousness has been imputed to the believer, he is still defective in the performance of his duty, and, "in many things offends" (James 3:2). By His death Christ purchased complete salvation for His people, but it is by His intercessory life in heaven that the present blessings of it are actually conferred upon them.

2. Its Character

"To intercede, means literally 'to pass between'. The term is used figuratively, to denote mediating between two parties with a view of reconciling differences, particularly in the way of supplicating in favour of one with another. In this sense, 'intercession' is frequently affirmed of Christ in the Scriptures: Rom. 8:34, Heb. 7:25. The verb employed in these passages when connected with the preposition that follows (huper) includes every form of acting in behalf of another; it is improper to limit it to prayer, as it denotes mediating in every possible way in which the interests of another can be promoted... But with reference to Christ there must be understood this difference, that **His** plea is not the innocence of His own clients, but His own merits; **His** appeal is not to absolute justice, but to sovereign mercy; what **He** sues for is not a legal right to which they are entitled, but a free favour to which in themselves they have no claim" (W. Symington).

Intercession is the correlate of atonement. They stand related to each other in much the same way as do creation and providence. The providence of God consists in upholding all things or maintaining in being the creatures He has made: it is best conceived of as a continual putting forth of the creative energy. So the intercession of Christ is the continued efficacy of His expiatory merit; on which account some of the older writers spoke of it as a perpetual oblation. If the providence of God were suspended, all created beings must be annihilated: and if Christ were not to make intercession, the merits of His atonement would be utterly unavailing: cf. 1 Cor. 15:17.

"In His incarnation, He came from the Father to acquaint us with His gracious purposes, and how far He had agreed with God on our behalf; and at His ascension He went from us to the Father, to sue out the benefits He had so dearly purchased. He drew up an answer upon the Cross to the bill (indictment), that sin by virtue of the law had drawn against us, and ascended to heaven as an advocate to plead that answer upon His throne, and rejoin to all the replies against it. When His offering was accepted, He went to heaven to the supreme Judge, to improve this acceptance of His sacrifice by a negotiation which holds and continues to this day. He has gone to heaven to appear in the presence of God for us Heb. 9:24" (S. Charnock). His advocacy is founded upon His oblation. He is our Advocate because He is our Propitiation (1 John 2:1, 2). The efficacy of His plea depends upon the purity and value of His sacrifice. Because He paid the debt as our Surety, He is qualified to plead the payment as our Attorney. By shedding His blood He purchased the remedy, by His intercession He applies it.

Christ's intercession needs to be viewed in connection with the **everlasting covenant**. As "Mediator of the covenant" (Heb. 9:15) every thing which Christ does as Priest has a relation to that Divine economy. The sacerdotal functions of oblation and intercession have regard respectively to the condition and the administration of that covenant. The stipulated **condition** of the covenant was that Christ should make satisfaction to the law and justice of God for the sins of those that are redeemed. The **administration** of the covenant comprehends whatever is concerned with putting and maintaining the covenant-children in possession of the blessings of redemption; and this takes its rise directly and immediately from the intercession of Christ. True it is, that the agency of the Spirit and the instrumentality of means are concerned in this object, but in the economy of our salvation the intercession of the Mediator is necessary alike to the operation of the one and to the efficacy of the other. Divine wisdom has so arranged it that **all** the good done to the souls of men should be commenced, continued, completed, and maintained throughout eternity, in relation to Christ's intercession.

Consider the present circumstances of God's people upon earth. Numerous and daily are their needs. Blessings to supply those needs were procured by the atoning sacrifice of the Redeemer. But who shall **apply** to God for the **bestowment** of those purchased benefits? They cannot themselves, for they have neither merit nor wisdom, yea, at first, no inclination for them. They are altogether unfit to appear in the presence of God for themselves; thus, Another must appear **for** them. To this it might be replied: God loves His people, has **determined** to confer on them the blessings purchased by His Son; wherein, then, is there any need or room for Christ's intercession? Such an objection would proceed on a mistaken conception concerning the **design** of our Saviour's intercession. Its object is not to awaken the Father's love; it is not to obtain a decree in favour of those who are its subjects. Far be the thought. No; the very existence of Christ's intercession is a **fruit** of God's love, an **evidence** of His gracious purpose.

God determines that His wondrous and infinite love shall be **displayed**, not only on earth at the cross, but also in His temple, in heaven. Moreover, He has ordained that His sovereign decree shall be fulfilled in a way most consistent with His glory, most compatible with the honour of His government, most productive of the good of His people. The intercession of Christ is the method which He has graciously and wisely selected to express His affection, and to fulfill His purposes of mercy to fallen man. An Israelite would have had no more valid reason for objecting against the **daily** sacrifice (Ex. 29:38-42) and accounting it needless in view of the annual atonement for **all** the sins of Israel (Lev. 16:21), than we now have for regarding the intercession of of Christ as being useless in view of His finished work at Calvery. The fact is that while the redeemed will enter heaven, freed from all sin, on the ground of Christ's atoning sacrifice, yet, while they are in this world, as sinful creatures, God requires Christ to mediate on their behalf. Moreover, no objection can be urged against the intercession of Christ on the ground of God's willingness **to bless** His people, which will not apply with equal force against **our** supplication **for** the supply of our need.

This leads us to say in the next place, that the intercession of Christ requires to be pondered in its relation to **the promises of God.** There are promises which the Father made to the Son in the everlasting covenant which are not yet fulfilled, and thus Christ (setting us an example!) turns them into petitions: having Himself performed the condition stipulated, He now pleads the reward assured Him. There were promises made by God to Christ as our Head and Representative "before the world began" (see Titus 1:1, 2, 2 Tim. 1:9), when He was "foreordained" to suffer (1 Peter 1:20). "Eternal life" was "**promised**" ere the world was created. Promised to whom? Not to any creature, for no creature then had a being. Therefore to Christ Himself, yet not for Himself, but for those whom God had given to Him. Thus, this "promise" and the "grace" which was given us in Christ, He now sues against as a feofee in trust for us; the added words "which God that cannot lie" (Titus 1:2) giving us an intimation of the **manner** of Christ's pleading—calling the veracity of God to witness the validity of the promise which He pleads.

An illustration, yea, a demonstration, of what we have just said is found in John 17. God had given unto Christ most definite assurance, before He came to this earth, that He would glorify Him (Isa. 53:10-12), and hence we find the Saviour pleading for the fulfillment of it, for God requires to be "inquired of" (Ezek. 36:37) even concerning those things which He solemnly pledged Himself to give. Therefore do we find the Mediator asking, "Father, glorify Thy Son" (John 17:1), and "glorify Thou Me with Thine own self with the glory which I had with Thee before the world was" (v. 5). So, too, God had infallibly guaranteed the security of His people (Jer. 32:40), nevertheless, we here find Christ praying, "Holy Father, keep through Thine own name those whom Thou hast given Me" (v. 11). It was the Surety requesting the fulfillment of that which God had agreed to grant. God proposed unto Him as the end of His sufferings and promised Him as the reward of His labours, that Christ should "bring many sons unto glory", and so for this He now sues (v. 24). The whole of John 17, from v. 5 onwards may be regarded as a copy of Christ's intercession on high. He continues to plead the fulfillment of all that has been promised Him.

Care needs to be taken that we do not **carnalize** the present intercession of Christ. We must not imagine Him, now in heaven, kneeling before the Father and thus supplicating Him on behalf of His people, for that would not be fitting unto His majesty at the right hand of God; nor is there the "strong cries and tears" now as in the "days of His flesh" (Heb. 5:7). As on the cross He died as a public person, in the room and stead of His people, so now He appears before God as a public person, representing all of His elect. Therefore does He make known His will and desire concerning them. He acts as our Advocate, pleading our cause before God, presenting those considerations which secured for us the pardon of our daily transgressions and continued supplies of Divine grace.

The petitions of our great High Priest partake of the nature of a claim or demand. It is not a petition for that which the Father is at liberty to grant or refuse, but that for which the Son has a **right** by way of purchase, and which God cannot in justice deny Him. Christ now claims the performance of God's promises as a debt due unto His meritorious obedience. That God appointed Christ to be our Surety, was an act of pure benignity and sovereign grace, but after He had appointed and accepted Him, upon the doing of His part in the work of redemption, Christ had a right to its application, and consequently to the office of Advocate, to see right done unto His people, to see their debts are paid, and to put justice in mind of the full payment He had made. Therefore do we find Him saying in John 17, "Father, **I will** that they also whom Thou hast given Me be with Me where I am; that they may behold My glory, hich Thou hast given Me" (v. 24). Let not be forgotten that Christ is no longer on the altar, but upon **the throne**. "All authority in heaven and earth" has been given to Him (Matt. 28:20) and this, as the royal Priest, He now exercises.

—ARTHUR W. PINK.

THE RADIO

Without here expressing any opinion as to whether the discovery of wireless communication was from God or the Devil, certain it is that the latter is using it not only as a medium for propagating error but as a means of ensnaring many professing Christians. So convinced are we of this, and to such an extent is this evil growing, we feel it a bounden duty to lift our feeble voice in warning God's dear people. We have been in a number of homes where the raido is installed, and several things have arrested our attention and saddened us.

First, there are some, how many we know not, who would not think of entering a Romish "church" (?) but who through curiosity to hear what her leaders have to say, do not hesitate to listen-in when some noted "Bishop" or "Cardinal" is giving an address. Now this is playing with fire! No matter how firmly established in the faith you deem yourself to be, it is written, "thou shalt not tempt the Lord thy God", and you **are** "tempting" Him if you listen to the mouthpieces of Satan and expect God to preserve you from all evil consequences. The same applies to listening-in to the "Russellites", "Christian Scientists" etc. "Be not deceived, evil communications corrupt good manners" (1 Cor. 15:33). "I would have you wise unto that which is good, and simple concerning evil" (Rom. 16:19).

Second, there are those known to us who would not enter a theatre or opera-house, but have no scruples against "tuning-in" and listening to their musical programmes, sometimes to the humorous dialogues which are broadcast. Possibly not a few of our readers may exclaim, I see no harm in this! But do you see any God in it? Is it pleasing to God? Is it honouring to Christ? Does it help you to walk in separation from the world which still despises and rejects the Lord Jesus? Does it aid you in pressing forward along the Narrow Way? Is an evening spent in this manner "**redeeming** the time" (Eph. 5:16)? The **honest** reader will have no difficulty in answering such questions. Moreover, this evil habit (like others) **grows** on one, unconsciously, insidiously, disastrously.

Third, the radio brings "the world" into your home, and Scripture says, "**be not** conformed to this world" (Rom. 12:2). No matter how many may disregard those plain words, they still mean what they say. Furthermore, Scripture faithfully warns us "whosoever therefore will be a friend of the world is the enemy of God" (James 4:4). And what will be the effect on your children for thus introducing the world into your home? Will it aid you in bringing them up "in the nurture and admonition of the Lord" (Eph. 6:4)? Will it cause them to have serious thoughts about another world? Will **God** bless it to them? Again we say, no **honest** soul will have any difficulty in answering such questions. O the tragedy of it, in how many homes has the "bedtime stories" of the wireless taken the place of Scripture-reading and prayer with the little ones.

Fourth, the Word of God bids us "give attendance **to reading**" (1 Tim. 4:13). There are thousands who used to, but they are doing so no longer. Even on the holy Sabbath listening in to the radio has, in numerous cases, taken the place of Bible-study and consulting helpful and edifying expositions thereon. Each year the demand for really spiritual books is steadily decreasing, the reason being that people now prefer to listen to the radio. No wonder their souls are so lean! No wonder they have before them such a low standard of Christian living! May it please the Lord to use these few lines to deliver some of His people from this twentieth-century curse.

—A. W. P.

"In all ways acknowledge HIM" (Prov. 3:6).
"Do all to the glory of God" (1 Cor. 10-31).

THE SUPREMACY OF GOD

Who is regulating affairs on this earth today—God or the Devil? That God reigns supreme in heaven, is generally conceded; That He does so over this world, is almost universally denied—if not directly, then indirectly. More and more are men in their philosophisings and theorisings, relegating God to the background. Take the material realm. Not only is it denied that God created everything, by personal and direct action, but few believe that He has any immediate concern in **regulating** the works of His own hands. Everything is supposed to be ordered according to the (impersonal and abstract) "laws of Nature". Thus is the Creator banished from His own creation. Therefore we need not be surprised that men, in their degrading conceptions, exclude Him from the realm of human affairs. Throughout Christendom, with an almost negligible exception, the theory is held that man is "a free agent," and therefore, lord of his fortunes and the determiner of his destiny. That Satan is to be blamed for much of the evil which is in the world, is freely affirmed by those who, though having so much to say about the "responsibility of man", often deny their **own** responsibility by attributing to the Devil what, in fact, proceeds from their own evil hearts (Mark 7:21-23).

But who is regulating affairs on this earth today—God or the Devil? Attempt to take a serious and comprehensive view of the world. What a scene of confusion and chaos confronts us on every side! Sin is rampant; lawlessness abounds; evil men and seducers are waxing "worse and worse" (2 Tim. 3:13). Today, everything appears to be out of joint. Thrones are creaking and tottering, ancient dynasties are being overthrown, democracies are revolting, civilization is a demonstrated failure; half of Christendom was but recently locked together in a death grapple; and now that the titanic conflict is over, instead of the world having been made safe for democracy, we have discovered that democracy is very unsafe for the world. Unrest, discontent, and lawlessness, are rife every where, and none can say how soon another great war will be set in motion. Statesmen are perplexed and staggered. Men's hearts are "failing them for fear, and for looking after those things which are coming on earth" (Luke 21:26). Do these things look as though God had control?

But let us confine our attention to the religious realm? After nineteen centuries of Gospel preaching, Christ is still "despised and rejected of men". Moreover, He (the Christ of Scripture) is proclaimed and magnified by very few. In the majority of modern pulpits He is dishonoured and disowned. Despite frantic efforts to attract the crowds, the majority of the churches are being emptied rather than filled. And what of the great masses of non-church goers? In the light of Scripture, we are compelled to believe that the "many" **are** on the Broad Road that leadeth to destruction, and that only a "few" are on the Narrow Way that leadeth unto life. Numbers are declaring that Christianity is a failure, and despair is settling on many faces. Not a few of the Lord's own people are bewildered, and their faith is being severely tried. And what of God? Does He see and hear? Is He impotent or indifferent? A number of those who are regarded as leaders of Christian-thought told us that, God could not help the coming of the late awful War, and that He was unable to bring about its termination. This was said, and openly, that conditions were beyond God's control. Do these things look as though God were ruling the world?

Who is regulating affairs on this earth today—God or the Devil? What impression is made upon the minds of those men of the world who, occasionally attend a Gospel service? What are the conceptions formed by those who hear even those preachers who are counted as "orthodox"? Is it not that a disappointed God is the One whom Christians believe in? From what is heard from the average evangelist today, is not any serious hearer obliged to conclude that he professes to represent a God who is filled with benevolent intentions, yet unable to carry them out; that He is earnestly desirous of blessing men, but that they will not let Him? Then, must not the average hearer draw the inference that the Devil has gained the upper hand, and that God is to be pitied rather than blamed?

But does not every thing seem to show that the Devil has far more to do with the affairs of earth than God has? Ah, it all depends upon whether we are walking by faith, or walking by sight. Are your thoughts, my reader, concerning this world, and God's relation to it, based upon what you **see?** Face this question seriously and honestly. And if you are a Christian, you will, most probably, have cause to bow your head with shame and sorrow, and to acknowledge that it is so. Alas, in reality, we walk very little "**by**

faith." But what does "walking by faith" signify? It means that our thoughts are formed, our actions regulated, our lives moulded by the Holy Scriptures, for "faith cometh by hearing, and hearing by the Word of God" (Rom. 10:17). It is from the Word of Truth, and that alone, that we can learn **what is** God's relation to this world.

Who is regulating the affairs of this earth today—God or the Devil? What saith the Scriptures? Ere we consider the direct reply to this query, let it be said that, the Scriptures predicted just what we now see and hear. The prophecy of Jude is in course of fulfillment. It would lead us too far away from our present inquiry to fully amplify this assertion, but what we have particularly in mind is a sentence in verse 8, "Likewise also these dreamers defile the flesh, despise dominion and speak evil of dignities". Yes, they "speak evil" of the Supreme Dignity, the "Only Potentate, the King of kings, and Lord of lords". Ours is peculiarly an age of irreverence, and as the consequence, the spirit of lawlessness, which brooks no restraint, and which is desirous of casting off everything which interferes with the free course of self-will, is rapidly engulfing the earth like some giant tidle-wave. The members of the rising generation are the most flagrant offenders, and in the decay and disappearing of parental authority we have the certain precursor of the abolition of civic authority. Therefore, in view of the growing disrespect for human law and the refusal to "render honour to whom honour is due", we need not be surpirsed that the recognition of the majesty, the authority, the sovereignty of the Almighty Lawgiver, should recede more and more into the background, and that the masses have less and less patience with those who insist upon them.

Who is regulating affairs on this earth today—God or the Devil? What saith the Scriptures? If we believe their plain and positive declarations, no room is left for uncertainty. They affirm, again and again, that **God** is on the throne of the universe; that the sceptre is in **His** hands; that He is directing all things "after the counsel of His own will". They affirm, not only that God created all things, but also that He is ruling and reigning over all the works of His hands. They affirm that God is the "Almighty", that His will is irreversible, that He is absolute sovereign in every realm of all His vast dominions. And surely it must be so. Only two alternatives are possible: God must either rule, or be ruled; sway, or be swayed; accomplish His own will, or be thwarted by His creatures. Accepting the fact that He is the "Most High", vested with perfect wisdom and illimitable power, and the conclusion is irresistible that He must be God in fact as well as in name.

In view of what we have briefly referred to above we say that, present-day conditions call loudly for a proclamation of God's omnipotency, God's sufficiency, God's sovereignty. From every pulpit in the land it needs to be thundered forth that God still lives, that God still observes, that God still reigns. Faith is now in the crucible, it is being tested by fire, and there is no fixed and sufficient resting-place for the heart and mind but in the throne of God. What is needed now, as never before, is a full, positive, constructive setting forth of the Godhead of God. Drastic diseases call for drastic remedies. People are weary with platitudes and mere generalizations; the call is for something definite and specific. Soothing-syrup may serve for peevish children, but an iron tonic is better suited for adults, and we know of nothing which is more calculated to infuse spiritual vigor into our frames than a scriptural apprehension of the full character of God. It is written, "The people that do know their God shall be strong and do exploits" (Dan. 11:32).

Without a doubt a world-crisis is at hand, and every where men are alarmed. But God is not! He is never taken by surprise. It is no unexpected emergency which now confronts Him, for He is the One who "worketh **all** things after the counsel of His own will" (Eph. 1:11). Hence, though the world is panic-stricken, the word to the believer is, "Fear not". "All things" are subject to His immediate control; "all things" are moving in accord with His eternal purpose, and therefore "all things" are working together "for good to them that love God, to them who are the called according to His purpose". It **must** be so, for "of Him, and through Him, and to Him are **all** things" (Rom. 11:36). Yet how little is this realized today! Many suppose that God is little more than a far-distant Spectator, taking no hand in the affairs of earth. It is true that man has a will, but so also has God. It is true that man is endowed with power, but God is all-powerful. It is true that, generally speaking, the material world is regulated by law, but behind that law is the law Giver and the law Administrator. Man is but the creature. God is the Creator, and endless ages before man existed, and ere the world was founded, God made His plans; and being infinite in power and man only infinite, His purpose and plan cannot be withstood or thwarted by the creatures of His own hands.

As we turn to the Word and are instructed thereout, we discover a fundamental principle which must be applied to every problem: Instead of beginning with man and his world and working back to God, we must begin with God and work down to man—"In the beginning God" (Gen. 1:1). Apply this principle to the present situation. Begin with the world as it is today and try and work back to God, and everything will seem to show that God has no connection with the world at all. But begin with God and work down to the world, and light, much light, is cast on the problem. Because God is holy, His anger burns against sin; because God is righteous, His judgments fall upon those who rebel against Him; because God is faithful, the solemn threatenings of His word are fulfilled; because God is omnipotent, none can successfully resist Him, still less overthrow His counsel, and because God is Omniscient, no problem can master Him and no difficulty baffle His wisdom. It is just because God is who He is and what He is that we are now beholding on earth what we do—the beginning of His outpoured judgments.

But let it be said very emphatically that the heart can only rest upon and enjoy the blessed truth of the absolute supremacy of God as **faith is in exercise.** Faith is ever occupied with God; that is the character of it, that is what differentiates it from intellectual theology. Faith endures, "as seeing Him who is invisible" (Heb. 11:27): endures the disappointments, the hardships, and the heart-aches of life, by recognising that all comes from the hand of Him who is too wise to err and too loving to be unkind. But so long as we are occupied with any other object than God Himself, there will be neither rest for the heart nor peace for the mind. But when we receive all that enters our lives as from **His** hand, then no matter what may be our circumstances or surroundings—whether in a hovel, a prison-dungeon, or a martyr's stake—we shall be enabled to say, "The lines are fallen unto me in **pleasant** places" (Psa. 16:6). But, that is the language of **faith,** not of sight or of sense.

But if instead of bowing to the testimony of Holy Writ, if instead of walking by faith, we follow the evidence of our eyes, and reason therefrom, we shall fall into a quagmire of virtual atheism. Or, if we are regulated by the opinions and views of others, peace will be at an end. Granted that there is much in this world of sin and suffering which appalls and saddens us, granted that there is much in the providential dealings of God which startle and stagger us, that is no reason why we should unite with the unbelieving worldling, who says, "If I were God, I would not allow this or tolerate that" etc. Better far, in the presence of bewildering mystery, to say with one of old, "I was dumb, I opened not my mouth; because Thou didst it" (Psa. 39:9). Scripture tells us that God's judgments are "unsearchable", and His ways "past finding out" (Rom. 11:33). It must be so if faith is to be tested, confidence in His wisdom and righteousness strengthened, and submission to His holy will fostered.

Here is the fundamental difference between the man of faith and the man of unbelief. The unbeliever is "of the world", judges everything by worldly standards, views life from the standpoint of time and sense, and weighs every thing in the balances of his own carnal mining. But the man of faith brings in **God**, looks at every thing from **His** standpoint, estimates values by spiritual standards, and views life in the light of eternity. Doing this, he receives whatever comes as from the hand of God. Doing this, his heart is calm in the midst of the storm. Doing this, he rejoices in hope of the glory of God. —ARTHUR W. PINK.

N. B. This article is an extract from the new edition of our work on "The Sovereignty of God, a work of over three hundred pages. It is published in Swengel at $2 postpaid, but may be obtained from the Editor at the same price. We could fill many pages were we to insert the scores of unsolicited letters which have come to hand from those who have given it a prayerful and careful reading, testifying to how God has been pleased to bless it to the enlightening of their understandings, the strengthening of their faith, and the rejoicing of their hearts. We are anxious that many more of the Lord's dear people might receive similar blessing. Do not miss this golden opportunity of securing what some have designated "a veritable treasure-house of the riches of God's grace, a real storehouse of strong meat for the soul". Send in your order at once, ask the Lord to enable your faith to lay hold of His truth in it, and thus be fortified against the final efforts which Satan is now making, ere this age ends, to cause many to "make shipwreck of the faith". —A.W.P.

A MIGHTY SAVIOUR

What are we to understand by the words "to save" (Isa. 63:1)? Certainly, most men, when they read these words, consider them to mean salvation from hell. They are partially correct, but the notion is highly defective. It is true Christ does save men from the penalty of their guilt. He does take those to heaven who deserve the eternal wrath and displeasure of the Most High; it is true that He does blot out "iniquity, transgression, and sin", and that the iniquities of the remnant of His people are passed over for the sake of His blood and atonement. But that is not the whole meaning of the words "to save". This deficient explanation lies at the root of mistakes which many theologians have made, and by which they have surrounded their system of divinity with mist. They have said that to save is to pluck men as brands from the burning—to save them from destruction if they repent. Now, it means vastly, I had almost said, infinitely more than this. "To save" means something more than just delivering penitents from going down to hell. By the words "to save", I understand the whole of that great work of salvation, from the first holy desire, the first spiritual conviction, onward to complete sanctification. All this done of God through Jesus Christ. Christ is not only mighty to save those who do repent, but He is able to make men repent; He is engaged not merely to carry those to heaven who believe, but He is mighty to give men new hearts and to work faith in them; He is mighty not merely to give heaven to one who wishes for it, but He is mighty to make the man who hates holiness love it, to constrain the despiser of His name to bend his knee before Him, and to make the most abandoned reprobate turn from the error of his ways.

By the words "to save", I do not understand what some men say they mean. They tell us in their theology that Christ came into the world to put all men into a salvable state—to make the salvation of all men possible by their own exertions. I believe that Christ came for no such thing—that He came into the world not to put them into a **salvable** state, but into a **saved** state; not to put them where they could save themselves, but to do the work in them and for them, from the first even to the last. If I believed that Christ came only to put you, my hearers, and myself into a state where we might save ourselves, I should give up preaching henceforth and for ever; for knowing a little of the wickedness of men's hearts, because I know something of my own—knowing how much men naturally hate the religion of Christ—I should despair of any success in preaching a gospel which I had only to offer, its effects depending upon the voluntary acceptance of it by unrenewed and unregenerated men. If I did not believe that there was a mighty going forth with the Word of Jesus, which makes men willing in the day of His power, and which turns them from the error of their ways by the mighty, overwhelming, force of a Divine and mysterious influence. I should cease to glory in the cross of Christ. Christ, we repeat, is mighty, not merely to put men into a salvable condition, but mighty absolutely and entirely to save them. . . I take it that the highest proof of Christ's power is not that He offers salvation, not that He bids you take it if you will, but that when you reject it, when you hate it, when you despise it, He has a power whereby He can change your minds, and make you think differently from your former thoughts, and turn you from the error of your ways. This I conceive to be the meaning of the text, "Mighty to save".

-Extract from a Sermon by C. H. Spurgeon, 1857.

"He and I in that bright glory,
One deep joy shall share—
Mine, to be forever with Him;
His, that I am there".
John 17:24

not only given us senses, but also that which gratifies them; and this too reveals His goodness. The earth might have been as fertile as it is without its surface being so delightfully variegated. Our physical lives could have been sustained without beautiful flowers to regale our eyes, and exhale sweet perfumes. We might have walked the fields without our ears being saluted by the music of the birds. Whence, then, this loveliness, this charm, so freely diffused over the face of nature? Verily, "The **tender** mercies of the Lord are over **all** His works." (Psa. 145:9).

The goodness of God is seen in that when man transgressed the law of His Creator a dispensation of unmixed wrath did not at once commence. Well might God have deprived His fallen creatures of every blessing, every comfort, every pleasure. Instead, He ushered in a regime of a mixed nature, of mercy and judgment. This is very wonderful if it be duly considered, and the more thoroughly that regime be examined the more will it appear that "mercy rejoiceth against judgment" (James 2:13). Notwithstanding all the evils which attend our fallen state, the balance of good greatly preponderates. With comparatively rare exceptions, men and women experience a far greater number of days of health, than they do of sickness and pain. There is much more creature-happiness than creature-misery in the world. Even our sorrows admit of considerable alleviation, and God has given to the human mind a pliability which adapts itself to circumstances and makes the most of them.

Nor can the benevolence of God be justly called into question because there **is** suffering and sorrow in the world. If man **sins against** the goodness of God, if he despises the "riches of His goodness and forbearance and longsuffering", and after the hardness and impenitency of his heart treasurest up unto himself wrath against the day of wrath (Rom. 2:4, 5), who is to blame but himself? Would God **be** "good" if He punished not those who ill-use His blessings, abuse His benevolence, and trample His mercies beneath their feet? It will be no reflection upon God's goodness, but rather the brightest exemplification of it, when He shall rid the earth of those who have broken His laws, defied His authority, mocked His messengers, scorned His Son, and persecuted those for whom He died.

The goodness of God appeared most illustrously when He sent forth His Son "made of a woman, made under the law, to redeem them that were under the law, that we might receive the adoption of sons" (Gal. 4:4, 5). Then it was that a multitude of the heavenly host praised their Maker and said, "Glory to God in the highest and on earth peace, **good-will** toward men" (Luke 2:14). Yes, in the Gospel the "grace (Gk. benevolence or goodness) of God that bringeth salvation hath appeared to all men" (Titus 2:11). Nor can God's benignity be called into question because He has not made every sinful creature to be a subject of His redemptive grace. He did not the fallen angels. Had God left all to perish it had been no reflection on His **goodness.** To any who would challenge this statement, we would remind him of our Lord's sovereign prerogative: "Is it not lawful for Me to do what I will with Mine own? Is thine eye evil, because I am good?" (Matt. 20:15).

"O that men would praise the Lord for His goodness, and for His wonderful works to the children of men" (Psa. 107:8). Gratitude is the return justly required from the objects of His beneficience; yet is it often withheld from our great Benefactor simply because His goodness is so constant and so abundant. It is lightly esteemed because it is exercised toward us in the common course of events. It is not felt because we daily experience it. "Despisest **thou** the riches of His goodness?" (Rom. 2:4). His goodness is "despised" when it is not improved as a means to lead men to repentance, but, on the contrary, serves to harden them from the supposition that God entirely overlooks their sin.

The goodness of God is the life of the believer's trust. It is this excellency in God which most appeals to our hearts. Because His goodness endureth forever, we ought never to be discouraged: "The Lord is good, a stronghold in the day of trouble, and He knoweth them that trust in Him" (Nahum 1:7). "When others behave badly to us, it should only stir us up the more heartily to give thanks unto the Lord, because **He** is good; and when we ourselves are conscious that we are far from being good, we should only the more reverently bless Him that **He** is good. We must never tolerate an instant's unbelief as to the goodness of the Lord; whatever else may be questioned, this is absolutely certain, that Jehovah is good; His dispensations may vary, but His nature is always the same" (C. H. Spurgeon).

—ARTHUR W. PINK.

STUDIES IN THE SCRIPTURES

"Search the Scriptures" John 5 : 39

Copyright in all English-speaking Countries.

Editor: Arthur W. Pink, 1339 Bates Ave., Los Angeles, Calif, U. S. A.
Hon. Agent in England: Mr. A. Winstone, "Shalom", Old Bath Road, Leckhampton, Cheltenham.
Hon. Agent in Australia: Mr. G. Ardill, The Christian Workers' Depot. Commonwealth and Reservoir Streets, Sydney.

THE PATIENCE OF GOD

Far less has been written upon this than the other excellencies of the Divine character. Not a few of those who have expatiated at length upon the Divine attributes, have passed over the patience of God without any comment. It is not easy to suggest a reason for this, for surely the longsuffering of God is as much one of the Divine perfections as is His wisdom, power, or holiness, and as much to be admired and revered by us. True, the actual term will not be found in a concordance so frequently as the others, but the glory of this grace itself shines forth on almost every page of Scripture. Certain it is that we lose much if we do not frequently meditate upon the patience of God and earnestly pray that our hearts and ways may be more completely conformed thereto.

Most probably the principal reason why so many writers have failed to give us anything, separately, upon the patience of God, was because of the difficulty of distinguishing this attribute from the Divine goodness and mercy, particularly the latter. God's longsuffering is mentioned in conjunction with His grace and mercy again and again, as may be seen by consulting Ex. 34:6, Num. 14:18, Psa. 86:15, etc. That the patience of God is really a display of His mercy, in fact is one way in which it is frequently manifested, cannot be gainsaid; but that they are one and the same excellency, and are not to be separated, we cannot concede. It may not be easy to discriminate between them, nevertheless, Scripture fully warrants us in predicating some things of the one which we cannot of the other. ,

Stephen Charnock, the Puritan, defines God's patience, in part, thus: "It is part of the Divine goodness and mercy, yet differs from both. God being the greatest goodness, hath the greatest mildness; mildness is always the companion of true goodness, and the greater the goodness, the greater the mildness. Who so holy as Christ, and who so meek? God's slowness to anger is a branch of His mercy: 'the Lord is full of compassion, slow to anger' (Psa. 145:8). It differs from mercy in the formal consideration of the subject: mercy respects the creature as miserable, patience respects the creature as criminal; mercy pities him in his misery, patience bears with the sin which engendered the misery, and giving birth to more".

Personally we would define the divine patience as that power of control which God exercises over Himself, causing Him to bear with the wicked and forebear so long in punishing them. In Nahum 1:3 we read, "The Lord is slow to anger and great in power", upon which Mr. Charnock said, "Men that are great in the world are quick in passion, and are not so ready to forgive an injury, or bear with an offender, as one of a meaner rank. It is a want of power over a man's self that makes him do unbecoming things upon a provocation. A prince that can bridle his passions is a king over himself as well as over his subjects. God is slow to anger **because** great in power. He has no less power over Himself than over His creatures".

It is at the above point, we think, that God's patience is most clearly distinguished from His mercy. Though the creature is benefitted thereby, the patience of God chiefly respects Himself, a restraint placed upon His acts by His will; whereas His mercy terminates wholly upon the creature. The patience of God is that excellency which causes Him to sustain great injuries without immediately avenging Himself. He has a power of patience as well as a power of justice. Thus the Hebrew word for the Divine longsuffering is rendered "slow to anger" in Nehemiah 9:17, Psa. 103:8 etc. Not that there are any passions in the Divine nature, but that

(Continued on Page 288)

IMPORTANT NOTICES

Please advise promptly of change of address, otherwise copies will be lost in the mails.

We are glad to send a sample copy to any of your friends whom you believe would be interested in such a publication.

Send to Mr. I. C. Herendeen, Swengel (Union County), Penna., for a list of our publications. He has published many of our books and booklets.

This magazine is published as a work of faith and labour of love. The Editor and his wife gladly give their services. It is freely sent to all who will read it. No charge is made for it.

Christians who feel definitely led to do so, may have fellowship with us in this ministry. Those outside the U. S. A., please send only INTERNATIONAL Money Orders made out to Los Angeles, California, U. S. A.

CONTENTS

The Epistle to the Hebrews	266
The Satisfaction of Christ	272
The Christian's Warfare	278
The Intercession of Christ	281
A Personal Word	286
Review	287

THE EPISTLE TO THE HEBREWS

36. The Perfect Priest. Heb. 8:1-5

"This chapter is a continuation of the argument which has been prosecuted in the previous chapters respecting the priesthood of Christ. The apostle had demonstrated that He was to be a priest, and that he was to be, not of the Levitical order, but of the order of Melchizedek. As a consequence, he had proved that this involved a change of the law, appointing the priesthood, and that in respect to permanency and happy moral influence, the priesthood of Christ far surpassed the Jewish. This thought he pursues in the chapter, and shows particularly that it involved a change in the nature of the covenant between God and His people. In the prosecution of this, he (1) states the sum or principal point of the whole matter under discussion—that the priesthood of Christ was real and permanent, while that of the Hebrew economy was typical, and was destined in its own nature to be temporary: vv. 1-3. (2) There was a fitness and propriety of His being removed to heaven to perform the functions of His office there—since if He had remained on earth He could not have officiated as priest, that duty being by the law of Moses entrusted to others pertaining to another tribe: vv. 4, 5. (3). Christ had obtained a more exalted ministry than the Jewish priests held, because He was the Mediator in a better covenant—a covenant that related rather to the heart than to external observances: vv. 6-13" (Albert Barnes).

The above is perhaps about as good an analysis of Heb. 8 as can be supplied. We too are satisfied that the passage which is before us is both a continuation and a summarization of the whole preceding discussion of the apostle. In the previous chapters he has produced indubitable proof that Jesus of Nazareth, the Son of God, is the great High Priest of God's people, infinitely superior to all the priests who went before Him. The closing verses of chapter 7 especially, supply, a conclusive demonstration that He was priest and exercised the priestly office, while He was here on earth, and which He is now continuing to do in heaven. First, The description given of Him **as** "High Priest" in 7:26 has no pertinency whatever if it treats of what He was here upon earth. Take the expression, "undefiled"—what is there **in heaven** to defile? Nothing whatever. But understanding it to describe one of Christ's perfections while He was here in the world, it is full of significance.

Rightly did Geo. Smeaton declare, "Heb. 7:26, 27 show Christ on earth, as both Priest and Sacrifice. The 'such' of v. 26 refers not back to vv. 1-25, but to v. 27 cf. 8:1. The qualifications described, 'holy harmless, undefiled, separate from sinners', are descriptive of what He was here on earth when brought into contact with sin and sinners". Again; mark well the expression, "made higher than the heavens" in 7:26. **Who** was? The first part of the verse tells us: our "High Priest"! Note also the last clause of v. 27, "this He did once, when He **offered up** Himself". Who did "this"? Who is the "He"? The Lord Jesus, of course. And in **what** specific character is He there viewed? Why, as "High Priest". As we are told in 2:17, "He was a merciful and faithful High Priest in things pertaining to God, **to make** propitiation (Gk.) for the sins of the people", and as Rom. 3:25 plainly declares, He made propitiation at the cross. So again, in 4:14 we read,

"Seeing then that we **have** a great High Priest that is passed into the heavens". He did not enter heaven to become a priest, He **was** "Priest" when He "passed into the heavens". Language could not be plainer.

There is no excuse whatever for a mistake at this point, and our only reason for labouring it is that many who have boasted so loudly of their orthodoxy have systematically denied it. That Christ's sacrifice was a **priestly** one is clear from Eph. 5:2, "Christ . . . hath given Himself for us an offering and a sacrifice to God": not only as a "sacrifice" but as "an offering", and none **offered** to God the sacrifices of Israel save the priests. That Christ did not become Priest **after** He entered into heaven is also unequivocally established by Heb. 9:11, 12, "But Christ being come **an High Priest** of good things to come, by a greater and more perfect tabernacle, not made with hands . . . by His own blood He entered in once into the holy place, having obtained eternal redemption for us". He passed into heaven **in the capacity** of High Priest. Therefore we say that they who teach Christ became priest after His ascension are unconsciously or consciously, ignorantly or maliciously, corrupting the Truth of God and denying one of the most cardinal articles of our holy faith.

The line of argument followed by the apostle in the opening verses of Heb. 8 is not easily perceived. So far as the Lord has deigned to open their meaning to us, we understand it to be thus: Since Christ has ascended to the right hand of God, and now sits there as a Priest upon His throne, proof has been given that He is not a Minister of the earthly and Jewish sanctuary, but of the antitypical and heavenly one. Having set forth in chapter 7 the pre-eminence of Christ's priesthood over the Aaronic order and His all-sufficient qualifications for the office, the apostle now proceeds to evince His faithful execution of the same, and this, to the end of 10:19. In chapter 7 it is the excellency of our High Priest's **person** which is demonstrated; here in 8 it is His **ministry** which is contemplated. Note how in v. 2 He is spoken of as "a Minister of the sanctuary", that in v. 3 He has "somewhat also to offer", and observe the word "serve" in v. 5 and "ministry" in v. 6. In chapter 8 we are further shown the excellency of our Redeemer's sacerdotal office, first, from the high Sanctuary in which it is now exercised (vv. 1-5); second, from its functions corresponding with the better Covenant with which it is connected (vv. 6-13).

"Now of the things which we have spoken this is the sum: We have such an High Priest who is set on the right hand of the throne of the Majesty in the heavens" (v. 1). The participle is in the present tense and should be rendered "of the things of which we are speaking" (cf. R. V.), the general reference being to the entire contents of the epistle, the specific to what is found in 4:14 to 10:18. "This is the sum" or crowning point: it is here that all the previous teaching of the epistle culminates, for the priesthood of Christ is, really, its distinguishing theme.

"We have **such** an High Priest", looks back, particularly, to 7:26. John Brown pointed out the very close connection which exists between the closing verses of 7 and the opening ones of 8, thus: "It is to be borne in mind that the high-priesthood of Jesus Christ is the great subject of discussion in the section of the epistle of which these words form a part; and that, after having shown the reality of our Lord's high priesthood by two arguments (chap. 5)—the one derived from His legitimate investiture with this office, the other from His successful discharge of its functions—the apostle proceeds to show the pre-eminent excellence and dignity of our Lord's high-priesthood. He, with much ingenuity, deduces four arguments for the superiority of our Lord's priesthood to that of Aaron and his sons from the ancient oracle recorded in Psa. 110:4: 'The Lord hath sworn and will not repent, Thou art a priest forever after the order of Melchizedek'. A fifth argument suggested by, though not so wholly grounded on, this ancient oracle, is entered on in 7:26, and is prosecuted, if we mistake not, down to the middle of the 6th verse of chapter 8, where a new argument for the superiority of our Lord to the Aaronical priests obviously commences, the substance of which is this:—The superiority of our Lord's priesthood above that of Aaron and his sons is evident from the superior excellence of the covenant with which His priesthood is connected.

"The substance of the argument contained at the middle of v. 6 of chapter 8, may be thus expressed:—To fit a person for the successful discharge of the priesthood in reference to man, certain qualifications are necessary. These qualifications are wanting in the Aaronical priesthood: they are to be found in the highest perfection in Christ Jesus. We, that is, **men**, need a high priest 'holy, harmless, undefiled, made higher than the heavens'. Jewish priests do not answer to this description: Jesus Christ does. In Him we, **Christians**, have such a High Priest; and the conclusion is, He has received 'a more excellent ministry'. In this way, I apprehend, everything hangs well together, and the apostle's argumentative illustration appears complete and satisfactory. Indeed, the recurrence of the phrase '**such** a high priest' (7:26), and 'we have **such** a high priest (8:1), seems intended for the express purpose of showing that the train of thought is continuous."

"We have such an high priest, who is set on the right hand of the throne of the Majesty in the heavens". These words point another contrast between Christ and the Levitical priests. It is true that our Lord Jesus entered for a season, a condition of deep humiliation, taking upon Him the form of a servant, being made in the likeness of sin's flesh; and this was necessary unto the sacrifice which He was to offer. But as to His **durable** and abiding state, wherein He continues to discharge His priestly office, He is incomparably exalted above Aaron and his successors. After the Jewish high priest had offered the annual sacrifice of expiation unto God, he passed within the veil with the blood, presenting it before Him. But he stood before the typical mercyseat with holy awe, and upon the fulfillment of his duty immediately withdrew. But Christ, after He had offered His sacrifice unto God, entered heaven itself, not to stand in humble reverence before the throne, but to sit at God's right hand; and that, not for a season, but for evermore.

The immediate design of the Holy Spirit was to comfort the hearts and establish the faith of the sorely-tried Hebrews, who were constantly represented by their unbelieving fellows for no longer having fellowship with the sacred rites of Judaism, and thus, in their esteem, being without any temple, priest or sacrifice. The apostle therefore reminds them again that "We **have** such an High Priest", who, though invisible, has been exalted in dignity and glory far above those who serve under the law of a carnal commandment. For Christians today the "**We** have such an High Priest" defines the relation of Christ to God's elect: fallen angels and reprobate sinners have no High Priest, that is one reason why their punishment shall be **eternal**—there will never be a Mediator to plead their cause.

The great object before the apostle in this epistle was to present that which was calculated to draw the hearts of the Hebrews away from the temple at Jerusalem, to the true Sanctuary of Christian worship on High. It is for that reason that the **ascension** of Christ occupies so prominent a place in it. One of the objections which carnal critics have advanced against the Pauline authorship of Hebrews is the fact that only once (13:20) is the **resurrection** of Christ directly referred to, whereas in all the other epistles of Paul it is given a place of great prominence. But the reason for this is easily accounted for. The emphasis in Hebrews is placed upon Christ's being at God's right hand (1:3, 4:14, 6:20, 7:26, 8:1, 9:24, 10:12, 12:2) for the purpose of assuring those who were deprived of the temple-services in Jerusalem, that they **had** the reality and substance of those things which were merely typical and temporary, and that the real Sanctuary was not on earth, but in heaven, and there Christ Himself is now officiating.

"Who is set on the right hand of the throne of the Majesty in the heavens". The exalted position which our great High Priest now occupies should commend both His person and His office in our esteem and assure us what abundant cause we have for expecting the successful discharge of its functions. Who is "set" or "seated": Acts 7:55 warns us against interpreting this in a carnal or literal manner. With 8:1 should be compared 1:3 (see our comments thereon) and 12:2. There are some verbal variations to be noted. In 1:3, where Christ's personal glory as "Son" is in view, there was no need to mention "the throne". In 12:2, where it is the reward of the man Christ Jesus, the "throne" is seen, but the "Majesty in the heavens" is not added. Here, in 8:1, where the dignity and glory of His priestly office is affirmed, we have mentioned both "the throne" and the "Majesty" of God.

"A Minister of the sanctuary" (v. 2). This is exceedingly blessed. "Having declared the glory and dignity which He is exalted unto, as sitting down at the right hand of the throne of the Majesty in heaven, what can be farther expected from Him? There He lives, eternally happy in the enjoyment of His own blessedness and glory. Is it not reasonable it should be so, after all the hardships and miseries which He, being the Son of God, underwent in this world? Who can expect that He should any longer condescend unto office and duty? Neither generally have men any other thoughts concerning Him. But where then would lie the advantage of the Church in His exaltation which the apostle designs in an especial manner to demonstrate"? (John Owen).

Our blessed Redeemer, in His exalted glory, still condescends to exercise the office of a public minister in the behalf of His Church. It is required that our faith should not only apprehend what Christ did for us while He was here on earth, but also appropriate what He is now doing for His people in heaven. Indeed, the very life and efficacy of the whole of His mediation depends upon His **present** work on our behalf. Nowhere does the marvelous grace and the wondrous love of the Saviour more gloriously appear than in the ministry in which He is now constantly engaged. As all the shame, suffering, and pains of death deterred Him not from making an oblation for His people, so all the honour and glory, dignity and dominion with which He is now invested, diverts Him not from presenting its virtues before God and pressing for its blessings to be bestowed upon those for whom it was offered. His attention is still concentrated on His poor people in this wilderness world.

The "Sanctuary" in which our great High Priest ministers is Heaven itself: cf. 9:24, 10:19. It is the place where the majesty and glory of God are most fully displayed. "He looked down from the height of His sanctuary, from heaven did the Lord behold the earth" (Psa. 102:19). Heaven is here called "the Sanctuary" because it is **there** really dwells and actually abides all that was typically prefigured in the holy places of Israel's tabernacle. In the heavenly Sanctuary does Christ now discharge His priestly office for the good of His Church. It was a joyful time for Israel when Aaron entered the holy of holies, for he carried with him the blood which made atonement for all their sins. So the presence of Christ in heaven, pleading the efficacy of His meritorious blood, should fill the hearts of His people with joy unspeakable: cf. John 14:28.

"And of the true tabernacle, which the Lord pitched, and not man" (v. 2). This is not, as so many have supposed, an amplification of the preceding clause, but instead, a quite distinct thing. The word "true" is not here used in opposition to what is false (the temples of the heathen), but in contrast from the tabernacle of Israel, which was typical, shadowy, temporary. It has the force of that which is real, solid, and abiding. Israel's tabernacle was but an effigy of the antitypical one. "Moses gave you not that bread from heaven, but My Father giveth you the **true** Bread from heaven" (John 6:32), gives the force of the term. But what is the "true **tabernacle**" here referred to?

We answer, the Redeemer's humanity, in which He ministers before God on high. In proof of this note, first, the metaphor of a "tabernacle" is used for the body of man in 2 Cor. 5:1 and 2 Peter 1:13. Second, the Holy Spirit has expressly used this term (in the Greek) in John 1:14, "The Word became flesh and **tabernacled** among us". Third, in Heb. 9:11 "tabernacle" manifestly refers to Christ's humanity—observe it is there distinguished from "the holy place" (sanctuary) in 9:12!

In addition to what has been said above, it should be pointed out that the tabernacle of Israel was the outstanding O. T. type of the incarnate Redeemer. We have more fully developed this wondrous and beautiful truth in our exposition of John 1:14, to which we would refer the interested reader. Here we must confine ourselves to only two or three details. God sanctified Israel's tabernacle as a place to dwell in (Ex. 29:44, 45); so in Christ "dwelleth all the fulness of the Godhead bodily" (Col. 2:9). God's glory was most conspicuously manifested in the tabernacle—"The glory of the Lord filled the tabernacle" (Ex. 30:34); so of Christ the apostle declared "we beheld His glory, the glory as of the only begotten of the Father" (John 1-14). In the tabernacle, sacrifices and incense were offered to God, and all holy services were performed; so Christ in His body offered up His own sacrifice, prayers, and all holy services (Heb. 5:7, 10:5). To the tabernacle the people brought all their offerings (Lev. 1:3), so must we bring all ours to Christ (Heb. 13:15).

"The true tabernacle, which the Lord pitched, and not man". Here there is a manifest reference to the virgin-birth, the supernatural character of our Lord's humanity, being parallel with "A body hast **Thou** prepared Me" (10:5). The verb, "pitched" is a word proper unto the erection and establishment of a tabernacle—the fixing of stakes and pillars, with the fastening of cords thereto, was the principal means of setting up one (Isa. 54:2). It is the **preparation** of Christ's humanity which is signified: a body which was to be taken down, folded up for a season, and afterwards to be erected again, without the breaking or loss of any part of it. "Which the Lord pitched" shows the Divine origin of Christ's humanity: cf. Matt. 1:20. The words "and not man" declare that no human father was concerned with His generation: cf. Luke 1: 34, 35.

"For every high priest is ordained to offer gifts and sacrifices: wherefore it is of necessity that this man have somewhat also to offer (v. 3). The opening word of this verse intimates that the apostle is here supplying a confirmation of what he had declared in vv. 1, 2. He argues from a general to a particular: **"every high priest is ordained to offer"** (that being the specific purpose for which God calls him to this office) therefore, Christ, the great High Priest, must also have been ordained for that end. Thus, the Lord Jesus has done and is still doing that which appertains to the antitypical Sanctuary.

In the opening verses of our chapter we behold the Redeemer in the heavenly sanctuary, ministering there before God on the behalf of His people. "But **how** did He enter into this sanctuary? The high priests under the law entered into their sanctuary after having offered a sacrifice: and **so also** did the great High Priest of our profession. 'For every high priest is ordained to offer gifts and sacrifices: wherefore it is of necessity that this man have somewhat also to offer'. No attentive reader can help being sensible that these words, taken by themselves, do not convey a distinct, complete, satisfactory meaning. The statement is obviously elliptical: and the following seems to be the most probable way of supplying the ellipsis: We have a High Priest which has entered into the heavenly sanctuary, the true holy of holies. Every high priest is appointed to offer up sacrificial gifts in order to his entrance into the earthly sanctuary: it was necessary, as the antitype must correspond to the type, that this illustrious Priest should have somewhat also to offer, for the purpose of opening His way into the true sanctuary.

"Christ's being there, in the heavenly sanctuary, is the proof at once that an expiatory sacrifice has been offered, and that that sacrifice has been effectual. And what was this 'somewhat' which it was necessary that He should offer in order to His entering into the true sanctuary? We have but to look back to find the answer. It was 'Himself', 'holy, harmless, undefiled, separate from sinners'. His perfect, cheerful obedience to the preceptive part of the Divine law, and His perfect, cheerful obedience to the sanctioning part of it, opened for Him, as a High Priest, His way into that true holy place, where in the presence of God He acts as a public functionary in the name of His redeemed ones.

"It is plain that He could not have the sacrifices prescribed by the law to offer, for He did not belong to that class of persons to whom the offering of those was by law restricted; but He had a better sacrifice: read Heb. 10:5-13" (John Brown). "The apostle intends to show (v. 3) that Christ's priesthood cannot co-exist with the Levitical priesthood. He proves it in this way:—The law appointed priests to offer sacrifices to God; it hence appears that the priesthood is an empty name without a sacrifice. But Christ had no sacrifice such as was offered under the law; it hence follows that His priesthood is not earthly or carnal, but one of a more excellent character" (John Calvin).

Thus far the Holy Spirit has affirmed that the great High Priest of Christians is enthroned in heaven (v. 1); that He is there a "Minister", serving in the antitypical Sanctuary, and that, in the "true tabernacle", His own humanity (v. 2); and that His right to entrance there was His own perfect sacrifice (v. 3). He now declares, "For if He were on earth, He should not be a priest, seeing that there are priests that offer gifts according to the law" (v. 4). The opening "For" looks back to what had been declared in vv. 1, 2, and introduces a further proof that the **continuation** of Christ's priestly ministry **must be** in the heavenly sanctuary. The earthly system, Judaism, had its own priests who offered gifts "according to the law." "This mere earthly, typical, inferior priesthood has been already provided for, its rules are fixed, and the order of men defined who fill its functions; and according to those rules, Christ Jesus could not be one of them, not being of the right tribe. The fact, therefore, that He has priestly functions, a fact before proved, shows that His priesthood is in a different sanctuary" (F. S. Sampson).

This 4th verse is the one that is most appealed to by those who deny that Christ entered the priestly office before His ascension. But if it be examined carefully in the light of its setting, nothing whatever is to be found in it which favours the socinian view. That which the apostle is treating of here in chapter 8 is the **full** execution of the **whole** of Christ's priesthood: thereunto belonged not only the once oblation of Himself, but His continual intercession as well. Now that intercession must be made in heaven, at God's right hand. We say "must" for the O. T. types require it. Aaron had to carry incense, as well as blood, into the holy of holies (Lev. 16). Had Christ remained on earth after His resurrection, only half of His priestly work had been performed. His ascension was necessary for the maintenance of God's governmental rights, for the vindication of the Redeemer Himself, and for the wellbeing of His people; that what He had begun on earth might be continued, consummated and fully accomplished in heaven. The expiatory sacrifice of Christ had been offered once for all, but He must take His place as an Intercessor at God's right hand, if His Church should enjoy the benefits of it.

In this 4th verse the apostle is not only confirming his statement in vv. 1, 2. but he is also anticipating the objecting Jews: But you Christians have no high priest on earth! True, says the apostle, and well it is that we do not. It is to be carefully noted that the Spirit does not here say that when Christ **was** on earth He was **not** a Priest—no, He would not flatly contradict what He had plainly affirmed in 2:17. 5:7-9, 7:26, 27. Instead, He says "If He **were** on earth," that is, had He remained here, He would not have completely discharged His sacerdotal functions. Had Christ stayed on earth, He had left His office imperfect, seeing that His people needed One to "appear in the presence of God" (9:24) for them. If Aaron had only offered sacrifice at the brazen altar, and had not carried the blood within the veil, he had left his work only half done.

"Seeing that there are priests that offer gifts according to the law" (v. 4). This states the reason **why** Christ had not been a perfect priest if He had not gone to heaven: there were already priests, and that, of a tribe which He was not of, that offered gifts on earth, yea, had done so long before He became incarnate. Therefore if the entire design of Christ's priesthood had been merely to be a priest on earth, they would plead possession before Him. But, as v. 5 immediately proceeds to tell us, those priests only served "unto the example and shadow of heavenly things." Nothing but a real priesthood in heaven could supercede and abolish theirs. This is brought out plainly in 9:8: the "first tabernacle" was to stand until a Priest went into heaven and executed that office there: so that if Christ is to be Priest alone, He must become a Priest interceding in heaven, or otherwise, the Levitical priests would share that office with Him.

To sum up. The first clause of v. 4 is not an absolute, but a relative statement: "For if He were on earth, He would not be a priest". And why? "Seeing that there are priests that offer gifts according to the law", that is, the place is already occupied. Yes, but **what** place? Why that of offering gifts **according to the law.** Since Christ was above the law, the ideal and perfect Priest, He could not officiate in the temple at Jerusalem, for not only did His fleshly descent from Judah hinder this, but the sanctuary in which He now presents His sacrifice must correspond in dignity to the supreme excellency of His office. Thus, so far from His absence from the earth casting any suspicion on Him it is the necessary consequence of His being who He is and of having done what He has done.

"Who serve unto the example and shadow of heavenly things, as Moses was admonished of God when he was about to make the tabernacle: for, See, saith He, thou make all things according to the pattern showed to thee in the mount" (v. 5). Here the apostle furnishes further proof of what he had said at the beginning of v. 4. The presence of the type necessarily implies the absence of the Antitype (cf. 9:8-10), because the very nature of a type is to symbolise visibly an absent and unseen reality. From the Divine viewpoint, Judaism was set aside, ended, when God rent the veil of the temple (Matt. 27:51); but from the human, it was not abolished till Titus destroyed Jerusalem in A. D. 70. Israel's priests still served, but the only significance of their ministry was a typical one.

The design of the Spirit in v. 5 is obvious. There was something above and beyond the material tabernacle which God prescribed to Moses: that which he built, only furnished a faint foreshadowing of spiritual and heavenly realities, which are now actualised by Christ on High. The entire ministry of Israel's priests had to do with earthly and carnal things, which provided but a dim outline of things above. The word "example" signifies type, and is rendered "figures" in 9:24. The term "shadow" means an adumbration, and is opposed to the substance or reality; see Col. 2:17, Heb. 10:1. "Shadows" are but fading and transitory, have no substance of themselves, and but darkly represent.

"See, saith He, thou make all things according to the pattern showed to thee in the mount". "This passage is found in Ex. 25:40, and the apostle adduces it here on purpose, so that he might prove that the whole service according to the Law was nothing more than a picture, as it were, designed to shadow forth what is found spiritually in Christ'" (John Calvin).

The practical application to us of the teaching of v. 5 is: Christians ought to exercise the utmost care and diligence to ascertain the revealed mind of God in what He requires from us in our worship of Him. Though Moses was learned in all the wisdom of Egypt, that was of no value or avail when it came to spiritual acts,. He must do **all** things precisely as Jehovah ordered. In connection with what is styled "Divine worship" today, the great majority of professing Christians follow the dictates of their own wisdom, or inclination of their fleshly lusts, rather than Holy Scripture. Others mechanically follow the traditions of their fathers, or the requirements of popular custom. The result is that the Holy Spirit is grieved and quenched by the worldly inventions of carnal men, and Christ is **outside** the whole thing. Far better not to worship God at all, than to mock Him with human "will worship" (Col. 2:23). Far better to worship Him scripturally in the seclusion of our homes, than fellowship the abominable mockery that is now going on in almost all of the so-called "churches".

—ARTHUR W. PINK.

THE SATISFACTION
("Atonement")
OF CHRIST

12. Its Application (Concluded).

We cannot do better than begin this article by transcribing the opening words from chapter 1, book 3 of Calvin's "Institutes." "We are now to examine how we **obtain** the enjoyment of those blessings which the Father has conferred on His only begotten Son, not for His own private use, but to enrich the poor and needy. And first it must be remarked, that as long as there is a separation between Christ and us, all that He suffered and performed for the salvation of mankind is useless and unavailing to us. To communicate what He received from the Father, He must, therefore, become ours, and dwell in us. . . The sum of all is this —that the Holy Spirit is the bond by which Christ efficaciously unites us to Himself."

The Satisfaction of Christ rendered absolutely certain the salvation of those for whom He transacted, whose federal Head He was. Yet something farther was necessary to make His people the actual participants of it: in the language of Acts 26:18 the Holy Spirit must be sent to "open their eyes, to turn from darkness to light, and the power of Satan unto God, that they may receive forgiveness of sins, and inheritance among them which are sanctified by faith". The beneficiaries of Christ's mediatorial work enter this world in a state of guilt and depravity, and it is the peculiar office of the Holy Spirit to bring them into a state of life and liberty. The persons of the Godhead have shared and distributed the whole work of the salvation of the elect amongst Themselves unto three several parts: election is appropriated to the Father, redemption to the Son, the application of both election and redemption to the Spirit. Here again we reach a vitally important aspect of truth concerning which few today have any light.

We showed in article ten, conclusively we hope, that the efficacy of the Atonement has not been left an open question, that the full accomplishing of God's design therein is not in anywise dependent upon man. What we would now press upon the reader is that the same God who ordained the end, also ordained all the means whereby that end is infallibly reached. The end God had before Him was the salvation of His people, their ultimate glorification, their being fitted to spend eternity in His holy presence. The means whereby that end was to be reached are the mediatorial work of Christ, and the operations of the Holy Spirit. As the three persons of the ever-blessed Trinity are undivided in Their Essence, so they are perfectly unanimous in their will and workings. Therefore those who have an interest in the good will of the Father and the redemption of the Son, are likewise the subjects of the Spirit's gracious influence.

It is a great mistake and a serious error to separate the present mission and ministry of the Holy Spirit from the Atonement of Christ, just as it is to contemplate the sacrifice of the Son apart from the purpose of the Father. All of the Three Divine persons concurred in the terms and arrangements of the Everlasting Covenant. It is the special work of the Spirit to make effectual unto the souls of God's elect the gracious purpose of the Father and the meritorious purchase of the Son. That which Christ did **for** His people, the Spirit stands pledged to make good **in** them. The Holy Spirit has been sent here to free those captives for whose liberty Christ paid the Father the ransom-price. This the Father promised His Son on condition of His performing the work assigned Him. It needs to be steadily borne in mind that "**all** the promises in Him (i. e. in Christ) are yea, and in Him Amen" (2 Cor. 1:20), and therefore that the promises made to Christ's seed, recorded in Scripture, are but the **transcripts** of the promises which God first made to their Head—cf. Titus 1:2! Let such passages as Isa. 44:3, Ezek. 36:25-27, Joel 2:18 be read in **that** light.

"Salvation is of the Lord" (Jonah 2:9), entirely so, from beginning to end. It is God's "great salvation", in its origination, in its effectuation, its application and in its consummation. Man contributes nothing to it whatsoever. All the Trinity are concerned and engaged in it. The Father is the Author of salvation from sin, Christ the Purchaser, the Spirit the Conveyor. It is the Father who begets the elect (James 1:17, 18); yet, they are declared to be the "seed" of Christ (Isa. 53:10), while they are "born" of the Spirit (John 3:6). Though it has many aspects, and may be considered from various angles, nevertheless, it is one and the same salvation. It is the third aspect of it we are here contemplating, namely, the Satisfaction of Christ made efficacious by the infallible **application** thereof to God's elect. To take this up in detail, let us note:

1. The Holy Spirit's Office

What we wish to look at now is the particular relation which the Holy Spirit sustains to the **economy** of Redemption. In this He is **subordinate to** Christ the Mediator. There are a number of passages which clearly teach this. John the Baptist declared concerning Christ, "He shall baptise you with the Holy Spirit" (Mark 1:8). The **communication of** the Spirit was to be the distinguishing mark of the Saviour's ministry, in respect of which He would prove to be greater and mightier than the herald who sent to prepare His way. In John 20:22 we find the risen Redeemer imparting this Divine gift to His apostles: "He breathed on, and saith unto them, Receive ye the Holy Spirit". In Rev. 3:1 He is spoken of as "He that **hath** the seven Spirits of God". These, and other passages which might be quoted, show that, in the administration of the Everlasting Covenant, the Spirit is now subject to Christ. Hence is He called, "The Spirit of Christ" (Rom. 8:9).

That the Holy Spirit **should be** subject to Christ, that the Saviour should direct the Spirit's operations, was promised Him in the Everlasting Covenant. In Acts 1:4 He is referred to as "The **promise** of the Father". Observe how when John the Baptist's prediction was fulfilled and Christ baptised His people with the Holy Spirit, Peter explained the supernatural phenomena attending it, by saying, "Therefore being by the right hand of God exalted, and having received of the Father the **promise** of the Holy Spirit, He hath shed forth this, which ye now see and hear (Acts 2:33)! So again in Gal. 3:14 we read, "That the blessing of Abraham might come on the Gentiles **through** Jesus Christ; **that** we might receive the **promise** of the Spirit through faith. So too we read that believers are "sealed with that Holy Spirit of **promise**" (Eph. 1:13).

In the next place, we would point out how that Christ has actually **purchased** the gift of the Holy Spirit for His people, that His coming to the redeemed is one of the consequences or fruits of Christ's Atonement. First, this is clearly implied in John 7:39: "But this spake He of the Spirit which they that believe on Him should receive: for the Holy Spirit was not (given) **because** that Jesus was not yet glorified." Whether we understand the "glorified" as referring to Christ's death (John 13:31) or to His exaltation (1 Tim. 3:16), the coming of the Spirit is clearly a result thereof; by this we are to understand that the obedience of Christ was the **meritorious** cause of God's sending His Spirit to indwell His people. Again; we may note that Christ's communication of the Spirit to His apostles in John 20:22 was not till after His blood had been shed. Again, observe the double "that" in Gal. 3:14 following Christ's being made a curse for us in v. 13; it is the relation of cause to effect.

"But when the fulness of the time was come God sent forth His Son, made of a woman, made under the law. To redeem them that were under the law, that we might receive the adoption of sons. And because ye are sons, God hath sent forth the Spirit **of His Son into** your hearts". (Gal. 4:4-6). Here we have three things: the Son's being sent forth to redeem God's elect; this, that they might receive the adoption of sons; in consequence thereof the Spirit's being sent into their hearts. The elect were adopted into God's family before the foundation of the world (Eph. 1:4-5), hence they "**are** sons" (Gal. 4:6), and this **before** they received the Spirit. The Spirit is not given to make them sons, for all the members of Christ were written in the book of life as sons and daughters before sin existed or time began. No, the Spirit was given to them because they are sons, and that, as the meritorious gift of Christ, purchased by His redemption.

To sum up this point. This choicest benefit we receive from God could not have come unless His justice had been fully satisfied, and His favour procured by a sufficient sacrifice. It was the death of Christ which appeased the anger of His holy Father, and opened those treasures of grace which by reason of our sins had otherwise been shut up from us. Wondrously is this brought out in the O. T. types: the Rock (Christ) must be **smitten** before the Water (the Spirit) could flow forth unto God's people (Ex. 17:6). The very design of the Spirit is to make manifest the fulness of God's love to His people, and how could that be until God had demonstrated it at the cross: Rom. 5:8! The Spirit is here to declare the means of salvation, and they are the obedience, death and resurrection of Christ.

We are now to consider the teaching of Christ in His paschal discourse on this most sacred and blessed subject. "But the Comforter, the Holy Spirit, whom the Father will send in My name" (John 14:26). Christ keeps the treasury of Grace in His own hands. He is so choice of it that He would not entrust its administration to angels. Angels were employed to strengthen Him, both at His temptation and in His agony in Gethsemane: and they are ministering spirits for the heirs of salvation, but they have not the custody of that which brings them into heirship. Christ employs none but the Spirit to be His Attorney and Deputy in this world. The Spirit is sent in **His** name: "But when the Comforter is come, whom **I** will send unto you from the Father" (John 15:26).

"Howbeit when He, the Spirit of truth, is come, He will guide you into all truth: for He shall not speak of Himself; but whatsoever He shall hear, shall He speak: and He will show you things to come. He shall glorify Me: for He shall receive of Mine, and shall show unto you" (John 16:13, 14). There are three things in these verses which need to be particularly noted in this connection. First, the Spirit would not speak of Himself, but only that which He should hear. He was to come as the Representative of Christ, and therefore He would reveal none other truth and communicate none other grace than what is in and by and from Christ Himself. Just as Christ declared, "I do nothing of Myself; but as My Father hath taught Me, I speak these things . . . I speak that which I have seen with My Father" (John 8:28, 38), so the Spirit would set His seal upon what Christ had taught. The Spirit was an equal participant in the councils of the Father and Son, being thoroughly cognisant of all that passed between them in the Everlasting Covenant. He has an infinite knowledge of Their designs, for He "searcheth all things, yea, the deep things of God" (1 Cor. 2:10); therefore does He make intercession for the saints "according to God" (Rom. 8:27).

Second, "He shall glorify Me," that is, the Lord Jesus. As Christ sought not His own glory, but ever had the glory of the Father before Him in all that He did, so the Spirit seeks not His own glory, but that of Him whom He now represents. This is the mission of the Holy Spirit, the design of His being sent here, the work He has come to do. "As the work of the Son was not His own work, but rather that of the Father who sent Him (John 5:17), and in whose name He performed it (Luke 2:49); so the work of the Spirit is not His own work, but rather the work of the Son whom He sent, and in whose name He doth accomplish it" (J. Owen).

"He shall receive of Mine, and shall shew it unto you". The things of Christ may be reduced to two heads: "Grace and Truth" (John 1:17). From Christ the Spirit receives these; to His redeemed He effectually communicates grace and personally reveals the truth. Just as Christ declared "The Father loveth the Son, and hath given all things unto His hand" (John 3:35), so hath Christ delivered all His interests into the Spirit's hand. Two great things accrue to us by Christ: **acquisition** of redemption, **application** of redemption. The one is wrought by His death, the other by his resurrection-life; the one was procured by Him immediately, the other is secured by the Spirit mediately.

2. The Spirit Regenerating

"That which is born of the Spirit is spirit" (John 3:6). And, what is **to be** born of the Spirit? It is to be vitally united to Christ, so that "he that is **joined unto** the Lord is one spirit" (1 Cor. 6:17). Therefore it is to be made the recipient of "eternal life" for "God hath given to us eternal life and this life is in His Son" (1 John 5:11). And this is given to us on the ground of Christ's Satisfaction. This is brought out plainly in John 3, though nearly all writers on that chapter have quite missed the point. There we find our Lord pressing upon Nichodemus the imperative necessity of the new birth:

"Marvel not that I said unto thee, Ye must be born again". The Pharisee was quite non-plussed, and asked, "How can these things be?" Christ's reply is found in vv. 14-16.

Now to say Christ here taught that regeneration is effected by faith in Him as "lifted up", is to miss the main point in His words. The key to those verses lies in connecting the "must" of v. 14 with the "must" of v. 7. To be born again is to be made partaker of a new life: it is to have "eternal life". Now the very design of Christ's being "lifted up" and of God's love in "giving" Him was, "that whosoever believeth in Him should not perish, but have **eternal life**" (v. 15). But no man could be born again, none could have eternal life, save as the result of a full satisfaction having been made to the claims of a holy and righteous God. Except the Corn of wheat "fall into the ground and die, it abideth alone" (John 12:24). The Holy Spirit could not regenerate except on the ground of the atoning death of Christ. Let us present some further proofs of this.

"For the law of the Spirit of life in Christ Jesus hath made me free from the law of sin and death" (Rom. 8:2). In v. 1 we read that believers are exempt from all condemnation because of their **legal** union with Christ. In v. 2 we are shown the fruit of this: the Holy Spirit makes it good to the soul in a **vital** way. The "law" of the Spirit refers both to His authority and power. But what we would call special attention to is that, in the economy of redemption, the authority and power of the Spirit is "of life **in Christ Jesus**"... In other words, the Spirit communicates to God's elect the very life which is in the Mediator. "The gift of God is eternal life through (or "in") **Jesus Christ** our Lord" Rom. 6:23). In Christ "dwelleth all the fulness of the Godhead" (Col. 2:9) therefore the Spirit both resides "in" and is dispensed "by" Him!

"And if Christ be in you, the body is dead because of sin; but the spirit is life because of righteousness" (Rom. 8:10). Because of our union with Christ, the whole body of sin (cf. 6:6, 7:24) is legally "dead". The "spirit" here refers to that which is born of the Spirit, and that is "life", and it is a life "**because of** righteousness", namely, the righteousness of Christ. The meritorious ground on which the Spirit imparts "life" to us is the Satisfaction of Christ. I live **because** Christ died and rose again for me.

"Not by works of righteousness which we have done, but according to His mercy He saved us, by the washing of regeneration, and renewing of the Holy Spirit; which He shed on us abundantly **through Jesus Christ** our Saviour; That being justified by His grace we should be **made heirs** according to the hope of eternal life" (Titus 3:5-7). Nothing could be plainer. Here, the **ground on which** the Spirit regenerates is clearly referred to as the Redeemer's mediation. Many have wondered how it was possible for the **Holy** Spirit to take up His abode in a fallen and depraved creature. He could not do so but for one thing, namely, that depraved creature has been legally cleansed by the precious blood of Christ. Beautifully was this foreshadowed in the O. T. types. The "oil" (emblem of the Spirit: 1 John 2:20, 27) was always placed upon the "**blood**": see Lev. 14:14-17.

Another beautiful type is found in Psa. 133:2, "Like the precious ointment upon the head, that ran down upon the beard, Aaron's beard: that went down to the skirts of his garments". Here Aaron foreshadowed our great High Priest receiving such a plenitude of that which spoke of the Holy Spirit, that all the members of His mystical body partake of the same. It is to this that Heb. 1:9 refers, "Therefore God, Thy God, hath anointed Thee with the oil of gladness above Thy fellows". Here the Mediator is in view, as the words "Thy God" plainly show. Though He, by virtue of His humanity being taken up into union with the second person of the Godhead, has been anointed "above" His fellows, yet they as His "fellows" receive the same gracious and holy unction as He did.

"How much more shall the blood of Christ, who through the eternal Spirit offered Himself without spot to God, purge your conscience from dead works to serve the living God" (Heb. 9:14). This verse brings before us another aspect of the believer's regeneration, namely, the purging of his conscience, so that he may worship God. It is the Spirit who removes from the conscience the intolerable load of guilt, by giving him to see that Christ bore it away for him. But what we would here emphasise is that this gracious operation of the Spirit is attributed to, is based upon, or is one of the fruits of, the "blood of Christ".

Now Christ, as Mediator, obtained for Himself a right to all the elect: "All Mine are Thine, and Thine are **Mine**" (John 17:10). They are His "peculiar people" (Titus 2:14). Thus, at God's appointed hour Christ is entitled to claim each of them for Himself. This right He exercises. "When, according to the determinate counsel of God, the time of the gracious visitation of every one of the elect is come, He actually delivers them, as His property, by an outstretched arm. And why should He not, seeing He can easily effect it by the power of the Holy Spirit, turning and inclining their heart? Is it credible that He should suffer those who are His lawful right, to be, to remain, the slaves of Satan? Shall He suffer any of those to perish whom He purchased for His own possession by His precious blood? Christ Himself has taught us thus to reason: 'Other sheep I have, which are not of this fold: them also I must bring, and they **shall** hear My voice' (John 10:16). Because these sheep were of right His property, it therefore becomes Him actually to lay hold of them as His own, and bring them into His fold" (H. Witsius). This is done by the Spirit.

To sum up this point. The coming of the Spirit in regenerating power to God's elect is both a Covenant-promise and an Atonement-purchase. The **cause** of the Spirit's working is jointly from the Father and the Son. Only as this is maintained do we ascribe the glory which belongs to Both by virtue of the Spirit's operations. The Spirit works from the Father's decree (2 Thess. 2:13), and the Son's redemption; in other words, He is sent to effectuate what was determined upon in the Everlasting Covenant. To all the Father elected, and to all for whom Christ died, the Spirit is given. "The Holy Spirit is the bond of union between us and Christ. We are united to Him because we have the same Spirit Christ had; there is the same Spirit in Head and members, and therefore He will work like effects in Him and in you. If the Head rise, the members will follow after, for His mystical body was appointed to be conformed to their Head, Rom. 8:29" (T. Manton, 1660).

3. Faith Imparted

That faith is, in some sense, essential unto salvation, it would with an open Bible before us, be worse than idle to deny. But the important question is, Did Christ **purchase** the gracious operations of the Spirit and **all** His fruits for those for whom He died? or, did He effect by His sacrifice nothing more than the removal of legal impediments out of the way of salvation, leaving them to provide their own faith and repentance? That Christ **must** have purchased these should be clear from the fact that, in their natural condition, the elect have no power to furnish any spiritual graces. It has been rightly pointed out that, "The Scriptures everywhere ascribe the **whole** ground and cause of our salvation to Christ. But if the differentiating grace which distinguishes the believer from the unbeliever is to be attributed to any cause external to Christ's mediation, then **that** cause, and not His redemption, is the real cause of salvation" (A. A. Hodge).

That faith is necessary in order to salvation is clear from such verses as Acts 16:31, Rom. 1:16, etc. God never gives the one without the other, therefore both are inseparably connected in His eternal purpose thereunto: "God hath from the beginning chosen you to salvation **through** sanctification of the Spirit (the new birth) **and** belief of the truth" (2 Thess. 2:13). Yet it is a mistake to say that faith is a "condition" of salvation in the sense of my paying for an article is the condition of obtaining the same. Every condition to the **right** of salvation has been fulfilled for us by Christ. Faith is rather the **connection** between the soul and God's salvation in Christ, and that connection is made by the Holy Spirit. The various steps in the outworking of God's eternal purpose are set forth in Rom. 8:29, 30. The actual **application** of redemption commences with the effectual Call of the Spirit, by which the elect are brought out of a state of nature into a state of grace.

There are two chief errors in connection with saving faith. The first is that fallen man is the author of it, that it is the product of the creature's will. This is a horrible delusion which must be firmly withstood. A dead man cannot believe. Believing in Christ in a spiritual and saving way is the result and fruit of "life" communicated to the heart. Christ declared that "No man can come to Me, except the Father which hath sent Me **draw** him" (John 6:44): this is accomplished in and by the Spirit's regeneration. It should be noted that John 1:12 is explained in 1:13, as that John 3:15, 16 are preceded by John 3:6, 7. Those who are born again believe. Those who believe **have been** born again: "Whosoever believeth that Jesus is the Christ **is** begotten of God" (1 John 5:1 R. V.).

The second error is in separating the Spirit's communication of faith from the merits of Christ's sacrifice. "Why did we at first believe? Why do we still exercise that faith and walk by it? Only because it was covenanted for on our behalf when Christ undertook to die for us. It should help us to pray better, 'Lord, increase our faith' when we remember at what a cost that faith was procured for us. And certainly this alone will keep us from one of the subtlest of all Satan's snares,—pride of faith. This is one of the greatest curses which Arminianism brings with it. The poor deluded worshipper of the free-will idol thinks that what separates him from others is that while they and he alike have heard the gospel, there was in him that principle of faith which the others lacked: and that, not because God had done anything for him that He had not done for them, for this it is his creed to deny... How easy it is to live proudly on faith! And where Arminianism prevails we are sure to see it. Faith will do as well as works for Satan's purpose of leading us to give to man the glory that is Christ's" (From Papers of the Sovereign Grace Union Conference, 1923).

In order that Christ may have **all the glory** even for our believing in Him, it is most necessary to recognise that faith is not only God's gift, Eph. 2:8, 9 (and therefore while we are saved "through" faith, we are **not** saved **for** faith), and that this faith is "of the operation of God" (Col. 2:12) i. e. of the Spirit's working, but also that the Spirit imparts it **on the ground of** Christ's redemption, i. e. that Christ **merited it** for us. It is because Christ appeased God's wrath and removed the obstacles from the outflow of His mercy toward us, that the Spirit is free to work in us. This is clearly stated in 2 Peter 1:1, "To them that have obtained a like precious faith with us **in the righteousness of** our God and Saviour Jesus Christ" (R. V.). God has treasured up all the store of grace and gifts in Christ, and it is out of His "fulness" the Spirit takes (John 16:14) and we "receive" (John 1:16). Only as this is held fast to is the righteousness of Christ exalted and magnified.

In Eph 1:3 we are told that God "hath blessed us with **all** spiritual blessings in the heavenlies **in Christ**", and not the least of these is **faith**! In Rom. 8:32 the question is asked, "He that spared not His own Son, but delivered Him up for us all, how shall He not with Him **also** freely give us **all** things?" Yes, "with" Christ, God freely bestows on us the Spirit, faith, repentance, and all that is needed for time and eternity. In Phil. 1:29 we read, "For unto you it is given **in the behalf of Christ**, not only **to believe** on Him, but also to suffer for His sake". In 1 Peter 1:3 it is said, "Blessed be the God and Father **of our Lord Jesus Christ,** which according to His abundant mercy hath **begotten us"**. It is **as** "the Father of our Lord Jesus Christ" that God begets us!

Salvation and all the blessings accompanying it were purposed, promised and purchased long before writer and reader first saw the light of day. Those for whom Christ died have an indefesable **right** to what He bought for them, and that, long before they come into actual possession of the same. If it be asked, This being so, why do not the elect enter upon the enjoyment thereof as soon as they are born into this world? The answer is this, Because God has reserved to Himself the right and liberty to discharge the debtor **when** and **as** He pleases. As in the parable: some are called at the first hour, some at the third, sixth, ninth, and some at the eleventh (Matt. 20).

4. Repentance Given

"Him hath God exalted with His right hand a Prince and a Saviour **for to give** repentance to Israel, and forgiveness of sins" (Acts 5:31). Impenitence and unbelief are the thick clouds which dissolve under the blessed beams of the Sun of Righteousness.

Every spiritual gift and blessing we receive argues or presupposes the vicarious work of Christ. The grace of God is "given you by Jesus Christ" (1 Cor. 1:4). It is by His having given Himself for our sins that we are delivered from "this present evil world" (Gal. 1:4). It is "**in Him** also we have obtained an inheritance" (Eph. 1:11). Christ died to procure for us a subjective as well as an objective sanctification, which is accomplished by His Spirit's indwelling us: Titus 2:14, Eph. 5:26, 27. It is because He has washed us from our sins in His own blood that "He hath made us kings and priests unto God and His Father" (Rev. 1:5, 6). God makes us "perfect in every good work to do His will, working in us that which is well-pleasing in His sight, **through Jesus Christ**" (Heb. 13:21).

Thus, all the graces of the Christian character and all the virtues of the Christian life which are wrought in us by the agency of the Holy Spirit, are imparted through Christ and received out of His meritorious fulness. Then, well may we join the saints in heaven in saying with a loud voice, "Worthy is the Lamb that was slain" (Rev. 5:12).

—ARTHUR W. PINK.

If new readers desire this magazine next year (D. V.), is it too much to ask for a few lines from them? If we hear not from you, be not surprised if your name is dropped from our list.

THE CHRISTIAN'S WARFARE

"For I delight in the law of God after the inward man; but I see another law in my members warring against the law of my mind, and bringing me into captivity to the law of sin which is in my members. O wretched man that I am! Who shall deliver me from the body of this death? I thank God through Jesus Christ our Lord. So then with the mind I myself serve the law of God, but with the flesh the law of sin" (Rom. 7:22-25).

A believer is to be known not only by his peace and joy, but by his warfare and distress. His peace is peculiar: it flows from Christ, it is heavenly, it is holy peace. His warfare is as peculiar: it is deep-seated, agonizing, and ceases not till death. I have chosen the subject of the Christian's warfare, that you may know thereby whether you are a soldier of Christ—whether you are really fighting the good fight of faith.

1. A Believer delights in the law of God: "I delight in the law of God after the inward man".

1. Before a man comes to Christ, he hates the law of God: his whole soul rises up against it—"the carnal mind is enmity against God, and is not subject to the law of God" (Rom. 8:7). (1) Unconverted men hate the law of God on account of **its purity**: "Thy Word is very pure, therefore Thy servant loveth it". For the same reason worldly men hate it. The law is the breathing of God's pure and holy mind. It is infinitely opposed to all impurity and sin. Every line of the law is against sin. But natural men love sin, and therefore hate the law, because it opposes them in all they love. As bats hate the light, and fly against it, so unconverted men hate the pure light of God's law, and fly against it. (2) They hate it for **its breadth**. "Thy commandment is exceeding broad" (Psa. 119:96). It extends to all their outward actions, seen and unseen; it extends to every idle word that men shall speak; it extends to the looks of their eye; it dives into the deepest caves of their hearts; it condemns the most secret springs of sin and lust that nestle there. Unconverted men quarrel with the law of God because of its strictness. If it extended only to my outward actions, then I could bear with it; but it condemns my most secret thoughts and desires, which I cannot prevent. Therefore ungodly men rise against the law. (3) They hate it for **its unchangeableness**. Heaven and earth shall pass away, but one jot or one tittle of the law shall in no wise pass away. If the law would change, or let down its requirements, or die, then ungodly men would be well pleased. But it is unchangeable as God: it is written on the heart of God with whom is no variableness nor shadow of turning. It cannot change unless God change; it cannot die unless God die. Even in an eternal hell its demands and curses will be the same. It is an unchangeable law, for He is an unchangeable God. Therefore ungodly men have an unchangeable hatred to that holy law.

2. When a man comes to Christ, this is all changed. He can say, "I delight in the law of God after the inward man". He can say with David, "O how love I thy law: it is my meditation all the day". He can say with the Lord Jesus, in the 40th Psa., I delight to do Thy will, O My God, yea, Thy law is within My heart". There are two reasons for this:—

1st., **the law is no longer an enemy**. If any of you who are trembling under a sense of your infinite sins, and the curses of the law which you have broken, flee to Christ, you will find rest. You will find that He has fully cancelled the demands of the law as a Surety for sinners, that He has fully borne all its curses. You will be able to say, "Christ hath redeemed me from every curse of the law, being made a curse for me, as it is written, Cursed is every one that hangeth on a tree" (Gal. 3:13). You have no more to fear, then, from that awfully holy law; you are not under the law but under grace. You have no more to fear from the law, than you will have **after** the Judgment Day. Imagine a saved soul after the Judgment Day. When that awful scene is past—when the dead, small and great, have stood before the great white throne—when the sentence of eternal woe has fallen upon all the unconverted, and they have sunk into the lake whose fires can never be quenched; would not that redeemed soul say, I have nothing to fear from the holy law; I have seen its vials poured out, but not a drop has fallen on me? So may you say **now**, O believer in Jesus. When you look upon the soul of Christ, scarred with God's thunderbolts, when you look upon His body, pierced for sin, you can say, He was made a curse for me; why should I fear that holy law?

2nd, **The Spirit of God writes the law on the heart**. This is the promise: "After those days, saith the Lord, I will put My law in their inward parts, and write it in their hearts; and will be their God, and they shall be My people" (Jer. 31:33).

Coming to Christ takes away the fear of the law, but it is the Holy Spirit coming into your heart that makes you love the law. The Holy Spirit is no more frightened away from that heart; He comes and softens it; He takes out the stony heart and puts in a heart of flesh; and there He writes the holy, holy, law of God. Then the law of God is sweet to that soul: he has an inward delight in it. "The law is holy, and the commandment holy, and just and good". **Now** he unfeignedly desires every thought, word, and action to be according to that law: "6 that my ways were directed to keep thy statutes: great peace have they that love Thy law, and nothing shall offend them". The 119th Psalm becomes the breathing of that new heart. Now also he would feign see all the world submitting to that pure and holy law. "Rivers of water run down mine eyes because they keep not Thy law". O that all the world but knew that holiness and happiness are one. Try yourselves by this. Can you say, "I delight in the law of God after the inward man"? Do you love it now? Do you long for the time when you shall live fully under it—holy as God is holy, pure as Christ is pure?

O come, sinners, give up your hearts to Christ, that He may write on it His holy law! You have long enough had the Devil's law graven on your hearts; come you to the Lord Jesus, and He will both shelter you from the curses of the law, and He will give you the Spirit to write all that law in your heart; He will make you love it with your inmost soul. Plead the promise with Him. Surely you have tried the pleasures of sin long enough. Come now, and try the pleasures of holiness out of a new heart. If you die with your heart as it is, it will be stamped a wicked heart to all eternity: "He that is unjust, let him be unjust still" (Rev. 22:11). O come and get the new heart before you die; for except you be born again you cannot see the kingdom of God.

II. A true believer feels an opposing law in his members: "I see another law in my members warring against the law of my mind, and bringing me into captivity to the law of sin which is in my members". When a sinner comes first to Christ, he often thinks he will now bid an eternal farewell to sin: now I shall never sin anymore. He feels already at the gate of heaven. But a little breath of temptation soon discovers his heart, and he cries out, "I see another law".

1. Observe what he calls it, **"another law";** quite a different law from the law of God—a law clean contrary to it. In v. 25 he calls it a "law of sin"—a law that commands him to commit sin—that urges him on by rewards and threatenings. In Rom. 8:2 it is called "a law of sin and death"— a law which not only leads to sin, but leads to death, eternal death: "the wages of sin is death". It is the same law which in Gal. is called the flesh: "the flesh lusteth against the spirit" (5:17). It is the same which in Eph. 4:22 is called "the old man", which is wrought according to the deceitful lusts. The same law which in Col. 3 is called "your members"—"mortify therefore, your members which are upon the earth" (v. 5). The same is called in Rom. 7:24 "this body of death". The truth then is, that in the heart of the believer there remains the whole members and body of an old man, or old nature; there remains the fountain of every sin that has ever polluted the world.

2. Observe again what this law is doing—**"warring"**. This law in the members is not resting quiet, but is always fighting. There can never be peace in the bosom of a believer. There is peace with God, but constant war with sin. This law in the members has got an army of lusts under him, and he wages constant war against the law of God. Sometimes, indeed, an army are lying in ambush, and they lie quiet till the hour of temptation, and then they war against the soul. The heart is like a volcano, sometimes it slumbers and sends up nothing but a little smoke; but the fire is slumbering all the while below, and will soon break out again. There are two great combatants in the believer's soul. There is Satan on the one side, with the flesh and all its lusts at his command; then on the other side there is the Holy Spirit, with all the new creature at His command. And so "the flesh lusteth against the spirit, and the spirit against the flesh; and these two are contrary the one to the other, so that ye cannot do the things which ye would."

Is Satan ever successful? In the deep wisdom of God the law in the members does sometimes bring the soul into captivity. Noah was a perfect man, and Noah walked with God, and yet he was led captive: "Noah drank of the wine, and was drunken". Abraham was "the friend of God" and yet he told a lie, saying of Sarah his wife, "She is my sister". Job was a perfect man, one that feared God and hated evil, and yet he was provoked to curse the day wherein he was born. And so with Moses, and David, and Solomon, and Hezekiah, and Peter and the apostles.

Have you experienced this warfare? It is a clear mark of God's children. Most of you, I fear, have never felt it. Do not mistake me. All of you have felt a warfare at times between your natural conscience and the law of God. But **that** is not the contest in the believer's bosom. It is a warfare between the Spirit of God in the heart, and the old man with his deeds.

If any of you are groaning under this warfare, learn to be humbled by it, but not discouraged. First, be **humbled** under it. It is intended to make you lie in the dust, and feel that you are but a worm. Oh! what a vile wretch you must be, that even after you are forgiven, and have received the Holy Spirit, your heart should still be a fountain of every wickedness! How vile, that in your most solemn approaches to God, in awfully affecting situations, you should still have in your bosom all the members of your old nature. Let this make you lie low. Second, let this **teach you your need of Christ.** You need His precious blood as much now as you did at the first. You can never stand before God in yourself. You must go again and again to Him to be washed. Even on your dying bed you must hide under Jehovah, our righteousness. You must also **lean** upon Christ. He alone can overcome for you. Cleave closer and closer to Him every day.

III. The feelings of a believer during this warfare:

1. He feels wretched. "Oh wretched man that I am" (v. 24). There is nobody in this world so happy as a believer. He has come to Christ, and found rest. He has the pardon of all his sins in Christ. He has near approach to God as a child. He has the Holy Spirit dwelling in him. He has the hope of glory. In the most awful times he can be calm, for he feels that God is with him. Still there are times when he cries, O wretched man! When he feels the plague of his own heart—when he feels the thorn in the flesh—when his wicked heart is discovered in all its fearful malignity—Ah, then he lies down, crying, O wretched man that I am! One reason of this wretchedness is, that sin discovered in the heart takes away the **sense** of forgiveness. Guilt comes upon the conscience, and a dark cloud covers the soul. How can I ever go back to Christ? he cries. Alas! I have sinned away my Saviour. Another reason is, the loathsomeness of sin. It is felt like a viper in the heart. A natural man is often miserable from his sin, but he never feels its loathsomeness; but to the new creature it is vile indeed. Ah! brethren, do you know anything of a believer's wretchedness? If you do not, you will never know his joy. If you know not a believer's tears and groans, you will never know his song of victory.

2. He seeks deliverance. "Who shall deliver me"? In ancient times, some of the tyrants used to chain their prisoners to a dead body; so that, wherever the prisoner wandered, he had to drag a putrid carcass after him. It is believed that Paul here alludes to this inhuman practice. His old man he felt to be a noisome putrid carcass which he was continually dragging about with him. His piercing desire is to be freed from it. Who shall deliver us? You remember once, when God allowed a thorn in the flesh to torment His servant, a messenger of Satan to buffet him, Paul was driven to his knees. "I besought the Lord thrice, that it might depart from me". Oh this is the true mark of God's children! The world have an old nature; they are old men together. But it does not drive them to their knees. How is it with you, dear souls? Does corruption felt within drive you to the throne of grace? Does it make you call on the name of the Lord? Does it make you say, like the importunate widow, "Avenge me of mine adversary"? Does it make you, like the Canaanitish woman, cry after the Lord Jesus? Ah, remember, if lust can work in your heart, and you lie down contented with it, you are none of Christ's!

3. He gives thanks for victory. Truly we are more than conquerors through Him that loved us; for we can give thanks before the fight is done. Yes, even in the thickest of the battle we can look up to Christ and cry, Thanks to God. The moment a soul groaning under corruption rests the eye on the Lord Jesus, that moment his groans are changed into songs of praise. In Christ you discover a fountain to wash away the guilt of all your sins. In Christ you discover grace sufficient for you—grace to hold you up to the end—and a sure promise that sin shall soon be rooted out altogether. "Fear not, I have redeemed thee. I have called thee by My name; thou art Mine" Ah, this turns our groans into songs of praise. How often a Psalm begins with groans and ends with praises! This is the daily experience of all the Lord's people. Is it yours? Try yourselves by this. O if you know not the believer's song of praise, you will never cast your crowns with them at the feet of the Lamb. Dear believers, be content to glory in your infirmities that the power of Christ may rest upon you.

—R. MURRAY M'CHEYNE, 1840.

THE INTERCESSION OF CHRIST

(Continued).

The wondrous plan of redemption originated in the sovereign wisdom and love of God from all eternity. The triune Jehovah determined to exhibit the excellencies of the Divine character and the exhaustless resources of the riches of His grace, by using sin as the dark background from which they might shine forth the more resplendently. God's permission of the fall and apostacy of man was in order to the fuller display of His attributes than had been the case if our first parents had remained obedient to their Maker. The entrance of sin into the world made possible the intervention of a third person, who stood in the most intimate relation to the parties which were at variance, and who restored His fallen people to communion with God.

In the Covenant of Grace, framed by the counsels of the Godhead, the second person of the Trinity was set up from everlasting as the Godman, in accordance with His own voluntary engagement as Mediator and Surety; and the work which He undertook to accomplish was that of mediation, namely, to bring sinners to God, and to be the perpetual medium of all intercourse and blessing between God and them; the entrance of sin having rendered mediation indispensable to reconciliation and fellowship with the thrice Holy One. A mere act of grace would not cancel the offence against heaven's Sovereign, and restore to favour the guilty. But for the Divine scheme of redemption the entire human race had perished without remedy, as did the rebel angels who had no Mediator.

The appointment of any mediator for the fallen sons of Adam lay with God alone, who had the sovereign right, according to the good pleasure of His imperial will, to admit a satisfaction for the violation of His law in the room of transgressors, or to leave them without one. It pleased the Most High to appoint His only begotten Son, as a Substitute and Surety for His guilty people, and in Him God found an adequate and glorious ransom. The Mediator is the God-man. As God, He is clothed with omnipotence; as man, he was susceptible of sympathy and compassion. Thus, all-sufficient help was laid upon One that was "mighty to save". Full and ample provision was made for repairing the injury done to the law and manifestative honour of God, and at the same time for securing the pardon of the guilty, and restoring the moral image of God to His fallen people.

The mediatory appointment was the central object of the Everlasting Covenant, for the office of Mediator displays throughout time and eternity the glory and sufficiency of this wondrous and rich provision of Divine mercy. In approaching unto the highest mount of blessing either on earth or in heaven, our greatest privilege is to come to "Jesus the Mediator of the new covenant" (Heb. 12:24), for this is at once the foundation and the capstone of all holy fellowship, and the security for the enjoyment of all favour and blessing. The mediation of Christ may be viewed in a two-fold aspect: as it relates to God, and as it regards His sinful people. He is the Mediator of reconciliation of sinners to God by His sacrifice and intercession. The one is the sure ground of the other. The death of the Substitute is the grand fundamental act of Christ's mediation, on the performance of which all His other acts of mediation are dependent. If our comfort and confidence, when conscious of sin, are that "we have an Advocate with the Father, Jesus Christ the righteous", the sure ground on which we have the warrant to entertain a joyful hope is, that "He is the **propitiation** for our sins" (1 John 2:1, 2).

Our Lord's mediation in heaven is by means of His intercession, and this is properly the **application** of the atonement. The atonement of Christ was required as a ransom for transgressors, as the payment to Divine justice of the sinner's great debt. His intercession in glory is needed to put the sinner in possession of the blessings which the atonement purchased. The two are inseparable and both are indispensable for the sinner if he is to realise the favour and friendship of God. Having made peace through the blood of His cross, Christ now, by His Spirit, enlightens the understandings of His people, renews their hearts, and reduces their wills and lives unto the obedience of faith. By His glorious power Christ quickens those who are spiritually dead, slays the enmity of the carnal mind, and transforms the moral nature into the Divine image and likeness

What has been said above gives a summary of that which has been before us in the preceding article—and carefully compare our exposition of Heb. 7:25 and the "Atonement" article in the Nov. issue. In further developing this transcendently important theme of our Redeemer's intercession let us now consider,

3. Its Subjects

As to who are the ones for whom Christ maketh intercession the unequivocal language of Rom. 8:33, 34 decides once and for all: "Who shall lay anything to the charge of **God's elect**? God that justifieth. Who is he that condemneth? Christ that died, yea rather . . . . who also maketh **intercession for us**". Against this plain statement there can be no appeal by any who are subject to the authority of Holy Writ. It is not for all sinners that the Saviour is now pleading before God, but for those who were given to Him by the Father before the foundation of the world. Every passage in Scripture bearing upon this aspect of our theme is equally explicit in restricting the advocacy of Christ to His own people.

If we revert to the types we find that Melchizedek, the high priest, blest none but Abraham (Gen. 14), the father of them that believe. When Aaron went into the tabernacle to appear before Jehovah, he bore on his breastplate the names of none save the twelve tribes of Israel. To imagine Aaron interceding on behalf of the Egyptians or Amelekites would be suited only to the brain of a madman. If we turn to O. T. prophecy we hear the Messiah saying that His goodness extendeth to "the saints that are in the earth" (Psa. 16:3), and then in sharp contrast, of reprobates He declared, "their drink offerings of blood will I not offer, nor take up **their names** into My lips" (v. 4). So again in Isa. 53:12 we are explicitly told that He "bare the sin of **many** (i. e. God's people, see v. 8) and made intercession for **the** transgressors".

If we turn to the great High Priestly prayer of Christ, found in John 17, we hear Him declaring, "I pray for them: I pray not for the world, but for them which Thou hast given Me; for they are Thine" (v. 9). And why would not Christ pray for the reprobate world? Because in all things He is subject to the good pleasure of the Father: "I came down from heaven, not to do Mine own will, but the will of Him that sent Me" (John 6:38). Nor has He changed. Christ can never run counter to His own Gospel and bless them whom the Gospel curses (Mark 16:16), nor save them whom the Gospel condemns (2 Thess. 1:8). It would be a contradiction to confirm the everlasting covenant by His death and then break it by His life; to walk according to the counsels of God when He was here upon earth, and to defeat them now He is in heaven. He that gave mercies to men's faith during the days of His flesh, will not give salvation to unbelief now He has entered into His glory.

"I pray for them: I pray not for the world, but for them which Thou hast given Me: **for they are Thine**": that, and that alone, is the reason why I take so deep an interest in and intercede for them. They are dear to Me, because they are dear to Thee. How precious and powerful was the truth of God's sovereign election to the heart of the Lord Jesus! He knew the whole of the Father's good will and pleasure towards all the elect. He knew that He Himself could not add one to the number. He knew that He was sent from the Father to live and die for them, and them only; and therefore, in perfect agreement therewith, He prayed for them only. In this also He has left us an example. We most certainly ought to pray according to the Truth of God, and intercede only for those whom Christ redeemed by His sore travail; and therefore we should qualify our requests for the salvation of any sinner with, "if he or she be one of them".

The intercession of Christ, be it remembered, is inseparably connected with His work of atonement, that work being the very ground and substance of it. His intercession is not a mere ministry of persuasive pleading, but the actual presenting of His atonement before the Father. Christ is "the Surety of the new covenant" or economy of redemption, and therefore His whole undertaking can only be on behalf of those who were given Him in that covenant. A definite number was given Him to be redeemed from among the sons of men: for them alone He died and purchased eternal life, for them alone He pleads continually and secures that life. As we have before pointed out, His pleading is not that of a supplicant, but a claimant, having rights and authority.

That the advocacy of the Redeemer is limited to those whom He saves, is evident from various considerations. His intercession for the elect only, is abundantly plain from the particularity of God's sovereign purpose of grace, and also from the definite character and discriminating design of redemption. The atonement and intercession are correlates, not only in nature, but in extent. Whomsoever and whatsoever Christ has procured by His blood, for them and for that does He plead before the throne of God. It is absurd and pernicious, as well as unscriptural, to suppose that Christ makes intercession for those who live and die in unbelief, who continue to disown His mediatory office.

In this connection weigh well the words of Christ in Matt. 11:25, "I thank Thee, O Father, Lord of heaven and earth, because Thou hast **hid these things** from the wise and prudent, and hast revealed them unto babes". It is here affirmed in positive language that there are some of mankind from whom the saving benefits of Christ's kingdom are "hid". Without insisting upon any specific definition of that solemn word, it cannot be successfully denied that it imparts some awful privation in the matter of the soul's eternal interests, nor is it possible to harmonise the fact of God's hiding these things from the wise and prudent with the theory that Christ procured those very things for them by His death. God would not act so glaringly inconsistent as to first purchase for men saving benefits (at the infinite cost of the precious blood of His own Son), and then deliberately hide those benefits from them for whom they were so expensively provided.

Rightly did John Owen conclude from Rom. 8:33, 34, "Whence also we cannot but observe, that those for whom He died may assuredly conclude He maketh intercession for them, and none shall lay anything to their charge; which breaks the neck of the general-ransom theory, for according to that, He died for millions that have no interest in His intercession, who **shall have** their sins laid to their charge, and perish under them".

Over what has been advanced, Arminians object that in Luke 23:34 we find Christ on the cross praying for the forgiveness of His murderers. To this it is sufficient reply to point out that we must distinguish between the prayers of Christ as a perfect man, and as Mediator. As He was a holy man, He cherished not any spirit of revenge, but desired only the good of His enemies. His prayer in Luke 23:34 was not a petition by virtue of His office as High Priest, but in discharge of His duty as He was subject to the law as a public person; which law enjoined the loving of His neighbour as Himself. Moreover, Christ did not pray for all His persecutors, but only for them who had sinned out of ignorance, as His words plainly show.

Coming now to the positive side of the subject. Christ intercedes for **His ministers.** In the great intercessory prayer of John 17 we find that after praying for Himself that He might be glorified, in order that He might glorify the Father, He next pleaded for His apostles, as the representatives of His future ministers; asking for them the blessings which they greatly need, and enforcing His petitions with the most weighty and affectionate pleas. Their spiritual illumination, preservation through His name, sanctification through the Truth, union to their living Head and to one another in faith and love, the success of their labours by the Truth which they preach and the power of their example, and their glorification with Him hereafter, are the great matter of His intercession for the heralds of the cross.

"How eminent is the office of the Christian minister, when it occupies the chief place in the intercession of the Mediator in glory! How high and honourable are its privileges and how abundant the assurance that the great ends for which the ministers of Christ are called shall, without fail, be effected, as these ever enter into the earnest and prevailing pleadings of the High Priest in heaven! What powerful and constraining motives are thus furnished to the members of the Church to put many prayers for ministers into the censer of the great High Priest, if they would have them kept in His name from the evil of the world, made eminently high and devoted, and rendered instrumental of blessing to the Church and to the world" (T. Houston).

Christ's advocacy is for **all believers.** In John 17:20 we read, "Neither pray I for these alone, but for them also which shall believe on Me through their word". Here it is the members of the Church of the Firstborn, a peculiar people, become such through believing on Christ through the preaching of His ministers. For all these He seeks substantially the same blessings as He sought for the apostles. The Saviour's intercession is continually presented for all those who have been, are, or shall yet be, gathered into one in Him, the Head. It secures for them the dispensation of the means of grace, and God's blessing upon the means, rendering them effectual to the heirs of salvation. As on Aaron's brestplate, worn by him when he entered into the most holy place, were engraven the names of **all** the tribes of Israel (little Benjamin's as much as Judah's), so on the heart of the Intercessor within the veil, are borne all the chosen of God. Out of the hand of the Angel of the Covenant ascends continually, amid the cloud of incense (His merits, fragrant to God), "the prayers of **all** saints" (Rev. 8:3).

Christ prays for **each Christian individually.** The intercession of our exalted Saviour is made not only for the entire election of grace comprehensively, or for the whole Church as a body, but it is for each saint severally. "I have prayed for **thee** that **thy** faith fail not" (Luke 22:32). "If any **one** sin, we have an Advocate with the Father, Jesus Christ the righteous" (1 John 2:1): "He that overcometh, I will not blot out his name out of the book of life, but I will confess **his** name before My Father, and before His angels" (Rev. 3:5): I will plainly and publicly own him as one that belongs to Me.

The scriptural marks of those for whom Christ prays are (a) "the transgressors" (Isa. 53:12): not angels, not sinless creatures, but violaters of God's law: for them He died, for them He lives. (b). Those who come unto God by Him (Heb. 7:25): they are those who fly to Christ for refuge, who renounce all dependence upon themselves, and who trust in His office and work for them. Thus, through Christ the one Mediator, by the Spirit, they have access unto the Father, Eph. 2:18. (c). Praying souls: Rev. 8:3. Do you, my reader, wish to know whether or not **you** are among the number for whom Christ intercedes? then ask God to help you answer the following questions: Do you value above all things **those** blessings for which Christ asks the Father?—that His people may be kept from evil (John 17:15), sanctified by the truth (John 17:17), have fellowship with the Father and with one another (John 17:21). Do you join your own repeated and earnest supplications for **these** things to His intercession? Do you rely wholly upon His unspeakable merits for the acceptance of your prayers? If so, you have good reason to believe that Christ **is** now pleading your cause before the Father.

It is unspeakably solemn to discover that Christ not only intercedes **for** His friends, but He also intercedes **against** His enemies. This awe-inspiring phase of our subject has been ignored by almost every writer upon this theme, nevertheless, it is plainly taught in the Scriptures. First, in the types. Of Elijah, who shadowed forth the Lord Jesus so remarkably and in so many respects, we read, "Wot ye not that the Scripture saith of Elijah? how he maketh intercession to God **against** Israel" (Rom. 11:2). Second, in Messianic prophecy we are told that He should cry, "Let their table become a snare before them: and for their welfare, a trap. Let their eyes be darkened, that they see not; and make their loins continually to shake. Pour out Thine indignation upon them, and let Thy wrathful anger take hold of them" (Psa. 69:22-24). **That** was the prayer of Him to whom they gave gall for meat and vinegar for drink (v. 21)!

Again, in the 2nd Psalm, God commissioned the Mediator to "Ask of Him" (v. 8), and then He adds, "Thou shalt break them with a rod of iron, Thou shalt dash them in pieces like a potter's vessel" (v. 9). This too is the fruit of His "asking". As God gives Him blessings for those who trust in Him, so He gives Him judgments for those who set themselves against Him (v. 12). As Christ had a love to shed His blood, so He hath a wrath to burn against them who kiss Him not with a kiss of fervent and affectionate homage: see Rev. 8:5. God has committed all judgment into the hands of His Son (John 5:22), and has exalted Him to His own right hand, until He makes His enemies His "footstool" (Heb. 1:13).

4. Its Properties

The pre-eminent fitness of the Lord Jesus Christ to be His people's Advocate is seen in His personal and official qualifications; and the properties of His intercession, as He continually carries it on, entitle Him to our fullest confidence. Consider,

First, its **purity**. He who enters into the Holiest of all, and whose work it is to present a flawless offering before the Lord of hosts, requires to be absolutely free from all impurity. Accordingly it is said of our High Priest, that He is "holy, harmless, undefiled, and separate from sinners" (Heb. 7:26); therefore, all that proceeds from Him is pure and holy. Blessed is it to see how jealously God guarded this in the types. In Ex. 30 God said of the incense, it shall be "pure and holy" (v. 35), and again, "it shall be unto you most holy" (v. 36). So "holy" (v. 37) was it to be unto them, that they were forbidden to make any of it for their own private use, under pain of being cut off from their people (v. 38). So too the altar of incense was overlaid with "**pure** gold" (Ex. 30:3), while a border of "gold" surrounded its top, thereby denoting that Christ would present no plea before God save that which had the Divine **glory** in view. The tendency of all which Christ asks for is to purify His people from all iniquity and to perfect holiness in the fear of the Lord.

Second, its **wisdom**. In our Intercessor are hid "all the treasures of wisdom and knowledge" (Col. 2:3). He is omniscient, and as such, possesses a perfect knowledge of the counsels of His Father and a perfect knowledge of the needs of His people. Nothing is hid from Him: "all things are naked and opened unto the eye of Him with whom we have to do" (Heb. 4:13). He is acquainted with the weaknesses, circumstances, trials and temptations of each of His people, and suits His pleas accordingly. He knows our cause better than we do ourselves, for "He needs not that any should testify of man, for He knows what is in man" (John 2:25). Our prayers are defective, for "we know not what we should pray for as we ought" (Rom. 8:26), but Christ is "of quick understanding in the fear of the Lord" (Isa. 11:3).

Third, its **authority**. Christ did not assume to Himself the office of Intercessor, but was called unto it by God: Jer. 30:21, Heb. 5:5. He has been given the right to see that all the stipulations of the covenant are fulfilled, all the debts of the covenant children discharged, and payment made of every purchased blessing. The very manner in which He conducts His intercession intimates this. As One seated upon the throne, He claims, rather than begs; seeks as a matter of right, more than of favour; demands rather than petitions. His "Father, I will" (John 17:24) shows this. Christ appears before God not only as our Friend, but as our Attorney, whom the high court of Heaven has admitted, and which the Judge of all cannot deny, for He is "Jesus Christ, **the righteous**" (1 John 2:1). Then how certain His suit, how prevailing must be His pleas, how sure His success.

Fourth, its **compassion**. The one who pleads the cause of poor sinners must not be hard-hearted, and impervious to suffering, and thus unable to enter into their circumstances and make their cause his own. No, the One whom God has appointed to be the Intercessor of His feeble, tried and weeping people, is He who Himself passed through this wilderness scene. Therefore are we assured, "We have not an High Priest which cannot be touched with the feeling of our infirmities; but was in all points tempted like as we are, sin excepted" (Heb. 4:15). And again, "For in that He Himself hath suffered being tempted, He is able to succour them that are tempted" (Heb. 2:18). He has tasted of all the sorrows of life. Of the sorest afflictions, bitterest temptations, most awful privations, He had full and frequent trial. Therefore has He the tenderest sympathy with all our weaknesses (but **not** our sins!) and an active disposition to help us in time of need.

Fifth, its **earnestness**. What a blessed and remarkable word is that concerning our Intercessor in Jer. 30:21, "He hath engaged His **heart** to approach unto Me, saith the Lord"! No perfunctory or mechanical praying is His. With greatest cordiality of spirit does He engage in His work of advocacy. Wondrously was this also typed out of old in "the censer full of **burning coals of fire**" (Lev. 16:12, 13) which the high priest took within the vail, representing as it did, the ardency of the affections of Christ's soul when He prays to the Father on our behalf. Let it also be remembered that the names of Israel's tribes were not only borne upon Aaron's shoulders (Ex. 28:12), but also upon his heart (v. 29) when he appeared before Jehovah. Great affections cannot be without earnestness in their cause. For what purpose did Christ take His human affections into heaven (Heb. 13:8), but to exercise them for us and to us!

Sixth, its **acceptableness**. Nothwithstanding the weakness and unworthiness of those for whom Christ intercedes, there is everything in His person and in the work in which He is engaged, calculated to secure for them acceptance. He is the Beloved of the Father, in whom He is ever well pleased. "He is the favourite of the Court wherein He pleads, acceptable to the Judge in His person, acceptable to Him in His office, acceptable to Him in the suit which He manages. His intercession is nothing else but the presenting to God the sacrifice which restored to Him the pleasure of His creation, gave Him a rest, and continues in it. The savour of that sacrifice in heaven, which was offered on earth, is grateful to the Judge of the world. It is as sweet to God as the Levitical incense (the type of it) could be to man (Ex. 30:34-36), a composition of the most aromatic spices" (S. Charnock).

Seventh, its **solitariness**. He is the alone Advocate: "There is **one** Mediator between God and men, the man Christ Jesus" (1 Tim. 2:5). Horribly have Romanists perverted this cardinal truth in the faith once delivered to the saints, by bringing in angels and fallen sinners to be His companions in this work, thereby snatching the glory from Christ to confer it upon the creature. Since our High Priest alone has the honour to sit at the right hand of God, He alone has the honour of this office of Advocacy. None else had the right to purchase for us, none else has the right to plead for us. This too was emphatically foreshadowed in the type: "And there shall be **no man** in the tabernacle of the congregation when he goeth in to make an atonement" (Lev. 16:17). The Levites served without, but none save the high priest ministered within the vail. It is the Saviour's supreme prerogative to be the "First and the

Last" (Rev. 1:11): as He was the Alpha in ransoming, so will He be the Omega in redeeming. As He was the sole Author of salvation by His passion, so He will be the sole Finisher by His intercession.

—ARTHUR W. PINK.

(To be continued, D. V.)

A PERSONAL WORD

"Thou crownest the year with Thy goodness; and Thy paths drop fatness" (Psa. 65:11). These are the words which have come to my mind and impress our heart as we took up our pencil to write a few lines at the close of another year. And as we review the Lord's dealings with us during the past twelve months, none seem more appropriate to our case. O how great is the Lord's goodness, and how abundant has been the manifestation of it toward us. Surely the least that we can do, ere we pass another milestone of life, is to offer Him a tribute of praise, by briefly placing on record some of His loving-kindnesses.

"Thou crownest the year with Thy goodness". On these words Spurgeon says in his Treasury of David, "We may understand the expression to mean that God's love encircles the year as with a crown; each month has its gems, each day its pearl. Unceasing kindness girdles all time with a belt of love. The providence of God in its visitations makes a complete circuit, and surrounds the year". Thus have we found it, both spiritually and temporally, during 1930. God has compassed all its days with His benignity and enclosed each month with His bounties. He has given us instances of His goodness in every thing that concerns us, so that on every hand we have met with tokens of His favour.

The Lord has been good to us personally. Throughout another year God has again graciously preserved the editor and his wife in good health. This is indeed a great blessing, for which we should be deeply thankful. Those who boast of possessing a constitution "as strong as iron" know not whereof they speak, for "**all** flesh is grass" (Isa. 40:6). They who imagine they are as "strong as an ox" have no more spiritual intelligence than one. All our strength comes from God. We may study closely and observe strictly the laws of health, be most particular in our diet, and careful to take plenty of openair exercise, but unless **God** is pleased to bless these means, sickness will be our portion. How wonderful it is that the great God is mindful of our puny bodies! Every night we definitely ask the Lord that, if it be His holy will, He will grant us a refreshing and reinvigorating sleep and awaken us in the morning in full health and strength. And He deigns to grant our request.

The Lord has been good in connection with the work which He has condescended to commit unto us. Were we given the opportunity, we would not exchange places with the President of the U. S. A. or with the Prime-minister of England. No, for by sovereign grace, we are far better occupied than in winning laurels of earthly fame. We are an ambassador of the King of kings. It is our blessed privilege to minister unto those who are joint-heirs with Christ. We are sowing Seed which will yield an eternal harvest, and month by month the Holy Spirit replenishes our basket. Though we endeavour to apply ourselves closely, constantly, to this written ministry, it never palls on us. There is a marvelous vitalizing power in God's eternal Word. Its pastures are ever "green" (Psa. 23:2), and fresh. Its refreshing wells are exhaustless.

Nor is our labour in vain. We might insert an equal number of unsolicited testimonies telling of help received, under God from the "Studies", as we gave in the "Welcome Tidings" in the August issue; but that is not necessary. Scarcely a day ever passes but what the Lord moves some soul to send us a word which draws out our hearts in praise unto the Giver of every good and perfect gift. These encouragements along the way are signal tokens of the Lord's tender mercy to us. A number of young preachers have written to say how that God has used our publications to establish them in the faith. This should make us abound in thanksgiving. Remember them, Christian readers, at the throne of grace, for they need their hands upheld against the modern Amalekites.

The Lord has been good in supplying our every financial need. Though the editor has received less than two hundred dollars (forty pounds) during the past two **years** for oral ministry, and though we never appropriate to ourselves anything that is sent in to and for the magazine, yet we have lacked no good thing, and owe no man anything. Though this year has been one of industrial depres-

that grace has snatched us as brands from the burning, giving us a place in God's family, and begotten us unto an eternal inheritance in glory; how miserably we requite Him. How shallow our gratitude, how tardy our obedience, how frequent our backslidings! One reason why God suffers the flesh to remain in the believer is that He may exhibit His "longsuffering **to usward**" (2 Peter 3:9). Since this Divine attribute is manifested only in this world, God takes advantage to display it toward "His own".

May our meditation upon this Divine excellency soften our hearts, make our consciences tender, and may we learn in the school of holy experience the "patience of saints", namely, submission to the Divine will and continuance in well doing. Let us earnestly seek grace to emulate this Divine excellency. "Be ye therefore perfect, even as your Father which is in heaven is perfect" (Matt. 5:48): in the immediate context Christ exhorts us to love our enemies, bless them that curse us, do good to them that hate us. God bears long with the wicked notwithstanding the multitude of their sin, and shall we desire to be revenged because of a single injury?

—ARTHUR W. PINK.

---

sion throughout the English-speaking world, and though the publishing and mailing out of the "Studies" costs one hundred dollars (twenty pounds) every month, we have never had to keep the Printer waiting twenty-four hours after his invoice has been received. These lines are being written quite a little before Dec. 31, but we believe that when that date is reached, D. V., we shall have a small balance (last year it was eighty-one dollars—sixteen pounds) to bring forward for 1931.

Following our custom we shall drop from our list the names of several hundreds to whom "Studies" have been sent for the last year or two. We do not feel justified to use the money of the Lord's stewards in wasting copies upon those who profit not from them, nor on those who take advantage of the generosity of others. We feel the freer to say this because we make it a rule to **return** all gifts sent in by those whom we have reason to fear are unsaved, as also from those who wish to "pay" for it. Spiritual things cannot be purchased with the dross of earth. On the other hand, those who desire to have fellowship with this work of the Lord's, or express their gratitude unto Him by a gift towards its continuation (but not otherwise) are free to do so.

In conclusion, let us once more earnestly solicit the prayers of God's people that we may be Divinely furnished unto all good works, and enabled to publish only that which will redound to God's glory, and be for the edification of His people. Pray that, if it be God's will, an increasing number may share with us these riches of His grace. Our circulation is a very restricted one. We hope to continue the "Atonement" articles throughout another year. We expect that henceforth this magazine will be printed in a bolder and more legible type. To God alone be all the praise for having crowned another year to us with His "Goodness". With hearty greetings to every Christian reader, yours by God's abounding mercy,

—A. W. AND V. E. PINK.

REVIEW

As the end of another year is at hand, the Christian should seek Devine help to compare his spiritual state now with what it was twelve months ago. Let him search his heart with such questions as these. Am I increasingly denying myself? Am I becoming more conformed to the image of Him who is "meek and lowly in heart"? Is the Spirit granting me clearer views of my inbred depravity and am I becoming viler in my own estimation? Is this making me appreciate the more the wondrous grace and forbearance of God? Is my confidence in God growing, so that I am leaving the future entirely in His hands? Am I more resigned to His blessed will, assured that He knows what is best for me? Are the details of my daily walk more strictly regulated by the precepts of Scripture than they were a year ago? Do I spend more time in secret prayer? Is my mind more frequently engaged in spiritual meditation? Am I gentler, kinder, more unselfish, toward my fellow-men? Am I less enthralled by the attractions of the world? These are some of the tests which each of us should apply to discover whether or not we are really growing spiritually—A. W. P.

God's wisdom and will is pleased to act with that stateliness and sobriety which becometh His exalted majesty.

In support of our definition above let us point out that, it was to this excellency in the Divine character that Moses appealed, when Israel sinned so grievously at Kadesh-Barnea and there provoked Jehovah so sorely. Unto His servant the Lord said, "I will smite them with the pestilence and disinherit them." Then it was that the typical mediator pleaded, "I beseech Thee let **the power** of my Lord be great according as Thou hast spoken, saying, The Lord is **longsuffering**" etc. (Num. 14:17). Thus, His "longsuffering" is His "power" of self-restraint.

Again, in Rom. 9:22 we read, "What if God, willing to show His wrath, and to make His **power** known, endured with much **longsuffering** the vessels of wrath fitted to destruction". Were God to immediately break these reprobate vessels into pieces, His power of self-control would not so eminently appear; by bearing with their wickedness and forebearing punishment so long, the power of His patience is gloriously demonstrated. True, the wicked interpret His longsuffering quite differently—"Because sentence against an evil work is not executed speedily, therefore the heart of the sons of men is fully set in them to do evil" (Eccl. 8:11)—but the anointed eye adores what they abuse.

"The God of patience" (Rom. 15:5) is one of the Divine titles. Deity is thus denominated, first, because God is both the Author and Object of the grace of patience in the creature. Second, because this is what He is in Himself: patience is one of His perfections. Third, as a pattern for us: "Put on therefore, as the **elect of God,** holy and beloved, bowels of mercy, kindness, humbleness of mind, meekness, **longsuffering**" (Col. 3:12). And again, "Be ye therefore followers (emulators) of God, as dear children" (Eph. 5:2). When tempted to be disgusted at the dulness of another, or to be revenged on one who has wronged you, call to remembrance God's infinite patience and longsuffering with yourself.

The patience of God is **manifested** in His dealings with sinners. How strikingly was it displayed toward the antideluvians. When mankind was uinversally degenerate, and all flesh had corrupted his way, God did not destroy them till He had forewarned them. He "waited" (1 Peter 3:20), probably no less than one hundred and twenty years (Gen. 6:3), during which time Noah was a "preacher of righteousness" (2 Peter 2:5). So, later, when the Gentiles not only worshipped and served the creature more than the Creator, but also committed the vilest abominations contrary to even the dictates of nature (Rom. 1:19-26), and hereby filled up the measure of their iniquity; yet, instead of drawing His sword for the extermination of such rebels, God "suffered all nations to walk in their own ways", and gave them "rain from heaven and fruitful seasons" (Acts 14:16, 17).

Marvelously was God's patience exercised and manifested toward Israel. First, He "suffered their manners" for forty years in the wilderness (Acts 13:18) Later, when they had entered Canaan, but followed the evil customs of the nations around them, and turned to idolatry; though God chastened them sorely, He did not utterly destroy them, but in their distress, raised up deliverers for them. When their iniquity was raised to such a height that none but a God of infinite patience could have borne them. He, notwithstanding, spared them many years before He allowed them to be carried down into Babylon. Finally, when their rebellion against Him reached its climax by crucifying His Son, He waited forty years ere He sent the Romans against them, and that, only after they had judged themselves "unworthy of eternal life" (Acts 13:46).

How wondrous is God's patience with the world today. On every side people are sinning with a high hand. The Divine law is trampled under foot and God Himself openly despised. It is truly amazing that He does not instantly strike dead those who so brazenly defy Him. Why does He not suddenly cut off the haughty infidel and blatant blasphemer, as He did Ananias and Sapphira? Why does He not cause the earth to open its mouth and devour the persecutors of His people, so that, like Dathan and Abiram, they shall go down alive into the Pit? And what of apostate Christendom, where every possible form of sin is now tolerated and practiced under cover of the holy name of Christ. Why does not the righteous wrath of Heaven make an end of such an abominations? Only one answer is possible: because God bears with "**much** longsuffering the vessels of wrath fitted to destruction."

And what of the writer and the reader? Let us review our own lives. It is not long since **we** followed a multitude to do evil, had no concern for God's glory, and lived only to gratify self. How patiently He bore with our vile conduct! And now

(Continued on Page 287)

Vol. X   JANUARY, 1931   No. 1

STUDIES IN THE SCRIPTURES

"Search the Scriptures" John 5:39

Copyright in all English-speaking Countries

EDITOR: Arthur W. Pink, 1339 Bates Ave., Los Angeles, Calif., U. S. A.
Hon. Agent in England: Mr. A. Winstone, "Shalom," Old Bath Road, Leckhampton, Cheltenham.
Hon. Agent in Australia: Mr. G. Ardill, The Christian Workers' Depot, Commonwealth and Reservoir Streets, Sydney.

THE GRACE OF GOD

This is a perfection of the Divine character which is exercised only toward the elect. Neither in the O. T. nor in the New is the grace of God ever mentioned in connection with mankind generally, still less with the lower orders of His creatures. In this it is distinguished from "mercy," for the mercy of God is "over all His works" (Psa. 145:9). Grace is the alone source from which flows the goodwill, love, and salvation of God unto His chosen people. This attribute of the Divine character was defined by Abraham Booth in his helpful book, "The Reign of Grace" (reprinted and obtainable for 50 cents) thus, "It is the eternal and absolute free favour of God, manifested in the vouchsafement of spiritual and eternal blessings to the guilty and the unworthy."

Divine grace is the sovereign and saving favour of God exercised in the bestowment of blessings upon those who have no merit in them and for which no compensation is demanded from them. Nay, more; it is the favour of God shown to those who not only have no positive deserts of their own, but who are thoroughly ill-deserving and hell-deserving. It is completely unmerited and unsought, and is altogether unattracted by anything in or from or by the objects upon which it is bestowed. Grace can neither be bought, earned, nor won by the creature. If it could be, it would cease to be **grace**. When a thing is said to be of "grace" we mean that the recipient has no claim upon it, that it was in nowise due him. It comes to him as pure charity, and, at first, unasked and undesired.

The fullest exposition of the amazing grace of God is to be found in the Epistles of the apostle Paul. In his writings "grace" stands in direct opposition to works and worthiness, all works and worthiness, of whatever kind or degree. This is abundantly clear from Rom. 11:6, "And if by grace, then is it no more of works: otherwise grace is no more grace. But if it be of works, then is it no more grace, otherwise work is no more work." Grace and works will no more unite than an acid and an alkali. "By grace are ye saved through faith; and that not of yourselves; it is the gift of God: not of works, lest any man should boast" (Eph. 2:8, 9). The absolute favour of God can no more consist with human merit, than oil and water will fuse into one: see also Rom. 4:4, 5.

There are three principal characteristics of Divine grace. First, it is **eternal**. Grace was planned before it was exercised, purposed before it was imparted: "Who hath saved us, and called us with a holy calling, not according to our works, but according to His own purpose and grace, which was given us in Christ Jesus before the world began" (2 Tim. 1:9). Second, it is **free**, for none did ever purchase it: "Being justified freely by His grace" (Rom. 3:24). Third, it is **sovereign**, because God exercises it toward and bestows it upon whom He pleases: "Even so might grace reign" (Rom. 5:21). If grace "reigns" then is it on the throne, and the occupant of the throne is sovereign. Hence "the **throne of grace**" (Heb. 4:16).

Just because grace is unmerited favour, it must be exercised in a **sovereign** manner. Therefore does the Lord declare, "I will be gracious to whom I will be gracious" (Ex. 33:19). Were God to show grace to all of Adam's descendants, men would at once conclude that He was righteously compelled to take them to heaven as a meet compensation for allowing the human race to fall into sin. But the great God is under no obligation to any of His creatures, least of all to those who are rebels against Him.

(Continued on Page 24)

IMPORTANT NOTICES

Please advise promptly of change of address, otherwise copies will be lost in the mails.

We are glad to send a sample copy to any of your friends whom you believe would be interested in such a publication.

Send to Mr. I. C. Herendeen, Swengel (Union County), Penna., for a list of our publications. He has published many of our books and booklets.

This magazine is published as a work of faith and labour of love. The Editor and his wife gladly give their services. It is freely sent to all who will read it. No charge is made for it.

Christians who feel definitely led to do so, may have fellowship with us in this ministry. Those outside the U. S. A., please send only INTERNATIONAL Money Orders made out to Los Angeles, California, U. S. A.

CONTENTS

The Epistle to the Hebrews - - - - 2
The Satisfaction ("Atonement") of Christ - - - - - - - - - - 9
The Intercession of Christ (Continued) 15
The Broken Heart - - - - - - - 21
God's Hold On Us - - - - - - - 22

THE EPISTLE TO THE HEBREWS

37. The Two Covenants: Heb. 8:6-9.

In the 7th chapter the apostle has demonstrated by irrefutable logic and upon the authority of Holy Scripture that the priesthood of Christ has superceded the Aaronic order. Here in chapter 8 he makes manifest the superior ministry of our great High Priest. First, He is "seated" (v. 1). Second, He is seated on the throne of Deity (v. 1). Third, He is a Minister of the heavenly sanctuary (v. 2). Fourth, His own person provides the antitype of the tabernacle (v. 2). Fifth, He is presenting before God a more excellent sacrifice (vv. 3-6). Sixth, He is Mediator of a superior covenant (v. 6). Seventh, that covenant has to do with "better promises" (v. 6). That upon which the Holy Spirit would here have us focalize our attention is the place where our High Priest ministers, and the immeasurable superiority of the economy which He is now administering.

This 8th chapter of Hebrews treats of two things: the sphere of our High Priest's ministry and the better covenant with which it is connected: the one being in suited accord with the other. The 6th verse gives the connecting link between them. The apostle's object in introducing the "new covenant" at this stage of his argument is obvious. It was to the old covenant that the whole administration of the Levitical priesthood was confined. The entire churchstate of the Jews, with all the ordinances and worship of it, and all the privileges connected with it, depended wholly on the covenant which God made with them at Sinai. But the introduction of the new Priesthood, necessarily abolished that covenant, and put an end to all the sacred ministrations which belong to it. This it is which the apostle here undertakes to prove.

"The question which troubled the minds and hearts of the Hebrews was their relation to the Levitical priesthood, and to the old dispensation. The temple was still in Jerusalem, and the Levitical ordinances appointed by Moses were still being observed. Although the Sun had risen, the moon had not yet disappeared. It was waning; it was ready to vanish away. Now it became an urgent necessity, for the Hebrew Christians to understand that Christ was the true and eternal High Priest in the heavenly sanctuary, and that the new and everlasting covenant with Judah and Israel was connected with the gospel promise, and not with the law. God Himself had made the first covenant old by promising the new. And now that Christ had entered into the holy of holies by His own blood, the old covenant had passed away; and yet the promises of God to His chosen people remained firm and unchanged" (A Saphir).

That God had "changed" the order of priesthood (7:12) was, as we have seen, clearly evidenced by His causing Christ to spring from the tribe of Judah (7:14). God's raising up of a Priest from that tribe necessarily excluded those belonging to the house of Aaron from the sacerdotal office, just as God's raising up David to sit upon the throne, forever set aside the descendants of Saul from the regal office. Herein we may discern one reason why Jehovah ordained and gave such strict regulations for the distribution of Israel into their tribes, namely, that He might provide for their instruction as to the continuance of the legal worship among them, which could no longer be continued than while the priesthood was reserved unto the tribe of Levi.

This Divine change in the order of priesthood necessarily entailed a change of covenant or economy, as a change of the royal family denotes a new dynasty, or as a new president involves a change of government. The economy with which Christ is connected as far excells the old order of things as His sacerdotal office exceeded that of Aaron's. Thus the apostle is here really advancing one more argument or proof for the pre-eminence of our Lord's priesthood. As a Minister or public functionary Jesus Christ is as far superior in dignity to the Levites as the dispensation over which He presides is of a far superior order than the dispensation in which they served.

In approaching the subject of the two covenants, the old and the new, it should be pointed out that it is not always an easy matter to determine whether the "old covenant" designates the Mosaic economy or the covenant of works which God made with Adam (Hos. 6:6 margin); nor to decide whether the "new covenant" refers to the Gospel dispensation introduced by Christ, or to the covenant of grace which was inaugurated by the first promise made to Adam (Gen. 3:15) and confirmed to Abraham (Gen. 17). In each case the context must decide. We may add that the principal passages where the two covenants are described and contrasted are found in 2 Cor. 3, Gal. 3 and 4, Heb. 8, 9 and 12.

"But now hath He obtained a more excellent ministry, by how much also He is the Mediator of a better covenant, which was established upon better promises" (v. 6). "This verse is a transition from one subject to another; namely, from the excellency of the priesthood of Christ above that of the law, to the excellency of the new covenant above the old. And herein also the apostle artificially compriseth and confirmeth his last argument, of the pre-eminence of Christ, His priesthood and ministry, above that of the law. And this He doth from the nature and excellency of that covenant whereof He was the Mediator in the discharge of His office" (John Owen).

"But now hath He obtained a more excellent ministry." The apostle here introduces his important assertion by a time-mark, the "But now" signifying at this season. It points a contrast from the period of the Mosaic dispensation, when Israel's priests served "unto the example and shadow of heavenly things" (v. 5). A close parallel is found in Rom. 3:21, "but now the righteousness of God without the law is manifested," which is defined in v. 26 as "to declare at this time His righteousness: that He might be just, and the Justifier of him which believeth in Jesus" (v. 26). God in His infinite wisdom gives proper times and seasons to all His dispensations toward His Church. The Lord hastens or consummates all His works of grace in their own appointed time: see Isa. 60:22. Our duty is to leave the ordering of all the concerns of His people, in the accomplishment of His promises, to God in His own good time: Acts 1:7.

That which is here ascribed unto Christ is "a more excellent ministry." The priests of old had a ministry, and an excellent one, for it was by Divine appointment they served at the altar (v. 5). So Christ has a ministry, and "a more excellent" one. In v. 2 He is designated "a Minister of the sanctuary." He is called such not with respect unto one particular act of administration, but because a standing office has been committed to Him. The service to which Christ has been called is of a higher order and more excellent nature than any which Aaron ever discharged. It is a "more excellent ministry" because it is the real and substantial one, of which the Levitical was but the emblem; it pertains to things in heaven, while theirs was restricted to the earthly tabernacle; it is enduring while theirs was but temporary.

This more excellent ministry Christ is here said to have "obtained." The way whereby the Lord Jesus entered on the whole office and work of His mediation has been expressed in 1:4 as by "inheritance": that is, by free grant and perpetual donation, made unto Him as the Son—compare our comments on that verse. There were two things which concurred unto His obtaining this ministry: first, the eternal purpose and counsel of God, decreeing Him thereunto (1 Peter 1:20, Rev. 13:8). Second, the actual call of God (Heb. 5:4, 5), which carried with it His unction of the Spirit above measure (Psa. 45:7), for the holy discharge of His whole office. Thus, Christ obtained this ministry not by any legal constitution, fleshly succession, or carnal ordination, as did the Levitical priests. The exaltation of the human nature of Christ into union with His Deity, for the office of this glorious ministry, depended solely upon the sovereign wisdom, grace, and love of God.

"But now hath He obtained a more excellent ministry, by how much also He is the Mediator of a better covenant." The particular point which the apostle here makes, or rather the conclusion which he here draws from the premises laid down, had been anticipated and intimated in what he said in 7:20, 22. There he had declared that the excellency of the covenant of which Christ has been made Surety and Mediator has a proportion with the pre-eminence of His priesthood above that of Aaron's. His being made a Priest by Divine oath (which the Levites were not) fitted Him to be the Surety of a better economy. Conversely, the covenant of which He is Surety must needs be better than the old regime because He who was the Surety of it had been made so by Divine oath. Thus, the dignity of Christ's priesthood is demonstrated by the excellency of the new covenant, and declaratively the new covenant sets forth the dignity of Christ's priesthood.

"He is the Mediator of a better covenant." It is most important to recognize that Christ is a **sacerdotal** Mediator. This is made clear by 1 Tim. 2:5, 6, "For there is one God, and one Mediator between God and men, the man Christ Jesus; Who gave Himself a **ransom** for all, to be testified in due time." The mediating Priest intervenes with sacrifice and intercession for the reconciling of God and sinners. As we shall (D. V.) yet see, Heb. 9:15 expressly declares that Christ's priestly work was the very purpose of His being appointed Mediator. So in 12:24 His sacrifice is again made prominent in connection with His mediation. Thus the **sacerdotal** character of His mediation cannot be scripturally gainsaid.

Christ has obtained a more excellent priestly ministry corresponding to the superior dispensation of which He is the Mediator. "But now (in this Christian dispensation) hath He (as 'Priest') obtained (from God) a more excellent ministry (than Aaron's) by how much also He is the Mediator of a better covenant." He is not only Priest, but Mediator; Priest because He is Mediator, Mediator because He is Priest. It is by His priestly office and work that He exercises His mediatorship, standing between two parties and reconciling them. He thus combines in His own person what was divided between two under the old economy, Moses being the typical mediator, Aaron the typical surety. As "Surety" Christ **pledged** Himself to see that the terms of the covenant were faithfully carried out; as "Mediator," He is **negotiating** for His people's blessing. The word "covenant" in this chapter signifies an arrangement or constitution of things, an economy or dispensation. The "old covenant" was that peculiar order of things under which the Jewish people were placed in consequence of the transactions at Sinai. The "new" or "better covenant" is that order of things which has been introduced by Jesus Christ, namely, the Christian dispensation.

"He is the Mediator of a better covenant." A mediator is a middle person between two parties entering into covenant, and if they be of different natures, a perfect mediator would have to partake of each of their natures in his own person. This Christ has done. Such mediation presupposes that the two parties are at such variance they cannot treat directly with the other; unless this were so, a go-between would be needless. See this fact illustrated in Deut. 5:23-27. In voluntarily undertaking to serve as Mediator, two things were required of Christ: first, that He should remove whatever kept the covenantors at a distance, taking away the cause of enmity between them. Second, that He should purchase and procure, in a way suited to the glory of God, the actual communication of all the good things prepared and proposed in this covenant (grace and glory) unto those on whose behalf He acts as Surety. Finally, He who is this Mediator must be accepted, trusted, and rested in by both parties entering into covenant. On God's part, He has openly declared that He is "well pleased" with Christ (Matt. 3:17); on the part of His elect, they are made willing "in the day of His power" (Psa. 110:3).

"Which was established upon better promises." Every covenant between God and man, must be founded on and resolved into promises. Hence, essentially, a promise and a covenant are all one, and God calls an absolute promise founded on an absolute decree, His covenant, Gen. 9:11. And His purpose for the continuation of the course of nature to the end of the world, He calls His covenant with day and night, Jer. 33:20. The being and essence of a Divine covenant lies in the promise. Hence are they called 'the covenants of promise,' Eph. 2:12. Such as are founded on and consist in promises. And it is necessary that so it should be" (John Owen).

"Which was established upon better promises." The word "established" here is important to note, for it plainly intimates to us that the apostle is **not** here treating of the Everlasting Covenant **absolutely**, and as it had been virtually administered from the foundation of the world in the way of a promise; but relatively, as it had been formally introduced on earth **as a new dispensation** or economy. In the Divine administration of the Everlasting Covenant it has now been reduced to a fixed statute or ordinance. The term "established" signifies **legally established,** formally established as by a law. All is now fixed in the Church by Divine arrangement and secured by inviolable sanctions. In 7:11 the Greek verb here rendered "established" is translated "received the law" —compare our comments thereon. "The covenant to which the priesthood of Christ refers has been also established by law. It has been promulgated by Divine authority. The truth with regard to it has been 'spoken by the Son of God, and confirmed to us by those who heard Him; and God has borne witness with signs and miracles, and gifts of the Holy Spirit,' according to His own will" (John Brown).

"Established upon better promises." Caution requires to be exercised and great care taken at this point lest we err in our understanding of the particular contrast which is here pointed by the word "better." "The promises in the first covenant pertained mainly to the present life. They were promises of length of days; of increase of numbers; of seed time and harvest; of national privileges, and of extraordinary peace, abundance and prosperity. That there was also the promise of eternal life, it would be wrong to doubt; but this was not the main thing. In the new covenant, however, the promise of spiritual blessings becomes the **principal** thing. The mind is directed to heaven; the heart is cheered with the hopes of immortal life; the favour of God and the anticipation of heaven are secured in the most ample and solemn manner" (A. Barnes). Observe well the two words which are emphasized in the above quotation. In O. T. times God "commanded the blessing, life **forever more**" (Psa. 133:3), not only temporal life in Canaan; while His people in N. T. times have "promise of the life that **now is,**" as well as "of that which is to come" (1 Tim. 4:8)!

Rightly did A. Saphir point out, "The contrast between the old and the new would be viewed in a false light, if we forgot that in the old dispensation spiritual reality and blessings were presented, and were actually embraced in faith by the people of God. The law had a positive or evangelical aspect, although herein also it was elementary and transitory, it acted as a guardian and a tutor; as the snow is not merely an indication of winter, and a contrast to the bright and genial sunshine, and the refreshing verdure of summer, but is also a beneficent protection, cherishing and preparing the soil for the approaching blessings from above. But now the winter is passed, the fullness has come."

The "better promises" are described in vv. 10-13: they are summed up in justification and sanctification, or more briefly still, in **redemption.** "But what he adds is not without some difficulty,— that the covenant of the Gospel was proclaimed on better promises; for it is certain that the fathers who lived under the Law had the same hope of eternal life set before them as we have, as they had the grace of adoption in common with us, then faith must have rested on the same promises. But the comparison made by the apostle refers to the **form** rather than to the substance; for though God promised to them the same salvation which He at this day promises to us, yet neither the manner nor the character of the revelation is the same or equal to what we enjoy" (John Calvin). Thus, the "promises" with which the new covenant is concerned are "better" in that they mainly respect spiritual and eternal blessings, rather than earthly and temporal ones; in that they have been ratified by the bloodshedding of Christ; in that they are now openly proclaimed to God's elect among the Gentiles as well as the Jews.

"For if that first covenant had been faultless then should no place have been sought for the second" (v. 7). The covenant which is here referred to is that into which Jehovah entered with Israel at Sinai: see Ex. 19:5; 34:27, 28; Deut. 4:13. Israel's response is recorded in Ex. 19:8, 24:3. It was ratified by blood: Ex. 24:4-8. This was not the "first" covenant absolutely, but the first made with Israel nationally. Previously, God had made a covenant with Adam (Hos. 6:6), and in some respects the Covenant at Sinai adumbrated it, for it was chiefly one of works. So too He had made a covenant with Abraham, which in some respects adumbrated the Everlasting Covenant, inasmuch as it was one purely of grace. Prior to Sinai, God dealt with Israel on the basis of the Abrahamic covenant, as is clear from Ex. 2:24; 6:3, 4. But it was on the ground of the Siniatic covenant that Israel entered Canaan: see Josh. 7:11, 15; Judges 2:19-21; 1 Kings 11:11; Jer. 34:18, 19.

"For if that first covenant had been faultless then should no place have been sought for the second." The connection between this and the preceding verse, intimated by the opening "For" is as follows: there the apostle had affirmed that the Christian covenant is superior to the Judaic; here, he demonstrates the same thing by arguing from the fact that the old covenant must have been defective, otherwise the new had been superfluous. It is an inference drawn from the facts of the situation. If there was need for a second, the first could not have been perfect, failing to secure that which was most desirable. A parallel is found in Gal. 3:21.

"For if that first covenant had been faultless, then should no place have been sought for the second." Wherein lay its "faultiness?" It was wholly external, accompanied by no internal efficacy. It set before Israel an objective standard, but supplied no power to measure up to it. It treated with men in the flesh, and therefore the law was impotent through the weakness of the flesh (Rom. 8:3). It provided a sacrifice for sin, but the value thereof was only ceremonial and transient, failing to actually put away sin. It was unable to secure actual redemption. Hence because of its inadequacy, a new and better covenant was needed.

"Every work of God is perfect, viewed in connection with the purpose which He means it to serve. In this point of view, the 'first covenant' was faultless. But when viewed in the light in which the Jews generally considered it, as a saving economy, in all the extent of that word, it was not 'faultless.' It could not expiate moral guilt; it could not wash away moral pollution; it could not justify, it could not sanctify, it could not save. Its priesthood were not perfected—they were weak and inefficient; its sacrifices 'could not take away sin,' make perfect as concerning the conscience, or procure 'access with freedom into the holiest of all.' In one word, 'it made nothing perfect'" (John Brown).

"For finding fault with them, He saith, Behold, the days come, saith the Lord, when I will make a new covenant with the house of Israel and with the house of Judah" (v. 8). The opening "For" denotes that the apostle now confirms what he had just affirmed in vv. 6, 7: the proof is found in what immediately follows. The "finding fault" may refer either to the old covenant, or to the people themselves who were under it: finding fault "with it" or "with them." In view of what is added in v. 9 the translation of the A. V. is to be preferred. It was against the people that God complained for their having broken His covenant.

"He saith, Behold, the days come," etc. The world "Behold" announces the importance of what follows, and calls to a diligent and admiring attention of the same. "Behold" bids us be filled with wonderment at this marvel of grace. It is indeed striking to observe that the apostle did not rely upon logical deductions and inferences, conclusive though they were. A change of priesthood necessarily involved a change of covenant, or dispensational administration. Nevertheless, obvious as this was, Paul rested not until he proved his assertions with a definite and pertinent "thus saith the Lord." He would not have the faith of the Hebrews stand in the wisdom of man, but in the power of God. Blessed example for God's servants today to follow. Alas that so many people are contented with the dogmatic assertions of some man who "ought to know what he is saying," instead of demanding clear proof from the Scriptures.

The text which the apostle here quotes in proof of his assertion is taken from Jer. 31:31. It is most blessed to note the time when God gave this precious promise to His people. Beautifully has A. Saphir pointed out, "It is in the night of adversity that the Lord sends forth bright stars of consoling hope. When the darkest clouds of woe were gathering above Jerusalem, and the prophet himself was in the lowest depths of sorrow, God gave to him the most glorious prophecies of Judah's great redemption and future blessedness. The advent and reign of Messiah, the Lord our righteousness, the royal dominion and priesthood of Israel's Redeemer, the gift of the Holy Spirit, the renewal and restoration of God's chosen people, the days of unbroken prosperity and blessedness—all the golden Messianic future was predicted in the last days of Jerusalem, when the magnificent fabric of its temple was about to sink into the dust, and its walls and palaces were about to be thrown prostrate on the ground."

This new covenant God promised to make with "the house of Israel and with the house of Judah." The word, "Israel" is used in the Scriptures in no less than four distinct senses. First, it is the name which God gave to Jacob when he wrestled with the angel and prevailed as a prince (Gen. 22:28). Second, it denotes his fleshly descendants, called "the children of Israel," that is, the Jewish nation. Third, it is employed of the ten tribes, the kingdom of Samaria or Ephraim, in contradistinction from the kingdom of Judah, and this, after the Nation was rent asunder in the days of Jeroboam. Fourth, it is applied spiritually to the whole of God's people (Gal. 6:16). To which we may add, fifth, in Isa. 49:3 (note the verses which follow) it appears to be applied to Christ Himself, as identified with His people. Personally, we believe that it is the second and the fourth of these usages that obtain in our present passage.

The law of first mention helps us here. The initial occurrence of any expression or word in Scripture defines its scope and fixes, very largely, its consequent significance. So it is in this case. The name "Israel" was first given to Jacob: from that point onwards he is the man with a double name, sometimes being referred to as Jacob, sometimes as Israel, according as the "old man" or "new man" was uppermost within him. This more than hints at the double application of this name; oftentimes it is applied to Jacob's natural descendants, at other times to his spiritual brethren. When Christ affirmed of Nathanael "Behold an Israelite indeed, in whom is no guile" (John 1:47), it was the same as though He had said, "Behold a true Israelite, a spiritual prince with God." To insist that "Israel" always signifies the fleshly descendants of Jacob betrays excuseless ignorance: why does the Holy Spirit speak of "Israel after the flesh" in 1 Cor. 10:18 if there be no Israel after the spirit!

The writer has no doubt whatever in his mind that the time is not far distant when God is going to resume His dealings with the Jewish people, restore them unto their own land, send back their Messiah and Redeemer, save them from their sins, and fulfill to them His ancient promise through Jeremiah. Nevertheless, we are fully assured that it is a serious mistake to limit the prophecy of Jeremiah (or any other prediction) to a single fulfillment. It is abundantly clear from 2 Cor. 3 that Christians in this dispensation are already enjoying the good of the new covenant which God has made with them. Moreover, are we not reminded at the Lord's table of our Saviour's words, "This cup is the new testament," or "covenant in My blood" (1 Cor. 11:25)?

It should be pointed out that O. T. Israel were typically and mystically significant of the whole Church of God. For that reason were the promises of grace under the old economy given unto the saints of God under the name of "Israel," "Judah," etc. (carefully compare Rom. 2:28, 29), because they were types of those who should really and effectually be made partakers of them. Hence it is that in 2 Cor. 1:20 we are told that "All the promises of God in Him (Christ) are Yea, and in Him Amen, unto the glory of God by us." Hence it is we read that "Jesus Christ was a Minister of the circumcision for the truth of God, to confirm the promises unto the fathers, and that the Gentiles might glorify God for His mercy" (Rom. 15:8, 9). And hence it is that the apostle Paul writing to Christians says, "Having therefore these promises"—the preceding verses quoting from Lev. 26:12, etc.! For the same reason in Heb. 13:5 the Christian is assured that the promise which the Lord made to Joshua belongs to him too.

Thus, by "the house of Israel" and the "house of Judah" in Heb. 8:8 we understand, first, the mystical and spiritual Israel and Judah; second, the application of this covenant to the literal and fleshly Israel and Judah in the day to come. In other words, we regard those expressions as denominating the whole Church of elect believers, typified of old, by the fleshly descendants of Abraham. Nor is it without reason that the Holy Spirit has here used both these names: we believe His (veiled) design was to take in God's elect among the Jews and the Gentiles. Our reason for believing this is because that in the very first inspired sermon preached after the new covenant had been established, Peter said to the convicted Jews, "the promise is unto you, and to your children (descendants) and to all that are afar off, as many as the Lord our God shall call" (Acts 2:39). It is indeed remarkable that the two emphasized words have a double reference. First, they applied to the literal house of Israel, who were then outside the land, in the dispersion (Dan. 9:7); second, to elect Gentiles, away from God: see Eph. 2:13!

At the time God announced His purpose and promise through Jeremiah, the fleshly descendants of Abraham were divided into two hostile groups. They had separate kings and separate centers of worship. They were at enmity with one another. As such they fitly adumbrated the great division between God's elect among the Jews and the Gentiles in their natural and dispensational state. There was a middle wall of partition between them (Eph. 2:14). There was "enmity" between them (Eph. 2:16). But just as God announced through Ezekiel (37:16, 17) that the diversified houses of Judah and Israel should "become one," so His elect among the Jews and the Gentiles are now one in Christ (Eph. 2:14-18)! Therefore are all born-again believers designated the "children" and "seed" of Abraham (Gal. 3:7, 29), and thus are they "blessed with faithful Abraham" (Gal. 3:9).

"Not according to the covenant that I made with their fathers in the day when I took them by the hand to lead them out of the land of Egypt; because they continued not in My covenant, and I regarded them not, saith the Lord" (v. 9). The contrast between the two covenants is first expressed negatively: "not according." The differences between them are many and great. The former was mainly typical, the latter has the substance. The one was administered under an imperfect priesthood, the latter under a perfect one. The one had to do, primarily, with that which was external; the other is, mainly, internal. The Mosaic covenant was restricted to one nation, the Christian is international in its scope.

The old covenant is spoken of as dating from the day when the Lord took Israel, "by the hand to lead them out of the land of Egypt." This language emphasizes the woeful and helpless condition that Israel was then in: unable to deliver themselves out of their bondage, like children incapable of walking unless supported and led. As Deut. 1:31 says, "The Lord thy God bare thee, as a man doth bear his son, in all the way that ye went." So in Hos. 11:3 God says, "I taught them to go, taking them by the arms." Such expressions also accentuate the infinite condescension of God toward His people: that He should (so to speak) bow down Himself to reach them in their lowly estate.

"But they continued not in My covenant, and I regarded them not, saith the Lord." "They soon forgat God's works, they waited not for His counsel" (Psa. 106:12). The principal reference is to Israel's conduct at Sinai, when, during the absence of Moses in the mount, they "thrust Him from them" (Acts 7:39), and made and worshipped the golden calf. That was but prophetic or indicative of their whole history. Their shameful conduct is mentioned here for the purpose of magnifying that marvellous grace that shall yet make the new covenant with such a people. "I regarded them not" refers to God's governmental dealings with Israel: the severity He exercised, consuming them in the wilderness. In view of which we may well heed that searching word, "Wherefore let him that thinketh he standeth take heed lest he fall" (1 Cor. 10:12).

—ARTHUR W. PINK.

THE SATISFACTION
("Atonement")
OF CHRIST

13. Its Results

Having sought to show from Scripture the **nature** of the Satisfaction which the Mediator offered unto God, and, by virtue of His acceptance of the same, its certain **efficacy** to procure and secure all that it was ordained to accomplish, we are now ready to contemplate in fuller detail some of the results which it has actually effected. By the "results" we mean the **consequences** which have flowed to the elect in their relation to God and His law. These are so many and so diversified that we shall not here presume an attempt to even enumerate them. Instead, following the emphasis of Scripture, we seek to direct attention unto the principal effects only. Once the Lord permits the regenerated soul to obtain a clear grasp of these, little difficulty should be experienced in apprehending the minor corollories with which they are accompanied.

God Himself had a specific end in view when appointing the great Atonement, and in consequence of its having been made, certain things are effectually fulfilled and accomplished by it. As we sought to show in the 9th article of this series, the **supreme** aim of God in the Satisfaction of Christ is the advancement of His own declarative honour, and that by the manifestation of His glorious attributes therein. God's **subordinate** aim in Christ's Satisfaction, which aim is subservient to and is effectual unto His ultimate intendment, is the deliverance of His people from the curse and the restoring of them to His image and fellowship. To effect this, God had to be propitiated, sin expiated, and the elect sinner reinstated in the Divine favour.

Perhaps the most comprehensive single statement in Scripture upon the design and result of the Satisfaction of Christ is found in 1 Peter 3:18. There we read that "Christ hath also once suffered for sins, the Just for the unjust, that He might bring us to God." Bringing us to God is a general expression for the accomplishment of the whole work of our salvation, both in the removal of all hindrances and in the bestowal of all requisites. More specifically, in order for the elect—viewed as fallen in Adam— to be brought unto God, it was necessary that all enmity between them should be removed; in other words, that **reconciliation** should be effected. So too it was necessary that the guilt of all their transgressions should be cancelled; in other words, that they should receive **remission** of sin. Further, it was necessary that they should be delivered from all bondage; in other words, that they should be **redeemed**. Finally, it was necessary that they should be made, both legally and experimentally, **righteous**.

In the four words emphasized in the closing sentences of the last paragraph we have summed up the essential **results** which have accrued from the Satisfaction of Christ. As those results bear upon sin, it has been expiated; as they bear upon the elect, they have been emancipated; as they bear upon God, He has been propitiated. Lest this statement should create a false impression, let us at once add that the Atonement produced no actual change in God, any more than do His acts of creation or providence. The efficient purpose existed in the Divine mind from all eternity. He acted upon it from the fall of Adam, as though the atonement was actually accomplished. The infinite justice and the infinite love which were exercised in the sacrifice of Christ, were in the Divine mind from the beginning. The effect of Christ's Satisfaction was to render possible the **concurrent** exercise of Justice and Love in their treatment of the same persons. As these four "results" named are of such incalculable value and importance we shall devote a separate article to the consideration of each one. And,

1. Reconciliation

In 2 Cor. 5 the Gospel of grace which God has called His servants to proclaim is spoken of thus: "And hath given to us the ministry of reconciliation" (v. 18), and "hath committed to us the Word of Reconciliation" (v. 19). This at once shows the great importance of having clear and scriptural views upon this mighty subject, for otherwise it is impossible to honour God in our preaching (which should ever be our first and chief concern), or to edify His people with wholesome doctrine. A mistake at this point seriously injures the whole of our evangelical ministrations and causes us to set forth a perverted presentation of God's saving truth. The realization of this ought to bow every minister of the Gospel before God in deep humility, earnestly entreating Him for Divine light and wisdom, that he may be so taught of the Lord that the Gospel trumpet may give forth no uncertain sound when it is placed to his lips. Far better not to preach at all, than to preach that which is contrary to Scripture, dishonoring to God, and injurious to souls. Let us now consider,

1. Its Nature

The word "reconcile" means to bring together again those who are alienated, to re-unite those who are at variance, to restore to amity and concord by removing that which hinders agreement and fellowship. It is most important to observe at the onset that the term "reconciliation" is itself objective in its signification. That is to say, reconciliation terminates upon the object, and not upon the subject. This is clear from Matt. 5:23, 24, where our Lord said, "If thou bring thy gift to the altar, and there rememberest that thy brother hath ought against thee; leave there thy gift before the altar, and go thy way; first be reconciled to thy brother." This is the first mention of the word in the N. T. Here the offender is not bidden to reconcile himself, but the person whom he has offended. The person who has done the injury is to make up the difference. He is to propitiate or reconcile his brother to himself, by a compensation of some kind. Christ did not say, Conciliate thy own displeasure towards thy brother, but remove his displeasure against thee.

The teaching of Matt. 5:23, 24 is of basic importance in connection with our present inquiry. Its plain meaning is that the one who has offended should go and seek to appease the anger of the one who has been offended, obtaining his forgiveness, regaining his favour and friendship, by humbling himself before him, asking his pardon, and satisfying him for any injury which may have been done him. In like manner when Scripture speaks of God's having reconciled us to Himself by the blood of Christ's cross (Col. 1:20) it does not refer to a subjective change which has been wrought in our hearts, producing our laying down of all enmity against God and our turning to Him in loving obedience; but it expresses one of the cardinal effects or results of His having graciously provided and accepted an atonement for us, so that instead of inflicting upon us the punishment we so richly deserve, we are, instead, received into his full favour on Christ's account. Thus we read in Rom. 11:15, "For if the casting away of them be the reconciling of the world": here the reconciling of the world is contrasted from the rejection of the Jews, which must evidently be understood as signifying the extension of God's favour unto the Gentiles.

In the application of the term to God, "reconciliation" has to do with that which is forensic. That is to say, it contemplates God in His character as the Judge of all the earth, as the moral Governor of the universe, administering law and maintaining order. It concerns our relationship to Him not as our Creator, nor as our Father, but as our King. Thus, to affirm that through Christ God is now reconciled to His people, does not mean that there has been any change in either His nature, will, or disposition—to so affirm would be blasphemy. No, "reconciliation" means that transgressors of the Divine law have been restored to the judicial favour of God, through Christ's having closed the breach which sin had made between them. Reconciliation affects no change in God himself, but it does in the administration of His government. His law now regards with approbation those against whom it was formerly hostile. There has been a change of relation between those for whom Christ died and the Judge of all. As this point is so little understood today, even by those claiming to be orthodox, we must amplify it a little further.

There is great need for exercising caution here, as in everything which pertains to our conceptions of the great God. Unless we are on our guard, our thoughts of Him will be but carnal. When one human being is reconciled to another there is an inward change: ill feelings are removed and good will is restored. But it is not so with the Lord God. It is greatly dishonouring to Him if we think of Him as possessing anything which corresponds to human passions. Reconciliation with God does not mean a change of heart in Him from an angry disposition to a friendly affection. Rather does it refer to an effect which has followed from that proper and full satisfaction which Christ offered to the violated law and offended justice of God. We repeat, it is God in His character of Judge, who insisting upon an atonement, has now no further demand to make, and therefore is most properly said to be appeased or reconciled to His sinful people. In order to understand this the better, let us next consider,

2. Its Implications

Conciliation is a state of peace, the mutual enjoyment of friendship. Reconciliation presupposes alienation and disfellowship. There is no occasion for reconciliation between parties who are in perfect accord with each other; but where that exists not, where instead there is discord and enmity, then the need for them to be reconciled is real. Thus, we say that the first implication in the term "reconciliation" is, that there has previously been a state of alienation. The second equally clear implication is that, there was harmony before the discord; that, originally, peace and amity existed before strife and enmity broke it, for reconciliation is the renewal of lost friendship, the re-uniting of those who have been at variance. Thus, this one word "reconciliation" comprehends by implication the threefold relation which has existed between the elect and God, considered as their Governor or Judge. First, they were in happy fellowship together. Second, that fellowship was disrupted by the fall, and sin produced mutual alienation. Third, as the result of Christ's satisfaction enmity is removed, peace is restored, and God and His people are re-united.

"God and man were once dear friends. Adam was the Lord's favourite. Till man was made, it was said of every rank and species of earthly creatures, 'God saw that it was good.' But when man was made, 'God saw every thing He had made, and behold, it was very good' (Gen. 1:31). God expressed more of His favour to him than to any other creature, except the angels: man was made after His own image (Gen. 1:26). He was fitted to live in delightful communion with his Maker. Man was His viceroy (Gen. 1:27). God entrusted him with the care, charge, and dominion over all the creatures; yea, he was capable of loving, knowing, or enjoying God. Other creatures were capable of glorifying God—of setting forth His power, wisdom, and goodness—objectively and passively; but man, of glorifying God actively" (T. Manton, Vol. 13, p. 255). Let it be carefully borne in mind that in Eden Adam stood not merely as a private person, but as the representative of the race, and that the elect were all in him.

The condition of Adam was happy, yet mutable. Though created sinless, yea, "upright" (Eccl. 7:29), yet was he capable of falling. Alas how quickly he fell. God had forbidden him to eat of the tree of the knowledge of good and evil, and warned him that in the day he did so, he would surely die. But he heeded not. He apostatised. He disobeyed his Maker, and dragged down all his posterity with him (Rom. 5:12). By his fall, all his spiritual privileges were forfeited: he lost the image, favour and fellowship of God. God drove him out of Eden and stationed the cherubim at its entrance with flaming sword to bar his return. Thus sin separated between man and God (Isa. 59:2). He, and all God's elect in Him, were "alienated from the life of God" (Eph. 4:18).

As the consequence of the fall and man's becoming by practice a sinful creature, there was a mutual antagonism between God and man. Of man it is written, "the carnal mind is enmity against God" (Rom. 8:7). Of Christians in their unregenerate state it is said, "and you, that were sometime alienated and enemies in your mind by wicked works" (Col. 1:21). The hatred of the sinner's heart for God was fully manifested when He became incarnate. Though He was full of grace and truth, went about doing good, preaching the Gospel, healing the sick, yet men despised and rejected Him, and were not satisfied until they hounded Him to death. Nor has the human heart changed one iota since then.

Sin has placed God and man apart from one another, so that all the harmony there was between them has been completely destroyed. By his sin man incurred the righteous hatred and wrath of God, which is "revealed from heaven against all ungodliness and unrighteousness of men" (Rom. 1:18). That God is alienated from the sinner and antagonistic to him is as clearly taught in the Scriptures as is man's enmity against God. "Thou hatest all workers of iniquity" (Psa. 5:5). "God is angry with the wicked every day" (Psa. 7:11). "Though the Lord be high, yet hath He respect to the lowly, but the proud He knoweth **afar off**" (Psa. 138:6). "But they rebelled, and vexed His Holy Spirit; therefore He was turned to be their **enemy,** He fought against them" (Isa.

63:10). Herein then lay the need for reconciliation: that the breach which sin had made should be healed, the anger of God appeased, and peace and amity be restored. We are now ready to consider,

3. Its Effectuation

Many, adopting the horrible heresy of the Sociaians ("Unitarians"), will not have it that the reconciliation is **mutual**; but God has been reconciled to His people, as truly as they to Him. Both there must be, for the alienation was mutual. God was angry with us, and we hated Him. As we have shown above, the Scriptures not only speak of enmity on man's part, but also of wrath on God's part, and that, not only against sin, but sinners themselves; and not only against the non-elect, but the elect too, for we "were by nature the children of wrath, even as others" (Eph. 2:3). Sin placed God and His people at judicial variance. We are the parties offending, God the party offended. Thus the alienation was on both sides, yet with this difference, that we were alienated in respect of affection, which is the ground and cause of Divine wrath; God in respect of the effects and issue of enmity and anger.

Now for Christ to make perfect conciliation it was required that He turn away the judicial wrath of God from His people. For this it was necessary for Christ to offer Himself a propitiatory sacrifice to God, Himself bearing that wrath which was due the sins of His people. This great fact was plainly typed out in the O. T. again and again. For example, when Israel sinned so greviously in the making of the golden calf, we find Jehovah saying to Moses, "Now therefore let Me alone, that My wrath may wax hot against them, and that I may consume them" (Ex. 32:10). But the immediate sequel shows us most blessedly how that the typical mediator interposed between the righteous anger of the Lord and His sinning people, turning away His wrath from them (vv. 11-14). Again, we read in Num. 16 that upon the rebellion of Korah and his company, the Lord said unto Moses, "Get thee up from among the congregation that I may consume them" (v. 5). Whereupon Moses said unto Aaron, "Take a censer, and put fire therein from off the altar, and put on incense, and go quickly unto the congregation, and **make an atonement** for them; **for there is wrath** gone out from the Lord, the plague is begun." Aaron did so, and we are told, "he stood between the dead and the living, and the plague was stayed" (v. 48)!

Nothing could be plainer than the above cases, to which many others might be added. All through the patriarchal and Mosaic economies we find that sacrifices were offered for the specific purpose of pacifying God's righteous vengeance, on sin, appeasing His judicial displeasure, and turning away His wrath; the effect of which was expressly termed a "reconciliation": see Lev. 16:20, 2 Chron. 29:24, etc. Surely none are so mad as to suppose that Israelites offered sacrifices to turn away their own anger from God. Then, inasmuch as those O. T. sacrifices were foreshadowings of Christ's Sacrifice, how can it be said that the great end of His work was to divert man's enmity from God, rather than to divert His wrath from us? But rather than rely upon mere reasoning, let us appeal to the clear teaching of the N. T. upon this vital point.

In Rom. 3:25 we read, "Whom God hath set forth a propitiation through faith in His blood to declare His righteousness." Now a "propitiation" is that which placates or appeases by satisfying offended justice. Nor is the force of this verse in any wise weakened by the fact that the Greek word for "propitiation" is rendered "mercy-seat" in Heb. 9:5, for the mercy-seat was a **blood-sprinkled** one! It was the place where the high priest applied the atoning sacrifice for the satisfying of God's justice against the sins of His people. The Hebrew word for "mercy-seat" signifies a "covering," and it was so designated for a double reason. First, because it hid from view the condemning law—the tables of stone being beneath it. Second, because the blood sprinkled upon it, covered the offences of Israel; from the eye of offended justice by an adequate compensation. That which it was fitly designed to typify was the averting of deserved vengeance by means of a **substitutionary** interposition.

Again, in Rom. 5:10 we are told, "For if, when we were enemies, we were reconciled to God by the death of His Son, much more, being reconciled, we shall be saved by His life." When we were "enemies," **God's** enemies, obnoxious to His righteous judgments. This word denotes the relation in which we stood to God as the objects of His displeasure, subject to the hostility of His law. We were "reconciled," that is, brought back again into His favour. And that, not by the Spirit's work in us, but "by the death," the propitiatory sacrifice, "of His Son." That this statement refers to the averting of God's anger from us, and the restoring us to His favour, may be seen by the following considerations:

First, in that the immediate context is commending the amazing love of God **to us** (v. 8), whereof "reconciliation" is one of the highest proofs or manifestations. But if v. 10 were referring to the laying down of **our** enmity to God, it would rather be an instance of our love for Him, than of His for us. Second, in that the terms of v. 10 are unmistakeably parallel with those of vv. 8, 9, and there we read, "while we were yet **sinners** Christ died for us," which can only mean, Christ died for us **as** "ungodly," to deliver us from the death which God's holiness required (vv. 6, 7), and died thus to bring us into the favour of God. Third, in that "reconciled to God by the death of His Son" is only another description of "being justified by His blood" in v. 9. Now to be "justified" is God's reconciliation to us, His acceptance of us into His favour, and not our conversion to Him; and that was in order that we should be "saved **from wrath**" (v. 9). Fourth, in that in the following verse we are said to have **"received** the reconciliation" (v. 11), which cannot be meant of the laying down of our arms of rebellion: we cannot be said to "receive" our **conversion**; but we can that which Christ's sacrifice has procured for us.

"All things are of God, who hath reconciled us to Himself by Jesus Christ" (2 Cor. 5:18). As this passage will come before us again (D. V.) in a later article, only a few words upon it can now be offered. "Who **hath** reconciled us." When did God do so? At the cross, as v. 21 clearly enough shows. By whom were we reconciled? Not by the work of the Spirit within, subduing our enmity, but "by Jesus Christ." How were we reconciled? By Christ's being "made sin for us" (v. 21), and thus receiving in Himself the penalty of the law, and thereby appeasing God's justice. It was by His sacrifice that the Lord Jesus reconciled us to God, for the design of a sacrifice was to propitiate God, and not to reform the offerer.

"And that He might reconcile both unto God in one body by the cross, having slain the enmity thereby" (Eph. 2: 15, 16). This important verse really calls for an exposition of its whole context, but we must content ourselves with a few brief words only. A careful analysis of vv. 11-15 reveals the fact that both a double alienation and a double reconciliation is under discussion. There is first an antagonism between Jews and Gentiles, vv. 11, 12. Second, there is a separation between God and His people, vv. 12, 13. Conversely, through the Satisfaction which Christ has made unto God, elect Jews and elect Gentiles have been united in "one new man" (v. 15), and both have been reconciled unto God (v. 16). Thus, the "Christ is our peace" of v. 14 is amplified in: between ourselves mutually (v. 15), between us and God (v. 16); and in consequence therefrom "Through Him we both have access by one Spirit unto the Father" (v. 18).

"That He," that is the incarnate Son of God. "Might reconcile," that is, restore to God's judicial favour. "Both," that is, elect Jews and elect Gentiles. "Unto God," that is, considered as the moral Governor of the universe. "In one body" that is, Christ's humanity— cf. Col. 1:22. "In the body of His flesh." Our Lord's humanity is here designated "one body," because the Spirit is emphasizing the One for the many, as in Rom. 5:17-19. It is the **representative** character of Christ's satisfaction which is here in view—Christ sustaining the responsibilities of all His people. It was in His humanity that He rendered obedience unto God; as it was His deity which gave value to all that He did. "Having slain the enmity thereby," that is, God's holy wrath, the hostility of His law. It should be carefully noted that the "enmity" of v. 16 cannot refer to that which existed between Jews and Gentiles, for that has been disposed of in vv. 14, 15. "Enmity" is here personified ("Slain"), as "sin" is in Rom. 8:3. Thus, the verse means that all the sins of God's people met upon Christ, and Divine justice took satisfaction from Him: in consequence, God's "enmity" has ceased, and they are restored to His favour. While the gracious provision originated in the love of God, the Atonement was the righteous means of removing His holy hatred against us.

Though the precise expression of "God's being reconciled to us" is not found in so many words in Scripture, phrases of precisely equivalent import most certainly are. Thus, "O Lord, I will praise Thee: though Thou wast angry with me, Thine anger is **turned away**" (Isa. 12:1). "Return, thou backsliding Israel, saith the Lord; I will not cause mine anger to fall upon thee, for I am merciful, saith the Lord, I will not **keep anger forever**" (Jer. 3:12). "And I will establish My covenant with thee; and thou shalt know that I am the Lord: That thou mayest remember, and be confounded, and never open thy mouth any more because of thy shame, when I am **pacified** toward thee for all that thou hast done, saith the Lord God" (Ezek. 16:63). To merely present a God who is **willing to be** reconciled to sinners is a wretched and wicked perversion of the Gospel.

Should it be humbly inquired, Why does Scripture throw the main emphasis on **our** being reconciled to God, we answer in the words of the Puritan, Thomas Manton, "First, because we are involved. It is the usual way of speaking amongst men: he that offendeth is said to be reconciled, because he was the **cause** of the breach; he needeth to reconcile himself and to appease him whom he hath offended, which the innocent party needeth not—**he** needeth only to forgive, and to lay aside his just anger. We offended God, not He us; therefore the Scripture usually saith, We are reconciled to God. Second, we have the **benefit**. It is no profit to God that the creature enters into His peace; He is happy within Himself without our love or service; but we are undone if we are not upon good terms with Him."

For Christ to make perfect reconciliation it was required that He should turn away the wrath of God from His people by removing their sins from before His face by means of a propitiatory sacrifice, as also that we should be brought to turn away from all our opposition to God and brought into voluntary and joyful obedience to Him. Until both of these are effected, reconciliation is not perfected. The one is secured by Christ's satisfaction, the other is accomplished by His sending His Spirit to renew us (Titus 3:5). A disposition must be produced in the rebel to return unto God and desire restoration to holiness and happiness in God, for "Can two walk together, except they be agreed?" (Amos 3:3). Hence the servants of God are bidden to go forth and beseech sinners to be reconciled to Him (2 Cor. 5:20), obedience to which consists of faith's entrance into the peace which Christ has made (Col. 1:20); yet this will not be, till we cease from all fighting against God. When they do so, they are said to "have now received the reconciliation" (Rom. 5:11).

4. Its Author

This is the Father Himself. We do not entertain the idea for a moment that Christ died in order to render God compassionate toward His people. Not so; it was the love of God which gave His Son to die for them. The satisfaction of Christ was in order to the removal of those legal obstacles which our sins had interposed against God's love flowing out to us in a way consistent with the honour of His justice. Reconciliation was not the procurement of God's grace, but an effect thereof. God's reconciling us to Himself does not imply any change either in His will or disposition toward us. His infinite displeasure with sin, His disapprobation of our persons considered as offenders, and the engagement of Divine justice against us as transgressors, are perfectly consistent with His everlasting love to us and with His eternal and immutable approbation of our persons as viewed in Christ. If we distinguish sharply between personal resentment and judicial condemnation, all difficulty at this point vanishes. "God loved us, in respect of the free purpose of His will to send Christ to redeem us and to satisfy for our sins; He was angry with us, in respect of His violated law and provoked justice by sin" (John Owen, Vol. 9, p. 172).

That the Father is the Author of reconciliation is plain from 2 Cor. 5:19, "God was in Christ reconciling the world unto Himself." After many hours of concentrated study upon it, we give it as our matured conviction that this expression covers the whole of our reconciliation, from its inception in the mind of God before the foundation of the world, till our final glorification in heaven. This expression "God was in Christ (a name of office, not of nature) reconciling" expresses the **agency** of the Father in the entire work of reconciliation. First, in choosing and appointing Christ for this work: Isa. 42:1, Rom. 3:25. Second, in the covenant and agreement with Him: Isa. 49:3-6, Psa.

89:3, 4. Third, in calling and sending Christ into this world: John 10:36, Heb. 5:4, 5. Fourth, in fitting Christ for this stupendous undertaking: Heb. 10:5, Isa. 11:1-3, John 3:34. Fifth, in His dealings with Christ at the cross: Isa. 53:6, 4. Sixth, in accepting His expiatory sacrifice: Rom. 4:24, 6-4. Seventh, in glorifying Christ: Matt. 28:18, Psa. 2:8.

5. Its Scope

"God was in Christ, reconciling a world unto Himself" (2 Cor. 5:19). In 2 Peter 2:5 we read of "the world of the ungodly." Here in 2 Cor. 5:19 it is the world of the godly or elect (as in John 6:33)—there is no "the" in the Greek. The expression is indefinite, though not universal. First, the "world" to show that men, and not angels (2 Peter 2.4), are intended—the sinning angels had neither Mediator nor Reconciler. Second, to show the amplitude of God's grace: confined not to the Jews—cf. Rom. 11:15. Third, to denote the ground of the Gospel tender. All who are concerned, should be awakened to seek after this privilege. The Gospel offer is made indefinitely to all sorts and conditions of men. The added words in 2 Cor. 5:19, "not imputing their trespasses unto them," is proof positive that all mankind are not included in the "world," for God does impute trespasses unto the wicked: Eph. 5:5, 6, etc.

"And having made peace through the blood of His cross, by Him to reconcile all things unto Himself; by Him, whether things in earth, or things in heaven" (Col. 1:20). The key to this verse lies in noting the particular epistle in which it is found. Here the apostle was refuting a false gnosticism with angelolatry and spirit emanations, which had been introduced by human philosophy to depose Christ as the only Mediator between God and men—see 2:18, etc. The Holy Spirit here shows the true relation of angels to Christ: they were created by Him (1:15, 16). Further, they too were the **gainers** by His Satisfaction (1:19-21). There had once been a union between angels and man, as fellow-citizens in one vast empire of God. But sin had dissolved that union. Sin is rebellion against God, and loyal angels could have no fellowship with sinners. But the great Atonement has restored the happy relationship between holy angels and God's elect: Eph. 1:10. They too have gained by it. Christ has restored the disrupted harmony of the universe. A clear proof and blessed illustration of this is found in Rev. 22:9, where an angel, speaking of himself to John, says, "I am thy **fellow-servant!**"

It may help some if we give a summary of the whole subject. 1. Its Origin was the love of God: Rom. 5:8, 2 Cor. 5:18. 2. Its Basis was the everlasting covenant, the "counsel of peace:" Zech. 6:13. 3. Its Procuring—cause was the satisfaction of Christ (Rom. 5:10), which has "made peace:" Col. 1:20. 4. Its Occasion was the legal alienation between God and His people through sin: Eph. 2:16. 5. Its Need lay in a satisfaction being required by Divine justice: Rom. 5:9, 10. 6. Its Nature is a restoring to God's judicial favour: Col. 1:21, 22. 7. Its Communicator is the Holy Spirit: Rom. 14:17. 8. Its Requirement is that sinners should be reconciled to God (2 Cor. 5:20), which means the embracing of His offer of reconciliation through Christ, and this, by ceasing all opposition to Him: Psa. 2:12. 9. Its Reception is by faith: Rom. 5:1, 11. 10. Its Consequence is sins remitted (2 Cor. 5:19) and access to God: Eph. 2:18. 11. Its Publication is by "the Gospel of peace": Eph. 6:14. 12. Its Extent is the re-uniting of all holy beings in the universe: Eph. 1:10.

—ARTHUR W. PINK.

THE INTERCESSION OF CHRIST (Continued)

In view of all that Christ has already done for His people it seems, to some, superfluous that He should now have to intercede for them. In view of the Son of God becoming incarnate, declaring the name of God and revealing the whole counsel of His will, and giving us the great example of love and holiness in His life; in view of His fulfilling all righteousness for us, making full atonement for our sins, redeeming us by His blood, and confirming His truth and acceptation with God, in all these things, by His resurrection from the dead, wherein He was declared to be the Son of God with power; does it not seem that He might well have left us to deal for ourselves and to build our eternal safety on the foundation which He laid? Alas!

when all this was done, if Christ had only ascended into His own glory, to enjoy His majesty, honour and dominion, without continuing His life and office on our behalf, we had been left poor and helpless, so that we had fallen a prey to our subtle and powerful Adversary.

It was not without reason that our blessed Saviour, when almost on the point of leaving this world, assured His sorrowing disciples that He would not leave them "orphans" (John 14:18), but instead, that He would still be their Patron, continue to act for them, and exercise His office of Mediator and Advocate with the Father on their behalf. Unless He did, they would be "orphans" —unable to defend themselves, incompetent to provide for themselves, insufficient of themselves to secure the right unto their inheritance. It was "expedient" for them that He should ascend the throne, otherwise He could not send the Holy Spirit unto them (John 16:7), that Paraclete or Helper, who should, in answer to Christ's prayers for them, supply their every need.

What is it that Christ intercedes for? In general, it may be said that His requests for believers are as wide as the intent of His death for them. Whatsoever blessing or privilege He purchased for them upon the cross, He sues for upon His throne. His intercession is the plea, based upon His satisfaction, which was the payment. The subject-matter of the Redeemer's intercession must ever be unto God's people a theme of the utmost importance. It comprehends their deliverances, supplies, and comforts in the present life, and their final salvation and eternal bliss. The Scriptures, in a great number and variety of statements, make known unto us the things for which Christ constantly pleads on behalf of His saints. In a previous article we called attention to the fact that the intercession of Christ needs to be contemplated in connection with the Everlasting Covenant and the promises which God made to the Mediator therein, and this needs to be carefully borne in mind when reverently endeavoring to ascertain the scope and contents of the Saviour's requests.

"The intercession of Christ as His people's High Priest in heaven, is intimately connected with His Surety-engagements in the covenant of redemption, and the stipulations made with Him as Mediator for the salvation of all who were given Him from eternity to be redeemed from among men. The covenant —the plan of sovereign wisdom and grace devised in the counsels of the Trinity—is the rich and unfathomable source of human salvation, and renders its enjoyment sure and unfailing to those whose names were inscribed 'in the Lamb's book of life before the foundation of the world.' It to them 'ordered in all things and sure' and is 'all their salvation and desire' (2 Sam. 23:5).

"The covenant of redemption—the eternal compact between the Father and the Son as the Representative and Surety of elect sinners—has been justly designated a **'Charter of free promises of grace and glory.'** These promises are the expression of the Divine decrees or purposes concerning the salvation of elect sinners, flowing from the sovereign grace of the Godhead, in the person of the Father, who stands as the covenant Head on His part. The conditional part of the covenant was to be perfected by Christ the Surety, who was set up from everlasting, and willingly became His people's Representative; and the promissory part was the Father's. He engaged to confer all blessings upon the fulfillment of the conditions by the Surety. This effected, became strictly meritorious of the blessings promised, so that their bestowment can be claimed, not only on the footing of God's faithfulness and truth, but likewise of His justice: see Psalm 89:35-37.

"The covenant from eternity guaranteed the certainty of the conditions being performed by the sinner's Surety, who could not 'fail nor be discouraged till He should set judgment in the earth' (Isa. 42:4). Hence it is presented to us **without** any condition to be performed by us. It is all **promise**, from beginning to end, and is often spoken of as one continued promise: 'In hope of eternal life, which God, that cannot lie, promised before the world began' (Titus 1:2). 'And this promise that He hath promised us, even eternal life' (1 John 2:25). Hence the promises of the covenant concerning the life and salvation of the elect are **absolute** and **unconditional**, all flowing from God's sovereign grace, and the condition being perfectly fulfilled by the sinner's Surety, God works in us to will and to do, the grace and all the duties which are connected with their acceptance. Therefore is the covenant spoken of in Scripture, by way of special emphasis, as 'The covenants of the promise' (Greek of Eph. 2:12).

"The covenant is one; but, from the time of its first publication in Paradise, immediately on the back of the fall, in the one grand fundamental promise of the Old Testament (Gen. 3:15), there were many renewals of it, and those were always in the form of a promise, enlarging and making clearer that which was first given to fallen man. The original phrase (Eph. 2:12) is, 'which covenants of the promise,' to signify that, as the covenant is one, so the promise is substantially the same in all ages and dispensations, only varied in reference to the external circumstances of the modes of its application" (T. Houston).

The great ends of the covenant, as they concerned the glory of God, the honour of Christ, and the salvation of elect sinners, are accomplished by the fulfillment of the promises. The Surety having met the condition of the covenant, in fulfilling all righteousness; He now takes up the promises made to Him, and pledged by the truth, holiness and justice of Jehovah, to confer and grant unto the promised seed, and pleads them before Him. The covenant-promises given to Christ may be regarded in a twofold aspect: first, those which were made to Him as Mediator, to be performed to Him personally. These we find Him pleading in John 17:1, 5; second, those which were given to Him as the Head of the elect, and which, in their fulfillment belonged to them as well as to Him. A brief but comprehensive summary of the nature and scope of those "exceeding great and precious promises" is furnished in 2 Peter 1:3, namely, "all things that pertain unto life and godliness:" compare Gal. 3:16, 2 Cor. 1:20.

The Saviour had, at all times, in His work of constant obedience and painful suffering, unwavering trust in the eternal promises: Psa. 22:10, Heb. 2:13. He pleaded them perpetually and rested always with assured confidence that, what God had promised, He was able and ready also to perform. This carried Him through every part of His arduous undertaking. This, too sustained Him in His last tremendous agony, when, "For the joy that was set before Him, He endured the cross, despising the shame" (Heb. 12:2). So now in heaven, the Saviour's perpetual work, as His people's Advocate and Intercessor, is His pleading the promises of the covenant for the advancement and triumph of His cause, and the salvation of His redeemed people. He finished the work of oblation which was given Him to do, when He made His soul an offering for sin, but He can only see of the travail of His soul with satisfaction, when the promise given Him by the Father is completely realized. The "pleasure of the Lord" prospers in His hands as the word of the oath receives its fulfillment. This leads us to consider, further, the intercession of Christ in,

5. Its Petitions

The intercession of Christ is eminently for **the Spirit to apply the purchased redemption.** In the counsels of the blessed Trinity from eternity, and in the covenant of grace, it was arranged that the whole applicatory part of salvation should be in the hands of the Spirit (Ezek. 36:27). Accordingly the Saviour, in view of His completed undertaking, asked the fulfillment of the covenant-stipulation in the mission and work of the Spirit. This was made a matter of special and repeated promise to His disciples in His great discourse of consolation in the upper room: "I will pray the Father and He shall give you another Comforter, that He may abide with you forever: the Spirit of truth; whom the world cannot receive, because it seeth Him not, neither knoweth Him: but ye know Him; for He dwelleth with you, and shall be in you" (John 14:16, 17). And again, "But the Comforter the Holy Spirit, whom the Father will send in My name, He shall teach you all things" (14:26)—the Spirit being sent in **Christ's** "name" signifies, on account of His merits and in His stead: to carry forward to completion the gracious work which He began.

In the economy of grace, the Son sends the Spirit as the Paraclete to be a Substitute for Himself on earth. It was necessary for Christ to go away, and profitable for His people that the Spirit should come to them and open exhaustless sources of spiritual consolation and strength to their souls: "It is expedient for you that I go away: for if I go not away, the Comforter will not come unto you; but if I depart, I will send Him unto you" (John 16:7). On the ground of His finished work, Christ asked the Father for the mission of the Spirit, and received His heart's desire (Acts 2:33), and, as a mediatorial "Prince and Saviour" (Acts 5:31) He sent Him forth.

Thus, the mission of the Spirit was the first fruit of Christ's office of advocacy, after His entrance into heaven, and therefore all the works which the Spirit begins and accomplishes in the souls of the elect, are fruits of it also. "He (the Spirit) shall receive of Mine," says Christ, "and show it unto you" (John 16:14): "Mine" by purchase, "Mine by plea, "Mine" by possession. More specifically, the petitions of our Intercessor concern:

1. The communications of saving grace to the elect in their **regeneration and justification**. By nature there is no difference between them and the world: they are in the same state of condemnation, they possess the same character of ungodliness, and they merit the same punishment. They are enemies to God in their mind by wicked works, rebels against the Divine authority, and sinners before the Lord exceedingly. Yet there is a difference, and that of immense importance: they are chosen of God, given to Christ to be redeemed, and the eye of the omniscient Saviour is upon them. When the hour fixed in the arrangements of infinite mercy for their salvation arrives, the Redeemer pleads His merits for the bestowment of spiritual life (Psa. 2:8). It is the intercession of our High Priest in heaven which, in every instance, procures the coming of the Spirit to dead sinners, to quicken them into newness of life. That which took place on the day of Pentecost, as recorded in Acts 2:32-42, has been repeated and continued (in varying scale or measure) until now.

So also is our justification equally a fruit of the advocacy of Him who was, "delivered for our offences and was raised again for our justification" (Rom. 4:25). When writing upon our justification by God, the apostle founded it upon the death of Christ, then with a "yea rather" upon the resurrection of Christ, and lastly with an "also" upon His intercession: Rom. 8:34. "Though our propitiation made on the cross by the blood of Christ be the meritorious cause of our justification, yet the intercession upon the throne made by the same blood of Christ, as a speaking blood, is the immediate moving cause. The propitiation Christ made on the cross, made God capable of justifying us in an honourable way; but the intercession of Christ as pleading that propitiation for us, procures our actual justification. The death of Christ accepted made justification possible, and the death of Christ pleaded by Him, makes justification actual. Righteousness to justify was brought in by Him on the cross, and righteousness justifying is applied by Him on His throne. Our justification was merited of God by His death, the merit of it acknowledged by God at His resurrection, and is conferred on us, when we believe, by His intercession" (S. Charnock).

2. **For the pardon of our daily sins.** The believer contracts daily debts by committing daily sins, and there is not an hour passes but we merit the total removal of justifying grace, and give God occasion to revive the memory of His former justice and cancel the grant of His lately conferred mercy. And how could we avoid it if Christ did not renew the memory of His propitation before God which first procured our acceptance, and which alone maintains our standing before Him? Every sin brings with it an obligation to punishment, therefore do we read, "If any one sin, we have an Advocate with the Father, Jesus Christ the righteous" (1 John 2:1). This advocacy of Christ answers the obligation which every sin brings upon us, as it answered all our obligations when we first came into His presence.

"In many things we all offend" (James 3:2), believers as well as unbelievers. Nor are our sins less criminal than those of others, for besides involving rebellion against the same authority, and a violation of the same holy, just and good law, they are aggravated by the peculiar obligations arising from the additional blessings we have received. The ground upon which God treats with us in mercy is the justifying righteousness of Christ, to which constant efficacy is given by His intercession. Believers not only need to be warned against temptations to sin, but to be furnished with consolation when they are despondent as the result of its committal. We are invited to "Come boldly (freely) to the throne of grace that we may obtain mercy, and find grace to help in time of need," and that invitation is based upon the fact that "we have a great High Priest that is passed into the heavens, Jesus the Son of God" (Heb. 4:14, 16). The "fountain" which has been opened "for sin and uncleanness" (Zech. 13:1) remains open, and flows out continually by virtue of Christ's intercession.

3. **For their deliverance from temptation.** "We have an enemy industrious to entrap us, and we have an Advocate as

industrious to protect us, who will either solicit for us a reasonable strength to resist his invasion, or strength to improve it to our spiritual advantage if He suffers the temptation to meet with some success in its attempt. Satan desires to sift us, Luke 23:31. . . Christ doth not solicit for such a strength whereby a temptation may be wholly successless, but whereby it may not be wholly victorius. He prayed for Peter against Satan, that his faith might not fail, but He did not pray positively that the temptation might wholly fail. He implies by that expression 'when thou are converted strengthen thy brethren,' that he should fall so foully as that not a grain of grace should be visible in him; that he should appear like one in an unregenerate state, so that his return should be as a new conversion. His intercession is not always for keeping off a temptation from us, for He many times suffers fierce ones to invade us, for gracious ends, both for His own glory and our good; but He solicits that a temptation may not utterly sink us and mortify our grace" (S. Charnock).

The Christian's hope and confidence that he shall endure to the end of his earthly course rests securely on the efficacy of Christ's continual intercession. Left to himself, or given over unto temptation, or left unaided by fresh supplies of grace, the believer would apostatise and utterly perish. But there is ample provision made in the Covenant of Grace, through union to Christ our living Head and by the indwelling of the Spirit, to secure his standing in grace and endurance to the end. The assured word of promise is all-encouraging. The inheritance unto which the Christian has been begotten is "reserved in heaven" for him, and meanwhile, he is "kept by the power of God through faith" (1 Peter 1:4, 5). He who has begun a good work in us will perform it unto the day of Christ (Phil. 1:6). As it was wholly by Christ's prayer that Peter was recovered, so each of His people are being saved "unto the uttermost" by His constant intercession (Heb. 7:25).

We have only to read attentively the 17th of John to find how earnestly Christ prays for the preserving of believers in grace. "Holy Father, keep . . . those which Thou has given me" (v. 11). "I pray not that Thou shouldest take them out of the world, but that Thou shouldest keep them from the evil" (v. 15). This petition of our High Priest's is answered by the Holy Spirit delivering each of them from committing the unpardonable sin, from not suffering them to be "utterly cast down" by Satan, from not allowing them to be completely engulfed by the world. The Spirit so strengthens them in the inner man that their faith never completely fails; He so convicts them of their sins that they are brought to repent of and confess their daily transgressions. He works in them both to will and to do of God's good pleasure, that they are kept (as to the general course and tenor of their lives) in the path of obedience to God.

4. **For their sanctification.** "As Christ is a Priest set on the right hand of the throne of the Majesty on high, He preserves the stability of the new covenant, and perpetuates the fruit of it: justification, in blotting out the memory of our sins, and sanctification in writing the law in our hearts: Heb. 8:1, 6, 10, 12. He is the Author of our first sanctification by His intercession, as the first fruits of it was the sending that Spirit by whose powerful operations the soul is reformed according to the Divine image; and He is the Author of our repeated sanctification by the exercise of His advocacy: 'Sanctify them through Thy truth' (John 17:17). The end of His intercession is not for sharpness of wit, a pompous wealth, a luxurious prosperity, or a lazy peace; but for faith, holiness, growth in grace. His intercession is not employed for low things, but for such as may fit us for honour in another world. Mortification of sin and holiness of conversation, are therefore called 'things above' where Christ sits at the right hand of God: Col. 3:1 compared with v. 5—things which come from above by virtue of Christ's session there" (S. Charnock).

Christ "gave Himself for us, that He might redeem us from all iniquity, and purify unto Himself a peculiar people, zealous of good works" (Titus 2:14). Through His atoning death believers are delivered from the guilt of sin, and through the Holy Spirit's indwelling and imparting the life of Christ to their souls, they are gradually freed from its power and pollution. As the oil which descended from Aaron's head ran down to the skirts of his garments (Psa. 133:2), so out of the fullness of grace that is perpetually in our great High Priest (John 1:16), there are conveyed to the members of His mystical body, even to the least, continuous supplies of grace for sanctification and comfort. The holiness of the redeemed consists in separation from the evil that is in the world, the exercise of all holy graces in heart and life, and the consecration of the whole man to the service of God. This is accomplished by the Holy Spirit applying the Truth in power to them.

5. For **the acceptance of their services.** "As our Advocate, Christ not only preserves our graces, but presents to God our services, and by His intercession maintains life in the one and secures credit for the other. He is as powerful a Soliciter for the acceptance of our duties, as He was a grateful Sacrifice for the expiation of our sins. Our prayers are both imperfect and blemished, but His merit applied by His intercession both purifies and perfects them. Our Advocate, by His skill, puts them into form and language according to the methods of the court of heaven, as an attorney doth the petitions and cause of his client, and by his interest secures a speedy hearing. Our works are no more the cause of the recording our petitions than they are of the justification of our persons. When Christ told His disciples that He had ordained them to bring forth fruit, He added a clause to prevent their imaginations of meriting the answer of their prayers by the present of their fruits, namely, that whatsoever they asked, they must expect only to obtain in His name: John 15:16" (S. Charnock).

1st., the acceptance of our persons is through the intercession of Christ. In themselves, saints, while on earth, are imperfect in all their graces: they are defiled in heart and life, their very righteousnesses still being as "filthy rags" (Isa. 64:6). How, then, is it possible for such persons to find acceptance with God? Only through the perfect sacrifice of the Mediator, and its continual presence as a memorial in heaven: see Heb. 9:14; 10:19, 20. 2nd, the acceptance of our **prayers.** As of old, the high priest of Judaism, after he had offered the sin-offering for the people, filled his hands with fragrant incense and put it in the golden censer with coals of fire, and passed within the vail, covering the propitiatory with its cloud, so our blessed Intercessor mingles the prayers of His saints with the much incense of His mediation and renders them accepted: Rev. 8:3. 3rd., the acceptance of their **sacrifices.** What is true of their prayers, is true also of their works of faith and labour of love, their songs of praise and tears of repentance, their deeds of mercy and holy acts of obedience: Phil. 4:18, 1 Peter 2:5. Nothing that we can offer is agreeable to God, save as it comes to Him through the hands and on the recommendation of our powerful Advocate, who is so beloved of Him. Christ is the antitype of Aaron bearing the "iniquity" of our "holy things" (Ex. 28:38) when he presents himself in the heavenly Sanctuary for the interests of His people. When Aaron stood to minister as Israel's representative, he wore the mitre on which was inscribed "Holiness to the Lord," concerning which we read, "And it shall be always upon his forehead, that they may be accepted before the Lord" (Ex. 28:38).

6. For **our salvation.** This is the main end of His intercession: Heb. 7:25. The main design of His death was satisfaction respecting God, the main design of His intercession is salvation respecting us. He lives in heaven to sue out for His people the possession of that which He purchased for them on earth: Rom. 5:10. By His death, as an atoning sacrifice, He reconciled us unto God; by His life, as a diligent Advocate, He carries forward and completes our salvation. "What He begins, He completes, nor rests till He has secured for His redeemed, perfect acquittal beyond the reach of accusations, deliverance from all temptation, immaculate holiness, and uninterrupted and perfect peace" (W. Symington).

7. For **our continuance in glory.** After Christ had prayed for what was necessary for His people during the period of their earthly pilgrimage, He closed with, "Father, I will that they also, whom Thou hast given Me, be with Me where I am; that they may behold My glory, which Thou hast given Me" (John 17:24). This respects the topstone of salvation and bliss. After this He concluded His prayer, as having nothing more to beg for them. Thus, the permanent continuance of the redeemed in glory stands connected with the mediation of our great High Priest. "Not a ray of light, not a smile of favour, not a thrill of gladness, not a note of joy, for which the inhabitants of heaven are not indebted to the Angel of the Covenant, standing with the golden censer full of incense before the Throne" (W. Symington). Christ "ever liveth to make intercession" (Heb. 7:25), for He is an "High Priest **forever** after the order of Melchizedek" (Heb. 6:20). Hallelujah!

—ARTHUR W. PINK.

THE BROKEN HEART

"The sacrifices of God are a broken spirit: a broken and a contrite heart, O God, Thou wilt not despise" (Psa. 51:17).

No Psalm expresses more fully the experience of a penitent, believing soul. First, his humble confession of sin: verses 3, 4, 5. Second, his intense desire for pardon through the blood of Christ: v. 7. Third, his longing after a clean heart: v. 10. Fourth, his desire to render something to God for all His benefits. He says, I will teach transgressors, Thy ways. My lips shall show forth Thy praise. He will give a broken heart: vv. 16, 17. Just as, long ago, they used to offer slain lambs in token of thanksgiving, so he says he will offer up to God a slain and broken heart. Every one of you, who has found the same forgiveness, should come to the same resolution—offer up to God this day a broken heart.

I. The natural heart is unbroken.

The law, the Gospel, mercies, afflictions, death, break not the natural heart. It is harder than stone: there is nothing in the universe so hard. "Ye stouthearted, that are far from righteousness" (Isa. 46:12). "They have made their faces harder than a rock" (Isa. 32:10). "Careless women... women that are at ease" (Isa. 32:10, 11).

Why? 1st, the vail is upon their hearts. They do not believe the Bible, the strictness of the law, the wrath to come; the face of a covering is over their eyes. 2nd, Satan has possession, and carries away the good Seed. 3rd, they are dead in trespasses and sins. The dead hear not, feel not, they are "past feeling." 4th, they build a wall of untempered mortar. They hope for safety in some refuge of lies—that they pray, or give alms, etc.

II. The awakened heart is wounded, not broken.

The law makes the first wound. When God is going to save a soul, He brings the soul to reflect on his sins. "Cursed is every one that continueth not in all things which are written in the book of the law to do them" (Gal. 3:10). "For I was alive without the law once: but when the commandment came (in power to the conscience), sin revived (became more accutely real), and I died (to my own self-righteousness—A. W. P.), Rom. 7:9. Life and heart appear in awful colours.

The majesty of God makes the next wound. The sinner is made sensible of the great and holy Being whom he has wronged. "Against Thee, Thee only have I sinned and done this evil in Thy sight" (Psa. 51:4).

The third wound is from his own helplessness to make himself better. Still the heart is not broken; the heart yet rises up against God. 1st, because of the strictness of the law. 2nd, because faith is the only way of salvation, and is the gift of God. 3rd, because God is sovereign, and may save or not as He will. Such risings against Him shows the unbroken heart. There is no more miserable state than this. It is one thing to be awakened and another thing to be saved. Do not rest in convictions.

III. The believing heart is broken two ways.

1. It is broken from its own righteousness. When the Holy Spirit leads a man to the Cross, his heart there breaks from seeking salvation by his own righteousness. All his burden of performances and contrivances drops. 1st, the work of Christ appears so perfect—the wisdom of God and the power of God—Divine righteousness. "I wonder that I should ever think of any other way of salvation. If I could have been saved by my own duties, my whole soul would now have refused it. I wonder that all the world did not see and comply with this way of salvation by the righteousness of Christ" (Brainard). 2nd, the grace of Christ appears so wonderful. That all this righteousness should be free to such a sinner! That I so long neglected, despised, hated it, put mountains between, and yet that He has come over the mountains! "That thou mayest remember and be confounded and never open thy mouth any more, because of thy shame, when I am pacified toward thee for all that thou hast done" (Ezek. 16:63). Have you this broken heart—broken within sight of the Cross? It is not a look into your own heart, or the heart of hell, but into the heart of Christ that breaks the heart. Oh, pray for this broken heart. Boasting is excluded. To Him be glory! Worthy is the Lamb! All these struggles of a self-righteous soul are to put the crown on your own head instead of at the feet of Jesus.

2. Broken from love of sin. When a man believes on Christ, he then sees sin to be hateful. 1st, it separated between him and God, made the great gulf, and kindled the fires of hell. 2nd, it cruci-

fied the Lord of glory—weighed down His soul—made Him sweat, and bleed and die. It is the plague of his heart now. All my unhappiness is from my being a sinner. Now he mourns sore like a dove. That he should sin against so much light. "Then shall ye remember your ways, and all your doings wherein ye have been defiled, and shall loathe yourselves in your own sight."

IV. **Advantages of a broken heart.**

1. **It keeps you from being offended at the preaching of the Cross.** A natural heart is offended every day at the preaching of the Cross. Many of you, I have no doubt, hate it. The preaching of Another's righteousness—that you must have it or perish—many, I have no doubt are often enraged at this in their hearts. All the offense of the Cross is not ceased. But a broken heart cannot be offended. Ministers cannot speak too plainly for a broken heart. A broken heart would sit forever to hear of the righteousness without works. Many of you are offended when we preach plainly against sin. But a broken heart hates sin worse than ministers can make it. Many are like the worshippers of Baal, "Bring forth thy son that he may die" (Judges 6:30). But a broken heart loves to see the idol stamped upon and beaten small.

2. **A broken heart is at rest.** The unconverted heart is like the troubled sea—"Who will show us any good?" It is going from creature to creature. The awakened soul is not at rest—sorrows of death, pains of hell, attend those who are forgetting their resting-place. But the broken heart says, "Return unto thy rest, O my soul." The righteousness of Christ takes away every dread—"casts out fear." Even the plague of the heart cannot truly disturb, for he casts his burden upon the Lord.

3. **Nothing can happen wrong to it.** To the unconverted, how dreadful is a sick-bed, poverty, death-tossed like a wild beast in a net. But a broken heart is satisfied with Christ. This is enough—he has no ambition for more. Take away all, Christ remains. He is a weaned child. —R. MURRAY M'CHEYNE, 1840.

GOD'S HOLD ON US AND OUR HOLD ON HIM

It is said, truly, that since the Christian can do all things in Christ's strength, he need never sin; and it is said, with equal truth, that, as a matter of fact, the Christian is always sinning.

There is, you will observe, no contradiction in those two statements. But then some just reverse them, change the theory into a fact, and the fact into a theory, and say: the one, that the Christian cannot help sinning; the other, that there are Christians who do not sin; both of which are untrue as the two former statements are true.

It is most important to keep this distinction clearly in sight. The Christian need not, in any particular instance you can name, sin, because he can do all things through Christ; but he does actually sin continually, because he does not do all things through Christ. We cannot do all things through Christ, except by a constant act of Divine grace; and, as a matter of fact, that is not constantly put forth. The evil heart which remains even in the regenerate, is not prevented from showing itself. God does leave His people to themselves that they may know what is in their hearts. He did so with His saints of old, He does so with His people now. And so invariably is this the case, that the apostle even says, "If we say we have no sin, we deceive ourselves, and the truth is not in us."

If Elijah, under the power of the Spirit, with his loins girt up, running in triumph before Ahab to the entrance of Jezreel, had any such thought in his mind, it was speedily dissipated. That same evening he began to know what was in his heart. While on the road to Beersheba he seems to have thought of nothing but the danger he was in from Jezebel. The whole of that journey was a flight, and though there was no pursuer, for Jezebel's purpose was answered, the same servant who had been with him on Carmel, and seen the rain come in answer to his prayers, now saw his master hastening away, and not resting till he found himself safe in a city belonging to Judah. He was a man of like passions with us, subject to the same temptations, with the same evil, treacherous heart. And the moment the hand of the Lord was taken off from him, that moment Elijah ceased to glorify God.

Some men think that they can keep their hand on God as long as they please. But He takes care to teach His children that it is not they who hold Him, but

He who holds them. That is a lesson which we all must learn sooner or later. And when a man has learned it, instead of being inclined to say, "My mountain standeth so fast I shall never be moved," he will rather say, "Hold Thou me up, and I shall be safe."

It is to teach us watchful dependence, that this part of Elijah's history is recorded. And if you are a young believer, beginning to think "I shall never again find as I have found the lustings of my evil nature, I am so strong now that I shall always conquer," do not forget Elijah! It needs no apostle to speak the converse of St. James' words, and to say that you are subject to like passions with Elijah. Where he fell, it is little to say that you may fall. Beware of the moment of temptation; when the heart is lifted up, when you are ready to say, "I am rich and increased with goods," when you think you are strong, then it is that you are in danger, and before you are aware may dishonour your God.
—Elijah the Prophet, by Garrett.

Now the grace of God is manifested in and by and through the Lord Jesus Christ. "The law was given by Moses, grace and truth came by Jesus Christ" (John 1:17). This does not mean that God never exercised grace toward any before His Son became incarnate—Gen. 6:8, Ex. 33:19, etc., clearly show otherwise. But grace and truth were fully revealed and perfectly exemplified when the Redeemer came to this earth, and died for His people upon the cross. It is through Christ the Mediator alone that the grace of God flows to His elect. "Much more the grace of God, and the gift by grace which is by one man, Jesus Christ. . . much more they which receive abundance of grace and of the gift of righteousness shall reign in life by one Jesus Christ. . . so might grace reign through righteousness unto eternal life by Jesus Christ our Lord" (Rom. 5:15, 17, 21).

The grace of God is proclaimed in the Gospel (Acts 20:24), which is to the self-righteous Jew a "stumbling block," and to the conceited and philosophising Greek "foolishness." And why so? Because there is nothing whatever in it that is adapted to gratify the pride of man. It announces that unless we are saved by grace, we cannot be saved at all. It declares that apart from Christ, the unspeakable Gift of God's grace, the state of every man is desperate, irremediable, hopeless. The Gospel addresses men as guilty, condemned, perishing criminals. It declares that the chastest moralist is in the same terrible plight as is the most voluptuous profligate; that the zealous professor, with all his religious performances, is no better off than the most profane infidel.

The Gospel contemplates every descendant of Adam as a fallen, polluted, hell-deserving and helpless sinner. The grace which the Gospel publishes is his only hope. All stand before God convicted as transgressors of His holy law, as guilty and condemned criminals; awaiting not sentence, but the execution of sentence already passed on them (John 3:18; Rom. 3:19). To complain against the partiality of grace is suicidal. If the sinner insists upon bare justice, then the lake of fire must be his eternal portion. His only hope lies in bowing to the sentence which Divine justice has passed upon him, owning the absolute righteousness of it, casting himself on the mercy of God, and stretching forth empty hands to avail himself of the grace of God now made known to him in the Gospel.

The third Person in the Godhead is the **Communicator** of grace, therefore is He denominated "the Spirit of grace" (Zech. 12:10). God the Father is the Fountain of all grace, for He purposed in Himself the everlasting covenant of redemption. God the Son is the only Channel of grace. The Gospel is the Publisher of grace. The Spirit is the Bestower. He is the One who applies the Gospel in saving power to the soul: quickening the elect while spiritually dead, conquering their rebellious wills, melting their hard hearts, opening their blind eyes, cleansing them from the leprosy of sin. Thus we may say with the late G. S. Bishop, "Grace is a provision for men who are so fallen that they cannot lift the axe of justice, so corrupt that they cannot change their own natures, so averse to God that they cannot turn to Him, so blind that they cannot see Him, so deaf that they cannot hear Him, and so dead that He Himself must open their graves and lift them into resurrection."
—ARTHUR W. PINK.

Eternal life is a **gift**, therefore it can neither be earned by good works, nor claimed as a right. Seeing that salvation is a "gift," who has any right to tell God on whom He ought to bestow it? It is not that the Giver ever **refuses** this gift to any who seek it whole-heartedly, and according to the rules which He has prescribed. No; He refuses none who come to Him empty-handed and in the way of His appointing. But if out of a world of impenitent and unbelieving, God is determined to exercise His sovereign right by choosing a limited number to be saved, who is wronged? Is God **obliged** to force His gift on those who value it not? Is God compelled to save those who are determined to go **their own** way?

But nothing more riles the natural man and brings to the surface his innate and inveterate enmity against God than to press upon him the eternality, the freeness, and the absolute sovereignty of Divine grace. That God should have formed His purpose from everlasting, without in anywise consulting the creature, is too abasing for the unbroken heart. That grace cannot be earned or won by any efforts of man, is too self-emptying for self-righteousness. And that grace singles out whom it pleases to be its favoured objects, arouses hot protests from haughty rebels. The clay rises up against the Potter and asks, "Why hast Thou made me thus?" A lawless insurrectionist dares to call into question the justice of Divine sovereignty.

The **distinguishing** grace of God is seen in saving that people whom He has sovereignly singled out to be His high favourites. By "distinguishing" we mean that grace discriminates, makes differences, chooses some and passes by others. It was distinguishing grace which selected Abraham from the midst of his idolatrous neighbors and made him "the friend of God." It was distinguishing grace which saved "publicans and sinners," but said of the religious Pharisees, "Let them alone" (Matt. 15:14). Nowhere does the glory of God's free and sovereign grace shine more conspicuously than in the unworthiness and unlikeliness of its objects. Beautifully was this illustrated by James Hervey, (1751):—

"Where sin has abounded, says the proclamation from the court of heaven, grace doth much more abound. **Manasseh** was a monster of barbarity, for he caused his own children to pass through the fire, and filled Jerusalem with innocent blood. Manasseh was an adept in iniquity, for he not only multiplied, and to an extravagant degree, his own sacriligious impieties, but he poisoned the principles, and perverted the manners of his subjects, making them do worse than the most detestable of the heathen idolators: see 2 Chron. 33. Yet, through this superabundant grace, he is humbled, he is reformed, and becomes a child of forgiving love, an heir of immortal glory.

"Behold that bitter and bloody persecutor **Saul**; when, breathing out threatenings and bent upon slaughter, he worried the lambs and put to death the disciples of Jesus. The havoc he had committed, the inoffensive families he had already ruined, were not sufficient to assuage his vengeful spirit. They were only a taste, which, instead of glutting the bloodhound, made him more closely pursue the track, and more eagerly pant for destruction. He is still athirst for violence and murder. So eager and insatiable is his thirst, that he even **breathes out** threatening and slaughter (Acts 9:1). His words are spears and arrows, and his tongue a sharp sword. 'Tis as natural for him to menace the Christians, as to breathe the air. Nay, they bled every hour in the purposes of his rancorous heart. It is only owing to want of power, that every syllable he utters, every breath he draws, does not deal out deaths, and cause some of the innocent disciples to fall. Who, upon the principles of human judgment, would not have pronounced him a vessel of wrath, destined to unavoidable damnation? Nay, would not have been ready to conclude that, if there were heavier chains and a deeper dungeon in the world of woe, they must surely be reserved for such an implacable enemy of true godliness? Yet, admire and adore the inexhaustible treasures of grace—**this** Saul is admitted into the goodly fellowship of the prophets, is numbered with the noble arm of martyrs and makes a distinguished figure among the glorious company of the apostles.

"The **Corinthians** were flagitious even to a proverb. Some of them wallowing in such abominable vices, and habituated themselves to such outrageous acts of injustice, as were a reproach to human nature. Yet, even these sons of violence and slaves of sensuality were washed, sanctified, justified (1 Cor. 6:9-11). 'Washed,' in the precious blood of a dying Redeemer; 'sanctified,' by the powerful operations of the blessed Spirit; 'justified,' through the infinitely tender mercies of a gracious God. Those who were once the burden of the earth, are now the joy of heaven, the delight of angels."

(Continued on Page 23)

STUDIES IN THE SCRIPTURES

"Search the Scriptures" John 5:39

Copyright in all English-speaking Countries

EDITOR: Arthur W. Pink, 1339 Bates Ave., Los Angeles, Calif., U. S. A.
Hon. Agent in England: Mr. A. Winstone, "Shalom," Old Bath Road, Leckhampton, Cheltenham.
Hon. Agent in Australia: Mr. G. Ardill, The Christian Workers' Depot, Commonwealth and Reservoir Streets, Sydney.

THE MERCY OF GOD

"O give thanks unto the Lord: for He is good, for His mercy endureth forever" (Psa. 136:1). For this perfection of the Divine character God is greatly to be praised. Three times over in as many verses does the Psalmist here call upon the saints to give thanks unto the Lord for this adorable attribute. And surely this is the least that can be asked for from those who have been such bounteous gainers by it. When we contemplate the characteristics of this Divine excellency, we cannot do otherwise than bless God for it. His mercy is "great" (1 Kings 3:6), "plenteous" (Psa. 86:5), "tender" (Luke 1:78), "abundant" (1 Peter 1:3); it is "from everlasting to everlasting upon them that fear Him" (Psa. 103:17). Well may we say with the Psalmist, "I will sing aloud of Thy mercy" (59: 16).

"I will make all My goodness pass before thee, and I will proclaim the name of the Lord before thee; and will be gracious to whom I will be gracious, and will show mercy on whom I will show mercy" (Ex. 33:19). Wherein differs the "mercy" of God from His "grace"? The mercy of God has its spring in the Divine goodness. The first issue of God's goodness is His benignity or bounty, by which He gives liberally to His creatures as creatures; thus has He given being and life to all things. The second issue of God's goodness is His mercy, which denotes the ready inclination of God to relieve the misery of fallen creatures. Thus, "mercy" presupposes sin.

Though it may not be easy at the first consideration to perceive a real difference between the grace and the mercy of God, it helps us thereto if we carefully ponder His dealings with the unfallen angels. He has never exercised mercy toward them, for they have never stood in any need thereof, not having sinned or come beneath the effects of the curse. Yet, they certainly are the objects of God's free and sovereign grace. First, because of His **election** of them from out of the whole angelic race (1 Tim. 5:21). Second, and in consequence of their election, because of His **preservation** of them from apostacy, when Satan rebelled and dragged down with him one-third of the celestial hosts (Rev. 12:4). Third, in making Christ their **Head** (Col. 2:10, 1 Peter 3:22), whereby they are eternally secured in the holy condition in which they were created. Fourth, because of the exalted **position** which has been assigned them: to live in God's immediate presence (Dan. 7:10), to serve Him constantly in His heavenly temple, to receive honourable commissions from Him (Heb. 1:14). This is abundant **grace** toward them; but "mercy" it is not.

In endeavoring to study the mercy of God as it is set forth in Scripture, a threefold distinction needs to be made, if the Word of Truth is to be "rightly divided" thereon. First, there is a **general** mercy of God, which is extended not only to all men, believers and unbelievers all alike, but also to the entire creation: "His tender mercies are over all His works" (Psa. 145:9): "He giveth to all life, and breath, and all things" (Acts 17:25). God has pity upon the brute creation in their needs, and supplies them with suitable provision. Second, there is a **special** mercy of God, which is exercised toward the children of men, helping and succouring them, notwithstanding their sins. To them also He communicates all the necessities of life: "for He maketh His sun to rise on the evil and on the good, and sendeth rain on the just and on the unjust" (Matt. 5:

(Continued on Page 48)

IMPORTANT NOTICES

Please advise promptly of change of address, otherwise copies will be lost in the mails.

We are glad to send a sample copy to any of your friends whom you believe would be interested in such a publication.

Send to Mr. I. C. Herendeen, Swengel (Union County), Penna., for a list of our publications. He has published many of our books and booklets.

This magazine is published as a work of faith and labour of love. The Editor and his wife gladly give their services. It is freely sent to all who will read it. No charge is made for it.

Christians who feel definitely led to do so, may have fellowship with us in this ministry. Those outside the U. S. A., please send only INTERNATIONAL Money Orders made out to Los Angeles, California, U. S. A.

CONTENTS

The Mercy of God	25
The Epistle to the Hebrews	26
The Satisfaction (Atonement) of Christ	33
The Intercession of Christ	39
Sound the Alarm	44

THE EPISTLE TO THE HEBREWS

38. The Two Covenants. Heb. 8:10-13

The subject of the two covenants supplies the principal key which unlocks for us the meaning of God's dispensational dealings with His people here on earth. Its importance and blessedness is not surpassed by anything within the entire range of Divine revelation. Yet, sad to say, it is something which is scarcely known at all today by the majority of professing Christians. Covenant-relationship has always been the basis on which God has dealt with His people. The foundation of all is the Everlasting Covenant, a compact or agreement which God made with Christ as the Head and Representative of the whole election of grace.

We would refer the interested reader unto two articles upon it, which appeared in the Jan. and Feb. 1930 issues of this magazine. What we shall here endeavour to treat of is the administration of that covenant, as it was made known by God, and the various forms in which it was established among His saints.

There was an original covenant made with Adam and all mankind in him: see Hos. 6:6 margin. This consisted of an agreement between God and man concerning obedience and disobedience, reward and punishment. To that covenant were annexed promises and threatenings, which were expressed in visible signs or symbols the first, in the tree of life; the latter in the tree of the knowledge of good and evil. By these did God establish the original law of creation as a covenant. On the part of man, it was required that he should accept of this law. It was a covenant of works, and had no mediator. That arrangement or constitution formed the basis on which God dealt with Adam, but it ceased as soon as sin entered the world. God had provided a way of salvation for His own elect apart from their personal obligation to sinless obedience as the condition of life, and that through their Surety discharging all their responsibilities in His own person. This was made known in the first promise God proclaimed: Gen. 3:15. All who receive the grace which is tendered through the promises of the gospel, are delivered from the curse of that covenant which Adam, their legal representative, broke.

But though this first earthly covenant is no longer administered as a "covenant," nevertheless, all those of Adam's descendants who receive not the grace of God as it is tendered to them in the promises of the Gospel, are under the law and curse of the Adamic covenant, because the obedience which it requires of the creature unto the Creator, and the penalty which it threatens and the curse it pronounces upon the disobedient, has never been met for them by a substitute. Therefore, if any man believe not, the wrath of God (not "cometh," but) abideth on him (John 3: 36), and this, because the command and curse, which result from the relation between man and his Maker, and the inflexible righteousness of God as the supreme Governor and Judge of all mankind, must be fulfilled.

Now the children of Israel were not formally placed under the Adamic covenant absolutely, as a **covenant of life**, for, from the days of Abraham the **promise** (a renewal of Gen. 3:15; see Gen. 12:1-3, 17:6-8, etc.) was given unto him and his seed. Let it be carefully noted that in Gal. 3:17 the apostle proves that **no** "law" would afterwards be given, nor covenant made, that should or could disannul that promise. Had Israel been brought under the Adamic covenant of works it **would** have disannuled the promise, for that covenant and the promise of Grace are diametrically opposed. Moreover, had Israel come formally under the Adamic covenant of works they were all under the curse, and so had all perished eternally.

That there were other **federal transactions between** God and His **Church before** the giving of the law at Sinai, is abundantly clear from the book of Genesis. God entered into covenant with Abraham, making him promises on behalf of his descendants, and appointing a solemn outward seal for its confirmation and establishment. That covenant contained the very nature and essence of what is termed the "new covenant." Proof of this is found in the fact that the Lord Jesus is said to be "a Mediator of the circumcision, for the truth of God to **confirm** the promises made to the fathers" (Rom. 15:8). As He was the Mediator of the new covenant, so far was He from recinding the promises which God made to Abraham, Isaac, and Jacob, that it belonged to His office to ratify and establish them. But it was at Sinai that the Lord entered formally into covenant with Israel as a nation (Heb. 8:9), a covenant which had all the institutions of Divine worship annexed to it (Heb. 9:1-6).

In contrast from the covenant which God made with Israel at Sinai, Christ is made "the Mediator of a better covenant" (Heb. 8:6). This is the covenant of grace, being so called in contrast from that of works, which was made with us in Adam. For these two, grace and works, do divide the ways of our relation to God, being opposite the one to the other (Rom. 11:6). Of this covenant of grace Christ was its Mediator from the beginning of the world, namely, from the giving of the first promise in Gen. 3:15, for that promise was given in view of His incarnation and all that He should accomplish by His future and actual mediation. Christ was as truly the Surety of Abel as He was of the apostle Paul, and God had "respect unto" (was favourable toward and accepted) the one on the ground of Christ's suretyship as much as He did the other. To this it may be replied, If such be the case, then wherein lies the superior privilege of the Gospel-dispensation over that of the Mosaic?

In seeking an answer to the above question, it is needful to recognize (as was pointed out in our last article) that the "new covenant" referred to in Heb. 8 is not the new covenant **absolutely** considered, and as it had been **virtually** administered from the days of Gen. 3:15 in a way **of promise**. For considered thus it was quite consistent with the covenant that God made with Israel at Sinai: in Gal. 3:17 the apostle proves that the renewal of the covenant (as a promise) to Abraham, was in no way abrogated by the giving of the law. Instead, in Heb. 8 the apostle is treating of such **an establishment** of the new covenant as demanded the revocation of the Siniatic constitution. What this "establishment" was, is made clear in Heb. 9 and 10: it was the **ordinances of worship** connected with it.

When Christianity had been formally established by God, not only was the old covenant annulled, but the entire system of sacred worship whereby it was administered, was set aside. When the "new covenant" was first given in the way of a promise (Gen. 3:15), renewed Gen. 12:17, etc.), it did not introduce a system of worship and privileges expressive of the same. But the **promise** of the new covenant **was** included in the Mosaic covenant, nor was it inconsistent with its rights and ceremonies, nay not even with them composed into a yoke of bondage. And why? Because all those rites and ceremonies were added **after** the making of the covenant in Ex. 19 and 24; nevertheless what was added did not and could not overthrow the promise. As the Mosaic system was completed, then all the worship of the Church was to proceed from it and to be conformed to it.

No sinner was ever saved but by virtue of the new covenant and the mediation of Christ therein. The new covenant of grace (in contrast from the old covenant of works made with the human race in Adam) was extant and effectual throughout the O. T. era. Then what is the "better covenant" with its "better promises" which the death of Christ has inaugerated? We say again, it is not a new covenant **absolutely** considered. There are many plain passages in the Psalms and the Prophets which show that the Church of old knew and believed the blessed truth of justification and salvation by Christ, and walked with God in the faith thereof: compare Rom. 4:3-9. Let those who have access to the incomparable and immortal "Institutes" of Calvin read carefully chapters nine to eleven in book 2.

"The Church under the Old Testament, had the same promise of Christ, the same interest in Him by faith, remission of sins, reconciliation with God, justification and salvation by the same way and means that believers have under the New. And whereas the essence and substance of the covenant consists in these things, they are not said to be under another covenant, but only a different **administration** of it. But this was so different from that which is established in the Gospel after the coming of Christ, that it hath the appearance and name of another covenant" (John Owen).

The leading differences between the two **administrations** of the covenant of grace may be reduced to the following heads. First, the **manner** in which the love of God in Christ is made known. The miracle recorded in Mark 8:23, 24 illustrates and adumbrates the two states. The O. T. saints had sight, but the Object set before their faith was seen at a distance, and through clouds and shadows. The N. T. saints "with open face behold the glory of God in a mirror" (2 Cor. 3:18). Second, in its **more plentiful** communication of grace unto the Church: John 1:16. O. T. believers had grace given to them (Gen. 6:8, etc.), but we an "abundance of grace" (Rom. 5:17). Third, in our **access** to God. The revelation of God at Sinai filled the people with terror; His revelation of Himself in Christ, fills us with joy. They were shut out from the holy place; we have freedom to approach His throne (Heb. 4:16). Fourth, the **extent** of the dispensation of Divine grace. Under the O. T. it was restricted to one nation; now it extends to all nations.

The covenant of grace was the same, as to its **substance**, from the beginning. It passed through the whole dispensation of times before the law, and under the law, of the same nature and efficacy, unalterable, everlasting, "ordered in all things and sure." The covenant of grace considered absolutely was the promise of grace in and by Christ Jesus (2 Tim. 1:9, Titus 1:2), and that was the **only** way and means of salvation unto the elect from the entrance of sin. Absolutely, in O. T. times, the covenant consisted only in **promise**, and as such is referred to in Acts 2:39 Heb. 6:14-16. The full and lawful "establishment" of it (Heb. 8:6), whence it became **formally** a "covenant" unto the whole Church, was future only. Two things were needed to change the "promise" into a "new covenant": the shedding of the blood of the only Sacrifice which belonged to it, and the institution of that worship in keeping therewith.

Whilst the O. T. Church enjoyed all the **spiritual** benefits of the promise, wherein the **substance** of the covenant is contained, before it was confirmed and made the sole rule of worship unto the Church, it was not inconsistent with the holiness and wisdom of God to bring His people under any other covenant, or prescribe unto them what forms of worship He pleased, for they did not render ineffectual the promise before given. Nor did the institutions of the Mosaic covenant divert from, but rather led to, the future establishment of the promise. Yea, the laws and worship of the Mosaic economy were of present use and advantage to the Church while it remained in its state of minority (Gal. 4). For much of the above we are indebted, under God, to the writings of John Owen (1670 A. D.). We now turn again to our passage.

"For this is the covenant that I will make with the house of Israel after those days, saith the Lord; I will put My laws into their minds, and write them in their hearts: and I will be to them a God, and they shall be to Me a people" (v. 10). "The design of the apostle, or what is the general argument which he is in pursuit of, must still be borne in mind, while considering the testimonies which he produceth in the confirmation of it. His design is to prove that the Lord Christ is the Mediator and Surety of a **better** covenant, than that wherein the service of God was managed by the high priests according to the law. For hence it follows, that His priesthood is greater and far more excellent than theirs. To this end he doth not only prove that God promised to make such a covenant, but also declares the nature and properties of it, in the words of the prophets. And so, by comparing it with the former covenant, he manifests its excellency above it. In particular, in this testimony, the imperfection of that covenant is demonstrated from its issue. For it did not effectually maintain peace and mutual love between God and the people; but being broken by them, they were thereon rejected of God. This rendered all the other benefits and advantages of it, useless. Wherefore, the apostle insists from the prophet, on those promises of this other covenant, which infallibly prevent the like issue, securing the people's obedience forever, and so the love and relation of God unto them as their God" (John Owen).

The apostle is here contrasting the Christian dispensation from the Mosaic. Having in the previous verse declared in general the abrogation of the old covenant, because of its inadequacy through the weakness of the flesh, he here describes the new covenant which has supplanted it. He shows it to be so excellent in its constitution that none should object against its substitution in place of the old: such is the force of the opening "For." The formal "this is the covenant" announces that it is the duty of Christians to make themselves distinctly and fully informed in the privileges belonging unto them. It was for this very end that the writings of the evangelists and apostles were added to those of the prophets. This new covenant is made with "the house of Israel," which we understand mystically, comprising under it all the people of God. It is taken spiritually for the whole Church, the "Israel of God" (Gal. 6:16). In the Millennium, this covenant shall yet be made with the fleshly descendants of Abraham.

"After those days" is in antithesis from "in the day" of v. 9, which was an indefinite expression covering the interval between God's sending Moses into Egypt and the arrival of Israel before Sinai. "After those days" means, following the O. T. era. The dispensation which succeeds that is called "the time of reformation" in 9:10. Now just as God's making of the first covenant with Israel was preceded by many things that were preparatory to the solemn establishment of the same—such as His sending of Moses to announce unto them His designs of grace, His delivering them out of the house of bondage, His miraculous conducting of them through the Red Sea, His making known His law at Sinai—so the new covenant was gradually made and established, and that by sundry acts preparatory for it or confirmatory of it. As this is so little understood we must enter into details.

First, the introduction of the new covenant was made by the ministry of John the Baptist (Luke 16:16). He was sent to prepare the way of the Lord. Until his appearing the Jews were bound absolutely unto the covenant at Sinai, without any alteration or addition to any ordinance of worship. But John's ministry was "the beginning of the Gospel" (Mark 1:1, 2). He called the people off from resting in the privileges of the old covenant (Matt. 3:8-10), and instituted a new ordinance of worship, baptism. He pointed away from Moses to the Lamb of God. Thus, his ministry was the beginning of the accomplishment of God's promise through Jeremiah. Second, the incarnation and ministry of the Lord Jesus was a further advance unto the same. His appearing in the flesh laid an axe to the root of the whole Mosaic dispensation (Matt. 3:10), though the tree was not immediately cut down. By His miracles and teaching Christ furnished abundant proof that He was the Mediator of the new covenant.

Third, the way for the introduction of the new covenant having been prepared, it was solemnly enacted and confirmed in and by Christ's death: thereby the "promise" became a "testament" (Heb. 9:14-16). From that time onwards, the old covenant and its administration had received its full accomplishment (Eph. 2:14-16, Col. 2:14, 15), and it continued to abide only in the longsuffering of God, to be taken out of the way in His own time and manner. Fourth, the new covenant was further established in the resurrection of Christ. The old covenant could not be abrogated till its curse had been borne, and that was discharged absolutely when Christ was "loosed from the pains of death" and delivered from the grave. Fifth, the new covenant was promulgated and confirmed on the day of Pentecost, answering to the promulgation of the law at Sinai, some weeks after Israel had been delivered out of Egypt. From Pentecost onwards the whole Church of God was absolved from any duty with respect unto the old covenant and the worship of it (although it was not manifest as yet unto their consciences), and the ordinances of worship and all the institutions of the new covenant now became obligatory upon them. Sixth, the question was formally and officially raised as to the continuance of the obligatory form of the old covenant, and the contrary was expressly affirmed by the apostles under the infallible superintendence of the Holy Spirit: Acts 15:1-29.

But at this point a difficulty, already noticed, may recur to our minds: Were not the things mentioned in Heb. 8:10-13, the grace and mercy therein expressed, actually communicated to God's elect both before Sinai and afterwards? Did not all who truly believed and feared God enjoy these same identical blessings? Unquestionably. What then is the solution? This: the apostle is not here contrasting the internal operations of Divine grace in the Old and N. T. saints, but as Calvin rightly taught, the "reference is to the economical condition of the Church." The contrast is between that which characterized the Judaic and the Christian dispensations in the outward confirmation of the covenant. While there were individuals like David and Daniel, perhaps many such, in whom the Spirit wrought effectually, yet it is evident that the great majority of Abraham's natural descendants had no experimental acquaintance with the external revelation God had given.

"I will put My laws into their minds, and write them in their hearts." That this is not an experience peculiar to Christians or millennial Israelites is clear from Psa. 37:30, 31, "The mouth of the righteous speaketh wisdom, and his tongue talketh of judgment. The law of his God is in his heart." So, too in Psa. 19:7, 8, we read, "The law of the Lord is perfect converting the soul . . . the statutes of the Lord are right, rejoicing the heart." But that the major portion of Israel, or even a considerable number of them, were regenerated, at any period in the lengthy history of that nation, there is nothing whatever to show; instead, there is very much to the contrary. This experience is enjoyed by none save God's elect, and in every age they have been but a "little flock."

"I will put My laws into their minds." These words have reference to the effectual operations of the Spirit in His supernatural and saving illumination of our understandings, whereby they are made habitually conformable unto the whole law of God, which is our rule of obedience in the new covenant. The carnal mind is enmity against God, and is not subject to His law, neither indeed can be (Rom. 8:7). But when we are renewed by the Spirit, He works in us a submission to the authority and revealed will of God. As the Lord opened the heart of Lydia "that she attended unto the things which were spoken of Paul" (Acts 16:14), so in the miracle of the new birth, the Christian is given an ear to heed and a mind to perceive the holiness, justice, and goodness of God's law. Yea, that law is effectually applied to him, so that it becomes the former of his thoughts, the subject of his meditation, and the regulater of his ways.

The preacher may announce the law of God to the outward ear, but only the Spirit can engrave it on the mind. The realization of this fact ought to drive every minister to his knees. No matter how diligently he has prepared his sermon, no matter how clearly and faithfully he expounds God's truth, no matter how solemnly and searchingly he endeavors to press it on the individual's conscience, unless God Himself gives His Word an entrance into the soul, nothing spiritual and eternal is accomplished. Nowhere is the deadness of the "churches" more plainly evidenced today than by the absence of concerted and definite prayer immediately before and immediately after the Word is preached: the "song service" has been substituted for the prayer service. O that God's own people might be aroused to the need of their coming together and crying, "Lord, open the eyes of these men" (2 Kings 6:20).

"And write them in their hearts." It is this which renders the former part actually effectual. The "heart" as distinguished from the "mind" comprises the affections and the will. First, the understanding is informed, and then the heart is reformed. An active principle of obedience is imparted, and this is nothing else than a love for God Himself. Where there is a real love for God, there is a genuine desire and determination to please Him. The heart of the natural man is "alienated" from God and opposed to His authority. That is why, at Sinai, God wrote the commandments upon stones—not so much to secure the outward letter of them, as to represent the hardness of the hearts of the people unto whom they were given. But at regeneration God takes away the heart of stone, and gives a heart of flesh (Ezek. 36:26)—pliable, living, responsive.

Let each reader pause here and lift up his or her heart to God, asking for grace and wisdom to honestly examine themselves in the light of this verse. You may sit under a sound and scriptural ministry every Sabbath, but **what effect** has it upon your inner man? You may be well acquainted with the letter of the Word, but how far is it directing the details of your daily walk? Does your mind dwell most on temporal or eternal things, material or spiritual? What engages your thoughts in your seasons of recreation? Is your heart fixed upon God or upon the world? There are thousands of professing Christians who can talk glibly of the Scriptures, but whose lives give no evidence that God has written His laws in their hearts. Are you one of this class?

"And I will be to them a God, and they shall be to Me a people." This expresses covenant-relationship. It is placed in the center of these promises because it is the spring from which the grace of the other blessings doth proceed. The wicked are living in this world "without God, and without hope" (Eph. 2:12), but unto the righteous He says, "I am thy Shield, thy exceeding great Reward" (Gen. 15:1). "Happy is that people, that is in such a case, happy is that people, whose God is the Lord" (Psa. 144:15). When He says "I will be to them a God" it means that He will act toward His people according to all that is implied in the name of God. He will be their Lawgiver, their Counsellor, their Protector, their Guide. He will supply all their needs, deliver from all dangers, and bring them unto everlasting felicity. He will be faithful and longsuffering, bearing with their frailties, never leaving nor forsaking them. "And they shall be My people" expresses both a dignity and a duty. Their dignity is set forth in 1 Peter 2:9; their duty in the verses which follow.

"And they shall not teach every man his neighbor, and every man his brother, saying, Know the Lord: for all shall know Me, from the least to the greatest" (v. 11). These words point a contrast from the general spiritual ignorance which obtained among the Jews: cf. Isa. 1:3, etc. "The words in the 11th verse are not to be understood absolutely, but comparatively. They intimate, that under that covenant there shall be a striking contrast to the ignorance which characterized the great body of those who were under the Old Covenant; that the revelation of the Divine will shall be far more extensive and clear under the new than under the old economy; and that there shall be a correspondingly enlarged communication of the enlightened influences of the Holy Spirit. They probably also are intended to suggest the idea, that that kind of knowledge which is the peculiar glory of the New Covenant is a kind of knowledge which cannot be communicated by brother teaching brother, but comes directly from Him—the great Teacher, whose grand characteristic is this, that whom He teaches, He makes apt to learn" (John Brown).

"And they shall not teach every man his neighbor, and every man his brother, saying, Know the Lord." During the Mosaic economy, and particularly in the last century before Christ, there was an external teaching of the Law, which the people trusted and rested in without any regard for God's teaching by the inward circumcision of the heart. Such teaching had degenerated into rival schools and sects, such as the Pharisees, Sadducees, Herodians, Essenes, etc., and they made void the Word of God through their traditions (Mark 7:13). It was against such the last of Israel's prophets had announced. "The Lord will cut off . . . the master and the scholar out of the tabernacles of David" (Mal. 2:12). Or, our verse probably has more direct reference to the general knowledge of God which obtained during the Mosaic economy, when He revealed Himself under types and shadows, and was known through "parables and dark sayings." These were now supplanted by the full blaze of the Gospel's light.

"For all shall know Me, from the least to the greatest." God is now known in the full revelation which He has made of Himself in the person of His incarnate Son: John 1:18. As we are told in 1 John 5:20, "And we know that the Son of God is come, and hath given us an understanding, that we may know Him that is true": "know Him" in the sense that we recognize, own, and practically obey Him as God. This spiritual, experimental, vital, saving knowledge of God is now communicated unto all of His elect. As the Saviour announced, "They shall all be taught of God" (John 6:45): taught His will and all the mysteries of godliness, which by the Word are revealed. This "knowledge" of God cannot be imparted by any external teaching alone, but is the result of the Spirit's operations, though He frequently, yea generally, uses the oral and written ministry of God's servants as His instruments therein.

"For I will be merciful to their unrighteousness, and their sins and their iniquities will I remember no more" (v. 12). "This is the great foundational promise and grace of the new covenant. For though it be last expressed, yet, in order of nature, it precedeth the other mercies and privileges mentioned, and is the foundation of the communication of them unto us. This the casual 'for' at the beginning of the verse doth demonstrate. What I have spoken, saith the Lord, shall be accomplished, 'For I will be merciful,' etc., without which there could be no participation of the other things mentioned. Wherefore, not only an addition of new grace and mercy is expressed in these words, but a reason also is rendered why, or on what grounds, He would bestow on them those other mercies" (John Owen).

In v. 12 a reason is given why God bestows the wondrous blessings enumerated in vv. 10, 11. The word here rendered "merciful" is propitious, for it is not absolute mercy without any satisfaction having been taken by justice, but grace shown on the ground of a propitiation: cf. Rom. 3:24, 25. Christ died to render God propitious toward sinners (Heb. 2:17), and in and through Him alone is God merciful toward the sins of His people. Just so long as Christ is rejected, the sinner is under the curse. But as soon as He is received, the blessings described in vv. 10-12 become his. Note there are just seven blessings named, which exemplifies the perfection of the new covenant.

It is to be noted that no less than three terms are used in v. 12 to describe the fearful evils of which the sinner is guilty, thus emphasizing his obnoxiousness to the holy God, and magnifying the grace which saves him. "Unrighteousness" signifies a wrong done unto God, against man's sovereign Ruler and Benefactor. "Sin" is a missing of the mark, the glorifying of God, which is what ought ever to be aimed at. "Iniquity" has the force of lawlessness, a setting up of my will against God's a living to please self rather than for His glory. How marvelous is the propitious favour of God toward those who are guilty of such multiplied enormities! The apostle's object was to point another contrast between the covenants. That which characterized Judaism was a reign of law and justice: that which distinguishes Christianity is the "Throne of Grace." Note that no "conditions" are here stipulated. But does not the new covenant require repentance and faith? Assuredly: Mark 1:15. But He who requires these has promised also to work them in His people: Acts 5:31.

"In that He saith, A new, He hath made the first old. Now that which decayeth and waxeth old is ready to vanish away" (v. 13). That the translators failed to perceive the drift of the apostle's reasoning here is evident from their adding the word "covenant" in italics. This was not only unnecessary, but its introduction serves to hide the force of the first half of this verse. In it the apostle draws an inference from what God had said through Jeremiah. He singles out one word, "new," and on it bases an argument: because Christianity is the "establishment" of the new covenant, then the preceding economy must have grown "old," and "old" is significative of that which draws near its end! How this shows us, once more, that every jot and tittle of Scripture is authoritative, full of meaning, and of sufficient evidence for what may be deduced from it!

"Now that which decayeth and waxeth old is ready to vanish away." Here is the conclusion of the apostle's argument. If the first covenant had been adequate no place had been sought for a second (v. 7). But place was sought for the second (v. 8), therefore the first covenant was not faultless. The old covenant had continued for fifteen hundred years, from Moses to Christ; but its purpose had now been served. God gave Israel more than a hint that the Mosaic economy would not last forever, when His providence permitted the nation to be carried down into Babylon. Upon their return from captivity, neither the temple nor its priesthood were ever restored to their pristine glory. And now, as the apostle wrote, in less than ten years Jerusalem and the temple were completely destroyed. If then the Jewish covenant was abolished because it was "old," how much more ought the "old man" to be put off (Eph. 4:24), and the "old heaven" purged out (1 Cor. 5:7)!

—ARTHUR W. PINK.

THE SATISFACTION
("Atonement")
OF CHRIST

14. Its Results (Continued)

At the beginning of our last article we pointed out that the principal results secured by the Satisfaction which Christ offered unto God, may be summed up in these four words: reconciliation, remission, redemption, and righteousness. It is indeed remarkable, and calls for our profoundest admiration, that God caused each of them to be shadowed forth on this earth-plane at the very time of our Lord's passion. Just as the nature of that unparalleled transaction which was taking place in the unseen between the Judge of all the earth and the Mediator was outwardly adumbrated in all the details of Christ's "trial" before Caiaphas, Herod, and Pilate, so also were the leading effects secured by that transaction illustrated in concrete and visible form. A wonderful field of study, which has been entered by scarcely any, is here opened for our reverent exploration. Perhaps the few hints now dropped will be sufficient to bestir some to prayerfully investigate it.

Reconciliation is the bringing together again of two parties who have been alienated. Christ has, by His Satisfaction, re-united the Governor of the universe unto His sinning people. Strikingly was this adumbrated by what we read of in Luke 23:10, 11, "and Herod with his men of war set Him at nought, and mocked and arrayed Him in a gorgeous robe, and sent Him again to Pilate. And the same day Pilate and Herod were made friends together: for before they were at enmity between themselves." Why has the Holy Spirit recorded this detail? Is it nothing more than a mere historical allusion? Of what interest to us is the relations which existed between Pilate and Herod? Why introduce this statement in v. 12 right after what is said in v. 11? For what reason does the Spirt emphasize "the same day?" The spiritually-minded should have no difficulty in supplying answers to these questions. It was God causing the glorious consequence of Christ's death to be tangibly imaged before the eyes of men.

Remission is the cancellation of guilt. Christ has, by His Satisfaction, propitiated the offended justice of God. He has made complete amends to the law for every injury which the sins of His people had wrought. He has, by His sacrifice, perfectly healed the breach which our transgressions had made. Christ has repaid all the wrongs which the iniquities of His people had done to the manifestative holiness of God: "I restored that which I took not away" (Psa. 69:4). In the light of this fact read what is recorded in Luke 22:50, 51, "And one of them smote the servant of the high priest, and cut off his right ear. And Jesus answered and said, Suffer ye thus far. He touched his ear and healed him." What a picture of Christ, on the very eve of His death, neutralizing the damage which His erring people had done!

Redemption is the liberating of sin's captives. Christ has, by His Satisfaction, emancipated those who were the slaves of sin, the helpless serfs of Satan. He has delivered from prison those who were bound. He has brought from death unto life those who were cast in the sepulchre by Adam's transgression. "By one man sin entered into the world, and death by sin; and so death passed upon all men" (Rom. 5:12). From that dreadful state Christ has freed His people. God caused this too to be adumbrated in connection with Calvary, for in Matt. 27:50-52 we read, "Jesus, when He had cried again with a loud voice, yielded up the spirit. And, behold, the veil of the temple was rent in twain from the top to the bottom; and the earth did quake, and the rocks rent; and the graves were opened; and many bodies of the saints which slept arose."

Righteousness is that which qualifies the saint to stand in the presence of the thrice holy God. It is that which fits him for the Court of Heaven. As we read in Isa. 61:10, "I will greatly rejoice in the Lord, my soul shall be joyful in my God; for He hath clothed me with the garments of salvation, He hath covered me with the robe of righteousness." Such a righteousness cannot be wrought out by man, therefore was it secured for His people by the perfect obedience of Christ. This is the "best robe" of Luke 15:22, namely, the righteousness of Christ imputed. This also was shadowed forth on earth at the time our Saviour died. The soldiers took His garments. Among them was His coat, "without seam, woven from the top throughout"—emblem of the flawless unity of His life, lived out by power from above. That perfect robe became the property of one whose wicked acts were instrumental in crucifying the Lord of glory (John 19:23, 24). O my readers, what a truly **marvelous** book is the Bible! Having considered the first of the four consequences of Christ's Satisfaction, let us now turn to,

2. Remission

That reconciliation and remission of sins are closely connected is clear from 2 Cor. 5:19, "God was in Christ, reconciling the world unto Himself, not imputing their trespasses unto them." That which was the ground of reconciliation is equally the ground of pardon. Necessarily so. Reconciliation implies in its very nature a release from the punishment of sin: on God's part it is the laying aside of His anger, and that was possible only because our sins were put away; on our part, of laying aside enmity and disobedience, which is possible only by an utter renunciation of sin. Again; the fruit of reconciliation is fellowship, and **that is** only promoted by the remission of sins, for two cannot walk together except they be agreed. In taking up this most blessed subject of remission, let us consider,

1. Its Nature

Remission is the sovereign prerogative of God as Judge, whereby He acquits the believing sinner from all liability to suffer punishment as a satisfaction to His law, and that on account of the Satisfaction of Christ, applied by the Spirit and appropriated through repentance and faith. Remission is God's declining to deal with His people according as justice required for their sins, and that because He has received full compensation for them from Christ in their stead. Because the Divine Creditor has received full payment from their Surety, the debtors are discharged. Thus, remission of sins is a cancellation of their guilt, a legal discharge, a removal of obligation to suffer the wrath of God. It is the verdict of the Lawgiver; a sentence of "not guilty."

The Greek word for remission, "aphesis," signifies "a sending away." It is translated "delverance" and "liberty" in Luke 4:18, and "forgiveness" in Acts 13:38 Eph. 1:7, etc. Thus remission of sins means that God refuses to charge them to the account of him who truly believes in Christ. It is a deliverance from the curse of the law, which holds us fast under its death-sentence until Divine grace revokes it. It is the privative or negative side of justification, whereby the sinner who flees to Christ for refuge is delivered from every claim which Divine justice had upon him. This is clear from Rom. 4, where the apostle is expounding the truth of justification before God, and, after citing the case of Abraham, he appeals to the language of David in further proof: "Blessed are they whose iniquities are forgiven, and whose sins are covered. Blessed is the man to whom the Lord will **not impute** sin" (vv. 7, 8).

There are other expressions used in the New Testament of equivalent import. Thus, "When He had by Himself **purged** our sins" (Heb. 1:3). The word "purged" is here used in a sacrificial way, and refers to the removal of them from before the face of the Judge: cf. Psa. 51:7, and its context. Again, in Heb. 10:10 we read, "By the which will we are **sanctified** through the offering of the body of Jesus Christ once for all," and cf. 13:12. Here too, "sanctified" is used in a **sacrificial** sense. "The blood of Jesus Christ His Son **cleanseth** us from all sin" (1 John 1:7). By contracting guilt, the sinner is defiled, and becomes unclean in the sight of an holy God; but when his guilt is removed, he is said to be "cleansed."

It is important to note that 1 John 1:7 has no reference whatever to the purifying of the unholy nature which still remains within the believer: this is quite clear from the next verse. No, it predicates the taking off of the guilt of sin and our obligaton unto wrath. Sin is the whole cause of God's displeasure against us, and that which makes us odious in His sight. Therefore when we are freed from sin by faith's appropriation of the death of Christ, we are said to be "cleansed." The same term was used in connection with Israel's annual day of atonement: "On that day shall the priest make an atonement for you, to **cleanse** you, that ye may be **clean** from all your sins before the Lord" (Lev. 16:30). Most certainly that does not and cannot mean that any internal purification was effected in their souls through Aaron's offering.

Three things are to be considered, and sharply distinguished, in connection with sin. First, its **fault.** This consists of a criminal **action,** a failing to render unto God that which is due Him, a transgression of His law. Now this is not taken away by the blood of Christ, nor, in the nature of the case, could it be. That which is done, cannot be undone. The sins we have committed, cannot be uncommitted. But though our sins as faulty and criminal actions are not annihiliated, they are—blessed be God—"passed over" (Rom. 3:25, margin) and "passed by" (Micah 7:18) as the ground of guilt. That is to say, God no longer imputes them to the believer.

Second, its guilt. This is the condemnation of the law. Sin is "sin" simply because the law of God forbids it; when committed, it entails "guilt" because the law must punish it. Guilt is the law binding its transgressor to suffer its righteous penalty. Now remission does not mean that the offender is made intrinsically innocent, for having committed offences he is still an offender. God never reputes a sinner to be in himself one who never omitted a duty or committed a transgression. Thus, guilt is not a quality, but a relation, an obligation to punishment which the law has made the sinner's due, but which relation and obligation ceases when his sins are remitted.

Third, its punishment. When the believing sinner is pardoned neither his criminal actions themselves are destroyed, nor his personal desert of punishment removed, but because of Christ's sacrifice he is discharged from all obligation to punishment. Sin is no longer imputed unto condemnation. Nay more, the offender is dealt with (not "regarded") before the tribunal of the Divine Judge as if he were pure from all sin. He still deserves (in himself) to be accursed, but the penitent and brokenhearted culprit is accepted unto pardon and is exempted from eternal punishment. "He that heareth My Word, and believeth on Him that sent Me, hath everlasting life, and shall not come into condemnation: but is passed from death unto life" (John 5:24).

Neither the root nor the being of sin is removed from the believer when God pronounces sentence of forgiveness upon him. It is simply the guilt or obligation to punishment which is remitted; it is the revoking of the law's sentence against the sinner. He is legally discharged. And this because God is "not imputing their trespasses unto them" (2 Cor. 5:19). This expression "not imputing" means that God is not laying them to the charge of His people, not reckoning them to their account. It is a metaphor taken from commercial transactions. Sin is a debt: Matt. 6:12. God is yet going to call sinners to account (Rom. 14:12), and charge their debt upon them: Matt. 25:19. Yes, people may now be gay and careless, but a day of reckoning lies ahead of them. But in that day of accounts, God will not impute the trespasses of them who are reconciled to Him by Christ—"Blessed is the man unto whom the Lord imputeth not iniquity" (Psa. 32:2).

"There is therefore now no condemnation to them which are in Christ Jesus" (Rom. 8:1). "Condemnation" here means the damnatory sentence of the law. It is not a question of our hearts not condemning us (1 John 3:21), nor of us finding nothing within which is worthy of condemnation; instead it is the far more blessed fact that God Himself condemns not the one who has trusted in Christ to the saving of his soul. Because, by faith, they are in Christ, having fled to Him for refuge (Heb. 6:18), they shall never be adjudged guilty, nor shall a sentence of eternal death be passed upon them, for sins being remitted (guilt removed), no ground remains for it. "As far as the east is from the west, so far hath He removed our transgressions from us" (Psa. 103:12).

2. Its Ground

As the moral Governor of His universe, it becomes God's justice to deal with sin according to its deserts. Thus He spared not the angels that sinned, but "cast them down to hell and delivered them into chains of darkness" (2 Peter 2:4). Now all of God's elect are sinners: they were so in Adam, they have been and are so in themselves. How then shall Divine justice deal with them? Shall it ignore their sins and acquit from punishment? Where then would be that inflexible righteousness which banished our first parents from Eden? What would become of God's own declaration that He "will by no means clear the guilty" (Ex. 34:7)? On the other hand, if they receive their due reward and are punished, how shall grace be shown them? On what ground are their sins remitted? Not on the basis of a belated reformation, for that would be no atonement for their past crimes. Not because of their repentance, for if sins could be pardoned at so cheap a rate then was there no need for Christ to die.

"He that believeth not is condemned already" (John 3:18). Condemnation is a word of tremendous import, and the better we understand it, the more shall we appreciate the wondrous grace which has delivered us from its power. In the halls of a human court the sentence "condemned to death" falls with a dreadful knell upon the ear of a convicted murderer, and fills the spectators with sadness and horror. But in the Court of divine Justice it is vested with a meaning and content infinitely more solemn and awe-inspiring. And to that Court every member of Adam's fallen race is cited. "Conceived in sin and shapen in iniquity" each one enters this world under condemnation—an indicted criminal, a rebel manacled. How then is it possible for anyone to escape the execution of the dread sentence? There was only one way, and that was by the **removal** from us of that which called forth the sentence.

That which entailed and demanded the sentence of the curse was the guilt which was inseparable from our sins. Let the guilt be removed and there could be no condemnation. But how could guilt be "removed?" Only by its being legally **transferred** to another. Divine holiness could not ignore it, but divine grace could and did transfer it. As we are told, "The Lord hath laid on Him (the Surety and Substitute of His people) the iniquity of us all" (Isa. 53:6). The punishment due His Church was visited upon its Sponsor. Christ, by virtue of His federal union with His people, which of His own accord He entered into, was dealt with by Divine wrath as though He had personally been the transgressor. God charged upon Christ and imputed unto Him all the sins of His elect, and proceeded against Him accordingly.

"There is therefore now no condemnation to them which are in Christ Jesus" (Rom. 8:1). The "therefore" here is an inspired and infallible inference drawn from the whole of the apostle's preceeding discussion. Because Christ has been "set forth a propitiation through faith in His blood" (3:25), because He was "delivered (to justice) for our offenses and arised again for our justification" (4:25), because by "the obedience of One, many (saints of all ages) are made righteous," legally constituted so (5:19), because they have judicially, "died to sin" (6:2), and "died" to the condemning power of the law (7:4), there is **therefore** no condemnation resting upon them. This is further opened in 8:3: "God sending His own Son in the likeness of sinful flesh, and for sin, condemned sin in the flesh." That which was the cause of condemnation is now condemned. The no condemnation of v. 1 is explained by the "condemned" of v. 3. Both must not be condemned: if sin itself be judged, punished, the believing sinner shall not.

How marvelous are the ways of God! As death was destroyed by death, the death of Christ, so sin by sin. By the greatest sin that was ever committed—the murder of the Son of God—sin itself was put away. By God's imputing the trespasses of His people unto their Surety, Christ was condemned so that they might be acquitted. Christ first took our guilt upon Him, and then He bore its punishment, for guilt is obligation unto punishment. This is the very nature of suretyship: he takes the debt of another upon himself, and upon the debtor's insufficiency, becomes liable to payment thereof. By Christ's offering up of Himself in the stead of believers, all their sins were expiated. In consequence thereof we are able to triumphantly exclaim, "who shall lay anything to the charge of God's elect"? (Rom. 8:33).

Just as Rom. 8:1 is explained in 8:3, so 2 Cor. 5:19 is amplified in 5:21. "God was in Christ reconciling the world unto Himself, not imputing their trespasses unto them." And why? Because "He hath made Him to be sin for us, who knew no sin; that we might be made the righteousness of God in Him." The nonimputation of sin to the believer is not only a consequent result of Christ's sacrifice, but was the cause of His death. Trespasses are not imputed to the members of His body, because they were imputed to the Head. "He," that is God the Father; "made Him" that is, Christ the Mediator; "made Him sin" legally constituted Him so, in accordance with the mutual agreement between Them in the everlasting covenant. "Made Him sin" means, appointed Him as the great Sinbearer, officially liable to wrath. Christ was "made sin for us" by the reckoning of our guilt to His account, not in mere semblance, but in dread reality. Because of this, divine Justice took satisfaction from Him; because of this He died "the Just for the unjust."

Throughout His life and His death, the Lord Jesus was repaying all that injury which the sins of His people had done unto the manifestative justice of God. Therefore God now remits the sins of His believing people because He **has** received a vicarious but full satisfaction for them from the person of their Surety. Through Christ we are delivered from the wrath to come. Necessarily so, for an **accepted** Sacrifice obtained (not merely "made possible"), purchased, the remission of sins. Vividly and blessedly was this typed out in Lev. 5:5, 6, 10, "When he shall be guilty in one of these things, that he shall confess that he hath sinned in that thing. And he shall bring his trespass offering unto the Lord for his sin which he hath sinned. . . and the priest shall make an atonement for him, concerning his sin. . . and **it shall be forgiven him**." So Christ's blood was shed "**for** the remission of sins" (Matt. 26:28). To this great and grand truth all the prophets bore witness (Acts 10:43). In Christ every claim of the law against the believer has been perfectly met. Thus grace reigns not at the expense of righteouness, but "**through** righteousness unto eternal life by Jesus Christ our Lord" (Rom. 5:21). Hallelujah!

3. Its Scope

"Who His own self bear our sins in His own body to the tree" (1 Peter 2:24). Whose sins? Believers. Which sins? Not a few of them, not the majority of them, but **every one** which was on the docket against them. "Having forgiven you **all** trespasses" (Col. 2:13). Christ came here to "finish the transgression, and to **make an end of** sins, and to make reconciliation for iniquity" (Dan. 9:24). Rightly did James Wells say, "There is no mischief that sin hath done which He hath not repaired; there is no debt that sin has incurred that He has not paid; there is no foe under which sin has brought us that He hath not conquered; there is no fiery wrath which sin hath lighted up which He hath not quenched; there is no curse which sin hath entailed that He hath not borne; there is no mountain that sin hath rolled in upon us which He has not overturned; there is no distance between us and God which He has not filled up."

"There is no condemnation to them which are in Christ Jesus" (Rom. 8:1). "Thou hast in love to my soul delivered it from the pit of corruption: for Thou hast cast all my sins behind Thy back" (Isa. 38:17)—as we turn our backs upon anything which we do not wish to behold. All our sins have been removed from the judicial eyes of God. God Himself declares that He "will not remember thy sins" (Isa. 43:25). Here our sins are likened unto a debt which has been cancelled; an act of oblivion has been passed upon them. "I have blotted out, as a thick cloud, thy transgressions, and, as a cloud, thy sins" (Isa. 44:22). Just as a dark cloud empties itself upon the earth and then melts away under the rays of the sun, so our sins have been dried up by Divine mercy, following the storm of judgment which was poured out at the cross.

"Who is a God like unto Thee, that pardoneth iniquity, and passeth by the transgression of the remnant of His heritage. . . and Thou wilt cast all their sins into the depths of the sea" (Micah 7:18, 19) — as the Egyptians were drowned in the Red Sea. God lays not aside our sins gently, but flings them away with violence, as things which He cannot endure the sight of, and which He is resolved never to take note of any more. Observe, "into the **depths** of the sea." Things cast into the depths of the ocean never appear again! Rivers may be turned and dried, but who could lave out the ocean? So Christ hath appeared "to **put away** sin by the sacrifice of Himself" (Heb. 9:26). "As far as the east is from the west, so far hath He removed our transgressions from us" (Psa. 103:12). Hallelujah!

4. Its Application

This brings us to the most difficult aspect of our subject. When were the Christian's sins put away? This question is capable of more than one answer, according as it is viewed from different standpoints. Vicariously his sins were remitted when his Surety was raised from the dead. At His birth Christ assumed the full burden of His peoples' liabilities and responsibilities; and He was not released from the same until God delivered Him from the grave. But **personally** we are not forgiven till we believe. We need to distinguish sharply between the results secured by Christ's death for God's elect, and their being, individually, made **partakers** of those effects. Christ purchased and procured a **right** unto our receiving forgiveness, but we do not enter into the **enjoyment** of this blessing until our faith is placed in Him. This may be illustrated by a young man who has been left an estate, but who cannot enter into possession of the same until he is thirty. Prior to that age he has a legal title to it, but he is not permitted to receive his inheritance: cf. Gal. 4:1-7.

"The blood of Jesus Christ His Son cleanseth us from all sin" (1 John 1:7). The blood of Christ needs to be considered three ways: as shed, as pleaded, as sprinkled. As **shed**. This was necessary by way of satisfaction and merit, to **obtain** for us God's pardon of our sins, for "without shedding of blood is no remission of sins" (Heb. 9:22). It is **pleaded** by Christ in heaven. This is the very basis of His intercession. "By His own blood He entered in once into the holy place" (Heb. 9:12), and its merits He continually presents to the Father. It is also to be pleaded **by us** when we beg any blessing, especially the pardon of our sins: "Having therefore, brethren, boldness to enter into the Holiest **by the blood of Jesus**" (Heb. 10:19). But it is not enough that His blood be shed and pleaded, it must be actually sprinkled or applied to our conscience: "The blood of **sprinkling** which speaketh better things than that of Abel" (Heb. 12:24).

We must also distinguish between the general pardon received the moment we believe, and the specific forgiveness which we stand in need of repeatedly. To say that there is no need for Christians to pray for forgiveness because all their sins were atoned for at the cross, betrays great confusion of thought and flatly contradicts Scripture. As well might an Israelite have argued against the offering of the daily lamb, because all his iniquities were remitted on the annual day of atonement (Lev. 16:21). So far as the Satisfaction of Christ has been offered once for all and is eternally valid before God, it allows of no repetition or addition. But considering forgiveness as the act of God as the moral Governor of the world, it is **continuous** unto the same persons. In the nature of the case sin cannot be formally pardoned before it is committed. As we daily commit trespasses, we are to daily ask for their forgiveness: Matt. 6:11, 12—note the "And" at the beginning of v. 12!

"Sins to come cannot be properly said to be pardoned, for till they are committed we are not guilty of them. This would not be so much a pardon as an indulgence and license to sin, such as the pope gives to his superstitious adherents—indulgencies for so many years to come. Thus a man once converted could no otherwise than frivolously pray 'Forgive us our sin.' It would take away care of avoiding sin to come, and repentance for what is past. Daily sins displease God, and deserve death" (T. Manton, vol. 22, p. 52). At conversion we receive the Divine forgiveness of all our **past** sins (2 Peter 1:9!) but forgiveness of present sins must be sued for daily. Keep short accounts with God, Christian reader! Constantly plead the promise of 1 John 1:9, "If we confess our sins, He is faithful and just to forgive us our sins, and to cleanse us from all unrighteousness."

5. Its Requirements

First, turning from sin unto God: "Let the wicked forsake his way, and the unrighteous man his thoughts: and let him return unto the Lord, and He will have mercy upon him; and to our God, for He will abundantly pardon" (Isa. 55:7). God will not remit the guilt while a man's heart remains in love with sin and he continues in the practice of it; if He did, He would compromise His holiness and encourage us in evil doing. "Christ died not to reconcile God to our sins, or to pardon our sins while we remain in them, but to bring us back again to the service and enjoyment of God" (T. Manton). The prodigal must leave the far country ere he can turn his face toward the Father's house.

Second, repentance: "Repent therefore of this thy wickedness, and pray God, if perhaps the thought of thine heart may be forgiven thee" (Acts 8:22). Repentance toward God signifies a willingness to return to the duty, love and obedience which we owe Him as our Creator, and from whence we have fallen by our folly and sin. "Him hath God exalted with His right hand to be a Prince and a Saviour, for to give repentance to Israel and forgiveness of sins" (Acts 5:31): as we must distinguish between God's viewing His elect in the purpose of His grace and in the sentence of His law, so we must between Christ's having purchased pardon and His now dispensing it according to the laws of His mediatorial kingdom.

Third, faith. The price of our forgiveness was paid when Christ died, but our actual admission into and possession of the privilege is not ours until we are planted into Him by a living faith. "Whosoever believeth in Him shall receive remission of sins" (Acts 10:43): cf. 13:38, 39; 26:18. "By faith alone we obtain and receive the forgiveness of sin; for notwithstanding any antecedent act of God concerning us in and for Christ, we do not actually receive a soul-freeing discharge until we believe" (John Owen). Faith is as necessary in an **instrumental** way as Christ's satisfaction was in a **meritorious** way. Faith is the link of connection between the blessings purchased by Christ and the soul's enjoyment of them. Faith is that which appropriates the benefits of Christ unto itself.

What are the marks, or true evidences, of a pardoned man? First, genuine affection for God and Christ: "her sins, which are many, are forgiven; for she loved much" (Luke 7:47): the latter was the effect of the former. Second, a reverential awe for God: "There is forgiveness with Thee, that Thou mayest be feared" (Psa. 130:4): a pardoned soul will no longer rush heedlessly into sin. Third, a spirit without guile (Psa. 32:2), that is, a heart that is sincere in seeking the glory of God and desires to please Him in all things—cf. Eph. 6:24. Where God pardons, He places His law in the heart (Heb. 8:10-12). Fourth, mourning for sin: where the heart is unbroken and unmelted, the condemnation of God rests upon it: cf. Luke 7:38. Fifth, the power of indwelling sin is broken: "He will **subdue** our iniquity, and Thou wilt cast all their sins into the depths of the sea" (Micah 7:19): God never does the one without the other—justification and sanctification are inseparable. Sixth, praise and thanksgiving unto God: "Bless the Lord, O my soul. . . who forgiveth all thine iniquities" (Psa. 103:2, 3). Seventh, a genuine spirit of forgiveness toward those who wrong us: "Forgive us our sins, for we also forgive every one that is indebted to us" (Luke 11:4).

—ARTHUR W. PINK.

THE INTERCESSION OF CHRIST

The intercession of Christ is not for the purpose of reminding God of that which He would otherwise forget, still less is it to inform Him of what He would not otherwise know. Nor is its object to incline God unto that to which He would otherwise be averse. No; its design is to exemplify the Divine majesty and holiness, by emphasising the distance which still remains between the Creator and the creature, between the Judge and transgressors of His law. Its design is to display the grace, the compassion and the merits of the Mediator, by His continuing to be constantly occupied with the interests of His redeemed: having loved His own which were in the world, He loves them unto the end (John 13:1). It is designed to impress upon His people their obligation to deep and lasting gratitude, to manifest to them the exceeding riches of God's grace toward them, and to establish their hearts, deepen their hopes, increase their consolation. No matter how dark may be the night, how rough the road, how severe their trials, there is One above whose prayers prevail to keep them from making shipwreck of the faith.

The intercession of the Redeemer is essential to the perfection of His priesthood. As Aaron both offered a sacrifice for the sins of his people and made supplication for them within the veil, so Christ's oblation of Himself is accompanied and followed by His advocacy on behalf of those for whom He obeyed and died. The two functions are inseparably conjoined; and, without the performance of both His glory as Priest could not be fully displayed, nor would His interference for the salvation of His people be of any avail. So too, the covenant of redemption, in which Christ was set up as Mediator, rendered His intercession necessary for the bestowment of the blessings which it provided. The grand condition of the covenant was the atoning death of Christ as a satisfaction to Divine justice; but once this was offered, it was further required that the covenant should be administered in applying the redemption purchased. This could only be done by Him to whom the whole dispensation of covenant-blessings is entrusted; and this is effected directly and perpetually by His all-powerful intercession.

The priesthood of Christ is ever represented as perpetual and unchanging; and to the acts which He performs in heaven are ascribed the deliverances and blessings which we receive, namely, the carrying on and completing of our salvation. We are freed from condemnation because Christ is risen: Rom. 4:25. Our standing before God is preserved by

Christ's being at His right hand: Rom. 8:33, 34. We are saved unto the uttermost because He ever liveth to make intercession for us: Heb. 7:25. Christ is a Priest upon His throne: Zech. 6:13, and "continueth ever," and that, because He has an unchanging priesthood (Heb. 7:24). By His oblation on earth as Priest, He offered once for all; by His priestly work in heaven, He carries into effect all the desires of His loving mercy to ransomed sinners, and puts them into possession of all the benefits which were obtained for them by His death. The blood of the Lamb was shed to make an atonement for sin, but it must be sprinkled on the mercy-seat in Glory to speak in God's ear and to the sinner's conscience, before the "better hope" of pardon and peace can be recognized.

The intercession of Christ as our exalted High Priest occupies in some respects a more conspicuous place than any other of His priestly acts. His work of atonement was limited to the brief period of His manifestation in the flesh on earth, but He was actually engaged as an Advocate and Intercessor from the first revelation of mercy in our world till His incarnation (Zech. 1:12, etc.). He pleaded for His people while He obeyed and suffered (Luke 22:31), and now that He has entered into the holy place not made with hands, He continues to intercede. The advocacy of our Surety is carried on to the end of earth's history, and when this world shall be no more, it will continue to be unceasingly conducted for ends the most beneficient and glorious, as the great work of His everlasting priesthood.

When God purposed to have a people who should show forth his praises throughout eternity, He determined that their salvation should be accomplished in a way that glorifies Him, and on such terms as would be for His honour. These terms are declared in the Gospel: those who should be saved, must be both justified and sanctified—justified, because none can be reconciled to Him unless the sentence of condemnation passed on all sinners be reversed; sanctified, since without holiness no man shall see the Lord. In order to their justification, they must have faith; in order to be sanctified, they must be born again and conformed to the Divine image. Both these Christ purchased by His blood, but He works them by His Spirit, and in order that the Spirit might be given for these purposes, He prays. All that the Spirit does in His people is in answer to Christ's intercession. This leads us to consider,

6. ITS SUPREMACY.

1. The potency of Christ's intercession was typified in O. T. times. First, in the fact that the high priest of Judaism not only bore the names of Israel's tribes upon his heart—the place of affection, but also upon his "shoulders" (Ex. 28:12)—the place of strength: cf Isa. 9:6. Second, in the fact that when Aaron entered into the holy of holies and approached the mercy-seat, he was heard on behalf of the whole congregation. When he sprinkled the blood and pleaded for them, and received the blessing for them in answer to prayer (emblemised by the incense), he communicated the same when he returned, and with uplifted hands, blest the people in the name of the Lord. Third, in that Jehovah gave express instructions that each of the altars should have "horns" upon their four corners (Ex. 27:2, 30:2)—the "horn" in scripture being the symbol of strength and dignity: the horns on the brazen altar speaking of the power of Christ's death; those on the incense altar, of the excellency of His intercession.

2. The efficacy of Christ's intercession was clearly prophesied in the O. T. Scriptures. In Psa. 2:8 God says to His mediatorial King, "Ask of Me and I will give Thee." In Psa. 21:2 we read, "Thou hast given Him His heart's desire, and hast not withholden the request of His lips." In Isa. 53:10 we are told, "When Thou shalt make His soul an offering for sin, He shall see His seed, He shall prolong His days, and the pleasure of the Lord shall prosper in His hands." That which Christ now has in hand is the saving of His people unto the uttermost, which is effected by His continued intercession for them, and this "shall prosper"! To mention only one more ancient prediction, in Isa. 62:1 we hear Christ declaring—the verses that immediately follow show He is the Speaker—"For Zion's sake will I not hold My peace, and for Jerusalem's sake I will not rest, until the righteousness thereof go forth as brightness, and the salvation thereof as a lamp which burneth."

3. The prevalency of Christ's intercession is assured by the dignity of His person. He is infinitely more excellent than all the angels, for in Him "dwelleth

all the fulness of the Godhead bodily" (Col. 2:9). He is equal with God, and so cannot be refused by God. As the Divine nature of the Mediator gave value to His satisfaction, so it gives efficacy to His advocacy. Though He does not intercede with God, as Himself is God, but as Mediator in His human nature, yet His pleading as man receives power and dignity from Him as God, which causes the sufficiency of it. It is a privilege due unto the greatness of His person to have His suit granted, as it is His duty, as the High Priest of His Church, to present it in the holy of holies. Nothing can be denied Him, for "all authority in heaven and earth" has been given to Him (Matt. 28:18).

The Intercessor is the Son; the One sought unto is the Father. "To whom should He grant anything if He refused the Son, and His Son upon the same throne as Himself? If an earthly father knows how to give good gifts unto his children that ask him, then a heavenly Father does much more, and most of all to an only-begotten and only-beloved Son, for whose sake He loves all His other children. It is a consideration that discovers the sincerity and tenderness of Divine mercy. Had not God intended to honour Him in all His requests for us, He would never have appointed One so nearly allied to Him to plead our cause; One that He could not deny without some dishonour to so near a relation, and a reflection upon His own affection, as He might have done to some inferior person. God would not love His Son according to His own greatness, if He did not express it in the most signal marks of His favour" (S. Charnock).

How blessed it is for the Christian to realize that the one who is His Advocate in heaven is the "great High Priest" (Heb. 4:14)! Melchizedek was designated "priest of the most high God"; Aaron was Israel's "high priest"; Christ alone is spoken of as "a **great** High Priest." It is this very fact which the Holy Spirit presses upon those who are "partakers of the heavenly calling" in Heb. 4:14-16, and this for their consolation and confidence, that they might come boldly to the throne of grace. He is there said to be "great" because He is the Son of God, and therefore is great in prevailing with His Father, as He Himself declared, "Thou hearest Me **always**" (John 11:42).

4. The efficacy of Christ's intercession is guaranteed by **the preciousness of His blood**: "the blood of sprinkling that speaketh better things than that of Abel" (Heb. 12:24). "Even the blood of the wickedest man on earth, if innocently shed, doth cry, and hath a power with justice, against him who slew him. Had Abel murdered Cain, Cain's blood would have cried, and called upon God's justice against Abel; but Abel's blood (there is an emphasis in that), who was a saint, and the first martyr in God's calendar; and so his blood cries according to the worth that was in him. Now 'precious in the sight of the Lord is the death of His saints'; and the blood of one of them cries louder than the blood of all mankind besides. Now from this I argue, if the blood of the saint cries so, what must the blood of the **'King** of saints' (Rev. 15:2), then do? If the blood of one member of Christ's body, what will then the blood of the Head, far more worth than that whole body? How doth it fill heaven and earth with cries, until the promised intent of its shedding be accomplished!" (Thos. Goodwin).

The presentation of the memorials of Christ's sacrifice is like a constant renewal of the one perfect offering whereby God is propitiated and sinners reconciled, and it is of potent efficacy for the application of redemption. As the Lamb stands before the Throne, He puts the Father in remembrance of Surety-engagements perfectly fulfilled, of promises of life and salvation given to the covenant-seed, of obedience offered and suffering endured, that brought a revenue of glory to all the Divine perfections; and, in consequence, the claims which He advances are the highest and irresistible. If, when God beheld the bow in the cloud (Gen. 9:16), He remembered the everlasting covenant, and declared that He would not again destroy the earth with a flood; if the blood sprinkled upon the Israelitish homes, was the mark to the angel of destruction that he should not enter and slay the firstborn; how much more must the precious memorial of Christ's atoning sacrifice, constantly living and fresh (Heb. 10:20), bring before God the purpose and stipulations of the covenant of peace, and present the most powerful and prevailing appeals to His character to grant whatever the Intercessor asks, to confer on the ransomed of the Lord all blessings of grace and glory!

5. The efficacy of Christ's intercession is guaranteed by **the union existing**

between the Redeemer and the redeemed. It is not for aliens and strangers that Christ pleads, but for those whom the Father blest in Him with all spiritual blessings before the foundation of the earth, and whom He gave to Christ to be members of His mystical Body. As one with Himself, legally and vitally, they are clothed with all the acceptableness to God as is Christ Himself. As the shewbread, consisting of twelve loaves continually renewed and fresh, perfumed with the sweet incense (Lev. 24:7), represented the whole Israel of God, so the High Priest of the covenant ever presents His people before the Father. Guilty and polluted in themselves, their best services defiled, they can only meet with rejection and condemnation. But presented before God as one with Christ, joined to Himself (1 Cor. 6:17), they are well pleasing in His sight, and are loved by the Father as is His Son (John 17:23).

7. ITS CONTINUANCE.

The constancy of Christ's advocacy was plainly foreshadowed in the O. T. types. As the continual daily sacrifices pointed to the lasting virtue of the Redeemer's death, so the constant burning incense signified the perpetuity of His intercession: "a perpetual incense before the Lord throughout your generations" (Ex. 30:8). This is plainly affirmed in Heb. 7:25, which announces that Christ "ever liveth to make intercession for them." Israel's high priests were removed by reason of death, but Christ "continueth ever" (Heb. 7:23, 24). We are obliged to spend much of our time in sleep, but He who is the Keeper of Israel never slumbers (Psa. 121:3). There are occasions when our souls are so cast down that we cannot pray; how blessed to know that there is One above who ever pleads for us!

The oblation of Christ was a transcient act, but His appearance in heaven for us is a permanent act. Though He has personally been exalted and crowned with honour, yet His mediatorial glory is not consummated. He has a mystical self to be perfected, a "fulness" to be enriched with (Eph. 1:23). Some of His redeemed are yet dead in sins, and must be quickened; others who have been regenerated are backsliders, and must be recovered; still others are passing through fiery trials and need Divine support. Until the last of "His own" has been brought safely Home, there is need for the Advocate to sue for their sustenance and maintenance in grace. While ten righteous remain in Sodom, the antitypical Abraham must continue pleading for their deliverance.

And what of the Eternal State? After all of His bloodwashed people shall be perfectly conformed to Christ's image, will their great High Priest cease to mediate on their behalf? No, indeed: He "ever liveth to make intercession for them." "There is a work that is necessary still to be performed for them. This is securing the permanence of their state of felicity, and the acceptance of the lofty worship which in glory they render to the heavenly King. So great and awful is the Majesty in the heavens—so bright and overpowering His glory, and so transcendent His infinite purity—that creatures, the most excellent, are not worthy to stand before Him. The 'heavens are not clean in His sight, and His angels hath He charged with folly.' The seraphim, when they draw nigh to worship, veil their faces, in token of creature distance; and cover their feet, as acknowledging their holiest services to be unworthy of Divine regard and acceptance.

"The ancient high priest, as He entered within the veil, and afterwards came forth to bless the congregation of Israel presided over the house of God, whether the tabernacle in the wilderness, or the magnificent temple in Jerusalem. So Christ takes the lead in the services of the sanctuary, whether of the church militant on earth, or triumphant in heaven. In the Temple above, where the vials of prayer are supplanted by the golden harps of praise, He leads the worship, accentuates the melody of the new song of the redeemed, and obtains acceptance for the highest kind of creature worship. The sweet incense of His mediation perfumes all the celestial services of the saints in glory; and throughout the roll of endless ages, Christ at the head of the host of the redeemed will bring unspeakable 'glory to God in the highest', and full and overflowing joys to His ransomed ones in heaven" (T. Houston).

Even when we reach the new Jerusalem, which comes down onto the new earth, we read of "the throne of God **and of the Lamb**" (Rev. 22:1). Throughout eternity Christ will continue to plead on behalf of His people. Never shall they cease to be the objects of His care;

never shall their names be erased from His heart; never shall their cause be taken from His lips; never shall the golden censer drop from His hand; nor shall His blessed merits ever cease to rise up in a cloud of fragrance before the Father. He is "a Priest forever." Faintly as we may now apprehend the needs-be and blessedness of this, when we shall see no longer through a glass darkly, but face to face, we shall fall down before Him in adoring worship, saying "Worthy is the Lamb."

Let us now point out the **practical application** of this glorious truth. 1. How we should admire the loving kindness of Christ to lost sinners that He "ever liveth to make intercession for them": that this should be one of the chief ends of His resurrection-life: to free us from misery, to promote and secure our eternal happiness. Though we be but worms and grasshoppers in His sight, His heart is fixed upon us. He has already lived one life for us and lost it for us; and when a new life was given Him, He lives it for us too. It was amazing condescension that the Lord of glory should have become man; still more wonderful was it that at His exaltation He did not cast off human nature. And why did He retain it? For our sakes, to mediate between God and men. O what praise, what love, what worship are due unto Him!

2. It should teach us to live for Christ. Shall He live eternally for us, and we refuse to live a few years for Him? If Christ carries our names on His heart, as a signal proof of His affection to us, we should carry His name upon our hearts, in a way of grateful return. Ought not His infinite love for us constrain us to live wholly for Him? How? After the example and method He has shown us. His living in heaven for us was preceded by His death; He was made a sacrifice before an Advocate. So there is something for us to die to, before we can live for Him. We must sacrifice our worldly, carnal, selfish interests. We must deny self, take up our cross and follow Him. Only to the extent that we are (in a practical way) dead to sin, dead to the world, dead to self, can we really live for Christ.

This is what we are called unto: "I beseech you therefore, brethren, by the mercies of God, that ye present your bodies a living **sacrifice**, holy, acceptable unto God, your reasonable service" (Rom. 12:1). How this "reasonable service" is to be performed, is explained in the next verse: "And be not conformed to this world: but be ye transformed by the renewing of your mind that ye may prove what is that good, and acceptable, and perfect will of God." We are not to emulate the men of the world, who live for themselves, but are to live for God, by learning, doing, and thus "proving" the excellency of His will. And this, because of Christ's dying and living for us. There is most cogent reason from Christ's example that we should live for and to Him.

3. It should teach us to be ever prayerful. The work of our High Priest within the veil is to present the offerings of saints on earth, and those are chiefly their sacrifices of prayer and thanksgiving. He pleads only for those who, by faith and supplication, come unto God by Him. He collects in His censer the prayers of all saints, and presents them for acceptance on the altar before God: Rev. 8:3. Our safety and deliverance lie in employing an Advocate who is ever present in court, who has the ear of the Judge, who is skillful to plead our cause. Our great duty and highest interest is to have recourse to our great Intercessor continually. If Christ's life in heaven is employed in constant intercession, ours on earth should be one of praying always without fainting. We have His own full assurance of an answer: "If ye ask anything in My name, I will do it" (John 14:14).

4. It should fill us with comfort and peace. His great mediatorial prayer was offered on the eve of His last agony, that His disciples should be consoled: "These things I speak in the world, that ye might have My joy fulfilled in yourselves" (John 17:13)! The same gracious design is still carried into accomplishment by the work of the Saviour's advocacy in heaven. If it affords comfort to a weak and afflicted soul to have a Christion friend pleading his cause at the throne of grace, how much greater consolation to have the Lord Jesus pleading for him in heaven! Depending upon the priestly life of our Redeemer, we are assured that past guilt shall not bring us into condemnation, that accusations of the enemy shall not prevail against us, and that under the strongest temptations our faith shall not fail. May the realization of this enable the writer and reader to say from the heart, "Whom have I in heaven but Thee? and there is none upon earth that I desire beside Thee" (Psa. 73:25). A.W.P.

SOUND THE ALARM

The "alarm" about what? The people of God having fellowship with "the unfruitful works of darkness" (Eph. 5:11), by remaining in "churches" from which God's Word bids them come out. The ministry to which God has called His servants is many-sided in its character and scope. To "preach the Word" comprehends very much more than proclaiming the Gospel to the unsaved and ministering comfort to sorrowing saints. It includes reproving and rebuking (2 Tim. 4:2), warning and exposing (1 John 4:1-3), denouncing (Jude 11) and anathematizing (Gal. 1:8). God's order to His servants is, "Cry aloud, spare not, lift up thy voice like a trumpet, and show My people their transgression" (Isa. 58:1). And again, "And thou shalt speak My words unto them, whether they will hear, or whether they will forbear: for they are most rebellious" (Ezek. 2:7). Those commands, though given thousands of years ago, are not obsolete, but part of that Word which "liveth and abideth forever." As a matter of fact they are most pertinent to these Perilous Times.

The passages quoted above were spoken in the days of Israel's apostacy, and history has repeated itself, therefore are they God's commands today in view of an apostate Christendom; and if the servant of God ignores them, he fails in a most important part of his work. That they are a living word will quickly be proved by any who dare to carry them out: the true servant of God will no more be popular now than Isaiah, Jeremiah, Ezekiel or Daniel were of yore. And just as those bearing the name of the Lord were the very ones who took the lead in denouncing and persecuting the prophets for their unpalatable messages, so professing Christians will be the first to condemn and persecute those who now denounce the wickednesses of "pre - millennarians," "fundamentalists," etc. But the faithful servant fears his Lord too much to be afraid of anything that men may do to him: he neither seeks their patronage nor fears their frowns.

Quite recently we were invited to occupy the pulpit of a "Baptist church," whose pastor is taking his "vacation." We knew nothing whatever about this "church," but concluding it was neither better nor worse than thousands of others, we declined. Our visitor left with us a recent issue of this church's (?) "bulletin," or printed program. The Sunday morning service began with a "voluntary," which was the "Boat Song" by Mendelssohn. Do any of our readers suppose the Holy Spirit of God would indite prayer in the heart of a preacher following that item? If so they must be blinded by Satan. The next item reads, "Audience (most suitable word!—not 'Congregation') rise as Choir enters." Why pay homage to it? What would be the difference between this and the order of service in a Romish cathedral? Later, is an "anthem," which only too often is "rendered" by those who six days a week trample upon the very things which they sing about on the seventh. During the "Offertory," Friml's "Melodie" is played. Next follows a "solo." Then comes the "sermon" — but in what frame of soul would the people be in to hear God's Word?

On the next page are the "Announcements." Among them is the following: "The Ladies union will hold a penny social Friday evening. Admittance to the social will be one penny per inch waist measurement. Games and refreshments." Now the "pastor" of this "church" (?) is a "Fundamentalist," who preaches Salvation by Grace alone. It is just such men who are guilty of the terrible sin of Jude 4, "Turning the grace of our God (note not 'their God' for they are strangers to Him!) into lasciviousness." Such men would do far less harm if they would openly preach salvation by works. Why? Because those who (notwithstanding all the worldliness he tolerates) feel it to be their bounden duty to "stand by the pastor" so long as he preaches the Truth—though often his life gives the lie to what he says in the pulpit—would then (perhaps) separate themselves from these religious clubs which are such an abomination unto God, and ought to be so unto all His people.

"Be ye not unequally yoked together with unbelievers: for what fellowship hath righteousness with unrighteousness? and what communion hath light with darkness?" (2 Cor. 6:14). What could be plainer than that? It needs no "interpreting." It just means what it says. "Having a form of godliness, but denying the power thereof from such turn away" (2 Tim. 3:5). How could language be made more unequivocal? These are Divine commands. But thousands of professing Christians, among them we fear a few real ones, are so tardy in obeying, that

God permits things to become so rotten that they are ultimately forced to get out. Recently, one who has had this magazine from the beginning, but who was, until a few weeks ago, a member of a "Baptist church" (?) wrote us to say he had withdrawn. During a recent Evangelistic Meeting, the "pianist" of his "church" (?) never attended, but on the contrary, one night she put on a "dance," and is now one of the candidates for queen at a "carnival." One of the S. S. teachers is a "Christian Scientist," and another refuses to believe in eternal punishment. The "treasurer of the church" boasts that he is a "Modernist." A member of the finance committee and a trustee does not believe in the inspiration of the Bible.

The one referred to above wrote us, "The pastor is clear and sound on all these truths and preaches them, but aside from that he never raises a finger to correct conditions in the church." This preacher is a fair sample of a large class today who wish to pose as "orthodox." Personally we have far more respect for the "Modernist," for he is more honest and consistent. The others run with the hare and hunt with the hounds. Miserable compromisers! Christ calls them "hirelings," and such they are, holding an easy job at a goodly wage, willing to wink at anything, so long as their "salary" is paid. It is just such imposters who have utterly disgusted thousands of thinking men and women, and led them to the logical conclusion that the whole of religion is a sham, and that all the preachers are after is your money. And, it is greatly to be feared that, ninety-nine times out of a hundred the man of the world is right in his conclusion.

Personally, if the writer were compelled (thank God he is not so) to choose between these two alternatives, conduct Bible conferences in such "churches" as the above, or, return to England and hire himself as a bar-tender at a beer and whisky saloon, without the slightest hesitation he would select the latter. Why? Because, though a most pernicious thing, the saloon is not run under the holy name of the Lord Jesus, and these so-called churches, with their worldliness and hollow hypocrisy are. It is no use mincing words today. The Lord of glory is on the eve of spueing out the whole filthy mess which is now sheltering under the cloak of His blessed name. He is nauseated by the blasphemous pretense which is now, on every side, masquerading under the name of "Christian."

"So then because thou art lukewarm, and neither cold nor hot, I will spue thee out of My mouth" (Rev. 3:16). The meaning of the figure which is used here should be easily perceived, yet many quite fail to get its significance. It is that of an emetic, which is a mixing together of two liquids of different temperatures. Thus, the "lukewarm" here refers not to a waning of affection or cooling off in zeal, but to a combining of elements that are foreign to each other, which combination is nauseating, repellent, to the Son of God. What that combination is, none should have any doubt about. It is the horrible mingling of the things of God with the things of the world, which is now to be witnessed in almost every section of Christendom. It is the (vain) attempt to retain sufficient of the "form of godliness" to satisfy those who are "religious," with enough of fleshly attractions to draw and hold the worldling.

This unholy mixture assumes a variety of forms, but in essence it is one and the same. Sometimes the preacher himself combines the two contrary elements in his pulpit ministrations. There is enough humor in his sermons to make the people laugh and enough pathos to make them weep, sufficient "anecdotes" to hold their attention and also sufficient quotations or reference to Scripture to cause some of his dupes—professing "Christians"—to leave the service consoling themselves with, "Well, he did bring in the Gospel." In other cases, where the preacher abominates levity in the pulpit, only too often he resorts to giving sensational clippings from the newspapers on the doings of Mussolini, the growing power of the Papacy, or the fearful increase in crime, under the pretence of edifying his hearers with the latest "Signs of the Times," sufficient "prophecy" being quoted to lead many to think that they have heard a Scriptural address.

In other cases, where little exception can be taken to the sermon, other parts of the service are an abomination to God and "quench the Spirit." Either the "church" is in debt or determined to run into debt by competing with their neighbors in building an up-to-date meeting-house (though their present one easily accommodates the congregation), and then there is much begging for money and resorting to all sorts of anti-scriptural ways and means of raising it. Or, where this is not the case, a group of bobbed-haired girls serves as a "choir," and other attractions are added to please music lovers. Almost everywhere the Sunday-night Gospel meeting starts with a thirty minutes "song service," instead of a united waiting upon God, earnestly supplicating His blessing. In places where "prayer" does have a more prominent place, "Faith-healing" testimonies, or "tongues" are supplied to satisfy the sensational-monger.

Now all such unholy mixtures are expressly forbidden by the Word of God. At the beginning He divided the light from the darkness. When He took Israel unto Himself, He separated His people from the heathen, and built a wall around them. He forbade them to sow with "divers seed" (Deut. 22:9), which, being interpreted spiritually, condemns the mingling of Scripture with science, art, and politics. He forbade them to plow with "an ox and ass together" (Deut. 22:10), which reprehends the unequal yoke. He forbade them to wear a garment "of woolen and linen together" (Deut. 22:11), which reprimands mixed principles of conduct. Mixtures are of Satan. He, and not God, is the author of confusion. It was the devil who sowed his tares among the wheat, and introduced his corrupting leaven in the pure meal. And he is still engaged in the same work.

"I would that thou wert cold or hot" (Rev. 3:15). How these words of Christ's condemn those who excuse much that is contrary to Scripture by arguing that "the end justifies the means." So long as the "young people" can be held, a some of them induced to make a lip profession of receiving Christ as their Saviour, many refuse to protest against the worldly devices that are employed to draw them. But the only "end" which Holy Scripture sets before us is the glory of God, and the only "means" prayer and the preaching of the Word, backed up by a godly daily life. "I would that thou wert cold or hot," one thing or the other: out and out Christians, or out and out worldlings. "If the Lord be God, follow Him, but if Baal, then follow him" (1 Kings 18:21).

In view of the appalling conditions now existing in almost all of the "churches," what is the duty of the real child of God? Are you willing for Scripture to answer that question, my reader? If so, none need remain in any doubt as to the Divine will in the matter. "<u>Thou</u> shalt not follow a multitude to do evil" (Ex. 23:2). "Have no fellowship with the unfruitful works of darkness, but rather reprove" (Eph. 5:11). "Be ye not unequally yoked together with unbelievers" (2 Cor. 6:14). Those are God's commands to you. What others do about it, is none of your concern. If some who you look up to as being wiser and more spiritual than yourself, refuse to separate themselves from what Christ condemns, that will not help you any when you are called on to give an account before God for your disobedience! It is your solemn responsibility to walk according to God's Word if every one else in the whole world scorns it.

It is impossible for any of us to honour God while we support or remain associated with anything that is dishonouring to Him. Most probably many of our readers will say, But what are we to do? The answer is, do as God bids you: "Behold, to obey is better than sacrifice, and to hearken than the fat of rams" (1 Sam. 15:22). "But we must go somewhere." Then go to the "secret place" of the Most High, and thou shalt abide "under the shadow of the Almighty" (Psa. 91:1). Go direct to the Word, and thou shalt find in it food for thy soul, waters to refresh thy weary heart, light for thy path. Go to the Lord Himself, He will not fail you: Cast all your care upon Him, for He careth for you. But does not Scripture say, "Not forsaking the assembling of ourselves together" (Heb. 10:25)? It does, but that verse certainly does not bid you associate with company of religious worldlings, nor does it contradict 2 Cor. 6:14, 17. 2 Tim. 3:5 plainly says, "From such turn away."

"But my friends will not understand me." Probably not; the Lord Himself was not understood; they said He was "mad" (John 10:20); and if they do not say the same of you, it is because you are treading a different path than the one He walked. "But fellow-Christians will condemn me, say that I am a Pharisee, claiming to be holier than others." Perhaps so, but what of that, if you receive Christ's well done thou good and faithful servant!" Ah, that is just it: are you really living to please Him, or yourself and your friends? Are you walking by faith or sight—having the things of this world, or the things of the world to come before you? Do you wish to be among the "spued out?" In all probability that will be your portion, unless you "Come out" (2 Cor. 6:17). May the honour of Christ constrain you so to do.

We do not say that it is the duty of every Christian to "come out," for we are not personally acquainted with every "church." Yet this we do say, if there are any "churches" which are scriptural in their membership, in their maintenance of discipline, in their preaching, and in all that concerns their public services, we do not know where to find them. We have travelled completely around the world, and ministered the Word in many places, but there is no church known to us where we could hold membership. But if you are a member of a church where Scripture is followed in all its arrangements, and its pastor and officers are God-fearing men and honour Him by their daily walk, then praise Him with all your heart, and do everything in your power to strengthen their hands. This article is not intended as an attack upon the true servants of God. Nor is it designed as a brief for those known as the "Plymouth Brethren," for if there is not so much of the world, there is as much of the "flesh" in many of their gatherings as we have proved (on three continents) by painful experience. The "form of godliness" is still maintained in some of their "assemblies," but the "power thereof" is noticeably lacking. But enough. We commit this article into the hands of our God, and leave it with each reader to ponder before Him and examine by the light of Holy Writ. "Prove all things; hold fast that which is good."

—ARTHUR W. PINK.

---

a hope is a viper, which if cherished in their bosoms will sting them to death. God is a God of justice as well as mercy, and He has expressly declared that He will "by no means clear the guilty" (Ex. 34:7). Yea, He has said, "The wicked shall be turned into hell, all the nations that forget God" (Psa. 9:17). As well might men reason: I do not believe that if filth be allowed to accumulate and sewerage become stagnant and people deprive themselves of fresh air, that a merciful God will let them fall a prey to a deadly fever. The fact is that those who neglect the laws of health are carried away by disease, notwithstanding God's mercy. Equally true is it that those who neglect the laws of spiritual health shall forever suffer the Second Death.

Unspeakably solemn is it to see so many abusing this Divine perfection. They continue to despise God's authority, trample upon His laws, continue in sin, and yet presume upon His mercy. But God will not be unjust to Himself. God shows mercy to the truly penitent, but not to the impenitent (Luke 13:3). To continue in sin and yet reckon upon Divine mercy remitting punishment is diabolical. It is saying, "Let us do evil that good may come," and of all such it is written, "whose damnation is just" (Rom. 3:8). Presumption shall most certainly be disappointed; read carefully Deut. 29:18-20. Christ is the spiritual Mercy-seat, and all who despise and reject His Lordship shall "perish from the way, when His wrath is kindled but a little" (Psa. 2:12).

But let our final thought be of God's spiritual mercies unto His own people. "Thy mercy is great unto the heavens" (Psa. 57:10). The riches thereof transcend our loftiest thoughts. "For as the heaven is high above the earth, so great is His mercy toward them that fear Him" (Psa. 103:11). None can measure it. The elect are designated "vessels of mercy" (Rom. 9:23). It is mercy that quickened them when they were dead in sins (Eph. 2:4, 5). It is mercy that saves them (Titus 3:5). It is His abundant mercy which begat them unto an eternal inheritance (1 Peter 1:3). Time would fail us to tell of His preserving, sustaining, pardoning, supplying mercy. Unto His own, God is "the Father of mercies" (2 Cor. 1:3).

"When all Thy mercies, O my God,
My rising soul surveys,
Transported with the view I'm lost,
In wonder, love, and praise."

—ARTHUR W. PINK.

45). Third, there is a **sovereign** mercy which is reserved for the heirs of salvation, which is communicated to them in a covenant way, through the Mediator.

Following out a little further the difference between the second and third distinctions pointed out above, it is important to note that the mercies which God bestows on the wicked are solely of a **temporal** nature; that is to say, they are confined strictly to this present life. There will be no mercy extended to them beyond the grave: "It is a people of no understanding: therefore He that made them will not have mercy on them, and He that formed them will show them no favour" (Isa. 27:11). But at this point a difficulty may suggest itself to some of our readers, namely, Does not Scripture affirm that "His mercy endureth forever" (Psa. 136:1)? Two things need to be pointed out in that connection. God can never cease to be merciful, for this is a quality of the Divine essence (Psa. 116:5); but the **exercise** of His mercy is regulated by His sovereign will. This must be so, for there is nothing outside Himself which obliges Him to act; if there were, that "something" would be **supreme**, and God would cease to be **God**.

It is pure sovereign grace which alone determines the exercise of Divine mercy. God expressly affirms this fact in Rom. 9:15, "For He saith to Moses, I will have mercy on whom I will have mercy." It is not the wretchedness of the creature which causes Him to show mercy, for God is not influenced by things outside of Himself as we are. If God **were** influenced by the abject misery of leprous sinners, He would cleanse and save all of them. But He does not. Why? Simply because it is not His pleasure and purpose so to do. Still less is it the merits of the creature which causes Him to bestow mercies upon them, for it is a contradiction in terms to speak of **meriting** "mercy." "Not by works of righteousness which we have done, but according to His mercy He saved us" (Titus 3:5)—the one standing in direct antithesis from the other. Nor is it the merits of Christ which moves God to bestow mercies on His elect: that would be putting the effect for the cause. It is "through" or because of the tender mercy of our God that Christ was sent here to His people (Luke 1:78). The merits of Christ make it possible for God to righteously bestow spiritual mercies on His elect, justice having been fully satisfied by the Surety! No, mercy arises solely from God's imperial pleasure.

Again; though it be true, blessedly and gloriously true, that God's mercy "endureth forever," yet we must observe carefully the objects **to whom** His "mercy" is shown. Even the casting of the reprobate into the Lake of Fire is an act of **mercy**. The punishment of the wicked is to be contemplated from a threefold viewpoint. From God's side, it is an act of **justice**, vindicating His honour. The mercy of God is never shown to the prejudice of His holiness and righteousness. From their side, it is an act of **equity**, when they are made to suffer the due reward of their iniquities. But from the standpoint of the redeemed, the punishment of the wicked is an act of unspeakable **mercy**. How dreadful would it be if the present order of things should continue forever, when the children of God are obliged to live in the midst of the children of the Devil! Heaven would at once cease to be heaven if the ears of the saints still heard the blasphemous and filthy language of the reprobate. What a mercy that in the New Jerusalem "there shall in nowise enter into it any thing that defileth, neither worketh abomination" (Rev. 21:27)!

Lest the reader might think that in the last paragraph we have been drawing upon our imagination, let us appeal to Holy Scripture in support of what has been said. In Psa. 143:12 we find David praying, "And of Thy **mercy** cut off mine enemies, and destroy all them that afflict my soul: for I am Thy servant." Again; in Psa. 136:15 we read that God "Overthrew Pharaoh and his hosts in the Red Sea: for His **mercy** endureth forever." It was an act of vengeance upon Pharaoh and his hosts, but it was an act of "mercy" unto the Israelites. Again, in Rev. 19:1-3 we read, "I heard a great voice of much people in heaven, saying, Alleluia; Salvation, and glory, and honour, and power, unto the Lord our God: for true and righteous are His judgments: for He hath **judged** the great whore, which did corrupt the earth with her fornication, and hath **avenged** the blood of His servants at her hand. And again they said, **Alleluia**. And her smoke rose up forever and ever."

From what has just been before us, let us note how vain is the presumptuous hope of the wicked, who, notwithstanding their continued defiance of God, nevertheless count upon His being merciful to them. How many there are who say, I do not believe that God will ever cast me into Hell; He is too merciful. Such

(Continued on Page 47)

THE LOVE OF GOD

There are three things told us in Scripture concerning the *nature* of God. First, "God is spirit" (John 4:24). In the Greek there is no indefinite article, and to say "God is *a* Spirit" is most objectionable, for it places Him in a class with others. God is "spirit" in the highest sense. Because He is "spirit," He is incorporeal, having no visible substance. Had God a tangible body, He would not be omnipresent, He would be limited to one place; because He is "spirit," He fills heaven and earth. Second, "God is light" (1 John 1:5), which is the opposite of darkness. In Scripture "darkness" stands for sin, evil, death; and "light" for holiness, goodness, life "God is light" means that He is the *sum* of all excellency. Third, "God is love" (1 John 4:8). It is not simply that God "loves," but that He *is* Love itself. Love is not merely one of His attributes, but His very nature.

There are many today who talk about the love of God, who are total strangers to the God of love. The Divine love is commonly regarded as a species of amiable weakness, a sort of good-natured indulgence; it is reduced to a mere sickly sentiment, patterned after human emotion. Now the truth is that on this, as on everything else, our thoughts need to be formed and regulated by what is revealed thereon in Holy Scripture. That there is urgent need for this is apparent not only from the ignorance which so generally prevails, but also from the low state of spirituality which is now so sadly evident everywhere among professing Christians. How little real love there is for God. One chief reason for this is because our hearts are so little occupied with His wondrous love for His people. The better we are acquainted with His love—its character, fulness, blessedness—the more will our hearts be drawn out in love to Him.

1. The love of God is *uninfluenced*. By which we mean, there was nothing whatever in the objects of His love to call it into exercise, nothing in the creature to attract or prompt it. The love which one creature has for another is because of something in them; but the love of God is free, spontaneous, uncaused. The only reason why God loves any is found in His own sovereign will: "The Lord did not set His love upon you, nor choose you because ye were more in number than any people; for ye were the fewest of all people: but *because* the Lord loved thee" (Deut. 7:7, 8). God has loved His people from everlasting, and therefore nothing of the creature can be the cause of what is in God from eternity. He loves from Himself: "according to His own purpose" (2 Tim. 1:9).

"We love Him, because He first loved us" (1 John 4:19). God did not love us because we loved Him, but He loved us before we had a particle of love for Him. Had God loved us in return for ours, then it would not be spontaneous on His part; but because He loved us when we were loveless, it is clear that His love was uninfluenced. It is highly important if God is to be honoured and the heart of His child established, that we should be quite clear upon this precious truth. God's love for me, and for each of "His own," was entirely unmoved by anything in them. What was there in me to attract the heart of God? Absolutely nothing. But, to the contrary, everything to repel Him, everything calculated to make Him loathe—sinful, depraved, a mass of corruption, with *"no good thing"* in me.

"What was there in me that could merit esteem,
Or give the Creator delight?
'Twas even so, Father, I ever must sing,
Because it seemed good in Thy sight."

(*Continued on Page* 72)

IMPORTANT NOTICES

Please advise promptly of change of address, otherwise copies will be lost in the mails.

We are glad to send a sample copy to any of your friends whom you believe would be interested in such a publication.

Send to Mr. I. C. Herendeen, Swengel (Union County), Penna., for a list of our publications. He has published many of our books and booklets.

This magazine is published as a work of faith and labour of love. The Editor and his wife gladly give their services. It is freely sent to all who will read it. No charge is made for it.

Christians who feel definitely led to do so, may have fellowship with us in this ministry. Those outside the U. S. A., please send only INTERNATIONAL Money Orders made out to Los Angeles, California, U. S. A.

CONTENTS

The Love of God	49
The Epistle to the Hebrews	50
The Satisfaction ("Atonement") of Christ	56
Profiting from the Word	62
Subjection to God	67
Faith Triumphant	69

THE EPISTLE TO THE HEBREWS

39. *The Typical Tabernacle.* Heb. 9:1-5.

The principal design of the apostle in this epistle was to prove and make manifest that the "old covenant" which Jehovah made with Israel at Sinai, with all the ordinances of worship and the privileges connected therewith, had been Divinely annulled. This involved a complete change in the church-state of the Hebrews, but so far from this being a thing to deplore, it was to their unspeakable advantage. A "new covenant" had been inaugurated, and the blessings connected with it so far excelled those which had belonged to the old dispensation, that nothing but blind prejudice and perverse unbelief could refuse the true light which now shone, and prefer in its stead the dark shadows of a previous night. God never asks anybody to give up any thing without proffering something far better in return; and they who despise His offer are the losers. But prejudice is strong, and never harder to overcome than in connection with religious customs. Therefore does the Spirit labour so patiently in His argument throughout these chapters.

The chief obstacle in the way of the Hebrews' faith was their failure to perceive that every thing connected with the ceremonial law — the tabernacle, priesthood, sacrifices—was *typical* in its significance and value. Because it was typical, it was only preparatory and transient, for once the Antitype materialized its purpose was served. The shadows were no longer needed when the Substance was manifested. The scaffolding is dispensed with, taken away, as soon as the finished building appears. The toys of the nursery become obsolete when manhood is reached. Everything is beautiful in its proper season. Heavy garments are needed when the cold of winter is upon us, but they would be troublesome in summer's sunshine. Once we recognize that God Himself has acted on this principle in His dispensational dealings with His people, much becomes plain which otherwise would be quite obscure.

The apostle had closed the 8th chapter by pointing out, "Now that which decayeth and waxeth old is ready to vanish away." In those words the Spirit had intimated the unescapable inference which must be drawn from the oracle given through Jeremiah. He had predicted a *"new"* covenant," which received its fulfillment in the establishing of Christianity. The ushering in of the new order of Divine worship necessarily denoted that the previous economy was "old," and if so, its end must be nigh. The force of 8:13 is as follows: "In that *He* says a 'new' ": God would not have done so unless *He* had made the first "old." The "He hath made the first old" has an active significance and denotes an authoritative act of God upon the old economy, whereby the calling of the other "new" was the sign and evidence. God did not call the Christian dispensation *"another"* covenant," or a *"second"* covenant," but a "new" one, thereby declaring that the Judiac covenant was obsolete.

The connecting link between the closing verses of chapter 8 and the opening verses of 9 may perhaps be set forth thus: although the old covenant or

Mosaic economy was "ready to vanish away," nevertheless, it yields, even for Christians, important and valuable teachings. It is full of most blessed *typical* import, the record of which has been preserved both for the glory of its Author and the edification and joy of His saints. Wonderful indeed were the pictorial foreshadowings which the Lord gave in the days of Israel's kindergarten. The importance of them was more than hinted at by God when, though He took but six days to make heaven and earth, He spent no less than forty days when instructing Moses concerning the making of the tabernacle. That clearly denoted that the work of redemptive grace, which was prefigured in Jehovah's earthly dwelling place, was far more glorious than the work of creation. Thereby are we taught to look away from the things which are seen, and fix our minds and affections upon that sphere where the Son of God reigns in light and love.

"The general design of this chapter is the same as the two preceding, to show that Christ as High Priest is superior to the Jewish high priest. This the apostle had already shown to be true in regard to His *rank*, and to the *dispensation* of which He was the Mediator. He proceeds now to show that this was also true in reference to *the efficacy of the sacrifice* which He made: and in order to do this, he gives an account of the ancient Jewish sacrifices, and compares them with that made by the Redeemer. The essential point is, that the former dispensation was mere shadow, type, or figure, and that the latter was real and efficacious."— (A. Barnes).

"Then verily the first had also ordinances of the Divine service, and a worldly sanctuary" (v. 1). Having in the former chapter given further proof of the excellency of Christ's sacerdotal office, by describing the superior covenant that was ratified thereby, the apostle now prepares the way to set forth the *execution* of that office, following the same method of proceedure in so doing. Just as he had drawn a comparison between Aaron and Christ, so he now sets over the ministrations of the one against the Other, and this in order to prove that that of Christ's was most certainly to be preferred. He first approaches the execution of the Levitical priests' office by mentioning several rites and types which appertained thereto.

"Then verily the first had also ordinances of Divine service, and a worldly sanctuary." The apostle here begins the comparison which he draws between the old covenant and the new with respect to the services and sacrifices whereby the one and the other was established and confirmed. In so doing he is still dealing with what was to all pious Israelites a most tender consideration. It was in the services and sacrifices which belonged to the priestly office in the tabernacle that they had been taught to place all their confidence for reconciliation with God. If the apostle's previous contention respecting the abolition of the legal priesthood was granted, then it necessarily followed that the sanctuary in which they served and all the offerings which Moses had so solemnly appointed, became useless too. It calls for our closest attention and deepest admiration to observe how the Spirit led the apostle to approach an issue so startling and momentous.

First, he is so far from denying that the ritual of Judaism was of human invention, that he declares, "verily (of a truth) the first covenant had also ordinances of *Divine* service." Thus he follows the same method employed in the preceding chapters. In drawing his comparisons between Israel's prophets and Christ, the angels and Christ, Moses and Christ, Joshua and Christ, Aaron and Christ, he had said nothing whatever in disparagement of the inferior. So far from reviling the first member in each comparison, he had dwelt upon that which was in its favour: the more they could be legitimately magnified, the greater the glory accruing to Christ when it was proved how far He excelled them. So here: the apostle granted the principal point which an objector would make—why should the first covenant be annulled if God Himself had made it? Before giving answer to this (seemingly) most difficult question, he allows and affirms that the service of Judaism *was* of Divine institution. Thus, in the earliest ages of human history God had graciously appointed means for His people to use.

The expression "ordinances of divine service" calls for a word or two by way of explanation. The word which is here rendered "ordinances" (margin "ceremonies") signifies rites, statutes, institutions. They were the appointments of God, which He had the alone right to prescribe, and which His people were under solemn bonds of observing, and that without any alteration or deviation.

These "ordinances" were of "divine service" which is a single word in the original. In its verbal form it is found in 8:5, "to serve unto the example and shadow of heavenly things." In the N. T. it is always found in connection with religious or divine service: in Acts 24:14, Phil. 3:3 it is translated "worship." It signifies to serve in godly fear or trembling, thus implying an holy awe and reverence for the One served—cf. Heb. 12:28. Thus, the complete clause means that under the Mosaic economy God gave His people authoritative enactments to direct their worship of Him. This law of worship was a hedge which Jehovah placed around Israel to keep them from the abominations of the heathen. It was concerning this very thing that God had so many controversies with His people under the old covenant.

Care needs to be duly paid to the tense which the apostle here used: he said not "verily the first covenant *has* also ordinances, of divine service," but "*had*." He is obviously referring to the past. The Mosaic economy had those ordinances from the time God covenanted with Israel at Sinai. But *that* covenant was no longer in force; it had been Divinely annulled. The "verily the first covenant had *also* ordinances of Divine worship," clearly intimates that the new covenant too has Divine "ordinances." We press this because there are some who now affirm that even Christian baptism and the Lord's supper are "Jewish" ceremonies, which belong not to this present dispensation. But this error is sufficiently refuted by this word "also"—found in the very epistle which was written to prove that Judaism has given place to Christianity!

"And a worldly sanctuary." The reference is (as the next verse plainly shows) to the Tabernacle, which Moses made in all things according to the pattern shown him in the mount. Many have been sorely puzzled as to why the Holy Spirit should designate the holy sanctuary of Jehovah a "worldly" one. Yet this adjective should not present any difficulty. It is not used invidiously, still less as denoting anything which is evil. "Worldly" is not here opposed to "spiritual," but as that which belongs to the earth rather than to the heavens. Thus the force of "worldly" here emphasises the fact that the Mosaic economy was but a transient one, and not eternal. The tabernacle was made here in this world, out of perishing materials found in the world, and was but a portable tent, which might at pleasure be taken down and set up again; while the efficacy of its services extended only unto worldly things, and procured not that which was vital and eternal. Note how in 9:24 the "holy places made with hands" are set in antithesis from "heaven itself."

We cannot but admire the wisdom given to the apostle in handling a matter so delicate and difficult. While his object was to show the immeasurable superiority of that which has been brought in by Christ over that which Judaism had enjoyed, at the same time he would own that which was of God in it. Thus, on the one hand, he acknowledges the service of the Levitical priests as "divine," yet, to pave the way for his further proof that Christ is a Minister of the heavenly sanctuary (8:1, 2), he points out that the tabernacle of Judaism was but a "worldly" one. "The antithesis to worldly is heavenly, uncreated, eternal. Thus in the epistle to the Galatians, the apostle, speaking of the legal parenthetical dispensation, says we were then in bondage under the 'elements of the world' (4:2); and in the epistle to the Colossians he contrasts with the 'rudiments of the world' (2:20) the heavenly position of the believer who has died with Christ, and 'is no longer living in the world,' but seeking the things above" (A. Saphir).

"For there was a tabernacle made; the first, wherein was the candlestick, and the table, and the shewbread; which is called the sanctuary" (v. 2). "The subject spoken of is the tabernacle: that which is in general affirmed of it is that it was 'made.' There is a distribution of it into two parts in this and the following verse. These parts are described and distinguished by, first, their names; second, their situation with respect unto one another; third, their contents or sacred utensils. The one is described in this verse, by its situation: it was the 'first,' that which was first entered into; then by its utensils, which were three; then by its name; it was called the sanctuary" (J. Owen).

"For there was a tabernacle made." A full description of it is to be found in the book of Exodus. The "tent" proper was thirty cubits, or forty-five feet in length, ten cubits, or fifteen feet in breadth, and the same in height. In shape it formed an oblong square. It was divided by a veil into two parts of unequal size. This continued to form God's house of worship until the days of Solomon, when it was replaced by the more permanent and magnificent temple. It is pertinent to ask at this point, Why should the Holy Spirit here refer to the "tabernacle" rather than to the temple, which was still standing at the time the apostle was writing? The word "tabernacle" is found ten times in this epistle, but the "temple" is not mentioned once. This is the more remarkable because Paul, more than any of the apostles, emphasized the resurrection of Christ, and the temple particularly foreshadowed Him in His resurrection (and millennial) glory; whereas the tabernacle principally prefigured Christ in His humiliation and lowliness. Yet the difficulty is easily solved: the temple was not erected till after Israel were thoroughly settled in their inheritance, and the Holy Spirit is here addressing a people who were yet in the wilderness!

The Holy Spirit now makes a bare allusion to the holy vessels which occupied the two compartments of the tabernacle. But what *rule* has been given us to guide in and fix with certainty the interpretation of the mystical signification of these things? Certainly God has not left His people to the worthless devisings of their own imaginations. No, in this very epistle, He has graciously informed us that the tabernacle, and all contained in it, were typical of Christ, yet not as He may be considered absolutely, but as the Church is in mystical union with Him, for throughout Hebrews He is viewed in the discharge of His *mediatory* office. Thus the tabernacle, its holy vessels and services, supplied a representation of the person, work, offices and glories of Christ as the Head of His people. That it did so is clear from 8:2 — see our comments thereon. The *"true* tabernacle" there mentioned (our Lord's humanity) is not opposed to what is false and erroneous (the shrines of the heathen), but to the tabernacle of Moses, which was but figurative and transitory. In the Lord Jesus we have the substance of what Israel had only the shadow.

"For there was a tabernacle made: the first (compartment) wherein was the candlestick." It is to be noted that no mention is here made of the outer court. In this omission, as in so many others, the anointed eye may clearly discern the absolute control of the Spirit over the sacred writers, moving and guiding them in every detail. In our articles upon Exodus (1926 etc.) we have attempted a much fuller exposition than can here be given. Suffice it now to say that everything connected with the outer court was fulfilled by Christ in the days of His flesh. The very fact that it *was* the "outer" court, accessible to all the people and unroofed, at once denotes to us Christ here in the world, openly manifested before men. Its brazen altar spoke of the cross, where God publicly dealt with the sins of His people. Its fine-linen hangings spoke of Christ meeting the claims of God's righteousness and holiness. Its sixty pillars tell of the strength and power of Christ, "mighty to save." Its laver foreshadowed Christ cleansing His Church with the washing of water by the Word (John 13).

Now as the outer court viewed Christ on earth, so the holy places pointed to Him in heaven. The holy place was a chamber which was entered by none save the priestly family, where those favoured servants of Jehovah ministered before Him. It was therefore the place of *communion*. In perfect keeping with this, each of the three vessels that stood therein spoke of *fellowship*. The lampstand foreshadowed Christ as the *power* for fellowship, as supplying the light necessary to it. The table with its twelve loaves, prefigured Christ as the *substance* of our fellowship, the One on whom we feast. The incense-altar typified Christ as the *maintainer* of fellowship, by His intercession securing our continued acceptance before the Father. The reason why the "incense-altar" is not mentioned here in Heb. 9 will be taken up when we come to v. 4.

"For there was a tabernacle made: the first (compartment) wherein was the candlestick," or better, "lampstand." There was no window in the tabernacle, for the light of nature cannot reveal spiritual things. It was therefore illuminated from this holy vessel, which was placed on the south side, near the veil which concealed the holy of holies. A full description of it is given in Ex. 25:31-36. It was made of beaten gold, all of one piece, with all its lamps and ornamentations, so that it was without either joints or screws. Pure olive oil was provided for it.

The very fact that the lampstand stood in the holy place, at once shows that it is *not* Christ as "the Light of the world" which is typified. It is strange that many of the commentators have erred here. The words of Christ on this point are clear enough: "as long as I am in the world, I am the light of the world" (John 9:5 and cf. 12:35, 36): only then was He manifested here as such. But men loved darkness rather than light. They rejected the Light, and so far as they were concerned, extinguished it. Since Christ was put to death by wicked hands, the world has never again gazed on the Light. He is now hidden from their eyes. But He who was slain by the world, rose again, and then ascended on high, it is there in the Holy Place, in God's presence, that the Light now dwells. And while there— O marvelous privilege—the saints have access to Him.

Black shadows rest upon the world which has cast out the Light of Life: "the way of the wicked is as darkness" (Prov. 4:19). It is now night-time, for the "Dayspring from on high" is absent. The lampstand tells of the gracious provision which God has made for His own beloved people during the interval of darkness, ere the Sun of righteousness shall rise once more, and usher in for this earth that morning without clouds. Its seven branches and lamps constantly fed by oil, represented the fullness of light that is in Christ Jesus, and which by Him is communicated to His whole Church. The "oil" was poured *into* its lamps and then shed forth light *from* them. Such was and is the economical relation of the Spirit unto the Mediator. First, Christ was "anointed" with the Spirit "above His fellows" (Psa. 45:7 and cf. John 3:34), and then He sent forth the Spirit (Acts 2:33). Objectively the Spirit conveys light to us through the Word; subjectively, by inward and supernatural illumination.

"And the table and shewbread" (v. 2). Though intimately connected, yet these two objects may be distinguished in their typical significance. The natural relation of the one to the other, helps us to perceive their spiritual meaning: the bread was placed upon and thus was supported by the table. The "table" speaks of *communion*. A beautiful picture of this is found in 2 Sam. 9. There David asks, "Is there yet any that is left of the house of Saul, that I may show him kindness for Jonathan's sake?" (v. 1). A lovely illustration was this of the wondrous grace of God, showing kindness to those who belong to the house of His enemy, and that for the sake of His Beloved. There *was* one, even Mephibosheth, lame on his feet; him David "sent and fetched" unto himself. And then, to show he is fully reconciled to this grandson of his foe, David said, "but Mephibosheth thy master's son shall eat bread always at my table" (v. 10)—evidencing that he had been brought into the place of most intimate fellowship. 1 Cor. 10:20, 21 also shows the spiritual significance of the "table."

The "shewbread," or twelve loaves on the table, also spoke of Christ. "My Father giveth you the true bread from heaven" (John 6:32). The word "shewbread" is literally "bread of faces," faces being put by a figure for *presence*—pointing to the Divine presence in which the bread stood; "shewbread *before Me* alway" (Ex. 25:30). The twelve loaves, like the twelve precious stones in the high priest's breastplate, pictured the twelve tribes of Israel being represented before God. Thus, in type, it was the Lord Jesus identifying Himself with His covenant people.

"And after the second veil, the tabernacle which is called the holiest of all" (v. 3). The first veil was the "hanging" over the entrance into the tabernacle, shutting off from view what was inside from those who were in the outer court. It is described in Ex. 26:36, 37. The second veil, described in Ex. 26:31-33 and explained in Heb. 10:20, was a heavy curtain which concealed the contents of the holy of holies from those in the holy place. The Levitical family ministered in the holy place, but none save the high priest was allowed within the holiest of all, and he only one day in the year. Three things have been mentioned as occupying a place in the first tabernacle; seven objects are now mentioned in connection with the holiest of all.

"Which had the golden censer" (v. 4). First, we would note the minute accuracy of the wording here. In v. 2 it was said, "*Wherein was* the candlestick," etc., for the objects there mentioned belonged properly to the first compartment. But here it is, "*which had* the golden censer." Why? Because this utensil did not form part of the furniture of the holy of holies. To what then is the reference? Plainly to what is recorded in Lev. 16:12, 13, "And he shall take a censer full of burning coals of fire from off the (brazen) altar before the Lord, and his hands full of sweet incense beaten small, and bring *within the veil*: And he shall put the incense upon the fire before the Lord, that the cloud of the incense may cover the mercyseat that is upon the testimony, that he die not."

For three hundred and fifty-nine days in the year Aaron ministered at the golden or incense altar, which stood in the holy place; but on the remaining day, the annual "Day of Atonement," he did not.

Instead, he used the "golden censer" of incense, passing with it within the veil. It is *this* which explains why there is no mention of the "golden altar" in v. 2, for the Holy Spirit is here treating (see the later verses) of the Judaic ritual on the Day of Atonement, and the fulfillment of the type by the Lord Jesus. That which was represented by the "golden censer" was the acceptability of Christ's person to God and the efficacy of His intercession. the beautiful type of Lev. 16:12, 13 denotes that, in consequence of the satisfaction which Christ made unto God, completed at the cross, His mediatory intercession is a sweet savour unto the Father, and effective unto the salvation of His Church. The fact that the smoke of this perfume covered the ark and the mercyseat, wherein was the law, and over which the symbol of the Divine presence abode, denoted that Christ has magnified the law, met its every requirement, and is the end of the law for righteousness unto everyone that believeth.

"And the ark of the covenant overlaid round about with gold, wherein was the golden pot that had manna, and Aaron's rod that budded, and the tables of the covenant" (v. 4). The ark, with the mercyseat which formed its lid or cover, was the most glorious and mysterious vessel of the tabernacle. It was the first thing made (Ex. 25:10, 11), yea, the whole sanctuary was built for no other end but to be, as it were, a house and habitation for the ark (Ex. 26:33). The ark was the outstanding symbol that God Himself was present among His people and that His covenant-blessing was resting upon them. It was the coffer in which the tables of the law were preserved. Its preeminence above all the other vessels was shown in the days of Solomon, for the ark alone was transferred from the tabernacle to the temple.

The ark was an outstanding figure of the incarnate Son of God. The wood of which it was made, typified His sinless humanity. "Shittim" wood never rotted, and the Septuagint translation of the O. T. renders it "incorruptible wood." The wood was overlaid, within and without, with gold, prefiguring Christ's Divine glory. The two materials of which the ark was made symbolised the *union* of the two natures in the Godman—"God manifest in flesh" (1 Tim. 3:16). The ark formed God's throne in Israel: "Thou that dwellest between the cherubim" (Psa. 80:1). Christ is the only One who perfectly enthroned God, honouring His government in all things. Each of the seven names given to the ark in the O. T. set forth some excellency in the person of Christ. Everything connected with its most remarkable history, as in Num. 10: 33, 14:44, Josh. 3:5-17, 6:4-20, etc., received its antitypical fulfillment in the Godman.

"Wherein was the golden pot that had manna." Some have imagined a contradiction between this statement and what is said in 1 Kings 8:9, "There was nothing in the ark save the two tables of stone." But there is no conflict between the two passages, for they are not treating of the same point in time. Heb. 9:4 is speaking of what was in the ark during the days when it was lodged in the tabernacle, whereas 1 Kings 8:9 tells of what comprised its contents after it came to rest in the temple. It is important to note this distinction, for it supplies the key to the spiritual interpretation of our verse: Heb. 9:4 makes known God's provisions in Christ for His people while they are journeying through the wilderness. Thus, the "manna" was Israel's food from Egypt to Canaan: type of Christ as the heavenly sustenance for our souls. The preservation of the manna in the golden pot, speaks of Christ in glory at God's right hand.

"And Aaron's rod that budded." The reference is to what is recorded in Num. 17. In the preceding chapter we read of a revolt against Moses and Aaron, occasioned by jealousy at the authority which God had delegated to His two servants. The revolt of Korah and his company was visited by summary judgment from on high, and was followed by a manifest vindication of Aaron. The form that vindication took is most instructive. The Lord bade Moses take the twelve tribal rods, writing the name of Aaron on Levi's, laying them up before the ark, and affirming that the one which should be made to blossom would indicate which had been chosen of God to be the priestly tribe. Next morning it was found that Aaron's rod had "brought forth buds, and blossomed blossoms, and yielded almonds." Afterwards God ordered Moses to place Aaron's rod before the ark "to be kept for a token against the rebels." The lifeless rod being made to blossom was a figure of God's vindication of His rejected Son by raising Him from the dead. Thus it speaks of the resurrection-power of our great High Priest.

"And the tables of the covenant." The reference is to Deut. 10:1-5. The preservation of the two tables of stone (on which were inscribed the ten commandments) in the ark, foreshadowed Christ magnifying the law and making it honourable (Isa. 42:21). The fulfillment of this type is stated in Psa. 40:7, 8, where we hear the Mediator saying, "Lo, I come: in the volume of the book it is written of Me; I delight to do Thy will, O My God; Yea, *Thy law is within My heart.*" The Representative of God's people was "made under the law" (Gal. 4:4), and perfectly did He "fulfill" it (Matt. 5:17). Therefore is it written, "by the obedience of One shall many be made righteous" (Rom. 5:19). Thus may each believer exclaim, "In the Lord have I righteousness and strength" (Isa. 45:24).

"And over it the cherubims of glory shadowing the mercyseat; of which we cannot now speak particularly" (v. 5). At either end of the mercyseat was the form of a cherub with outstretched wings, meeting in the center, thus overshadowing and as it were protecting God's throne. That there is some profound significance connected with their figures is clear from the prominent place which they occupy in connection with the description of the mercyseat given in Ex. 25:17-22: mention is there made of the cherubim, in either the singular or plural number, no less than seven times. The mention of them in Gen. 3:24 suggests that they are associated with the administration of God's judicial authority. In Rev. 4:6-8 (cf. Ezek. 1:5-10) they are related to God's throne. Here in Heb. 9 they are called the "cherubim of glory" because the Shekinah abode between them.

The mercyseat, or better, "propitiatory," was the throne upon which the high priest placed the expiatory blood. It was *not* the place where propitiation was made—that was at the brazen altar—but where its abiding value was borne witness to before God. Rom. 3:25 gives us the antitype: by the Gospel God now "sets forth" (Gal. 3:1) Christ as the One by whom He has been placated, as the One by whom His holy wrath against the sins of His people has been pacified, as the One by whom the righteous demands of His law were satisfied, as the One by whom every attribute of Deity was glorified. Christ Himself is God's restingplace. in whom He now meets poor sinners in all the fulness of His grace because of the propitiation made by Him on the cross.

The last clause of the verse is translated more literally in Bagster's Interlinear thus: "concerning which it is not now (the time) to speak in detail"—the "concerning which" is not to be restricted to that which is found here in v. 5, but takes in all that has been mentioned in vv. 2-5. It would have led the apostle too far away from his subject of the high priest's service, to give an interpretation of the spiritual meaning of the tabernacle and everything in it. Nevertheles, he plainly intimates that every part of it had a specific significance as typical of the Lord Jesus and His ministry. A. W. P.

THE SATISFACTION
("Atonement")
OF CHRIST

15. *Its Results (Continued)*

In previous articles we have pointed out the importance of distinguishing between the work which Christ performed and the results which that work produced. The need for so doing is great if we are to obtain anything more than a confused view of it. Unfortunately many have sadly failed at this point, so that neither they nor their readers have been able to apprehend separately the various parts of the vast whole. Noticeably has this been the case with that aspect of our theme which is now to be before us. Though the work of the Lord Jesus was one and indivisible, yet, as we saw when pondering its nature, it needs to be viewed from various angles. For this reason, among others, the typical altar of sacrifice was not round, but foursquare (Ex. 27:1). In like manner, though the result secured by Christ's work was also one and indivisible, namely, securing the eternal *salvation* of all for whom He transacted, yet that composite "result," that glorious "salvation," can best be understood when we contemplate its several sides. We now take up,

3. *Redemption*

Not a few have regarded "atonement" and "redemption" as being synonymous terms, but they are not so. Though closely, yea inseparably connected, they are, nevertheless, capable of being considered separately; the one being the cause, of which the other is the effect. Because Christ offered unto God a full and accepted satisfaction, the redemption of His people is the certain fruit, consequence, and reward of the same. The "result" of Christ's mediation and the character of the salvation which He secured for God's elect, can be most easily grasped when set out under these four words: reconciliation, remission, redemption, righteousness. By saying above that the "result" of Christ's satisfaction is as indivisible as the work itself, we mean that when one of these blessings is imparted, the other three always accompany it.

Near the beginning of our last article we pointed out how close is the connection between reconciliation and remission of sins (2 Cor. 5:19), and to link up this one with the preceding, we would note how intimate is the relation existing between remission and redemption. In Eph. 1:7 we read, "In whom we have redemption through His blood, the forgiveness of sins." Sins are "forgiven" or "remitted" by the redeeming blood. The preposition should be duly noted here: it is not "*through*" whom we have redemption" (which presents another phase altogether), but "*in* whom." Redemption was the Christian's right, not only when the Spirit applied it to him at his regeneration, but also when Christ died. Just as we had condemnation in Adam before we were born into this world, so the elect have redemption in Christ since the time that He was raised from the dead: note that "believing" is not mentioned in Eph. 1 till v. 12! "Redemption through His blood" is our forgiveness. Not that we are *actually* pardoned in the blood of His cross before we believe, but that the pardon was procured by the redeeming blood, the grant of it was then sealed, and security given that it should in due time be made unto us.

The greatness of redemption may best be perceived by contemplating the person of the Redeemer. To none other than the Son of God was entrusted that work which was to secure redemption for His people. The greater the person who is employed in a work, the greater is that work; it is thus in the reckoning and ways of men, how much more shall it be so in the wisdom and ways of God! Kings do not send their sons out on petty errands or trivial services, but only upon that which is high and weighty; and can it be imagined that the King of kings would send forth His Son to redeem, unless that had involved a work of transcendent magnitude? The creating of the universe was a vast enterprise, but God dispatched it with a single fiat: He spake and it was done (Psa. 33:9). But to effect redemption, God sent His own Son from heaven to earth, to live and die. O how great a work was this; the greatest that Himself ever undertook. In approaching this blessed subject of redemption, let us consider,

1. *Its Signification*.

"The term redemption is borrowed from certain pecuniary transactions among men, as the release of an imprisoned debtor by liquidating his debt, or the deliverance of a captive by paying a ransom. These are transactions with which mankind in general, and especially the Jews and primitive Christians, have been perfectly familiar. Accordingly, both in the Hebrew and Greek Scriptures, the deliverance of man from sin is frequently represented by language borrowed from such negotiations. The term before us is of this nature. It involved all the ideas included in atonement. It supposes sin, which is the cause of imprisonment or captivity. It supposes deliverance by a substitute, the captive or debtor being unable to effect his own escape. And, of course, it supposes also a clear emancipation or restoration as the result of the ransom being paid." (W. Symington).

The terms "ransom" and "redemption" when used in connection with the work of Christ are correlative in their import, the former denoting the price paid for the liberation of a prisoner, the latter marking the deliverance which is thus effected. The use of them in connection with our salvation, shows that this is brought about by the interposition of a Substitute, who procures the emancipation of the captive by the tendering of his ransom. By their sins men are brought under obligations to the law and justice of God, which He will not gratuitously fail to demand, and which they are quite incapable of discharging. To the law of God they are debtors; of the justice of God the prisoners. Their deliverance or salvation is not a manumission without price, that is, a simple discharge without compensation. Their salvation is not by an act of power only, effected by the intervention of an arm full of might to secure their escape. Both gratuitous favour (grace) and power *are* concerned, yet there was more. A price had to be paid, a ransom laid down, every way equivalent to the redemption for which it was offered.

Thus, "redemption" is *deliverance by ransom*. It is possible to conceive (in human affairs) of a price being paid and then, through some mis-carriage of justice, the prisoner not being freed; but in that case it would not be a "redemption," even though a ransom had been accepted. So also we may suppose a case where a captor, moved by compassion, freed his prisoner; yet though emancipated, he could not be said to have been "redeemed." Two things are absolutely necessary to a "redemption," a ransom paid, and the setting free of the object or person purchased. The two things, though intimately related, are clearly distinguished in Jer. 31:11, "For the Lord hath redeemed Jacob, *and* ransomed him from the hand of him that was stronger than he." And again, "I will *ransom* them from the power of the grave; I will *redeem* them from death" (Hos. 13:14). Thus, we say again, Redemption is the payment of a ransom and the *release* of the ransomed. Hence it is strictly limited to the people of God. In no sense are the reprobate "redeemed." Election and redemption are of the same extent: they relate to the same individuals, to all such, and to none else. To affirm that any whom Christ redeemed are now in Hell is a flat contradiction in terms, for Hell is a *prison* (Matt. 5:25, 1 Peter 3:19); and we may add, the most horrible and terrible blasphemy.

The deliverance or redemption which the ransom-price paid by Christ to Divine justice has effected, consists of three parts. First, there is a complete delivering of His people from the guilt or penalty of sin. This is their Justification. This is set forth in such Scriptures as the following: "Being justified freely by His grace through the redemption that is in Christ Jesus" (Rom. 3:24), "Christ hath redeemed us from the curse of the law, being made a curse for us" (Gal. 3:13). Second, there is, in this life, a blessed deliverance from the dominion and bondage of sin. This is their Sanctification. This is set forth in such passages as these: "Who gave Himself for our sins, that He might deliver us from this *present* evil world" (Gal. 1:4), "Forasmuch as ye know that ye were not redeemed with corruptible things, as silver and gold, from your vain conversation ... but with the precious blood of Christ" (1 Peter 1:18, 19). Third, there is, at the second coming of Christ, a final deliverance from the very presence of sin. This is their Glorification. This is contemplated in Luke 21:28, "Lift up your heads, for your redemption draweth nigh," and "waiting for the adoption, the redemption of our body" (Rom. 8:23).

Redemption is the *setting free* of those who have been ransomed. The Greek word for "redemption" is actually rendered "delivered" in Heb. 11:35: "Not accepting deliverance," which means, they refused to accept release from their afflictions on the terms offered by their persecutors, namely, upon the condition of renouncing their faith. Christ is therefore denominated not only "the Redeemer," but "the Deliverer" (Rom. 11:26). That from which He has emancipated His people is set forth in the following passages: "Christ hath redeemed us from the curse of the law" (Gal. 3:13). "Who hath delivered us from the power of darkness" (Col. 1:13). "Which delivered us from the wrath to come" (1 Thess. 1:10). "That through death He might destroy him that had the power of death, that is, the devil; and deliver them who through fear of death were all their lifetime subject to bondage" (Heb. 2:14, 15). Let us next consider.

2. Its Implication.

Redemption necessarily supposes *previous possession*. It denotes the restoring of something that has been lost, and that by the paying of a price. Thus we find Christ saying by the Spirit of prophecy, "I *restored* that which I took not away" (Psa. 69:4)! This was strikingly illustrated in the history of Israel, who, on the farther shores of the Red Sea, sang, "Thou in Thy mercy hast led forth Thy people which Thou hast *redeemed*" (Ex. 15:13). First, in the book of Genesis, we see the descendants of Abraham, sojourning in the land of Canaan; cf. Heb. 11:9. Later, we see the chosen race in cruel servitude, in bondage to the Egyptians, groaning amid the brick-kilns under the whip of their taskmasters. Then a ransom was provided in the blood of the pascal lamb, following which, the Lord by His mighty hand brought them out of serfdom and brought them into the promised inheritance.

In the above type we see three things: a people who were the Lord's; a people in bondage, lost to Him; a people recovered and restored to Him. Says someone, "But how can all these things hold good in the antitype? I can see that Christians were once the Devil's captives, now freed by Christ; but how were they His *before* He freed them?" Ah, that is a question which no Arminian can answer. Yet Scripture supplies a satisfactory explanation. The type is just as true and accurate in the first point, as it is in the second and third. The redeemed belonged to Christ long before He shed His precious blood to ransom them. They were His by the eternal election of God, His by the Father's love gift: "Thine they were and Thou gavest them Me" (John 17:6). Yes, they were "chosen in Him before the foundation of the world" (Eph. 1:4). But, "in Adam *all* died" (1 Cor. 15:22), therefore did He come "to seek and to save that which was *lost*" (Luke 19:10). But through His blood He recovered them: "The church of God, which He hath *purchased* with His own blood" (Acts 20:28).

Thus, the implication of "redemption" is a double one. First, all the members of Christ's Church belonged to Him in eternity past. Second, through the Fall, they were brought into bondage. All men in their unrenewed state are slaves to sin and Satan, and under the wrath of God. "Whosoever committeth sin is the servant of sin" (John 8:34). Ere Christians were regenerated, "*serving* divers lusts and pleasures" (Titus 3:3) described their awful state. In the bondage of our ignorance, we supposed that we were free, imagining that liberty consisted of the power to do as we liked, instead of as we ought. Little did we dream that we were in the "snare of the Devil, who are taken captive by him at his will" (2 Tim. 2:26). Nor could we free ourselves. Sin's chains were far too strong for human might to snap. Satan saw to it that we should not break out of his prisonhouse.

Man as a fallen creature is no more a "free agent" than he is a sinless being. "If the Son therefore shall *make you free* ye shall be free indeed" (John 8:36) would be quite meaningless, if the natural man already possessed liberty. But people will no more bow to this flesh-humbling truth today than they would when Christ Himself uttered it—"we be Abraham's seed and were never in bondage to any man" (John 8:33) was the haughty but lying boast of the Jews. Hence it is that so very, very few seek the redemption which is in Christ Jesus: knowing not that *they* are bound; they suppose they are already free. This is one of the outstanding marks of these Laodicean days: men boasting that they are rich and increased with goods, and in need of nothing, knowing not that they are "wretched and miserable and poor and blind and naked" (Rev. 3:17). Yes, redemption presupposes bondage; happy the one who has had his or her eyes opened to see the need for a mightier hand than their own striking off the shackles of self-will, self-love and self-righteousness, which, by nature, bound and held them fast. We now turn to consider,

3. *Its Effectuation*

Sin is a debt, whereof God is the Creditor: Matt. 6:12. Debts render men liable to imprisonment for non-payment, so sin has caused God to "shut them all up in unbelief" (Rom. 11:32), nor can any escape till the uttermost farthing has been paid (Matt. 5:26). Man, by his disobedience to God, has been brought into a state of abject wretchedness, such wretchedness as Scripture often expresses it by *captivity* Isa. 61:1, Psa. 126:4, 2 Tim. 3:6. The Lord, because of our rebellion, both in Adam and personally, did, as the supreme Judge and Governor, deliver us unto Satan, and left us under the power of sin and death. Satan, as the jailor, led us captive at his will, making use of sin and the world as fetters to increase and continue our misery: "Wherein in time past ye walked according to the course of this world, according to the prince of the power of the air, the spirit that now worketh in the children of disobedience: among whom also we all had our conversation in times past in the lusts of our flesh" (Eph. 2:2, 3). From this dreadful state none but Christ could deliver us.

In every place in Scripture where our redemption in and by Christ is mentioned, there is an allusion to the law of redemption among the Jews. This law is set forth, most fully, in Lev. 25, where we find regulations laid down for a twofold redemption, of persons and possessions. None had a right to redeem but either the person himself, who had made the alienation, or some other that was near of kin to him. But inasmuch as none of Adam's race ever was, or ever will be, able to redeem himself, Another must interpose on his behalf if ever he is to be delivered. This is expressly affirmed by God: "None of them can by any means redeem his brother, nor give to God a ransom for him" (Psa. 49:7). Thus, poor sinners were entirely shut up to the merciful intervention of Christ. It was by Him and Him alone, this blessed promise was to be fulfilled: "Thus saith the Lord, Even the captives of the mighty shall be taken away, and the prey of the terrible shall be delivered:

for I will contend with him that contendeth with thee, and I will save thy children" (Isa. 49:25).

The Redeemer must be *Kinsman*: "The man is near of kin to us, one that hath 'he *right* to redeem" (Ruth 2:20 margin). Thus the *covenant-oneness* of Christ and His people underlies the truth of redemption: "For both He that sanctifieth and they who are sanctified are all of one: for which cause He is not ashamed to call them brethren" (Heb. 2:11)—one from all eternity, one by His having been appointed their Head. But not only must the Redeemer be federally united to those He redeems, but He must also take upon Him their nature and enter their circumstances, therefore are we told, "Forasmuch then as the children are partakers of flesh and blood, He also Himself likewise took part of the same; that through death He might destroy him that had the power of death, that is, the Devil; and *deliver* them" (Heb. 2:14, 15). So we read again, "God sent forth His Son made of a woman, made under the law, *to redeem* them that were under the law" (Gal. 4:4, 5).

The incarnation of the Son of God most strikingly fulfilled another O. T. type of redemption. The Mosaic law provided that, in case any person was found murdered, then the nearest to him in blood was to prosecute the murderer and bring him to justice, and this nearest relation, thus avenging the murder, is called by the name of (Ga'al) *redeemer*, rendered "revenger" in Num. 25:19. "Satan was the murderer from the beginning (John 8:44) who had given both body and soul a mortal wound of sin, which was certain death and eternal misery, and the Redeemer came to avenge the murder. He took our cause in hand, as being our nearest kinsman, and it cost Him His own life to avenge ours" (Wm. Romaine, 1750). To which we may add, through His death, Christ "destroyed (rendered null) him that *had* the power of death" (Heb. 2:14).

Having accepted the office of Redeemer, having become one with His people in taking upon Him their nature, it was required that He should pay the ransom-price which Divine justice required. Now a "ransom" is something given in the stead of what is ransomed, and this was the vicarious life and death of the Lord Jesus: "the Son of man came, to give His life a ransom for many" (Matt. 20:28). Redemption views Christ as our "Surety" (Heb. 7:22), taking upon Him the liabilities of God's elect, and paying to God the price of their remission. Christ is the great Paymaster of His people's debts: "That by means of death, for the redemption of *the transgressions* under the first testament, they which are called might receive the promise of eternal inheritance" (Heb. 9:15). "Being justified freely by His grace through the redemption that is in Christ Jesus" (Rom. 3:24): in the first clause the inestimable blessing of justification is ascribed to the free grace of God, being altogether apart from our works, either before or after faith; in the second clause it is attributed to Christ's "redemption:" though we are justified gratuitously, yet it is through the purchase of the Son of God.

Believers are said to have been "bought with a price" (1 Cor. 6:20). *To whom* was the ransom-price paid? It seems strange that any Christian should experience difficulty in answering such a question, yet even some able Bible students have erred seriously on this point. Arguing that sinners were never in bondage to God, and that they are the captives of the Devil, a theory has been invented that the price of our ransom was paid to Satan himself, which theory can only be rightly denominated "diabolical redemption." Once this theory is held up in its naked hideousness, every renewed soul ought to shrink from it in horror. Surely there is a vast difference between sinners being the captives of the Devil, and his having any legitimate property-rights over them. That man is a slave of Satan is only a secondary result of his bondage. *Who* delivered him over to Satan, on account of his sins? Only one answer is possible: God Himself.

It is by Divine justice that the sinner is bound over to punishment. The Devil is only the *executioner* of God's righteous sentence. It is to God Himself the debt of obedience and suffering is due. It is God alone who has the right to detain him in prison. The detaining power is the equity of the Divine law and government, but for which, Satan could not hold him in thraldom a single moment. Therefore it was *to God*, to His inflexible justice, that Christ paid the ransom-price. Man had not sinned against Satan, but against the divine Lawgiver, to whom alone it belongs to condemn or absolve. And God being satisfied, the Devil has no power over the redeemed, but is put out of office, as the executioner has nothing to do when the judge and the law is satisfied. To say that Christ offered Himself a ransom unto Satan is the most horrible blasphemy. Satan was to be conquered, not satisfied. Our enslaving foe, was but the subordinate instrument of God's righteous judgment; why, he cannot so much as tempt men without the immediate permission of God, how much less could he demand from God the precious, precious blood of Christ.

The ransom which was paid for our redemption was the blood of Christ (1 Peter 1:19): this is sometimes set forth as a "price," sometimes as a "sacrifice." These are but one and the same thing under several notions. Now as the "sacrifice" was offered *unto God* (Eph. 5:2), so was the "price" paid to God, paid to His justice, paid to Him in His character of Judge and Governor. "Who hath delivered us from the power of darkness, and hath translated us into the kingdom of His dear Son: in whom we have redemption through His blood" (Col. 1:13, 14). The latter verse explains the particular nature of the "deliverance" in the previous one. It is not a mere release, as of a slave liberated, by the compassion of his master, nor that of a debtor set free at his constant entreaties by his creditor; nor by the exercise of force only, as Abraham delivered Lot and David his followers from the Amalekites at Ziglag. But this "deliverance" from Satan's dominion is a *redemption*, a discharge by a ransom-price paid down; there was a rendering all that was due the law by a Substitute and Surety. The shedding of His blood was the last and greatest act of His mediatorial work on earth.

Thus Christ purchased His people out of the hands of vindictive Justice. Thereby He fulfilled that remarkable Messianic prophecy in Isa 45:13, "I have raised Him up in righteousness, and I will direct all His ways: He shall build My city, and He shall let go My captives, not for price nor reward, saith the Lord of hosts:" the last clause signifies, it was not for personal gain that Christ did this: it was not "for price," though He effected it *by* price. Because Christ "bought" us (1 Cor. 6:20), we are out of debt, free. There is not a single charge on the heavenly docket against any of His people. No debtor's prison now awaits them. "Though shalt by no means come out thence, till thou hast paid the uttermost farthing" (Matt. 5:26): these terrible and hope-destroying words shall never be spoken to any of the *redeemed*.

Because the Representative of God's people was siezed by the law, those whom Christ represented *must* go free. Beautifully was this adumbrated in John 18:8: "if therefore ye seek Me, let *these go* their way." Christ's death was the believer's discharge: "Who is he that condemneth? It is Christ that died" (Rom. 8:33). "On that day shall the priest make an atonement for you, to cleanse you, that ye may be clean from *all* your sins before the Lord" (Lev. 16:30): if the typical blood so effectively cleansed the people ceremonially, how much more must the antitypical Sacrifice perfectly and eternally deliver from sin! The outcome of the ransom-price paid by Christ is the certain and actual redemption of His people.

There is *no unavailing* redemption in any of the O. T. types. If land was "redeemed," *restoration* to its original owner was the *certain* outcome; if persons were "redeemed," then liberty was actually enjoyed by them. "*Deliver* him from going down to the Pit, I have found a *ransom*" (Job 33:24), is God's authoritative fiat. Payment God cannot twice demand, first at my bleeding Surety's hand, and then again at mine. Because Christ paid to the full the whole debt which His people owed, Justice *demands* that the debtors should be liberated. Therefore the unqualifying word goes forth, "And the ransomed of the Lord *shall* return, and come to Zion with songs and everlasting joy upon their heads" (Isa. 35:10).

4. *Its Application.*

"Blessed be the Lord God of Israel, for He hath visited and redeemed *His people*" (Luke 1:70). "The *Church of God* which He hath purchased with His own blood" (Acts 20:28). It is never said in Scripture that Christ died to purchase "salvation:" it is always His flock, His people, His Church. "The Lord's portion is His people, Jacob is the lot of His inheritance" (Deut. 32:9), and the elect are not only God's inheritance, but His "*purchased* possession" (Eph. 1:14). By His death Christ paid the ransom-price, and made His people, whom sin had taken prisoners, His own. Therefore does the Father say to Him, "As for Thee, by the blood of Thy covenant I have sent forth *Thy* prisoners out of the pit wherein is no water" (Zech. 9:11). Christ has a legal right to their persons, and therefore does God, by His strong arm (in His own appointed time), bring them forth. "He *sent* redemption unto His people" (Psa. 111:9).

Redemption is *unto an inheritance*: Gal. 4:5-7, Eph. 1:14. Now just as an earthly parent reserves to himself the right to say (in his will) at what age his heir shall enter upon his estate, so God has appointed the time when each of His redeemed ones shall be freed from the dominion of sin, and when the whole election of grace shall enter their inheritance. As we have seen, the deliverance which Christ has procured for His people is threefold, so also is its application. First, they are freed from the guilt of sin when the Spirit first works faith in them and they are enabled to believe in Christ (Gal. 5:1). Second, they are gradually delivered from the power of indwelling sin, as through the Spirit they are led to *"mortify* the deeds of the body" (Rom. 8:13). Third, they are completely emancipated from the presence of sin when "there shall come out of Zion the Deliverer, and shall turn away ungodliness from Jacob" (Rom. 11:26, etc.). Each of these is redemption by *power*, in contrast from by price: cf. Ex. 6:6, Neh. 1:10, Psa. 77:15; for the same reason the resurrection of the body, by an act of Divine power, is called a "redemption" (Rom. 8:23).

5. *Its Manifestation.*

Redemption is unto *a life of godliness*. "Being now made free from sin, and become servants to God, ye have your fruit unto holiness, and the end everlasting life" (Rom. 6:22). Those whom Christ has ransomed are given grace to live a holy life, freed from the bondage of their former corruptions: "redeemed . . . *from* your vain conversation . . . with the precious blood of Christ" (1 Peter 1:18). Those who are not delivered from their previous vain manner of life are not redeemed from hell and damnation, unless God gives them repentance. Let every reader test himself or herself by this sure and certain rule: you have not savingly believed that Christ laid down *His* life for you, unless *you* are now yielding up your life to Him: note the words, "in time past" in Eph. 2:2. Christ has redeemed none that they might continue in a course of self-pleasing.

"That we being delivered out of the hand of our enemies might serve Him without fear, in holiness and righteousness before Him, *all* the days of our life" (Luke 1:74, 75). "Whenever God pardons sin, He subdues it (Micah 7:19). Then is the condemning power of sin taken away, when the commanding power of it is taken away. If a malefactor be in prison, how shall he know that his prince hath pardoned him? If a jailor come and knock off his chains and fetters, and let him out of prison, then he may know that he *is* pardoned: so if we walk at liberty (Psa. 119:45) in the ways of God, this is a blessed sign He has pardoned us" (Thos. Watson, 1690).

Let none make any mistake on this point. Scripture says "who gave Himself for our sins, that He might *deliver us from* this *present* evil world" (Gal. 1:4). If, then, you are still in love with the world, a slave to its fashions, a follower of its ways, a companion of its people, you are yet in your sins. "Christ gave Himself for us that He might redeem us from all iniquity, and purify unto Himself a peculiar people, *zealous of good works"* (Titus 2:14). Christ offers Himself to none as a Saviour who are unwilling to submit to Him as their Lord. True, He has redeemed us from the "curse of the law," but most certainly not from the *righteous requirements* of the law. The people of God have been redeemed from their misery, but not from their duty. We have been redeemed *"to God"* (Rev. 5:9). Renunciation of the world, denial of self, and a daily walk to the glory of God, are the sure marks of *all* the "redeemed."

A. W. P.

PROFITING FROM THE WORD

4. *The Scriptures and Prayer.*

A prayerless Christian is a contradiction in terms. Just as a still-born child is a dead one, so a professing believer who prays not is devoid of spiritual life. Prayer is the breath of the new nature in the saint, as the Word of God is its food. When the Lord would assure the Damascus disciple that Saul of Tarsus had been truly converted, He told him, "Behold, he prayeth" (Acts 9:11). On many occasions had that self-righteous Pharisee bowed his knees before God and gone through his "devotions," but this was the first time he had ever really *prayed*. This important distinction needs emphasizing in this day of powerless forms (2 Tim. 3:5). They who content themselves with formal addresses unto God, know Him not; for "the spirit of grace *and* of supplications" (Zech. 12:10) are never separated. God has no dumb children in His regenerated family: "shall not God avenge His own elect, which cry day and night unto Him?" (Luke 18:7). Yes, "cry" unto Him, not merely "say their prayers."

But will the reader be surprised when the writer declares it is his deepening conviction that, probably, the Lord's own people sin more in their effort to pray than in connection with any other one thing they engage in. O what hypocrisy there is, where there should be reality. O what presumptuous demandings, where there should be submissiveness. O what formality, where there should be brokenness of heart. How little we really *feel* the sins we confess, and what little *sense* of deep need for the mercies we seek. And even where God grants a measure of deliverance from these awful sins, how much coldness of heart, how much unbelief, how much self-will and self-pleasing have we to bewail. Those who have no conscience upon these things are strangers to the spirit of holiness.

Now the Word of God should be our directory in prayer. Alas, how often have we made our own fleshly inclinations the rule of our asking. The holy Scriptures have been given to us "that the man of God may be perfect, throughly furnished unto *all* good works" (2 Tim. 3:17). Since we are required to "pray in the Spirit" (Jude 20), it follows that our prayers ought to be according to the Scriptures, seeing that He is their Author throughout. It equally follows that according to the measure in which the Word of Christ dwells in us "richly" (Col. 3:16) or sparcely, the more or the less will our petitions be in harmony with the mind of the Spirit, for "out of the abundance of the heart the mouth speaketh" (Matt. 12:34). In proportion as we hide the Word in our hearts, and it cleanses, moulds and regulates our inner man, will our prayers be acceptable in God's sight. Then shall we be able to say, as David did in another connection, "Of Thine own have we given Thee" (1 Chron. 29:14).

Thus, the purity and power of our prayer-life is another index by which we may determine the extent to which we are profiting from our reading and searching of the Scriptures. If our Bible-study is not, under the blessing of the Spirit, convicting us of the sin of prayerlessness, revealing to us the place which prayer ought to have in our daily lives, and is actually bringing us *to* spend more time in the secret-place of the Most High; unless it is teaching us how to pray more acceptably to God, how to appropriate His promises, and plead them before Him, how to appropriate His precepts and turn them into petitions; then, the time we have spent over the Word has not only been to little or no soul enrichment, but the very knowledge we have acquired of its letter will only add to our condemnation in the Day to come. "Be ye *doers* of the Word, and not hearers only, deceiving your own selves" (James 1:22), applies to its prayer-admonitions as to everything else contained in it. Let us now point out seven criteria.

1. We are profited from the Scriptures when we are brought to realize *the deep importance of prayer*. It is greatly to be feared that many present-day readers (and even students) of the Bible have no deep convictions that a definite prayer-life is absolutely essential to a daily walking and communing with God, as it is for deliverance from the power of indwelling sin, the seductions of the world, and the assaults of Satan. If such a conviction really gripped their hearts, would they not spend far more time on their faces before God? It is worse than idle to reply. A multitude of duties which have to be performed crowd out prayer, though much against my wishes. But the fact remains that each of us takes time for any thing we deem to be imperative. Who ever lived a busier life than our Saviour? Yet who found more time for prayer! If we truly yearn to be supplicants and intercessors before God and use all the available time we now have, He will so order things for us that we shall have more time.

This lack of a positive conviction of the deep importance of prayer is plainly evidenced in the corporate life of professing Christians. God has plainly said, "My house shall be called the house of prayer" (Matt. 21.13). Note, not "the house of preaching and singing," but of *prayer*. Yet, in the great majority of even the so-called orthodox churches, the ministry of prayer has become a negligible quantity. There are still evangelistic campaigns, and Bible-teaching conferences, but how rarely one hears of two weeks set apart for special prayer! And how much good do these "Bible conferences" accomplish if the prayer-life of the "churches" is not strengthened? But when the Spirit of God applies in power to our hearts such words as, "Watch ye and pray, lest ye enter into temptation" (Mark 14:38), "In every thing by prayer and supplication with thanksgiving, let your requests be made known to God" (Phil. 4:6), "Continue in prayer and watch in the same with thanksgiving"

(Col. 4:2), then are we being profited from the Scriptures.

2. We are profited from the Scriptures when we are made to feel that *we know not how to pray*. "We know not what we should pray for as we ought" (Rom. 8:26). How very few professing Christians really believe this. The idea most generally entertained is, that people know well enough what they should pray for, only they are careless and wicked, and so fail to pray for what they are fully assured is their duty. But such a conception is at direct variance with this inspired declaration in Rom. 8:26. It is to be observed that that flesh-humbling affirmation is made not simply of men in general, but of the saints of God in particular, among which the apostle hesitated not to include himself: "*we* know not what we should pray for as we ought." If this be the condition of the regenerate, how much more so of the unregenerate! Yet, it is one thing to read and mentally assent to what this verse says, but it is quite another to have an experimental realization of it, for the heart to be made to feel, that what God requires from us He must *Himself* work in and through us.

"I often say my prayers,
But do I ever pray?
Or do the wishes of my heart,
Dictate the words I say?
I might as well kneel down
And worship gods of stone,
As offer to the living God,
A prayer of words alone."

It is many years since the writer was taught these lines by his mother—now "present with the Lord"— but their searching message still comes home with force to him. The Christian can no more *pray* without the direct enabling of the Holy Spirit than he can create a world. This must be so, for real prayer is a felt need awakened within us by the Spirit, so that we ask God, in the name of Christ, for that which is in accord with His holy will. "If we ask anything acording to His will, He heareth us" (1 John 5:14). But to ask for something which is not according to God's will, is not praying, but presuming. True, God's revealed will is made known in His Word, yet not in such a way as a cookery-book contains recipes and directions for the preparing of various dishes. The Scriptures frequently enunciate principles, which call for continuous exercise of heart and Divine help to show us their application unto different cases and circumstances. Thus, we are being profited from the Scriptures when we are taught our deep need of crying "Lord, *teach* us *to* pray" (Luke 11:1), and are actually constrained to beg Him for the spirit of prayer.

3. We are profited from the Scriptures when we are made conscious of *our need of the Spirit's help*. First, that He may make known to us our real wants. Take, for example, our temporal needs. How often we are in some external strait, things from without press hard upon us, and we long to be delivered from these trials and difficulties. Surely *here* we "know" of ourselves *what* to pray for. No, indeed; far from it. The truth is that, despite our *natural* desires for relief, so ignorant are we, so dull is our discernment that (even where there is an exercised conscience) we know not who submission unto His pleasure God may require, or how He may sanctify these afflictions to our inner good. Therefore does God call the petitions of most who seek for relief from external trials, "howlings," and not a crying unto Him with the heart: see Hos. 7:14. "For who knoweth *what* is good for man in this life?" (Eccl. 6:12). Ah, heavenly wisdom is needed to teach us our temporal "needs" so as to make them the matter of prayer according to the mind of God.

Perhaps a few words need to be added to what has just been said. Temporal things *may be* scripturally prayed for (Matt. 6:11, etc.), but with this threefold limitation. First, *incidentally* and not primarily, for they are not the things which Christians are principally concerned in: Matt. 6:33. It is heavenly and eternal things (Col. 3:1), which are to be sought first and foremost, as of far greater importance and value than temporal things. Second, *subordinately*, as a means to an end. In seeking material things from God it should not be in order that we may be gratified, but as an aid to our pleasing Him better. Third, *submissively*, not dictatorially, for that would be the sin of persumption. Moreover, we know not whether any temporal mercy would really contribute to our highest good (Psa. 106:18), and therefore we must leave it with God to decide.

We have inward wants as well as outward. Some of these may be discerned in the light of conscience: such as the guilt and defilement of sin, of sins against the light of nature and the plain letter of the law. Nevertheless, the knowledge which we have of ourselves by means of the conscience is so dark and confused that, apart from the Spirit, we are no ways able to discover the true fountain of cleansing. The things about which believers do and ought to treat, primarily, with God in their supplications, are the inward frames and spiritual dispositions of their souls. Thus, David was not satisfied with confessing all known transgressions and his original sin (Psa. 51:1-5), nor yet with an acknowledgment that none can understand his errors, whence he desired to be cleansed from "secret faults" (Psa. 19:12); but he also begged God to undertake the inward searching of his heart to find out what was amiss in him (Psa. 139:23, 24); knowing that God principally requireth "truth in the inward parts" (Psa. 51:6). Thus, in view of 1 Cor. 2:10-12 we should definitely seek the Spirit's aid that we may pray acceptably to God.

4. We are profited from the Scriptures when the Spirit teaches us *the right end on praying.* God has appointed the ordinance of prayer with at least a threefold design. First, that the great Triune God might be honoured, for prayer is an act of worship, a paying homage; to the Father as the Giver; in the Son's name, by whom alone we may approach Him; by the moving and directing power of the Holy Spirit. Second, to humble our hearts, for prayer is ordained to bring us into the place of dependency, to develope within us a sense of our helplessness, by owning that without the Lord we can do nothing, and that we are beggars upon His charity for everything we are and have. But how feebly is this realized (if it be at all) by any of us until the Spirit takes us in hand, removes pride from us, and gives God His true place in our hearts and thoughts. Third, as a means or way of obtaining for ourselves the good things for which we ask.

It is greatly to be feared that one of the principal reasons why so many of our prayers remain unanswered, is because we have a wrong, an unworthy, end in view. Our Saviour said, "Ask, and ye shall receive," (Matt. 7:7); but James affirms of some, "Ye ask, and receive not, because ye ask amiss, that ye may consume it upon your pleasures" (James 4:3). To pray for anything, and not expressly unto the end which God has designed, is to "ask amiss," and therefore, to no purpose. Whatever confidence we may have of our own wisdom and integrity, if we are left to ourselves, our aims will never be suited to the will of God. Unless the Spirit restrains the flesh within us, our own natural and distempered affections immex themselves in our supplications, and thus they are rendered vain. "Whatsoever ye do, do all to the glory of God" (1 Cor. 10:31), yet none but the Spirit can enable us to subordinate all our desires unto God's glory.

5. We are profited from the Scriptures when we are taught *how to plead God's promises.* Prayer must be in faith (Rom. 10:14), or God will not hear it. Now faith respects God's promises (Heb. 4:1, Rom. 4:21), if therefore we understand not what God stands pledged to give, we cannot pray at all. The promises of God contain the matter of prayer and define the measure of it. What God has promised, all that He has promised, and nothing else, are we to pray for. "Secret things belong unto the Lord our God" (Deut. 29:29), but the declaration of His will and the revelation of His grace belong unto us, and is our rule. There is nothing that we really stand in need of, but God has promised to supply it, but yet in such a way and under such limitations as will make it good and useful to us. So too there is nothing that God has promised but we stand in need of it, or are some way or other concerned in it as members of the mystical body of Christ. Hence, the better we are acquainted with the Divine promises and the more we are enabled to understand the goodness, grace and mercy that is prepared and proposed in them, the better equipped are we for acceptable praying.

Some of God's promises are general, rather than specific; some are conditional, others unconditional; some are fulfilled in this life, others in the world to come. Nor are we able of ourselves to discern either which promise is most suited to our particular case and present emergency and need, or to appropriate by faith and rightly plead it before God. Wherefore we are expressly told, "For what man knoweth the things of a man, save the spirit of man which is in him? even so the things of God knoweth no man, but the Spirit of God. Now we have received, not the spirit of the world, but the Spirit which is of God; that we might know the things that are freely given to us of God" (1 Cor. 2:11, 12). Should someone reply, If so much be required unto acceptable praying, if we cannot supplicate God aright without much less trouble than you indicate, then few will continue long in this duty. Then we answer, such an objector knows not what it is to pray, nor seems willing to learn.

6. We are profited from the Scriptures when we are brought to *complete submission unto God*. As stated above, one of the Divine designs in appointing prayer as an ordinance was that we might be humbled. This is outwardly denoted when we bow the knee before the Lord. Prayer is an acknowledgment of our helplessness, and a looking to Him from whom all our help cometh. It is an owning of His sufficiency to supply our every need. It is a making known our "requests" (Phil. 4:6) unto God; but "requests" are very different from *demands*. "The throne of grace is not set up that we may come and there vent our sudden distempered passions before God" (Wm. Gurnall, Puritan). We are to spread our case before God, but leave it to His superior wisdom to prescribe how it shall be dealt with. There must be no dictating, nor can we "claim" anything from God, for we are beggars dependent upon His mere mercy. In all our praying we must add, "Nevertheless, not as I will, but as Thou wilt."

But may not faith plead God's promises and expect an answer? Certainly; but it must be *God's* answer. Paul besought the Lord thrice to remove his thorn in the flesh; instead of so doing, the Lord gave him grace to endure it (2 Cor. 12). Many of God's promises are promiscuous, rather than personal. He has promised His Church, pastors, teachers and evangelists, yet many a local company of His saints has languished long without either. Some of God' promises are indefinite and general, rather than absolute and universal: as for example Eph. 6:2, 3. God has not bound Himself to always give in kind or specie, to grant the particular thing we ask for, even though we ask in faith. Moreover, He reserves to *Himself* the right to determine the fit time and season for bestowing His mercies. "Seek ye the Lord, all ye meek of the earth . . . it *may be* ye shall be hid in the day of the Lord's anger" (Zeph. 2:3). Just because it "may be" God's will to grant a certain temporal mercy unto me, it is my duty to cast myself upon Him, plead for it, yet with entire submission to His good pleasure for the performance of it.

7. We are profited from the Scriptures when prayer becomes *a real and deep joy*. To merely "say our prayers" each morning and evening is an irksome task, a duty to be performed which brings a sigh of relief when it is done. But to really come into the conscious presence of God, to behold the glorious light of His countenance, to commune with Him at the mercyseat, is a foretaste of the eternal bliss awaiting us in Heaven. The one who is blest with this experience says with the Psalmist, "It is good for me to draw near to God" (73:28). Yes, good for the heart, for it is quietened; good for faith, for it is strengthened; good for the soul, for it is blest. It is the lack of this soul-communion with God which is the root cause of our unanswered prayers: "Delight thyself also in the Lord; and He *shall* give thee the desires of thine heart" (Psa. 37:4).

What is it which, under the blessing of the Spirit, produces and promote this joy in prayer? First, it is the heart's delight in God as the Object of prayer, and particularly, the recognition and realization of God as *our Father*. Thus, when the disciples asked the Lord Jesus to teach them to pray, He said, "After this manner, pray ye: Our Father which art in heaven." And again, "God hath sent forth the Spirit of His Son into your hearts, crying, Abba (the Heb. for 'Father'), Father" (Gal. 4:6), which includes a filial, holy delight in God, such as children have in their parents in their most affectionate addresses unto them. So again in Eph. 2:18 we are told, for the strengthening of faith and the comfort of our hearts, "For through Him (Christ) we both have access by one Spirit unto *the Father*." What peace, what assurance, what freedom this gives to the soul: to know we are approaching our Father!

Second, joy in prayer is furthered by the heart's apprehension and the soul's sight of God as on the throne of *grace*. A "sight" or prospect, not by carnal imagination, but spiritual illumination, for it is by faith we "see" Him which is invisible (Heb. 11:27); faith being the "evidence of things not seen" (Heb. 11:1), making its proper object evident and present unto them that do believe. Such a sight of God upon *such* a "throne" cannot but thrill the soul. Therefore are we exhorted, "Let us therefore come boldly unto the throne of grace, that we may obtain mercy, and find grace to help in time of need" (Heb. 4:16).

Thirdly, and drawn from the last-quoted Scripture, freedom and delight in prayer is stimulated by the consciousness that God is, through Jesus Christ, *willing and ready* to dispense grace and mercy to suppliant sinners. There is no reluctance in Him which we have to overcome. He is more ready to give, than we are to receive. So He is represented in Isa. 30:18, "And therefore will the Lord wait, that He may be gracious unto you." Yes, He waits to be sought unto; waits for faith to lay hold of His readiness to bless. His ear is ever opened to the cries of the righteous. Then let us "draw near with a true heart, in *full assurance* of faith" (Heb. 10:23), and "in *everything* by prayer and supplication, with thanksgiving, let your requests be made known unto God," and we shall find that peace which passeth all understanding guarding our hearts and minds through Christ Jesus (Phil. 4:6, 7). A. W. P.

SUBJECTION TO GOD

Obedience to the Lord is one of the chief characteristics of a genuine Christian (Rom. 6:22). By nature, we are not in subjection to God, for man is "born like a wild ass's colt" (Job 11:12). Therefore is it written, "the carnal mind is enmity against God: for it is not subject to the law of God, neither indeed can be" (Rom. 8:7). As they contemplate their unregenerate days, the Lord's people sorrowfully confess, "all we like sheep have gone astray; we have turned every one to *his own* way" (Isa. 53:6). Yes, that is the very quintessence of sin: the determination to have our own way. Thus it was at the beginning: our first parents in Eden chafed at the Divine restraint and took matters into their own hands. Thus it has been ever since: the history of the human race has been one of revolt and rebellion against God.

Now true conversion is a being brought into subjection to God. First, the conscience is convicted of insubordination to God and is made to tremble for having so long and so grievously defied Him. His claims are now recognized and felt, and there is a broken-hearted repentance for having ignored those claims. Second, there is a breaking of our wills, a subduing of the fleshly principle within, and a being made willing for God to rule us (Psa. 110:3). Self-love, self-will and self-righteousness receive their death-wound. Third, there is wrought in the heart a readiness to submit to God's way of salvation (Rom. 10:3), so that we come as empty-handed beggars to receive out of the fulness of His grace. Fourth, there is a receiving of Christ Jesus as *Lord* (Col. 2:6).

The true and normal Christian life consists of being in subjection to God. The attitude of the renewed heart is, "Lord, what wouldst Thou have me to do?" No longer is there the determination to have our own way, but instead, the dominating longing is to please, to honour, to obey, the Lord in all things. We are now able to say, "For to me to live is Christ" (Phil. 1:21): that is, to be ruled by Him, to seek only His glory. It is a taking of Christ's "yoke" upon us and learning of Him (Matt. 11:29): learning from the example He has left us, that we should "follow His steps" (1 Peter 2:21). It is a "living *by* (not only 'on') *every* word that proceedeth out of the mouth of God" (Matt. 4:4): searching it diligently from end to end to discover His revealed will, and bringing all our ways into conformity therewith.

In His Word God has made known the details of this subjection which He requires from us, and that, as it concerns every aspect and relationship of our lives. The church is to be in subjection to its glorious Head in all things (Eph. 5:24). As sojourners on earth, we are to be in subjection to the powers that be (Rom. 13:1) etc., paying our taxes and obeying the laws of the country in which we reside. Christian employees are to be in subjection to their masters (1 Peter 2:18-20), and that, as the servants of Christ, doing the will of God from the heart (Eph. 6:6). Children are to be in subjection to their parents in the Lord (Eph. 6:1). And wives are to be in complete subjection to their husbands (Eph. 5:22-24). It is upon *this* aspect of the subject that we would now a little enlarge upon.

Genuine Christianity is intensely practical, and should ennoble and beautify every earthly relation in which we are placed; above all, it ought to *transform the home*. "Likewise ye wives be in subjection to your own husbands" (1 Peter 3:1). The opening word of this verse is very searching. It looks back to what is said in 1 Peter 2:18, where servants are bidden to be in subjection to their masters, which is enforced by an appeal to the example of the Lord Jesus. There we see none other than the Beloved of the Father in perfect subjection to God, not taking matters into His own hands, but meekly committing His cause to Him that judgeth righteously (2:23). And *why* is the Christian wife to be "in subjection to" her husband? Because God has *commanded* it. It is thus that she honours

Him: by submitting to *His* ordinance and respecting His authority in such an injunction. But suppose the husband be an unsaved man, is subjection to *him* required? Yes, for the remainder of this verse says, "that if any (of the husbands) obey not the Word (and therefore are unsaved), they also may without the Word be *won* by the conversation (behaviour) of the wives."

"Likewise ye wives be in subjection to your own husbands." "The head of the woman is the man" (1 Cor. 11:3). On the day that sin entered into the world, the Lord God said unto the woman, "thy desire shall be subject to thy husband, and he shall rule over thee" (Gen. 3:16). This Divine statute has never been repealed, and even though, in this day of lawlessness and defiance of God, it be wellnigh almost universally disregarded, it still holds good. The N. T. reiterates the same Divine command: "Wives submit yourselves unto your own husbands, as unto the Lord" (Eph. 5:22). There is only one exception to be made in the application of this rule, namely, when the husband commands what *God* forbids, or where he forbids what God commands; in such a case (which in the merciful providence of God is very rare), "whether it be right in the sight of God to hearken unto you more than to God, judge ye" (Acts 4:19) is pertinent.

"While they behold your chaste conversation (or 'manner of life') with fear" (1 Peter 3:2). Ungodly husbands may not pay much heed to what you *say*, they may turn a deaf ear to your giving them the Gospel—and in such case, it is your duty to desist (Prov. 23:9, Matt. 7:6); but they *will* "behold" your daily walk, the manner in which you conduct yourself, the spirit in which you endure (perhaps) their sneers, taunts, unreasonable demands—whether retaliating, or meekly bearing them. Let them "*see* your good works" (Matt. 5:16), for they will be far more potent than your words. Seek grace from God that your life in the home may be glorifying unto Him. "Your *chaste* conversation:" purity, modesty, retiringness; the absence of that boldness, masculinity and immodesty so noticeable in many worldlings. "Your chaste conversation with fear," that is, in the fear of God, with the consciousness that *His* holy eye is observing all things.

What is said in 1 Peter 3:3 is to be taken relatively, and not absolutely. On the one side, slovenliness is to be avoided; on the other side, an undue attention to the things which perish is to be eschewed: excessive absorption of mind and heart over modern "fashions" of bodily decoration ill-becomes one who is clothed with the righteousness of Christ (Isa. 61:10). Let your husband see that *your* heart is set upon something higher than gratifying the "lust of the eyes." V. 4 gives the positive side: "But let it be the hidden man of the heart, in that which is not corruptible, of a meek and quiet spirit, which is in the sight of God of great price." Here the Christian wife is shown what *is to be* prayerfully aimed at and cultivated. It is the "hidden man of the heart," the spiritual life within, which is to be the object of care and study, evidenced outwardly by a "meek and quiet spirit," which signifies yieldedness, foregoing your own desires and interests for Christ's sake. Though a "meek and quiet spirit" is despised by the unregenerate, and may not be appreciated by the husband, yet is it of "great price" in the sight of God.

"For after this manner in the old time the holy women also, who trusted in God, adorned themselves, being in subjection unto their own husbands" (1 Peter 3:5). Those who are to be copied are the "holy women" of "old time," and not the godless rebels and giddy worldlings who dress like butterflies. "*Subjection* unto their own husbands" is the true and spiritual "*adornment*." What a word is this! How little is it really believed by the majority of women who now bear the name of Christ! Ah, it is much easier to speak to others about Christ, than it is to *live* Christ, particularly so, in the *home*. How did *He* live? In complete subjection. As a growing Boy, we are told of Him, "And He went down with them to Nazareth, and was *subject unto* them" (Luke 2:51). Yes, He "pleased not Himself" (Rom. 15:3). He was the perfect *Servant* (Isa. 42:1, Phil. 2:6).

"Even as Sarah obeyed Abraham, calling him lord: whose daughters ye are, as long as ye do well, and are not afraid with any amazement" (1 Peter 3:6). Willing and loving subjection to their husbands, out of respect for the authority of God, is what characterizes the daughters of Sarah; as walking by faith in the path of obedience to God, is that which marks all of Abraham's sons (John 8:39, Gal. 3:7). Where the fear of God is ruling the heart (v. 2), the wife will not be "afraid" of her husband, nor will the Lord allow her to be the loser because of obedience to her earthly head, either in this life or the life to come, for His promise is, "them that honour Me, I will honour" (1 Sam. 2:30).

Many are deploring the fact that this is an age of lawlessness, yet few seem to recognize the real cause of it. The Lord's people are the "salt" of the earth—that which stays the carcass from going to utter putrefaction. But where the salt *loses* its "savour," there corruption proceeds apace. Lawlessness in the world is the inevitable outcome of lawlessness in professing Christendom. The Divine commands for the regulating of church and home life have been flouted on every side; little wonder then that where practical subjection to God has been lacking, we now behold insubordination to the laws of men. It cannot be otherwise. One generation sows the winds, and the next one reaps the whirlwind. O may the Holy Spirit search the hearts and consciences of writer and reader, to discover how far *our* disobedience is responsible for the terrible condition now prevailing all around us. Remember that one disobedient Jonah brought a storm on every one in the ship where he was!

"Be not deceived, God is not mocked: for whatsoever a man soweth, that shall he also reap" (Gal. 6:7). In many, many instances, disobedient children is the sure consequence of the disobedience of their mothers. No mother has any scriptural ground to count upon God's being merciful to her children while she is herself refusing to obey His commands in the home. O that every Christian woman who reads this article may remind herself anew of those searching words, "ye are *not your own*, but bought with a price" (1 Cor. 6:19, 20). Therefore it is for Him to say what you shall do, and how you shall act; and *He* says, "Wives submit yourselves unto your own husbands, as unto the Lord" (Eph. 5:22). A. W.P.

FAITH TRIUMPHANT

"Behold, God is my salvation: I will trust, and not be afraid" (Isa. 12:2). God must be known, before He is trusted. He must be known as a personal Saviour, before He will be fully trusted. And where He is known, not in theory, but in experimental reality, *as* our Saviour, then it ought to be an easy, natural, spontaneous thing, for us to have implicit confidence in Him; confidence that He will supply every real need, both temporal and spiritual, for time and eternity. "He that spared not His own Son, but delivered Him up for us all, how shall He not with Him *also* freely give us all things?" (Rom. 8:32). He who gives a valuable jewel to a friend, will not begrudge a little case to carry it away in. So He who withheld not the Darling of His heart, will not refuse food and raiment to those who trust in Him.

We are not unmindful of the fact that these lines will be read by not a few who are faced by a grave financial situation. Yea, it is because of this that we have earnestly besought the Lord to graciously give a word of cheer to encourage His tried people. There is a fear which, especially in the Christian, is grievously dishonouring to the Lord, such as is spoken of in Luke 21:26, "men's hearts failing them for fear, and for looking after those things which are coming on the earth." Not a little of this is in evidence today. Yet the very "hard times" with which a holy God is now chastening the Nations—for their disregard of Him, their pleasure-loving madness, and the wicked manner in which they have squandered their money the last few years — afford a golden opportunity for His saints to demonstrate that they possess a peace, a rest, a confidence, a joy, which the loss of no temporal prosperity can disturb, still less destroy.

Only today we received a letter from a Brother in New York City, in which he said, "Some time ago I noticed a statement outside a bank which read, 'Have two good names on your checks: yours and ours.' This was one of the branches of the Bank of —— which *failed* last week and involved millions. This, it is said, is the largest bank failure in this country. Thus we learn the inadequacy of man's 'good names'." This has recalled to us, "The *name of the Lord* is a strong tower: the righteous runneth into it, and *is safe*" (Prov. 18:10).

O reader, if you really be a Christian, then "my God *shall* supply all your need according to His riches in glory by Christ Jesus" (Phil. 4:19). No matter how dark may be your outlook, no matter how grave the situation you are facing, that Scripture "*cannot* be broken" (John 10:35)! "Trust in the Lord, and do good; so shalt thou dwell in the land, and verily thou *shalt be* fed" (Psa. 37:3). I care not how urgent your case may be, or how extreme and desperate it may yet become, *that* is the unerring word of Him that *cannot* lie. Then seek grace to rest your soul entirely upon it.

God sometimes allows His children to be brought face to face with distressing situations and trying emergencies before He interposes on their behalf. He sometimes permits the oil in the cruse to run low and the meal in the barrel to be almost exhausted, ere He shows Himself strong on the behalf of those whose hearts are perfect toward Him. Faith must be *tested* to prove its reality. The greater our extremity, the more favourable the opportunity for God to make *His* power *manifest*. Sometimes He allows us to come right up to the jaws of death: He did Job, Hezekiah, Jonah, Daniel—but He saved each of them! "But we had the sentence of death in ourselves, that we should not trust in ourselves, but in God which raiseth the dead" (2 Cor. 1:9), that is, in Him who worketh miracles.

"And He said unto Abram, Know of a surety that thy seed shall be a stranger in a land that is not theirs and shall serve them; and they shall afflict them four hundred years; And also that nation, whom they shall serve, will I judge: and afterward *shall they* come out with great substance" (Gen. 15:13, 14). Now read Ex. 1:8-14. Did it *look* as though there was any likelihood of God's promise to Abram being fulfilled? See the patriarch's descendants groaning amid the brick-kilns of Egypt, helpless under the iron rule of their merciless taskmasters. Ah, faith is opposed to sight. "Who is among you that feareth the Lord, that obeyeth the voice of His Servant, that walketh in darkness, and hath no light? let him trust in the name of the Lord, and *stay upon* his God" (Isa. 50:10). When every thing outward seems against you, when you have come to the *end* of your own resources, when every human creature fails you, turn to the Lord, cast yourself on Him, plead His promises, trust Him fully, and HE will *not* fail you. He failed not the Israelites, but faithfully kept His word to Abram: read Ex. 12:41.

Christian reader, no one has ever *trusted* the Lord and been confounded. "By faith Abraham, when he was called to go out into a place which he should after receive for an inheritance, obeyed; and he went out, not knowing whither he went" (Heb. 11:7). Did God mock his faith? No, indeed. Elijah counted on God's faithfulness by the brook Kerith, that the *ravens* would feed him (1 Kings 17:4): was he disappointed? No, indeed. Daniel trusted in the living God when they cast him into the den of lions: did the Lord fail him in that urgent hour of need? No, indeed. *And God is unchanged*. The wonders He wrought in days gone by were but samples of what He has been doing (as the writer can bear personal witness) for His people ever since, and will continue doing to the end of time.

"Is anything too hard for Me?" (Jer. 32:27) is His own challenge. All power is His. Infinite resources are at His disposal. He who provided a way of deliverance for Noah from the world-destroying flood, who made a way through the Red Sea for the sorely-pressed Israelites, who miraculously fed that vast host for forty years in the wilderness, who delivered the three Hebrews from Babylon's fiery furnace, *still lives*, and is ready to come to the aid of those who trust in Him with all their hearts. Then, "Have faith in God" (Mark 11:22).

"And Asa cried unto the Lord his God, and said, Lord, it is nothing with Thee to help, whether with many, or with them that have no power: help us, O Lord our God, for we *rest on Thee*, and in Thy name we go against this multitude. O Lord, Thou art our God; let not man prevail against Thee. So the Lord smote the Ethiopians before Asa" (2 Chron. 14: 11, 12). Of course He did! He *never* disappoints those who "rest on" Him. "O our God, wilt Thou not judge them? for we have no might against this great company that cometh against us; neither know we what to do: but our eyes are *upon Thee*. And all Judah stood before the Lord with their little ones, their wives, and their children" (2 Chron. 20: 12, 13). Read vv. 14-25 for the sequel!

To "trust" in God means to "cast thy burden upon the Lord" (Psa. 55:22) when it is too heavy for our own shoulders; to "dwell in the secret place of the Most High" (Psa. 91:1), when we know not where to lay our heads upon earth; to "lean on" our Beloved (Song of Sol. 8:5); to "stay" ourselves, when sinking, on the Lord our God (Isa. 26:3). In a word, trust in God is that exercise of faith whereby the soul, looks unto Him alone and casts itself on His goodness, His faithfulness, His power, His promises, and is thereby lifted above carnal discouragements and fears. "Trust in Him *at all times*, ye people, pour out your heart before Him: God is a *refuge* for us" (Psa. 62:8).

Will the reader now turn to page 94 in the April issue and prayerfully read the short article on Faith. Then *re*-read this one, and turn it into prayer. The Lord be pleased to add His blessing for His name's sake. A.W.P.

6. It is *holy*. God's love is not regulated by caprice, passion, or sentiment, but by principle. Just as His grace reigns not at the expense of, but "through righteousness" (Rom. 5:21), so His love never conflicts with His holiness. "God is light" (1 John 1:5) is mentioned *before* "God is love" (4:8). God's love is no mere amiable weakness, or effeminate softness. Scripture declares "whom the Lord loveth He chasteneth, and scourgeth every son whom He receiveth" (Heb. 12:6). God will not wink at sin, even in His own people. His love is *pure*, unmixed with any maudlin sentimentality.

7. It is *gracious*. The love and favour of God are inseparable. This is clearly brought out in Rom. 8:32-39. What that "love" is from which there can be no "separation," is easily perceived from the design and scope of the immediate context: it is that goodwill and grace of God which determined Him to give His Son for sinners. That *love* was the impulsive power of Christ's incarnation: "God so loved the world that He gave His only begotten Son" (John 3:16). Christ died not in order to make God love us, but because He did love His people. Calvary is the supreme demonstration of Divine love. Whenever you are tempted to doubt the love of God, Christian reader, go back to Calvary.

Here then is abundant cause for trust and patience under Divine affliction. Christ was beloved of the Father, yet *He* was not exempted from poverty, disgrace and persecution. *He* hungered and thirsted. Thus, it was *not* incompatible with God's *love* for Christ when He permitted men to spit upon and smite Him. Then let no Christian call into question God's love when he is brought under painful afflictions and trials. God did not enrich Christ on earth with temporal prosperity, for "He had not where to lay His head." But He *did* give Him the Spirit "without measure" (John 3:34). Learn then that *spiritual* blessings are the principal gifts of Divine love. How blessed to know that when the world hates us, God loves us!

—ARTHUR W. PINK.

PRAISE THE LORD

In the "Personal Word" of December last (p. 286), we stated our belief that by the end of the year "there would be a small balance for us to bring forward for 1931." Nor has our confidence in the living God been put to confusion. Owing to the fact that these Magazines are, for the benefit of those in foreign countries, printed some six weeks ahead of time, we close our books each year on the evening of November 17. Through lack of space in the last two issues, we were unable to state that, by the abounding goodness of our faithful God, we were enabled to finish 1930 with a *credit* balance of $2.50 (ten shillings) after every bill had been paid. The last gift, which enabled us to do this, came in that very morning. Truly, God *never* suffers those who look alone to Him to be confounded. We trust that this brief notice will lead many of our prayer-helpers to lift up their hearts in fervent thanksgiving to Him who is the God of all grace.

Will our readers kindly note that we can now supply the 1930 issues of this magazine, neatly and strongly bound, for permanent use and reference, at $1 (4/3) postpaid. This volume contains the first twelve of the "Atonement" articles, and the first twelve on the Divine Attributes.

"Though like a sheep estranged I stray,
Yet have I not renounced Thy way.
Thine hand extend; Thine own reclaim;
Grant me to live, and praise Thy name."

2. It is *eternal*. This of necessity. God Himself is eternal, and God *is* love; therefore, as God Himself had no beginning, His love had none. Granted that such a concept far transcends the grasp of our feeble minds, nevertheless, where we cannot comprehend, we can bow in adoring worship. How clear is the testimony of Jer. 31:3, "I have loved thee with an everslasting love, therefore with lovingkindness have I drawn thee." How blessed to know that the great and holy God loved His people before heaven and earth were called into existence, that He had set His heart upon them from all eternity. Clear proof is this that His love is spontaneous, for He loved them endless ages before they had any being.

The same precious truth is set forth in Eph. 1:4, 5 "According as He hath chosen us in Him *before* the foundation of the world, that we should be holy and without blame before Him. *In love* having predestinated us." What praise should this evoke from each of His children! How tranquilizing for the heart: since God's love toward me had no beginning, it can have no ending! Since it be true that "from everlasting to everlasting" He is God, and since God is "love," then it is equally true that "from everlasting *to* everlasting" He loves His people.

3. It is *sovereign*. This also is self-evident. God Himself is sovereign, under obligations to none, a law unto Himself, acting always according to His own imperial pleasure. Since God be sovereign, and since He be love, it necessarily follows that His love is sovereign. Because God *is* God, He does as He pleases; because God is love, He loves whom He pleases. Such is His own express affirmation: "Jacob have I loved, but Esau have I hated" (Rom. 9:13). There was no more reason in Jacob why he should be the object of Divine love, than there was in Esau. They both had the same parents, and were born at the same time, being twins; yet God loved the one and hated the other! Why? Because it pleased Him so to do.

The sovereignty of God's love necessarily follows from the fact that it is uninfluenced by anything in the creature. Thus, to affirm that the cause of His love lies in God Himself, is only another way of saying, He loves whom He pleases. For a moment, assume the opposite. Suppose God's love were regulated by anything else than His own will, in such a case He would love by rule, and loving by rule He would be under a law of love, and then so far from being free, God would Himself be *ruled by law*. "In love having predestinated us unto the adoption of children by Jesus Christ to Himself, according to"—*what?* Some excellency which He foresaw in them? No; what then: "according to the good pleasure of His will" (Eph. 1:4, 5).

4. It is *infinite*. Everything about God is infinite. His *essence* fills heaven and earth. His *wisdom* is illimitable, for He knows everything of the past, present and future. His *power* is unbounded, for there is nothing too hard for Him. So His love is without any limit. There is a depth to it which none can fathom; there is a height to it which none can scale; there is a length and breadth to it which defies measurement, by any creature-standard. Beautifully is this intimated in Eph. 2:4: "But God, who is rich in mercy, for His *great* love wherewith He loved us:" the word "great" there is parallel with the "God *so* loved" of John 3:16. It tells us that the love of God is so transcendent it cannot be estimated.

"No tongue can fully express the infinitude of God's love, or any mind comprehend it: it 'passeth knowledge' (Eph. 3:19). The most extensive ideas that a finite understanding can frame about Divine love, are infinitely below its *true* nature. The heaven is not so far above the earth as the goodness of God is beyond the most raised conceptions which we are able to form of it. It is an *ocean* which swells higher than all the mountains of opposition in such as are the objects of it. It is a *fountain* from which flows all necessary good to all those who are interested in it" (John Brine, 1743).

5. It is *immutable*. As with God Himself there is "no variableness, neither shadow of turning" (James 1:17), so His love knows neither change nor diminution. The worm Jacob supplies a forceful example of this: "Jacob have I loved," declared Jehovah, and despite all his unbelief and waywardness, He never ceased to love Him. John 13:1 furnishes another beautiful illustration. That very night one of the apostles would say, "Show us the Father;" another would deny Him with cursings; all of them would be scandalized by and forsake Him. Nevertheless, "having loved His own which were in the world, He loved them *unto the end*." The Divine love is subject to no vicissitudes. Divine love is "strong as death . . . many waters cannot quench it" (Song of Sol. 8:6, 7). Nothing can separate from it: Rom. 8:35-39.

> "His love no end nor measure knows,
> No change can turn its course,
> Eternally the same it flows,
> From one eternal source."

(*Continued on Page* 71.)

STUDIES IN THE SCRIPTURES

"Search the Scriptures" John 5:39

Copyright in All English-speaking Countries

EDITOR: Arthur W. Pink, 1339 Bates Ave., Los Angeles, Calif., U. S. A.
Hon. Agent in England: Mr. A. Winstone, "Shalom," Old Bath Road, Leckhampton, Cheltenham.
Hon. Agent in Australia: Mr. G. Ardill, The Christian Workers' Depot, Commonwealth and Reservoir Streets, Sydney.

THE WRATH OF GOD

It is sad indeed to find so many professing Christians who appear to regard the wrath of God as something for which they need to make an apology, or at least they wish there were no such thing. While some would not go so far as to openly admit that they consider it a blemish in the Divine character, yet they are far from regarding it with delight, they like not to think about it, and rarely hear it mentioned without a secret resentment rising up in their hearts against it. Even with those who are more sober in their judgment, not a few seem to imagine that there is a severity about the Divine wrath which is too terrifying to form a theme for profitable contemplation. Others harbour the delusion that God's wrath is not consistent with His goodness, and so seek to banish it from their thoughts.

Yes, many there are who turn away from a vision of God's wrath as though they were called to look upon some blotch in the Divine character, or some blot upon the Divine government. But what saith the Scriptures? As we turn to them we find that God has made no attempt to conceal the fact of His wrath. *He* is not ashamed to make it known that vengeance and fury belong unto Him. His own challenge is, "See now that I, even I, am He, and there is no god with Me: I kill, and I make alive; I wound, and I heal; neither is there any that can deliver out of My hand. For I lift up My hand to heaven, and say, I live forever. If I whet My glittering sword, and Mine hand take hold on judgment; I will render vengeance to Mine enemies, and will reward them that hate Me" (Deut. 32:39-41). A study of the concordance will show that there are *more* references in Scripture to the anger, fury, and wrath of God, than there are to His love and tenderness. Because God is holy, He hates all sin; and because He hates all sin, His anger burns against the sinner: Psa. 7:11.

Now the wrath of God is as much a Divine perfection as is His faithfulness, power, or mercy. It *must be* so, for there is no blemish whatever, not the slightest defect in the character of God; yet there *would be* if "wrath" were absent from Him! Indifference to sin is a moral blemish, and he who hates it not is a moral leper. How could He who is the Sum of all excellency look with equal satisfaction upon virtue and vice, wisdom and folly? How could He who is infinitely holy disregard sin and refuse to manifest His "severity" (Rom. 9:22) toward it? How could He who delights only in that which is pure and lovely, loathe and hate not that which is impure and vile? The very nature of God makes Hell as real a necessity, as imperatively and eternally requisite, as Heaven is. Not only is there no imperfection in God, but there is no perfection in Him that is less perfect than another.

The wrath of God is His eternal detestation of all unrighteousness. It is the displeasure and indignation of Divine equity against evil. It is the holiness of God stirred into activity against sin. It is the moving-cause of that just sentence which He passes upon evil-doers. God is angry against sin because it is a rebelling against His authority, a wrong done to His inviolable sovereignty. Insurrectionists against God's government shall be made to know that God *is* the Lord. They shall be made to feel how great that Majesty is which they despise, and how dreadful is that threatened wrath which they so little regarded. Not that God's anger is a malignant and malicious retaliation, inflicting injury for the sake of it, or in return for injury received. No; while God will vindicate His dominion as the Governor of the universe, He will not be vindictive.

(Continued on Page 96)

IMPORTANT NOTICES

Please advise promptly of change in address, otherwise copies will be lost in the mails.

We are glad to send a sample copy to any of your friends whom you believe would be interested in such a publication. Send to Mr. I. C. Herendeen, Swengel (Union County), Penna., for a list of our publications. He has published many of our books and booklets.

This magazine is published as a work of faith and labour of love. The Editor and his wife gladly give their services. It is freely sent to all who will read it. No charge is made for it.

Christians who feel definitely led to do so, may have fellowship with us in this ministry. Those outside the U. S. A. please send only INTERNATIONAL Money Orders made out to Los Angeles, California, U. S. A.

CONTENTS

The Wrath of God	73
The Epistle to the Hebrews	74
The Satisfaction ("Atonement") of Christ	80
Husbands	87
Regeneration, or, The New Birth	90
Pride	93
Faith	94

THE EPISTLE TO THE HEBREWS

40. *The Contrasted Priests*: Heb. 9:6-10.

At the commencement of our last article we stated that, the principal design of the apostle in this epistle was to prove and make manifest that the "old covenant" which Jehovah made with Israel at Sinai, with all the ordinances of worship and privileges connected therewith had been Divinely annulled. This involved a complete change in the church-state of the Hebrews, but so far from this being a thing to be deplored, it was to their unspeakable advantage. In prosecuting this design, the Holy Spirit through Paul does, as it were, remove the veil from off the face of Moses. In 2 Cor. 3:13 we read, "And not as Moses, which put a veil over his face, that the children of Israel could not steadfastly look to the end of that which is abolished." These words direct attention to a profound spiritual truth which God (in keeping with His dispensational ways) caused to be mystically adumbrated or shadowed forth by a material and visible object.

In 2 Cor. 3:7 the apostle had spoken of the brightness of Moses' face as a symbol of his ministry: the revelation which he received was a divine and glorious one. But because the truth communicated through Moses was in an *obscure* form (by types and emblems) he veiled himself. Paul, as a minister of the "new covenant" used "great plainness of speech" (2 Cor. 3:12) i. e. employing no "dark parables" or enigmatic prophecies, still less mysterious ceremonies. Moses wore a veil "that the children of Israel could not steadfastly look to the end of that which is abolished" (3:7) i. e. to prevent their seeing the termination or fading away of the celestial brightness of his countenance. The mystical meaning of this was, God would not allow Israel to know at that time that the dispensation of the Levitical or legal ministry would ultimately cease. The publication of that fact was reserved for a much later date.

"But their minds were blinded: for until this day remaineth the same veil untaken away in the reading of the old covenant; which veil is done away in Christ" (2 Cor. 3:14). Yes, that "veil" which lay so heavily over the Mosaic types is now "done away in Christ," for He is their Antitype, the key which unlocks them, the sun which illuminates them. This, it is the great purpose of the Hebrews' epistle to demonstrate. Here is *doctrinally* removed the "veil" from off the Mosaic institutions. Here the Spirit makes known the nature and purpose of the "old covenant." Here He declares the significance and temporal efficacy of all the institutions and ordinances of Israel's worship. Here He announces that the Levitical rites and ceremonies made a representation of heavenly things, but insists that those heavenly things could not themselves be introduced and established without the removal of what had adumbrated them. Here He shows that the glory of God shines in the face of Jesus Christ.

Three things there were which constituted the glory of the old covenant, and which the Jews so rested in they refused the Gospel out of an adherence unto them: the priestly office; the tabernacle with all its furniture, wherein that office was exercised; the duties and worship of the priests in that tabernacle by sacrifices, especially those wherein there was a solemn expiation of the sins of the whole congregation. In reference to them, the apostle proves: first, that none of them could make perfect the state of the Church, nor really effect assured peace and confidence between God and the worshippers. Second, that they were but typical, ordained to represent that which was far more sublime and excellent than themselves. Third, that the Lord Jesus Christ, in His person and mediation, was really and substantially, all that they did but prefigure, and that He was and did what they could only direct unto an expectation of.

In Heb. 7 the apostle has fully evidenced this in connection with the priestly office. In the 8th chapter he has done the same in general unto the tabernacle, confirming this by that great collateral argument taken from the nature and excellency of that covenant whereby the incarnate Son was the Surety and Mediator. Here in the 9th, he takes up the services and sacrifies which belonged unto the priestly office in the tabernacle. It was in them that the Jews placed their greatest confidence for reconciliation with God, and concerning which they boasted of the excellency of their Church-state and worship. Because this was the chief point of difference between the Gospel-proclamation and those who repudiated it, and because it was that whereon the whole doctrine of the justification of sinners before God did depend, the apostle enters into minute detail, declaring the nature, use and efficacy of the sacrifices of the law, and manifesting the nature, glory and efficacy of the sacrifice of Christ, whereby those others had been put an end to (condensed from John Owen).

"Now when these things were thus ordained, the priests went always into the first tabernacle, accomplishing the service of God" (v. 6). Having made a brief reference to the structure of the tabernacle in its two compartments, and the furniture belonging to each of them respectively, the apostle now turns to consider the uses for which they were designed unto in the service of God. First, he says "these things were thus ordained," or as the R. V. more correctly renders it, "thus prepared," for the Greek word (translated "made" in v. 2), signifies to dispose and arrange. When the things mentioned in vv. 2-5 had been made and duly ordered, they stood not for a magnificent show, but were designed for constant use in the service of God. Hereby we are taught that, for any service to be acceptable to God, it must be in strict accord with the pattern He has given us in His Word: carefully ponder (1 Chron. 15:12, 13). Everything was duly prepared for Divine service *before* that service was performed. So in public service or Divine worship today there must be fit persons who, under the Spirit, are to lead it—"*able* ministers of the new testament" (2 Cor. 3:6); fit arrangements and order (1 Cor. 14:40), not mere human tradition (Matt. 15:9); a fit message unto edification (1 Cor. 14:26).

"The priests went always into the first tabernacle." They only were allowed in the holy place that were the sons of Aaron; but even these were suffered to penetrate no farther, being barred from entrance into the holy of holies. This was in contrast from the high priest who entered the inner sanctuary, yet only on one day in the year. The word "always" is translated "continually" in 13:15. It signifies constantly, at all times as occasion did require. Christians have been made "kings and priests unto God" (Rev. 1:6), and they are bidden to "give thanks *always* for all things unto God and the Father in the name of our Lord Jesus Christ" (Eph. 5:20); to "rejoice *evermore*" and "pray *without ceasing*" (1 Thess. 5:16, 17).

"Accomplishing the service of God." The translators have rightly added the last two words, for the "service" here is a Divine one. "Accomplishing the service of God" means that they officiated in the ministry of the sacred ceremonies. The *daily* services of the priests were two: the dressing of the lamps of the candlestick: supplying them with the holy oil, trimming their wicks, etc.; this was done every evening and morning. Second, the service of the golden altar, whereon they burned incense every day, with fire taken from off the brazen altar, and this immediately after the offering of the evening and morning sacrifices. Whilst this service was being performed, the people without gave themselves unto prayer (Luke 1:10). Their *weekly* service was to change the shewbread on the table, which was done every Sabbath, in the morning. All of this was typical of the *continual application* of the benefits of the sacrifice and mediation of Christ unto His people here in the world.

The *practical* application to Christians now of what has just been before us, should be obvious. There ought to be family worship, both in the morning and in the evening. The replenishing of the oil in the lamps for continuous light, should find its counterpart in the daily looking to God for needed light from His Word, to direct our steps in the ordering of home and business life to *His* acceptance and praise. God has declared, "Them that honour Me I will honour, and they that despise Me shall be lightly esteemed" (1 Sam. 2:30). If God be not honoured in the home by the family "altar," then we cannot count upon Him blessing our homes! The burning of the incense should receive its antitype in morning and evening praise and prayer unto God: owning Him as the Giver of every good and every perfect gift, thanking Him for spiritual and temporal mercies, casting all our care upon Him, pleading His promises, and trusting Him for a continuance of His favours. The Greek word here for "accomplishing" is a compound, which signifies to "completely finish"—rendered "perfecting" in 2 Cor. 7:1—denoting their service was not done by halves. May we too serve God wholeheartedly.

"But into the second went the high priest alone once every year, not without blood, which he offered for himself, and the errors of the people" (v. 7). That to which the apostle here refers is the great anniversary—sacrifice of expiation, whose institution and solemnities are described at length in Lev. 16. On the tenth day of the seventh month (which corresponds to our September) Israel's high priest, unattended and unassisted by his subordinates, entered within the holy of holies, there to present propitiating sacrifices before Jehovah. Divested of his garments of "glory and beauty" (Ex. 28:2 etc.) and clad only in "the holy linen" (Lev. 16:4), he first entered the sacred precincts bearing a censer full of burning coals and his hands full of incense, which was to be placed upon the coals, so that a cloud of incense should cover the mercyseat (Lev. 16:12, 13); which spoke of the fragrant excellency of Christ's person unto God, when He offered Himself an atoning sacrifice. Second, he took of the blood of the bullock, which had been killed for a sin-offering for himself and his house (Lev. 16:11), and sprinkled its blood both upon and before the mercyseat (16:14). Third, he went out and killed the goat which was a sin-offering for the people, and did with its blood as he had with that of the bullock's (16:15).

When the high priest's work within the veil had been completed, he came forth and laid both his hands on the head of the live goat, and confessed over him "all the iniquities of the children of Israel and all their transgressions in all their sins, putting them upon the head of the goat," which was then sent away "unto a land not inhabited" (Lev. 16:21, 22); all of which was typical of the Atonement made by the Lord Jesus, and of the plenary remission of sins through His blood. In the shedding of the victims' blood and offering it by fire on the altar, there was a representation made of the vicarious imputation of guilt to the sacrifice, and the expiation of it through death. In the carrying of the blood into the presence of Jehovah and the sprinkling of it upon His throne, witness was borne to His *acceptance* of the atonement which had been made. In the placing of the sins of Israel upon the live goat and its carrying of them away into a land uninhabited, there was a foreshadowing of the blessed truth that, as far as the east is from the west so far hath God removed the transgressions of His people from before Him.

"Into the second veil went the high priest *alone*:" "There shall be no man in the tabernacle of the congregation when he goeth in to make an atonement" (Lev. 16:17). This denoted that Christ alone was qualified to appear before God on behalf of His people: none other was fit to mediate for them. "*Once* every year," to foreshadow the fact that Christ entered heaven for His people once for all: Heb. 9:12. "Which he offered for himself," for he too was a sinner, and therefore incompetent to make real, efficacious and acceptable atonement for others; thereby intimating that he must yet give place to Another. "And for the errors of the people," which is to be interpreted in the light of the O. T. expression "sins of ignorance" (Lev. 4:2; 5:15; Num. 15:22-29), which are contrasted from deliberate or presumptuous sins (see Num. 15:30, 31). Under the dispensation of law God graciously made provision for the infirmities of His people, granting them sacrifices for sins committed unwillingly and unwittingly. But for determined and open rebellion against His laws, no atoning sacrifice was available: *see* Heb. 10:28.

The distinction pointed out above is the key to Psa. 51:16, "For Thou desirest not sacrifice, else would I give it." There is no room for doubt that David knew full well the terrible character of the sins which he committed against Uriah and his wife. Later, when he was convicted of this, he realized that *the law* made no provision for forgiveness. What, then, did he do? Psa. 51:1-3 tells us: he laid hold on God Himself and said, "The sacrifices of God are a broken spirit: a broken and a contrite heart, O God, Thou wilt not despise" (v. 17). It was faith, penitently, appropriating the mercy of God in Christ.

"The Holy Spirit this signifying, that the way into the holiest of all was not yet made manifest, while as the first tabernacle was yet standing" (v. 8). The apostle now makes known the use which he intended to make of the description which had been given of the tabernacle and its furniture in vv. 2-5: from the structure and order of its services he would prove the pre-eminence of the priesthood and sacrifice of Christ above those which had belonged to the tabernacle. He points out that the Holy Spirit had provided instruction for Israel in the very disposal of their ancient institutions. Inasmuch as none but the high priest was permitted to pass within the veil, it was plainly intimated that under the Mosaic dispensation the people were *barred* from the very presence of God. Such a state of affairs could not be the ultimate and ideal, and therefore must be set aside before that which was perfect could be introduced.

"The Holy Spirit this signifying:" the reference is to the arrangements which obtained in the tabernacle, as specified in the preceding verses. Here we learn that the third person of the blessed Trinity was immediately concerned in the original instructions given to Israel. This intimates in a most striking way the perfect union, unison and co-operation of the persons of the Godhead in all that They do. 2 Peter 1:21 declares that, "holy men of old spake, moved by the Holy Spirit," prominent among whom was Moses. In Ex. 35:1 we read, "Moses gathered all the congregation of the children of Israel together, and said unto them, These are the words which the Lord hath commanded"—the Holy Spirit moving Him to give an accurate record of all that he had heard from the Lord.

"The Holy Spirit this signifying," or making evident, that "the way into the holiest of all was not yet made manifest." *How* did He thus "signify" this fact? By the very framework of the tabernacle: that is, by allowing the people to go no farther than the outer court, and the priests themselves only into the first compartment. "For things in His wisdom were thus disposed, that there should be the first tabernacle whereinto the priests did enter every day, accomplishing the Divine services that God required. Howbeit in that tabernacle there were not the pledges of the gracious presence of God. It was not the especial residence of His glory. But the peculiar habitation of God was separated from it by a veil, and no person living might so much as look into it on pain of death. But yet, lest the church should apprehend, that indeed there was no approach, here, nor hereafter, for any person into the gracious presence of God; He ordained that once a year the high priest, and he alone, should enter into that holy place with blood. Hereby he plainly signified, that an entrance *there was to be*, and that with boldness, thereinto. For unto what end else did He allow and appoint, that once a year there should be an entrance into it by the high priest, in the name of and for the service of the church? But this entrance being *only* once a year, by the high priest only, and that with the blood of the covenant, which was always to be observed whilst that tabernacle continued, he did manifest that the access represented was not to be obtained during that season; for all believers in their own persons were utterly excluded from it" (J. Owen).

"The way into the holiest of all was not yet made manifest." The apostle is not now speaking of the second compartment in the tabernacle (as in v. 3), but of that which was typified by it. "Now, in that most holy place, were all the signs and pledges of the gracious presence of God; the testimonies of our reconciliation by the blood of the atonement, and of our peace with Him thereby. Wherefore, to enter into these holies is nothing but to have an access with liberty, freedom and boldness, into the gracious presence of God, on the account of reconciliation and peace made with Him. This the apostle doth so plainly and positively declare in 10:19-22 that I somewhat wonder so many learned expositors could utterly miss of his meaning in this place. The holies then is the gracious presence of God, whereunto believers draw nigh, in the confidence of the atonement made for them, and acceptance thereon: see Rom. 5:1-3, Eph. 2:14-18, Heb. 4:14, 15" (J. Owen).

But let us observe more closely this expression "the *way* into the holiest of all." This way is no other but the sacrifice of Christ, the true High Priest of the Church: as He Himself declared, "I am the Way, the Truth and the Life, no man cometh unto the Father but by Me" (John 14:6). Thus the ultimate reference here in "the holiest of all" is to Heaven itself, yet having a present and spiritual application unto access to and communion with God. The "way" into this is through faith in the sacrifice of Christ. Marvelously was this adumbrated here on earth at the moment of His death, for then the veil of the temple was rent in twain from the top to the bottom (Matt. 27:51), thereby opening a way into the holy of holies.

But this access to God, or way into the holiest of all, "was not yet made manifest, while as the first tabernacle was yet standing." It is to be very carefully noted that the apostle did *not* say that there was then no way "provided" or "made use of," but only that it was not, during O. T. times, "made manifest." There *was* an entrance into the presence of God, both unto grace and glory, for His elect, from the days of Abel and onwards, but that "way" was not openly and publicly displayed. By virtue of the everlasting covenant (the agreement between the Father and the Son), and in view of Christ's satisfaction in the fulness of time, salvation was applied to saints then, and they were saved by faith as we are now, for the Lamb was slain from the foundation of the world. But the open manifestation of these things waited for the actual exhibition of Christ in the flesh, the full declaration of His person and mediation by the Gospel, and the introduction and establishment of all the privileges of Gospel worship.

"While as the first tabernacle was yet standing." The references here is *not* to the first compartment or holy place, into which the priests entered and where they served, but is used synecdochially (a part put for the whole) for the entire legal system, which included the temples of Solomon and Zerubbabel. The "first tabernacle" is here spoken of in contrast from the "true tabernacle" of 8:2, namely, the humanity of Christ, which was the antitype and succeeded in the room of the type—cf. Rev. 13:6! The apostle is here treating of what had its standing before God whilst the "first covenant" and Aaronic priesthood remained valid. He cannot be here referring to the "first tabernacle" as a building, for *that* had become a thing of the past, long centuries before he wrote this epistle. Yet the temples that succeeded it had their standing on the basis of the old covenant. This had now been annulled, and with it the whole system of worship which had so long obtained in Judaism.

"Which was a figure for the time then present, in which were offered both gifts and sacrifices, that could not make him that did the service perfect as pertaining to the conscience" (v. 9). Having briefly pointed out the emblematic significance of the *two* compartments of the tabernacle, the apostle now approaches his leading object in this paragraph, namely, to demonstrate that Christ had "obtained a more excellent ministry" than that which had belonged to the Levitical priesthood. This he does by giving a brief summary of the imperfections of the tabernacle and all its services, wherein the *administration* of the old covenant did consist. By calling attention to the defects or inadequacy of the Judaic system, the apostle adopted the most effective method of exposing the unreasonableness of the rejection of the more glorious Gospel by the majority of the Jews, and at the same time showed what folly and wickedness it would be for the believing Hebrews to return to that system.

The apostle's design in vv. 9, 10 is to show that, notwithstanding the outward excellency and glory of the tabernacle-system (through Divine appointment), yet, in the will and wisdom of God, that system was only designed to continue for a season, and that the time of its expiation had now arrived. That the Levitical priesthood and their services were never intended by God to occupy a *perpetual* place in the worship of His church, was evident from the fact that they were utterly unable to effect for His saints that which He had purposed and promised. Not only did the presence of the veil, which excluded all save Aaron from the presence-chamber of Jehovah, intimate that the ideal state had not yet come; not only did the annual *repetition* of the great atoning-sacrifice indicate that, as yet, the all-efficacious Sacrifice had not yet been offered; but all the gifts and sacrifices combined failed to "perfect as pertaining to the conscience." They were only "a figure for the time then present," an institution and provision of God "until the time of reformation."

"Which was a figure for the time then present." The "which was" includes the tabernacle in both its parts, with all its vessels and services. The Greek word for "figure" here is not the same as the one rendered "type" in Rom. 5:14 and "examples" in 1 Cor. 10:6, 11, but is the term commonly translated "parable," as in Matt. 13:3, 10 etc. It is used here for one thing representing another. It signifies "figurative instruction." By means of obscure mystical signs and symbols God taught the ancient church. The great mystery of our redemption by Christ was principally made known by a parable, which was addressed to the eyes rather than to the ears. That was the method which God was pleased to employ, the means He used under the law, of making known things to come. "Which was a figure," is the Holy Spirit's affirmation that the structure, fabric, furniture and rites of the tabernacle were all vested with a Divine and spiritual significance. That the truly regenerate among Israel were acquainted with this fact is illustrated by the prayer of David, "Open Thou mine eyes, that I may behold wondrous things out of Thy law" (Psa. 119:18).

"Which was a figure for the time then present." The verb here is of the preter-imperfect tense, signifying a time that *was* then present, but is *now* past. The reference is to what had preceded the establishment of the new covenant, before the full Gospel revelation had been made. The figurative instruction which God gave to the early Church was not designed to be of permanent duration. Nevertheless, a sovereign God saw fit to continue that obscure and figurative representation of spiritual mysteries for no less than fifteen hundred years. His ways are ever the opposite of man's. "It is the glory of God to *conceal* a thing" (Prov. 25:2)! But how thankful we should be that "the darkness is past, and the true light now shineth" (1 John 2:8). Still, let it not be overlooked that the revelation God made through the tabernacle was sufficient for the faith and obedience of Israel had it been diligently attended unto.

"In which were offered both gifts and sacrifices." The Greek word for "sacrifices" is derived from a verb which means to kill, thus the reference here is to those oblations which were slaughtered. As distinguished from these, "gifts" were without life and sense, such as the meal-offering, oil, frankincense and salt which were mingled therewith (Lev. 2), the first-fruits, tithes, and all free-will offerings, which were presented by the priests. These were "offered" unto God, and that in the tabernacle, for there alone was it meet to offer them. So also was the "tabernacle" (8:2) of Christ alone suited for its designed end. And what is the particular message this should have for the Christian's heart? Surely to remind him of that word, "I beseech you therefore, brethren, by the mercies of God that ye present your bodies a living sacrifice, holy, acceptable unto God, which is your reasonable service" (Rom. 12:1).

"That could not make him perfect as pertaining to the conscience." These words are not to be understood as restricted to the officiating priest, rather do they look more directly to the person in whose stead he presented the offering to God. Here the apostle points out the imperfection of the whole tabernacle-order of things, and its impotency unto the great end that might be expected from it. To "perfect" a worshipper is to fit him, legally and experimentally, for communion with God, and for this there must be both justification and sanctification, and neither of these could the Levitical priests procure. They could neither remit guilt from before God, nor remove the stains of it from the soul. Where those are lacking, there can be no peace or assurance in the heart, and then the real spirit of worship is absent. As this (D. V.) comes before us again in 10:2, we will not here further enlarge.

Ere passing on to the next verse, it may be enquired, If then the Levitical sacrifices failed at this vital point, why were they ever appointed by God at all? To this question two answers may be returned. First, those sacrifices availed to remove the temporal governmental consequence of Israel's sins; when rightly offered, they freed from political and external punishment, so that continuance in the land of Canaan was preserved; but they cancelled not the wages of sin, removed not the eternal punishment which was due unto every sin by the law. Second, they directed the faith of the regenerate forward to the perfect sacrifice of Christ (which the Levitical offerings typically represented), the virtue and value of which was available to faith's appropriation from the beginning.

"Which stood only in meats and drinks, and divers washings, and carnal ordinances, imposed until the time of reformation" (v. 10). To convince those to whom he was writing that the Levitical ceremonies were incapable of perfecting the conscience, the apostle here demonstrates the truth of this by pointing out their inadequate nature and character. The ordinances of Judaism corresponded closely with the old covenant, which was made with man in the flesh: its sanctuary and furniture were material—things of sight and sense; its ministry was not spiritual, but had to do only with external rites; its ablutions effected nothing more than a ceremonial cleansing, and entirely failed to purify the heart, as faith does (Acts 15:9).

The "service" of the tabernacle-system "stood only in meats and drinks." This expression refers to the sacrifices and libations, which consisted of flesh and bread, oil and wine. "And divers washings": first, that of the priests themselves (Ex. 29:4 etc.), for whose use the "laver" was chiefly intended (Ex. 30:18, 31:9 etc.); second, of the various parts of the burnt-offering sacrifice (Lev. 1:9, 13); third, of the people themselves when they had contracted defilement (Lev. 15:8, 16 etc.). "And carnal ordinances" which refers, most probably, to the whole system of laws pertaining to diet and manner of life. "Which stood *only* in," this is emphatic; the rites of Judaism were *solely* external and fleshly, there being nothing spiritual joined with them. Thus their insufficiency to procure spiritual and eternal blessings was evident: legal meats and drinks could not nourish the soul; ceremonial washings could not purify the heart.

"Imposed until the time of reformation." "The word for 'imposed' is properly 'lying on them,' that is, as a burden. There was a weight in all these legal rites and ceremonies, which is called a yoke, and too heavy for the people to bear (Acts 15:10). And if the imposition of them be principally intended, as we render the word 'impose,' it respects the bondage they were brought into by them. Men may have a weight lying on them, and yet not be brought into bondage thereby. But these things were so 'imposed' on them, as that they might feel their weight, and groan under the burden of it. Of this bondage the apostle treats at large in the epistle to the Galatians. And it was impossible that those things should perfect a church-state, which in themselves were such a burden, and effective of such a bondage" (John Owen).

The institutions of the Levitical service possessed a general character of externality and materialty: as v. 13 of our chapter says, they sanctified "to the purifying of the *flesh*," but they reached not the dire needs of the soul. Therefore they were not designed to continue forever, but for a determined and limited season, namely, "unto the time of reformation," which expression respected the appearing of the promised Messiah to inaugurate the new and better covenant: see Luke 1:68-74. "But when the fullness of the time was come, God sent forth His Son, made of a woman, made under the law; to redeem them that were under the law, that we might receive the adoption of sons" (Gal. 4:4, 5). A.W.P.

THE SATISFACTION
("Atonement")
OF CHRIST

16. *Its results (continued)*

Numerous and fearful have been the errors into which many have fallen when treating of the results of the perfect Satisfaction which Christ offered unto God on behalf of his people. Reconciliation has, on the one hand, been restricted to sinners throwing down the arms of their rebellion, whereas Scripture also plainly speaks of Christ's having "slain the enmity" of the Divine justice (Eph. 2:16); while on the other hand, some affirm that all (including the Devil himself) have been reconciled to God, when the word declares there are many who shall be "punished with everlasting destruction *from* the presence of the Lord" (2 Thess. 1:9). The remission of sins which Christ actually obtained for all He represented, has been whittled down to a mere *possibility* of forgiveness, which may or may not be procured by men according as their wills shall determine. While so terribly has the glorious truth of redemption been perverted that thousands believe there are multitudes in Hell for whom Christ shed His precious blood as a ransom-price. May it please the Lord to use the preceding articles to dissipate the fogs of heresy from the minds of many of our readers.

4. *Righteousness.*

This is, perhaps, the most wonderful of all the "results" obtained by the arduous Work of our blessed Saviour. Yet is it today, in most professing Christian circles, the least understood. If it be true that the blessed truths of reconciliation, remission and redemption have been grievously and grossly misrepresented by many who have posed as teachers sent from God, that which is now to be before us has been flatly denied, held up to ridicule, and branded as a serious error, by not a few of those who wished to be regarded as the champions of orthodoxy. It is indeed painful to find the writings of men who staunchly upheld the Divine inspiration of the Scriptures, the deity of Christ, His virgin birth and substitutionary death, defiled by a vicious repudiation of the principal consequence of His atoning sacrifice. But Satan is very subtle, and the higher the reputation of a man for soundness in the faith, the happier is the Enemy to employ him in his awful work of opposing God.

But today that inestimably blessed truth which we now desire to set before the reader (as the Lord is pleased to enable), is not so much denied, as it is *ignored*. That which is the crowning glory of the Gospel (Rom. 1:17), that by which God has supremely displayed His infinite wisdom (1 Cor. 2:7), that which should most of all render the Redeemer precious to His people (Psa. 71:14-16), and that which ought to be the chief object of the believer's joy (Isa. 61:10), is now left out of almost all so-called evangelical ministry. Even where Christ is presented as the sinner's only hope, and His blood as the only cleanser of sin, that which secures a title for Heaven, that which alone can render a sinner acceptable before the Judge of all the earth, that which is the ground upon which He pronounces the ungodly *justified*, is missing from the best preaching and writings of this degenerate age. At best, only a half Gospel is being proclaimed, only the negative side of what Christ earned for His people is being set before them. Whether or not this criticism be too sweeping we leave the reader to decide after he has read the remainder of this article.

1. *Its Nature.*

Following our usual custom, let us first show the connection between our present theme and that which was before us in our last article. "Being justified freely by His grace through the redemption that is in Christ Jesus" (Rom. 3:24): here we are shown the intimate relation which exists between the believer's righteousness and his redemption. To "justify" is the opposite of to "condemn": see Deut. 25:1, Rom. 8:33, 34 etc. Now to "condemn" a man is not to infuse evil into him, but is to pronounce him a transgressor. As the condemning of a man does not *make* him guilty, but simply announces that he *is* so, to "justify" a man is not to *make* him good, nor to infuse goodness into him, but is to declare that he *is* "just." Justification is that formal sentence of the divine Judge whereby He pronounces the one before Him righteous. The *ground* upon which God pronounces this sentence is the "redemption which is in Christ Jesus."

As we showed in the last article, redemption is the consequence of a ransom-price having been paid. The ransom-price which the Lord Jesus offered unto the justice of God was that perfect Satisfaction which He gave to the divine law, which consisted of the entire course of His virtuous and meritorious life, culminating in the laying down of His life at the cross in obedience to His Father's command: John 10:18, 14:31. Christ, then, "magnified the law and made it honourable" (Isa. 42:21), by keeping it in heart and life, in thought and word and deed; and therefore God, in His character of Law-administrator, the Judge of all the earth, has imputed the Saviour's obedience to all who believe on Him; and because they have that reckoned to their account, they are "justified," declared righteous in the High Court of heaven. The Christian is justified freely by God's "grace," because it was sovereign benignity which provided the Mediator and His ransom; yet that justification is not at the price of setting aside the claims of the law, but "*through* the redemption that is in Christ Jesus." Thus, grace reigns not at the expense of righteousness, but "*through* righteousness unto eternal life by Jesus Christ our Lord" (Rom. 5:21).

Old Testament prophecy not only announced that the Messiah and Mediator should "make reconciliation for iniquity," but also that He would "bring in everlasting righteousness" (Dan. 9:24). The two were equally needed by us: the one to deliver from Hell, the other to entitle unto Heaven. The taking away of our sins was not sufficient. In this world offenders are sometimes pardoned, so as to be no longer liable to punishment, yet without being at the same time received into favour, admitted to fellowship, and placed in a position of honour and privilege. But not so is it when a believing sinner is justified "through the redemption which is in Christ Jesus": he obtains not only pardon from God, but favour and acceptance; not only exemption from the penalty of sin, but a title to the reward of righteousness. Accordingly it is written, "Therefore being justified by faith, we have peace with God through our Lord Jesus Christ: by whom *also* we have access by faith into this *grace* (favour) wherein *we stand*" (Rom. 5:1, 2). And again, "That being justified by His grace, we should be *made heirs* according to the hope of eternal life" (Titus 3:7).

Two things were required in order to our acceptance by God: the removal of our sins, the making us righteous in the sight of His law. Man was impotent to effect the one as much as the other. We were no more able to get rid of our guilt, than the Ethiopian can change his skin or the leopard his spots. Equally powerless were we to render unto God that perfect obedience which His justice demands, and that because of the *weakness* ("without strength" Rom. 5:6) of the flesh (Rom. 8:3). "Therefore by the deeds of the law (that is, *our own* performances) shall no flesh be justified in His sight" (Rom. 3:20). Hence, if ever we were to be saved, One must come here and meet *both* these needs on our behalf: not only suffer the penalty which our transgressions entailed, but also render to the law active and positive obedience so as to merit righteousness for us. It is of the utmost importance to understand the distinction between obeying the law and enduring punishment. The mere suffering its penalty can never bring in righteousness, as the damned in Hell shall discover to their eternal anguish.

Christ, in the room and stead of His people, lived here a life of complete obedience to every demand of that law which they were responsible to keep, and then, in His death, He paid the full and entire penalty of that law which they had broken; and in this way He wrought out a complete righteousness for His church. Thus the *authority* of the law was fully vindicated, and its *breach* was fully avenged. There is a *double* exchange of place: Christ took ours, and we are given His. "For ye know the grace of our Lord Jesus Christ, that, though He was rich, yet for your sakes He became poor, that ye through His poverty might be rich" (2 Cor. 8:9). There was therefore a twofold identification: Christ was made one with us (Heb. 2:11, 14), we are made one with Him (Eph. 5:30). We had no righteousness of our own; now, as believers, we have received a perfect righteousness, by imputation, from Christ. "*Their* righteousness is *of Me*, saith the Lord" (Isa. 54:17).

To affirm that the sufferings of Christ was all that Divine justice required in order to redeem His people, is to blankly deny the force and teaching of many scriptures. For example, "As by one man's disobedience many were made sinners, so by the *obedience* of One shall many be made righteous" (Rom. 5:19). Just as light and heat are always united in the sun, so the righteousness of Christ's life and the efficacy of His death are conjoined in our justification. The blood of Christ ought never to be thought of as independent of or detached from His life of obedience: it was their *united* value which purchased our redemption. In their agency they were inseparable, though in our meditation, distinguishable. Christ yielded perfect obedience to the preceptive part of the law, and full satisfaction to its penal, on purpose that the merit of *all* might be made over to them who believe. This is the distinguishing glory of the Gospel: the blessed truth of free justification through the righteousness of Christ. Just as God transferred the guilt of His people to Christ, so does He transfer His obedience to them. Christ has not only made us accepted, but acceptable to God (Heb. 10:14)—accepted, because acceptable.

2. *Its Necessity.*

"The claims of God's holy government in relation to man were made known at Sinai. There He promulgated His law, a law whose claims cannot be remitted or lowered, because they are founded on His own essential and unchanging holiness. The great *mandatory* commandment of that law is, Thou shalt love God perfectly, and manifest that love in thought and action. Perfectly and always. The great *prohibitory* commandment is, Thou shalt not covet (Rom. 7:7) —that is, thou shalt not desire anything of evil, anything that is forbidden by God.

"The law pronounced blessing and eternal life on any who should keep it; but it pronounced curse and judgment on all who should violate it even once, if only in thought: 'Cursed is every one that continueth not in all things which are written in the book of the law to do them' (Gal. 3:10). From Mount Gerizim was pronounced the blessing; from Ebal, the curse. The law cannot remit or lower its claims; for its claims are founded on the essential and unchanging holiness of God. And the law having been promulgated, must be fulfilled: 'Verily I say unto you, Till heaven and earth pass, one jot or tittle shall in no wise pass from the law till all be *fulfilled*' (Matt. 5:18).

"The law demanded: 1. The absence of all wilful transgression. 2. The absence of sins of ignorance. 3. Perfectness in the inner man. 4. Perfectness of developed character in unreserved and unremitting devotedness to God. But we naturally have none of these things. Instead of being without wilful transgressions, and without sins of ignorance, in both we abound. Instead of perfectness in the inner man, unfathomable depths of corruption are therein. Instead of perfectness of character, the things that ought to be absent are present, and the things that ought to be present are absent. Instead of being unreservedly devoted to God, we are unreservedly devoted to ourselves. Such is our condition. And all this moral leprosy has come upon us as the result of the Fall. It is the result of Adam's first sin, for with him we had, by God's appointment, *a legal oneness*. He sinned, and his transgression brought upon him and upon us 'Judgment unto condemnation':—one of the first and chief results of that judgment being the presence and dominance in us of indwelling Sin, whereby all power of doing good is supplanted by the abiding presence of energetic evil. Who can tell the thrill of anguish and horror that must come on the soul, when, in eternity, it too late discovers the truth of these things?

"We are thus shut up into utter hopelessness. We find ourselves heirs of wrath, strong for evil, powerless for good. 'The law worketh wrath.' 'If there had been a law which could have given life. . . . But Scripture hath concluded all *under sin*' (Gal. 3:21, 22). The law can stir up the workings of sin within us: it can work 'all manner of concupiscence' (Rom. 7); but it cannot deliver from those workings. 'The law entered that the offense might abound.' 'By the law is the knowledge of sin.' It is the prerogative of God alone to determine, and by His law to make known unto us, what is, and what is not, sin. Man is full of sin, yet he knows it not. 'I had not known sin but by the law, for I had not known lust (concupiscence, or desire) except the law had said, thou shalt not covet (Rom. 7:7). In our flesh there is nothing but evil desire: 'the flesh lusteth against the Spirit,' and that evil desire is *sin*. Men refuse to acknowledge this. Wilful disobedience is the only form of sin they recognise.

"There never could have been any hope for such as we if God, in the infinitude of His grace, had not been pleased to declare that His holy courts admitted the principle of *substitutionary service*. For He announces that He has appointed for all 'who are of faith' a *Surety or Sponsor*, who, undertaking all their responsibilities is their *alter ego*, their other self, and accepted in their stead all that is needed to supply a valid and sure title of life and glory" (from "Atonement Saveth," by B. W. Newton). Here then was the desperate need. The law could not abate its demand: flawless and continuous obedience. We have no ability to meet its demand: "There is none righteous, no not one" (Rom. 3:10), sounds the doom of the most punctillious moralist, equally as it does the most abandoned profligate. Therefore if ever rebellious and guilty criminals were to be saved, it could only be by Another assuming their responsibilities and satisfying the law in their stead. This brings us to consider,

3. *Its Procurement.*

"Atonement Saveth. The truth expressed by these words is the great keystone of our hopes for time and eternity. Atonement brings to all those who are under it (not salvability, but) *salvation*. All who are of the family of faith are under it. What then do we mean by Atonement? Atonement, or appeasement, is a priestly work of the Lord Jesus *directed toward God*, whereby, by one oblation, finished on the cross, He has settled forever the claims of the Divine Government and procured for all His believing people, not only pardon, but *acceptableness and rewardableness* according to the value of His own meritorious obedience, which has been presented to God, and accepted by God for them. . . .

"The eternal Son voluntarily undertook to be the Sponsor of His people. Humbling Himself to be born of a woman and made under the law (that so He might fulfill the law), He formally assumed the responsibilities of all the family of faith, engaging to do everything and to suffer everything that was necessary *Godward*, in order to deliver them from wrath and secure to them an inalienable title to life and glory. His appointment to this Suretyship was founded upon the Justice of God, which required that all sin must be punished; and it was founded also on the Love of God, which determined not only to deliver from wrath, but to bring also to His own bosom and into His glory, those who personally deserved wrath. It was necessary, therefore, that the Substitute should, in the stead of His people (even all who should believe), meet every requirement of God's law, which demanded perfectness of obedient service; and likewise that He should bear all the penalties appointed to Him as the Substitute, because of our disobedience; for we owe unto God a *double* debt—a debt of obedience, and because of failure in that, a debt of penal suffering. Both must be paid. The penalty must be borne; and the perfect obedience rendered, otherwise, there could be no Atonement, and, in consequence, no salvation" (B. W. Newton, from "A t o n e m e n t Saveth").

The above quotation contains a succient statement upon this important aspect of our theme. In seeking to amplify it a little, let us emphasize the fact that when the Beloved of the Father became Surety for us insolvent wretches, He made Himself subject to the *whole* law of God. Though its threatenings were set in terrible array, and though its commands peremptorily insisted on the very perfection of obedience, He asked for no mitigation of its severity, nor any abatement of its demands; but instead, with full but joyous submission to the Judge of all, He cried "Lo, I come. . . . I delight to do Thy will, O My God: yea, Thy law is within My heart" (Psa. 40:7, 8)—yes, "come" to pay the uttermost farthing of their debt, and to perform every jot and tittle of their duty. That perfect righteousness imputed to them, which is the ground upon which God justifies believing sinners, was *inaugurated* when God sent forth His son to be born under the law (Gal. 4:4); it was *perpetuated* throughout the whole course of the Saviour's life, when He did always those things which pleased the Father (John 8:29); it was *consummated* when Immanuel bowed His blessed head and cried with triumphant voice, "It is finished" (John 19:30). Let us examine this in fuller detail.

"What the law could not do, in that it was weak through the flesh, God sending His own Son in the likeness of sinful flesh, and for sin, condemned sin in the flesh: that the righteousness of the law might be fulfilled in us" (Rom. 8:3, 4). The last clause quoted states the ultimate end God had in view (so far as His elect were concerned) in sending His Son here, namely, that "the righteousness of the law," its holy and just demands, should be fulfilled for us in the person of our Representative, so that in the accounting of God *they* had themselves fulfilled it. "Righteousness" is a *judicial* term, and refers *not* to a state of mind or disposition of heart, but instead, to a *legal status* before the tribunal of God. The "righteousness of the law" signifies the full answering of all the requirements of the law, coming up to a perfect conformity to it, and that, by doing all its enjoins. It is this alone which gives title to enjoy its reward, namely, life everlasting. This "righteousness of the law" was and is "fulfilled in us" as we were and are *viewed in Christ*, just as v. 1 affirms, "there is therefore now no condemnation *to them which are in Christ Jesus".!*

Now in order to this "righteousness" being wrought out for us by Christ it was necessary that He should, first, be "made under the law" (Gal. 4:4). "Christ was holy and righteous not as a private person, not for Himself alone, but for us sinners and our justification" (R. Haldane). Yet at this point great caution needs to be exercised lest we sully the honour and glory of the Mediator. There have been those who most erroneously affirmed that when the Son of God became incarnate it was obligatory upon Him *to* fulfil the law, that as Man, this was His personal *duty*. Not so. Had that been the case, His obedience had been of such a character that its merit could not have been imputed to others, for He would merely have been paying His own creature-debt to the law. Such is horrible blasphemy, proceeding from an altogether inadequate and faulty view of our Lord's manhood. As this error is now so fearfully prevalent, even in circles where few would expect to find it, something further needs to be said in order to its refutation.

The manhood of Christ never had an existence separate from the Godhead of the Son. When the "Word became flesh" (John 1:14), the second person of the adorable Trinity took into union with Himself an immaculate human nature, consisting of spirit and soul and body. We say "an immaculate human *nature*," for it was *not* a human *person*; instead, it was a Divine person who assumed that human nature. Carefully has the Holy Spirit guarded this very point in Luke 1:35, where it was said unto Mary, "that holy *thing* which shall be born of thee shall be called the Son of God"—so denominated because that just as when a woman is united to a man in marriage she takes his name, so the humanity of the Saviour being taken into union with the second person of the Trinity, is called "the Son of God." Thus, because the holy manhood of the Redeemer became a part of the *person* of the Lord of glory, He was not only exempted from the common condemnation of all other men (inherent sin as the result of the Fall), but He was *not obligated* to be in subjection to the law as all other men are.

Let it be said with all possible emphasis that it was not as a private person, but as the public and *official* Representative of His people that the God-man was "made under the law." It was purely a voluntary act on His part, and in no sense compulsory. Therefore was His obedience infinitely meritorious, and capable of being imputed to His people. True, His being subject to the law and meeting its every requirement had been proposed to Him by the Father in the everlasting covenant, yet it must be expressly insisted upon that it was by His own free consent that those terms were accepted by Him. It was for the sake of His people, and not for Himself, that He became under the law. Even after He had become incarnate, the Saviour explicitly declared, "The Son of man is *Lord* also of the sabbath" (Mark 2:28), and if Lord of the Sabbath, therefore "Lord" of the whole law. The law had *no* claims upon *Him*. That obedience which He rendered to it was entirely voluntary, free, and on the behalf of and in the stead of His insolvent people.

"And being found in fashion as a man, *He* humbled Himself, and *became* obedient" (Phil. 2:8). Weigh well these momentous words, and stand in awe at the amazing phenomenon which they present. *Who* "humbled" Himself? None other than the Maker of heaven and earth. When did He "humble" Himself? First, when He left the glory of heaven and entered into the virgin's womb. Unparalleled stoop was this; unprecedented condescension was that. But more; having assumed human nature unto Himself, He "humbled" Himself still further, and "became obedient." Notice the active, rather than the passive voice: it is not "He was humbled," but "He humbled Himself." It was an act of His own, a voluntary act, *not* a duty, compulsorily laid upon Him! He "became obedient." Why? To render to God and His law that perfect service which was required in order to our being (legally) "made righteous." But not until we rightly estimate the surpassing dignity and excellency of the Surety's *person* shall we be able to value aright the *worth* of His obedience.

Think of *whose* obedience it is! "The obedience of CHRIST—the obedience of Him who walketh in the circuit of the skies (Job 22:14), and all the kingdoms of the world are reputed as nothing before Him! The obedience of *Him* who doeth according to His will in the army of heaven and among the inhabitants of the earth (Dan. 4:35). The obedience of Him who is Alpha and Omega, the Beginning and the Ending, which is, and which was, and which is to come, the Almighty (Rev. 1:8). Doubtless, *such* obedience must be deserving, truly deserving, of all that Grace and Glory which are, and will be communicated to His people, in every period of time and throughout all ages of eternity. *Worthy* is the Lamb that was slain. No wonder that *such* obedience shall 'justify the ungodly' (Rom. 4:5); should make us poor fallen creatures righteous,—perfectly righteous in the sight of *God*—without the concurrence of any good works or any holy duties of our own.

"The infinitely most noble obedience of *Jesus Christ*. To this obedience I would have our thoughts continually directed. This surpasses the services of both angels and men, in all their various and wonderful orders. 'Tis true, compared with our duties, *Abraham's* obedience is like Saul's stature, who, from his shoulders upward, was higher than any of the people. But when the righteousness of *Christ* comes into view, it is somewhat like that magnificent Personage described in Rev. 10. Should such a sublime and majestic Being appear amidst an assembly of the most renowned monarchs of the world, how would their splendour be eclipsed, and all their grandeur dwindle into meanness! Before such an illustrious Potentate of heaven, who would take notice of Caesar, or bestow a look upon Alexander? So the righteousness of *Christ*, being the righteousness of Him who lay in the bosom of the Father from eternity, the righteousness of Him who now sits on the right hand of the throne of the Majesty in the heavens; this righteousness, being in itself most consummately perfect and unspeakably ennobled by the dignity of the Performer, all other kinds, degrees, or forms of righteousness, shrink before it into the littleness of pygmies, of worms, of mites. Could they speak, the language of each would be, 'Look not upon me for I am dim, yea, I am black. But look upon your *Lord*, for His works are marvelous, and *He* is glorious in His holiness" (James Hervey, Vol. 4, 1750, A. D.).

"Think not that I am come to destroy the law, or the prophets: I am not come to destroy, but to fulfil" (Matt. 5:17). As in Rom. 8:3, 4, here again we are informed what was the great objective before the Son of God in coming into this world. Having been, by His own free consent, "made under the law" (Gal. 4:4) not only to undergo its penalty and bear its curse, but also to keep its precepts (which is the principal part of it), Christ Himself here announces that He came to "fulfil" it. But the enemies of the truth have struggled hard, though quite unsuccessfully, to evacuate the meaning of that important word. They have affirmed that this term "fulfil" simply means Christ "filled out," or brought to light the hidden depths of the law's meaning, and revealed its searching holiness. But let it be duly noted that Christ here spoke of both the "law" and the "prophets"—did He "fill out" them? No, He *"fulfilled"* them!

Others say that Christ "fulfilled" the law in that He *expounded* it, which is contradicted by the whole tenor of His ministry: see particularly John 1:17. No, "fulfil" is here to be taken in its strict and obvious sense: just as "he that loveth another has *fulfilled* the law" (Rom. 13:8) means, he has met its requirements, he has kept its precepts. It is to be noted that Christ did not say, "think not I am come to destroy the law *and* the prophets," but "the law *or* the prophets . . . but to fulfil." Two separate and distinct things were here predicated by Christ. Its obvious meaning was, the O. T., in all its parts and elements, *referred to* Himself and was *accomplished by* and in Himself. Thus, "the law" here stands for the whole Jewish law (including its types —the sacrifices of the law), though having primary reference to the *moral* law, as is unmistakeably clear from the next twenty-seven verses. To obey its commands, to keep them in thought, word and deed, was the great end for which Christ became incarnate. This was man's duty, our duty; but we had failed to perform it, therefore did Christ come and discharge it for us.

In Matt. 5:20-42 Christ's main purpose was not to teach His people "Christian ethics" (*that* we have in the Epistles), but to arouse the consciences of His legalistic hearers. In this section of the Sermon on the Mount, our Lord expounded the law with the object of making men to see their *need* of a perfect righteousness (cf. Matt. 19:17), a righteousness which would fully meet the requirements of the thrice holy God, a righteousness in which *His* piercing eye could discern no flaw or blemish. It was *ignorance* of the law which was the real source of Phariseeism, for they claimed to fulfil it in the outward letter; therefore would Christ awaken their conscience by pressing its true inner import and exacting holy demands. It will be found that the "Sermon" perpetually returns to one main thought, applied with various modifications and peculiar terms; to awaken in men a sense of their depravity, to shut them up to the righteousness *of God*: see especially vv. 28, 44!

Matt. 5:20 is the sum and substance of all that follows to the end of that chapter. What then is the "righteousness" there spoken of? It is that justifying righteousness of God which fully meets the need of a divinely-convicted sinner. Its opening "for" plainly points back to v. 17. That "righteousness" which *exceeded* the punctillious outward performances of the Scribes and Pharisees is what the incarnate Son of God, acting as the Surety of His people, vicariously wrought out for them, and which upon their believing, is imputed to them; so that the flawless obedience of Christ to the whole will of God is reckoned to their account in such a way that *they* are legally regarded as having perfectly fulfilled the law in their own persons. God did not recede from His rights, but enforced them. The law *has been* fulfilled, by our Sponsor, and the transcendent merits of "the Just" (Acts. 3:14) are transferred to each of those for whom He acted. *This* is the "best robe" with which the returning prodigal is clothed! *This* is the "Court-dress" which fits for the King's palace. Thus can every true Christian not only say, "the blood of Christ has cleansed me from all sin," but also *"in the Lord* have I *righteousness"* (Isa. 45:24). Hallelujah! Much more remains yet to be said, but we must leave it (D.V.) for the next article.—A.W.P.

HUSBANDS

One of the perfections of Holy Writ lies in its blessed *balance* of Truth. If the duties of employees to their employers be pointed out, the obligations of masters to their servants are also insisted upon. If children be commanded to honour their father and mother, the parents are also reminded of the responsibilities which they have to their offspring. If wives are bidden to be in subjection to their husbands, the husbands are likewise exhorted to render unto their wives that which is due unto them. The scales of Divine justice are held evenly, for God is no respecter of persons. Nor is there anything lacking from His Word, for it contains that which "thoroughly furnishes unto all good works." May Divine grace enlarge the hearts of both writer and reader that we may run in the way of His commandments (Psa. 119:32).

The principle to which we have just called attention is exemplified in Eph. 5, Col. 3 and 1 Pet. 3. In each of those chapters the Holy Spirit has made known the will of God respecting the attitude which He requires the wife to take unto her husband. And, in each of those chapters He has also pressed upon the husband his obligations to his wife. Christian husbands have duties as well as rights, and while they have important claims upon their wives, their wives also have equally important claims upon them. Generally we are far more concerned about what others should be and do, than what *we* should be and do to others. But this ought not to be, and will not be so if due heed be given to *all* God has commanded. If the wife properly heeds what God has said to her, the husband will have no just ground for complaint; if the husband conducts himself toward his wife as God bids him, she will have no legitimate warrant for murmuring.

Putting it on its lowest ground, common gratitude surely requires that a recompense of true affection is due unto the one who has left her parents and relatives, to cleave unto her husband and share with him in all conditions until death. Moreover, human prudence teaches that the interests and comforts of the marriage-state require that the husband continue to cherish and care for his wife, for while love remains fresh, all things go sweetly; but when love fails, everything is soon out of joint—strife, unhappiness, and often divorce, being the certain outcome. Yet how often is the loving devotion on the part of the wife only, the husband taking it as his due, without any reciprocal return of affection and unselfish care. But God's Word gives no sanction to the husband conducting himself as an independent despot; instead, it affirms that he is under obligations no less strict than his wife. His headship is to be held not in wilfulness and selfishness, but in loving devotion; it is to be exercised not in arbitrary authority, but in seeking the welfare of his wife in all things.

"Husbands, love your wives, even as Christ also loved the church, and gave Himself for it" (Eph. 5:25). So far from Scripture warranting the husband being a domestic tyrant, it insists that his dominion is to be a reign of love. As in the preceding verse the subjection of the Church to Christ is set before the wife as the model for her conduct, so the example of Christ, in His relation to the Church, is held up before the husband. The husband's love for his wife is to be a reflection of Christ's love for His Church—pure and faithful, ardent and devoted, tender and self-abandoning, sacrificial and securing the highest happiness of its object. Just as the wife is to continue in subjection to her husband no matter how manifold his imperfections, so the husband is to continue loving his wife notwithstanding all her infirmities. Thus, his supremacy of place is to be justified practically by a more ardent affection.

"Husbands, love your wives, even as Christ also loved the Church and gave Himself for it." There is not a weightier, more comprehensive, and heart-searching injunction in all the Bible than this one, or one that calls for more earnest and daily seeking from God the grace needed to comply therewith. Christ loved His church with an intense inward affection which naught could quench. But more: He made full outward demonstration of His love by giving Himself for it. Such is the example and model of the husband's love for the wife which the Holy Spirit here holds up before him. His love is to be evidenced by protecting her from danger (Gen. 20:16), providing for her during his lifetime (1 Tim. 5:8), and, as far as he may, for the time after his death (Prov. 6:6-8), and by daily attentions and efforts to lighten her load and brighten her lot.

"Husbands *love* your wives." Love is the heart finding its delight in the object of its affections: thus we hear the

Saviour exclaiming anticipatively, "My *delights* were with the sons of men" (Prov. 8:31). Therefore does Scripture say, "Rejoice with the wife of (not merely "in") thy youth as the loving hind and pleasant roe; let her breasts satisfy thee at all times, and be thou ravished always with her love" (Prov. 5:18, 19). But more: love not only finds its delight in the object of its affections, but there flows from it a deep desire for its highest good, and unsparing efforts to promote this to the utmost extent of our power. Love is practical, and must be operative: "Let us not love in word, neither in tongue; but in deed and in truth" (1 John 3:18).

"Husbands, love your wives, and be not bitter against them" (Col. 3:19). In all the husband's intercourse with his wife he must ever be on his guard against sharpness of speech, severity of demeanor, or yielding to a spirit of being hard to please. His duty is to think less of exercising his authority than of manifesting his affection. Surliness is reprehensible. Even in times of provocation, the husband must not act hastily or speak harshly and cruelly; he is to overlook his wife's comparative frailty, and display his strength by controlling his temper. Let the patience of an unalterable love have its perfect work, overcoming evil with good, ever remembering, that "a soft answer turneth away wrath" (Prov. 15:1).

"Husbands, love your wives, and be not bitter against them." Allow no place to a bitter disposition which is provoked by trifles. Be not guilty of bitter words and speeches, which quickly destroy love and breed disaffection. Refrain from all bitter deeds which are unbecoming a Christian, and are unlike Christ's dealings with His Church. Instead of being bitter against the partner of your bosom, heed that word in Prov. 31:30, "A woman that feareth the Lord, she shall be *praised*." Forget not to praise her thriftiness, her cooking, her thoughtfulness for your wellbeing: note how in Rev. 2 and 3 Christ Himself praises every thing good which He found in the churches in Asia. When she needs admonishing, do it tenderly and in the fear of God.

"Likewise ye husbands, dwell with them according to knowledge, giving honour unto the wife, as unto the weaker vessel, and as being heirs together of the grace of life; that your prayers be not hindered" (1 Pet. 3:7). For some inexplicable reason the English translators have departed from the order of words in the Greek, quite changing their meaning. That the wife should be sympathised with and kindly help given her because she is the "weaker vessel," would be understandable, but to render her "honour" for *that* reason sounds paradoxical. The Bagster Interlinear rightly renders this verse as follows, "Husbands likewise, dwelling with (them) according to knowledge, as with a weaker (even) vessel, with the female, rendering (them) honour as also (being) joint heirs of (the) grace of life; so as not to be cut off your prayers." We shall follow this order of rendition.

"Likewise ye husbands dwell with." It has been pointed out by John Brown in his admirable commentary on this Epistle, that these words seem naturally to suggest that each married couple should have their own separate house to live in. This is confirmed by Eph. 5:31. It is an arrangement seldom disregarded without uncomfortable consequences. Years ago we heard it said, No house is large enough for two families, and we have lived to see the truth of this verified in more than one instance. But the words "dwell with" include something more. In all ordinary circumstances husbands are bound to make their houses their homes. The very word "husband" means "house-band," binding all the house together. This shows his place and what is required of him, reprimanding the man who is seldom in his household, who leaves it to the wife and servants to order.

There are exceptions to every rule. There may be times when duty obliges the bread-winner to be absent from his family for several days, yet this is to be avoided whenever possible, and God can make it possible where He is prayerfully sought unto. "It is *not good* that the man should be alone" (Gen. 2:18). And again it is written, "As a bird that wandereth from her nest, so is a man that wandereth from his place" (Prov. 27:8). The husband's place is by the side of his wife. How can a man who is away from home discharge his duties to his household? Family worship, family instruction, family discipline, must all, so far as he is concerned, be neglected. This same passage also condemns the man who, in his hours of recreation, seems fonder of almost any society than that of his wife. She is to be "dwelt with" as his chosen companion and confidential friend, her presence being the best refreshment after his toils, his loving attentions the alleviation of her burdens and anxieties. By a constant interchange of kindly offices, he will increase both in her and in himself that confidential esteem which makes all relative duties easy and pleasant.

"Dwelling with them according to knowledge, as with a weaker vessel." This last expression is no disparagement of her sex, nor is it contravened by any *exceptionally* strong-minded or strong-bodied member of it. "It is no insult to the vine to say that it is weaker than the tree to which it clings, or to the rose to say that it is weaker than the bush that bears it. The strongest things are not always the best, neither the most beautiful or the most useful" (John Lillie). God has not given to the woman the frame and constitution which fits her to rough it in the world, and in most instances where this fact is ignored, sooner or later she pays a heavy price. This relative weakness of the wife ought to engage the husband's superior strength on her behalf, and be a perpetual appeal unto his patience and tenderness. As the guardian of her earthly good, the husband is to be concerned about everything which relates to her health, comfort, and reputation. Holy discernment is called for if the fair flower which God has intrusted to him be not injured.

"Giving them honour as being heirs together of the grace of life." Not only is the husband to treat his wife as a consort and companion, rather than as his slave, pondering her counsel (Gen. 21:12, 1 Sam. 1:23), remembering that it is *hers* to look well to "the ways of her household" (Prov. 31:27), but also to view her as his spiritual equal, standing on the same level with himself in Christ, in whom there is "neither male nor female" (Gal. 3:28). He is to love her because Christ loves her. He is to respect her as one of those for whom Christ died. If this be properly realised then loth will they be to despise one another that are both bought with the precious blood of the same Redeemer, and loth will they be to grieve one another.

"That their prayers be not hindered" (1 Pet. 3:7). This is the final motive presented by the Holy Spirit for the husband to let love sweeten the yoke which God has placed upon the wife. "It is here plainly taken for granted that Christians habitually engage in prayer. The heirs of life cannot live without prayer. Having the spirit of adoption they cry 'Abba Father.' They pray in secret, and where two of these heirs are brought together in the closest of human relations, they pray together, and a great deal of their improvement and happiness depends on their prayers together and apart. Anything which hinders the latter, materially interferes with the former. The temper that leads him to neglect his duty to his wife, unfits him for his duty to his God; and though human unkindness, even from our best human friend, should lead us to go with greater alacrity to Him who is a friend at all times, yet the jars and contentions of husband and wife are in their own nature calculated so to embitter the spirit of both as to unfit for prayer, which should always be presented with holy hands, and must be offered without wrath if it is to be offered without doubting.

"There seems in these words a direct reference to family prayers. How can they be attended to at all, if the husband do not dwell with his wife? How can they be usefully attended to, if they dwell not together in unity? If family prayers are hindered, what hope of family prosperity, in the best sense of the words? And if conjugal duty is neglected, how can they but be hindered? Let, then, Christian husbands, and wives too, guard against everything which may hinder family prayer. Let their whole conduct toward each other look back and forward to the family altar. Let it be consistent with devotion, preparatory to it, indicative of its influence.

"The passage before us is merely a particular application of a great general principle: the connection between holy conduct and devotional exercises. They act and re-act on one another. The more conscientiously we perform our various duties, the more shall we be disposed for, the more enjoyment shall we find in, and the more advantage shall we derive from, our devotional exercises. Calling on the name of the Lord, and departing from iniquity, are closely conjoined" (John Brown). Wilful indulgence in a course of sinning, in any direction whatever, not only paralizes a spirit of true devotion, but "*cuts off*" the soul's communion with God. Nor is there any social sin that more directly tends to this fatal result than the disregard and violation of what a man owes in that tenderest of all his social relations—his relation to his wife.

How all of this should speak to young Christians who are seriously contemplating matrimony, to see well to it that the partner they choose for life, is one who will be a true help-meet, and not a hinderer of spiritual life and communion with God. "*Be not* unequally yoked together with unbelievers" (2 Cor. 6:14). A.W.P.

REGENERATION, or, THE NEW BIRTH

Two chief obstacles lie in the way of the salvation of any of Adam's fallen descendants: bondage to the guilt and penalty of sin, bondage to the power and presence of sin; or, in other words, their being bound for Hell and their being unfit for Heaven. These obstacles are, so far as man is concerned, entirely insurmountable. This fact was unequivocally established by Christ, when, in answer to His disciples' question, "Who then can be saved?" he answered, "with men this is *impossible*." A lost sinner might more easily create a world than save his own soul. But (forever be His name praised), the Lord Jesus went on to say, "with *God* all things *are* possible" (Matt. 19:25, 26). Yes, problems which completely baffle human wisdom, are solvable by Omniscience; tasks which defy the utmost efforts of man, are easily accomplished by Omnipotence. Nowhere is this fact more strikingly exemplified than in God's saving of the sinner.

As intimated above, two things are absolutely essential in order to salvation: deliverance from the guilt and penalty of sin, deliverance from the power and presence of sin. The one is secured by the mediatorial work of Christ, the other is accomplished by the effectual operations of the Holy Spirit. The one is the blessed result of what the Lord Jesus did *for* God's people; the other is the glorious consequence of what the Holy Spirit does *in* God's people. The one takes place when, having been brought to lie in the dust as an empty-handed beggar, faith is enabled to lay hold of Christ, God now justifies from all things, and the trembling, penitent, but believing sinner receives a free and full pardon. The other takes place gradually, in distinct stages, under the Divine blessings of regeneration, sanctification and glorification. In regeneration, indwelling sin receives its death-wound, though not its death. In sanctification, the regenerated soul is shown the sink of corruption that dwells within, and is taught to loathe and hate himself. At glorification both soul and body will be forever delivered from every vestige and effect of sin.

Now a vital and saving knowledge of these Divine truths cannot be acquired by a mere study of them. No amount of pouring over the Scriptures, no painstaking examination of the soundest doctrinal treatises, no exercise of the intellect, is able to secure the slightest spiritual insight into them. True, the diligent seeker may attain a natural knowledge, an intellectual apprehension of them, just as one born blind may obtain a notional knowledge of the colourings of the flowers or the beauties of a sunset; but the natural man can no more arrive at a *spiritual knowledge* of spiritual things, than a blind man can a true knowledge of natural things, yea, than a man in his grave can know what is going on in the world he has left. Nor can anything short of Divine power bring the proud heart to a felt realization of this humbling fact; only as God supernaturally enlightens, is any soul made conscious of the awful spiritual darkness in which it naturally dwells.

The truth of what has just been said is established by the plain and solemn declaration in 1 Cor. 2:14, "But the natural man receiveth not the things of the Spirit of God: for they are foolishness unto him: neither can he know them, because they are spiritually discerned." Alas that so many evade the sharp point of this verse by imagining it applies not to them, mistaking an intellectual assent to spiritual things for an experimental acquaintance of them. An external knowledge of Divine truth, as revealed in Scripture, may charm the mind and form ground for speculation and conversation, but unless there is a Divine *application* of them to the conscience and heart, such knowledge will be of no more avail in the hour of death than the pleasing images of our dreams are of any satisfaction when we awake. How awful to think that multitudes of professing Christians will awaken in Hell to discover that *their* knowledge of Divine truth was no more substantial than a dream.

While it be true that no man by searching can find out God (Job 11:7), and that the mysteries of His Kingdom are sealed secrets until He deigns to reveal them to the soul (Matt. 13:11), nevertheless, it is also true that God is pleased to use means in the conveyance of heavenly light to our sin-darkened understandings. It is for this reason that He commissions His servants to preach the Word, and, by voice and pen, expound the Scriptures; nevertheless, their labours will produce no eternal fruits, unless He condescends to bless the seed they sow and give it an increase. Thus, no matter how faithfully, simply, helpfully, a sermon be preached or an article written, unless the Spirit *applies* it to the heart, the hearer or reader is no spiritual gainer. Then will you not humbly entreat God to open *your* heart to receive whatever is according to His holy Word in this article.

In what follows, we shall, as God enables, seek to direct attention to what we have referred to at the beginning of this article as the second of those two humanly insurmountable obstacles which lies in the way of a sinner's salvation, and that is, the fitting of him for Heaven, by the delivering of him from the power and presence of sin. Such a work is a Divine one, and therefore is it *miraculous*. Regeneration is no mere outward reformation, no mere turning over a new leaf and endeavouring to live a better life. The new birth is very much more than going forward and taking the preacher's hand: it is a supernatural operation of God upon man's spirit, a transcendent wonder. All of God's works are wonderful. The world in which we live is filled with things which amaze us. Physical birth is a marvel, but, from several standpoints, the new birth is more remarkable. It is a marvel of Divine grace, Divine wisdom, Divine power, and Divine beauty. It is a miracle performed upon and within ourselves, of which we may be personally cognizant; it will prove an eternal marvel.

Because regeneration is the work of God, it is a *mysterious* thing. All God's works are shrouded in impenetrable mystery. Life, natural life in its origin, its nature, its processes, baffles the most careful investigator. Much more is this the case with spiritual life. The Existence and Being of God transcends the finite grasp; how then can we expect to understand the process by which we become His children? Our Lord Himself declared that the new birth was a thing of mystery: "the wind bloweth where it listeth, and thou hearest the sound thereof, but *canst not tell* whence it cometh, and whither it goeth, *so* is every one that is *born* of the Spirit" (John 3:8). The wind is something about which the most learned scientist knows next to nothing. Its nature, the laws which govern it, its causation, all lie beyond the purview of human inquiry. So it is with the new birth: it is profoundly mysterious.

Regeneration is an intensely *solemn* thing. The new birth is the dividing line between Heaven and Hell. In God's sight there are but two classes of people on this earth: those who are dead in sins, and those who are walking in newness of life. In the physical realm there is no such thing as being *between* life and death. A man is either dead or alive. The vital spark may be very dim, but while it exists, life is present. Let that spark go out altogether, and, though you may dress the body in beautiful clothes, nevertheless, it is nothing more than a corpse. So it is in the spiritual realm. We are either saints or sinners, spiritually alive or spiritually dead, children of God or children of the Devil. In view of this solemn fact, how momentous is the question, Have I been *born again?* If not, and you die in your present state, you will wish you had never been born at all.

I. *Its Necessity*

1. *The need for regeneration lies in our natural degeneration.* In consequence of the fall of our first parents, all of us were born alienated from the Divine life and holiness, despoiled of all those perfections wherewith man's nature was at first endowed. Ezek. 16:4, 5 gives a graphic picture of our terrible spiritual plight at our entrance into this world: cast out to the loathing of our persons, rolling ourselves in our own filth, impotent to help ourselves. That "likeness" of God (Gen. 1:26) which was at first stamped on man's soul has been effaced, aversion from God and an inordinate love of the creature having displaced it. The very fountain of our beings is polluted, continually sending forth bitter springs, and though those streams take several courses and wander in various channels, yet are they all brackish. Therefore is the "sacrifice" of the wicked an abomination to the Lord (Prov. 15:8), and his very ploughing "sin" (Prov. 21:4).

There are but two states, and all men are included therein: the one a state of spiritual life, the other a state of spiritual death; the one a state of righteousness, the other a state of sin; the one saving, the other damning; the one a state of enmity, wherein men have their inclinations contrary to God; the other a state of friendship and fellowship, wherein men walk obediently unto God, and would not willingly have an inward motion opposed to His will. The one state is called darkness, the other light: "For ye were (in your unregenerate days, not only in the dark, but) darkness, but now are ye light in the Lord" (Eph. 5:8). There is no medium between these conditions; all are in one of them. Each man and woman now on earth is either an object of God's delight or of His abomination. The most benevolent and imposing works of the flesh cannot please Him, but the faintest sparks proceeding from that which grace hath kindled are acceptable in His sight.

By the fall man contracted an *unfitness* to that which is good. Shapen in iniquity and conceived in sin (Psa. 51:5), man is a "transgressor from the womb" (Isa. 48:8): "they go astray as soon as they be born, speaking lies" (Psa. 58:3), and "the imagination of man's heart is evil from his youth" (Gen. 8:21). He may be civilized, educated, refined, and even religious, but at heart he is "desperately wicked" (Jer. 17:9), and all that he does is vile in the sight of God, for nothing is done from love to Him, and with a view to His glory. "A good tree cannot bring forth evil fruit, neither can a corrupt tree bring forth good fruit" (Matt. 7:18). Until they are born again, all men are "unto every good work reprobate" (Titus 1:16).

By the fall man contracted an *unwillingness* to that which is good. All motions of the will in its fallen estate, through defect of a right principle from whence they flow and a right end to which they tend, are only evil and sinful. Leave man to himself, remove from him all the restraints which law and order impose, and he swiftly degenerates to a lower level than the beasts, as almost any missionary will testify. And is human nature any better in civilized lands? Not a whit. Wash off the artificial veneer and it will be found that "as in water face answereth to face, so the heart of man to man" (Prov. 27:19). The world over it remains solemnly true that "the carnal mind is enmity against God: for it is not subject to the law of God neither indeed can be" (Rom. 8:7). Christ will prefer the same charge in a coming day as when He was here on earth: "Men loved darkness rather than light" (John 3:19). Men *will not* come to Him that they might have life."

By the fall man contracted an *inability* to do that which is good. He is not only unfitted and unwilling, but *unable* to do that which is good. Where is the man that can truthfully say he has measured up to his own ideals? All have to acknowledge there is a strange force within dragging them downward, inclining them to evil, which, notwithstanding their utmost endeavours against it, in some form or other, more or less, conquers them. Despite the kindly exhortations of friends, the faithful warnings of God's servants, the solemn examples of suffering and sorrow, disease and death on every side, and the vote that their own conscience gives, yet they yield. "They that are in the flesh (in their natural condition) *cannot please God*" (Rom. 8:8:).

Thus it is evident that the need is imperative for a radical and revolutionary change to be wrought in fallen man before he can have any fellowship with the thrice holy God. Since the earth must be completely changed, because of the curse now resting on it, before it can ever again bring forth fruit as it did when man was in a state of innocency; so must man, since a general defilement from Adam has seized upon him, be renewed, before he can "bring forth fruit to God" (Rom. 7:4). He must be grafted upon another stock, united to Christ, partake of the power of His resurrection; without this he may bring forth fruit, but not unto God. How can any one turn to God without a principle of spiritual motion? How can he live to God who has no spiritual life? How can he be fit for the kingdom of God who is of a brutish and diabolical nature?

2. *The need for regeneration lies in man's total depravity*. Every member of Adam's race is a fallen creature, and every part of his complex being has been corrupted by sin. Man's heart is deceitful above all things and desperately wicked (Jer. 17:9). His mind is blinded by Satan (2 Cor. 4:4) and darkened by sin (Eph. 4:18), so that his thoughts are only evil continually (Gen. 6:5). His affections are prostituted, so that he loves what God hates and hates what God loves. His will is enslaved from good (Rom. 6:20) and opposed to God (Rom. 8:7). He is without righteousness (Rom. 3:10), under the curse of the law (Gal. 3:10) and is the captive of the Devil. His condition is truly deplorable, and his case desperate. He cannot better himself, for he is "without strength" (Rom. 5:6). He cannot work out his salvation, for there dwelleth no good thing in him (Rom. 7:18). He needs, then, to be born of God, "for in Christ Jesus neither circumcision availeth anything, nor uncircumcision, but *a new creation*" (Gal. 6:15).

Man is a fallen creature. It is not that a few leaves have faded, but that the entire tree has become rotten, root and branch. There is in every one that which is radically wrong. The word "radical" comes from a Latin one which means "the root," so that when we say a man is radically wrong, we mean that there is in him, in the very foundation and fiber of his being, that which is intrinsically corrupt and essentially evil. Sins are merely the fruit, there must of necessity be a root from which they spring. It follows, then, as an inevitable consequence that man needs the aid of a Higher Power to effect a radical change in him. There is only One who can effect that change: God created man, and God alone can re-create him. Hence the imperative demand, "Ye *must* be born again" (John 3:7). Man is spiritually *dead* and naught but all-mighty power can make him alive.

"By one man sin entered into the world, and death by sin; and so death passed upon all men" (Rom. 5:12). In the day that Adam ate of the forbidden fruit, he died spiritually, and a person who is spiritually dead cannot beget a child who possesses spiritual life. Therefore, all by natural descent enter this world "alienated from the life of God" (Eph. 4:18), "dead in trespasses and sins" (Eph. 2:1). This is no mere figure of speech, but a solemn fact. Every child is born entirely destitute of a single spark of spiritual life, and therefore if ever it is to enter the kingdom of God, which is the realm of spiritual life (Rom. 14:17), it must be *born* into it. A.W.P.

To be continued, D.V.

PRIDE

Pride is the greatest of all evils that beset us, and, of all our enemies, it is that which dies the slowest and hardest; even the children of the world are able to discern this. Madame De Staël said, on her death-bed, "Do you know what is the last to die in man? It is self-love." God hates pride above all things, because it gives to man the place that belongs to Him who is above, exalted over all. Pride intercepts communion with God, and draws down His chastisement, for God resists the proud. He will destroy the name of the proud, and we are told that there is a day appointed when the loftiness of man shall be bowed down, and the haughtiness of man laid low. I am sure, then, you will feel, my dear friend, that one man cannot do another a greater injury than by praising him, and feeding his pride. "He that flattereth his neighbour, spreadeth a snare for his feet," and "a flattering mouth worketh ruin." Be assured, moreover, that we are far too short-sighted to be able to judge of the degree of our brother's piety; we are not able to judge it aright without the balance of the sanctuary, and that is in the hand of Him who searches the heart. Judge nothing, therefore, before the time, until the Lord come, and makes manifest the counsels of the heart, and renders to every man his praise. Till then, let us not judge of our brethren, whether for good or for evil, but with becoming moderation, and remember that the surest and best judgment is what we form of ourselves when we esteem others better than ourselves.

If I were to ask you how you know that I am one of the most advanced in the Christian career, and an eminent servant of God, you would, no doubt, be at a loss to reply. You would, perhaps, cite my published works, but you do not know, my dear friend and brother, you, who can preach an edifying sermon as well as I can, that the eyes see further than the feet go, and that unhappily, we are not always, nor in all things, what our sermons are; that we have this treasure in earthen vessels, that the excellency of the power may be of God, and not of us. I will not tell you the opinion I have of myself, for, in doing so, I shall probably, all the while, be seeking my own glory; and while seeking my own glory, appear humble, which I am not. I had rather tell you what our Master thinks of me—He that searches the heart, and speaks the truth, who is the Amen, the Faithful Witness, and has often spoken in my inmost soul, and I thank Him for it; but, believe me, He has never told me I am an "eminent Christian, and advanced in the ways of Godliness." On the contrary, He tells me very plainly that if I knew my own place, I should find it that of the chief of sinners, and least of all saints. His judgment, surely, my dear friend, I should take rather than yours.

The most eminent Christian is one of those of whom no one has ever heard speak, some poor labourer, or servant, whose whole is Christ, and who does all for His eye, and His alone. The first shall be last. Let us be persuaded, my dear friend, to praise the Lord alone. He only is worthy of being praised, revered, and adored. His goodness is never sufficiently celebrated. The song of the blessed (Revelation 5) praises none but Him who redeemed them with His blood. It contains not one word of praise for any of their own number—not a word that classes them into eminent, or not eminent—all distinctions are lost in the common title, the redeemed, which is the happiness and glory of their whole body. Let us strive to bring our hearts into unison with that song in which we all hope that our feeble voices will one day mingle. This will be our happiness, even here below, and contribute to God's glory, which is wronged by the praise that Christians too often bestow on each other. We cannot have two mouths—one for God's praise, and one for man's. May we then, do now, what the seraphim do above, who with two wings cover their faces, as a token of their confusion before the holy presence of the Lord; with two cover their feet, as if to hide their steps from themselves; and with the remaining two fly to execute their Lord's will, while they cry, "Holy, holy, holy, Lord God of hosts, all the earth is full of Thy glory." J. N. Darby.

FAITH

"But without FAITH it is impossible to please Him" (*Heb.* 11:6).

No matter how much light we may have, no matter how zealous we may be, no matter how well-thought of by the true people of God, only as faith is really *in operation* do we "please" God. This is very searching and should lead to frequent self-examination. "Man looketh on the outward appearance, but God looketh on the heart." Our outward conduct may be blameless, but the heart (which man cannot see) may be far from the Lord. It is the childlike trustful confidence of our inner being that He desires. Then how earnestly should we beg God, each day, to *stir into exercise* the faith which He has given us!

Not only is it true that the un-regenerate cannot originate faith by any efforts of their own, or produce it by any resolution of mind or determination of will, but it is also true (though very few realize it) that the regenerate cannot *call into action* the faith which God has already bestowed upon them. This is very humbling, yet it is God's truth nevertheless. Even the apostle Paul had to say, "For to will *is* present with me, *but* to perform that which is good I find not" (Rom. 7:18). As a regenerated man he had the "will" or desire to do that which is good, to please God, but the *power* to "perform" or carry-out his desire, he had not. No; Christ has told us plainly, "Without Me ye can do nothing" (John 15:5). These words are far reaching. Apart from Christ's direct enabling we can not even call into exercise the faith which we have.

What, then, are we to do? First, humbly acknowledge and confess to God our sinful inability, our excuseless lack of power. Second, beg Him to *work in us* what we are unable to do of ourselves. Say unto Him, "Lord, Thou has said in Thy Word, 'Without faith it is impossible to please' Thee. I long *to* please Thee. I *want* to honour and glorify Thee in daily walking by faith; but of myself I am unable to do so. O God, for *Christ's* sake, work in me by the power of Thy blessed Spirit that which *is* 'pleasing' in Thy sight. Stir up Thine own gift of faith within me into *exercise and act;* yea, Lord, increase my faith." Third, *expect* Him to do so. Count upon Him hearing and answering your petitions.

Pay no attention to your feelings. The devil will attack you at this very point. He will say, "You have asked God to call into exercise, unto action, the faith He has given you, and to increase it; but He has not done so, the proof being that you *feel* no difference." But faith is something that we cannot "feel:" it is *spiritual*, and therefore lies outside the range of our *natural* senses. Faith has to do with God, and He cannot be known through our natural faculties or feelings. Real faith looks away from self with its emotions and reasonings; looks to God, eyes His promises, and *trusts* Him to fulfill them.

But it is altogether contrary to the "flesh" (man in his fallen condition) *to* look to God. By nature we look to and trust in any one and anything rather than to and in the living God. *That* is why we need to cry and ask Him to put forth *His* power and produce in and through us a super-natural (above nature) faith with its supernatural fruit! May the Lord graciously make each one of us more conscious of our deep need of crying to Him *daily*, "Lord, stir up into exercise and call forth into action the faith which Thou hast given me." A. W. P.

"If thou Lord, shouldest mark (impute) iniquities, O Lord, who shall stand?" (Psa. 130:3). Well may each of us ask this question, for it is written "the ungodly shall not stand in the judgment" (Psa. 1:5). How sorely was *Christ's* soul exercised with thoughts of God's marking the iniquities of His people when they were upon Him! He was "amazed and very heavy" (Mark 14:33). His awful agony, His bloody sweat, His strong cries and supplications (Heb. 5:7), His reiterated prayers "If it be possible, let this cup pass from Me," His last dreadful cry "My God, My God, why hast Thou forsaken Me?," all manifest what fearful apprehensions He had of *what it was for God to* "mark iniquities." Well may poor sinners cry out, Lord *who* shall "stand" when the Son of God Himself so trembled beneath the weight of His wrath. If thou, my reader, hast not "fled for refuge" to Christ, the only Saviour, "how wilt thou do in the swelling of Jordan?" (Jer. 12:5).

"When I consider how the goodness of God is abused by the greatest part of mankind, I cannot but be of his mind that said, the greatest miracle in the world is God's patience and bounty to an ungrateful world. If a prince hath an enemy got into one of his towns, he doth not send them in provision, but lays close siege to the place, and doth what he can to starve them. But the great God, that could wink all His enemies into destruction, bears with them, and is at daily cost to maintain them. Well may He command us to bless them that curse us, who Himself does good to the evil and unthankful. But think not, sinners, that you shall escape thus; God's mill goes slow, but grinds small; the more admirable His patience and bounty now is, the more dreadful and unsupportable will that fury be which ariseth out of His abused goodness. Nothing smoother than the sea, yet when stirred into a tempest, nothing rageth more. Nothing so sweet as the patience and goodness of God, and nothing so terrible as His wrath when it takes fire" (Wm. Gurnall, 1660). Then "flee" my reader, flee to Christ; "flee *from* the wrath to come" (Matt. 3:7) ere it be too late. Do not, we earnestly beseech you, suppose that this message is intended for somebody else. It is *to you!* Do not be contented by *thinking* you *have* already fled to Christ. Make *certain!* Beg the Lord to search your heart and show you yourself. A. W. P.

N. B. *A word to Preachers.* Brethren, do we in our oral ministry, preach on this solemn subject as much as we ought? The O. T. prophets frequently told their hearers that their wicked lives provoked the Holy One of Israel, and that they were treasuring up to themselves wrath against the day of wrath. And conditions in the world are no better now than they were then! Nothing is so calculated to arouse the careless and cause carnal professors to search their hearts, as to enlarge upon the fact that "God is angry with the wicked every day" (Psa. 7:11). The forerunner of Christ warned his hearers to "Flee from the wrath to come" (Matt. 3:7). The Saviour Himself bade his auditors "Fear Him, which after He hath killed, hath power to cast into Hell; yea, I say unto you, Fear Him" (Luke 12:5). The apostle Paul said, "Knowing therefore the *terror* of the Lord, we persuade men" (2 Cor. 5:11). Faithfulness demands that we speak as plainly about Hell as Heaven.

The series of expositions of the Epistle to the Hebrews began Jan., 1928. At the end of each year we have the twelve issues nicely bound, for those who desire them in more permanent form. The first six volumes have been out of print for some time past, and will not be reissued. But we can still supply the 1928, 1929, 1930 volumes, the three for $3 (12/6) postpaid. We cannot break a set, as we have fewer of 1928 than the later years. Any desiring a single volume may have either the 1929 or 1930.

"If today He deigns to bless us
    With a sense of pardoned sin;
He tomorrow may distress us,
    Make us feel the plague within;
All to make us
    Sick of self and fond of Him."

That Divine wrath *is* one of the *perfections* of God is not only evident from the considerations presented above, but is also clearly established by the express declarations of His own Word. "For the wrath of God is revealed *from heaven*" (Rom. 1:18). "It was revealed when the sentence of death was first pronounced, the earth cursed, and man driven out of the earthly paradise; and afterwards by such examples of punishment as those of the Deluge and the destruction of the Cities of the Plain by fire from heaven; but especially by the reign of death throughout the world. It was proclaimed in the curse of the law on every transgression, and was intimated in the institution of sacrifice. In the 8th of Romans, the apostle calls the attention of believers to the fact, that the whole creation has become subject to vanity, and groaneth and travaileth together in pain. The same creation which declares that there is a God, and publishes His glory, also proclaims that He is the Enemy of sin and the Avenger of the crimes of men. But above all, the wrath of God was revealed from heaven when the Son of God came down to manifest the Divine character, and when that wrath was displayed in His sufferings and death, in a manner more awful than by all the tokens God had before given of His displeasure against sin. Besides this, the future and eternal punishment of the wicked is now declared in terms more solemn and explicit than formerly. Under the new dispensation there are two revelations given from heaven, one of wrath, the other of grace" (Rob. Haldane).

Again; that the wrath of God is a Divine perfection is plainly demonstrated by what we read of in Psa. 95:11, "Unto whom I sware in My wrath." There are two occasions of God "swearing:" in making promises (Gen. 22:16), and in denouncing threatenings (Deut. 1:34). In the former, He swares in mercy to His children; in the latter, He swares to terrify the wicked. An oath is for solemn confirmation: Heb. 6:16. In Gen. 22:16 God said, "*By Myself* have I sworn." In Psa. 89:35 He declares, "Once have I sworn *by My holiness*." While in Psa. 95:11 He affirmed, "I sware *in My wrath*." Thus the great Jehovah Himself appeals to His "wrath" as a perfection equal to His "holiness:" He swares by the one as much as by the other! Again; as in Christ "dwelleth all the fulness of the Godhead bodily" (Col. 2:9), and as all the Divine perfections are illustriously displayed by Him (John 1:18), therefore do we read of "the *wrath* of the Lamb" (Rev. 6:16).

The wrath of God is a perfection of the Divine character upon which we need to frequently meditate. First, that our hearts may be duly impressed by God's holy detestation of sin. We are ever prone to regard sin lightly, to gloss over its hideousness, to make excuses for it. But the more we study and ponder God's abhorrence of sin and His frightful vengeance upon it, the more likely are we to realize its heinousness. Second, to beget a true fear in our souls for God: "Let us have grace whereby we may serve God acceptably with reverence and godly fear: for our God is a consuming fire" (Heb. 12:28, 29). We cannot serve Him "acceptably" unless there is due "reverence" for His awful Majesty and "godly fear" of His righteous anger, and these are best promoted by frequently calling to mind that "our God is a consuming fire." Third, to draw out our souls in fervent praise for having delivered us *from* "the wrath to come" (1 Thess. 1:10).

Our readiness or our reluctancy to *meditate* upon the wrath of God becomes a sure test of how our hearts really stand affected toward Him. If we do not truly rejoice in God, for what He is in Himself, and that because of *all* the perfections which are eternally resident in Him, then how dwelleth *the love of God* in us? Each of us needs to be most prayerfully on his guard against devising an image of God in our thoughts which is patterned after our own evil inclinations. Of old the Lord complained, "Thou thoughtest that I was altogether as *thyself*" (Psa. 50:21). If we rejoice not "at the remembrance of His *holiness*" (Psa. 97:12), if we rejoice not to know that in a soon-coming Day God will make a most glorious display of His *wrath*, by taking vengeance on all who now oppose Him, it is proof positive that our hearts are *not* in subjection to Him, that we are yet in our sins, on the way to the everlasting burnings.

"*Rejoice*, O ye nations (Gentiles) His people: *for* He will avenge the blood of His servants, and will render vengeance to His adversaries" (Deut. 32:43). And again we read, "I heard a great voice of much people in heaven, saying Alleluia; Salvation, and glory, and honour, and power, unto the Lord our God; *For* true and righteous are His judgments: for He hath judged the great whore, which did corrupt the earth with her fornication, and hath avenged the blood of His servants at her hand. And again they said Alleluia" (Rev. 19:13). Great will be the rejoicing of the saints in that day when the Lord shall vindicate His majesty, exercise His awful dominion, magnify His justice, and overthrow the proud rebels who have dared to defy Him.

(Continued on Page 95)

VOL. X   MAY, 1931   No. 5

STUDIES IN THE SCRIPTURES

"Search the Scriptures" John 5:39

Copyright in all English-speaking Countries

EDITOR: Arthur W. Pink, 559 Dupont Ave., York, Penna., U. S. A.
Hon. Agent in England: Mr. A. Winstone, "Shalom," Old Bath Road, Leckhampton, Cheltenham.
Hon. Agent in Australia: Mr. G. Ardill, The Christian Workers' Depot, Commonwealth and Reservoir Streets, Sydney.

THE CONTEMPLATION OF GOD

For the past sixteen months we have had in review some of the wondrous and lovely perfections of the Divine character. From this most feeble and faulty contemplation of His attributes, it should be evident to us all that God is, first, an *incomprehensible* Being, and, lost in wonder at His infinite greatness, we are constrained to adopt the words of Zophar, "Canst thou by searching find out God? canst thou find out the Almighty unto perfection? It is high as heaven; what canst thou do? deeper than hell; what canst thou know? The measure thereof is longer than the earth, and broader than the sea" (Job 11:7-9). When we turn our thoughts to God's eternity, His immateriality, His omnipresence, His almightiness, our minds are overwhelmed.

But the incomprehensibility of the Divine nature is not a reason why we should desist from reverent inquiry and prayerful strivings to apprehend what He has so graciously revealed of Himself in His Word. Because we are unable to acquire perfect knowledge, it would be folly to say we will therefore make no efforts to attain to *any* degree of it. It has been well said that, "Nothing will so enlarge the intellect, nothing so magnify the whole soul of man, as a devout, earnest, continued, investigation of the great subject of the Deity. The most excellent study for expanding the soul, is the science of Christ and Him crucified and the knowledge of the Godhead in the glorious Trinity" (C. H. Spurgeon). To quote a little further, from this prince of preachers:

"The proper study of the Christian is the Godhead. The highest science, the loftiest speculation, the mightiest philosophy, which can engage the attention of a child of God, is the name, the nature, the person, the doings, and the existence of the great God which he calls his Father. There is something exceedingly improving to the mind in a contemplation of the Divinity. It is a subject so vast, that all our thoughts are lost in its immensity; so deep, that our pride is drowned in its infinity. Other subjects we can comprehend and grapple with; in them we feel a kind of self-content, and go on our way with the thought, 'Behold I am wise.' But when we come to this master science, finding that our plumbline cannot sound its depth, and that our eagle eye cannot see its height, we turn away with the thought 'I am but of yesterday and know nothing' " (Sermon on Mal. 3:6).

Yes, the incomprehensibility of the Divine nature should teach us humility, caution and reverence. After all our searchings and meditations we have to say with Job, "Lo, these are parts of His ways: but how little a portion is heard of Him!" (26:14). When Moses besought Jehovah for a sight of His glory, He answered him "I will proclaim the name of the Lord before thee" (Ex. 33:19), and, as another has said, "the name is the collection of His attributes." Rightly did the Puritan John Howe declare, "The notion therefore we can hence form of His glory, is only such as we may have of a large volume by a brief synopsis, or of a spacious country by a little landscape. He hath here given us a true report of Himself, but not a full; such as will secure our apprehensions—being guided thereby —from error, but not from ignorance. We can apply our minds to contemplate the several perfections whereby the blessed God discovers to us His being, and can in our thoughts attribute them all to Him, though we have still but low and

(Continued on Page 120)

IMPORTANT NOTICES

Please advise promptly of change of address, otherwise copies will be lost in the mails.

We are glad to send a sample copy to any of your friends whom you believe would be interested in such a publication.

Send to Mr. I. C. Herendeen, Swengel (Union County), Penna., for a list of our publications. He has published many of our books and booklets.

This magazine is published as a work of faith and labour of love. The Editor and his wife gladly give their services. It is freely sent to all who will read it. No charge is made for it.

Christians who feel definitely led to do so, may have fellowship with us in this ministry. Those outside the U. S. A., please send only INTERNATIONAL Money Orders made out to York, Penna., U. S. A.

CONTENTS

The Contemplation of God	97
The Epistle to the Hebrews	98
The Satisfaction ("Atonement") of Christ	104
Regeneration, or, The New Birth	111
Profiting from the Word	115

THE EPISTLE TO THE HEBREWS

41. *Eternal Redemption:* Heb. 9:11-14

In 8:6 the apostle had affirmed, "He is the Mediator of a better covenant." Such a declaration would raise a number of important issues which are here anticipated and settled. Who is the High Priest of the new covenant? What is the tabernacle wherein He administered His office? What are the particular services He performed, answering to those which God appointed unto Aaron and his successors? Wherein do the services of the new High Priest excel those of the Levitical? These were pressing questions, and it was necessary for them to be Divinely answered, not only for the silencing of objectors, but that the faith of believing Jews might be established. Thus, in 9:11, 12 we have the actual ministry of Christ declared, in vv. 13, 14 the proofs that it was "more excellent."

The 9th chapter of Hebrews contains a particular exemplification of this general proposition: Christ is the substance of the Levitical shadows. The general proposition was stated in 8:1, 2: Christians have an High Priest who is a Minister of the true tabernacle. Here in chapter 9 confirmation is given of what was pointed out at the close of 8, namely, that Christ's bringing in of the new covenant did abrogate the old. In exemplifying this fact mention is made in 9:1-10 of sundry shadows of the law, in v. 11 and onwards it is shown that the antitypical accomplishment of them was in and by Jesus Christ. The contents of vv. 1-10 may be reduced to two heads: ordinances of Divine service, and a worldly sanctuary in which they were observed. In vv. 11 to 28 the Spirit magnifies the excellency of Christ's priesthood by showing that He brought in what the Aaronic rites were unable to secure (condensed from W. Gouge, 1650).

The contents of these verses which are now to be before us set forth the ministry of Christ as "the Mediator of the new covenant." They describe His initial work as the High Priest of His people. They set forth the inestimable value of His sacrifice, and what it procured. They magnify His precious blood and the character of that redemption which was purchased thereby. Each verse calls for a separate article, and every clause in them demands our closest and most reverent attention. May the Spirit of God deign to open unto us something of their blessed contents, and apply them in power to our hearts. We purposely cut down our introductory comments that more space may be reserved for the exposition.

"But Christ being come an high priest of good things to come, by a greater and more perfect tabernacle, not made with hands, that is to say, not of this building; Neither by the blood of goats and calves, but by His own blood, He entered in once into the holy place, having obtained eternal redemption for us" (vv. 11, 12). "These words naturally call attention to two things: The official character with which our Lord is invested, and the ministry which He has performed in that official character. His official character: He is 'come an high priest of good things to come.' His ministry in that official character: 'He has obtained eternal redemption for His people'" (John Brown).

"But Christ being come an High Priest." The opening word emphasises a contrast: the legal high priest "could not make him that did the service perfect, as pertaining to the conscience" (v. 9): "*But Christ*"—could. The title here given the Saviour deserves particular notice. He is referred to in a considerable variety of ways in this epistle, and many different designations are there accorded Him. Each one is used with fine discrimination, and the reader loses much by failing to distinguish the force of "Jesus," "Christ," "Jesus Christ," "our Lord," "The Son," etc. Here (and also in 3:6, 14; 5:5; 6:1; 9:14, 24, 28; 11:26) it is "Christ," the Messiah (John 1:41), His official designation, a term that means "The Anointed," see Psa. 2:2 and cf. Acts 4:26. Great emphasis is placed by the Holy Spirit upon this title: "the Christ" (John 20:31), "that Christ" (John 6:69), "very Christ" (Acts 9:22), "The Lord's Christ" (Luke 2:26), "The Christ of God" (Luke 9:20).

"But Christ being come an High Priest." Under the name of the Messiah or Anointed One, He had been promised unto Israel for many centuries, and now the accomplishment had arrived. In a moment of doubt, His forerunner, in prison, sent unto Him asking, "Art Thou He that should come?" (Matt. 11:3). Upon the fulfillment of God's promises that He would send the Messiah, give a perfect revelation of His will, and bring in "perfection," the faith of the Jewish church was built. And now God's Word was verified, the true Light s h o n e. The awaited One had come: "in the character in which He was promised, having done all that it was promised He should do" (John Brown). Therefore does the Holy Spirit here given the Redeemer His official, and distinctively Hebrew, title. "But Christ being come" no doubt looks back, especially to Psa. 40:7.

"But Christ being come an High Priest." True, He came also as Prophet (Deut. 18:15, 18), and as King (Matt. 2:2), but here the Holy Spirit especially emphasises the sacerdotal office of Christ, because it was in the exercise of *that* He offered Himself as a sacrifice unto God. The words which we are now considering begin a new division of this Epistle, though it is intimately related to what has gone before. In 9:11 to 10:22 the Holy Spirit sets before us the antitype of Lev. 16, which records the work of Israel's high priest on the annual day of atonement. There we behold Aaron officiating both outside the veil and within it. So the priestly functions of Christ fall into two great divisions, as they were performed on earth and as they are now continued in heaven. Before our great High Priest could enter the Holiest on high and there make intercession before God, He had first to make an atonement for the sins of those He represented, which was accomplished in His state of abjection here below, being consummated by His offering Himself a sacrifice unto God: 7:27, 8:3, 9:26.

A priest is one who officiates in the name of others, who approaches to God in order to make atonement for them by sacrifice. The design of his ministry is to render the Object of their worship propitious, to avert His wrath from men, to procure their restoration to His favour: see Lev. 16. Thus, the work of the priest is mediatory. Since the fact of sin is a cardinal one in the case of man, the function of a mediating priest for man must be mainly expiatory and reconciling: Heb. 8:3. It should serve as a most solemn warning unto all today that, while the Jews believed their Messiah would be both a prophet and king, they had no expectation of His also being priest, who should redeem sinners unto God. One who should go forth in the terror of His power, subjugating the nations and restoring the kingdom to Israel, appealed to their carnality; but for One to minister at the altar, employ His interest with God on behalf of transgressors, draw near to the Divine Majesty in their name, and mediate peace between them and an offended Creator, seems to have had *no* place in their thoughts. Hence it is that the *priesthood* of Christ is given such a prominent place in this epistle to the *Hebrews*.

"But Christ being come an High Priest." As to the *time* of His investiture with this office, it was clearly co-incident to the general office of *Mediator*. At the same moment that God appointed His Son "Mediator," He was c o n s t i t u t e d the Prophet, the Priest, and the Potentate of His Church. Prospectively, that took place in the eternal councils of the blessed Trinity, when in the "everlasting covenant" the Father appointed the Son and the Son agreed to be the Mediator between Him and His people. Historically, the Son became the Mediator at the moment of His incarnation: there is "one Mediator between God and men, the *Man* Christ Jesus" (1 Tim. 2:5); as soon as He was born, He was hailed as *"Christ, the Lord"* (Luke 2:11). Formally, He was officially consecrated to this office at His baptism, when He was *"anointed* (Christed) with the Holy Spirit and with power" (Acts 10:38).

"But Christ being come an High Priest," and this according to the eternal oath of the Father, which "oath" was afterwards made known to the sons of men in time. This was before us when we considered 7:20-25. It was "by the word of the oath" that the Son is consecrated to His priestly office (7:28), the "oath" denoting God's eternal purpose and unchanging decree. In Psa. 2:7 we read that God said, "I *will declare* the decree," and accordingly in Psa. 110:4 we are told, "The Lord hath sworn, and will not repent, Thou are a priest forever after the order of Melchizedek"—there it was openly published. That God's "oath" *preceded* Christ's entrance upon and discharge of His sacerdotal office is clear from Heb. 7:20-25, otherwise the force of the apostle's reasoning there would be completely overthrown.

"But Christ *being come* an High Priest," otherwise He *could not* have "offered" Himself a sacrifice to God. As we saw when pondering 5:6, 7, Christ was exercising His sacerdotal functions in "the days of His flesh," i. e., the time of His humiliation. So too it was as "a merciful and faithful High Priest" that Christ "made propitiation for the sins of the people" (2:17). The types foreshadowed the same thing, especially Lev. 16. Aaron was not constituted a priest by entering the holy of holies; he was such before, or otherwise he could not have passed within the veil. Every passage which speaks of Christ's *one* oblation or His "offering" Himself *once* are conclusive as to His being a priest here on earth, for that word "once" cannot possibly be understood of what He is now doing in heaven; it must refer to His death as an historical fact, completed and finished here below: it is in designed contrast from His *continuous* intercession which is based upon it. The priestly sacrifice which He offered is emphatically described as co-incident with His death: 9:26. Any one of the common people could slay the sin-offering (Lev. 4:27-29), but none save the priest could *offer* it to God (Lev. 4:30)! Thus, every verse which speaks of Christ "offering" Himself to God emphasises the *priestly* character of His sacrifice.

"An high priest of good things to come." The reference here is to that more excellent dispensation which the Messiah was to inaugurate. Old Testament prophecy had announced many blessings and privileges which He would bring in, and accordingly the Jews had looked forward to better things than they had enjoyed under the old economy. The apostle here announces that this time had actually arrived, that the promised blessings had been procured by the High Priest of Christianity. As the result of Christ's advent, life and death, righteousness had been established, peace had been made, and a new and living way opened, which gave access to the very presence of God. Different far were *these* blessings from what the carnal Jews of Christ's day desired. Of course the "good things to come" are not to be restricted to those blessings which God's people already enjoy, but include as well those which yet await them. The "good things" are summed up in "grace and glory," and are in contrast from "the wrath to come" (Matt. 3:7).

"By a greater and more perfect tabernacle." This repeats what was said in 8:2. The reference is to the human nature which the Son of God took unto Himself. "The Word became flesh and (Greek) *tabernacled* among us" (John 1:14). Christ officiated in a much more glorious habitation than any in which Aaron and his successors served. Most appropriately was the humanity of the Saviour called a "tabernacle" for "in Him dwelleth all the fulness of the Godhead bodily" (Col. 2:9). Additional confirmation that the "greater and more perfect tabernacle" here referred to Christ's body, is supplied by Heb. 10:20, where the Holy Spirit again applies to Him the language of the Mosaic tabernacle and shows that in the Lord Jesus is found the antitype —"through the *veil*, that is to say *His flesh*."

"By a greater and more perfect tabernacle." There is both a comparison and a contrast between the tent which Moses pitched and the human habitat in which the Son of God abides: for the comparison we refer the reader to our comments upon 8:2. The contrast is first pointed by the word "greater," the Antitype far surpassing the type both in dignity and worth. The humanity of Christ, in its conception, its framing, its gracious endowments by the Holy Spirit, and particularly because of its union to and subsistence in the divine person of the Son, was far more excellent and glorious than any earthly fabric could be. "The human nature of Christ doth thus more excel the old tabernacle, than the sun does the meanest star" (John Owen). Of old God declared, "I will make a man more precious than fine gold; even a man than the golden wedge of Ophir" (Isa. 13:12) —a prophecy which obviously had its fulfillment in the Man Christ Jesus.

"And more perfect tabernacle": this points the second contrast between the type and the Antitype. As the word "greater" refers to the superior dignity and excellency of the humanity of Christ over the materials which comprised the tabernacle of Moses, so the "more perfect" respects its sacred use. The body of Christ was "more perfectly fitted and suited unto the end of a tabernacle, both for the inhabitation of the divine nature, and the means of exercising the sacerdotal office in making atonement for sin, than the other was. So it is expressed in 10:5, 'Sacrifice and burnt-offering Thou wouldst not, but a body hast Thou prepared Me.' This was that which God accepted, wherewith He was well pleased, when He rejected the other to that end" (John Owen). Probably the Holy Spirit has used this expression "more perfect" here because it was also through Christ's service in this "tabernacle" that His people had been "perfected forever."

"Not made with hands, that is to say, not of this building." Further reference is here made to the humanity of Christ by a double negation: "Not made with hands" is set in opposition to the Jewish tabernacle, which was made by the hands of men (Ex. 36:1-8). The humanity of Christ was the product of Him that hath no hands, even God Himself. Thus the expression here is the same as "which the Lord pitched, and not man" in 8:2. Then how much "greater" was the "more perfect Tabernacle"! The temple of Solomon was a most sumptuous and costly building, yet was it erected by human workmen, and therefore was it an act of infinite condescension for the great God to dwell therein: "But will God indeed dwell on the earth? behold, the heaven and heaven of heavens cannot contain Thee; how much less this house that I have builded?" (1 Kings 8:27). Reference to the supernatural humanity of Christ was made in Dan. 2:45: He was to be a "Stone," cut out of the same quarry with us, yet "without hands," i. e., without the help of nature, begotten by a man.

"That is to say, not of this building," words added to further define the preceding clause—the term rendered "building" is translated "creature" in 4:13. The humanity of Christ belonged to a totally different order of things than ours: there is no parallel in the whole range of creation. "Although the substance of His human nature was of the same kind with ours, yet the *production* of it in the world, was such an act of Divine power, as excels all other Divine operations whatever. Wherefore, God speaking of it, saith 'The Lord hath created a new thing in the earth, A woman shall compass a Man' (Jer. 31:22) or conceive Him without natural generation" (John Owen). How blessed to see that God is so far from being confined to natural means for the effecting of His holy counsels, that He can, when He pleases, dispense with all the ordinary methods and "laws" by which He works, and act contrary to them.

"Neither by the blood of goats and calves, but by His own blood He entered in once into the holy place, having obtained eternal redemption for us" (v. 12). Having shown that in Christ's person we have the antitype of the tabernacle, the apostle now proceeds to set forth that which was foreshadowed by the entrance of Israel's high priest into the holy of holies on the day of atonement: this he does both negatively and positively, that the difference between the shadow and the substance might more evidently appear. The design of this verse is to display the pre-eminence of Christ in the discharge of His priestly office above the legal high priest. This is seen, first, in the excellency of His sacrifice, which was His own blood; second, in the holy place whereinto He entered by virtue of it, which was Heaven itself; third, in the effect of it, in that by it He procured "eternal redemption."

"Neither by the blood of goats and calves": it was by means of these that Aaron entered the holy of holies on the day of atonement (Lev. 16:14, 15)—the apostle here uses the plural number because of the annual repetition of the same sacrifice. In Lev. 16, the "calf" or young bullock (of one year old) is mentioned first; perhaps the order is here reversed because the "goat" was specifically for the people, and it is Christ redeeming His people which is the dominant thought. It was by virtue of the blood of these animals that Aaron entered so as to be accepted with God. The reference here is *not* directly to what the high priest brought with him into the holiest—or the "incense" too had been mentioned — but to the *title* which the sacrifices gave him to approach unto the Holy One of Israel.

"But by His own blood He entered in once into the holy place." Here we are brought directly unto the great mystery of the priestly work of Christ, especially as to the sacrifice which He offered unto God to make an atonement for the sins of His people. The "holy place"—called in 9:8 "the Holiest of all"—signifying Heaven itself, the dwelling-place of God. This is unequivocally established by 9:24 "into heaven itself." There never was any place to which this title of "holy place" so suitably belonged: thus it is designated in Psa. 20:6 "His holy heaven." And *when* was it that Christ entered Heaven by virtue of the merits of His own blood? Almost all of the commentators take the reference here as being to His ascension. But this we deem to be a mistake, and one from which erroneous conclusions of a most serious nature have been drawn. The writer is fully satisfied that what is affirmed in this verse took place immediately after Christ, on the cross, triumphantly cried "It is finished." Some of our reasons for believing this we give below.

First, the typical priest's entrance within the veil took place immediately after the victim's death: its body being carried without the camp to be burned in a public place, its blood being taken into the holiest, to be sprinkled on the propitiatory, covering the ark. Those closely-connected acts in the ritual were so related that the burning followed last in order. Now Heb. 13:11 clearly establishes the fact that that typical action coincided with Christ's sacrifice outside Jerusalem: therefore, to make Christ's entrance into heaven occur forty days after His death, destroys the type. In pouring out His blood on the cross and surrendering His spirit into the hands of the Father, Christ expiated sin, and at that very moment the veil of the temple was rent, to denote His entrance into the presence of God. No sooner had He expired, than He entered Heaven, claiming it for Himself and His seed. His resurrection testified to the fact that God *had* accepted His sacrifice, that justice had been fully satisfied, and that He was now entitled to the reward of His obedience. His resurrection was the antitype of Aaron's *return* from the holy of holies unto the people, which was designed as a proof that Divine wrath had been averted and forgiveness secured.

Second, Aaron began by laying aside his robes of glory (Lev. 16:4), putting on only linen garments: *that* was far more in keeping with Christ's abasement at the cross, than His triumph and glory at His ascension. Third, when Aaron entered the holy of holies, atonement was not yet completed: that awaited his sprinkling of the blood upon the propitiatory. Therefore, if the antitype of this occurred not until the ascension of Christ, His sacrifice waited forty days for God's acceptance of it. Fourth, while Aaron was within the veil, the people without were full of fear for the high priest, lest he fail to appease God. Similar was the state of Christ's disciples during the interval between His death and resurrection: they remained in a state of suspense and doubt, dejection and dread. But far different were they immediately after His ascension: contrast Luke 24:21 and 24:52, 53! Fifth, God's rending of the veil at the moment of Christ's death was deeply significant: it was the Divine imprimature upon the Son's "It is finished." It was the outward adumbration in the visible realm to image forth what had taken place in the spiritual—Christ's entrance into heaven. In like manner, Christ's appearance to the disciples after His death, and His "peace be unto you," evidenced that peace *had* been made, that the atonement was completed.

"By His own blood He entered in," entered heaven as the Surety of His people, as their "Forerunner" (6:20). That which gave Him the right to do so was the perfect satisfaction which He had made, a satisfaction which honoured God more than all our sins dishonoured Him, which magnified the law and made it honourable. It was *not* the shedding of His blood alone which constituted His satisfaction or atonement, any more than a heart-belief in His resurrection (Rom. 10:9) without "faith in His blood" (Rom. 3:25) would save a sinner. He "became obedient *unto* death, even the death of the cross" (Phil. 2:8), and what He there voluntarily endured was the climax and consummation of His redemptive work. "His *own* blood" emphasises its inestimable value. It was the blood of the "Son" (Heb. 1:2, 3). It was the blood of "God" incarnate (Acts 20:28). Well might the Holy Spirit call it "precious" (1 Pet. 1:19). No greater price could have been paid for our redemption. How vile and accursed, then, must *sin* be, seeing it can only be expiated by so costly a sacrifice! What *claims* Christ has upon His own! Well might He say, "Whosoever he be of you that forsaketh not all that he hath, he cannot be My disciple" (Luke 14:33).

"He entered in once into the holy place." The word "once" is that which has led so many to conclude that the reference was to the Saviour's ascension. But this, we have endeavored to show above, is a mistake. As we shall (D.V.) yet see, Heb. 9 and 10 contemplate a *double* entrance of Christ into heaven in fulfilment of the *double* type—Aaron and Melchizedek. That Christ *did* enter heaven at death is clear from His words to the thief (Luke 23:43); 2 Cor. 12:2, 4 places "paradise" in the third heaven. In every other passage where the term "once" occurs concerning the atoning work of Christ, it is always used contrastively with the *frequent* repetitions of the O. T. sacrifices: see 7:27; 9:25, 26; 10:11, 12. That which is contemplated is Christ's *presenting* His satisfaction unto God. His ascension was for the purpose of intercession, which is *continuous*, and not completed.

"Having obtained eternal redemption," and this before He entered Heaven. To "redeem" is to deliver a person from a state of bondage, and that by the payment of an adequate ransom-price. Four things were required unto our redemption. It must be effected by the expiating of our sins. It must be by such an expiation that God, as the supreme Ruler and Judge, should accept. It must be by rendering such a satisfaction to the Law, that its precepts are fulfilled and its penalty endured, so that its curse is removed. It must annul the power of Satan over us. How all of this was accomplished by the Redeemer, we have shown in our articles upon His "Satisfaction." This "redemption" is *eternal*, which is in contrast from Israel's of old — after their deliverance from Egypt they became in bondage to the Philistines and others. As the blood of Christ can never lose its efficacy, so none redeemed by Him can ever again be brought under sin's dominion.

"For if the blood of bulls and of goats, and the ashes of an heifer sprinkling the unclean, sanctifieth to the purifying of the flesh: How much more shall the blood of Christ" (vv. 13, 14). Having again demonstrated the pre-eminence of our Priest in vv. 11, 12, the apostle now exhibits the superior efficacy of His sacrifice. By a synedoche *all* sacrifices of expiation and all ordinances of purification appointed under the law are here summarized: the blood of lambs, etc., being included. The particular reference in the "ashes of an heifer" being to Num. 19:2-17, with which should be carefully compared John 13:1-15. It is principally the *use* of the ordinance of Num. 19 which is here in view. An heifer having been burned, its ashes were preserved, that, being mixed with pure water, they might be sprinkled on persons who had become legally unclean. When an Israelite, through contact with death, became ceremonially defiled, he was cut off from all the public worship of Jehovah; but when he carried out the instructions of Num. 19 he was restored.

Those "ashes," then, were a most merciful provision of God; without them, all acceptable worship had soon ceased. They had *an* efficacy, for they availed to the purifying of the flesh, which was a temporary, external and ceremonial cleansing. Typically, they pointed to that spiritual, inward and eternal cleansing which the blood of Christ provides. "The spiritual defilements which befall believers are many, and some of them unavoidable whilst they live in this world; yea, the best of their services have defilements adhering to them. Were it not that the blood of Christ, in its purifying virtue, is in a continual readiness unto faith, that God therein had opened a fountain for sin and uncleanness, the worship of the church would not be acceptable unto Him. In a constant application thereunto, doth the exercise of faith much consist" (John Owen).

"How much more shall the blood of Christ," etc. If the blood and ashes of beasts, under the appointment of God, were efficacious unto an external and temporary justification and sanctification—that is, the removal of both guilt and ceremonial pollution—how much more shall the sacrifice of Him who was promised of old, was the Anointed and therefore the One ordained and accepted of God, effectually and eternally cleanse those to whom it is applied. "The blood of Christ is comprehensive of *all* that He did and suffered in order unto our redemption, inasmuch as the shedding of it was the way and means whereby He offered Himself (in and by it) unto God" (John Owen).

"Who through the eternal Spirit offered Himself." There has been considerable difference of opinion as to whether the "eternal Spirit" has reference to the Divine nature of Christ animating and sustaining His humanity, or to the third Person of the Trinity. That which settles the point for us is this: Christ "offered *Himself*" to God: that is, in His entire person, while acting in His mediatorial office. As the mediator, He took upon Him the "form of a servant," and therefore was He filled and energised by the Spirit in all that He did. Christ was "*obedient* unto death:" as He was subject to the Spirit in going into the wilderness (Matt. 4:1), so the Spirit led Him a willing victim to the cross. This wondrous statement shows us the perfect co-operation of the Eternal Three, concurring in the great work of redemption.

Christ offered Himself "without spot," to God. There is a double reference in these words: unto the purity of His person, and to the holiness of His life. There is both a moral and a legal sense to the expression. It speaks of Christ's fitness and meetness *to be* a sacrifice for our sins. Not only was there no blemish in His nature and no defect in His character, but there was every moral excellence. He had *fulfilled* the law in thought, word and deed, having loved the Lord His God with all His heart and His neighbour as Himself. Therefore was He fully qualified to act for His people.

"Purge your conscience from dead works." This is one of the effects produced by Christ's sacrifice, an effect which the legal ordinances were incapable of securing. Because Christ's sacrifice has expiated our sins, when the Spirit applies its virtues to the heart, that is, when He gives faith to appropriate them, our sense of guilt is removed, peace is communicated, and we are enabled to approach God not only without dread, but as joyous worshippers. The "conscience" is here specially singled out (cf. 10:22 for the larger meaning) because it is the proper seat of the *guilt* of sin, charging it on the soul, and hindering an approach unto God. By "dead works" are meant our sins as unto their guilt and defilement—cf. our comments on 6:1. True believers are delivered from the curse of the law, which is *death*.

"To serve the living God," not simply in outward form but in sincerity and in truth. This is the advantage and blessing which we receive from our conscience being purged. Christians have both the right and the liberty *to* "serve God." The "living God" cannot be served by those who are dead in sins, and therefore alienated from Him. But the sacrifice of Christ has purchased the gift of the Spirit unto all for whom He died, and the Spirit renews and equips the saint for acceptable worship. "This is the end of our purgation: for we are not washed by Christ that we may plunge ourselves again into new filth, but that our purity may serve to glorify God" (John Calvin). Under the word "serve" is comprised all the duties which we owe unto God, not only as His creatures, but as His children. Then let us earnestly seek grace to put Rom. 12:1 into daily practise. A.W.P.

THE SATISFACTION
("Atonement")
OF CHRIST

17. *Its Results*: (*Righteousness continued*)

In our last article we sought to show that in order to the justification of His people God required from Christ something more than a sacrifice which would blot out their sins. It has been rightly said that, "There are few questions of more importance than the one which has reference to the way in which a sinner becomes perfectly righteous before God. If he be not completely righteous, he cannot enter heaven" (J. C. Carson). When man fell from his sinless condition he was no more able to procure for himself a righteousness which would meet the inflexible demands of God's justice and holiness, than he could eradicate the sinful nature which now vitiates all his faculties. His only hope lay in a substitute who was able both to keep the law for him and to suffer the penalty for his breach of it. Both of these were indispensible if sinners were to be saved from hell and given a valid title to heaven. "If thou wilt enter into life, keep the commandments" (Matt. 19:17). Life is not to be obtained unless all is done that the law requires: it *must* be kept either by us or a surety.

"There is the same need of Christ's obeying the law in our stead, in order to the reward, as of His suffering the penalty of the law in our stead in order to our escaping the penalty; and the same reason why one should be accepted on our account, as the other. This is certain, that that was the reason why there was need that Christ should suffer the penalty for us, even that the law might be answered; for this the Scripture plainly teaches. This is given as the reason why Christ was made a curse for us, that the law's threatening a curse to us: Gal. 3:10, 13. But the same law that fixes the curse of God as the consequent of not continuing in all things written in the law to do them (v. 10). has as much fixed *doing* those things *as an antecedent of living in them* (v. 12). There is as much of a connection established in one place as in the other . . . We have not eternal life merely on the account of being void of guilt, but on the account of Christ's activeness in obedience and doing well" (Jon. Edwards Vol. 4, P. 92).

"I am not ashamed of the Gospel of Christ for it is the power of God unto salvation to every one that believeth . . . For therein is *the righteousness of God* revealed" (Rom. 1:16, 17). It is indeed pitiable to discover the evasive subterfuges to which men have resorted in their unworthy efforts to rob the Gospel of its distinguishing glory. Many who ought to have known better (some we fear, did) defined this expression as "God's *method* of justifying sinners." That the Gospel reveals the consummate wisdom of God in devising a way whereby *all* His attributes are illustriously displayed in the saving of His people, is perfectly true. That the Gospel exhibits the perfect consistency between the grace and righteousness of God, His mercy and justice, is a most blessed fact. Yet, *this* is not at all the meaning of that expression "the righteousness of God." Let such a definition be applied to 2 Cor. 5:21 and its fallacy is at once exposed: "He hath made Him to be sin for us, who knew no sin; that we might be made God's method of justification in Him!"

"The righteousness of God. This is one of the most important expressions in the Scriptures. It frequently occurs both in the O. T. and in the New; it stands connected with the argument of the first five chapters of the Roman epistle, and signifies that fulfilment of the law which God has provided, by the imputation of which sinners are saved" (Rob. Haldane). We are bold to affirm that the competency or incompetency of a man to expound the epistle to the Romans largely turns upon his understanding of this key expression. If he errs in his apprehension of "the righteousness of God," his whole scheme of interpretation is bound to be faulty and erroneous. Nor can any man fully preach the Gospel, so as to exalt Christ as He ought to be exalted, while he fails to unfold the blessedness of this vitally important term. Nor can any believer be fully established in the faith, nor is he capable of rendering to God that praise which is His due, while he remains ignorant of what is meant by "even the righteousness of God by faith of Jesus Christ unto all and upon all them that believe"(Rom. 3:22). What then, is meant by this expression?

The "righteousness of God" is that perfect conformity to the divine law in heart and life which the holiness of God requires, which the grace of God has provided, which the incarnate Son of God has wrought out, and which the justice of God imputes to every one that believes. Let us enlarge upon this statement. First, the "righteousness of God" is that perfect conformity to the law in heart and life which the holiness of God requires. God cannot relinquish His rights, nor recede from His just claims. For Him to set aside the demands of the law for full obedience to it, would be as much as saying He had given a law which was *not* "holy and just and good" (Rom. 7:12). This could never be. Divine love gave the law; divine wisdom drew it up; divine justice requires the perfect performance of it. Therefore, second, divine grace *provided* a satisfaction unto its righteous claims. Unfallen man failed to keep it; fallen man cannot keep it; so the God-man—forever be His name praised—came here to keep it in the stead of and in the behalf of His people.

It was by a *special* Divine constitution that Christ became subject to the law. Men are born under the law as the *natural* descendants of Adam. But not so the Lord Jesus Christ. As His humanity was produced in a supernatural manner (that is, not according to the settled order of nature, but by the intervention and power of the Holy Spirit), so He was "made under the law" (Gal. 4:4) by a special Divine appointment. Christ, as Man, by virtue of the personal union of His manhood with the second person of the Godhead, was raised high above the condition and state of a mere creature. "Being found in fashion as a man, He *humbled Himself* and became obedient unto death" (Phil. 2:8). He was under no *personal* obligation to the law, but voluntarily placed Himself under it, that He might work out for His people a perfect and vicarious righteousness. May our hearts truly be drawn out to Him in profoundest admiration and adoration for such an amazing condescension.

The unremitting and perfect obedience which Christ rendered unto the law proceeded from supreme love to God and unfeigned affection to men. "His delight in *God* was conspicuous even from His early years. The sacred solemnities of the sanctuary were more engaging to His youthful mind than all the entertainments of a festival. When He entered upon His ministry, *whole nights* were not too long for His copious devotions. The lonely retirements of the desert, as affording undisturbed communion with God, were more desirable to Christ than the applauses of an admiring world. So ceaseless and transcendent was His love to God, that He *never* sought any separate pleasure of His own, but *always* did those things which were pleasing in His Father's sight. 'Wist ye not that I must be about My Father's business'? was the rule of His childhood and the leading maxim of His whole life. In doing this, He took unspeakable satisfaction; in doing this, He was absolutely indefatigable. It was His 'meat and drink,' refreshing as the richest food, delightful as royal dainties, to finish the work that was given Him to do (John 4:34).

"How wakeful and jealous was His concern for the divine honour! I hear the vilest reproaches cast upon His own character. I see the most horrible indignities possible to His own person. Yet no resentful emotion reddened in His cheek; nor one angry syllable starts from His mouth. But when m e r c e n a r y wretches profaned the Temple, and turned His 'Father's house' into a den of thieves, then His bosom throbs with zeal, then He makes His tongue like a sharp sword, and having first severely rebuked, afterwards resolutely expels, the sacrilegious intruders. Indeed, His zeal for the house of *the Lord* and for the purity of His ordinances, is represented by the evangelical historian as *eating Him up* (John 2:17). Like a heavenly flame glowing in His breast, it sometimes fired Him with a graceful indignation, sometimes melted Him to godly sorrow, always broke forth and exerted itself in a variety of vigorous efforts, till it even consumed His vital spirits. . . .

"Who can declare the *charity of Jesus Christ?* It was ardent, it was unintermitted, it was unbounded. Though always serene and serious, He was never sullenly grave. His conversation was affability itself, and the law of kindness dwelt on His lips. What fretted and chagrined the disciples, made not the least ruffling impression on their *Lord*. The rude and troublesome behaviour of some, the weak and impertinent talk of others, served only to display the unalterable mildness of His temper. Nothing could imbitter His spirit. Even the wicked and unthankful were partakers, ample partakers of His benevolence. Whoever applied to Him in vain? When did He dismiss any needy petitioner without the desired blessing? What heavy burden did He not unloose? What afflictive evil did He not relieve? He even 'took their infirmities and bear their sicknesses,' Matt. 8:17. In all their afflictions He was afflicted.

"He not only relieved when His aid was implored, but anticipated the expectations of the distressed. He 'went about doing good' (Acts 10:38), seeking the afflicted and offering His assistance. With great fatigue (John 4:6) He travelled to remote cities; with no less condescension, He visited the meanest villages, that all might have the honour and benefit of His healing Presence and heavenly instructions. He gave sight to the blind, health to the diseased. He delivered the wretched soul from the dominion of darkness and from the tyrrany of sin. He made His followers partakers of a divine nature, and prepared them for a state of never-ending bliss. Nor were these righteous acts His 'strange work,' but His repeated, His hourly, His almost incessant employ. When ridiculed and affronted, He kindly bore and kindly overlooked the insult. When contradicted by petulant and presumptuous sinners, He endured, with the utmost serenity of temper, their unreasonable cavils and their obstinate perverseness.

"When His bloody sweat tinged the stones, when His bitter cries pierced the clouds, and were enough to awaken the very rocks into compassion, His disciples slept, stupidly and repeatedly slept. But did their Divine but slighted Master resent the unkindness? Did He refuse to *admit* an excuse for their disobedience and neglect? Nay; He *made* their excuse, and that the most tender and gracious imaginable: 'the spirit indeed is willing, but the flesh is weak' (Matt. 26:41). When His *enemies* had nailed Him to the cross, as the basest slave and most flagitious malefactor, when they were glutting their malice with His sorrows, His torments, and His blood: nay, when they spared not to insult and revile Him, even in His last expiring agonies; far, very far from being exasperated, this *Hero of heaven* repaid all their contempt and barbarity with the most fervent supplications in their behalf: 'Father, *forgive* them, for they know not what they do' (Luke 23:34) was His plea. Divine, adorable compassion" (Jas. Hervey).

Now as the Christian bows in admiration and adoration before the Holy Spirit's description of the exquisitely lovely ways of our Lord, let him not miss that which is most evangelical of all in the four Evangelists, namely, that the perfect life of Christ was not only, nor even primarily, a pattern for our *imitation*, but was also, and supremely, in order to our *justification*. To present to a ruined and impotent creature the flawless life of the Holy One of God, is *no* "glad tidings," but as another has said, "only a consummate Copy for a *withered* hand to transcribe." But O my brethren, when our faith is enabled to lay hold of the blissful fact that, from Bethlehem to Calvary, Christ acted as our Surety and Representative, that by *all* He did, He wrought out for us a perfect righteousness, which in the construction and judgment of the law is *really ours;* that God Himself imputes that righteousness to us, and will forever deal with us according to its deserts, *then* we behold the light of the *glorious* Gospel and enter into the "unsearchable riches of Christ."

"And is this righteousness designed for *us?* Is this to be our wedding-dress, this our beautiful array, when we enter the regions of eternity? Unspeakable privilege! Is this what *God* has provided, to more than supply our loss in Adam? Boundless benignity! Shall *we* be treated by the Judge of the world as if *we* had performed all this unsinning and perfect obedience? Well might the prophet cry out, like one in astonishment, '*How great* is His goodness!' How great indeed! Since all that *the Lord Jesus* did and suffered, was doing and suffering for us men and our salvation, is imputed to us for righteousness, and is the sole and infinitely sufficient cause of our justification; is not your heart enamoured with a view of this incomprehensibly rich grace? What so excellent, what so comfortable, what so desirable, as this gift of a *Saviour's* righteousness? Though delineated by this feeble pen, methinks it has dignity and glory enough to captivate our hearts and fire our affections: fire them with ardent and inextinguishable desire after a personal interest and propriety in it? O may the eternal Spirit reveal our Redeemer's righteousness in all its heavenly beauty and divine lustre. Then, I am persuaded, we shall esteem it *above everything*. We shall regard it as the 'one thing needful.' We shall count *all* things in comparison of it, worthless as the chaff, empty as the wind" (Jas. Hervey).

It is that perfect obedience which Christ rendered to God, His absolute conformity to the law, which makes Him competent to save. Thus saith the Lord God, He *shall* "justify many". On what consideration? Why this: because He is "My *righteous* Servant" (Isa. 53:11). It is because of His perfect obedience in life and in death that "Judah shall be saved" from eternal damnation, and "Israel shall dwell safely," having been given an indefeasible title to life and glory; for it is on this very account, namely, that God raised unto David "a *righteous* Branch" and that He is owned as "the Lord our righteousness" (Jer. 23:5, 6). It is this which renders His intercession so prevalent. He is an Advocate, a successful Advocate, with the Father. Why? Because He is "Jesus Christ *the righteous*" (1 John 2:1)! Has the Lord Jesus risen on His people with "healing in His wings"? It is because He is "the Sun *of righteousness*" (Mal. 4:2). So various, so efficacious, so extensive, are His beneficent influences, that like a "sun" (the monarch of the material creation), He enlightens and enlivens; like "wings," He cherishes and protects; like an all-powerful remedy, He "heals" and restores. And all this by virtue of His *righteousness*.

Pitiable indeed, though perhaps needful it is, that we should now turn away from this glorious object, and briefly look at some of the objections which a carping unbelief has brought against it. Not a few who have been looked upon as exceptionably able students of the Word, have dogmatically affirmed that "the righteousness of Christ" is an expression of human invention, and is nowhere to be found in Holy Scripture. It is sufficient refutation to quote 2 Peter 1:1—"to those who have obtained like precious faith with us in the righteousness of our God and Saviour Jesus Christ" (R. V. and also margin of A. V.)! This inspired sentence is the key to all those texts in the N. T. and many in the Old, which mention the "righteousness *of God.*" It is not the essential righteousness of an absolute God, but the *vicarious* righteousness of an *incarnate* God! Just as "the Church *of God* which He hath purchased with His own blood" (Acts 20:28) means, and can only mean, that church of God who became incarnate, the church of *Christ.*

It has been objected that God would have been unjust to require Christ to perfectly obey the law, and after having done so, inflict upon Him the penalty which the law enforces upon the *disobedient.* Such an objection had held good if Christ acted only in the capacity of a *private* person, that is, as a single or isolated individual. But He did not. He came here as the federal Head of His people (Rom. 5:14 last clause, 1 Cor. 15:45, 47), made one with them (Heb. 2:11, 14). To say that the law requires no man to obey and die too, is specious reasoning, quite beside the point at issue. The real question is, Did the law require a *transgressor* to obey and die? There is a *twofold* debt which sinners owe to God: as *creatures,* perfect obedience to the law; as *criminals,* liability to suffer its punishment. The claims of the law cannot be relaxed at either point. In coming here as the Sponsor of His people, Christ assumed *all* their debts, and discharged their full responsibilities both as creatures and criminals. It needs to be steadily borne in mind that Christ was "made under" (Gal. 4:4) a *broken* law, and consequently, under its curse: therefore justice required that He should not only fulfill its precepts, but suffer its penalty.

Had the Surety died only, He had delivered us from punishment, but that would have afforded no claim to "life," no title to the "reward" (Rom. 10:5). Scripture declares of the Divine commands that "in *keeping* of them there is great *reward*" (Psa. 19:11), but it nowhere affirms that in undergoing their curse there is the same reward. God's elect, fallen in Adam, not only needed to be made negatively guiltless, but positively righteous. To "reign in life" (Rom. 5:15), to be entitled to the "crown" (2 Tim. 4:8), required the *obedience* of Christ to be imputed to us. Just as in sanctification there is *both* the putting off of the "old man" and the putting on of the "new man" (Eph. 4:22-24), so the Divine sentence of justification proceeds on the *double* basis that there is "no condemnation" resting upon those in Christ, and *also* that His righteousness has been "imputed" to their account (Rom. 4:11). Rom. 4:25 unites the two: Christ was "delivered (to death) for our *offences* (remission) *and* was raised again for our *justification*"—righteousness. "This is the heritage of the servants of the Lord, and *their* righteousness is *of Me,* saith the Lord" (Isa. 54:17).

John Bunyan, in the account which he gave of the Lord's dealings with him, recorded with artless simplicity the establishment of his soul in this most glorious truth. "Now I saw that Christ Jesus was looked upon by God, and should be looked upon by us, as that common or *public* person, in whom all the whole body of His elect are always to be considered and reckoned: that *we fulfilled the law by Him,* died by Him, rose from the dead by Him, got the victory over sin, death, the devil, and hell, by Him; when He died we died; and so of His resurrection etc." (Grace Abounding). May it please the Lord to grant a like precious faith unto many readers of this article. To have the heart established in this blessed truth is worth infinitely more than the riches, honours, pleasures of this perishing world.

Returning now to the objections which Satan has moved men to make against this precious truth. One of the favourite "arguments" of the Romanists against the teachings of the Reformers upon this subject was: If God has transferred the righteousness of Christ to believers then they are sinless, holy, righteous in their own persons, as righteous as Christ is righteous. But this is a confounding things that differ. The saints of God may be considered either as to what they still are *in themselves* or as justified *in Christ.* That this distinction is not one of human invention, is capable of being established from many scriptures. Take one passage only from either Testament: "I am black, but comely" (Song of S. 1:5). Yes, "black" in myself, as a fallen descendant of Adam, and such I continue to the end of my earthly course; but "comely," as I am in Christ (Col. 2:10). "Purge out therefore the old leaven, that ye *may be* (experimentally) a new lump, as ye *are* (judicially, in Christ) un-leavened" (1 Cor. 5:7). They who make not this distinction are ignorant of "the *mystery* of the Gospel" (Eph. 6:19).

Others have objected—though it is not likely many will echo it in these days of lawlessness—if Christ has fully kept the law for His people, then *they* are freed from all obligation to personally keep it. The answer is, True, God does not require His people to keep the law for the *same* ends and upon the same accounts that Christ fulfilled it, namely, to satisfy Divine justice and purchase a title to everlasting life and an inheritance in heaven. But for *other* ends, God *does* require His people to obey the law, namely, as creatures in subjection to His holy will, and out of loving gratitude for all He has done for them. Christ kept the law to earn eternal life for us—carefully ponder Rom. 5:21, 1 John 4:9; Christians are to keep it from a desire to please Christ: "If ye love Me, *keep* My commandments" (John 14:15.) Nor do we have to keep the law by our own power: "In the Lord have I righteousness *and* strength" (Isa. 45:24).

Again, it has been objected that such a thing as *vicarious obedience*, the transferring of moral merits from one to another, is quite unknown in human history. What of that? That only goes to prove the *uniqueness* of Christ's Work. Many things which are impossible to men, are possible to God. Those who refuse to believe in the vicarious obedience of Christ (most probably to their own eternal damnation) because of its unprecedented character, have the same ground for rejecting His miraculous birth, His impeccability (incapableness of yielding to temptation), His unique life, His raising Himself from the dead; for none of these have any parallel in human history either! But this particular objection overlooks entirely the unique *relation* which existed between Christ and His people, namely, their federal union: in the eyes of God's law, what Christ did, His people did.

"For as by one man's disobedience, many were made (legally constituted, as in 2 Cor. 5:21), sinners, so by the obedience of One shall many be made (legally constituted) righteous" (Rom. 5:19). One had thought this was plain enough for any who profess to bow to Scripture, yet there have been those who, doing manifest violence to the Greek (see Bagster's Interlinear), have insisted it should be renderd "one obedience," which they limit to Christ's willingness to be crucified. As though anticipating this very perversion, in Phil. 2:8 the Spirit has expressly declared that, Christ "became obedient *unto* death," not merely *"in* death." Death was the final act of His obedience, referring us back to all the previous virtues and duties of His righteous walk. Just as Jehovah's promise "and even *to* hoar hairs will I carry you" (Isa. 46:4) does not exclude God's sustaining grace in youth and manhood, so "obedient unto death" does not exclude the vicarious obedience of Christ's *life*. In like manner, "justified by His blood" (Rom. 5:9) was the climax or consummation of the complete satisfaction which Christ offered to God. Let us now briefly consider,

4. Its *Typification*.

The double value of Christ's Work was shadowed forth as soon as sin entered the world: see Gen. 3:21. Two things are to be noted there. To procure those "skins" blood must be shed, life must have been taken. Very, very striking was this. The first blood ever spilt on this earth, was shed not by the hand of man, but by the hand of God! The first life taken in this world was not Abel's (as many suppose), but that of sinless sacrifices. Their blood pointed forward to that of Christ's, which cleanseth the believer from all sin. But more: the skins taken from those slain animals "*clothed*" Adam and Eve, thereby foreshadowing that "robe of righteousness" (Isa. 61:10) with which the believer is covered.

"The name of Christ not only cancels the sin; it supplies in the place of that which it has cancelled, its own everlasting excellency. We cannot have its nullifying power only: the other is the sure concomitant. So was it with every typical sacrifice in the law. It was stricken; but as being spotless it was also burned on the altar for a sweet-smelling savour. That savour ascended as a memorial before God: it was accepted for, and its value was attributed or imputed to, him who had brought the vicarious victim. If, therefore, we reject the imputation of righteousness, we reject sacrifice as revealed in Scripture; for Scripture knows of no sacrifice whose efficacy is so exhausted in the removal of guilt, as to leave nothing to be presented in acceptableness before God" (B. W. Newton).

How beautifully was the imputation of the perfect righteousness of Christ to all whom He represented, typed out by what is recorded in Psalm 132:2. The costly and fragrant ungent which poured upon Aaron's head and which ran down his beard, descended to the very skirts of his clothes. So the merits of our great High Priest have passed to and upon all who are members of His mystical Body. Again; when Aaron (as the representative) presented the names of the children of Israel before God, he did not *barely* present them, but he bore their names on his breastplate, engraved on *precious* stones (Ex. 28:17-20), thereby adumbrating, as far as earthly things can, the splendid and exalted nature of the Redeemer's righteousness *in which* we are presented to God.

Let the reader carefully and prayerfully ponder the wonderful incident portrayed in Zech. 3:1-5. There we behold a "brand plucked out of the fire" (v. 2). Observe particularly the *two* things done for and to him. First the command is, *"Take away* the filthy garments from him" (v. 4), figuring the removal of our sins. Second, "they set a *fair* mitre upon his head and *clothed* him with garments" (v. 5), emblemising that vicarious and immaculate righteousness of Christ, which is not only "unto" but also *"upon* all them that believe" (Rom. 3:22).

5. *Its Imputation.*

"To him that worketh not, but believeth on Him that justifieth the ungodly, his faith is counted for righteousness" (Rom. 4:5). Here again the enemies of the truth have fought hard to rob God's children of the comfort and assurance which the blessed teaching of this chapter is designed to give them. Many have argued that God imputes to faith itself an intrinsic value which He accepts *in lieu of* perfect obedience to His law. But this is a most horrible perversion, invented by Romanists, and now echoed by those who ought to hate it. Faith is an emptying thing, which causes the pauper to gladly receive God's gracious gift, and possesses no more merit than does the appeal of a beggar for charity. The "his faith is counted *for* righteousness," does *not* mean "in the stead of," for the Greek preposition is "eis" and not "anti," and signifies "unto" as in Rom. 10:10: "with the heart man believeth *unto* righteousness."

Our Surety gave full satisfaction to the law, but we are not credited with this by God's gracious imputation until we have faith in Christ. "The righteousness of God by faith of Jesus Christ unto all and upon all *them that believe*" (Rom. 3:22). "For Christ is the end of the law for righteousness to everyone *that believeth*" (Rom. 10:4). Therefore is this righteousness also called "the righteousness of faith" (Rom. 4:13). It is denominated the "righteousness of God" because God required, ordained, provided, accepted and imputed it. It is a righteousness which exalts God's justice, magnifies His law, manifests His grace, and displays *all* His awful and lovely attributes in their full lustre. It is designated the "righteousness of Christ" (2 Peter 1:1), because He wrought it out without the co-operation of His creatures. It is the "righteousness of faith" because faith apprehends it.

From the jesuitical way in which certain men have spoken of "the imputation of righteousness" many have deemed them orthodox on this vital subject, but their blank denial of the imputation of *Christ's* righteousness thoroughly exposes their heterodoxy, to all who bow to the authority of Holy Writ. "That righteousness might be imputed to them" (R o m . 4 : 1 1). W h a t righteousness? *Whose* righteousness? The only possible scriptural answer is: that perfect satisfaction which Christ rendered to *all* the demands of the law, and which God places to the credit of every true believer in Him. So truly is Christ's righteousness placed to their account, it is said to be *"upon* all them that believe" (Rom. 3:22). Such persons actually *possess* it. They *wear* it as their "robe" (Isa. 61:10).

"That we might be made the righteousness of God in Him" (2 Cor. 5:21). Yes, *in Him,* as our Proxy and Head, and this because He wrought out a justifying-righteousness not only in our nature, but in our name, not only as our Benefactor, but as our Representative. "*In the Lord* (not in themselves) shall all the seed of Israel be justified" (Isa. 45:25). In the Lord Jesus, believers have a righteousness without spot or blemish, perfect and all glorious; a righteousness which has not only expiated all their sins, but satisfied every requirement of the law's precepts. "That I may win Christ, and be found in Him, *not* having *mine own* righteousness which is of the law, but that which is through the faith of Christ, the righteousness which is *of God* by faith" (Phil. 3:9, 10).

God's imputation of Christ's righteousness to the believer, is not an esteeming him to be righteous when really he is not so. Nor is it a naked pronunciation of any one to be righteous *without* a just and sufficient foundation for the judgment of God declared therein. God pronounces none righteous who are not so. Nor is it a *transfusion* of Christ's righteousness into those who are to be justified, so that they should be inherently righteous thereby. No; it is a Divine and legal grant whereby God, out of His mere love and grace, on the alone consideration of the whole mediation of Christ, makes an effectual donation of a real and true righteousness, even that of Christ Himself, unto all who believe; and so accounting is as *theirs*, on His own gracious act, as not only to absolve them from all sin, but granting them the right to eternal life and the title to an everlasting inheritance in heaven. The meritorious obedience of Christ is so truly transferred to believers that they are called "the righteous" (Matt. 25:40). Surely the Christian has cause to say, "my mouth shall show forth *Thy* righteousness, Thy salvation all the day" (Psa. 71:15)—the one being founded upon the other, the latter deriving its origin from the former; there could be no "salvation" without a proper, real, law-*fulfilling* righteousness. A.W.P.

REGENERATION, or,
THE NEW BIRTH

The more clearly we are enabled to discern the imperative *need* of regeneration and the various reasons *why* it is absolutely essential in order to a fallen creature being fitted for the presence of the thrice holy God, the less difficulty are we likely to encounter when we endeavour to arrive at an understanding of the *nature* of regeneration, *what* it is which takes place within a person when the Holy Spirit renews him. For this reason particularly, and also because such a cloud of error has been cast upon this vital truth, we feel that a further article needs to be devoted to the consideration of this particular aspect of our subject.

Jesus Christ came into this world to glorify God and to glorify Himself by redeeming a people unto Himself. But what glory can we conceive that God has, and what glory would accrue to Christ, if there be not a vital and fundamental difference between His people and the world? And what difference can there be between those two companies but in a *change of heart*, out of which are the issues of life (Prov. 4:23): a change of nature or disposition, as the fountain from which all other differences must proceed—sheep and goats differ in nature. The whole mediatorial work of Christ has this one end in view. His priestly office is to reconcile and bring His people unto God; His prophetic, to teach them the way; His kingly, to work in them those qualifications and bestow upon them that comeliness which is necessary to fit them for holy converse and communion with the thrice holy God. Thus does He "purify unto Himself a peculiar people zealous of good works" (Titus 2:14).

"Know ye not that the unrighteous shall not inherit the kingdom of God? Be not deceived" (1 Cor. 6:9). But multitudes *are* deceived, and deceived at this very point, and on this most momentous matter. God has warned men that "the heart is deceitful above all things, and desperately wicked" (Jer. 17:9), but few will believe that this is true of *them*. Instead, tens of thousands of professing Christians are filled with a vain and presumptuous confidence that all is well with them. They delude themselves with hopes of mercy while continuing to live in a course of self-will and self-pleasing. They fancy they are fitted for Heaven, while every day that passes finds them the more prepared for Hell. It is written of the Lord Jesus that "He shall save His people *from* their sins" (Matt. 1:21), not *in* their sins; save them not only from the penalty, but also from the power and pollution of sin.

To how many in Christendom do these solemn words apply, "For he flattereth himself in his own eyes, until his iniquity be found to be hateful" (Psa. 36:2). The principal device of Satan is to deceive people into imagining that they can successfully combine the world with God, allow the flesh while pretending to the Spirit, and thus "make the best of both worlds." But Christ has emphatically declared that, "no man can serve two masters" (Matt. 6:24). Many mistake the real force of those searching words: the true emphasis is not upon "two," but upon "serve"—none can *serve* two masters. And God requires to be "served"—"feared, submitted unto, obeyed; *His* will regulating the life in all its details, see 1 Sam. 12:24, 25. "Thou shalt worship the Lord thy God, and Him *only* shalt thou *serve*" (Matt. 4:10).

3. *The need for regeneration lies in man's unsuitedness to God.* When Nicodemus, a respectable and religious Phar-

Isee, yea, a "master in Israel," came to Christ, He told him plainly that "except a man be born again" he could neither see nor enter the "kingdom of God" (John 3:3, 5)—either the Gospel-state on earth or the Glory-state in Heaven. No ie can enter the spiritual rea'..n unless he has a spiritual nature, which alone gives him an aptitude for and capacity to enjoy the things pertaining to it; and this, the natural man has not. So far from it, he cannot so much as "discern" them (1 Cor. 2:14). He has no love for them, nor desire after them (John 3:19). Nor can he desire them, for his will is enslaved by the lusts of the flesh (Eph. 2:2, 3). Therefore, before a man can enter the spiritual kingdom, his understanding must be supernaturally enlightened, his heart renewed and his will emancipated.

There can be no point of contact between God and His Christ with a sinful man until he is regenerated. There can be no lawful union between two parties who have nothing vital in common. A superior and an inferior nature may be united together, but never contrary natures. Can fire and water be united, a beast and a man, a good angel and a vile devil? Can Heaven and Hell ever meet on friendly terms? In all friendship there must be a similarity of disposition; before there can be communion there must be some agreement or oneness. Beasts and men agree not in a life of reason, and therefore cannot converse together. God and men agree not in a life of holiness, and therefore can have no communion together (Condensed from S. Charnock).

We are united to the "first Adam" by a likeness of nature; how then can we be united to the "last Adam" without a likeness to Him from a new nature or principle? We are united to the first Adam by a living soul, we must be united to the last Adam by a quickening Spirit. We have nothing to do with the heavenly Adam without bearing an heavenly image (1 Cor. 15:48, 49). If we are *His* members, we must have the same nature which was communicated to Him, the Head, by the Spirit of God, which is *holiness* (Luke 1:35). There must be one "spirit" in both: thus it is written, "he that is joined to the Lord is one spirit" (1 Cor. 6:17). And again God tells us, "If any man have not the Spirit of Christ he is none of His" (Rom. 8:9). Nor can anything be vitally united to another without life. A living head and a dead body is inconceivable.

There can be no communion with God without a renewed soul. God is incapable on His part, with honour to His Law and holiness, to have fellowship with such a creature as fallen man. Man is incapable on his part, because of the aversion rooted in his fallen nature. Then how is it possible for God and man to be brought together without the latter experiencing a thorough change of nature? What communion can there be between Light and darkness, between the living God and a dead heart? "Can two walk together, except they be agreed?" (Amos 3:3). God loathes sin, man loves it; God loves holiness, man loathes it. How then could such contrary affections meet together in an amicable friendship? Sin has alienated from the life of God (Eph. 4:18), and therefore from His fellowship; life, then, must be restored to us before we can be instated in communion with Him. Old things must pass away, and all things become new (2 Cor. 5:17).

Gospel-duties cannot be performed without regeneration. The first requirement of Christ from His followers is that they shall *deny self*. But that is impossible to fallen human nature, for men are "lovers of their own selves" (2 Tim. 3:2). Not until the soul is renewed, will self be repudiated. Therefore is the new-covenant promise, "I will take the stony heart out of their flesh, and will give them an heart of flesh" (Ezek. 11:19). All Gospel-duties require a pliableness and tenderness of heart. Pride was the condemnation of the Devil (1 Tim. 3:6), and our first parents fell through swelling designs to be like unto God (Gen. 3:5). Even since then, man has been too aspiring and too well opiniated of himself to perform duties in an evangelical strain, with that nothingness in himself which the Gospel requires. The chief design of the Gospel is to beat down all glorying in ourselves, that we should glory only in the Lord (1 Cor. 1:29-31); but this is not possible till grace renews the heart, melts it before God, and moulds it to His requirements.

Without a new nature we cannot perform Gospel-duties *constantly*. "They that are after the flesh do mind the things of the flesh" (Rom. 8:5). Such a mind cannot long be employed upon spiritual things. Prickings of conscience, terrors of hell, fears of death, may exert a temporary influence, but they do not last. Stony-ground may bring forth blades, yet for lack of root, they quickly wither away (Matt. 13). A stone may be flung high into the air, but ultimately it falls back to the earth; so the natural man may for a time mount high in religious fervour, but sooner or later it shall be said of him, as it was of Israel, "their *heart* was not right with Him, neither were they *steadfast* in His covenant" (Psa. 78:37). Many seem to begin in the Spirit, but end in the flesh. Only where *God* has wrought in the soul, will the work last forever (Eccl. 3:14, Phil. 1:6).

As regeneration is indispensably necessary to a Gospel-state, so it is to a state of heavenly glory. "It seems to be typified by the strength and freshness of the Israelites when they entered into Canaan. Not a decrepit and infirm person set foot in the promised land: none of those that came out of Egypt with an Egyptian nature, and desires for the garlic and onions thereof, with a suffering their old bondage, but dropped their carcasses in the wilderness; only the two spies who had encouraged them against the seeming difficulties. None that retain only the old man, born in the house of bondage; but only a new regenerate creature, shall enter into the heavenly Canaan. Heaven is the inheritance of the sanctified, not of the filthy: 'that they may receive an inheritance among them which are sanctified through faith that is in Me' (Acts 26:18). Upon Adam's expulsion from paradise, a flaming sword was set to stop his re-entering into that place of happiness. As Adam, in his forlorn state, could not possess it, we also, by what we have received from Adam, cannot expect a greater privilege than our root. The priest under the law could not enter into the sanctuary till he was purified, nor the people into the congregation: neither can any man have access into the Holiest till he be sprinkled by the blood of Jesus: Heb. 10:22" (S. Charnock).

Heaven is a prepared place for a prepared people. Said Christ, "I go to prepare a place for you" (John 14:2). For whom? For those who have, in heart, "forsaken all" to follow Him (Matt. 19:27). For those who love God (1 Cor. 2:9), and they who love God, love the things of God: they perceive the inestimable value and beauty of spiritual things. And they who really love spiritual things, deem no sacrifice too great to win them (Phil. 3:8). But in order to love spiritual things, the man himself must be made spiritual. The natural man may hear about them and have a correct idea of the doctrine of them, but he receives them not spiritually in the *love* of them (2 Thess. 2:10), and finds not his joy and happiness in them. But the renewed soul longs after them, not by constraint, but because God has won his heart. His confession is, "Whom have I in heaven but Thee? and there is none upon earth that I desire beside thee" (Psa. 73:25). God has become his chief good, His will is his only rule, His glory his chief end. In such an one, the very inclinations of the soul have been changed.

The man himself must be changed before he is prepared for heaven. Of the regenerate it is written, "giving thanks unto the Father, which hath *made us meet* to be partakers of the inheritance of the saints in light" (Col. 1:12). None are "made meet" while they are unholy, for it is an inheritance of the *saints;* none are fitted for it while they are under the power of darkness, for it is an inheritance *in light.* Christ Himself ascended not to heaven to take possession of His glory till after His resurrection from the dead, nor can we enter heaven unless we have been resurrected from sin. "He that hath wrought (polished) us *for* the selfsame thing (to be clothed with our heavenly house) is God," and the proof that He has done this is, the giving unto us "the earnest of the Spirit" (2 Cor. 5:5); and where the Spirit of the Lord is "there is *liberty*" (2 Cor. 3:17), liberty from the power of indwelling sin, as the verse which follows clearly shows.

"Blessed are the pure in heart: for they shall see God" (Matt. 5:8). To "see" God is to be introduced into the most intimate intercourse with Him. It is to have that "thick cloud" of our transgressions blotted out (Isa. 44:22), for it was our iniquities which separated between us and our God (Isa. 58:2). To "see" God, here has the force of *enjoy,* as in John 3:36. But for this enjoyment a "pure heart" is indispensable. Now the heart is purified by faith (Acts 15:9), for faith has to do with God. Thus, a "pure" heart is one that has been cleansed from sin and has a holy Object before it. A "pure" heart is one that has its affections set upon things above, being attracted by "the beauty of holiness." But how could he enjoy *God* who cannot now endure the imperfect holiness of His children, but rails against it as unnecessary "strictness" or puritanic fanaticism? God's face is only to be beheld in righteousness (Psa. 17:15).

"Follow peace with all and holiness, without which no man shall see the Lord" (Heb. 12:14). None can dwell with God and be eternally happy in His presence unless a radical change has been wrought in him, a change from sin to holiness. This change *must* be, like that introduced by the Fall, one which reaches to the very roots of our beings, affecting the entire man: removing the darkness of our minds, awakening and then pacifying the conscience, spiritualising our affections, converting the will, reforming our whole life. And this great change must take place here on earth. The removal of the soul to heaven is no substitute for regeneration. It is not the *place* which conveys likeness to God. When the angels fell, they were in heaven, but the glory of God's dwellingplace did not restore them. Satan entered heaven (Job 2:1), but he left it again unchanged. There must be a likeness to God wrought in the soul by the Spirit before it is fitted to enjoy heaven.

"Flesh and blood cannot inherit the kingdom of God" (1 Cor. 15:50). If the body must be changed ere it can enter heaven, how much more so the soul, for "there shall in no wise enter into it anything that defileth" (Rev. 21:27). And *what is* the supreme glory of heaven? Is it freedom from toil and worry, sickness and sorrow, suffering and death? No: it is, that heaven is the place where there is the full manifestation of Him who is "glorious in holiness"—that holiness which the wicked, while presumptuously hoping to go to heaven, despise and hate here on earth. The inhabitants of heaven are given a clear sight of the ineffable purity of God and are granted the most intimate communion with Him. But none are fitted for this unless their inner beings (as well as outer lives) have undergone a radical, revolutionising, supernatural change.

Can it be thought that Christ will prepare mansions of glory for those who refuse to receive Him into their hearts and give Him the first place in their lives down here? No, indeed; rather will He laugh at their calamity and mock when their fear cometh (Prov. 1:26). The instrument of the heart must be tuned here on earth to fit it to produce the melody of praise in heaven. God has so linked together holiness and happiness (as He has sin and wretchedness) that they cannot be separated. Were it possible for an unregenerate soul to enter heaven, it would find there no sanctuary from the lashings of conscience and the tormenting-fire of God's holiness. Many suppose that nothing but the *merits* of Christ are needed to qualify them for heaven. But this is a great mistake. None receive remission of sins through the blood of Christ, who are not first "turned from the power of Satan unto God" (Acts 26:18). God subdues their iniquities whose sins He casts into the depths of the sea (Micah 7:19). Pardoning sins and purifying the heart are as inseparable as the blood *and* water which flowed from the Saviour's side (John 19:34).

Our being renewed in the spirit of our mind, and our putting on of the new man "which after God is created in righteousness and true holiness" (Eph. 4:23, 24), is as indispensable to a *meetness* for heaven, as an having the righteousness of Christ imputed to us is for a *title* thereto. "A malefactor, by pardon, is in a *capacity* to come into the presence of a prince and serve him at his table, but he is not in the *fitness* till his noisome garments, full of vermin be taken off" (S. Charnock). It is both a fatal delusion and wicked presumption for one who is living to please self to imagine that *his* sins have been forgiven by God. It is the "washing of regeneration" which gives evidence of our being justified by grace (Titus 3:5-7). When Christ saves, He *indwells* (Gal. 2:20), and it is impossible for Him to reside in a heart which yet remains spiritually cold, hard, and lifeless. The supreme Pattern of holiness cannot be a Patron of licentiousness.

Justification and sanctification are inseparable: where one is absolved from the guilt of sin, he is also delivered from the dominion of sin, but neither the one nor the other can be until the soul is regenerated. Just as Christ's being made in the likeness of sin's flesh was indispensable for God to impute to Him His people's sins (Rom. 8:3), so it is equally necessary for us to be made new creatures in Christ (2 Cor. 5:17) before we can be, legally, made the righteousness of God in Him (2 Cor. 5:21). The need of our being made "partakers of the Divine nature" (2 Pet. 1:4) is as real and as great as Christ's taking part in human nature, ere He could save us (Heb. 2:14-17). "Except God be born, He cannot come into the kingdom of sin. Except a man be born again he cannot see the kingdom of righteousness. And Divine power—the power of the Holy Spirit, the plenipotentiary and executant of all the will of Godhead—achieves the incarnation of God and the regeneration of man, that the Son of God may be made sin, and the sons of men made righteous" (H. Martin).

How could one possibly enter a world

of ineffable holiness who has spent all of his time in sin, i. e., pleasing *self?* How could he possibly sing the song of the Lamb if his *heart* has never been tuned unto it? How could he endure to behold the awful majesty of God *face to face*, who never before so much as saw Him "through a glass darkly" by the eye of faith? As it is excruciating torture for eyes that have been long confined to dismal darkness, to suddenly gaze upon the bright beams of the midday sun, so will it be when the unregenerate behold Him who is Light. Instead of welcoming such a sight "*all* kindreds of the earth shall *wail* because of Him" (Rev. 1:7); yea, so overwhelming will be their anguish, they will call to the mountains and rocks, "Fall on us, and hide us from the face of Him that sitteth on the throne, and from the wrath of the Lamb" (Rev. 6:17). And, my reader, *that* will be *your* experience, unless God regenerate you! A.W.P.

PROFITING FROM THE WORD

5. *The Scriptures and Good Works.*

The Truth of God may well be likened unto a narrow path skirted on either side by a dangerous and destructive precipice: in other words, it lies between two gulfs of error. The aptness of this figure may be seen in our proneness to sway from one extreme to another. Only the Holy Spirit's enabling can cause us to duly preserve the balance; failure to do which inevitably leads to a fall into error, for "error" is not so much the denial of Truth, as the perversion of Truth, the pitting of one part of it against another. The history of theology forceably and solemnly illustrates this fact. One generation of men have rightly and earnestly contended for that aspect of Truth which was most needed in their day. The next generation, instead of walking therein and moving forward, warred for it, intellectually, as the distinguishing mark of *their* party, and usually, in their defense of what was assulted, have refused to listen to the balancing truth which often their opponents were insisting upon; the result being, they lost their sense of perspective and emphasised what they believed *out of* its *scriptural proportions.* Consequently, in the next generation, the true servant of God is called on to almost ignore what was so valuable in their eyes, and emphasise that which they had, if not altogether denied, almost completely lost sight of.

It has been said that "Rays of light, whether they proceed from the sun, star, or candle, move in perfect straight lines: yet so inferior are our works to God's, that the steadiest hand cannot draw a perfectly straight line; nor, with all his skill has man ever been able to invent an instrument capable of doing a thing apparently so simple" (T. Guthrie, 1867). Be this so or no, certain it is that, men, left to themselves, have ever found it impossible to keep the even line of Truth between what appear to be conflicting doctrines: such as the sovereignty of God and the responsibility of man; election by grace, and the universal proclamation of the Gospel; the justifying faith of Paul and the justifying works of James. Only too often, where the absolute sovereignty of God has been insisted upon, it has been to the ignoring of man's accountability; and where unconditional election has been held fast, the unfettered preaching of the Gospel to the unsaved has been let slip. So, on the other hand, where human accountability has been upheld and an evangelical ministry been sustained, the sovereignty of God and the truth of election have generally been whittled down or completely ignored.

Many of our readers have witnessed examples which illustrate the truth of what has just been said, but few seem to realize that exactly the same difficulty is experienced when an attempt is made to show the precise relation between faith and good works. If, on the one hand, some have erred in attributing to good works a place which Scripture does not warrant, certain it is that, on the other hand, some have failed to give to good works the province which Scripture assigns them. If, on the one side, it be serious error to ascribe our justification before God to any performances of ours; on the other side, they are equally guilty who deny that good works are absolutely *necessary* in order to our reaching Heaven, and to allow nothing more than that they are merely evidences or fruits of our justification. We are well aware that we are now (shall we say?) treading on thin ice, and running a serious risk of ourselves being charged with heresy; nevertheless we deem it expedient to seek Divine aid in grappling with this difficulty, and then commit the issues thereof to God Himself.

In some quarters the claims of faith, though not wholly denied, have been disparaged because of a zeal to magnify good works. In other circles, reputed as orthodox (and they are what we now have chiefly in mind), only too rarely are good works assigned their proper place, and far too infrequently are professing Christians urged with apostolic earnestness to maintain them. No doubt this is due at times to a fear of under-valuing faith, and encouraging sinners in the fatal error of trusting to their own doings, rather than to and in the righteousness of Christ. But no such apprehensions should hinder a preacher from declaring *"all the counsel of God."* If his theme be faith in Christ as the Saviour of the lost, let him fully set forth that truth without any modification, giving to this grace the place which the apostle gave it in his reply to the Philippian jailor (Acts 16:31). But if his subject be good works, let him be no less faithful in keeping back nothing that Scripture says thereon; let him not forget that Divine command, "affirm constantly that they which have believed in God might be careful to maintain good works" (Titus 3:8).

The last-quoted Scripture is a most pertinent one for these days of looseness and laxity, of worthless profession and empty boasting. This expression "good works" is found in the N. T., in the singular or plural number, no less than thirty times; yet from the rareity with which many preachers, who are esteemed sound in the faith, use, emphasize, and enlarge upon them, many of their hearers would conclude that those words occur but once or twice in all the Bible. Speaking to the Jews on another subject, the Lord said, "what therefore God hath joined together, let not man put asunder" (Mark 10:9). Now in Eph. 2:8-10 God has joined two most vital and blessed things together which ought never to be separated in our hearts and minds, yet they are most frequently parted in the modern pulpit. How many sermons are preached from the first two of these verses, which so clearly declare salvation to be by grace through faith and not of works. Yet how seldom are we reminded that the sentence begun in them is only completed in v. 10, where we are told, "For we are His workmanship, created in Christ Jesus unto good works, which God hath before ordained that we should walk in them."

We began this series of articles (in the May 1930 issue) by pointing out that the Word of God may be taken up from various motives and read with different designs, but that 2 Tim. 3:16, 17 makes known for what these Scriptures are really "profitable," namely, for doctrine or teaching, for reproof, correction, instruction in righteousness, and all of these that "the man of God may be perfect, thoroughly furnished unto all good works." Having dwelt upon its teaching about God and Christ, its reproofs and corrections for sin, its instruction in connection with prayer, let us now consider how these furnish us unto all "good works." Here is another vital criterion by which an honest soul, by the help of the Holy Spirit, may ascertain whether or not his reading and study of the Word is really benefiting him.

1. We are profited from the Word when we are thereby taught the *true place of good works.* "Many persons in their eagerness to support orthodoxy as a system, speak of salvation by grace and faith in such a manner as to undervalue holiness and a life devoted to God. But there is no ground for this in the Holy Scriptures. The same gospel that declares salvation to be freely by the grace of God through faith in the blood of Christ, and asserts, in the strongest terms, that sinners are justified by the righteousness of the Saviour imputed to them on their believing in Him, without any respect to works of law, also assures us, that without holiness no man shall see God; that believers are cleansed by the blood of atonement; that their hearts are purified by faith, which works by love, and overcometh the world; and that the grace that brings salvation to all men, teaches those who receive it, that denying ungodliness and worldly lusts, they should live soberly, righteously, and godly, in this present world. Any fear that the doctrine of grace will suffer from the most strenuous inculcation of good works on a scriptural foundation, betrays an inadequate and greatly defective acquaintance with Divine truth, and any tampering with the Scriptures in order to silence their testimony in favour of the fruits of righteousness, as *absolutely necessary* in the Christian, is a perversion and forgery with respect to the Word of God" (A. Carson, 1847).

"For we are His workmanship, created in Christ Jesus unto good works, which God hath before ordained that we should walk in them" (Eph. 2:10). God has designed and commanded that those who believe in Christ should live in, walk in, abound in, good works, and all duties of obedience unto Him. To this end are precepts, counsels, motives, and encouragements, everywhere multiplied in the Scriptures. Wherefore "good works," as including the purifying of our hearts, growth in grace, practical godliness and fruitfulness, are necessary from the very ordination of God, that is, from His revealed will and command; necessary in order to our being granted an entrance into eternal glory and felicity, equally necessary as are repentance and faith, for Christ is "the Author of eternal salvation unto all them that *obey* Him" (Heb. 5:9).

But what force (ask some) has this ordination or command of God unto good works, when notwithstanding it, though we fail to diligently apply ourselves unto obedience, we shall nevertheless be justified by the imputation of Christ's righteousness, and so may be saved without them? Such a senseless objection proceeds from utter ignorance of the believer's present state and relation unto God. To suppose that the hearts of the regenerate are not as much and as effectually influenced with the authority and commands of God unto obedience, as if they were given in order unto their justification, is to ignore what true faith is, and what are the arguments and motives whereby the minds of Christians are principally affected and constrained. Moreover, it is to lose sight of the inseparable connection which God has made between our justification and our sanctification: to suppose that one of these may be without the other is to overthrow the whole Gospel. The apostle deals with this very objection in Rom. 6:1-3.

2. We are profited from the Word when we are thereby taught the *absolute necessity of good works*. If it be written that "without shedding of blood is no remission" (Heb. 9:22) and "without faith it is impossible to please Him"(Heb. 11:6), the Scripture of Truth also declares, "Follow peace with all, and *holiness* without which no man shall see the Lord" (Heb. 12:14). The life lived by the saints in heaven is but the completion and consummation of that life, which after regeneration, they live here on earth. The difference between the two is not one of kind, but degree. "The path of the just is as the shining light, that shineth more and more unto the perfect day" (Prov. 4:18). If there has been no walking with God down here, there will be no dwelling with God up there. If there has been no real communing with Him in time, then there will be none with Him in eternity. Death effects no vital change to the heart. True, at death, the remainders of sin are forever left behind by the saint, but no new nature is then imparted. If then he did not hate sin and love holiness before death, he certainly will not do so afterwards.

No one really desires to go to Hell, though there are few indeed who are willing to forsake that broad road which inevitably leads there. All would like to go to Heaven, but who among the multitudes of professing Christians are really willing and determined to walk that Narrow Way which alone leads thereto? It is at *this* point we may discern the precise place which good works have in connection with salvation. They do not merit it, yet they are inseparable from it. They do not procure a title to Heaven, yet they are among the *means* which God has appointed for His people's getting there. In no sense are good works the procuring cause of eternal life but they are part of the means (as are the Spirit's work within us and repentance, faith and obedience by us) conducing to it. God has appointed the way wherein we must walk in order to our arriving at the inheritance purchased for us by Christ. A life of daily obedience to God is that which alone gives actual *admission* to the enjoyment of what Christ hath purchased for His people—admission now by faith, admission at death or His return in full actuality.

3. We are profited from the Word when we are taught thereby *the design of good works*. This is clearly made known in Matt. 5:16, "Let your light so shine before men, that they may see your good works, and glorify your Father which is in heaven." It is wothy of our notice that this is the *first* occurrence of the expression, and, as is generally the case, the initial mention of a thing in Scripture intimates its consequent scope and usage. Here we learn that the disciples of Christ are to authenticate their Christian profession by the silent but vocal testimony of their lives (for "light" makes no noise in its "shining"!) that, men may *see* (not hear boastings about) their good works, and this, that their Father in heaven may be glorified. Here, then, is their fundamental design: for the honour of God.

As the contents of Matt. 5:16 are so generally misunderstood and perverted, we add a further thought thereon. Only too commonly the "good works" are confounded with the "light" itself, yet they are quite distinct, though inseparably connected. The "light" is our *testimony* for Christ, but of what value is this unless the life itself exemplifies it? The "good works" are not for the directing attention to ourselves, but to Him who has wrought them in us. They are to be of such a character and quality, that even the ungodly will know they proceed from some higher source than fallen human nature. Supernatural fruit requires a supernatural root, and as this is recognized, the heavenly Husbandman is glorified thereby. Equally significant is the *last* reference to "good works" in Scripture: "Having your conversation honest among the Gentiles: that, whereas they speak against you as evil-doers, they may by your good works, which they shall behold, glorify God in the day of visitation" (1 Peter 2:12). Thus the first and final allusions emphasize their design: to glorify God because of His works through His people in this world.

4. We are profited from the Word when we are taught thereby *the true nature of good works*. This is something concerning which the unregenerate are in entire ignorance. Judging merely from the external, estimating things only by human standards, they are quite incompetent to determine what works are good in God's esteem, and what are not. Supposing that what men regard as good works, God will approve of them too, they remain in the darkness of their sin-blinded understandings; nor can any convince them of their error, till the Holy Spirit quickens them into newness of life, bringing them out of darkness into God's marvelous light. Then it will appear that only those are good works which are done in obedience to the will of God (Rom. 6:16), from a principle of love to Him (Heb. 10:24), in the name of Christ (Col. 3:17), and to the glory of God by Him (1 Cor. 10:31).

The true nature of "good works" was perfectly exemplified by the Lord Jesus. All that He did was done out of obedience to His Father. He "pleased not Himself" (Rom. 15:3), but ever performed the bidding of the One who had sent Him (John 6:38). He could say, "I do always those things that please Him" (John 8:29). There were no limits to Christ's subjection to the Father's will: He "became obedient unto death, even the death of the cross" (Phil. 2:8). So too all that He did proceeded from love to the Father and love to His neighbour. Love is the fulfilling of the law; without love, compliance with the law is naught but servile subjection, and that cannot be acceptable to Him who is Love. Proof that all Christ's obedience flowed from love is found in His words, "I *delight* to do Thy will, O My God" (Psa. 40:8). So also all that Christ did had in view the glory of the Father: "Father, glorify *Thy* name" (John 12:28) revealed the object constantly before Him.

5. We are profited from the Word when we are taught thereby *the true source of good works*. Unregenerate men are capable of performing works which are, in a natural and civil, though not in a spiritual sense, good. They may do those things which, externally, as to matter and substance of them are good—such as reading the Bible, attending the ministry of the Word, giving alms to the poor; yet the mainspring of such actions, their lack of godly motive, renders them as filthy rags in the sight of the thrice Holy One. The unregenerate have no power to perform works in a *spiritual* manner, and therefore is it written, "there is none that doeth good, no, not one" (Rom. 3:12). Nor are they able to: they "are not subject to the law of God, neither indeed can be" (Rom. 8:7). Hence, even "the ploughing of the wicked is sin" (Prov. 21:4). Nor are believers able to think a good thought or perform a good work of themselves (2 Cor. 3:5): it is God who works in them "both to will and to do of His good pleasure" (Phil. 2:13).

When the Ethiopian can change his skin and the leopard his spots, "then may they also do good, that are accustomed to do evil" (Jer. 13:23). Men may as soon expect to gather grapes of thorns or figs of thistles, as good fruit to grow upon or good works to be performed by the unregenerate. We have first to be "created in Christ Jesus" (Eph. 2:10), have His Spirit put within us (Gal. 4:6), and His grace implanted in our hearts (Eph. 4:7, 1 Cor. 15:10), before there is any capacity for good works. Even then, we can do nothing apart from Christ (John 15:5). Often we have a will to do that which is good, yet how to perform it, we know not (Rom. 7:18). This drives us to our knees, begging God to make us "perfect in every good work," *working in* us "that which is well pleasing in His sight through Jesus Christ" (Heb. 13:21). Thus are we emptied of self-sufficiency, and brought to realise that *"all"* our springs" are in God (Psa. 87:7); and thus we discover that we can do all things through Christ strengthening us (Phil. 4:13).

6. We are profited from the Word when we are taught thereby the great *importance of good works*. Condensing as far as possible: "good works" are of great importance because by them God is glorified (Matt. 5:16), by them the mouths of those who speak against us are closed (1 Peter 2:12), by them we evidence the genuineness of our profession of faith (James 2:13-17). It is highly expedient that we *"adorn* the doctrine of God our Saviour in *all* things"(Titus 2:10). Nothing brings more honour to Christ than those who bear His name *living* constantly (by His enablement) in a Christ-like way and spirit. It was not without reason that the same Spirit who caused the apostle to preface his statement concerning Christ's coming into this world to save sinners with "This is a *faithful saying*," etc., also moved him to write, "This is a *faithful saying* . . . that they which have believed in God might be careful to maintain good works" (Titus 3:8). May we indeed be "zealous of good works" (Titus 2:14).

7. We are profited from the Word when we are taught thereby *the true scope of good works*. This is so comprehensive as to include the discharge of our duties in every relationship in which God has placed us. It is interesting and instructive to note the first "good work" reported in Holy Writ, namely, the anointing of the Saviour by Mary of Bethany (Matt. 26:10, Mark 14:6). Indifferent to either the blame or praise of men, with eyes only for the "Chiefest among ten thousand," she lavished upon Him her precious ointment. Another woman, Dorcas (Acts 9:36) is also mentioned, "full of good works": after worship comes service, glorifying God among men and benefiting others.

"That ye might walk worthy of the Lord unto all pleasing, being fruitful in *every* good work" (Col. 1:10). The bringing up (not "dragging" up!) of children, lodging (spiritual) strangers, washing the saints' feet (ministering to their temporal comforts) and relieving the afflicted (1 Tim. 5:10), are spoken of as "good works." Unless our reading and study of the Scriptures is making us better soldiers of Jesus Christ, better citizens of the country in which we sojourn, better members of our earthly homes (kinder, gentler, more unselfish), "thoroughly furnished unto *all* good works," it is profiting us little or nothing.

—Arthur W. Pink.

---

in man the gift of reason, and an immortal spirit, by which he is allied to a higher order of beings who are placed in the superior regions. Over the world which He has created, He sways the scepter of omnipotence. 'I praised and honoured Him that liveth forever, whose dominion is an everlasting dominion, and His kingdom is from generation to generation: and all the inhabitants of the earth are reputed as nothing: and He doeth according to His will in the army of heaven, and among the inhabitants of the earth: and none can stay His hand, or say unto Him, What doest Thou?', Dan. 4:34, 35" (John Dick).

A creature, considered as such, has no rights. He can demand nothing from his Maker; and in whatever manner he may be treated, has no title to complain. Yet, when thinking of the absolute dominion of God over all, we ought never to lose sight of His moral perfections. God is just and good, and ever does that which is right. Nevertheless, He exercises His sovereignty according to His own imperial and righteous pleasure. He assigns each creature his place as seemeth good in His sight. He orders the varied circumstances of each according to His own counsels. He moulds each vessel according to His own uninfluenced determination. He has mercy on whom He will, and whom He will He hardens. Wherever we are, His eye is upon us. Whoever we are, our life and every thing is held at His disposal. To the Christian, He is a tender Father; to the rebellious sinner He will yet be a consuming fire. "Now unto the King eternal, immortal, invisible, the only wise God, be honour and glory for ever and ever. Amen." (1 Tim. 1:17). A.W.P.

defective conceptions of each one. Yet so far as our apprehensions can correspond to the discovery that He affords us of His several excellencies, we have a present view of His glory."

As the difference is indeed great between the knowledge of God which His saints have in this life and that which they shall have in Heaven, yet, as the former should not be undervalued because it is imperfect, so the latter is not to be magnified above its reality. True, the Scripture declares that we shall see "face to face" and "know" even as we are known (1 Cor. 13:12), but to infer from this that we shall then know God as fully as He knows us, is to be misled by the mere sound of words, and to disregard that restriction of the same which the subject necessarily requires. There is a vast difference between the saints being glorified and their being made Divine. In their glorified state, Christians will still be finite creatures, and therefore, never able to fully comprehend the infinite God.

"The saints in heaven will see God with the eye of the mind, for He will be always invisible to the bodily eye; will see Him more clearly than they could see Him by reason and faith, and more extensively than all His works and dispensations had hitherto revealed Him; but their minds will not be so enlarged as to be capable of contemplating at once, or in detail, the whole excellence of His nature. To comprehend infinite perfection, they must become infinite themselves. Even in Heaven, their knowledge will be partial, but at the same time their happiness will be complete, because their knowledge will be perfect in this sense, that it will be adequate to the capacity of the subject, although it will not exhaust the fulness of the object. We believe that it will be progressive, and that as their views expand, their blessedness will increase; but it will never reach a limit beyond which there is nothing to be discovered; and when ages after ages have passed away, He will still be the incomprehensible God" (John Dick, 1840).

Second, from a review of the perfections of God, it appears that He is an *all-sufficient* Being. He is all-sufficient in Himself and to Himself. As the First of beings, He could receive nothing from another, nor be limited by the power of another. Being infinite, He is possessed of all possible perfection. When the Triune God existed all alone, He was all to Himself. His understanding, His love, His energies, found an adequate object in Himself. Had He stood in need of anything external, He had not been *independent*, and therefore would not have been God. He created all things, and that "for Himself" (Col. 1:16), yet it was not in order to supply a lack, but that He might communicate life and happiness to angels and men, and admit them to the vision of His glory. True, He demands the allegiance and services of His intelligent creatures, yet *He* derives no benefit from their offices, all the advantage redownds to themselves: Job 22:2, 3. He makes use of means and instruments to accomplish His ends, yet not from a deficiency of power, but oftentimes to more strikingly display His power through the feebleness of the instruments.

The all-sufficiency of God makes Him to be the Supreme Object which is ever to be sought unto. True happiness consists only in the enjoyment of God. His favour is life, and His loving kindness is better than life. "The Lord is my portion, saith my soul; therefore will I hope in Him" (Lam. 3:24): our perceptions of His love, His grace, His glory, are the chief objects of the saints' desire and the springs of their highest satisfaction. "There be many that say, Who will show us any good? Lord, lift Thou up the light of *Thy* countenance upon us. Thou hast put gladness in my heart, more than in the time that their corn and their wine increased" (Psa. 4:6, 7). Yea, the Christian, when in his right mind, is able to say, "Although the fig tree shall not blossom, neither shall fruit be in the vines; the labour of the olive shall fail, and the fields shall yield no meat; the flock shall be cut off from the fold, and there shall be no herd in the stalls: *yet* I will rejoice *in the Lord*, I will joy in the God of my salvation" (Hab. 3:17, 18).

Third, from a review of the perfections of God, it appears that He is the *Supreme Sovereign* of the universe. It has been rightly said that, "No dominion is so absolute as that which is founded on creation. He who might not have made any thing, had a right to make all things according to His own pleasure. In the exercise of His uncontrolled power, He has made some parts of the creation mere inanimate matter, of grosser or more refined texture, and distinguished by different qualities, but all inert and unconscious. He has given organization to other parts, and made them susceptible of growth and expansion, but still without life in the proper sense of the term. To others He has given not only organization, but conscious existence, organs of sense and self-motive power. To these He has added

(*Continued on Page* 119)

Vol. X   JUNE, 1931   No. 6

STUDIES IN THE SCRIPTURES

"Search the Scriptures" John 5:39

Copyright in All English-speaking Countries

EDITOR: Arthur W. Pink, 559 Dupont Ave., York, Penna., U. S. A.
Hon. Agent in England: Mr. A. Winstone, "Shalom," Old Bath Road, Leckhampton, Cheltenham.
Hon. Agent in Australia: Mr. G. Ardill, The Christian Workers' Depot, Commonwealth and Reservoir Streets, Sydney.

THE SATISFYINGNESS OF CHRIST

For the past seventeen months we have been occupied in these front-page articles with the attributes of the Divine nature and character, that is, with those excellencies which pertain to God—Father, Son, and Holy Spirit—as God. It is fitting then that we should turn now to contemplate the excellencies of Christ the Mediator, for "the light of the knowledge of the glory of God" is to be seen "in the face of Jesus Christ" (2 Cor. 4:6). The fullest and clearest revelation that God *is* and *what* He is, is made in the person of Christ, "No man hath seen God at any time; the only-begotten Son, which is in the bosom of the Father, He hath declared" (John 1:18). But this "knowledge" of God is not a mere matter of intellectual apprehension, which one man can communicate to another; but a spiritual discernment, imparted by the Holy Spirit. God must shine in our hearts to give us *that* "knowledge."

When the materialistic Philip said, "Lord, show us the Father" the Lord Jesus replied, "he that hath seen *Me* hath seen the Father" (John 14:9). Yes, He was "the Brightness of His glory, and the express Image of His person" (Heb. 1:3). In the eternal Word become flesh "dwelleth all the fulness of the Godhead bodily" (Col. 2:9). Amazing and glorious fact, it is in the perfection of manhood that the fulness of the Godhead is in Christ revealed to our faith. We could not ascend to God, so He descended to us. All that men can ever know of God is presented to them in the person of His incarnate Son. Hence, "That I may know Him" (Phil. 3:10) is the abiding longing of the most mature Christian.

It will be our prayerful design in the ensuing articles (D.V.) to declare some part of that glory of our Lord Jesus Christ which is revealed in Scripture, and proposed there as the object of our faith, love, delight, admiration and adoration. But alas, after our utmost endeavours and most diligent inquiries we have to say, "How little a portion" (Job. 26:14) it is of Him that we understand! His glory is incomprehensible; His praises unutterable. Some things a Divinely-illuminated mind can conceive of, but what we express, in comparison with what that glory is in itself, is even less than nothing. Nevertheless, that view which the Spirit grants from the Scriptures of Christ and His glory to faith, however weak and obscure be the knowledge which we obtain of it, is yet inexpressibly to be preferred above all other knowledge, understanding or wisdom whatsoever. So it was declared, by him who was favoured to know Him as few ever have been, "Yea doubtless, and I count all things but loss for the excellency of the knowledge of Christ Jesus my Lord" (Phil. 3:8).

It has been well said that "The revelation made of Christ in the blessed Gospel, is far more excellent, more glorious, more filled with rays of Divine wisdom and goodness than the whole creation, and the just comprehension of it, if attainable, can contain or apprehend. Without the knowledge hereof, the mind of man, however priding itself in other inventions and discoveries, is wrapped up in darkness and confusion. This therefore deserves the severest of our thoughts, the best of our meditations, and our utmost diligence in them. For if our future blessedness shall consist in living where He is, and beholding of His glory; what better preparation can there be for it, than in a constant previous contemplation of that glory, in the revelation that is made in the Gospel unto this very end, that by a view of it we may be gradually transformed into the same glory" (John Owen).

Certain it is that the grandest of all privileges which believers are capable of, either in this world or the world to come, is the beholding of the glory (the per-

(Continued on Page 144)

IMPORTANT NOTICES

Please advise promptly of change in address, otherwise copies will be lost in the mails.

We are glad to send a sample copy to any of your friends whom you believe would be interested in such a publication.

Send to Mr. I. C. Herendeen, Swengel (Union County), Penna., for a list of our publications. He has published many of our books and booklets.

This magazine is published as a work of faith and labour of love. The Editor and his wife gladly give their services. It is freely sent to all who will read it. No charge is made for it.

Christians who feel definitely led to do so, may have fellowship with us in this ministry. Those outside the U. S. A. please send only INTERNATIONAL Money Orders made out to York, Penna., U. S. A.

CONTENTS

The Satisfyingness of Christ	121
The Epistle to the Hebrews	122
The Satisfaction ("Atonement") of Christ	128
Regeneration, or, The New Birth	134
Caring for the Children	138
Communion	142

THE EPISTLE TO THE HEBREWS

42. The Mediator: 9:15.

The proposition which the apostle is occupied with proving and illustrating in this section of the epistle is that which was laid down in 8:6, "But now hath He obtained a more excellent ministry, by how much also He is the Mediator of a better covenant, which was established upon better promises." In the verses which were before us in the last article, the superiority of Christ over Aaron was brought out in the following respects. First, in that He officiated in a more excellent tabernacle (v. 11). Second, in that He offered to God a superior sacrifice (vv. 11, 14). Third, in that He has entered a more glorious sanctuary (v. 12). Fourth, in that He secured a more efficacious redemption (v. 12). Fifth, in that He was moved by a more excellent Spirit (v. 14). Sixth, in that He obtained for His people a better cleansing (v. 14). Seventh, in that He made possible for them a nobler service (v. 14).

Christ has "obtained eternal redemption" for His people. As we pointed out in our last article, to "redeem" signifies to liberate by the paying of a ransom-price: "If the Son shall make you free, ye shall be free indeed" (John 8:36). The freedom which the Christian has is, first, a *legal* one: he has been "redeemed from the curse of the law" (Gal. 3:13). Because of this, second, he enjoys an *experimental* freedom from the power of sin: "sin shall not have dominion over you" (Rom. 6:14). Justification and sanctification are never separated: where God imputes the righteousness of Christ, He also imparts a principle of holiness, the latter being the fruit or consequence of the former; both being necessary before we can be admitted into heaven. Because the blood of Christ has fully met every claim of God upon and against His people, its virtues and purifying effects are applied to them by the Spirit. Both of these were foreshadowed under the Levitical types of the old economy, and are seen in 9:13.

"The blood of bulls and of goats and the ashes of an heifer sprinkling the unclean" sanctified "to the purifying of the flesh." There is here both a comparison and a contrast. The comparison is between the type and the Antitype; the contrast, between what the one and what the other effected. Those typical rites procured only a temporary "redemption" from the governmental consequences of sin; Christ's sacrifice has secured an "eternal redemption" from all the consequences of sin. A double type is referred to in 9:13. No single sacrifice could adequately represent the power and efficacy of the blood of Christ. By the *"blood of bulls and goats"* the *guilt* of Israel's sins were temporally removed; by the sprinkling of the *"ashes of an heifer"* they were ceremonially purified from the *defilements* of the wilderness. We quote below a valuable footnote from A. Saphir:

"The ashes of an heifer. It was to take away the defilement of death. The institution is recorded in the book of Numbers as relating to the provision God makes for His people in their wilderness journey. As no blood of the slain victim was 'incorruptible,' it was necessary, in order to show the cleansing by blood from defilement through contact with death, to have as it were the essential principle of blood presented in a permanent and available form. The red heifer, which had never been under the yoke, symbolizes life in its most vigorous, perfect, and fruitful form. She was slain without the camp (Heb. 13:11, Num. 19:3, 4). She was *wholly* burnt, flesh, skin, and blood, the priest casting cedar-wood, hyssop, and scarlet into the fire. The ashes of the burnt heifer, put into flowing water, were then sprinkled with hyssop for ceremonial purification. . . . Christ is the fulfillment. For the blood of Christ is not merely, so to speak, the key unlocking the holy of holies to Him as our High Priest and Redeemer, it is not merely our ransom by which we are delivered out of bondage, and, freed from the curse, are brought nigh unto God; but it also separates us from death and sin. It is incorruptible, always cleansing and vivifying; through this blood we are separated from this evil world, and overcome; by this blood we keep our garments white (John 6:53, Rev. 7:14).

"What had necessarily to be separated in the types, is here in unity and perfection. Likewise, what *really* and *potentially* is given to us when we are first brought into the state of reconciliation and access, of justification and sanctification, is in our actual experience continually repeated. We have been cleansed and sanctified once and forever; the same blood, remembered and believed in, cleanseth us continually. The difference between this continual cleansing and the first (according to John 13:10) must never be forgotten, or we fall into a legal condition, going back from the holy of holies into the holy place. But, on the other hand we must not forget the *living* character of the blood, which by the Spirit is continually applied to us, and by which we have peace, renewal of the sense of pardon, and strength for service (1 Pet. 1:2)."

Having pointed out what God's people are redeemed *from*, the Holy Spirit next makes a brief notice of what Christ has redeemed *unto*. He has delivered us from the curse of the law and the bondage of sin; He has also procured for us an "eternal inheritance": His satisfaction has merited for us the favour and image of God and everlasting bliss in His presence. In referring to this, the Spirit also takes occasion to bring out the fact that the sacrifice of Christ was necessary in order for God to make good His promises of old. Herein too He once more meets the Jewish prejudice — why must this great High Priest *die?* The death of Christ was requisite in order to the accomplishing of God's engagements to Abraham and his (spiritual) seed, to confirm His covenant-pledges, which, once more, brings into view the relation which Christ sustains to the everlasting covenant.

"And for this cause He is the Mediator of the new testament, that by means of death, for the redemption of the transgressions under the first testament, they which are called might receive the promise of eternal inheritance" (v. 15). Each word in this verse requires to be duly weighed and carefully considered both in the light of what immediately precedes and follows, otherwise we are certain to err. The opening "And" is plain intimation that no new subject begins here, which at once disposes of the figment that this and the next verses require to be placed in a parenthesis. The apostle continues to treat of what was before him in the verses which we considered in the last article. He is still showing the excellency of our High Priest and the superior efficacy of His sacrifice. That the contents of this verse are by no means free from difficulty is readily allowed, yet its leading thoughts are plain enough.

"And for this cause He is the Mediator of the new testament." The Greek words for "for this cause" are rendered "therefore" in 1:9 and other places. They signify, because of this, or for this reason. There has been a great deal of discussion as to precisely what is referred to in "for *this* cause": some insisting that it looks back to what has been affirmed in the previous verses, others contending that it points forward to that which is declared in the second half of this verse. Personally, we believe that *both* are included. There is a fulness to God's words which is not to be found in man's, and whenever an expression is capable of two or more meanings, warranted by the context and the analogy of faith, both should be retained. Let us then look at the two thoughts here brought together.

"For this cause": because of the superior nature and efficacy of the sacrifice which Christ was to offer, God appointed Him to be the Mediator of the new covenant. It was out of (prospective) regard unto the fitness of Christ's person and the excellency of His offering, that God ordained Him to make mediation between Himself and His fallen people. Because He should make an effectual atonement for their sins and provide a way whereby their troubled consciences might have peace, God decreed that His Son, becoming incarnate, should interpose between poor sinners and the awful Majesty they have offended. "For this cause": and also, because it was only by means of death that the transgressions under the first testament could be redeemed and the called receive the promise of eternal inheritance, Christ was appointed Mediator of the new covenant.

With his usual sagacity John Owen combined both ideas: "It is evident there is a reason rendered in these words, of the necessity of the death and sacrifice of Christ, by which alone our consciences may be purged from dead works. And this reason is intended in these words, 'For this cause.' And this necessity of the death of Christ, the apostle, proves both from the nature of His office, namely, that He was to be the Mediator of the new covenant, which, being a testament, required the death of the testator; *and* from what was to be effected thereby, namely, the redemption of transgressions, and the purchase of an eternal inheritance. Wherefore, *these* are the things which he hath respect unto in these words."

"He is the Mediator of the new testament." It seems strange that some of the best of the expositors understand this to mean that *after* Christ had "offered Himself without spot to God" He became "the Mediator," which is indeed a turning of things upside down and a putting an effect for a cause. A mediator is one who stands between two parties, and two parties at variance, and that with the object of settling the difference between them, that is, of effecting a reconciliation. Hence we read, "For there is one God, and one Mediator between God and men, the man Christ Jesus; Who gave Himself a ransom for all, to be testified in due time" (1 Tim. 2:5, 6). The second half of our verse ought to have prevented such a blunder: "He is the Mediator of the new testament, that *by means of death*. . . they which are called might receive the promise of eternal inheritance."

As we pointed out in our comments upon 8:6, it is most important to recognise that Christ is a *sacerdotal* Mediator, that is, one who has interposed His sacrifice and intercession between God and His people in order to their reconciliation. In voluntarily undertaking to serve as Mediator between God and His people considered as fallen creatures, two things were required from Christ. First, that He should completely remove that which kept the covenanters at a distance, that is, take away the cause of enmity between them. Second, that He should purchase and procure, in a way suited unto the glory of God, the actual communication of all the good things—summed up in "grace and glory" (Psa. 84:11)—which belong to those whose Surety He was. *This* is the foundation of the "merits" of Christ and of the grant of all blessings unto us for His sake.

In what has just been pointed out, we may perceive an additional signification to the opening "And" of our verse. Christ is not only "High Priest" (vv. 11 to 14), but "Mediator" too. He undertook office upon office in order to our greater good. Christ is, in the "new covenant" or "testament," the Mediator, Surety, Priest and Sacrifice, all in His own person. In order that we may have something like a definite conception of these, let us consider, separately, the various relations which our blessed Redeemer sustains to the everlasting covenant. First, He is the *Surety* of it: Heb. 7:22. As such He engaged to render full satisfaction to God on behalf of His people, to do and suffer for them all that the law required. He transferred to Himself all their obligations, undertaking to pay all their debts. In other words, He substituted Himself in their place and stead, in consequence of which there was a double imputation: God reckoning to Christ all their liabilities, God imputing to them His perfect righteousness (2 Cor. 5:21).

As the "Surety" Christ most blessedly fulfilled the type of Gen. 43:9, being Sponsor to His Father for all His beloved Benjamin's: Heb. 2:13, Isa. 49:5, 6, John 10:16. Second, as the *Mediator* of the covenant (Heb. 12:24), He took His place between God and His people, undertaking to maintain the interests and secure the honour of both parties, by perfectly reconciling the one to the other. As the "Mediator" Christ has blessedly fulfilled the type of Jacob's "ladder," uniting heaven and earth. Third, as the *Messenger* (Mal. 3:1) or "Angel" of the covenant (Rev. 8:3-5) He makes known God's purpose and will to His people, and presents their requests and worship to Him. Fourth, as the *Testator* of the covenant (Heb. 9:16) He has ratified it and made bequests and gifts to His people. Finally, and really first, as the *Head* of the whole election of grace, the covenant was made with Him by God: Psa. 89:3, etc.

"For this cause He is the Mediator of the new testament." Here again there has been an almost endless controversy as to whether this last word should be rendered "covenant" or "testament," that is, "will." The same Greek word has been translated by both these English terms, some think wrongly so, for a "covenant" is, strictly speaking, an agreement or contract between two parties: the one promising to do certain things upon the fulfilment of certain conditions by the other; whereas a "testament" or "will" is where one bequeaths certain things as gifts. Thus there seems to be little or nothing in common between the two concepts, in fact, that which is quite contrary. Nevertheless, our English translators have rendered the Greek word *both* ways, and we believe, rightly so. Nevertheless it remains for us to enquire, *why* should the same term be rendered "covenant" in 8:6 and "testament" in 9:15? Briefly, the facts are as follows.

First, the word "diatheke" occurs in the Greek N. T. thirty-three times, having been translated (in the A. V.) "covenant" twenty times (twice in the plural number) and "testament" thirteen times, four of the latter being used in connection with the Lord's supper. Second, in the Sept. version (the translation of the Heb. O. T. into Greek) this word "diatheke" occurs just over two hundred and fifty times, where, in the great majority of instances, it is used to translate "berith." Third, the Greek word "diatheke" is not that which properly denotes a covenant, compact, or agreement; instead, the technical terms for *that* is "syntheke," but the Spirit never once uses this word in the N. T. Fourth, on the other hand, it should be noted that the Hebrew language has no distinctive word which means a will or testament. Fifth, the most common use of the term "diatheke" in the N. T., particularly in 2 Cor. 3 and in Hebrews, neither denotes a "covenant" proper (a stipulated agreement) nor a "will," but instead, an economy, a dispensational arrangement or ordering of things.

Now it needs to be very carefully noted that from Heb. 9:15 to the end of the chapter, the apostle argues from the nature of a will or "testament" among men, as he distinctly affirms in v. 16. His manifest object in so doing was to confirm the Christian's faith in the expectation of the benefits of this "covenant" or "testament." Nor did he violate the rules of language in this, straining neither the meaning of the Heb. "berith" nor the Greek "diatheke," for there is, actually, a close affinity between the two things. There are "covenants" which have in them free grants or donations, which is of the nature of a "testament"; and there are "testaments" whose force is resolved into conditions and agreements—as when a man wills an estate to his wife on the stipulation that she remains a widow— which is borrowed from the nature of a "covenant."

If we go back to the O. T. and study the various "covenants" which God made with men, it will be found again and again that they were merely declarations whereby He would communicate good things unto them, which has more of the nature of a "testament" in it. Sometimes the word "covenant" was used simply to express a free promise, with an effectual donation and communication of the thing promised, which also has more of the nature of a "testament" than of a "covenant." Thus, once more, we perceive a fulness in the words of the Holy Spirit which definitions from human dictionaries do not include. That which *was* a "covenant," has become *to us* a "testament." The "covenant" was made by God with Christ. By His death that which God pledged Himself to do unto the heirs of promise in return for the work which Christ was to perform, is now *bequeathed* to us as a free gift: what was a legal stipulation between the Father and the Mediator, comes to us purely as a matter of grace.

Some have insisted that "the Mediator of the new covenant" is understandable, but that "Mediator of the new testament" is no more intelligible than the "testator of a covenant" would be. Our answer is that, the Spirit of God is not tied by the artificial rules which bind human grammarians. Rom. 8:17 tells us that Christians are "heirs of God," that is of the Father, yet He has not *died!* No figure must be pressed too far. Some have argued that because the Church is the Body of Christ, it cannot also be His "Bride," but such carnal reasoning is altogether inadmissible upon spiritual and Divine things; as well might we argue that because Christ calls us "brethren" (Heb. 2:12), therefore we cannot be His "children" (Heb. 2:13); or that because Christ is the "everlasting Father" of Israel (Isa. 9:6), He cannot also be their "Husband" (Isa. 54:6). The truth is, that Christ is both the Mediator of the new covenant, and the Mediator of the new testament, looking at the same office from two different angles. God has so confirmed the promises in Christ (2 Cor.

1:20), that at His death He made a legacy of them and bequeathed them to His people in a testamentary form.

To sum up what has been said on this difficult but important subject: throughout the N. T. the Holy Spirit has intentionally used only the one word "diatheke"—though there was another in the Greek language ("syntheke") which more exactly expressed a "covenant"—because it was capable of a double application, and that, because the Son of God is not only the Mediator of a new covenant, but also the Testator of His own gifts. Thereby God would fix our gaze on the *cross* of Christ, and see there that what had up to that day existed as a "covenant," then became for the first time, a "testament"; and that while the covenant between the Father and the Son is from everlasting, the "new *testament*" dates only from Calvary.

"For the redemption of the transgressions under the first testament." This states one of the principal ends which God had in view when appointing Christ to be the "Mediator," namely, to deliver His people from all the bondage they were subject to as the result of their violations of His law, and that by the payment of a satisfactory price. But, it may be asked, why not "the redemption of the transgressors" rather than "transgressions"? Did Christ purchase sins? The reference is to His expiation of His people's iniquities, and they were "debts," and Christ's death was a *discharge* of that debt. "The discharge of a debt is a buying it out. Thus to redeem sins is no more harsh a phrase than to be 'delivered for our offences' (Rom. 4:25), or 'who gave Himself for our sins' (Gal. 1:4), or to be 'merciful to their unrighteousness,' Heb. 8:12" (Wm. Gouge).

"For the redemption of the transgressions under the first testament." In these words the Spirit makes a further exhibition of the virtue and efficacy of Christ's death, by affirming that it paid the price of remitting the sins of the O. T. saints. Here again the apostle is countering the Jewish prejudice. The death of Christ was necessary not only if sinners of N. T. times should be fitted to serve the living God (v. 14), but also to meet the claims which God had against the O. T. saints. The efficacy of Christ's atonement was retrospective as well as prospective: cf. Rom. 3:25. The true (in contrast from the typical), spiritual (in contrast from the ceremonial), and eternal (in contrast from the temporal) "redemption" of the O. T. saints was effected by the sacrifice of Christ. The same thing is clearly *implied* in Heb. 9:26: had not the one offering of Christ—as the Lamb "foreordained before the foundation of the world" (1 Pet. 1:19, 20)—been of perpetual efficacy from the days of Abel onwards, then it had been necessary to *repeat* it constantly in order to redeem believers of each generation. It was God's eternal purpose that Christ's atonement, settled in the "everlasting covenant," should be available to faith from the beginning. Hence, the apostle said, "Through this Man is preached unto you the forgiveness of sins (cf. Gal. 3:8, Heb. 4:2), and by Him *all* that believe—O. T. saints as truly as the N. T.—are justified from all things" (Acts 13:38, 39).

"Now, if any one asks, whether sins under the Law were remitted to the fathers, we must bear in mind the solution already stated,—that they *were* remitted; but remitted *through Christ*. Then notwithstanding their external expiations, they were always held guilty. For this reason Paul says that the law was a handwriting against us (Col. 2:14). For when the sinner came forward and openly confessed that he was guilty before God, and acknowledged by sacrificing an innocent animal that he was worthy of eternal death, what did he obtain by his victim, except that he sealed his own death as it were by this handwriting? In short, even then they only reposed in the remission of sins, when they looked to Christ. But if only a regard to Christ took away sins, they could never have been freed from them, had they continued to rest in the law" (J. Calvin).

"For the redemption of the transgressions under the first testament." It remains for us to ask, Why *this* limitation? for Christ atoned for the sins of those who were to believe as much as for they who had, before He became incarnate, looked in faith to Him. First, because a measure of doubt or uncertainty could exist only concerning them. Some have taught, and possibly some in the apostle's day thought, that nought but earthly blessings would be the portion of those who died before the present dispensation. Therefore to remove such a doubt, it is affirmed that O. T. believers too were redeemed by Christ's blood. Second, because the apostle had pressed so hard the fact that the Levitical sacrifices could not remove moral guilt from those who lived under the Mosaic economy, he shows Christ's sacrifice had. Third, because by just consequence it follows that, if those who trusted Christ of old had redemption of *their* transgressions through Him, much more they who are under the new testament. "The blood of Jesus Christ His Son cleanseth us from all sin" (1 John 1:7): it was just as efficacious in taking away the transgressions of believers before it was actually shed, as it is of cleansing believers today, nineteen centuries after it was shed.

"They which are called might receive the promise of eternal inheritance." Here the "heirs" are designated by character rather than by name, by this qualification (Greek) "they which have been called," that is, effectually so, or truly converted to God. In John 1:12 this privilege of heirship is settled upon "believers," such as do heartily accept of Christ and His grace. In Acts 26:18 and Col. 1:12 the heirs are described as "sanctified," that is, as personally dedicated to God and set apart to live unto Him. This expression "the called" is a descriptive appellation of the true spiritual people of God, and looks back to the "call" of Abraham (Heb. 11:8), who, in consequence of the mighty workings of divine grace in his heart, turned his back upon the world and the things of the flesh (Gen. 12:1), and entered the path of faith's obedience to God. Only those possessing these marks are the spiritual "children" of Abraham, such as have been "called with a *holy* calling" (2 Tim. 1:9).

"Might receive the promise of eternal inheritance." This is the goal toward which the apostle has been steadily moving, as he has passed from clause to clause in this verse. That the called of God might receive the promise of eternal inheritance was the grand ultimate object of the "everlasting covenant" so far as men are concerned, and the chief design of the new testament. But an obstacle stood in the way, namely, the transgressions or sins of those who should be "called." In order to the removal of that obstacle, Christ must die that death which was due unto those transgressions. For the Son of God to die, He must be appointed unto a mediatorial position and become incarnate. Because He was so appointed, because He did so die, because He has redeemed from all transgressions, the "eternal inheritance" is sure unto all His people, His heirs, the "called" of God.

"Might receive the promise of eternal inheritance." The children of Israel received from God an external call which separated them from the heathen, and when they were redeemed from Egypt they received promise of a temporal or earthly inheritance. But inside that Nation was "a remnant according to the election of *grace*," and they, individually, received from God an inward call, which made them the heirs of an eternal inheritance. It is of these latter that our verse speaks, yet as including also the saints of the present dispensation. Promise of an "eternal inheritance" had the O. T. saints. They had the Gospel preached unto them (Heb. 4:2). They were saved through "the grace of the Lord Jesus Christ" (Acts 15:11) as well as we. They "did all eat the *same* spiritual meat and did all drink the same spiritual drink," even Christ (1 Cor. 10:3, 4). And therefore did they "desire a better country, that is, an *heavenly*" (Heb. 11:16). How all of this sets aside the preposterous figment of the modern "dispensationalists," who relegate "Israel" to an inferior inheritance from that which belongs to "the Church"!

"Might receive the promise of eternal inheritance." What is meant by the first four words here? First, let us very briefly define the "eternal inheritance." By it we understand God's "great salvation" (Heb. 2:3), considering it in its most comprehensive sense, as including justification, sanctification and glorification. It is that blessed estate which Christ has purchased for "His own," here called an "inheritance" to remind us that the way whereby we come unto it is by a gratuitous adoption, and not by any merits of our own. Now as the state of those who are to receive it is twofold, namely, in this life and in that which is to come, so there are two parts of this inheritance: "grace and glory." Even now "eternal life" is communicated to those who are called according to God's purpose. But "grace" is only "glory" begun: the best "wine" is reserved for the time to come. For the future aspect of the "eternal inheritance" see 1 Peter 1:3-5.

The way whereby God conveys this "eternal inheritance" is by "promise": see Gal. 3:18 and Heb. 6:15-18. And this for a threefold reason at least. First, to manifest the absolute *freeness* of the grant of it: the "promise" is everywhere opposed unto everything of "works" or desert in ourselves: Rom. 4:14, etc. Second, to give *security* unto all the heirs of it, for the very veracity and faithfulness of God is behind the promise: Titus 1:1, etc. Since God has "promised" *to* bestow the "inheritance," nothing in, of, or from the heirs can possibly be an occasion of their forfeiting it: 1 Thess. 5:24. Third, that it might be *by faith*, for what

God promises necessarily requires faith, and faith only, unto its reception: Rom. 4:16. To *"receive* the promise" has a double force. First, it is to "mix faith" with it (Heb. 4:2), to *appropriate* it (Heb. 11:13, 17), so as not to stagger at it in unbelief (Rom. 4:21, 22). Second, it is to receive the *fulfillment* of it. As unto the *foundation* of the whole inheritance, in the sacrifice of Christ, and all the grace, mercy and love, with the fruits thereof, these are communicated to believers in this life: Gal. 3:14. As unto the *consummation*, the future state in glory, we "receive the promise" by faith, rest thereon, and live in the joyous expectation of it: Heb. 11:13.

In conclusion, let us sum up the contents of this remarkable verse, adopting the analysis of John Owen. 1. God has designed an "eternal inheritance" unto certain persons. 2. The way in which a right or title is conveyed thereunto is by "promise." 3. The persons unto whom this inheritance is designed, are the "called." 4. The obstacle which stood in the way of their enjoyment of this inheritance was their "transgressions." 5. That this obstacle might be removed, and the inheritance enjoyed, God made a "new covenant," because none of the sacrifices under the first covenant could expiate sins. 6. The ground of the efficacy of the "new covenant" unto this end was, that it had a Mediator, a great High Priest. 7. The means whereby the Mediator of the new covenant did expiate the sins against the first testament was by "death," and this of necessity, seeing that this new covenant, being also a "testament," required the death of the Testator. 8. The death of this Mediator has taken away sins by "the redemption of transgressions." Thus, the promise is sure unto all the seed. A.W.P.

THE SATISFACTION
("Atonement")
OF CHRIST

18. *Its Effects.*

Having dwelt at length upon the principal "results" which the Satisfaction of the Mediator has secured, we turn now to look at some of its leading "effects." The distinction we have in mind is not very clearly intimated by these two terms, so we must define what we intend by their use. In treating of the "results" we have almost (though not quite) confined our attention to the objective or external benefits which Christians derive from the work of their great High Priest. Here, we desire to point out the subjective or internal blessings which accrue to us from it. In this article we shall endeavour to take up and follow out in fuller detail what was briefly touched upon in Article 12, division 2, where, under the "Application" of the Atonement we mentioned, The Spirit regenerating.

That aspect of Truth which is now to be before us has received but scant notice even by many who wrote most helpfully upon the true nature and character of the Satisfaction of Christ. There has been a sad failure to duly hold the balance of Truth. Not a few have so stressed the *legal* results secured by our Saviour's sacrifice, and have so failed to proportionately emphasize the *experimental* effects which it purchased, that it is greatly to be feared multitudes have been deceived into supposing that *they* had a saving interest therein, when, in fact, they lacked the Scriptural marks of those who have passed from death unto life. Christ died to "save His people from their sins" (Matt. 1:21): not only from the guilt and penalty of them, but also from their pollution and power.

It is because there has been such a one-sided calling unto faith without an equal insistence for repentance, and because there has been such an emphasis laid upon the Grace which is revealed in the Gospel without a proportionate exposition of its Holiness, that ground has been given for the enemies of the Truth to charge the Gospel with immoral tendencies, to affirm that it encourages careless living and releases men from the due performance of their duties, that it is unfriendly to the producing of good works. And the deplorable thing is that the lives of many who profess to have been saved by grace through the righteousness of Christ, has tended to confirm their contentions, until not a few who have had dealings with professing Christians, have said (and with much cause), If that is what Christianity produces I want nothing to do with it.

It needs to be loudly affirmed, trumpeted forth from every "orthodox" pulpit in the land, that the mediatorial work and sufferings of the Lord Jesus not only obtained for God's people redemption from the penal consequences of their sins, but has also secured *their personal sanctification*. Well did Thomas J. Crawford say, in his splendid work "The Doctrine of Holy Scripture Respecting the Atonement" (1874), "In speaking or thinking of the 'salvation' which Christ has purchased, there are many who seem to attach to it no farther idea than that of mere *deliverance from condemnation*. They forget that *deliverance from sin*—the cause of condemnation—is a no less important blessing comprehended in it. Assuredly it is just as necessary for fallen creatures to be delivered from the pollution and moral impotency which they have contracted, as it is to be exempted from the penalties which they have incurred; so that, when reinstated in the favour of God, they may at the same time be made capable of loving, serving, and enjoying Him forever. And in this respect the remedy which the Gospel reveals is fully suited to the exigencies of our sinful state, providing for our complete redemption from sin itself, as well as from the penal liabilities it has brought upon us.

"Nay, it would seem as if the former of these deliverances—that is to say, our deliverance from sin itself—were represented in some passages of Scripture as the grand and ultimate consummation of redeeming grace, to which the latter, though in itself inestimably precious and important, is preparatory. Witness these plain and forcible declarations: 'He died for all, *that* they who live should not henceforth live unto themselves, *but unto Him* who died for them and rose again' (2 Cor. 5:15). 'Christ also loved the Church, and gave Himself for it, that He might *sanctify it and cleanse it* with the washing of water by the Word, and that He might present it to Himself a glorious Church not having spot or wrinkle or any such thing; but that it should be holy and without blemish' (Eph. 5:25-27). 'He gave Himself for us, that He might redeem us from all iniquity, and purify unto Himself a peculiar people, *zealous of good works*' (Titus 2:14). 'The blood of Jesus, who through the eternal Spirit offered Himself without spot unto God, should purge your conscience from dead works, *to serve the living God*' (Heb. 9:14). These statements seem to indicate that our redemption from the guilt and penal consequences of sin was intended to be the means to an ulterior end—that end being our personal sanctification."

Certain it is that the inestimable blessings of justification and sanctification are represented in the Word of God as *inseparable* results of the Saviour's mediation. Nor ought we to have any difficulty in apprehending how the Satisfaction of Christ, in obtaining for us the former blessing, should thereby secure our attainment of the latter. For our redemption by the blood of Christ binds us to His service as a purchased or peculiar people: "Ye are not your own, for ye are bought with a price; therefore glorify God in your body and in your spirit, which *are* God's" (1 Cor. 6:19, 20). Furthermore, it has (as we have shown in Article 12), procured for the redeemed the grace of the Holy Spirit "which He shed on us abundantly" (Titus 3:6), and by which His purchased people are renewed in the whole man after the image of God, and are enabled more and more *to die* unto sin and to live *unto righteousness*.

The sanctifying power of "the redemption that is in Christ Jesus" is practically displayed in and by the character and conduct of true believers. There is as marked a difference between the children of God and the children of this world, as there is between light and darkness. There is as real a distinction, *outwardly manifested*, between the blood-bought and the blood-washed, people of Christ and those whose iniquities are not purged, as there is between life and death. Even in this life, according to the measure of their growth in grace, those who have been born again are witnesses to the present efficacy of Christ's Satisfaction. Still more so will they be in the life to come, when they are freed from all those infirmities and blemishes which now cleave to them.

"Never, then," (to quote again from T. Crawford) "was there a more unfounded calumny than the assertion that personal holiness is disparaged or dispensed with in the scheme of our redemption. So far from being so, it is magnified and honoured. True, it is not the *foundation* on which we are called to build; but it is a prominent part of the *stately edifice*, for the erection of which that foundation has been laid. It is not our *remedy*, but it is the completion of *the actual cure* which that remedy is designed to accomplish. It is not in any respect or in any degree *the means of salvation*, but it is one of the most essential and most precious elements of *salvation itself*."

What is that salvation which Christ has purchased for His people? Of what does it consist? What are its prime elements?

Someone answers, Deliverance from the everlasting burnings, which our sins justly deserved. True, yet that is only one part of the answer. A valid title to everlasting bliss in Heaven, says another. Equally true, yet that answer also fails to cover all the ground. What about the *present!* What is the precious portion which the redeemed enjoy even now? Or, suppose we put it in another way. Multitudes profess to have been saved by Christ, yet, though quite sincere in their profession, when measured by the Scriptures, it is evident that they are mistaken. How, then, may the writer and the reader be sure that he is not mistaken? Who are the *legitimate* claimants of this privileged state? Salvation is an experience, a personal experience, which is begun in this life. And it is this we shall now seek to describe.

1. *Emancipation.*

"If the Son therefore shall make you free, ye shall be free indeed" (John 8:36). Free *from what?* First, from the power of *indwelling sin*. Not that the sinful nature is eradicated or even slain, but that the *heart* is delivered from its dominion. "Being now made free from sin" (Rom. 6:22). That which was once loved, is now hated. Those solicitations which were gladly heeded, are now resisted. "The fear of the Lord is the *beginning* of wisdom" (Prov. 9:10). None have been made wise unto salvation (2 Tim. 3:15) unless there has been implanted in their hearts a filial respect for God. And, "the fear of the Lord is to *hate* evil" (Prov. 8:13), and "by the fear of the Lord men *depart from* evil" (Prov. 16:6). The heart of a saved person is set upon pleasing God.

Second, the Christian is delivered from the power of *the world.* "The friendship of the world is enmity with God, whosoever therefore will be a friend of the world is the enemy of God" (James 4:4). The friendship of the world consists of indulging worldly lusts, following worldly vanities, fellowshipping with worldlings. It is for the heart to find its satisfaction in the perishing things of time and sense. From this the grace of God delivers its favoured subjects, by fixing their hearts upon One who is "altogether lovely." Before Christ saves him, a man seeks happiness in the pleasures, honours, or riches of this world; but when He delivers *"from* this present evil world" (Gal. 1:4), his affections are drawn unto things above. "For whatsoever is born of God *overcometh* the world" (1 John 5:4). The heart of a saved person finds its delight in God.

Third, the Christian is delivered from the power of *the Devil.* For this purpose did Christ leave Heaven: "to proclaim liberty to the captives and the opening of the prison to them that are bound" (Isa. 60:1), and when the Spirit of God applies the Gospel in power to the heart, then is that individual "delivered from the power of darkness and translated into the kingdom of His dear Son" (Col. 1:13). It was "in *time past*" that Christians "walked according to the course of this world, according to the prince of the power of the air" (Eph. 2:2). When Christ saves a soul, He breaks Satan's chains, delivers his captive, and brings him into the place of liberty. True, the Devil still tempts, harasses and wounds the Christian, but destroy him or take him prisoner again he cannot. Concerning all God's children it is written, "they *overcame* him (the Devil) by the blood of the Lamb" (Rev. 12:11). The heart of a saved person is occupied with serving God.

"That the righteousness of the law might be fulfilled in us, who walk not after the flesh, but after the spirit" (Rom. 8:4). The first part of this verse has been before us in previous articles, the second half is what we will now consider. There we have described those unto whom God has imputed the righteousness of Christ. It is by these marks they may be clearly identified: they walk not after the flesh, they walk after the spirit. A course of godly living, of spiritual behaviour, is both the inseparable concomitant of union with Christ and an infallible evidence thereof. The "walk" is that which is open to the observation of others, and is plainly seen by them. It is not any particular act which is here specified, but the general course and uniform tenor of the life that is referred to.

"Who walk not after the flesh." The principle of evil is still within, active, powerfully opposing (Gal. 5:17); nevertheless, the Christian has been freed from its dominion, so that it is no longer the controlling power in his heart and life. The best of God's children offend in many things (James 3:2), yet the prayer of their heart is, "Order my steps in Thy Word: and let not any iniquity have dominion over me" (Psa. 119:133). Sometimes real saints have sad falls into outward and open sins, yet they do not continue therein, but are brought to repent and forsake them. To walk after the flesh is to follow a course of self-will, self-pleasing, self-gratification (Isa. 53:6), and this no *saved* person does or can do.

They walk "after the spirit." This gives us the positive side, for when grace works within the heart its subject is enabled to "overcome evil with good." When God saves a sinner he is not only so far delivered from the power of indwelling sin that his walk—his regular course of conduct—is no longer controlled by fleshly principles and lustings, but he is also enabled to live a spiritual and godly life. Christians are not only effectually taught to deny "ungodliness and worldly lusts" but also to "live soberly, righteously, and godly, in this *present* world" (Titus 2:12). To "walk after the spirit" is to respond unto the promptings of that new nature received at regeneration; it is to be controlled by new and unworldly principles; it is for a person to be dominated by the Holy Spirit, so that he loves God, serves God, and glorifies God. How this is brought about we shall now see under,

2. *Regeneration*.

As we wish to be as concise as possible we shall here limit ourself to one aspect of this miracle of grace, namely, the Holy Spirit reversing that depraved state of soul spoken of in Rom. 8:7, "The carnal mind is enmity against God: for it is not subject to the law of God, neither indeed can be." When God renews His people He deals directly with the will, powerfully bringing it into a conscious subjection to *His* will. There is what may be called a transfer of the moral law from the tables of stone to the fleshly tables of the heart: "I will put My laws into their mind, and write them in their hearts" (Heb. 8:10). God secures the intelligent acquaintance of the Christian with His law and a cordial acquiesence in it. But let it be emphatically affirmed that this transfer is *not* of such a nature that the law of God is no more to be found outside and above the will of the Christian.

At regeneration the law of God does not disappear as an authoritative code of duty, because it has become the desire of the Christian's heart and the purpose of his will to please God. Not so: that which the Holy Spirit has secured is a changed heart, which lives in the recognition of God's authority, and is able to say, "I delight in the law of God after the inward man" (Rom. 7:22). Instead of salvation having freed its subject from subjection to God, from obedience to Him, from obligation to keep His law, it has subdued his enmity against God's law and bestowed a love for it—a love that finds expression not only in endearing words, but in practical submission to the authority of the Ruler of heaven and earth.

It is at this very point that the modern Antinomians have erred. Infected by that spirit of lawlessness which is so rife in the world, and misled by an erroneous conception of the *nature* of spiritual "liberty," they have insisted that Christians are entirely delivered from the claims of God's law. They suppose that an inward consent to the holiness of His commands presents a higher ideal of spiritual freedom, than subjection to an external code. But the reverse is the fact. The withdrawal of objective law is really the denial of responsibility, and *liberty* is infringed, when responsibility is infringed. Spiritual liberty is not the power to do as we please (*that* is licentiousness), but the power to do as we *ought;* it is the being delivered from that bondage of sin which prevented us from serving God. The true nature of spiritual liberty is clearly enough defined in Psa. 119:45: "I will walk at liberty: *for* I seek Thy precepts."

When a sinner is regenerated, he is made "willing" (Psa. 110:3) to be under the law of God, to be in subjection to his Maker. The obedience of the Christian is not that of a slave, for the law of God is within his heart in the character of a holy tendency, as well as standing over him with its commandments. Nor is his obedience the operation of a *mere* mental tendency or spiritual mechanism working out its own bias—as of a vessel languidly drifting with the stream. No, it is the obedience of a loving and loyal *subject*, adoring his King and saying, "Lord, what wilt Thou have me to do?" It is the renewed heart gladly, *owning* the rightful authority and supremacy of its Maker. And *this* is the highest ideal of *liberty* that can be framed. It is the liberty of Heaven itself, for there God does not abdicate His *throne*, nor cease to issue His *commands* (Psa. 103:20).

It is equally vain to assert that a subjective view of the Law—love in the heart dispensing with the need of external commands—presents a higher ideal of Grace. Grace is not a species of lawlessness, or mercy dispensed by ignoring the claims of justice. Grace reigns through righteousnss (Rom. 5:21), and that at *every* stage. Not only has Christ met every claim of the law against His people, but, by the workings of His Spirit, He places in their hearts a new principle, which causes them to cry, "O how *love* I Thy law" (Psa. 119:97). The triumph of Grace is that it effects a *reconciliation* between the blatant rebel and the righteous Governor of all, and makes an insurrectionist a loyal subject. Well might the apostle say, "Do we then make void the law through faith? God forbid: yea, we *establish* the law" (Rom. 3:31).

3. Sanctification.

This is another fruit of the Cross of Christ. The Lord Jesus not only rendered a perfect obedience unto the law for the justification of His people, but He also merited and procured for them those supplies of His Spirit which were essential unto their sanctification. To deliver us from the guilt of sin is an unspeakable mercy, yet would it not be a perfect favour unless He also purged from the venom of sin which has infected our nature. Had the believer been pardoned without being "purified" (1 Pet. 1:22), he had still been unfit for converse with God. But God not only satisfied His *justice* in the sacrifice of Christ, but also magnified His *holiness* by providing for the renewing of His people in His own image. Personal holiness is just as essential a part of "salvation" as is forgiveness. Therefore did the satisfaction of our Surety not only secure for His people a perfect legal standing before God, but also provided for their perfect experimental fitness for His presence.

To "sanctify" is to set apart unto, to dedicate or devote to, God. Where polluted man is concerned, he must be *purified* (both judicially and experimentally) before he is meet for the Lord's use (2 Tim. 2:21): note how in Eph. 5:26 "sanctify" is defined by "cleanse." Now there is a double sanctification pertaining to the Christian: judicial and experimental. *Christ* is the believer's sanctification as truly as He is his righteousness, see 1 Cor. 1:30; but unless such a bare statement be defined and amplified, it conveys no definite concept to us. The satisfaction of Christ is the *meritorious* cause of the Christian's sanctification, but the work of the Spirit is the *efficacious* cause thereof, hence we read of the "sanctification of the Spirit" (2 Thess. 2:13). That takes place at the new birth, when the regenerated soul is set apart unto God, separated from those dead in sin. That aspect of our experimental sanctification is absolute and complete. But there is another side to the Christian's experimental sanctification which is relative or progressive, and which, because of sin indwelling us, is never perfected in this life.

This practical (in contrast from positional) and progressive (in contrast from absolute) sanctification consists of two branches: mortification and renovation. A complete summary of these is given to us in Titus 2:12. There, mortification is comprehended under two words, answering to the two tables of the law: *denying* "ungodliness," which comprehends the first four commandments; denying "worldly lusts" which covers the last six commandments. Then, that renovation which the grace of God produces is to "*live*" soberly," which respects ourself; "righteously" or "justly" in all our dealings with our neighbours; and "godly" in connection with God. When Divine grace "brings" *salvation* to a person, his heart is inclined unto obedience, and he is made fruitful in his life unto the glory of God.

Now the heart of the Christian is made holy by regenerating grace purifying it from the pollution (*not* presence) of sin, implanting a hatred of and a striving against it; and by renewing us after God's image. In that spiritual life which was communicated at the new birth, there is contained in embryonic form all spiritual graces and fruits which, by the operations of the Spirit through the Word, are developed and matured. By the Spirit, the renewed heart is kept under the influence of efficacious grace, and it is disposed and enabled to fear the Lord, walk in His statutes, and be conformed to His law. The more the Christian *feels* his own utter inability to serve God acceptably, and the more earnestly and constantly he beseeches Him to work in him "both to will and to do of His good pleasure," the clearer evidence has he of his experimental and progressive sanctification, and in *this* way is he assured of his justification.

As the Christian finds that he is becoming less and less disposed to confer with flesh and blood (either his own wisdom or that of others), and more and more consults the Holy Scriptures, because he is desirous of learning his duty; as he denies self, takes up his cross, and seeks to follow Christ; as every fresh discovery of God's will commands his attention and fills him with holy reverence; as he is more ready, more cheerful, more determined in his obedience; as his supreme desire is really to glorify God, and this becomes the *prevailing* state of his heart and mind; then, though he is increasingly conscious of the plague of his own heart, and mourns more deeply and frequently than ever his *many* failures, both of omission and commission; nevertheless, it is evident that the work of sanctification is advancing in his soul.

The *rule* of our sanctification is God's written Word (John 17:17), for by it alone does the Spirit work, forming in the saint those dispositions which it both promises and requires. The Holy Scriptures are the one rule by which all of our conduct is to be regulated. Practical holiness is a personal conformity of heart and life to what God's Word enjoins. The "commandments of men" (Matt. 15:9) are of no weight or value whatsoever. *Their* "touch not, taste not, handle not" (Col. 2:21) are to be resolutely refused. No creature is to be allowed to dictate unto the Lord's freeman. Our one concern must be to obey, serve, and please *God*.

While it be true that the whole work of sanctification is of God, it needs to be steadily borne in mind that His work is only carried forward in us by *our* use of the means which He has appointed to this end, and *His blessing* of those means. If we become more or less prayerless, our souls will necessarily languish. If we fail to desire and drink in the pure milk of His Word, we shall not grow thereby. If we are slothful and fail to walk in the path of duty, if we are careless and presume upon God's goodness, then we provoke His Spirit, and He withholds His aids and assistances. And were such a sad state persisted in to the end of our earthly course, that would be clear proof, no matter what our pretensions, that we had *never* been justified and sanctified by God.

To sum up this division. Sanctification may be considered, first, as an *act* of God the Spirit (1 Pet. 1:2) already completed, when the Christian is set apart unto God by His life-giving operation, by His begetting us with the Word of truth (James 1:18), from which root the fruits of practical holiness grow. Second, as a *state* of acceptance with God, into which salvation brings us: 1 Cor. 6:11. Third, as a *growth*, an increasing conformity to God in heart, mind, and life: 2 Cor. 7:1. Fourth, as a *longing*, an (as yet) unrealized desire, a panting after and praying for complete conformity to the image of God's son: 1 Thess. 5:23; which desire is realized at the moment of the soul's entrance into Heaven, and consummated at the resurrection of his glorified body. Each and all of these four aspects of one sanctification are the *fruits* of Christ's satisfaction — purchased for His people. By that perfect sacrifice which He offered unto God, the Lord Jesus procured for us all that we need for time and eternity, and *He* is only fully honoured when we perceive that every gift, operation, blessing, and fruit of the Holy Spirit comes to us on the ground of the Redeemer's merits.

4. *Preservation.*

This too is another of the precious fruits produced by the tree of Calvary. "By one offering He hath perfected *forever* them that are sanctified" (Heb. 10:14). Herein lies one of the main differences between the perfect satisfaction of Christ and the typical offerings under the law. The atonement made by Israel's high priests availed only for one year: twelve months later it must needs be repeated. But the sacrifice of Christ was once for all: its virtue and efficacy is eternal. "There is therefore now no condemnation to them which are in Christ Jesus" (Rom. 8:1), nor can anything ever separate His people from the love of God (Rom. 8:35-39). "Wherefore He is able also to save them *to the uttermost* that come unto God by Him, seeing He ever liveth to make intercession for them" (Heb. 7:25). A perfect, unforfeitable, eternal salvation, has Christ procured for His own.

Yet on this point also we need to carefully remember that the Lord does not deal with us as stocks and stones, but as rational creatures; not as irresponsible automatons, but as accountable beings. He preserves His people through means which He inspires them to use. He preserves in the path of practical godliness, not in a course of carnal carelessness. The hearts of believers are like gardens, wherein there are not only flowers, but weeds also; and as the former must be watered and cherished, so the latter must be curbed and nipped. If nothing but the dews and showers of God's promises fell on our hearts, though they tend to the nourishing of our graces, yet the weeds of corruption would grow with them, and in the end choke them, unless they be nipped by the severity of the Divine threatenings.

Although God has pledged Himself to secure those for whom Christ died, and that in the use of means, therefore they cannot apostatise; nevertheless, He has plainly warned us that there is an infallible connection between sin and destruction (1 Cor. 6:9), and that the one must be avoided, if the other is to be escaped. We *must* "watch and pray" if temptations are to be escaped from. We are "kept by the power of God *through faith*" (1 Pet. 1:5). We are not only saved by faith at the outset of our spiritual career, but we are supported and sustained by it through all our consequent experience: "the just shall *live* by faith" (Heb. 10:38). As it is by faith we enter that narrow way which leadeth unto life, so it must be by faith we walk all the journey through, for it is only "through faith and perseverance" that we "inherit the promises" (Heb. 6:12).

The life of the Christian, between his being delivered from Hell and his actual entrance into Heaven, is not a picnic, but a warfare. There is armour to be put on, weapons to be used, enemies to be vanquished, if the fight is to be won. Therefore are we bidden to make our "calling and election *sure*" (2 Pet. 1:10), and that, by *adding to* our faith, virtue, knowledge, temperance, perseverance, g o d l i n e s s, brotherly-kindness, and love. Therefore are we requird to "show the same diligence to the full assurance of hope *unto the end*" (Heb. 6:11). God calls His people unto glory and eternal bliss via a path of self-denial and holy obedience. If we *neglect* our duties, there is no promise that God will perfect that which concerneth us. They who deny not the flesh, who refuse not the friendship of the world, who press not forward along the highway of practical holiness, evidence that they have *no* spiritual life, no matter what their profession may be. But they who deny self, take up their cross, and follow Christ, no matter how weak and unprofitable they may feel, are assured that He who has begun a good work in them "*will* finish it" (Phil. 1:6). A.W.P.

REGENERATION, or, THE NEW BIRTH

When the Lord Jesus said "That which is born of the flesh is flesh" (John 3:6) He not only intimated that every man born into this world inherits a corrupt and fallen nature and therefore is unfit for the Kingdom of God, but also that this corrupt nature can never be anything else but corrupt, so that no culture can fit it for the kingdom of God. Its tendencies may be restricted, its manifestations modified by education and circumstances, but its sinful tendencies and affections are still there. A corrupt tree cannot bring forth good fruit, prune and trim it as you may. For good fruit, you must have a good tree or graft from one. Therefore did our Lord go on to say, "And that which is born of the Spirit is spirit." This brings us to consider,

II. Its Nature.

We have now arrived at the most difficult part of our subject. Necessarily so, for we are about to contemplate the workings of *God*. These are ever mysterious, and nothing whatever can really be known about them, save what He Himself has revealed thereon in His Word. In endeavouring to ponder what He *has* said on His work of regeneration two dangers need to be guarded against: first, *limiting* our thoughts to any isolated statement thereon or any single figure the Spirit has employed to describe it. Second, reasoning from what He has said by *carnalizing* the figures He has employed. When referring to spiritual things, God has used terms which were originally intended (by man) to express material objects, hence we need to be constantly on our guard against transferring to the former erroneous ideas carried over from the latter. From this we shall be preserved if we diligently compare *all* that has been said on each subject.

In treating of the nature of regeneration much damage has been wrought, especially in recent years, by men confining their attention to a single figure, namely, that of the "new birth," which is only one out of many expressions used in the Scriptures to denote that mighty and miraculous work of God within His people which fits them for communion with Him. Thus, in Col. 1:12, 13, the same vital experience is spoken of as God's having "*made us meet*" to be partakers of the inheritance of the saints in light: Who hath delivered us from the power of darkness, and hath translated us into the kingdom of His dear Son." Regeneration is the commencement of a new experience, which is so real and revolutionising that the one who is the subject of this Divine begetting is spoken of as "a new creature: old things are passed away, behold, all things are become new" (2 Cor. 5:17). A new spiritual life has been imparted to the soul by God, so that the one receiving it is vitally implanted into Christ.

The nature of regeneration can, perhaps, be best perceived by comparing and contrasting it with what took place at the Fall, for though the person who is renewed by the Spirit receives more than what Adam lost by his rebellion, yet, the one is, really, God's answer to the former. Now it is most important that we should clearly recognise that no faculty was lost by man when he fell. When he was created, God gave unto man a spirit, and soul and body. Thus, man was a tripartite being. When man fell, the Divine threat "In the day that thou eatest thereof, thou shalt surely *die*" was duly executed, and man died spiritually. But that does not mean that either his spirit or soul, or any part thereof, ceased to be, for in Scripture "death" never signifies annihilation, but is a state of separation. The prodigal son was "dead" while he was in the far country (Luke 15:24), because he was separated from his father. "*Alienated from* the life of God" (Eph. 4:18) describes the fearful state of one who is unregenerated, so does "she that liveth in pleasure is dead while she liveth" (1 Tim. 5:6): that is, dead spiritually, dead Godwards, while alive in sin —the spirit, soul and body, each being *active against* God.

That which took place at the Fall was not the destruction of either portion of man's threefold being, but the vitiating or corrupting of them. And that, by the introduction of a new principle within him, namely, *sin*, which is more of a quality than a substance. By the Fall man became possessed of a sinful "nature." But let it be stated very emphatically that a "nature" is *not* a concrete entity, but rather that which characterises and impells an entity or creature. It is the nature of gravitation to attract, it is the nature of the wind to blow, it is the nature of fire to burn. A "nature" is not a tangible thing, but a *principle of operation*, a power impelling to action. Thus, when we say that fallen man possesses a "sinful nature," it must not be understood that something as substantial as his soul or spirit was *added* to his being, but instead, that a principle of evil *entered* into him, which polluted and defiled every part of his constitution, as frost entering fruit spoils it.

At the Fall, man lost none of the faculties with which the Creator had originally endowed him, but he lost the power to *use* his faculties *Godwards*, All desire Godwards, all love for his Maker, all real knowledge of Him, was lost. Sin possessed him: sin as a principle of evil, as a power of operation, as a defiling influence, took complete charge of his spirit and soul and body, so that he became the "servant" or slave "of sin" (John 8:34). As such, man is no more capable of producing that which is good, spiritual, and acceptable to God, than frost can burn or fire freeze: "they that are in the flesh (remain in their natural and fallen condition) *cannot* please God" (Rom. 8:8). They have no power to do so, for all their faculties, every part of their being, is completely under the dominion of sin. So completely is fallen man beneath the power of sin and spiritual death, that the things of the Spirit of God are "foolishness" unto him, "neither can he know them" (1 Cor. 2:14).

Now that which takes place at regeneration is the *reversing* of what happened at the Fall. The one born again is, through Christ, and by the Spirit's operation, *restored to* union and communion with God; the one who before was spiritually dead, is now spiritually alive: John 5:24. Just as spiritual death was brought about by the entrance into man's being of a principle of evil, so spiritual life is the introduction of a principle of holiness. God communicates a *new principle*, as real and as potent as sin. Divine grace is now imparted. A holy disposition is wrought in the soul. A new temper of spirit is bestowed upon the inner man. But no new faculties are created within him, rather are his original faculties enriched, ennobled, and empowered. Just as man did not become less than a threefold being when he fell, so he does not become more than a threefold being when he is renewed. Nor will he in Heaven itself: his spirit and soul and body will simply be *glorified*, i. e., completely delivered from every taint of sin, and perfectly conformed to the image of God's Son.

At regeneration a "new nature" is imparted by God. But again we need to be closely on our guard lest we carnalize our conception of what is denoted by that expression. Much confusion has been caused through failure to recognise that it is a *person*, and not merely a "nature," which is born of the Spirit: "*ye* must be born again" (John 3:7), not merely something *in* you must be; "*he* which is born of God" (1 John 3:9). The *same* person who was spiritually dead—his whole being, alienated from God—is now made spiritually alive: his whole being, reconciled to God. This must be so, or otherwise there would be no preservation of the *identity* of the individual. It is the person, and not simply a nature which is born of God: "Of His own will begat He *us*" (James 1:18). It is a new birth *of* the individual himself, and not of something *in* him. The nature is never changed, but the person is—relatively, but not absolutely.

The *person* of the regenerate man is essentially the same as the person of the unregenerate: each having spirit, and soul and body. But just as in fallen man there is *also* a principle of evil which has corrupted every part of his threefold being, which "principle" is his "sinful nature" (so called because it expresses his evil disposition and character, as it is the "nature" of swine to be filthy), so when a person is born again another and new "principle" is introduced into his being, a new "nature" or disposition, a disposition which propells him Godwards. Thus, in both cases "nature" is a quality rather than a substance. "That which is born of the Spirit is *spirit*" must not be conceived of as something substantial, distinct from the soul of the regenerate, like one portion of matter added to another; rather is it that which *spiritualises* all his inward faculties, as the "flesh" had carnalized them.

Again; "that which is born of the Spirit is spirit" is to be carefully distinguished from that "spirit" which every man has in addition to his soul and body: see Num. 16:22, Eccl. 12:7, Zech. 12:1. That which is born of the Spirit is not something tangible, but that which is spiritual and holy, and that is a quality rather than a substance. In proof of this, compare the usage of the word "spirit" in these passages: in James 4:5 the inclination and disposition to envy is called "the *spirit* that dwelleth in us lusteth to envy." In Luke 9:55 Christ said to His disciples, "ye know not what manner of *spirit* ye are of," thereby signifying, ye are ignorant of what a fiery *disposition* is in your hearts. See also Num. 5:14, Hos. 4:12, 2 Tim. 1:7. That which is born of the Spirit is a principle of spiritual life, which renovates all the faculties of the soul.

Some help upon this mysterious part of our subject is to be obtained by noting that in such passages as John 3:6, etc., "spirit" is contrasted from the "flesh." Now it should scarcely need saying that "the flesh" is not a concrete entity, being quite distinct from the body. When the term "flesh" is used in a moral sense the reference is always to the *corruption* of fallen man's nature. In Gal 5:19-21 the "works of the flesh" are described, among them being "hatred" and "envyings," in connection with which the body (as distinguished from the mind) is *not* implicated—clear proof that the "flesh" and the "body" are not synonymous terms. In Gal. 5 the "flesh" is used to designate those evil tendencies and affections which result in the sins there mentioned. Thus, the "flesh" refers to the *degenerate state* of man's spirit and soul and body, as the "spirit" refers to the regenerate state of the spirit and soul—the regeneration of the body being yet future.

The privative (darkness is the privative of light) or negative side of regeneration, is that Divine grace gives a mortal wound to indwelling sin. Sin is not then eradicated nor totally slain in the believer, but it *is* divested of its *reigning* power over his faculties. The Christian is no longer the helpless slave of sin, for he resists it, fights against it, and to speak of a *helpless* victim "fighting," is a contradiction in terms. At the new birth sin receives its death-blow, though its dying struggles within us are yet powerful, and acutely felt. Proof of what we have said is found in the fact that while sin's solicitations were once agreeable to us, they are now hated. *This* aspect of regeneration is presented in Scripture under a variety of figures, such as the taking away of the heart of stone (Ezek. 36:26), the binding of the strong man (Matt. 12:29) etc. The absolute dominion of sin over us is destroyed by God (Rom. 6:14).

The positive side of regeneration is that Divine grace effects a complete change in the state of the soul, by infusing a principle of spiritual life, which renovates all its faculties. It is this which constitutes its subject a "new creature," *not* in respect of his essence, but of his views, his desires, his aspirations, his habits. Regeneration or the new birth is the Divine communication of a powerful and revolutionising principle into the soul and spirit, under the influence of which all their native faculties are exercised in a different manner from that in which they were formerly employed, and in *this* sense "old things are passed away; behold, all things are become new" (2 Cor.

5:17). His thoughts are "new," the objects of his choice are "new" his aims and motives are "new," and thereby the whole of his external deportment is changed.

"By the grace of God I am what I am" (1 Cor. 15:10). The reference here is to *subjective* grace. There is an objective grace, inherent in God, which is His love, favour, goodwill for His elect. There is also a subjective grace which terminates on them, whereby a change is wrought in them. This is by the infusion of a principle of spiritual life, which is the spring of the Christian's actions. This "principle" is called "a new heart" and a "new spirit" (Ezek. 36:26). It is a supernatural habit, residing in every faculty and power of the soul, as a principle of holy and spiritual operation. Some have spoken of this supernatural experience as a "change of heart." If by this expression be meant that there is a change wrought in the fallen nature itself, as though that which is natural is transformed into that which is spiritual, as though that which was born of the flesh *ceased to be* "flesh," and became that which is born of the Spirit, then, the term is to be rejected. But if by this expression be meant, an acknowledgment of the reality of the Divine work which is wrought in those whom God regenerates, it is quite permissible.

When treating of regeneration under the figure of the new birth, some writers have introduced analogies from natural birth which Scripture by no means warrants, in fact disallows. Physical birth is the bringing forth into this world of a creature, a complete personality, which before conception had no existence whatever. But the one who is regenerated *had* a complete personality before he was born again. To this statement it may be objected, Not a *spiritual* personality! What is meant by this? Spirit and matter are opposites, and we only create confusion if we speak or think of that which is *spiritual* as being something concrete. Regeneration is not the creating of a person which hitherto had no existence, but the renewing and restoring of a person whom sin had unfitted for communion with God, and this by the communication of a nature or principle or life, which gives a new and different bias to all his old faculties. It is an altogether erroneous view to regard a Christian as made up of two distinct personalities.

As "justification" describes the change in the Christian's *objective* relationship to God, so "regeneration" denotes that intrinsic *subjective* change which is wrought in the inclinations and tendencies of his soul Godwards. This saving work of God *within* His people is likened unto a "birth" because it is the gateway into a new world, the beginning of an entirely new experience, and also because as the natural birth is an issuing from a place of darkness and confinement (the womb) into a state of light and liberty, so is the experience of the soul when the Spirit quickens us. But the very fact that this revolutionising experience is *also* likened unto a *resurrection* (1 John 3:14) should deliver us from forming a one-sided conception of what is meant by the "new birth" and the "new creature," for resurrection is not the absolute creation of a new body, but the restoration and glorification of the old body. Regeneration is also called a Divine "begetting" (1 Pet. 1:3), because the image or likeness of the Begetter is conveyed and stamped upon the soul. As the first Adam begat a son in his own image and likeness (Gen. 5:3), so the last Adam has an "image" (Rom. 8:29) to convey to His sons: Eph. 4:24, Col. 3:10.

It has often been said that in the Christian there are two distinct and diverse "natures," namely, the "flesh" and the "spirit" (Gal. 5:17). This is true, yet care must be taken to avoid regarding these two "natures" as anything more than two *principles* of action. Thus, in Rom. 7:23 the two "natures" or "principles" in the Christian are spoken of as, "I see another *law* in my members, warring against the *law* of my mind." The flesh and the spirit in the believer must be conceived of as something very different from the "two natures" in the blessed person of our Redeemer, the Godman. Both the Deity and humanity *were* substantial entities in Him. Moreover, the "two natures" in the saint result in a necessary conflict (Gal. 5:17), whereas in Christ there was not only complete harmony, but "*one* Lord."

The faculties of the Christian's soul remain the same in their essence, substance, and natural powers as before he was "renewed," but these faculties *are* changed in their properties, qualities and inclinations. It may help us to obtain a clearer conception of this if we illustrate by a reference to the waters at Marah (Ex. 15:25, 26). Those "waters" were the same waters still, both before and after their cure. Of themselves, in their own nature, they were "bitter," so as the people could not drink of them;

but in the casting of a tree into them, they were made sweet and useful. So too with the waters at Jericho (2 Kings 19:20, 21), which were cured by the casting of salt (emblem of grace: Col. 4:6) into them. In like manner the Christian's affections continue the same as they were in their nature and essence, but they are cured or healed by grace, so that their properties, qualities and inclinations are *renewed* (Titus 3:5), the love of God now being shed abroad in the heart by the Holy Spirit (Rom. 5:5).

What man lost by the fall was his original *relation to* God, which kept all his faculties and affections within the proper exercise of that relation. At regeneration the Christian received a new life, which gave a new direction to his faculties, presenting new objects before them. Yet, let it be said emphatically, it is not merely the restoration of the life which Adam lost, but one of unspeakably higher relations: he received the life which the Son of God has in Himself, even "eternal life." But the old personality still remains. This is clear from Rom. 6:13, "but yield yourselves unto God, as those that are alive from the dead, and *your* members as instruments of righteousness unto God." The members of the same individual are now to serve a new Master. A.W.P.

(To be continued, D. V.)

CARING FOR THE CHILDREN

Having sought in the last two issues to present some of the teachings of Holy Writ upon the subjection of the wife to her husband, and the responsibilities of the husband to his wife, it seems meet, if we are to complete the subject of the Christian home, to say a few words on the obligations of parents to their offspring. But ere doing so, at the risk of being misunderstood, we would seriously ask married readers to prayerfully ponder 1 Cor. 7:29. It has always been a solemn responsibility to beget and bear children, but perhaps never more so than in these "Perilous Times" (2 Tim. 3:1). The enjoyment of the marriage-relationship (as of every other) needs to be exercised in the fear of God, the spirit of prayer, and with God's glory in view: 1 Cor. 10:31. While God is to be trusted, He must not be tempted (Matt. 4:7). Let husbands and wives seek to be "temperate in *all* things" (1 Cor. 9:25) and heed that word, "let your *moderation* be known unto all men" (Phil. 4:5).

The Christian's home should be, as one has called it, "the masterpiece of the *applied* Gospel." It ought to be that sphere in which there is the loveliest manifestation and exemplification of the spirit of Christ. Alas, that it so often becomes the place where the Christian is most off his guard, where spiritual restraints are discarded, and where inconsistencies are allowed to grow into habits. We need to remind ourselves frequently that "The eyes of the Lord are in every place, beholding the evil and the good" (Prov. 15:3). That God takes particular note of our home-life, its arrangements and ordering, is clear from 1 Tim. 3:4, 12; Titus 1:6. There ought to be no need for hanging a motto on our walls "Christ is the head of this home": it should be *patent* to all who enter it, everything connected therewith should witness to His superintending presence.

Where children have been prayerfully sought from and given by God, they are to be looked upon and dealt with as "an heritage of the Lord" (Psa. 127:3), that is, belonging to the Lord. They are *His* creatures, and entrusted to your care, your guardianship, for a season—sometimes for a very short season; for being *His*, He has the right to take them from us when He pleases. These little ones are given unto you by Him, as a solemn trust, as a holy charge, to be reared *for Him*. Then ask Him for wisdom, for grace, for every needed help, *to* train them for His honour and glory.

Because children are "an heritage of the Lord," the first duty of Christian parents is to definitely and solemnly *dedicate* them unto Him. This ought to be done very shortly after they are born. There should be a turning unto God, a thanking Him for the gift, a yielding of it back again into His hands, an unreserved committal of it to Him to do with it as seemeth Him good, a consecrating of it to *His* service, and an earnest supplicating of His blessing upon its life. The last time we saw our own aged mother, she reminded the writer that she dedicated him to God's service before he was born. And by Divine grace she remained true to her vow: for though almost fourteen years passed without her seeing her first-born (and the only one of her three children which God had saved) she told us: "Having dedicated him to God, I would not ask Him to send him back to me while he was engaged in His service in foreign lands."

You long to see your little one saved, yet *you* cannot save it: "Salvation is of the Lord." Then, deliver it back again by faith into the hands of Him who gave it to you: say with David "of Thine own have we given Thee" (1 Chron. 29:14). Many a Christian is resting his own soul on, "I know whom I have believed, and am persuaded that He is able to keep that which I have committed unto Him against that day" (2 Tim. 1:12). And *what* is it that you have "committed" unto Him? You answer, My own soul. Very good; but why stop short with it? "*That* which I have committed" is just as wide and as large as faith is ready to make it. Each of us places his own limitation on that "that"! Why not "commit" the souls of your children into His hands as definitely and as trustfully as you first did your own! Why not?

"Then were there brought unto Him little children, that He should put His hands on them, and pray" (Matt. 19:13). Is not this recorded for our instruction? We have long felt that those who do not believe in the baptising of infants (and we are among the number) have failed at an important point, namely, the absence of any public dedicating of the children of saints unto God. While the duty of dedicating the children to God devolves first upon the parents, and should be done by them (and not delegated to any "priest") in private, yet it seems to us that there should also be a *public* presenting of the little one to the Saviour, *as* in Matt. 19:13, etc., and a seeking of the united prayers of God's people where this is possible. We say "possible," by which we mean, where there is access to a church in which the Lord is truly owned and honoured; but not otherwise.

But let it next be said that, your dedication of the child to God's service does not remove or diminish your personal responsibility thereto, it only increases it. You have presented your little one to God, now it is your duty and privilege to train it *for Him*. And let it be said emphatically, that "training" cannot begin too early. No greater mistake can be made than to permit the first few years to pass without definite and diligent efforts made to plant within it the incorruptible seed of God's Word. The first thing which a worldling usually teaches her child is "nursery rhymes,"

let it not be so with you, Christian mother. *Before* it learns to speak, read to it God's Word, and ask Him to bless it to its soul. Nothing is too hard for Him. As infancy is left behind for early childhood, instead of amusing the little one with lying "fairy tales," instruct it in the historical portions of Divine Truth.

"Train up a child in the way he should go (not in the way he "would" go!): and when he is old, he will not depart from it" (Prov. 22:6). Every Christian heart must feel deeply for the children which are growing up in such a deadly atmosphere as is abroad in the world today, and which is likely to become still worse, rather than better. But this only increases the responsibility of the parent to miss no opportunity for storing up the Word of God in their minds. In view of the increasing infidelity taught in the public schools, and blatant wickedness of their school-fellows, it is all the more essential that the characters of your children should be formed under the holy influences of a godly home. And the *first* essential of a godly home is that each of the parents should constantly set before their children *the example* of personal piety.

It should be duly taken to heart that Eph. 6:4 and Col. 3:20, 21 is *preceded* by the Holy Spirit's exhortations to the mothers and fathers—Eph. 5:22-25, Col. 3:18, 19! The parents themselves must be walking in obedience to God, before they are entitled to the obedience of their children. The parents' lives must be right with God, before they can count upon *His* blessing to train their children for Him. This order is also plainly intimated in that important passage in Deut. 6:5-9: "And thou shalt love the Lord thy God with all thine heart, and with all thy soul, and with all thy might. And these words, which I command thee this day, shall be in thine heart: *and* thou shalt teach them diligently unto thy children."

The order of truth presented in the above verses is indeed searching. First, the parent is to love the Lord with all *his* heart. Second, the words of God are to abide in his heart, ruling it, purifying it, hallowing it. Then, God's Word is to flow out from that heart in loving instruction to the children, and in holy converse in the bosom of the family, shining out in all the activities of daily life, so that all who come into your home may see that the Word of God is the standard for each and all, in *everything*. But *do* your children see God's Word shining out in your daily life, Christian parents? influencing your temper, controlling your habits, directing all your ways? O my reader, it is but a *mockery* for you to teach your children the holy Word of God if your own life is not governed by it.

"And thou shalt teach them *diligently* unto thy children." Yes, *"thou* shalt": that is God's command. And you are breaking His command, defying Him, if you allocate to some "sunday school" teacher the responsibility which God's Word has placed upon *you*. "But when is a busy working-man going to find time to do this?" This very scripture tells you: "when thou sittest in thine house" —at the meal-table! Begin the breakfast with five minutes reading of Scripture. Discuss the passage over the meal. Ask the little ones questions upon it, and invite questions from them. Spend ten minutes together around the Word after the evening meal. "And *where* shall I begin?" Just where the Word begins. Go over the first four chapters of the Bible with them again and again. The first three things they need to hear are all found there: creation, degeneration, salvation. First, the work of God in the making of heaven and earth (Gen. 1:2). Second, the disobedience and fall of man (Gen. 3). Third, the way back to God through the slain Lamb—Abel's sacrifice in Gen. 4.

"Remember the sabbath day to keep it holy" (Ex. 20:8). And how is this to be done? Negatively, "not doing thine own ways, nor finding thine own pleasure, nor speaking thine own words" (Isa. 58:13). Positively, by being occupied with Divine and spiritual things. Perhaps a further personal word will be permitted. The writer's father was a busy merchant, and in England we had a delivery of mail every Sunday morning, which often contained important business letters. But none were opened on the Lord's day! No Sunday newspapers ever entered our home, not even when the Boer War was on. When we were little, all our toys were put away Saturday night, and pictorial editions of Bunyan's Pilgrim's Progress, Fox's book of martyrs, etc. were brought out. And today, the writer is unfeignedly thankful to God, that he *was* brought up in a home where the holy Sabbath was so "strictly"—scripturally — kept. The day began by our father reading to us God's Word. In the morning the family attended preaching service. In the afternoon father and mother read to us out of spiritual books. Quite a little of the time was spent in the singing of hymns. And our father was not a preacher!

What we have said above has been written for the encouragement of fathers who may read this article. However difficult it may be for you to spend much time with your children during six days of the week, fail not to spend most of the Sabbath in praying with, reading to, instructing your little ones. God has said, "them that honour Me, I will honour; and they that despise Me, shall be lightly esteemed" (1 Sam. 2:30). The way in which you keep the Sabbath will very largely determine the measure in which God's blessing rests upon your family. Failure at *this* point is *certain* to bring down the chastening hand of God heavily upon you and yours.

"A Sabbath well spent,
Brings a week of content,
And strength for the toils of the morrow;
But a Sabbath profaned,
Whatever be gained,
Is a certain forerunner of sorrow."

Of Abram God said, "For I know that he will command his children and his household after him, and they shall keep the way of the Lord, to do justice and judgment; *that* the Lord may bring upon Abram that which He hath spoken of him" (Gen. 18:19). Note well the word we have placed in italics: God's blessing of Abram and his household turned upon the patriarch's preserving a godly government over it. Most strikingly is this confirmed by what God told Isaac: He declared that blessing should come upon him "*because* that Abraham obeyed My voice, and kept My charge, My commandments, My statutes, and My laws" (Gen. 26:4, 5)—a categorical refutation of the modern heresy that "the patriarchs were not under law"! Abraham *governed* his household according to the Divine commands and statutes, and in consequence the blessing of God rested not only upon him, but also upon his posterity! And this is recorded for our instruction and encouragement.

Contrast now the solemn case of Eli, the high priest of Israel in the days of Samuel. Of him God said, "I will *judge* his house forever for the iniquity which he knoweth, *because* his sons made themselves vile, and he *restrained them not*" (1 Sam. 3:13). How unspeakably solemn. The destroying hand of God fell upon those men because their father had failed to govern them. This is recorded for our warning! So too, of Adonijah, who revolted in the days of David, we read, "And his father *had not* displeased him at any time" (1 Kings 1:6). As a child he was allowed to have his own way; under no restraint at home, he grew up a self-willed young man. Note his *end*: he was slain as a rebel (1 Kings 2:25)!

In the training of the little one, it is most necessary to bear in mind from the outset that, "Foolishness is bound in the heart of a child, but the rod of correction shall drive it far from him" (Prov. 22:15). A sinful nature has been transmitted by the parents, and nothing but Divine grace can subdue it. And for this, the Divinely-appointed means must be used. First, they must be prayed for. Second, Divine wisdom is to be sought for the right portions of Scripture to be applied to the particular outbursts of the "flesh" which you see in the child. Third, he must be reasoned with, warned, admonished. Fourth, where these means fail to check disobedience, then the rod must be resorted to. "He that spareth his rod hateth his son: but he that loveth him chasteneth him betimes" (Prov. 13:24).

How the last-quoted passage exposes those who say "I love my children too much to beat them." Such language is a perversion of the word "love": that sacred word ought never to be on the lips of such people. God says "He that *loveth* him *chasteneth* him": then let God be true and every man a liar. The all-wise God says, "Chasten thy son while there is hope, and let not thy soul spare for his crying" (Prov. 19:18). And again, "withhold not correction from the child: for if thou beatest him with the rod, he shall not die" (Prov. 23:13). Dare not to pit your reasoning and maudlin sentimentality against these plain statements.

The above passages do not mean that the parental reign is to be one of terror and stern authority, but rather, one of love; yet love must not degenerate into weak indulgence. The "rod" is only to be applied as the last resort, and then in reason and moderation, never in sudden impulse and anger. At times it is well for the father not only to take an offending child apart and talk seriously with it (pressing upon him or her the fact that in disobeying the parents, *God* has been defied), but also to pray with him—telling God of the fault that has been committed, asking *Him* to bring home the guilt of it to the conscience, and to deliver from this sin.

"And ye fathers, provoke not your children to wrath" (Eph. 6:4): either by injustice, undue severity, or partiality. "But bring them up in the nurture and admonition of the Lord." "Nurture" means nourishment, feeding them on the pure milk of the Word. "Admonish" means to instruct, warn, discipline. "Fathers, provoke not your children, lest they be discouraged" (Col. 3:21). How these words show the tender solicitude of God for the children of His people! He would have their parents to remember and consider their weakness, the impatience of the flesh; to avoid unnecessary restrictions, and learn to distinguish between wilful offences and heedlessness. No father should make his children to dread him. Children need leading, not driving; treating as responsible beings, and not as brute creatures.

Much holy wisdom and Divine grace are called for at every stage. The father especially needs to be much on his guard against discouraging the children under the chilling feeling that it is impossible to please him, and make them think he has no confidence in their affections and fidelity. Forget not to commend that which is good, and praise them when they do well. Remember you too were a child not long ago, and you cannot put an old head on young shoulders. Your authority is not for your gratification, but for their good. Nevertheless, they must not be nurtured in self-will, nor pass undisciplined for disobedience. While the desire of the worldling is to fit his son or daughter to occupy a good position in the world, let your whole aim be to educate the child for heaven.

The supreme aim of family life should be household piety, every thing else being subordinate thereto. Husband and wife should go hand in hand to the Throne of Grace, and act together in every good work. The children must be taught to "honour"—love and obey—their parents. Authority must be sustained by rewards and penalties. Never make a threat you intend not to execute, nor a promise you mean not to perform. Teach the child self-control, self-restraint, unselfishness. Be careful of the pictures that hang on your walls, the literature which enters your home. Watch carefully the companionships of your children. Beware of allowing them to sleep away from home. Above all, remember the children will learn more from your *example*, than from your words. They soon forget what you say, but will long remember what you do! None are so quick as they to detect inconsistencies. If they see you given to worldliness, covetousness, or anger, admonish as earnestly as you may against these things, it will have no weight with them.

O what dependency upon God, what wisdom, what watchfulness, what patience, are needed! The family is the vineyard which the Christian parent is called on by God to tend and preserve! Say not that we have set too high a standard before you. Not so. It is *God's* standard at which each of us must ever aim, and what *we* have said comes far, far short of *His* requirements. Rather, bow before Him and acknowledge your failure. Ask His forgiveness. Seek His grace. Beg Him to make you what you ought to be, and then to bless those whom He has entrusted to you. A.W.P.

COMMUNION

"Casting *all* your care upon Him, for He careth for you" (1 Pet. 5:7). This means just what it says. Christian reader, there ought to be *no* restraint between you and the Lover of your soul. He would have you be on, and maintain, more intimate terms with Himself, than with any human creature. He is always accessible, and never changes in His feelings toward you. He would have you make Him your "Friend": not only your Counsellor, but your Confident — the One into whose ear (and the only one) you are to pour the very *secrets* of your heart. He would have you be quite artless and natural, just like a little child coming to its mother, pouring into her ear its every little woe, trouble, and disappointment. When harassed by any soul-troubles, such as a feeling of coldness of heart toward Him, burdened about a lack of faith, or because your thoughts so often wander when you try to meditate on Divine things, or in prayers;—come to Him, tell Him all about it, unburden yourself to Him: cast "*all* your care upon Him," keep back nothing.

When something has irritated you, disturbed your composure of mind and peace of soul; when someone has said or done something which causes a resentment to rise within you, and you find it hard to forgive them; go and tell the Lord about it: confess to Him that this ought not to be, that you are ashamed of yourself, and ask Him to lay His calming hand upon you, and to *give* you a forgiving spirit. Or suppose something in the household arrangements has "gone wrong," something which you could not help: perhaps the milkman or the baker late, or the stove not cooking as you wish, and you are disturbed; go to Him, tell Him about it; cast *this* "care" upon Him. You can *never* "weary" the Lord.

It is the Christian's holy privilege to cultivate the most familiar converse with Christ. Nothing more *honours* Him, nothing more delights Him, for this is giving Him His *true* place in your daily life. The "Christian life" is not the vague and mystical thing which the unsaved deem it to be, and which some preachers have made people think it is. No, it is an intensely *practical* and blessed thing. It is *pride* (quite unsuspected) which hinders so many from maintaining this simple and *childlike* converse and communion with Christ. People are ready to call upon Him when some *big* thing (as they think it) confronts them, some really *urgent* need comes up; but the little (?) things they seek to carry and work out themselves. But God's Word says, "in *everything* by prayer and supplication let your requests be made known unto God" (Phil. 4:6).

Above, we have said that it is "pride" which keeps back the Christian from casting *all* (every) his care upon Christ. The proof of this is intimated in the verse immediately preceding (1 Pet. 5:7): for there we read, "*Humble yourselves* therefore under the mighty hand of God, that He may exalt you in due time." It *is* an humbling thing to our haughty flesh, our self-sufficiency, our proud reason, to be made to feel the truth of Christ's words "without Me ye can do *nothing*" (John 15:5)—acceptably to God. But it is a blessed thing for the heart when we are brought to the place of complete conscious *dependency* upon the Lord for everything. That is the place of rest, joy, victory. May the Lord be pleased to add His blessing to these few lines. A.W.P.

Christ and Christ alone, can *satisfy the heart*. And when He *does* actually and truly satisfy, the language of the soul is, "Whom have I in heaven but Thee? and there is none upon earth that I desire beside Thee" (Psa. 73:25).

O how slight and shadowy, how petty and purile are those things from which the trials and distresses of men and women do arise! They all grow on the one root of the *over-valuation* of temporal things. Money cannot purchase joy of soul. Health does not insure happiness. A beautiful home will not satisfy the heart. Earthly friends, no matter how loyal and lovable, cannot speak peace to a sin-burdened conscience, nor impart eternal life. Envy, covetousness, discontent, receive their death-wound when Christ, in all His loveliness is revealed as the "chiefest among ten thousand" (Song of Solomon 5:10). A.W.P.

A PERSONAL WORD

"And Elisha shalt thou anoint to be prophet *in thy room*" (1 Kings 19:16). These were a part of the words which God addressed unto Elijah at the completion of his work. After his departure, another was to act in his stead as the mouthpiece of Jehovah unto Israel. In many respects Elijah was a striking type of Christ—the student will do well to follow out that hint for himself. So he was at this point. When the Lord Jesus returned to Heaven, God appointed men to witness for His Son in the place where He wrought.

In 2 Kings 2 we behold the path which God calls His servants to tread, and that path *must be* traversed if they are to be faithful and effective witnesses for their absent Master. Mark it well that this path begins at "Gilgal" (2 Kings 2:1), which was the first stoppingplace of Israel after they entered Canaan: Joshua 5:9. Gilgal speaks of *consecration to God*—"circumcision" symbolizes the denial of the flesh, which is the distinctive mark of God's people: compare Col. 2:11 and 3:5. It is here that the path of Christ's representative must begin: until he is fully consecrated to Him, he is not "meet for the Master's use."

From Gilgal Elijah took Elisha to "Bethel" (2 Kings 2:2), which word means "the House of God." It was a place of hallowed memory. It was there that Jehovah appeared to Jacob and gave him that wondrous vision of the ladder connecting earth with heaven. But alas, that place was now defiled. The "House of God" had been corrupted, debased. A "golden calf" polluted it; false priests served there. An idolatrous "feast" was kept there. "Houses of ivory" and "great houses" had supplanted the simple "stone" which Jacob had there set up for a memorial. Read 1 Kings 12:28, 29, 32, 33; Amos 3:13-15, and unless you are blind, you will perceive an accurate (prophetic) portrayal of modern Christendom. Elisha had to visit corrupted "Bethel": the servant of God must take to heart the present *ruin* of the "House of God" if his ministry is to be effectual.

From Bethel they proceeded to "Jericho" (2 Kings 2:4). That city had once been "pleasant for situation," but now the curse of God rested upon it: see Joshua 6:26, 1 Kings 6:33, 34. Ah, is any interpreter needed? Jericho is a type of the world, awaiting the judgment of God. And today the "visible Church" and the "world" are *one!* The servant of God needs to enter deeply into this solemn fact: his heart must be impressed with the awful reality of it, or, otherwise, he will himself waste his energies in building up or maintaining what God will so soon destroy.

From Jericho they crossed the Jordan (2 Kings 2:6-8), and thus reached the Wilderness, where John the Baptist ministered at the beginning of this age! And mark it well, it was *there*, in the place which speaks of absolute *separation*, that Elisha received "a double portion" of Elijah's (type of Christ) spirit (v. 9)! Ah, it is only as the servant *dissociates* himself from everything which dishonours God, and on the outside of the corrupt systems and organizations, bears testimony for his absent Master, that the Holy Spirit will deign to use him.

Much like the above has been the writer's experience during the past three years. Leaving Sydney, Australia, where a corporate testimony for Christ had become impossible, we were called to spend a year in England. Then a year in Kentucky. Now a year in this most wicked city of all, Los Angeles. But our travels have not been profitless. We have learned more fully that the House of God on earth *is* a ruin. Now, the Lord has called us to York, Penna., where (D. V.) it will be our happy privilege to minister unto *small* groups (here and there) who are *outside* the camp. Please pray that a "double portion" of our Master's Spirit may rest upon us. A.W.P.

sonal and official excellencies) of Christ: beheld now by faith, beheld then by sight. And equally certain is it that, no man ever shall behold the glory of Christ by sight in heaven, who doth not in some measure now behold it by faith; for grace is a necessary preparation for glory and faith for sight. Where the soul has not been previously purified by grace and faith, it is altogether incapable of glory and the open vision. Those who pretend to be greatly enamoured by or to ardently desire that which they never saw or had actual experience of, only dote on their imaginations. The pretended desires of many (especially on their deathbeds) to behold the glory of Christ in heaven, who had no vision of it by faith whilst they are here in this world, are nothing but self-deceiving delusions.

There is no true rest for the mind nor satisfaction for the heart until we rest in Christ (Matt. 11:28-30). God has proposed unto us the "mystery of godliness," that is, the person of His incarnate Son and His mediatorial work, as the supreme and most glorious object of our faith and meditation; in which "mystery" we are called upon to behold the highest exhibition of the Divine wisdom, goodness, and condescension. The Son of God assuming manhood into union with Himself, thereby constituting the same individual person in two natures so infinitely distinct as those of God and man, whereby the Infinite became finite, the Eternal temporal, and the Immortal mortal, yet continuing still infinite, eternal and immortal, is that unique expression of omniscience and omnipotence which will be admired and adored unto all eternity.

It is not to be expected that they who are immersed in fleshly pleasures and drowned in the love of the world and present things, will have any true apprehension of Christ, or any real desire for it. But for those who have, through the miraculous agency and enablings of the Holy Spirit, "tasted that the Lord is gracious" (1 Pet. 3:3), how foolish and vile should we be if we gave all our time and devoted our best thoughts and strength to other things, to the neglect of the prayerful and diligent searchings of Scripture, to obtain a fuller knowledge of Him in whom the Father is "well pleased"! May it please the Holy Spirit to use these articles to stir up many to a renewed contemplation and meditation upon the manifold glories of Him who is "Altogether Lovely."

This is the one chief means which God has so graciously provided for delivering His people from those carking cares, life-sapping frettings, peace-disturbing anxieties and joy-obliterating worryings, which render miserable and wretched at heart those who know Him not. That man is "born unto trouble as the sparks fly upward" is declared in Scripture, but the same Scriptures reveal a Divinely-appointed *relief from* all the evils to which fallen man is heir, so that we may not faint under them, but gain the victory over them; so much so that we may be perfectly content if called upon to live in a hut or a cave, calm in a lion's den, happy in a prison, and sing praises unto God while burning at a martyr's stake.

Listen to the testimony of one who passed through a far deeper sea of trial and tribulation than has been the lot of the great majority of men. "We are troubled on every side, yet *not* distressed; we are perplexed, but not in despair; persecuted, but not forsaken; cast down, but not destroyed. . . For which cause we faint not; but though our outward man perish, yet the inward is renewed day by day. For our light affliction which is but for a moment, worketh for us a far more exceeding eternal weight of glory; While we look not at the things which are seen, but at the things which are not seen: for the things which are seen, are temporal, but the things which are not seen are eternal" (2 Cor. 4:8, 9, 16-18).

It is the beholding by faith those things which "are not seen" by the outward eye (which the spiritually poverty-stricken occupants of palaces and millionaire-mansions know nothing of!), the things that are spiritual and eternal, which alleviates all the Christian's afflictions, makes his burdens light, and preserves his soul from fainting under them. And of these unseen, spiritual and eternal things, the manifold and supernal glories of Christ are the principal. He who is enabled to retreat unto the contemplation of Him who is "the Lord of glory," will, when "all around gives way," be lifted out of himself, elevated above his surroundings and circumstances, and delivered from the prevailing power of every evil.

Not until the mind is enabled to arrive at a *fixed judgment* that all things here below are transitory and perishing, reaching only unto the outward man, that the best of them have in them nothing that is truly substantial and abiding, yea, that everything *under* the sun is but "vanity and vexation of spirit"; and that there are other things incalculably better that they, which *can* comfort, rejoice and satisfy the heart; and that *these* are to be made the one object and quest of our desires, thoughts, and pursuits; not till then will any of us ever be delivered from spending our lives in fears, distresses and sorrows. Christ, and Christ alone, can save; and

(Continued on Page 143)

Vol. X JULY, 1931 No. 7

STUDIES IN THE SCRIPTURES

"Search the Scriptures" John 5:39

Copyright in all English-speaking Countries

EDITOR: Arthur W. Pink, 559 Dupont Ave., York, Penna., U. S. A.
Hon. Agent in England: Mr. A. Winstone, "Shalom," Old Bath Road, Leckhampton, Cheltenham.
Hon. Agent in Australia: Mr. G. Ardill, The Christian Workers' Depot, Commonwealth and Reservoir Streets, Sydney.

THE DEITY OF CHRIST

What a truly amazing thing that a babe born in Bethlehem's manger, which grew in wisdom and stature in the carpenter's shop at Nazareth, and a few years later died upon the cross, should be at the same time "God blessed forever" (Rom. 9:5)! Yet O. T. prophecy had announced this very phenomenon centuries before He appeared before men: "For unto us *a child is born* . . . and His name shall be called Wonderful, Counsellor, The mighty God" (Isa. 9:6); and, "But thou, Bethlehem Ephratah, though thou be little among the thousands of Judah, out of thee shall He *come forth* unto Me, to be ruler in Israel, whose goings forth have been from of old, *from everlasting*" (Micah 5:2).

The Deity of Christ is evidenced by *the names* which are given Him in Scripture. In Psa. 45:6 we find the Father saying to the Son, "Thy throne O God, is forever and ever:" cf. Heb. 1:8, 9. In Num. 21:15 we read, "The people spake against *God* . . . and the Lord sent fiery serpents," while in 1 Cor. 10:9 we are told, "Neither let us tempt *Christ*, as some of them also tempted, and were destroyed of serpents." Once more; the ineffable name of "Jehovah" is ascribed again and again unto Christ. This name is peculiar to God, whereby He is distinguished from all creatures: "I am Jehovah: that is My name, and My glory will I not give to another" (Isa. 42:8). "Thou, whose name alone is Jehovah" (Psa. 83:18): cf. Amos 9:6. Now this very designation belongs to the eternal Son incarnate: "Prepare ye the way of Jehovah" (Isa. 40:3 and cf. Matt. 3:3). "Sanctify Jehovah of hosts Himself, and let Him be your fear . . . and He shall be for a sanctuary, but for a stone of stumbling and for a rock of offence" (Isa. 8:13, 14): for the N. T. proof that this passage refers to Christ, see 1 Pet. 2:6-8. In Psa. 110:1 He is addressed as "Adonai."

It was none other than *"God"* who was "manifest in flesh" (1 Tim. 3:16), and therefore did the angel tell Joseph that the Son his virgin-wife would bring forth, should be called "Immanuel," that is, "God with us" (Matt. 1:23). Most blessedly was this owned when Thomas addressed Him as "my Lord and my God" (John 20:28). In Heb. 3:12 He is styled "the living God:" note the whole of Psalm 95, quoted in the immediate context, refers to Christ. In Titus 2:13 He is owned as "the great God and our Saviour Jesus Christ:" cf. 2 Pet. 1:1. In 1 John 5:20 Christians are informed, "and we are in Him that is true, in His Son Jesus Christ. *This* is the *true God* and eternal life." While in Rev. 1:8 He is denominated "the Almighty."

Attributes of God, which are shared with no creatures, are found in and exercised by the Son. John 3:13 and Matt. 18:20 clearly demonstrate His *omnipresence*, for while He stood here upon earth, He was in heaven; and wheresoever two or three are gathered in His name, Christ is "in the midst of them." His *omniscience* is plainly evidenced in John 2:25; 21:17; Rev. 2:23, for God *"only* knoweth the hearts of all the children of men" (1 Kings 8:39). His *omnipotence* is expressly affirmed in John 5:19, "for what things soever He (the Father) doeth, these also doeth the Son likewise." He is "upholding *all* things by the Word of His power" (Heb. 1:3). In Heb. 13:8 we behold His *immutability*, for He is *"the same* yesterday and today and forever." His absolute

(Continued on Page 168)

IMPORTANT NOTICES

Please advise promptly of change of address, otherwise copies will be lost in the mails.

We are glad to send a sample copy to any of your friends whom you believe would be interested in such a publication.

Send to Mr. I. C. Herendeen, Swengel (Union County), Penna., for a list of our publications. He has published many of our books and booklets.

This magazine is published as a work of faith and labour of love. The Editor and his wife gladly give their services. It is freely sent to all who will read it. No charge is made for it.

Christians who feel definitely led to do so, may have fellowship with us in this ministry. Those outside the U. S. A., please send only INTERNATIONAL Money Orders made out to York, Penna., U. S. A.

CONTENTS

The Deity of Christ	145
The Epistle to the Hebrews	146
The Satisfaction ("Atonement") of Christ	152
Regeneration, or The New Birth	158
Welcome Tidings	163
Following Christ	165

THE EPISTLE TO THE HEBREWS

43. *The New Testament.* Heb. 9:16-22

Having affirmed (9:12, 14) that the blood of Christ is the means of the believer's redemption, in v. 15, the apostle proceeds to make further proof of this basic and vital truth. His argument here is taken from the design and object of Christ's priesthood, which was to *confirm* the covenant God had made with His people, and which could only be done by blood. First, he affirms that the Saviour was "the Mediator of the new testament." Many functions were undertaken by Him. Just as one type could not set forth all that the Lord Jesus did and suffered, so no single office could display all the relations which He sustained and all the benefits He procured for us. That which is done by a prophet, by a priest, by a king, by a surety, by a mediator, by a husband, by a father, that and more has been done by Christ. And the more clearly we observe in Scripture the many undertakings of Christ for us, as seen in His *varied relations*, the more will He be endeared to our hearts, and the more will faith be strengthened.

Christ's undertaking to be a "Mediator" both procured a covenant to pass between God and men, and also engaged Himself for the performance thereof on both parts. This could only be by a full satisfaction being rendered to Divine justice, by the shedding of blood infinitely valuable as His was. To assure His people of their partaking of the benefits of God's covenant, the cross of Christ has turned that covenant into a *testament*, so that the conditions of the covenant on God's part (its requirements: namely, perfect obedience rendered to His law, and thus "everlasting righteousness" being brought in: Dan. 9:24; and full satisfaction being taken by the law for the sins of His people) might be so many *legacies*, which being ratified by the death of the Testator, none might disannul.

Unspeakably blessed as are the truths expressed (so freely) above, there is another which is still more precious for faith to apprehend and rest on, and that is, that behind all offices (so to speak), lying at the foundation of the whole dispensation of God's grace toward His people, is the *mystical oneness* of Christ and His Church: a legal oneness, which ultimates by the Spirit's work in a *vital* union, so that Christ is the Head and believers are the members of one Person (1 Cor. 12:12, 13). *This*, and this alone, constituted the just ground for God to impute to Christ all the sins of His people, and to impute to them the righteousness of Christ for their justification of life. What Christ did in obeying the law is reckoned to them as though that obedience had been performed by them; and in like manner, what they deserved on account of their sins was charged to and endured by Him, as though they themselves had suffered it: see 2 Cor. 5:21.

The first spring or cause of the *union* between Christ and His Church lay in that eternal compact between the Father and the Son respecting the recovery and salvation of His people contemplated as fallen in Adam — for the nature and terms of that compact see our article "The Everlasting Covenant" in the Jan. 1930 issue. In view of the human nature which He was to assume, the Lord Christ was "predestinated" or "foreordained" (1 Pet. 1:20) unto grace and glory, and that by virtue of the *union* of flesh unto His Godhead. This grace and glory of the God-man was the exemplary cause and *pattern* of *our* predestination: Rom. 8:29, Phil. 3:21. It was also the cause and means of the communicating of all grace and glory unto us, for we were "chosen in Him before the foundation of the world" (Eph. 1:4). Christ was thus elected (Isa. 42:1) as Head of the Church, His mystical body. All the elect of God were then committed unto Him, to be delivered from sin and death, and brought unto the enjoyment of God: John 17:6, Rev. 1:5, 6.

In the prosecution of this design of God, and in order to the accomplishment of the "everlasting covenant" (Heb. 13:20), Christ undertook to be the "Surety" of that covenant (Heb. 7:22), engaging to answer for all the liabilities of His people and to discharge all their legal responsibilities. Yet was it as Priest that Christ acted as Surety: *God's* "Priest," *our* "Surety." That is to say, all the activities of Christ were of a sacerdotal character, having God for their immediate object; but as these activities were all performed on our behalf, He was a Surety or Sponsor for us also. As the "Surety" of the covenant, Christ undertook to discharge all the debts of those who are made partakers of its benefits. As our Surety He also merited and procured from God the Holy Spirit, to communicate to His people all needful supplies of grace to make them new creatures, which enables them to yield obedience to God from a new principle of spiritual life, and that faithfully unto the end.

When considering the *administration* of the "everlasting covenant" in time, we contemplate the *actual application* of the grace, benefits and privileges of it unto those for whose sakes it was devised and drawn up. For this the *death* of the Mediator was required, for only through His blood-shedding is the whole grace of the covenant made effectual unto us. This it is which is affirmed in 9:15, and which we considered at length in our last article. In the passage which is now to be before us, the apostle does two things: first, he refers to a well known fact which is everywhere recognised among men, namely, that a will or testament requires the death of the testator to give it validity. Second, he refers to an O. T. type which exemplifies the principle which he is here setting before us.

"For where a testament is, there must also of necessity be the death of the testator. For a testament is of force after men are dead: otherwise it is of no strength at all while the testator liveth" (vv. 16, 17). That which is found in vv. 16-23 is really of the nature of a parenthesis, brought in for the purpose of showing *why* it was necessary for the incarnate Son to die. In v. 24 the apostle returns to his proofs for the superiority of the ministry of Christ over Aaron's. What we have in vv. 16, 17, is brought in to show both the need for and the purpose of the death of Christ, the argument being drawn from the character and design of that covenant of which He is the Mediator. Because that covenant was also to be a "testament" it was confirmed by the death of the Testator. Appeal is made to the only use of a will or testament among men.

The method by which the apostle here demonstrates the necessity of Christ's death as He was "the mediator of the new testament" is not merely from the signification of the word "diatheke" (though we must not lose sight of its force), but as he is speaking principally of the two "covenants" (i. e. the two forms under which the "everlasting covenant" has been *administered*), it is the *affinity* which there is between a solemn covenant and a testament, that he has respect unto. For it to be carefully noted that the apostle speaks not of the death of Christ merely as it was a *death*, which is all that is required of a "testament" as such, without any consideration of the *nature* of the testator's death; but he speaks of it also (and primarily) as it was a *sacrifice* by the shedding of His blood (vv. 12, 14, 18-23), which belongs to a Divine *covenant*, and is in no way required by a "testament." Thus, we see again the needs-be for retaining the *double* meaning and force of the Greek word here.

There has been much needless wrangling over the Divine person alluded to under the word "Testator," some insisting it is Christ, some the Father, others arguing the impossibility of the latter because the Father has never died. We believe that, in this case, Saphir was right when he said, "The testator is, properly speaking, God; for we are God's heirs; but it is God in Christ." Had he referred the reader to 2 Cor. 5:19 his statement had been given scriptural confirmation.

The "everlasting covenant" or Covenant of Grace has the nature of a "testament" from these four considerations or facts. First, it proceeded from the *will* of God: He freely made it (Heb. 6:17). Second, it contained various legacies or gifts: to Christ, God bequeathed the elect as His inheritance (Deut. 32:9, Psa. 16:6, Luke 22:29); to the elect themselves, that they should be joint-heirs with Him (Rom. 8:16, Rev. 3:21). Third, it is unalterable (Gal. 3:15), "ordered in all things and sure" (2 Sam. 23:5); having been duly witnessed to (1 John 5:7); hence, being of the nature of a "testament" there are *no* stipulations for men to fulfil (Gal. 3:18). Fourth, the death of Christ has secured the administration of it.

A deed is not valid without a seal; a will cannot be probated until the legatee dies, nor was God's covenants with men (the historical adumbrations of the "everlasting covenant") ratified except by blood-shedding. Thus it was with His covenant with Abraham (Gen. 15:9, 18); thus it was with His covenant with Israel at Sinai (Ex. 24;6). Thus, unto the confirmation of a "testament" there must be the *death* of the testator; unto the ratification of a "covenant" the *blood* of a sacrifice was required. Thereby does the apostle prove conclusively the necessity for the sacrificial death of Christ as the Mediator, both as the Mediator of a "covenant" and as the Mediator of a "testament": for through His sacrificial death, both the *promises* contained in the "covenant" and the *bequeathments* of the "testament," are made irrevokably sure to all His seed. We trust, then that we have been enabled to clear up the great difficulty which the word "diatheke" has caused so many, and shown that it has a *double* meaning and force in *this* passage.

It remains for us to point out that the O. T. supplies us with a most striking type which blessedly illustrates the principle enunciated in this 16th verse. But note first of all that v. 15 opens with "For" and that this comes right after the mention of "the Mediator of the new testament," and the promise of "eternal inheritance" in v. 15. Now the "mediator" of the "old testament" was Moses, and it was not until his *death*, though immediately after it, that Israel entered their inheritance, the land of Canaan! Looked at from the standpoint of God's government, the death of Moses was because of his sin (Numb. 20:10-12); but considered in relation to his *official* position, as "the servant over the house of God," it had another and deeper meaning, as Deut. 3:26 shows: "the Lord was wrath with me *for your sakes*"—how blessedly did this foreshadow the reason why God's wrath was visited upon Christ: Christ, as Moses, must die before the inheritance could be ours.

In v. 17 it is not of the making of a testament which is referred to, but its execution: its efficacy depends solely on the testator's death. The words "is of force" mean, is firm and cannot be annulled; it must be executed according to the mind of the one who devised it. The reason why it is of "no strength" during his lifetime, is because it is then subject to alteration, according to the pleasure of him who made it. All the blessings of "grace and glory" were the property of Christ, for He was "appointed Heir of all things" (Heb. 1:2): but in His death, He made a bequeathment of them unto all the elect. Another analogy between a human testament and the testamentary character of Christ's death is that, an absolute grant is made without any conditions. So is the kingdom of heaven bequeathed to all the elect, so that nothing can defeat His will. Whatever there is in the Gospel which prescribes conditions, that belongs to it as it is a "covenant" and not as a "testament." Finally, the testator assigns the time when his heirs shall be admitted into the actual possession of his goods; so too has Christ determined the season when each shall enter both into grace and glory.

Perhaps a brief word should be added by way of amplification to the bare statement made above respecting the conditions which the Gospel prescribes unto those who are the beneficiaries of Christ's "testament." Repentance and faith are required by the Gospel; yet, strictly speaking they are *not* "conditions" of our entering into the enjoyment of Christ's gifts. Faith is a *means* to receive and partake of the things promised, repentance is a *qualification* whereby we may know that *we* are the persons to whom such promises belong. Nevertleless, it is to be remembered that He who has made the promises works in His elect these graces of repentance and faith: Acts 5:31, Phil. 1:29.

"It is a great and gracious condescension in the Holy Spirit to give encouragement and confirmation unto our faith, by a representation of the truth and reality of spiritual things, in those which are temporal and agreeing with them in their general nature, wherby they are presented unto the common understandings of men. This way of proceeding the apostle calls, a speaking 'after the manner of men' (Gal. 3:15). Of the same kind were all the parables used by our Saviour; for it is all one whether these representations be taken from things real, or from those which, according unto the same rule of reason and right, are framed on purpose for that end" (John Owen).

"Whereupon neither the first was dedicated without blood. For when Moses had spoken every precept to all the people according to the law, he took the blood of calves and of goats, with water, and scarlet wool, and hyssop, and sprinkled both the book, and all the people, saying, This is the blood of the testament which God hath enjoined unto you. Moreover he sprinkled with blood both the tabernacle, and all the vessels of the ministry. And almost all things are by the law purged with blood; and without shedding of blood is no remission" (vv. 18-22). In these verses the apostle is still pressing upon the Hebrews the necessity for the blood-shedding of Christ. Their national history witnessed to the fact that when God entered into covenant with their fathers, that covenant was confirmed by solemn sacrifice.

In the verses upon which we are now to comment, the apostle is not merely proving that the old covenant or testament was confirmed with blood, for had that been his only object, he could have dispatched it in very few words; rather does he also declare what was the *use* of blood in sacrifices on all occasions under the law, and thereby he demonstrates the use and efficacy of Christ's blood as unto the ends of the new covenant. The ends of the blood under the old covenant were two, namely, purification and pardon, both of which were confirmed in the expiation of sin. Unless the main design of the Spirit in these verses be steadily kept in view, we miss the deeper meaning of many of their details.

What has just been said above, supplies the explanation of what has seemed a problem to some, namely, that in these verses the apostle mentions five or six details which are not found in the historical narrative of Ex. 24. But the Holy Spirit is not here limiting our view to Ex. 24, but gathers up what is found in various places of the law; and that, because He not only designed to prove the dedication of the covenant by blood, but also to show the whole use of the blood under the law, as unto purification and remission of sin. And He does this with the purpose of declaring the virtue and efficacy of the blood of Christ under the new testament, whereunto He makes an application of all the things in the verses which follow. The "Moreover" at the beginning of v. 21 is plain intimation that the Spirit is here contemplating something *in addition to* that which is found in Ex. 24.

V. 18. The opening word is usually rendered "therefore" or "wherefore": it denotes the drawing of an inference; it confirms a general rule by a special instance. In v. 16 the general rule is stated; now, says the apostle, think it not strange that the new testament was confirmed by the death of the Testator, for this is so necessary that, the first one also was confirmed in the same manner; and that, not only by death, but not "without *blood,*" which was required for the ratification of a solemn covenant. That to which reference is made, is the "first" testament or covenant. Here the apostle makes clear what he intended by the first or old covenant, on which he had discoursed at large in chapter 8: it was the covenant made with Israel at Horeb. Just a few words on the character of it.

Its terms had all the nature of a formal covenant. These were the things written in the book (Ex. 24:4, 7) which were an epitome of the whole law, as contained in Ex. 20-23. The revelation of its terms were made by Jehovah Himself, speaking with awful voice from the summit of Sinai: Ex. 19, 20. Following the fundamental rule of the covenant, as contained in the Ten Commandments, were other statutes and rites, given for the directing of their walking with God. The same was solemnly delivered to Israel by Moses, and proposed unto them for their acceptation. Upon their approbation of it, the book was read in the hearing of all the people after it had been duly sprinkled with the blood of the covenant (Ex. 24:7). Thereupon, for the first time, Jehovah was called "The God of Israel" (Ex. 24:10), and that by virtue of the covenant. This formed the foundation of His consequent dealings with them: all His chastening judgments upon Israel were due to their breaking of His covenant.

While there is a contrast, sharp and clear, between the old testament and the new, yet it should not be overlooked that there was also that which bound them together. This was ably expressed by A. Saphir: "The promise given to Abraham, and not to Moses, was not superseded or forgotten in the giving of the law. When God dealt with Israel in the wilderness, He gave them the promise that they should be a peculiar treasure unto Him above all people; 'for all the earth is Mine'; and that they should possess the land as an inheritance (Ex. 19:5, 6; 23:30; Deut. 15:4). Based upon this promise, and corresponding with the Divine election and favour, is the law which God gave to His people. As He had chosen and redeemed them so that they were to be a holy people, and to walk before Him, even as in the Ten Commandments the gospel of election and redemption came first: 'I am the Lord thy God, which brought thee out of Egypt.' Hence this covenant or dispensation, although it was a covenant, not of grace and Divine gifts and enablings, but of works, was connected with and based upon redemption, and it was dedicated, as the apostle emphatically says, not without blood.

"Both the book, or record of the covenant, and all the people, were sprinkled with the blood of typical sacrifices. For without blood is no remission of sins, and the promises of God can only be obtained through atonement. But we know that this is a figure of the one great Sacrifice, and that therefore all the promises and blessings under the old dispensation, underlying and sustaining it, were through the prospective death of the true Mediator. When therefore the spiritual Israelite was convinced by the law of sin, both as guilt and as a condition of impurity and strengthlessness, he was confronted by the promise of the inheritance, which *always* was of grace, unconditional and sure, and in a righteous and holy manner through expiation."

V. 19. The one made use of for the dedication of the covenant was Moses. On God's part he was immediately called unto this employment: Ex. 3. On the part of the people, he was desired and chosen to transact all things between God and them, because they were not able to bear the effects of His immediate presence: Ex. 19:19, Deut. 5:22-27; and this choice of a spokesman on their part, God approved (v. 27). Thus Moses became in a general way a "mediator" between God and men in the giving of the law (Gal. 3:19). Thereby we are shown that there can be no covenant between God and sinful men, but in the hands of a Mediator, for man has neither meetness, merits, nor ability to be an undertaker of the terms of God's covenant in his own person.

Moses spake "every precept unto the people." This intimates the particular character of the old testament. It consisted primarily of commandments of obedience (Eph. 2:15), promising no assistance for the performance of them. The "new testament" is of another nature: it is one of *promises*, and although it also has precepts requiring obedience, yet is it (as a covenant) wholly founded in the promise, whereby strength and assistance for the performance of that obedience are given to us. Moses' reading "*every* precept unto the people" emphasizes the fact that all the good things they were to receive by virtue of the covenant, depended on their observance of all that was commanded them; for a curse was denounced against every one that "continued not in all things written in the law to do them" (Deut. 27:26). Obviously, *such* a "covenant" was never ordained for the saving of sinners: its insufficiency for that end is what the apostle demonstrates in the sequel.

We are again indebted to the exposition of J. Owen for much of the above, and now give in condensed form some of his observations on the contents of v. 19. Here, for the first time, was any part of God's Word committed to writing. This book of the law was written that it might be read to *all* the people: it was not to be restricted to the priests, as containing mysteries unlawful to be divulged. It was written and read in the language which the people understood and spake, which condemns Rome's use of the Latin in her public services. Again; God never required the observance of any rites or duties of worship, without a previous warrant from His Word. How thankful should we be for the *written* Word!

That which Moses performed on this occasion was to sprinkle the blood. Ex. 24:6 informs us that he took "half of the blood" and sprinkled it "on the altar" (on which was the book); the other half on the people. The one was *God's* part; the other *theirs*. Thereby the *mutual* agreement of Jehovah and the people was indicated. Typically, this foreshadowed the twofold efficacy of Christ's blood, to make salvation Godwards and to save manwards; or, to the remission of our sins unto justification, and the purification of our persons unto sanctification. The "scarlet wool," probably bound around the "hyssop" (which was a common weed), was employed as a sprinkler, as that which served to *apply* the blood in the basons upon the people; "water" being mixed with the blood to keep it fluid and aspersible. In like manner, the communication of the benefits of Christ's death unto sanctification, is called the "sprinkling of the blood of Jesus Christ" (1 Pet. 1:2). To avail us, the blood must not only be "shed," but "sprinkled."

The mingling of the "water" with the "blood" was to represent the "blood *and* water" which flowed from the pierced side of the Saviour (John 19:34, 35). The spiritual "mystery" and meaning of which is profound and blessed. In 1 John 5:6 the Holy Spirit has particularly emphasized the fact that the Christ came "by water and blood." He came not only to make atonement for our sins by His blood that we might be justified, but also to sprinkle us with the efficacy of His blood in the communication of the Spirit unto sanctification, which is compared unto "water": see John 7:38, 39, Titus 3:5. The application of the blood to the "book" of the covenant was an intimation that atonement could be made by blood for the sins against its precepts, and the application of the "water" to it told of its purity. The sprinkler pointed to the humanity of Christ, through which all grace is communicated to us: the "scarlet wool" speaking of His personal glory (Dan. 5:7 etc.), and the "hyssop," the meanest of plantlife (1 Kings 4:33), being a figure of His lowly outward appearance.

V. 20. In these words Moses reminded Israel of the foundation of their acceptance of the covenant, which foundation was the authority of God requiring them so to do; the word "enjoined" also emphasised the nature of the covenant itself: it consisted principally not of promises which had been given to them, but of "precepts" which called for hearty obedience. By quoting here these words of Moses "this is the blood of the testament," the apostle proves that not only death, but a sacrificial death, was required in order to the consecration and establishment of the first covenant. The blood was the confirmatory sign, the token between God and the people of their mutual engagements in that covenant. Thus did God from earliest times teach His people, by type and shadow, the supreme value of the blood of His Son. These words of Moses were plainly alluded to by the Saviour in the institution of His "supper": "This is My blood of the new testament" (Matt. 26:28) i. e., this represents My blood, by the shedding of which the new testament is confirmed.

V. 21. The apostle now reminds the Hebrews that, not only was the old testament itself dedicated with blood, but that also all the ways and means of solemn worship were purified by the same. His purpose in bringing in this additional fact was to prove that not only was the blood of Christ in sacrifice *necessary*, but also to demonstrate its *efficacy* in the removing of sins and thereby qualifying sinners to be worshippers of the most holy God. The historical reference here is to what is found in Lev. 16:14, 16, 18. The spiritual meaning of the tabernacle's furniture being sprinkled with blood was at least twofold: first, in themselves those vessels were holy by God's institution, yet in the use of them by polluted men, they became defiled, and needed purging. Second, to teach the Israelites and us that, the very means of grace which we use, are only made acceptable to God through the merits of Christ's sacrifice.

What we have just sought to point out above, brings before us a most important and humbling truth. In all those things wherein we have to do with God, and whereby we approach unto Him, nothing but the blood of Christ and the Spirit's application of it unto our consciences, gives us a gracious acceptance with Him. The best of our performances are defiled by the flesh; our very prayers and repentances are unclean, and cannot be received by God except as we plead before Him the precious blood of Christ. "The people were hereby taught that, God could not be looked to for salvation, nor rightly worshipped, except faith in every case looked to an intervening blood. For the majesty of God is justly to be dreaded by us, and the way to His presence is nothing to us but a dangerous labyrinth, until we know that He is pacified towards us through the blood of Christ, and that this blood affords to us a free access. All kinds of worship are then faulty and impure until, Christ cleanses them by the sprinkling of His blood... If this thought only came to our mind, that what we read is not written so much with ink as with the blood of Christ, that when the Gospel is preached, His sacred blood distils together with the voice, there would be far greater attention as well as reverence on our part" (John Calvin).

V. 22. "By the law" signifies "according unto the law," that is, according to its institution and rule, in that way of faith and obedience which the people were obligated unto. This has been shown by the apostle in the verses preceding. His design being to prove both the necessity for the death of Christ and the efficacy of His blood unto the purging of sins, whereof the legal institutions were types. The qualifying "almost" takes into consideration the exceptions of "fire" (Num. 31:23) and "water" (Lev. 22:6, 7 etc.): but let it be carefully noted that these exceptions were of such things as wherein the worship of God was *not* immediately concerned, nor where the conscience was defiled; they were only of external pollutions, by things in their own nature indifferent, having nothing of *sin* in them; yet were they designed as *warnings* against things which *did* defile. The "almost" also takes note of the exception in Lev. 5:11.

The last clause of v. 22 enunciates an axiom universally true, and in every age. The curse of the law was, and still is, "the soul that sinneth it shall die" (Ezek. 18:20). But whereas there is no man "that sinneth not" (Eccl. 7:20), God, in His grace, provided that there should be a testification of the remission of sins, and that the curse of the law should not be immediately executed on them that sinned. This He did by allowing the people to make atonement for those sins by the blood of sacrifices: Lev. 17:11. Thereby God made known two things. First, to the Israelites that, by the blood of animals there should be a *political* or temporal remission of their sins granted, so that they should not die under the sentence of that law which was the rule of government over their nation. Second, that a real spiritual and eternal forgiveness should be granted unto faith in the sacrifice of Christ, which was represented by the slain animals. The present application of this verse is that, no salvation is possible for any soul that rejects the sacrifice of Christ. A.W.P.

THE SATISFACTION
("Atonement")
OF CHRIST

19. *Its Extent.*

Considering all the ground which has already been carefully gone over, there really ought to be no need for a separate discussion of this phase of our subject. The question, *For whom* did Christ make satisfaction? for whose sins did He atone? has been clearly anticipated and definitely answered in almost every aspect of our theme which has been before us. If we go back to the very foundation, namely, the everlasting covenant, there we find that the Father promised the Son a specific reward (Isa. 53:10-12) upon His performance of the work assigned Him. The Son perfectly accomplished that work (John 17:4), therefore He *must* "see of the travail of His soul and be satisfied." If a single one of those for whom He died be not regenerated, justified, sanctified, and glorified by God, then the Father's promise to His Son would be nullified.

The *nature* of Christ's satisfaction determines to a demonstration those who are the beneficiaries of it. First, it was a *federal* work. There was a legal oneness between Christ and those for whom He acted. The Saviour stood as the Surety, and if a single one whose debts He paid, receive not a full discharge from the law, then Divine justice would be reduced to a farce. Second, it was a *substitutionary* work. Christ acted not only on the behalf of, but in the stead of, those who had been given to Him by the Father; hence all whose sins He bore must of necessity have their sins remitted—God cannot punish twice, once on the Substitute and then again on the subject. Third, it was a *penal* work: every requirement of the law, both preceptive and punitive, was fulfilled by Christ, therefore all for whom He acted *must* receive the reward of His obedience, which is everlasting life. Fourth, it was a *priestly* work: His sacrifice being accepted by God, its efficacy and merits *must be* imputed to all those for whom He offered it.

The *design* of Christ's satisfaction as made known in Scripture reveals its scope. To suppose that the greatest and grandest of all God's works was without design would be to be guilty of blasphemous thoughts. That design was framed by infinite wisdom, so that there can be no flaw or failure in it. That design is executed by omnipotence, so that it is impossible to thwart it. What that design was, has been shown (in part) in the 9th article of this series. It was not an indefinite and undefined one. Scripture has made known in plain and unmistakable terms that the mediatorial work of Christ was in order to God's being magnified, the God-man glorified, and God's elect saved. The eternal Son of God became incarnate in order to *"save* His people from their sins" (Matt. 1:21).

But, without reviewing any further the preceding articles, let us now say why we deem it expedient to devote a separate paper to the more specific stating and proving of what has come before us previously in only a more or less incidental or subordinate way. It is because a right (Scriptural) view of *this* point is absolutely essential, if God is to be honoured and Christ is to be glorified by us therein. The enmity of the Serpent against the Seed of the woman has been inveterate throughout the ages, and perhaps at no other one point has he so persistently attacked the glory of Christ. While it is impossible for Satan to either undo the finished work of the Saviour, or to destroy any of its fruits, yet he is permitted to *misrepresent* it, and nowhere has his subtlety been more exercised and manifested than in the means employed here. He has indeed appeared as an "angel of light." His very attempts to *discredit* the satisfaction of Christ have been made under the guise of *magnifying* it, and that is why he has succeeded in getting many men reputed as "orthodox" to do some of his foul work for him.

Perhaps it will enable most of our readers to grasp more readily what we have just referred to in the above paragraph, if we frame the following questions. Which seems to have the greater tendency to *exalt* Christ: to say that He died because He desired and sought to make possible the salvation of all mankind? or to say that He died only for God's elect, the "little flock"? Which seems to display the more His compassion for sinners? Which seems to bring out the more the value of His blood: to say that it avails only for the "few"? or to say that its merits are so infinite that every member of Adam's race would be redeemed did he or she but put their trust in it? The very fact that every one of us would answer the questions in the *wrong* way until we are taught aright from Scripture, not only evidences the worthlessness of carnal reasoning upon spiritual things, but also shows to what a terrible extent our minds have been poisoned by the venom of the Serpent. If it can yet be clearly shown that, in *reality*, the wider view actually *dishonours* Christ, then the consummate guile and malice of the Devil therein should be plainly apparent.

Before exposing the futility of the above reasoning, let us prepare the way by giving other illustrations or examples of our inability to think aright where spiritual things are concerned. Does it not seem to us that a greater revenue of glory had accrued to God had sin never invaded His dominions and corrupted His creatures? Yet *He* deemed otherwise, or else He had not suffered it so to be. Again; does it not seem to the Christian, *every* Christian, that he could glorify God more in this present life if the sinful nature were eradicated from his being? Yet if this were so, God *would* take the "flesh" completely out of our beings when He regenerated us. And does it not seem to many a reader that he or she could accomplish more for Christ, if better health, different circumstances and surroundings, or more money, were given to them by God? And so we might continue. The fact is that the wisest Christian is utterly incapable of thinking rightly about Divine things until his thoughts are formed by Scripture.

But coming now to a closer answering of the questions raised above. First, many imagine the glory of God is exceedingly exalted by affirming that He truly desires the salvation of every member of Adam's fallen race, and that they who teach His free grace is restricted to the elect, grievously dishonor His benevolence. Now to maintain aright the glory of God we must speak in the language of His Word. Only that is glorious in God which He ascribes unto Himself. "Our inventions, though never so splendid in our own eyes, are unto Him an abomination, a striving to pull Him down from His eternal excellency, to make Him altogether like unto us" (J. Owen). "God is dishonoured by that honour which is ascribed to Him beyond His own prescription" (Jerome). To assign unto God any thing which He has not assumed, is only to deify our own imaginations.

Many objects present a fair appearance when viewed at a distance, but their defects become apparent when examined at close quarters. So it is here. The assertion that God's design in sending His Son to this earth was that every sinner might be saved by Him, may at first glance seem to conduce unto the magnifying of His goodness and grace, but a little reflection thereon should quickly show the contrary. It certainly is not to the glory of God to suppose that the success of Christ's costly undertaking should be left contingent on the creature's will—*that* can never be the measure of *His* honour. And it certainly is not to the glory of God to suppose that He designed to save any that perish, for that would show His benevolent purpose was frustrated and would proclaim a disappointed and defeated Deity. The truth is that the glory of God's grace consists not in the number of objects to whom it is shown, but in its being *free* and *undeserved*, thus tending to lay the highest of all obligations on those who are concerned therein.

The fact is that those who advocate the scheme of a general redemption, are so far from magnifying the grace of God, that they, really, degrade both Divine grace and Christ's sacrifice. For according to their theory God has only provided a precarious salvation, which is offered to the caprice of man's acceptance, a mere possibility, which can only become actual through the sinner's compliance with certain conditions; a possibility, which when properly examined, is seen to be an impossibility. How vast the difference between a precarious salvation, and an infallible one! How immeasurably superior a redemption which secures the certain salvation of every one for whom it was made, and a suppositionary redemption which *guarantees* the salvation of *none*, leaving everything uncertain, dependent upon fickle man! How infinitely greater the glory which comes to God by that plan, through which grace *efficaciously* works in and applies the saving benefits to all for whom Christ died, than a method which would exalt the power of the creature and set the crown upon his free-will!

If it be still contended that we magnify the grace of God far more by proclaiming its universality rather than by insisting upon its particularity, by affirming that it extends to all mankind rather than to an elect remnant, then to carry out such an argument to its logical conclusion, we should be obliged to believe that God *will save all*, for He certainly will do that which is for His highest glory —*this* being the paramount consideration before Him in *all* that He does: see Psa. 29:9, Prov. 16:4, Rev. 4:11. Moreover, such an argument would require, yea demand, that Divine grace be extended unto the fallen angels as well as to all mankind. Will men pretend to reflect on God's goodness because He has not extended His grace to all who might have been the objects of it had He so pleased? Has he not a right to do what He wills with His own?

Which exalts Christ the more? which demonstrates the more the value and efficacy of His atonement: that which effectually secures the actual salvation of every one for whom it was made? or that which ends in the great majority of those for whom He shed His precious blood being eternally punished in hell? Surely none with any spiritual discernment can fail to see which view is more glorifying to the Redeemer. And if we call to mind the *nature* of His satisfaction, that it was a specific bearing of the sins of definite persons, that it was a paying of their debts, a suffering the law's curse in their stead, in order that they might go free; and when we remember that the Judge of all *accepted* this atonement, was satisfied with the price the Sponsor paid,— then, where would be God's honour, His justice, His faithfulness, were He, notwithstanding, to yet punish millions of those for whom His Son bled and died? If Christ died for all men universally, then all men universally *must be saved*. There is no other possible alternative, except to say that God will punish *twice*, first in the person of the Surety, and then in many of the persons in whose place He is supposed to have stood.

We sincerely trust that neither writer nor reader is lacking in compassion to his fellow-creatures, yet we must not allow our pity for men to lead us to adopt any principle which is dishonouring to the Divine perfections and subversive of Christ's satisfaction. Others may speak for themselves, but the writer would not dare to trust his salvation to a Saviour who was unable to save most of those for whom He died. If it were true that Christ shed His blood for those who are now in hell, what guarantee would be left me that I shall not go there? An atonement that *fails* to atone, a sacrifice which fails to deliver, is worthless. To say that salvation is possible to all, *if* all would receive Christ, is to ignore those unequivocal words of the Saviour in John 6:44, "No man *can* come to Me, except the Father which hath sent Me draw him." To say that salvation turns upon the sinner's own acceptance of Christ would be like offering a sum of money to a blind man upon the condition that he would see, or offering to ransom a prisoner on the proviso that he burst his way out of his steel-walled cell.

"Many divines say that Christ did something when He died that enabled God to be just, and yet the Justifier of the ungodly. What that *something* is they do not tell us. They believe in an atonement made for everybody; but then, *their* atonement is just this; that Judas was atoned for as much as Peter, that the damned in hell were as much an object of Jesus Christ's satisfaction as the saved in heaven. Though they do not say it in proper words they must mean that, in the case of multitudes, Christ died in vain, for they say He died for all, and yet so ineffectual was His dying for them, that many are damned afterwards. Now, such an atonement I *despise*—I reject it. I may be called Antinomian or Calvinist, for preaching a limited atonement; but I had rather believe a limited atonement that is *efficacious* for all for whom it was intended, than an universal atonement that is not efficacious for anybody, except the will of man be joined with it. Why, my brethren, if we were only so far atoned for by the death of Christ that any one of us might afterwards save himself, Christ's atonement were not worth a farthing, for there is no man of us can save himself—no, not under the Gospel" (C. H. Spurgeon on Isa. 53:10).

But is not a true believing on the Lord Jesus Christ required *in order to* a receiving of God's great salvation? Certainly it is, but it is the office of the Holy Spirit to *give* saving faith to *every one* of those for whose sins Christ atoned. There is an infallible connection insured between the one and the other. The costly price of redemption was far too precious in the sight of God for it to be cast away on souls that perish. Therefore did He predestinate that the Spirit should communicate life to all for whom Christ died. "Who was delivered for our offences, and was raised again for our justification" (Rom. 4:25): that is clear enough—all whose "offences" Christ bore, *must be* "justified"! There are inseparable and saving benefits bestowed upon all them whom Christ loved and gave Himself for. "For if, when we were enemies, we were reconciled to God by the death of His Son, much more, being reconciled, we *shall be* saved by His life" (Rom. 5:10): these go together, hence, as the greater part of men are *not* "saved" by His life, that is proof positive that they were *not* "reconciled by His death."

"Christ hath redeemed us from the curse of the law. . . . That we might receive the promise of the Spirit through faith" (Gal. 3:13, 14): to each of those whom He redeemed, Christ gives His Spirit. "For He hath made Him to be sin for us, who knew no sin; that we might be made the righteousness of God in Him" (2 Cor. 5:21): as inevitably as Christ was "made sin" for those for whom He died, so inevitably must those for whom He was made sin be "made the righteousness of God in Him"! "He that spared not His own Son, but delivered Him up for us all, how shall He not with Him *also* freely give us all things?" (Rom. 8:32): if God delivered up Christ for all mankind, then He will, He *must* to make good His word here, freely bestow (not "offer," but actually "*give*") repentance, faith, and every spiritual blessing. It is this sure and certain connection between Christ's *purchase* of salvation and the actual *enjoyment thereof* by those for whom it was wrought, which the advocates of a universal redemption lose sight of. Hear that prince of the Puritans, John Owen:

"Redemption is the freeing of a man from misery by the intervention of a ransom. Now, when a ransom is paid for the liberty of a prisoner, does not justice *demand* that he should have and enjoy the liberty so purchased for him by a valuable consideration? If I should pay a thousand pounds for a man's deliverance from bondage to him that detains him, who hath power to set him free, and is contented with the price I give, were it not injurious to me and the poor prisoner that his deliverance be not accomplished? Can it possibly be conceived that there should be a redemption of men, and those men not redeemed? that a price should be paid, and the purchase not consummated? Yet all this must be made true, and innumerable other absurdities, if universal redemption be asserted. A price would be paid for all, yet few delivered; the redemption of all consummated, yet few of them redeemed; the judge satisfied, the jailer conquered, and yet the prisoners inthralled! '*Universal*' and "*redemption*' are as irreconcilable as '*Roman*' and '*Catholic*'."

The difference then, between truth and error on this vital subject, lies in the returning of scriptural answers to these questions: What was the purpose of God in the mission of Christ? Was it to make the salvation of all Adam's race possible? or was it to make the salvation of His own people certain? Was it to simply remove those "obstacles" which stood in the way of the Divine righteousness pardoning any one? or was it to remove the *sins* of those whom God had predestinated unto eternal glory? Was it simply to "open a way" whereby sinners *may* approach unto the Holy One? or did Christ die the Just for the unjust that "He might *bring us to God*" (1 Pet. 3:18)? That the second of each of these alternatives is the true one, consider:

1. *The purchase of Christ.* By the term "purchase" Scripture signifies that Christ meritoriously procured for His people the actual bestowment upon them of all those good things which He earned for them, which may be summed up under "life," "salvation," and an "eternal inheritance." Now these blessings were not purchased for His people "conditionally," but *absolutely*, just as when a surety pays a debt, the debtor is necessarily discharged, or as when a ransom is given for the redeeming of a captive, the captive must be freed. Christ's work was not of such a nature that the will of God is still *conditional* as to whether or not the reward of His satisfaction should be bestowed upon certain ones. No, He has *absolutely* obtained for His people peace with God and the remission of their sins, and that by purchasing for them that very faith with which they believe, appropriate, and enjoy, the salvation which He wrought out for them.

Scripture is most explicit in demonstrating that Christ's purchase and the Spirit's application of the purchased blessings have for their objects the *same* individuals: that for whomsoever Christ obtained any spiritual blessings by His death, unto them it shall most certainly be communicated. For whomsoever He wrought reconciliation *with* God, in them doth He (by His Spirit) work reconciliation *unto* God. The one is not extended to any, to whom the other does not reach. It is true that no sinner obtains any of the saving benefits of Christ's satisfaction until he repents and believes, but it is equally true that Christ has purchased these very graces for His people, and is now exalted on High to administer them: Acts 5:31 etc. The Scriptures perpetually conjoin together the benefits *purchased* by Christ and the benefits *bestowed* on those for whom they were purchased, so that we cannot sever the one from the other. "The chastisement of our peace was upon Him, and with His stripes we are healed" (Isa. 53:5): His chastisement and our peace, His wounding and our healing, are inseparably associated.

Thus the *design* of Christ's satisfaction is infallibly made known by the *results* of it. The intendment of God *in* the atonement is plainly evident through what is accomplished *by* it, for whatsoever He has purposed must be effected (Isa. 46:10); hence, what *is* secured by the sacrifice of Christ makes manifest what God planned it *should* procure. "If there be anything plainly taught in Scripture, it is that the sacrifice of Christ was made for those only who shall eventually be saved by it. If the wisdom of men cannot reconcile this with *their* views of what is right, let them be prepared to dispute the matter with the Almighty in the day of judgment" (Alex. Carson).

2. *The rectitude of the Divine character.* God's justice indispensably requires that all the benefits of Christ's sacrifice should be imputed and imparted to every one for whom it was offered and accepted. "Shall not the Judge of all the earth do right? A God of truth, and without iniquity, just and right is He. The Supreme Being gives to every one his due. This principle cannot be violated in a single instance. He cannot, according to this, either remit sin without satisfaction, or punish sin where satisfaction for it has been received. The one is as inconsistent with perfect equity as the other. If the punishment for sin has been borne, the remission of the offence follows of course. The principles of rectitude suppose this, nay peremptorily demand it: justice could not be satisfied without it. Agreeably to this it follows that, the death of Christ being a legal satisfaction for sin, *all* for whom He died *must* enjoy the remission of their offences.

"It is as much at variance with strict justice or equity that any for whom Christ has given satisfaction should continue under condemnation, as that they should have been delivered from guilt without a satisfaction being given for them at all. But it is admitted that all are not delivered from the punishment of sin, that there are many who perish in final condemnation. We are therefore compelled to infer, that for such no satisfaction has been given to the claims of infinite justice—no atonement has been made. If this is denied, the monstrous impossibility must be maintained, that the infallible Judge refuses to remit the punishment of some for whose offences He has received a full compensation; that He finally condemns some, the price of whose deliverance from condemnation has been paid to Him; that, with regard to the sins of some of mankind, He seeks satisfaction in their personal punishment after having obtained satisfaction for them in the sufferings of Christ; that is to say, that an infinitely righteous God takes double payment for the same debt, double satisfaction for the same offence, first from the Surety, and then from those for whom the Surety stood. It is needless to add that these conclusions are revolting to every right feeling of equity, and must be totally inapplicable to the procedure of Him who 'loveth righteousness and hateth wickedness'" (W. Symington).

Christ made full satisfaction unto the law of God (Matt. 5:17, Gal. 4:4, 5), but how could He have made satisfaction for the sins of those on whom the law will take satisfaction for ever? How can the justice of God have been appeased in the case of those against whom its flaming sword will awake to all eternity? Christ expiated offences (Rom. 4:25), but how can those offences for which the guilty perpetrators shall suffer endlessly, have been expiated? How did Christ redeem from the curse of the law (Gal. 3:13) those who are to be kept in everlasting thraldom and misery? The Arminian scheme postulates a Saviour of those who are never saved, a Redeemer of those who are never redeemed, a Deliverer of millions who are never delivered.

To reply to the above by saying that, Christ made a sufficient atonement for the sins of all men universally, but that many are not saved by it because they *trust not* in it, is to lose sight of the fact that half of the human race have never heard the Gospel, and so *could not* believe it! Whatever blame may rest upon Christians for their dilatoriness and selfishness, the Holy Spirit would most certainly have stirred up some to carry the glad tidings to those who have perished in heathen darkness *had* Christ purchased their salvation. To say otherwise would be rank blasphemy. The special mission *of* the Spirit is *to* apply the saving benefits of Christ's salvation to *all* for whom it was made. The One who is able to "raise up children" out of "stones" (Matt. 3:9) *cannot* be checkmated by the cold-heartedness of His people.

3. *The declarations of Holy Writ.* As we have shown in previous articles, the Satisfaction of Christ had its origin in the sovereign will of God, hence His mere good pleasure decided and determined *who* should be saved by it. A favoured section of Adam's race were chosen to be its beneficiaries: herein, we behold the "goodness" of God. Fallen angels and the remainder of Adam's family were not to be redeemed by it, but were predestinated to suffer the due reward of their iniquity: therein we behold the "severity of God" (Rom. 11:22)! The same contrastive principles are adumbrated in the material creation: nature, no more than Scripture, knows anything of a God who is mighty to save and yet not mighty also to destroy—witness tidal waves, tornadoes, earthquakes, famines and pestilences.

In keeping with what has just been said, we find that Scripture divides mankind into two classes: the Church and the world, the "friends" of God and His "enemies," the "sheep" and the "goats." And let it be properly noted that whatever is affirmed distinctively of the one class, is implicitly denied of the other. Every assertion that Christ died for "His people," is a repudiation of the theory that He died for all mankind. Just as when it is said that a certain man toils to provide food for his family, and nobody is foolish enough to conclude that he is *also* labouring to provide food for all mankind, so when the Word declares that Christ "loved the Church and gave Himself for it" (Eph. 5:25), all should see that such discriminative language is meaningless, if He also loved and gave Himself for the entire human race.

"Not every one that saith unto Me, Lord, Lord, shall enter into the kingdom of heaven; but he that doeth the will of My Father which is in Heaven. Many will say to Me in that day, Lord, Lord, have we not prophesied in Thy name? and in Thy name have cast out demons? and in Thy name done many wonderful works? And then will I profess unto them, I never knew you: depart from Me, ye that work iniquity" (Matt. 7:21-23). Here a broad line of distinction is drawn between two classes of the human family, with respect to one of which the Saviour makes the solemn affirmation, "I *never knew* you." The import of those words, according to Scripture usage, is too plain to be misunderstood; the antithetical "The Lord *knoweth* them that are *His*" (2 Tim. 2:19), shows that He *never* had a *saving cognizance* of those to whom He shall say "depart from Me."

"Our Lord speaking of those for whom He died, calls them sheep: 'I lay down My life for the sheep' (John 10:15). He explains who His sheep are by saying, that they are such persons as 'hear His voice and follow Him' (vv. 3, 4), and He adds, 'I give unto them eternal life, and they shall never perish.' Does it not plainly follow from His words that those for whom He died *shall be* saved, that He died for none but those upon whom the gift of faith should be bestowed? And does He not signify, by particularizing them as the persons for whom He laid down His life, that He did *not die* for others of an opposite character? If He died for all, there would be no meaning in saying that He died for His 'sheep,' because in this case there would be nothing *peculiar to them*, nothing by which they were distinguished from any other description of men" (J. Dick, 1850). To this we may add, the name "sheep" is synonymous with "elect," for such are "sheep" *before* they believe, yea, before they are born (see John 10:16); and that in this very same passage Christ affirmed there were some who are *not* His "sheep" —*see* 10:26.

"*All* that the Father giveth Me *shall* come to Me" (John 6:37): but this would not be true if the enmity of the carnal mind, the stubbornness of the unrenewed will, or the oppositions of Satan, were able to successfully resist the "drawing" (John 6:44) of the Father! Christ expressly said, "I pray *not* for the world" (John 17:9), therefore He *died not* for the world, for His sacrifice and His intercession have *the same* objects: (Rom. 8:34). "Feed *the Church* of God, which He hath purchased with His own blood" (Acts 20:28): if the atonement be of universal extent, if Christ's blood be shed for all, then such discriminating language would not only be unnecessary, but altogether misleading. "The Son of man came not to be ministered unto, but to minister, and to give His life a ransom for *many*" (Matt. 20:28): *no* satisfactory reason can be given why Christ should say only "many" if all mankind were also included: cf. Heb. 9:28. "Who gave Himself *for us*, that He might redeem us from all iniquity and purify unto Himself a peculiar people, zealous of good works" (Titus 2:14): those for whom Christ died are "a *peculiar people*," and not the whole Adamic race indiscriminately.

Those passages which are appealed to by those who advocate the doctrine of universal redemption will be carefully considered in the next article, D. V. A.W.P.

REGENERATION, OR THE NEW BIRTH

All men are by nature the children of wrath, and do belong unto the world, which is the kingdom of Satan (1 John 5:19), and are under the power of darkness. In this state men are not the subjects of Christ's kingdom, and have no meetness for Heaven. From this terrible state they are unable to deliver themselves, being "without strength" (Rom. 5:6). Out of this state God's elect are supernaturally "called" (1 Pet. 2:9), which call effectually delivers them from the power of Satan and translates them into the kingdom of God's dear Son (Col. 1:13). This Divine "call," or work of grace, is variously denominated in Scripture: sometimes by "regeneration" (Titus 3:5), or the new birth, sometimes by illumination (2 Cor. 4:6), by transformation (2 Cor. 3:18), by spiritual resurrection (John 5:24). This inward and invincible call is attended with justification and adoption (Rom. 8:30, Eph. 1:5). and is carried on by sanctification in holiness. This leads us to consider:

III. Its Effects.

"The wind bloweth where it listeth, and thou hearest the sound thereof, but canst not tell whence it cometh, and whither it goeth: so is every one that is born of the Spirit" (John 3:8). Though the wind be imperious in its action, man being unable to regulate it; though it be mysterious in its nature, man knowing nothing of the cause which controls it; yet its presence is unmistakeable, its effects are plainly evidenced: so it is with *every one* that is born of the Spirit. His secret but powerful operations lie beyond the reach of our understanding. Why God has ordained that the Spirit should quicken this person and not that, we know not, but the transforming results of His working are plain and palpable. What these are, we shall now endeavor to describe.

1. *The illumination of the understanding*. As it was in the old creation, so it is in connection with the new. "In the beginning God created the heaven and the earth" (Gen. 1:1). That was the original creation. Then came degeneration: "And the earth became without

form and void (a desolate waste) and darkness was upon the face of the deep." Next came restoration: "And the Spirit of God moved upon the face of the waters, and God said, Let there be light: and there was light." So it is when God begins to restore fallen man: "For God who commanded the light to shine out of darkness, hath shined in our hearts, to give the light of the knowledge of the glory of God in the face of Jesus Christ" (II. Cor. 4:6).

This Divine illumination which the mind receives at the new birth is not by means of dreams or visions, nor does it consist in the revelation of things to the soul which have not been made known in the Scriptures. Not so, the only means or instrument which the Holy Spirit employs is the written Word: "The entrance of Thy words giveth light; it giveth understanding unto the simple" (Psa. 119:130). Hitherto, God's Word may have been read attentively, and much of its teaching intellectually apprehended; but because there was a "vail" upon the heart (2 Cor. 3:15) and so no spiritual discernment (1 Cor. 2:14), the reader was not inwardly affected thereby. But now the Spirit removes that vail, opens the heart to receive the Word (Acts 16:14), and powerfully applies to the mind and conscience some portion of it. The result is that, the one renewed is able to say, "One thing I know, that, whereas I was blind, now I see" (John 9:25). To particularize:

The sinner is now enlightened in the knowledge of his own terrible condition. He may, before this, have received much scriptural instruction, subscribed to a sound creed, and believed intellectually in "the total depravity of man"; but now the solemn declarations of God's Word concerning the state of the fallen creature are brought home in piercing power to his own soul. No longer does he compare himself with his fellows, but measures himself by the rule of God. He now discovers that *he* is unclean, that his heart is "desperately wicked," and that he is altogether unfit for the presence of the thrice holy God. He is powerfully convicted of his own awful sins, feels that they are more in number than the hairs of his head, and that they are high provocations against Heaven, which call for Divine judgment on him. He now realizes that there is "*no* soundness" (Isa. 1:6) in him, and that all his best performances are only as "filthy rags" (Isa. 64:6), and that he is deserving of nought but the everlasting burnings.

By the spiritual light which God communicates in regeneration the soul now perceives the infinite demerits of sin, that its "wages" can be nothing less than eternal death, or the loss of Divine favor and a dreadful suffering under the wrath of God. The equity of God's law and the fact that sin righteously calls for such terrible punishment is humbly acknowledged. Thus his mouth is "stopped" and he confesses himself to be guilty before God, and justly liable to His awful vengence, both for the plague of his own heart and his numerous transgressions. He now realises that his whole life has been lived in utter independence of God, having had no respect for His glory, no concern whether he pleased or displeased Him. He now perceives the exceeding sinfulness of sin, its awful malignity, as being in its nature contrary to the law of God. How to escape the due reward of his iniquity, he knows not. "What must I do to be saved?" is his agonising cry. He is convinced of the absolute impossibility of contributing anything to his deliverance. He no longer has any confidence in the flesh; he has been brought to the end of himself.

By means of this illumination the renewed soul, under the guidance of the Spirit through the Word, now perceives how well-suited is Christ to such a poor, worthless wretch as he feels himself to be. The prospect of obtaining deliverance from the wrath to come through the vicarious life and death of the Lord Jesus, keeps his soul from being overwhelmed with grief and from sinking into complete despondency because of the sight of his sins. As the Spirit presents to him the infinite merits of Christ's obedience and righteousness, His tender compassion for sinners, His power to save, desires for an interest in Christ now possess his heart, and he is resolved to look for salvation in no other. Under the benign influences of the Holy Spirit, the soul is drawn by some such words as, "Come unto Me all ye that labor and are heavy laden, and I will give you rest," or "him that cometh to Me I will in no wise cast out," and he is led to apply to Him for pardon, cleansing, peace, righteousness, strength.

Other acts besides turning unto Christ flow from this new principle received at regeneration, such as *repentance*, which is a godly sorrow for sin, an abhorring of it as sin, and an earnest desire to forsake and be completely delivered from its pollution. In the light of God, the renewed soul now perceives the utter vanity of the world, and the worthlessness of those paltry toys and perishing trifles which the godless strive so hard to acquire. He has been awakened from the dream-sleep of death, and things are now seen in their true nature. Time is precious and not to be frittered away. God in His awesome Majesty is an object to be feared. His law is accepted as holy, just and good. All of these perceptions and actions are included in that holiness without which no man shall see the Lord. In some these actions are more vigorous than in others, and consequently, are more perceptible to a man's self. But the fruits of them are visible to others in external acts.

2. *The elevation of the heart.* Rightly does the Lord claim the first place: "he that loveth father or mother more than Me is not worthy of Me" (Matt. 10:37). "My son, give Me thine heart" (Prov. 23:26) expresses God's claim: they "first gave their own selves to the Lord" (2 Cor. 8:5) declares the response of the regenerate. But it is not until they are born again that any are spiritually capacitated to do this, for by nature men are "lovers of their own selves" and "lovers of pleasure more than lovers of God" (2 Tim. 3:2, 4). When a sinner is renewed, his affections are taken off his idols and fixed on the Lord (1 Thess. 1:9). Hence it is written "with the heart (the affections) man believeth unto righteousness" (Rom. 10:10). And hence, also, it is written, "If any man *love not* the Lord Jesus Christ let him be accursed" (1 Cor. 16:22).

"And the Lord thy God will circumcise thine heart, and the heart of thy seed, *to love the Lord thy God with all thy heart*" (Deut. 30:6). The "circumcising" of the heart is the "renewing" of it, severing its love from all illicit objects. None can truly love God supremely till this miracle of grace has been wrought within him. Then it is that the affections are refined and directed to their proper objects, He who once was despised by the soul, is now beheld as the "altogether lovely" One. He who was hated (John 15:18), is now loved above all others. "Whom have I in heaven but Thee? and there is none upon earth that I desire besides Thee" (Psa. 73:25) is now their joyous confession.

The love of God has become the governing principle of the life (2 Cor. 5:13).

What before was drudgery is now a delight. The praise of man is no longer the motive which stimulates action; the approbation of the Saviour is the Christian's highest concern. Gratitude moves to a hearty compliance with His will. "How precious also are *Thy* thoughts unto me O God" (Psa. 139:17) is now his language. And again, "the desire of our soul is to Thy name, and to the remembrance of Thee. With my soul have I desired Thee in the night; yea, with my spirit within me will I seek Thee early" (Isa. 26:8, 9). So too the heart is drawn out to all the members of His family, no matter what their nationality, social position, or church-connections: "We know that we have passed from death unto life, because we love the brethren" (1 John 3:14).

3. *The emancipation of the will.* By nature, the will of fallen man is free in only one direction: away from God. Sin has enslaved the will, therefore do we need to be "made free" (John 8:36). The two states are contrasted in Rom. 6: "free from righteousness" (v. 20), when dead in sin; "free from sin" (v. 18), now that we are alive unto God. At the new birth the will is liberated from the "bondage of corruption" (Rom. 8:21 and cf. 2 Peter 2:19) and rendered conformable to the will of God (Psa. 119:97). In our degenerate state the will was naturally rebellious, and its practical language was, "Who is the Lord, that I should obey Him?" (Ex. 5:2). But the Father promised the Son, "Thy people *shall be willing* in the day of Thy power" (Psa. 110:3), and this is accomplished when God "worketh in us both to will and to do of His good pleasure" (Phil. 2:13 and cf. Heb. 13:21).

"A new heart also will I give you, and a new spirit will I put within you: and I will take away the stony heart out of your flesh, and I will give you an heart of flesh. And I will put My Spirit within you, and cause you to walk in My statutes, and ye shall seek My judgments, and do them" (Ezek. 36:26, 27). This is a new-covenant promise (Heb. 8:10), and is made good in each renewed soul. The will is so emancipated from the power of indwelling sin as to be enabled to answer to the Divine commands according to the tenor of the new covenant. The regenerated freely consent to and gladly choose to walk in subjection to Christ, being anxious now to obey Him in all things. His authority is their only rule, His love the constraining power:

"If a man love Me, he *will* keep My words" (John 14:23).

4. *The rectification of the conduct.* A tree is known by its fruits. Faith is evidenced by works. The principle of holiness manifests itself in a godly walk. "If ye know that He is righteous, ye know that every one that doeth righteousness is born of Him" (1 John 2:29). The deepest longing of every child of God is to please his heavenly Father in all things, and though this longing is never fully realised in this life—"*Not* as though I had *already* attained, either were already perfect" (Phil. 3:12)—nevertheless he continues "reaching forth unto those things which are before."

"Ye have obeyed from the heart that form of doctrine *whereto* ye were delivered" (Rom. 6:17 mar.). The Greek word for "form" here signifies "mould." Observe how this figure also presupposes the *same* faculties after the new birth as before. Metal which is moulded remains the same metal as it was previously, only the fashion or form of it is altered. That metal which before was a dish, is now turned into a cup, and thus a new name is given to it: cf. Rev. 3:12. By regeneration the faculties of the soul are made suitable to God and His precepts, just as the mould and the thing moulded fit one another. As before the heart was at enmity against every commandment, it is now moulded to them. Does God say, "fear Me," the renewed heart answers, "I desire *to* fear Thy name" (Neh. 1:11). Does God say, "remember the sabbath day to keep it holy," the heart answers, "the sabbath day is my *delight*" (Isa. 58:13). Does God say, "love one another," the new creature finds an instinct begotten within it to *do* so, so that real Christians are said to be "taught of God" *to love* one another" (1 Thess. 4:9).

A change will take place in the deportment of the most moral unconverted man as soon as he is born from above. Not only will he be far less eager in his pursuit of the world, more scrupulous in the selection of his company, more cautious in avoiding the occasions to sin and the appearances of evil, but he realises that the holy eye of God is ever upon him, marking not only his actions, but weighing his motives. He now bears the sacred name of Christ, and his deepest concern is to be kept from every thing which would bring a reproach upon it. His aim is to let his light so shine before men that they may see his good works and glorify his Father which is in heaven.

That which occasions him the deepest distress is not the sneers and taunts of the ungodly, but that he fails to measure up to the standard God has set before him, and that conformity to it after which he so much yearns. Though Divine grace may preserve him from outward falls, yet he is painfully conscious of many sins within: the risings of unbelief, the swellings of pride, the oppositions of the "flesh" to the desires of the "spirit." These occasion him deep exercises of heart and lead to humble and sorrowful confessions unto God.

It is of great importance that the Christian should have clear and scriptural views of what he is *both* as the subject of sin and of grace. Though the regenerate are delivered from the absolute dominion of sin (Rom. 6:14), yet the principle of sin, the "flesh," is not eradicated. This is clear from Rom. 6:12, "Let not sin therefore reign in your mortal body, that ye should obey it in the lusts thereof": that exhortation would be meaningless if there were no indwelling sin seeking *to* reign, and no lusts demanding obedience. Yet this is far from saying that a Christian *must* go on in a course of sinning: "Whosoever is born of God doth not commit sin; for His seed remaineth in him: and he cannot sin, because he is born of God" (1 John 3:9), the reference there being to the regular practice and habit of sinning. Nevertheless, prayerful heed needs to be constantly paid to this word, "Awake to righteousness, and sin not" (1 Cor. 15: 34).

The experiences of Paul, both as the subject of sin and of grace, are recorded in Rom. 7. A careful reading of vv. 14-24 reveals the fact that grace had neither removed nor purified the "flesh" in him. And as the Christian today compares his own inner conflicts, he finds that Rom. 7 describes them most accurately and faithfully. He discovers that in his "flesh" is no good thing and he cries, "O wretched man that I am." Though he longs for fuller conformity to the image of Christ, though he hungers and thirsts after righteousness, though he is under the influence and reign of grace, and though he enjoys real fellowship with God, yet, at seasons (some more acutely felt than others) he feels that though with the mind he serves the law of God, yet with the flesh the law of sin. Yea, every experience of reading the Word, prayer, meditation, proves to him that he is, in his fallen nature, "carnal, sold under sin," and that when he would do good, evil is present with him. This is a matter of great grief to him, and causes him to "groan" (Rom. 8:23) and yearn the more for release from this body of death.

But ought not the Christian to "grow in grace"? Yes, indeed. Yet let it be said emphatically that growing "in grace" most certainly does not mean an increasing satisfaction with myself. No, it is the very opposite. The more I walk in the light of God, the more plainly can I see the vileness of the "flesh" within me, and there will be an ever-deepening abhorence of what I am by nature. "For to will is present with me, but how to perform that which is good I find not" (Rom. 7:18) is not the confession of an unbeliever, nor even of a babe in Christ, but of the most enlightened saint. The only relief from this distressing discovery and the only peace for the renewed heart is to look away from self to Christ and His perfect work for us. Faith empties of all self-complacency and gives an exalted estimate of God in Christ.

A growth "in grace" is defined, in great part, by the words that immediately follow: " and in the knowledge of our Lord and Saviour Jesus Christ" (2 Pet. 3:18). It is the growing realization of the perfect suitability of Christ to a poor sinner, the deepening conviction of His fitness to be the Saviour of such a vile wretch as the Spirit daily shows me I am. It is the apprehension of how much I need His precious blood to cleanse me, His righteousness to clothe me, His arm to support me, His advocacy to answer for me on High, His grace to deliver me from all my enemies both inward and outward. It is the Spirit revealing to me that there is *in Christ* everything that I need both for earth and heaven, time and eternity. Thus, growing in grace is an increasing living *outside of* myself, living *upon* Christ. It is a looking to Him for the supply of *every* need.

The more the heart is occupied with Christ, the more the mind is stayed upon Him by trusting in Him (Isa. 26:3), the more will faith, hope, love, patience, meekness, and all spiritual graces, be strengthened and drawn forth into exercise and act to the glory of God. The *manifestation* of growth in grace and in the knowledge of Christ is another thing. The actual process of growing is not perceptible either in the natural or in the spiritual sphere; but the results of it are, mainly so to others. There are definite *seasons* of growth, and generally the Christian's spiritual graces are growing the most while the soul is in distress through manifold temptations, mourning on account of indwelling sin. It is when we are *enjoying* God and are in conscious communion with Him, feasting upon the perfections of Christ, that the fruits of the Spirit in us are *ripened*. The chief *evidences* of spiritual growth in the Christian are a deepening hatred of sin and loathing of self, a higher valuation of spiritual things, and yearning after them, a fuller recognition of our deep need and dependency on God to supply it.

Regeneration is substantially the same in all who are the subjects of it: there is a spiritual transformation, the conforming of the soul unto the image of God: "that which is born of the Spirit *is spirit*" (John 3:6). But although every regenerated person is a new creature, has received a principle of faith and holiness which acts on every faculty of his being, and is indwelt and led by the Holy Spirit, yet God does not communicate the same measure of grace (Rom. 12:3, 2 Cor. 10:13, Eph. 4:16) or the same number of talents to all alike. God's children differ from each other as children do at their natural birth, some of whom are more lively and vigorous than others. God, according to His sovereign pleasure, gives to some fuller knowledge, to others stronger faith, to others warmer affections—natural temperament has much to do with the form and colour which the *manifestation* of the "spirit" takes through us. But there is no difference in their state: the same work has been performed in all, which radically differentiates them from worldlings.

"Do ye not know that the saints shall judge the world?" (1 Cor. 6:2). Does not this clearly denote, yea, require, that the "saints" shall exercise a distinguishing holiness and live quite otherwise than the world? Could one who now takes the Lord's name in vain be righteously appointed to sit in judgment upon those who profane it? Could one who lives to please self be a fit person to judge those who have loved pleasure more than God? Could one who has despised and ridiculed "puritanic strictness of living" sit with Christ as a judge on those who lived in rebellion against Him? Never; instead of being the judges of others, all such will find themselves condemned and executed as malefactors in that Day.

"The Lord will give grace and glory: no good thing will He withhold from them that walk uprightly" (Psa. 84:11).

"Grace and glory" are inseparably connected: they differ not in nature, but in degree. "Grace" is glory begun; "glory" is grace elevated to its acme and perfection. 1 John 3:2 tells us that the saints shall be "like Him," and this, because they will "see Him as He is." The immediate vision of the Lord of Glory will be a transforming one, the bright reflections of God's purity and holiness cast upon the glorified will make them perfectly holy and blessed. But this resemblance to God, His saints do *here*, in measure, bear upon them: there are some outlines, some lineaments of God's image stamped upon them, and this too is through *beholding* Him. True, it is (comparatively speaking) through a glass darkly, yet "beholding" we "*are* changed into the *same* image from glory to glory (from one degree of it to another) as by the Spirit of the Lord" (2 Cor. 3:18).

In conclusion, let both writer and reader test and search himself in the presence of God, by these questions. How stands my heart affected toward sin? Is there a deep humiliation and godly sorrow after I have yielded thereto? Is there a genuine detestation of it? Is my conscience tender, so that my peace is disturbed by what the world calls "trifling faults" and "little things"? Am I humbled when conscious of the risings of pride and self-will? Do I loathe my inward corruption? What engages my mind in seasons of recreation? Are my affections dead toward the world and alive toward God? Do I find spiritual exercises pleasant and joyous or irksome and burdensome? Can I truthfully say, "How sweet are Thy words unto my taste! yea, sweeter than honey to my mouth" (Psa. 119:103)? Is communion with God my highest joy? Is the glory of God dearer to me than all the world contains? A.W.P.

WELCOME TIDINGS

Once again the season has arrived for us to record our annual testimony to the abounding grace and goodness of God. First, in connection with the manifold blessings which He has showered upon the work He has condescended to commit unto us. As we take up our pencil we are reminded anew of the swift flight of time. How rapidly one year succeeds another! In view of this we are constrained to cry, Lord, "So teach us to number our days, that we may apply our hearts unto wisdom" (Psa. 90:12). One way of so doing, is to live each day as though we knew it would be our last: doing with our "might" whatsoever our hands find to do; doing it with the realization that we must soon render an account of our stewardship unto the Judge of all the earth; doing whatsoever we do, "heartily as to the Lord, and not unto men" (Col. 3:23), seeking His glory only.

In attempting to give our dear friends some idea of the manner and measure in which the Lord is graciously blessing and multiplying the "Bread" by which we are seeking to feed His blood-bought people, our chief difficulty is to make a selection from the many evidences to hand that God is deigning to use this little monthly messenger as a means of deepening His work of grace in the hearts of not a few of "His own." This is (by His mercy) more and more our aim: not only to *expound* God's holy Word, but to make *practical application* of it to our daily lives and walk. To know the Truth is a holy privilege, but to be "*doers* of the Word" (James 1:22) is what God requires, and what is the principal test as to whether we are truly profiting from what we read or hear.

Before giving some quotations from letters to hand during the last few months, we joyfully record once more, to the glory of our faithful God, that despite the worldwide industrial depression, the Lord continues to freely move His stewards to have financial fellowship with us in this work. We mention this also because we desire to make it clear to all that, these lines are *not* an indirect appeal for funds. No one engaged in *the Lord's* work ever has need to solicit any help from man. Whenever there is any *begging* (directly or indirectly) for money or gifts, it is a *certain* sign that the one begging is *not* in the will of God, and is working in the energy of the flesh. And we would earnestly exhort every Christian to have *no* fellowship with such work. No, we have no need to ask for a cent from any one. Every bill is paid, and a goodly sum is now on hand. Praise God!

One encouraging feature which is illustrated by the letters received is to find how God has blest one series of articles to one, and a different series to another. Numbers have been much helped by those on the Atonement. Others on the expositions of Hebrews. A Brother in England writes, "Your expositions of Hebrews has indeed been a rich feast of good things, and we hope that by God's grace you will be enabled to continue them during the coming days." Another Brother has received such blessing from the cover-page series on the Attributes of God, that he is paying for a whole edition of them to be printed in separate, booklet form. We hope that many will order them.

How those on the Intercession of Christ were used by God is illustrated by the following: "Rising early yesterday morning to have some time with the Word and prayer before commencing household duties, I took up the 'Nature of His Intercession.' Words fail to describe the joy as the Holy Spirit witnessed that Jesus was *my* Advocate. The Holy Spirit applied it to my soul as I pondered it, and told me every word was for me. My heart is too full, neither can I find words to describe my experience; but I truly had fellowship with the Triune God." That Australian Sister sought God *first* (Matt. 6:33). O that others would do likewise: rising early and *beginning* the day with Him!

The Lord was pleased to bless the "Xmas" article to open the eyes of a number to the sinfulness of joining in with the world in the celebrating of that Pagan and Papal custom. A number have expressed thanks for the "Radio" warning, and have written to say that this evil has been removed from their home. Praise God! A Sister who lives right out in the country, with *no* near neighbours, was sick some time ago. The doctor who visited her said, "Where is your radio?" She replied, "I don't want one." He answered, "Why it brings *the world* to your feet!" And she answered, "I don't want *that*."

"I find your Magazine very beneficial to my soul and useful in giving so many suggestions in my service for the Lord" —Missionary in San Salvador. It always rejoices us when we find a servant of God putting the needs of his *own* soul before that of those to whom he ministers. It is so easy to slide into the snare of reading (shall we say ?) professionally, vicariously—seeking material for sermons, but failing to cultivate the garden of our own hearts. It is much to be feared that "they made me the keeper of the vineyards, but mine *own* vineyard have I *not kept*" (Song of S. 1:6), will be the lament of many in a soon-coming Day.

"Take heed *unto thyself*" (1 Tim. 4:16) needs to be prayerfully heeded by every servant of God.

"During by brief ministry of six years, I have read with delight the articles you have written. Some of your books have been read and re-read, and have helped to establish the faith of this young preacher" (Bapt. pastor in W. Va.) What cause for praise is this! It is indeed occasion for thanksgiving when God deigns to use our pen to root and ground in His holy Truth one who is a teacher of others. We wish that those of our readers who are preachers would, in addition to this Magazine, purchase from the B. T. D. Swengel, Union Co., Pa., some of our other works, particularly our verse by verse exposition of John's gospel, in the preparing of which we spent ten years of hard work.

"Your writings have been the source of much inspiration and real spiritual blessing to me, and I am sure through me to my people here." (Pastor in Iowa). "I have received the Studies since the beginning of their publication and have been greatly helped in the understanding of the Scriptures, and consequently have passed on the truths there learned to others in private and public to small groups of Christians in the suburbs of Sydney, Australia." "Many thanks for your periodical which I have received during the last year. If it is possible send it to me this year also: I will be very obliged. I am a missionary among Russian refugees in Finland." "Studies comes regularly and continues to be a great blessing to us. Truly they make us masticate well, for it is meat and not milk you are feeding us. We are so grateful" (Missionary in Honduras).

"I send an uplift thanks for your Magazine: I have received much knowledge of God. Your exposition of 'The Satisfaction of Christ' has brought much light" (Bro. in Sweden). "Have been reading your Studies with great interest and spiritual profit" (Missionary in Bulgaria). "I am so grateful to you for all the help I have gotten from 'Studies' these past years. May the Lord continue to use you in an even greater way" (Missionary in Guatemala). "Hearty t h a n k s, dear Brother, for the good food and instruction of your paper. I am as glad as a little child every time it enters my home" (Brother in Norway). "I make continual use of the expositions" (Missionary in China).

"I appreciate your exhaustive labours

in preparing these Studies for ignorant and unlearned men like myself to feed upon. You will not know till eternity what a good work you are doing. God bless you, and keep you faithful. I shall pray for you (we wish every Christian reader would do so. A.W.P.) I will be grateful to you and to God for all exhortations you send me" (Young preacher in No. Carolina). How rare it is today to find any, especially any Preachers, who welcome *love's* "exhortations"! Yet the Word says, "But *exhort* one another daily" (Heb. 3:13). Psa. 141:5 is ever the language of those whose hearts are right with God.

"I am thankful for the help I have received from the subjects which the Lord has led you to take up and write on, though I may say they have caused me much buffeting; but this has only driven me to my knees" (Brother in Wales). "Many thanks for Studies. The precious truths in them have made me groan and cry unto the dear Lord many times to be made right and kept right. At other times I have felt comforted by them" (Brother in England). Yes, it is written, "Blessed are they that *mourn*: for *they* shall be comforted" (Matt. 5:4). God has ordained that the Lamb shall be eaten "with *bitter* herbs" (Ex. 12:8)!

"Am writing to thank you in the Lord for the Magazine which we have received quite safely through the past year. The messages have been wonderful and inspiring. Placed as we are in this lonely spot, it is glorious to get God's Truth, and we do thank Him for your ministry and writings. God grant that we, and all who read with true desire, may profit from the Word, and that your joy may be increased as you labour for Him" (Brother and Sister in Canada). We wish that every Christian reader would join us in crying to the Lord that He would graciously bring us into touch with more *isolated* sheep.

"The last year has been a time of trouble and testing for me, and the Lord has graciously used the 'Studies' to show me His will for me. I am resting in Him" (Sister in N. Y.). "Your article on the 'Patience of God' has been a great blessing to me, especially the last paragraph. One who professed to be a friend did me an injury some months ago, and since then had kept well out of my way. But that last paragraph made me seek him out and give him my hand; and both he and I are happier as the result" (Brother in England). Praise God! Two practical testimonies like these mean far more than a hundred mere eulogies. Let every reader turn to Matt. 5:23, 24.

We trust that these tokens of the Lord's grace will cause every prayer-helper to present fervent thanksgivings to God. Though the days are evil, the Lord is still at work, silently, yet *surely*, nevertheless! Continue in prayer (Col. 4:2) that He will cause this magazine to bring forth still more fruit to His glory. Ask the Lord to fit the editor for more *acceptable* service to God. Ask that we may be guided and helped in the preparation of every article. Ask Him for an *increased circulation*: though it goes to the ends of the earth, we have barely one thousand readers! Are you doing what *you* can to make the Studies known to those likely to value them? Please accept our hearty thanks for all co-operation and fellowship. A.W.P.

FOLLOWING CHRIST

"He that followeth Me shall not walk in darkness, but shall have the light of life" (John 8:12). How easy it is to *read* these words, but how difficult it is to truly put them into practice! It is much, very much to be thankful for, if the Holy Spirit has wrought a real desire in the heart of the reader *to* "follow" Christ, for such a desire surely cannot be within multitudes of those who bear His name and with their lips sing His praises. Daily does the Christian need to beseech God to *strengthen* this desire until it actually becomes the uppermost longing of his soul and the dominant purpose of his life.

It is much, very much to be thankful for when the Holy Spirit makes us to realise that, of ourselves, we are *unable* to carry out that desire *and* "follow" Christ. As He Himself tells us, "without *Me* ye can do nothing" (John 15:5). This fact ought to deeply humble us as we are made to feel our inability to do that which is right, and should forever remove all pride and boasting from us. We are apt to think that this inability is merely a "weakness" or lack of strength; but in reality, it is *sin* within us, the "flesh," that awful and depraved nature with which we were born into this world.

"The carnal mind is enmity against

God: for it is not subject to the law of God, neither indeed can be" (Rom. 8:7). While that "enmity" receives its death-blow at regeneration, it is not altogether dead in the Christian. At times the remainder of this "enmity" slumbers, and Satan seeks to delude us into thinking it is completely slain, thus taking us off our guard. No, the "flesh" remains in us to the end of our earthly course, and its unchanging tendency is to draw us away *from* "following" Christ. How this should make us "abhor" ourselves (Job 42:6): that there is that in us, that which is part and parcel of our very being, which is *opposed* to Christ!

Now while the realization of indwelling sin should humble us, it ought not to *paralyse us*, nor must we allow the thought that to continue in any course of sin is inevitable. No, it ought to drive us to our knees and earnestly seek *help* from above. We must daily beg God to *restrain* the workings of the "flesh" and to "subdue" our iniquities (Micah 7:19). We need to daily plead the promise "He shall save His people *from* their sins." God says, "Awake to righteousness, and sin not" (1 Cor. 15:34), and our bounden duty is to diligently and constantly seek grace that we may be *preserved from* all sinning.

"Then said Jesus unto His disciples, If any man will (determines to) come after Me, let him deny himself, and take up his cross, and follow Me" (Matt. 16:24). Here we learn what must *precede* a real and true "following" of Christ. First, there has to be the denying of self: our own wisdom, will, desires and interests, have to be set aside. We "should not henceforth live unto ourselves, but unto Him which died for us, and rose again" (2 Cor. 5:15). Second, there has to be the living of our daily lives in complete subjection to God. The "cross" which we are to "take up" stands for entire and loving obedience to the Lord: of Him it is written that, He "became obedient unto death, even the death of the cross." It is only as self is repudiated and as the heart is dominated by the spirit of Calvary, that we are prepared *to* "follow" Christ.

Now to "follow" Christ is to *take* His "yoke" upon us (Matt. 11:29). It is to enlist under the banner of the "Captain" of our salvation. It is to completely yield to His Lordship. It is to obey His commandments, and thus truly *serve* Him. It is to seek and do only those things which are pleasing in His sight. For this, Divine strength is needed. "*Draw me*" (Song of Sol. 1:3) must be our daily prayer. Only as we "receive" from *His* "fullness" John 1:16) are we enabled to follow "the example" which He has left us.

As we *are* thus enabled *to* "follow" Him, we shall "not walk" in darkness." No, we shall be in fellowship with Him who is "the true Light." Nor must we be dismayed because we do not fully enter into this blessed experience all at once: "the path of the just is as the shining light, that shineth *more and more* unto the perfect day" (Prov. 4:18). The way to get more strength and light, is to *use* what has already been given us.

To "follow" Christ is to tread the path of Divine blessing. True, it is a narrow path, and oftentimes a lonesome one, for "few" (Matt. 7:14) there are who tread it. True, it is sometimes a rough and thorny path, yet God has provided shoes for our feet (Luke 15:22; Eph. 6:15). Yet is it also a most blessed path. It is there that we *enjoy* the Lord's accompanying presence. It is there that we are favoured with the rich *compensations* which are given to those who turn their backs upon self-pleasing and the world. The Lord will be no man's debtor: "Verily I say unto you, There is no man that hath left house, or brethren, or sisters, or father, or mother or wife or children, or lands, for My sake, and the Gospel's, but he shall receive an hundredfold, *now* in this time ... and in the world to come eternal life" (Mark 10:29, 30).

"For they have wholly followed the Lord" (Numb. 32:12). The reference is to Caleb and Joshua, in contrast from the other ten spies who gave way to an evil heart of unbelief and offered evil advise to the people. Their hearts were set upon the Lord: they had full confidence in Him, had respect to all the intimations of His will and persevered in obedience, overcoming trial and temptation. Having put their hand to the plough, they looked not back. Consequently, instead of perishing in the wilderness as did their disobedient fellows, they entered the promised land. "For they have *wholly* followed the Lord." This is written for our encouragement. They were men of like passions with us, yet (by grace) they triumphed. O let us not be content with following Christ spasmodically, half-heartedly, or afar off; but forgetting the things behind, let us "reach forth" unto those things which are before. A.W.P.

earth, *made* also the other to dwell in heaven. There is still a proportion between them, they agree in something. But what are all the nothings of the world, to *the God* infinitely blessed for evermore!" (J. Owen).

Distinction and inequality in respect of *office* in Christ, does not in the least take away His absolute equality with the Father in nature and essence. As the Mediator, as the One who took upon Him "the form of a servant" (Phil. 2:7), He could say, "My Father is greater than I" (John 14:28); but as the second person of the Trinity, He could say "I and Father are one" (John 10:30). As God the Son, He is essentially and eternally self-existent with the Father and the Spirit, co-equal and co-glorious. But as the One who became Surety for His people, made under the law, (Gal. 4:4), He was economically, positionally, and by office, inferior to the Father; yet even then, *not so* in His essential being. In becoming man, He ceased not to be God.

It has been well pointed out that, If Christ were a mere *creature*, even though far superior to the arch-angel, then, the gulf between God and men has never been bridged, and therefore *communion* between them is impossible. The distance which separates *Him* who called all things out of nothing (Heb. 11:3) and the *things* thus "called" or created, is impassible to all but God. Second, that if Christ be a creature, then, infinite sin has never found an infinite sacrifice. Sin against man, a finite creature, is a finite offence; but against God, an infinite Being, it is an infinite offence; and therefore nothing could atone for it save a sacrifice possessing infinite value. Third, that if Christ were only a creature, His claims to Godhead were blasphemy. Thus, those who deny His Godhead are blasphemers, unregenerate souls, and on their way to the eternal burnings: see John 8:24, 1 John 2:23.

Let us, in conclusion, seek to point out some of the corollaries of this wondrous and blessed truth, some of the practical consequences which it necessarily involves. First, fellow-Christians, our Saviour *is Divine!* The One who loved us, and gave Himself for us, was none other than the second person of the Holy Trinity: co-eternal, co-equal, co-glorious, with the Father and the Holy Spirit. Though very Man of very man, He is also very God of very God. Let us frequently remind ourselves of this fundamental fact. Let us seek to form the constant habit of thinking of Him not only as the One who is touched with the feeling of our infirmities, but also as the One who created all things and who now sustains and directs all things. True, when He became incarnate, He was in all things "made like unto His brethren," yet He ever was, is, and will always remain, "the mighty God."

Second, since Christ be God, His *authority* is absolute and His claims upon us supreme. He is entitled to unreserved *submission* from us. He says, "Ye call Me Master and Lord: and ye say well; for so I am" (John 13:13). He has the unqualified right to command, to say what we shall not do, and what we must do. O how the apprehension of His Godhead ought to awe our hearts and prompt to absolute obedience, responding to *every* intimation of His will unto us!

Third, since Christ be God, He is worthy of our fullest *confidence*. Everything is subject to His imperial pleasure; all power in heaven and earth is His; *nothing* is too hard for Him. Let us remember this when we bow the knee before Him and make known our needs and requests. Nothing honours Him more than our faith, and nothing is more calculated to deepen our faith and strengthen our hearts in prayer, than the realisation of His Godhead. It was thus that believers acted during the time that He tabernacled among men. Those who recognise in Him the promised Messiah, brought their sick and dying to Him, and He *never* mocked them. O what great things we should *expect* from Him who is God the Son!

Finally, since Christ be God, He is entitled to our adoration and *worship*. "Worthy is the Lamb that was slain *to receive* power and riches, and wisdom, and strength, and honour, and glory, and blessing" (Rev. 5:12). See to it then, dear brethren and sisters, that you definitely give to Him the same homage and praise that you do unto the Father. "That all men should honour the Son, *even as* they honour the Father. He that honoureth not the Son, honoureth not the Father which hath sent Him" (John 5:22). It is impossible to make too much of Christ.
A.W.P.

sovereignty was seen in His rebuking of the winds and stilling of the storm; so also in His blasting of the fig tree. His *incomprehensibility* is affirmed in Matt. 11:27.

He received, and is to receive, *worship*. Now worship is due unto none but God: "Thou shalt worship the Lord thy God and *Him only* shalt thou serve." Therefore do we find that Peter (Acts 10:25, 26), Paul and Barnabas (Acts 14:11-15), and an angel (Rev. 22:8, 9) refused the worship of men. How different with Christ: when the leper fell down and worshipped Him (Matt. 8:2) He did not say, "see thou do it not," but *received* the Divine honors paid Him. Nay more, He Himself taught that "all should honour the Son, *even as* they honour the Father" (John 5:23). So too do we find the Father giving orders concerning His Son "Let all the angels of God *worship* Him" (Heb. 1:6).

"All things were made by Him; and without Him was not anything made, that was made" (John 1:3). Christ, the eternal Word, made *all* that ever was made: therefore He Himself *never* was "made." "All things that the Father hath are Mine" (John 16:15): what is more peculiarly *the Father's* than His own nature, essence, Deity? "The church *of God*, which He hath purchased with His own blood" (Acts 20:28), with which should be compared "Hereby perceive we the love of God, because *He* laid down His life for us" (1 John 3:16). Deity was absolutely essential if His sacrifice were to possess *infinite* value: hence the emphasis of "the blood of Jesus Christ *His Son* cleanseth us from all sin" (1 John 1:7).

The Deity of Christ also appears in Scriptural allusions which are more of the nature of incidental references than formal statements, but which to the anointed eye are equally convincing and conclusive. For example, "Prepare ye the way of the Lord, make His paths straight" (Matt. 3:3). Neither Moses, any of the prophets, nor the apostles ever had an herald to go before and announce his coming. Again, though a landsman, we never read of Christ *following* His disciples as they boarded a ship: instead, we are told, "and when He was entered into a ship, His disciples followed Him" (Matt. 8:23 and cf. Mark 8:10, Luke 8:22)! Mark His "*your* (not "our") fathers did eat manna" (John 6:49) and contrast "all *our* fathers were under the cloud" (1 Cor. 10:1). How His divine glory shines forth in such an utterance as this, "he that loveth father or mother more than *Me* is not worthy of Me" (Matt. 10:37): no mere creature, no matter how exalted in the scale of being, could rightfully make such a claim as that.

"Kiss the Son lest He be angry, and ye perish from (or "in") the way, when His wrath is kindled but a little. Blessed are all they that put their *trust in Him*" (Psa. 2:12). Let the last clause of that verse be carefully weighed. How often Scripture forbids us to put our trust in *any* but GOD: "Put not your trust in princes, nor in the son of man, in whom is no help . . . Happy is he that hath the God of Jacob for his help, whose hope is in the Lord his God" (Psa. 145:3, 5). "Thus saith the Lord, Cursed is the man that trusteth in man . . . Blessed is the man that trusteth in the Lord" (Jer. 17:5, 7). If then God pronounces a curse on those who put their trust in a mere creature, and since He declares "blessed" they who put their trust in His Son, it is conclusively established that Christ is infinitely more than a creature, that He is in truth the Lord God Almighty.

The *claims* made by Christ manifest His absolute Deity. "The Son of man is Lord also of the sabbath" (Mark 2:28). There we hear Him affirming His personal and inherent authority over the law: we say "inherent," for God never delegated such authority to any creature. "Come unto Me, all ye that labour and are heavy laden, and I will give you rest" (Matt. 11:28). Who but the eternal God could truthfully say that! "He that hath seen Me, hath seen the Father" (John 14:9). Christ could never have said that unless He were of the *same* nature, essence and being as the Father: that this *was* what He here claimed, is clear from His next words, "Believest thou not that I am in the Father, and the Father in Me?"

It matters not what degree of *creature*-eminence be conceded to the Lord Jesus, if His absolute Deity be denied; for, after all, whatever be the difference and distance between the finite and Infinite, between the creature and the Self-existent One, must then exist between God and Christ. "If any one should ask now, with those in the Song of Solomon, What is in the Lord Jesus, our 'Beloved,' *more than* in any other 'beloveds' that should make Him so desirable and worthy of all acceptation? What is *He* more than others? I ask, what is a king more than a beggar? Much every way. Alas, this is nothing: they were born alike, must die alike, and after that is the judgment. What is an angel more than a worm? A worm is a creature, an angel is no more; He that made the one to creep in the

(Continued on Page 167)

STUDIES IN THE SCRIPTURES

"Search the Scriptures" John 5:39

Copyright in All English-speaking Countries

EDITOR: Arthur W. Pink, 559 Dupont Ave., York, Penna., U. S. A.
Hon. Agent in England: Mr. A. Winstone, "Shalom," Old Bath Road, Leckhampton, Cheltenham.
Hon. Agent in Australia: Mr. G. Ardill, The Christian Workers' Depot, Commonwealth and Reservoir Streets, Sydney.

THE CONDESCENSION OF CHRIST

For the sake of accuracy of thought a distinction should be drawn between the condescension and the humiliation of Christ, though the majority of writers have confounded them. This distinction is clearly made by the Holy Spirit in Phil. 2:7, 8: first, He "made Himself of no reputation"; second, He "humbled Himself." The condescension of God the Son consisted in His assumption of our nature, the Word becoming flesh. His humiliation lay in the consequent abasement and sufferings which He endured in our nature. The assumption of human nature was not, of itself, a part of Christ's humiliation, for He still retained it in His glorious exaltation. But for God the Son to take into union with Himself a created nature, animated dust, was an act of unparalelled and infinite condescension. May the Holy Spirit graciously awe us, and draw out our hearts in wonderment and worship, as we seek to reverently contemplate this holy mystery.

"Who, being in the form of God, thought it not robbery to be equal with God: But made Himself of no reputation, and took upon Him the form of a servant, and was made in the likeness of men: And being found in fashion as a man, He humbled Himself, and became obedient unto death, even the death of the cross. Wherefore God also hath highly exalted Him, and given Him a name which is above every name" (Phil. 2;6-9). These verses trace the path of the Mediator from highest glory to deepest humiliation, and back again to supremest honour. What a wondrous path was His! And how terrible that this Divine description of His path should have been made the battle-ground of theological contention. At few points has the awful depravity of man's heart been more horribly displayed than by the blasphemies which have been vented upon these verses. We shall not sully these pages by mentioning them, but proceed, as the Holy Spirit enables, to a positive exposition of them.

A glance at the context (Phil. 2:1-5) will at once show that the practical design of the apostle was to exhort Christians unto spiritual fellowship among themselves: to be likeminded, to love one another, to be humble and lowly, to esteem other better than themselves. To enforce this, the example of Christ Jesus our Lord is proposed in the verses we are now to consider. We are bidden to have in us the same mind that was in Him: the mind, spirit, habit, of self-abnegation, the mind of self-sacrifice, and of obedience to God. We must humble ourselves beneath the mighty hand of God, if we are to be exalted by Him in due time (1 Pet. 5:6). To set before us the example of Christ in its most vivid colours, in its most heart-affecting features, the Holy Spirit takes us back to the position which our Mediator occupied in a past eternity, shows us that supreme dignity and glory was His, and then reminds us of those unfathomable depths of condescension and humiliation into which He descended for our sakes.

"Who being in the form of God." First of all, this affirms the absolute Deity of the Son, for no mere creature, no matter how high in the scale of being, could ever be "in the form *of God."* Three words are used concerning the Son's relation to the Godhead. First, He subsists in the "form" of God: God is to be seen in Him alone. Second, He is "the *Image* of the invisible God" (Col. 1:15), which expression tells of His *manifestation* of God *unto us:* cf. 2 Cor. 4:6. Third, He is the "Bright-

(Continued on Page 192)

IMPORTANT NOTICES

Please advise promptly of change in address, otherwise copies will be lost in the mails.

We are glad to send a sample copy to any of your friends whom you believe would be interested in such a publication.

Send to Mr. I. C. Herendeen, Swengel (Union County), Penna., for a list of our publications. He has published many of our books and booklets.

This magazine is published as a work of faith and labour of love. The Editor and his wife gladly give their services. It is freely sent to all who will read it. No charge is made for it.

Christians who feel definitely led to do so, may have fellowship with us in this ministry. Those outside the U. S. A. please send only INTERNATIONAL Money Orders made out to York, Penna., U. S. A.

CONTENTS

The Condescension of Christ	169
The Epistle to the Hebrews	170
The Satisfaction ("Atonement") of Christ	176
Regeneration, or The New Birth	182
Sound the Alarm	186
Is Christ Your Lord?	189

THE EPISTLE TO THE HEBREWS

44. *The Great Sacrifice*: Heb. 9:23-28.

Our present passage is so exceeding full that it is expedient we should reduce our introductory remarks. Perhaps about all it is necessary to say is, that here in Hebrews the apostle is treating of the priestly ministry of Christ, and demonstrating the immeasurable superiority of His sacerdotal functions over those of the legal priests. In the verses which are now to be before us, the apostle makes a definite application of that which has been treated of in the preceding section. A contrast is now drawn between the types and their Antitype. Therein we are shown that inasmuch as the Great Sacrifice which Christ offered unto God was the substance of all the O. T. shadows, it was efficacious, allsufficient, final.

In 9:1-10 a declaration is made of sundry types and shadows of the law. In 9:11-28 a manifestation of the accomplishment of them is seen in the person and work of the Lord Jesus. In this second section we are shown the excellency of Christ's priesthood in the effecting of those things and the securing of those blessings which Aaron and his sacrificing of animals could not effect and secure. First, the affirmation is made that Christ has entered into the true tabernacle, Heaven itself; that He did so on the ground of His own infinitely meritorious blood, the value of which is evidenced by the fact that it has "obtained eternal redemption" (vv. 11, 12). Second, confirmation of this is then made: inasmuch as the blood of beasts purified the flesh, much more can the blood of Christ purge the conscience (vv. 13, 14). Moreover the Mediatorial office which Christ undertook guaranteed our salvation (v. 15). So too the validity of the covenant-testament insured the same (vv. 16, 17); as also the types pledged it (vv. 19-22).

In 9:23 (which properly belonged to our last section) the apostle concludes the main point he has been discussing, namely, that the typical things being purged with animal's blood, there must needs be a more excellent way of purifying and consecrating heavenly things, and that was by the precious blood of the incarnate Son of God Himself. Having established this fact, he now returns to the other points of difference between the legal priests and Christ. Those priests entered only an earthly tabernacle, but Christ has gone into Heaven itself (vv. 24, 25). The entrance of Israel's high priest into the holy of holies was repeated year by year, but Christ entered once for all (vv. 25, 26). This is confirmed by the fact that men die but once, still less could the God-man suffer death repeatedly (vv. 27, 28). Hence the blessed issue to all who rest upon the Great Sacrifice is, that He shall appear unto them "without sin unto salvation" (v. 28).

"Therefore (it was) necessary that the patterns of things in the heavens should be purified with these; but the heavenly things themselves with better sacrifices than these" (v. 23). The opening word denotes that a conclusion is now drawn from the premises just established, a conclusion which has respect unto *both* parts of the assertion made. In this verse the apostle brings to a head, or sums up, his previous argument concerning the typical purification of all things under the law, and the spiritual purification which has been effected by the sacrifice of Christ. "The general principle involved in these words is, plainly, that in expiation the victim must correspond in dignity to the nature of the offences expiated, and the value of the blessings secured. Animal blood might expiate ceremonial guilt and secure temporary blessings, but in order to the expiation of moral guilt and the attainment of eternal blessings, a nobler victim must bleed" (John Brown).

"Therefore necessary (it was)": the reference is both to the type and the Antitype. It was so from God's institution and appointment. There was nothing in the nature of the typical objects themselves which demanded a purgation by sacrifice, but, inasmuch as God designed to foreshadow heavenly things by them, it was requisite that they should be purged with blood. Likewise, inasmuch as God ordained that the heavenly things should be purified, it was necessary that a superior sacrifice should be made, for the typical offerings were altogether inadequate to such an end. Such "necessity" was relative, and not absolute, for God was never under any compulsion. His infinite wisdom deemed such a method fitting and suited to His glory and the good of His elect.

The "patterns" or "figures" (v. 24) were the things which the apostle had been treating of, namely, the covenant, the book, the people, the tabernacle and all its vessels of ministry. The "things in the heavens" were the everlasting covenant, the Church, and its redemption by Jesus Christ. The "heavenly things" had been designed in the mind of God in all their order, causes, beauty, and tendency unto His own glory, from all eternity; but they were "hid" in Himself (Eph. 3:8-10). Of these was God pleased to grant a typical resemblance, a shadowy similitude, an earthly adumbration, in the calling of Israel, His covenant with them, and the appointing of the tabernacle with its priesthood. By this means He deigned to instruct the early Church, and in their conformity to that typical order of things did their faith and obedience consist; the spiritual meaning of which the O. T. saints did, in measure, understand (Psa. 119:18).

"The heavenly things." "By heavenly things, I understand all the effects of the counsel of God in Christ, in the redemption, salvation, worship, and eternal glory of the Church; that is, Christ Himself in all His offices, with all the spiritual and eternal effects of them on the souls and consciences of men, with all the worship of God by Him according unto the Gospel. For of all these things, those of the law were the patterns. God did in and by them give a representation of all these things" (John Owen). More specifically Christ Himself and His sacrifice were typified by the legal rites. So also all the spiritual blessings which His mediation has secured are "heavenly things": see John 3:12, Eph. 1:3, Heb. 3:1. The Church too (Phil. 3:20) and Heaven itself as the abode of Christ and His redeemed are included (John 14:1-3). But here a difficulty presents itself: how could such objects as those be said to be "purified"?

Of all the things mentioned above not one of them is capable of real purification from uncleanness excepting the Church, that is, the souls and consciences of its members. Yet the difficulty is more seeming than real. The term "purification" has a twofold sense, namely, of external dedication unto God and internal purification, both of which are, generally included in the term "sanctification" as it is used in Scripture. Thus, the covenant, the book of the covenant, the tabernacle, and all its vessels were "purified" in the first sense, that is, solemnly dedicated unto God and His service. In like manner were all the "heavenly things" themselves "purified." Christ was consecrated, dedicated unto God in His own blood: John 17:19, Heb. 2:10 etc. Heaven itself was dedicated to be an habitation forever unto the mystical body of Christ, in perfect peace with the angels who never sinned: Eph. 1:10, Heb. 12:22-24.

Yet there was also an internal "purification of most of these "heavenly things." The souls and consciences of the members of the Church were *really* cleansed, purified and sanctified with an inward and spiritual purification: Eph. 5:25, 26, Titus 2:14. It has been "washed" in the blood of Christ (Rev. 1:5) and is thereby cleansed from all sin (1 John 1:7). And Heaven itself, was in some sense purified—as the tabernacle was, because of the sins of the people in whose midst it stood (Lev. 16:16). When the angels apostatised, sin entered Heaven itself, and therefore was not pure in the sight of God (*see* Job 15:15). And upon the sin of man, a breach was made, enmity ensued, between the holy angels above and fallen men below; so that Heaven was no meet place for an habitation unto them both, until they were reconciled, which was only accomplished in the sacrifice of Christ (Eph. 1:10, Col. 1:20).

One other detail needs to be considered: "But the heavenly things with better sacrifices." It is the use of the plural number here in connection with the sacrifice of Christ which has occasioned dificulty to some. It is a figure of speech known as an "enallage," the plural being put for the singular by way of *emphasis*. It is so expressed because the great sacrifice not only confirmed the signification, virtue, and benefits of all others, but exceeded in dignity, design and efficacy all others. Again; under the law there were five chief offerings appointed unto Israel: the burnt, the meal, the peace, the sin, the trespass (see Lev. 1-5), and in Christ's great Sacrifice we have the antitype of all five, and hence His has superseded theirs. Thus, the plural, "sacrifices" here emphasises the one offering of Christ, expresses its superlative excellency, and denotes that it provides the substance of the many shadows under the law.

If the reader will read straight on through Heb. 9:18-23 he will then be in a position to appreciate the lovely sequel which is recorded in Ex. 24:8-11. A most glorious type was that. There we have a scene for which there is nothing approaching a parallel on all the pages of inspiration until the incarnation of the Son of God be reached. What we have there in Ex. 24 might well be termed the O. T. Mount of Transfiguration. There we see not only Moses and Aaron, Nadab and Abihu, but also seventy "elders" (representatives of the people) in the very *presence of God*, perfectly at ease, eating and drinking there. The key-word to that marvelous incident is the "Then" at the beginning of v. 9, which brings out the inestimable value of the *blood* which had been sprinkled, and shows the grand privilege which it had procured, even making possible *communion* with God. The antitype of this is presented in Heb. 10:22.

"For Christ is not entered into the holy places made with hands, the figures of the true; but into heaven itself, now to appear in the presence of God for us" (v. 24). The opening "For" denotes that a further reason is being advanced to demonstrate the superiority of Christ's sacrifice over those which were offered under the law. In v. 23 this was shown by its power to "purify" *better objects* than the typical offerings could dedicate or cleanse. Here the proof is drawn from the *place* which Christ entered after He had offered Himself a sacrifice unto God, namely, into Heaven itself. That which was the peculiar dignity of the high priest of Israel, and wherein the principal discharge of his duty did consist, was that he entered that sacred abode where the typical and visible representation of the presence of God was made. The antitype of this is what is here before us.

"For Christ." The Mediator is again denominated by His official title. In addition to our notes thereon under v. 14, we may point out that this title "The Anointed" imports three things. First, the *offices* or functions which the Son of God undertook for the salvation of His people. These were three in number, and each was foreshadowed of old: the prophetic (1 Kings 19:16, Psa. 105:15), the priestly (Lev. 8:12, 30; Psa. 133:2), the kingly (1 Sam. 10:1, 16:13). Second, the *right* which He has to undertake those functions: He who "anointed" Christ was the Father (Acts. 10:38), thereby appointing and authorising Him (Heb. 5:5). Third, His *ability* to perform those functions whereunto He was anointed: therefore did He declare "the Spirit of the Lord is upon Me, *because* He hath *anointed* Me to preach" etc. (Luke 4:18). That expression "the Spirit of the Lord is upon Me" referred to that Divine enduement which had been conferred upon Him: cf. John 3:34.

"For Christ is not entered into the holy places made with hands, the figures of the true." The negative is first expressed in order to emphasise the contrast which follows. Three things are here said of the place in which Aaron and his successors ministered. First, with respect to its institution, it was the "holy of holies," and that, because it had been dedicated as the chamber where the special pledges of God's presence were given. Second, as to its fabric, though framed by Divine command, it was but of human workmanship, "made with hands." Third, as to its principal end or design, it was a resemblance or figure of heavenly things. From the Sept. translation of "holy of holies" by "the holy places," it seems that they used the plural number to supply the lack in the Greek language of a suitable superlative.

"But into Heaven itself." This entrance of Christ into the celestial Sanctuary is to be distinguished from His entering "once into the holy place" of v. 12. In our exposition of that verse we sought to show at some length that the reference there is to what took place immediately after the Saviour expired upon the cross, when, in fulfilment of the type of Lev. 16:14, He appeared before the Father to present to Him the memorial of His completed satisfaction. Aaron's entrance into the holy of holies was not for the purpose of making atonement—*that* was effected outside (Lev. 16:11)—but to *present* to God an atonement already accomplished. Nor could Aaron's passing within the veil, clad only in his "linen" garments (Lev. 16:4 and contrast Ex. 28:2—etc.), possibly be a figure of Christ's triumphant admission into heaven with all the jubilation belonging to a coronation day. We must constantly distinguish between Christ as the antitype of Aaron, and Christ as the antitype of Melchizedek. Aaron pointed to nothing after Christ's *resurrection;* Melchizedek did. The "once" of 9:12 emphasises the finality of Christ's sacrifice. His "entrance" here in 9:24 was for the purpose of intercession, which is *continuous*: 7:25.

The entrance of our royal High Priest into heaven was necessary for rendering His sacrifice effective in the *application* of the benefits of it to the Church. As J. Owen pointed out, the entrance of Christ into heaven on His ascension, may be considered two ways. "1. As it was *regal*, glorious and triumphant; so it belonged to His kingly office, as that wherein He triumphed over all the enemies of the Church: see it described in Eph. 4:8-10 from Psa. 68:18. Satan, the world, death and hell being conquered, and all power committed to Him, He entered triumphantly into heaven. So it was regal. 2. As it was *sacerdotal.* Peace and reconciliation being made by the blood of the cross, the covenant being confirmed, eternal redemption obtained, He entered as our High Priest into the holy place, the temple of God above, to make His sacrifice effectual to His Church, and to apply the benefits of it thereunto."

Christ entered Heaven as the great High Priest of His Church, as the Mediator of the new covenant, as the "Forerunner" of His people (6:20), as their "Advocate" (1 John 2:1), and the "Firstborn of many brethren." His design in so doing was "to appear in the presence of God for us." This He does "now," at the present season, and always. What the typical priest did was of no continuance. But this "now" is expressive of the whole season and duration of time from the entrance of Christ into heaven to the consummation of all things. Absolutely, His entrance into Heaven had other ends in view (John 17:5, Heb. 1:3 —"upholding" etc.), but to appear before God for His people as their High Priest, was the only end or object of His entering Heaven, considered *as* God's "Temple," where is the "throne of grace." How this manifests Christ's full assurance of the success of His undertaking, His complete discharge from all that guilt which had been imputed to Him. Had He not made a full end of our sins, He could not have appeared with confidence as our Surety in the presence of God!

"To appear in the presence of God for us." This is an act of His sacerdotal office. Not only *is* it our High Priest who doth so "appear," but He doth so *as* the High Priest of His Church. Nevertheless, it is such an act as necessarily implies the offering of Himself as a sacrifice for sin antecedent thereto, for it was *with* the blood of the atoning sacrifice that Aaron entered into the holy place (Lev. 16) as the head and representative of the people. In this appearance Christ presents Himself to God "as a lamb that had been slain" (Rev. 5:6)! It is *that* which gives validity and efficacy to His "appearing." The word "appear" is a forensic one, as of an Attorney before the Judge. He has gone there to seek from God and dispense to His people those blessings which He purchased for them. He has gone there to plead the infinite merits of His sacrifice, as a permanent reason why they should be saved: Rom. 8:34, Heb. 7:25. This supplies the great testimony to the continuance of Christ's love, care and compassion toward the Church: it is their interests which He promotes.

"Nor yet that He should offer Himself often, as the high priest entereth into the holy place every year with blood of others" (v. 25). In this verse the apostle doth two things: meets an objection which might be made, and continues to demonstrate the superior excellency of the Great Sacrifice. The objection could be framed thus: If Aaron's entrance into the holy of holies was a type of Christ's entering heaven, then must He, like the legal high priest, enter oft. This the apostle here denies. Such a conclusion by no means follows, in fact, is utterly erroneous. God did not require this from Christ, there was no need of it, and, as he shows in the next verse, it was impossible that He should.

Such is the absolute perfection of the one offering of Christ, that it stands in need of, that it will admit of, *no* repetition in any kind. Therefore does the apostle declare that if *it* be despised or neglected, "there remaineth no more sacrifice for sins" (10:26). This absolute perfection of the one offering of Christ arises from, first, the dignity of His person: Acts 20:28. It was the God-man who obeyed, suffered and died: nothing superior, nothing equal, could again be offered. Second, from the nature of the sacrifice itself. In the internal gracious workings of Christ, grace and obedience could never be more glorified than they had been by Immanuel Himself. So too, in the punishment He underwent: He suffered to the full, the whole curse of the law; hence, any further offering or atonement would be highly blasphemous. Third, from the love of the Father unto Him and delight in Him. In His one offering God was well pleased, and in it *He* rests. Hence the impossibility of any repetition —condensed from J. Owen.

"Nor yet that He should offer Himself often." In these positive and pointed words the Holy Spirit has plainly anticipated and repudiated the blasphemous practice of the Papists, who in their daily "mass" pretend to sacrifice Christ afresh, and by their "priests" present Him as an offering to God, claiming that the bread and wine are transubstantiated into the real flesh and blood of Christ. Therefore are they guilty of the unspeakably dreadful sin of crucifying *to themselves* the Son of God afresh, and putting Him to an open shame (Heb. 6:6), for by their pretended "real sacrifice of Christ" they, through their daily repetition of it, deny its sufficiency and finality (Heb. 10:2), degrading it below that of the annual atonement of Israel, which was made by the blood of beasts.

"As the high priest entereth into the holy place every year with blood of others." On these words W. Gouge beautifully pointed out that, "Herein we have an evidence of God's tender respect to man in sparing his blood. Though man were ordained a priest to typify Christ's priesthood, though man in that function were to appear before God, though he were to bear their names, yea, and their sins (Ex. 28:38), all of which Christ did, yet when it came to the shedding of his blood, as Christ did His, God spared him, and accepted the blood of beasts, as He accepted the ram for Isaac (Gen. 22:13). How this magnifies God's love to us, who was so tender of *man*, and yet spared not His own *Son* (Rom. 8:32)!"

"For then must He often have suffered since the foundation of the world: but now once in the end of the world hath He appeared to put away sin by the sacrifice of Himself" (v. 26). This verse consists of two parts. First, a reason is given confirming the assertion made in v. 25: had Christ been obliged to "offer Himself often" to God, then must He have "suffered' afresh "from the foundation of the world," that is, died afresh in each generation of human history. Second, a confirmation of that reason taken from the appointment of God: only once, and that in the fulness of time, did Christ come to earth to be a sacrifice for the sins of His people. Thus the apostle exposes the gross absurdity of the objection he met in v. 25: to admit that, would be to say Christ's blood had no more efficacy than that which the Jewish high priest offered.

The force of the apostle's argument rests upon two evident suppositions. First, that the "offering" (v. 25) and "suffering" (v. 26) of Christ are inseparable. It was in and by His suffering that the Lord Jesus offered Himself unto God, and that because He was Himself both the Priest and the Sacrifice. Aaron "offered" repeatedly, yet he never once "suffered," for *he* was not the sacrifice itself. It was the bullock which was slain, that suffered. But Christ being both Priest and Sacrifice could not "offer" without "suffering," and herein does the force of the argument principally consist. The very especial nature of Christ's offering or sacrifice, which was by the shedding of His blood in death, precluded a repetition thereof.

Second, the apostle's argument here is also built on the fact that there *was* a necessity for the expiation of the sin of all that were to be saved from the foundation of the world. Sin entered the world immediately after it was founded, by the apostasy of our first parents. Notwithstanding, numbers of sinners, as Abel, Enoch, Noah, Abraham and the spiritual remnant in Israel had their sins pardoned and were eternally saved; yet no sacrifice which they offered could remit moral guilt or redeem their souls. No; *their* salvation was also effected by virtue of the sacrifice of Christ. Hence it follows unavoidably that unless the merits of His own one offering extended unto the taking away of all their sins, then either He must have suffered often, or they perish. Contrariwise, seeing that elect sinners *were* saved through Christ "from the foundation of the world," much more will the virtues of the Great Sacrifice extend unto the end of the world.

"But now," not at the beginning of human history; "once," that is, once for all, never to be repeated; "in the end of the world," or in "the fullness of time" (Gal. 4:4). This expression "end of the world" or more literally, "consummation of the ages" is here used antithetically from "since the foundation of the world" which usually has reference to the first entrance of sin into the world, and God's dispensation of grace in Christ thereon; as "before the foundation of the world" (Eph. 1:4 etc.) expresses eternity and God's counsels therein. The Divine distinctions of time with respect to God's grace toward His Church, may be referred to three general heads: that before the law, during the law, and since the incarnation of Christ unto the end of the world. This last season, absolutely considered, is called the "fulness of times" (Eph. 1:10), when all that God had designed in the dispensation of His grace was come to a head, and wherein no alteration should be made till the earth was no more.

"Hath He appeared to put away sin by the sacrifice of Himself." He "appeared" here on earth (the Greek word is quite different from the one used in v. 24): of old He had been obscurely shadowed forth in types, but now He was *"manifest* in flesh" (1 Tim. 3:16). The end or purpose of this appearing of Christ was to "put away sin"—the Greek word is a very strong one, and is rendered "disannuling" in 7:18. Let it be carefully noted that this declaration is made only as it respects the Church of Christ. He made a complete atonement for all the sin of all His people, receiving its wages, expiating its guilt, destroying its dominion. The results are that, when God *applies* to the penitent believer the virtues of Christ's sacrifice, all condemnation is removed (Rom. 8:1), and its reigning power is destroyed (Rom. 6:14).

"And as it is appointed unto men once to die, but after this the judgment: so Christ was once offered to bear the sins of many; and unto them that look for Him shall He appear the second time without sin unto salvation" (vv. 27, 28). In these verses the apostle concludes his exposition of the causes, nature, designs and efficacy of the sacrifice of Christ, wherewith the new covenant was dedicated and confirmed. In them a three-fold confirmation is made of the uniqueness and sufficiency of the Saviour's atonement. First, a comparison is drawn: pointed by the "as" and "so." Second, a declaration is made as to why Christ died: it was to "bear the sins of many." Third, the resultant consequence of this is stated at the end of v. 28.

First, the comparison. This is between the death of men by the decretory sentence of God, and the offering of Christ by God's appointment. "It is appointed unto men once to die." That "appointment" was a *penal* one, being the sentence and curse of the broken law (Gen. 2:19), consisting of two parts: temporal death and eternal judgment. Death is not the result of chance, nor is it a "debt of nature," a condition to which man was made subject by the law of his creation. Death is something more than the result of physiological law: the same God who sustained Methusalah for wellnigh a thousand years, would have sustained Adam's body for all eternity had he never fallen. Sinless angels are immortal. Death is the wages of *sin* (Rom. 6:23). The cases of Enoch and Elijah, Lazarus and that generation of believers alive on earth at the return of Christ (1 Cor. 15:51), are only exceptions to the common rule, by mere acts of Divine sovereignty.

"After this the judgment." This, by the same Divine, unalterable constitution, is also "appointed" unto all: Acts 17:31. Death does not make an end of man, but is subservient to something else, which is equally certain and inevitable in its own season. As death leaves men, so shall judgment find them. This "judgment" is here opposed to the "salvation" of believers at the second appearing of Christ. It is the judgment of the wicked at the last great day: Rom. 2:5. It will be the executing upon them of the condemnatory sentence of the law, the irrevocable curse of God—eternal banishment from Him, for indescribable and eternal torments to be inflicted upon them.

"So Christ was once offered." As the death-sentence, as a penal infliction, was passed upon all of Adam's descendants (Rom. 5:12) viewed as criminals, as having broken the law in the person of their federal head, *so* Christ was "appointed" or sentenced by God, the Judge of all, to undergo the curse of the law, on the behalf and in the stead of those whom He represented.

"So Christ was once offered to bear the sin of many." Here we see that deliverance from the curse which the wisdom and grace of God provided for His elect. The Anointed One, *as* the High Priest of His people, presented to God an all-sufficient and final satisfaction for all the sins of all who have been, from eternity, given to Him by the Father. Thus vv. 27, 28 present the antithesis of the Law and the Gospel, as it relates to "men" indefinitely, and to the "many" specifically. The sins of many He "bare"—had imputed to Him, received the punishment of, and fully expiated—in His own body on the tree (1 Pet. 2:24).

"And unto them that look for Him shall He appear the second time without sin unto salvation." This needs to be interpreted in harmony with its context, and as furnishing the antitype of what is found in Lev. 16. The word for "appear" here is not the one commonly used for the return of Christ—it means "to be seen." When Aaron disappeared within the veil, the people waited with eager expectation until he came out again to bless them. So Christ, having made atonement, and gone into heaven, shall yet re-appear and be seen by those who wait for Him. As men after death, must yet appear the "second time" in their body, to undergo condemnation therein; so Christ shall appear the second time, to bestow on God's elect eternal salvation.

"Unto them that look for Him:" that is, all the redeemed, the "many" whose sins He bore. Though the vision tarry, they wait for it (Heb. 2:3). Five things are included in this word "look for." First, the steadfast faith *of* His appearing, resting with implicit confidence on His promise in John 14:2, 3. Second, a real love unto it: 2 Tim. 4:8. Third, an ardent longing after it, so that they cry, "Even so, come, Lord Jesus" (Rev. 22:20). Fourth, a patient waiting for it, in the midst of many discouragements: James 5:7, 8. Fifth, a personal preparation for it: Matt. 25:10, Luke 12:35-37.

"Without (imputed) sin, unto salvation." Hereby Christ's second advent is contrasted from His first. When He appeared the first time, it was *with* "sin" upon Him (John 1:29) as the Surety of sinners. Therefore was He the Man of sorrows, and afflicted from His youth up (Psa. 88:15). But He will re-appear in a very different state: as the Conqueror of sin and Satan, the Saviour of His people, the King of kings and Lord of lords. At His return, the efficacy of His once-for-all offering will be openly manifested. The question of His peoples' sins having been finally settled at the cross, He will then *glorify* His redeemed. "For our conversation is in heaven: from whence also we look for the Saviour, the Lord Jesus Christ: Who shall change our vile body, that it may be fashioned like unto His glorious body, according to the working whereby He is able even to subdue all things unto Himself" (Phil. 3:20, 21).

A. W. P.

THE SATISFACTION
("Atonement")
OF CHRIST

20. *Its Extent*.

That aspect of our subject which is now before us has been a very vexed question among theologians, especially so during the last century, for Christ's death for God's people only was never denied till the basic truth of Election was rejected; and that rejection only became common about one hundred and fifty years ago. Were it not so vitally important that we should be quite clear about this branch of our theme, we should avoid the discussion of it as too controversial. But inasmuch as the extent of the Atonement depends upon its *nature*, and directly concerns the honour of God and the glory of His Son, we feel called upon to give our best attention to the same.

In our last article we endeavoured to present some of the evidence which proves that the atonement of Christ was a *real* one, a *definite* one, an *efficacious* one, that whatsoever it was designed to effect must be accomplished. Appeal too was made to some of those Scriptures which expressly make known *for whom* Christ died, namely, His "Church," His "people," the "sheep." Yet clear and plain, full and frequent, as are the declarations of Holy Writ concerning the purpose and design of God in the death of Christ, so that he who runs ought to be able to read, yet, scarcely any truth of Scripture is now more frequently called into question than is this one. A theory diametrically opposed thereto has been advanced by the enemies of the Truth, and, sad to say, is now being promulgated by many who imagine they are the friends of Christ—as to whether or not they are, God alone can infallibly determine.

On practically every side where there is any pretense of honouring Christ to-day, it is taught that the love of God extends to all mankind, that Christ gave Himself a ransom for the whole human race, and that the Holy Spirit is now seeking to woo and win every sinner to Him. So uniform has this preaching become, so fervently has it been advocated, so widely has it been accepted, that for any one to affirm the contrary, is to be looked upon as a setter forth of "novelties," and for him to *press* the same, is to invite his being denounced as a narrow-minded and harsh-hearted bigot, a hyper-Calvinist, a heretic of the worst sort. Yet such an one can always console himself with, "If I yet pleased men, I should not be the servant of Christ" (Gal. 1:10).

Ere we turn and examine those passages which are appealed to by those who proclaim a universal redemption, three things should be carefully considered. First, since all of Adam's race are not pardoned and saved, and never will be, then Christ cannot have made an atonement for their sins: this was shown at length in our last. Second, the Holy Scriptures cannot contradict themselves. Being the inspired Word of God, there cannot be any inconsistencies in them: they cannot teach that Christ died for God's elect only, and also affirm that He died for all mankind as well: one or the other is an erroneous deduction which men have drawn from them. Third, seeing they explicitly teach the former, then there must be some honest and legitimate way of interpreting those passages which may, at first glance, seem to teach the latter.

Now the Word of God does not yield up its meaning to lazy people. Salvation is free; but "Truth" has to be "bought" (Prov. 23:23); yet few indeed are willing to pay its stipulated price. Not only do the Scriptures have to be "searched" (John 5:39), and searched "daily" (Acts 17:11); not only does passage have to be carefully compared with passage (1 Cor. 2:13); not only must all this be done in meekness (Psa. 25:9) and complete dependency upon God (Prov. 3:6); but there must also be a fervent crying "after knowledge" and an importunate "lifting up of the voice for understanding," and seeking her "as silver" (which entails hard labour and diligent perseverance), yea, a searching for her as for "hid treasure" (Prov. 2:1-5).

It is at the above point that so many have failed. The meaning of God's Word cannot be ascertained as easily as can that of a newspaper article, nor can any enter into the "*mystery* of the Gospel" (Eph. 6:19) as readily as one may solve a problem in mathematics. If a person approaches Holy Writ with prejudice, his mind is closed against *its* teachings. If he regards any passage as plain and simple and is satisfied that he already understands it, he is not likely to cry unto God for or receive light from it. If he assumes that he is now in possession of practically all that the Bible teaches on a subject (contrary to 1 Cor. 8:2), or blindly follows some man unto whom he credits the same thing, then God will take the wise in their own craftiness (1 Cor. 3:19) and suffer them to remain in darkness. It is because of this that so many are misled by the mere *sound* of certain words.

Our last statement has received many a solemn illustration. Take the controversy which has been waged in certain quarters as to whether or no man remains in a state of consciousness after he passes out of this world. How many who deny that he *does* so, have appealed to such passages as "the dead praise not the Lord" (Psa. 115:17), "the dead know not any thing" (Eccl. 9:5). But the matter cannot be settled so easily. Those passages must be studied in the light of their contexts, the dispensation under which they were given, and then interpreted in harmony with other passages of a different, but not conflicting, nature. Take again the great controversy between the Reformers on transubstantiation: how easy it was to be deceived by the mere *sound* of those words, "This *is* My body!" The same principle applies to our present subject. The issue raised between Calvinists and Arminians cannot be settled by an appeal to such words as "God so loved *the world*" and Christ "died for *all*" (2 Cor. 5:15). Such expressions need to be *studied* and interpreted in keeping with the Analogy of Faith.

Incalculable damage has been wrought by unequipped men undertaking to preach the "simple (?) Gospel" and expound the Holy Scriptures. There has been a zeal which was not proportioned with spiritual knowledge. Men with the merest smattering of Scripture consider themselves qualified to pass judgment on the teachings and writings of those who have devoted a lifetime to the continuous and concentrated study of God's Word. To a multitude of evangelists and preachers of today, we would say, "O that ye would altogether hold your peace! and it should be your wisdom" (Job 13:5). Rightly has it been said, "Modern theology is largely based upon the sound rather than the sense of Scripture. And it is an every-day practice for men to expound texts who cannot even quote—much less expound—the contexts" (J. M. Sangar). "Not a novice" (1 Tim. 3:6) has been deliberately ignored, and "Be not many of you teachers" (James 3:1. R. V.) has been defiantly disobeyed.

When men say that God has provided an atonement which is designed for all mankind, they need to be asked, Do you mean that Christ's sacrifice procured for all sinners that quickening grace of the Holy Spirit which is indispensably needed to bring men to a cordial and saving reception of the atonement? Do you mean that an atonement has been made by Christ so as to infallibly secure that all shall be saved by it? If so, be honest, and declare yourself a "Universalist." But if you do not mean this, then cease using *empty* words which can only deceive souls and dishonour Christ. The real issue between Calvinists and Arminians is not so much upon the scope of the atonement, as it is upon the *efficacy* of it!

Let us now briefly set forth that position which is popularly maintained in these degenerate times. We are told that there is such a *fulness* in the atonement, that the value of Christ's sacrifice is *sufficient* for the salvation of the entire race, were all men to believe in Him. But this means that the sufficiency of the atonement is a *conditional* one—conditional upon the whole world believing. But that "condition" is not so easily performed. Almost all preachers today speak of faith in Christ as a comparatively easy matter, but the Scriptures teach quite otherwise: *see* Matt. 19:25, 26; John 5:44, 6:44; Eph. 1:19; 1 Pet. 4:18. The Word of God represents the fallen children of Adam as being spiritually bound with chains, shut up in death, securely held in prison, so that nothing short of a *miracle* of grace, the putting forth of Divine omnipotence can free them. In his masterly treatise on "Particular Redemption" W. Rushton (1831) illustrated this *conditional* sufficiency of the atonement thus:

"A wealthy and philanthropic individual visits Algiers and approaches a dungeon in which a wretched captive lies bound with chains and fetters, and strongly secured within walls and doors and bars. He proclaims aloud to the captive that he has brought gold *sufficient* for a ransom, on condition that the captive will liberate himself from his chains, burst open his prison doors and come forth. Alas, exclaims the wretched man, your kindness *does not reach* my case. Unless your gold can *effect* my deliverance, it can be of no service to me. To *offer* it on *such* terms can do me no good. Now man by nature is *spiritually* as unable to believe in Christ, as the Algerian captive is *physically* unable to break his chains and the prison doors; so that all this boasted sufficiency of the atonement is only an empty offer of salvation on certain terms and conditions; and *such* an atonement would be much too weak to meet the desperate case of a *lost* sinner.

"But how different is *the salvation of God!* 'By the blood of Thy covenant, I have *sent forth* Thy prisoners out of the pit wherein is no water' (Zech. 9:11). The Lord Jesus, by His death, hath paid the ransom, and made the captives His own. Therefore He has a *legal right to* their persons, and with His own right arm He brings them forth. It is His glory 'to *bring out* the prisoners from the prison, and them that sit in darkness *out of* the prison house' (Isa. 42:6, 7)." Yes, Scripture affirms that "He *sent* (not 'offered!') redemption unto His people" (Psa. 111:9).

Turning now to the principal passages which Arminians appeal to, let us begin with John 3:16: "For God so loved the world that He gave His only begotten Son" etc. To a superficial mind this declaration appears to settle the controversy once for all. We do not use that term "superficial" in any invidious sense, but common honesty will not allow us to substitute another for it. Anyone who has examined a concordance and looked up the passages where "world" occurs, soon discovered that this word is used in the N. T. in quite a number of ways and with widely different latitudes, so that nothing can be determined for certain by the occurrence of this term in John 3:16. Sometimes the "world" signifies the unbelieving as in John 15:18, at others it includes none but believers as in Rom. 11:12, etc. Sometimes the "world" denotes a material system, created by Christ (John 1:10), at others it is applied to a mere handful of people as in John 7:4 and 12:19. In the great majority of instances it is a general and indefinite expression which has reference to *the Gentiles* in contradistinction from Israel after the flesh.

Now it is a fundamental and unvarying rule of interpretation that both definite and indefinite phrases or terms must be understood and defined in strict accordance with *the subject* about which they are employed. So it is with John 3:16. The subject of that verse is *the love of God*, to which the indefinite expressions "World" and "whosoever" are joined. Therefore, if we would discover to a certainty *who* are the objects of God's love, we have to diligently compare and examine other passages where the love of God is mentioned. Then we learn that His love is *eternal*: Jer. 31:3, Eph. 1:4, 5. That it is *uninfluenced*. Nothing in its object calls it into exercise, prompts or attracts it (Deut. 7:7, 8): it proceeds simply from the spontaneous will of God. It is *immutable* or unchanging (Song of Sol. 8:6, 7). Those whom God loves, He loves forever (John 13:1), *nothing* can ever separate from it, nothing can ever cause God to cease loving those on whom He set His love (Rom. 8:35-38). It is *sovereign* (Rom. 9:13): there was no more cause in Jacob why *he* should be the object of the Divine love, than there was in Esau.

The love of God is known by its *manifested effects*. There is an infallible connection (as there is between cause and effect) between the *love* of God and His *ordination* of its objects to life and salvation: hence we read, "We are bound to give thanks always to God for you brethren, *beloved of the Lord*, because God hath from the beginning *chosen you to salvation*" (2 Thess. 2:13). So also, those whom God loves, He regenerates. "Behold, what manner of *love* the Father hath bestowed upon us, that we should be called the *sons* of God" (1 John 3:1)—making them "sons" is the certain effect of His having loved them from all eternity. Those whom God loves, He "draws" to Himself (Jer. 31:3). Those whom God loves, He "chastens" (disciplines) so that they become actual *"partakers* of His holiness" (Heb. 12:6, 10). It therefore follows that those who are *not* made His "sons," who are not made "partakers of His holiness," were never the objects of His love.

The same love of God which was the cause of sending Christ to die for the salvation of His people, is *also* the same cause which "freely gives" all things *with* Christ (Rom. 8:32), i.e., the Spirit to regenerate, faith to receive Him, love to be devoted to Him: compare 2 Pet. 1:3. Were it otherwise, God's love would be incomplete, inadequate, deficient, unefficacious. God's love for me would be vain, if it did not actually save me, deliver me, and win my heart to Him. John 3:16 simply states the *design* of God's love, and that is, that all who *believe* in Christ should be saved by Him, which believers, in their unbelieving state, are found "scattered abroad" (John 11:52) throughout the earth, among the Gentiles as well as the Jews.

The popular interpretation of John 3:16 is repudiated by all the *facts* of history. First, take the history of the human race *before* Christ was born. Unnumbered millions lived and died *"without* God and without hope" (Psa. 9:17). If God, "loved" them, where is the least evidence of it? He "suffered all nations to walk in *their own* ways" (Acts 14:16). He "gave them over to a reprobate mind" (Rom. 1:28). He announced to Israel "you *only* have I known of all the families of the earth" (Amos 3:2). Second, take the history of the race *since* Christ was born. Remember the "dark ages" which lasted not for a few days, but for a thousand years, when the Papacy dominated almost all Christendom and the Bible was withheld from the peoples. And since the great Reformation, what untold millions have died in heathendom without ever hearing of Christ! It would be inexplicably strange if God should "love" multitudes to whom He never so much as *signified* His love—leaving them in entire ignorance of the Son of His love! Third, take the coming Day of Judgment. To whom will God's *love* then be exercised?

To sum up our comments on John 3:16. We understand "the world" here to mean men of *all nations*, with an especial reference to the Gentiles, whom Nicodemus (as all Jews) considered to be accursed. To those who reject this explanation, and say, We keep by the plain declaration "God so loved the world," we ask them to apply the same principle to the following passages: "on *the Gentiles* also was poured out the gift of the Holy Spirit" (Acts 10:45), "God also *to the Gentiles* granted repentance unto life" (Acts 11:18), "declaring the conversion of *the Gentiles*" (Acts 15:3). Is that expression "the Gentiles" in these passages a general and indefinite one, or a universal and specific one? is it a relative or an absolute one? That is, does it take in *all*, or refer only to *some?* Acts 15:14 answers the question: "God has visited the Gentiles to *take out of them* a people for His name!"

2 Pet. 3:9. The last clause of this verse is frequently quoted, but without any attention being given to the first part of it. Is that honest? The *"any"* whom the Lord is "not willing" should perish, is clearly defined: v. 8 shows that it is God's "beloved" who are here addressed and referred to. The "promise" which He is *"not* slack" in fulfilling, has reference to the return of Christ (v. 4), which "scoffers" (v. 3) suppose will never be fulfilled. The great reason why God has not yet sent back His Son is because the last of His elect have not been regenerated: all of *them* shall come to repentance before human history can be wound up and v. 10 fulfilled. Thus, the "any" looks back to the "us-ward" in the previous part of the verse!

"Behold the Lamb of God, which taketh away the sin of the world" (John 1:29). John the Baptist was the herald of a new dispensation. One of the leading distinctions between the Old and N. T. dispensations was with regard to its *scope*. The former was greatly restricted, being, for two thousand years, almost exclusively confined to a single nation; and to that limitation the members of the Church had become thoroughly accustomed. But the new dispensation possessed an opposite character. At the cross, the "middle wall of partition," by which the Jews were kept separate from all other nations, was broken down, so that henceforth there should be no difference between Jew and Gentile, bond and free. But the previous regime had given rise to a deeply-seated prejudice in favour of exclusive privilege, which it was no easy matter to uproot.

Although the Saviour had manifested a regard for a Roman centurion, a woman of Canaan, and had even plainly declared "other sheep I have which are not of this fold" (John 10:16), still the exclusive sentiment retained a firm hold even upon the minds of His disciples. They were Jews, and were manifestly reluctant to descend to a common level with others, in regard to the enjoyment of religious privilege. Clear proof of this is seen in the case of Peter (Acts 10:14): God had to work a miracle before he was willing to preach the Gospel to Cornelius. The jealous antipathy of the Jews comes out even more noticeably in 1 Thess. 2:15, 16. This one consideration accounts for and throws much light upon the use of terms of an *extensive* import when speaking of the *new* economy. To mark the contrast from Judaism, the strongest language that could be used became necessary: hence the employment of "the world" and "all men" to denote men in general without regard to national distinction.

From what has been said above, it is not to be surmised that the Holy Spirit moved men to employ language which was *not* strictly true or accurate. Far from it. Nothing is more common, either in the writings of men or in the Word of God, to use a *general* designation when it is intended to express a general principle, but which does *not* include *every* individual comprehended in the general designation employed. When we read that a certain city is smitten with a small-pox epidemic, no one concludes that *every* individual in it has contracted that disease. So when we read in Ex. 9:6 that *"all* the cattle of Egypt died," we must not take those words absolutely, as Ex. 9:9, 19, 25 plainly show.

A critical examination of the terms of John 1:29 obliges us to take into account the undeniable fact that a very considerable portion of the human race was already in hell when the Son of God became incarnate. This one consideration is sufficient to show that we are *compelled* to understand that the "world" here is far less extensive in its scope than the whole human family. Again, that Christ *did not* "take away the sin of," bear the guilt of, suffer for, the iniquities of all alive on earth in His own day, is abundantly clear from His own words to the Pharisees, "Ye shall die in your sins" (John 8:24 and cf. 9:41). The best commentary upon John 1:29 is the song of the redeemed, "Thou wast slain, and hast redeemed us to God by Thy blood *out of every* kindred, and tongue, and people, and nation" (Rev. 5:9)!

"Who gave Himself a ransom for all, to be testified in due time" (1 Tim. 2:6). What has been said above concerning the signification of the term "world" when used in connection with the objects of God's love or the subjects of Christ's redemption, applies with equal force and pertinancy to the word "all." That Christ gave Himself a ransom for "all" *without distinction* of nationality, social status, age or sex, is blessedly true; but to say that He died in the stead of "all" *without exception* cannot be maintained without involving the most palpable absurdities and contradictions. Nor is there anything elsewhere in Scripture which *obliges* us to give to "all" in this and similar verses an absolute and unlimited meaning.

The word "all" is employed in Scripture with considerable latitude and variety of meaning; very rarely indeed is it used without limitation. Mark 1:5 says that, "*all* the land of Judea and they of Jerusalem were all baptised" of John, yet Luke 7:30 shows the Pharisees and lawyers were "not baptised of him." When the Saviour told His disciples that "ye shall be hated of *all* men for My name's sake" (Matt. 10:22), it is obvious that those who believed on Him must be excluded. When we read that "*all* men came unto" Christ (John 3:26), we can only understand that many of the Jews attended upon His ministry. When Christ declared He would "draw all unto" Himself (John 12:32), He had in mind the "all that the Father giveth Me" of John 6:37. So here in 1 Tim. 2:6 the "ransom for all" is defined by the "ransom for many" of Matt. 20:28. The "all" of 1 Tim. 2:4 and 6 is simply emphasising the *contrast from* the Jewish nation only.

1 John 2:2. Here again many have been deceived by the mere sound of terms. The very first word of this verse shows that Christ is the "propitiation" of those *only* for whom He is an "Advocate with the Father" and John 17:9 proves that He prays for none but the elect. Again, if the closing words of this verse expressed an unlimited universality, then the previous clause would be quite superfluous: if the "whole world" takes in all the race, then it would be meaningless to say that Christ is the propitiation "for *our* sins" and *also* for every body's—the "our" would be included. Instead, the "our" refers to *Jewish* Christians, for John was an apostle to the "circumcision" (Gal. 2:9) and his epistle was written (first) to such (see 2:7); the "whole world" signifies God's elect scattered among the Gentiles. Rom. 3:25 shows that Christ's "propitiation" is *limited to* those who put their faith in it.

Scripture always interprets Scripture: if the reader really desires to know the meaning of 1 John 2:2 let him compare John 11:51, 52 and 17:20, carefully noting the "also." That this expression the "whole world" is *not* an unlimited one, is clear from the last clause of Rev. 13:3, compared with Rev. 20:4; or Rev. 12:9 with Matt. 24:24. To affirm that Christ shed His blood for the sins of all mankind, is to be guilty of charging Him with rebellion against the sovereign will of God. But how far from the truth is such a concept! "Every part of our Lord's conduct on earth was an act of *obedience to* the Father's will (John 6:38). How then could He lay down His life for any but those who were given Him of the Father to be redeemed from among men? Had He laid down His life for all mankind, He would have *gone beyond* His commission" (James Haldane).

It remains to be pointed out that there is a (relative) universality to Christ's sacrifice in three respects. First, in *time*: its efficacy was not limited to one generation or dispensation. Being "foreordained before the foundation of the world" (1 Pet. 1:20), His merits extended to *all* believers from Abel onwards. Second, in *place*: the efficacy of Christ's death was not to be limited to any one nation: Rev. 5:9. Third, in *virtue*: "The blood of Jesus Christ His Son cleanseth us from *all* sin" (1 John 1:7). Christ's sacrifice made atonement for Noah's drunkenness, Lot's incest, David's murder, Peter's denial, Paul's persecution of the Church. In *these* three respects there is *no* limitation to His sacrifice.

Luke 19:41-44. Christ's weeping over Jerusalem is often regarded as His lamentation over lost sinners. Such was not the case. Verses 43, 44 show plainly that He had before Him the destruction of the city. As He foresaw the awful siege and contemplated the unparalelled temporal calamities, He was deeply moved. As a nation, the doom of the Jews was sealed: the things belonging to their civic peace were now hid from their eyes. But so far from their spiritual state being hopeless, or Christ bewailing *that*, He knew full well that in a few weeks at most thousands of them would believe to the saving of their souls!

Space will only allow us to notice briefly a few more texts. The "all men" of Rom. 5:18 is explained by 1 Cor. 15:22. 1 Cor. 8:11 asks a question, not states a fact: it warns against the evil *tendency* of uncharitable conduct. The "all" for whom Christ died (2 Cor. 5:15) are in that same verse said to "live unto . . . Him which died for them." The "world" of 2 Cor. 5:19 are those unto whom God is "not imputing their trespasses," and that is certainly *not* the "world of the ungodly" (2 Pet. 2:5). The "living God" of 1 Tim. 4:10 is the Father (see Matt. 16:16) and "Saviour" there means Preserver—in a temporal way. Christ "Tasted death for every" (Heb. 2:9): there is *no* word for "man" in the Greek, and the next verse shows it is "every" *son*. That some whom the Lord "bought" (2 Pet. 2:1) shall be damned, presents no difficulty: He *bought* "the field" Matt. 13: 43, 44), but "redeemed" only His people; as Man (Acts 17:31) He has acquired the *right* to judge and dispose of all.

To reason as some have done from the second half of Heb. 9:26 that Christ made atonement for no man's sins in particular, but only for sin in general, is really too purile for serious consideration. Yet this is what is being taught in many places today. The cross is looked upon as little more than an honouring of the moral government of God, a satisfying of His justice abstractly considered. Such a theory involves this absurdity: that Christ died not for *sinners*, but for *sin*. Sufficient to point out in refutation that "sin" has no existence apart from *sinners!* Sin is not a mere non-entity, or metaphysical abstraction, but a moral quality, which like all other moral qualities, necessarily supposes a moral agent to which it belongs. Separate sin from sinners and it ceases to be. Surely the Son of God died for something else than a mere abstraction!

To say that in the atonement of Christ God has laid a sufficient and suitable basis for the salvation of all men, *if so be* they would avail themselves of it, may sound very plausible, yet is it, in reality, meaningless jargon. Such an assertion ignores the eternal and sovereign *election* of the Father. It *dissevers* the work of the Spirit from the work of Christ. It repudiates the *lost* condition of men. While professing to widen the extent of the atonement, it compromises its reality and efficacy. To say that everything turns on the sinner's acceptance, is to affirm that Christ did nothing more for those who are saved than He did for those who are lost. It is not faith which gives Divine efficacy to the blood; it was the blood which efficaciously purchased faith. To make the eternal salvation of sinners turn upon an act of their own wills, would not only be leaving the success of the redemptive work of Christ, contingent upon the fickle caprice of men, but would allow them to divide the honours with Christ!

To talk of God's "offering assistance to sinners" while He leaves them in a state of *un*-regeneracy, is the veriest trifling. To say that Christ died for all the sins of all who hear the Gospel, and that the *only* thing which can now damn them is their unbelief, is to fly in the face of Eph. 5:5, 6 etc. Moreover, such a statement is, really, a contradiction in terms. Either their unbelief is a *sin*, or it is not. If *not*, then why are they punished for it? If it *be*, then, according to their own affirmation, Christ atoned for it, and there is nothing more in their unbelief than there is in their other sins to hinder them from partaking of the fruits of Christ's sacrifice. Let such silly triflers choose which horn of the dilemma they please.

Seeing that Christ died for the elect only, *how* is the Gospel to be preached to sinners indiscriminately? This question will be carefully considered and answered at length (D. V.) in the Oct. issue.
—A. W. P.

REGENERATION, or THE NEW BIRTH

Regeneration is that which alone fits a fallen creature to fulfil his one great and chief duty, namely, to glorify his Maker. This is to be the aim and end in view in all that we do: "Whether therefore ye eat, or drink, or whatsoever ye do, do all to the glory of God" (1 Cor. 10:31). It is the motive actuating us and the purpose before us which gives value to each action: "When thine eye (figure of the soul looking outward) is single (having only one object in view —the glory of God), the whole body is full of light; but when thine eye is evil, the body is full of darkness" (Luke 11: 34). If the intention be evil, as it certainly is when the glory of God is not before us, there is nothing but "darkness," *sin*, in the whole service.

Now fallen man has altogether departed from what ought to be his chief end, aim, or object, for instead of having before him the honour of God, *himself* is his chief concern; and instead of seeking to please God in all things, he lives only to please himself or his fellow-creatures. Even when, through religious training, the claims of God have been brought to his notice and pressed upon his attention, at best he only parcels out one part of his time, strength and substance to the One who gave him being and daily loadeth him with benefits, and another part for himself and the world. The natural man is utterly incapable of giving supreme respect unto God, until he becomes the recipient of a spiritual life. None will truly aim at the glory of God until they have an affection for Him, none will honour Him supremely whom they do not supremely love. And for this, the love of God must be shed abroad in the heart by the Holy Spirit (Rom. 5-5), and this only takes place at regeneration. Then it is, and not till then, that self is dethroned and God is enthroned; then it is that the renewed creature is enabled to comply with God's imperative call, "My Son, give *Me* thine heart" (Prov. 23:26).

The salient elements which comprise the *nature* of regeneration may, perhaps, be summed up in these three words: impartation, renovation, subjugation. God *communicates* something to the one who is born again, namely, a principle of faith and obedience, a holy nature, eternal life. This though real, palpable, and potent, is nothing material or tangible, nothing added to our essence, substance or person. Again; God *renews* every fac-faculty of the soul and spirit of the one born again, not perfectly and finally, for we are "renewed day by day" (2 Cor. 4:16), but so as to enable those faculties to be exercised upon spiritual objects. Again; God *subdues* the power of the sin indwelling the one born again. He does not eradicate it, but He dethrones it, so that it no longer has dominion over the heart. Instead of sin ruling the Christian, and that by his own willing subjection, it is resisted and hated.

Regeneration is *not* the improvement or purification of the "flesh," which is that principle of evil still with the believer. The appetites and tendencies of the "flesh" are precisely the same after the new birth as they were before, only they no longer *reign* over him. For a time it may seem that the "flesh" *is* dead, yet in reality it is not so. Often its very stillness (as an army, in ambush) is only awaiting its opportunity for a gathering up of its strength for a further attack. It is not long ere the renewed soul discovers that the "flesh" is yet very much alive, desiring to have its way. But grace will not suffer it to have its sway. On the one hand the Christian has to say, "For to will is present with me, but how to perform that which is good I find not" (Rom. 7:18). On the other hand, he is able to declare, "Christ liveth in me, and the life which I now live in the flesh I live by the faith of the Son of God, who loved me, and gave Himself for me" (Gal. 2:20).

Some people find it very difficult to conceive of the *same* person bringing forth good works who before brought forth nothing but evil works, the more so when it be insisted upon that no new faculty is added to his being, that nothing substantial is either imparted or taken from his person. But if we rightly introduce the factor of *God's* mighty power into the equation, then the difficulty disappears. We may not be able to explain, in fact we are not, *how* God's power acts upon us, how He cleanses the unclean (Acts 10:15) and subdues the wolf so that it dwells with the lamb (Isa. 11:6), any more than we can thoroughly understand His working upon and within us without destroying our own personal agency; nevertheless, both Scripture and experience testifies to each of these facts. It may help us a little at this point if we contemplate the workings of God's power in the natural realm.

In the natural realm every creature is not only entirely dependent upon its Maker for its continued existence, but also for the *exercise* of all its faculties, for "in Him we live, and move (Greek 'are moved') and have our being" (Acts 17:28). Again; as the various parts of creation are linked together, and afford each other mutual support—as the heavens fertilize the earth, the earth supplies its inhabitants with food, its inhabitants propagate their kind, rear their offspring, and co-operate for the purpose of society—so also the whole system is supported, sustained and governed by the directing providence of God. The influences of providence, the manner in which they operate on the creature, are profoundly mysterious; on the one hand, they are not destructive of our rational nature, reducing us to irresponsible automatons; on the other hand, they are all made completely subservient to the Divine purpose.

Now the operation of God's power in regeneration is to be regarded as of the same kind with its operation in providence, although it be exercised with a different design. God's energy is one, though it is distinguished by the objects on which, and the ends for which, it is exerted. It is the same power which creates as which upholds in existence: the same power which forms a stone and a sunbeam, the same power which gives vegetable life to a tree, animal life to a brute, and rational life to a man. In like manner, it is the same power which assists us in the natural exercise of our faculties, as it is which enables us to exercise those faculties in a spiritual manner. Hence "grace" as a principle of Divine operation in the spiritual realm, is the same power of God as "nature" is His process of operation in the natural world.

The grace of God in the application of redemption to the hearts of His people is indeed *mighty*, as is evident from the effects produced. It is a change of the whole man: of his views, motives, inclinations and pursuits. Such a change no human means are able to accomplish. When the thoughtless are made to think, and to think with a seriousness and intensity which they never formerly did; when the careless are, in a moment, affected with a deep sense of their most important interests; when lips which were accustomed to blaspheme, learn to pray; when the proud are brought to assume the lowly attitude and language of the penitent; when those who were devoted to the world, give evidence that the object of their desires and aims is a heavenly inheritance; and when this revolution, so wonderful, has been effected by the simple Word of God, and by the very Word which the subjects of this radical change, had often heard unmoved, it is proof positive that a mighty influence has been exerted, and that that influence is nothing less than *divine*—God's people have been made willing in the day of His *power* (Psa. 110:3).

Many figures are used in Scripture, various expressions are employed by the Spirit, to describe this saving work of God within His people. In 2 Peter 1:4 the regenerated are said to be "partakers of the Divine nature," which does *not* mean of the very essence or being of God, for that can neither be divided nor communicated—in Heaven itself there will still be an unmeasurable distance between the Creator and the creature, otherwise the finite would become infinite. No, to be "partakers of the Divine nature" is to be made the recipients of inherent grace, to have the lineaments of the Divine image stamped upon the soul: as the remainder of the verse shows, being "partakers of the Divine nature" is the antithesis of "the *corruption* that is in the world through lust."

In 2 Cor. 3:18 this transforming miracle of God's grace in His people is declared to be a "changing" into the image of Christ. The Greek word there for "change" is the one rendered "transfigured" in Matt. 17:2. At Christ's transfiguration no new features were added to the Saviour's face, but His whole countenance was irradiated by a new light; so in 2 Cor. 4:6 regeneration is likened unto a "light" which God commands to shine in us—note the whole context of 2 Cor. 3:18 is treating of the Spirit's work by the Gospel. In Eph. 2:10 this product of God's grace is spoken of as His "workmanship," and is said to be "created," to show that He, and not man, is the Author of it. In Gal. 4:19 this same work of God in the soul is termed Christ's being "formed" in us—as the parents' seed is formed or moulded in the mother's womb, the "likeness" of the parent being stamped upon it.

We cannot here attempt a full list of the numerous figures and expressions which the Holy Spirit has employed to set forth this saving work of God in the soul. In John 6:44 it is spoken of as a being "drawn" to Christ. In Acts 16:14 as the heart being "opened" by the Lord to receive His Truth. In Acts 26:18 as an opening of our eyes, a turning us from darkness unto light, and the power of Satan unto God. In 2 Cor. 10:5 as the "casting down imaginations, and every high thing that exalteth itself against the knowledge of God, and bringing into captivity every thought to the obedience of Christ." In Eph. 5:8 as being "light in the Lord." In 2 Thess. 2:13 it is designated the "sanctification of the Spirit." In Heb. 8:10 as God's putting His laws into our mind and writing them on our hearts—*contrast* the figure in Jer. 17:1! Thus it should be most apparent that we lose much by limiting our attention to only one figure of it. All we have given, and still others not mentioned, need to be taken into consideration, if we are to obtain anything approaching an adequate conception of the *nature* of that miracle of grace which is wrought in the soul and spirit of the elect, enabling them to henceforth live unto God.

As man was changed in Adam from what he was by a state of creation, so man must be changed in Christ from what he is by a state of corruption. This change which fits him for communion with God, is a Divine work wrought in the inclinations of the soul. It is a being renewed in the spirit of our minds (Eph. 4:23). It is the infusion of a principle of holiness into all the faculties of our inner being. It is the spiritual renovation of our very persons, which will yet be consummated by the regeneration of our bodies. The whole soul is renewed, according to the image of God in knowledge, holiness and righteousness. A new light shines into the mind, a new power moves the will, a new object attracts the affections. The individual is the same, and yet not the same. How different the landscape when the sun is shining, than when the darkness of a moonless night is upon it—the same landscape, and yet not the same. How different the condition of him who is restored to fulness of health and vigour after having been brought very low by sickness; yet it is the same person.

The very fact that the Holy Spirit has employed the figures of "begetting" and "birth" to the saving work of God in the soul, intimates that the reference is only to the *initial* experience of Divine grace: "He which hath *begun* a good work in you" (Phil. 1:6). As an infant has all the parts of a man, yet none of them come to maturity, so regeneration gives a perfection of parts, which yet have need to be developed. A new life has been received, but there needs to be a growth of it: "*grow* in grace" (2 Pet. 3:18). As God was the Giver of this life, He only can feed and strengthen it. Thus, Titus 3:5 speaks of "the renewing" and not the "renewal" of the Holy Spirit. But it is our responsibility and bounden duty to *use* the Divinely-appointed means of grace which promote spiritual growth: "*desire* the sincere milk of the Word that ye may grow thereby" (1 Pet. 2:2); as it is our obligation to constantly avoid everything which would hinder our spiritual prosperity: "Make not provision for the flesh to the lusts" (Rom. 13:14), and cf. Matt. 5:29, 30, 2 Cor. 7:1.

God's consummating of the initial work which we experience at the new birth, and which He renews throughout the course of our earthly lives, only takes place at the second coming of our Saviour, when we shall be perfectly and eternally conformed to His image, both inwardly and outwardly. First, regeneration; then our gradual sanctification; finally our glorification. But between the new birth and glorification, while we are left down here, the Christian has both the "flesh" and the "spirit", both a principle of sin and a principle of holiness, operating within him, the one opposing the other: see Gal. 5:16, 17. Hence his *inward* experience is such as that which is described in Rom. 7:7-25. As life is opposed to death, purity to impurity, spirituality to carnality, so is now felt and experienced within the soul a severe conflict between sin and grace. This conflict is perpetual, as the "flesh" and "spirit" strive for mastery. From hence proceeds the absolute necessity of the Christian being sober, and to "watch unto prayer."

Finally let it be pointed out that the principle of life and obedience (the new "nature") which is received at regeneration is not able to preserve the soul from sins, nevertheless, there is full provision for continual supplies of grace made for it and all its wants in the Lord Jesus Christ. There are treasures of relief in Him, whereunto the soul may at any time repair and find necessary succour against every incursion of sin. This new principle of holiness may say to the believer's soul, as did David unto Abiathar when he fled from Doeg: "Abide then with me, fear not; for him that seeketh my life, seeketh thy life; but with me thou shalt be in safeguard" (1 Sam. 22:23). Sin is the enemy of the new nature as truly as it is of the Christian's soul, and his only safety lies in heeding the requests of that new nature, and calling upon Christ for enablement. This we are exhorted to in Heb. 4:16. "Let us therefore come boldly unto the throne of grace, that we may obtain mercy, and find grace to help in time of need."

If it ever be a time of need with the soul, it is so when it is under the assults of provoking sins, when the "flesh" is lusting against the "spirit." But at that very time there is suitable and seasonable help in Christ for succour and relief. The new nature begs, with sighs and groans, for the believer *to* apply to Christ. To neglect Him, with all His provision of grace, whilst He stands calling on us, "*Open* to Me. . . . for My head is filled with dew and My locks with the drops of the night" (Song of Sol. 5:2), is to despise the sighing of the poor prisoner, the new nature, which sin is seeking to destroy, and cannot but be a high provocation against the Lord.

At the beginning, God entrusted Adam and Eve with a stock of grace in themselves, but they cast it away, and themselves into the utmost misery thereby. That His children might not perish a second time, God, instead of imparting to them *personally* the power to overcome sin and Satan, has laid up their portion in Another, a safe Treasurer; in Christ are their lives and comforts secured (Col. 3:3). And how must Christ regard us, if, instead of applying to Him for relief, we allow sin to distress our conscience, destroy our peace, and mar our communion? Such is not a sin of infirmity which cannot be avoided, but a grievous affront of Christ. The means of preservation from it is at hand. Christ is always accessible. He is ever ready to "succour them that are tempted" (Heb. 2:18). O to betake ourselves to Him more and more, day by day, for *everything*. Then shall each one find, "I *can* do all things through Christ which strengtheneth me" (Phil. 4:13).—A. W. P.

SOUND THE ALARM

To sound an alarm is rarely, if ever, a pleasant task, yet mercy unto others often makes it necessary. In the case of servants of God, faithfulness to their Master, as well as love for their brethren, makes this, at times, a bounden duty. In the mind of the writer there is not a shadow of doubt but that the conditions now prevailing so widely in what is known as the orthodox section of Christendom render it imperative that some voice, however feeble, should be raised in warning. Wolves are none the less wolves because they hide beneath sheep's clothing, yea, they are the more dangerous on that very account; and the more necessary does it become for the under-shepherds of Christ to warn His flock against them.

None of the Lord's people would knowingly attend and have fellowship with a "church" (?) where the fundamentals of the faith were verbally repudiated. A denial of the Holy Trinity, the atoning sacrifice of Christ, or the Divine inspiration and authority of the Scriptures, would at once drive the sheep away. But *verbal* repudiation is not the only way in which the Truth of God may be denied. Satan is very subtle, and is oftentimes "transformed into an angel of light" (2 Cor. 11:14), and therefore we are told "it is no great thing if his ministers also be transformed as the ministers of righteousness; whose end shall be according to their works" (v. 15). Please note very carefully that it does *not* say "whose end shall be according to their *words*," but "their works"!

The principle expressed in the first half of Titus 1:16 illustrates what we now have in mind: there are those who "profess that they know God, but in *works* they deny Him." They preach one thing and practice another. They urge their people to tithe, yet they themselves fail to set the example. They ask for reverence in the pew, but themselves indulge in levity in the pulpit. They talk about the glory of the Lord, yet refuse to exercise a discipline which glorifies Him. They preach on full consecration, yet themselves belong to secret orders and are members of social clubs. They preach grace, and yet their own homes are often a disgrace.

Thank God there are still a *few* Godly men in the pulpit, and there may yet be some churches left to which a child of God can *scripturally* belong. We do not profess to be able to diagnose the spiritual state of a church by a brief visit thereto. There is an old saying—and a true one it is—that you have to *live* with a person before you know him. The same is true of a church. Of course there are exceptions. One hour in the company of some people is quite sufficient to discover that a deeper acquaintance with them is undesirable. So, to be present at a single service in some churches is quite sufficient to chill and sicken a true Christian. To unite with any church is a very sacred and solemn step to take, and one ought—especially in these days—to go very slow (Isa. 28-16), and seek to be quite sure that he is not uniting with one that a few months later he will have to leave.

Since our February article we have received the following from a Brother in Minnesota: "Your message 'Sound the

Alarm' is very much needed in this day and age. In your letter of Sept., 1927, you advised me to go slow in joining another organization. I am sorry that I did not take your good advice. We joined the —— Baptist church, but came out of that organization about a year ago. As I read your article it seemed almost as though you were describing the —— church and its pastor." A few days ago we got this word from another reader, "We are again without a church home: there were conditions within the —— church which we could not overlook and not dishonour our Lord": and that church was a "Fundamental" one! The sad, sad thing is that so many *are* dishonouring their Lord by *refusing* to "come out" from that which is a disgrace to His holy name.

A Brother in Australia has written us, "We have been meeting for the last twelve months with a little company of ——. They built a Hall quite close to us. There is the form of godliness, but that is all. Much feverish activity in what they are pleased to call 'the Gospel,' with a looseness in walk that brings the truth into disrepute. One gets heart-sick of it all. With all the activity in service, there is a marked disinclination to study the Word of God, and their 'Bible readings' are shallow and perfunctory to the last degree. If you go along quietly with them, you appear to be acquiescing in their doings (it is more than 'appear to be'—Silence gives consent! A.W.P.); if, on the other hand, you raise your voice in protest you are a disturber of the peace." How much worse will things have to get before those who hold the Lord's honour so lightly will *cease* having "fellowship with the unfruitful works of darkness" (Eph. 5:11)?

This week we have received a letter from a Brother in Scotland who states: "I am afraid those who desire to honour God in all their ways must stay at home. Most of the Meetings are corrupted. May God help us all to see our condition before Him, that we may not be deluded by Satan and wake up in Hell." But where are those who (by grace) *are* determined to "honour God in *all* their ways"? They are few indeed, or they could not remain associated with that which so glaringly dishonours Him. Alas, "The *fear of man* bringeth a snare" (Prov. 29:25). When this solemn issue is pressed on people, many will answer, But what would my friends and relatives think? Such need to ask themselves, What does the Lord Jesus think of my unfaithfulness *to Him!*

While composing this article a letter has come to hand from another preacher, in which he says. "I was called to a Baptist Church in Illinois. The young people danced; the older folks, with the exception of a few, played cards. Had seven deacons, only one ever attended prayer-meetings, and he was far from being a spiritual man. Had suppers, bazaars, and what not. I only lasted nine months there." He then goes on to say that, one of the Fundamentalist leaders, hearing of his predicament, had him called to his present charge, concerning which he says: "Here I found a church split in two. Half of the members not born again. Previous preacher gave the people nothing. Had suppers and food sales. Allowed Fraternals to have their funerals here. O what a confusion! Have had a *back*-door revival of about fortyeight people. Had a blessed visitation of the Holy Spirit."

Referring to our Feb. article on "Sound the Alarm" this preacher asks, "What would happen if we all would do the same thing (come outside the camp) in this day and age?" We answered him, in part, by saying: "Much would depend upon *why* they took such a step. If they separated from a church merely to please some man, or in imitation of others, then no good will come of it. But if they came out of Christ-dishonouring churches (?) because *His* honour and glory was dearer to them than anything else, and because they saw that God's Word *required* it of them, then God would certainly bless their obedience to Him and loyalty to His Son." But why be concerned over such a question? Our *only* concern must be to *obey God*: we may quite safely leave with Him all the consequences!

If all God's people who are yet inside the present-day ecclesiastical "Babylon" heeded the clarion call of Rev. 18:4, "Come out of her, My people, that ye be not partakers of her sins, and that ye receive not of her plagues," then the line of demarkation would once more be drawn *between* the world and those who belong to that Church for which the Son of God died. But while the children of God remain in worldly "churches" (?), that line of separation is obliterated. It is *not* sufficient for us to lift up our voices in protest against the unscriptural methods, customs, and ways which now have such a prominent place in the religious clubs, wrongly called "churches." Actions speak louder than words! While I remain inside, my so doing *neutralizes* all my verbal protestings. Moreover, my remaining on the inside is, in all probability, encouraging others to do so too; and for that, an account will yet have to be rendered to Christ.

Christendom is reaping today the evil sowings of the last two or three generations, particularly the unscriptural "evangelistic" methods that have been employed — the demand for visible "results," the lusting after *numbers*. Thousands have been pressed into "making a profession" and rushed into "joining the church." Consequently, a very large percentage of the present-day members are *un*-regenerate. Nor will the Holy Spirit work in their midst. God requires reality. Alas, it is now as it was in our Lord's day: "This people draweth nigh unto Me with their mouth, and honoureth Me with their lips; but their heart is far from Me" (Matt. 15:8). Nothing is more calculated to "quench the Spirit" (1 Thess. 5:19) than hypocrisy! Nor will God hearken to the cries of His own while they remain yoked with the unsaved.

We are constantly receiving letters from individual saints who write, "There are so very few with whom we can have fellowship any more." This is true almost everywhere. It is our firm conviction that as the population of the earth has increased, the number of real Christians have decreased—God's thoughts and ways are ever the opposite of ours! Certain it is, that those who give evidence of being indwelt by *Christ* are few and far between. There must be *oneness of heart* before there can be real "fellowship"! And *what* oneness of heart is there between those who are truly striving to please the Lord, and those who are obviously living to please self? "Can two walk together, except they be agreed?" (Amos 3:3). Since, then, the fellowship is *not* real, why keep up the pretense? Turn away from those who only hinder you!

A favourite bait which Satan is using to keep many of God's children inside the camp (the place from which the presence of God has departed) is their "service for Christ," their "usefulness." They have a Sunday school or Bible-class, where they are allowed to give out the Truth. But it is *never* right to disobey God, and *He* says, "Be ye *not* unequally yoked together with unbelievers: for what fellowship hath righteousness with unrighteousness? and what communion hath light with darkness?" (2 Cor. 6:14). Surely the *honour* of Christ should come first. Sever your connection with every organization or company which dishonours Him, and start a Class in your own home, on the "outside" (Heb. 13:13). We greatly fear that in many cases it is (unsuspected and secret) *pride* rather than devotedness to the Lord, which is causing many to esteem their "service" so highly.

The fact is that things are far worse inside "the camp" than many of God's children suspect. Nor can they *see* this for themselves while they remain inside it. No matter how good your eyes may be, you *cannot* see things clearly in a *dark* place. And a spiritually "dark place" the vast majority of the "churches" is today, for He who is "the true Light" has *withdrawn* from them (Rev. 3:20). It is only when one obeys the command of 2 Tim. 3:5 and *"turns away* from" those having naught but the empty "form of godliness," that he is able to see things as they really are.

We could here quote one personal testimony after another from those who *have* withdrawn from the "mixed multitude" in the churches, bearing witness that they are *now* able to discern far more clearly the Christ-dishonouring place which they left. They also write of the increased inward peace and joy of heart which is now theirs, and of the precious seasons which they have each Sabbath in the quiet of their own homes apart from "the strife of tongues" (Psa. 31:20). Instead of going to bed feeling sick at heart, they retire full of praise unto Him who has failed not to honour those who honour Him (1 Sam. 2:20).

O gracious God our Father, speak the word of power to Thy dear children and deliver them from the fear of man. O Lord Jesus, draw forth Thy blood-bought people from those associations which are dishonouring to Thee. O Thou blessed Holy Spirit, so deepen Thy work of grace in the hearts of those whom Thou dost indwell, that they will turn away in sorrowful but holy loathing from all that the Scripture condemns. O Thou Triune Jehovah, for the glory of Thy great name, bring forth unto Thyself outside the camp those of Thine own who are still found within it. Amen. A.W.P.

IS CHRIST YOUR LORD?

We do not ask, Is Christ your "Saviour," but is He, really and truly, your *Lord?* If He be not your Lord, then most certainly He is *not* your "Saviour." Those who have not received Christ Jesus as their "Lord," and yet suppose Him to be their "Saviour," are deluded, and their hope rests on a foundation of sand. Multitudes are deceived on this vital point, and therefore, if the reader values his or her soul, we implore you to give a most careful reading to this little tract.

When we ask, Is Christ your Lord, we do *not* inquire, Do you believe in the Godhead of Jesus of Nazareth? The demons do that (Matt. 8:28, 29), yet perish notwithstanding! You may be firmly convicted of the Deity of Christ, and yet be in your sins. You may speak of Him with the utmost reverence, accord Him His Divine titles in your prayers, and yet be unsaved. You may abominate those who traduce His person and deny His Divinity, and yet have no spiritual love for Him at all.

When we ask, Is Christ your LORD? we mean, does He in very deed occupy the throne of your heart, does He actually rule over your life? "We have turned every one to his *own* way" (Isa. 53:6) describes the course which *all* follow by nature. Before conversion, every soul lives to please self. Of old it was written, "every man did that which was right in his own eyes," and why? "In those days there was *no king* in Israel" (Judges 21:25). Ah, *that* is the point we desire to make clear to the reader. Until Christ becomes your *King* (1 Tim. 1:17, Rev. 15:3), until you bow to His sceptre, until *His* will becomes the rule of your life, SELF dominates, and thus Christ is disowned.

When the Holy Spirit begins His work of grace in a soul, He first convicts of sin. He shows me the real and awful nature *of sin.* He makes me realize that it is a species of insurrection, a defying of God's authority, a setting my will against His. He shows me that in going my "own way" (Isa. 53:6), in pleasing *myself,* I have been fighting against God. As my eyes are opened to see what a lifelong rebel I have been, how indifferent to God's honour, how unconcerned about *His* will, I am filled with anguish and horror, and made to marvel that the thrice Holy One has not long since cast me into Hell. Reader, have you ever gone through *this* experience? If not, there is very grave reason to fear you are yet spiritually *dead!*

Conversion, true conversion, *saving* conversion, is a turning from sin to God in Christ. It is a throwing down the weapons of my warfare against Him, a *ceasing* to despise or ignore His authority. New Testament conversion is described thus: "Ye turned to God from idols to *serve* (be in subjection to, *obey*) the living and true God" (1 Thess. 1:9). An "idol" is any object to which we give what is due alone unto God—the supreme place in our affections, the moulding influence of our hearts, the dominating power of our lives. Conversion is a right-about-face, the heart and will *repudiating* sin, self, and the world. Genuine conversion is always evidenced by, "Lord, what wilt *Thou* have me to do?" (Acts 9:6): it is an unreserved surrendering of ourselves to *His* holy will. Have *you* so yielded yourself to Him (Rom. 6:13)?

There are many people who would like to be saved from Hell, but who do *not* want to be saved from self-will, from having their own way, from a life of (some form of) worldliness. But God will not save on *their* terms. To be saved, we *must* submit to HIS terms. Listen to His terms, "Let the wicked *forsake* his way, and the unrighteous man his thoughts, and let him return unto the Lord (having revolted from Him in Adam), and He will have mercy upon him" (Isa. 55:7). Said Christ, "Whosoever he be of you that *forsaketh not* all that he hath (all that is opposed to Me), He cannot be My disciple" (Luke 14:33). Men must be turned "from darkness to light, *and the power of Satan* unto God," before they can "receive forgiveness of sins and inheritance among them which are sanctified" (Acts 26:18).

"As ye have therefore received Christ Jesus the Lord, walk ye in Him" (Col. 2:6). That is an exhortation to Christians, and its force is, *Continue* as you began. But *how* had they "begun"? By receiving "Christ Jesus *the Lord*": by surrendering to Him, by subjecting themselves to *His* will, by ceasing to please themselves. His authority was now owned, His commands now became their rule of life, His love constrained them to a glad and unreserved obedience. They "gave their own selves to *the Lord*" (2 Cor. 8:5). Have *you*, my reader, done so? *Have* you? Do the details of your life *evidence* it? Can those with whom you come into contact *see* that you are no more living to please self (2 Cor. 5:15)?

O my reader, make no mistake upon

this point: a conversion which the Holy Spirit produces is a very *radical* thing. It is a *miracle* of grace. It is the *enthroning* of Christ in the life. And such conversions are rare indeed. Multitudes of people have just sufficient "religion" to make them miserable. They are vainly striving to serve two masters. They refuse to forsake *every* known sin—and there is no true peace for any soul until he does. They have never "received Christ Jesus *the Lord*" (Col. 2:6). Had they done so, "the *joy of the Lord*" would be their "strength" (Neh. 8:10). But the language of their hearts and lives (*not* their "lips") is, "We will not have this Man to *reign over* us" (Luke 19:14). Is that *your* case?

The great miracle of grace consists in changing a lawless rebel into a loving and loyal subject. It is a "renewing" of the heart and mind, so that the favoured subject of it has come to loathe what he loved, and the things he once found irksome are now winsome (2 Cor. 5:17). He *delights* "in the law of God after the inward man" (Rom. 7:22). He discovers that Christ's "commandments are *not* grievous" (1 John 5:3), and that "in keeping of them there is great reward" (Psa. 19:11). Is *this* your experience? It would be, if you received Christ Jesus THE LORD!

But to receive Christ Jesus *the Lord* is altogether beyond unaided human power. That is the *last* thing which the unrenewed heart *wants* to do. There must be a supernatural *change* of heart before there is even the desire for Christ to occupy its throne. And that change, none but God can work (1 Cor. 12:3). Therefore, "*Seek ye* the Lord while He may be found" (Isa. 55:6). Reader, you may have been a professing Christian for years past, and you may have been quite sincere in your profession. But if God has condescended to use this tract and show that you have *never* really and truly "received Christ Jesus *the Lord*," if now in your own soul and conscience you realize that SELF has ruled you hitherto, will you not now get down on your knees, and *confess* to God your self-will, your *rebellion* against Him, and beg Him to so *work in you* that, without further delay, you may be enabled to *yield yourself* completely to His will, and become His subject, His servant, His loving slave, in deed and in truth. A.W.P.

IMPORTANT NOTICE

We feel that there is great need for the above message to be brought to the notice of a wider circle. So many have been taught *all* which was necessary in order to their being saved was that they "believe in Christ" or "rest upon His finished work," that multitudes are deceived, and imagine that all is well with them when they have never been truly broken down before God. It is impossible for any sinner to savingly believe in Christ until he first *repents*: see Matt. 21:32, Mark 1:15, Acts 20:21. No one ever *actually* rests upon the finished work of Christ till he sees his awful condition, mourns bitterly for his sins, and *turns from them* in loathing. Christ died not to make it possible to go on in a course of self-will and self-pleasing, and then go to Heaven when we die. No, He died to "save His people *from* their sins" (Matt. 1:21). Unless there be in my heart a genuine, deep, lasting, and efficacious desire and determination to *please* Christ in all things, then I have no Scriptural warrant for regarding myself as a saved person.

An edition of this message "Is Christ your Lord?" has been printed in tract form, for free but prayerful and careful distribution. We are anxious for it to reach church-members and others who think they are Christians. It has been published by the Bible Truth Depot of Swengel (Union Co.), Penn., and as we feel led of the Lord, we shall be glad to supply our readers with copies of the same. We covet the earnest prayers of God's children that this message may be used by the Holy Spirit to the enlightening, convicting and converting of many now blinded by Satan.

We are praying that God will make it possible for the four articles on *Regeneration* to be re-issued in booklet form. This message is also sorely needed today, almost everywhere. We are deeply thankful that God, in His great grace, has recently granted the writer a clearer view of this blessed and vital truth than he had before; and we long to share this additional light with others. We hope to see it issued without any price on it, so that none of the "poor of the flock" may be debarred from obtaining it through lack of funds. We would like to send copies to hundreds of young students in seminaries, Bible-schools, etc. Pray with us about this, but *please* do *not* regard this notice as an appeal for funds. A.W.P.

impossible that there should be *any* equality. "To whom then will ye liken Me, or shall I be equal? saith the Holy One" (Isa. 40:25) is God's own challenge. Thus, for *any creature* to deem himself "equal with God" would be the highest robbery and supremest blasphemy of which any could ever be guilty.

"But made Himself of no reputation." The meaning of these words is explained in those which immediately follow. So far was the Son from tenaciously insisting upon His personal rights as a Member of the blessed Trinity, He voluntarily relinquished them. He willingly set aside the magnificent distinctions of the Creator, to appear in the form of a creature, yea, in the likeness of a fallen apostate. He abdicated His *position* of supremacy, and entered that of servitude. Though equal in majesty and glory with God, He joyfully resigned Himself to the Father's will: John 6:38. Incomparable condescension was this. He who was by inherent right in the form of God, suffered His glory to be eclipsed, His honour to be laid in the dust, and Himself to be humbled to a death most shameful.

"And took upon Him the form of a servant." In so doing, He did not cease *to be* all that He was before, but He assumed to Himself something He had not previously. There was no change in His Divine nature, but the uniting to His Divine person of a human nature. "He who is God, can no more be not God, than he who is not God, can be God" (John Owen). None of Christ's Divine attributes were relinquished, for they are as inseparable from His Divine person as heat is from fire, or weight is to a substance. But His majestic glory was, for a season, obscured, by the interposing vail of human flesh. Nor is our last statement negatived by John 1:14—"*we* beheld His glory" (explained by Matt. 16:17), is in contrast from the unregenerate masses before whom He appeared as "a root out of a dry ground," having "no form nor comeliness" (Isa. 53:2).

It was *God Himself* who was "manifest in flesh" (1 Tim. 3:16). The One born in Bethlehem's manger was "The mighty God" (Isa. 9:6), and heralded as, "Christ the Lord" (Luke 2:11). Let there be no uncertainty on this point. Had He been "emptied" of any of His personal excellency, had His Divine attributes been laid aside, then His satisfaction or sacrifice *would not* have possessed *infinite* value. The *glory* of His person was not in the slightest degree set aside or diminished when He became incarnate; though it was (in measure) concealed by the lowly form of the servant which He had assumed. Christ was still "equal with God" when He descended to earth. It was "The Lord of Glory" (1 Cor. 2:8) whom men crucified!

"And took *upon* Him the form of a servant." *That* was the Great Condescension, yet is it not possible for us to fully grasp the infinitude of the Son's stoop. If God "humbleth Himself to behold the things that are in heaven, and in the earth" (Psa. 113:6) how much more so to actually *become* "flesh" and be found amongst the most lowly! He entered into an *office* which placed Him below God: John 14:28, 1 Cor. 11:3. He was, for a season, "made lower than the angels" (Heb. 2:7). He was "made under the law" (Gal. 4:4). He was made lower than the ordinary condition of man, for He was "a reproach of men, and despised of the people" (Psa. 22:6).

What point all this gives to, "Let this mind be *in you*, which was also in Christ Jesus" (Phil. 2:5)! How earnestly should the Christian seek grace to be contented with the lowest place which God and men may assign him; to be ready to perform the meanest service; to be and do *anything* which brings glory to God! Let us be provoked unto humility and lowliness of mind, and thus follow the example which Christ has left us. A.W.P.

The Lord has graciously granted us many tokens that we were led of Him to move from Los Angeles to York, Pa. We know that many will rejoice with us that God is now opening doors for us to minister His blessed Word to little companies of His hungry sheep. He is granting some blessed seasons of refreshment, which we fondly hope are but the earnest of still greater showers of blessing. We ask for the supplications of Christian readers that we may be Divinely guided step by step, and used in blessing unto needy souls. There are many "churches" which we dare not enter (Eph. 5:11), and though some are offended because of this, yet we are comforted by the realisation that the Lord knows our heart. We want to be in those places and in that experimental condition where *He* can use us. A.W.P.

ness of His glory and the express Image of His person" (Heb. 1:3), or more exactly, the "effulgency (outshining) of His glory and the exact Expression of His substance" (Bagster Interlinear), which perhaps combines both of the concepts suggested by "form" and "image," namely, that the whole nature of God is in Christ, and that by Him God is declared and expressed to us.

"Who being" or subsisting (it is hardly correct to speak of a Divine person "existing": He is self-existent, He always *was*) in "the form of God." "Form" (the Greek word is only found elsewhere in the N. T. in Phil. 2:7 and Mark 16:12) is that which is apparent, and "the form of God" is an expression which seems to denote His visible glory, His displayed majesty, His manifested sovereignty. From eternity the Son was clothed with all the insignia of Deity, adorned with all Divine splendour. "The Word *was* God" (John 1.1).

"Thought it not robbery to be equal with God." Almost every word in this verse has been made the occasion of contention. Making no pretentions to scholarship, the writer has sufficient confidence in the superintending providence of God, to be satisfied that the translators of our authorised version were preserved from any serious mistake on a subject so vitally important. As the first clause of our verse refers to an objective delineation of the Divine dignity of the Son, so this second clause affirms His subjective consciousness thereof. The word "thought" is the same (in the Greek) as "esteem" in v. 3, except there the present tense is used, here the aorist, which indicates a definite point in time past. The word rendered "robbery" denotes not the spoil or prize, but *the act* of taking the spoil. The Son reckoned not equality with the Father and the Holy Spirit an act of usurpation.

"Thought it not robbery to be equal with God." This is only the negative way of saying that Christ considered equality with God as that which justly and essentially pertained and belonged to Him. It was His by indisputable right. Christ esteemed such equality as no invasion of Another's prerogative, but regarded Himself as being entitled to all Divine honors. Because He held the rank of one of the Three co-eternal, co-essential, and co-glorious Persons of the Godhead, the Son reckoned that His full and perfect equality with the other Two was His own unchallengable portion. In this second clause of v. 6 there is no doubt a latent reference to Satan's fall: he, though "the anointed cherub" (Ezek. 28:14), was infinitely below God, yet did he grasp at an equality with Him. To this Isa. 14:14 refers: "I will ascend above the heights of the clouds, *I will be like* the Most High."

However the Greek word for "robbery" be translated, it is evident that the emphatic and vital term of this clause is "equal," for if that signifies a real and proper equality, then the proof for the absolute Deity of the Saviour is irrefragable. How, then, is the exact significancy of this term to be determined? Not by having recourse to Homer, nor any other heathen writer, but by discovering the meaning of its cognate. If we can fix the precise rendering of the adjective, then we may be sure of the adverb. Now the adjective is found in Matt. 20:12, Luke 6:34, John 5:18, Acts 11:17, Rev. 21:16 and in each passage the reference is not to a resemblance or likeness only, but to a *real* and proper equality! Thus the force of this clause is parallel with, "I and Father *are* one" (John 10.30).

"My Father is greater than I" (John 14:28) must not be allowed to negative John 10:30. There are *no* contradictions in Holy Writ. Each of these passages may be given its *full* force, without there being any conflict between them. The simple and sufficient way to discover their perfect consistency is to remember, that Scripture exhibits our Saviour in *two* chief characters: as God the Son, the second Person of the Trinity; as Mediator, the God-man, the Word become flesh. In the former character, He is described as possessing all the perfections of Deity; in the latter, as the Servant of the Godhead. Speaking of Himself according to His essential Being, He could unqualifiedly say, "I and Father are one"—one in essence or nature. Speaking of Himself according to His mediatorial *office*, He could say, "My Father is greater than I"—not essentially, but economically.

Each expression that is used in Phil. 2:6 is expressly designed by the Holy Spirit to magnify the Divine dignity of Christ's person. He is the Possesser of a glory equal with God's. He possesses unquestioned right to that glory, deeming it no robbery to challenge it. His glory is not an accidental or phenomenal one, but a substantial and essential one: subsisting in the very "form of God." Between that which is Infinite and that which is finite, that which is Eternal and that which is temporal, He who is the Creator and that which is the creature, it is utterly

(Continued on Page 191)

STUDIES IN THE SCRIPTURES

"Search the Scriptures" John 5:39

Copyright in all English-speaking Countries

EDITOR: Arthur W. Pink, Millmont, Union Co., Penna., U. S. A.

Hon. Agent in England: Mr. A. Winstone, "Shalom," Old Bath Road, Leckhampton, Cheltenham.

Hon. Agent in Australia: Mr. G. Ardill, The Christian Workers' Depot, Commonwealth and Reservoir Streets, Sydney.

THE CONDESCENSION OF CHRIST

In this article we propose to continue our exposition of Phil. 2:6, 7. Our reason for doing so is twofold: first, the vital importance of what is there revealed. A right understanding of that passage is essential if we are to interpret it so as to honour the person of Christ. In order to do this there must be a correct apprehension of the precise character of our Lord's condescension, *wherein* it did not and wherein it did consist. A mistake at this point inevitably produces a concept which is most derogatory to His glory. Second, we are constrained to continue our contemplation of this wondrous and blessed subject because such awful errors upon it have been vigorously propagated during the last two or three generations, mainly under what is known as that "Kenosis theory." As far as possible, we shall avoid technicalities.

"Who, being in the form of God" (v. 6). The verb which is here used proves that it is no transient thing which is in view: the Son subsists in "the form of God" eternally. The same construction is found in John 1:18, "The only begotten Son, which is in the bosom of the Father, He hath declared Him"—words denoting the Son's unique relation to the Father, the verb again affirming an *abiding* relationship. It is *not* that He "was" in the bosom of the Father, and left it, but that He is *there always* in that intimate filial relationship. Incarnation did not change this: though on earth, He still subsisted in Heaven—"who is" in John 3:13 is the same Greek verb.

"Thought it not robbery to be equal with God" (v. 6). This was His personal right as the eternal Son: oneness in authority and dominion, oneness in Lordship and dignity, was that to which Jehovah's "Fellow" (Zech. 13:7) was justly entitled. Thus by combining the two expressions we learn that the *"form of God"* has reference to the Divine essence as *clothed with* glory and majesty. As the "form of a servant" in the next verse was no mere phantasm, but a subjective and objective reality, so Christ's being in "the form of God" denotes He was from all eternity true God, adorned with Divine splendour and majesty.

"But (or 'nevertheless' as in Rom. 5:14) made Himself of no reputation" (v. 7). In the light of what immediately follows, these words also fix to a certainty the force of the terms used at the close of v. 6, proving that Christ was *really* "equal with God." Had that *not* been the case, had the Son been in His own essential person, in any way inferior to the Father, then it had been *no* act of self-abnegation in declining to *display* for a time that equality; nor could what He did have been set before us as an example (v. 5). It would be a strange recommendation of lowliness to say that a mere creature (no matter how high in the scale of being) grasped not at "equality with God"!

"But made Himself of no reputation," or "But Himself emptied." What is meant by this is clearly signified in what immediately follows. He laid aside the robes of His incomprehensible glory, divested Himself of His incommunicable honours. In other words, when He entered upon His mediatorial state, instead of acting in the grand capacity of an universal Sovereign, He "took upon Him the form of a servant." And even *this* "form" was not like unto that of those minis-

(Continued on Page 216)

IMPORTANT NOTICES

Please advise promptly of change of address, otherwise copies will be lost in the mails.

We are glad to send a sample copy to any of your friends whom you believe would be interested in such a publication.

Send to Mr. I. C. Herendeen, Swengel (Union County), Penna., for a list of our publications. He has published many of our books and booklets.

This magazine is published as a work of faith and labour of love. The Editor and his wife gladly give their services. It is freely sent to all who will read it. No charge is made for it.

Christians who feel definitely led to do so, may have fellowship with us in this ministry. Those outside the U. S. A., please send only INTERNATIONAL Money Orders made out to Mifflinburg, Penna., U. S. A.

CONTENTS

The Condescension of Christ	193
The Epistle to the Hebrews	194
The Satisfaction ("Atonement") of Christ	200
Depravity	206
Repentance	208
Preservation and Perseverance	213

THE EPISTLE TO THE HEBREWS

45. *The Typical Sacrifices:* 10:1-4.

The 10th chapter of our epistle has two main divisions: the first is occupied with a setting forth of the sufficiency of Christ's sacrifice unto those who believe, vv. 1-20; the second is devoted to the making of a practical application of the doctrine of the first section unto faith, obedience, and perseverance, vv. 21-39. The principal design of the Spirit therein is to exhibit the excellency and efficacy of Christ's satisfaction, and this, not so much Godwards, as saintwards, showing the inestimable blessings which it has procured for the favoured members of the household of faith. The method which the apostle was inspired to follow in carrying out this design, was to, once more, set in antithesis the typical sacrifices of the Mosaic dispensation with the one Sacrifice of Christianity, contrasting the shadow with the Substance, and this, in order to bring out the inadequacy of the one and the sufficiency of the other to provide a perfect standing before God, with the resultant privilege of drawing near to Him as accepted worshippers.

Because the sacrifices under the old covenant were incapable, in and of themselves, to satisfy the claims of a holy God, they were also unable to meet the needs of those who brought them. Because that, of themselves, they could not make peace with God, neither could they give peace to the conscience of the offerer. Because they failed to make real atonement for sin, they could not cleanse the sinner. Therefore does the apostle point out that the Aaronic offerings were but "shadows," that the repetition of them intimated their insufficiency, that the fact of *un*expiated sin was recalled to memory each time a victim was slain, and that inasmuch as it was merely the blood of *beasts* which was shed, it was impossible that such a medium or offering could either placate the wrath of God or procure His blessing upon those who presented such sacrifices.

The connection between Heb. 10 and what immediately precedes is very blessed. In the closing verse of chapter 9 two things are joined together: the cross of Christ and His second coming. And *what* intervenes between Calvary and the actual entrance into Glory of those who were there redeemed and reconciled to God? This: the Christian-life on earth, and it is *this* which is mainly in view in the closing chapters of our epistle. It is the *present* status, privileges, walk, discipline and responsibilities of the saints which are therein set forth. That which is exhibited in the first twenty verses of Heb. 10 is the *perfect standing* before God which the regenerated believer now has, and his blessed privilege as a worshipper of entering in spirit within the Heavenly courts while waiting down here for the promised return of his Saviour. Having shown in chapter 9 that atonement has been accomplished, that the heavenly places were purified when the Redeemer entered the Holiest, the Spirit now emphasises the fact that the believer has been fitted to draw nigh unto God Himself as a purged and accepted worshipper.

In previous sections the apostle has contrasted the priests of the Levitical dispensation with our great High Priest, he has opposed the vastly different covenants or economies to which each belonged, he has shown the immeasurable superiority of Christ's one offering of Himself over the many sacrifices of old, he has placed in antithesis the respective "tabernacles" in which Aaron and Christ officiated. Each and all of these was designed to press upon the wavering Hebrews the deficiency of Judaism and the excellency of Christianity. Now he shows that not only are the two systems with all that pertains to them as different as a flickering candle and the shining of the sun, but that the *privileges enjoyed* by the individuals belonging to the one and the other are as widely separated as is light from darkness. The Mosaic system, as such, was neither able to impart permanent peace to the conscience nor give access into the **presence of God, but the Satisfaction of** Christ *has* procured these precious blessings unto those who flee to Him for refuge.

The order of thought which is followed in the first main division of our present chapter ought not to be difficult to grasp. First, we have an affirmation and demonstration of the deficiency of the legal sacrifices to "perfect" the worshipper: vv. 1-4. Second, we have a manifestation and exemplification of the sufficiency of Christ's sacrifice to "perfect forever" (v. 14) those for whom He made satisfaction unto God: vv. 5-20. Thus the apostle proves again the imperative need for the supplanting of all the unefficacious offerings of Judaism by the all-sufficient offering of Christ. In the developing of the first point, an assertion is made of the inadequacy of the Levitical sacrifices to expiate sin and meet the dire needs of the offerer (v. 1). A confirmation of the truth of this assertion is drawn from the frequency of their repetition (v. 2). It is shown that the annual typical propitiation was only a constant re-opening of the question of sin (v. 3). From these facts the inevitable conclusion is drawn that it was impossible for such sacrifices to remove sins.

"For the law having a shadow of good things to come, not the very image of the things, can never with those sacrifices which they offered year by year continually make the comers thereunto perfect" (v. 1). Three questions are suggested to the thoughtful reader of this verse. First, exactly what is the contrast pointed by "shadow" and "image"? Second, what is meant by the comers being made "perfect"? Third, why did God appoint sacrifices that were so unefficacious? These shall be our points of focus as we endeavour to expound this verse.

"For the law having a shadow of good things to come." The opening "For" intimates that what is introduced thereby is an inference drawn from what had previously been stated. Having shown that the sacrifice of Christ had met all the demands of God and had confirmed the new covenant, the apostle concludes from thence that, inasmuch as the Levitical sacrifices could not effect those ends which had been accomplished by Christ's, they must be taken out of the way. The "law" here is not to be restricted to the ceremonial, as the words *"having* a shadow" warn us; still less is it the *moral* law, which, absolutely considered, had no sacrifices belonging to it. No, the reference is to the whole of the Mosaic economy, or more specifically, to the covenant which God made with Israel at Sinai, with all the institutions of worship belonging thereto.

"Shadow is put first emphatically; only a shadow or outline of the substantial and eternal blessings promised. A shadow has no substance; but brings before the mind the form of the body from which it is projected! The 'image' itself is given to us in Christ, a full and permanent embodiment of the good things to come" (A. Saphir). We believe this presents the correct idea: it is clearly borne out by Col. 2:17, "which are a shadow of things to come, but the body is of Christ." The apostle is there speaking of the same things as he treats of here in 10:1: the Mosaic economy, with all its ordinances and institutions of worship, gave only an earthly adumbration or representation, and did not possess the substance, reality, or "body": *that* is found only in Christ Himself, to whom the O. T. shadows pointed. A "shadow" gives a representation of a body, a more or less just one of its form and size, yet only an obscure and imperfect one—compare our remarks on 8:5.

The "good things to come" (future, not when this epistle was written, but at the time that the Mosaic economy was instituted) has reference to all those blessings and privileges which have come to the church in consequence of the incarnation of Christ and the discharge of His office. Well might they be designated *"good* things," for there is no alloy or mixture of evil with them; other things are "good" relatively, but these things absolutely. The "image" or substance of them is found in Christ, and set forth in His Gospel: for a similar use of the term "image" cf. Rom. 8:29. "This therefore is that which the apostle denies concerning the law. It had not the actual accomplishment of the promise of good things; it had not Christ exhibited in the flesh; it had not the true real sacrifice of perfect expiation: it represented these things; it had a shadow of them, but enjoyed not, exhibited not the things themselves. Herein was its imperfection and weakness, so that by none of its sacrifices could it make the Church perfect" (J. Owen).

"Can never with those sacrifices which they offered year by year continually make the comers thereunto perfect." In these words we have the inference or conclusion for which the "For" at the beginning of the verse prepares us: if the law contained in it nothing better than a "shadow," it is obvious that its sacrifices could not possibly make perfect those who offered them. J. Owen has most helpfully pointed out that the Greek word here rendered "continually" signifies "forever," occurring elsewhere in this epistle only in 7:3, 10:12, 14 (Bagster's Interlinear gives "in perpetuity") and that it should be connected not with the clause preceding, but with the one following, thus: "the law by its sacrifices could not perfect forever, or unto the uttermost, the comers thereto."

Three things are affirmed in the second half of our verse. First, the impotency of the "law" or old covenant, or Mosaic economy. It could *never* "make perfect." It could by no means, in no way do so; it was impossible that it should. This is stated so emphatically in order to remove from the minds of the Hebrews *all* expectations of perfection from Judaism. Second, that with respect unto which this impotency of the law is here ascribed was its "sacrifices," which was the very thing in which most of the Jews had chiefly placed their hopes. But not only is that affirmed of the sacrifices in general, but also in particular of the great sacrifice on the day of atonement, which was offered "year by year": if *that* was ineffectual, how much more so the minor offerings! Third, that wherein its impotency lay was its inability to "perfect" the "comers."

Concerning the meaning of "perfect" here, we would refer back to our exposition of 7:11. For the benefit of those who do not have access to the Aug. 1930 issue, we would point out that the term "perfect" is one of the key-words of this epistle, close attention needing to be paid to its contexts. It has to do more with *relationship* than experience. It concerns the *objective* side of things rather than the subjective. It looks to the judicial and vital aspect, more than to the practical. "Perfection" means the bringing of a thing to that completeness of condition designed for it. Doctrinally if refers to the producing of a satisfactory and final relationship between God and His people. It speaks of that unchanging standing in the favour and blessing of God which Christ has secured for His saints. See also our notes on 2:10; 5:9; 6:1.

That "perfection" which God requires is absolute conformity to His moral law, so that not only is there no guilt of transgression resting upon us, but a full, flawless, and rewardable obedience to our account. How impossible it was for the slaying of beasts to secure *this* is self-evident. The "comers thereunto" are defined in v. 2 as "the worshippers": it was those who made use of the Levitical sacrifices in the worship of God. This term "come" in the Hebrews' epistle has its root in the "bring" of Lev. 1:2, the Hebrew word there signifying those who "draw nigh" with an oblation, coming thus to the altar. Though the slaying of beasts procured a temporary expiation, it did not secure an eternal forgiveness, it did not perfect "continually" or "for ever." Hence, the effect produced on the conscience of the offerer was only a transient one, for a sense of sin returned upon him, forcing him unto a repetition of the same sacrifices, as the apostle declares in the next verse. This brings us to our third question: Why did God appoint unto Israel sacrifices so ineffectual?

Many answers might be returned to this question. Though the Levitical offerings failed to procure an eternal redemption, yet were they by no means useless and without value. First of all, they served to keep in the minds of Israel the fact that God is ineffably holy and will not tolerate evil. They were constantly reminded that the wages of sin is death. They were taught thereby that a constant *acknowledgment* of their sins was imperative if communion with the Lord was to be maintained. In the second place, by means of these types and shadows God was pointing out to them the direction from which true salvation must come, namely, in a sinless Victim enduring in their stead the righteous penalty which their sins called for. Thereby God instructed them to look forward in faith to the time when the Redeemer should appear, and the great Sacrifice be offered for the sins of His people. Third, there was an efficacy in the O. T. sacrifices to remove temporal judgment, to give ceremonial ablution, and to maintain external fellowship with Jehovah. They who despised the sacrifices were "cut off" or excommunicated; but those who offered them maintained their place in the congregation of the Lord.

Ere passing on to the next verse let us seek to make practical application unto ourselves of what has been before us. In coming to God, that is, drawing nigh unto Him as worshippers, the first qualification in us is that we are legitimately assured of the perfect expiation (cancellation) of our sins. When this foundation is not laid in the soul and conscience, all attempts to approach God as worshippers are highly presumptuous, for no guilty person can stand before Him. To offer thanksgiving and praise to Him *before* we know we have been forgiven and accepted by Him, is to repeat the highhanded sin of Cain. The very first things proposed to us in the Gospel are that we own our undone condition, judge ourselves unsparingly, turn from our sins, and appropriate to our deep need the grace of God as it is tendered to us in Jesus Christ. Only as the heart is truly contrite and faith lays hold of the atoning blood of the Lamb, is any sinner entitled to draw nigh unto the Holy One.

"For then would they not have ceased to be offered? because that the worshippers once purged should have had no more conscience of sins" (v. 2). The contents of this verse enable us to grasp more clearly the particular aspects of Truth which our present chapter is dealing with. It is not so much what the sacrifices effected Godwards, as manwards: it is their purifying effects upon the worshipper which is mainly in view. This is quite evident from the expressions "once purged" and "no more conscience of sins." In like manner, the principal thing in the verses which follow is the setting forth of what Christ's atonement has secured for *His people*: see vv. 10, 14, 19.

"For then would they not have ceased to be offered?" "This verse is added as a proof of the reason concerning the impotency of the foresaid legal sacrifices. The reason was taken from the *reiteration* of those sacrifices, whereby it was made manifest that they could not make perfect. The argument may be framed thus: That which makes perfect ceaseth when it hath made perfect; but the sacrifices which were offered year by year, ceased not; therefore they could not have made perfect" (W. Gouge). In reply it might be opposed: The repetition of the sacrifice was not through any inherent defect in it, but because the offerer had acquired fresh guilt; the offering expiated all sin up to the time it was offered, but new sins being committed, another sacrifice became necessary. Let us face this difficulty.

There *was* a defect in the sacrifices themselves, as will be seen more plainly when we reach v. 4; *they* were altogether inadequate for meeting the *infinite* demands of God, they were altogether insufficient to compensate for the wrong done to God's manifestative glory and could not repair the loss of His honour. None save a sacrifice which possessed intrinsic merits, having an *infinite* value, could make real and final satisfaction. That Sacrifice has been offered, and so perfect is it that it stands in no need of addition. The Atonement of Christ is of perpetual efficacy unto God, and is ever available to faith. No matter how often application be made unto it, its power never wanes and its preciousness never diminishes.

"Because that the worshippers once purged should have had no more conscience of sins." The final words fix for us the meaning, or rather scope, of the "once purged" here. That sacrificial term may denote either (or both) the removal of the guilt of sin or the pollution thereof: the one is taken away by justification, the other by sanctification. The one is the effect of the sacerdotal actings of Christ toward God, in making atonement for sin; the other is by the Spirit's application of the virtues of that Sacrifice to our souls and consciences, whereby t h e y a r e cleansed, renewed, and changed. It is the former *only* which is before us here, namely, such a purging of sin as takes away its condemning power from the conscience on account of the *guilt* of it. But this the Levitical sacrifices failed to do, as the next verse shows.

"No more conscience of sins." This does *not* mean that the one who has been "purged" or justified has no further *consciousness* of sins, for no one is more painfully aware of them and of the indwelling "flesh" than is a regenerated soul. *That* is his great burden and sorrow. No, the one who is insensible to the evil and demerit of indwelling sin is a deluded soul: "If we say we have no sin, we deceive ourselves, and the truth is not in us" (1 John 1:8). Nor do the last words of Heb. 10:2 in anywise intimate that there is no need for a Christian's being deeply exercised over his sins and that God does not require him to repent for and confess them, and make repeated application to the Throne of Grace for "mercy" through the sacrifice of Christ. "He that covereth his sins shall not prosper: but whoso confesseth and forsaketh them shall have mercy" (Prov. 28:13): this holds good in *every* dispensation.

"No more conscience of sins" signifies freedom from an apprehensive or terrifying sense of what they deserved. It means complete deliverance from the fear of God's ever imputing them to us. It is the blessed recognition that "there is therefore now no condemnation to them which are in Christ Jesus" (Rom. 8:1). Faith has laid hold of the precious testimony of God unto the efficacy of the blood of Christ as having satisfied His every demand. If we really believe that the wages of sin were paid to our sinless Substitute, how can we be fearful that they will yet be paid to us! The word "conscience" is compounded from two words meaning "with knowledge," that is, a *joint*-knowledge of good and evil. Conscience is the eye of the soul, discerning right from wrong, yet is it dependent—as the eye is—on light. To and through the conscience God speaks as Light (1 John 1:5). When His light first breaks in and shows me what I am, I get a bad conscience; when it is purged by blood (through faith laying hold of its efficacy) I obtain a cleansed one.

It is important to observe that our verse does not say the worshipper should have "no conscience of sins," but "no *more* conscience" of them. This confirms the idea that the "continually" ("forever") of the previous verse is to be connected not with the "sacrifices," but with "perfect." It would be a great mistake to suppose that the Levitical sacrifices altogether failed to remove sins from before God: Lev. 4:2, 31; 16:21, 22 show otherwise. Nor was it that those sacrifices failed to remove the load of conscious guilt from those who offered them: in such case we should never have read of them *rejoicing* before God. No, what the apostle is here insisting upon is that those sacrifices only gave peace of conscience *pro tem*: they were unable to lay a foundation for permanent rest and abiding peace.

But what of the sins of the Christian *after* he has been "purged" or justified? John 13:10 makes answer: "he that is washed (Greek, "has been bathed") needeth not save to wash his feet, but is clean every whit." By the blood of Christ the Christian has been completely cleansed once for all, so far as the judicial and eternal consequences of sin are concerned: "By one offering He hath perfected *forever* them that are sanctified" (Heb. 10:14), thereby providing for them such stable peace and consolation as that they need not a fresh sacrifice to be made for them day by day. The Gospel makes known how those who sin every day may enjoy peace with God all their days, and that is by a daily confession of sins to God (judging themselves for them and truly repenting of them) and a daily appropriation to themselves of the cleansing power of Christ's precious blood for the defilements of their daily walk.

"But in those sacrifices there is a remembrance again of sins every year" (v. 3). The first word of this verse denotes the nature of the argument insisted upon. In the second verse it had been pointed out that, had the worshippers been legally perfected they would have had no more conscience of sins; *but*, says the apostle, it was *not* so with them: God appointed nothing in vain, and He had not only prescribed the repetition of those sacrifices, but also that in each offering there should be a "remembrance" made of sin, as of that which was to be expiated. It was by God's own institution (Lev. 16:21, 22) that there should be an "express remembrance," or a remembrance expressed by acknowledgment: See Gen. 41:9; 42:21. By an appeal to this patent fact did the apostle confirm what had been declared in vv. 1, 2.

But at this point a real difficulty confronts us: the first four verses of this chapter are designed as a background to bring out more plainly the glorious truth presented in what follows: in other words, a contrast is pointed by showing what the Levitical sacrifices could not procure, Christ's *has*—"By one offering He hath perfected forever them that are sanctified" (v. 14). Yet, notwithstanding, the fact remains that Christians ought not only once a year, but every day, call to remembrance and penitently confess the same, yea, our Lord Himself has taught us to pray every day for the pardon of our sins: Luke 11:3, 4. Wherein, then, lies the *difference* between the Levitical sacrifices and Christ's, seeing that after *both* of them there is equally a remembrance of sin again to be made? Though the problem seems intricate, yet is its solution simple.

Those under the Mosaic economy confessed their sins preparatory for and in order to a *new atonement* of them; not so the Christian. Our "remembrance" and confession respects only the *application* of the efficacy and virtue of that perfect Atonement which has been made once for all. With them, their remembrance looked to the curse of the law which was to be answered, and the wrath of God which was to be appeased; with us, that which is involved is the *imparting* of the benefits of Christ's sacrifice unto our conscience, whereby we have assured peace with God. Confession of sin is as necessary under the new covenant as under the old, but with an entirely different *end in view*: it is not as a part of the compensation for the guilt of it, nor as a means of pacifying the conscience so that we may still go on in sin; but to fill us with self-abasement, to induce greater watchfulness against sin, to glorify God for the mercy available, and to obtain a *sense of* His pardon in our own souls.

"For it is not possible that the blood of bulls and of goats should take away sins" (v. 4). Here the apostle brings to a head that which has been set forth in the preceding verses: seeing that the law contained only a "shadow" of real redemption and could not perfect unto perpetuity the worshippers (v. 1), and seeing that "conscience of sins" remained (v. 2) as was evidenced by the very design of the annual and typical propitiation (v. 3), it therefore inevitably followed that it was "impossible" such sacrifices should "take away" or properly expiate sins. Such, we take it, is the force of the opening "For" here.

There is a necessity of sin being "taken away," both from before the Governor of the world and from the conscience of His people. But this, the blood of beasts could not effect. Why not? First and foremost because God had not instituted animal sacrifices for *that* purpose. All the virtues and efficacy of the ordinances of Divine worship depend upon the end unto which *God* has instituted them. The blood of animals offered in sacrifice was designed of God to *represent* the way in which sin was to be removed, but not by itself to *effect* it. Nor did it comport with the Divine will and wisdom that it should. God had declared His severity against sin, with the necessity of its punishment to the glory of His righteousness and sovereign rule over His creatures. A most solemn demonstration of this was made at Sinai, in the giving of the fiery law: Ex. 19:16-24: but what consistency had there been between that and the satisfying of God's awful justice, and the removal of sin by such beggarly means as that of the blood of bulls and goats? In such case there had been no manner of proportion manifested between the infinite demerits of sin and the feeble instruments of its expiation.

It was impossible for any mere creature to satisfy the demands of the allmighty Governor of the universe. The highest angel could never have adequately made compensation for the tremendous wrong which sin had done God, nor repair the loss of His manifestative glory; yea, had not Christ's sinless and holy humanity—in which He performed the stupendous work of redemption—been united in His deity, *that* could not have met the claims of God nor merited eternal salvation for His people. Far less could the blood of beasts vindicate the honour of an infinite Majesty, pacify His righteous wrath, meet the requirements of His holy law, nor even cleanse the conscience and heart of man. "The blood of bulls and goats were external, earthly, and carnal things; but to take away sin was an internal, Divine, and spiritual matter" (W. Gouge). Though the Levitical sacrifices possessed, by God's institution, an efficacy to remove an outward and ceremonial defilement, they could not take away an inward and moral pollution.

This 4th verse enunciates and illustrates a deeply important principle which exposes the great error of Ritualists. As we have pointed out above, all ordinances of Divine worship derive their value from God's institution: they can only effect that which He has appointed, they have in them no inherent efficacy. While they may usefully *represent* spiritual truths, they have no spiritual virtue of their own, and cannot of and by themselves secure spiritual results. The offerings of Judaism had a Divinely appointed meaning and value, but they could not take away sins. The same holds good of the two ordinances of Christianity. Baptism and the Lord's Supper have been ordained of God. They have a symbolical significance. They represent blessed realities. But they h a v e no inherent power either to remove sin, regenerate souls, or impart spiritual blessing. It is only as faith looks beyond the symbol to Him who is symbolized that the soul receives blessing.

Ere closing, perhaps we ought to anticipate a question which is likely to have arisen in the minds of the readers. In view of what is affirmed in the verses which have been before us, are we to conclude that *none* of the Old Testament saints had a perfect and permanent standing before God? No, indeed, for such an inference would manifestly clash with many plain O. T. passages and with the promises which the Church had under the old covenant. The apostle is not here denying absolutely that no one had spiritual access to God and real peace of conscience before Him, but is merely affirming that *such* blessings could not be secured *by means of* the Levitical sacrifices. But those who belonged to the "remnant according to the election of grace" (Rom. 11:5) had faith given them to look beyond the shadow to the Substance: see Job 19:25; Psa. 23:6; Song of Sol. 2:16; Isa. 12:2; Dan. 12:2, etc. A. W. P.

THE SATISFACTION
("Atonement")
OF CHRIST

21. *Its Typification.*

Christ has been greatly dishonoured and His atonement grievously misrepresented by the attempts which have often been made to illustrate it from supposed analogies in human relations. Rightly has it been said that, "The plan of redemption, the office of our Surety, and the satisfaction which He rendered to the claims of justice against us, *have no parallel* in the relations of men to one another. We are carried above the sphere of the highest relations of created beings into the august counsels of the eternal and independent God. Shall we bring *our own* line to measure *them?* We are in the presence of Father, Son and Holy Spirit; one in perfections, will and purpose. If the righteousness of the Father demands a sacrifice, the love of the Father provides it. But the Love of the Son runs parallel with that of the Father; and not only in the general undertaking, but in every act of it we see the Son's full and free consent" (Waymarks Vol. 6).

But while no parallel to the Great Transaction, or to the relation of the Father, Son and Holy Spirit to its accomplishment, can be found in any of the relations of mere creatures to one another, God has graciously adapted a series of *types*, historical and ceremonial, to the illustration of His wondrous plan, and especially to portray the various aspects of the office and work of Christ. In them the Divine wisdom is signally displayed, and it is the part of human wisdom to devote our closest attention to the same. By the typical system, God was not only educating His people for the "good things to come," but was also preparing human language to be a fit medium for the revelation of His grace in Christ. It is to the types we must turn if we would define aright the sacrificial terms of the N. T.

But an impression obtains in some quarters that instruction by the types belongs to an inferior dispensation, and was only designed for the Church in the days of its infancy. Scripture teaches otherwise. It is true that "the typology of the Pentateuch is the Divine kindergarten," yet it is also true that "Whatsoever things were written aforetime were written for *our* learning" (Rom. 15:4), and that God's dealings with Israel were "*our* types" (1 Cor. 10:6 margin). Yea, so far from the study of the types being an elementary one, Heb. 5:10-12 shows that they furnish our "strong meat."

While it is true that the "typology of the Pentateuch is the Divine kindergarten," this does not mean either that the teaching of the types is to be lightly esteemed, or that the instruction which they furnish is inferior in quality to that which is given in the Epistles. No school-child is really qualified to take in the teaching of the higher grades until he is thoroughly familiar with and has more or less mastered the lessons of the lower grades. So none are fully equipped to receive the evangelical teachings of the N. T., if the key-phrases of the O. T. types are neglected. Not only has the sacrificial work of Christ as many aspects as there are great sacrifices in the Pentateuch, but the doctrinal statements of the Epistles are frequently couched in the language of the types, and can only be rightly interpreted in the light which they furnish.

"A type is something emblematic or symbolic, used to express, embody, represent or forecast, some person, truth or event. It is an image or similitude of something else, sustaining to doctrinal teaching some such relation as a picture does to a precept or promise, representing to the eye or imagination a concept addressed to the ear or understanding. It is one of the most frequent forms of figurative teaching in Scripture, but being sometimes more obscure than obvious demands keener insight and closer study" (A. T. Pierson). The types were prophecies, forecasts of things to come, and therefore do they furnish one of the most striking and conclusive proofs of the Divine inspiration of the Scriptures, for only He who knew the end from the beginning could have so accurately, so fully, and so marvellously anticipated and adumbrated Calvary thousands of years before Christ died.

"The O. T. types were a mode of instruction of the way in which God was to be approached, and were peculiarly suited to the human mind struggling with a sense of guilt; and they have furnished to the Church of all times, a vocabulary or nomenclature, without which men could not with sufficient precision have been able to hold intercourse with each other on the subject of the Atonement. It deserves special notice that prophecy and the sacrifices are always found together, and throw light upon each other; and that they run in parallel lines through the entire O. T. economy. Nay, the sacrifices may be regarded as a sort of prophecy, or a guarantee to which the veracity of God was pledged, for the shadow must one day be a reality" (Geo. Smeaton). "A type is a *prophetic symbol*, and since prophecy is the prerogative of Him who sees the end from the beginning, a real type, implying as it does a knowledge of the Reality, can only proceed from God" (Liddon's Bampton Lectures).

The O. T. types supply incontrovertible evidence that the Gospel was no novel invention of N. T. times. When the risen Saviour would make known to His disciples the meaning of His death, we read that, "Beginning at Moses and all the prophets, He expounded unto them in all the scriptures the things concerning Himself" (Luke 24:27). So far from the evangel of the apostle's being any (absolutely) new thing, every element in it was revealed long centuries before their birth, not only in words, but in visible representations: there was both a wondrous anticipation of and preparation for the Gospel. Thus a reverent contemplation of the types supplies a blessed confirmation of faith, for they attest the Divine authorship of both Testaments. Moreover, they stimulate adoration; even when we know a person, we enjoy looking at his picture; so here. It is *Christ* that is before us in them.

The *Divine* origin of sacrifices is self-evident. Whoever would have dreamed of the device of offering animal sacrifices to God as a method of acceptable worship? That Abel should have "brought of the firstlings of his flock and of the fat thereof" (Gen. 4:4), can only be satisfactorily accounted for on the ground that he knew this was what God required from him. And this is precisely what the N. T. affirms: Heb. 11:4 declares that it was "by faith" that Abel offered his sacrifice, and Rom. 10:17 says "faith cometh by hearing, and hearing by the word of God." Thus, Abel had received a revelation from God, and *believing* what he had "heard," acted accordingly. Moreover, the acceptance of Abel's sacrifice by a Divine testimony of approval (Gen. 4:4), which, no doubt, was given by the descent of consuming fire from heaven — Lev. 9:24, Judges 6:21, 1 Kings 18:38—intimates the same thing. *That* solemn testimony of reception would only have terrified the offerer, had he himself *invented* this mode of worship! "The lightning shooting round the altar, and consuming the victim, would have conveyed the impression of an angry God: how, then, could they have apprehended by this means that they were reconciled? How could they have known without a Divine revelation that this consuming fire was a token of Divine *acceptance?*" (G. Smeaton).

The great sacrifice of Christ was foreshadowed from the beginning. He who predestinated the salvation of His elect, did also appoint the means thereto: the Lamb was "foreordained before the foundation of the world" (1 Pet. 1:20). Then what memorial could be devised more opposite than that of animal sacrifices? By such a means was exemplified the *death* which had been denounced upon man's disobedience, and in the shedding of the victim's blood and the violent character of its death, was portrayed something of the awfulness of that death which was the "wages of sin." At the same time a fit representation was also made of that death that was to be undergone by the Redeemer, and thus there was connected in one view the two cardinal facts in the history of men — the *fall* and *recovery* from it. The O. T. sacrifices were a "showing forth of the Lord's death" till He came.

It is both important and blessed to note that the Gospel-covenant was revealed by God immediately after the Fall. The promise that the woman's Seed should bruise the serpent's head (Gen. 3:15) and the institution of the types (Gen. 3:21), were to the very end that faith and hope might be preserved in what God had so graciously purposed. God did not leave even our first parents in ignorance of His merciful designs, but made known the nature of His eternal counsels. Soon after, a further revelation was made unto Cain and Abel, and still later to others. The infinite wisdom of God so contrived the types that they might in the most intelligible manner (that material things can describe spiritual) signify the Redeemer, and life and salvation through Him. "From the time of the Fall, there has been but one way open to Heaven, and that was through Christ; and all believers, before and under the law, hoped for pardon of sin and salvation through Him. In hopes of that pardon and salvation they observed the typical services" (W. Romaine).

That the O. T. saints perceived something at least of the mystical and spiritual meaning of the types is clear from a number of passages; that they had a much clearer and fuller apprehension of them than is commonly supposed, is the writer's firm conviction. The Lord Jesus declared that, "Abraham rejoiced to see My day: and he saw, and was glad" (John 8:56). Heb. 11:13 tells us that the patriarchs confessed themselves to be "strangers and pilgrims on the earth," which shows they knew that their true "inheritance" was in Heaven; while Heb. 11:14, 16 expressly states they sought and desired "an heavenly" country. Job said, "I know that my Redeemer liveth" (19: 25), and the Hebrew word there for "Redeemer" signifies one who is a redeemer by right of affinity or kinship—not only a Redeemer in act, but by office. So also David acknowledged, "my flesh longeth for Thee . . . to see Thy power and Thy glory, so as I *have seen* Thee in the sanctuary" (Psa. 63:2), that is, by means of the figures and shadows of the vessels of the tabernacle and the Levitical services and sacrifices.

"First the blade, then the ear and then the full corn in the ear" enunciates one of the principles of the Divine work in everything, the types not excepted. The further we proceed, the profounder their meaning, and the fuller their detail. In the Divine clothing of our first parents with "coats of skins" (Gen. 3:21), there was illustrated the facts that: fallen man needed an external covering to fit him to stand before God; that he could not produce this by his own labours; that the life of an innocent victim must be taken, in order to provide a suitable covering for him; that God himself must provide it. In the offering of Abel and God's acceptance of the same (Gen. 4:4), we learn that God can only regard any sinner with favour by virtue of his acceptance in Christ. The *Divine* origin of sacrifices is again intimated in that before flesh was eaten by man, the distinction between clean and unclean animals was quite familiar (Gen. 8:20). The power of an accepted sacrifice to remove the Divine curse was plainly signified in Gen. 8:21. The principle of substitution was strikingly manifested in Gen. 22:13.

What may be termed the first *great* sacrifice was the "Passover," recorded in Ex. 12. There we behold the efficacy of the Lamb's precious blood to deliver those sheltering beneath it from that judgment of God which their sins deserved. What virtue, an infidel might ask, had the blood of a poor animal to secure the life of Israel's first-born from the sword of a mighty and invisible angel? Was the blood on the door a necessary mark for the angel, because he had not understanding enough to distinguish between the houses of Egyptians and Israelites? Could not God have signified His pleasure to the angel without such a mark as that? The answer to these, and all such questions is, God's design was to furnish a type of *Christ*, and instruct the faith of His people in things to come.

The following is a bare outline of the points in the Passover-type which may be profitably studied by the reader. First, Divine judgment was pronounced: *"all the firstborn (the representative of the family) in (not 'of') the land of Egypt shall die"* (Ex. 11:5). Second, God "put a difference between the Egyptians and Israel" so that not one of His own people were hurt (Ex. 11:7). Third, not by Israel's choice or Moses' recommendation, but by Divine appointment every Israelitish household was to take an unblemished lamb, kill it, and apply its blood to the outside of his house (Ex. 12:3-7). Fourth, the Divine promise was, "when I see the blood, I will pass over you" (12:13). Fifth, the angel entered not such houses, for death had *already* done its work there—a substitute had been slain. Here is *redemption;* deliverance from judgment.

At Sinai God made known His will much more fully respecting the sacrifices which He required. A great deal of instruction therein is to be found in the first seven chapters of Leviticus, into most of which we cannot now enter: much deeply important teaching is to be found therein in a typical form. The Levitical sacrifices emphasised the enormity of sin and the punishment which must be visited upon it, as well as set forth the dependence of the forgiving grace of God on an expiatory offering. Under the Mosaic economy an elaborate system was developed to show that in many ways man offends God and is worthy of death. The sacrifices vividly evidenced the fact that the Divine punishment incurred was inevitable, yet that that punishment could be borne by a substitute, and on that ground the offender could be restored to favour. The principal thing they were designed to exhibit was the indispensable necessity of atonement by vicarious expiation: the one great truth they illustrated was that God could not sacrifice His holiness to His love.

That the Mosaic sacrifices all pointed forward to Christ and had their end in Him, was evidenced by the fact that very soon after He had come and shed His blood, God caused the shadows to pass away. Within a very few years the temple was destroyed, and with it all the Jewish sacrifices ceased. And though a century or two later Julian the Apostate gave the Jews permission to rebuild their temple, and that for the very purpose of restoring the ancient rites, yet God from Heaven blasted all their attempts in a miraculous and extraordinary manner.

The Levitical sacrifices made clear to men the ground on which the Divine pardon could be obtained. It was not an act of absolute mercy, nor was it bestowed on the sole condition of penitence, but on the consideration of something quite distinct from both. "And it shall be, when he shall be guilty of one of these things, that he shall confess that he hath sinned in that thing. And he shall bring his trespass offering unto the Lord for his sin . . . and the priest shall make an atonement for him concerning his sin . . . and it shall be forgiven him" (Lev. 5:5, 6, 10). If we compare these verses with Lev. 17:11, which informs us that "it is the blood which maketh an atonement for the soul," then the proof is conclusive that the sacrifice presented by the offender was the appointed means of obtaining forgiveness for his transgression.

The burnt offering (Lev. 1) and the sin offering (Lev. 4) claim particular attention, for not only were *they* the most important sacrifices of the Levitical dispensation (as Psa. 40:6 intimates), but they represented the sufferings of our great High Priest under two distinct aspects. The burnt offering principally shows Christ as He was to God, the sin offering as He is to men. In both He was represented as a sin-bearer, for in both of these sacrifices transfer was made of sin by the priest laying his hand on the head of the victim (Lev. 1:4, 4:4); in both the victim's blood was shed and sprinkled (Lev. 1:5; 4:4-6); in both atonement was made for sin (1:4, 4:20); and both were burnt, either wholly or in part upon the altar (1:9; 4:9, 10). These points of union were sufficiently close to show that they corresponded in representing the sacrifice offered by our High Priest on the cross.

But there were also distinctive differences between them of a character sufficiently marked to show that they represented Christ's sacrifice under *different* aspects. Thus, the burnt offering was voluntary (Lev. 1:2, 3), the sin offering was compulsory (Lev. 4:2, 3). The burnt offering was flayed, cut into pieces, and the inwards and legs washed in water; but none of these three things were required of the sin offering. The blood of the burnt offering was merely sprinkled round about upon the altar (1:11), but the blood of the sin offering was put upon the horns of the altar, sprinkled seven times before the Lord, before the veil of the sanctuary, and poured out at the bottom of the altar of burnt offering (4:6, 6). Other differences we now pass over, desiring to direct attention merely to the first one mentioned.

The *voluntariness* of Christ's death is clearly brought out in Psa. 40:7, 8 and Eph. 5:25; John 10:17, 18 also shows He freely laid down His life for His sheep. But, when in the councils of eternity, ratified by the everlasting covenant "ordered in all things and sure," Christ had undertaken to be our Surety, *then* what was before purely free and voluntary became in a sense *compulsory*. Just as when God binds Himself by oath, He is obliged to fulfil His word, so Christ once He had bound Himself to stand in His peoples' place and stead, was no longer free — though, not that He wished to be free. Just as the type was bound with cords "unto the horns of the altar" (Psa. 118: 27), so Christ was held fast to the cross not only by love to His people, which floods could not quench, but by His own eternal covenant-engagement.

The substitution of Christ in the sinner's place was most distinctly shown in the types, particularly in the sin offering. Before the animal was slaughtered, the sacrificing priest laid his hand upon its head (Lev. 4:3, 4). That act represented the transferring of sin from the transgressor to the victim (Lev. 16:21): it identified the one with the other. It showed the substitution of the victim for the offender, and declared by a visible sign that it bare his sins and endured their death-penalty. In this way was the solemn yet blessed truth of *imputation* foreshadowed. It was because God transferred to Christ the guilt of His elect, constituting Him "sin for us," that the sword of Divine justice smote Him as He bare our sins in His own body on (or "to") the tree.

The most important of all the types is that which is found in Lev. 16: the appointed ritual for the great day of atonement. The type of Lev. 16 goes much farther than does the one in Ex. 12: the Passover illustrated the *redemptive* character of Christ's sacrifice; that of Lev. 16 its *propitiatory* nature. In Ex. 12 we see the blood sheltering from judgment those who are under it; in the early chapters of Lev., we see the power of the blood restoring to communion the penitent transgressor; but in Lev. 16 we behold the blood opening a way into the very presence of God, entitling the penitent and believing worshipper to come with boldness unto His very throne.

By a careful comparison of Deut. 27 and Lev. 16 we may discover how the law was, and still is, a "schoolmaster" unto Christ (Gal. 3:24). In the former chapter, we see that the law demanded implicit and complete obedience to its demands (v. 10); and how that the Levites pronounced with "a loud voice" a *curse* on the transgressor of it (vv. 14, 15). That curse was repeated twelve times, according to the number of Israel's tribes, and on each pronouncement thereof "all the people" were required to say "Amen": the final word being "Cursed be he that confirmeth not all the words of this law to do them" (v. 26)—cf. Gal. 3:10. The law required sinless perfection under the penalty of eternal damnation, and thus it revealed the imperative need of an *atonement*. While in Lev. 16 we see how that the law by its great sin-offering, with its blood of atonement, pointed forward to Christ.

The sacrificial system of Judaism reached its climax on the great day of atonement. As the ark was the chief object in the tabernacle, so the annual Day of Propitiation was the chief one in Israel's religious calendar. On that auspicious occasion the high priest divested himself of his robes of "glory and beauty" (Ex. 28), and put on "the holy linen" garments (Lev. 16:4). The spotless white in which he was clothed spoke of the perfect *righteousness* of Christ, which, tested as it was both by man (John 8:46) and Satan (John 14:30), and then passing through the infinitely searching scrutiny of God under the fiery trial of the cross, insured the Divine acceptance of that satisfaction which He made to God on behalf of His people.

Two young goats were selected "for a sin-offering"; though there were two animals, it was but one offering. Two goats were selected in order that a fuller representation might be given: the one being designed more expressly to exhibit the *means*, the other the *effect* of the atonement. They were brought and presented together before the Lord (v. 7). The Lord determining by lot which of them was to be slain. The other animal stood by and was atoned for (Heb. of v. 10) by the dying victim, and then bore away the sins laid upon it into the land of eternal forgetfulness (vv. 21, 22): a blessed figure of that *remission* of our sins when we believe on the Lord Jesus Christ unto salvation.

Passing by what was done with the bullock, we confine our attention unto the two goats. After the one had been killed, the high priest took its blood within the veil and sprinkled it upon the mercy-seat once, but seven times before it (v. 15 and cf. v. 14): once was sufficient for God, but seven times "before" Him to provide a *perfect* standingground for His people. The antitype of this is seen in Heb. 9:12, "But by His own blood He entered in once into the holy place, having obtained eternal redemption" (Heb. 9:12). The consequence of this is that "Having therefore, brethren, boldness to enter into the holiest by the blood of Jesus, by a new and living way which He hath consecrated for us" (Heb. 10:19, 20).

After the high priest had finished his work inside the sanctuary, we are told, "he shall bring the live goat, and Aaron shall lay both his hands upon the head of the live goat and confess over him all the iniquities of the Children of Israel . . . and shall send him away by the hand of a fit man into the wilderness: and the goat shall bear upon him all their iniquities into a land not inhabited" (vv. 20-22). That was a continuation and completion of the ceremony concerning the sin-offering, so that this symbolic transfer of their sins to the head of the scapegoat, which bore them away, plainly signified that the atonement effected by the sacrifice of the first goat was the complete removal of all their transgressions from before the face of God.

"And Aaron shall come into the tabernacle of the congregation, and shall put off the linen garments, which he put on when he went into the holy place, and shall *leave* them there" (Lev. 16:23). Why? To denote that his work was *finished*. The blessed antitype of this we see in Luke 24:12: on the resurrection morning, those who came to Christ's empty sepulchre "beheld the *linen clothes*" lying there, a token that He was risen from the dead, and so of atonement completed, and accepted by God.

One other important feature in the types, often overlooked, claims our notice, namely, the *burning* of the victim's body on the altar (Lev. 1:10 etc.). The animal was first slain as a just judgment for the sin which had been transferred to it by the laying on its head of the hand of the offerer; and then, after guilt had been borne, its flesh was laid on the altar and burned, and went up with acceptance unto God, a "sweet-smelling savour." In this was represented the glorious truth that, not only was Christ our sin-bearer, but that He is also our *righteousness* before God (Jer. 23:6, 2 Cor. 5:21). We are identified with Him not only in His *death* for us, but also in the *fragrance* of it before God.

In Num. 19 there is yet another most important type upon which we can only now say a few words. In it we see how the death of Christ has made full provision for those defilements which His people contract while passing through this evil world. In it too we behold again the steady progress in the types, and the deeper instruction which God gave to Israel from time to time. They were yet in the land of Pharaoh when the passover was instituted: the doom of Egypt and their own deliverance therefrom were the thoughts then presented to their souls. Later, they were brought nigh to God, Himself tabernacling in their midst, and in Lev. 16 they are shown the high demands of His holiness. Now in Num. 19, they are taught that even the unavoidable contact with death (the world lying in the Wicked one) defiles. But God has provided cleansing from it.

In closing, we call attention to one other deeply important value of the types and the use to which they may be put: they furnish an infallible rule by which can be *tested* any man's (our own included) *interpretation* of the N. T. Scriptures concerning the Atonement! He who denies the penal and vicarious nature of Christ's death, repudiates the clear testimony of the types, he who sets aside the efficacy of His sacrifice by reducing it to a merely "making possible" the salvation of men, does likewise, for the types know nothing of an ineffectual sacrifice. So too in them we see plainly the *limitation* of God's love to His elect people, for no lamb was provided for the Egyptians, nor did Aaron make any atonement for the sins of the Midianites and Ammonites! A.W.P.

DEPRAVITY

"The wicked are estranged from the womb, they go astray as soon as they are born, speaking lies. Their poison is like the poison of a serpent; they are like the deaf adder that stoppeth her ear, which will not hearken to the voice of charmers, charming never so wisely" (Psa. 58:3:5).

It has been supposed by some interpreters that this Psalm was written as a prophetic description of the unjust judges who condemned our Lord Jesus Christ. It begins by reproving them for their unjust judges: "Do ye indeed' (v. 1). It opens up the dark recesses of their heart and history: "the wicked are estranged from the womb" (v. 3). It shows their coming destruction: "the righteous shall rejoice when he seeth the vengeance; he shall wash his feet in the blood of the wicked" (v. 10). However this may be, they were of the same nature with us. The Scribes and Pharisees who condemned our Lord had hearts of the same kind as ours, so that we may learn this day the awful depravity of the heart of man.

I. *Original Depravity.*

"The wicked are estranged from the womb." The expression "from the womb" occurs frequently in Scripture, and means from the very first period of our existence. The angel of the Lord said to the wife of Manoah, "The child shall be a Nazarite unto God from the womb" (Judges 13:5); that is, from the very first point of its existence. God said to Jeremiah, "Before I formed thee in the belly I knew thee; and before thou camest forth out of the womb I sanctified thee; and ordained thee a prophet unto the nations" (1:5). Jeremiah was set apart as a prophet before he was born. Paul says, "But when it pleased God, who separated me from my mother's womb, and called me by His grace, to reveal His Son in me" (Gal. 1:15). Paul was set apart by God for the work of the ministry from the very first. So, in the words before us, it is declared that from the very first we are estranged from God. Now, this estrangement is twofold.

1. *Of the head.* The whole mind is estranged from God. "At that time ye were without God" (Eph. 2:12). The natural man is ignorant of God from the very womb. God is a stranger to him, so that he does not know Him. He has no true discovery of God's infinite purity, of His immutable justice, and of the strictness of His law. He does not know the love of God, nor how freely He has provided a Saviour. "God is not in all his thoughts" (Psa. 10:4). Either he does not turn his mind upon God at all, or else he thinks Him altogether such an one as himself. "There is none that understandeth" (Psa. 14:2).

2. *Of the heart.* A new born child will naturally feel after its mother's breast: it naturally seeks the breast. But it does not in the same manner feel after God: "There is none that seeketh after God" (Rom. 3:11). From the very first we dislike God. A child soon comes to relish the presence of its earthly parents, and of other children. But it does not relish the presence of God. The natural tendency of the heart is to go away from God, and to remain out of His sight. A natural man does not like the presence of a very eminent saint. If he has full liberty, he will leave the room, and seek other company more suited to his taste. This is the very way he treats God. God is too holy for him, he is too pure, and therefore, he does all he can to leave His company. This is the reason why you cannot get unconverted men to pray in secret. They would rather spend half an hour in the tread-mill every morning than go to meet God. This is the true condition of every one of you who is now unconverted; indeed it was the condition of us all, but some of you have been brought out of it. From the time you were in the womb, till now, your whole head and heart have been turned away from God: "the imagination of man's heart is evil from his youth" (Gen. 8:21). "Who can bring a clean thing out of an unclean, not one" (Job. 14:4). Your *whole nature* is totally depraved. You are accustomed to think that you have some parts good; that though some part was depraved, yet some is not. But the whole heart is faint and sick. Your *whole history* remains unsound, your whole head is covered with sin. You are accustomed to think that a great part of your life has been innocent. You admit that some pages of your life are stained with crimson and scarlet sins—some pages you blush to look back upon—but surely you have some fair leaves also. Learn that you are "estranged from the womb." Every moment you have spent without God, and in turning away from God. *Every* page of your life has got this written at the top of it: This day God was not in all his thoughts,

he did not like to retain God in his knowledge. "Every imagination of the thoughts of his heart was only evil continually."

II. Actual sin.

"They go astray as soon as they be born, speaking lies." There are two paths from which every natural man goes astray as soon as born.

1. *The way of God's commandments.* This is the pure way in which holy angels walk. They do His commandments, hearkening to the voice of His word. It is a pure way, having ten paths in which the feet of the upright love to go. "Blessed are the undefiled in the way, who walk in the law of the Lord." "Make me to go in the path of Thy commandments: for therein do I delight." From this we go astray as soon as born, speaking lies. One of these paths says, "Thou shalt not bear false witness against thy neighbour"; but this is one of the very first that is forsaken—speaking lies. "All we like sheep have gone astray, we have turned every one to his own way" (Isa. 53:6).

2. *The way of pardon.* Christ saith unto him "I am the way," and again, "Straight is the gate and narrow is the way that leadeth unto life." The same is in view in Isa, 35:9, "The redeemed shall walk there." But from this way also "they go astray as soon as they be born, speaking lies." Life is given to sinners that they may enter upon this Way, but they spend it in going further and further away. The parable of the lost sheep shows the true state of every unconverted soul, wandering away from the good shepherd. "They are all gone out of the way." "Destruction and misery are in their ways, and the way of peace have they not known" (Rom. 3:12). And, oh! what fearful meaning does this give to the declaration "speaking lies," for it is written, "who is a liar, but he that denieth that Jesus is the Christ?" (1 John 2:22). And again, "he that believeth not God, hath made God a liar." No man can go away from Christ without speaking lies.

Learn the fearful condition of those of you who are natural men. First, from the day you were born you have gone astray from the path of God's commandments. Every year, month, week, day, hour, minute, has been filled up with sin. Every day has seen you go farther from holiness, farther from God, nearer to hell. You are treasuring up wrath against the day of wrath. Oh! what a treasure—heeping up fuel to burn you throughout eternity. If any of you live in drinking or swearing, or any other sin, you are heeping up fuel for your eternal hell. You are getting farther on in your sin. You are wreathing your chains more and more round you. By a law of human nature, every time you sin, the habit becomes stronger, so that you are every day becoming more completely like the Devil. It is every day more hard to turn. Experience shows that most people are converted when young. Dear young people, every day you live in sin it will be more impossible to turn. "They that seek Me early shall find me." Second, from the day you were born you have gone astray from Christ. Every day you remain unsaved, you are wandering away from Him. Every day you are getting nearer to hell and farther from Christ. Unbelief gets stronger every day.

III. *The deadly enmity of natural man to God*—"their poison."

1. *Because they are the children of the old Serpent, the Devil.* All natural men are the seed of the Serpent (Gen. 3:15). All who oppose and dislike the children of God, do so because they are the seed of the Serpent, and the poison of the Serpent remains in them. John the Baptist said to the Pharisees, "O generation of vipers" (Matt. 3:7). In a still more dreadful manner did our blessed Lord say, "Ye serpents, ye generation of vipers" (Matt. 23:33). The Pharisees and Sadducees were not of a different nature, from us; they had the same flesh and blood, and the same wicked heart; they were children of their father, the Devil, and the lusts of their father they would do (John 8:44).

2. *Because they had a mortal enmity to God.* The poison of the serpent is deadly poison. When it darts its envenomed sting into a man it seeks to kill him. Such is the cruel venom of the natural heart against God. He is a mortal enemy to God's holy government. It has been said, "If the throne of God were within your reach, and ye knew this, it would not be safe one hour." Man is a mortal enemy to the very being of God. "The fool has said in his heart—no God" (Psa. 14:1). It is in his heart he says this, such is the secret desire of every unconverted bosom. If the breast of God were within the reach of men,

it would be stabbed a million times in one moment. When God was manifest in flesh, He was altogether lovely; He did not sin; He went about continually doing good: and yet they took Him and hung Him on a tree; they mocked Him and spit upon Him. And this is the way men would do with God again.

Learn first, the fearful depravity of your heart. I venture to say that there is not an unconverted man present who has the most distant idea of the monstrous wickedness which is now within his breast. Stop till you are in hell, and it will break out unrestrained. But let me tell you what it is:—you have a heart that would kill God if you could. If the bosom of God were now within your reach, and one blow would rid the universe of Him, you have a heart fit to do the deed. Second, the amazing love of Christ — "while we were enemies, Christ died for us."

IV. Deaf to the voice of the Gospel.

It is a well known fact that many kinds of serpents can be tamed by the power of music. This is referred to in Eccl. 10:11 and Jer. 8:17. Many travellers in Egypt and India have seen this. But there is said to be one kind of serpent which is either deaf, so that it cannot hear the music, or it has the power of making itself deaf for the time, so that it is not charmed. So it is with unconverted men. Christ is the great charmer. His voice is like the sound of many waters. Never man spake like this Man. When Andrew and Peter heard it, they left all and followed him; so did James, and John, and Matthew. When the bride hears Him, she cries, "The voice of my Beloved"! When the sheep hear His voice, they follow Him; when the dead hear His voice, they live; when the heavy-laden hear it, they find rest.

But unconverted men will not hear. They are like Manasseh—they will not hearken; they are like the Jews when Stephen preached—they stopped their ears and ran. Ah, how many of you are doing the same thing—stopping your ears. How many of you stop your ears with the noise of the world, its business and care—some with a favourite lust. The voice of the great Charmer has been often heard in this place, and some have heard it and followed Him; and why are you left behind?

Learn, first, the folly of this. He is charming you to bless you, to bring you to peace, pardon, holiness. "There is none other name under heaven given among men whereby we must be saved." Second, the guilt of this. It is the highest sin of all, to refuse Him that speaketh from heaven: Heb. 12:25. It is unpardonable. All manner of sin and blasphemy may be forgiven you, but if you will not hear the voice of Christ, you must perish. Some would feign lay the blame off themselves, but God washed Himself clear of the unbeliever's guilt. It is you that stopped your ear; ye do always resist the Holy Spirit. You will one day find that, "He that believeth not shall be damned" (Mark 16:16).

—R. M. Cheyne, 1845.

REPENTANCE

One of the Divinely predicted characteristics of the "perilous times" in which we are now living is that "evil men and seducers shall wax worse and worse, deceiving, and being deceived" (2 Tim. 3: 13). The deeper reference of these words is to *spiritual* seducers and deceivers Men with captivating personalities, men who occupy a prominent place in Christendom, men with an apparently deep reverence for Holy Writ, are beguiling souls with fatal error. Not only are evolutionists, higher critics and modernists deluding multitudes of our young people with their sugar-coated lies, but some who pose as the champions of orthodoxy and boast of their ability to "rightly divide the Word of Truth," are poisoning the minds of many to their eternal destruction.

Such a charge as we have just made is indeed a serious one, and one which is not to be readily received without proof. But proof is easily furnished. The Word of God teaches plainly that in this dispensation, equally with preceding ones, God requires a sincere and deep repentance *before* He pardons any sinner. Repentance is absolutely necessary in order to salvation, just as necessary as is faith in the Lord Jesus Christ. "Except ye repent, ye shall all likewise perish" (Luke 13:3). "Then hath God also to the Gentiles granted repentance *unto life*" (Acts 11:18). "For godly sorrow worketh repentance *to salvation* not to be repented of" (2 Cor. 7:10). It is impossible to frame language more explicit than that. Therefore, in view of these verses, and others yet to be quoted, we cannot but sorrowfully regard those who are now affirming that repentance is *not*, in this dispensation, essential unto salvation, as being deceivers of souls, blind leaders of the blind.

A careful comparison of the prominent place which is given to repentance in the New Testament with the very small place it has in present-day teaching, even in so-called "orthodox" pulpits, brings to light one of the most significant and solemn "signs of the times." Some of the most prominent of those who are pleased to style themselves "teachers of *dispensational* truth" insist that repentance belongs to a past period, being altogether "Jewish," and deny in toto that, in this age, God demands repentance from the sinner before he can be saved, thus blankly repudiating Acts 17:30: "But *now* commandeth all men every where to repent." When it is borne in mind that these men are most diligent students of Scripture, we can but sorrowfully see in them the fulfilment of those words "ever learning, and never able to come to the knowledge of the truth" (2 Tim. 3:7).

Others, in their recoil from salvation by reformation, have failed to duly preserve the balance of truth, and give proper place to such Scriptures as "He that covereth his sins shall not prosper: but whoso confesseth and forsaketh them shall have mercy" (Prov. 28:13), and "Let the wicked forsake his way, and the unrighteous man his thoughts, and let him return unto the Lord, and He will have mercy upon him" (Isa. 55:7). It is not that there is anything meritorious in a sinner's compliance with this righteous demand of God, but that the claims of the Holy One must be pressed on those who have transgressed against Him. Yet that is just the thing which the haughty rebel desires to hear about least of all, and the sad thing is that so many are now, wittingly or unwittingly, withholding that which is unpalatable to men but which is honouring to God. How widespread this withholding is, may be quickly discovered by an examination of present-day tracts purporting to explain *how* a sinner may be saved: in most of them not a word is said about repentance! Alas, in the past, our own tracts have failed sadly to sufficiently emphasize this point.

Even where it *is* held that repentance is necessary before a sinner can be saved, only too often the most shallow and superficial views are entertained of what repentance really is. In many circles it is assumed that if a person sheds tears or appears to be heart-broken on account of the evil course he has followed, this is clear proof that a saving work of Divine grace has begun in that person's heart. But this by no means follows. The prickings of an uneasy conscience are not the same as the conviction of sin which is produced by the Holy Spirit. Esau wept, and wept bitterly, yet was he not regenerated. Felix trembled under the preaching of Paul, but there is no hint in Scripture that he has gone to heaven. Multitudes are deceived on this very point, and there is very little in present-day ministry which is calculated to undeceive them. Every one of us who values his soul and is concerned about his eternal destiny, will do well to carefully examine his repentance in the light of scripture and ascertain whether it be of man or from God, natural or supernatural.

The first occurrence of the word "repent" furnishes the key to its meaning and scope. In Gen. 6:6 we read, "And it repented the Lord that He had made man on the earth." The language is figurative, for He who is infinite in wisdom and immutable in counsel never changes His mind. This is plain from "God is *not* a man that He should lie, neither the son of man that He should repent" (Num. 23:19), and "The Strength of Israel will not lie *nor repent*, for He is not a man that He should repent" (1 Sam. 15:29); and again, "with whom is *no* variableness, neither shadow of turning" (James 1:17). Thus, in the light of these definite statements we are compelled to conclude that in Gen. 6:6 (and similar passages) the Almighty condescends to accommodate Himself to our mode of speaking, and express Himself after a human manner—as He also does in Psa. 78:65; 87:6; Isa. 59:16 etc.

Now by carefully noting the setting of this word in Gen. 6:6 and attentively observing what follows, we discover: first, that the *occasion* of repentance is *sin*, for in Gen. 6:5 we read that "God saw that the wickedness of man was great in the earth": thus repentance is a realization of the exceeding sinfulness of sin.

Second, that the *nature* of repentance consists in a *change of mind*: a new decision is formed in view of the deplorable conditions existing—"it *repented* the Lord that He had made man." Third, that genuine repentance is *accompanied by* a real sorrow for sin, for that which necessitated the change of mind: "and it *grieved* Him at His heart"—cf. 2 Cor. 7:10. Fourth, that the *fruit* or consequence of repentance appears in a determination to *undo* (forsake, and rectify as far as possible) that which is sorrowed over: "and the Lord said I will *destroy* man" (v. 7). All of these elements are found in a repentance which has been produced in the heart by the gracious and supernatural operation of the Holy Spirit. Let us now consider,

1. *Its Necessity.*

This is discovered by a contemplation of the Law, for "by the law is the knowledge of sin" (Rom. 3:20). Where there is no enforcing and expounding of the holy law of God there can be no true, deep, saving knowledge of sin. As the apostle Paul so plainly affirms, "I had not *known* sin, but by the law" (Rom. 7:7). The exceeding sinfulness of sin (Rom. 7:13) is only exposed when the Spirit turns the light of God's law upon our conscience and heart. But this is preeminently an age of lawlessness, and that in every respect. And it cannot be otherwise: where the law of God is flouted, where thousands of preachers are declaring that the law has no place in this dispensation of grace, we cannot expect people to have much respect for human law. God has caused the people to reap that which they have sown: having sown the wind, they are now reaping the whirlwind. Bolshevism and anarchy are the inevitable rebound from having slighted and rejected the Ten Commandments!

Practical godliness consists in a conformity of heart and life to the *Law* of God, and in a sincere compliance with the *Gospel* of Christ. But it is only as we rightly understand both the Law and the Gospel that we can discern wherein a conformity to the one and a compliance with the other really consists. Now the requirements of the Law are summed up in that word, "Thou shalt love the Lord thy God with all thine heart, and with all thy soul, and with all thy might" (Deut. 6:5 and cf. Matt. 22:37). Observe carefully the three things here specified: first, the duty required, namely, love to God. Second, the ground or reason for this, namely, because He is the Lord our God. Third, the measure or extent of this duty, namely, to love Him with *all* the heart. Nothing other than this, nothing less than this, will ever meet the righteous claims of God upon us.

Now that which is implied in and required unto a real love to God is, first, a true *knowledge of Him*. If our apprehensions of God are wrong, if they are not formed by Scripture, then it is obvious we have but a false image of Him, framed by our own fancy. By a true knowledge of God (John 17:3, 1 John 5:20) we mean far more than a correct theoretical notion of His perfections: there must be a heartfelt realization of His personal loveliness, His ineffable glory. And where *that* truly exists, there will be a *delighting* of ourselves in Him (Psa. 37:4) and a desire and a determination to *please* Him. And self-love naturally causes us to magnify self and seek to promote our own interests, so a true love to God causes us to put Him first and seek His interests.

In repentance *sin* is the thing to be repented of, and sin is a transgression of the law (1 John 3:4). And the first and chief thing required by the law is *supreme love to God*. Therefore, the lack of supreme love to God, the heart's disaffection for His character and rebellion against Him (Rom. 8:7) is our great wickedness, which we have to repent of. But it will never be in our hearts to repent, unless we truly see our blame. And we can never truly see our blame, until we perceive that which chiefly renders us *to* blame. It is the excellency of God, the infinite perfections of His glorious being, which renders Him worthy of and entitled to our supreme love and fullest obedience; and this it is which chiefly renders us to blame, for *not* having loved and served Him. Not to love so loveable an Object as the God of love is the crime of crimes.

What is *sin?* Sin is a saying, I renounce the God who made me; I disallow His right to govern me. I care not what He says to me, what commandments He has given, nor how He expostulates: I prefer self-indulgence to His approval. I am indifferent unto all He has done to and for me; His blessings and gifts move me not: I am going to be lord of myself. Sin is rebellion against the Majesty of Heaven. It is to treat the Almighty with contempt. Oh how vastly different a thing is *sin* from what the world supposes! How insensible are the unregenerate to the glory of God and that which is due unto Him from us!

The natural man supposes that the great evil of sin consists in its being so injurious *to us*. For a creature which is absolutely dependent, to assume an attitude of haughty independence, is the sin of sins. To despise One who is infinitely glorious and infinitely worthy of honour, love and obedience, is an awful abomination. To be more concerned about pleasing fellow-rebels than to seek the favour of God, is turpitude of the blackest dye. O reader, if you have never seen the *great evil* of sin, then are you a stranger to God and blind to His surpassing loveliness; you are under the *blinding* power of sin.

Weigh well what is now being presented if you value your soul, dear friend. The *"deceitfulness* of sin" (Heb. 3:13) may hitherto have closed your eyes to the terrible condition you are in. If so, are you now willing to be undeceived? Are you willing to really see *yourself?* Then make no mistake upon this point: never was any sinner pardoned while he was impenitent; and never was a soul truly penitent, while insensible of the great evil of sin; and never did a sinner perceive the great evil of sin till he became acquainted with the infinitely great and glorious God against whom he has sinned. You may indeed have been sorry for sin on *other* accounts— as exposing you to shame before men, as having injured your reputation, or because it has brought down God's chastening hand upon your body or temporal affairs. But if you have never seen the great evil of sin as it is against that God who is infinitely glorious in Himself, then your repentance was not genuine, and *God* has not pardoned you.

"Against Thee, Thee only, have I sinned, and done this evil in Thy sight" (Psa. 51:4). A sense of the great evil of sin is essential to true repentance. We cannot be suitably affected toward things unless we see them as they are. No matter how lovely a thing or person may be, if their excellency be not perceived the heart is untouched. Even the infinite glory of God will not excite our esteem and love, if we have no sense of it. So, on the other hand, let sin be never so evil, yet if this be not *realized* we are not suitably affected toward it. Though it deserves to be hated with perfect hatred, and though there be every reason why we should be horrified on account of it and abase ourselves before God, mourning it in bitterness of heart, fearing it, watching against it as the greatest of all evils, yet we shall never do so until we see sin in its real hideousness. Thus a deep sense of the infinite evil of sin is plainly essential to repentance, yea, it is from this that repentance immediately springs.

The evil of sin arises from our obligations to do otherwise, namely, our being under obligation to love and serve Him who is infinitely glorious. But unless I clearly *see* this, there will be, there cannot be any deep repentance. The language of every sinner's heart is, I care not *what* God requires, I am going to have *my own* way. I care not what be God's claims upon me, I refuse to submit unto His authority. I care not what He has threatened to do unto those that defy Him, I will not be intimidated. His eyes may be upon me, but I am not going to be restrained thereby; I care not what *He* loves and what He hates I shall please myself. But when the Holy Spirit enlightens and convicts a soul, his language is—"Against Thee, Thee only, have I sinned, and done this evil in Thy sight."

Thus, true repentance issues from a realization in the heart, wrought therein by the Holy Spirit, of the sinfulness of sin, of the awfulness of ignoring the claims of God and defying His authority. It is therefore a holy horror and hatred of sin, a deep sorrow for it, an acknowledgment of it before God, and a complete heart-forsaking of it. Not until this is done will God pardon us. Whoever will take the trouble to search through the Scriptures on this point, will find that it is plainly and uniformly taught by Moses and the Prophets, by Christ and His Apostles. Begin with what God demanded on the Day of Atonement: "whatsoever soul it be that shall not be *afflicted* in that same day," so far from the sacrifice removing *his* sins, "he shall be cut off from among his people" (Lev. 23:29).

Weigh well the teaching of these verses: "If they shall bethink themselves in the land whither they were carried captives, and *repent*, and make supplication unto Thee in the land of them that carried them captives, saying, We have sinned, and have done perversely, we have committed wickedness; And *return* unto Thee with *all* their heart, and with all their soul, in the land of their enemies, which led them away captive, and *pray* unto Thee . . . *Then* hear Thou their prayer and their supplication . . . and *forgive* Thy people that they have sinned against Thee" (1 Kings 8:47-50). No change of dispensation has wrought any change in the character of the thrice holy God. His claims are ever the same.

For the teachings of the Prophets *see* Psa. 32:3-5, Prov. 28:13, Jer. 4:4, Ezek. 18:30-32, Hosea 5:15, Joel 2:12:18. John the Baptist, the forerunner of Christ, preached saying, "Repent ye, for the kingdom of heaven is at hand" (Matt. 3:2). This was as though he said, "Such is the nature of the Messiah's kingdom, so holy is it, that no impenitent sinner, while such, can be a member of it and share its blessings. The promised One is on the eve of making His appearance: therefore repent ye, and thus be prepared to receive Him." Thus did John preach, and many did he turn unto the Lord their God: Luke 1:16, 17.

The Lord Jesus taught and constantly pressed the *same* truth. His call was, "Repent ye, and believe the Gospel" (Mark 1:15): the Gospel cannot be savingly believed until there is genuine repentance—as the ground must be ploughed before it is capable of receiving the seed, so the heart must be melted ere it will welcome *the Lord and* Saviour Jesus Christ. Therefore did He declare, "Blessed are they that *mourn*, for they shall be comforted" (Matt. 5:4), and announce that He had been sent "to heal the *broken*-hearted" (Luke 4:18). He came here to "call sinners to repentance" (Luke 5:32), and insisted that "*Except ye repent,* ye shall all likewise perish" (Luke 13:3, 5). He illustrated this truth at length in the parable of the prodigal son, who "came to himself," repented, *left* the "far country," returned to the Father, and so obtained His forgiveness (Luke 15:17-20).

When risen from the dead, Christ commissioned His servants, "that repentance *and* remission of sins should be preached in His name among *all* nations" (Luke 24:47), and Acts 5:31 tells us that He has been exalted on high to communicate these blessings in the *same order*, namely, "to give repentance to (the *spiritual*) Israel *and* forgiveness of sins." Accordingly we find the apostles, who were filled with the Holy Spirit, thus carrying out His command. On the day of Pentecost when many were "pricked in their hearts" and asked "what shall we do?", Peter did not say, Do nothing, but rest upon the finished work of Christ. Instead, he said, "*Repent*, and be baptised every one of you in the name of Jesus Christ, for the remission of sins" (Acts 2:38). Again, in Acts 3:19 we find him saying, "Repent ye therefore and be converted *that* your sins *may be* blotted out"!

When Paul was converted and sent to preach the Gospel to the Gentiles, it was to "open their eyes and to *turn them from* darkness to light and from the power of Satan unto God, *that* they might receive forgiveness of sins" (Acts 26:18); hence we find he went everywhere and preached to men that "they should repent and turn to God and do works meet for repentance" (Acts 26:20), "testifying to both Jews *and also* to the Greeks, repentance toward God and faith toward our Lord Jesus Christ" (Acts 20:21). As to those who shut their eyes, stopped their ears, hardened their hearts, and were given up to destruction in the days of the Prophets (Isa. 6:10), of Christ (Matt. 13:15), and of the Apostles (Acts 28:27), their sentence ran thus: "lest they should see with their eyes, hear with their ears, understand with their hearts, and be converted, and I should heal them," which compared with Mark 4:12 signifies, "and their sins should be forgiven them."

Against these clear and consistent testimonies of Holy Writ, certain men have insisted that the Divine call to repentance was never made to any except those who were in covenant relationship with God. But as we have shown, Acts 17:30 and 26:20 clearly expose this error. Some have pointed out that the word "repent" is not once found in all John's Gospel, and in view of 20:31 have *reasoned* that it is not necessary unto salvation. But John's Gospel is plainly addressed unto those who *are* saved (see 1:16). It is that Gospel which sets forth the Son in relation to the sons of God. John 20:31 obviously means that this Gospel is written to *strengthen* the faith of Believers; as 1 John 5:13 (addressed to those who already *knew* they were saved: see 2:3 etc.) signifies the purpose of that Epistle was to *deepen* assurance. Others have drawn a false inference from the very infrequent mention of repentance in the Epistles, but they also are addressed to the saints; yet 2 Cor. 7:10, 2 Tim. 2:25, 2 Pet. 3:9 manifestly confirm the fact that repentance *is* required throughout *this* dispensation.

"There is no *new* thing under the sun" (Ecc. 1:9), nor is the present-day denial of the necessity of repentance for salvation any twentieth century novelty. In proof of this statement we could fill page after page with quotations from Antinomians and others who lived long before "dispensational truth" was first heard of. No, it is an old devise of Satan's, yet under a new dress. But woe be unto those who accept his lie. God must cease to exist before He will lower His claims and cease demanding repentance from all who have rebelled against Him. Make no mistake upon this point, dear reader: *it is turn or burn*—turn from your course of self-will and self-pleasing; turn in broken-heartedness unto God, seeking His mercy in Christ; turn with full purpose to please and serve Him, or be tormented day and night forever and ever in the Lake of Fire. A.W.P.

PRESERVATION AND PERSEVERANCE

The precious truth of Divine preservation is designed for the deepening of the Christian's gratitude. It makes known to him the fullness of that grace which God bestows upon His people. It declares that He who has begun a good work in them, will continue and complete it (Phil 1:6). It assures us that nothing shall ever separate them from the love of God which is in Christ Jesus their Lord (Rom. 8:35-39). It reveals the blessed fact that the power of God is engaged to protect them from evil and deliver them from their foes: God "hath raised up an horn of salvation for us . . . that we should be saved from our enemies" (Luke 1:69, 71). What a song of thanksgiving should this raise in the hearts of the redeemed!

Again, this blessed truth of the saints' security is intended as a Divine tonic for our drooping spirits. Fighting the good fight of faith, yet how often the battle seems to be going against us! Were it not for the comforting assurance of God's promises we might well be in doubt as to the ultimate issue. Living in a hostile world, Satan and his hosts seeking to bring about our destruction, having no might of our own, despair would fill our hearts were God to leave us to ourselves. But blessed be His name, He does not. His ear is open to our cries, His arm ever ready to defend us. "The angel of the Lord encampeth round about them that fear Him, and delivereth them" (Psa. 34:7).

Now like every other truth revealed in Scripture, the Divine preservation of the saints is capable of being perverted and "wrested" to men's destruction (2 Peter 3:16). Religious hypocrites, empty professors, baptised worldlings, make a wrong use of it, whereby, the Truth of God is dishonoured. They draw from it a peace and joy to which they are not entitled. They assume, without warrant that *they* are saved, and though they have none of the marks of regeneration and bear no spiritual fruit, nevertheless they persuade themselves that God will carry them through to heaven. Satan has deceived them into thinking that some time in the past, years ago, they believed in Christ, and discovering that the Bible teaches, "Once saved, always saved," they go on in a carnal confidence from which the great majority are never aroused, until they awake in hell.

Because this blessed truth of God's preservation of His children has been so perverted by multitudes who are not His children, not a few have concluded it is a "dangerous doctrine," and that it is better for the pulpit to be silent thereon. But this is a pitting of their worthless reason against the infinite wisdom of God. *He* has published it plainly enough in His Word, and so should His servants. Moreover, to follow such a course would be withholding from the children part of their necessary bread. The abuse of a doctrine is no proof that it is a harmful one. If all men were gluttons, that would be no argument for my declining to eat any food, but it would be a caution for me to use it temperately.

God Himself has safeguarded the truth of Divine preservation by inseparably linking with it the complementary truth of human perseverance. Nowhere has God promised to preserve anybody while he is following a course of self-will and self-pleasing. It is not in the path of fleshly indulgence and conformity to this world, but in the Highway of Holiness that His protecting grace is to be found. If I deliberately drink poison no praying will deliver me from its deadly effects. If I neglect the means of grace then my soul will starve. If I presume upon God's goodness and expect Him to shield me when I deliberately run into the place of temptation, then I shall be justly left to reap as I have sown.

The little word "if" is often used as the Spirit's sentinel to protect this precious truth. "*If* ye continue in My Word then are ye My disciples indeed" (John 8:31). "We are made partakers of Christ *if* we hold the beginning of our confidence steadfast unto the end" (Heb. 3:14). "*If* ye do these things, ye shall never fall" (2 Pet. 1:10). "*If* that which ye have heard from the beginning remain in you, ye also shall continue in the Son, and in the Father". (1 John 2:24). It is not these things which conduct us into Christ, but they *evidence* that we *are* in Him. It is because there is a spurious faith, a false profession, an imitation of God's work of grace, that the Spirit so often emphasises the fact it is only as we press forward along the Narrow Way of practical godliness that our perseverance proves our faith to be genuine.

Walking in obedience to God's commands and precepts is no meritorious condition of earning salvation, but it is the proof that we are saved. Bringing forth fruit to the glory of God does not unite us to the true Vine, but makes it manifest that we *are* united to Him. Denying ungodliness and worldly lusts, mortifying our members which are upon the earth, taking up the cross and following Christ, do not secure a title to heaven, but show that we *are* journeying heavenward. A steady perseverance in the use of the Divine means of grace, in running the race that is set before us, and in pressing onwards to a closer walk with Christ, are the *evidences* that we are blest with persevering grace, and "are not of them who draw back unto perdition, but of them that believe to the saving of the soul" (Heb. 10:39).

We need to be on our guard against a one-sided view of Salvation. While it be true that one who is born of the Spirit has been saved, it is equally true that, from another standpoint his salvation is yet future: see Rom. 13:11, Heb. 9:28, 1 Pet. 1:5. The Christian has been saved from the penalty of sin, but he is now being saved from the power and pollution of sin. He has been "delivered from the wrath to come," but he now needs delivering from the assaults of Satan, from the temptations of an enticing world, from the solicitations of the "flesh" which still dwells within him. The Christian is yet in the place of danger. Not yet has he entered his eternal rest; so far from it, he is called upon to "fight the good fight of faith," and to take unto him "the whole armour of God."

It is the fact that the Christian is yet in the place of danger which gives force to the *warnings* of Scripture. These are as necessary to him as are the promises and precepts. There are certain danger-signals the Spirit has set up, and which it is the part of wisdom to heed. "For if ye live after the flesh, ye shall die" (Rom. 8:13): here we learn what would be the inevitable end were a certain line of conduct persisted in. Such a word as this can only be disregarded at our imminent peril. Carnal presumption may ignore and defy it, but the righteous will heed it. Though every true saint has the infallible assurance that "The Lord *will* perfect that which concerneth me," nevertheless he at once adds, "forsake not the works of Thine own hands" (Psa. 138:8).

God's promises are the foundation of our prayers, being the ground upon which faith rests. But these promises were never designed to render the means of grace needless. Rather are they given to stir us up to make a diligent use of them. A regenerate heart *does* make such use of them, but a corrupt heart turns even the grace of God into lasciviousness, nor will any legal terrors prevent this. The thunders and lightnings, and the earthquake which shook mount Sinai, greatly terrified Israel, yet a few days later we find them dancing merrily around the golden calf. Such is fallen human nature: almost killed with fear at some awful providence, yet laughing at that fear as soon as the shock is over. Nothing but the grace of God can set the heart right and keep it settled.

The doctrine of Divine preservation affords a stable prop to upright hearts, yet it lends no wanton cloak to corrupt hearts. It brings a cordial to revive the faint, but has a guard to chech the froward. That guard, as we have seen, is the qualifying "if": "to present you holy and unblamable and unreproveable in His sight, *if* ye continue in the faith grounded and settled, and be not moved away from the hope of the Gospel" (Col. 1:22, 23). When Christ says that He gives unto His sheep "eternal life, and they shall never perish" (John 10:28), He affirms their everlasting security. But when the Holy Spirit announces that it is through "faith and patience" we "inherit the promises"

(Heb. 6:12), we are thereby taught that actual perseverance in the way of faith and holiness must be our *evidence* that we are of His sheep. A belief in the doctrine of Divine preservation is worthless and useless if it be unaccompanied with the grace of perseverance.

The doctrine of Divine preservation provides no shelter to either laziness or licentiousness. If preservation is promised to the saint, then I must be found pressing forward along the path of duty, using the means of grace, or else the doctrine will *condemn* me. Christians are exhorted to make their "calling and election *sure*" (2 Pet. 1:10), and this, not by taking any thing for granted, but by using "all diligence" so as to be *assured by* adding unto faith, courage, knowledge, self-control, patience, godliness, brotherly-kindness, love. We are to prove our grace by a growth in grace. We are to evidence that we are good-ground hearers by bringing forth fruit. There is real need for such exhortations as the above: *appearances* of grace and faith are often found, which sparkle and flash for a time, like meteors in the sky, and then vanish away.

There are some who, like the foolish virgins, bear a lighted lamp and keep up a Christian profession, and yet have no oil in their vessels—no grace in their hearts. There are stony-ground hearers who receive the Word with eagerness, yea with joy, and yet have no root in themselves. There are some to whom God gives *another* heart, as He did to Saul (1 Sam. 10:9), but not a *new* heart; and such may prophecy for a season, as Saul did, and taste the joy which prophets taste, and yet be rejected from the kingdom as Saul was. "Many are called, but few chosen" (Matt. 20:16).

No dependence can be placed upon a past experience, nor a present reformation of life, nor upon short-lived impressions either of sorrow or joy: a steady and continuous *growth* in grace and in the (experimental) knowledge of the Lord Jesus must be sought as the crowning evidence of regeneration. But may not a real Christian backslide and then be restored? Yes, he may, but *not without* a deep and bitter repentance for his fall. "And it come to pass, when he heareth the words of this curse, that he bless himself in his heart, saying, I shall have peace, though I walk in the imagination of mine heart, to add drunkenness to thirst: The Lord will not spare him, but then the anger of the Lord and His jealousy shall smoke against that man, and all the curses that are written in this book shall lie upon him" (Deut. 29:19, 20). On the other hand, "whoso confesseth and forsaketh his sins shall have mercy" (Prov. 28:13). A.W.P.

---

ent unto death" but that He should die "the death of *the cross*" ought indeed to completely overwhelm our hearts, and bring us to His feet as adoring worshippers. When we try to think of *what* that "death of the cross" was in itself—the Holy One of God nailed to a felon's gibbet; the Lord of glory stripped naked, exposed to the contempt of a jeering crowd; the true Light now opposed by "the power of darkness"; the One who is "God blessed forever" now "made a curse"; the sword of Divine justice smiting Him, the full penalty of His people's sins being exacted of Him—ah, the apprehension of this (however feebly), my fellow-Christians, must indeed fill us with "wonder, love, and praise." In all these things did the Beloved of the Father lay aside the privilege of His infinite dignity.

The *manifestation* of His essential and personal glory was indeed eclipsed while the Son tabernacled for thirty-three years in this dark world. His perfect equality with God was hidden by the vail of flesh which He had taken upon Him. Therefore, as He was on the eve of completely accomplishing the work which had been committed to Him, He prayed, "And now, O Father, glorify Thou Me with Thine own self with the glory (His *displayed* Lordship) which I had with Thee before the world was" (John 17:5)—let that visible outshining of My personal dignity, which has been concealed by My abasement, wherein I descended for the suffering of death, be again conspicuously displayed. The Father's response to this is seen in Phil. 2:9, 10, which will come before us (D. V.) in a later paper. A.W.P.

tering spirits, whose very duty is dignity itself; but, stooping far below the nature of angels, He assumed a body of animated dust, and was "made in the likeness of men"—after the similitude of those inferior and depraved creatures who had revolted against God. Wondrous, amazing condescension was this!

To understand by "made Himself of no reputation" that He "emptied Himself of His Divine attributes," is horrible blasphemy. In such a case He would not have been "*God* manifest in flesh" (1 Tim. 3:16). How the Spirit has anticipated and refuted this error by affirming that the Virgin's Son should be called "Immanuel"—"*God* with us" (Matt. 1:23)! Nor is it correct to say that He suspended "the exercise of His inherent omnipotence and omniscience," for a careful reading of the four Gospels reveals the fact that, every essential attribute of Deity was evidenced by the Lord Jesus Christ during the days of His humiliation. That in two or three passages some of His miraculous works are attributed to the Spirit and some to *the Father*, no more proves that they were not wrought by His *own* Divine power, than His resurrection being ascribed to the Father and the Spirit disproves John 10:18! Instead, we behold a blessed co-operation and fellowship of the Eternal Three!

If all the remaining terms of this passage (vv. 5-11) be properly weighed, there should be no difficulty in arriving at the right understanding of the "made Himself of no reputation." For example, notice the one thing emphasised in v. 8: it is not that He became either "feeble" or "fallible," but "obedient"—*that* neither required the relinquishing or suspending of His omnipotence and omniscience; but it did require the abnegation of dominion and sovereignty! Again; does not the particular character of His *reward* intimate the nature of His "emptying"? God's response to the Son's perfect obedience is seen in two things: the *position* accorded Him, and all creatures yet owning Him as "*Lord*."

"But made Himself of no reputation." This was in order to His becoming a "Servant," but *that* did not in anywise necessitate or require either the "emptying" or "suspending" of His Divine wisdom or power. From being Lord of all, He descended to the place of obedience, though He still remained the "Lord of glory" as 1 Cor. 2:8 clearly proves, yet His *external* habit and appearance was that of "a man of sorrows." In His person He remained *all* that He was previously, but in the new position He entered, His glory was outwardly obscured. He entered the sphere of servitude, yet without the slightest injury to His Godhead.

He "made Himself of no reputation" *must* be understood relatively and not absolutely. The Son could not part with His essential perfections. "Neither by any thing that He did, nor any thing that He suffered, nor any condition He underwent, did He really forego, nor was it possible that He should do so, any thing of His Divine glory. He was no less Son when He died, than when He was declared to be the Son of God with power, by the resurrection from the dead" (John Owen). If it still be replied, He emptied Himself of His Divine glory, we answer, in these two senses only: with respect to His infinite condescension in the *position* which He took, and with respect to the *manifestation* of Himself here in this world.

It was in the taking *upon* Him of "the form of a *servant*" that His unparalelled condescension consisted: it was in *that* that He "made Himself of no reputation." Thus in comparison with the *positional* glory which he had in "the *form* of God" wherein He was "equal with God," He "emptied" Himself. The Word's becoming "flesh" was an unspeakable, unconceivable condescension. Moreover, it is to be steadily borne in mind that in becoming flesh, He did not immediately take to Heaven that human nature which He had assumed, but first became a *servant* in it, a "servant" to God, to do His will, and that in the most difficult service that was ever performed in this world. In that service, too, He "made Himself of no reputation." The work He did was stupendous and honourable, but the manner in which it was accomplished exposed Him to the scorn of the world.

Moreover, in that servant-work which the Son of God performed, He not only subjected Himself to the will of God, but He did so to the fullest possible degree: He "became obedient unto death." Had He only become Man, and as God-man had sat on the throne governing the world, *that* had been infinite condescension. And had He, as the God-man, *served* at all, that had been amazing self-abnegation. But that He did not stop short at this, that He did not ascend to heaven from the mount of transfiguration, that He should actually enter the portals of *death* itself, ought truly to fill us with deep admiration and wonderment.

Finally, that He, the Prince and Author of life, should not only become "obedi-
(Continued on Page 215)

Vol. X   OCTOBER, 1931   No. 10

STUDIES IN THE SCRIPTURES

"Search the Scriptures" John 5:39

Copyright in All English-speaking Countries

EDITOR: Arthur W. Pink, Millmont, Union Co., Penna., U. S. A.
Hon. Agent in England: Mr. A. Winstone, "Shalom," Old Bath Road, Leckhampton, Cheltenham.
Hon. Agent in Australia: Mr. G. Ardill, The Christian Workers' Depot, Commonwealth and Reservoir Streets, Sydney.

THE HUMANITY OF CHRIST

It has been truly said that, "Right views concerning Christ are indispensable to a right faith, and a right faith is indispensable to salvation. To stumble at the foundation, is, concerning faith, to make shipwreck altogether; for as Immanuel, God with us, is the grand Object of faith, to err in views of His eternal Deity, or to err in views of His sacred humanity, is alike destructive. There are points of truth which are not fundamental, though erroneous views on any one point must lead to God-dishonouring consequences in strict proportion to its importance and magnitude; but there are certain foundation truths to err concerning which is to insure for the erroneous and the unbelieving, the blackness of darkness forever" (J. C. Philpot, 1859).

To know Christ as God, to know Him as man, to know Him as God-man, and this by a Divine revelation of His glorious person, love and blood to our souls,—this is indeed to have eternal life in our hearts. Nor can He be savingly known in any other way than by Divine and special revelation: "But when it pleased God, who separated me from my mother's womb and called me by His grace, to *reveal* His Son in me" (Gal. 1:15, 16). A notional conception of His person may be obtained through diligently studying the Scriptures, but a vital knowledge of Him must be communicated from on high (Matt. 16:17). A theoretical and theological knowledge of Christ is what the natural man may acquire, but a saving and soul-transforming (2 Cor. 3:18) view of Him is only given by the Spirit to the regenerate (1 John 5:20).

"But made Himself of no reputation, and took upon Him the form of a servant, and was made in the likeness of men" (Phil. 2:7). The first clause of this verse (and the whole of the preceding one) has been before us in the last two papers. The two expressions which we are here to consider balance with (and thus serve to explain) those used in v. 6. The last clause of v. 7 is exegetical of the one immediately preceding. "Made in the likeness of men" has reference to the human *nature* which Christ assumed; the "form of a servant" denotes the position or *state* into which He entered. So "equal with God" has reference to the Divine nature, the *"form* of God" signifies His manifested glory in His position of Lord over all.

Coming now more immediately to our subject. 1. The humanity of Christ was *unique*. History supplies no analogy, nor can it be illustrated by any thing in Nature. The humanity of Christ is incomparable, not only with our fallen human nature, but with unfallen Adam's too. Not only was the Lord Jesus born into circumstances totally different from those in which Adam first found himself, but the sins and griefs of His people were on Him from the first. His humanity was produced neither by natural generation as is ours, nor by special creation as was Adam's. The humanity of Christ was, under the immediate agency of the Holy Spirit, supernaturally "conceived" (Isa. 7:14) of the Virgin. It was "prepared" of God (Heb. 10:5), yet "made of a woman" (Gal. 4:4).

The uniqueness of Christ's humanity also appears in this: that it never had a separate existence of its own. The eternal Son assumed (at the moment of Mary's conception) a human *nature*, but *not* a human person. This distinction is important and calls for careful consideration. By a "person" is meant an intelligent

(Continued on Page 240)

IMPORTANT NOTICES

Please advise promptly of change in address, otherwise copies will be lost in the mails.

We are glad to send a sample copy to any of your friends whom you believe would be interested in such a publication.

Send to Mr. I. C. Herendeen, Swengel (Union County), Penna., for a list of our publications. He has published many of our books and booklets.

This magazine is published as a work of faith and labour of love. The Editor and his wife gladly give their services. It is freely sent to all who will read it. No charge is made for it.

Christians who feel definitely led to do so, may have fellowship with us in this ministry. Those outside the U. S. A. please send only INTERNATIONAL Money Orders made out to Mifflinburg, Penna, U. S. A.

CONTENTS

The Humanity of Christ	217
The Epistle to the Hebrews	218
The Satisfaction ("Atonement") of Christ	224
Profiting from the Word	230
Repentance	234
A Personal Word	238

THE EPISTLE TO THE HEBREWS

46. *The Divine Incarnation.* Heb. 10:5-7.

In the first four verses of our present chapter the apostle was moved to press upon the Hebrews the insufficiency of the Levitical sacrifices to bring about those spiritual and eternal effects that were needed in order for poor sinners being fitted to stand before God as accepted worshippers. His design in so doing was to pave the way for setting before them the dire need for and the absolute sufficiency of Christ's sacrifice. First, he affirmed that the old covenant provided a "shadow" of the future "good things," but not the substance itself (v. 1). Under the Mosaic economy men were taught that ceremonial guilt, acquired through breaking the ceremonial law, severed from ceremonial fellowship with God, and that the offering of the prescribed sacrifices procured ceremonial forgiveness (Lev. 4:20) and restored to external fellowship, and thereby temporal punishment was averted. In this way there was adumbrated in a lower sphere what Christ's sacrifice was to accomplish in a higher.

That there was an insufficiency to the typical sacrifices was plainly intimated by their frequent repetition (v. 2). Had the offerer been *so* "purged" as to have "no more conscience of sins," that is, had his moral guilt been fully and finally expiated, then no further offering had been needed. Even though God's people continually commit fresh sins a new sacrifice is not required. Why? Because the one perfect Sacrifice *has made* complete satisfaction unto God, and is of perpetual efficacy before Him: therefore is it ever available to penitence and faith, for application unto fresh pardons. But no such sufficiency pertained to the typical sacrifices: a temporary and outward cleansing they could effect, but nothing more. "For though thou wash thee with nitre, and take thee much soap, thine iniquity is marked before Me, saith the Lord God" (Jer. 2:22).

There was no proportion between the infinite demerits of sin, the demands of God's justice, and the slaying of *beasts*. Whether the matter be viewed in the light of God's nature, of man's soul, or of the exceeding sinfulness of sin, it was obvious that the blood of bulls and goats could not possibly make atonement (v. 4). Nor was this fact altogether unknown in Old Testament times: did not one of Jehovah's prophets declare, "Wherewith shall I come before the Lord, and bow myself before the high God? shall I come before Him with burnt offerings, with calves that are a year old? Will the Lord be pleased with thousands of rams, with ten thousands of rivers of oil? shall I give my firstborn for my transgression, the fruit of my body for the sin of my soul?" (Micah 6:6, 7)! But later this light was lost to the carnal Jews, who, like the darkened Gentiles, came to believe that a real and efficacious atonement *was* made by the offering of animal blood unto God.

"It was therefore necessary that the patterns of things in the heavens should be purified with these; but the heavenly things themselves with *better* sacrifices" (Heb. 9:23). Yet patent as this now is to any renewed mind, it was an exceedingly difficult matter to convince the Jews of it. The Levitical sacrifices were of Divine institution and not of human invention. Their fathers had offered them for fifteen centuries; thus, to affirm at this late date that they were set aside by God made a big demand upon their faith, their prejudices, their affections. Nevertheless, the logic of the apostle was invincible, the force of his arguments unanswerable. But it is blessed to observe that he did not rest his case here; instead, he referred once more to an authority against which no appeal could be allowed.

As we have passed from chapter to chapter, and followed the inspired unfolding of the pre-eminency of Christianity over Judaism, we have been deeply impressed by the fact that, at *every* crucial point, *proof* has been furnished from the Old Testament Scriptures. When affirming the excellency of the Son over angels (1:4), appeal was made to Psa. 97:7 (1:6). When insisting on the exaltation of the humbled Messiah over all the works of God's hands (2:6-9), Psa. 8:4-6 was cited. When declaring the superiority of Christ's priesthood over Aaron's, Psa. 110:4 was given in substantiation of it (6:20). When pointing out the superseding of the old covenant by the new, Jer. 31:31 was shown to have taught that very thing (8:8). And now that the all-important point has been reached for showing the imperative necessity of the abolition of the Levitical offerings, another of their own Scriptures is referred to as announcing to the Hebrews this identical fact. How all this demonstrates the inestimable worth and the final authority of Holy Writ!

"Wherefore when He cometh into the world, He saith, Sacrifice and offering Thou wouldst not, but a body hast Thou prepared Me: In burnt offerings and sacrifices for sin Thou hast had no pleasure. Then said I, Lo, I come (in the volume of the book it is written of Me), to do Thy will, O God" (vv. 5-7). These verses contain a direct quotation from the 40th Psalm, which, equally with the 2nd, 16th, 22nd, 110th, etc., was a Messianic one. In it the Lord Jesus is heard speaking, speaking to His Father; and well does it behoove us to give our utmost attention to every syllable that He here utters.

The citation which is here made from the O. T. Scriptures is introduced with, "Wherefore when He cometh into the world, He saith." The precise force of the opening "Wherefore" is not easily determined: it seems to signify, In accord with the facts pointed out in the first four verses; or, in proof thereof, listen to the prophetic language of Christ Himself. J. Owen suggested: "It doth not give an account why the words following were spoken, but why the things themselves were so ordered and disposed." The "Wherefore" is a logical particle intimating that by virtue of the impotency of the O. T. sacrifices, Christ came not to offer those fruitless sacrifices, but to do the will of God in their room. The Mosaic worship, with all its complicated ritual, was superseded by something better coming in its stead. Christ took away the first, that He might establish the second.

The passage which is here before us calls for a whole book to be written thereon, rather than a single article: so blessed, so wondrous, so important are its contents. In it we behold the amazing grace and wisdom of the Father, the matchless love and obedience of the Son, and the federal agreement which was between the Father and the Son with reference to the work of redemption and the salvation of the Church. In it too we see demonstrated again the perfect harmony which exists between the Old and the New Testament and the declaration of these things. In it we are taken back to a point before the foundation of the world, and are permitted to learn something of the august counsels of the Eternal Three. In it we are shown the means which the Divine wisdom appointed for the carrying out of those counsels. It is both our duty and privilege to prayerfully inquire and diligently search into the mind of the Holy Spirit therein.

"Wherefore when He cometh into the world." The One who is here before us is the second person in the Holy Trinity. It is He who had been the Father's delight from all eternity. It is none other than the One by whom and *for* whom all things were created "that are in heaven, and that are in earth, visible and invisible" (Col. 1:16); who is "over all, God blessed forever" (Rom. 9:5). This ineffably blessed and glorious One condescended not merely to behold, or even to send an ambassador, but to personally come into this world. And, wonder of wonders, He came here not "in the form of God," bearing all the manifested insignia of Deity, nor even in the appearance of an angel, as occasionally He did in O. T. times; but instead, He came in "the form of a *servant*," and was actually "made under the law." May our hearts be truly bowed in wonderment and worship at this amazing and unparalelled marvel.

"When the fulness of the time was come" (Gal. 4:4), when the sinfulness of man and his utter helplessness to extricate himself from his dreadful misery had been completely demonstrated; when the insufficiency of Judaism and the powerlessness of the Levitical sacrifices had been made manifest; then it pleased the Son to become incarnate, execute the eternal purpose of the Godhead, fulfill the terms of the everlasting covenant, make good the prophecies and promises of the O. T. Scriptures, and perform that stupendous work which would bring an incalculable revenue of praise to the Triune God, glorify Him above all His other works, put away the sins of His people, and provide for them a perfect and everlasting righteousness which would entitle and fit them to dwell forever in the Father's House. So transcendent are these things that only those whom the Spirit of Truth deigns to illuminate and instruct are capable, in any measure, of apprehending and entering into their ineffable meaning and preciousness. May it please Him, in His sovereign grace, to shine now upon the hearts and understandings of both writer and reader.

"Wherefore when He cometh into the world, He saith, Sacrifice and offering Thou wouldst not, but a body hast Thou prepared Me." Here we behold the perfect intelligence of the Son concerning the mind and will of the Father. In the eternal purpose of the Triune God, Christ, as Mediator had been "set up from everlasting" (Prov. 8:23). The Lord had "possessed Him," He was "by Him, as One brought up with Him" (Prov. 8:22, 30). As such, nothing was concealed from Him; all the counsels of Deity were made known to Him. Therefore did He declare, after His incarnation, "The Father loveth the Son, and showeth Him all things" (John 5:20). An illustration of this fact is before us in our present passage.

"He saith, Sacrifice and offering Thou wouldst not, but a body hast Thou prepared Me." But here a difficulty presents itself: the Levitical sacrifices had been instituted by God Himself, how then could it be said that He willed them not? The solution is simple: the language here (as is not infrequently the case in Scripture) is to be taken relatively, and not absolutely. There was one real sense in which the O. T. sacrifices were acceptable to God, and another in which they were not so. The reference here is not to the actual appointment of the sacrifices, for Heb. 10:8 tells us they were "offered according to the law" which God had given to Israel. Nor is the reference to the obedience of the people concerning them during the Mosaic economy, for God both required and approved them at their hands. Nor is it that the apostle is merely speaking from the *present* viewpoint (as some have superficially supposed), i. e., that the sacrifices were *no longer* pleasing to Him. No, our text strikes much deeper: God willed not those sacrifices for the *ends* which He ordained the Sacrifice of Christ to effect.

"*But* a body hast Thou prepared Me." The first word of this clause serves to define the preceding one: the body of Christ is placed over against, substituted in the stead of, replaces, the Levitical offerings. Let the reader recall the whole context: there the Holy Spirit has shown the utter inadequacy of the blood of bulls and goats, the impossibility of its meeting the highest claims of God and the deepest need of sinners. God had not appointed animal sacrifices for *those* ends: He *never* took pleasure in them with reference thereto; according to the will of God they were altogether insufficient for any such purpose. From all eternity it was Christ, the "Lamb," who had been "foreordained" to make satisfaction unto God for His people (1 Peter 1:20). The Levitical sacrifices were never designed by God as anything more than a temporary means to shadow forth the great Sacrifice. This, the Mediator Himself was fully cognizant of from before the foundation of the world.

"But a body hast Thou prepared Me." The term "a body" is a synedochial expression (a part put for the whole, as when we say a farmer has so many "head" of cattle, or a manufacturer employs so many "hands") of the whole human nature of Christ, consisting of spirit and soul and body. As to some of the reasons why the Holy Spirit here threw the emphasis on Christ's "body" rather than on His "soul" (as in Isa. 53:10) we would humbly suggest the following. First, to emphasise the fact that the offering of Christ was to be by *death*, and this the body alone was subject to. Second, because the new covenant was to be *confirmed* by the offering of Christ, and this was to be by blood, which is contained in the body alone. Third, to make more evident the conformity of the Head to His members who were "partakers of flesh and blood." Fourth, to remind us that Christ's whole human *nature* (that "holy *thing*," Luke 1:35) was not a distinct *person*.

"But a body hast Thou prepared Me." The verb has a double force: the humanity of Christ was both foreordained and created by the Father. The first reference in the "prepared" here is the same as in Isa. 30:33. "Tophet is *ordained* of old, for the king it is *"prepared"*; "the things which God hath *prepared* for them that love Him" (1 Cor. 2:9); "the vessels of mercy, which He hath afore *prepared* unto glory" (Rom. 9:23). In His eternal counsels, God had resolved that the Son should become incarnate; in the everlasting covenant the Father had proposed and the Son had agreed that, at the appointed time, Christ should be made in the likeness of men. The second reference in the word "prepared" is to the actual creating of Christ's humanity, that it might be fitted for the work unto which it was designed.

"But a body hast Thou prepared Me." Commentators have needlessly perplexed themselves and their readers by discovering a discrepancy between these words and Psa. 40:6 which reads, "Mine ears hast Thou opened" or "digged" (margin). Really, there is no discord whatever between the two expressions: one is figurative, the other literal; both having the same sense. They refer to an act of the Father towards the Son, the purpose of the action being designed to make Him meet to do the will of God in a way of obedience. The metaphor used by the Psalmist possessed a double significance. First, the "ear" is that member of the body whereby we hear the commands we are to obey, hence nothing is more frequent in Scripture than to express obedience by hearing and hearkening. Here too the part is put for the whole. In His Divine nature alone, it was impossible for the Son, who was co-equal with the Father, to come under the law; therefore did He prepare for Him another nature, in which He *could* render submission to Him.

It is impossible that anyone should have ears of any use but by having a body, and it is through the ears that instruction unto obedience is received. It is to this the incarnate Son made reference when, in the language of prophecy, He declared, "He wakeneth morning by morning, He wakeneth Mine ear to hear as the learned. The Lord God hath opened Mine ear, and I was not rebellious, neither turned away back" (Isa. 50:4, 5). Thus the figure used in Psa. 40:6 intimated that the Father did so order things toward the Messiah that He should have a nature wherein He might be free and able to be in subjection to the will of God; intimating, moreover, the quality of it, namely, in having ears to hear, which belong only to a "body."

The second significance of the figure used in Psa. 40:6 may be discovered by a comparison with Ex. 21:6, where we learn of the provision made by the law to meet the case of a Hebrew servant, who chose to remain in voluntary servitude rather than accept his freedom, as he might do, at the seventh year of release. "Mine ears hast Thou digged" announced the Saviour's readiness to act as God's "Servant:" Isa. 42:1, 53:11. Only it is to be duly noted that in Ex. 21:6 it is "ear," whereas in Psa. 40:6 it is "ears"— in *all* things Christ has the "pre-eminence!" There was never any devotion either to Master or Spouse which could be compared with His: there was (so to speak) an over-plus of willingness in Him. "A body hast Thou prepared Me" presents the same idea, only in another form: His human nature was assumed for the very purpose of being the vehicle of service. Christ came here to be the substance of all the O. T. shadows, Ex. 21:1-6 not excepted. In becoming Man, the Son took upon Him "the form of a servant" (Phil. 2:7).

"A body hast Thou prepared Me." "The origin of the salvation of the Church is in a peculiar manner ascribed unto the Father—*His* will, His grace, His wisdom, His good pleasure, His love, His sending of the Son, are everywhere proposed as the *eternal springs* of all acts of power, grace and goodness, tending unto the salvation of the Church. And therefore doth the Lord Christ on all occasions declare that He came to do the Father's will, seek His glory, make known His name, that the praise of *His* grace might be exalted" (J. Owen). It was by the Holy Spirit that the human nature of the Redeemer was created. His body was "prepared" not by the ordinary laws of procreation, but by the supernatural power of the third person of the Trinity working upon and within Mary. There is thus a clear allusion here to the Virgin-birth of the Lord Jesus.

"He prepared Him such a body, such a human nature, as might be of the same nature with ours, for whom He was to accomplish His work therein. For it was necessary that it should be cognate and allied unto ours, that He might be meet to act on our behalf, and to suffer in our stead. He did not form Him a body out of the dust of the earth, as He did that of Adam, whereby He could not have been of the same race of mankind with us; nor merely out of nothing, as He created the angels whom He was not to save (2:14-16). He took our flesh and blood proceeding from the loins of Abraham. He so prepared it, as that it should be no way subject unto that depravation and pollution, that came on our whole nature by sin. This could not have been done, had His body been prepared by carnal generation—the way and means of conveying the taint of original sin, which befell our nature, unto all individual persons—for this would have rendered Him every way unmeet for His whole work of mediation (7:26) . . . This body or human nature, thus prepared for Christ, was exposed unto all sorts of temptations from outward causes. But yet was it so sanctified by the perfection of grace, and fortified by the fullness of the Spirit dwelling therein, that it was not possible it should be touched with the least taint or guilt of sin" (J. Owen).

Summing up this important point: though the actual operation in the production of our Saviour's humanity was the immediate work of the Holy Spirit (Luke 1:35), nevertheless, the preparation thereof was also the work of the Father in a real and peculiar manner, namely, in the infinitely wise and authoritative contrivance of it, and so ordering of it by His counsel and will. The Father originated it in the decreetive disposition of all things, the Holy Spirit actually wrought it, and the Son Himself assumed it. Not that there was any distinction of time in these separate actings of the Holy Three in this matter, but only a disposition of *order* in Their operation. In the *same* instant of time the Father authoritatively willed that holy humanity into existence, the Holy Spirit efficiently created it, and the Son personally took it upon Him as His own.

"In burnt offerings and sacrifices for sin Thou hast had no pleasure" (v. 6). These words amplify and define the central portion of the preceding verse. There we hear the Son, just prior to His incarnation saying to the Father, "Sacrifice and offering Thou wouldest not."

Against this a carping objector might reply, True, God never willed those sacrifices and offerings which our idolatrous fathers presented to Baal, nor those which the heathen gave to their gods; but that is a very different thing from saying that no animal sacrifice satisfied Jehovah. Such an objection is here set aside by the plain declaration that even the Levitical offerings contented God not. "In burnt offerings and sacrifices for sin Thou hast had no pleasure." In these words Christ comprehended *all* the sacrifices under the Mosaic economy which had respect to the expiation of sin and also the worship of God. In v. 5 the term "sacrifice" includes all those offerings which the Israelites brought to the Lord for the purpose of obtaining His pardon; under the word "offering" was embraced all the gifts which they brought with the object of expressing thanksgiving for blessings received at His hands. Here in v. 6 the latter are, by a synedoche, referred to by "burnt offerings," and the former by sacrifices "for sin." Concerning both of them Christ said to the Father "Thou wouldest not" (v. 5) and "Thou hast had no pleasure."

The difference between "Thou wouldest not" and "Thou hast had no pleasure" is, the former declares that God had never *designed* the Levitical offerings should make a perfect satisfaction unto Himself; the latter, that He *delighted not* in them. Such language is to be understood relatively and not absolutely. God *had* required sacrifices at the hands of Israel: He had "imposed" them "until the time of reformation" (Heb. 9:10). Absolutely they could neither be said to be wholly nugatory in themselves nor displeasing to God, but as they could not produce any real atonement for sin, they did not correspond in the proper sense of the term either to the Divine pleasure nor to the law of God, but only foreshadowed what was to come. God had ordained a satisfaction possessing such moral obedience and personal excellency that there would need no more repetition thereof. These words "in burnt offerings and sacrifices for sin Thou hast had no pleasure" serve as a background to bring out in more vivid relief the blessedness of "This is My beloved Son in whom I *am* well pleased" (Matt. 3:17)!

Once more we would point out how that the teaching of these verses supply a timely warning against our making a wrong use of symbolic ordinances. "Whatever may be the use or efficacy of any ordinances of worship, yet if they are employed or trusted unto for *such* ends as God hath *not* designed them unto, He accepts not of our persons in them, nor approves of the things themselves. Thus He declares Himself concerning the most solemn institutions of the old Testament. And those under the New have been no less abused in this way, than those of old" (J. Owen).

"Then said I, Lo, I come (in the volume of the book it is written of Me), to do Thy will, O God" (v. 7). Those words express the readiness and willingness of the Son to do all that had been ordained unto the making of a full satisfaction to God and the salvation of His people. They contain the second branch of the antithesis pointed in the quotation which is here made from the Messianic Psalm. They record the response of the Son's mind and will to the design and purpose of the Father. They conduct us back to the eternal counsels of the Godhead, in which the Father had expressed His determination to have an adequate compensation for the insult to His honour which sin should give, His disapproval of animal sacrifices as the means thereof, His decision that the Son should become incarnate and in human form magnify the law and make it honourable; with the Son's free and perfect acquiescence therein.

"Lo, I come to do Thy will, O God." That "will" was not only to "take away sins" (v. 4), which the Levitical offerings had not effected, but was also to make His people "perfect" (v. 1 and cf. v. 14). It was the gracious design of God not only to remove all the effects of sin, original and personal, which provoked His judicial hatred of us (Eph. 2:3), but also to provide for and give to them such a righteousness as would occasion Him more cause to love us than ever, and loving to delight in us. His "will" meant not only peace and pardon to us, but grace and favour: as the angels announced to the Bethlehem shepherds, the coming of Christ meant not only "glory to God in the highest, and on earth peace," but also "good-will toward men." He had predestinated not only to forgive us, but to have us adopted and graciously "accepted," and that "to the praise of the glory of His grace" (Eph. 1:5, 6).

The "will" of God which the Son came here to execute was that "eternal purpose which He had purposed in Christ Jesus our Lord" (Eph. 3:11). Had He so pleased, God could have "taken away sin" by taking away sinners, and so made a short work of it, by removing them both at one stroke—as Ezekiel speaks (23:48). But instead, He purposed to take away sins in such a way that favoured sinners should stand justified before Him. Again, had He so pleased, God could have taken off the sins of His people by a sole and sovereign act of pardon. To *hate* sin is an act of His *nature*, but to *express* His hatred *by punishing* sin is an act of His *will*, and therefore might be wholly suspended. Were it an act of the Divine nature to punish sin, then whosoever sinned would die for it immediately; but being an act of His will, He oftentimes suspends the punishment. Seeing He is prepared to forebear for a while, He *could* have foreborne forever. But His wisdom—the *"counsel* of His own will" (Eph. 1:11) deemed it best to require an adequate satisfaction.

What has just been said receives plain confirmation in the words used by the suffering Saviour in Gethsemane: "And He said, Abba, Father, *all* things *are possible* unto Thee: take away this cup from Me; nevertheless, not what I will, but what Thou wilt." Here the incarnate Son lets us know that the reason why it was not possible for the awful cup of wrath to pass from Him was because God had *ordained* that He *should* drink it, and *not* because there was *no* other alternative. We indeed can perceive none other, and *relatively* speaking there was none other *after* the everlasting covenant had been sealed; yet *absolutely* considered, speaking from the viewpoint both of God's infinite wisdom and sovereign pleasure, He *could*, had He so pleased, have saved us in another way. Never allow the thought that sin has produced a situation which in anywise limits or restrains the *Almighty*. It was *by* His will that sin entered!

Had God so pleased, He *could* have accepted the blood of beasts as a full and final atonement for our sins. The *only* reason why He did not was because He had decreed that *Christ* should make atonement. He determined in Himself that if He had satisfaction it should be a full and perfect one. *Everything* must be resolved into and traced up to the *sovereign* pleasure of Him who "worketh *all* things after the counsel of His own *will"* (Eph. 1:11). It is in the light of what has just been said that we must interpret Heb. 10:4: it was "not possible" because of the eternal purpose of the Triune Jehovah. God would have satisfaction to the full, or none at all. This the Son knew, and to it He fully consented.

The Son was in perfect accord with the will of the Father from before the foundation of the world. As Zech. 6:13 tells us "and the covenant of peace shall be between Them *Both*": the reference being to the "everlasting covenant" (Heb. 13:20). The "counsel of peace" signifies that compact or agreement which was between the Father and the Son. It was, then, by His own voluntary consent that the Son was made "Surety of a better covenant" (Heb. 7:22), a title which necessarily imports a definite undertaking on His part, namely, His agreeing to yield that obedience to the law which His people owed, to make reparation to Divine justice on behalf of their sins, and thus discharge the whole of their debt.

By a free act of His own will, the Son consented to execute that stupendous work which the Father had proposed unto Him.

This consent of the Son to His Father's proposal to Him before the foundation of the world, was, *renewed* by Him at the moment of His incarnation: "Wherefore *when He cometh into the world*, He saith . . . a body hast Thou prepared Me . . . *Then* said I, Lo, I come . . . to do Thy will O God." He freely acquiesced in assuming to Himself a human nature, to take on Himself the "form of a servant," to be "made unto the law," to become "obedient unto death." He told the Father so in the above words, which are recorded for His glory and for our instruction, wonderment and joy. The further consideration of them, as well as the meaning of "in the volume of the book it is written of Me" we must defer (D. V.) till our next article. A.W.P.

THE SATISFACTION ("Atonement") OF CHRIST

22. *Its Proclamation.*

We have now arrived at what is, from some standpoints, the most difficult aspect of our subject. Exactly what is it which the servant of God ought to preach? Or, more specifically, what constitutes the main item in his message to the unsaved, and in what is he to instruct the saints? To many it appears that he who clearly apprehends the limitation of God's love to His elect, and the satisfaction of Christ being made for them only, is to be fettered in the preaching of the Gospel; yea, not a few suppose that if a preacher really believes such doctrines as these, he will have no message at all for the unsaved. But such is far from being the case: those who draw such conclusions err grievously. No honest mind can ponder the epistles of Paul without seeing that he believed firmly in the sovereign love and discriminating grace of God, and the restricted design of the atonement; yet none can read through the Acts without discovering that the same Paul was a most zealous evangelist and preached a Gospel which was as free as the air we breathe.

That Christ died only for those who shall be infallibly saved, is a doctrine which seems to have an adverse bearing towards the world at large, and to embarrass the free proclamation of the Gospel. A feeling arises that there is something very much like an inconsistency or incompatability between the restricted design and efficacy of the Great Propitiation to a predetermined and limited number of the race, and the commission which Christ has given to His servants. In seeking to grapple with this difficulty, let us begin by inquiring, Is an *un-*limited atonement necessary in order to warrant ministers of the Gospel tendering Divine pardon to all men without exception, and inviting and exhorting them to come to Christ? In seeking answer to this question, it should be evident that our conduct in preaching the Gospel and addressing our fellow-men with a view to their salvation, should not be regulated by any *inferences* of our *own* from the nature and extent of the provision actually made for saving them, but is to be governed solely by the instructions which *God has given*. It is not for us to reason and argue, but to *obey*.

The commission which Christ has given to His servants is too plain to be misunderstood. They are commanded to "preach the Gospel to every creature" (Mark 16:15). They are required to proclaim to their fellow-men, of whatever character, and in all variety of circumstances, glad tidings of great joy. They are bidden to preach "repentance and remission of sins" in His name "among all nations" (Luke 24:47). They are enjoined to say, "All things are ready, come unto the marriage," and to go forth into the very highways, and as many as they shall find "bid to the marriage" (Matt. 22:4, 9). They are to invite men to come to Christ, and beseech their hearers to be "reconciled to God" (2 Cor. 5:20). They are to freely announce that, "The Gospel of Christ is the power of God unto salvation *to every one that believeth*" (Rom. 1:16), and that "*Whosoever* shall call upon the name of the Lord shall be saved" (Rom. 10:13). Nothing could be clearer than this, and no philosophical reasonings or theological sophistries must be allowed to negative their marching-orders.

God's *revealed* will is our only rule to walk by, and must ever be held as sufficient warrant for all that we do. In seeking to know our duty as to whom we should preach to and as to what we are to say unto our fellow-men, Holy Writ is to be our sole guide and authority. Denominational customs, creedal prejudices, the example of eminent preachers, are no criterion at all. "To the Law and to the Testimony" (Isa. 8:20), must be our one and only recourse. Our business is to "preach the Word" (2 Tim. 4:2), leaving God to *apply* it according to His eternal purpose. We are to "sow beside *all* waters" (Isa. 32:20). Thus our duty is clearly defined. Like the Sower in the parable (Matt. 13), we are to scatter the Seed on the stony as well as on the good ground.

The servants of God are to "preach the Gospel" (Mark 16:15), which is a proclamation of mercy through Christ. The Gospel is a Divine revelation of the way of salvation by free grace through the Lord Jesus. It announces deliverance from condemnation and the bestowment of eternal life upon all who comply with its terms. The Gospel presents not a system of philosophy, but the person of the God-man as the Object *of faith*. It makes known how the thrice holy God may be just and yet the Justifier of lawbreaking sinners. The things of our eternal concernment are therein proposed to us. A compliance with this Divine revelation is made by means of "repentance toward God and faith toward our Lord Jesus Christ" (Acts 20:21). Remission of sins is freely promised to *all* who thus comply with it. But it also implies and denounces tidings of the very opposite nature to all who neglect it: "he that believeth not shall be damned" (Mark 16:16); "the Lord Jesus shall be revealed from heaven with His mighty angels, in flaming fire taking vengeance on them that know not God, and that *obey not the Gospel*" (2 Thess. 1:7, 8).

Now in preaching the Gospel to a single individual (which is, usually, more difficult than preaching to a crowd) it is in nowise necessary for me to say to him, Christ died for *you*, He bore *your* sins on the cross. Neither the Lord Jesus nor the apostles adopted such a mode of procedure. Take one pertinent illustration from each of them. In His discourse to Nicodemus, Christ did not say, "As Moses lifted up the serpent in the wilderness even so shall the Son of man be lifted up *for you*," but "even so shall the Son of man be lifted up that whosoever *believeth in Him* should not perish" (John 3:14), thus pressing the responsibility of His hearer. So too when the Philippian jailer cried, "What must I do to be saved?" Paul said, "Believe on the Lord Jesus Christ," but he did *not* add "who died for *you*." It is not until *after* we have truly believed, that we learn we are among that favoured company for whom the incarnate Son shed His precious blood.

The Gospel declares that, "Christ died for the ungodly" (Rom. 5:6), and that the most ungodly wretch there is out of Hell who repents and believes shall be saved. "This is a faithful saying, and worthy of all acceptation, that Christ Jesus came into the world to save *sinners*" (1 Tim. 1:15), yea, even the "chief" of sinners. That great fact supplies a *warrant* to preach the Gospel unto all men, but it is only as the individual sinner *believes* on Christ it becomes known that Christ died for *him*. Thus, to preach the Gospel to every creature and call on them to believe and be saved, is quite consistent, for it is a Divinely-revealed truth that "whosoever believeth" *shall be* saved! Any man who experiences a difficulty in freely preaching the Gospel because he cannot announce that Christ died for every individual of the human race, does not clearly understand what the "Gospel" is. The Gospel message is that Christ died for the most guilty who repent and believe.

Nor is God guilty of the slightest deception in sending forth His servants to tender salvation to *all* sinners on the terms that they repent and believe, for He *is* true to His Word. He *does* save *every* sinner who complies with His terms; nor does He withhold His Spirit from any who truly desire Him to work in them a saving repentance and faith. Even viewing the matter from the Arminian's standpoint, it is impossible for him to show any greater (seeming) inconsistency between God's sovereign election of some men to salvation and His sovereign reprobation of others, with His good faith in the *indiscriminate* tendering of salvation of all who hear the Gospel, than with the infallible *foreknowledge* of God which the Arminians admit. If God certainly foreknows that the Gospel will be only "a savour of death unto death" (awfully aggravating the doom) of the vast majority of those who hear it, then why does He send the Gospel unto them at all?

The ground on which a sinner is bidden to believe unto the saving of his soul is neither God's decree of election, nor that Christ died for him in particular, but the plain declaration of the Gospel itself, namely, "he that believeth and is baptised shall be saved" (Mark 16:16). It cannot be said too emphatically that the *only* warrant for personal faith in Christ which *any* man has, is that which the indiscriminate commands, invitations and promises of the *Gospel* hold forth. If we were assured of the absolute universality of redemption, or if we were permitted to read every name recorded in the Lamb's book of life, the case would be no plainer and more certain than it now is. The One who "cannot lie" most solemnly declares that *"whosoever* believeth" in His Son shall not perish, but have everlasting life. Christ Himself expressly announces, "him that cometh unto Me I will in no wise cast out" (John 6:37). Any other warrant than this would be entirely inconsistent with the nature of *faith*: to demand it is sheer rebellion.

Neither God's sovereign foreordination of an elect company unto salvation, nor the limitation of Christ's atonement to that company, in anywise alters the fact or militates against the truth of the indiscriminate tender of pardon which is made by and through the Gospel. It is *every* man's duty *to* "repent and believe the Gospel." It is God's gracious purpose to receive and save *all* who do thus repent and believe. The proclamation which God is making through the Gospel is real and sincere. The reason why so many do not benefit from that proclamation and avail themselves of its proffered mercy, is their own wilful refusal of it. The door of Divine mercy stands *wide* open: over its portals stands written "whosoever will may come." If those invited insist upon making "excuse," then, their blood is upon their own heads. Their very refusal to come to Christ that they "might have life" (John 5:40) only makes manifest the inveteracy of their sin, and will yet most fully justify the righteous judgment of God in the day to come—Psa. 51:4, Matt. 22:12, Rom. 3:19.

"An indiscriminate offer of an interest in the Atonement has been made for two thousand years since Christ died. But remember that the same indiscriminate offer was made for four thousand years *before* He died! The offer then was that *if* men would 'believe' upon a Christ to be sacrificed hereafter they *should be* saved. Now, is it sense or nonsense to believe that at the end of those four thousand years Christ died for the purpose of saving those who had *already rejected* Him, and who had consequently gone to their own place? Would it not have met the precise case of all who lived on earth before His advent if He had promised them that at the end of time He would die to save all those who had previously believed? Would there have been any propriety in His promising to die also for those who had previously *rejected* His kind offers and been lost? As far as the design of the Atonement, the purpose to be attained by His death, is concerned, what conceivable difference does it make whether the sacrifice of Christ be offered at the beginning, the middle, or the end of human history? If He had died at the end, He certainly could not die for those who had previously rejected His offers and perished therefor. And since He did die in the middle, why may not the Gospel be offered on the same terms to all men, as well after as before His death?

"The only difficulty lies in the fact that finite creatures are utterly unable to comprehend the sovereign will and the unchangeable all-knowledge of God, which absolutely shuts out all contingency in relation to the hopes, the fears, the doubts, the responsibilities, the struggles, of human beings. Events are contingent in themselves. But there is no contingency in relation to the Divine purpose. One event is conditioned upon another, but there are no conditions in the Divine decree. God's purpose, His design of redemption, like every other Divine purpose, is timeless. What has been and what will be, who have believed and who will believe, are all the same to Him. To Him the believers and the elect are identical. His design in the Atonement may with absolute indifference be stated either as a design to save the elect, or as a design to save all who have believed or who would believe on His Son" (A. A. Hodge).

"The preachers of the Gospel in their particular congregations, being utterly unacquainted with the purpose and secret counsel of God, being also forbidden to pry or search into it (Deut. 29:29) may from hence justifiably call upon every man to believe, with assurance of salvation to every one in particular upon his so doing, knowing and being fully persuaded of this, that there is enough in the death of Christ to save every one that shall so do; leaving the purpose and counsel of God, on whom He will bestow faith, and for whom in particular Christ died (even as they are commanded), to Himself" (J. Owen).

Nothing but confusion can disturb our minds if we fail to distinguish sharply between God's eternal purpose and man's present duty: the two things are quite distinct, and have *no* connection between them. The purpose or decree of God is *not* the rule of our duty, nor is the performance of our duty in doing what we are commanded any declaration of God's eternal counsels that it should be done. There is no sequel between the universal precepts of the Word and God's purpose in Himself concerning specific persons. The business of the preacher is to urge the fact that God "now commandeth all men every where to repent" (Acts 17:30), leaving it with the Spirit to work a saving repentance in whom He pleases. When I tell an individual sinner, "this is His command, that we should believe on the name of His Son Jesus Christ" (1 John 3:23), I know not whether God has decreed to work a saving faith in him, nor is that any of my business; my duty is to discharge the commission Christ has given me, and the duty of my hearers is to comply with God's demands. God Himself will see to the accomplishment of His foreordination.

Coming now to a closer answer to the questions raised at the beginning of this article: the supreme business of God's servants is to preach *Christ*. Now to do this there must be a scriptural setting forth of His glorious person, as the eternal Son, the Maker of heaven and earth. There must be an exposition of His two natures: His absolute Deity, His holy humanity. There must be an explanation of His offices: a Prophet to reveal the will of God, a Priest to offer Himself a sacrifice to God, a King to rule over the people of God. There must be a declaration of the two states in which He exercises His offices. First of humiliation: His condescension in becoming flesh, the reasons for this, and the glorious consequences of it. Second His glorification: His exaltation to the right hand of God, His headship over the Church, His intercessory ministry. But supremely, there must be the preaching of His obedience to the law, His perfect righteousness, His vicarious death, the all-sufficiency of His merits to those who trust in Him.

"I determined not to know any thing among you, save Jesus Christ, and Him crucified" (1 Cor. 2:2). We are not only to open up the mystery of His person, the manifold glories of His many offices, the perfections of His character, but, above all, we are to expound the meaning of the Cross. It is only by dwelling much on the varied significations of Calvary that the truth can be fully told out, whether the sinfulness of man's sin, or the greatness of God's love. To illustrate the various aspects of the sacrificial work of the Redeemer, a close study needs to be given to and then a free use made of the O. T. types.

But it is not sufficient to barely "preach" Christ, there must also be an *application* made of what is revealed in Scripture concerning Him to the use of God's people, that their hearts may be drawn out to Him, and that they may see their interest in Him. To "preach" is to *woo*. The servant of God is not only an advocate pleading his Master's cause, refuting the objections of opposers, but he also is a witness, telling out of his own experience the preciousness of Christ. Thus he is to attract, allure, and win souls to Him. That which best fits any minister to "preach" Christ is to himself *walk* and commune *with Him!* A part of some of the typical sacrifices was reserved as a feast for the offerer and his friends. So we must teach the saints to look away from self to Christ, to *feed on* Him, to live by Him, to be occupied with His perfections.

Because men are by nature *opposed to* Christ, the servant of God must needs begin with *the Law,* so as to discover to them the dreadful state they are in. The claims of God upon us as His creatures must be pressed. The perfect and constant obedience which He requires from man must be clearly set forth. Then the utter failure of man to meet God's righteous claims upon him, and the exceeding sinfulness of his disobedience. A way must be made *for* the Gospel, by showing and convincing people they are out of Christ, under the condemnation of a holy God, and of themselves utterly unable to liquidate their debts. The ministry of John the Baptist must precede that of Christ! The contents of Rom. 1:18 to 3:20 must be stressed before the good news of Rom. 3:21-26 is proclaimed. What need of a physician till we know we are sick? What need of a Saviour till we know we are lost? What need of Christ to cleanse till we see our filthy defilement?

At the outset, the preacher needs to recognize and realize that "The carnal mind is enmity against God" (Rom. 8:7). No arguments of his can overcome, no inducements melt the heart of stone. Paul may plant, and Appolos may water, but God only can give the "increase." Nothing short of the supernatural working of the Spirit can bring a sinner to Christ. Therefore both the preacher and his Christian hearers need to be much in prayer, *seeking* the Holy Spirit's grace and power to quicken, convict and convert the lost. We are fully assured that one principal reason why there are so few genuine conversions today, is because there is so little real and importunate praying unto God.

"We are to dwell largely on the being and perfections of God, and our original obligations to Him, who is by nature our Creator. We are particularly to explain the nature and reasonableness of the Divine law, and to answer the sinner's objections against it. We are to exhibit to his view the sin which he stands charged with in the Divine law, and the curse he is under for it, and the only way of obtaining pardon through the blood of Christ. In a word, we are to open to his view the whole plan of the Gospel, the infinite riches of God's grace, the nature and sufficiency of Christ's atonement, the readiness of God to forgive repenting sinners who come to Him in the name of Christ, the calls and invitations of the Gospel, the dreadfulness of eternal misery in the lake of fire and brimstone; the glory and blessedness of the heavenly state, the shortness and uncertainty of time, the worth of his soul, the dangers which attend him, from the world, the flesh and the devil, the inexcusable guilt of final impenitence, etc," (Jos. Bellamy, 1759).

It is most important for us to recognize and constantly bear in mind the fact that the Gospel is *addressed to* the sinner's *responsibility*. It is true from one viewpoint that the Gospel comes to men who are not on probation, but under God's condemnation, yet from another viewpoint (equally true) it is delivered to their accountability. It bids men to be reconciled to God (Cor. 5:20), by which is meant, the throwing down of the weapons of their warfare against Him. It calls upon them to "forsake" their way and thoughts and return unto the Lord, and announces to all who do so that He will "have mercy upon" them (Isa. 55:7). It bids them "Repent and be converted," which means a right-about-face, a turning from sin and self-pleasing unto God, and this, in order that their "sins may be blotted out" (Acts 3:19). It commands all men to believe in Christ and receive Him as their Lord. It announces that failure to believe is adding sin to sin and increasing their condemnation (John 3:18).

The preaching of the Gospel is both a declaration of God's revealed will to pardon all who comply with its terms, and an insistence upon the duty devolving on all who hear it. The business of Christ's servants is to present what Scripture teaches concerning the salvation of men and the way which God has ordained in order to their obtaining of it. We are to constantly press the fact that God has inseparably connected salvation with repentance and faith. Many today are labouring under the delusion that the *only* relation between God and men is that of Creditor and debtors, and that Christ paid the whole debt, and therefore none are under any obligations of *duty* and that *all* God now requires from any sinner is for him to believe that Christ *has* done all, and that faith is merely and simply a resting and relying in that fact. But such a concept is a fatal delusion, and grossly dishonouring to God.

The God of the N. T. is *not* another God from Him who is revealed in the O. T.! God is there set forth as the Lawgiver, as the Ruler over all, requiring perfect conformity to His demands. Now those requirements of God were neither unjust nor tyrannical, but instead, righteous and merciful. Nor did Christ come here to abrogate the law, but rather to "magnify the law, and make it honourable" (Isa. 42:21). And when the Holy Spirit begins a saving work in the soul, He presses the requirements of God's law, convicts of failure to meet those requirements, and produces a deep and lasting sorrow for such failure. Further, He creates in the heart which He renews a *love* for the law (Rom. 7:22) and a holy longing and determination to please and serve God. Thus, the work of the Spirit in those who are truly saved is *not* to the setting aside of that *duty* which every man owes to God—his Maker, Sustainer, and Governor—but is the imparting of a delight unto and power for the performance of that duty!

Thus the *first* duty of the evangelist is to call upon all men to *repent*: see Mark 1:15. This is his very commission from Christ: see Luke 24:47. It was thus that Peter (Acts 2:38, 3:19) and Paul evangelised: see Acts 17:30, 20:21. Our business is to show *why* God requires this repentance, namely, for us to acknowledge the righteousness of His claims upon us. Our business is to show *what* repentance consists of: see Prov. 28:13, Acts 3:19, 1 Thess. 1:9, etc. Our business is to emphasize the fact that God never has and never will pardon any sinner until he *does* repent: see Lev. 23:29; 26:40-42; 1 Kings 8:46-50; Psa. 32:3-5; Jer. 4:4; Ezek. 18:30-32; Luke 5:32; 13:3; Acts 3:19; 11:18; 2 Cor. 7:10.

The next great duty of the evangelist is to call on his hearers to "believe on the Lord Jesus Christ." That this call may be something much more than a mere *uttering* of the *word* "Believe!", "Believe!"; we must carefully define and explain *what* saving faith consists of. That it is, first, a sincere renunciation of all other ways and means of salvation: Acts 4:12. Second, that it is the free and full consent of the heart *to* God's way of salvation: Rom. 10:9. Third, that it is a personal trusting in Christ and relying upon the sufficiency of His satisfaction unto God: Acts 16:31. Saving faith is more than a bare belief of the Truth. The dying Israelites might have been fully assured that a look at the brazen serpent would give healing, but until they *actually* "looked," in full confidence in God's promise, they had not benefited one whit!

None receive a soul-freeing discharge from the power and penalty of sin till they believe in Christ. Though the law of God has been satisfied and every demand of His justice met as to the sins of the elect, yet this has not hindered God from ascribing such a *way* from their coming to Him as is suited to the exalting of His glory and the honour of Christ. This the spirit accomplishes by preparing the soul of the sinner for the enjoyment of God, and that, by the "law of faith." The *benefits* of Christ's death are only *applied* when we believe. The personal state of those for whom He shed His blood is not actually changed by His death itself, for they still lie under the curse whilst they are unregenerate (Eph. 2:3). That which Christ has procured for His own is left in the hands of the Father, for Him to bestow when He sees fit. Repentance and faith are necessary not to add anything to Christ's atonement, nor to merit forgiveness, but only to the actual *receiving* of it.

That which God calls the sinner to "believe" is *the Gospel*. The first act of faith does not consist in believing that Christ died for me, but that He died for *sinners*. Christ is presented as an Object of *faith*. The Gospel announces that the Lord Jesus stands ready to receive every sinner who will throw down the arms of his rebellion, and trust in Him alone for salvation. As I do this, and *am* saved by Him, I obtain clear evidence of my election unto salvation: John 6:37, 2 Thess. 2:13. The business of the preacher is *not* to "offer" Christ to sinners, but to "*preach*" Him, expounding the *doctrine* of the Gospel. Our duty is to give the general call; the Holy Spirit will see to its effectual application unto God's elect.

The Gospel is a Divine fan: by it the wheat is separated from the chaff. "The Gospel is addressed equally to the seed of the woman and the seed of the serpent. To the one, it is the savour of life,—to the other the savour of death; hence it is depicted as a two-edged sword, proceeding out of the Redeemer's mouth. It resembles the pillar interposed between the Egyptians and Israel: 'It was a cloud and darkness to them, but it gave light by night to these.' If our Gospel, says the apostle, be hid, it is hidden to them that are lost; if men receive not the atonement made upon Calvary, as the only ground of their hope,—if they do not take shelter under the Saviour's wings, then there remaineth no more sacrifice for sins, but a certain fearful looking for of judgment and fiery indignation, which shall devour them as the implacable enemies of God" (James Haldane).

While pressing on all their bounden *duty* to repent and believe, let not the servant of God be slack in plainly teaching that both repentance and faith are Divine *gifts*: Eph. 2:8, 9; Acts. 5:31. The natural man can no more savingly repent and believe than he can create a world: John 6:44. "We may as well melt a flint, or turn a stone to flesh, as repent in our own strength. It is far above the power of nature, nay, most contrary to it. How can we hate sin, which naturally we love above all? forsake that which is as dear as ourselves? It is the almighty power of Christ which only can do this: we must rely on, seek to Him for it: Jer. 31:18, Lam. 5:21" (D. Clarkson, 1690).

Finally, let the servant of God see to it that his zeal in preaching the Gospel to the unsaved, does not cause him to withhold from "the children" their needed *bread*. The reprobate may vomit it out, but the regenerate will be nourished thereby. Every preacher is under bonds to see to it that, at the close of his pastorate he can say, "I have not shunned to declare unto you *all* the counsel of God" (Acts 20:27). Only by so doing will he fulfil his commission, preserve the balance of Truth, establish God's saints in the faith, and glorify his Master.—A.W.P.

PROFITING FROM THE WORD

6. *The Scriptures and Obedience.*

All professing Christians are agreed, in theory at least, that it is the bounden duty of those who bear His name to honour and glorify Christ in this world. But as to *how* this is to be done, as to *what* He requires from us to this end, there is wide difference of opinion. Many suppose that honouring Christ simply means to join some "church," take part in and support its various activities. Others think that honouring Christ means to speak of Him to others and be diligently engaged in "personal work." Others seem to imagine that honouring Christ signifies little more than making liberal financial contributions to His cause. Few indeed realise that Christ is honoured only as we *live holily* unto Him, and that, by walking in subjection to His revealed will. Few indeed really believe that word, "Behold, *to obey* is better than sacrifice, *to hearken* than the fat of rams" (1 Sam. 15:22).

We are not Christians at all unless we have fully surrendered ourselves to and "received Christ Jesus *the Lord*" (Col. 2:6). O dear reader, we would plead with you to diligently ponder that statement. Satan is deceiving so many today by leading them to suppose that they are savingly trusting in the "finished work" of Christ while their hearts remain unchanged, and self still rules their lives. Listen to God's Word: "Salvation is far from the wicked: *for they seek not* My statutes" (Psa. 119:155). Do you really *seek* His "statutes"? Do you diligently search His Word to discover what He has commanded? "He that saith, I know Him, and *keepeth not* His commandments, is a liar, and the truth is not in him" (1 John 2:4). What could be plainer than that?

"And why call ye Me, Lord, Lord, and *do not* the things which I say?" (Luke 6:46). Reality in the life, not glowing words from the lips, is what Christ requires. What a searching and solemn word is that in James 1:22, "But be ye doers of the Word, and not hearers only, deceiving your own selves"! There are many "hearers" of the Word, regular hearers, reverent hearers, interested hearers; but alas, what they hear is not *incorporated* into the life: it does not regulate their ways. And *God* says, they who are not *doers* of the Word, are "deceiving" their own selves!

Alas, how many such there are in Christendom today. They are not downright hypocrites, but deluded. They suppose that because they are so clear upon salvation by grace alone, *they* are saved. They suppose that because they sit under the ministry of a man who has "made the Bible a new book" to them, that they have grown in grace. They suppose that because their store of Biblical knowledge has increased, they are more spiritual. They suppose that the mere listening to a servant of God or reading his writings is *feeding on* the Word. Not so! We only "feed" on the Word when we personally appropriate, masticate, and *assimilate into our lives* what we hear or read. Where there is not an increasing conformity of heart and life to God's Word, then increased knowledge will only bring increased condemnation! "And that servant, which *knew* his Lord's will, and prepared not, neither *did* according to His will, shall be beaten with *many stripes*" (Luke 12:47).

"Ever learning, and never able to come to the knowledge of the truth" (2 Tim. 3:7). This is one of the prominent characteristics of the "perilous times" in which we are now living. People hear one preacher after another, attend this Convention and that Conference, read book after book on Biblical subjects, and yet never attain unto a vital and practical acquaintance with the Truth, so as to have an impression of its power and efficacy on the soul. There is such a thing as spiritual *dropsy*, and multitudes are suffering from it. The more they hear, the more they want to: they drink in sermons and addresses with avidity, but their lives are unchanged. They are puffed up with their knowledge, not humbled into the dust before God. The faith of God's elect is "the acknowledgment (in the life) of the truth which is *after godliness*" (Titus 1:1), but to this, the vast majority of professing Christians are total strangers.

God has given us His Word not only with the design of instructing us, but for the purpose of *directing* us: to make known what He requires us to *do*. The first thing *we* need is a clear and distinct *knowledge* of our duty; and the first thing *God* demands of us is a conscientious *practice* of it, corresponding to our knowledge. "What doth the Lord require of thee, but to do justly, and to love mercy, and to walk humbly with thy God?" (Micah 6:8). "Let us hear the conclusion of the whole matter: Fear God, and keep His commandments: for this is the whole duty of man" (Eccl. 12:13). The Lord Jesus affirmed the same thing when He said, "Ye are My friends, if ye do whatsoever I command you" (John 15:14).

1. Now a man is profited from the Word as he discovers *God's demands upon him*, His undeviating demands, for HE changeth not. It is a great and grievous mistake to suppose that in this present dispensation God has *lowered* His demands, for that would necessarily imply His previous demand was a harsh and unrighteous one. Not so, "The law is holy, and the commandment holy, and just and good" (Rom. 7:12). The sum of God's demands is, "Thou shalt love the Lord thy God with *all* thine heart, and with all thy soul, and with all thy might" (Deut. 6:5); and the Lord Jesus repeated it in Matt. 22:37. The apostle Paul enforced the same when he wrote "If any man *love not* the Lord Jesus, let him be *anathema*" (1 Cor. 16:22).

To proceed a step further. 2. A man is profited from the Word when he discovers how entirely and how sinfully he has *failed to meet* God's demands. And let us point out for the benefit of any who may take issue with the last paragraph, no man, *can* see *what* a sinner he is, how infinitely short he has fallen of measuring up to the standard God has given, until he has a clear sight *of* the exalted demands of God upon him! Just in proportion as preachers *lower* God's standard of what He requires from every human being, to that extent will their hearers obtain an adequate and faulty conception of their sinfulness! and so, the less will they perceive their need of an all-mighty Saviour! But once a soul really perceives *what are* God's demands upon him, and how completely and constantly he has failed to render Him His due, then does he recognize what a desperate situation he is in. The Law must be preached before any are ready for the Gospel.

To proceed further. 3. A man is profited from the Word when he is taught therefrom that God, in His infinite grace has fully *provided for* His people's meeting His own demands. At this point too practically all present-day preaching is seriously defective. There is being given forth what may loosely be termed a "half Gospel," but which, in reality, is virtually *a denial of* the Gospel. Christ is brought in, yet only as a sort of make-weight. That Christ vicariously met every demand of God upon all who believe on Him is blessedly true, yet is it only a part of the truth. The Lord Jesus has not only vicariously satisfied for His people the requirements of God's righteousness, but He has also secured that *they* shall *personally* satisfy them too. Christ has procured the Holy Spirit to make good *in* them, what the Redeemer wrought *for* them!

The grand and glorious miracle of salvation is that the saved are *regenerated*. A transforming work is wrought within them. Their understandings are illumined, their hearts are changed, their wills are renewed. They are made "*new* creatures" in Christ, so that "old things are passed away; behold, all things are become new" (2 Cor. 5:17). God refers to this miracle of grace thus: "I will put My *laws* into their mind, and write them in their hearts" (Heb. 8:10). The heart is now inclined to God's law; a disposition has been communicated to it which *answers to* its demands; there is a sincere desire to perform it. And thus the quickened soul is able to say, "when Thou saidest, *Seek ye* My face; my heart said unto Thee, Thy face, Lord, *will I* seek" (Psa. 27:8).

Christ not only rendered a perfect obedience unto the law for the justification of His believing people, but He also merited for them those supplies of His Spirit which were essential unto their sanctification, and which could alone transform carnal creatures and enable them to render acceptable obedience unto God. Though Christ died for the "ungodly" (Rom. 5:6), though He *finds* them "ungodly" (Rom. 4:5) when He justifies them, yet He *leaves them not* in that abominable state. On the contrary, He effectually teaches them by His Spirit to "*deny* ungodliness and worldly lusts" (Titus 2:12). Just as weight cannot be separated from a stone, or heat from fire, so cannot justification and sanctification.

When God really pardons a sinner in the court of his conscience, under the sense of that amazing grace, the heart is purified, the life is rectified, and the whole man is sanctified. Christ "gave Himself for us that He might redeem us *from* all iniquity, and *purify* unto Himself a peculiar people (*not* "careless about," but) *zealous of* good works" (Titus 2:14). Just as a substance and its properties, causes and their necessary effects, are inseparably connected, so are a saving faith *and* conscientious obedience unto God. Hence we read of "the obedience of faith" (Rom. 16:26).

Said the Lord Jesus, "He that hath My commandments, and keepeth them, *he it is* that *loveth* Me" (John 14:21). Neither in the O. T., the Gospels, or the Epistles, does God own any one as a lover of Him, save he who *keeps* His commandments. Love is something more than a sentiment or emotion: it is a principle of action, and it expresses itself in something more than honied expressions, namely, by deeds which please the object loved. "For this *is* the love of God, that we *keep* His commandments" (1 John 5:3). O my reader, you are deceiving yourself if you think you love God, and yet have no deep desire and make no real efforts to walk obediently before Him.

But what is *obedience to God?* It is far more than a mechanical performance of certain duties. I may have been brought up by Christian parents, and under them, acquired certain moral habits; and yet my abstaining from taking the Lord's name in vain, and being guiltless of stealing, may be no *obedience* to the third and eighth commandments. Again: obedience to God is far more than conforming to the conduct of His people. I may board in a home where the Sabbath is strictly observed, and out of respect for them or because I think it is a good and wise course to rest one day in seven, I too may refrain from all unnecessary labour on that day, and yet not *keep* the fourth commandment at all! Obedience is not only subjection to an external law, but it is the surrender of my will to the authority of another. Thus, obedience to God is the heart's recognition of His Lordship: of His right to command, and my duty to comply. It is the complete subjection of the soul to the blessed yoke of Christ .

That obedience which God requires can proceed only from a heart which *loves* Him. "Whatsoever ye do, do *heartily*, as to the Lord" (Col. 3:23). That obedience which springs from a dread of punishment is servile. That obedience which is performed in order to procure favours from God is selfish and carnal. But spiritual and acceptable obedience is cheerfully given: it is the heart's free response to and gratitude for the unmerited regard and love of God to us.

4. Now we are profited from the word when we not only see it is our bounden duty to obey God, but when there is wrought in us *a love for* His commandments. The "blessed" man is the one whose "*delight* is in the law of the Lord" (Psa. 1:2). And again we read, "Blessed is the man that feareth the Lord, that delighteth greatly in His commandments" (Psa. 112:1). It affords a real test for our hearts to honestly face the question, Do I really value His "commandments" as much as I do His *"promises?* Ought I not to do so? Assuredly, for the one proceed as truly from *His love* as do the other. The heart's compliance with the voice of Christ is the foundation of all practical holiness.

Here again we would earnestly and lovingly beg the reader to attend closely to this detail. Any man who supposes that he is saved and yet has no genuine *love for God's* commandments, is deceiving himself. Said the Psalmist, "O how love I Thy law!" (119:97). And again, "Therefore I love Thy commandments above gold; yea, above fine gold" (119:127). Should some one object *that* was under the O. T.! We ask, Do you intimate that the Holy Spirit produces *less* of a change in the hearts of those whom He now regenerates than He did of old! But a N. T. saint also placed it on record, "I *delight* in the law of God after the inward man" (Rom. 7:22). And, my reader, unless *your* heart *delights* in the "law of God" there is something radically wrong with you; yea, it is greatly to be feared that you are spiritually dead.

5. A man is profited from the Word when his heart and will is yielded to *all* God's commandments. Partial obedience, is no obedience at all. A holy mind declines whatsoever God forbids, and chooses to practice all that He requires, without any exception. If our minds submit not unto God in all His commandments, we submit not to *His* authority in any thing He enjoins. If we do not approve of our duty in its *full* extent, we are greatly mistaken if we imagine that we have any *liking* unto *any* part of it. A person who has *no* principle of holiness in him may yet be disinclined to many vices and be pleased to practice many virtues, as he perceives the former are unfit actions and the latter are, in themselves, comely actions, but his disapprobation of vice and approbation of virtue arise *not* from any disposition to *submit to the will of God.*

True spiritual obedience is *impartial*. A renewed heart does not pick and choose from God's commandments: the man who does so, is not performing *God's* will, but his own! Make no mistake upon this point: if we do not sincerely desire to please God in *all* things, then we do not truly wish to please *Him* in any thing. Self must be denied; not merely some of the things which may be craved, but self itself! A wilful allowance of *any* known sin breaks the whole law: James 2:10, 11. "Then shall I not be ashamed, when I have respect unto *all* Thy commandments" (Psa. 119:6). Said the Lord Jesus, "Ye are My friends, if ye do *whatsoever* I command you" (John 15:14): if I am not His "friend," then I must be His *enemy*, for there is no other alternative—see Luke 19:27!

6. We are profited from the Word when the soul is moved to *pray earnestly for enabling grace*. In regeneration the Holy Spirit communicates a nature which is fitted for obedience according to the Word. The heart has been won by God. There is now a deep and sincere desire to please Him. But the new nature possesses no inherent power, and the old nature or "flesh" strives against it, and the Devil opposes. Thus, the Christian exclaims, "for to will *is* present with me, but to *perform* that which is good I find not" (Rom. 7:18). This does not mean that he is the slave of sin, as he was before conversion; but it means that he finds not how to *fully* realize his spiritual aspirations. Therefore does he pray, *"Make me to go* in the path of Thy commandments, for therein do I delight" (Psa. 119:35). And again, "Order my steps in Thy Word, and let not any iniquity have dominion over me" (119:133).

Here we would reply to a question which the above paragraphs has probably raised in many minds: Are you affirming that God requires *perfect* obedience from us in this life? We answer, Yes. God will not set any lower standard before us than that: see 1 Pet. 1:15. Then does the real Christian measure up to that standard? Yes, and No. Yes, in *his heart*, and it is at *that* God looks (1 Sam. 16:7). In his heart, every regenerated person has a real love for God's commandments, and genuinely *desires* to keep all of them completely. It is in *this* sense, and this alone, that the Christian is experimentally "perfect." The word "perfect" both in the O. T. (Job 1:1, Psa. 37:37) and in the New (Phil. 3:15) means upright, sincere, in contrast from hypocritical.

"Lord, Thou hast heard the *desire* of the humble" (Psa. 10:17). The "desires" of the saint are the language of his soul, and the promise is, "he *will* fulfil the desire of them that fear Him" (Psa. 145:19). The Christian's desire is to obey God in all things, to be completely conformed to the image of Christ. But this will only be fully realized in the resurrection. Meanwhile, God, for Christ's sake, graciously accepts the will for the deed (1 Pet. 2:5). He who knows our hearts and sees in His child a genuine love for and a sincere desire *to keep* all His commandments, accepts the fervent longing and cordial endeavour in lieu of an exact performance (2 Cor. 8:12). But let none who are living in wilful disobedience draw false peace and pervert to their own destruction what has just been said for the comfort of those who *are* heartily desirous of seeking to please God in all the details of their lives.

If it be asked, How am I to know that *my* "desires" are really those of a regenerated soul? we answer, saving grace is the communication to the heart of an habitual *disposition unto* holy acts. The "desires" of the reader are to be *tested* thus. Are they constant and continuous, or only by fits and starts? Are they earnest and serious, so that you really "hunger and thirst after righteousness" (Matt. 5:6) and "pant after" God (Psa. 42:1)? Are they operative and efficacious? Many desire to escape from Hell, yet their desires are not sufficiently strong to bring them to hate and turn from that which must inevitably bring them to Hell, namely, wilfully sinning against God. Many desire to go to Heaven, but not so that they enter upon and follow that "narrow way" which alone leadeth thereto. True spiritual "desires" *use* the means of grace and spare no pains to realize them, and continue prayerfully *pressing* forward unto the mark set before them.

7. We are profited from the Word when we are, even now, *enjoying the reward of* obedience. "Godliness is profitable unto all things" (1 Tim. 4:8). By obedience we purify our souls (1 Peter 1:21). By obedience we obtain the ear of God (1 John 3:22), as disobedience is a barrier to our prayers: (Isa. 59:2, Jer. 5:25). By obedience we obtain precious and intimate manifestations of Christ unto the soul (John 14:21). As we tread the path of Wisdom (complete subjection to God) we discover that "her ways are ways of pleasantness, and all her paths are peace" (Prov. 3:17). "His commands are *not* grievous" (1 John 5:3), and "in keeping of them there *is* great reward" (Psa. 19:11). A.W.P.

REPENTANCE

2. *Its Nature.*

"Except ye repent, ye shall all likewise perish" (Luke 13:3). In view of these solemn words it is tremendously important that each of us should seek and obtain from God the repentance which *He* requires, not resting content with anything short of this. Hence, there needs to be the most diligent and prayerful examination as to the *character* of our repentance. Multitudes are deceived thereon. Many are perplexed by the conflicting teaching of men on this subject; but instead of that discouraging, it should stir up to a more earnest searching of the Scriptures. Before turning to the positive side of this branch of our theme, let us first point out some of the features of a non-saving repentance.

Trembling beneath the preaching of God's Word is not repentance. True there are thousands of people who have listened unmoved to the most awe-inspiring sermons, and even descriptions of the torments of the damned have struck no terror to their hearts. Yet, on the other hand, many who *were* deeply stirred, filled with alarm, and moved to tears, are now in Hell. I have seen the faces of strong men pale under a searching message, yet next day all its effects had left them. Felix "trembled" (Acts 24:25) under the preaching of Paul!

Being "almost persuaded" is not repentance. Agrippa (Acts 26:28) is a case in point. A person may give full assent to the messages of God's servant, admire the Gospel, yea, "receive the Word with joy," and after all, be only a stony-ground hearer (Matt. 13:20, 21). Not only so, he may be conscious of his evil-doing and acknowledge the same. Pharaoh owned "I have sinned against the Lord your God" (Ex. 10:16). A man may realise that he *ought* to yield himself to the claims of God and become a Christian, yet never be more than "*almost* persuaded."

Humbling ourselves beneath the mighty hand of God is not repentance. People may be deeply moved, weep, go home and determine to reform their lives, and yet return to their sins. A solemn example of this is found in Ahab. That wicked king of Israel coveted Naboth's vineyard, plotted to secure it, and gained his end by causing him to be murdered. Then the servant of God met him and said, "Hast thou killed and also taken possession?" And we are told that "he rent his clothes, and put sackcloth upon his flesh, and fasted . . . and went softly" (1 Kings 21:27-29) Yet in the very next chapter we find him again rebelling against God, and that he was cut off by Divine judgment. Ah, my reader, you may have humbled yourself before God for a time, and yet remain the slave of your lusts. You may be afraid of Hell, and yet not of sinning. If Hell were extinguished, so would be the repentance of many church-members. O mistake not fear of the wrath to come for a holy hatred and horror of sin.

Confessing sins is not repentance. Thousands have gone forward to the "altar" or "mourners' bench" and have told God what vile creatures they were, enumerating a long list of transgressions, but without any deep realization of the unspeakable awfulness of their sins, or a spark of holy hatred of them. The sequel has shown this, for they now ignore God's commandments as much as they did before. O my reader, if you do not, in the strength of God, *resist* sin, if you do not *turn from it*, then your fancied repentance is only whitewash—paint which decorates, but not the grace which transforms into gold.

You may even do works meet for repentance, and yet remain impenitent. A sinner may be convinced of the evil of his ways, turn from them, and go so far as to make restitution for the harm which he has wrought, and yet perish notwithstanding. A clear proof of this is furnished in the New Testament. Judas confessed his sins to the priests, and returned their money (Matt. 27:3-5), and then he went out from the presence of those evil men. Was he saved? No, he went and hanged himself! O how this ought to make each of us tremble and search our hearts.

The Greek "metanoeo," which occurs most frequently as the word rendered "repent," signifies a change of mind: Matt. 21:29 both illustrates and confirms that definition. Yet let it be said very emphatically that saving repentance means far more than a mere change of opinions: it is a *changed* mind, which leads to action. Now this changed mind is not brought about by any intellectual process, but is the result of the understanding being wrought upon by the conscience, and that, as the conscience has been supernaturally ploughed up by the Holy Spirit. In consequence of this there is a judging or condemning of self, a taking sides with God against myself.

Fallen man is not now on trial, but is a criminal already under sentence (John 3:18). "There is none righteous, no, not one: There is none that understandeth, there is none that seeketh after God. They are all gone out of the way, they are together become unprofitable; there is none that doeth good, no, not one" (Rom. 3:10-12). *That* is God's indictment against each of us. No pleading will avail, no excuses will be accepted. The present issue between God and the sinner is, Will man bow to, or endorse with his heart, God's righteous verdict.

It is just here that the Gospel meets us. It comes to us as those who are already *lost*, as those who are "ungodly," "without strength," at "enmity" with God." When the Gospel first comes to the sinner it finds him in a state of apostacy from God, both as sovereign Ruler and as our supreme Good, neither obeying and glorifying Him, nor enjoying and finding satisfaction in Him. Hence the demand for "repentance toward God" *before* "faith toward our Lord Jesus Christ" (Acts 20:21). True repentance toward God *removes* this disaffection of our minds and hearts toward Him, under both these characters. In saving repentance the whole soul turns to Him and says: I have been a disloyal and rebellious creature: I have scorned Thy high authority and most rightful law. I will live no longer thus. I now desire and determine with all my might to serve and obey Thee as my only Lord. I subject myself unto Thee, to submit to Thy will.

Nor is the above all that a truly penitent soul says unto God. He goes on: Hitherto I have been a miserable and forlorn creature, destitute of anything which could satisfy or make me truly happy. My heart has been set upon a vain world, which could not meet my real needs: it has flattered and mocked me often, but never contented me; it has "pierced me through with many sorrows." I forsook the Fountain of living waters, and turned to broken cisterns which held none. I own and bewail my folly; I unsparingly condemn myself for my madness. I now betake myself to Thee as my present and everlasting Portion.

The Gospel proclaims the amazing *grace* of God, which is the guilty and condemned sinner's *only* hope. Yet that grace will never be welcomed until the sinner really bows beneath God's sentence against him. This is why both repentance *and* faith are demanded of us. The two must never be separated. When our Lord was speaking to the chief priests and elders about their rejection of John's message, the charge He preferred against them was: ye "repented not afterward, *that ye might believe* in him" (Matt. 21:32). Repentance is the heart's acknowledgment of the justice of God's sentence of condemnation; faith is the heart's glad acceptance of the grace and mercy which are extended to us through Christ. Repentance is not simply the turning over of a new leaf and a vowing that I will mend my ways: rather is it a setting to my seal that God is true when He declares I am *"without strength"*: that in myself, my case is hopeless, that I am no more capable of "doing better" than I am of creating a world. Not until this is believed on the authority of God's Word shall I really turn to Christ and welcome Him—not as a Helper, but as Saviour!

Repentance is more than a conviction of sin or terror of the wrath to come. This is clear from Acts 2:37, 38. Under Peter's searching message, the Jews were made to realise their awful guilt before God: they were made conscious of the fearful fact that they had murdered the Prince of life, and so were in terrible fear of being cast into Hell. Nevertheless, though already "pricked in their hearts," when they cried out "What shall we do?" Peter said, "Repent." To a superficial mind, such a demand might appear needless: yet was it seasonable counsel. Their being "pricked in their heart" was *legal terror*, whereas saving "repentance" is an *evangelical* judging of self, mourning over sin out of a sense of God's grace and goodness.

A prayerful and careful pondering of Acts 2:37, 38 should correct more than one error which is now current in various circles. When the hearers of Peter were affrighted by their awful crime and fearful of eternal wrath, pricked in the heart—as though a sword had been run through their vitals—they cried out in anguish "What shall we do?" The apostle did not say, "Be passive, there is nothing you can do," thus encouraging the fatal inertia of hyper-Calvinists. Nor did he say, "Believe your sins *are* blotted out," which is the counsel of many "physicians of no value" in our day. No, his reply was far otherwise, in substance amounting to this: Take all the blame which belongs to you. Own the whole truth unto God. Do not gloss over, but confess your awful wickedness; let your uncircumcised hearts be truly humbled before Him. And then look by faith to the free grace of God through the blood of Christ for pardon, and in token that all your dependance is on His mediation and merits, be baptised in His name, and that shall be to you an *external sign* of the remission of your sins.

"It is manifest from the nature of the case, that he who hath his eyes opened to see the glory of the Divine nature, the beauty of the Divine law, the infinite evil of sin, the need of an infinite atonement, and so to see his need of Christ: and at the same time, views God as the supreme, all-sufficient Good, ready to receive every sinner that returns to Him through Christ; it is manifest, I say, that every one who is thus taught of God, will repent and return to God as his sovereign Lord and supreme Good, and return through Jesus Christ, who is the way to the Father, and the only way, in the view of one thus Divinely enlightened. For in the clearer light the glory of the Divine nature and law is seen, in exact proportion will be the sense of the infinite evil of sin, and the need of Christ's infinite atonement and perfect righteousness. And so 'repentance toward God and faith toward our Lord Jesus Christ' will be naturally and inseparably connected. Yea, they will be necessarily implied in each other.

"He who repents in the view of the Glory of God, the glory of the law, and of the atonement, will in his repentance look only to free grace through Jesus Christ for mercy, and he who looks only to free grace through Jesus Christ for mercy, in a view of the glory of God, law, atonement, will in doing so, take the whole blame of his disaffection to the Divine character, as exhibited in the law, and on the cross of Christ, to himself, *judging and condemning himself*, and in the very act of faith, repent and be converted. When therefore it is said 'Believe on the Lord Jesus Christ, and thou shalt be saved' (Acts 16:31), *the same* (inclusive) *thing is meant* as when it is said, 'Repent ye therefore and be converted that your sins may be blotted out' (Acts 3:19). For the apostolic faith implies repentance in its own nature, and their repentance implies faith in its nature. Sometimes they only mention faith, and sometimes only repentance, and sometimes both together; but the *same thing* is *always* intended. For in the view of the apostles, repentance and faith were mutually implied in each other" (Jos. Bellamy, 1750).

Giving a more full and formal definition of repentance, we would say: Repentance is a supernatural and inward revelation from God, giving a deep consciousness of what I am in *His* sight, which causes me to loathe and condemn myself, resulting in a bitter sorrow for sin, a holy horror and hatred for sin, and a turning away from or forsaking of sin. It is the discovery of God's high and righteous claims upon me, and of my lifelong failure to meet those claims. It is the recognition of the holiness and goodness of His law, and my defiant insubordination thereto. It is the perception that God has the right to rule and govern me, and of my refusal to submit unto Him. It is the apprehension that He has dealt in goodness and kindness with me, and that I have evilly repaid Him by having no concern for *His* honour and glory. It is the realisation of His gracious patience with me, and how that instead of this melting my heart and causing me to yield loving obedience to Him, I have *abused* His forebearance by continuing in a course of selfwill.

Evangelical repentance is a heart-apprehension of the exceeding sinfulness of sin. It is the recognition of the *chief* thing wherein I am blameworthy, namely, in having so miserably failed to render unto God that which is His rightful due. As the Holy Spirit sets before me the loveliness of the Divine character, as I am enabled to discern the exalted excellency of God, then I begin to perceive that to which He is justly entitled, namely, the homage of my heart, the unrestricted love of my soul, the complete surrender of my whole being to Him. As I perceive that, from the moment I drew my first breath, God has sought *only my good*, that the One who gave me being has constantly ministered to my every creature need, and that the least I can do in return is to acknowledge His abounding mercies by doing that which is pleasing in His sight; I am now overwhelmed with anguish and horror as I realize I have treated Him more vilely than my worst enemy.

Oftentimes example is better than the most accurate definition. The N. T. furnishes quite a number of concrete instances, even where the term itself is not found. When the "publican" stood afar off and would not so much as lift up his eyes unto heaven, but smote upon his breast, saying, "God be merciful to me a sinner" (Luke 18:13), we behold repentance *in action*. He recognised that awful moral distance which sin had taken him from God; he was deeply conscious of his utter unworthiness to gaze upon the Holy One; he unsparingly judged himself; he realised that his only hope lay in the sovereign mercy of God. So too the thief on the cross: in his words to his hardened companion, "Dost not thou fear God, seeing thou art in the same *condemnation*, and we indeed *justly;* for we receive the due reward of our deeds" (Luke 23: 40-41). There was no self-extenuation, but a ready owning of his sinnership and his desert to be punished.

Mark carefully the expressions of penitence used by David in Psa. 51. He talks not of his "failures," "mistakes" or "infirmities," but instead of "my transgression" (v. 1), "my sin" (v. 2), "this evil" (v. 4), "my iniquity" (v. 9), and expressly mentions the worst feature of his crime, namely, his "bloodguiltiness" (v. 14). True repentance abhors gentle names for sin, nor does it seek to cloak wickedness. That which, while being tempted, is thought of as no great offence, when (later) is truly repented of, is acknowledged to be heinous. Sin before its commission often appears unto the mind as a very small evil, but when grace acts in a way of repentance for it, then the false glamour disappears and it is viewed in its dreadful malignity and loathed accordingly.

True repentance is always accompanied by a deep longing and a sincere determination to forsake that course which is displeasing to God. With what *honesty* could any man seek God's pardon while he continued to defy Him and would not part with that which He forbids? Would any king pardon a traitor, though he seemed never so humble, if he saw that he would be a traitor still? True, God is infinitely more merciful than any human king, yet in the very passage where He first formally proclaimed His mercy, He at once added "that will by no means clear the guilty" (Ex. 34:5-7) i.e., the guilty-hearted, those with false and disloyal hearts toward Himself, who would not be subject to Him in all things, and declined to have their every thought brought into captivity to obedience unto Him (2 Cor. 10:5).

What has just been said needs to be strongly emphasised in this day of lawlessness, when, on every side, the very "grace of God" is being "turned into lasciviousness" (Jude 4). Many are the Scriptures which set forth this truth, that there must be a *forsaking* of sin before God will pardon offenders. "There is forgiveness with Thee, *that* Thou mayest be feared" (Psa. 130:4). Were God to grant pardon unto those in whom there was no change of heart *to* fear and obey Him, then there would be mercy with Him that He might be *insulted* and dishonoured still further! God's mercy is never exercised at the expense of His holiness! God never displays one of His attributes so as to dishonour another. To pity a thief, while continuing a thief, would be folly, not wisdom. Well did the Puritan T. Goodwin say, "Resolve either to leave every known sin and submit to every known duty, or else never look to find mercy and favour with God."

Of old it was announced that should any "bless himself in his heart, saying, I shall have peace, though I walk in the imagination of mine heart to add drunkenness to thirst (that is, one sin to another): the Lord *will not* spare him" (Deut. 28:19, 20). So, on the other hand it was declared, "If My people, which are called by My name, shall humble themselves, and pray, and seek My face, and *turn from* their wicked ways; *then* will I hear from heaven, and will forgive their sin, and will heal their land" (2 Chron. 7:14 and cf. 2 Chron. 6:26). And the principles of God's government have not changed! The death of Christ has not caused God to *lower* His standard—how unspeakably horrible and dreadful that any one should suppose it has! No, what God demanded of old, He demands now.

Thus, repentance is the *negative side* of conversion. Conversion is a wholehearted turning unto God, but there cannot be a turning *unto* without a turning *from*. Sin must be forsaken, ere we can draw nigh unto the Holy One. As it is written, "ye turned to God *from idols* to serve (live for) the living and true God" (1 Thess. 1:9). Thus, repentance is the sinner *making his peace with God*. We are not unmindful of the fact that that expression is derided by many, yet it is a scriptural one: "let him take hold of My strength, that he may make peace with Me" (Isa. 27:5). It is blessedly true that *Christ* "made peace through the blood of His cross" (Col. 1:20), yet it is equally true that no sinner ever enters into the saving good of Christ's blood until he makes *his* peace with God; in other words, till he throws down the weapons of his warfare and ceases fighting against God. The Lord Jesus Himself plainly taught this in Luke 14; let the reader *carefully* ponder vv. 28-33, paying special attention to v. 32 and the "so likewise" of v. 33! A.W.P.

A PERSONAL WORD

"Now these are the journeys of the children of Israel. . . . And the children of Israel removed from —— and pitched in ——. And they departed from —— and pitched in ——" (Num. 33). These are the words which have come to mind as we sat down to write a few lines acquainting our friends with the Lord's most recent dealings with us. If the reader will glance through Num. 33 he or she will at once perceive that God's people of old were frequently called upon to change their tenting-place. Nor should we be surprised at this: they were pilgrims, as yet not having entered their inheritance. The Lord employs various means to forcibly remind His people they have not yet reached their eternal Home. With us it has been "journeyings oft."

"The Lord shall lead you" (Deut. 4:27). What a precious promise is this! We are not left in this trackless desert without a Guide. No, the Lord Himself directs the steps of His own. "He led them forth" (Psa. 107:7). He still does so. He may bring us into deep waters and a fiery furnace, but blessed be His name He does not leave us there. "He led them safely" (Psa. 78:53). What an inestimable privilege it is to have the protecting arms of the Almighty around us! The editor and his wife have been called upon to travel many thousands of miles the last few years, both by land and by sea, yet no harm has befallen us. This is much to be thankful for.

"He led them forth by the right way" (Psa. 107:7). To Israel of old, the way the Lord led them must have seemed a strange one: through the Red Sea, out of one wilderness into another: backwards and forwards, to the one side and then to the other. Yet it was the *best* way for them. Our path too has twisted and turned again and again, yet we are fully assured that God has had our highest interests in view, and we thank Him for *"all* the way" (Deut. 8:2) in which He has conducted us. Had we consulted the ease of the flesh or carnal reason we had remained much more stationary, but when the "cloud" of Divine Providence moves, it is our bounden duty to follow it.

Our last address in York was but a temporary one, in the home of kind Christian friends, where we could quietly wait upon our God to ascertain His mind as to exactly where *He* would have us next locate. When we left California, God made it plain that He was calling us back to Pennsylvania (after an absence of over six years), but which part of that State we knew not. But He graciously made very clear to us His will, and has provided us with a peaceable habitation in Millmont. Here we shall (D. V.) devote most of our time to prayerful study and writing, going forth, occasionally, to minister the Word orally to little groups who yearn after a closer walk with God.

"O magnify the Lord with me, and let us exalt His name together" (Psa. 34:3) —for journeying mercies; for the loving friends He gave us in York, where our every temporal need was generously ministered unto for eight weeks; for preserving us in full health and strength, and sparing us any financial anxiety; for continuing to prosper the work of this little magazine. Please continue to hold up our hands in prayer, that God will fit us to be a greater blessing to His dear people. A.W.P.

---

we are "shapen in iniquity" and conceived "in sin" (Psa. 51:5). Though Christ truly became partaker of our nature, yet was He "holy, harmless, undefiled, separate from sinners" (Heb. 7:26). For this reason He could say, "The prince of this world cometh, and hath *nothing* in Me" (John 14:7)—there was nothing in His pure and holy humanity which could respond to sin or Satan.

And now let us attempt a word or two by way of application. It was truly remarkable when man was made in the image of God (Gen. 1:26), but O my soul bow in wonderment and worship at the amazing condescension of God being made in the image of man! How this made manifest the greatness of His love and the riches of His grace! It was for His people and their salvation that the eternal Son assumed human nature and abased Himself to the sorrows of death. He drew a veil over His glory that He might remove our reproach. Surely, pride must be forever renounced by the followers of such a Saviour!

Inasmuch as "the Man Christ Jesus" (1 Tim. 2:5) lived in this world for thirty-three years He has left "an *example* that ye should follow His steps" (1 Pet. 2:21). He "did no sin," nor should we (1 Cor. 15:34). "Neither was guile found in His mouth," nor should it be in ours (Col. 4;6). "When He was reviled, He reviled not again," nor must His followers. He was weary in body, but not in welldoing. He suffered hunger and thirst, yet never murmured. He "pleased not Himself" (Rom. 15:3), nor must we (2 Col. 5:15). He did *always* those things which pleased the Father (John 8:29): this too must ever be our aim (2 Cor. 5:9). Let us earnestly endeavour after and fervently pray for more and more conformity to His perfect image.   A.W.P.

Experience alone can beat this truth into men's minds. A man will lie broken at the foot of the precipice, every bone dislocated by the fall, and yet hope to save himself. Piles of sin will fall upon him and bury him, and yet his self-trust will live. Crushed to atoms, every particle of our nature reeks with conceit. Ground to powder, our very dust is pungent with pride. Only the Holy Ghost can make a man receive that humbling sentence, *"Salvation is of the Lord"*.—C. H. Spurgeon.

being subsisting by himself. The second person of the Trinity assumed a human nature and gave it subsistence by union with His Divine personality. It *would* have been a human "person," if it had not been united to the Son of God; but being united to Him, it cannot be called a "person," because it never subsisted by itself, as other men do, each of whom has an independent existence. Hence the force of "that holy *thing* which shall be born of thee" (Luke 1:35). It was not possible for a Divine person to assume another "person," subsisting of itself, into union with Himself: for that two persons, remaining two, could become one person, is a contradiction. "A body hast Thou prepared Me" (Heb. 10:5): the "Me" denotes the Divine Person, the "body" the nature He took unto Himself.

2. The humanity of Christ was *real*. "Forasmuch then as the children are partakers of flesh and blood, He also Himself likewise took part of the same. . . . Wherefore in all things it behoved Him to be made like unto His brethren" (Heb. 2:14, 17). He assumed a *complete* human nature, spirit and soul and body. Christ did not bring His human nature from heaven (as some have strangely and erroneously concluded from 1 Cor. 15:47), but it was composed of the very substance of His mother. In clothing Himself with flesh and blood, Christ also clothed Himself with human feelings, so that He differed not from His brethren, sin only excepted.

"While we always contend that Christ is God, very God of very God, let us never lose the firm conviction He is most certainly and truly a man. He is not a God humanized, nor yet a human being deified; but, as to His Godhead, pure Godhead, equal and co-eternal with the Father; as to His manhood, perfect manhood, made in all respects like unto the rest of mankind, sin alone excepted. His humanity is real, for *He was born*. He lay hidden in the Virgin's womb, and in due time was born into a world of suffering. The gate by which we enter upon the first life, he passed through also; He was not created, nor transformed, but His humanity was begotten and born. As He was born, so *in the circumstances of His birth*, He is completely human; He is as weak and feeble as any other babe. He is not even royal, but human. Those who were born in marble halls of old were wrapped in purple garments, and were thought by the vulgar to be a superior race; but this Babe is wrapped in swaddling clothes and hath a manger for His cradle, that the true humanness of His being may come out. More a man than He is a Prince of the House of David, He knows the woes of a peasant's child.

"As He grows up, the very *growth* shows how completely human He is. He does not spring into full manhood at once, but He grows in wisdom and stature, and in favour with God and man. When he reaches man's estate, He gets the common stamp of manhood upon His brow. 'In the *sweat* of thy brow shalt thou eat bread' is the common heritage of us all, and He receives no better. The carpenter's shop must witness to the toils of a Saviour, and when He becomes the preacher and the prophet, still we read such significant words as these—'Jesus, being weary sat thus on the well.' We find Him needing to betake Himself to rest in *sleep*, He slumbers at the stern of the vessel when it is tossed in the midst of the tempest. Brethren if *sorrow* be the mark of real manhood, and 'man is born unto trouble as the sparks fly upward,' certainly Jesus Christ has the truest evidence of being a man. If to hunger and to thirst be signs that He was no shadow, and His manhood no fiction, you have these. If to associate with His fellow-men, and eat and drink as they did, will be proof to your mind that He was none other than a man, you see Him sitting at a feast one day, at another time He graces a marriage-supper, and on another occasion He is hungry and 'hath not where to lay His head' " (C. H. Spurgeon).

They who deny Christ's derivation of *real* humanity through His mother undermine the atonement. His very fraternity (Heb. 2:11), as our *Kinsman*-Redeemer, depended on the fact that He obtained His humanity from the substance of Mary. Without this He would neither possess the natural nor the legal union with His people, which *must* lie at the foundation of His *representative* character as the "last Adam." To be our Goel (Redeemer), His humanity could neither be brought from heaven nor immediately created by God, but must be derived, as ours was, from a human mother; but, with this difference: His humanity never existed in Adam's covenant to entail guilt or taint.

3. The humanity of Christ was *holy*. Intrinsically so, because it was "of the Holy Spirit" (Matt. 1:20); absolutely so, because taken into union with God, the Holy One. This fact is expressly affirmed in Luke 1:35, "that *holy* thing," which is contrasted from "But we all as an *unclean* thing" (Isa. 64:6), and that because

(Continued on Page 239)

Vol. X   NOVEMBER, 1931   No. 11

STUDIES IN THE SCRIPTURES

"Search the Scriptures" John 5:39

Copyright in all English-speaking Countries

EDITOR: Arthur W. Pink, Millmont, Union Co., Penna., U. S. A.
Hon. Agent in England: Mr. A. Winstone, "Shalom," Old Bath Road, Leckhampton, Cheltenham.
Hon. Agent in Australia: Mr. G. Ardill, The Christian Workers' Depot, Commonwealth and Reservoir Streets, Sydney.

THE PERSON OF CHRIST

Well may we with fear and trembling enter upon this high and holy subject. Christ's name is called "Wonderful" (Isa. 9:6), and even the angels of God are commanded to worship Him (Heb. 1:6). There is no salvation apart from a true knowledge of Him (John 17:3): "whosoever denieth the Son (either His true Godhead, or His true and holy humanity) hath not the Father" (1 John 2:23). Thrice blessed are they unto whom the Spirit of Truth communicates a supernatural revelation of the ineffable Being of Christ (Matt. 16:17): it will lead them on in the only path of wisdom and joy (for in Him "are hid all the treasures of wisdom and knowledge" Col. 2:3) until they shall be taken to be where He is, and behold His supernal glory for ever and ever (John 17:24). An increasing apprehension of the Truth concerning the person of Christ should be our constant and prayerful aim.

"Without controversy great is the mystery of godliness: God was manifest in flesh" (1 Tim. 3:16). In view of such a Divine declaration as this, it is both useless and impious for any man to attempt an *explanation* of the wondrous and unique person of the Lord Jesus. He cannot be fully comprehended by any finite intelligence: "none knoweth the Son, but the Father" (Matt. 11:27). Nevertheless it is our privilege to grow "in the knowledge *of* our Lord and Saviour Jesus Christ" (2 Peter 3:18). So too it is the bounden duty of His servants to hold up the person of the Godman as He is revealed in Holy Scripture, as well as to warn against those errors which becloud His glory.

The one born in Bethlehem's manger was "the mighty God" (Isa. 9:6), "Immanuel" (Matt. 1:23), "the great God and Saviour" (Titus 2:13). He is also true Man, having a spirit, a soul and a physical body, for these are essential to human nature, so that none could be real man without all three. Nevertheless, the humanity of Christ (that holy *thing*, Luke 1:35) is *not* a distinct person, separate from His Godhead, for it never had a separate existence before it was taken into union with His Deity. He is the God-man, yet *"one Lord"* (Eph. 4:5). As such He was born, lived here in this world, died, rose again, ascended to heaven, and will continue thus for all eternity. As such He is entirely unique, and the Object of lasting wonder to all holy beings.

The person of Christ is a composite one. Two separate natures are united in His one peerless Person, but they are not fused into each other, instead, they remain distinct and different. The human nature is not Divine, nor has it been, intrinsically, deified, for it possesses none of the attributes of God. The humanity of Christ, absolutely and separately considered, is neither omnipotent, omniscient, nor omnipresent. On the other hand, His Deity is not a creature, and has none of the properties pertaining to such. The taking unto Himself of human nature did not effect any change in His Divine Being. It was a Divine *person* who wedded to Himself a holy humanity, and though His essential glory was partly veiled, yet it never ceased to be, nor did His Divine attributes cease to function. As the God-man, Christ is the "one Mediator" (1 Tim. 2:5). He alone being fitted to stand between God and men and effect a reconciliation between them.

It is to be firmly maintained that the two natures are united in the one person of Christ, but that each of them retains its separate properties, just as the soul

(Continued on Page 264)

IMPORTANT NOTICES

Please advise promptly of change of address, otherwise copies will be lost in the mails.

We are glad to send a sample copy to any of your friends whom you believe would be interested in such a publication.

Send to Mr. I. C. Herendeen, Swengel (Union County), Penna., for a list of our publications. He has published many of our books and booklets.

This magazine is published as a work of faith and labour of love. The Editor and his wife gladly give their services. It is freely sent to all who will read it. No charge is made for it.

Christians who feel definitely led to do so, may have fellowship with us in this ministry. Those outside the U. S. A., please send only INTERNATIONAL Money Orders made out to Mifflinburg, Penna., U. S. A.

CONTENTS

Th Person of Christ	241
The Epistle to the Hebrews	242
The Satisfaction ("Atonement") of Christ	248
Love: Divine and Human	254
Repentance	257
The Mighty Breaker	261
Prayer	262

THE EPISTLE TO THE HEBREWS

47. Christ's Dedication. Heb. 10:7-10

"As in all our obedience there are two principal ingredients to the true and right constitution of it, namely, the *matter* of the obedience itself, and the *principle* and fountain of it in us: whereof the one, the apostle calls the 'deed,' the other the 'the will' (2 Cor. 8:12)—which latter God accepts in us, oftentimes without, always more than, the deed or matter of obedience itself—even so in Christ's obedience, which is the pattern and measure of ours, there are those two eminent parts which complete it. First, the obedience itself, and the worth and value of it in that it is *His*—so great a person's. Second, the willingness, the readiness to undertake and the heartiness to perform it. The dignity of His person gave the value and merit to the obedience performed by Him. But the will, the zeal in His performance gives the acceptance, and hath besides a necessary influence into the worth of it, and the virtue and efficacy of it to sanctify us. All of which you have in Heb. 10:7-10.

"The 'offering of the body of Jesus Christ:' there is the matter, His becoming 'obedient unto death' (Phil. 2:8). Then there is the readiness by which He did so, 'Lo, I come to do thy will, O God,' This calls for not only a distinct but a more eminent consideration, both necessarily concurring to our sanctification and salvation. Now the story of His willingness to redeem and save is of four parts. 1. His actual consent and undertaking to the work, made and given to the Father from everlasting. 2. The continuance of His will to stand to it from everlasting unto the time of His incarnation. 3. The renewal of this consent when He came into the world. 4. The steadfast continuance of that will all along in the performance, from the cradle to the cross.

"It was necessary that Christ's *consent* should be then given, even from everlasting, and that as God made a promise to Him for us, so also that He should give consent unto God. Yea; and indeed it was one reason why it was necessary that our Mediator should be God, and existent from eternity, not only to the end that He might be privy to the first design and contrivance of our salvation, and know the bottom of God's mind and heart in it, and receive all the promises of God from God for us, but also in this respect, that His own very consent should go to it from the first, even as soon as His Father should design it. And it was most meet it should be so; for the performance and all the working part of it was to be His, to be laid upon His shoulders to execute, and it was a hard task, and therefore reasonable He should both know it from the first, seeing He was extant together with His Father. It was fit that both His heart and head should be in it from the first. And you have all in one Scripture, Isa. 9:6, where, when Christ is promised, 'Unto us a Child is born, unto us a Son is given,' observe under *what* titles He is set forth unto us:

"'Wonderful Counsellor, the mighty God, the everlasting Father,' where everlastingness, which is affixed to one, is yet common to those other two. The 'everlasting Counsellor,' as well as 'everlasting Father,' for He was both *Counsellor* and *Father*, in that He was the *Mighty God*, and all alike from everlasting. For, being God, and with His Father as a Son from everlasting, He must needs be a *Counsellor* with Him, and so privy unto all God meant to do, especially in that very business, for the performance of which He is there said to be *given* as a Son, and born as a Child, and the effecting of which is also said to be laid wholly on His shoulder. Certainly in this case, if God could hide nothing from Abraham He was to do, much less God from Christ, who was God with Him from everlasting. And as He was for this cause to be privy to it for the cognisance of the matter, so to have given His actual *consent* likewise thereunto; for He was to be the Father and Founder of all that was to be done in it. And in that very respect and in relation to that act of will, then passed, whereby He became a 'Father' of that business for us, it is He is styled the 'everlasting Father.' For it is in respect of that everlastingness He is God, and so 'Father' from everlasting, as well as God from everlasting; a "Counsellor' for us with God, a 'Father' of us in our salvation. God's 'Counsellor,' because His wisdom was jointly in that plot and the contrivement of it; and 'Father' both of us and this design, because of *His* will in it, and undertaking to effect it. In that His heart and will were in it as well as the Father's He was therefore the 'Father' of it as well as God, and brought it to perfection" (Adopted, with slight variations, from T. Goodwin, 1600-1680).

Concerning the *continuance* of the Son's willingness to the Father's purpose, from everlasting to the time when His humanity was conceived in the Virgin's womb, we have more than a hint in that remarkable passage found in Prov. 8. There (by the Spirit of prophecy) we are permitted to hear Him say of the Father, "Then I was by Him, as One brought up with him." But not only so, He added, "And I was daily His delight, *rejoicing always* before Him; rejoicing in the habitable part (that portion where His tabernacle was to be placed) of His earth; and My delights were *with* the sons of men" (vv. 30, 31). Thus we see how His heart was more set upon the redeeming of His people than all other works. The theophanic manifestations which He made of Himself from time to time during the O. T. period, illustrated the same fact: see Gen. 12:7, Ex. 3:2-9, Dan. 3:25 etc.

But it is the *renewing* of His consent when Christ came into the world which we would particularly contemplate. This may well be called the will of *consecration* of Himself by a vow to this great work, then solemnly made and given. This was the *dedication* of His holy "Temple" (John 2:19), foreshadowed of old by Solomon in the dedication of the temple which he erected unto God. This took place at the moment that His humanity was conceived by the Virgin: "*When* He cometh into the world, He saith . . . a body (a vehicle of service) hast Thou prepared Me. . . . Lo, I come, to do Thy will, O God." How truly marvellous and blessed that it pleased the Holy Spirit (the Divine Secretary of Heaven, and Recorder of the everlasting covenant) to write down for our learning the very words which the Son uttered to His Father at the moment when He condescended to take our nature and become incarnate! Equally wonderful is it that we are permitted to hear the very words which the Father addressed to the Son on His return to Heaven: "The Lord said to My Lord, Sit Thou at My right hand, till I make Thine enemies Thy footstool" (Psa. 110:1).

"When He cometh into the world, He saith." The Speaker is none other than the second person in the Divine Trinity. *He* was the One who took that "body" into everlasting union with Himself—an infinitely greater condescension than for the noblest king to marry the meanest servant-girl. The ineffably glorious Son of God was personally humbled far more and gave much more away than did that humanity when it was humiliated by being nailed to the cross. Therefore was His willingness to this tremendous stoop eminently requisite, and recorded for our comfort and praise. Thus, at the very moment that the human nature was a-making, and not yet capable of giving its *own* consent, He who was the Brightness of the Father's glory and the express Image of His person, announced *His* readiness. Inexpressibly blessed is this; may the contemplation thereof bow us in worship before Him. "Worthy is the Lamb!"

"Then said I, Lo, I come (in the volume of the book it is written of Me), to do Thy will, O God" (v. 7). There is a *double* reference (as is so often the case with the words of God) in the parenthetical clause. The "book" He mentioned *primarily* regarded the archives of God's eternal counsels, the scroll of His decrees. Secondarily, it concerned the Holy Scriptures, which are a partial transcript of that record of the Divine will which is preserved on High (Psa. 119:89). In that "book," drawn up by the Holy Spirit, it is written of Christ, the God-man Mediator for *He* is the Sum and Substance of all the Divine counsels (Eph. 3:11), as well as the Depository of all the Divine promises (2 Cor. 1:20). The Son was perfectly cognisant of all that was written in that book, for He had been "Counsellor" with the Father. The term "volume" is the right translation of the Hebrew word "magillah" in Psa. 40:7, but the Greek word "kephalis" ought most certainly to be rendered "head" — "kephale" occurs seventy-six times in the N. T., and is *always* rendered "head" elsewhere.

A most wondrous and blessed revelation is here made known to us: "in the head of the book" of God's decrees, at *the beginning* thereof, it is "written of" Christ! In that book is recorded the names of all God's favoured children: Luke 10:20, Heb. 12:23; but at the *head* of them is *Christ's*, for "in *all* things" *He* must have the "pre-eminence" (Col. 1:18). Thus, the first name on that heavenly scroll of the Divine decrees is that of the Mediator Himself! So too in the Holy Scriptures, which give us a copy, in part, the *first* name in the O. T. is that of Christ as Creator (Gen. 1:1 cf. John 1:1-3), and the *first* name in the N. T. is "Jesus Christ" (Matt. 1:1)! Yes, "in the *head* of the Book" it is written of *Him.*

The Man Christ Jesus was the *first* one chosen of God; chosen to be taken into everlasting union with the second person of the Trinity. Therefore does the Father say to us, "Behold My Servant, whom I uphold, Mine *Elect* in whom My soul delighteth" (Isa. 42:1). The Church was chosen in Christ (Eph. 1:4) and then given to Christ (Heb. 2:13). The Man Christ Jesus, taken into union with God the Son, was appointed to be the Head of the whole election of grace, and they to be members of His mystical Body (Eph. 1:23, 24; 5:30). "Christ be My first elect He said; Then chose our souls in Christ our Head."

Precious too is it to discover that the *human* nature of Christ *also* consented to the terms of the everlasting covenant, for it was something distinct from the Divine nature of God the Son, and so had a distinct will, and was directly concerned in the Great Transaction, for *it* was to be made the subject of all the sufferings and was to be the sacrifice offered up. The fundamental consent was the Divine person's, and this He gave when assuming our nature; but there was also an accessory consent of the human nature, now married into one person with the Divine. How soon then, *when* was it that the human nature gave *its* consent? No doubt many will deem this a question which it is impossible for us to answer, and that any effort so to do would be a prying into "secret things." Not so: it belongs to those things which *are* revealed.

Ere turning to the consideration of this marvelous detail, we must not overlook the *willingness* of the virgin Mary to be —in such an unprecedented manner, and in a way which (humanly speaking) seriously endangered her own moral reputation—the mother of our Lord's sacred humanity. This is most blessedly shown us in the inspired record of Luke's Gospel. There we learn that this amazing honour, yet sore trial, was proposed to her (*not* forced upon her, for God never violates human accountability!) by the angel: "Behold, thou shalt conceive in thy womb, and bring forth a Son, and shalt call His name Jesus" (v. 31). Mark now her meek response: "Behold the handmaid of *the Lord*"—I give myself up to Him—"*be it* unto me *according* to thy word" (v. 38). Not until *after* she had herself acquiesced, did she "conceive"— note the word "before" in Luke 2:21 and compare with Luke 1:31-38. Thus does God make His people "willing" in the day of His power (Psa. 110:3).

Returning now to the willingness of our Lord's *humanity* in consenting to God's eternal purpose: "This may safely be affirmed, that as soon as, or when first He began to put forth any *acts of reason*, that then His will was guided to direct its aim and intentions to God as His Father, from Himself as the Mediator. And look, as in infant's hearts, *if they had been born in innocency*, there would have been sown the notion of God, whom they should *first* have known, whatever else they knew; and the moral law being written in their hearts, they should have directed their actions to God and His glory, through a natural instinct and tendency of spirit. Thus it was in Christ when an infant, and such holy principles guided Him to that, which was that will of God for Him, and to be performed by Him; and which was to sway and direct all His actions and thoughts, that were to be the matter of our justification, which were to be exerted more and more according to the capacity of reason as it should grow" (T. Goodwin).

There was a meetness, yea a needs-be for this. For what Christ did as a Child had a meritoriousness in it, as much as what He did when a full-grown Man. So too what He suffered, even in His very circumcision, is made influential unto the sanctification of His people through the virtue of it, equally with what He suffered on the cross. His coat was *"without seam"* (John 19:23): the righteousness He wrought out for His Church was a *unit*—beginning at Bethlehem's manger, consummated at Calvary. It is the 22nd Psalm which furnishes a definite answer to our question, and reveals *how* early the Saviour was dedicated to God. Hear His gracious and unique words: "Thou art He that took Me out of the womb: Thou didst make Me hope upon My mother's breasts. I was cast upon Thee *from the womb*: Thou art My God from My mother's belly" (vv. 9, 10). O my brethren and sisters, prostrate your souls in adoration before this Holy One, who from the very first instant after He entered this world was unreservedly dedicated and consecrated to God, owning Him, relying wholly upon Him.

In this we may behold the fulfilment of a lovely and striking type, namely, that of the Nazarite, to which Matt. 2:23 directly, though not exclusively, refers. The "Nazarite" was one who, voluntarily, separated and devoted himself entirely unto the Lord (Num. 6:12). Samson is the outstanding illustration of this in the O. T.: the parallels between him and Christ are remarkable. 1. An angel announced to his mother her conception (Judges 13:2-3). 2. The prophecy of the angel is recorded. 3. He was sent to a woman utterly barren, to show her conception was extraordinary. 4. Her son was to be a Nazarite, that is, "holy to the Lord" (Num. 6:8). 5. He was to be "a Nazarite unto God *from the womb*" (Judges 13:5). 6. It was declared that her son should be a deliverer of Israel (v. 5). 7. Israel was then subject to the Gentiles (the Philistines), as the Jews were to the Romans when Christ was born. 8. It was in his *death* that he wrought his mightiest victory!

Equally striking, equally blessed, are the first words which the N. T. records as being uttered by our Saviour: "know ye not that in the (affairs) of My Father it behoves to be Me" (Bagster Interlinear). The Greek is very emphatic, the last word before "Me" signifying to be completely and continuously given up to it, and is rendered "wholly" in 1 Tim. 4:15. The reader is familiar with the context of Luke 2:49. The Saviour's mother appears to have chided Him, and, in substance, He said: True you are My earthly parent, and I have been subject to you hitherto in your particular province, but do you not know that I have another Father, far higher than you, who hath commanded Me, by virtue of My office of Mediator, other manner of business? I am the Christ, devoted to the Father's interests; His will and law is written in My heart; I am not Mine own!

Let us revert for a moment to the 40th Psalm. There we hear the Saviour saying, "Mine ears hast Thou digged" (v. 6): that figurative language applied only to His humanity. The metaphor employed is taken from Ex. 21:1-6. The Hebrew servant was entitled to, "go out free" at the end of the sixth year, but an exception was allowed for: "If the servant shall plainly say, I love my master, my wife, and my children; I will not go out free: then . . . his master shall bore his ear through with an aul, and he shall serve him for ever" (vv. 5, 6). The antitype of this is seen in Christ. As creatures, *we* are *necessarily* born "under the law," subjects of the government of God. With the Man Christ Jesus, it was otherwise. His humanity, having been taken into union with the second person in the Trinity, was altogether exempt from any servile subjection, just as a woman ceases to be a *subject* when married to a king. It was an act of unparalleled condescension, by His own voluntary will, that the God-man entered the place of service; and *love*, love to His God, to His Church, His people, was the moving-cause.

Observe another thing in the prophetic language of the Mediator in Psa. 40: "Then said I, Lo, I come: in the volume of the book it is written of Me; I delight to do Thy will, O My God: yea, Thy law is within My heart" (vv. 7:8). When the appointed hour arrived the Son volunteered to fulfil every jot and title which had been recorded of Him in the Book of God's decrees—transcribed (in part) on the pages of Holy Writ. He carried all of it written in His heart. This was even more than to have His ear "bored"—to give free consent to the Father's purpose; it was, as it *would* have been *if* infants had been born in innocency, to have God's law (the *expression* of His *will*!) as the moulding principle and controlling factor of His human nature, dwelling in the very centre of His affections. Thus could He say, "My *meat* (My very sustenance and substance) is to do the will of Him that sent Me, and to finish His work" (John 4:34) i.e. *actualize* what the Father had *ordained.*

Our theme is exhaustless; eternity will be too short to contemplate it. Bear with the writer, dear reader, as he endeavours to follow it a step further. "But I have a baptism to be baptised with; and how am I straitened till it be accomplished!" (Luke 12:50). What words were those! The Lord Jesus knew the unspeakable *bitterness* of that baptism, a baptism such as no mere creature could have endured; nevertheless, He panted after it. His very heart was contracted by the delay. Never woman desired more to be delivered than did He to finish His travail, to pass over that "brook" (Psa. 110:7), that sea of wrath into which He should be immersed. Note His remarkable word to Judas: "that thou doest do *quickly*" (John 13:27).

Again, mark how when He first announced to His disciples His forthcoming sufferings and death (Matt. 16:21), and Peter "took Him (aside as a friend out of natural affection) and began to rebuke Him, saying, Pity thyself, Lord" —Thou who art going about doing good, ministering to the needy, allow not Thyself to suffer such indignities, such an ignominious end. And how did Christ receive this word? Did He appreciate it? No, never did He take any word so ill; never did His holy zeal flash forth more vividly than then. He turned and said unto Peter, "Get thee behind Me, Satan; thou art an offense unto Me." Never such a word was spoken unto saint, before or since. The word "offense" means an occasion of stumbling; Peter's counsel had that tendency in it —to turn Him aside from that great work upon which His heart was so fully set.

There is a remarkable word in the "Pascal Discourse" which it is impossible to explain or account for except on the ground of that holy impatience or zeal which consumed the Saviour to make an end of the work the Father had assigned Him. After Judas had gone out to betray Him, the Saviour redeemed the time by speaking at length to the Eleven, and in the midst of so doing He said, "But that the world may know that I love the Father; and as the Father gave Me commandment, even so I do. Arise, let us go hence" (John 14:31). He was in haste to be gone, lest the band headed by the betrayer should miss Him in the garden. Then He looked (as it were) at the hour-glass of His life, and seeing that the sands of time had not yet completely run out, He resumed and completed His address.

The closer he drew to the final conflict, the more blessedly did appear the perfectness of His consecration to God. When the moment of arrest arrived, and Peter drew his sword and attempted resistance, the Saviour exclaimed, "The cup which My Father hath given Me, shall I not drink it?" (John 18:11). When conducted to the hall of judgment, He was *not dragged,* as an unwilling victim, but was *"led* as a sheep to the slaughter" (Acts 8:32). Hear His own words— spoken centuries before by the Spirit of prophecy—"The Lord God hath opened Mine ear, and I was *not* rebellious, neither turned away back. I *gave* My back to the smiters, and My cheeks to them that plucked off the hair: I *hid not* My face from shame and spitting" (Isa. 50:5, 6). *That* (excepting the cross itself) was the hardest part of what had been assigned Him, yet He rebelled not. O blessed Saviour grant us more of Thy spirit.

He never showed the slightest sign of reluctancy till Gethsemane was reached, when He took (as it were) a more immediate look into the awful cup which He was to drink, and saw in it the wrath of God and His being made a "curse." Then, to exhibit the *holiness* of His nature, shrinking from being "made sin" (2 Cor. 5:21), to demonstrate the *reality* of His humanity—trembling, horrified, in anguish at what awaited Him; and to *manifest* His unquenchable love to us, by making known more clearly *what* He suffered on our behalf, He cried, "If it be possible, let this cup pass from Me." Yet instantly He was quieted: "Nevertheless, *not* My will be done. but Thine." Thus we are shown again His full and perfect acquiescence to the Father's purpose, and that the *one* and *only* object before Him was the doing of *the Father's* will!

Yet one more thought on this precious subject: "Lo, I come to *do* Thy will, O God." Weigh well the verb. It was not merely that the Son consented to passively endure whatever the Father was pleased to lay upon Him, but also that He desired to actively perform the work which had been alloted to Him. Though that work involved immeasurable humiliation, untold anguish, though it entailed not only Bethlehem's manger but Calvary's cross, He hesitated not. As a child, as a Man, in life and in death, He was "obedient" to His God. *Our* disobedience was voluntary, so the satisfaction which He made for us was voluntary. Though what He did was done out of love for us, *yet chiefly* in subjection to God's will and out of love to Him. "I love the Father; and as the Father gave Me commandment, even so I do" (John 14:31)!

Let us pause long enough to make one word of application. In view of all that has been before us, of what surpassing *value* must be *such* obedience! When we remember that the One we have been contemplating is none other than the Almighty, who, "hath measured the waters in the hollow of His hand and meted heaven with a span" (Isa. 40:12), then is it not obvious that *this* humiliation and consecration must possess a dignity and efficacy which has more than compensated God for all the dreadful disobedience of His people! It was the Divine excellency of Christ's person which gave infinite worth to all that He did as the God-man-Mediator; therefore is He able to "save unto the uttermost them that come unto God by Him." O Christian reader look away from self with its ten thousand failures, to Him who is "Altogether Lovely." No matter how black and foul thy sins, the precious blood of *such* an One cleanseth from them all. And what wholehearted devotion is due unto Him from us! O may His love truly constrain us to obey and please Him.

"Above when He said, Sacrifice and offering and burnt offerings and offering for sin Thou wouldst not, neither hadst pleasure therein, which are offered by the law; Then said He, Lo, I come to do Thy will, O God. He taketh away the first, that He may establish the second" (vv. 8, 9). In these words we have the apostle's inspired comment upon the remarkable quotation given from Psa. 40. Repetition is here made that the conclusion drawn might the more plainly appear. That to which attention is now directed is to the *order* of statement, and what that order necessarily intimated. The first word of v. 8 ("Above") and the first of v. 9 ("Then") are placed in opposition, and it is to them that the "first" and the "second" at the end of v. 9 looks.

Granting that the Levitical sacrifices were "offered by the law," nevertheless, God rejected them as the means of making real expiation of sin and the saving of His church. This He had made known as far back as the days of David; nor was it a new decision that God formed then, for what He spoke through His prophets in time was but the revelation of what He had decreed in eternity. This the Son, the Mediator, was cognizant of, therefore did He say, "Lo I come to do Thy will, O God." "Lo" Behold! a word signalizing what a glorious spectacle was then presented to God, to angels, and to men. "I come" from Heaven to earth, from the "form of God" to the "form of a servant;" come forth like the rising of the sun, with light and healing in his wings, or as a giant rejoicing to run his race. To "do Thy will," to perform Thy counsels, to execute what Thou requirest, to render that entire service of love which Thy people owed unto the law, to perform the great work of redemption. Thus, the perfect obedience of Christ is placed in direct contrast from the whole of the Levitical offerings: His accomplishing what theirs could not.

"He taketh away the first, that He may establish the second." This inference is patent; no other conclusion could be drawn. The Levitical offerings were unefficacious to accomplish the purpose of God; the satisfaction of the incarnate Son had. The Greek word for "taketh away" is even stronger than the term applied to the old covenant—"made old" and "vanish away" (8:13). It is usually applied to the taking away of life (Acts 16:27). Dead things are not only useless, but prove harmful carrion, fit only to be *buried!* Thus it was with the Mosaic shadows. So also an equally emphatic and final word is used in connection with the one offering of our Lord's: it has "established" the will of God concerning the Church. That is, it has placed it on such an immutable foundation that it shall never be moved or altered.

"By the which will we are sanctified through the offering of the body of Jesus Christ once for all" (v. 10). This is a commentary upon the whole passage. "By," or better *"in which will"* refers not to Christ's, for the preceding verse speaks of the will of the Father, purposing that Christ should offer the perfect and acceptable sacrifice. Moreover, the "will" is *distinguished from* the "offering" of the Redeemer. The "Thy will" of v. 9 refers to the eternal agreement between the Father and the Son in connection with the covenant of redemption, the performing of His "commandment" (John 10:19). *"In* which will" gives the sphere or element in which the great sacrifice was offered and in which the elect are "sanctified."

"In the which will we are sanctified through the offering of the body of Jesus Christ once for all." "Sanctified" positionally, restored to God's favour, standing accepted before Him. The death of Christ was a "sacrifice" (7:27, 9:23), by which He put away sin (9:26) and provided for the purging of our conscience (9:14) and the setting apart of our persons unto God (10:14). All these passages affirm that the death of Christ was a sacrifice by which the elect are separated as a peculiar people unto the worship of the living God. It is important to see the type realized in the Antitype. "As the ancient sacrifices, as symbols in the lower sphere, freed the worshipper from merited (temporal) punishment, because the guilt passed over to the victim, so the death of Christ, in a higher sphere, not only *displayed* the punishment due to us for sin, but the actual *removal* of that punishment. It puts us in the position of a people near to God, a holy people, as Israel were in a typical (or ceremonial) sense" (G. Smeaton).

"In the which will we are sanctified through the offering of the body of Jesus Christ once for all." "Sanctified" is here to be taken in its widest latitude, as including a full expiation of sin, a complete dedication to God, a real purification of our natures, a permanent peace of conscience unto which belongs the privilege of immediate access to God. Faith is the instrumental cause, whereby we enter into the good of it. The Spirit's work within is the efficient cause, whereby we are enabled to believe and lay hold of it. The redemptive work of Christ is the meritorious cause, whereby He earned for us the gift of His Spirit to renew us. But the sovereign and eternal will of the Father is the supreme and originating cause. All that the will of God ordained for the good of His Church is communicated to us through the satisfaction or offering of Christ, but this is only apprehended by an understanding enlightened and a heart opened by the Holy Spirit. A.W.P.

THE SATISFACTION
("Atonement")
OF CHRIST

23. Its Reception.

"What must I do to be saved?" is the earnest and urgent inquiry of one who has been truly awakened by the Holy Spirit and made to feel his lost condition and deserts of eternal punishment. Where such an inquiry is sincerely made, the comforting answer furnished by Scripture is simple and plain: "Believe on the Lord Jesus Christ, and thou shalt be saved." Yet this does not mean that the preaching of the Gospel is an easy matter, for which every Christian is qualified. Far, far from it. From the Divine side, none. but those called of God and supernaturally taught by Him, are fitted for such a blessed and solemn task; from the human side, a life's constant study is required to prepare a servant of Christ's for proclaiming His "unsearchable riches." Incalculable damage has been wrought by novices running into evangelical activities without being sent of God. To all such we would say, "O that ye would altogether hold your peace! and it should be your wisdom" (Job 13:5).

In the last article we sought to indicate, though in little more than outline form, something of what is comprehended by or included in the proclamation of the Atonement. Briefly stated it is this: an exposition and explanation of the teaching of Scripture concerning the wondrous person of the God-man, of His relation to the Church as Sponsor and Surety, of His varied offices, of His perfect work; freely setting Him forth as an all-sufficient Saviour, ready to receive any who truly feel their need of Him and who trust in Him. In this paper our aim is to set forth how the virtue of His sacrifice actually becomes ours, in what way we are made the recipients of those priceless blessings which He purchased for His people. O may the Spirit so guide us into the Truth that we may be enabled to treat of this important section of our subject in such a way as to truly honour God, edify His people, and help exercised souls.

In taking up the *reception* of the Atonement two things need to be kept quite distinct and treated of separately, namely, the operation of the Spirit, and the act of the awakened sinner. Some of the older writers distinguished these two things by employing the terms the *application* of the Atonement and the *appropriation* of it: probably we cannot improve upon them. The one speaks of the benefits of Christ's satisfaction being brought to those for whom it was made; the other, having reference to us laying hold of them and making them ours. It is very much like the two-fold mention of the tabernacle's furniture in Exodus, or the order of the five great offerings in the opening chapters of Leviticus. God began with the "ark" (Ex. 25:10), then the "mercyseat" (25:17), the "table" (25:23), the "candlestick" (25:31), and then the brazen altar (27:1); but it was the very opposite with Aaron (the representative of the people): he had to commence at the altar of sacrifice, and came last of all to the ark. So the *Divine* order of the offerings was the burnt, meat, peace, and the sin and trespass; but as *men* used them (according to their needs) they had to begin with the sin-offering.

The great Satisfaction or Atonement originated in the mind of God, and was formulated in the terms of the everlasting covenant, which was drawn up between the Father and the Mediator. It was accomplished here on earth by Christ, the incarnate Son, who by His perfect obedience and sufferings met every demand of the law and procured the eternal salvation for that people which had been given to Him and whose Sponsor He was. It is proclaimed and propounded in the Gospel, and is expounded by the true servants of the Lord Jesus. The particular aspect of this mighty theme which is now to engage our attention is, How is the Atonement made good to those for whom it was offered? Through what Divinely-appointed channel do the virtues of Christ's redemptive work actually reach the individual soul? In other words, what is required before a sinner today personally receives the saving benefits of that wondrous transaction which was consummated at the cross almost two thousand years ago?

The answer which is now generally returned to this question is, that it is by means of *the Gospel* salvation is conveyto the soul. But obviously *this* answer is quite inadequate, for the great majority of those who hear the glad tidings which are published by the servants of Christ, are not saved thereby. To some the Gospel is "a savour of life unto life," to others it is "a savour of death unto death." What, then, is it which makes the difference? To the Thessalonians Paul wrote, "For our Gospel came not unto you in word only, but also *in power*, and in the Holy Spirit, and in much assurance" (1 Thess. 1:5). The reference here is to the gracious and invincible operations of the third Person of the Trinity. God the Father is the Author of our salvation; God the Son is the Purchaser of it; God the Spirit is the Conveyer.

The imperative need for the work of the Spirit in order to make effectual the Atonement unto the actual saving of sinners is little perceived in these degenerate times, even by professing Christians. That man is a fallen creature is still allowed in some circles, nor has the term "total depravity" entirely disappeared from present-day preaching; yet as to the terrible consequences which sin has wrought in the human constitution, scarcely any now have more than the vaguest conceptions. So long as a man obeys the laws of his country, discharges with measureable faithfulness his human obligations, and does not grossly defy the commandments of God, it is popularly assumed that there is little wrong with him. That his *heart* is desperately wicked, that his *mind* is filled with enmity against God, that his *will* is antagonistic to Him, that he is altogether unconscious of the deadly virus of sin which has corrupted every part of his inner being, and which has completely unfitted him for any communion with the thrice Holy One, is something which is altogether unknown to the vast majority of those now bearing the name of Christian.

The truth is that the natural man is *dead* in trespasses and sins. Because of this he is oblivious to the righteous claims of God upon him, and therefore knows not that in view of his failure to meet those claims the wrath of God abides upon him. Because there is no spiritual life within him, he has no *spiritual* relish of or appetite for Divine things, though he may (through religious education) have an intellectual and theoretical interest in them. Because the natural man is alienated from the life of God, he is completely under the dominion of sin, so that the pleasing of self (having his own way) is the governing principle of his whole life. Tell him that *he* is, on his way to the everlasting burnings, and that they are his *just* due, and he believes it not. Either he thinks that he has done nothing which deserves such terrible punishment, or he supposes that he *has been* "delivered from the wrath to come." Having *no* spiritual perception, his understanding being "darkened" (Eph. 4:18), it is *impossible* that he *should* be conscious of his dreadful condition or see his dire need.

Only the Spirit of God can awaken any sinner from the sleep of death: only He can impart spiritual life to the soul, supernatural light to the understanding, and sight to the eyes of the heart. This is what He is sent to do. He is "the Servant" of the Godhead who is here *to bring in* "the poor, the maimed, the halt, and the blind." He is the One who has been given to "compel to come in" that the Father's House may be filled with the appointed guests (Luke 14:21, 23). He compels by His sweet constraints, making the unwilling willing, creating in their hearts a desire for the Feast, making them to be conscious of their deep need of the Bread of life. The Holy Spirit is the One who shines into the sin-darkened mind so that it is made conscious of its vileness. He is the One who so searches the conscience that the individual is made to feel he is the greatest sinner out of Hell. He is the One who subdues the principle of self-love and self-will, so that the soul is brought into subjection to God. He is the One who communicates faith, so that the heart is enabled to embrace Christ as a personal Lord and Saviour.

"The Holy Spirit is as indispensable to your believing, as is Christ in order to your being pardoned. The Holy Spirit's work is direct and powerful; and you will not rid yourself of your difficulties by trying to persuade yourself that His operations are all indirect, and merely those of a Teacher presenting truth to you. Salvation *for* the sinner is Christ's work; salvation *in* the sinner is the Spirit's work. Of this internal salvation He is the beginner and the ender. He works in you, in order to your believing, as truly as He works in you after you have believed.

"This doctrine, instead of being a discouragement, is one of unspeakable encouragement to the sinner; and he will acknowledge this, if he knows himself to be the thoroughly helpless being which the Bible says he is. If he is *not* totally depraved, he will feel the doctrine of the Spirit's work a hindrance, and an insult, no doubt, just as an able-bodied traveller would feel that you were both hindering and insulting him, if you told him that he cannot set out on his journey without taking your arm. But as, in that case, he will be able to save himself without much assistance, he might just set aside the Spirit altogether, and work his way to heaven alone! The truth is, that without the Spirit's direct and almighty help, there could be no hope for a totally depraved being at all . . .

"If you understand the genuine Gospel in all its freeness, you will feel that the man who tries to persuade you that you have strength enough left to do without the Spirit, is as great an enemy of the cross, and of your soul, as the man who wants to make you believe that you are not altogether guilty, but have some remaining goodness, and therefore do not need to be wholly indebted for pardon to the blood and righteousness of Immanuel. 'Without strength' is as literal a description of your state, as 'without goodness.' If you understand the Gospel, the consciousness of your total helplessness would just be the discovery that you are the very sinner to whom the great salvation is sent; that your inability was all foreseen and provided for, and that you are in the very position which needs, which calls for, and which shall receive, the aid of the Almighty Spirit.

"Till you feel yourself in this extremity of weakness, you are not in a condition (if I may say so) to receive the heavenly help. Your idea of remaining *ability* is the very thing that repels the help of the Spirit, just as any idea of remaining goodness thrusts away the propitiation of the Saviour. It is your *not seeing that you have no strength* that is keeping you from believing. So long as you think you have some strength, you will be trying to use that strength in *doing* something,—and especially in performing, to your own and Satan's satisfaction, that great act or exercise of soul called 'faith.' But when you find out that you have no strength left you will, in blessed despair, cease to work,—and (ere you are aware)—believe! For, if believing be not a ceasing from work, it is at least the necessary and immediate result of it. You expended your little stock of imagined strength in holding fast the ropes of self-righteousness, but now, when the conviction of having no strength at all is forced upon you, you drop into the arms of Jesus. But this you will never do so long as you fancy that you have strength to believe" (From "God's way of Peace" by H. Bonar).

O that there were many preachers today honouring the third person of the Trinity by thus magnifying and emphasizing *His* part in the work of salvation. O that the modern evangelist would faithfully press upon his unsaved hearers their utter powerlessness to turn unto God of themselves, and their inability to receive Christ as their Lord and Saviour until a miracle of Divine grace has been wrought in them. The Lord Jesus (our Exemplar) did not hesitate to plainly say to a promiscuous crowd "No man can come to Me, except the Father which sent Me draw him" (John 6:44). The Father draws to Christ by the operation of the Spirit. It is written, "Not by works of righteousness which we have done, but according to His mercy He saved us, *by* the washing of regeneration and renewing of *the Holy Spirit*" (Titus 3:5).

Believing is necessary, indispensably necessary, before any sinner receives Divine forgiveness. But Scripture is very emphatic in declaring that no sinner can savingly believe apart from the powerful operations of the Holy Spirit. A miracle of grace has to be wrought in his heart before he is capacitated to lay hold of Christ. This must be so, for the human heart is fast closed against Him and will not come to Him that it might have life (John 5:40). The eyes of our understanding are blind, so that we see in Christ no beauty that we should desire Him. It is with the heart that man believeth unto righteousness (Rom. 10:10), and the heart must first be wooed and won by Christ (through the Spirit's operations) before it will turn to Him. "The love of God is shed abroad in our hearts by the Holy Spirit" (Rom. 5:5). Until this takes place, the Lord has to say of us all, "I know you, that ye have not the love of God in you" (John 5:42).

In the application of the Atonement to the elect, each of them is entirely passive. Until the Holy Spirit has performed His initial work of grace in the soul, not only is each individual utterly incapable of seeking after Christ (see Rom. 3:11), but he has no desire toward Him and no sense of his real need of Him. Not until he has been Divinely quickened and brought out of that grave into which the fall of Adam brought us all (Rom. 5:12), is any man capable of performing any spiritual actions. There cannot be the manifestations of life before life itself is imparted. A bitter fountain cannot send forth sweet waters, neither can a corrupt heart delight in a holy object. An evil tree cannot bring forth good fruit, neither can the unregenerate hate sin or love God. "It is the Spirit that quickeneth, the flesh profiteth nothing" (John 6:63).

For one who by sinful instinct loved and idolised self, making everything subservient to having his own way, to be brought to deny and loathe himself (Job 42:6), and to forsake his own ways (Isa. 55:7), is something which nothing short of Omnipotence can bring about. For one who naturally hates God (desiring rather to think about and be occupied with any one or any thing else) to be brought to love Him and delight in Him—love Him with all the heart and delight in Him supremely—is indeed a miracle of grace. Yet, let it be pointed out that true love to God is not begotten by fears of Hell nor by hopes of Heaven—the promptings of self-preservation will produce the one, as the workings of self-love will inspire the other. No, unless I love God for *what He is in Himself*, I do not love Him at all, but only lie to Him with my lips. Yet it is only the Spirit who can cause any soul to say from the heart, "Who is like unto Thee, O Lord glorious in holiness!" (Ex. 15:11).

Thus, each person of the Godhead is due His own particular praise. The Father for having chosen us in Christ before the foundation of the world, and predestinated us unto the adoption of children. The Son for having served as our Surety, fulfilled our obligations, and paid our debts. The Spirit for having brought us from death unto life, convicted us of our lost condition, awakened us to our need of Christ, and drawn us to Him. If the Father is to be adored because of His predestination, and the Son because of His propitiation, equally so is the Spirit for His regeneration. We are indebted to the One as much as to the Others. The work of Christ had been in vain, were it not for the work of the Spirit in us. "Thanks be unto God for

His unspeakable Gift" (2 Cor. 9:15) applies as much to the Comforter as it does to the Redeemer.

The embracing of Christ by faith presupposes both a true knowledge of ourselves and of the Saviour Himself. There has to be a Divine conviction given to us of that sin and wretchedness, thraldom and bondage, unto which we are reduced by the Fall. The law must be our schoolmaster unto Christ. Without a discovery to us of sin and misery by the law, the sinner will never flee unto Him who is "the end of the law for righteousness" (Rom. 10:4). A man at sea sailing in a shattered boat close unto a great rock, will refuse to leave his boat and cast himself upon the rock for safety, so long as he believes his boat is strong enough to carry him to land. But when the winds and waves beat into his frail craft and break her in pieces, and not till then, will he be glad to avail himself of the rock. So while the poor sinner imagines that his own doings and good intentions are sufficient to carry him through to Heaven, he will never betake himself to the Rock of ages.

The powerful wind of the Spirit is needed to demolish that "refuge of lies" (Isa. 28:17) in which the sinner shelters, if ever he is to perceive that a continuing to rest upon his own fancied goodness and righteousness must inevitably sink him into Hell. Not until the Spirit strips him of his own worthless doings, and makes him to stand naked in all his shame and filthiness before God, will he truly cry, "What must I do to be saved?" As the apostle declared, "I was alive (in my own estimation) without the law once, but when the commandment came (when God applied it in power unto my understanding and conscience, and showed me how far short I came of its righteous demands) sin revived (I then had a real apprehension of the exceeding sinfulness of sin and of my utter unfitness to stand for a moment before the thrice holy God), and I died"—saw myself as utterly lost (Rom. 7:9).

Until the Spirit *does* press upon the soul the claims of God and its lifelong disregard of the same, until He applies to us that holy standard which bids us love God with all our heart, mind and strength, and our neighbor as ourself, and convicts us of the fact that not only have we made no honest attempt to do so, but have had no sincere *desire* to keep it, we are utterly blind to our dreadful sins of *omission*. Until the Spirit brings home to the heart our true state, notwithstanding all our selfish wishes to be delivered from Hell and taken to Heaven, yet the heart remains blind to the glory of God and what is due Him from us. So far from the unregenerate sinner being willing to repent of his sins, he knows nothing whatever about the worst of his sins. So far from desiring to humble himself before God, he is totally ignorant of the reason *why* he should humble himself. So far from being anxious to be made spiritually alive, he is quite oblivious to the fact that he is spiritually dead. And so far from seeking the gracious enablement of the Spirit to reconcile him to God, he is quite unawares that he is the enemy of God. But all of this is wellnigh wholly lost sight of today by preachers and evangelists. The general assumption is (even though it be not plainly formulated), there is so little wrong with the fallen descendants of Adam that all they need to do is read the Bible and hear the Gospel preached, and they will easily be turned to Christ. A little information, plus a little earnest persuasion, and almost anybody can be induced to sign a card and "accept Christ as his personal Saviour." Consequently, the humble, dependent, fervent, united, and patient waiting upon God for the power of His Spirit is a thing of the past; and so too (with *very* rare exceptions) are *genuine* miracles of grace. This Laodicean age "has need of nothing" (Rev. 3:17), least of all does it feel its dire and desperate need of the Spirit of God to awaken the dead, to pull down strongholds and cast down every high thing that exalteth itself against the knowledge of God (2 Cor. 10, 4, 5).

Not until the sinner has been emptied of his self-sufficiency, convicted that he is an outlaw against God, and brought into the dust before Him, is he ready to appreciate Christ. Nor will he, nor can he, savingly embrace the Redeemer until the Spirit has revealed Christ *in* him. (Gal. 1:16). None can trust in a Saviour they know not; and to *know* Christ as a living reality is a vastly different thing from having heard about Him from the pulpit, or even to have read of Him through the Scriptures. "For God who commanded the light to shine out of darkness hath shined in our hearts, to give the light of the knowledge of the glory of God in the face of Jesus Christ"

(2 Cor. 4:6): *this* is what *must* take place before any soul truly trusts Him. Have *you*, my reader, experienced this supernatural revelation of Christ to your *heart?* Once the Holy Spirit really reveals Christ to the soul, he needs no urging to receive Him: "They that *know* Thy name *will* put their trust in Thee" (Psa. 9:10).

Now it is not only the Spirit's province to apply the law, convict of sin, empty of pride, break down self-will, subdue self-love, but it is also His blessed office to take of the things of Christ and show them unto (John 16:14) those for whom He died. He is here to teach those whom He awakens from the sleep of spiritual death who the Redeemer is, the wondrous offices which He sustains, the great purpose for which He come into this world. He is here to slay their enmity against Christ, to destroy their unbelief, and to impart a saving faith. He is here to bring them into a saving knowledge of the truth: as the Lord Himself declared, "They shall all be taught of God. Every man therefore that hath heard, and *hath learned* of the Father (by the Spirit) cometh unto Me" (John 6:45). The Spirit is here not to magnify Himself, but to glorify the Redeemer (John 16:14). He is here to reveal His lovely perfections unto God's elect, to win their hearts to Him, to conform them unto His blessed image.

Various motives have induced us to dwell at such length upon the *application* of the Atonement as it is received by men. First, because *this* is the side of the Truth which most honours God, inasmuch as it gives to Him His proper place in the saving of sinners. Second, because of the appalling ignorance thereon which now so widely prevails. Third, so that the Christian reader may the better perceive *how much* he owes to the gracious operations of the Spirit. Fourth, to make clear to preachers and evangelists the urgent need of using the plough of the law *before* they attempt to sow the seed of the Gospel. It is of no avail to keep on saying to people "Believe on Christ" until you have employed that scriptural material which the Spirit can use to convict souls of their *awful need of* Christ.

We turn now to consider, very briefly, the *appropriation* of the Atonement, or the sinner's own act in becoming a personal partaker of the saving virtues of Christ's satisfaction. As we showed in our last article, the Gospel is addressed to human responsibility: "This is a faithful saying, and worthy of all *acceptation*, that Christ Jesus came into the world to save sinners" (1 Tim. 1:15). The business of God's servants is to preach and press the righteous demands of the Divine law, to call upon sinners to repent of their transgressions and turn from their wicked ways; to present Christ as a Saviour from the curse of the law, and bid their hearers lay down the weapons of their warfare against Him, and receive Him as their Lord and Saviour. Not until Christ is cordially received as Prophet, Priest and King, is forgiveness of sins to be obtained. As Prophet to reveal to us the righteousness and grace of God. As Priest who offered a sacrifice, the blood of which is sufficient to cleanse the foulest who trusts in it. As King to rule over us.

The object or design in our first coming to Christ is to be saved by Him, to be saved *from self*, to be delivered from rebelling against God. He is the great Physician, and can allay the fever and cleanse the leprosy of sin. He who comes to Christ *without* a disposition to be *reconciled to* God, is only seeking deliverance from Hell, and does not desire that salvation which the Gospel proclaims, namely, deliverance from the power and condemnation of *sin*. Saving faith implies in its very nature both repentance and conversion, or a "turning to God from idols to serve the living and true God" (1 Thess. 1:9).

A mediator must be accepted by *both* parties that are at variance, and each must stand to what He doth. God has declared Himself fully satisfied; it rests now with the individual sinner to also give the assent of *his* heart to Christ's dying in the stead of the ungodly and rest upon the sufficiency of His sacrifice. Saving faith is that act of the soul whereby one who is hopeless, helpless and lost in himself, does in a way of expectancy and trust seek for all help and relief in Christ alone. Faith is a going out of ourselves unto God in Christ, finding in Him all that we need for time and eternity. Faith is the one link between the sinner and the Sin-bearer. Faith is a receiving into our hearts the testimony of God concerning His Son, and a setting to our seal that He is true (John 3:33).

Should these lines be read by a sin-burdened soul, distressed by the plague of his own heart, and fearful that he or she has sinned beyond the hope of Divine pardon, we would point you to Him who is "mighty to save." Christ died not for righteous people, but for the ungodly (Rom. 5:6). He came here to save the *lost* (Luke 19:10). His promise is, "him that cometh to Me I will in no wise cast out" (John 6:37). "He is able also to save them to the uttermost that come unto God by Him" (Heb. 7:25). Then look away from your ruined self, fly to Christ for refuge, trust in His precious blood, and He will save you with an everlasting salvation. A.W.P.

LOVE: DIVINE AND HUMAN

Everything in this poor world is tottering. Men blame God and their fellows for it; but in spite of this the children of God can praise and magnify the Lord and exclaim, God *is* love! The love of God: how different from the love (so-called) of man or natural love! Both are known in Scripture. The first: godly, Divine. It is the love which is a part of God's nature, of what He is in Himself. God is love (1 John 4:8). It is that which He bestows upon His children (1 John 3:1). It is also that which is imparted to the sinner who is born again: "whosoever believeth that Jesus is the Christ is born of God, and everyone that loveth Him that begat, loveth him also that is begotten of Him" (1 John 5:1). To the religious Jews the Lord said, "But I know you, that ye have not the love of God in you" (John 5:42). Thus, the spring of godly love in the heart of the regenerated sinner is God. This love, which is Divine, goes out from him, first toward God, and secondly to all who are born of God. It is righteous, charitable, joyful, toward them who are of the household of faith. It is manifested in righteousness, pity and mercy to those who are outside.

God is love, but God is also "light" (1 John 1:5), and these attributes of God are inseparable. If we walk in the light, as He is in the light, we have (but only then) fellowship one with the other. It is *thus* that God's children can worship Him in spirit and in truth (John 4:24). It is *thus* that they are able to manifest their love to the brethren by works, for faith without works is dead (James 2:20). It is *thus* that they are able to show mercy and pity to them who are outside the household of faith—"he shall have judgment without mercy, that showeth no mercy" (James 2:13). But this love is first righteous, then charitable.

"Love not the world, neither the things that are in the world; if any man love the world, the love of the Father is not in him" (1 John 2:15). Loving the world and the things that are in the world means, not only to love them for our fleshly pleasure, but also showing love toward the world and the things of it. We cannot show "love" toward a world which murdered and hates still our Lord. This would be treason. The love of God is to His children only (John 17:9) His *pity* and *mercy* extend unto *all* His creatures. The godly love which the child of God possesses, which dwells in his heart, extends only to God Himself and His children; but His pity and mercy to *all* creatures, even animals. God must have the first place in everything, and all we do must be done heartily as to the Lord, and not to man (Col. 2:23). We are called saints, holy men of God, are of the Royal Family, and as such our walk and actions should be toward God, toward our brethren, and toward all men; —holy, because God is holy (1 Peter 1:16).

God does not wink at sin; His love is not sentimental, neither weakness; but strong, sober, righteous. Proof of this is seen at Calvary, where God gave His only begotten Son for His chosen people, to bring them into the full favour of His love. God gave His only begotten Son for us—*what* have we given to Him? They who are truly God's children are (should be) prepared unto anything which the Lord demands from them: to suffer anything for His honour, and manifest His name amongst brethren and in the world. Are we? Have we?

This urges the need for God's children to pray continually that God may increase their faith and lead them in the path of obedience. Our faith may be weak, because everything around is dark, and like Peter we may fear to sink down in the waves of the raging storm, but—we must obey. We do not see a way of escape: we are closed in on all sides; nevertheless, *obey*. Go, do it; or, stand still, wait and see. Here, as in many other cases, the children of Satan show more wisdom than the children of God. In the last terrible slaughter of the great war, German storm-troops were commanded, in their closed ranks, to storm the deadly and destructive machine-guns of the enemy. Used to obedience, they asked no questions but went. No doubt most of their hearts were full of fear; they were convinced they would never come back again. But the command was given: Go —and they went. Obey and die!

"He that believeth on Me, as the Scripture hath said, out of his belly shall flow rivers of living water" (John 7:38). If the children of God quench their thirst at the pure Fountain, which is Christ, living faith (and actions conformed thereto), expressed as godly love, shall flow as rivers of living water from them, purifying, elevating, refreshing to all who are truly His that they come into contact with. This is also the true love which leads to service. It is ridiculous for a child of God to enter His service if the love of God is not manifested by him through living faith and the works which belong to it. Very sad indeed it is, but the fact remains, that many of God's people have entered His service on their own account. There was not developed the love of God in faith by works, because there was no drinking, constant drinking, at the Fountain of life. There may have been plenty of head-knowledge of the Truth; there may have been running after a God-sent teacher, but there was not the much-needed *secret communion* with God; there was not the needed deep searching of self; there was not the bringing into subjection of self to the will of God. The solemn words spoken by our Lord, "Not My will, but Thine be done," are a strange sound to them. They acknowledge the Lord, but in their pride like to be a bit lordly themselves. Their hidden motive (perhaps never known to themselves) was *pride* and a fleshly desire to be somewhat. They were never called by God unto His service. And when the Lord in mercy blocks their path or restrains their self-will, then they get rebellious, kick against the pricks, and end by being cast forth as withered branches, stupefied by all their head-knowledge. Alas, how is the fine gold become dim!

I repeat, the spring of the love which flows forth from the child of God is God Himself: "I in them, and Thou in Me" (John 17:23). "Hereby perceive we the love of God . . . and we ought to lay down our lives for the brethren" (1 John 3:16). "Marvel not My brethren, if the world hate you" (1 John 3:13). Marvel not. Why do we love God? Because He first loved us (1 John 4:10). If we love the world, the world will love us. But if we do not love the world, then the world will not love us. And for the same reason the world hates the true children of God: just as we first hated God, were at enmity with Him, so is the world at enmity with God's people now. In *this* the children of God are manifested, and the children of the devil. The one does righteousness, the other does not.

And what is the spring of *human* love, *natural* love?—if we may use the word "love" here. The spring is the deceitful and desperately wicked heart: Jer. 17:9, Mark 7:20-23. Man having lost by the fall his God-consciousness, became self-conscious. His object was no longer God, but *self*. He was no longer God-occupied, but self-occupied. This SELF is the main factor, the dominating power in man since he fell. It is plain therefore that what is called human or natural love finds its object in *pleasing self*. Just as the object of godly love in the saint is the pleasing of God. This may come to many as a shock, as a surprising and astounding thing, nevertheless it is according to God's truth, and according to what *He* thinks and says of human love. This is very little known, and still less acknowledged in these days, wherein words are losing their proper meaning and facts their true value. Multitudes, and most of God's children, are totally ignorant of this fact, and know not that the secret motive of their natural or human love is *selfishness*.

The reason of their ignorance is that they never took the trouble or had the courage to search their poor selves in a honest way, and far less test the result of this searching by God's Holy Word. This proves again that the natural man is as stupid as the ox that eateth grass, and that he is also a coward. This natural love expresses and manifests itself in innumerable and different ways, from the most refined and kind motives and appearances, to the lowest and most beastly. It may be seen in gentleness, pity, gratitude; or in art, science, heavy toil, patriotism, religion, music, self-preservation etc., or in love of kindred; or on the other hand, delighting in cruelty, drunkenness, vice and crime—but however highly estemed, or basely exhibited, whether it reaches the height of virtue, or sinks to criminalty, the spring of all this is: the human depraved heart, and the hidden motive is the *pleasing of self*—selfishness.

It may be objected that human or *natural* "love" is in certain cases approved of by God, and lawful in itself. This is perfectly true, for the Holy Scriptures describing the awful degeneration and degradation of people in the last days says there are those who are "without natural affection," and in the class with blasphemers and traitors (2 Tim. 3:1-5). But this does not prove (and no where in Scripture are we told) that human nature is anything more than human nature. God's Word tells us that God in His mercy and goodness to the human race sends His rain and sunshine upon the just and the unjust, and approves of many things which in themselves are lawful, but *not spiritual*. What is lawful and moral is not always Divine; far from it: but what is Divine, is always moral. For instance, marriage is honourable (Heb. 13:4). The powers that be are ordained of God (Rom. 13:1). The kindness of the barbarian people which they showed to the beloved apostle Paul (Acts 28:2); the ploughing of the farmer etc. But, at the same time, multitudes of marriages are a compact of Satan himself. Our governments all over the world are ungodly, and some are even cruel and barbarous. The ploughing of the wicked is sin (Prov. 21:4), and the sacrifice and the way—*every* way—of the wicked is an abomination to God (Prov. 15:8, 9). But here is shown the goodness, and pity of God to this poor world; for without this natural love, it could not exist. God now and then approves of His saints being fed by ravens, but this does not change those ravens into saints, neither their good works into godly love. That which is born of the flesh *is* flesh (John 3:6), and in the flesh "there dwelleth *no* good thing" (Rom. 7:18).

Narrowing the manifestation of natural love down to that of kindred, and to fellow-men, there is no getting away from the solemn fact that this never will be, (and never can be) anything other than *natural*, and therefore never has any other object but the pleasing of *self*, and not of God. This is the awful consequence of the Fall. In the beginning, it was not so; but alas! man *is* a fallen creature. His heart is no longer God-conscious, but self-conscious. Praise God there is a love of kindred amongst some of God's people which *is* godly, just as there are some saints who plough for the glory of God. But in these cases it is not self-will nor selfishness which is the dominating power, but the Holy Spirit: because they are born of God, are subject to His will, and know Him and bow to Him as LORD.

God's people should bear constantly in mind the great difference between *godly* love and human or *natural* love. This will lead them to a closer scrutinising of *self* and a more prayerful study of God's Word. Thereby they will find out that many of their actions, many a worship, many a prayer, many a service, which posed as godly, was indeed nothing else than a work of the flesh—natural, sensual, selfish. We need to find out the hidden secret motive of everything we do or not do. This will prove how vile we are by nature; it will lead us to godly repentance before Him who loved us ere the world was. Then we shall wonder and sink in the dust before a holy God who gave His only begotten Son, and wonder and adore for His precious blood which was shed for us. A. Klooster.

N. B. The above article was sent us in a private letter, but we felt its message was so important that we desired to share it with our friends. It is written by a dear Brother, connected with no organization or "church," who is devoting all his time to colportage work and preaching the Gospel by the wayside in Holland. We earnestly beg the daily prayers of God's saints for him. Should any feel led to have financial fellowship with him, remit to us and we shall be happy to forward it to him. A.W.P.

Are there not other Christians who would enjoy the contents of this little magazine did they but know of it? There *are* starved sheep asking for bread and being mocked with a stone. Perhaps the reader knows of one or two such. If so, you would be doing them and us a favor to send us their names and addresses. Drop them a line yourself, telling of the help *you* have received from "Studies," and urge them to apply to us personally for them. In this way we shall be able to "send portions unto them for whom nothing is prepared" (Neh. 8:10). This is a selfish age, and one way to counteract its evil effects on *our* hearts is to cultivate the habit of thinking about and seeking the good of others. A.W.P.

REPENTANCE

III. Its Implications.

"If God is an absolutely perfect, an infinitely glorious and amiable Being, infinitely worthy of supreme love and honour, and of universal obedience; and if our disaffection to the Divine character and rebellion against God, is altogether inexcusable and infinitely criminal, agreeable to the voice of the Divine law, and to the import of the cross of Christ; if God the great Governor of the universe views things in this light, and in this view calls unto us from heaven to confess our sins, repent and turn unto Him with all our hearts; if these things are so, and they are; then the meaning of God's words is certain, the ideas designed to be conveyed by them are determinate. To repent, beyond dispute, is to change our minds as to the Divine character, to lay aside our prejudices, to open our eyes, and begin to look upon God as He is, an absolutely perfect, an infinitely glorious and amiable Being, infinitely worthy of supreme love and honour, and of universal obedience; and in the light of this glory to begin to view our disaffection and rebellion as altogether inexcusable and infinitely criminal, and in the view, cordially take all that blame to ourselves which God lays upon us, and to be affected accordingly.

"Repentance is a saying 'righteous art Thou, O Lord, when Thou speakest, and clear when Thou judgest. Should justice take place, no iniquity should be imputed unto Thee. It would not be a blemish, but a beauty in Thy character, and all heaven ought forever to love and adore Thy glorious majesty, should I receive my just deserts and perish forever. But Thou canst have mercy on whom Thou wilt, through Jesus Christ. To Thine infinite grace and self-moving goodness through Him I look. God be merciful to me a sinner.' Repentance stands then in opposition to all our former prejudices against the Divine character; and in opposition to that sin-extenuating, self-justifying, law-hating, God-blaming disposition which reigns in every impenitent soul. God is seen in His beauty; the Divine law, as a ministration of condemnation and death, appears glorious, our disaffection and rebellion infinitely criminal. We justify God, approve His law, condemn ourselves, accept the punishment of our iniquity as worthy of God; and thus we confess, repent, and turn unto the Lord, looking only to free grace through Jesus Christ for pardon." (J. Bellamy, 1750.)

Repentance, then, presupposes, first, a recognition and *acknowledgment of God's claims* upon us as our Creator, Governor, Provider and Protector. Because God is who and what He is, namely the Sum and Source of all moral and spiritual excellency, and because of our relation to Him as creatures completely dependent upon Him, He is infinitely entitled to be loved with all our hearts, worshipped with fullest adoration, and served with joyous, perfect and unremitting obedience. Until there is at least some measure of a clear and definite (we do not say *full*) recognition of this, the mind is yet under the blinding power of Satan (2 Cor. 4:4) and the heart is yet alienated from God (Eph. 4:18). Thus, repentance necessarily presupposes *regeneration*, in which the favoured soul is "given an understanding that we may know Him that is true" (1 John 5:20). The first *evidence* that this supernatural enlightenment has been given, is the inward apprehension of God's excellency and supremacy, accompanied by a horrified consciousness of how dreadfully I have failed, all through my life, to give Him His rightful place in my heart and life.

In the second place, true repentance presupposes *a hearty approval of God's law* and a full consent to its righteous requirements. "The law is holy, and the commandment is holy, and just, and good" (Rom. 7:12): it cannot be otherwise, for *God* is its Author, and nothing unholy, unjust, or evil, could ever proceed from Him. It therefore follows that *such* a law can never be altered or repealed. Those who affirm that the law of God *has been* abolished, cast the greatest reproach upon all the perfections of the Divine character. Upon His *holiness*, whereby He loves the right and hates the wrong: for a repeal of the law would suppose God releasing His creatures from doing right and allowing them to do wrong. Upon His *justice*, whereby He gives to every one his due: supposing Him to rescind His righteous claims. Upon His *immutability*: supposing Him to have been in one mind in the past, and another in the present. Upon His *goodness*: supposing Him to have cancelled that which was designed for our highest wellbeing.

If the reader will only make a determined effort to grasp the fact that the requirements of God's law are all summed up in "thou shalt *love* the Lord thy God with all thine heart etc." (Deut. 6:5), he ought to have no difficulty in perceiving how frightful is the teaching that the law has been abrogated. Men must indeed have strange conceptions of Divine grace and of the Gospel, if they suppose that God is now demanding something other or something less than the supreme place in men's affections and lives. Do they think for a moment that in Old Testament times God was asking for more love than was His due? Do they imagine that God does not now deserve as much love as He once did? Such a thought would be the most awful blasphemy. Or, do they suppose that God has relinquished His rights and now freely allows His creatures to despise Him? that He has made a concession to their evil hearts by lowering His standard? Is not the *real* source of opposition to God's law the "enmity of the carnal mind" (Rom. 8:7)!

Perhaps the reader is inclined to reply, But did not *Christ* come here to fulfill the law for us, and does not *His* obedience *free us* from its demands? Pause, dear friend, and weigh well such a question, and endeavour to see what such a concept plainly involves. Surely you do not mean that the Son of God became incarnate for the purpose of procuring an abatement of the law, or to purchase lawless liberty for His rebellious subjects. What! could He esteem His Father's interest and glory, the honour of His law and government, so lightly? Did He shed His precious blood so as to persuade the great Govenor of the world to slacken the reigns of government and grant an impious license to lawlessness? Perish the thought. Such a terrible concept would make the ineffably holy Christ the enemy of God and the friend of sin.

So far from the Son coming to earth for such a purpose, He expressly declared, "Think not that I am come to destroy the law, or the prophets: I am not come to destroy, but to fulfil. For verily I say unto you, Till heaven and earth pass, one jot or one tittle shall in no wise pass from the law, till all be fulfilled" (Matt. 5:17, 18). If the verses which follow this quotation be carefully pondered, it will be seen that our Lord denounced the Pharisees because they had, by their own traditions and inventions, nullified God's law: while allowing that it condemned some external and gross acts of sin, they denied that it reprehended the first strivings of corruption in the heart. Therefore did Christ say, "Except your righteousness shall exceed the righteousness of the scribes and Pharisees, ye shall in no case enter into the kingdom of heaven" (Matt. 5:20).

That the law of God was never to be repealed is taught again and again in Psalm 119: "Thy righteousness is an everlasting righteousness and Thy law is the truth . . . The righteousness of Thy testimonies *is everlasting.* . . . Concerning Thy testimonies, I have known of old that Thou hast founded them *forever* . . . Thy Word is true from the beginning, and every one of Thy righteous judgments endureth forever" (vv. 142, 144, 152, 160). It was as though the Psalmist said, "The duty required by Thy law is right and good, everlastingly right and good; and therefore, as Govenor of the world, Thou hast by law for ever settled and established it as duty and law never to be altered, but to endure for ever; and for ever; therefore, will it endure."

So far from Christ having died to disannul the law, so that now it wholly ceases to be a rule of life to believers, one great and declared design of His coming into the world was to *recover* His people unto a *conformity thereto*: see Titus 2:11-13. O how men love their corruptions and hate God's law, desiring to have it cashiered so that they may live as they please, and yet escape the reproaches of their consciences here and eternal punishment hereafter. But God "sitteth King for ever" (Psa. 29:10) and will assert the *rights* of His crown, maintain the honour of His majesty and the glory of His great name, and vindicate His injured law. He shall yet say, "But those Mine enemies, which would not that I should reign over them, bring hither, and slay before Me" (Luke 19: 27).

Herein we may see plainly the imperative and absolute *need for regeneration*, if ever a fallen creature is to be won to God, and a defiant rebel transformed into a loving subject. "Because the carnal mind is enmity against God; for it is not subject to the law of God, neither indeed can be" (Rom. 8:7)—such is the terrible condition of every man and woman by nature. Nothing but the supernatural operation of the all-mighty Spirit of God can produce a change of heart, so that one can truthfully say, "I *delight* in the *law* of God after the inward man"

(Rom. 7:22). But such teaching as this never has been and never will be popular in the world. The false prophets who cry "peace, peace" will be loved, but they who press the high and unchanging claims of a righteous God will be hated and denounced as "legalists" etc.

Christ came into this world and died to answer all the demands of the law, and this, not only that sinners might be saved, but that the law itself might be the more firmly "established," i. e., in the consciences and hearts of the redeemed. Therefore did the apostle write, "Do we then make void the law through faith? God forbid: yea, we establish the law" (Rom. 3:31). In this very epistle of the Romans the apostle, moved by the Holy Spirit, lays it down as a first principle that "the wrath of God is revealed from heaven against all ungodliness and unrighteousness of men who hold the truth in unrighteousness" (Rom. 1:18). From this premise, he goes on to prove that, "now we know that what thing soever the law saith, it saith to them who under the law: *that* every mouth may be stopped, and all the world may become guilty before God" (3:19). But is it not clear as a sunbeam that if the law had been repealed at the cross that none *could* stand "guilty" before God, for "sin is not imputed when there is no law" (Rom. 5:13)!

If the law were repealed, what need was there for such a long train of argument to prove that "by the deeds of the law there shall no flesh be justified in His sight" (3:20)? In such case, it had been quite sufficient to say that a repealed law could neither justify nor condemn anybody. Instead, the apostle shows that the law requires a "patient continuance in well doing" and threatens "tribulation and anguish upon every soul of man that doeth evil" (Rom. 2:5, 7). This shows that both Jews and Gentiles have sinned and therefore are condemned by the law—brought in guilty—and so the apostle draws the inevitable conclusion that none can be cleared or justified by the law. Is it not obvious then that all this inspired reasoning supposes that the law is as much enforced as ever! Accordingly he goes on to show Christ's death answered the demands of the law, and that, *not* to make it void, but to "*establish*" it.

Hence it is that we find the New Testament Scriptures uniformly speak of those who have no saving interest in Christ's righteousness by faith, as being as much under the wrath of God and the curse of the law as though He had never died. As we have seen, Rom. 1:18 declares "the wrath of God is (not "was") revealed from heaven against *all* ungodliness and unrighteousness of men." Again, in Gal. 3:10 we are told, "For as many as are of the works of the law *are* under the curse: for it is written: Cursed is every one that continueth not in *all* things which are written in the book of the law to do them": compare 2 Thess. 1:7-9. But if the law had been repealed by the death of Christ, then all the world would have been *freed* from the curse, for a repealed law can neither bless the righteous nor curse the wicked!

Therefore it is we find that when Christless sinners are *really* awakened by the Holy Spirit to see and feel what a dreadful state they are in, they are always convinced that *they are under* the wrath of God and the curse of His law: see Rom. 7:9-11, and thereby are they made to understand their dire need of a Saviour. But how could the Holy Spirit *use* the law if it had been repealed? And what of those who are never awakened and convicted by the Spirit, and who continue to despise the claims of God and flout His holy law? Ah, they shall find that after their hardness and impenitent heart they have but treasured up unto themselves "wrath against the Day of Wrath and revelation of the righteous judgment of God" (Rom. 2:6).

God the Father, as the Govenor of the world, *gave* the law. God the Son *magnified* it (Isa. 42:21) by expounding its purity, by obeying its precepts, by enduring its penalty. God the Holy Spirit honours the law by pressing upon the *sinner* its holy demands, and using it as a "schoolmaster" to bring him to Christ (Gal. 3:24). It is the special work of the third person of the Trinity to communicate unto each of the elect a sense of the infinite glory of God, the equity of His law, and the righteousness of His claims upon them. He begets within them a disposition which conforms them unto the discharge of their duties, and this He does by putting the *law* into their minds and writing it in their hearts (Heb. 8:10). In this way it becomes their very nature *to love* God with all their heart so that they "might serve Him without (servile) fear in holiness and righteousness before Him, all the days of our life" (Luke 1:74, 75). Thus do both the Son and the Spirit honour the Father as Supreme Govenor, and join in the same design to discountenance sin, humble the sinner, magnify the law, and glorify grace.

But this enforcing of the infinite glory of God, of His governmental supremacy, of His holy law, of His righteous claims, of His demand for loving obedience and an implicit compliance with all His commands, is what is *left out* of every false religion in the world. And today there are, perhaps, as many false religions *inside* of Christendom as there are outside —denials of the Truth, perversions of the Truth, half-truths twisted and mangled, lawlessness proclaimed under the pretense of exalting grace. "Pretence" we say, for God's grace never reigns at the expense of righteousness but "through righteousness" (Rom. 5:21). Divine grace teaches us that "denying ungodliness and worldly lusts, we should live soberly, righteously, and godly, in this present world" (Titus 2:13). It is the ministers of Satan, "deceitful workers" (2 Cor. 11:13), who are now by their one-sided teaching causing many to "turn the grace of our God into lasciviousness" (Jude 4).

Here, then, is the explanation why true repentance is so little preached today. The sense of God's governmental supremacy has been lost, the claims of His righteousness are ignored, the unchanging demands of His holy Law are no longer recognised, hence, the unregenerate, not knowing God, having no sense of His infinite glory, and there being practically nothing in present-day preaching to instruct them therein, it follows that all their fancied reverence for and devotion to God takes its rise from merely *selfish* considerations, nothing but self-love (the *natural* instinct of self-preservation) lying at the bottom of modern "Christianity." As it is natural for unregenerate men to suppose they deserve something for their duties, so it is natural for them to be insensible of the infinite evil of their sins. And hence it is that new gospels are invented, new notions of "the way of salvation" are contrived, to *suit* the depraved taste of unhumbled and impenitent sinners, who are concerned about *their own* interests and care not what becomes of God's glory.

In the third place, true repentance presupposes a frank and *broken-hearted acknowledgment of our wicked failure* to keep God's righteous law. When the Holy Spirit opens the eyes of a sinner to see, in some measure, the supreme excellency and loveliness of the Divine character, and shows him how infinitely worthy God is of our sincere adoration: when He assures us of the righteousness and goodness of God's law, and how justly He is entitled to be loved by us with *all* our hearts; and when He convicts us of our wretched and lifelong failure to respond unto His most just claims upon us; when He makes us feel that so far from having delighted ourselves in this infinitely glorious God, we have sought to dismiss Him from our thoughts, and set our hearts upon the perishing things of time and sense, seeking our satisfaction in *them;* and that so far from having owned His rightful supremacy over us and His just claim for our lives to be governed by Him, we have scorned His authority, ignored His commandments, and acted only in self-will,—then it is, for the first time, we begin to *perceive* the infinite evil of sin, and are filled with self-loathing, horror and grief at our terrible course of conduct.

What we have just endeavoured to set forth is as different from what the strivings of an uneasy conscience produces as light is from darkness. One who has never been the subject of the supernatural and gracious operations of the Spirit may blame himself for sabbath-breaking, taking the Lord's name in vain, lying, drunkenness, who has never felt himself to blame for being disaffected to the Divine character. Even the wicked king Saul once acknowledged, "I have sinned, I have played the fool, and have erred exceedingly" (1 Sam. 26:21). So has many another since then, who was yet altogether blind to *the chief thing* wherein he was to blame. While men are ignorant of the beauty of God's character, of how absolutely worthy He is of being loved; while they perceive not the equity and blessedness of His law, of how absolutely entitled it is to implicit, unremitting, and joyous obedience; it is impossible that they should *repent* because of their failure to render *this* to Him.

Just as the absence of love to God, together with disaffection to His holy character, lies at the root of and influences the whole course of wickedness which mankind generally live in, so when Scripture calls upon men to repent of particular sins and turn to God, it is their *lack of love* for God and their *enmity against* His law, as manifested in and by their particular sins, which they are required to repent of. There is no sin whatsoever that any man is guilty of, but what it proceeds from a disrespect of God's character and a disregard of His authority. Thus it was said of David's sin that he not only had "despised the commandment of the Lord," but had "despised *Me*," the Lord (2 Sam. 12:9, 10). Therefore in repentance we are required not only to judge our particular sins, but also that *insubordination to God* which produced them: we are to unsparingly and bitterly condemn ourselves because we have treated the Lord of glory, the King of the universe, with contempt. *That* is *the* crime for which we are, above all things else, to blame. Not until we have realised that our rebellion against God was *such* that nothing but the *death of Christ* could possibly atone for it, have we truly repented.

Thus, genuine and saving repentance is a taking sides with God *against myself*. It is *not* that our repentance expiates our sins, for there is nothing meritorious about it. It makes *no* amends for our past vile conduct, nor does it move God to mercy. Yet is repentance required, yea demanded of us, and Divine mercy is not shown where no repentance is. No, repentance is designed to make the heart *loathe* sin, and that through a deep sense of its infinite enormity and dreadful pollution; it is to make us *dread* sin through a heart-realisation of its awful guilt. Only thus is the stubborn will broken and the heart made contrite and prepared to turn unto the Lord Jesus and seek salvation through Him by grace alone. A.W.P.

THE MIGHTY BREAKER

"The breaker is come up before them: they have broken up, and have passed through the gate, and are gone out by it: and their king shall pass before them, and the Lord on the head of them" (*Micah* 2:13).

Pause, my soul, over this precious scripture, and ask thine own heart who this Almighty Breaker can be, except the Lord Jesus Christ; for He, and He alone, answers to such a Divine character. Was it not He which came up as the Breaker from everlasting; when, in the council of peace, the Divine decree was broken open, and the Son of God stood forth the sinner's Surety? Was it not He whom John saw by vision, who alone was found worthy in heaven to open the book, and loose the seals thereof? Was it not the same precious Holy One, who, when in the volume of the book it was found written of Him, that He should fulfil the law of Jehovah for sinful man, cried out, "Lo, I come?" And was it not Christ, even thy Christ, my soul, that in the fulness of time came up as the Breaker, to break down the dreadful bar of separation which sin had made between God and man, and to open the new and living way for the sinner to God by His blood? And when He had broken down the fence sin had made in disobedience to the Divine law, the accusations of Satan, the dominion of death and the grave, by sustaining the whole weight and burden of all in His own precious person; did He not, as the Almighty Breaker, burst asunder the bars of death, and prove Himself thereby indeed to be this Almighty Breaker in such a palpable evidence, that it was impossible His Holy body could be holden by it? And hath He not broken through all intervening obstacles, ascended up on high, led captivity captive, entered into glory, and there ever liveth and appeareth in the presence of God for us? Is not Jesus then this Almighty Breaker?

But, my soul, look yet further. It is also said in this blessed scripture, that the Breaker is not only come up before them, (that is, His people) but that "they have broken up, and have passed through the gate, and are gone out by it; and their King shall pass before them, and the Lord on the head of them." And so they are, if so be this Almighty Breaker hath broken down the strongholds of sin and Satan in which they lay bound; broken down the natural hatred and enmity of their own heart against God and His Christ in which they were born, and in which they lived, and must have died, but for His sovereign grace manifested in them and towards them; burst open the prison-doors of Satan, and broke off his cursed chains, and brought them out! If these things are wrought and accomplished in the people, may they not be said, in His strength, to have broken up, and have passed through the gate of Satan's dominions, and are gone out by it into the glorious liberty of the sons of God?

Is it so, my soul, in thy experience? Dost thou indeed know Jesus for thy Almighty Breaker, by such sweet tokens of His love and power? Hath thy King passed thus before thee, and thy Lord on the head of thee? Oh, then, be ever on the look out for all the renewed visits of His grace, in which He still acts as thine Almighty Breaker, in breaking down all remaining obstacles which thy unbelief and fears, and doubts, are continually raising up against thine own happiness, in His precious manifestations. Look up to Him daily, hourly, minutely, if possible, that He may break down all the remains of indwelling corruption in thy nature, by which these fears and this unbelief gets fast hold in thy soul; and be often on the look out also for that glorious day of God, when this Almighty Breaker shall finally and fully come, and break through the clouds to judgment, to break down every remaining evil that keeps thee now from everlasting enjoyment of thy Lord! Hasten, blessed Jesus! come, my Beloved, and, with a glory infinitely surpassing all conception, manifest Thyself as the Almighty Breaker, in this full display of Thy sovereignty and power. And then, as Samson (the type in this instance) carried with him the gates of his prison, so wilt Thou break up and carry away all the gates of Thy people's graves, and take away all Thy redeemed home with Thee to glory, that where Thou art, there they shall be also. Hail, Thou Almighty Breaker! Jesus omnipotent reigneth! (Rob. Hawker, 1825.)

PRAYER

"What things soever ye desire when ye pray believe that ye *receive* them, and ye shall have them" (Mark 11:24). By the words "believe that ye receive them" we understand, *expect* God to give them to you. But it is at this point that so many of God's people fail oftenest in their prayer-lives. There are three chief things to be attended to in prayer.

First, make sure that you are asking for some thing which is in accordance with God's Word: see 1 John 5:14. But right here the Devil will foil you unless you are upon your guard. He will come as an "angel of light" and preach a sermon to you on *submission to* God's holy will. O yes, the Devil is quite capable even of *that!* It is our privilege and duty to know *what* God's will is! "Wherefore be ye *not* unwise, but *understanding* what the will of the Lord *is*" (Eph. 5:17). It is the *revealed* will of God which is in view in these passages, for with His "secret" will *we* have nothing to do; that is none of our business. God's revealed will is made known in His *Word*. Fix this in your mind, and never allow Satan to inject a thought (Eph. 4:27) to shake you thereon, that *every* thing God has commanded you to do, every precept and exhortation addressed to you, *is* "God's will" for *you*, and is to be turned into prayer for enabling grace. It *is* God's will that you should be "sanctified" (1 Thess. 4:2), that you should "rejoice" (Phil. 4:4), that you should "make your calling and election sure" (2 Pet. 1:10), that you should "grow in grace and in the knowledge of the Lord" (2 Pet. 3:18).

Second, having made sure that what you are praying for *is* according to God's revealed will, then *plead* His promises, such as Matt. 7:7, Phil. 4:19 etc. Plead them in the Name of Christ, asking God *to* give you the "desires of thine heart" (Psa. 37:4) for Christ's sake, that *He* may be honoured in and by a godly walk from you, and that His people may be helped and encouraged by your example. *Those* are "pleas" which God cannot deny.

Third, and this is what we would earnestly and lovingly press upon the Christian reader: EXPECT God *to* do as you have asked. Unless there is this expectancy, faith is not fully in exercise. It is this expecting from Him which honours and pleases God, and which *always* draws down from Him answers of peace. There may be some difficulty, problem, trial, looming ahead of you, which assumes the proportions of a mountain. Never mind that: do not let it depress, discourage, or dismay you. Praise God it stands written in the eternal Word of *Truth*, "Verily I say unto you, If ye have faith and *doubt not*. . . . ye shall say unto this mountain *be thou removed*, and be thou cast into the sea; It *shall* be done" (Matt. 21:21). Notice carefully that it is not "If thou doubt not and hast faith," but "If ye *have* faith" and then (while you are *awaiting* God's answer) "doubt not," but continue to *expect* the fulfillment of His promise. When you first get down on your knees beg God in the name of Christ and for His own glory's sake, to work in you by His Spirit that expectancy of faith which will *not* take "NO" from Him; which reverently but confidently says, "I will not let Thee go, except Thou bless me" (Gen. 32:26). *That* is what honours God, *that* is what pleases Him, *that* is what obtains answers from Him. A.W.P.

N.B. "A friend at court!" No doubt that expression is more or less familiar to the older readers, but it has almost dropped out of use in this generation. It denoted that one had a friend possessing influence with another in authority, and using it on my behalf. How unspeakably blessed to know that the Christian has a Friend at Court, the Court of Heaven; "A Friend that sticketh closer than a brother." He has the ear of God, for on earth He declared "Thou hearest Me *always*" (John 11:42). Then, *make use of Him*, fellow-saints. Bring thy petitions to Him, and ask Him to present them to His Father and your Father, accompanied by His own all-prevailing merits; and, if they are for God's glory and thy (real) good, be fully assured that they *shall* be granted. Thus will Christ be honoured and your faith strengthened. A.W.P.

---

fire"—placed itself in a bush (a thing of the earth), where it burned, yet was not the bush consumed. Remarkable foreshadowment was this of the "fullness of the Godhead," dwelling in Christ (Col. 2:9). That this *is* the meaning of the type is clear from Deut. 33:16, where we read of "The goodwill of Him that dwelt in the bush."

The great mystery of the Trinity is that one Spirit should subsist eternally as three distinct Persons; the mystery of the person of Christ is that two separate spirits (Divine and human) should evermore constitute but one person. The moment we deny the unity of His person we enter the bogs of error. Christ is the God-man. The humanity of Christ was not absorbed by His Deity, but preserves its own characteristics. Scripture hesitates not to say, "Jesus increased in wisdom and stature, and in favour with God and man" (Luke 2:52). Christ is both infinite and finite, self-sufficient and dependent at the same time, because His person embraces two different natures, the Divine and the human.

In the incarnation the second person of the Trinity established a personal union between Himself and a human spirit and soul and body. His two natures remained and remain distinct, and their properties or active powers are inseparable from each nature respectively. "The union between them is not mechanical, as that between oxygen and nitrogen in our air; neither is it chemical, as between oxygen and hydrogen when water is formed; neither is it organic, as that subsisting between our hearts and brains; but it is a union more intimate, more profound, and more mysterious than any of these. It is *personal*. If we cannot understand the nature of the simpler unions, why should we complain because we cannot understand the nature of the most profound of all unions?" (A. A. Hodge, to whom we are also indebted for a number of other thoughts in this article.) A.W.P.

> "Is there a thing beneath the sun
> That strives with Thee my heart to share?
> O tear it thence, and reign alone,
> The Lord of every motion there.
> Then shall my heart from earth be free,
> When it has found repose in Thee."

and body of men do, though united together. Thus in His Divine nature, Christ has nothing in common with us—nothing finite, derived or dependent. But in His human nature, He was made in all things like unto His brethren, sin excepted. In that nature He was born in time, and did not exist from all eternity: He increased in knowledge and other endowments proper thereto. In the one nature He had a comprehensive knowledge of all things; in the other, He knew nothing but by communication or derivation. In the one nature He had an infinite and sovereign will; in the other, He had a creature will, which though *not* opposed to the Divine will, yet its conformity thereunto was of the same kind with that which is in perfect creatures.

The necessity for the two natures in the one person of our Saviour is self-evident. It was fitting, requisite, that the Mediator should be both God and man, that He might partake of the nature of both parties and be a middle person between them, filling up the distance and bringing them near to each other. Only thus was He capacitated to communicate unto us His benefits: and only thus could He discharge our obligations. As Witsius the Dutch theologian (1690) pointed out: "None but God could restore us to true liberty. If any creature could redeem us we should be the peculiar property of that creature: but it is a manifest contradiction to be free and yet at the same time be the servant of any creature. So too none but God could give us eternal life: hence the two are joined together—'the true God and eternal life' (1 John 5:20)".

Equally necessary was it that the Mediator should be Man. He was to enter our law-place, be subject to the law, keep it, and merit by keeping it. Therefore we read, "But when the fullness of the time was come, God sent forth His Son, made of a woman, made under the law" (Gal. 4:4). Note the order: He must first be "made of a woman," before *He* could be "made under the law." But more; He had to endure the curse of the law, suffer its penalty. He was to be "made sin" for His people, and the wages of sin is death. But that was impossible to Him till He took upon Him a nature capable of mortality: "Forasmuch then as the children are partakers of flesh and blood, He also Himself likewise took part of the same; that through death He might destroy him that had the power of death, that is, the Devil" (Heb. 2:14).

Thus, the person of the God-man is unique. His birth has had no precedent and His existence no analogy. He cannot be explained by referring Him to a class, nor can He be illustrated by an example. The Scriptures while clearly and fully revealing all the elements of His person, yet never present in one formula an exhaustive definition of that person, nor a connected statement of the elements which constitute it and their mutual relations. The "mystery" is indeed great. How is it possible that the same person should be at the same time infinite and finite, omnipotent and helpless? He altogether transcends our understanding. How can two complete spirits coalesce in one person? How can two consciousnesses, two understandings, two memories, two wills, constitute one person? No one can explain it. Nor are we called upon to do so. Both natures act in concert in one person. All the attributes and acts of both natures are referred to one person. The *same* person who gave His life for the sheep, possessed glory with the Father before the world was!

This amazing Personality does not center in His humanity, nor is it a compound one originated by the power of the Holy Spirit when He brought those two natures together in the womb of the virgin Mary. It was not by adding manhood to Godhead that His personality was formed. The Trinity is eternal, and unchangeable. A new person is not substituted for the second member of the Trinity, neither is a fourth added. The person of Christ is just the eternal Word, who in time, by the power of the Holy Spirit, through the instrument of the virgin's womb, took a human nature (not at that time a man, but the *seed* of Abraham) into personal union with Himself. The Person is eternal and Divine; His humanity was introduced into it. The center of His personality is always in the eternal and personal Word, or Son of God.

Though there exists no analogy by which we may illustrate the mysterious person of Christ, there is a most remarkable type in Ex. 3:2-6. The "flame of fire" in the midst of the "bush," was an adumbration or emblem of the presence of God indwelling the Man Christ Jesus. Observe that the One who appeared there to Moses is termed, first, "the Angel of the Lord," which declares the relation of Christ to the Father, namely, "the Angel ('Messenger') of the covenant." But secondly, this Angel said unto Moses, "I am the God of Abraham": *that* is what He was absolutely in Himself. The fire—emblem of Him who is a "consuming

(Continued on Page 263)

STUDIES IN THE SCRIPTURES

"Search the Scriptures" John 5:39

Copyright in All English-speaking Countries

EDITOR: Arthur W. Pink, Millmont, Union Co., Penna., U. S. A.
Hon. Agent in England: Mr. A. Winstone, "Shalom," Old Bath Road, Leckhampton, Cheltenham.
Hon. Agent in Australia: Mr. G. Ardill, The Christian Workers' Depot, Commonwealth and Reservoir Streets, Sydney.

THE SUBSISTENCE OF CHRIST

The ground upon which we are now to tread is quite unknown even to the majority of God's people (so great has been the spiritual and theological deterioration of the last century), though it was thoroughly familiar to the better-taught saints of the Puritans' times and of those who followed them. That the Son of God is co-equal with the Father and the Spirit, and that nearly two thousand years ago the Word became flesh and was made in the likeness of men, is still held firmly (and will be) by all truly regenerated souls; and that it is the union of the Divine and human natures in His wondrous person which fits Him for His mediatorial office, is also apprehended with more or less clearness. But that is about as far as the light of nearly all Christians can now take them. That the God-man subsisted in Heaven before the world was is a blessed truth which has been lost to the last few generations.

A thoughtful reader who ponders such a verse as John 6:62 must surely be puzzled: "What and if ye shall see the Son of man ascend up where He was before?" Mark it well that our Redeemer there spake of Himself not as the Son of God, but as "the Son *of man*," and affirmed that *as such* He had been in Heaven *before* He became incarnate. But ignorant as we may be of this precious truth, the O. T. saints were instructed therein, as is evident from the 80th Psalm, where we find Asaph praying, "Let Thy hand be upon *the Man* of Thy right hand, upon the Son of man whom Thou madest strong for Thyself" (v. 17)! Yes, the Man Christ Jesus, taken into union with Himself by the second person of the Trinity, subsisted before the Father from all eternity, and was the Object of the O. T. saints' faith.

When first presented to the attention of a Christian, the last statement made by us appears to be mysticism run wild, or downright heresy. It *would be* had we said that the soul and body of the Son of man had any *existence* before He was born at Bethlehem. But *this* is *not* what Scripture teaches. What the written Word affirms is that the Mediator (Christ in His *two* natures) had a real *subsistence before God* from all eternity. First, He was "foreordained before the foundation of the world" (1 Pet. 1:20). He was chosen by God to be the Head of the whole election of grace: see Isa. 42:1. But more; it was not only *purposed* by God that the Mediator (the man Christ Jesus wedded to the eternal Word—John 1:1, 14) should have an historical existence when the "fulness of time" (Gal. 4:4) had duly arrived, but He had an *actual subsistence* before Him long, long before that. But *how* could this be?

In seeking the answer to our last question, it will help us to contemplate something which though not strictly analogous, yet, on a lower plane serves to exemplify and illustrate the principle. In Heb. 11:1 we are told that "faith is the substance of things hoped for." The Greek word for "substance" more properly signifies "a real subsistence": it is opposed to that which is only an image of the imagination, it is the antithesis of phantasy. Faith gives a real subsistence in the mind and heart of things which are yet to be, so that they are enjoyed now, and so that their power is experienced in the soul. Faith lays hold of the things which God has promised, so that they become actually present and the heart is influenced thereby.

(Continued on Page 288)

IMPORTANT NOTICES

Please advise promptly of change in address, otherwise copies will be lost in the mails.

We are glad to send a sample copy to any of your friends whom you believe would be interested in such a publication.

Send to Mr. I. C. Herendeen, Swengel (Union County), Penna., for a list of our publications. He has published many of our books and booklets.

This magazine is published as a work of faith and labour of love. The Editor and his wife gladly give their services. It is freely sent to all who will read it. No charge is made for it.

Christians who feel definitely led to do so, may have fellowship with us in this ministry. Those outside the U. S. A. please send only INTERNATIONAL Money Orders made out to Mifflinburg, Penna, U. S. A.

CONTENTS

The Subsistence of Christ	265
The Epistle to the Hebrews	266
The Satisfaction ("Atonement") of Christ	272
Repentance	278
Profiting from the Word	282
A Personal Word	285

THE EPISTLE TO THE HEBREWS

48. The Perfecting of the Church; 10:11-14.

The connection between our present passage and the verses preceding is so close, the relation between them so intimate, that what is now to be before us cannot be understood, and appreciated apart from the other. The design of the whole is to show the superlative excellency of the sacrifice of Christ and what it has procured for His people, with the inevitable setting aside of all the typical offerings. This great change in the outward worship of God's saints on earth was no temporary expediency in view of the failures of fleshly Israel, but was ordained by the Divine counsels before the foundation of the world, recorded in the Book of God's decrees, and, in due time, transcribed upon the pages of Holy Scripture; the 40th Psalm having announced the alteration which was to be brought about by the incarnation and advent to this earth of the Son of God.

Most blessedly does that Messianic Psalm acquaint us with what passed between the Father and the Son and of the covenant agreed upon by Them. Most blessedly are we there shown not only the Son's acquiescence to the Father's purpose, but also His readiness and joy to execute the same. The strenuous undertaking was to rest upon *His* shoulder, the burden and heat of the day was to be borne by Him, the humiliation and pains of death were to be His portion; yet so far from rebelling against this frightful ordeal, He exclaimed "I *delight* to do Thy will, O My God" (Psa. 40:8). So dear to Him was the Father's glory, so filled with zeal was He to accomplish His counsels, so deep was His longing to magnify His law and make it honourable, that His very "meat" was to do and accomplish His will. Never did famished mortal so crave food to satisfy hunger, as did the God-man Mediator to perform the Father's pleasure.

He too knew full well that the blood of bulls and goats could never repair the damage which sin had wrought. He too had heartily concurred in the august Council of the Trinity that, if satisfaction were to be made unto Divine justice, then an *adequate* one should be given, one which should be suited in every way to meet *all* the aspects of the case. Inasmuch as it was man who had revolted against the Divine government and broken the Divine law, He was willing to become Man, and in the same nature which had apostatized from God render perfect obedience to Him. Inasmuch as "the Law" was the rule of obedience (Jer. 31:33), comprehending all God's demands, the entire service of love which creatures owe unto their Maker, the Son consented to be "made under the law" (Gal. 4:4) and "fulfil" its precepts (Matt. 5:17). Inasmuch as the penalty of that law was death unto the transgressor, He agreed to be "made a curse for us."

It was *not* that all of this was *forced on* the Son, but that He freely agreed thereto. If there are verses which tell us the Father "sent" the Son, there are other passages which declare that the Son "came." Blessedly was this foreshadowed in Gen. 22, where we behold an earthly adumbration of that "counsel of peace" which was between "Both" the Father and the Son (Zech. 6:13). There we are shown a human father willing to sacrifice his beloved son upon the altar, and there too we see a human son (then fully grown) willing to be slain! Marvelously did that set forth the *mutual* consent of the Divine persons with regard to the Great Transaction. Mark attentively, those precious words, "So they went *both* of them *together*" (Gen. 22:8)! As we follow Isaac upon mount Moriah, his actions said, Lo, I come to do *Thy* will, O my God."

In man three things combine to the doing of a thing. First, there is the exercise of *will*, which is the *prime* mover and spring of all the rest. Second, there is the exercise of *wisdom*, by which he plans and arranges. Third, the putting forth of *strength* to accomplish the same. So it is in the Divine Trinity in connection with the salvation of the Church and all that that entails. "Will" is more generally ascribed to the Father: Matt. 11:26, Eph. 1:11, etc. "Wisdom" is more eminently attributed to the Son, the "Wonderful Counsellor," called so often "Wisdom" in the book of Proverbs Luke 7:35, 11:49 etc. "Might" to the Holy Spirit—Luke 1:35, where He is designated "the Power of the Highest." The Father contrived the great work of redemption, the Son transacted it, and the Holy Spirit applies the same. Here in Heb. 10 things are traced back to the first great cause of our salvation, namely, the sovereign will of the Father.

The closer the whole passage be read, the more will it appear that the apostle was moved to ascend in thought to the originating source of redemption. In v. 5 we hear the Lord Jesus saying to the Father concerning the legal sacrifices, "Thou wouldest not," i. e. they were not what Thou didst eternally purpose should take away sins. To this He adds, "But a body hast Thou *prepared* Me," which (as we have shown) in its deepest meaning signifies: a human nature hast Thou *ordained* for Me, to be the meet vehicle of service in which I should render an adequate satisfaction. Next, He makes reference to the Book of God's eternal decrees, in view of which He declares, "I come to do Thy *will*, O God." Finally, the Holy Spirit sums up the whole by affirming "in the which will we are sanctified through the offering of the body of Jesus Christ once."

We feel it a bounden duty to enlarge upon this fundamental truth, the more so in view of the present almost universal denial of the absolute sovereignty of God. The Holy Spirit has Himself here emphasised the fact that God's imperial pleasure was the sole moving-cause even in that greatest of all the Divine works, through which is communicated the chiefest glory to God and highest good to His people. God was under *no* necessity to save any. He "spared not the angels that sinned, but cast them down to hell" (2 Peter 2:4); and had it so pleased Him, He had done the same with the whole human race. There was *no* necessity in His *nature* which compelled or even required Him to show mercy; had there been, mercy had been bestowed on the fallen angels! The Almighty is under *no* restraint either from anything outside or anything inside Himself; to affirm the contrary, would be to repudiate the absolute freedom of His will.

Still less was God under any necessity of giving His own beloved Son if He chose to redeem a part of Adam's race. He who declares, "All nations before Him are as nothing: and they are *counted to Him* less than nothing, and vanity. To whom then will ye liken God?" (Isa. 40:17, 18) is not to be measured by human reason nor limited by our unbelief. Had God so pleased He had made this earth a thousand times bigger than it is; and had He so pleased, He had created it a thousand times smaller. In like manner, He was absolutely free to use whatsoever means *He* determined in order to save His people from their sins. The sending forth of His Son to be made of a woman and to die upon the cross, was *not* a work of His *nature*, but of His *will*; as He now begets us "of His own will" (James 1:18). True it "became" Him so to do (Heb. 2:10), and He is infinitely honoured thereby, yet He could have refused had He so pleased.

Thus, the "will" of God referred to throughout Heb. 10 is that eternal, gracious, free purpose, by which God determined in Himself to recover His elect out of lost mankind, to remove their sins, sanctify their persons, and bring them nigh unto the everlasting enjoyment of Himself. This act of the will of God was without any meritorious cause foreseen in them, and altogether apart from anything outside Himself to dispose Him thereto. It was His own free and uncaused act by which God purposed so to do. Nor have we the smallest occasion to regard this supremacy of the Most High with any aversion. God is no Tyrant, nor does He act capriciously. *His* will is a wise and holy one, therefore do we read of Him working "all things after the *counsel* of His own will" (Eph. 1:11), and therefore did He devise a plan whereby His *grace* might be most magnified.

It was for this reason He determined that His people should be saved in such a way as to remove *all* ground for boasting in themselves, and to glory only in God Himself. Therefore did He appoint His own Son to be their Saviour, and that by rendering to Him such a satisfaction as would meet every requirement of justice and every demand of the most enlightened conscience. God's end and aim in giving Christ to die was to advance the glory of His *grace*, which consists in having the monarchy and *sole* prerogative in saving sinners attributed unto it; the highest of whose honour and eminency is this, that *it* alone "reigns" (Rom. 5:21), and hath not and could not have any competitor therein. As it is the excellency of God that He is God alone, and there is none beside Him, so it is of His Son that He is Saviour alone and there is none beside Him (Acts 4:12).

Unto God the Son, made Man, has been assigned an office which no creature in earth or heaven could possibly fill. The fullest trial and manifestation of this is made in a case of less difficulty (than that of making satisfaction to Divine justice for sin) in Rev. 5. There we read of a challenge given, "Who is worthy to open the book"—which was sealed and held in the hand of God seated on His throne—"and to loose the seals thereof?" Waiving the question as to *what* "book" this was, we note the response: "And no one in heaven, nor in earth, neither under the earth, was able to open the book, neither to look thereon" (v. 3). Even the beloved John was discouraged, and "wept much because no one was found worthy to open and to read the book" (v. 4). Mark the unspeakably blessed sequel: "One of the elders saith unto me, Weep not; behold, the Lion of the tribe of Judah, the Root of David, *hath* prevailed to open the book and to loose the seals thereof. And I beheld, and, Lo, in the midst of the throne . . . stood a Lamb as it had been slain . . . and He came and took the book out of the right hand of Him that sat upon the throne" (vv. 5-7). If then no mere creature was fit to *reveal* redemption, how much less to *effect* it!

Thus, the *origin* of our salvation is found in the sovereign will of God; the *means*, in the satisfaction made by His incarnate Son. The two things are brought together in v. 10, "In the which will we are sanctified through the offering of the body of Jesus Christ once." "In the which will" has reference to what is recorded in the Book of God's decrees. That "will" was that His people should be "sanctified" unto Him, set apart with acceptance to Him. This was to be effected through "the offering" of Christ, which began at the first moment of His birth and ended when on the cross He cried, "It is finished." This was "once for all."

It was an absolute necessity that there should be these two things: the originating will of God the Father, the consenting will of the Mediator to make full satisfaction for sin. Necessary it was that the Father should be willing and call His Son to this work, for *He* was the person unto whom the satisfaction was to be made. Had Christ performed all that He did, freely and gladly, yet, unless the Father had first decreed that He *should* and had "called" Him unto it, then had He rejected the whole, asking "who hath required this at Thy hand?". Therefore has the Spirit insisted upon this foundational fact again and again in the course of this epistle: see 2:10; 3:4; 5:4, 5; 6:17 etc. Thus does 10:10 ascribe as much, yea more, to God's appointing and accepting of Christ's sacrifice, as to the merits of Christ unto the sanctification of His people.

"And every priest standeth daily ministering and offering oftentimes the same sacrifices, which can never take away sins: But this Man, after He had offered one sacrifice for sins, for ever sat down on the right hand of God; from henceforth expecting, till His enemies be made His footstool. For by one offering He hath perfected forever them that are sanctified" (vv. 11:14). "These words are an entrance into the close of that long blessed discourse of the apostle, concerning the priesthood and sacrifice of Christ, their dignity and efficacy; which he shuts up and finisheth in the following verses, confirming the whole with the testimony of the Holy Spirit before produced by Him.

"Four things doth he here instruct us in, by way of recapitulation of what he had declared and proved before. 1. The state of the legal priests and sacrifices, as unto the recognition of them, by which he had proved before their utter insufficiency to take away sin (v. 11). 2. In that one offering of Christ, and that once offered, in opposition thereunto (v. 12). 3. The consequence thereof on the part of Christ; whereof there are two parts. First, His state and condition immediately ensuing thereon (v. 12), manifesting the dignity, efficacy, and absolute perfection of His offering. Secondly, as unto the continuance of His state and condition afterwards (v. 13). 4. The absolute effect of his sacrifice, which was the sanctification of the Church (v. 14)" (J. Owen).

"And every priest standeth daily ministering and offering oftentimes the same sacrifices, which can never take away sins" (v. 11). The opening "And" links this verse with the 10th, for the purpose of accentuating the blessedness of what is there declared. Once more the Holy Spirit emphasises the contrast between the all-sufficient offering of Christ and the unefficacious offerings under the law. This is brought out under five details, upon which there is little need for us to enlarge at length.

First, under the law the sacerdotal office was filled by *many*: attention is called to this by the "*every* priest," which is set over against the "this Man" of v. 12, who was competent by Himself to do all God required. Second, the Levitical priests *stood*. This was was true both of the high priest and of all under him. No chair or seat was provided for them in either the tabernacle or temple, for their work was never ended. Third, they were employed *daily*, which showed they were unable to do immediately and once for all that which would satisfy God. Fourth, they oftentimes presented "the *same* sacrifices": true, they varied in detail and design, nevertheless they had this in common, that, they were irrational creatures, incapable of offering intelligent and acceptable obedience to God. Fifth, they could not meet the infinite demands of justice, expiate sins, nor provide a permanent resting-place for an exercised conscience.

An improvement should be made of what has just been before us, by pointing out the utter worthlessness of all human devices for appeasing God and comforting the conscience. If the Levitical offerings, which were of Divine appointment, were unable to really meet either the full requirements of God or the deepest need of sinners, how much less can the contrivances of men do so! How vain are the Romish inventions of confession, absolution, indulgencies, masses, penances, purgatory, and the like tom-fooleries! Equally vain are the austerities of some Protestants: the signing of a temperance-pledge, giving up of tobacco, and other reformations, with tears, fastings, and religious performances designed to make peace with God. The salvation of the Lord does not come to a soul via any such things. "Not by works of righteousness which we have done, but according to His mercy He saved us, *by* the washing of regeneration and renewing of the Holy Spirit; which He shed on us abundantly *through* Jesus Christ our Saviour" (Titus 3:5, 6).

"But this man, after He had offered one sacrifice for sins for ever sat down on the right hand of God" (v. 12). The opening word denotes that a contrast is here presented from what was before us in v. 11: it is the Holy Spirit placing in antithesis the one perfect and efficacious offering of Christ from the unavailing sacrifices of the law. The word "Man" ought to be in italics: if any word is to be supplied it should be that of "Priest." The Greek simply reads, "But He," the pronoun being emphatic. It is the sacerdotal work of the Mediator which is in view. He came and once for all laid Himself on the Divine altar as an atonement to God — the entire course of His obedience terminating and being consummated at the cross.

There is both a comparison and a contrast here between Christ and Aaron and his successors. Both were priests; both offered a sacrifice for sins; but there the analogy between them ends. They were many; He alone. They offered numerous sacrifices; He, but one. They continued to offer sacrifices; His is complete and final. Their offerings were unefficacious; His, has actually removed sins. They stood; He has sat down. They ministered *unto* God; He is seated at the right hand *of* God. The typical high priest entered the holiest only for a brief season, one day in the year; Christ has gone on High "forever." He has not ceased to be a Priest, nor to exercise that office; but He is now "a Priest upon His *throne*" (Zech. 6:13). The position He occupies witnesses to the supreme excellency of His work, and attests the acceptance of His sacrifice by God.

The glorious place which our once humiliated Saviour has been accorded, supplies conclusive evidence of the value and finality of His redemptive work. "The very fact that Christ is in heaven, accepted by His Father, proves that His work must be done. Why, beloved, as long as an ambassador from our country is at a foreign court, there must be peace; and as long as Jesus Christ our Saviour is at His Father's court, it shows that there is real peace between His people and His Father. Well, as He will be there for ever, that shows our peace must be continued and shall never cease. But that peace could not have been continual, unless the atonement had been wholly made, unless justice had been entirely satisfied" (C. H. Spurgeon).

Commentators have been divided as to whether the "for ever" is to be connected with the Saviour's one sacrifice or to His sitting down at God's right hand. The Greek, while hardly conclusive, decidedly favours the latter. Perhaps the double thought is designed. They who insist that the "for ever" *must* be joined to the first clause, argue that it *cannot* be so with the second because 1 Thess. 4:16, Rev. 19:11 etc. show that the Saviour will yet leave Heaven. As well might appeal be made to Christ's "standing" to receive Stephen (Acts 7:55). But the difficulty is self-created through *carnalizing* the metaphor used. "For ever sat down" is in designed contrast from the "standeth daily" of v. 11. Christ has ceased for ever from the priestly work of making oblation: He will never again be engaged in such a task; but He has *other* characters to fill beside that of Maker of atonement.

"For ever sat down on the right hand of God." Four times in this epistle is reference made to Christ's being seated on High, yet is there no repetition. On each occasion the reference is found connected with an entirely different line of thought. First, in 1:3 it is His seat of personal glory which is in view: the whole context before and after showing that. Second, in 8:1 it is the seat of priestly pre-eminence which He occupies, namely, His superiority over all others who filled the sacerdotal office. Third, here in 10:12 it is the seat of sacrificial acceptance, God's witness to the value of His satisfaction. Fourth, in 12:2 it is the seat of the Victor, the prize given for having successfully run His race.

The One born in Bethlehem's manger, who on earth had not where to lay His head, who died upon the cross, and whose body was laid in a borrowed grave, is now in Heaven. He has been given a place higher than that of the arch-angel, He has been exalted above all created things. There is a *glorified Man* at God's right hand! Christ is the *only one* among all the hosts above who *deserves* to be there! It is naught but Divine *favour* which gives holy angels and redeemed sinners a place in the Father's House; but the Man Christ Jesus has *merited* that high honour!

"The highest place that Heaven affords,
Is His by sovereign *right*,
King of kings and Lord of lords,
He reigns there in the Light."

Unspeakably blessed is this; the more so when it be realized that Christ has entered heaven *for His people*. He has gone there in His *official* character. He has gone there as our Representative; to appear before God "for us" (Heb. 9:24). He is there as our great High Priest, bearing our names on His breastplate. Wondrous and precious are those words, "Whither the *fore-runner* is *for us* entered, even Jesus" (Heb. 6:20). There the mighty Victor sits "crowned with glory and honour." He occupies the Throne of universal dominion, of allmighty power, of sovereign and illimitable grace. He is making all things work together for the good of His own. The kingly scepter shall He wield until all His redeemed are with Him in glory.

"From henceforth expecting till His enemies be made His footstool" (v. 13). In these words we have the seventh and last N. T. reference made to the 110th Psalm. There we read, "The Lord said unto my Lord, Sit Thou at My right hand, until I make Thine enemies Thy footstool" (v. 1). Allusion is here made to that promise of the Father to the Son for the purpose of supplying additional confirmation of what had just been declared. In vv. 10, 12 (also in 14), the utter *needlessness* for any repetition of Christ's sacrifice is shown, here the *impossibility* of it. From the beginning, a state of glory and position of honour had been appointed the Mediator following on the presentation of His offering to God. He was to take His place on the throne of heaven, till His foes were completely subjugated: therefore to enter the place of service and die again He was no longer capable!

The suffering Saviour has been invested with unlimited power and dominion, and nothing now remains but the accomplishing of all those effects which His sacrifice was designed to procure. These are twofold; the saving of His elect, the subjugating of all revolters against God, for "He hath appointed a day in the which He will judge the world in righteousness by that Man whom He hath ordained" (Acts 17:31). The Redeemer having perfected His great work, now calmly awaits the fulfilment of the Father's promise: cf. 1 Cor. 15:25-27. Christ will yet put forth His mighty power and overthrow every proud rebel against Him. He will yet say, "I will tread them in Mine anger, and trample them in My fury, and their blood shall be sprinkled upon My garments . . . for the day of vengeance is in Mine heart" (Isa. 63:3, 4): cf. Rev. 14:20. Then will men experience the terribleness of "the wrath of the Lamb" (Rev. 6:16).

The *"wrath* of the Lamb" is as much a perfection as is the *"love* of Christ." In His overthrow of God's adversaries, His glory shines as truly as when He conducts the redeemed into the Father's House. He is equally to be adored when we behold His vesture stained with the blood of His enemies, as when we see His life ebbing from His side pierced for us. Each was an intrinsic part of that work assigned Him of the Father. Though in our present state we are apt to shrink-back with horror, as we contemplate Him saying to those who despised and rejected Him. "Depart from Me, ye cursed," yet in that day we shall praise Him for it. "Oh! what a triumph that will be, when men, wicked men, persecutors, and those who opposed Christ, are all cast into the lake that burneth" (C. H. Spurgeon).

A remarkable adumbration (shadowing forth) of what has just been before us was made by God in A. D. 70. During the days of His flesh, the enemies of Christ pursued Him with relentless hatred. Nor was their enmity appeased when they had hounded Him to death: their rage continued to vent itself upon His followers. No one can read through the book of Acts without discovering many an evidence of the rancour of apostate Judaism against the early Christians. Loudly did the Jews boast of their triumph against Jesus of Nazareth, and for a time it looked as though they would prevail against His church. Though the issue hung in suspense for some years, God made a complete end to the same by utterly destroying them as a nation, and thereby gave a pledge of the eternal destruction of those who obey not the Gospel. In sending the Romans to burn their city and raze their temple, we discover a solemn foreshadowing of that which shall yet take place when Christ says, "But those Mine enemies, which would not that I should reign over them, bring hither and slay before Me" (Luke 19:27).

But let our final thought of this 13th verse be one of a different tenor. In the word "expecting" we have manifested again the lovely moral perfections of the Mediator. Christ is able to destroy all His enemies in a moment, yet for nineteen centuries He has bided His time. Why? Because, even in Heaven, He meekly and gladly bows to the Father's pleasure. His final triumph is still postponed, because He calmly *waits* that day which God has "appointed" (Acts 17: 31). Therefore do we read of "the kingdom and *patience* of Jesus Christ" (Rev. 1:9). In this too He sets us an example. Whatever be our lot and condition, however the forces of evil rage against us, we are to possess our souls in patience (Luke 21:19), knowing that there is a *"set time"* to favour Zion (Psa. 102:13). Ere long, every enemy of Christ and of His church shall be overthrown—overthrown, *not* "reconciled": "His enemies be made His footstool" plainly gives the lie to the dreams of Universalists!

"For by one offering He hath perfected for ever them that are sanctified" (v. 14). Three things claim our attention here: first, the relation of this verse to the context; second, what is meant by "perfected for ever"?; third, who are the "sanctified"? The link between our verse and what precedes is contained in the opening "For," which has a double force. First, it intimates that what is now said furnishes additional proof for the thesis of the whole passage: the very fact that the one offering of Christ has "perfected for ever" (contrast 7:19!) those sanctified by God, gives further demonstration of the efficacy and sufficiency of it, and the needlessness of any repetition. Second, the same fact manifests the meetness of the Mediator's sitting at God's right hand until His enemies are made His footstool—His work having accomplished such a blessed result, He is entitled both to rest and reward.

"For by one offering He hath perfected for ever them that are sanctified." The word for "perfected" literally means "completed" or "consummated." It is more of an objective than a subjective perfection which is here in view, as the immediate context and the whole epistle shows. This verse is not speaking of the Church's eternal state in Glory, but of its present standing before God. By His sacrifice Christ has procured for His people the full pardon of sin and peace before God thereon. The "one offering" of the Lord Jesus possesses such infinite merits (being that of an infinite or Divine person in a holy humanity), that it has wrought out a complete expiation and secured for "His own" personal acceptance with and access to God, a priestly standing and covenant nearness before Him.

Because their salvation has been accomplished by the vicarious obedience and vicarious suffering, in life and in death, by no less a person than Immanuel, because He glorified God's law by keeping it fully and enduring its curse, His people are both perfectly justified and perfectly sanctified, that is, a complete righteousness and complete fitness to worship in the Temple of God is theirs, not in themselves, but through Christ their Head. Their *title* to heaven is founded alone on the righteousness of Christ imputed to them. Their *fitness* is given when the Holy Spirit regenerates them. Their present *enjoyment* of the same is determined by the maintenance of communion with God day by day. Their perfect and eternal enjoyment thereof will issue from their *glorification* at the return of the Saviour.

The word "perfected" here is to be understood in a sacrificial rather than in an experimental sense. It has reference to the Christian's *right* to stand in the holy presence of God in unclouded peace. Our title so to do is as valid now as it will be when we are glorified, for that title rests alone on the sacrificial work of our Substitute, finished on the cross. It rests on something altogether external to ourselves, altogether apart from what God's sovereign grace works in us or through us, either when we first believe or afterwards. We are precious in the sight of God according to the preciousness of Christ: see Eph. 1:6, John 17:22, 23. Yet, let it be added that, this perfect objective sanctification (our consecration to God by *Christ*) in no wise renders the less requisite our need of being constantly cleansed, experimentally, by the Spirit's use of the Word: John 13:10, 1 Pet. 1:2 etc.

Those perfected by the "one offering" of Christ are "them that are sanctified," or more literally, simply "the sanctified," the reference being to those who were *eternally set apart* by the Father (Jude 1). The persons of the elect are variously designated in this epistle. They are referred to as "heirs of salvation" (1:14), "sons" (2:10), "brethren" of Christ, (2:12), "partakers of the heavenly calling" (3:1), "heirs of promise" (6:17), "the house of Israel" and "of Judah" (8:8); but here "the sanctified," because the Spirit's object in the whole of this passage is to trace everything to its originating source, namely, the imperial will of a sovereign God.—A.W.P.

THE SATISFACTION
("Atonement")
OF CHRIST

24. *Its Rejection.*

All the race of Adam are guilty before God, and, consequently, none of them can by any works of their own, find acceptance with Him. Almost every page of Scripture bears testimony to this truth. The whole scheme of revelation takes it for granted. The plan of salvation taught in the Word could have no place on any other supposition. The Son of man came here to save that which was *lost*. Were we not exposed to danger, there could be no salvation. When the Lord Jesus called Paul and sent him forth to preach to men, it was "to open their eyes," and to turn them from darkness to light, and from the power of Satan unto God" (Acts 26:18). Here we have the character of the whole Gentile world: they are as ignorant of the true character of God and of the way of acceptance with Him, as blind men are ignorant of the real nature of the objects of sight. They walk, "In the vanity of their mind, having the understanding darkened, being alienated from the life of God through the ignorance that is in them, because of the blindness of their heart" (Eph. 4:17, 18).

That the world is guilty before God, is not only declared by Scripture, but is also to be seen by the present state of man with regard to happiness. It is obvious to any impartial observer that the human race is *miserable*, even amidst its mirth and dissipation. Men are *seeking* happiness (a proof that they do not *have* it) from the enjoyment of earthly things, according to their various tastes and appetites; but they find it not. From the highest to the lowest, there is that which *mars* their peace and enjoyment. The very things which the poor regard as evidences of the happiness of the rich, are but so many devices to drive away sorrow. If they would honestly express themselves, the millionaire in his mansion and the king on his throne would declare, "*all* is vanity and vexation of spirit." True happiness is to be found in God alone.

In such a state of guilt and misery is placed the whole human race. It is indeed a melancholy truth, but one which is altogether incontestible. Instead, then, of disputing the Divine testimony, let us inquire from the same authority, whether there be any way of escape. Is the fate of fallen men as hopeless as that of fallen angels? No, blessed be God, it is not. The same Word of Truth which tells of man's ruin, announces the Divine remedy; the same Book which describes human guilt and wretchedness, tells of a way of deliverance therefrom. The One, who, in the exercise of His high sovereignty, reserved the sinning angels in everlasting chains of darkness unto the judgment of the great day, has, in His abounding mercy, provided salvation for undone sinners of Adam's race.

The Divine way of salvation is the most stupendous monument of Divine wisdom and grace, of sovereignty and power, of justice and mercy, that ever was exhibited in this world. God has provided a Saviour, who, by His virtuous life and vicarious death, has made atonement for sin, by which all His people obtain eternal life. The whole scope of revelation, from the first intimation made in Eden (Gen. 3:15) to the end of the New Testament, bears witness to this marvellous and precious way of salvation. The Divine promises declared it, the types illustrated it, the prophets foretold it. When the Son of man was here, He announced that He "came to give His life a ransom for many" (Matt. 20:28): almost everybody knows that a "ransom" is a price paid for the recovery of anything that is lost to its original owner. The uniform teaching of the Epistles is, that "Christ Jesus came into this world to save sinners."

The Scriptures are both full and clear in making known the way in which guilty sinners are interested in the atonement of Christ. "Even the righteousness of God which is *by faith* of Jesus Christ unto all and upon all them that *believe*: for there is no difference; for all have sinned and come short of the glory of God; Being justified freely by His grace through the redemption which is in Christ Jesus: Whom God hath set forth to be a propitiation *through faith* in His blood, to declare His righteousness for the remission of sins that are past, through the forbearance of God; To declare at this time His righteousness: that He might be just, and the justifier of him which *believeth* in Jesus. Where is boasting then? It is excluded. By what law? of works? Nay: but by the law of *faith*" (Rom. 3:22-27). In this passage the apostle not only establishes the guilt of man and the atonement of Christ, but also clearly asserts that *faith* is the medium through which sinners are interested in the work of Christ.

"But to him that *worketh not*, but believeth on Him that justifieth the ungodly, his faith is counted for righteousness" (Rom. 4:5). Can any thing be more explicit? Can any thing be more directly to the point? Salvation must be given gratuitously, that no flesh may glory in God's presence. The "reward" of the man that "worketh," the apostle says, is *not* of "grace," but of "debt." It therefore follows that works of *no* kind whatever can give a title to the atonement of Christ or the favour of God.

But let it be said with emphasis that a saving reception of Christ's atonement is by *such* a faith which effectually changes the heart and the mind, so that the desires and pursuits of its recipient are entirely different than formerly. There has ever been a need to press this fact, for the enemies of the Gospel charge it as unfriendly to good works. But in these terrible days, when multitudes who profess to be saved by grace through the redemption of Christ, are giving the lie to their profession by continuing in a course of self-will and self-indulgence, the need for making clear this fact is doubly evident. Saving faith is that which *"purifieth* the heart" (Acts 15:9). "Therefore if any man be in Christ, he is a *new* creature: old things are passed away; behold, all things are become new" (2 Cor. 5:17).

Formerly, the Christian sought for happiness in the pleasures, honours, or riches of this world; now he seeks it in those things which are above. He abhors the things in which he once delighted, and delights in what he once abhorred. "For I *delight* in the *law* of God" says the apostle, "after the inward man" (Rom. 7:22). Many things in the commandments of Jesus Christ are so disagreeable to flesh and blood, that they are (figuratively) called the cutting off of a right hand, or the plucking out of a right eye: yet the Christian not only acquiesces, but finds pleasure in yielding obedience to Christ in such things. True, he still has a corrupt nature to struggle against, yet his delight is decidedly in the law of his God. Saving faith is that which "overcometh the world" (1 John 5:4). But we must now make a closer approach to our immediate theme.

The proclamation of mercy through the atonement of the incarnate Son of God is called the Gospel, or good news, because it announces deliverance from condemnation and eternal life to every believer. But it also necessarily implies and plainly denounces tidings of a very opposite nature to all who reject it, and in general to all the workers of iniquity. If it proclaims life to those who receive it, then death must be the portion of all who neglect it. This solemn fact is made prominent throughout the New Testament in the most awful and striking manner. Many are sheltering behind a profession of Christianity, and fondly hope that there is a sort of general impugnity in sin on account of the death of Christ; but all such are fatally deluded, for the Gospel denounces wrath against all who do not receive it, and against all evildoers.

In the great commission which our Lord gave first to His apostles, He asserted as expressly as that they who believed the Gospel shall be saved, that they who believed it not shall be *damned* (Mark 16:16). What the Gospel is was shown in our last article, and Gal. 1:8 announces that any deviation from that Gospel, any substitution of another, brings down the curse of Heaven upon the one who proclaims it, and by parity of reason, on those who accept it. What would be thought of *this* by those who pride themselves in their liberality of sentiment? who make the belief or rejection of the Truth a matter of trifling consideration? Here is the Truth, *God's* Truth: the rejection of the Gospel means the perdition in Hell of both soul and body forever.

"I am not ashamed of the Gospel of Christ: for it is the power of God unto salvation to every one that believeth. . . . For therein is the righteousness of God revealed from faith to faith. . . . For the wrath of God is revealed from heaven against all ungodliness and unrighteousness of men" (Rom. 1:16-18). If the whole of these three verses be read attentively, it will be seen that the Gospel contains both a revelation of the "righteousness" of God and also of His "wrath." In like manner, the same chapter which tells us that "God so *loved* the world that He gave His only begotten Son, that whosoever believeth in Him should not perish, but have everlasting life" (John 3:16), also declares, "He that believeth not the Son shall not see life, but the *wrath* of God abideth on him" (v. 36).

The condemnation of all who are ignorant of the true God and who reject the Gospel of Christ, is made known in 2 Thess. 1:7-9, "the Lord Jesus shall be revealed from heaven with His mighty angels, in flaming fire taking vengeance on them that know not God, and that obey not the Gospel of our Lord Jesus Christ: who shall be punished with everlasting destruction from the presence of the Lord, and from the glory of His power." This language is so terrible and decisive that nothing but the blindness and hardness of a depraved heart could defy it. To know God and receive His Son is "eternal life" (John 17:3), but to be ignorant of the true character of God and reject His Gospel entails eternal damnation.

"Therefore we ought to give the more earnest heed to the things which we have heard lest at any time we should let them slip. For if the word spoken by angels was steadfast, and every transgression and disobedience received a just recompense of reward: How shall we escape if we neglect so great salvation" (Heb. 2:1-3). Let those who trifle with their souls and refuse to seriously attend unto the Gospel, learn from this that God is in earnest in what He declares in the Scriptures. It seems incredible that people can hear and read unmoved the awful denunciations which the Word of Truth hurls against them. They surely cannot believe that such threatenings proceed from Him who cannot lie. Too late shall they discover that every word in them shall be faithfully executed.

Perhaps some are inclined to ask at this point, How can God justly punish men for rejecting a Saviour who never died *for them?* Many have regarded this as an insoluable problem; yet it is capable of a simple solution. First, let us duly attend to the plain and solemn declaration of Christ Himself: "He that believeth on Him is not condemned; but he that believeth not is condemned already, because he hath not believed in the name of the only begotten Son of God" (John 3:18). Nothing could be plainer than that: if any find it difficult to fit that verse in to their theology, then something is wrong with their theology—Christ is "despised *and rejected* of men."

It is quite true that every man lies under the condemnation of God before the Gospel first comes to him: the judgment for Adam's offence rests upon him (Rom. 5:12-19), to which is added the guilt of his own transgressions. But it is also true that *additional* guilt and condemnation comes to those who spurn the advances of Divine mercy made unto them through the Gospel. There are *degrees* of criminality, as there will be of punishment. Clear proof is furnished in those solemn words of Christ's: "And thou Capernaum, which art exalted unto heaven, shalt be brought down to hell. . . . It shall be more tolerable for the land of Sodom in the day of judgment, than for thee" (Matt. 11:23, 24). So too, more tolerable shall it be in the Day of Judgment for the unevangelised section of Heathendom, than it will for multitudes in Christendom who refuse to obey the Gospel.

Christendom's sins are going to be punished (the more severely) for having scorned that glad tidings which was "worthy of (entitled to) all acceptation." And let us emphasise once more the fact that the Gospel message is *not* that Christ died for *me*, but that He died for *sinners*. The Gospel is addressed to human responsibility, and presents a Saviour who is ready to save all who will comply with its terms. If men will not come to Christ that they "might have life" (John 5:40), then their blood is upon their own heads. Therefore will God yet say to them, "Because I have called, and ye refused; I have stretched out My hand, and no man regarded; but ye have set at nought all My counsel, and would none of My reproof: I also will laugh at your calamity; I will mock when your fear cometh; when your fear cometh as desolation, and your destruction cometh as a whirlwind; when distress and anguish cometh upon you. Then they shall call upon Me, but I will not answer; they shall seek Me early, but they shall not find Me: for that they hated knowledge, and *did not choose* the fear of the Lord" (Prov. 1:24-29).

The preaching of the Gospel unto men at large becomes a searching test of their state of heart. It *ought* to have a powerful influence upon them in breaking their hearts on account of sin. Why did the Son of God leave His heavenly glory and enter a life of unspeakable humiliation here on earth? Why did He suffer such frightful indignities at the hands of men, so that His face was spat upon, His hair plucked out, His back scourged? Why was He nailed to the cross of woe, where His life's blood was poured out? The answer is, for *sin*. And can that be thought upon with any seriousness, and the heart not be broken before God? What will melt the hard heart of man and thaw it into godly sorrow for sin, if the contemplation of Christ's sacrifice will not do it?

O my readers, the shedding of the precious blood of Immanuel ought surely to melt the most adamantine heart that is yet out of Hell. Would men but ponder the Saviour's passion, both in the character and degree of it, viewing its bitter ingredients and heightened circumstances, and then also consider that it was human transgressions which brought Him to Calvary, surely they would be far more deeply affected for sin than they now are. It is written, "they shall look upon Me whom they have pierced" and *what* follows? This: "and they shall *mourn* for Him as one mourneth for his only son, and shall be *in bitterness* for Him" (Zech. 12:10). Ah, *that* is true penitence —a broken heart from viewing the broken body of Christ. What then must be the state, and what must be the punishment, of them concerning whom the Saviour has to ask, "Is it *nothing* to you, all ye that pass by? behold, and see if there be any sorrow like unto My sorrow" (Lam. 1:12).

Again; the proclamation of the Gospel and the serious consideration of the Saviour's sufferings ought to have a powerful effect in turning men *from sin*. Behold my reader, the Lord of glory dying as a sacrifice, making His soul "an offering for sin" (Isa. 53:10). Will you deliberately elect to continue living in that for which the Son of God died? Will you regard as a "sweet morsel" that which was more bitter than gall to the Beloved of the Father? God Himself *condemned* sin at the cross (Rom. 8:3), dare you, then, approve of it? O will you not condemn it too, repudiate it, turn from it in loathing, and seek grace from above to have nothing more to do with it? When you are tempted to sin, recall the bleeding wounds of the suffering Saviour. Nothing is more calculated to slay our love for sin than a contemplation of the awful wages which it paid to the Redeemer.

Oh what an indescribably dreadful state must they be in (as the writer and the Christian reader once were!) who turn a deaf ear to God's call through the Gospel, and in so doing "despise and reject" His Son! What a dreadful and unmistakable evidence is this that "the carnal mind *is* enmity against God" (Rom. 8:7)! Ah, that explains *why* it is that all men "make excuse" (Luke 14:18) when they are bid to come to the rich feast that Divine mercy has spread. It is not carelessness or indifference; no, the real root of the trouble lies much deeper: it is a desperately wicked heart (Jer. 17:9) which is opposed to the thrice holy God, that is the source of impenitence and unbelief. Men prefer material and temporal things to spiritual and eternal ones, the "pleasures of sin for a season" (Heb. 11:25), rather than those "pleasures for evermore" (Psa. 16:11) which are at God's right hand.

What has just been said above is no theoretical reasoning of ours, but the plain teaching of Christ Himself. After He had so solemnly declared, "he that believeth not is condemned already because he hath not believed in the name of the only begotten Son of God" (John 3:18), He at once (by way of explanation) added, "And this is the condemnation, that light is come into the world, and men loved darkness rather than light, because their deeds were evil. For every one that doeth evil hateth the light, neither cometh to the light, lest his deeds should be reproved" (vv. 19, 20). No matter what (seemingly) plausible "excuses" men and women may make for their present rejection of the Gospel, He who cannot err insists that behind those excuses is a *love* of darkness (sin) and a *hatred* of of the Light!

Let men say what they will with respect to their rejection of the Gospel, all their objections are founded in their disaffection to *truth and holiness*. They may claim to respect and believe God's Word, and that they want to be saved, or profess they *are* saved, but in truth they "hate the Light because their deeds are evil." They will not part with their idols. They will not *forsake* that pleasant but Broad Road which leadeth to destruction. They will not *deny* "self," and submit to Christ as their *Lord*. They are willing to be saved their own way, but not God's. They wish to serve two masters, and make the best of both worlds. They may be good members of society, and be virtuous and pious, but the real language of their hearts is "we will *not* have this Man to *reign* over us" (Luke 19:14).

When people are told that they *despise* as well as "reject" Christ, they feel the charge is not true of them. When it is insisted upon that they *hate* Christ (John 15:18), they suppose the indictment is far too severe. Nay, they imagine they have a high estimate of Christ, that they sincerely own Him to be the most excellent One that has ever walked this earth, and that they are earnestly desirous of being saved by Him. But a *"deceived* heart has turned them aside" (Isa. 44: 20). Had the Jewish nation been told one year before Christ began His public ministry that they would not only scorn Him, but put Him to death, would not *they* have indignantly denied such a charge? Most assuredly, they would. They would have answered: All our hopes center in Him, we are eagerly awaiting His promised advent, and shall gladly receive Him the moment He appears. And in so speaking, they would have been perfectly sincere. Yet God's infallible Word declares that Christ was the one "whom the nation *abhorreth*" (Isa.

49:7). And *why* did they? Because when He stood before them, He was *different* from what they expected.

Ah, my reader, in what has just been said above, we have the Divine explanation to the solemn situation which is confronting us today. History has repeated itself. The Jews would have willingly received a Messiah patterned after their own carnal desires. Had Christ presented Himself only as a Deliverer from their temporal troubles, gratified their fleshly lusts, and not interfered with *their* selfish plans, He had received a royal welcome from them. But for the *Holy* One of God they had no heart. For One who required repentance, for One who came to save them from the *present* dominion of sin, for One who demanded unqualified submission to God's will, for One who must be received as *Lord and Master*, they had no love. To forsake all and follow Him, suited them not. To abandon their idols, mortify the flesh, and enter the path of *obedience to* His commands and precepts, was altogether foreign to their every thought and desire.

And is it any different today? Not a whit. Present to men One who was filled with compassion for the suffering, who ministered to the needy, fed the poor, healed the sick, and, as a public Benefactor and Philanthropist, He is universally admired. Or, proclaim Him as a Deliverer from the wrath to come, as One who is willing to save from Hell and take to Heaven, and the movings of self-interest will induce multitudes to welcome Him as such. But, my reader, the Lord Jesus Christ cannot be *halved* in any such manner as this. He must be received just as He is, a *whole* Christ as the Scriptures present Him to us. As a Prophet to reveal God's will, and that, in order for us to walk therein. As a priest to mediate, offering Himself as a sacrifice to God, presenting our sacrifices of praise to Him. As a King to occupy the throne of our hearts, to rule us by His precepts, to subdue our enemies. But *as such* the unregenerate see in Him no beauty that they should desire Him.

Thousands of professing Christians are willing to believe in Christ for salvation, but not to conform to Him in obedience. They desire the "rest" which He gives, but not His "yoke"—just as of old the multitudes sought Him for the loaves and fishes, yet had no heart for His searching teachings. People want the justification which the Gospel proclaims, but not the mortification of the old man which it enjoins. But this cannot be. In order to "come" to Christ, the sinner must turn from sin and all else that competes for his heart. The truth is that the vast majority of those now bearing His name love their worldly and fleshly lusts far more than they do Christ.

"Thus it is now with the carnal professors of the Gospel: because Christ answers not their expectation, they entertain prejudice against Him as represented in the Gospel, and are unwilling to come to Him. They want a Saviour that will let them live quietly in their sins, be indulgent to them in their fleshly courses, and yet bring them to heaven when they can live in sin no longer. But when the Gospel represents Christ as One who requires strictness and holiness in all of His followers, who calls for separation from the world in all that come to Him, who tells them they must suffer any evil rather than sin, and take up the cross if they will have Him for *their* Christ; when the Gospel offers One whom nothing will please but that holiness and strictness which the world derides; One whom persecutions and reproaches will attend all His followers; then prejudice seizes on their souls. Thus we see *why* so many will not come to Christ, and *who* they are" (D. Clarkson, 1680).

And "what shall the end be of them that *obey not* the Gospel of God?" (1 Pet. 4:17). What *can* it be. What *must* be the portion of those who love darkness and hate the Light? Only one answer is possible. And Scripture does not leave us in ignorance thereof. "If they escaped not who refused Him that spake on earth, much more shall not we escape, if we turn away from Him that speaketh from Heaven" (Heb. 12:25). Escape they shall not. The Angel that hath a rainbow about His head, hath pillars of fire for His feet (Rev. 10:1) to consume them who refuse His peace. "He hath appointed a day, in the which He will judge the world in righteousness by that Man whom He hath ordained" (Acts 17:31). And in that Day He shall say, "But those Mine enemies, which would not that I should reign over them, bring hither, and slay before Me" (Luke 19:27).

Oh my reader, if you value your soul at all, weigh thoroughly what has just been before you. Pass it not on to some one else, but take it home to thyself.

Christ cannot be imposed upon, and soon it will be too late to undeceive yourself. "A diabolical life and a believing heart are contradictions. No man can with any reason lay claim to a faith in Christ who prefers the pleasures of the world before the sweetness of a Redeemer, that which is an offense to Him before that which is His delight. How can they believe in Christ that are carried down with the violent current of their own lusts, and regard not one tittle of His law? If faith be full of good works, then the lack of such clearly implies the absence of faith" (S. Charnock, 1680). May the Lord deign to add His blessing to these pages for His name's sake. A.W.P.

REPENTANCE

We trust that sufficient has been said in the previous sections to enable any exercised and prayerful reader to distinguish between a false and a true repentance, between a non-saving and a saving one. There are three kinds of repentance spoken of in Scripture. First, that of desperation: Esau, Pharaoh, Ahitophel, and Judas are illustrations. Second, that of reformation: Ahab's and that which was brought about under the preaching of Jonah, are illustrations. Third, that which is unto salvation: Acts 11:18, 2 Cor. 7:10. It is most important that we learn to discriminate between legal conviction and evangelical repentance. Multitudes are deceived at this point: they suppose that because they have been terrified through contemplating the wrath to come and have abandoned many of their evil ways, they have repented. This by no means follows. A legal conviction fears *Hell*, evangelical repentance reveres *God*: the one dreads *punishment*, the other hates *sin;* the one informs the mind, the other melts the heart. Evangelical repentance makes no excuses and has no reserves, but cries "I have dishonoured Thy name, grieved Thy Spirit, abused Thy patience."

When a sinner is brought to truly realise that he is in great danger, he earnestly desires and diligently seeks deliverance, but that is from the natural instinct of self-preservation, and not because of supernatural grace at work in his heart. Tell him that *nothing* is required from him except to believe in Christ, rest on His finished work, and like a stony-ground hearer he at once receives the Word with joy, and no human being can make him doubt his salvation. Yet his heart has never been broken before God, nor has he any true love for Him. Such people mend their ways and become quite zealous religionists. They pray earnestly, read the Bible frequently, and sometimes become active workers in warning their fellows. But tell such that notwithstanding their tears, zeal, and believing the letter of Scripture, they deserve to be damned as much as ever they did, and that God can justly *refuse* them mercy, and their enmity against Him is likely to become swiftly apparent.

Thousands of deceived souls in Christendom, deluded by the false gospellers of the day, love a God who has no existence except in their own disordered imaginations. And terrible beyond words will be their disillusionment in the next world. "How sad and dreadful a thing will it be for such poor sinners when they come to die, and enter into the world of spirits, there to find that the God they once loved and trusted in, was nothing but an image framed in their own fancy! They hated the God *of Scripture*, and hated His *law*, and therefore would not believe that either God or His law were indeed what they were. They were resolved to have a God and a law more to their own minds. How dreadful will their disappointment be! How terrible their surprise! They would never own that *they* were enemies to God; now they will see that their enmity was so great as to make them resolutely —notwithstanding the plainest evidence— even to deny Him to be what He was. And how righteous will the ways of the Lord appear to be unto them then, in that He gave such over to strong delusion to believe a lie, because they would not love nor believe the truth, but had pleasure in unrighteousness" (Jos. Bellamy).

While God be considered *merely* as Creditor and sinners as debtors and Christ is regarded as paying the *whole* debt of all who believe, it cannot but be that souls will be fatally misled. Because Christ obeyed the law as well as suffered its penalty, it by no means follows that we are discharged from doing our duty. Yet, it is now being taught on every side that Christ *has* done *all*, and that there is nothing to do but firmly believe in Him, that Christians have *nothing* to do with the law, no not as a rule of life, that they have been freed from all obligations to any *duty*. But Scripture affirms that Christ died to "purify unto Himself a peculiar people, zealous of good works" (Titus 2:14), and that so far from the Christian being discharged from duty, his obligations are immeasurably increased by the grace of the Gospel: Rom. 12:1. But everything is viewed in a false light today, and instead of Christ being regarded as the Friend of *holiness*, He is made the Minister of *sin*.

"Repentance to be sure must be *entire*. Many will say, Sir, I will renounce this sin and the other, but there are certain darling lusts which I must keep. O sirs, in God's name let me intreat you: it is not the giving up of any one sin, nor fifty sins, which is true repentance; it is the solemn renunciation of *every* sin. If thou dost harbour one of these accursed vipers in thy heart, thy repentance is but a sham, if thou dost indulge in but one lust, and dost give up every other, that one lust, like one leak in a ship, will sink thy soul. Think it not sufficient to give up thy outward vices, fancy it not enough to cut off the more corrupt sins of thy life; it is all or none which God demands. 'Repent' says He, and when He bids you *repent*, He means repent of *all* thy sins, otherwise He can never accept thy repentance as being real. He says, 'Guild thee as thou wilt, O sinner, I abhor thee! Aye, make thyself gaudy, like the snake in its azure scales, I hate thee still, for I know thy venom, and I will flee from thee when thou comest to Me in thy most specious garb. All sin must be given up, or else you shall never have Christ; all transgression must be renounced, or else the gates of heaven must be barred against thee. Let us remember this, that repentance to be sincere, it must be *entire*.

"True repentance is a turning of *the heart*, as well as of the life, it is the giving up of the whole soul to God, to be His for ever and ever; it is a renunciation of the sins of the heart, as well as of the crimes of the life. Ah, dear hearers, let none of us fancy we have repented, when we have only a false and fictitious repentance; let none of us take that to be the work of the Spirit, which is only the work of poor human nature; let us not dream that we have savingly turned unto God, when perhaps we have only turned to ourselves, let us not think it enough to have turned from vice to virtue; let us remember it must be a turning of the whole soul to God, so as to be made anew in Christ Jesus; otherwise we have not met the requirements of the text.

"Lastly, upon this point, true repentance must be *perpetual*. It is not my turning to God during today that will be a proof I am a true convert; it is forsaking my sins throughout the entire course of my life, until I sleep in the grave. You must not fancy that to be upright for a week will be a proof that you are saved, it is a perpetual abhorrence of evil. The change which *God* works is neither a transitory not superficial one; not a cutting off the top of the weed, but an eradication of it; not the sweeping away of the dust of one day, but the taking away of that which is the cause of the dust. You may today go home and pretend to pray, you may today be serious, tomorrow honest, and the next day you may pretend to be devout; but yet, if you *return*—as Scripture has it, like the dog to its vomit and like the sow to its wallowing in the mire— your repentance shall but sink you deeper into hell, instead of being a proof of Divine grace in your heart" (From Spurgeon's sermon on Psa. 7:12). Would that such faithful sermons were being preached in the so-called orthodox and "fundamentalist's" pulpits today.

"To learn *by* heart that which others say *from* the heart—to get the outline of a believer's experience, and then to adopt it skillfully to one's self as our *own* experience—this is a thing so simple, that instead of wondering there are hypocrits, I often marvel that there are not ten times more. And then again, the graces —the real graces within—are very easy to counterfeit. There is a repentance that needs to be repented of, and yet it approaches near as possible to true repentance. Does repentance make men hate sin? they who have a false repentance may detest some crimes. Does repentance make men resolve that they will not sin? so will this false repentance, for Balaam said, 'If Balak would give me his house full of silver and gold, I will not go beyond the word of the Lord.' Does true repentance make men humble themselves? so does false repentance, for Ahab humbled himself before God, and yet perished. There is a line of distinction so fine, that an eagle's eye hath not seen it; and only God Himself, and the soul that is enlightened by His Spirit, can tell whether our repentance be real or no" (Spurgeon on Luke 13:24). To help the exercised reader identify true repentance, consider:

IV. Its Fruits.

First, a real *hatred of sin* as sin, not merely its consequences. A hatred not only of this or that sin, but of all sin, and particularly of the root itself: self-will. "Thus saith the Lord God, Repent, and turn from your idols; and turn away your faces from *all* your abominations" (Ezek. 14;6). He who hates not sin, loves it. God's demand is, "Ye shall loathe yourselves in your own sight for all your evils that ye have committed" (Ezek. 20:43). One who has really repented can truthfully say, "I hate *every* false way" (Psa. 119:104). He who once thought a course of holy living was a gloomy thing, has another judgment now. He who once regarded a course of self-pleasing as attractive, now detests it and has purposed to forsake all sin forever. This is the change of mind which God requires.

Second, a *deep sorrow for sin*. The non-saving repentance of so many is principally a distress occasioned by forebodings of Divine wrath; but evangelical repentance produces a deep grief from a sense of having offended so infinitely an excellent and glorious a Being as God. The one is the effect of fear, the other of love; the one is only for a brief season, the other is the habitual practice for life. Many a man is filled with regret and remorse over a misspent life, yet has no poignant sorrow of heart for his ingratitude and rebellion against *God*. But a regenerated soul is cut to the quick for having disregarded and opposed his great Benefactor and rightful Sovereign. This is the change of heart which God requires.

"Ye sorrowed to repentance: for ye were made sorry after a godly manner . . . for godly sorrow worketh repentance to salvation" (2 Cor. 7:9, 10). Such a sorrow is produced in the heart by the Holy Spirit and has *God* for its object. It is a grief for having despised *such* a God, rebelled against *His* authority, and been indifferent to *His* glory. It is this which causes us to "weep bitterly" (Matt. 26:75). He who has not grieved over sin takes pleasure therein. God requires us to "afflict" our souls (Lev. 16:29). His call is, "Turn ye even to Me with all your heart, and with fasting, and with weeping, and with mourning: and rend your hearts and not your garments, and turn unto the Lord your God: for He is gracious and merciful" (Joel 2:12, 13). Only that sorrow for sin is genuine which causes us to *crucify* "the flesh with the affections and lusts" (Gal. 5:24).

Third, a *confessing of sin*. "He that covereth his sins shall not prosper" (Prov. 28:13). It is "second nature" to the sinner to *deny* his sins, directly or indirectly, to minimise, or make excuses for them. It was thus with Adam and Eve at the beginning. But when the Holy Spirit works in any soul, his sins are brought to light, and he, in turn, acknowledges them to God. There is no relief for the stricken heart until he does so: "When I kept silence, my bones waxed old through my roaring all the day long, for day and night Thy hand was heavy upon me: my moisture is turned into the drought of summer" (Psa. 32:3, 4). The frank and broken-hearted owning of our sins is imperative if peace of conscience is to be maintained. This is the change of attitude which God requires.

Fourth, an actual *turning from sin*. "Surely there is no one here so stupified with the laudanum of hellish indifference as to imagine that he can revel in his lusts, and afterward wear the white robes of the redeemed in Paradise. If you imagine you can be partakers of the blood of Christ, and yet drink the cup of Belial; if you imagine you can be members of Satan and members of Christ at the same time, ye have less sense than one would give you credit for. No, you know that right hands must be cut off and right eyes plucked out—that the most darling sins must be renounced—if you would enter the kingdom of God" (From Spurgeon on Luke 13:24).

Three Greek words are used in the N. T. which present different phases of repentance. First, "metanoeo," which means a change of mind: Matt. 3:2, Mark 1:15 etc. Second, "metanolomai," which means a change of heart: Matt. 21:29, 32, Heb. 7:21 etc. Third, "metanoia," which means a change of course or life: Matt. 3:8; 9:13; Acts. 20:21. The three must go together for a genuine repentance. Many experience a change of mind: they are instructed, and know better, but they continue to defy God. Some are even exercised in heart or conscience, yet they continue in sin. Some amend their ways, yet not from love to God and hatred of sin. Some are informed in mind and uneasy in heart, who never reform their lives. The three *must* go together.

"He that covereth his sins shall not prosper, but whoso confesseth and *for-*

saketh them shall have mercy" (Prov. 28:13). He who does not, fully in his heart's desire, and increasingly so in his life, turn from his wicked ways, has not repented. If I really hate sin and sorrow over it, shall I not abandon it? Note carefully the "wherein in time *past*" of Eph. 2:2 and *"were* sometimes" of Titus 3:3! "Let the wicked *forsake* his way, and the unrighteous man his thoughts, and let him return unto the Lord, and He will have mercy upon him" (Isa. 55:7). This is the change of course which God requires.

Fifth, accompanied by *restitution* where this is necessary and possible. No repentance can be true which is not accompanied by a *complete* amendment of life. The prayer of a genuinely penitent soul is, "Create in me a clean heart, O God, and renew a right spirit within me" (Psa. 51:10). And where one really desires to be right with God, he does so with his fellow-men too. One who, in his past life, has wronged another, and now makes no determined effort to do everything in his power to right that wrong, certainly has not repented! John G. Paton tells of how after a certain servant was converted, the first thing he did was to restore unto his master all the articles which he had stolen from him!

Sixth, these fruits are *permanent*. Because true repentance is preceded by a realisation of the loveliness and excellency of the Divine character and an apprehension of the exceeding sinfulness of sin for having treated with contempt so infinitely a glorious Being, contrition for and hatred of all evil is abiding. As we grow in grace and in the knowledge of the Lord, of our indebtedness and obligations to Him, our repentance deepens, we judge ourselves more thoroughly, and take a lower and lower place before Him. The more the heart pants after a closer walk with God, the more will it put away every thing which hinders this.

Seventh, yet repentance is *never perfect in this life*. Our faith is never so complete that we get to the place where the heart is no more harrassed with doubtings. And our repentance is never so pure that it is altogether free from hardness of heart. Repentance is a lifelong act. We need to pray daily *for* a deeper repentance.

In view of all that has been said, we trust it is now abundantly clear to every impartial reader that those preachers who *repudiate* repentance are, to poor lost souls, "physicians of *no* value." They who leave out repentance, are preaching "another gospel" (Gal. 1:6) than Christ (Mark 1:15; 6:12) and His apostles (Acts 17:30; 20:21) proclaimed. Repentance is an evangelical duty, though it is not to be rested in, for it contributes *nothing* unto salvation. Those who have never repented are yet in the snare of the Devil (2 Tim. 2:25, 26), and are treasuring up to themselves wrath against the Day of Wrath (Rom. 2:4, 5).

"If, therefore, sinners would take the wisest course to be the better for the use of the means of grace, they must try to fall in with God's design and the Spirit's influences, and labour to see and feel their sinful, guilty, undone state. For this end they must forsake vain company, drop their inordinate worldly pursuits, abandon everything which tends to keep them secure in sin and quench the motions of the Spirit; and for this end must they read, meditate and pray; comparing themselves with God's holy law, trying to view themselves in the same light that God does, and pass the same judgment upon themselves; so that they may be in a way to approve of the Law and admire the grace of the Gospel; to judge themselves and humbly apply to the free grace of God through Jesus Christ for all things, and return through Him to God" (J. Bellamy).

N.B. A *summary* of what has been before us may be helpful to some. 1. Repentance is an evangelical duty, and no preacher is entitled to be regarded as a servant of Christ's, if he be silent thereon (Luke 24:47). 2. Repentance is required by God in *this* dispensation (Acts 17:30) as in all preceding ones. 3. Repentance is in nowise meritorious, yet without it the Gospel cannot be savingly believed (Matt. 21:32, Mark 1:15). 4. Repentance is a Spirit-given realisation of the exceeding sinfulness of sin and a taking sides with God against myself. 5. Repentance presupposes a hearty approval of God's law and a full consent to its righteous requirements, which are all summed up in "thou shalt love the Lord thy God with all thy heart etc." 6. Repentance is accompanied by a genuine hatred of and sorrow for sin. 7. Repentance is evidenced by a forsaking of sin. 8. Repentance is known by its permanency: there must be a continual turning away from sin and grieving over each fall thereinto. 9. Repentance, while permanent, is never complete or perfect in this life. 10. Repentance is to be sought as a gift from Christ (Acts 5:31). A.W.P.

PROFITING FROM THE WORD

7. *The Scriptures and the World.*

Not a little is written to the Christian in the N. T. about "the world" and his attitude toward it. Its real nature is plainly defined, and the believer is solemnly warned against it. God's holy Word is a light from Heaven, shining here "in a dark place" (2 Pet. 1:19). Its Divine rays exhibit things in their true colours, penetrating and exposing the false veneer and glamour by which many objects are cloaked. That world upon which so much labour is bestowed and money spent, and which is so highly extolled and admired by its blinded dupes, is declared to be "the enemy of God"; therefore are His children forbidden to be "conformed" to it and to have their affections set upon it.

The present phase of our subject is by no means the least important of those that have already been before us, and the serious reader will do well to seek Divine grace to measure himself or herself by it. One of the exhortations which God has addressed to His children is, "as newborn babes, desire the sincere (pure) milk of the Word that ye may *grow* thereby" (1 Pet. 2:2), and it behoves each one of them to honestly and diligently examine himself so as to discover whether or not this be the case with him. Nor are we to be content with an increase of mere head-knowledge of Scripture: what we need to be most concerned about is our *practical* growth, our experimental conformity to the image of Christ. And one point at which we may test ourselves is, Does my reading and study of God's Word make me less worldly?

1. We are profited from the Word when our eyes are opened to *discern the true character* of the world. One of the poets wrote, "God is in Heaven, all's well with the world." From one standpoint that is blessedly true, but from another it is radically wrong, for "the whole world lieth in the Wicked one" (1 John 5:19). But it is only as the heart is supernaturally enlightened by the Holy Spirit, we are enabled to perceive that that which is so highly esteemed among men, is, really, "abomination in the sight of God" (Luke 16:15). It is much to be thankful for when the soul is able to see that the "world" is a gigantic fraud, a hollow bauble, a vile thing which must one day be burned up.

Before we go further, let us define that "world" which the Christian is forbidden to love. There are few words found upon the pages of Holy Writ used with a greater variety of meanings than this one. Yet careful attention to the context will usually determine its scope. The "world" is a system or order of things, complete in itself. No foreign element is suffered to intrude, or, if it does, it is speedily accommodated or assimilated to itself. The "world" is fallen human nature acting itself out in the human family, fashioning the framework of human society in accord with its own tendencies. It is the organized kingdom of the "carnal mind" which is "enmity against God," and which is "*not* subject to *the law* of God, neither indeed can be" (Rom. 8:7). Wherever the "carnal mind" is, there is "the world"; so that worldliness is the world without God.

2. We are profited from the Word when we learn that the world is *an enemy to be resisted and overcome*. The Christian is bidden to "Fight the good fight of faith" (1 Tim. 6:12), which implies that there are foes to be met and vanquished. As there is an holy Trinity, the Father, the Son, and the Holy Spirit, so also is there an evil trinity—the flesh, the world, and the Devil. The child of God is called unto a mortal combat with them; "mortal," we say, for either they will destroy him, or he must get the victory over them. Settle it, then, in thy mind, my reader, that the world is a deadly enemy, and if thou dost not vanquish it in thine heart then thou art no child of God, for it is written, "For whatsoever is born of God *overcometh* the world" (1 John 5:4).

Out of many, the following reasons may be given as to why the world *must* be "overcome." First, all its alluring objects tend to divert the attention and alienate the affections of the soul from God. Necessarily so, for it is the tendency of things seen to turn the heart away from things unseen. Second, the spirit of the world is diametrically opposed to the spirit of Christ, therefore did the apostle write, "Now we have received, not the spirit of the world, but the spirit which is of God" (1 Cor. 2:12). The Son of God came into the world, but "the world knew Him not" (John 1:10), therefore did its "princes" or rulers crucify Him (1 Cor. 2:8). Third, its concerns and cares are hostile to a devout and heavenly life. Christians, like the rest of mankind, are required by God to labour six days in the week;

but while so employed they need to be constantly on their guard, lest covetous *interests* govern them rather than the performance of *duty*.

"This is the victory that overcometh the world, our faith" (1 John 5:4). Nought but a God-given faith *can* overcome the world. But as the heart is occupied with invisible yet eternal realities, it is delivered from the corrupting influence of worldly objects. The eyes of faith discern the things of sense in their real colours, and see that they are empty and vain, and not worthy to be compared with the great and glorious objects of eternity. A felt sense of the perfections and presence of God, makes the world appear as less than nothing. When the Christian views the Divine Redeemer dying for his sins, living to intercede for his perseverance, reigning and over-ruling things for his final salvation, he exclaims, "there is none upon earth that I desire besides Thee"; and, amidst the storms of this present life, he "endures as seeing Him who is invisible" (Heb. 11:27).

And how is it with *you*, dear reader? You may cordially assent to what has just been said in the last paragraph, but how is it with you *actually*? Do the things which are so highly valued by the unregenerate, charm and enthrall you? Take away from the worldling those things in which he delights, and he is wretched; is this so with you? Or, is your *present* joy and satisfaction found in objects which can *never* be taken from thee? Treat not these questions lightly, we beseech you, but ponder them seriously in the presence of God. The *honest* answer to them will be an index to the real state of your soul, and will indicate whether or not you be deceived into supposing yourself to be "a new creature in Christ Jesus."

3. We are profited from the Word when we learn that Christ died to *deliver us from* "this present evil world" (Gal. 1:4). The Son of God came here not only to "fulfil" the requirements of the law (Matt. 5:17), to "destroy the works of the Devil" (1 John 3:8), to deliver us "from the wrath to come" (1 Thess. 1:10), to save us, "from our sins" (Matt. 1:21), but also to free us from the bondage of this world, to deliver the soul from its enthralling influence. This was foreshadowed of old in God's dealings with Israel. They were slaves in Egypt, and "Egypt" is a figure of the world. They were in cruel bondage, spending their time in "making bricks" for Pharaoh. They were unable to free themselves. But Jehovah, by His mighty power, emancipated them and brought them forth out of the "iron furnace." Thus does Christ with His own. He breaks the power of the world over their hearts. He makes them independent of it, so that they neither court its favours nor fear its frowns.

Christ gave Himself a sacrifice for the sins of His people that, in consequence thereof, they might be delivered from the damning power and governing influence of all that is evil in this present world: as from Satan, who is its prince; from the lusts which are predominant in it; from the vain conversation of the men who belong to it; and from the awful conflagration which awaits it. Now the Holy Spirit indwelling the saints, co-operates with Christ in this blessed work. He turns their thoughts and affections away from earthly things to Heavenly. By the working of His power, He frees from the demoralizing influence of that which surrounds us, and conforms to the Heavenly standard. And, as the Christian grows in grace, he recognises this, and acts accordingly. He *seeks* yet fuller deliverance from this "present *evil* world," and begs God to completely free him from it. That which once charmed him, now nauseates. He longs for the time when he shall be taken out of this scene where his blessed Lord is so grievously dishonoured.

4. We are profited from the Word when our *hearts are weaned from it*. "Love not the world, neither the things in the world" (1 John 2:15). "What the stumbling-block is to the traveler in the way, the weight to the runner, the lime-twigs to the bird in its flight, so is the love of the world to a Christian in his course —either wholly diverting him from, greatly enticing him in, or forcably turning him out of it" (Nath. Hardy, 1660). The truth is that until the heart be purged from this corruption, the ear will be deaf to Divine instruction. Not until we are lifted above the things of time and sense, can we be subdued unto obedience to God. Heavenly truth glides off a carnal mind as water from a spherical body.

The world has turned its back upon Christ, and though His name is professed in many places, yet will it have nothing to do with Him. All the desires and designs of worldlings are for the gratification of *self*. Let their aims and pursuits be as varied as they may, self being supreme, everything is subordinated to the pleasing thereof. Now Christians are in the world, and cannot get out of it; they have to live their Lord's appointed time in it. While here they have to earn their living, support their families, and attend to their worldly business. But they are forbidden to *love* the world, as though it could make them happy. Their "treasure" and "portion" is to be found elsewhere.

The world appeals to every instinct of fallen man. It contains a thousand objects to charm him: they attract his attention, the attention creates a desire for and love of them, and insensibly yet surely make deeper and deeper impressions on his heart. It has the same fatal influence on *all* classes. But attractive and appealing as its varied objects may be, all the pursuits and pleasures of the world are designed and adopted to promote the happiness of *this* life ONLY—therefore, "what shall it profit a man if he should gain the whole world, and lose his own soul." This the Christian is taught by the Spirit, and through His presenting of Christ before the soul, his thoughts are diverted from it. Just as a little child will readily drop a dirty object when something more pleasing is offered to it, so the heart which is in communion with God will say, "I count all things loss for the excellency of the knowledge of Christ Jesus my Lord . . . and do count them dung, that I may win Christ" (Phil 3:8).

5. We are profited from the Word when we *walk in separation from* the world. "Know ye not that the friendship of the world is enmity with God? whosoever will be the friend of the world is the enemy of God" (James 4:4). Such a verse as this ought to search every one of us through and through, and make us to tremble. How can I fraternize with or seek my pleasure in that which condemned the Son of God? If I do, that at once identifies me with His enemies. O my reader, make no mistake upon this point, it is written, "If any man love the world, the love of the Father is not in him" (1 John 2:15).

Of old it was said of the people of God that they "shall dwell alone, and shall not be reckoned among the nations" (Num. 23:9). Surely the disparity of character and conduct, the desires and pursuits, which distinguish the regenerate from the unregenerate *must* separate the one from the other. We who profess to have our citizenship in another world, be guided by another Spirit, be directed by another rule, and be journeying to another Country, cannot go arm in arm with those who *despise* all such things! Then let everything in and about us exhibit the character of Christian *pilgrims*. May we indeed be "men wondered at" (Zech. 3:8) because "*not* conformed to this world" (Rom. 12:2).

6. We are profited from the Word when we *evoke the hatred of* the world. What pains are taken in the world to save appearances and keep up a seemly and goodly state! Its conventionalities and civilities, its courtesies and charities, are so many contrivances to give an air of respectability to it. So too its churches and cathedrals, its priests and prelates, are needed to gloss over the corruption which seethes beneath the surface. And to make good weight "Christianity" is added, and the holy name of Christ is taken upon the lips of thousands of those who have never taken *His* "yoke" upon them. Of them God says, "This people draweth nigh unto Me with their mouth, and honoureth Me with their lips; but their heart is far from Me" (Matt. 15:8).

And what is to be the attitude of all real Christians toward such? The answer of Scripture is plain: "from such turn away" (2 Tim. 3:5), "come out from among them and be ye separate, saith the Lord" (2 Cor. 6:17). And what will follow when this Divine command is obeyed? Why, then we shall prove the truth of those words of Christ's: "If ye were of the world, the world would love his own: but because ye are not of the world, but I have chosen you out of the world, therefore the world *hateth* you" (John 15:19). *Which* "world" is specifically in view here? Let the previous verses answer: "If the world hate you, ye know that it hated Me before you" *What* "world" hated Christ and hounded Him to death? The *religious* world, those who pretended to be most zealous for God's glory. So it is now. Let the Christian turn his back upon a Christ-dishonouring Christendom, and his fiercest foes and most relentless and unscrupulous enemies will be those who claim to be Christians themselves! But "Blessed are ye, when men shall revile you and persecute you . . . for My sake; rejoice, and be exceeding glad" (Matt. 5:11, 12). Ah, my brother, it is a healthy sign, a sure mark that you *are* profiting from the Word, when the religious world hates you. But if, on the other hand, you still have a "good standing" in the "churches" or "assemblies," there is grave reason to fear that you love the praise of men more than that of God!

7. We are profited from the Word when we are *elevated above* the world. First, above its *customs and fashions*. The worldling is a slave to the prevailing habits and styles of the day. Not so the one who is walking with God: his chief concern is to be "conformed to the image of His Sön." Second, above its *cares and sorrows*: of old it was said of the saints that they "took joyfully the spoiling of their goods," knowing that they had "in heaven a better and an enduring substance" (Heb. 10:34). Third, above its temptations: what attraction has the glare and glitter of the world for those, who are "delighting themselves in the Lord"? None whatever. Fourth, above its *opinions and approval*. Have you learned to be independent of and defy the world? If your whole heart is set upon pleasing God, you will be quite unconcerned about the frowns of the godless.

Now my reader, do you really wish to measure yourself by the contents of this article? Then seek honest answers to the following queries. First, what are the objects before your mind in times of recreation? What do your thoughts most run upon? Second, what are the objects of your *choice*? When you have to decide how to spend an evening or the Sabbath afternoon, *what* do you select? Third, which occasions you the most sorrow—the loss of earthly things, or lack of communion with God? Which causes the greater grief (or chagrin): the spoiling of your plans, or the coldness of your heart to Christ? Fourth, what is your favourite topic of conversation? do you hanker after the news of the day, or to meet with those who talk of the "altogether lovely" One? Fifth, do your "good intentions" materialise, or are they nothing but empty dreams? Are you spending more or less time than formerly on your knees? is the Word sweeter to your taste, or has your soul lost its relish for it?—A.W.P.

A PERSONAL WORD

The present issue of this little monthly messenger completes not only another year, but the first decade of its history. For ten years we have been engaged in seeking to proclaim the unsearchable riches of Christ, expound His glorious gospel, and feed some of His blood-bought sheep. It is therefore fitting on this occasion that we should raise our "Ebenezer" and acknowledge the abounding grace and mercy of our faithful God. We praise Him for having ministered "Seed to the sower" (2 Cor. 9:10), and enabled us to bring forth from the rich storehouse of His Word physic for the sick in soul, food for the hungry, a reviving cordial for the faint. None but those engaged in a similar work have any idea of what is involved in the preparation of four or five articles every month, year by year; but we have proved here too that God's grace is sufficient, and that He is ready to supply all the need of those who count upon His so doing.

As we review the past ten years, we are devoutly thankful to find that no fundamental changes have occurred in our views of God's Truth. Fuller light has led to both modifications and amplifications, and has often made us ashamed of our dullness and slowness to apprehend spiritual things. We have indeed *no* cause for boasting, for we have nothing good, but what we "first received" (1 Cor. 4:7). But we have *much* cause for humiliation: that we have so often failed to commend the message to the reader's conscience (2 Cor. 4:2) as we ought, that the pure water of the Word has been so much defiled by our fleshly handling of it, and that we did not preserve the balance of truth as we should. How longsuffering the Lord is with His unworthy servant: may our (imperfect) realization thereof move us to greater diligence and carefulness.

The past year has been one of severe testing unto many, but to the praise of the glory of God's grace we are able to record the fact that He has not only preserved us from all anxiety, but spared us any experience calculated to occasion worry. The God of Elijah is ministering to and freely meeting our every need. He who declares, "The silver is Mine, and the gold is Mine" (Hag. 2:8) has again moved His people to have both prayerful and financial fellowship with this work, so that every bill up to the Oct. issue has been paid within twenty-four hours of its receipt. We are, of course, writing these lines before payment of the Nov. and Dec. numbers falls due; but we have every reason to believe that on Nov. 18 we shall (D.V.) close our books again with a credit balance. Join the writer, dear reader, in praising God for His abounding goodness to us.

We take this opportunity to heartily thanking all who have sent in gifts to support this publication. Every cent that has been received for the magazine, has been devoted to the expenses of printing and postage; the editor and his wife take out nothing for themselves, being more than glad to give their humble services freely. Still more grateful are we for the prayers of God's people. Many have written us to say they desired to send in a thank-offering, but were unable to do so. To all such we would say, God knows your heart, dear friend, and accepts the will for the deed: His Word declares "if there be first a willing mind, it is accepted according to that a man hath, not according to that he hath not" (2 Cor. 8:12). And let us say at this point, we earnestly hope no one who is (under God) receiving any help from this magazine will ask us to cease sending it merely because they are unable to forward any money—that would be *Pride!* You are more than welcome to the "Studies." As the Lord enables, we gladly send this paper *free* to all whom we have reason to believe are profited from it.

During the last twelve months, many new names have been added to our mailing list: most of them being sent in by old readers. Few of these have written us personally, so we have (in the majority of instances) no means of knowing whether they value it or no. At the close of each year, we drop from our list hundreds of new names, for we must not waste copies on those who consider it too much trouble to drop us a line. But we are always glad to re-enter their names upon a personal application, providing we are satisfied they are not taking an unfair advantage of the generosity of others. We can truthfully say that we would far rather send these "Studies" to one hundred of the "poor of the flock" who are unable to send in a gift, than to twenty people who donate five dollars each, and then rarely read the magazine. A ten cent gift sent in gratitude and love is as acceptable as ten dollars.

Our most difficult task at the end of each year is to know whose names to retain and whose to drop, and our readers would make it much simpler if they send us a few lines to say whether or not God has made the "Studies" a blessing to them. If you really wish to receive the magazine during 1932, and do not, the fault is most probably yours—through failing to just ask for them. May we also request that you *promptly* notify us of any change of address: the postal authorities forward letters to a new one, but *not magazines*. We often send two, four, or six copies to an old address before a reader lets us know they have moved and are not getting the magazine. This should not be, for those copies are lost in the mails, and each one so lost means practically seven cents *wasted*.

We are again having the twelve current issues neatly and strongly bound, for those desiring them for permanent use and reference. These we supply at one dollar post paid, which is virtually what they actually cost us. We still have a *few* of the 1928, 1929, and 1930 bound volumes left, containing the exposition of Hebrews from the beginning; they are also one dollar each. Those of our readers who have been helped by the Studies, and are able to purchase other works, would do well to send for a list of our writings. May we specially mention our verse by verse exposition of John's Gospel, in four volumes of 350 pages each; the purchaser being allowed to take them one at a time to suit his own convenience.

As we grow older, we feel the great need of a deeper experimental acquaintance with God, and so of the Holy Spirit's applying His Word in power to our hearts. More and more we are learning that there is a vast difference between a theoretical knowledge of the truth and and inward experience of it. Our great need is for the Lord to write His Word upon our hearts, to thoroughly search our innermost being therewith, to make us feel the power of it in our conscience. Only thus are we personally fitted to be of any *spiritual* help to others. We must ourself be taught how to overcome the flesh, the world and the devil, before we can communicate the secret of it to others. Pray, Brethren and Sisters, that the writer may be pruned and purged, and thus be a fitter vessel for the Master's use. We hope to throw increasing emphasis on that which is calculated to expose a worthless profession, and to promote a closer walk with God.

Though it is now almost three and a half years since we left the pastorate and quit the Bible-Conference platform, the Lord has unfailingly ministered to our personal needs. Once again both of us have been permitted to journey through another year without any sickness. In the good providence of God, we are now having more opportunities to give out the Word orally to a few who crave a fuller fellowship with Christ. Christian friends who were unable to find an edifying ministry closer to hand, have journeyed one hundred, five hundred, and eight hundred miles in order to spend a few days in our humble home (an unpainted wooden house, which is quite good enough for a "stranger and pilgrim" in this world), and we have had blessed seasons together before the Throne and over the Word. We also minister to a little group two nights a month in Glenholden, Penna.

We are thankful to say that our 1931 list is a little larger than that of the previous year, but we are still much exercised over it. We long so much to have the privilege of reaching a larger number of God's hungry people and sharing with them some of the wondrous riches of His grace. Will not each reader who *is* receiving help from these Studies, make a real effort to bring them to the attention of other Christians—sample copies are gladly forwarded to all names sent in. Please join us in daily intercession that God will increase the circulation of this magazine. "Ye also helping together by prayer for us, that the gift bestowed upon us by the means of many persons, thanks may be given by many on our behalf"(2 Cor. 1:11). With all good wishes from A. W. and V. E. Pink.

"Glorify Thou Me with Thine own self with the glory which I had with Thee before the world was" (John 17:5). The "glory" which is there expressly in view is that exalted place which had been given to Him as the Head of all creation. In the timeless transactions of the everlasting covenant, in the unique honour which had been accorded Him as the "Beginning" of God's "way," the "Firstborn of all creation," He *had* this, "glory" and for the open *manifestation* of it He now prayed—answered at His ascension.

"When there were no depths, I was brought forth" (v. 24): "brought forth" out of the womb of God's decrees; "brought forth" into covenant-subsistence before the Divine mind; "brought forth" as the Image of the invisible God; "brought forth" as the Man Christ Jesus, after whose likeness Adam was created. Though Adam was the first man by open manifestation on earth, Christ had the priority as He secretly subsisted in Heaven. Adam was created in the "image" and after the "likeness" of Christ as He actually but secretly subsisted in the person of the Son of God, who, in the fulness of time, was born openly.

"Then I was by Him, as one brought up with Him" (v. 30). Gesenius says that the Hebrew verb here is connected with one which means "to prop, stay, sustain," and hence "such as one may safely lean on." Therefore is it rendered "nurse" in Ruth 4:16, 2 Sam. 4:4. As men commit their children unto a nurse to cherish and train, so God committed His counsels unto Christ. The Hebrew word for "brought up" also signifies a "master-builder," and is so rendered in the R. V. Christ took the fabric of the universe upon Himself, to contrive the framing of it with the most exquisite skill. It is akin to the Hebrew word "amen," which has the same letters as the verb to which Gesenius refers, only with different vowel-points. How blessedly it describes Him who could be relied upon to carry out the Father's purpose!

"And I was daily His delight, rejoicing always before Him" (v. 30). "It is not absolutely the mutual eternal delight of the Father and the Son, arising from the perfection of the same Divine excellency in each person that is intended. But respect is plainly had unto the counsels of God concerning the salvation of mankind by Him who is His 'Wisdom' and 'Power' unto that end. The counsel of peace' was between Jehovah and the Branch (Zech. 6:13), or the Father and the Son *as* He was to become incarnate. For therein was He 'foreordained before the foundation of the world' (1 Pet. 1:20), namely, to be a Saviour and Deliverer, by whom all the counsels of God were to be accomplished, and this by His own will and concurrence with the Father. And such a foundation was laid of the salvation of the Church in those counsels of God, as transacted between the Father and the Son, that it is said, 'eternal life' was 'promised before the world began,' Titus 1:2" (J. Owen). A.W.P.

Now if faith possesses the power to give reality to that which as yet has no historical actuality, if faith can enjoy in the present that whose existence is yet future, how much more was God Almighty able to give to the Mediator a covenant-subsistence endless ages before He was born. In consequence of God's so doing, Christ was the Son of man in Heaven, secretly before God, before He became the Son of many openly and manifestatively in this world. As Christ declared of His Father, by the language of prophecy, "in the shadow of His hand hath He hid Me, and made Me a polished shaft; in His quiver hath He hid Me" (Isa. 49:2)—note that the verses which follow have reference to the everlasting covenant. The "quiver" of God is a fine expression to denote the secrecy and security in which the purpose of God in Christ was concealed.

Many are the passages which speak of this wondrous subject. Perhaps the clearest, and the one that enters into most detail, is that found in Prov. 8. Not a few are aware that the term "Wisdom" (in v. 12 etc.) is one of the names of Christ: see 1 Cor. 1:24. That "Wisdom" in Prov. 8 has reference to a *person* is clear from v. 17, and to a *Divine* person is seen by v. 15. Numbers have recognised that the whole passage (vv. 13-36) has Christ in view, but in *what character*, has not been so clearly discerned. While it be evident that what is said in vv. 15, 16, 32-36 could only apply to a *Divine* person, it should be equally plain that some of the terms used in vv. 23, 24 etc., *cannot* be predicated of the Son of God absolutely considered. Contemplated only as co-eternal and co-equal with the Father, it could not be said that Christ was ever "brought forth."

If the Christian reader will carefully ponder all the terms used in Prov. 8:13-36 it should be apparent to him that some of them are impossible to understand of Christ's Deity separately considered, as others of them cannot be of His humanity only. But the difficulties disappear once we perceive that the whole passage contemplates the Mediator, the God-man in His two natures. The Man Christ Jesus, as united to the second person of the Godhead, was "possessed" (v. 22), by the Triune God from all eternity. Let us attempt a few brief comments on this marvelous passage.

"The Lord possessed Me in the beginning of His way, *before* His works of old" (v. 22). The Speaker is the Mediator, who had a covenant-subsistence before God ere the universe was called into being. The Man Christ Jesus, taken into union with the eternal Son, was "the Beginning" of the Triune God's "way." It is difficult for us to speak of eternal matters as first, second, and third, yet God has set them forth in the Scriptures for us, and it is permissible for us to use such distinctions as an aid to our understanding. The *first* act or counsel of God had respect to the Man Christ Jesus. He was appointed to be not only the Head of His Church, but "the Firstborn of all creation" (Col. 1:15). The predestination of the Man Christ Jesus unto the grace of Divine union and glory was the first of God's decrees: "in the *head* (Greek) of the book" it was written of Him (Heb. 10:7)—cf. Isa. 42:1, Rev. 13:8.

The person of the God-man Mediator was *the foundation* of all the Divine counsels: *see* Eph. 3:11 and 1:9, 10. He was ordained to be the Cornerstone, on which all creation was to rest. As such, the Triune Jehovah "possessed" or "embraced" Him as a Treasury, in which all the Divine counsels were laid up, as an efficient Agent for the execution of all His works. As such, He is both "the Wisdom of God" and "the Power of God" *executively*, being a perfect Vehicle through which to express Himself. As such, He was "the Beginning" of God's way. The "way" of God, signifies the outworking of His eternal decrees, the accomplishing of His purpose by wise and holy dispensations: cf. Isa. 55:8, 9.

"I was set up from everlasting" (v. 23). This could not be spoken of the Son Himself, for as God He was not capable of being "set up." Yet *how* could He be "set up" as the God-*man* Mediator? By mediatorial settlement, by covenant-constitution, by Divine subsistence before the mind of God. From the womb of eternity, in the "Council of Peace" (Zech. 6:13), before all worlds, was Jesus Christ in His official character "set up." Before God planned to create any creature, He first "set up" Christ as the great Archetype and Original. It is to be carefully borne in mind that there was an *order* in God's counsels as well as creation, and *Christ* has "the pre-eminence" in *all* things.

The Hebrew verb for "set up" is *"anointed,"* and should have been so translated. The reference is to the appointing and investing of Christ with the mediatorial office. This was done in the everlasting covenant: all the glory which our Lord possesses as Mediator was *then* granted to Him, on the condition of His obedience and sufferings, and therefore when He had finished His work He prayed,

(Continued on Page 287)

ted in the United States of America

www.ingramcontent.com/pod-product-compliance
Lightning Source LLC
Chambersburg PA
CBHW072018240426
43667CB00043B/1475